ANACONDA'S TAIL
The Civil War on the Potomac Frontier, 1861-1865

ANACONDA'S TAIL

The Civil War on the Potomac Frontier, 1861-1865

Donald Grady Shomette

Millstone Publishing
Dunkirk, Maryland

Published in the United State by Millstone Publishing

Manufactured in the United States of America
First Edition

Shomette, Donald Grady, 1943–
Anaconda's Tail: The Civil War on the Potomac Frontier, 1861-1865
p. cm.
ISBN 978-0-578-61322-2
Includes bibliographic references and index.
1. Civil War on the Potomac Frontier—History. I. American Civil War in Southern
Maryland and Northern Neck of Virginia, 1861-1865. II. Title.

Millstone Publishing
Dunkirk, Maryland 20754

For Carol

Hark to the wand'ring son's appeal.
Maryland!
My mother State, to thee I kneel,
Maryland!
For life and death, for woe and weal,
Thy peerless chivalry reveal,
And gird they beauteous limbs with steel,
Maryland! My Maryland!

Maryland
Second Stanza
1861

CONTENTS

ACKNOWLEDGMENTS

History, like a wild river rushing to the sea, often has many undiscovered tributaries flowing into it that often confuse and sometimes overwhelm the unwary explorer searching for its headwaters. From time to time its shores may change, and finding its main channel sometimes becomes frustrated by false leads. For those who travel its path upstream there are, to be sure, shoals and rapids, snags and weather that can hamper the journey at countless points along the way. But assisted by navigational aids and a good waterman or two who know the true course, arrival at one's destination is assured.

In attempting to fairly and accurately navigate the little known history of Southern Maryland and its Potomac frontier during the Civil War, I have traveled cautiously along a challenging and often unexplored route. Here, within the grand tableau of that momentous conflict, I have attempted to portray that all but forgotten regional story on a human scale, for it is indeed a tale well worth the telling. To do so, fortunately, I have been assisted by a number of wonderful individuals and institutions that have helped pilot a course up this meandering waterway of time.

I would first and foremost like to thank my longtime friend and colleague Dr. Ralph E. Eshelman for "hooking" me into this project many years ago, and for critical readings of the manuscript. I am equally grateful to Dr. Robert Browning, Chief Historian (retired) of the U.S. Coast Guard and noted scholar on the Civil War at sea for his critical assessment of the text. I would like to recognize fellow author and historian Kenneth Schaaf for his detailed review and valuable comments on the work while in progress. Acknowledgment must be extended the late Paul Berry, Head Librarian of the Calvert Marine Museum, Solomons, Maryland, a dear friend, as well as to the museum's former Maritime Curator Richard Dodds for generously providing me with the fruits of their own research on relevant aspects of the conflict. I am also truly indebted to the late Edwin Beitzell for his incredible pioneering work on the history of St. Mary's County, Maryland, and in particular on Camp Hoffman, the camp for Confederate prisoners of war at Point Lookout. His works have served as an inspiration for my own research on this long overlooked component of our nation's history. I would like to thank Jonathan Beasley for the use of his wonderful library and personal collections on the Civil War, and Janet and Bill Brown for access to their records collections on the people and places of St. Mary's County. Special thanks is also due to George Miller for his unending support.

No work of this regional nature could have been completed without the aid of the many Maryland archival repositories that house and conserve the very core documents of history itself. These included: the Maryland Historical Society, Baltimore; the Southern Maryland Studies Program, College of Southern Maryland, La Plata; the Charles County Historical Society, La Plata; the St. Mary's County Historical Society, Leonardtown; the Anne Arundel County Historical Society, Annapolis; the Prince George's County Historical Society, Riverdale; and the Calvert County Historical Society, Prince Frederick. Special acknowledgement must be extended to Leila Boyer and the late Karen Sykes, both of the latter institution, and to Colleen Puterbaugh, Research Librarian, James O. Hall Research Center, of the

Surratt House Museum, Clinton, for going well out of their way to facilitate my research. And, of course, no such history could be completed without the enormous archival resources and dedicated staffs of the National Archives and Record Administration, Washington, D.C., the Naval History and Heritage Command Library, Washington Navy Yard, and, of course, the Library of Congress, my former home for more than two decades.

Finally, I must thank my lovely wife and partner Carol Ann Shomette for editing my often-fragmented manuscripts, listening patiently to endless readings and rewrites of chapters as they slowly emerged in the rough, and for her unstinting and loving support throughout the long birthing process of this work.

PROLOGUE
"An elegant and comfortable retreat"

It is unknown just when William Cost Johnson first viewed the remote shores of Point Lookout in pastoral St. Mary's County, Maryland. But one thing is certain – he liked what he saw. To the undiscerning eye the land appeared to be little more than a narrow, sandy, foot-shaped peninsula jutting into waters at the junction of the Potomac River and Chesapeake Bay, varying in width from one to five hundred yards. It was a place where no one arrived by accident, except perhaps shipwreck. Yet the sparsely populated tract had a number of strategic attributes that made it extremely desirable to Johnson: it was equidistant from Baltimore, Maryland, Washington, D.C. and Norfolk, Virginia, and, most importantly, accessible to the largest steamers of the day; the property was available; and it was inexpensive. By the mid-19th century Point Lookout was known as "a watering place, frequented only by those residing in this latitude and notable for its picturesque scenery, splendid bathing and fine fish and oysters." [1] It was indeed an isolated spot, remote and largely inaccessible except by water, and surrounded by a deeply agrarian and thinly populated countryside. Here the sweet, pungent smell of tobacco curing in barns, and the ancient and powerful patrimonies to which it had given rise, remained unchanged and unchallenged for more than two centuries.

Despite its natural attractions the only noteworthy development at Point Lookout was a lighthouse, a one-and-a-half-story residence with the light tower standing proud above the roof, built in 1830 by one John Donahoo on a tract one acre and forty-four square perches in size.[2] The point upon which it was ensconced was seldom visited by outsiders beyond the surrounding countryside of St. Mary's, "the Mother County of Maryland." Nevertheless, the lighthouse had been of incalculable benefit to mariners, with the abrupt bends in the river and extent of shoals projecting into the bay rendering navigation most hazardous without this solitary beacon of warning.[3] Where others saw only isolation, William Cost Johnson saw opportunity.

Born in 1806 near the tiny hamlet of Jefferson in Frederick County, Maryland, Johnson had studied law. In 1831, at the age of twenty-five, he was admitted to the bar and as a delegate to the Maryland State Legislature. The following year he was elected on an anti-Jacksonian ticket to the Twenty-third Congress of the United States, and later to three more terms as a Whig. Serving until 1843 as member of the Committee on Public Lands, and Chair of the Committee on the District of Columbia, he had ample opportunity to scrutinize many aspects of land use and real estate development during his tenure.[4] At the age of thirty-seven, upon his re-entry into private life as a practicing attorney, he was finally able to put his congressional experience and connections to good personal use.

Johnson had visions of economic development in Southern Maryland well beyond the tobacco farming that had held the region in its sway for centuries. By 1856 he had taken a special interest in St. Mary's County, more specifically its Chesapeake coastline lying between the outets of the bucolic Patuxent and Potomac rivers. It was perhaps not coincidental that about this time a speculator, Augustus Dudley Mann, the recently retired Assistant Secretary of State (1853-1855), proposed a plan for the development of a direct trade route "by means of mammoth steamers between the waters of the Chesapeake and Milford Haven in England." Johnson not only publicly endorsed the scheme but in January 1857 also proceeded to advocate the advantages of that portion of the Chesapeake shore near Point Lookout as the American terminus of Mann's proposed ocean route. He avidly espoused the advantages to inland access offered by both the neighboring Patuxent and St. Mary's rivers, the latter being a nearby tributary of the Potomac, as a component of a transportation network employing the point as its central hub.[5] Though the plan continued to gather adherents, and one transportation company even contemplated establishing a major coal depot for steamers at the point, it was William Cost Johnson who first zealously seized the initiative at actual commercial development.[6]

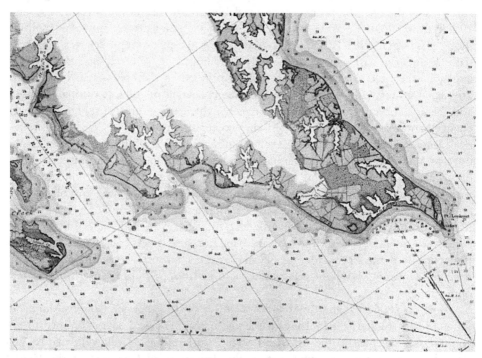

Point Lookout before development, 1856. Detail from "Potomac River. Sheet No. 1. Entrance to Piney Point Maryland. U.S. Coast Survey." Geographic and Map Division, Library of Congress, Washington, D.C.

By the summer of 1857 Johnson had purchased over 400 acres of land at Point Lookout from four sets of property owners, William M. and Rebecca Taylor, William A. Smith, Robert and Ann Ford, and Richard H. Clarke. His objective was to erect something new to the Chesapeake – a seaside resort unlike any in the country. Having interested a number of "Southern capitalists" in the project he proceeded to contract one Henry T. Garnett to sell subscriptions for the erection of waterfront cottages, which could be sold or leased with renewal rights to subscribers for a period of twenty years. The architectural firm of Lind & Murdoch of Baltimore was awarded the contract for designing and carrying out the plan. Johnson also determined to build a majestic hotel as the resort hub, wharfage for the reception of daily passenger steamer traffic, and all the necessary support outbuildings to accommodate subscribers, owners and visitors. "This situation is a very beautiful one," reported one of his early promotional stories planted in the Baltimore press, "and the projectors will make all their improvements on the most extensive scale. The ground contains some three hundred acres; on one side of which flows the water of the Chesapeake; on the other is washed by the Potomac River. There are three lakes of fresh water, one of which is a quarter of a mile long. The company proposes to erect at once seven hundred cottages of a neat and substantial character." [7]

The cottages were to be arranged in blocks, each block having a large square attached, which was to be laid off and landscaped "in handsome style" with streets and ornamental shrubbery. Broad avenues sixty feet in width, totalling twelve miles in overall length, were announced as one of the major attributes to be built. And "for those fond of indulging in that kind of sport, there will be bowling alleys, billiard saloons, shooting galleries, arching grounds, and a hippodrome." A ten-acre grove of pines on the northwest end of the property was to be set aside for the recreational facilities and also as a site for the erection of the more elegant and expensive summer houses replete with handsome walks for the very well-to-do. Fronting on the Chesapeake, the great hotel, at first planned for one hundred apartments, with reading, smoking and reception rooms and a large ball and dining room, was to be constructed for the benefit of short term visitors from Baltimore, Washington, Richmond and elsewhere. Connected with the hotel a garden covering two acres, landscaped with ornamental shrubbery and laced with veins of discrete strolling paths throughout, would provide fragrantly romantic lanes for after dinner walks. Along the shores of both the Chesapeake and Potomac, the former of which would be for surf bathers and the latter for stillwater bathers, convenient beachfront changing houses were to be built for the use of subscribers and hotel patrons. The estimated cost for the project was placed at a stunning half million dollars.[8]

By the end of February 1858 subscriptions for two-thirds of the cottage sites had been taken, but a downward revision of cottage numbers had also been determined. In early March it was announced that only a little over one hundred cottages of different sizes, to be sold at prices ranging from $300 to $600, were to be constructed and completed "at the earliest possible date." At least forty-five cottages had already been secured by notables from Washington, D.C., Maryland and Virginia, and even from as far away as Louisiana. Among the more illustrious purchasers were Supreme Court Justice Roger Brooke Taney and famed industrialist Cyrus B. McCormick of Chicago. There was also a liberal smattering of both Washington society and Southern Maryland plantation aristocracy.[9]

Though the building project was far from complete, by mid-April 1859 public notices touted the convenient location, equidistant from the great cities of the Chesapeake Tidewater, "affording an elegant and comfortable retreat for surf and still water bathing, with all the luxuries of Salt Water, Fish, Oysters, &c.; affording elegant and beautiful drives in the distance of fifteen miles, surrounding the peninsular, through a handsomely cultivated country." It was advertised that the resort, with its one hundred and nine cottages and handsome hotel would be ready for occupancy on July 1.[10]

Notwithstanding such optimistic predictions by developers and promoters, construction proceeded slower than anticipated, unquestionably influenced by the early and untimely death of the project's principal champion and promoter, William Cost Johnson. But it did not stop. Before his demise Johnson had mortgaged the property and all therein to one William Allen of 265 East Baltimore Street, Baltimore, and development continued. By the end of September 1859, though all of the cottages, now numbering 106, had been completed and sold and excursion steamers had already begun irregular service from Baltimore, only the center component of the hotel, containing thirty-eight rooms, had been finished. Work on the long steamer pier was still underway.[11]

The delay had some, including promoters of newly minted or rival watering places such as at Piney Point farther up the Potomac, questioning the timetable for not only completion of construction, but landscaping and amenities. Some challenged the wisdom of having selected the site itself for a resort. Though improvement of the grounds was being pushed forward, it was not without its difficulties and critics.

"Several years must necessarily elapse before it can afford any degree of comfort during the summer season," wrote one observer,

"except in the way of bathing. Nature having supplied it with nothing in the way of shade trees, they must be placed there by the hand of man; and as the Point is formed of nothing scarcely but a body of loose sand of unknown depth, the growth of trees when planted will, unless the roots are supplied with soil from elsewhere, be very slow. The most wealthy and influential farmers and others in St. Mary's County, seem to take a lively interest in the experiment, and appear very anxious to see it go into operation. Some of the more timid who have purchased cottages, have been offering them for sale again, which has caused others to look upon the matter as a mere speculation, and stand aloof from it." [12]

Ignoring such critics, on June 12, 1860 the very heart of the late William Cost Johnson's dream, the magnificent bayside Pavilion Hotel, was opened for business. The establishment was replete with comfortable accommodations for 750 guests. All was to be managed by Logan O. Smith, formerly proprietor of the City Hotel in Alexandria, Virginia, and the United States Hotel, in Washington, D.C. under the overall proprietorship of Hefelbower & Co. And who could resist?

"Point Lookout besides being deservedly the most famous place in all America for fine Oysters, Hog Fish, Soft Crabs, Sheephead, Mackerel, and all other salt water luxuries," read one advertisement,

"possesses finer facilities for Surf Bathing than even Cape May, while the back country immediately adjoining it – including the Drives, Partridge and Woodstock Shooting, &c., &c., – offer advantages together, superior of those of any other watering places on this continent. The Water Views from the pavilion and from all the cottages are extensive, varied, and charming. The health of the point is unexcelled by that of mountain regions, and the access to it by steamers from Baltimore, Washington, Norfolk, and Richmond, will probably be daily to and from each of those cities. He [the proprietor] has spared no expense in providing a fine Band, Carriages, Horses, Pleasure Boats, &c., for hire, or in stocking his cellars with the best Wines, Liquors, &c. In short his patrons will find at their command every luxury and comfort obtainable at any other American watering place." [13]

One of the significant draws to the point was the surrounding countryside, the inhabitants of which welcomed the new resort with open arms, as one happy visitor from Washington reported in describing his holiday. "Immediately at the rear of the first half mile of the peninsula's point," he wrote,

"the agricultural settlements of St. Mary's county, Md., commence. The land there is very fertile, and is the property of wealthy proprietors, the juniors of whose families are much given to driving down to the Point nightly, in parties of from a dozen to a hundred, and taking part in the festivities occurring among the guests there as regularly (except on Sundays) as night draws her curtains around the hotel and cottages. These Marylanders, besides being a well-to-do set of people, add greatly to the pleasures of society at the Point, as they are a frank, refined, and chivalrous community, as much devoted as any others, the world over, to the pleasures of the table, the dance, and social intercourse generally." [14]

Those pleasures, unhappily, were to be short lived indeed.

It seemed perhaps of little consequence that on the same day that the late William Cost Johnson's great Point Lookout "watering place" was formally opened for business, that 870 miles away in Springfield, Illinois, at the photographic studio of Thomas A. Hicks, a tall, gangly looking politician sat to have his formal portrait taken. Less than a month earlier, the self-educated attorney and former U.S. Congressman had been nominated by the young Republican Party as its candidate for President of the United States. It is likely that no one at the resort, or indeed throughout the alluvial fields and countryside of surrounding Southern Maryland, could foresee the impact that his subsequent election to office would engender upon their society, their personal lives, or indeed their very existence.

Few guests who arrived that day aboard steamer or stage coach could have imagined how such a scene of serenity and pleasure encountered upon disembarking would within but a year become one of conspiracy, intrigue and outright rebellion against the established government of the United States. Fewer still could have fathomed that within but a short time after that it would again be transformed almost overnight into a vast Golgotha of misery and death, a military prison where thousands of battle-scarred men would suffer and perish as a consequence of one of the bloodiest conflicts in history, the American Civil War. And none could have prognosticated the social and fratricidal cataclysm, insanity and change that would sweep across the length and breadth of Southern Maryland, along its Potomac frontier and into the adjacent pastoral hinterland of the Northern Neck of Virginia.

This is the story of that great upheaval.

"Night Watch on the Potomac." Prints and Photographs Division, Library of Congress, Washington, D.C.

1

NIGHT VIGILANTS
"The supper was a very elegant and substantial one."

No one can say for certain what was running through the mind of Captain Mason Locke Weems on that Thursday in April 1861 when his elegant sidewheel steamer *Mary Washington* passed the imposing sand and clay cliffs rising above the Chesapeake Bay shores of Calvert County, Maryland. As he steamed down the great estuary bound for the entrance of the Patuxent River eighty miles south of Baltimore, his thoughts may well have briefly dwelled on the tumultuous news of the day. Having departed the great port that same morning, a city bustling with talk of rebellion, mobs, war, and the startling turn of events only a few days before in Charleston Harbor, South Carolina, it must have been difficult for the captain to maintain his concentration.

For the moment at least Captain Weems had more on his mind. There were of course the almost mechanical motions he was obliged to go through, just as he had done countless times over the past few decades. With the ease that comes from years of experience he deftly guided his ship alongside the long wharf at Millstone Landing, her first stop on the Patuxent in the heart of the rolling tobacco lands of St. Mary's County. Built of timber pilings driven into the muddy river bottom with its rough cut top stringers planked over, neither the wharf nor the small cluster of sheds, buildings and a modest hotel on the adjacent shore were much to look at, but they were adequate for the business at hand. There were the normal procedures to address after docking, the disembarking of passengers, the welcoming of others coming aboard who were bound upriver, and the loading and offloading of cargoes. Just business as usual.

Launched in 1846 *Mary Washington* was nearing her seniority as a bay steamer, but she was still robust. With her sturdy keel of white oak, cedar frames and bottom, of course coppered to protect her from the Chesapeake's voraciously hungry shipworms, she had for years withstood storms, shoals, and every obstacle nature could throw at her. Originally built by John H. Robb for a rival line, the Baltimore & Rappahannock Steam Packet Co., Captain Weems had acquired her in December 1855 for his own company, the Weems Line, one of the oldest on the bay. His small but quite profitable fleet had served the Baltimore-Patuxent route for decades. It now numbered four ships, which, besides *Mary Washington*, included *George Weems*, *Patuxent* and *Planter*. But *Mary Washington* was his pride and joy for she was a marvelously outfitted craft famed throughout the Chesapeake Tidewater for her splendid appointments, excellent cuisine and personal service. Moreover, Weems himself was a well-known fixture on the bay, popular with his passengers and a personal friend of many of the planters on the river, large and small alike, as well as the townsfolk who populated the villages and hamlets all along his route.[1]

One of the Weems Line's most admired features was its reputation for reliability in keeping to its schedule as advertised, except in extreme weather conditions. *Mary Washington* would leave her pier at Baltimore every Thursday morning promptly at 6 a.m. Her first stop on the Patuxent, though not advertised as such, was at Millstone

Landing. Her last was forty-five miles upriver at Hills Landing, close to the old riverport of Upper Marlboro, the seat of government for Prince George's County since 1706 and northernmost accessible and navigable point on the ever-silting waterway. There the river channel was narrow, barely wide enough for a vessel such as *Mary Washington* to come about. The following day she would depart the landing at 6 a.m. bound south for the town of Benedict, the only Charles County port on the river. She would remain there until Saturday morning at 6 a.m. for the return trip to Baltimore. Her sister ships *Patuxent* and *Planter* would follow an alternate day schedule but make callings that also serviced Fair Haven, a little Anne Arundel County fishing village on the Chesapeake several miles below Annapolis, as well as Benedict, Lyons Creek, and Hills Landing on the Patuxent, with miscellaneous other short stops along the way.[2] From time to time the Weems Line steamers had made incursions into the territory of rival lines such as the Baltimore Steam Packet Company, the Merchant and Miners Transportation Company, the Eastern Shore Steamboat Company, and the Individual Enterprise Company. Yet it was the Patuxent upon which the Weems Line had long relied for most of its business, indeed ever since *Eagle*, its first steamboat, began to call at the river landings in 1822.[3]

The captain must have watched intently as his officers and deckhands went about their normal tasks preparatory to landing. As all the lower tier crewmen – stokers, deckhands, roustabouts, oilers, chambermaids, and dining room waiters – were his personal slaves, it was only normal that he maintain a watchful eye especially in these times.[4] With northern abolitionists and even free blacks introducing what many in the South considered an "infection," slave escapes had been on the rise. Only his officers (with the exception of the pilot who was black), the master, mate, engineer, quartermaster, and purser were white and could be trusted absolutely.

Weems, like most Marylanders, was well aware that the possibility of slave revolt was ever present, especially in the rural tobacco lands of Southern Maryland, albeit masked by the genteel, crinolined surface of deeply rooted white Tidewater culture. Indeed, from time to time several of the southern counties of the state had instituted harsh measures to counter the threat of such a possibility. Following the bloody Nat Turner slave rebellion in Virginia in August 1831, waves of insurrection scares had from time to time temporarily paralyzed adjacent Charles County and other parts of Maryland as well. As early as the 1840s special paramilitary police forces were regularly organized under local court appointed committees of vigilance to insure the security of the slaveholders as well as that of the white population at large, which was generally smaller in number than the slaves they owned. Concerned about abolitionist influence exerted upon the slave population by local freemen of color, both from within the county and beyond, a number of plantation owners petitioned in 1856 that curfews for all blacks be instituted. The move was approved and passes were required for any black man, woman or child to walk about after sunset, ostensibly "for the welfare of both masters and servants." The penalty for writing a pass for a slave other than one's own was usually fifteen lashes or more for the slave in question administered by the county sheriff. In nearby Prince George's

County the government passed an act appointing three men in each election district to manage "the obstreperous Negro" in any way they deemed necessary.

Companies of white "patrollers" appointed by county sheriffs were formed to "deal rigidly" with violators, and punishments were usually brutal. Similar actions were instituted in other Southern Maryland counties. Not infrequently, of course, slaves and freemen innocent of violations were sometimes punished for simply being in the wrong place at the wrong time.[6] "We all thought, " said Dennis Sims, a slave belonging to the Thomas Mason plantation on Goose Bay on the Potomac River in Charles County, "of running off to Canada or to Washington, but feared the patrollers." [7]

Concerns about the spread of abolitionist sentiments to the local slaves of Southern Maryland by the region's small number of free black inhabitants and from beyond continued to engender unending actions to silence or intimidate them. Acting within the legal guidelines of the Maryland "Black Code," public meetings were held in 1857 in adjacent Charles County's Nanjemoy District to draft resolutions requiring all black freemen to purchase or secure homes and satisfy an appointed committee of whites regarding their gainful employment. The resolutions were ostensibly generated by concerns over the idleness of unemployed freemen who, with "time on their hands," were believed to have nothing better to do than

"The Plantation Police or Home Guard, Examining Negro Passes." The plantation police, or patrol, was an institution peculiar to the slave states. As in Maryland, they were semi-official organizations raised and supported by the planters but recognized by state authorities. Their principal duty was to visit the various plantations and patrol the roads at night, arresting all negroes and others not having proper passes. Though the above is a picture of an inspection in Louisiana, it would have been much the same in Maryland. *Frank Leslie's Illustrated Newspaper*, New York Public Library.

spread the infection of abolitionist rhetoric among those held in bondage. Non-compliance by anyone not procuring a residence and having steady employment by July 17 of the same year required the violator to be set up in some public place and his or her services sold to the highest bidder. Notes and security bonds were to be held by the committee and kept to the end of the year, after which they were to be handed over to the subject in question, provided he or she had not absconded or "voluntarily" withdrawn from the service of the employers. When the appointed deadline arrived, forty free blacks were summarily rounded up and paraded before the committee. Seven who met the terms of the resolution were released. The remaining thirty-three were hired out, or indentured, like it or not, to the highest bidders for the rest of the year. When one of the parties "intimated" that he would appeal to authorities in Port Tobacco, the county seat, he received five lashes of the whip for his trouble.[8]

Well before the famed October 1859 failed attempt by the firebrand abolitionist John Brown and twenty-one of his followers to seize the Federal Arsenal at Harpers Ferry, Virginia, to facilitate a massive slave insurrection, talk of civil war between the southern slave states and northern free states had been simmering. Though three companies of volunteer militia from the city of Baltimore, the City Guard, Laws Greys, and Shields Guard, and three from Frederick, Maryland, the United Guards, Junior Defenders and Independent Riflemen, were part of the force that helped put down the uprising, it had only fanned the flames of discontent among many Maryland whites. Then with the November 1860 election of the Illinois "rail splitter" Abraham Lincoln as sixteenth President of the United States, the proverbial pot began to boil over.

The question of extending or prohibiting slavery into the new territories of the American west had been a divisive one for a decade between the industrial northern states, whose economies were not dependent upon slavery, and the agriculture-based southern states such as Maryland that were. For white Marylanders, as throughout the South, fears were manifest that Lincoln's election was a victory for abolition and a direct threat to their property, namely their slave holdings, and would result in the elimination of the institution of slavery altogether. Indeed, by 1860 the anti-slavery movement, reinforced by widely spread opposition to the Fugitive Slave Law of 1850 in the northern states, had become one of the pre-dominant issues of the election.

A total of 92,441 votes were cast in Maryland for the four presidential can-didates, John C. Breckinridge, a Southern Democrat and standing Vice President of the United States, John Bell, a Constitutional Unionist, Stephen A. Douglas, a Democrat, and Lincoln, a Republican. Only 2,294 votes, a little over two percent of the total, had gone to Lincoln. Nowhere in the state, which counted 87,189 of its inhabitants in 1860 as slaves, was the so called white "Black Republican" candidate so roundly despised as in Maryland's southern counties. In the state capital of Annapolis he had received only one vote and in surrounding Anne Arundel County only two. Though Breckinridge had captured Maryland's eight electoral votes, Lincoln had been elected with only forty percent of the national vote. Hostilities were so great in Charles County towards the President Elect that a public meeting was held in the village of Middletown, convened by the county leaders, to censure those citizens who voted for the Republican ticket. They promptly issued a notice to one of the censured, Nathan Burman, "a Black republican emissary," that he must leave the county by January 1, 1861.[9]

On December 20, 1860 the State Legislature of South Carolina passes its Ordinance of Secession, unilaterally withdrawing from the Union by a vote of 169 to nothing. The Federal garrisons at Fort Moultrie and Castle Pinckney in Charleston Harbor were forced to strategically retire six days later to Fort Sumter. Talk of war had quickly morphed into contagious rebellion. At first everyone, North and South, believed that if hostilities broke out the conflict would be resolved within a matter of weeks. But the seizures of Moultrie and Pinkney and the blockade of Sumter itself had served as a catalyst for like actions throughout the South. Six more states, convinced of the constitutionality of secession, departed from the Union in quick succession. On December 30 the U.S. arsenal in Charleston was taken. On January 3, 1861 Forts Pulaski and Jackson and the U.S. arsenal in Savannah, Georgia were seized. Under the lame duck administration of President James Buchanan Federal reaction in Maryland was minimal. On January 5, 1861 as Forts Morgan and Gaines and the U.S. arsenal at Mobile, Alabama were occupied by that state's militia, the Secretary of the Navy took limited action. Forty U.S. Marines commanded by Captain Algernon S. Taylor were sent to Fort Washington, a run-down and neglected defense work a few miles below Washington, D.C. on the Maryland side of the Potomac River in Prince George's County, "to protect public property" and prevent a similar surprise attack by secessionists.

The dilapidated brick and masonry works, built adjacent to the ruins of old Fort Warburton, which was once captured by the Royal Navy without a fight during the War of 1812, had been abandoned to caretaker status in 1853. Its sole garrison, until Taylor's arrival, had been but a single watchman who, it was said, could be bought for a bottle of whiskey. Soon after his arrival Taylor wrote to Marine Corps Commandant Colonel John Harris regarding the "defenseless and pregnable condition" of the works and requested reinforcements immediately. On January 9 another small U.S. Marine detachment, just thirty men strong under First Lieutenant Andrew J. Hays, was sent to secure the strategically and symbolically significant Fort McHenry guarding the entrance to Baltimore Harbor. But that was all.[10]

Each new sunrise, it seemed, brought with it news of Federal military facilities, navy yards and ships throughout the South being taken or fired upon by secessionists. On January 8, 1861 Forts Johnson and Caswell at Smithville on Cape Fear, North Carolina were captured. The State of Mississippi left the Union the following day. At the same time the *Star of the West* was fired upon by rebel batteries in Charleston Harbor while attempting to bring reinforcements to besieged Fort Sumter. Then in quick succession forts Jackson and St. Philip on the Mississippi River below New Orleans were occupied by Louisiana troops while Florida and Alabama militia seized Fort Barrancas, the Pensacola Navy Yard, and Fort McRee, Florida. Alabama formally seceded from the Union on January 11 by a vote of sixty-one to thirty-nine followed soon afterwards by Georgia. On January 20 Fort Massachusetts on Ship Island, Mississippi, a key to control of the Mississippi River, was taken by rebel troops. Six days later Louisiana left the Union followed on February 1 by Texas. Only the Border States of Kentucky, Missouri, Tennessee,

Arkansas, Virginia, North Carolina and Maryland continued to hold back, but it seemed simply a matter of time before more than half of them also joined the infant Southern Confederacy. The cost to the Federal Government was staggering. All told, fortifications pierced for 1,099 guns and ready to be manned by 5,430 soldiers, as well as other federal property valued at $5,947,000 had fallen into secessionist's hands without a contest. The military implications were overwhelming as hundreds, then thousands, of U.S. Army and Navy officers and men, mostly southerners supportive of secession, resigned and traveled south to take up arms against the Union.[11]

Washington, D.C., sandwiched between Maryland and Virginia, and serving not only as the seat of the Federal Government but also as home to the strategically important Washington Navy Yard, was virtually without defenses. Amidst the gathering storm a growing sense of panic had begun to grip the government. On February 1 three companies of a regiment of artillery, part of a force sent to Fort McHenry in Baltimore, was dispatched to the capital, leaving only two artillery companies to defend the fort itself. The outgoing Buchanan Administration was paralyzed.[12]

"Balloon View of Washington, May, 1861." *Harper's Weekly*, Prints and Photographs Division, Library of Congress, Washington, D.C.

Acting upon intelligence that the Washington Navy Yard, along with its arms and armory, was in danger of seizure by a mob intent on preventing the March 4 inauguration of President Elect Lincoln, plans were initiated to defend that station. Two hundred seamen from receiving ships as well as the yard's U.S. Marine guard and even the civilian mechanics belonging to the Ordnance Department were mustered and readied for combat. The yard's commandant, Franklin Buchanan, an

Eastern Shore Marylander, personally sympathetic to the Southern cause, struggled to resolve his true loyalties. Outwardly adamant that the facility be prepared, he declared that "this yard shall not be surrendered to any person or persons except by order from the honorable Secretary of the Navy." In the last extremity should its defenders be overpowered, he pledged, on his order the armory and magazine would be blown up if need be. Within a short time all of the powder from the magazine had been transferred to Fort Washington nine miles downstream on the Potomac River, surrounded by rural Prince George's County farmland and well beyond the mob's reach. The best arms and war materiel were moved secretly to the attic of the armory, which could be defended if it came to that better than any other place in the yard. Eventually howitzer batteries were erected to secure the three entrances to the yard and five more guns were dispersed to protect other vulnerable or strategic points within. But it was a desperate move that served to do little more than briefly lift morale.[13]

With every cascading event, Southern Marylanders along the Patuxent-Potomac axis, whose sentiments and culture were deeply allied to the South, and especially Virginia, took heart. Indeed well before February 1861 the secessionist movement had firmly gripped all of the southern counties lining both rivers – Prince George's, Anne Arundel, Calvert, Charles, and St. Mary's – which had already begun to prepare for the coming day of reckoning by forming home guard infantry and cavalry units. The undertaking was daunting given the region's land area, just under 2,000 square miles. White inhabitants numbered barely 38,000 men, women and children, but the black population was well over 51,000, eighty percent of whom were slaves.

In St. Mary's, at a citizens' meeting held at the Washington Hotel in the bucolic county seat of Leonardtown, it was determined "for the purpose of patrolling, guarding the village, &c." to organize an armed paramilitary unit dubbed the "Night Vigilants." As no Federal military authority was yet evident in the region it was presumed by most that the Night Vigilants, composed of seven squads of eight men each, would serve as a police force to maintain order in the town. Their primary purpose, however, was to prohibit, in the event of war, a potential uprising by the county's more than 6,500 slaves who provided the free labor that kept the economy alive. Then on January 18 the St. Mary's County Commissioners appointed Committees of Vigilance for the county's six election districts, St. Inigoes, Factory, Leonardtown, Chaptico, Charlotte Hall, and Patuxent, numbering twenty-five men in each. The committees were ostensibly formed to serve as an additional police force to patrol and maintain order in the county. The action, it was reported, was initially undertaken because of the late January discovery of an alleged insurrection plot "on the part of a gang of slaves and free negroes," but unquestionably also agitated by the secessionist news from the South.[14]

The fear of violent slave insurrection was not limited to St. Mary's and Charles counties. On January 11 the citizens of Upper Marlboro in Prince George's also convened a large meeting and took action regarding the danger of a black revolt. A resolution was passed requesting that all stores in the town be closed at 7 p.m. No slave from the adjoining neighborhood was to be allowed to visit the village after that hour unless he possessed a pass. A curfew of 9 p.m. was to be authorized for those living in the village who, unless they were on special business, were forbidden to walk the streets after that hour. As the stance of both state and local governments were as yet uncertain, a committee of seven town and county leaders were appointed to "supply the place of local government and to carry out the resolutions of the meeting." The committee was comprised of: Dr. James Harper, General Thomas Fielder Bowie, Dr. R. H. Osborn, William A. Jarboe, George Wilson, Fielder Suit, and Samuel B. Hance. A committee of five, consisting of: Dr. John H. Boyle, Washington J. Beall, Dr. Frederick Sasscer, Charles Clagett, and Richard O. Mullikan, was appointed to organize a home guard.[15]

In neighboring Anne Arundel County units such as the Magothy Home Guard were formed and handsomely outfitted with full dress uniforms produced by the Baltimore firm of Patterson and Fields. The attire was splendid and consisted of a coat of blue cloth, heavily trimmed with gold lace. The pants were of the same material and color, and ornamented with a broad stripe of orange upon the outer seam.[16]

Such undertakings, like many major white civic initiatives in the region, were often carried out amidst an air of social festivity that belied the cause of such actions. Leonardtown hosted "a handsome entertainment, in the large Hall over the store of Messrs. Simms & Maddox," located on Main Street near the courthouse, to commemorate the formation of the Night Vigilants. The gathering was designated by the only newspaper in the county, the *St. Mary's Beacon*, as a cause for general celebration. The officers of the Riley Rifles, another recently formed paramilitary unit, and the Night Vigilants were invited as special guests, swelling the party to about seventy-five persons. The Honorable Henry G. S. Key, Chief Judge of the First Judicial Circuit Court, and a patron of all the county "Guard" units, was among the local dignitaries in attendance.

"The supper," it was later reported, "was a very elegant and substantial one, and the delicacies of the scene, such as wild duck &c., were served up in the best style and great abundance." Lieutenant James T. Blackistone, who had served for fourteen years in the Maryland State Senate, attended as the presiding officer. Late that night the "company after partaking freely of savory viands and singing several National and convivial airs, left for their homes highly gratified with the style and spirit of the entertainment." Notwithstanding the genial atmosphere and camaraderie of the evening, the causal factors for the creation of the two armed units were hardly spoken of. However, the underlying tensions and excitement of the momentous events unfolding everywhere, both near and far, could not be denied.[17]

All in Southern Maryland, especially in Anne Arundel County, did not share the predominance of sympathy for the secessionists though the greater portion of white citizens provided a nodding approval. Opposition to outright secession was afforded by several key political leaders and supported by the editor of the *Annapolis Gazette*, Thomas J. Wilson. With weekly regularity Wilson aggressively denounced secessionists, buoyed Unionist sentiments in the pages of the paper, and influenced many hitherto neutral county inhabitants to veer from the Southern cause, while helping to quell public support for the South. Labeling southern supporters as "Hotspurs" and "Slave Barons," he attributed the national drift towards civil war almost entirely to audacious Southern politicians. These, he noted, included men in high office in Annapolis who had sworn to uphold the Constitution but were explicitly and publicly advocating rebellion against the State and Federal Government.[18] Almost all were of the ancient Maryland landholding aristocracy, and the principal slave owners of the state.

But soon even Wilson and his anti-secessionist rhetoric would be lost in the tidal wave of events sweeping across the Maryland Tidewater.

***

Captain Weems watched intently as his crewmen and the black stevedores began to unload *Mary Washington*'s cargo at Millstone Landing, even as numerous passengers started to disembark. Many were familiar faces of friends or longtime clients of the line. Others belonged to strangers who mostly kept to themselves and were bound for parts unknown. Some, it was rumored, were headed for the Deep South and a rebel army and navy said to be forming across the Potomac River somewhere in Virginia. One among them had until recently been a captain in the U.S. Navy, a veteran sailor whose notable service had begun during the Barabary Wars.

Most of the cargo, from textiles and groceries to hardware and farm equipment, was bound for the shops, farms, and plantations of St. Mary's, without which many of the county residents would be sorely pressed. Indeed, without the Weems Line connection to Baltimore, fourth largest city in the nation and the unrivaled shipping and commercial hub of the state, the quality of life along the rural shores of the Patuxent and Potomac would have been drastically diminished. Overland connections between the few major urban areas of the Western Shore region of the state, namely Baltimore, Annapolis, and Washington, D.C., with Southern Maryland's towns, hamlets and farms were primitive at best. With only a little over 400 miles of "main" roads, all being little more than cleared dirt lanes and avenues, and frequently awash or impassable. There were few public roads in St. Mary's or elsewhere in Southern Maryland; passage was often blocked by nature or literally by dozens of gates. Some, such as the main road from Washington to Upper Marlboro, required a score of tolls paid to local property owners. The 200-mile-long Chesapeake Bay, which bisected both Maryland and Virginia into eastern and western sections, and its forty-two major and minor tributaries were in truth the only practical highways of the day. The vessels that plied them composed the most reliable mass transportation system in the region's history.[19]

The metronomic rhythm of arrivals and departures of *Mary Washington* and the other Weems Line steamers meant far more now than commerce and transportation to and from the county: they brought the news of the day from the outside world through newspapers, official reports and circulars, intelligence, gossip, and rumors alike. All were immediately picked up and published in the pages of the *St. Mary's Beacon* or in neighboring Charles County by the *Port Tobacco Times*. With the nation in turmoil it was unquestionably news that stirred the blood. And the Weems Line was the region's most important connection to a world that was now changing at breakneck speed.

Though Weems may not have known it as he greeted the passengers coming aboard at Millstone Landing, only the day before, April 17, Virginia had repealed its ratification of the U.S. Constitution that it had originally passed June 25, 1788. On May 6 the Commonwealth would join the Confederacy followed on May 20 by North Carolina and Arkansas, and immediately afterwards by Tennessee. The news would soon be spread and, though stunning in its implications, was not unexpected. And "whither goest Virginia," the common wisdom held, it was almost certain Maryland would follow. Eight days later the Convention of Virginia passed an Ordinance of Secession and formally joined the Southern Confederacy. Civil war was no longer simply in the offing. It was now guaranteed, and the Chesapeake Tidewater was to become a principal region of contention.

The celebrations throughout the rural length and breadth of the gentle rolling tobacco lands of Southern Maryland was indeed already well underway, as was the mobilization for war.

2

BLOOD HOUNDS
"She could not be coerced or forced, so she was attacked by him."

For white planters of Southern Maryland, many being slave owners born and bred to an ancient plantation aristocracy in a totally rural society where tobacco was king, the social order was largely unchanged since the days of the first settlers two centuries earlier. Slavery had been at its core, a constant substratum of Southern life since the beginning. Long allied to the agrarian culture of the South, its white society now echoed approvingly the rebellion that was rising just on the other side of the watery frontier that was the Potomac River. Yet in a state laced with myriad embayments, rivers and streams, Southern Maryland's links to the great and prosperous city of Baltimore to the north, where the Gospel of industry ruled supreme, were both economic and social in nature. They were connected primarily by arterial bonds of water, not land. Unlike their agrarian brethren in the southen counties, the merchants, manufacturers, tradesmen and ship builders of the dynamic, rowdy, maritime metropolis on the Patapsco River enjoyed an explosively expanding economy. It was a dynamic based upon substantially free market labor that nearly outstripped the rest of the state in its entirety. Its linkage to the rest of Maryland was enormous, though challenged subcutaneously by a creeping sectionalism, and facilitated by geographic, economic and political differences throughout. Yet, while many residents in northern and western parts of the state were sympathetic to those in the southern and Eastern Shore counties and the very institution of slavery, the majority were guarded or opposed in their views regarding actual secession. Much of the city's heart, its political sympathies, societal web and a significant degree of its commerce was tied to the South. Baltimore, however, was a young and industrially self-sufficient world class entity that presented a dramatic contrast to the much older agricultural-based society that had dominated Southern Maryland for hundreds of years.

Baltimore Mayor George William Brown, though a proponent of gradual emancipation of slavery within the State of Maryland, in many ways maintained throughout his life what was a predominantly Southern paternalistic – some would say self-serving – view of the institution. Like Brown, some pro-slavery advocates had justified their positions by recalling that seven of Lincoln's fourteen predecessors who served as the nation's chief executive had kept slaves as servants and laborers, including Presidents Washington and Jefferson. Abolitionists, however, were ready to point out that the institution blindly ignored the cruel reality of life in bondage wherein the black man was legally deemed subhuman, without rights, and held as chattel property that could be bought and sold like cattle or furniture.

"I knew that slavery had existed almost everywhere in the world, and still existed in some places," Brown wrote in 1887, twenty-two years after the end of the Civil War,

> "and that, whatever might be its character elsewhere, it was not in the Southern States 'the sum of all villainy.' On the contrary, it had existed materially in the development of the race. Nowhere else, I believe, had negro slaves been so well

treated, on the whole, and had advanced so far in civilization. They had learned the necessity, as well as the habit, of labor; the importance – to some extent at least – of thrift; the essential distinctions between right and wrong, and the inevitable difference to the individual between right-doing and wrong-doing; the duty of obedience to law; and – not least – some conception, dim though it might be, of the inspiring teachings of the Christian religion. They had learned also to cherish a feeling of respect and good will towards the best portion of the white race, to whom they looked up, and whom they imitated." [1]

It was a popular and characteristically patrician view shared by many of Brown's generation that had justified and maintained the racial baggage and bias of the institution of slavery since colonial days, particularly in, but not limited to, the Southern states.

Between 1820 and 1850 the population of Baltimore, the largest and northern-most Southern entrepôt below the Mason-Dixon Line, had expanded from 62,785 to over 169,000 residents. Ten years later, on the eve of rebellion, the city populace numbered 266,553 (constituting well over a third of the state total of 687,049). Of these, 29,911 were free blacks, the largest such population in the nation. Between 1840 and 1860 the city had literally doubled its economic growth rate. In the thirty years prior to 1850, 130,000 mostly Irish and German immigrants had entered through the Port of Baltimore to work in the harbor, the shipyards, factories, on the B&O Railroad, or to farm the surrounding countryside, greatly displacing the need for slave labor. By 1860 the city held sixty-eight percent of the state's foreign born population, fueling in part the labor needs of its great industrial expansion. The nation's capital, Washington, D.C., counted a population of just 61,122 residents, including 10,983 blacks, or eighteen percent of the whole, of which only 1,774 were slaves. By comparison the capital of Maryland, the little town of Annapolis, could boast of just 4,539 inhabitants including 1,301 free blacks and 475 slaves. Yet the five counties of Southern Maryland, sandwiched between the banks of the Potomac, Patuxent and Chesapeake, had a total 1860 population of 37,945 whites, 40,622 slaves, and 10,837 free people of color, or 89,404 souls in all. This area, where nearly fifty-eight percent of the population was black and accounted for barely thirteen percent of the state's total inhabitants, had experienced only an eight percent economic growth in the previous two decades.[2]

The governing factor that had held the counties of Southern Maryland in fiscal stagnation was land ownership. The greatest holdings were concentrated in a relatively small number of hands, the rural landed gentry, in a plantation landscape totally dependent upon the manual labor of slaves to support the single crop tobacco-based economy. The often misleading appearance of wealth and stability of Southern Maryland was perhaps best personified by those same great and minor manoral establishments belonging to the landed aristocracy that permeated the region but contained a minority of the white population. Each had its main house and satellite support buildings serving as the hub for the surrounding estate and social order, in essence small, self-reliant, isolated villages. As John C. Calhoun once quite accurately remarked: "The Southern States are an aggregate . . . of com-munities, not of individuals. Every plantation is a little community, with the master at its head . . . These small communities aggregated make the State in all." Southern Maryland was no exception.[3]

Owing to the decentralized white manorial system that had grown up around early colonial economic dependence upon tobacco culture, major urban centers had failed to take hold in Southern Maryland. More than 130 early towns in the colony had been created, most as ports of entry, by edict, legislative order or executive fiat between 1668 and 1751 to facilitate the management and taxation of the tobacco trade. Fifty-two had been designated in the five counties of Southern Maryland. Most had either failed to take root or had long since fallen by the wayside owing to wars, silting river systems, opposition by the lords of the manors, or a multitude of other causes. Those few towns that survived were usually small governmental or religious centers, or were situated at crossroads or on still navigable deep-water landings well suited for maritime commerce. It was thus that the manor or plant-ation was still the core of Southern Maryland life for both white and slave cultures, and the cultivation of tobacco was its reason for being.

Tobacco was without question the most valuable and difficult crop to grow in Maryland, the planting and harvesting of which required exhaustive labor and time. Unlike corn or wheat, though vital products that needed only two seasons from planting to harvest, tobacco took most of a year. Beginning in January cultivation commenced with the preparation of the fields for planting, mending tools and equipment, and laying out seedbeds. In March the loamy soil was usually ready for transplant of seedlings to field. Months later, in mid-summer, as the crop was growing, constant attention and care was necessary to maintain the fragile product. At harvest time backbreaking labor was required to pick, bundle, cure and later pack and ship the product to market. The process of cultivating and curing tobacco, which included fallowing, hilling, cutting of hills, planting and replanting, topping, suckering, weeding, cutting, picking up, removing out of the ground, hanging, strik-ing, stripping, stemming, and prizing, demanded an enormous amount of manual labor. The dedicated and unrelenting toil of a single individual might produce two to three acres of tobacco per year, at least under optimum conditions.[4]

By the onset of the Civil War some great tobacco estates were still quite sub-stantial in extent. The Thomas Mason plantation on Goose Bay, just south of Chicamuxen Creek, said to be 10,000 aces, and the 3,500 acre Silas Dorsey property near Pisgah, both in Charles County, perhaps exemplified the more notable. Others such as the Richard and Charles Contee farm on South River in Anne Arundel County, where more than 100 of the county's 7,332 slaves labored in bondage, were somewhat smaller in size but no less representative of the total domination by the white social order. Many landowners such as the Contees were descendents of the earliest settlers in Maryland; pedigrees and acreage usually defined social status in the agrarian economy of the region. The main or manor houses on the more sub-stantial estates, as exemplified by the Mason plantation in Charles County, or the great Sotterley estate of the Briscoe family in St. Mary's County, were usually large wooden or brick affairs adorned with porches on the side or back and brick chimneys. Many, such as the Burton Stafford manor on a cove off the Potomac River not far from Chicamuxen, were situated on or close to navigable or once navigable waters. Some were connected by old rolling roads over which produce was still carried to landings as in colonial days and shipped to Baltimore for distribution to world markets.[5]

Not all great land holdings were engaged solely in agricultural practices. Many of the landed gentry supplemented incomes by holding public offices and command positions in militia establishments. Oxon Hill, Harmony Hall, Battersea and other grand estates like them often served as social centers where relatives, neighbors, friends and the elites of the aristocracy comprised the community network that dominated Southern Maryland white society and government. Captain Oden Bowie's Fairview domain, centered on its fine old two-story brick Georgian mansion built ca. 1745 in a region called the "Forest." It was a few miles west of Collington in the upper part of Prince George's County and perhaps best exemplified the epitome of Southern Maryland gentility. Here Bowie, the first president of the Maryland Jockey Club, and his son William Booth Bowie raised and stabled a string of racehorses with such posh names as Dickens, Catespy, Crickmore, and others, that were famed throughout the state.[6]

Burton Stafford's estate, dubbed "Blood Hound Manor" by his slaves, encompassed a largely marshy tract of land at the edge of the Potomac, much of it ill-suited for tobacco. But its rolling terrain was well situated for the purpose of his main livelihood, commercially raising and training bloodhounds, at least a hundred at a time, exclusively for the purpose of chasing runaway slaves. Stafford's customers were slaveholders and professional slave catchers from Maryland and Virginia, and some from as far away as Mississippi and Louisiana, who traveled to Charles County specifically to purchase or lease his hounds. [7]

Page Harris, a slave born and raised on the plantation, would recall many years later just how his master went about his business: "Mr. Stafford had about 50 slaves on his farm," he recalled.

> "He had an original method in training young blood hounds. He would make one of the slaves traverse a course, [and] at the end, the slave would climb a tree. The younger dogs led by an old dog, sometimes by several older dogs, would trail the slave until they reached the tree, then they would bark until taken away by the men who had charge of the dogs. Mr. Stafford's dogs were often sought to apprehend runaway slaves. He would charge according to the value and worth of the slave captured. His dogs were often taken to Virginia, sometimes to North Carolina, besides being used in Maryland. I have been told that when a slave was captured, besides the reward paid in money, that each dog was supposed to bite the slave to make him anxious to hunt human beings." [8]

At the top of the plantation hierarchy was the owner of the estate and master of all that dwelled therein. The majority of the inhabitants of a Southern Maryland tobacco plantation or farm, of course, were the slaves themselves, the backbone of the labor force. A few owners viewed their slaves, though legally their chattel property, paternalistically but also condescendingly as lesser beings. Silas Dorsey, judging from the words of Charles Cole, one of his seventy-five slaves, regarded his blacks as part of a family group. He "was a man of excellent reputation and character, was loved by all who knew him, black and white, especially his slaves. He was never known to be harsh or cruel to any of his slaves . . . he and his wife were very considerate in all their dealings." Others such as Thomas Mason, a man of weak mental disposition whose mother managed the affairs of his estate, was considered kind but quite simple. The real boss, the elderly Mistress Mason, "had good disposition and never permitted slaves to be punished." But for the majority, though "many slave masters were kind and considerate . . . to most slaves they were just a driver and the slaves were work horses for them." [9]

An overseer, usually an unmarried white man who resided on the plantation, but occasionally a trusted male slave, administered the day-to-day operations of work in the fields. Bill Mack was a black overseer on the large McPherson farm in Charles County where he had charge of the entire plantation and continued in that role until he was too old to work and was replaced by his wife's brother Caleb. An old maid named Sally McPherson owned all. The whole Mack family, all slaves, were to be no exception to the rule when it came to work despite the important position held by the senior male member in the farm's administrative order. Mack's own son Richard, seventeen years old at the outbreak of the Civil War, observed that because tobacco was raised in Charles County on a large scale, "Men, women and children had to work hard to produce the required crops. The slaves did the work and they were driven at full speed sometimes by the owners and others by both owner and overseers." Richard's job, even as a small boy, was laboring in the tobacco fields and cutting wood for lumber and firewood. For all their hard labor slaves received no money.[10]

Escape from bondage was an alluring hope for many slaves but for most a dismal prospect at best. Not only were their chances of capture substantial, but for those who succeeded they would be leaving their families and loved ones perhaps forever. Moreover the Fugitive Slave Law of 1850, which allowed slave chasers to pursue and recapture slaves even in free states, made the prospects of flight still more remote. Many would nevertheless try and a few would achieve success through their own cunning, sometimes with the assistance of sympathetic whites and free blacks, or with the aid of the "Underground Railroad," even with standing rewards for their capture and return. In Prince George's County, which bordered on the District of Columbia, with a large free black population as well as slaves, the exodus from the county was perhaps more pronounced than elsewhere. In Anne Arundel County with a population of 23,900, including 4,864 free people of color, fights with patrollers and slaveholders were not uncommon, particularly in the northern sector where there were a fair number of anti-slavery advocates who often provided refuge and aid for runaways from Southern Maryland. The consequence was usually an increase in the number of patrollers fielded after such incidents.[11]

At least one successful Southern Maryland runaway born into slavery on a farm in Charles County near Port Tobacco would help change history. His name was Josiah Henson. Born in 1789, Josiah had as a youth been witness to a typically brutal punishment when his father defied his sadistic owner. After receiving one hundred lashes, his father then had his right ear nailed to the whipping post and cut off. The old man was soon afterwards sold to a new owner in Alabama and never heard from again. When Josiah's master died the Henson family, including all his brothers and sisters, were parceled out at auction to new owners. Young Josiah and his mother were moved to the farm of one Isaac Riley in Montgomery County, Maryland, and later to Kentucky. After having attempted to purchase his freedom and then been cheated by his owner, in 1830 Henson successfully escaped to Canada and founded a settlement and school for fugitive slaves. In 1849 he published his autobiography, *The Life of Josiah Henson, Formerly a Slave, Now an Inhabitant of Canada, as Narrated by Himself.* Three years later the abolitionist writer Harriet Beecher Stowe, reputedly inspired by Henson's narrative, published *Uncle Tom's Cabin.* In the moving novel a fugitive slave, George Harris, returned to Kentucky to rescue his wife and escaped across the Ohio River and eventually to Canada. The book proved to be a critical and popular triumph credited with sparking abolitionist sentiments throughout the North in the days before the war.[12]

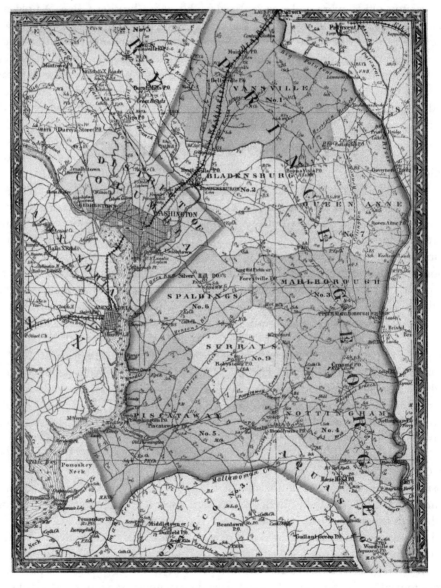

"Prince George's County." Simon J. Martinet, Baltimore, 1861. Geography and Map Division, Library of Congress, Washington, D.C.

Successful escapees such as Henson notwithstanding, professional slave chasers made their living pursuing runaway slaves for the bounty offered for captures. Relentless pursuit, pressing even into the heart of northern free states, was common. For fugitives apprehended by their masters, patrollers, or professional slave catchers, punishment for their efforts was often brutal. Southern Maryland patrollers who managed to catch a runaway would immediately administer a flogging, and then brand their unfortunate prisoner on the cheek with the letter "R" using a red hot iron. Repeat offenders were often sold away to owners in more southerly states such as South Carolina and Georgia where brutalization was even more common than in Maryland.[13]

Escape was not the only form of resistance to a slave's status. Feigned sickness, sabotage of tools, theft of food, clothing and other items, and countless forms of disobedience were common. Punishment for any reason, even the slightest infraction deemed by a master or overseer as suitable for retribution, was usually the result. The "Black Code" of Maryland law frowned upon overworking or causing injury to free black servants but provided no regulations regarding the treatment or management of slaves, which was the prerogative of the owner. On the Mason plantation, when the mistress of the house once slapped the aunt of young James Deane, the aunt slapped back. The aunt was immediately sold and taken south and never seen again.[14]

Few were the slaves who did not bear the scars from the punishments of their masters or from accidents in a day's labor. Dennis Simms, a young slave on the Contee plantation, observed that it was imperative to toe the mark or else be flogged with a rawhide whip. He recalled: "When we behaved we were not whipped, but the overseer kept a Pretty close eye on us, " Simms related after the war. "We all hated what they called the 'nine ninety-nine', usually a flogging until [you] fell over unconscious or begged for mercy." [15]

Most slaves owned by Contee remained close to their cabins after dark or face an unmerciful whipping. Those caught beyond the limits of the plantation without the company of a white person or without written permit of his master, could be whipped by any person who apprehended him with twenty lashes across the bare back. If a slave went to another plantation without a written permit from his master, on lawful business, the owner of the plantation would usually give the offender ten lashes. "We were never allowed to congregate after work, never went to church, and could not read or write for we were kept in ignorance. We were very unhappy." [16]

Occasionally brutality was met with brutality. Richard Mack recalled one such episode, an incident wherein a white master began to beat his slave with a whip. The slave retaliated with a knife, "splitting the man's breast open, from which he died. The slave escaped and was never captured. The white cappers or patrollers in all of the counties of Southern Maryland scoured the swamps, rivers and fields without success." [17]

Had the slave in question been captured, his punishment would have been hanging after having his hands cut off. Following the execution his head might be severed from the body. The body would be divided into four quarters and the parts set up in the most public places of the county where the act had been committed.[18] Usually, however, the slave owner administered the coup de gras himself in more mundane but equally bloody fashion. In August 1861, when Jackson Scroggins, one of Captain Samuel Cox's forty or fifty slaves, failed in an escape attempt he was bound and whipped to death by the captain. When another slave owner, Jackson Smoot of Charles County, ordered irons placed on the wrists and legs of one Nace Dorsey, the slave bolted. Smoot shot him in the head with buckshot, killing him instantly.[19]

With the closure of the legal importation of slaves in 1807, a reliance on slave breeding and auctions was adopted to keep the institution operative. Moreover, for the owners of smaller estates, farms and commercial establishments there was often a dependence on slaves hired from elsewhere. In Surrattsville (modern Clinton) in Prince George's County, John Surratt and his wife Mary, owners of a tavern that also served as their farmhouse and post office for the district, were small farmers who sometimes hired slaves from other owners. Though never possessing more than seven blacks at any given time, at least four of which were engaged in the Surratt household and in tavern duties, economic downturns had obliged them to hire from other owners rather than purchase slaves.[20]

Baltimore, though possessing the largest free black population in the country, was also one of the leading slave auction emporiums in the South. Young Rezin Williams recalled having unwittingly served as something of a Judas Goat in facilitating the sale of a large parcel of slaves in the city. He recalled late in life that a certain slave master had taken him to the wharf in the city, boarded a boat, and the slave dealer and the captain began negotiating a deal. Williams, not realizing that he was being used as a decoy, led a group of some thirty or forty blacks, men, women and children through a dark and dirty tunnel for a distance to a slave market pen where they were placed on the auction block. Williams was instructed to pacify the women who immediately set up a wail after they were separated from their husbands and children. "It was a pitiful sight to see them, half naked, some whipped into submission, cast into slave pens surrounded by iron bars," he said. "A good healthy negro man from 18 to 35 would bring from $200 to $800. Some women would bring about half the price of the men. Often when the women parted with the children and loved ones, they would never see them again." [21]

Southern Maryland was not without its own slave emporiums. One of the most prominent was Bryantown in Charles County, which prior to the war was known primarily as a market for slaves, tobacco, and grain. The village was modest in size, with several stores, the nearby St. Mary's Female Institute, and two or three taverns or inns which were well known in their day for their hospitality to guests and arrangements to house slaves destined to be sold. "There were two inns," noted Richard Mack, "both of which had a long shed, strongly built with cells downstairs for men and a large room above for women. All night the slave traders would bring their charges to the inns, pay for their meals, which were served on a long table in the shed, then afterwards, they were locked up for the night." [22] Slaves were brought in chained or handcuffed and others not.

While strong young men in good health could fetch a fair price at Bryantown, young women were also sought after, the more physically attractive being the most wanted. As Mack, who bore personal witness to such auctions during the war, would note in later years:

"The slave traders would buy young and able farm men and well developed young girls with fine physiques to barter and sell. They would bring them to the taverns where there would be the buyers and traders, display them and offer them for sale. At one of these gatherings a colored girl, a mulatto of fine stature and good looks, was put on sale. She was of high spirits and determined disposition. At night she was taken by the trader to his room to satisfy his bestial nature. She could not be coerced or forced, so she was attacked by him. In the struggle she grabbed a knife and with it, she sterilized him and from the result of injury he died the next day. She was charged with murder. Gen. Butler, hearing of it, sent troops to Charles County to protect her, they brought her to Baltimore, later she was taken to Washington where she was set free . . . This attack was the result of being good looking, for which many a poor girl in Charles County paid the price." [23]

The status of a female house slave was in a sense one of the better positions in the plantation slave hierarchy, where one might rise to some importance and trust within the master's household or even management of the house. Some would serve as companions or nurses for elderly or sick whites and nursemaids for not only their own offspring but the master's children as well. However, the position was also one of the most difficult for female slaves for they were the most likely to be obliged to protect themselves from sexual assault by their male owners, guests of the plantation, and even white male servants. Many times they were not able to defend themselves for fear of losing their positions. At the same time they were subjected to many impositions by the women of the household through jealousy, especially when the relationship between master and slave resulted in children. By example, Richard Mack recalled an event on a neighboring farm regarding the situation of one such female house servant. "There was a doctor in the neighborhood who bought a girl and installed her on the place for his own use, [and] his wife hearing of it severely beat her. One day her [the slave's] little child was playing in the yard. It fell down in a post hole filled with water and drowned. His wife left him; afterwards she said it was an affliction put on her husband for his sins." [24]

The societal makeup of Southern Maryland life, both black and white, was thus clearly, if brutally, defined. Yet even in the white community class distinction was often equally severe. For the free individual of color obliged to hire himself or herself out as labor or the propertyless white man obliged to fend for himself, life was in many ways not much better than black servitude on a plantation. As James Deane candidly noted: "The poor white people in Charles County were worse off than the slaves, because they could not get any work to do, on the plantation, the slaves did all the work." It was, indeed, much the same throughout all of Southern Maryland.[25]

With the major landowners possessing the largest number of slaves, the smaller landowners and tenant farmers were often obliged to secure labor from the few free blacks available to work their farms. The soils were increasingly depleted by tobacco agriculture; economic growth in Southern Maryland had been stymied for decades. Prince George's County, at the head of steamer navigation on the Patuxent and one of the richest counties in Maryland, was a case in point. By 1860, in the county where more slaves were owned than any other in the state, the four election districts

25

lining the west bank of the river – Queen Anne, Upper Marlboro, Nottingham, and Aquasco – were producing more than thirteen million pounds of tobacco annually. There amidst a total population of 10,382, just 378 slaveholders owned 6,491 slaves, almost ninety-two percent of the four districts' total black populace. Most were housed and labored on the property of the largest and richest estate owners. The remainder of the slave and free black inhabitants were generally employed as laborers or household servants for the small tenant farmers and landholders. A Baltimore *Sun* report on December 25, 1860 noted that a total of 1,084 farms throughout the whole county, on lands valued at $9,100,755, were producing little more than $100 per year in profit, while just a dozen manufacturing concerns were each generating just $500 a year. Perhaps not surprisingly, in these and adjacent election districts, citizens in many communities such as Queen Anne's Town, Upper Marlboro, Good Luck, Beltsville, Vansville, and Bladensburg would provide only limited direct or indirect support for the Southern cause during the war. Yet those in southern Anne Arundel, Calvert, Charles and St. Mary's, all counties farther from Washington, D.C., would provide far more aid and comfort to the Confederate cause than Prince George's, which bordered the nation's capital, ever could.[26]

In many ways, Maryland provided a dichotomy and at the same time a paradigm for the nation as a whole, illustrative of the societal chasm of division which defined both North and South. The rich, industrialized mercantile North, dramatically influenced by a growing and dynamic German and Irish immigrant population was on one side, and the far slower paced, economically limited, slave-dependent agrarian society of the South on the other. For Marylanders, the chasm was about to become visceral. With the arrival of *Mary Washington* at Millstone Landing and the news that she carried, the measured, almost fluid pace of the lives of the people of Southern Maryland, both black and white, were about to be changed dramatically forever after.

3

A PECULIAR POSITION

"The filthy cage of unclean birds must and will assuredly be purified by fire."

On the night of Monday, April 15, 1861, three days before the scheduled arrival of the steamer *Mary Washington*, news was received in Leonardtown that sparked an outbreak of "the wildest enthusiasm . . . huzzahs and congratulations." Major Robert Anderson, two days earlier after a 34-hour bombardment, had surrendered Fort Sumter in Charleston Harbor to his one-time artillery student at West Point, Louisiana born General Pierre Gustave Tountant Beauregard. All across St. Mary's County the citizenry immediately and openly expressed a wish for direct recognition of the Southern Confederacy, as it was being called, if not outright alliance. Soon the bells of Leonardtown were ringing out merry peals punctuated by volleys of gunfire orchestrated by the Riley Rifles. An outpouring of joy was reverberating through most of the county within hours, which, it was said, "never witnessed an excitement more general and intense than has prevailed in our midst since the news was received." Soon most of Southern Maryland was also reveling in the latest accounts eminatng from Baltimore, which, to the editor of the *St. Mary's Beacon*, "indicates in the most unmistakable manner that the sympathies of our people are exclusively with the South." [1]

The groundswell of elation rapidly manifested itself into political action, for three days later, even as *Mary Washington* was tying up at Millstone Landing, there was a countywide public call for a community meeting. "In view of the crisis now upon the country, a general wish has been expressed that every citizen of the County should assemble in County Meeting at Leonard Town on Tuesday next. The presence of every man in the county is earnestly solicited." [2]

Questionable intelligence, rumors, and solid information alike regarding the swiftly evolving events emanating from Baltimore and beyond was delivered in a continuing stream by the Weems Line steamers. The prospect of war was on everyone's lips. Two days after Sumter's surrender, it was learned from the news carried aboard *Mary Washington*, that to put down the insurrection President Lincoln had issued an astonishing call for 75,000 volunteers to serve for three months. To the dismay of many in St. Mary's, Maryland would be called upon to fill its quota of four regiments. Not surprisingly, it was a task that some Southern Marylanders vowed would never be accomplished. They simply would not allow it. Others, principally Unionists in Anne Arundel County, took the president's call to heart and by mid-summer would organize a loyal home guard. Yet with the state hovering on the brink of leaving the Union, the situation was growing increasingly precarious. Many pro-secessionist paramilitary units in Baltimore such as the Palmetto Guards, named in homage to South Carolina, and others were being openly organized, trained and formed into armed camps. Citizens loyal to the Union remained closeted for their own safety. Since Maryland and Virginia surrounded Washington, D.C., it seemed only a matter of time before the largely undefended capital city of the United States, unless reinforced quickly, would fall into rebel hands. Indeed, on the day before the surrender of Fort Sumter Confederate Secretary of War Leroy Pope

Walker, from the rebel capital at Montgomery, Alabama, predicted that the Stars and Bars would fly over the still unfinished U.S. Capitol dome by May 1. The *New Orleans Picayune* foresaw that the first fruits of the new rebel government would be the removal of Lincoln and his Cabinet. In Mississippi the *Vicksburg Whig* reported that a force of 5,000 men had been organized "to seize the Federal Capital the instant the first blood is spilled." [3]

The vulnerability of the city on the Potomac was not ignored by secessionists in Baltimore, railway hub of Maryland and the District of Columbia's vital and only landline of communication and supply from the north. On April 18, only hours after *Mary Washington* had departed from her berth bound for the Patuxent, four companies of the 1st Pennsylvania Volunteers, under the command of Major John C. Pemberton, accompanied by two artillery companies, set off for Washington to save the capital from rebel capture. The run by train on the Northern Central line from Harrisburg, Pennsylvania had been without incident. However, when they disembarked in Baltimore at Bolton Station to make their way to the Camden Street Station where they would re-embark aboard the Philadelphia, Wilmington & Baltimore line for the District of Columbia, events soured rapidly.

To many onlookers the 1st Pennsylvania Volunteers appeared to be anything but soldierly as some wore mismatched militia uniforms and others were still in their civilian clothes. Only a few were armed because they had set off so quickly; there was simply no time to visit their respective armories. As they marched the regiment was immediately surrounded by a hooting, yelling mob stirred to a fever pitch by earlier rallies protesting the possible movement of troops through the city. The Pennsylvanians marched between two lines of 120 Baltimore police officers to cars awaiting them at Camden Station, with the mob shouting "Stone them! Kill them!" Almost immediately the jeering escalated into brick and stone throwing. Nicholas Biddle, a sixty-five-year-old free black orderly wearing an honorary uniform awarded for his two decades of service in Captain James Wren's Washington Artillery of Pottsville, Pennsylvania, was soon spotted by the mob. Suddenly a cry rang out: "Nigger in uniform! Nigger in uniform." A volley of stones and bricks showered about him. One hit him in the face, sending him to the ground, blood spilling copiously onto his uniform. Saved by his comrades, Biddle would nevertheless be the first casualty of the war felled by enemy action but certainly not the last. The mob, which had grown to more than 2,000 men, continued to accost the Pennsylvanians until the train at Camden Station, filled with torn and injured soldiers, finally escaped at 4:00 p.m. bound for Washington.[4]

Both Governor of Maryland Thomas Holliday Hicks and Mayor of Baltimore George W. Brown quickly issued separate proclamations. Hicks, a square jawed, gray haired politician born in Dorchester County, was a member of the American Nativist Party (also known as the Know Nothing Party), who believed slaves were property rather than human beings. He addressed the "peculiar position" of Maryland and expressed the belief that it was not to be expected that its citizens would unanimously agree upon "the best mode of preserving the honor and integrity of the State" or maintaining the peace. He warned against taking rash steps in an emergency that was great, and issued a plea for the people to restrain themselves. He begged that they abstain "from all heated controversy upon the subject, and . . . avoid all things that tend to crimination and recriminations." Promising to use his executive powers to preserve the peace and the people of the state from civil war, he called upon the populace to obey the law. But most importantly, to allay concerns that the state militia might be employed by Lincoln to quell the rebellion in the South, he assured the mob "that no troops will be sent from Maryland, unless it is for the defence of the national capital . . . The people of the State will in a short time have the opportunity afforded them, in a special election for Members of Congress of the United States, to express their devotion to the Union, or their desire to see it broken up." [5]

In his own proclamation, Mayor Brown concurred with the governor, especially with "his resolution that no troops shall be sent from Maryland to the soil of any other State." He too expressed optimism that the great national questions of the day should be resolved at the ballot box, and that the threat of bloody civil war "will at least pass over our beloved State and leave it unharmed; but if they shall be disregarded, a fearful and fratricidal strife may at once burst forth in our midst." Cognizant of and entirely sympathetic to the significant secessionist leanings of many in his own city, he concluded: "Under such circumstances, can any good citizen doubt for a moment, the course which duty and honor alike require him to pursue?" [6]

Following the bloody attack on the Pennsylvania Volunteers, requests for restraint were unfortunately to go entirely unheeded. The next day, April 19, acting upon the advice of Lieutenant General Winfield Scott, a national hero of the War of 1812, Mexican-American War, and senior commander of the U.S. Army, President Lincoln authorized a total blockade of the states of South Carolina, Georgia, Alabama, Florida, Mississippi, Louisiana and Texas. Scott believed that the blockade, soon dubbed by the press the "Anaconda Plan," should envelop the insurgent states, strangling their trade and transportation, and help bring them to terms with less bloodshed than any other scheme. He rationalized that "the transportation of men and all supplies by water is a fifth of the land cost, besides an immense saving of time." Moreover it would be a key step in preventing international intervention in what the president asserted was a domestic problem (an action which quickly secured declarations of neutrality from Great Britain and other nations).[7] At the same time, the general, a Virginian whom many incorrectly thought would resign his commission and go south, issued General Order No. 3 at the direction of Secretary of War Simon Cameron. The order extended the Military Department of Washington to include Maryland, Delaware and Pennsylvania, all under the command of Major General Robert Patterson of Pennsylvania. To keep the lines of communication, reinforcement, and supply open between the capital and the northern states, Patterson was instructed to "post the volunteers of Pennsylvania all along the railroad from Wilmington, Del., to Washington City, in sufficient numbers and in such proximity as may give reasonable protection to the line of parallel [telegraph] wires, to the road, its rails, bridges, cars and stations." [8] That Maryland would thereby have a Union military presence, many calling it occupation, at least along the rail line, was now a given.

And so it began, precisely on the eighty-sixth anniversary of the fight on Lexington Green between the British Army and Massachusetts militia that began the

American Revolution that war and revolt came to Maryland. It was with some irony that it was to be the 6th Massachusetts, having departed from Lexington and Concord bound for Washington on the Philadelphia, Wilmington & Baltimore Line via the "City of Brotherly Love," that would provide the tinder. Well forewarned that troops passing through Baltimore would likely be assailed, the regiment's commander, Colonel Edward F. Jones, ordered his men to load their guns but to ignore any verbal attacks they might encounter. "You will undoubtedly be insulted, abused, and perhaps assaulted, to which you must pay no attention whatever, but march with your faces square to the front, and pay no attention to the mob, even if they throw stones, bricks, or other missiles; but if you are fired upon, and any of you are hit, your officers will order you to fire. Do not fire into any promiscuous crowds," he ordered, "but select any man whom you may see aiming at you, and be sure you drop him." [9]

"The Sixth Regiment of the Massachusetts Volunteers firing into the people in Pratt street, while attempting to pass through Baltimore en route for Washington, April 19, 1861." *Frank Leslie's Illustrated Newspapers.* Prints and Photographs Division, Library of Congress, Washington, D.C.

Upon arrival in the city at the President Street Station at 11:20 a.m. the first seven companies proceeded without confrontation to the Camden Street Station to re-embark for Washington. Then as the regimental band and companies C, D, I, and L, approximately 220 strong, were proceeding on foot under the command of Captain Albert S. Follansbee, they soon encountered a mob tearing up the tracks at Pratt Street and placing anchors on the tracks elsewhere to obstruct the passage of the cars being towed from the President Street Station. They immediately began a retro-march in double quick time in an attempt to return to the station at which they had offloaded. From the gathering crowd Confederate flags soon appeared even as rocks, bottles and other projectiles began to rain down upon the troops, wounding some. Suddenly a musket shot from the mob felled a soldier. For a moment pregnant with indecision the infantrymen stopped, but their orders were clear. Resolutely they shouldered their weapons and unleashed a fusillade of bullets into the crowd, killing and wounding several. In an instant all was pandemonium as a staccato of gunfire, shouts, curses and screams filled the air. In a desperate effort to quell the shooting, Mayor Brown joined the head of the Bay State column, but in vain. Though personally a strong supporter of secession, Police Chief George P. Kane and approximately fifty city policemen appeared between Light and Charles streets with drawn revolvers and formed a line in the rear of the column to provide protection until it finally reached the security of the train station from which it had marched.

Before the bloody incident was over four Massachusetts men were killed and thirty-six more were wounded. Between nine and twelve members of the mob as well as several innocent bystanders also died, and an unknown number were injured. The confrontation was immediately dubbed "The Pratt Street Riot." Though the main body of the 6th Massachusetts at the Camden Street Station was able to depart and reach Washington at 5 p.m. the same day, safe passage through Baltimore by other Federal troops was no longer deemed feasible. Those who had retreated to the train cars at the President Street Station were finally rescued by the police after a violent mob siege and sent back to Philadelphia. That same morning, as if to punctuate the bad news for Unionists, it was learned that the Federal arsenal at Harpers Ferry, along with 15,000 guns, had been destroyed to prevent capture and was then, without a fight, immediately occupied by Confederate forces. It would quickly become a major rallying point for secessionists bent on joining the rebel army.[10]

Mayor Brown and Governor Hicks immediately dashed off joint communiqués to President Lincoln informing him of the collision between the citizens of Baltimore and Massachusetts soldiers, and begged him to send no more. "The people are exasperated to the highest degree by the passage of troops," wrote the mayor, "and the citizens are universally decided in the opinion that no more troops should be ordered to come. Under these circumstances, it is my solemn duty to inform you that it is not possible for more soldiers to pass through Baltimore, unless they fight their way at every step." The governor promised that the state's militia, which he had immediately called up, would keep the peace. Yet the Rubicon had been crossed. Soon after the Massachusetts soldiers departed, Mayor Brown and Governor Hicks issued a citywide call for a meeting at Monument Square, asking the thousands of residents that assembled there at 4 p.m. for calm and for men of all parties to forget their differences. Viewed with disdain by many Baltimoreans, the governor sought to make his "peculiar position" clear: "I am a Marylander; I love my State and I love the Union, but I will suffer my right arm to be torn from my body before I will raise it to strike a sister State." To many Marylanders the disputed passage of Federal troops through Maryland territory was nothing less than a violation of state sovereignty. To others it constituted a virtual declaration of war.

To Federal authorities it seemed the only way possible to save the capital of the United States of America.[11]

But it was already too late. That same night word arrived that more and larger Federal forces were by then en route from Harrisburg and Philadelphia. With no response to their telegram forthcoming from the president, Mayor Brown and the Board of Police Commissioners ostensibly determined on their own, the mayor later stated in defense of the move, to head off another fatal clash. The action was in a manner that would soon be deemed by Federal authorities as nothing less than treason.

In Baltimore it was quickly agreed that a detachment of the city police force led by Chief Kane (to whom command of the existing state militia had been transferred by Governor Hicks) would be sent to burn all the railroad bridges north and east of the city and scuttle a ferryboat in the Susquehanna River to prevent the passage of Federal troops. Kane would lead a contingent of the Maryland Guard and two companies of axe-wielding firemen from the city fire department under the direction of Colonel Isaac Ridgeway Trimble, onetime chief engineer of the Baltimore and Susquehanna Railroad. The Bush and Gunpowder River bridges on the Philadelphia, Wilmington & Baltimore line, as well as three others on the North Central Railroad, leading to Harrisburg, Pennsylvania, would have to be demolished. In the meantime the streets of Baltimore were barricaded and protected "by armed men who swarmed in all directions," even as secessionist Maryland militia companies poured into the city from the surrounding counties. Rail and mail service between Washington and the North would thus be completely severed.[12]

The *Philadelphia Press* reported that the next day "a mob from Baltimore lying in wait for the train from Philadelphia, at Canton, fired a pistol at the engineer, who stopped the train. The crowd, compelling the passengers to leave the cars, occupied the train, and forced the engineer to take them back to Gunpowder Bridge. There the train was stopped, and the crowd set fire to the draw of the bridge and waited till that portion was burned; returning to Bush River Bridge, the draw was likewise burned. The mob then returned to Canton Bridge and burned that. The train then conveyed the mob to the President street station."

On April 20, Captain Wilson C. Nicholas, commander of a secessionist Maryland militia unit called the Garrison Forest Rangers, seized the Federal arsenal at Pikesville near Baltimore along with a deposit of ancient arms and a substantial supply of powder.[13]

From the windows, balconies, and rooftops throughout Baltimore, Confederate flags could now be seen fluttering in the breeze. On the day of the riot one expatriot Baltmorean, James Ryder Randall, was stirred by the resistance of his fellow Marylanders to pen an angry but sentimental poem. The words were soon placed to the tune of a college song, "Lauriger Horatius", by a beautiful young Baltimore socialite named Hetty Cary and renamed "Maryland! My Maryland." And so was born an anthem that would be embraced by Maryland secessionists and later become the official state anthem.

In the meantime telegraph communications between Washington and the North were cut off. Rail traffic to Baltimore from both the north and west was completely severed. The capital city of the United States was now totally isolated and virtually defenseless, as surmise and conjecture, fact and rumor, which had a thousand tongues, readily entwined. And it was just the beginning.

"Burning of the Gunpowder Creek Railroad bridge, on the Philadelphia and Baltimore Railroad, by the Maryland Secessionists." *Frank Leslie's Illustrated Newspapers.* Prints and Photographs Division, Library of Congress, Washington, D.C.

A third time Federal forces attempted to march to the rescue, this time with 2,000 Pennsylvania volunteers under General George C. Wynkoop; on April 21 they reached Cockeysville, Maryland, fourteen miles north of Baltimore. Between 400 and 500 armed Marylanders had gathered to oppose the "invasion." At that moment Mayor Brown and a small delegation of several prominent Baltimoreans, including Severn Teackle Wallis, George W. Dobins, and John C. Brune, were meeting with President Lincoln and General Scott to request that no new efforts be undertaken to send troops through Maryland. Then a telegram from John W. Garrett, president of the B&O Railroad, came in reporting that several thousand Northern troops were at Cockeysville. "Intense excitement prevails. Churches have been dismissed and the people are arming in mass. To prevent terrific bloodshed, the result of your interview and arrangement is awaited." Lincoln ordered Wynkoop to return to Harrisburg.[14]

The mob was not mollified. Word quickly spread that Fort McHenry would soon be attacked and that $500,000 had been placed at Mayor Brown's disposal by Baltimore industrialist Ross Winans to enhance the city defenses against the next Federal attempts to pass through. At the same time a corps of non-uniformed citizens was already being organized by Colonel Trimble and readied for a fight. Trimble was an imposing looking man whose rapidly receding hairline was countered by heavy, dark eyebrows and a massive drooping mustache that almost touched the bottom of his chin. It was said that by April 20 as many as 15,000 Marylanders, divided into three regiments of citizen militia, had enrolled under his command for the defense of Baltimore against Federal "incursion." At Winans' arms works the industrialist's entire labor force had set to making pikes for street fighting, and casting "balls of every description of cannon, the steam gun, rifles, muskets, etc., which they are turning out very rapidly." [15] Though its mayor blandly declared that all Baltimore was doing was simply maintaining its "armed neutrality," it seemed to many supporters of secession that the whole of Maryland would soon be joining the Confederacy.

The rabidly pro-secessionist *Richmond Examiner* echoed the prevailing sentiment of the South as a result of the riots, calling for the "cleansing and purification" of Washington, the "festering sink of iniquity, that wallow of Lincoln and Scott," by the capture of "Scott, the arch traitor" and Lincoln, the "Illinois Ape." There would be many carcasses, the paper predicted, "that will blacken the air upon the gallows," once the city had fallen.

> "The capture of Washington is perfectly within the power of Virginia and Maryland, if Virginia will only make the proper effort by her constituted authorities; nor is there a single moment to lose, the entire population pant for the onset; there never was half the unanimity among the people before, nor a tithe of the zeal upon any subject that is now manifested to take Washington, and drive from it every Black Republican who is a dweller there . . . From the mountain tops and valleys to the shores of the sea there is one wild shout of fierce resolve to capture Washington city at all and every human hazard. The filthy cage of unclean birds must and will assuredly be purified by fire." [16]

In Washington there were less than 1,000 U.S. Army troops and Marines under General Scott and John A. Dahlgren's command, and perhaps as many as 1,200 to 1,500 District of Columbia Volunteers available for the defense of the entire city. Panic and rumors soon prevailed. The majority of residents and government officialdom expected a massive rebel attack at any time, despite the arrival of the 600 to 700 Pennsylvania Volunteers from the recent Baltimore debacle. A mass exodus of many citizens was soon underway. It seemed quite clear that the capital was an untenable Federal enclave unless considerable help soon appeared.

It was to come by a most unlikely route.

Captain Philip Reybold was a Delaware ship owner quite familiar with the water routes between the Delaware and the Chesapeake. He suggested to the authorities in Philadelphia a most creative scheme to sidestep the secessionists in Baltimore and move Federal troops to the capital. A number of steamboats with dimensions suitable for traversing the Chesapeake and Delaware Canal, which connected Delaware Bay and the Chesapeake, might be temporarily employed to quickly move troops from Philadelphia to Annapolis. Once they reached the Maryland capital, they could proceed by railroad from that city to Washington. With canal locks being 220 feet long but only twenty-four feet wide, the big, beamy sidewheel steamers of the day were out of the question. But the new propeller steamers built specifically for such transits through the canal might be employed. A number of such vessels, sans passengers, could pass through the canal at night and converge at the little town of Perryville, Maryland, in the mouth of the Susquehanna River. There they could rendezvous with the point of the Federal spear, a number of Massachusetts troops brought in by rail. From there the troops could then board the vessels and steam directly for Annapolis, take and hold that city and secure the rail line to Washington until more powerful reenforcements could be sent by larger steamers via the Virginia Capes. Captain Samuel I. Du Pont, Commandant of the Philadelphia Navy Yard, immediately seized upon the concept, if not the actual practice, of bypassing Baltimore by water route from Perryville and set it into motion by commandeering all suitable steamboats in the vicinity of Philadelphia.[17]

The spear, however, was already sharpened and underway.

General Benjamin Franklin Butler, recently appointed by the Governor of Massachusetts to military command, had left Boston on April 18 with 724 militiamen belonging the 8th Massachusetts Volunteers. But with no direct rail access to Baltimore owing to the destruction of the bridges over the Gunpowder and Bush rivers he had been held up at Philadelphia. He nevertheless embraced the end run strategy suggested by Reybold and supported by Du Pont. Leaving Philadelphia by train on April 20 with cooked rations for three days, the New Englanders arrived without incident at Perryville on the north shore of the Susquehanna. With permission from the president of the Philadelphia, Wilmington, and Baltimore Railroad, Butler immediately commandeered the company's diminutive ferryboat *Maryland*. At midnight that same eve, with the 8th Massachusetts aboard, *Maryland* arrived in Annapolis Roads. Those aboard must have been stunned as they saw the town's houses lighted and the sky occasionally lit by rockets, perhaps announcing their arrival to rebels in the area.[18]

Major General Benjamin F. Butler. Brady National Photographic Art Gallery (Washington, D.C.), Prints and Photographs Division, Library of Congress, Washington, D.C.

Governor Hicks immediately sent a communication to the general advising him not to land as the "excitement here is very great, and I think you should take your men elsewhere," and then telegraphed the same advice to Secretary of War Simon Cameron. Having opposed the landing of troops, the governor now found himself strongly chastised by William L. W. Seabrook of Frederick County, Commissioner of the Maryland Land Office. Seabrook, it was said, asserted an enormous and almost mystical influence over the governor, and now accosted him for his actions. He strongly advised him that Butler and the Federal troops had as much right to be in Maryland as anyone, including himself, and hoped that he would not be influenced by the protests and would allow them to land. Hicks remained resolute.[19]

The governor did not limit his protests to Butler. He also assailed Superintendent of the U.S. Naval Academy George S. Blake, Secretary of State William H. Seward, and President Lincoln himself. Seward responded succinctly: "President [Lincoln] cannot but remember that there has been a time in the history of our country, when a General of the American Union, with forces designed for the defense of its Capital, was not unwelcome anywhere in the State of Maryland, and certainly not at Annapolis, then as now, the Capital of that patriotic State, and then also one of the Capitals of the Union." [20]

After conferring with Blake and ignoring the governor's protests, Butler quickly boarded the venerable sixty-five-year-old USS *Constitution*, then serving as a training ship for the Naval Academy, and wrestled her from the mud bottom in which she had become entrenched. With the aid of *Maryland* they proceeded to move her from the Severn River into Chesapeake Bay to prevent possible capture by rebels. At dawn the following day the 7th New York Regiment, known as the National Guard, commanded by Colonel Marshall Lefferts, arrived from Philadelphia aboard the steamer *Boston*. They found *Maryland* hard aground, possibly through complicity of her secessionist-leaning pilot, with Butler's troops still aboard with little food or water, after towing *Constitution* from the harbor.

The New Yorkers, many of them being prominent, well-heeled and well-connected businessmen, had left Manhattan amid great enthusiasm and with almost adoring support from the inhabitants. In every street therein "an immense innumerable throng cheered them on their way" as they marched to the train station for the trip to Philadelphia. When news of the fight in Baltimore was received just before their departure, every soldier was served out forty-eight rounds of ball cartridge. Upon their arrival in Annapolis Harbor they had cheered when they saw *Constitution* afloat with the stars and stripes flying above her, but were briefly shocked to see the glitter of bayonets, at first mistaken to be those of the enemy, moving about on the deck of *Maryland* where the Massachsuetts men were being drilled in the manual of arms. The first troops to land were the New Yorkers from aboard *Boston* since *Maryland* was still aground. But soon the New Englanders were offloaded and carried to the Naval Academy grounds as well.

Butler established headquarters in the City Tavern. The governor and local authorities, including Mayor John R. Magruder and a "Committee of the Government," and possibly Alderman Joshua Brown, superintendent of the Annapolis and Elkridge Railroad, met with the general to again protest the passage of troops over Maryland soil. The conference was not pleasant. The Marylanders declared the troopers couldn't come ashore because they simply could not get out of Annapolis, as the railroad company had taken up the tracks, which was the company's private property and within its rights to do. Moreover, they warned, if the troops passed over the railroad, it would be destroyed. Butler replied succinctly: "Sir, we came here not as citizens of Massachusetts, but as citizen soldiers of the United States, with no intention to invade any state, but to protect the Capitol of our common country from invasion. We shall give no cause of offence, but there must be no fugitive shots or any bricks on the way." He declared that his men "were not Northern troops, they are a part of the whole militia of the United States, obeying a call of the President." The landing on the grounds of the Naval Academy, which was U.S. Government property and not Maryland's sovereign territory, was "entirely proper and in accordance with your excellency's wishes." [21]

Though unwilling to agree, Hicks had to submit. "I content myself with protesting this movement," he said, "which, in view of the excited condition of the people of this State, I cannot but consider an unwise step on the part of the Government. But I most earnestly urge upon you that there shall be no halt made by the troops in this city." [22]

Butler was a balding, crosseyed, and altogether homely man bearing a drooping, most disagreeable looking mustache. He had nevertheless been a successful attorney before the war, and a failed 1860 Massachusetts gubernatorial candidate on the Breckinridge ticket, who rarely flinched. Once, while in college, he had written an essay denouncing "abolitionists for distributing incendiary publications" and exciting the rebellion of slaves. Now he set out with two companies of his regiment on a quickstep march from the waterfront to the Annapolis and Elkridge Railroad depot to help save the Union.

"The tracks had been torn up between Annapolis and the [Annapolis] Junction," which converged with the main B&O line between Baltimore and Washington, wrote one soldier belonging to the 7th New York. A locomotive found at the depot "had been taken to pieces by the inhabitants, in order to prevent our travel. In steps a Massachusetts volunteer [Private Charles Homans], looks at the piecemeal engine, takes up a flange, and says coolly, 'I made this engine, and I can put it together again.' Engineers were wanted when the engine was ready. Nineteen stepped out of the ranks. The rails were torn up. Practical railroad makers out of the regiment laid them again." The well planned sabotage had been substantial, as great sections of the track had been ripped up, with rails and wooden ties thrown off to the side, dumped in streams, or in the adjoining forest making recovery difficult if not impossible. Nevertheless, though lacking adequate tools, making do with what was at hand and replacing missing pieces from side switches, by the end of the day four miles of track had been completely repaired by the soldiers. Notwithstanding the rapid progress of Butler's small force, rumors regarding the landing at Annapolis were many.

One such unverified tale was reported in the pages of the *Richmond Enquirer* under the heading of "The New York Seventh Regiment Literally Cut to Pieces," purporting to carry a report carried by Lieutenant Charles Carroll Simms, USN, upon his arrival at Washington on April 22. The article alleged that Simms carried news "that the Seventh Regiment of New York was literally cut to pieces this morning, between Annapolis and Marlboro by the Maryland State troops." On April 25 a Washington newspaper reprinted the story, which was absolutely false, under the mocking headline "What Secession Feeds On." [23]

The occupation of Annapolis and seizure of the railroad had been a tactical victory for the Federal military intent on saving the capital of the United States, but for Governor Thomas Hicks it had proved a most embarrassing situation. On April 20, under intense pressure from a number of his constituents to call for a special session of the state legislature to resolve once and for all Maryland's allegiance, the governor was in a quandary. He was well aware that many if not all members of the legislature were sympathetic to the Confederacy. Some vocally supported Maryland secession at any cost, others advocated a peaceful withdrawal from the Union, and still others were dedicated to preserving peace and harmony within the Union. There were those, especially from the Southern Maryland delegation, who sought to maintain by law under the Constitution the continuance of the institution of slavery upon which their economy and very livelihoods depended. The decision to secede or remain was coming to a head, and much depended on the resolve of the President of the United States and Butler. Hicks made one more futile attempt to dissuade the general from proceeding. On April 23 he protested the actions regarding the railroad, this time declaring, "that such an occupation of said road will prevent the members of the Legislature from reaching this city" for the special session. [24]

Butler's response was direct and challenged the governor's rationale head on. If his troops could not pass via the railway line in one direction, he reasoned, how was it possible for the members of the legislature to pass in the oppposite direction? He had taken possession of the railroad specifically because the head railroad official in Annapolis had warned that if troops used trains the mob would destroy it. "I am endeavoring to save and not to destroy," he assured the governor, "to obtain a means of transportation, so I can vacate the capital prior to the sitting of the legislature, and not be under the painful necessity of occupying your beautiful city while the legislature is in session. " [25]

With unquestionable anguish Hicks determined to hold off as long as he could. Finally he set April 24 as the date for the extra session to convene.

The date set was perhaps of other significance as well, for it was the same moment that Federal authorities determined the danger to the U.S. Naval Academy as incontrovertible. The decision was made to order the operations of the Academy transferred to a "solid" northern state. Newport, Rhode Island was to become the new home of the Academy, and along with it went "Old Ironsides," the USS *Constitution*, the nation's most historic ship. On April 25, having offloaded her guns at the ancient fort on the Severn, the grand old frigate, manned by student mid-shipmen and faculty and laden with material for the new academy, got underway. With shoal waters befouling her progress she was taken under tow by the USS *R. R. Cuyler*, escorted by the USS *Harriet Lane*, and cleared for New York and Newport. On May 8 the steamer *Baltic* took aboard the Academy's officers, faculty, band, families and library and as much of the institution's property as possible. Both *Constitution* and *Baltic* arrived at Newport on May 9. [26]

***

Such a dangerous event as the Maryland General Assembly possibly voting for secession, in the very presence of Federal troops, seemed to Secretary of the Treasury Salmon P. Chase total anathema. If Maryland joined the Confederacy, he believed, the strength of the rebellion would be trebled. "Do not, I pray you, let this new success of treason be inaugurated in the presence of American troops," he implored Lincoln. "Save us from this near humiliation." Why not order General Scott to secure the state once and for all for the Union? "A word to the brave old commanding General will do the work of preservation, and you alone can give the word." [27]

Two days before the special legislative session was to begin, the determination of the Lincoln Administration to stand fast was reinforced when several delegations of citizen's committees from Maryland sought and secured an audience with the president. Their objective was to procure the executive countermanding of the order for troops to march through their state en route to the capital. One delegation, numbering thirty individuals from five Young Men's Christian Associations in Baltimore led by South Carolina-born slaveholder Richard Fuller, pastor of Baltimore's Seventh Baptist Church and president of the Southern Baptist Convention, had a prolonged interview "but made no impression" upon the chief executive. At that same moment, Confederate President Jefferson Davis, while informing Governor Letcher of Virginia that more troops were on the way to his state, was urging him to also "sustain Baltimore if practicable." Thus it was not surprising that Lincoln's response to the YMCA delegation was blunt: "You express your great horror of bloodshed, and yet would not lay a straw in the way of those who are organizing in Virginia and elsewhere to capture this city." Stressing that he still had no desire to invade the South, he was obliged to defend the capital of the nation. "Keep your rowdies in Baltimore," he added before dismissing the citizens committee, "and there will be no bloodshed." Nevertheless, reinforcing the views of the delegation, Hicks also presented a plea to the president, again urging the withdrawal of troops from Maryland, a cessation of hostilities, and the referral of the national dispute to the arbitration of Lord Lyons, the minister of Great Britain. Secretary Seward responded for the administration by succinctly reminding the governor that the troops had only been called out to suppress an insurrection and must come through Maryland as it was the route – the only fast and feasible route – to the capital and was chosen by the Commander in Chief himself. Moreover, he concluded, the nation's troubles were internal affairs and could not and would not be "referred to any foreign arbitration." [28]

Hicks found himself in an even more distressing situation than before. Should the legislature vote for secession and the Confederacy, as most expected it would, the strong Federal military presence in Annapolis would most certainly promulgate bloodshed if not outright rebellion in the state capital. In a play for more time he again changed the date of the special session to April 26 "to deliberate and consider the condition of the State, and take such measures as in their wisdom they may deem fit to maintain peace, order and security within our limits."

The mood in Annapolis was dour at best. A journalist, Charles Henry Webb of the *New York Times*, reported from the city on April 26: "Owing to the blockade of the Port and the seizure of the railroad, no provisions can be brought into

Annapolis, and the inhabitants apprehend famine. The leading hotel was unable, yesterday morning, to furnish breakfast for myself and a friend, and we were obliged to scout around town for a meal. Flour has been sold at $20 per barrel. The troops have provisions in plenty, and this irritates the inhabitants. Not a Union flag is to be seen, nor did I hear a loyal sentiment uttered in the City. They blame the North for all their troubles, and express hatred towards the troops." [29]

Myriad rumors had by now begun to race about the town regarding Federal intentions and the almost unanimous "impression" that the legislature was about to pass an ordinance of secession. But one tale, which began to circulate on April 23, that caused a particular stir was "that negroes across the Severn were in a state of insurrection," and that Butler had offered to place his troops at the command of Governor Hicks to quell the uprising – all of which was pure fiction. Whatever the truth was, however, the presence of so many soldiers was most unsettling to the citizens of Annapolis, even among those who were pro-Union. Many residents began to leave for the safer countryside. "The people of Annapolis are highly indignant at the occupation of our city," reported the *Annapolis Gazette*. "But, we are powerless to oppose them. Yielding to the advice of the more prudent, our people have refrained from any open demonstration against the troops . . . The excitement here is terrible. No man seems to know what should be done to avert the evil that has come upon us; and all admit that we are utterly powerless to offer any resistance." [30]

Undeterred by rumors, the unsettled grumblings of city residents and fearing attack by rebel sympathizers, Butler proceeded to consolidate his defensive posture in Annapolis. Occasional signal rockets observed on outlying roads, presumably sent up by the enemy, prompted the dispatch of 200 soldiers to the outskirts of town, backed by a number of watercraft on the adjacent waterways suitable to transport reinforcements if need be. Troops belonging to the 6th New York, which had just arrived, were stationed at old forts Madison and Nonsense, guarding the Severn and the town. The former, a semi-elliptical defense work built ca. 1808, was originally a thirteen-gun emplacement constructed on Carr Point, while the latter was an 80-foot diameter circular earthwork, constructed ca. 1810 on Bieman's Hill as an outer defense for Fort Madison, near what would one day become the Commandant's Quarters at the U.S. Naval Academy. Armed with four guns each, the steam ferry *Maryland* and an iceboat donated by the City of Philadelphia were sent out to maintain a patrol of the Severn. The narrow but strategic land bridge between Spa and College creeks was fortified with entrenchments even as earth-works were being thrown up a half mile from the town on the farm of Judge Nicholas Brewer to protect the rail line to Annapolis Junction and the West Street approach. The general's muscular defensive posture was to maintain 1,300 troops from New York and Massachusetts in Annapolis. As new troops came in, a line of 1,100 more men was to be deployed between the town and Annapolis Junction. To maintain his interior line of communication he ordered tracks be laid down between the town's railroad depot on the corner of Calvert and West streets to the reception wharf at the U.S. Naval Academy. The move would insure rapid offloading of reinforcements and materiel and the restoration of transit to Washington via Annapolis

Junction. No one, however, had any concept of the damage that had been caused by the rebels.[31]

On April 24 the New York volunteer regiments began the hazardous but successful operations to reopen the heavily sabotaged railroad connection between the city and Annapolis Junction, fifteen miles south of Baltimore. The operation, driven by necessity, was innovative. First, the tops of a pair of cattle cars were removed to make flat cars. The first car was armed with a howitzer loaded with grape shot and protected by sixteen soldiers. The gun's ammunition and six more soldiers were stacked on the second. Next came the locomotive that had been repaired and driven by Private Charles Homans, followed by a pair of small passenger cars each carrying a company of New York infantrymen. Thus outfitted the unique rail-mounted battery and transport began its journey from Annapolis. Approximately five miles from the city, the train encountered a gaggle of rebels engaged in ripping up the tracks. Within seconds of sighting the train the party scattered and vanished into the countryside. Soon the damage had been repaired and the first two cars, bearing the howitzer and ammunition, were detached. Drag lines were coupled to pull them along thereby avoiding the possibility of derailment where rebels had injured the tracks. Stopping from time to time to make repairs on the dismantled rails, the detachment finally arrived at the hamlet of Millersville at 2 p.m. Here the rebels had again savaged the line, this time by completely destroying a bridge. Undeterred, the New Yorkers set to work and by sunset a new bridge had been erected; they then continued their slow advance through the night. At 4 a.m. they finally arrived at Annapolis Junction. On the morning of April 25 the 7th New York began boarding a special train at Annapolis bound for the nation's capital. [32] In Washington unvarnished anxiety prevailed regarding their delayed arrival, and the much feared attack of the enemy at any moment. But what was now important was that the critical connection between Annapolis and Washington had finally been made. The great port on the Patapsco, however, was another matter!

It appeared to many in Baltimore that their city, if not entirely in the hands of secessionists, would soon be. Recruitment by Major George Steuart of the 1st Light Division, the city's official militia unit, had progressed rapidly, including a unit called the Guerilla Corps. They were soon outfitted with 3,000 stands of arms, primarily revolvers, collected from the citizenry by the Board of Police, although with their numbers now estimated at 15,000, they were poorly armed indeed. On April 22 Colonel Trimble, who had been actively organizing a corps of civilians from a plethora of avowed secessionists, while now acting under the direct orders of Mayor Brown and the Board of Police, set to establishing an embargo. Its purpose was to insure "that no provisions of any kind be transferred from the City of Baltimore to any point or place from this time, until further orders, without special permission." Thereafter no steamboat would be permitted to leave the city harbor without a permit. Though the Federals had succeeded on their end run around Baltimore, there would be no assistance in such future endeavors if Brown could help it.[33]

A Baltimore correspondent for the Washington *Daily National Republican*, an ardent Unionist publication, while on "a pleasant and agreeable ride of two hours and a half" over the Washington branch of the B&O Railroad, reported on April 24 of the chaotic situation still extant in the city on the Patapsco River.

Top. "Frank Pierce, a soldier of the Eighth Massachusetts Regiment, diving for a missing rail on the road from Annapolis to Washington." Prints and Photographs Division, Library of Congress, Washington, D.C. Bottom. "Annapolis Junction, on the Washington branch of the Baltimore and Ohio Railroad, in possession of the troops of the United States government." *Frank Leslie's Illustrated Newspapers.* Prints and Photographs Division, Library of Congress.

"Upon passing through the principal streets, citizen soldiers were to be seen in squads at almost every corner, and now and then five, ten, and fifteen recruits were observed moving in the direction of the Susquehanna Railroad Depot, where, it is stated, they are to be put through a regular course of Scott's Infantry tactics, preparatory to their reception into regular organized companies, for the purpose of preventing the passage of any more troops which may be sent from Pennsylvania or elsewhere to defend your city [Washington]. It is very evident that anarchy reigns supreme throughout the city, and that the mayor, who pretends to govern it, is no more nor less than a mere cat's-paw in the hands of a brutal, drunken mob, who would, in order to gratify their rabid appetites, and also for a 'change,' see the city a mass of smouldering ruins. Had Mayor Brown crushed this hydra-headed monster of mobocracy in the beginning, he would not have to succumb to it." [34]

In the meantime, well cognizant of the situation in Baltimore and fearing the outcome of a legislative meeting in Annapolis, on April 24 Hicks ordered the special session of the General Assembly to convene not in Annapolis, where Butler was likely to close it down, but in Frederick, in Western Maryland, far from the general's reach. The move was not unwarranted. The general had bluntly informed him that if the legislature undertook, with or without the governor's recommendation, to even discuss an ordinance of secession that it would be considered "an act of hostility to the United States." In no uncertain terms the general then threatened to "disperse that Legislature or more properly speaking, would shut them up together where they might discuss it all the time, but without any correspondence or reporting from the outer world." Hicks was unquestionably intimidated. Undoubtedly to help quell the general's animosity, and at the same time prevent the possibility of a writ of secession being issued by the assembly, the governor placed the Great Seal of Maryland in Butler's possession for the duration of the legislative session. Without the seal no binding legislation could be officially enacted into law.

The assembly dutifully convened in Frederick at 1 p.m. in the county court-house. In his message to the legislature the governor urged moderation and the avoidance of any strong statements in behalf of either the Union or Confederacy. Nevertheless, the Prince George's County delegation submitted a memorial requesting passage of an immediate act of secession, which was met by a rejoinder from the Committee on Federal Relations. On April 27 and 28, in spite of the back room politicking by pro-secessionists, the committee declared that the legislature lacked the constitutional authority to undertake any actions that might lead to departure from the Union. A decision to secede would have to be the result of a duly elected convention as prescribed by the Maryland Constitution of 1851. By a direct vote in the House of Delegates on April 29 the move to secede was defeated 53 to 13. The State Senate then published an address, signed by all its members, denying any intention of passing an ordinance of secession. But permitting Maryland to participate in the war was something else. On Thursday, May 9 the firebrand pro-secessionist Severn Teackle Wallis, Chairman of the Committee on Federal Relations of the Maryland House of Delegates, submitted a report and resolutions declaring "the war waged by the United States upon the people of the Confederate

States" unconstitutional, repugnant to civilization and sound policy, and subversive of free institutions.

A protest was entered against the war on the part of the State, that it would take no part directly or indirectly in its prosecution. An assertion was made that Maryland desired the peaceful and immediate recognition of the independence of the seceded states. The "present military occupation of the State of Maryland" was protested against as unconstitutional, oppressive, and illegal. The final resolutions asserted that under existing circumstances it was unexpected to call a "Sovereign Convention" at that time, or to take any measures for the immediate arming and organization of the militia. And finally, Wallis proposed adjournment of the legislature to a day to be named. The report was adopted—yeas 40, nays 11—and the resolutions made the order of the day for May. Soon after the General Assembly, by a vote in the House of 43-12, and in the Senate of 11 to 3, passed the series of resolutions protesting the war as unjust. The body then announced a determination to take no part in its prosecution, and expressed a desire for immediate recognition of the Confederacy.[35]

It was not secession, but it was definitely not pro-Union. The call for recognition of the Confederacy was deemed by many in the Federal establishment as nothing less than treason. Those who registered in the affirmative would soon pay an unwelcomed price for their vote.

The State would officially remain with the Union, but the heart of Southern Maryland was obviously another matter. By then a mass migration southward had already begun, even as the President of the United States was taking draconian measures. On April 27 Lincoln ordered the suspension of *habeas corpus* all along Maryland's railroad lines. It was an action that would soon be expanded to permit the arrest and imprisonment without charges, benefit of trial or right of defense of any suspected dissident in the State of Maryland. Henceforth, in the name of putting down the rebellion and maintaining the preservation of the Union, the suppression of the civil liberties of those accused of secessionist sympathies was but a taste of what was to come. Free public expressions deemed suspicious or unloyal, having friends or relatives who fled to the Confederacy, communications of any kind with anyone in the South, or even wearing colors that were the same as those in the Confederate flag were subject to possible arrest and imprisonment without benefit of charge or legal counsel. Military arrests, imposition of martial law in Border States, and the use of military courts to try offenders of military and martial law alike would become the order of the day. It was, indeed, to be with a heavy hand that Maryland would be retained in the Union. And for many, it was to be nothing less than a nightmare.

The Constitution of the United States of America, Southern Marylanders protested, had been seriously violated.

4

YOUR HONOR AND YOUR CHIVALRY
"To deport ourselves as soldiers of Honor."

At first, the counties bordering the Southern Maryland watersheds were unaware of the turn of events in Annapolis and would soon enough reel in horror from the countermeasures instituted by the Federal Government. Yet, inspired by the aggressive secessionist actions of the Baltimoreans and heartened by the still strong probability that Maryland would follow in the footsteps of her "Sister" states below the Mason-Dixon Line, they were emboldened to action as never before.

On April 23, even as Federal troops were readying to entrain at Annapolis for Washington, the meeting that had been called for in Leonardtown days earlier to address what that county's next move should be proved to be "decidedly the largest that ever convened in the county . . . composed of both Military and citizens." By some accounts between 800 to 1,000 individuals were in attendance.[1]

The St. Mary's militia and paramilitary groups turned out in full strength. Together with the citizenry from all over the county they began to pour into the town early in the morning. By noon the usually quiet streets "presented an appearance of sabre and bayonet that forcibly reminded the beholder of a field of battle." Captain Robert Neale's St. Mary's Guards were the first to arrive, followed soon after by Captain J. Edwin Coad's Clifton Guards and Captain Randolph Jones's St. Inigoe's Dragoons. All were received by the town's own Riley Rifles led by Captain James T. M. Raley. Although a full company from Charlotte Hall was unable to attend owing to the absence of its young commander, Captain Richard Thomas, who was away in Baltimore, several members were present and "attracted considerable notice by their soldierly appearance and handsome uniform." Another new company just in the process of being formed in the Clifton Factory District by Captain Reeves also sent a delegation "and came in for a liberal share of adulation." After a "very handsome parade" through the crowded village streets, the troops were dismissed for midday dinner.[2]

Then the largest public meeting ever held in St. Mary's County was formally convened "for the purpose of considering the present crisis and adopting measures for the defence of our rights, the security of our homes, and the maintenance of the honor of our State." The foremost men of the county, all men of great standing, stepped forward to conduct the proceedings. Colonel Benedict I. Heard was unanimously elected president, while Colonel Cornelius Combs, Chapman Billingsley, and Colonel John H. Sothoron, were elected vice presidents. Most were elder leaders of the county and well aware of the dangers they faced, some having witnessed or directly suffered from the British depredations in St. Mary's during the War of 1812. L. W. B. Hutchins and John P. King acted as secretaries. The Reverend Dr. James Bunting from Budds Creek then invoked "in fervent and eloquent terms the Divine blessing upon the cause for the furtherance of which the meeting was convened." [3]

The meeting followed the formal rules of parliamentary procedure in the strictest terms, which was for all present a general source of pride. On motion a committee of six, one from each election district in the county, was appointed by the chair to report resolutions expressive of the views of the meeting.[4] While the committee retired to confer, the assembly was regaled by speeches from six of the more notable men of the county, John H. Sothoron, Chapman Billingsley, Oscar Miles, J. Edwin Coad, Dr. Robert F. Neale, and James T. Blackistone, as well as Colonel Nathaniel Duke from neighboring Calvert County, who had served in the State Assembly. Stirring words were presented by all in forcible and eloquent terms and "in vindication of Southern rights and the honor of our State." Then, the chairman of the resolutions committee appeared and read the preamble and proposed resolutions. [5] The Preamble was clear and concise in presenting the agenda.

"In times of extraordinary political emergency like the present – when there is a sectional Administration of what is now called the United States of America – when there is a determined purpose on the part of those controlling such Administration to deprive nearly half of those States of their equal rights in the administration of the Government, and the enjoyment of equal privileges within the limits of the same in violation of the letter and spirit of the constitution of the United States – when eight States have determined, by the sovereign will of their people, that they have severed their connection with the said sectional Government, by invading their soil, blockading their ports, destroying their commerce and trade, and in every way aggressing their rights and Institutions with a view to force them to submission, it is due to the people of those States, that the people of all other States, friendly to Justice and Right, and to those principals [*sic*] of Freedom and Independence which promoted our Forefathers to resist aggression and wrong, should express their sympathy with this cause of Right, against the cause of might and tyranny.

Therefore, we, the citizens of Saint Mary's County, Maryland, in County meeting assembled, do earnestly and devotedly express our sympathies with the cause and people of the States which have seceded from the Union, and do pledge ourselves by every sacred obligation we can assume, to aid, by every means in our power, in securing the Independence of all those States, and that of such others as may join them." [6]

Three major resolutions were then offered up for consideration. The first was that a levy upon the assessable property of the people of St. Mary's County be authorized by the County Commissioners to raise $10,000 "for the purpose of purchasing arms and ammunition for our people, in order that they may be enabled to defend their rights, and the honor and interest of our State." The resolution passed unanimously.

The second resolution was that a committee of public safety consisting of twelve men be appointed to take the necessary steps to procure sidearms and munitions, which the County Commissioners were duly authorized to purchase and distribute. The committee would also be authorized by popular consent "to take such general steps for the public safety as in their judgment may be required" and to appoint a subcommittee of not more than three "to call the people of the county together, for consultation, at such time and place as in their judgment may be necessary." The committee of safety would include: Colonel Theophilus Harrison, Colonel John H. Sothoron, Dr. Robert F. Neale, Dr. James Waring, Richard H.

Reeder, Colonel Chapman Billingsley, Colonel Benjamin G. Harris, Francis J. Stone, Thomas Loker, Thomas O. Spencer, Dr. J. W. Forrest and Edward S. Abell, Dr. Walter Briscoe and William H. Thomas. Like the first resolution, the second passed unanimously.[7]

"St. Mary's County." Simon J. Martinet, Baltimore, 1861, Geography and Map Division, Library of Congress, Washington, D.C.

The final resolution was uncontested: "That we mourn over the graves of our fellow citizens who lost their lives in the city of Baltimore, while heroically and even without arms, defending our common right and the soil of our State from the pollution of the steps of the enemies of both – the mercenary soldiers of Massachusetts – and have taught that bigoted and fanatical people, that there can be a 'Lexington' elsewhere than on their soil, which now disgraces its sacred memory." [8]

A motion was then made and carried that a committee of three be appointed by the chair to meet with the County Commissioners to formally request them to levy the $10,000 requested for arms and ammunition. Benjamin G. Harris, Dr. Walter

Briscoe and William H. Thomas were appointed and immediately called upon the commissioners. "The Committee soon returned and reported that the Court had responded to the request to double the sum called for if necessary. As soon as it was known that this action had been taken, a patriotic citizen of this county promptly agreed to furnish the money to the amount of the levy." [9]

By 6 p.m. the throngs of citizens and militia that had gathered in the county seat of St. Mary's to define their loyalties in the impending conflict had departed for home, certain of the correctness of their course and zealous in their cause.[10]

The militaristic and, one could say, even romantically chivalrous zeal for union with the newly seceded states was never more symbolically expressed in Southern Maryland than after the meeting. With great ceremony the crinoline clad ladies of Leonardtown presented a handsome new flag to the Riley Rifles, among whose ranks contained some of the most ardent secessionists in the county. Boldly adopted from the new flag of the Confederate States, it "bore upon its folds eight stars and a portion of a ninth, intended to represent the seceded States, and Maryland just emerging from her, heretofore, doubtful position and allying her destiny with her sister States of the South," and was presented to the unit accompanied by great applause. By the first week in May the ladies had been given a new task, the manufacture of undress uniforms and "other campaign equipments" necessary for the unit and suitable for going to war.[11]

The sentiments of St. Mary's citizenry had never been a secret. Nor had their efforts to take steps to prepare for the eventuality of war as every motion was proudly reported in the pages of the *St. Mary's Beacon*. As early as March 1859 the first effort to organize a military unit called the St. Mary's Dragoons was readily achieved. Another company, the St. Inigoes Dragoons was formed in January 1860, followed less than a month later with the organization of the Clifton Rifles.

In April, soon after the Riley Rifles were founded, they had been suitably uniformed enough to hold a full dress parade in Leonardtown. With the end of the year and news of the pending secession of South Carolina, the citizenry in the county seat moved to organize the Leonardtown Home Guard. And still the call to arms sounded. In February 1861 residents of the Patuxent District formed an infantry company dubbed the Smallwood Vigilants.[12]

Martial ardor continued to soar as the New Year matured and more military organizations formed. Advertisements for recruits soon proliferated. "Volunteers wanted," read one such notice in the *St. Mary's Beacon*. "Citizens of the County desirous of uniting in formation of a Cavalry Company are requested to leave their name at the store of Messrs. Simms and Maddox in the village [of Leonardtown]." [13]

As the cusp of spring approached, war fervor in St. Mary's had exploded exponentially, and the sentiments of countians became ever more pronounced and public. The issues regarding the preservation of the Union, states' rights and questions regarding Federal supremacy and the possible abolition of slavery were no longer intangible subjects merely to be debated. Rhetoric and hyperbole had become inflammable properties embraced by all. At the annual Washington's Birthday celebration, convened in the heart of the county at Great Mills, expressions of support for the newly born Confederacy were abundant.

A deft display of military drill by the Clifton Guards who were hosting the affair and the St. Inigoes Dragoons was followed by an oration by George Thomas of Mattapany. Then glasses were raised in many toasts to states' rights and Maryland's sisterhood with Virginia. One of the local dignitaries, Captain J. Edwin Coad, offered a toast to "The Union and Constitutional rights of all the States, for the sake of the States, but under any circumstances, and under all circumstances, the Union of the South for the Sake of the South." Another was raised by Major John H. Milburn to "Our rights in the Union, if we can, but our rights in or out of the Union." Lieutenant Henry I. Carroll offered a toast to Jefferson Davis, "President of the Southern Republic." Perhaps the most arousing was presented by Thomas W. Gough of Medley Neck, one of the incorporators of the only major industrial operation in the county, the Clifton Manufacturing Company in Great Mills. "The State of Maryland and Virginia have grown together in prosperity, they should cling together in adversity," he said boldly, raising his cup high. "Like the Siamese Twins to divide them would be to kill them." Captain Randolph Jones, a physician from St. Inigoes, concluded: "Gentlemen, I have not been taught to dance or speak, but what I hope is better, I have been taught to stand shoulder to shoulder with brave friends ready to smite the enemy of my country." [14]

Within weeks several more new companies were being formed in the county, all belonging to the St. Mary's Light Infantry, Maryland Volunteers, whose barracks were to be in the "dwelling house at Mattapany," on Colonel Thomas's plantation, which could suitably quarter 200 men. At Charlotte Hall a company calling itself the St. Mary's Rangers, Captain Joseph Forrest commanding, had begun training and drilling in an encampment near the village, "familiarizing themselves with the hardships of camp life and perfecting themselves in the detail of drill, &c."

On Bedlam Neck in the Chaptico District the Oakley Rifles, Captain Walter Dent commanding, was organized from a base of thirty-five volunteers, which by May 9 was reported to be growing in strength by the hour. Citizens' support for provisions, uniforms, and money to obtain such necessities was readily solicited for the new units. But the needs were significant among forces that were becoming a blend of patricians and commoners, most being farmers with similar religious beliefs, ethnic ancestry, and political convictions despite their class status. "Some young men," it was advertised in one public appeal for assistance, "are willing to serve their country, but are absolutely unable to supply themselves with uniforms or camp equipage of any kind." [15]

The organization of military units in Southern Maryland was not limited to St. Mary's. In Calvert County two companies of cavalry, one dubbed the Southern Guards and the other the Calvert Cadets, each numbering forty men, had already formed. The Southern Guards, under Captain George D. Lyles, had been organized almost a year earlier as war clouds began to form, while the Cadets had been established in January 1861 under Captain Basil Duke Bond. Both were fully armed and equipped and by the time of the surrender of Sumter were already the toast of local society. Indeed, on March 16 a grand dinner at Plum Point on the Chesapeake Bay side of the Calvert peninsula was attended by over 300 ladies and gentlemen of the county. After dinner and speeches by captains Lyles and Bond, two of their lieutenants and several others, a grand military parade by the troops and entertainment were provided to the delight of all.[16]

In Charles County volunteer units began to drill and flash their military muscle, some long authorized under the state system, and others organized immediately before or inspired by the formation of the Confederates States at Montgomery, Alabama on February 6, 1861. As early as late December 1860 a meeting was assembled at Allen's Fresh to form a "permanent organized rifle company." A unit calling itself the Patuxent Mounted Guard of Patuxent City was formed and accoutered in uniform coats of fine blue cloth, lavishly trimmed with gold lace, and pants to match with a broad strip of orange on the outer seam, provided by the establishment of Thomas McCormick of Carroll Hall in Baltimore. In Anne Arundel Southern sympathy was visibly apparent when a spirited youth in Annapolis hoisted the Palmetto Flag of South Carolina near St. Anne's Church. Though Unionists pulled down the flag and the lad suffered injuries from the scuffle, the fractious division of sentiments were no longer limited to heated discussions.

In January 1861 a unit called the Mounted Volunteers, which had been drilling in the Charles County seat at Port Tobacco, began seeking public subscriptions for arms and ammunition and other accoutrements that the State had not furnished for them. Sixteen delegates were dispatched to the four county election districts to solicit funds. In Bryantown an infantry rifle company, the Bryantown Minute Men, convened to elect officers for the newly forming company. And in Nanjemoy the Nanjemoy Rifle Company was ordered to meet in the hamlet of Trappe. Another unit, the Smallwood Rifles (not to be confused with the Smallwood Vigilants of St. Mary's), captained by the owner and editor of the *Port Tobacco Times*, Elijah Wells, and armed with "Mini rifles" drilled every Saturday in the Port Tobacco town square under a flag presented by the ladies of Charles County. At the presentation the unit formally "Resolved, That we hereby pledge our services to the State of Maryland for the protection of her honor and fair game under the Constitution of the United States, as given to us by our forefathers in its original purity." Thereafter they began to parade monthly in the town.[17]

Even in Upper Marlboro, the seat of Prince George's, Captain F. B. Schaffer, formerly of the National Rifles of Washington, had begun a recruitment effort to organize a "secessionist company" that could be rallied to the Southern cause at a moment's notice. Another countian, John Contee, had already begun to organize a unit dubbed the Planter's Guard. In Vansville Captain Edward Herbert was organizing the Vansville Rangers, and in Piscataway Captain George R. W. Marshall mustered the Piscataway Rifles. In Upper Marlboro a unit of cavalry dubbed the Mounted Rifles was said to have been organized by Oden Bowie, Chairman of the Maryland Democratic Central Committee, veteran of the Mexican War, horse breeder, longtime Member of the Maryland House of Delegates, and first president of the infant Baltimore and Potomac Railroad. Other companies such as Captain John K. Pumphrey's Independent Guards and John H. Skinner's Patuxent Rifles, both of Nottingham, and the Potomac Riflemen, though new and untested, were almost certainly of secessionist sympathies. By April 21 it was being reported in the Baltimore press that the "light cavalry of Prince George" was "swarming to the very edge of the District." On that same day telegraph service to and from the city had been cut.[18]

Recruitment in the counties lining the lower Patuxent and Potomac was aggressive, particularly in St. Mary's and Charles. Those vested with organizing were not above employing the fair sex to facilitate the process. It was for many an attraction of great potency, a noble and chivalrous presentment wherein young men, imbued with the vision of gallantry and glory, could defend their cause and the very flower of womanhood against all odds for honor and state.

In one recruiting notice for a company of the St. Mary's Light Infantry was stated the names of several prominent young ladies of the county, all but one being unmarried, who had been placed in charge of the recruiting list for sign ups. A potential recruit could also enroll with any one of seventeen or more names of notable militia colonels and county patricians who were authorized to enlist men for service. This of course added a certain pedigree to the process. Moreover, the romantic notions of soldiering, evoking the chivalrous mythos of Sir Walter Scott, had an allure in Southern culture that was magnetic.

There was some intrinsic charm in that one of the favorite pastimes of Southern Maryland was embodied in the very storied concept of gallant and courtly combat on the field of honor in symbolic defense of virtuous womanhood itself. The sport of jousting, a tamer replication of medieval tournament jousting, wherein spearing a ring with a lance while on horseback rather than unseating an opponent from his steed was regularly held at colorful annual festivals throughout the region. At one such tournament held at Piscataway before the war the local press reported in an article celebrating the gaiety and chivalric mindset of the times. At the event, Compton Barnes, the winner, "carried the crown, solid gold, handsomely chased, surmounted with a star of gold with a large diamond in the center to the Forbidden Knight and made an appropriate address." The crowning of the queen and her court followed in glorious pagentry.[19]

It was perhaps a natural step to appeal to that same noble standard of sacrifice and glory in the recruitment advertisements appearing in the local press. "Young Marylanders," read one such appeal, "who are worthy of man's esteem or woman's love, rally now in the name of your honor and your chivalry; if it must be so, resolve, as did a brave old chief, to make a grave which shall be bloody work for your enemies to dig, and where the passing traveler may pause and say how gloriously you died." [20]

A typical enlistment form for Company A of the St. Mary's Light Infantry required only the name of the individual enrolling, his recruitment number, the name of his commanding officer, and a "promise to join the above company, organized for active service . . . To report for duty at head Quarters one day after signing" and "To deport ourselves as soldiers of Honor." Organizers were not without vision concerning the need for more than volunteers for service. An address to the possible requirement, if deemed necessary, for a general draft in St. Mary's County was handled with velvet gloves when "friends of Maryland, and particularly those of the better sex," were "invited to prepare a list as below, and obtain thereto the names of all young men worth having, who are not members of some company which is for active service." [21]

All along the lower Patuxent-Potomac-Chesapeake drainage axis young men and old, from prominent and lesser families alike, rapidly began to turn out to enlist in local units to defend their state, acting in the full belief that Maryland would join with her seceding sisters across the Potomac and beyond. Those in the agrarian southern counties accepted the potential growth of Federal military power in the urban centers of Washington, Annapolis and Baltimore almost as a challenge to the culture of self reliance, the dominant system of Southern patriarchy and even manhood itself. Well into the spring all hope of redeeming what was perceived as an assault on the very core of white virtues and values was heavily vested with the Maryland State Senate and House of Delegates, both well known as bastions of Southern ideals.

"The spirit of our people are in no wise daunted by the imposing military force in Washington," wrote James S. Downs, the defiant editor of the *St. Mary's Beacon*, "nor by the armed occupation of our State nor by the truculent threats of the [New York] *Post* and [New York] *Tribune* and other organs of Northern Sentiment. They place full confidence in the wisdom and integrity of the Legislature, and doubt not that it will make ample provision for arming the people of the State and will enable them, by authorizing the call of a Sovereign Convention, to elect whether they will make aggressive war upon their Southern sisters or manfully cast their destiny where both their honor and their interest demand they should go." [22]

And throughout all of Southern Maryland, still unfazed by the tumultuous turn of events as one historian so aptly noted, teenage boys whose lives would soon be violently altered forever after, as before every war, still went hunting and fishing, breaking colts, plowing fields, going to picnics, barn dances and other gatherings of youth with the same vim and enthusiasm as their ancestors. Most believed the war would be a short one and the South, with Maryland as a member state, would be forever free of the Union.[23] All trust for integration into the Southern Confederacy had been pinned on the Maryland Legislature.

Such hopes of immediate gratification were of course soon to be brutally demolished with the arrival of accounts of the proceedings of the special session of the Maryland Assembly in Frederick. Not only had the government been officially obliged to move against secession, the governor himself, once viewed by most as a stalwart of the Old South as recently as the Pratt Street Riot, now revealed himself as a Unionist. One of his first moves following the session was an attempt to prevent the organization and manning of paramilitary groups in the state.

The organization of unauthorized volunteer military units in Southern Maryland and elsewhere in Maryland, ostensibly raised for its defense (should a legislative move towards secession become more than a mere chimera), had been a serious concern of Federal military and loyal state civil authorities. Some control had to be established if they hoped to maintain Union command along the northern shores of the Potomac. From his temporary executive chamber in Frederick Governor Hicks issued the order on April 28 outright forbidding such activities.[24]

The proclamation, eventually published in St. Mary's County on May 9, was accepted by most white Southern Marylanders as little more than the work of a despicable traitor to his own state. For the secessionists who had counted upon the legislature to vote for joining the Confederacy it had been preceded by even more upsetting news. On April 27 President Abraham Lincoln had extended the "Anaconda Plan" blockade of southern states to include Virginia and North Carolina, both of which had just formally seceded and joined the Confederacy. From Washington, D.C. to the Rio Grande, the U.S. Navy was now charged with the strangulation of all Confederate maritime commerce and trade to destroy the South's economic ability to wage war. The northernmost extent of the great blockade would be the Potomac River, the southern frontier of Prince George's, Charles and St. Mary's counties. Now even crossing the waterway, which had been a significant commercial artery between Maryland and Virginia and the major outlet to the wider world of commerce, might be construed as treasonous.

That same day the War Department issued General Order No 12 creating a new military department headquartered in the state capital called the Department of Annapolis with General Butler as commander. As Hicks had feared the U.S. Army was now there to stay. The department included all territory twenty miles on each side of the railroad line between Annapolis and Washington. It extended at least as far as the town of Bladensburg, Maryland, terminus of the line on the eastern border of the District of Columbia. Included in the order was a directive placing Fort Adams in Rhode Island under the temporary control of the Secretary of the Navy to serve as the U.S. Naval Academy. Colonel Joseph K. F. Mansfield was detailed to command the newly designated Department of Washington. Thus, a veritable line of demarcation had been drawn symbolically and militarily separating Southern Maryland from the rest of the state. Four days later the U.S. Navy Department authorized the formation of the Potomac Flotilla, first as a component of the Atlantic Blockading Squadron and eventually as an independent unit, to patrol the waters between Southern Maryland and the Virginia shores. The City of Washington thus become the northern terminus of the Union naval blockade of the Confederacy, the "Anaconda's Tail" of General Scott's much ballyhooed and oft ridiculed effort to strangle the Confederacy by sea. The lower counties of Western Shore Maryland had overnight become an island of secessionists seemingly cut off from active participation in the rebellion.[25]

On May 3 President Lincoln issued a proclamation calling into the service 42,034 additional volunteers for a period of three years. He also ordered an increase of the regular army from 16,367 to 22,714 men, eight regiments infantry, one regiment cavalry, and one regiment artillery, as well as 18,000 new recruits for the U.S. Navy "for not less than nor more than three years." The total strength of the army including volunteers would thus increase to 156,861 and the navy to 25,000. Two days later General Scott ordered General Butler to occupy and fortify the strategic junction of the B&O Railroad at Relay, Maryland, eight miles from Baltimore. There the Washington branch crossed the Patapsco River and the main branch continued west to Harpers Ferry and Point of Rocks. The move effectively interrupted the heavy and steady stream of recruits and supplies to the Confederate Army that had been flowing west from Baltimore since the riots to link up with secessionist Maryland forces gathering there. The course to Richmond, a city with a population of only 37,910 inhabitants before the war, now lay for Marylanders intent on joining the Confederacy through the porous shoreline of Southern Maryland. [26]

Even as the move to save the capital and isolate Baltimore was underway, a committee of the Maryland State Legislature met with President Lincoln in a last ditch effort to assure him of the state's loyalty to the Union. However, as the interview progressed their motives became clear. The Federal military juggernaut was just getting started and it seemed certain that any immediate intervention from the Confederacy was growing increasingly unlikely. The Union's capacity for transit across Maryland was already being demonstrated. A general military occupation of state territory to insure fealty in the near future was now a distinct probability. There seemed little alternative but to vow their loyalty and humble themselves. They acquiesced directly to the president, reported the *New York Times,* to "both the right and the power of the government to bring troops through Baltimore or the State, and to take any measures for the public safety which, in the discretion of the President, might be demanded either by actual or reasonably apprehended exigencies. They expressed their belief that no immediate effort at secession or resistance of the federal authority would be attempted by the Legislature or State authorities, and asked that, in this view, the State should, as long as possible, be spared the evils of military occupation or a mere revengeful chastisement for former transgressions."

Lincoln demurred then replied "that their suggestions and representations should be considered, but that he should now say no more than that the public interests, and not the spirit of revenge, would actuate his measures." [27]

In Annapolis, unfortunately as elsewhere, untoward incidents threatened to turn into serious confrontations. It was on May 7, Hicks would complain to Butler that several free blacks had apparently arrived at the Maryland capital with the general's troops, either as servants or camp followers, and were "armed and insolent" or sought the company of slaves to corrupt them. Two of them "grossly insulted a storekeeper in Annapolis, and drew their pistols with threats to shoot him." The governor vigorously protested to the general that "the mere presence of these negroes in our state is a violation of our statutes." Even if they comported themselves responsibly, he declared, they should not be permitted by the Federal Government to violate the laws of Maryland by being permitted to accompany troops. "You can readily see," he concluded, "that there [*sic*] presence here will be provocative of disorder and ill feeling." [28] Butler ignored the complaint for by then he was already considering what to do about the rebellious city on the Patapsco.

***

At 3 p.m., May 9 the steamer *Maryland* with other transports in company arrived at Baltimore with 1,300 Federal troops that had boarded at Perryville. They landed at the Locust Point terminus of the Baltimore and Ohio Railroad, within a half mile of Fort McHenry. Awaiting them at the wharf were Mayor Brown, the Police Commissioner, and two hundred policemen, all of whom had crossed the harbor in a ferryboat ostensibly to insure there would be no further bloodshed. This time only a small crowd of curiosity seekers had watched the landing. Standing off the point with her gunports open was the navy warship *Harriet Lane.* Like it or not, Baltimore was to be occupied. Then, with the exception of 200 men left to take charge of horses, provisions, and baggage, the troops were transferred to two trains which immediately departed. The Federal colossus, it seemed to some, was now finally beginning to stir. If there were any doubts, on May 13 General Butler marched into Baltimore, arriving at Camden Station with a thousand men amidst a raging thunderstorm and soon occupied Federal Hill overlooking the city. The general justified his actions, undertaken without orders (for which he was scolded by General in Chief Scott), by stating that there were reports of a riot in the city and that several manufactories of arms and supplies meant for the rebels had been discovered. Massive fortifications on the hill would soon be constructed. By the end of the year fifty heavy guns would be mounted ostensibly to protect the city's inner harbor but, if necessary, easily turned upon the city itself. The move was almost certainly undertaken to remind the citizenry that Federal might could, if needed, also render Baltimore a smoldering ruin if further disturbances were to occur. The great metropolis on the Patapsco would remain under Federal control for the duration of the war.[29]

Almost immediately Butler began seizing suspected arms and citizens of questionable allegiance. One arrest of significance was State Senator Ross Winans, an avowed secessionist, noted industrialist and one of the richest men in Baltimore. During a meeting of anti-Union conspirators called the States Rights and Southern Rights Convention he had introduced a resolution urging Marylanders to "repel, if need be, any invader who may come to establish a military despotism over us," and pledged half a million dollars for the city's defense against the Yankees. As a major arms manufacturer, ship designer, and inventor of a remarkable steam powered gun (which was also captured), Winans had become a nationally known figure. Taken while en route home from the legislative session in Frederick, he was accused of high treason and incarcerated at Fort McHenry.[30]

Though Butler soon left Baltimore to take command of strategic Fort Monroe in Hampton Roads, leaving General George Cadwalader in charge of the Department of Annapolis, the arrests he had set in motion continued at an accelerated pace. One of the most noteworthy occurred on the morning of May 25 when John Merryman, a prominent gentleman farmer from Cockeysville, Maryland and past president of the Maryland State Agricultural Society, who had been a first lieutenant in a company of secessionist volunteers, was arrested two miles from the town. The arrest was made on a general order issued by Cadwalader at Fort McHenry. The order did not set forth a name or offence and was executed at night by a detachment under a Captain Yeo from the 1st Regiment, Pennsylvania Volunteers.[31] The charge was high treason for bearing arms "belonging to the United States Government for the purpose of using the same against the Government." Left unsaid, but certainly a major reason for the arrest, was his part in the bridge burnings outside of Baltimore that had temporarily isolated the city, and for his alleged recruitment efforts for a Confederate regiment. Merryman was taken into custody without a warrant having been issued or access to legal counsel allowed, and, like Winans, jailed at Fort McHenry.

The following day, however, U.S. Supreme Court Chief Justice Roger Brooke Taney, a native of Calvert County who had decided in the famous Dred Scott case and later swore in Abraham Lincoln as president, ruled that the military arrest of Merryman had violated the privilege of the writ of *habeas corpus*. Taney claimed in his writ that the military had "thrust aside the judicial authorities and officers to who the constitution has confided the power and duty of interpreting and administering the laws, and substituted a military government in its place, to be administered and executed by military laws." Congress alone and not the president, he declared, had the authority under the Constitution to suspend that privilege. General Cadwalader, commander of Fort McHenry, was thus ordered to produce the body of Merryman at the U.S. Circuit Court in Baltimore on May 3. The case immediately became a national issue when the general refused to surrender his prisoner by stating that the president had authorized him to suspend the writ. In time Lincoln defended the action by holding that he had the power of suspension on the grounds that the Constitution provided for such action in certain cases of insurrection or rebellion where public safety necessitated it. Though Merryman, like Winans, would be released in a few weeks, many Marylanders, both Unionists and secessionists, especially in the southern counties, were enraged by the suspension of *habeas corpus*.

A writ of attachment was delivered to Fort McHenry for contempt of court, but Cadwalader refused to accept it until he heard from Washington. On May 28, from the United States Court House on St. Paul Street, Baltimore, Taney released a public statement on the affair:

"I issued the attachment, yesterday, because upon the face of the return the detention of the prisoner was unlawful, upon two grounds:

First – The President, under the Constitution and laws of the United States cannot suspend the privilege of the writ of habeas corpus, nor authorize any military officer to do so.

Second – A military officer has no right to arrest and detain a person, nor subject him to the rules and article of war for an offence against the laws of the United States, except in aid of the judicial authority, and subject to its control, and if the party is arrested by the military, it is the duty of the officer to deliver him over immediately to the civil authority, to be dealt with accordingly.

I forebore yesterday to state orally the provisions of the Constitution of the United States Courts are here in full and free discharge of their functions, and the United States Marshal can execute processes without the slightest of obstruction in all parts of the territory occupied by her citizens. The Administration, in ordering these military arrests, and in suspending the privilege of the writ of *habeas corpus*, is not regarded here as being in any way justified by that *salus populi* which is supposed sometimes to overrule the Constitution." [32]

Lincoln was not swayed. On July 2 he authorized General Scott to suspend the writ on or near any military line between New York and Washington. The suspension would later be extended and maintained by the president for most of the war. As one observer fearfully noted after Justice Taney unsuccessfully ordered an attachment against Cadwalader: "If resistance is made we will have the *Judicial* arm of the Government against the *Executive* arm, the result of which of course will be the downfall of the former under the military power of the latter, & then what becomes of the three colors is the Emblem is trodden out of Existence by all the armed heel of one of the other two. The right of arbitrary imprisonment of all *suspected* persons is the necessary consequence, & you may look for numerous arrests in the future." [33]

So it was to be bullets that would defend the Constitution, many in the North believed, and not legal briefs. And many more in Southern Maryland, arrested and imprisoned without a warrant or access to legal counsel granted, would suffer the consequences.

Soon after the Merryman arrest, the U.S. Marshal in Baltimore seized possession of the Merrill & Thomas gun factory in the city and the Du Pont powder works in Delaware. It was only the beginning.

For many rural Southern Marylanders the results of the Merryman case and the dramatic events underway in Annapolis, Washington, and Baltimore in the spring of 1861 might well have taken place on the moon. Despite the formidable Federal mobilization north of the Annapolis-Washington line, and the troop buildups that would likely follow, the ardent secessionists of the lower Patuxent and Potomac region did not flinch from doing what they could for the rebel cause. Well before the news of the fall of Fort Sumter had begun to sink in, some inhabitants had already started laying the groundwork for an intricate series of routes to convey men, munitions, medical supplies, mail, food, and other materials to Virginia. The foundations were even laid for a sophisticated spy system later dubbed the "Secret Line" that would reach from Richmond through Maryland and as far north as the Great Lakes and the Canadian border. It would survive until the end of the war. At first the highway to the very heart of the rebellion via Southern Maryland was uncontested.

But not for long.

5

SLOW STEAM
"They are closing the coils around us, sir!"

It was an acknowledged fact that support for the Confederacy was entirely prevalent throughout the southern counties of Western Shore Maryland. That such support could be readily engaged to facilitate the transport of arms, supplies and troops for the South was also a fact recognized early on. Hard pressed Federal authorities were struggling to maintain the neutrality, if not the loyalty, of the whole state. Saving Washington, Baltimore and Annapolis, however, was their primary concern. Closure of the major roads, ferries, and rail lines west and south, and in particular those from Baltimore to Harpers Ferry, had rapidly crippled the southward movement of pro-secessionist Marylanders. Almost overnight rebel supporters had quickly turned their attentions to Southern Maryland from which men and materiel could be transported to Virginia across the as yet unpatrolled Potomac River. Prince George's, Charles and St. Mary's counties were to become the initial fulcrum of activity that would later be extended to both Anne Arundel and Calvert. Within a short time key landings and ports on the Patuxent River such as Millstone, Benedict, Spencer's Wharf and Nottingham, would also become way stations for the transit to the numerous Potomac crossings to Virginia. And in doing so, the riverine frontier between Southern Maryland and the Northern Neck of Virginia would become a highway of naval contention and conflict that would continue until the very end of the war.

The extent of the burgeoning rebel transport network operating from Southern Maryland quickly began to inflict considerable dismay among some Federal authorities. It was learned from a few loyal informants and the interrogation of a handful of rebel sympathizers such as George W. Smith, a prominent figure in Charles County affairs who had served since 1857 as county sheriff and owner of an ordinary in Bryantown. In January 1861 he had been nominated as captain of a rifle company called the Bryantown Minutemen.[1] When arrested and questioned in April the sheriff quickly revealed, in an apparent effort to escape prosecution and incarceration for treasonous actions, the names and activities of Confederate collaborators in Southern Maryland. He shamelessly pleaded that he was "guilty of no intentional wrong." He admitted that he had indeed acted erroneously but "did it innocently, having been persuaded that there was no wrong in what he did" in regards to the men he had named. To his interrogators he "most piteously" begged to be discharged by taking the oath of allegiance, and declared he would be true and "give information of anything that may be done against the Government in that region."[2]

The machinations of enemy activities gleaned from Smith's interrogation was not only revealing but also extremely disturbing to Federal authorities. A complex network of transportation and communication, it was learned, was already forming between pro-secessionist elements in the state operating between Baltimore, Annapolis, and Southern Maryland with connections across the Potomac to the Northern Neck of Virginia and the Eastern Shore. Many of those engaged in moving supplies and volunteers to the Confederacy were leaders in civic affairs and men prominent in Southern Maryland, state society and government. And with no Federal troops or ships readily available to intercede, passage across both the Patuxent River and then the Potomac quickly became of central importance to the system.

George Smith's chief interrogator, one T. B. Robey, was the first to inform Washington on the specifics of the grim news. One of the "principal leaders in the secession party and those who have aided against the Government" in Charles County was James A. Mudd, who lived a mile outside of Bryantown. Like Smith, Mudd was well known in the county and active in local affairs and politics. He had served, like many prominent county men of substance, as a petit juror in the county court, as a participant in local civic meetings, and as a judge at the Charles County Agricultural Society fair, the largest and most important annual social event in the region, usually held in early November. In January 1861 at a meeting of the Mounted Volunteers of Charles County, captained by Samuel Cox and convened in Port Tobacco, it was made known that the State of Maryland had refused to furnish arms and accoutrements for the unit. Mudd was one of four men from the Fourth Election District appointed to solicit public subscriptions for their support.[3]

Smith soon revealed that Mudd had been conveying men and boxes "supposed to contain munitions of war from Baltimore and different counties in the State" to Pope's Creek on the Potomac. From there they would be ferried across the river at night in small boats. The boxes, containing the guns and ammunition, had been brought down from Anne Arundel County. With the boxes carried by a wagon belonging to a cavalry company from Bryantown, no fewer than 200 men "from Baltimore and other places" were transported at Mudd's personal expense to the Pope's Creek crossing to join the Confederate Army and Navy.[4]

Pope's Creek was by most measures perhaps the perfect starting point for a crossing from Southern Maryland to the Confederacy. "It is nowhere more than forty or fifty feet wide," noted Thomas Austin Jones, manager of a ferry operation at the site and now one of the principal conductors on the route, which was bordered on both sides by an extensive marsh. Between the marsh and the river lay a sixty-foot wide strip of land that formed a natural causeway between the two bluffs separated by the marsh. A public road approached the adjacent steamboat landing from two opposite directions. "The boldness of the water and comparative narrowness of the river at Pope's Creek, together with its accessibility, made it a much used point of departure for those wishing to cross to Virginia. Besides, nearly every one in the neighborhood was known to be in sympathy with the South. It was, therefore, when the war had put an end to intercourse at Washington and above it with Virginia, that hundreds of people came to the neighborhood of Pope's Creek to get put across the river." [5]

Other Charles County residents such as Hileary Burch of Benedict, Zachariah V. Posey, owner of the Farmers and Planters Hotel in Port Tobacco [6] and Luther Martin of Allen's Fresh,[7] had also been conducting almost daily overland wagon transport of passengers, arms, munitions and other supplies from the riverport of Benedict on the Patuxent to Pope's Creek. From there two of Charles County's leading figures, the aforementioned Thomas A. Jones, foster brother of Samuel Cox, and Thomas D. Stone, conveyed them on dark, moonless nights to Virginia in small boats which they supplied, manned by their own slaves. Jones, born on October 2, 1820 near Port Tobacco, was a well known landowner of five hundred acres of farmland adjoining the steamboat and ferry landings at Pope's Creek, about sixty miles from Washington by water though not more than forty by land. He also knew the river there better than anyone alive. The great waterway bound his farm on the southwest. With his residence being situated near the mouth of the creek, the site was most strategically seated for his operations. "My small, one-story frame house," he would later write, "was built upon a bluff about eighty feet high. I could stand in my back yard and look up the river until my view was cut off by Maryland Point, seven or eight miles distant; while down the river I could see the water almost as far as the eye could reach," to Laidler's Ferry at Lower Cedar Point. Between Pope's Creek and Mathias Point Neck in King George County, Virginia, the river narrowed to two miles in width, with both coasts providing excellent places to hide and launch small boats.[8]

Jones and Stone were men of prominence. The former had served on both petit and grand juries in the county court, as a tax collector, and in June 1857 as a delegate to the county Democratic Party convention in Port Tobacco. The latter had served as a committeeman for the county Agricultural Society in 1855 and 1860. Since 1857, he too had been a staunch member of the county Democratic Party and served as a delegate from the Second Election District to the county party conventions in Port Tobacco in both 1857 and 1861. As an orator his political views were frequently aired at party meetings and rallies. In November 1860 he had delivered a particularly stirring oration regarding his "attachment to the Constitution and the Union." In December 1860 he was appointed during a meeting at Allen's Fresh as fourth lieutenant of a permanent rifle company, and was among many who signed a letter declaring hostility to the incoming Republican administration of Abraham Lincoln. By the spring of 1861 his attachment to the Constitution and the Union had been entirely shattered and his allegiance subverted.[9]

Perhaps one of the most notorious of the contraband movers was E. H. Jones who resided at a place then known as the Old Factory in St. Mary's. He had been a major force in a campaign to bully Union supporters to leave the county, and for good measure, it was noted in one Federal report, "on all occasions [he] cursed and abused the Government." Jones had been in Baltimore in April when the riots erupted and it is altogether possible he had been a participant. Emboldened by the challenge to Federal authority there he returned home bringing with him no less than 800 stands of arms that were promptly transported across the Potomac. Thereafter, well into the fall of 1861, he conducted a regular transport of contraband goods using his own horses and wagons while hauling them from the Patuxent to the Potomac. Federal authorities later learned that he had also converted his home into a headquarters and refuge for rebel spies passing to and from Virginia, and personally "enlisted, equipped and forwarded a large number of men for the Confederacy." [10]

From the beginning Federal efforts to stifle the smuggling routes and rebel lines of communication through Southern Maryland proved inadequate. Major concerns focused on securing military control and neutralizing secessionists in the major urban centers of Washington, Baltimore and Annapolis, and consolidating Federal supremacy in the strategic triangle between the three cities. As a consequence, throughout much of the early spring of 1861 Southern Maryland was left untouched. Additional smuggling routes south were soon opened from landings at the mouth of the Wicomico River, St. Clement's and Breton Bays, the St. Mary's River, Upper Cedar Point, Nanjemoy, Smith's Point in Charles County, Budd's Ferry, Piscataway and Fox's Landing in Prince George's.[11]

All types of military necessities flowed southward from Baltimore to Virginia through the lower counties of Maryland regardless of eventual Federal occupation and the early but pitiful attempts by the few Union blockaders. Military cloth was readily to be had from the shop of Wethered Brothers, Charles and John, on German Street. Other firms such as Whitley, Stone & Company openly advertised fulled gray cloth "suitable for Uniforms," as well as blankets, shirts and other items of military attire. Military headgear and caps were to be obtained from the store of Joseph Bernhard at 208 West Pratt Street. Baltimore tailors such as John H. Rea & Company, John Mullen and Thomas McCormick, and Charles Sisco advertised themselves as prepared to manufacture uniforms for military units in any quantity, and military trimmings of every description.[12]

For revealing the actions of his compatriots to Union officials, George W. Smith's interrogator, T. B. Robey, recommended his prisoner's release "as I think this is all that can be made out of him, and he can be used hereafter if necessary." Not so fortunate were some of the men that Smith had exposed to the inquisitor to face arrest and imprisonment. Yet as would soon be proved, for every one incarcerated another would soon take his place in the field.

***

On April 15, the same day as the president's call for 75,000 volunteers, his new Secretary of the Navy, Gideon Welles, a Connecticut man who had just taken office on March 7, began the first of countless moves to secure naval control of the Potomac and eventually the Southern Maryland shoreline. The Washington Navy Yard, like most Federal facilities across the nation, was largely bereft of defenses and even armed vessels. Many Unionists concurred: Washington was in imminent danger of capture by Confederates lurking just across the Potomac at the port of Alexandria and in adjacent Fairfax County, Virginia. Insurrection by rebel supporters in Maryland was possible if not probable. Thus Welles dispatched orders to immediately redirect ships from other areas to Washington as quickly as possible. One such order went out to the New York Navy Yard to immediately send back a warship even then en route there from the capital. The USS *Pocahontas*, a small, second class steam screw sloop, under Commander John P. Gillis, was ordered back to the Navy Yard as soon as she arrived in the East River. Others were to follow.[13]

Summoning ships was one thing but providing for the defense of their vulnerable main base of operations, the Washington Navy Yard itself, was another as difficulties at the facility abounded. On the day of Lincoln's call for volunteers, Captain John A. Dahlgren, commander of the Ordnance Department at the yard, complained bitterly to Commandant Franklin Buchanan. The commandant was a heroic, hawk-faced forty-seven-year veteran of the navy from Easton, Maryland, esteemed co-founder and first superintendent of the U.S. Naval Academy, and flagship captain in Commodore Perry's expedition to Japan in 1853. Twenty-six of his mechanics, Dahlgren grumbled, were mysteriously absent. Producing and preparing ordnance for naval vessels was his job, and the president's call for volunteers had not helped matters. "I understand," he noted in exasperation, "that this [absenteeism] arises from most of them, if not all, having been mustered into military service." He was already having difficulties providing howitzers for the navy's warships. With so many of his best hands gone precisely when he was preparing to increase the number of orders to meet the national emergency it appeared he might have to suspend work altogether. The only solution, he informed the commandant, was that it would be necessary to excuse from military service men employed in his department supplying ships of war. With no men to manufacture them there would be no guns for the navy. It was quite simple.[14]

"Washington Navy Yard, 1861." Alfred R. Waud Collection, No. 488, Prints and Photographs, Library of Congress, Washington, D.C.

Buchanan did not reply for four days. Finally on April 19, even as President Lincoln was calling for a total blockade of Southern ports, the commandant informed Secretary Welles of the problem. "Very important work is delayed in consequence, particularly in the Ordnance Department. An Act of Congress dated September 30, 1850, prohibits a person from receiving the pay performing two duties for the Government, consequently I can not pay the men as mechanics while they receive their pay as soldiers." Three days later, the commandant, in a short note to Dahlgren, revealed the real reason for his recalcitrance. [15]

"I have this day," he wrote, "resigned my commission as a captain in the navy and consider myself only temporarily in command here, you will carry out all the instructions you have received in preparing the steamers for war service, as directed by my order to you this morning, and superintend the defense of the yard when necessary. I shall not take any part in the defense of this yard from this date." [16]

Franklin Buchanan, late commandant of the Washington Navy Yard, assumed his beloved Maryland was about to secede, and resigned his commission on April 22. He was not alone, for 311 other junior and senior naval and Marine Corps officers and engineers in the Washington-Annapolis-Baltimore triangle were already departing to join the armed forces of the Confederacy. Many more would follow in their wake. But there had been clues as to his course of action. Only nineteen days earlier on April 3, Lincoln had attended the wedding of Buchanan's daughter Nannie at the Washington Navy Yard. When the president attempted to shake the hand of Elizabeth Buchanan, another of the commandant's daughters, she refused. Though he called her a "little rebel," however, even she succumbed to the president's wit and charm after he presented her with a bribe of bonbons. It must have seemed even then that the Buchanan family's true loyalties were evident. [17]

Left: Secretary of the Navy Gideon Welles. Brady National Photographic Art Gallery (Washington, D.C.). Prints and Photographs Division, Library of Congress, Washington, D.C. Right: General Winfield Scott. Prints and Photographs, Library of Congress, Washington, D.C.

The departure of Buchanan and other naval and military personnel was not undertaken in isolation. A veritable exodus of Southern politicians and men, women and children from every station of society was already underway. A cloud of incredible desperation lay over Washington, a city fearful of imminent invasion or bloody mob rule even as those in command struggled to hold things together as one disaster followed another. When the Gosport Navy Yard at Portsmouth, Virginia, and ten of the navy's major though mostly aged warships were destroyed on April 20 to prevent capture by rebel forces, the importance of the Washington Navy Yard was suddenly magnified a hundredfold. The bony fingers of panic that had gripped Capitol Hill now began to tighten even more forcefully.

General Winfield Scott, Commander in Chief of the U.S. Army, a seventy-five-year-old national hero of two earlier wars, though dubbed "Ole Fuss and Feathers" by his detractors and in ill health, was not given to fear and sought to maintain an air of military composure. "He was the country's 'Grand Old Man' and greatly esteemed by everyone," noted one observer about this time, "but he was now very infirm, pompous, and with many of the affectations which sometimes go with extreme age and it was extremely difficult to engage his attention. His mind was centered on the makeup of an army as he had always known it and he did not care for innovations." On the afternoon of April 21 he queried the Inspector General of the District of Columbia Militia, Colonel Charles P. Stone, on the city's defense status.

The general began the query roughly. "Gosport Navy Yard has been burned!"

"Yes, General!" replied Stone.

"Harper's Ferry bridge has been burned!"

Again Stone replied: "Yes, General."

"The bridge at Point of Rocks was burned some days since!"

"Yes, General."

"The bridges over Gunpowder Creek beyond Baltimore have been burned!"

Stone replied once more: "Yes, General."

Solemnly the general declared: "They are closing their coils around us, sir!"

Still Stone replied, in the same tone: "Yes, General."

"Now," asked the general candidly, "how long can we hold out here?"

Stone replied positively: "Ten days, General, and within that time the North will come down to us."

"How will they come? The route through Baltimore is cut off."

"They will come by all routes," the colonel answered. "They will come between the Capes of Virginia, up through Chesapeake Bay, and by the Potomac. They will come, if necessary, from Pennsylvania through Maryland directly to us; and they will come through Baltimore and Annapolis."

"Well, sir, how many men have you," asked Scott.

"In all, General, there are four thousand nine hundred. But the number includes the battery of artillery near your headquarters, and the Ordnance men at the Arsenal, under my command, and who will have enough to do to guard the arsenal."

"How many miles of picket line between your outposts?"

"Eighteen miles of picket line and less than five thousand men!"

"Then you must, in case of attack, fight [with] your pickets!" said the general with some despair.

Then followed a discussion regarding Stone's plans for defending the city in the last extremity until a rescue could be made. If it became necessary to abandon all else, Scott declared, it would be absolutely imperative to "occupy, strongly and effectively, the Executive Square, with the idea of finally holding only the Treasury building and, perhaps, the State Department building, properly connected. The seals of the several departments of the Government must be deposited in the vaults of the Treasury. They must not be captured and used to deceive and create uncertainty among public servants distant from the Capital."

Then speaking more impressively, he said: "Should it come to the defense of the Treasury building as a citadel, then the President and all the members of his cabinet must take up their quarters with us in that building! They shall not be permitted to desert the Capital!" [18]

Washington was, for the most part, anything but auspicious in appearance. As one Massachusetts volunteer, Private Warren Lee Gross, noted, the city was little more than an overgrown country village though one with wide streets stretching out from a common center like a spider's web. The Capitol building was as yet incomplete, with an unfinished dome. The Patent Office, the Treasury, and other public buildings, "were in marked and classic contrast with the dilapidated, tumble-down, shabby look of the average homes, stores, groceries, which increased in shabbiness and dirty dilapidation as they approached the suburbs. The climate in Washington was congenial, but in the winter months the mud was fearful . . . In the lower quarter of the city there was not a piece of sidewalk. Even Pennsylvania Avenue, with its sidewalks was extremely dirty; and the cavalcade of teams, artillery caissons, and baggage wagons, with their heavy wheels, stirred the mud into a stiff batter for the pedestrian." [19]

The city's vulnerability had for months been recognized but not until the secession of South Carolina was immediate action deemed necessary. At the beginning of 1861 the only regular troops near the capital were several hundred U.S. Marines at the Marine Barracks and fewer than a hundred enlisted artillerymen at the Washington Arsenal. The only volunteer organizations included: a company of riflemen, the Potomac Light Infantry at Georgetown, which was a fairly well drilled and armed unit believed to be of reliable loyalty; the National Rifles in Washington (whose secessionist commander would soon be obliged to depart for Southern Maryland after publicly announcing that the unit's only purpose was "to guard the frontier of Maryland and help to keep the Yankees from coming down to coerce the South!"); approximately 160 men of the Washington Light Infantry Battalion; and a small unit called the National Guard Battalion, composed almost entirely of older volunteers, but all Washington residents faithful to the government.[20]

As the crises rapidly grew Inspector General Stone vigorously set to work increasing volunteers units for the preservation of the city. By the middle of February he was able to report "thirty-three companies of infantry and riflemen and two troops of cavalry were on the lists of the District volunteer force; and all had been uniformed, equipped, and put under frequent drill." [21]

Desperate calls continued to be circulated for men to defend the capital and were enlarged upon with the president's national call for volunteers. Then within the enclosed space on the north side of the War Department, spirited enlistments in a number of volunteer companies commenced the same day as his call to arms. Thus it was that the first citizen troops called into the service by Lincoln's summons were those of the District of Columbia. Units such as the Turner Rifles, the Metropolitan Rifles, the Putnam Rifles, the Henderson Guards, the National Rifles, the Andrews Rifles, the Washington Zouaves, and the Constitutional Guards, as well as already formed companies in the National Guard Battalion, usually identified by the names of their individual captains, began to grow around the nucleus of loyal Washingtonians. On Tuesday, April 16 Washington's Mayor Henry Addison invited all citizens over the age of forty-five "who are willing to render military service to their country, and particularly to defend the District of Columbia against the aggression of rebels" to enroll their names at his office. A company of men over the age of forty who called themselves the "Fossil Guards," and another composed of elderly citizens, veterans of the War of 1812 known as the "Silver Greys," were soon being mustered on Capitol Hill. A few days later a gathering of French and Italian immigrants met at the European Hotel to form the Garibaldi Guards. By April 18 Cassius Marcellus Clay of Kentucky, an early and devoted member of the Republican Party, though recently appointed Minister to Russia, formed his own unit. They were assigned to patrol the downtown area near Willard's Hotel at Pennsylvania Avenue and Fourteenth Street, hub of all things Republican. Republican Senator James H. Lane of Kansas formed the Frontier Guards specifically for the protection of the White House, which soon took on the appearance of a barracks. Now it was estimated that at least 1,000 men had been taken into service. Word soon spread that more volunteers from as far away as Chicago, Illinois and St. Paul, Minnesota were mustering to make the trek eastward to defend the capital, though even the news of the arrival of Butler's troops at Annapolis seemed unable to lift the spirits of most of the city population. At 7 p.m. on the 18th the battered and bedraggled 1st Pennsylvania Volunteers arrived in the city, earning their place in history as the first reinforcements to reach the capital. Thereafter they would bear the title "First Defenders." [22]

As Washington did its best to prepare for the probability of imminent attack, Navy Secretary Welles worked diligently to utilize what little forces he had in hand. When the great steam sloop-of-war *Pawnee*, appeared off the Washington Arsenal, news of the Baltimore riots was fresh on everyone's lips. But word of an even more disastrous nature was soon to add even more concern. The U.S. Naval base at Portsmouth, Virginia had fallen.

A relatively new state-of-the-art, purpose-built, 1,289-ton, twin-screw steam-powered sloop-of-war launched in 1859, *Pawnee* was now the sole major naval defense of the capital. For her officers and crew, the three previous weeks had been a devestating experience. They had spent the first three months of 1861 in relative quiet at the Washington Navy Yard, even as the national crisis began to erupt. Then, on April 6, they had been dispatched on an expedition to Charleston, South Carolina in a last desperate effort to relieve the garrison at Fort Sumter. The voyage had been doomed to failure owing to a storm which delayed their arrival at the last critical moment. After their return to the capital they had been immediately dispatched to the Gosport Navy Yard to secure ships and stores of the Atlantic fleet, most of which had been tied up in ordinary or in drydock. Arriving on the night of April 20 they had found the entire squadron, with the exception of the USS *Cumberland*, scuttled to prevent capture. Though managing to save the great frigate, they were unable to destroy the dry dock and naval stores before capture by rebel forces. Now, as one of the few major warships in Union hands left in the Chesapeake, *Pawnee's* importance to Federal control of the all important Tidewater waterways was enormous. Armed with eight 9-inch guns and a pair of 12-pounders she was still a match for anything the Confederates could mount against her either ashore or on the water. Her importance did not go unnoticed by Confederate authorities.[23]

Though *Pawnee*'s arrival had also strengthened the city's defense at a critical juncture, the situation was nevertheless dismal. The District of Columbia, it was now clear, had been cut off from reinforcements by rail from the north. If the rebels mounted batteries at choke points along the Potomac, either on the Southern Maryland or Virginia side, or sank obstructions in the channel, the capital would be completely isolated. The city would have to hold on with the few loyal volunteers at hand until regular troops could somehow get through.[24]

Welles did not flinch. He promptly ordered twenty U.S. Marines, fully equipped, to board one of the few vessels in hand, the little 4th-rate screw steamer *Anacostia*, Lieutenant Commander Thomas S. Fillebrown commanding, to proceed down the Potomac to Kettle Bottom Shoals, near a strategic narrows on the river. There she was to protect the channel from being obstructed by the rebels. Fillebrown was instructed to "take prizes or prisoners if you meet with any interference," and to cruise under "slow steam" above and below the shoals to observe all suspicious movements.[25]

In the meantime Colonel Charles F. Smith, U.S. Army, reported to Secretary Welles that he had commandered the commercial steamers *Baltimore*, *Mount Vernon*, *Philadelphia*, and *Powhatan*, belonging to the Potomac Steamboat Company. All were well known on the river, having regularly plied between the capital and Aquia Creek, Virginia, the terminal point of the Richmond, Fredericksburg and Potomac Railroad [R.F.& P.]. The railroad, which connected Fredericksburg with Richmond, was now in rebel hands. All four ships were immediately turned over to the navy and ordered outfitted and armed at the Washington Navy Yard for service either as transports or warships. Although deemed harsh measures at the time, the confiscations helped deprive Virginia (which was also commandeering anything afloat) the use of the ships for potential naval or transport duty, or even as a war squadron on the Potomac. It also improved the navy's hitherto negative capacity to interdict rebel transportation running across the river from Southern Maryland.[26]

Nevertheless, the Navy Secretary was desperate for vessels. Almost anything afloat upon which a gun or two could be mounted would do to meet the rigorous demands set by Lincoln's blockade proclamation, not only for the Potomac but the Chesapeake Tidewater in its entirety. On April 21 he dispatched instructions to the Commandant of the Philadelphia Navy Yard, Captain Samuel F. Du Pont, to immediately procure "five staunch steamers from ten to twelve feet draught, having particular reference to strength and speed and capable of carrying a nine-inch pivot gun . . . for coastal service." Similar orders were dispatched to the commandants of both the New York and Boston Navy Yards. He also took measures to secure vulnerable navy vessels from danger. Thus orders were sent to Commander William S. Hunter to move the Receiving Ship *Allegheny* from the Baltimore waterfront to the protective shadow of Fort McHenry.[27]

Moved to action by the president's declaration of a blockade, Lieutenant James Harmon Ward, skipper of the Receiving Ship *North Carolina*, then stationed at the New York Navy Yard, offered a proposal destined to have a significant impact on the security of the Potomac and Federal efforts to suppress rebel support from

Southern Maryland. "I have the honor to press upon your attention," Ward wrote, "an organization I proposed of a flying flotilla, to be composed of one larger and two smaller steamers and three light draft schooners." The larger steamer would be commanded by himself, while the two smaller vessels would be under the charge of Lieutenant Daniel L. Braine, U.S. Navy and Sailing Master William Budd of the U.S. Coast Survey. The steamers would be armed and fast. None would draw, when fully laden, more than seven feet of water. "Every arrangement exists," he noted, "for immediately chartering and speedily equipping the light flying force with a view to service in the Chesapeak[e] and its tributaries." Its mission would be: to interrupt the enemy's communications while maintaining those of the Union; clear the region of rebel shipping; maintain a threat to the rebel coast in the Tidewater at all points; protect loyal citizens, convoy, tow and transport troops and intelligence "with dispatch"; and attack the foe at any desired or important point at deemed necessary. Ward's proposal was immediately endorsed by the base commandant, Samuel L. Breese.[28]

James Ward, was a heavyset man, some might say stocky in stature, who resembled a baker more enamored with his bread than a naval man of action. His face was broad, the roundness of which was accentuated in the popular style of the day by thick sideburns that circumnavigated his cheeks to join a mustache under his nose, but leaving his cleft chin naked. The beginnings of jowls pressed his collar outward making him look uncomfortable in uniform. Yet such looks were deceiving. Born in Hartford, Connecticut in 1806, he had graduated at the age of sixteen from the American Literary Scientific and Military Academy in Norwich, Vermont and entered the U.S. Navy as a midshipman in March 1823. His subsequent career aboard the USS *Constitution* in the Mediterranean, followed by scientific studies at Washington College in Connecticut, was capped with a return to sea duty off the coast of Africa and in the West Indies. Then it was another return to academia, this time not as a student but as an instructor in ordnance and gunnery at the Naval School in Philadelphia. Publication of his curriculum as *An Elementary Course of Instruction in Ordnance and Gunnery* and his assignment to the faculty of the newly opened Naval School, soon to be known as the U.S. Naval Academy, in Annapolis in 1845 as an instructor of gunnery and engineering soon led to his reputation as one of the most scholarly officers in the navy. At the outbreak of the Mexican War he was assigned command of the USS *Cumberland* and in 1848 to the steamer *Vixen*. Later, he was awarded command of the USS *Jamestown* and returned to the coast of Africa to hunt slave ships. Somehow during that service he found time to write *A Manual of Naval Tactics*, published in 1859. The following year, while at the New York Navy Yard, he published a major treatise on steam engineering entitled *Steam for the Millions*, and developed a unique pivot gun mount for naval gunnery.[29]

Ever since the firing on Fort Sumter, Ward had been eager to enter the fight and aggressive in his desire to engage the rebels head on. His wish would soon become a historic reality. Breese immediately dispatched Sailing Master Budd to Washington to personally deliver Ward's proposal to the Navy Secretary. By April 27 Welles was convinced of the utility of the proposal and instructed Commandant Breese to detail Ward and Braine "to carry into effect the expedition proposed."

Budd was detached from service with the U.S. Coast Survey and detailed to the navy to be "connected to the expedition." The parameters of the establishment and fielding of the little flotilla were succinct, leaving much leeway for its new commander. "In the further completion of a flying flotilla," read Welles' instructions to Breese, "you will be governed by the details set forth in the communication above cited [Ward's memo] and you will afford every facility to these officers to expedite the same." Ward, Braine, and Budd, upon reaching the Chesapeake, were to report directly to Flag Officer Garrett J. Pendergrast, Commander of the still-forming Atlantic Blockading Squadron at Hampton Roads or the senior naval officer on the bay.[30]

The Navy Department's approval of Ward's scheme for the fielding of a small flotilla for service in the Chesapeake and its tributaries had set in motion the creation of an infant force of just six vessels, three small steamers and three schooners, that would initially be attached to the Atlantic Blockading Squadron. It would, it was hoped, eventually prove valuable to the river's defenses and a serious obstruction to rebel activities in Southern Maryland. It wasn't much, but it was a start.

For the moment everything depended on the acuity and capabilities of Captain John A. Dahlgren who had assumed command of the Navy Yard. The new commandant, whose receding hairline, close set eyes and eternal frown, exaggerated by a full mustache that swept into deep sideburns, was imposing. Yet his appearance seemed to portray a troubled man, not the tireless, organizer who would play a most significant roll in the coming days of the war as Commander of the South Atlantic Blockading Squadron. A thirty-five year veteran of the navy and founder of the Ordnance Department, he now found himself working with deficiencies in every area, from manpower and weaknesses in the yard's defenses to armaments and ships. The indefatigable officer proved equal to the task.

One of his initial moves was to begin preparing the four vessels confiscated from the Potomac Steamboat Company for naval service. *Mount Vernon*, which had been seized at Alexandria, Virginia, was the first: she was hastily fitted as a dispatch steamer armed with a 32-pounder and breech loading rifles for her extremely small crew, composed of a pilot and six seamen. Lacking any available senior officers, a boatswain named George Willmuth was placed in command. The commandant's next address was to secure an adequate number of river and bay pilots that would inevitably be needed for the service and then to address as best he could the defenses of the Navy Yard. When Secretary Welles requested from Secretary of War Simon Cameron a corporal's guard for the yard's protection, Dahlgren was adamant that nothing less than "a reliable battalion" would be necessary.

"This yard is of importance," he reminded the secretary, "not only because of its furnishing the Navy so largely with naval stores, but also as a position in the general defense of the city. Near it is a bridge easily reached and passed whenever an attack may be conducted by crossing from Alexandria, then over the low heights opposite the yard." There were, he noted, just three companies of militiamen, 268 strong, thirty-seven U.S. Marines, and thirty-four men from the Ordnance Department, 339 in all, to defend the great expanse of the yard and its approaches. The militia companies were thinly distributed along its borders, which were also patrolled by the small body of marines at hand. Cannon and howitzers were planted with their muzzles pointed down stream. At the Long Bridge, hitherto guarded by just four militia dragoons from the city, he placed another howitzer, ten men and a corporal's guard of marines to improve the admittedly weak defenses. On April 23 the arrival of the 1,364-ton sidewheeler *Keystone State*, belonging to the Ocean Steam Navigation Company but pressed into service by the navy, helped improve the situation somewhat as she had 134 marines aboard as well as four 12-pounders. Dahlgren retained the marines at the yard as they were considered "very necessary to its defense and its approaches and will relieve a corresponding number of volunteers." Welles concurred and did his best to secure further reinforcements.[31]

Although the greatest danger of an attack on Washington, before the arrival of reinforcements, was by land from either the Maryland or the Virginia sides, or both, the security of the Potomac and water access to the capital for men and supplies was vital. Of key importance to that security were the maintenance and protection of navigational aids, adequate pilotage, and the prevention of the installation of obstructions and rebel batteries at strategic points along the nearly 100-mile stretch of waterway between the city and the Chesapeake. Along many sectors of the river on both sides there were promontories that could readily lend themselves to fortification by rebel forces. If heavy guns, hundreds of which had been recovered by the rebels from the wreckage of the Gosport Navy Yard, could be brought up it was very possible the enemy might not only harass Union shipping but could close the river to maritime traffic. Washington might thus be severed from all critical seaborne support and communications.

As rumors flew thick about the city, it was not surprising that some reached the ears of General Scott. One such account was circulated that a rebel battery was already under construction four miles below Mount Vernon at White House Point on the Virginia shore at the same spot where American artillery had been mounted during the War of 1812 and promulgated a spirited fight with the Royal Navy. "A battery at this point," it was later determined, "would command the approach to it [the city] for more than 3 miles, and vessels of more than 12 feet draft can not pass more than three-eights of a mile from it. The deepest water is near the bluff." Scott took heed and requested the navy to investigate. Thus on April 22 Secretary Welles initiated the first of countless patrols, ordering Dahlgren to immediately dispatch a ship to reconnoiter the river, render assistance to any vessel requiring it, and defend against enemy assault. The inhabitants along the Maryland shoreline were dangerously secessionist in sympathy, and the enemy's machinations along the openly rebel coast on the other side of the river were still unknown. Welles pointedly ordered the reconnaissance ship to "observe if guns are planted on either shore." [32]

***

On the same day the first Potomac patrol of the war was dispatched, *Pocahontas*, after a three day voyage from New York, arrived at the Washington Navy Yard. Almost as soon as the warship tied up at the Navy Yard, she received instructions from Welles to sail immediately back down the Potomac to reconnoiter White House Landing, seize any vessels carrying troops or provisions for the enemy, "disperse hostile gatherings or preparations that may be discovered," and of course repel all attacks.[33]

The same evening at 11:30 p.m. *Mount Vernon* also sailed under the command of Boatswain Willmuth, with one gunner, a pilot, an engineer, several firemen, four marines and ten men from the Navy Yard Ordnance Department as crew. It was indeed a small complement of men with which to sail into unknown enemy territory. Dahlgren had attempted to reinforce the ship with a company of militia assigned to the defense of the yard, but the unit's captain flatly refused on the grounds that he considered the little steamer unsafe and her ancient 32-pounder likely to explode. Having no direct authority over the militia the commandant had little choice but to accept the captain's decision and the steamer sallied forth, both weakly manned and armed. Her specific mission was to ascertain whether or not the navigational aids on the river off Lower Cedar Point had been disturbed. Her secondary objective was to see if Fort Washington, the sole regular defense work lying between Washington and Southern Maryland's Potomac coast, was in need of anything.

After stopping briefly at Fort Washington where she encountered *Pawnee, Keystone State* and *Anacostia, Mount Vernon* came to anchor adjacent to some of the most dangerous shoals on the river at one of its narrowest channels. Shortly after noon on April 24 she came about southwest of the Lower Cedar Point Lightship, a permanently manned and moored navigational aid. Here a lightship of one kind or another had been on station more or less continuously since 1821. The last was brought up from an earlier station in Pamlico Sound, North Carolina as recently as 1860. Lacking a pilot familiar with the ever shifting shoals below that point, Willmuth was unable to press farther, but as events would soon prove it didn't matter. After coming to, he was startled to observe smoke rising from the direction of the lightship. Soon afterwards twenty men in a 40-foot longboat, equal in number to his own, were seen leaving the vessel. Then flames appeared. The lightship, one of the principal navigational aids on the river, had been stripped of her valuable Costan Lamp and set ablaze by rebels who had also taken her crew as captives. *Mount Vernon*'s men opened fire with their muskets in an unsuccessful effort to bring the enemy boat about. Then a shell was shot across her bow but to no effect. The raiders soon landed unhurt on the Virginia shore.[34]

Even as the effort was underway to halt the rebel boat from escaping, Willmuth also observed a well known river steamer named *James Guy* maneuvering "in a suspicious manner and communicating with the shore" and ordered her hove to. Upon discovering lady passengers aboard, however, he allowed her to proceed on her way. Chivalry had trumped logic, as it would again and again in Southern Maryland throughout the early days of the war.

As *James Guy* steamed away, *Mount Vernon* returned to the lightship, lowered a boat, and went alongside. Upon "finding her a perfect wreck," the expeditionaries returned to Fort Washington only to discover that the fort's extremely skittish commander, Major Joseph A. Haskins, a distinguished but aged one-armed veteran of the Mexican War, was expecting a rebel attack at any moment. Willmuth ordered his steamer to remain at wharfside throughout the night. The following morning she returned downriver, passed the wrecked lightship, observed that the other navigational aids in the river had not been moved, and examined the shoreline for batteries. None were found. After stopping again for the night at the fort, the little warship tied up at the Navy Yard on the morning of April 25.[35]

When *Anacostia* returned only hours earlier from a similar reconnaissance, she too brought confirmation that as yet no rebel obstructions had been planted in the river, nor had batteries been erected between Lower Cedar Point and Washington. But there was bad news as well. One of the Potomac Line vessels that had not been confiscated by the army, reported Lieutenant Fillebrown, had been seized by rebels at Alexandria and now lay near the R. F. & P Railroad terminus on Aquia Creek. The ship in question was *George Page*, an eight-year-old, 410-ton sidewheeler, home ported at Alexandria and well known on the river. As there was not a sufficient depth of water to allow his own ship's entry into the waterway it had been possible to determine if the rebels had yet erected any defenses there.[36]

***

By April 23 Washington was well aware that several large contingents of Federal troops would soon be arriving in the city, from both Annapolis where General Butler was completing the repairs on the rail line and by several ships laden with volunteers from New York. The news that the rebels now had a vessel that might be converted into a man of war that could intercept incoing vessels was more than a little disturbing, but that enemy forces were now massing below Alexandria was even more frightening. Moreover the ongoing exodus from the capital was appalling. Both Confederate sympathizers (including U.S. Supreme Court Justice John A. Campbell of Alabama, who, it was alleged, had provided Jefferson Davis with a stream of intelligence regarding the city) and simple civilians alike were departing in droves. Many simply feared an immediate rain of destruction. It was critical that the capital receive reinforcements as soon as possible, and Welles did not wish to leave any details to chance. Thus he directed Dahlgren to dispatch Commanders Stephen Clegg Rowan of *Pawnee* and Gillis of *Pocahontas* to proceed back down the river to White House Point to await troop laden transports from New York. When met, they were to convoy them to any convenient point of landing "so that they may reach the capital." If the troop ships did not appear by April 26, both *Pawnee* and *Pocahontas* were to return to their anchorage. In the meantime Rowan was sternly instructed to "detain everything you meet with arms and armed men and bring them to the yard." The following day Gillis's orders were expanded. He was now directed to steam into the Chesapeake itself as far south as necessary, to intercept the in- coming troop transports and inform them to proceed to Washington via the Poto- mac and not Annapolis as originally ordered.[37]

Salvation, however, had already set out. At 10 a.m. April 25 the 7th New York entrained at Annapolis for Washington. If they arrived safely, they would be the first major Federal reinforcement, besides the few hundred Pennsylvanians, to reach the capital since it had been cut off by the destruction of the bridges north and east of Baltimore barely a week earlier. To some it had seemed like a year. Four hours later they marched past the White House beneath the smiling gaze of President Lincoln. Washington might be saved after all. The capital of the United States was indeed no longer defended by just city militiamen, elderly volunteers and those poorly equipped soldiers who had passed through Baltimore before the Pratt Street Riot. Soon the city and its immediate environs would be swarming with tens of thousands of Union soldiers and the Potomac River with U.S. Navy gunboats. In the mean-time, for lack of an immediate designated bivouac area, the 7th New York would find quarters in the chambers of the House of Representatives in the U.S. Capitol Building.[38]

But the business at hand still had to be addressed. *Anacostia* set sail on her next mission, again to the Kettle Bottoms, only two hours before the 7th Regiment arrived in the city.[39]

It would then be Southern Maryland's turn to be isolated. And soon the first Federal efforts to stem the flow of men, arms and supplies to the Confederate States of America via the backdoor to Virginia would be underway. As if to accentuate the difficulties ahead, it was learned, even as *Anacostia* was departing on her mission, that the rebels had finally removed all of the buoys on the river as well as all of the light vessels, including the Smith Point Lightship at the entrance to the Potomac.[40]

As the little warship was passing Indian Head and the modest little hamlet of Glymont, she was boarded by Captain D. Pierson, skipper of the schooner *John McAdam* of St. George, Maine, who desperately sought his protection. Lieutenant Fillebrown later informed Secretary Welles of the incident: "He [Pierson] reports that he was ordered by citizens of Charles County, Md., to leave that place or his vessel would be burned tonight. His cargo consists of timber destined for the U.S. navy yard, Charlestown, Mass., and has other to take from the navy yard here." [41]

Though *Anacostia* took the big lumber schooner in tow and anchored her under the guns of Fort Washington it was apparent that at least some Southern Mary-landers had not been intimidated by the events transpiring elsewhere in the state. And their secessionist loyalties were quite obvious.

Trust, it appeared, was now an extremely diminishing commodity on the Potomac, and there seemed no shortage of secessionist saboteurs to make it even more rare. On Monday, April 29 the *National Intelligencer* reported on treachery at the Washington Navy Yard that only increased the rampant paranoia that had envelop-ed the nation's capital.

"A day or two since," stated the paper, "it was discovered that a large quantity of bombshells which the Ordinance [*sic*] Department was manufacturing, had been filled with a mixture of sand and sawdust. It is supposed to have been done by William Thompson, a pyrotechnist, who left the yard a few days since and enlisted in the Southern army. A man named Ludwig, keeper of the magazine at the Navy Yard, also left the city to join the Southern army, and is supposed to know something concerning the matter." [42]

It is unknown whether the two suspects were ever caught, but it appeared now that no one knew for certain just who might be a rebel in their midst.

6

ESCALATION

"The mettle of this Bombastes Furioso will be tried in a few days."

When Jefferson Davis presented his war message to the Confederate Congress at Montgomery, Alabama on April 29, 1861 it was thereafter assumed by both Unionists and secessionist that only a major armed conflict could now resolve the issues at hand. Without delay the Montgomery Congress passed an act declaring war between the Southern Confederacy and the United States Government, excepting North Carolina, Tennessee, Kentucky, Arkansas, Missouri, and Delaware, the territories of Arizona and New Mexico, the Indian Territory south of Kansas, and significantly the State of Maryland. The preamble to the act recited the alleged wrongs suffered by the seceding states and argued the necessity of war upon the Federal Government.[1]

***

John A. Dahlgren was now the new Commandant of the Washington Navy Yard. Though the navy's needs elsewhere demanded much of his time and energy, the necessity of keeping the Potomac open to navigation had assumed a priority status that now occupied much of his daily regimen. The destruction of buoys and lightships on the river by Confederates now required him to frequently send out vessels to replace or secure the all important navigational aids. Regular reconnaissance patrols were of necessity now deployed to keep watch for the erection of enemy batteries along the river's choke points. Every possible opportunity to maintain continuous observation of rebel motions was to be employed; all naval vessels passing to and from the city were instructed to keep a lookout for enemy activity on both the Southern Maryland and Virginia shores.

On April 28 the warship *Powhatan*, Lieutenant J. Glendy Spronston commanding, carried on board a number of buoys, sinkers, and spars, and set out from the Navy Yard on one such mission. Hugging the inshore channel past White House Point, she moved cautiously to make observations regarding potential enemy works in the area. Farther down, she anchored for the night without incident. In the distance, Spronston later reported, was heard "the sound of wheels, as if a steamer had gone up Aquia Creek." It was soon determined that the sound emanated from the steamboat *George Page*, which had recently been commandeered by the newly authorized Confederate States Navy, was now moving about inside the creek.[2]

Powhatan got underway again at dawn the next day, rounded Maryland Point and prepared buoys and spars for launching. Throughout the day navigational aids were set out to replace those recently removed by the rebels at Lower Cedar Point, Yates Bar, Montgomery Bluff Point, Swan Point, two on Kettle Bottom Shoals, and three more below the shoals. Then in an effort to insure that the buoys remained in place, Sproston visited several watermen's boats on the river, and after purchasing some fish left them with a warning that if the markers were removed he would stop all fishing on the river.[3] At the warship steamed up and anchored in Machodoc Creek, Virginia, where it was learned that the men who burned one of the lightboats resided in the neighborhood. At daylight, *Powhatan* weighed anchor and steamed down along the settlement of Madrick. Observing a number of people seining, Spronston pulled on shore, bought a parcel of fish, and "held a conversation of a civil character." In the meantime a friend of *Powhatan*'s pilot came on board and reported that two schooners, having been observed on the creek the previous day, had bodies of armed men on board, though neither were any longer present. Upon departing the creek, the warship steamed to the opposite side of the river and anchored off Ludlow's Ferry, inside Lower Cedar Point. In a little nearby inlet, Spronston discovered one of the channel buoys and the longboat of the lightship and towed them off after determing the local inhabitans to all be little more than "rank secessionists." [4]

While Spronston was busily occupied in deploying navigational aids, Lieutenant Fillebrown in *Anacostia* was ordered to drop down to Aquia Creek to look for signs of batteries or "supposed hostile gatherings" reported in the area. The reconnaissance seemed to indicate little more than normal activity at the R. F. & P. railroad facilities on the waterway. Three days later *Anacostia* and *Mount Vernon* were sent to the creek on yet another scouting mission, with the same results. It seemed hardly worth the effort.[5]

And so it continued, there being almost daily cruises from the Navy Yard down river. There appeared little to suggest enemy activity on the creek or on either shore of the river save for occasional quixotic reports or sightings here and there of elusive rebels or mariners of questionable loyalties. Aquia appeared to be nothing more than a sleepy backwater of minimal interest to the rebels. Union shipping, both commercial and military, though often under convoy, began to increase substantially on the river without molestation. On May 5, without opposition, the USS *Pocahontas* escorted in the transport steamer *Star of the South*, carrying 600 troops from Brooklyn, New York and four supply-laden steamers. The soldiers were the first to arrive at the capital city by water.[6]

***

As Washington continued to prepare for the worst, fifty-two miles to the southeast in Leonardtown a public meeting of an organization called the Southern Rights' Men of St. Mary's County convened at the courthouse on Saturday evening, May 6. On motion, Dr. Robert Neale of the Chaptico Election District was called to the chair and John F. King appointed secretary. The purpose of the meeting was stated by the chairman to be the selection of delegates to represent the county in the next Congressional Convention to be held at Upper Marlboro, Maryland on June 5 to select candidates favorable to secession for the special congressional election ordered by Governor Hicks. A resolution offered by Colonel Benjamin G. Harris was unanimously adopted.

"Resolved, That the course of our representative in Congress, Hon. George W. Hughes, receives our cordial approbation."

It was then moved and carried that the meeting proceed to elect three delegates and three alternatives to represent St. Mary's County at the convention. Colonel Theophilius Harrison, Henry G. S. Key of Leonardtown and J. Edwin Coad were selected as delegates, with Robert Ford, Dr. L. J. Sutton and James Roach chosen as alternates.

Power was given to such of the delegates as should be present in the Convention to cast the whole vote of the county. Three weeks later the Southern Right's Party of Charles County, with Judge Francis H. Digges as chairman and Charles H. Wills as secretary, would follow suit, selecting Frederick Stone, Dr. Stouten W. Dent and Dr. Thomas A. Carrico as delegates. Calvert, Charles, Anne Arundel and Prince George's counties would do likewise for their own delegations.[7]

***

By the first week of May the city of Washington began to welcome an almost continuous stream of troops. Within a short time three passenger trains and one freight train were running from Baltimore with troops even though the route was not entirely secure. Critical telegraph lines were still being cut, sometimes twice in a single day, while sabotage to the tracks was an ongoing problem. The Secretary of War recommended to General Scott that a regiment be stationed along the line as a permanent guard. One company was to be posted every four miles for protection and patrols were to be sent out from these with regularity.[8]

On Tuesday, May 14 General Butler issued orders from Baltimore designed to blunt all rebel activity in that city but to also insure the continuance of normal business as usual. He began by assuring that no loyal or well disposed citizen would be disturbed in his occupation or buiness and that private property would not be interferred with unless used to afford aid and succor to the rebels. All property, munitions of war, or aid and support for the rebellion was to be seized and held subject to confiscation. All manufacturers of arms and munitions of war were requested to report in "so that the lawfulness of their occupations may be known and understood, and all misconstructions of their doings avoided." No transportation of articles itended for aid or support of the enemy was to be tolerated, and discovery of such was to be considered as proof of the "illegal intention on the part of the consignors, and will render the goods liable to seizure and confiscation." All public assemblages, with the exception of the police, and Maryland militiamen acting under the orders of the governor "for drill or other ppurposes" was strictly forbidden. Butler also informed that the government was ready to arrange for contracts with local owners and manufacturers of equipment, clothing, munitions and provisions "in order that their workshops may be employed for loyal purposes, and the artisans of the city resume and carry on their wonted profitable occupations." To kick off the process, he informed the public that the Acting Assistant Quartermaster and Commissary of Subsistence stationed in the city had been instructed to procure and furnish, at fair prices, forty thousand rations for the use of the U.S. Army, and that "further supplies will be drawn from the city to the full extent of its capacity, if the patriotic and loyal men choose to furnish supplies. "[9]

The Federal juggernaut was now in continuous motion. Between Baltimore and Perryville train of steamers were now constantly shuttling, maintaining a line of water communication with Philadelphia "for all purposes of trade and travel" until the bridges so recently destroyed were repaired.[10] The railroad line from Annapolis to Bladensburg via Annapolis Junction also provided additional logistical support for the capital city although the route passed through dangerously hostile territory such as Bladensburg itself, deemed by the Secretary of War as "not a loyal district."

76

He recommended two companies be assigned to occupy the town. Eventually the diminutive, once thriving port on the Anacostia River, now the strategic nexus of rail traffic on the eastern rim of the District of Columbia, would be occupied by many thousands of troops.

The reestablishment of the railroad link between Annapolis, Bladensburg and Baltimore was fraught with difficulties, not the least of which was "certain reported irregularities committed by troops guarding [the] road from Annapolis to [Annapolis] Junction." Though the specifics of the irregularities were not described in Union military communiqués, they were most likely abuses by Federal troops against the civilian population. To reinforce the small detachment of the 5th New York Volunteers, which had been strung out all along the route, it was strongly "suggested" to General Scott that fifty mounted men be posted at Millersville, halfway between Annapolis and Annapolis Junction. Another guard of infantry would be stationed at the Annapolis depot, and a third infantry unit at Beltsville. Mounted patrols ranged between these points specifically "to secure the police of the road, especially as it has to be passed by working parties after each heavy train to repair breaks, &c." It seemed the only way "the discipline of the troops may be improved and the opportunities for irregularities lessened." [11]

The impact on the cities of both Washington and Annapolis and their inhabitants by the soon steady influx of troops was of course substantial. The first troops to arrive in the capital, the 7th New York Regiment, was initially quartered in the Capitol Building but soon after moved to a camp north of the city at an estate on Columbia Heights dubbed "Camp Cameron." The well ordered encampment quickly began to draw visitors and curiosity seekers from both the city and countryside. "Yesterday afternoon," noted one keen observer. "Fourteenth street presented a very gay appearance, with many carriages *en route* for the camp, and the many others who chose to foot it out. The regiment have a drill near the road every afternoon, at five o'clock." [12]

The 1st Rhode Island Volunteers, composed largely of college students, were quartered at the Patent Office where, with the 2nd Rhode Island, they were drilled and presented regular dress parades for the public. With several companies armed with the newest breech loading carbines these blue clad soldiers were soon known best for serenading the young ladies. The 12th New York "arrived without any uniforms and looked very shabby with their equipments buckled over their varicolored citizens' clothes." They were put into camp in the central part of the city at Franklin Park and shortly afterwards issued regular service uniforms. In a few weeks they were dubbed Butterfield's Regulars, after their commanding officer, Lieutenant Colonel Daniel Butterfield. Their manual of arms was faultless, and they were soon deemed one of the finest regiments in the city.[13]

As Washington's population burgeoned with mostly blue clad soldiery, some units stood out, distinguished not by their military expertise but by their substantially ethnic uniforms. They provided something of a colorful offset and an almost festive air that helped subdue tensions and raise morale among the inhabitants. There were three regiments whose uniforms were described as "particularly handsome and gay," the 39th, 69th, and 79th New York. The first, which dubbed itself the Garibaldi Guards (not to be confused with the Washngton

Garibaldi Guards) were uniformed as Italian light infantry or Bersagliari in a very dark greenish-blue cloth with flat brimmed round top hats set off with cock's feathers. The 69th was an all Irish regiment that wore coats conspicuously set off with crimson and green and carried a green flag with the harp of Erin embroidered thereon. The 79th was the colorful Highland Regiment, commanded by a brother of Secretary of War Simon Cameron. The Highlanders were noted as "very showy in their kilts," but well drilled. Regiments from Wisconsin, Minnesota, Connecticut and other New England states arrived abundantly armed and splendidly equipped, some of the latter bringing with them full regimental wagon trains. Many of these units wore a most serviceable gray uniform that would subsequently be put aside for the national blue. These organizations, the Washington press corps crowed, were composed of fine material, "handsome, stalwart, intelligent men, who could turn their minds and hands to any occupation," and who a few weeks afterwards would begin work in surrounding the city with a cordon of strong fortifications.[14]

Perhaps the most colorful unit was the 11th New York, the Fire Zouaves, "made up of vigorous men from the fire department of New York City," who arrived 1,100 strong on May 2 with a full drum corps. The unit was under the command of Colonel Elmer E. Ellsworth, a young, aggressive man who had recruited and organized it. They carried with them a magnificent national flag of silk and a crimson regimental standard upon which was embroidered in white letters "U.S. National Guards - First Regiment Zouaves, New York." Both flags were six feet by ten feet in size and mounted upon black oak staffs topped with silver spearheads that had been presented to them at New York by Mrs. John Jacob Astor, Jr. and General John A. Dix.[15]

The arrival of the rough and tumble Fire Zoauves immediately endeared them to the city. "As they appeared last night," remarked one Washington newspaper,

"no class of men could be better calculated to go through the fatigue of a campaign than Colonel Ellsworth's Zouaves. Thick set, rigged, and tough fellows they are, capable of bearing any amount of hardship. For activity, bravery, and hardihood, none can compare with these very fine boys, and if they do not give a good account of themselves in battle, it will not be from a lack of any of these qualities. Their uniform consists of a gray jacket trimmed with blue and red cord, gray pants, and red shirt, red cap with a blue band, and regulation overcoat. They are all armed with Sharp's breech loading rifles, worth $67 a piece, and huge bowie knives which can be attached to the muzzles of their rifles, to answer the purpose of bayonets. Their knapsacks are made of rubber cloth, and in case of rain they can be used so as to protect the entire body from the wet. A blanket, tin plate, knife, fork, and various other articles, can be carried in each knapsack without any inconvenience. A fatigue cap of gray felt, and a tin cup strapped on the outside of the knapsack, and a stout pair of shoes, completes the outfit." [16]

As would become custom, the arrival of new regiments usually resulted in formal reviews before the president, his cabinet and other officials. Different regiments of New Jersey troops, 3,500 strong, which had sailed in a fleet of sixteen propeller steamers to reach Washington via Annapolis, drawn up in a formation two miles long on Pennsylvania Avenue, undertook one such review on the afternoon of

May 7. At 4:30 p.m. they took up their line of march to the White House and were there appraised by President Lincoln and the Secretary of State, "who seemed to be forcibly struck with the number, precision of movement, and soldierly bearing of the men, and frequently took occasion to express their pleasure of the manifestation here given, of New Jersey's determination to preserve the Union of the States, if the service of her sons could effect it." [17]

"President Lincoln and Genl. Scott Reviewing 3 years regiment on Penn Ave. 1861." Alfred R. Waud Collection, No. 701, Prints and Photographs, Library of Congress, Washington, D.C.

An almost holiday atmosphere began to engulf the District of Columbia as the ever growing military presence continued to daily swell the city's population, slowly alleviating the sense of doom so recently felt. Even as the New Jersey troops paraded in splendid array in front of the Executive Mansion another military unit, the city's Metropolitan Rifles, entertained the public with its own display of prowess as it marched to a park on Seventh Street and engaged in a contest of competitive target practice before all. Free military concerts were soon being held with regularity on the grounds of the White House, usually beginning at 5 p.m. and ending two hours later. General Joseph K. F. Mansfield, appointed to the command of the newly created District Military Department covering the District, Maryland and Virginia, was of the opinion that the rebels might field no less than 10,000 men on the shores of the Potomac and that bombardment of the city was a strong possibility. Yet the immediate public fear of rebel occupation of the nation's capital had already begun to dissipate ever so slightly.[18]

Federal confidence continued to increase, even as secessionist Governor Letcher of Virginia issued an escalatory proclamation on May 3. The declaration authorized the commanding general of the military forces of his state to "call out, and to cause to be mustered into the service of Virginia, from time to time, as the public exigency may require, such additional number of volunteers as he may deem necessary." Twenty-two places of rendezvous for recruits were designated, including three either on or contiguous to the Potomac: Alexandria, Fredericksburg and King George County Court House.[19] The principal mustering area for troops under Brigadier General Philip St. George Cocke of Virginia, who had just been appointed to the command of the newly minted Potomac Department of the State of Virginia, and Colonel Daniel J. Ruggles of the Provisional Army of Virginia, was at Fredericksburg.

General Cocke issued his own clarion call at Fredericksburg for the support of all Virginians, invoking not only the sacred name of George Washington, but God and womanhood. "The capital of the United States has never been threatened and it is not now threatened," he proclaimed, despite the Confederate declaration of war on April 29 and numerous announcements of officials doing just that throughout the South. The North, he declared without reference to the attack on Fort Sumter, had decalred war on the south. "We make no war on them, but should Virginia soil or the grave of Washington be polluted by the tread of a single man in arms from the North of the Potomac, it will cause an open war. Men of the Potomac border, men of the Potomac Military Department; to arms! . . . Women of Virginia, cast from your arms all cowards; and breathe the pure and holy, the high and glowing inspirations of your nature, into the hearts and souls of lover, husband, brother, father, friend!" [20]

The response to Cocke's proclamation in one Washington newspaper was perhaps reflective of a new energy in the city: "The mettle of this Bombastes Furioso" stated the defiant *Daily National Republican* on May 9, "will be tried in a few days."

***

Regardless of the public sense of relief that some Washingtonians were beginning to feel, the Federal military command was anything but comfortable, especially with the situation along the southern Potomac frontier. On May 6 it was announced that the government had chartered the steamer *William B. Raney*, Captain Gallagher, to convey a military force from Annapolis down the Chesapeake as far as Dividing Creek, between the Great Wicomico and Rappahannock River, to retake the Smith Point Lightship recently hijacked by rebels. Onboard *Raney*, which was armed with four guns, was a force of seventy men under the command of Lieutenant Peirce Crosby, USN. Their mission was to recover the lightship and return it to its old position in order to again render the Potomac's entrance safe for navigation. Though failing in his first objective, Crosby returned to Annapolis not with the Smith Point Lightship but with the Windmill Point Lightboat. The lieutenant had discovered the vessel, normally stationed off the Rappahannock, while searching for the Smith Point Lightship a dozen miles up the Great Wicomico River after three armed schooners at the mouth of that river had taken possession of her. The crew had barely escaped leaving everything behind including a warm breakfast. When

Crosby recaptured the boat he observed no less than two hundred rebel cavalry in arms on the shore and in the surrounding countryside. Unfortunately, while en route up under tow of *Raney* she had exploded her boiler at the mouth of the Patuxent, severely scalding one man.[21]

In Annapolis, General Butler was disturbed to learn that the Smith Point Lightship, still sequestered somewhere in the Great Wicomico, had yet to be recovered. He promptly "ordered" Lieutenant Charles W. Flusser of the U.S. Navy, with the chartered steamer *William Underwood*, thirty seamen from the U.S. Coast Survey vessels *Alleghany* and *Foreward*, and a detachment of twenty-five men and two guns from the 8th and 100 men from the 13th New York Volunteers at Annapolis to find and recapture her. The order was followed even though the general had no direct authority over naval personnel. Upon the steamer's discovery of the lightship in Mill Creek on the Great Wicomico River, the same that had earlier evaded Lieutenant Crosby, a force of some thirty concealed rebels, believed to belong to a unit called the Lancaster Greys, opened a brisk fire upon the expeditionaries, but failed to deter them. The resolute New Yorkers found their prize stripped of everything that could be removed yet the vessel itself was retrieved in good condition and brought safely to Annapolis on May 18.[22]

Armed secessionists were becoming active in Southern Maryland, at least in small groups. The first indication of organized resistance was made apparent about midnight on May 9 when a squad of approximately fifty mounted rebels fired some twenty shots on the picket guard at the newly erected Camp Butler on the Severn River. It was later reported that the garrison "regretted that the marauders did not dismount and give an account of themselves. Similar squads are roving about, but their acts are disowned by the citizens." Violence was in the air. The following day, a person atired in civilian clothes stabbed a sentinel in the yard of the Naval Academy.[23]

Beyond the protection of military units, intimidation of anyone engaged in Union-related activities in Southern Maryland was on the rise. In one such case a contractor named Robert Spear, who was to provide a large quantity of ship timbers lying on the banks of the Potomac, had dispatched several vessels to take the material away. However, the crews, claiming they had been warned of dangers near the landing, departed without completing their assigned task. One of the vessels, manned by pro-secessionists, was taken to the Virginia shore and abandoned in a creek. The second boat supposedly retreated to safety elsewhere. Navy assistance was sought but the effort to recover the timber proved in vain.[24]

The occupation of Alexandria by General Cocke's rebel troops only increased the danger for river traffic bound to or from Washington, and occasional firing on passing vessels from the shore provided harassment too worrisome to ignore. Dahlgren was obliged to deploy *Pawnee* to take up position near the town to intimidate the foe with her heavy broadside if need be, as the smaller naval boats on the river would be unable to resist grapeshot from the wharves. [25]

Yet not all the news was bad. Samuel L. Breese, Commandant of the New York Navy Yard, had acted immediately upon Navy Secretary Welles's orders to facilitate the fitting out of a small flotilla for the Potomac River. On May 1 he informed the secretary: "I have this day agreed to purchase two very fast screw steamers selected by Commander W[ard] as adapted to his purpose. They are entirely new and will mount 24-pounder howitzer. One larger is being sought." The cost of each vessel had been $15,000. Eleven days later Breese was able to report to Welles that the core of the flying squadron, now increased to three vessels, was almost fitted out. Ward's flagship, *Thomas Freeborn*, carried two 32-pounders and was manned by forty-two officers and crew. The 269-ton, 143-foot 4-inch-long wooden sidewheeler had been purchased at New York for $32,000. The wooden screw steamers *Resolute* and *Reliance*, also procured at New York, were manned by twenty men each and armed with not only a 24-pounder smoothbore but also a 12-pounder. The three schooners were still to be acquired.[26]

"The Potomac Flotilla gunboat *Reliance*." Alfred R. Waud Collection, No. 1043, Prints and Photographs Division, Library of Congress, Washington, D.C.

Commander Ward's selection of *Resolute* and *Reliance* would serve as a model for the types of vessels needed for the work ahead, not just in the Chesapeake Tidewater but along many sections of General Scott's "Anaconda" blockade as suggested by an article in the December 1861 issue of *Scientific American* under the headline "Kinds of Gunboats Wanted."

"There are a great number of inland seas in the South, separated from the ocean by narrow necks of land, in which there are many shallow gaps, by which vessels of light draft can pass in and out and carry on an illicit trade. Two gunboats *Resolute* and *Reliance*, drawing only from six to seven feet, are the very kind adapted for this service, and fifteen of such are needed. Each is 93 feet in length, 16 feet in breadth, draft of water 6 feet 5 inches, tonnage 100 tons. Their hulls are very strong; they are heavily coppered, and their sterns are protected by thick boiler iron. They are supplied with vertical direct acting engines; the cylinders are 17 by 17 inches. The diameter of their propellers is 7 feet 8 inches, pitch 14 feet, and 4 blades. The boilers are return tubular 15 feet in length, by 6 feet ten inches in breadth, height 8 feet. Each boat consumes only about one tun of coal in four hours, and the boilers can steam at a pressure of 100 pounds, and the engine and boilers do not weight quite twenty tuns. They are stanch and very fleet gunboats – perfect little bull dogs of war, and are a terror to all the smuggling, sailing schooners on the 'secceh' coast of Virginia where they have been cruising." [27]

***

On May 17 Commander James H. Ward set out for Chesapeake Bay aboard *Thomas Freeborn* accompanied by one of the two propeller steamers, with the other following soon afterwards. The squadron would arrive at the Washington Navy Yard three days later amidst a flurry of disturbing news: the rebels were erecting their first major defense works on the Potomac River at Aquia Creek.[28]

The first indication of enemy activity on the creek had been discovered a few days earlier during a cruise by *Mount Vernon*. Lieutenant Spronston, commander of the gunboat, was a cautious officer. When on May 13 he brought his ship to for the night off Aquia Creek, he expected it to be no different than previous evenings in dangerous territory. Shortly after dropping anchor he heard the beating of drums at the creek landing but decided to hold fast. At midnight the wind picked up and a rainstorm assaulted the Potomac Valley, obliging him to let go his second anchor. Then with the daylight, the crisp sounds of reveille were heard from the same quarter as the drums had been the previous evening. After getting underway, Spronston determined to investigate and stood into the creek towards a long wharf, projecting from the south shore. Informed by his pilot that the channel was very narrow with but ten or twelve feet of water and not enough room in which to turn the ship, he nevertheless pressed cautiously on.

Spronston was perhaps not entirely surprised at what he then saw. He had been informed by the pilot that a young mariner named Henry Hainey, who had been driven out of Alexandria for his Unionist sentiments, had recently come up from Aquia and reported seeing a four-gun battery there. Then the lieutenant confirmed Hainey's report and observed an earthen fortification inshore of the wharf and adjacent to a house. Approaching to within a third of a mile from the works, all the while keeping his guns trained on them, he focused his glass upon the semicircular mound. Quickly he counted four embrasures. In one of the embrasures closest to the house he observed a 32-pounder trained directly on him – with an officer holding the lock string prepared to fire. Another gun was being mounted in the second embrasure even as he watched. In the third embrasure was a field gun pointed to the opposite end of the wharf upon which, judging from the number of men there, were two additional field pieces, both concealed. Perhaps as many as twenty men were also engaged in cutting down trees in front of the main fort, permitting both its big guns and small arms a better field of fire. The silent standoff continued for ten to fifteen minutes with neither side fully prepared for battle or daring to open fire, but taking close observations of each other. Spronston scrutinized with concern the steamer *George Page* just below the bend of the creek, fortunately with no signs of having her steam up.

Suddenly the spell was broken when *Pocahonta*s, then en route to the Rappahannock, was sighted steaming down the river. Spronston immediately ordered *Mount Vernon* to back round and steam out of the creek to communicate with her sister ship.

On May 18 *Anacostia*'s commander, having finally been apprised of the rebel operations underway on the waterway, was the first to reach Washington and to

83

formally report to Dahlgren: "a battery at Aquia Creek; four guns and one heavy caliber. Work not completed. About 200 men about it," some armed and others laboring on the earthworks. The works being thrown up were immediately adjacent to a hotel at the terminus of the R. F. & P. Railroad. A small Confederate flag waved over the engine house, and *George Page* lay at anchor a half mile above the battery. The following day, while en route back to Washington, *Mount Vernon* confirmed the news.[29]

While in the Great Wicomico, after boarding a schooner bound from the Port of Philadelphia to Fredericksburg, *Mount Vernon*'s new commander, John P. Gillis, provided Secretary Welles with his opinion of what to do about the new threat. "If a storming party were in an armed steamer of light draft, with boats to land, the battery could be taken and destroyed."[30] Though aggressive in intent, the scheme would soon be found anything but practical.

The much feared rebel threat to river traffic was now becoming a reality, and the potential for a rebel amphibious incursion into Southern Maryland a quite distinct possibility.

***

By mid-May the Federal presence in Maryland north of the rail line between Annapolis and Bladensburg, at the edge of the District of Columbia, was burgeoning. In Annapolis a short railway running from the city wharf through the Naval Academy grounds and then up to the main depot had been completed under the superintendence of Captain John Maralees, thereby reconnecting the capital of the nation with the capital of Maryland. Eight hundred men of the 2nd New York Volunteers were now stationed along the railway on guard, from Annapolis Junction to Washington. Freight cars loaded at Philadelphia could now proceed to Perryville by rail and from there by steamer to the Annapolis pier and then carried safely to Washington by train, providing a logistical circumvention around Baltimore. By May 13 the Northern Central Raiload had been thoroughly repaired, and through freight trains to Baltimore and then directly to the District of Columbia commenced operations immediately. Now two arms of communications and transport had been opened to the capital.[31]

At Annapolis two large 32-pounders were mounted in a round earthwork called Fort Stevens, at the lower end of the Naval Academy grounds, to command the Severn River's entrance to the bay below the city. The men manning the guns were daily drilled should some chance be offered to test their efficiency against the secessionist threat, which seemed to be diminishing by the hour. More than 2,000 troopers, the 13th and 20th New York Volunteers, and a light artillery company, all of whom would soon be rotated to Washington upon the arrival of the next reinforcements, temporarily occupied the city. Indeed, the Annapolis waterfront seemed alive with steamers and schooners unloading their cargoes, everything from railroad iron and coal to stores and newly minted soldiers. At least one or more warships would soon be ever present to protect the fulcrum of support so necessary to preserve Washington and Maryland for the Union.[32]   ***

It was 2 p.m., May 20, when *Thomas Freeborn* arrived at the Washington Navy Yard, undoubtedly much to Commandant Dahlgren's relief, bringing with her a small craft that had been encountered and taken en route under suspicion of nefarious activity.[33]

"Commander James H. Ward, USN." Naval Historical and Heritage Command, Washington, D.C.

Ward's entrance came none too soon, as the few naval vessels in the region were already stretched to their limits in constant cruising. The day after *Freeborn*'s arrival, Commander Gillis in *Pocahontas*, while patrolling off Machodoc Creek, observed the steamer *James Guy* exiting the little waterway, obviously having engaged in some illicit operation. This time, without delay he took the vessel into Federal custody and escorted her to the Navy Yard. The owner loudly professed that *he* had brought her to Washington under *convoy* of *Pocahontas* "to save his vessel," despite Gillis's report to the contrary. Dahlgren referred the matter to Secretary Welles. Within days, the little 156-ton *James Guy* would be engaged in Union military operations on the Potomac, transporting troops, helping to run down spies, and stem contraband traffic in Southern Maryland.[34] But for the moment they seemed the least of the Navy Department's worries for it was now determined that the rebels were definitely engaged in something serious on Aquia Creek.

***

Officially designated as belonging to the Atlantic Blockading Squadron headquartered in Hampton Roads, Ward was obliged to report to his squadron commander, Flag Officer Pendergrast, aboard the USS *Cumberland*, to receive his first assignment. Thus only two days after arriving at the Washington Navy Yard *Thomas Freeborn* departed for Fort Monroe, Virginia, now the only Federal military asset still in Federal hands on the lower Chesapeake.[35] The voyage proved from the outset to be both troublesome and educational. As the ship sailed south Ward decided to make the most of it by taking observations of potential enemy strong-points along the way. Then having progressed only as far as Tomkins Shoal off Maryland Point, and barely five miles above Mathias Point, the pilot ran the ship aground, attributing the stranding to the latest removal of buoys by the rebels. Employing the aid of a Washington-bound armed tug, *Freeborn* was eventually refloated but not before Ward took the opportunity of personally visiting the Maryland shore. The locals professed to be strong Unionists who had no intercourse with Virginia. Yet he was also informed that others maintained a constant communication between Port Tobacco and Mathias Point. "Disaffected Marylanders," they told him, "go over that way to join the Virginia forces," along with supplies that were sent via the same route. Vowing to inform his flag officer of the findings, Ward believed it was probable that he might be directed to return to this region of the Potomac as he had originally proposed, "in which event I shall be pretty sure to know something about." [36]

Two days after Ward's departure a military operation was undertaken that would immeasurably influence the war on the Potomac, the safety of Washington and serve to discourage secessionists in Southern Maryland – namely the invasion and occupation of the city of Alexandria and the heights of Arlington, Virginia. Though troops had been flowing into the capital for days, Union military planners had been uncertain what rebel forces were up to. The close proximity of Alexandria, within eyesight of the Capitol of the United States, and the danger of rebel batteries being mounted on Arlington Heights, had become psychologically unbearable. Strategically, with Alexandria serving as the railhead terminus for the Orange and Alexandria Railroad, the Loudon and Hampshire, and the Washington and Alexandria Railroad, the city had become a visible threat while in rebel hands. With the gunboat *George Page* on the river and Alexandria under their control, Con-federates might effectively blockade the capital's water communications with a combination of batteries and the warship. If reinforced, they might even launch an assault on Washington, or an invasion of Southern Maryland to facilitate a statewide secessionist insurrection. If the loyalty of Alexandrians was of any question, on May 23, the inhabitants cast their final votes in the statewide referendum confirming Virginia's joining the Confederacy. The vote of 958 for to 106 in the town against removed all Unionist objections towards armed Federal occupation.[37]

At 2:00 a.m., May 24, even before the votes were counted, a well organized surprise Union invasion of Northern Virginia, planned in utmost secrecy to capture Alexandria and Arlington Heights, began in earnest. Federal troops thrust faultlessly and without loss into rebel territory across the Potomac via the Long Bridge from Washington, the Potomac Aqueduct from Georgetown, and the Chain Bridge, three miles above Georgetown. A flanking assault by water from Giesboro Point to the docks of Alexandria aboard the steamers *Baltimore*, *Mount Vernon* and *James Guy* under the protection of the USS *Pawnee* was directed by Commander Rowan. At 4:20 a.m., with his ship's powerful broadside aimed directly at the Alexandria waterfront, Rowan dispatched Lieutenant Reigert B. Lowry to the shore before the three steamers landed their troops to demand the surrender of the town from Major Alexander H. Terrett, the Confederate commander in charge. Standing in an open street in the predawn darkness, surrounded by excited Virginia soldiers, the two officers conferred in civil fashion. In Rowan's name, Lowry ordered the surrender of the town and the garrison therein, stating that resistance was useless and that the demand was actuated "simply by a desire to spare the shedding of blood of women and children." After some negotiation it was agreed that Terrett and his garrison of no more than 500 men, if permitted to retire unmolested and without opposition, would relinquish the town to Federal troops by 8:00 a.m.[38]

The only casualty in the entire operation had been Colonel Elmer Ellsworth of the Fire Zouaves, killed by a well known secessionist named James Jackson, owner of the Marshal House Hotel on King Street, when the colonel attempted to remove a Confederate flag from the hotel roof. In the melee Jackson was also shot dead.[39]

On the day following the shootings, funeral services for Colonel Ellsworth were held in the East Room of the White House where both the president and Mrs. Lincoln attended.

Both North and South now had their first martyrs.

7

A SHEET OF FLAME
"Much agitation prevails along the Potomac coast."

Despite the Union's stunning surprise occupation of Alexandria, rebel activities on the Virginia side of the Potomac frontier from Quantico Creek as far south as the Northern Neck opposite Charles and St. Mary's counties were becoming increasingly provocative. The only truly notable Union strong point on the Southern Maryland shore was Fort Washington, which had been strengthened with a muscular new battery. It was reported on May 27 that "32-pounders are all mounted, the furnaces for heating shot are in apple pie order, the magazines are full, the hand grenades are ready for use at a moment's notice, the bombs are 'lying around loose,' and the artillerists sleep nightly beneath their guns. It is the intention of the Government to erect a battery on the hill, immediately behind the fort." [1]

The Washington press reported the following day that the Virginians had obstructed the mouth of Coan River, a tributary of the lower Potomac nearly seven miles southwest of Point Lookout, by sinking vessels in the channel to prevent the ingress of Federal warships. The little waterway, it was believed, afforded substantial access to Northumberland County, Virginia, "and a large district of country in that section of the State." Though the sunken ships were reported to be plainly visible and said to reach entirely across the channel, effectively protecting the waterway from seaborne access via the Potomac to the thriving town of Heathsville, the veracity of the story was unverified but worrisome. And opposite Budd's Ferry, in the vicinity of Quantico Creek, a small U.S. Navy steamer from the Washington Navy Yard had captured and burned a rebel schooner on the Virginia shore.[2]

Now that it was clear that enemy works were being built there, Aquia Creek was another matter. At about sunset between 6:30 and 7:00 p.m. on the evening of Wednesday, May 29, Commander Ward, recently returned from Hampton Roads, determined to challenge the new Railroad Battery on the little waterway and test its strength. The engagement was to provide the first of many stings to come from the "Anaconda's Tail," and the first land-sea engagement of the Civil War.

While steaming southward *Thomas Freeborn* and *Resolute* opened the contest with a desultory fire upon two batteries on the creek, one of which was adjacent to the long wharf. The other, a new one known as the Walker Battery, of four rifled 3-inch 6-pounder field guns, was situated in a hollow between two hills, about a mile below. The gunboat, simply testing range and seeking the degree of the enemy's response, slowly expended between twelve and fourteen shot and shell. A single rebel gun near the wharf replied in kind firing a pair of solid shot (inaccurately presumed by Federals to be 64-pound ball) and ten shells.[3]

The firing lasted less than an hour. [4] The cost to either side had been minimal. A single Confederate soldier, said to be a resident of Fredericksburg, was slightly wounded in the hand or arm by an exploding shell fragment, but that was all. The exchange had been little more than a feeling out process in which no casualties were registered. The Richmond press, however, in a typical exaggeration of facts adopted by both sides during the war, managed to enlarge upon the truth by lionizing the role of the battery "under the direction of one of the best gunners in the world, Mr. Cunningham, formerly of the Washington Navy Yard." According to the *Richmond Examiner* the gunner's shots "took effect in the foremost steamer's hull, and a shell burst upon her deck." A witness watching the exchange through a spyglass from the Maryland side of the river was quoted as having seen "the crew pick up from the deck of the steamer some twenty-five or thirty dead or wounded persons," which of course was false. But it certainly looked good to the citizens of Richmond.[5]

Having been notified that a fight was underway and fearing the worst lay ahead, namely a Union landing, Colonel Ruggles immediately assembled the whole force available to him, the 2nd Tennessee and a battalion of volunteers, 1,200 men in all, at Camp Mercer, near Fredericksburg. As soon as the troops were mustered he entrained 700 men, all that could be carried aboard, intending on sending the train back for the remaining 500, but arrived at Aquia well after the exchange had been terminated. With the affair apparently over, the general and his men promptly reboarded the train and returned to the town where they arrived about 5 a.m., May 30. Though neither side had gained an advantage he was still certain that it was the Union's intention to come ashore in Virginia. "Much agitation prevails along the Potomac coast," Ruggles reported, "from the apprehension that the enemy will land in large and small numbers to devastate and plunder." He thus recommended that 12-, 18-, and 32-pounders be furnished for establishing batteries at strategic points along the Potomac River shoreline "for surprising and harassing the enemy." [6]

While having reinforced his interest in further testing the Aquia defenses, Ward felt obligated to examine another worrisome point on the river before addressing the enemy works on the creek. The following day the commander landed at Mathias Point accompanied by Acting Master Budd, Master's Mate Lee and a small party of seamen. The site was one of the key Potomac River choke points at the edge of a very narrow channel, situated on the Virginia shore at a sharp bend in the waterway directly opposite the entrance to the Port Tobacco River. It had been one that Captain William F. Lynch of the Confederate Navy had already visited at the beginning of May, under the direction of Thomas H. Williamson, Chief Engineer of the Virginia State force, as a possible location for a semicircular ten-gun battery to prevent passage of Union vessels on the river. He had nevertheless recommended against the project as it would require more supporting troops than were at the time available. The proposed construction was thus postponed until more men were at hand. The guns originally earmarked for the battery were sent instead to Aquia Creek to defend the direct rail approaches to Fredericksburg, and the Mathias Point plan was temporarily set aside.

Ward found the site heavily forested with dense jungle-like ground cover twenty feet above the water that made a "minute" exploration of the whole point difficult. The party was only able to penetrate a belt 300 yards thick and three miles long without discovering evidence of enemy works. "I am," Ward informed Secretary Welles, "therefore able to speak with ocular certainty . . . to say that not a sign of a movement, the cutting of a sapling, driving a stake, or casting a shovelful of earth toward the erection of a battery exists." He felt secure now in turning his full attention to the Confederate Aquia Creek defenses.[7]

"Sighting a gun on board U.S.S. Thomas Freeborn, 1861." Naval Historical and Heritage Command, Washington, D.C.

By Friday, May 31 word of the little skirmish at Aquia had yet to reach Washington, and other far more newsworthy items regarding the war were dominating the conversations on Pennsylvania Avenue. It was noted with some interest locally that the converted merchant steamer USS *Monticello* (formerly *Star*), Captain Henry Eagle, had arrived at the Navy Yard on Thursday, May 30 bringing with her the schooners *Catherine* of Newbern, North Carolina, and *Iris* of Baltimore, loaded with naval stores. Both were prizes taken seventy miles south of the Virginia coast by the USS *Harriet Lane*, an ex-revenue cutter. *Monticello* had been on blockade duty, constantly under steam for forty-five days, and had been injured in a skirmish off Sewell's Point, Virginia. She was in need of repairs, and since the Gosport Navy Yard had fallen to the rebels, the closest naval facility was at Washington. Her arrival did not go unnoticed. "President Lincoln," it was announced, "accompanied by Ex-Gov. [Nathaniel P.] Banks of Mass., visited the steamer *Monticello* at the Navy Yard, and examined with much interest the effects of the shots from Sewall's Point last week." That same evening the three-masted steam propeller *Stars and Stripes* also arrived and tied up at the Arsenal to take on board a heavy battery, in order to rejoin the blockading squadron down the bay.[8]

***

It was already warm by 10:30 a.m. on the morning of Friday, May 31, 1861 when three Union warships steamed down the Potomac toward Aquia Creek. *Thomas Freeborn*, the "first class" former New York steam tug now serving as flagship of the little squadron, was in the lead, followed by *Resolute* and the recently

90

arrived *Anacostia*, as well as a diminutive transport schooner and a number of longboats and launches.[9]

The ships of the tiny flotilla were anything but imposing. Not until May 13 had *Thomas Feeborn* been armed with a pair of long 32-pounders mounted fore and aft and of a pattern first cast in 1819. Her most unique feature were the gun's pivot carriages, invented, built and installed by Commander Ward himself.[10] *Resolute*'s two smooth-bore howitzers, were reliable but less imposing. *Anacostia*, a 217-ton, 217-foot-long screw steamer, armed with two 9-inch Dahlgrens, had for some time been a familiar sight on the Potomac having been originally chartered by the navy in 1858 and subsequently purchased for service as a tender.[11]

Upon approaching the creek the squadron was immediately greeted by shots from rifled field guns of the Walker Battery. The first fire, which fell short, was issued from an eminence to the rear of the guns at the railroad terminus near the wharf but served as a warning of what was to come. As soon as the first rebel projectile had been sent, all of the battery garrison mounted the earthworks and cheered. Within seconds, as if summoned by the rebel yells, Yankee shells began to rain down on Confederate territory as the Union gunboats instantly opened a vigorous return fire. Concentrating at first on the field guns, they would later pay attention to the battery protected by sand berms near the long wharf a mile below.[12]

"Action between the U.S. vessels Pawnee and Freeborn and the rebel batteries at Acquia [*sic*] Creek." Alfred R. Waud Collection, 277, Prints and Photographs, Library of Congress, Washington, D.C.

Commander Ward, supposing that he possessed guns of superior range if not firepower, was aggressive but not foolish and for the most part kept his squadron out of reach of the enemy's artillery. He quickly discerned that the Walker Battery, nestled amidst hills overlooking the creek entrance, was simply too elevated for his naval guns to assail. Nevertheless, the exchange of fire was unrelenting as shot and exploding shells passed through the air in both directions, drawing both cheers and curses from the onlookers in the surrounding hills. Occasionally such observation points proved quite dangerous. The moment a company emerged from the woods to obtain a more satisfactory view of the fight, shells exploded over them though so miraculously scattered as to cause no injury. One of the ten-second exploding shells thrown by a rifled gun on *Anacostia* was at first believed to have done so much damage, it seemed to Ward, that "it is hardly possible the enemy can have escaped considerable loss." Two shots completely demolished a sand bunker in which Captain Lynch, the commander of Confederate naval defenses on the Potomac, and several of his officers were ensconced. Incredibly neither Lynch nor anyone else was killed.

As the artillery duel continued unabated, most of the rebel defenders remained defiant but also under cover. Displays of pluck were notable. The four 3-inch rifled guns of the Walker Battery were commanded by a young naval cadet from Nashville named Patton Robertson "who fired the cannon with remarkable precision, and displayed, for a young man, not yet of age, the most dauntless and cool bravery." Though it was reluctantly admitted by the rebels that some of the Union's shooting was well directed, one defender later remarked rather gleefully that the "only damage to our side was the death of a chicken, though a stray ball killed a horse on the opposite side of the creek." [13]

Captain Lynch's situation was difficult, for as long as the Union vessels remained circling about at a distance it was pointless to waste valuable ammunition. He thus did his best to economize, firing only when a warship dared narrow the range. During the entire battle, he later reported, his battery fired just fifty-six shots, only three of which had any effect (though one rebel observer reported as many as seventy-six shots had been fired). His restraint was in bold contrast to the hail of iron from the naval guns, which would deliver "before the close 592 shots, comprised of shell and balls of the largest dimensions." [14]

By noon the battery by the wharf had finally been silenced. Now the flotilla began to renew the attack on the Walker Battery "preparatory to engaging it with more effect, as it was about two miles from the vessels." [15] Only a short time before, the USS *Keystone State*, a third-rate, 1,364-ton sidewheeler en route from below to the Washington Navy Yard (and apparently mistaken by rebel observers to be *Pawnee*), stopped to observe the fight for several hours before bringing the first word of the engagement to the capital city. The Navy Department immediately dispatched *Pawnee* downriver to assist should combat be resumed the next day. The account first appearing in the press noted "the attacking vessels were from ½ to 1¼ mile from the nearest battery" and that the "guns at the batteries, judging from the shot, were not heavier than 32-pounders." It was also noted that from the motions of the *Anacostia*, which had quit the fight and turned upriver to secure more ammunition, that she had been struck by a ball, an injury later noted as undoubtedly slight "as she hauled down near the lower battery to engage" before turning upriver.[16]

The rebel firing continued though now only from the Walker Battery and with little effect other than knocking the hat off of one of the army officers of the 71st New York Regiment, some of whom had been brought along in the event a landing opportunity presented itself. By 1:30 p.m. it was all over.[17] "After an incessant discharge," Ward reported to Secretary Welles, "kept up for two hours by both our 32-pounders, and the expenditure of all the ammunition suitable for distant firing." Three batteries at the railroad terminus appeared to have been silenced. Yet, firing from the new batteries on the heights, "which reached us in volleys, dropping the shot on board and about us like hail for nearly an hour," had fortunately caused no injuries. Thus, he was obliged to order the squadron off, "as the heights proved wholly above the reach of our elevation." [18]

"The Attack on the Batteries at the Entrance of Aquia Creek, Potomac River, by the United States Vessels 'Pawnee,' 'Yankee,' 'Thomas Freeborn,' 'Anacostia' and 'Resolute,' June 1st, 1861." *Yankee*'s participation is not mentioned in official reports of the engagement. The steamer pictured inside the creek is presumable the *George Page*. *Frank Leslie's Illustrated Newspaper*, Naval Historical and Heritage Command, Washington, D.C.

In the meantime word of the contest had been sent to Fredericksburg where Colonel Ruggles was again informed. Without delay he roused what available forces he could from the immediate vicinity as well as Colonel William B. Bate's Tennessee Legion, a brigade composed of Tennesseans and Virginians (also known as Walker's Legion). As before, they arrived soon after the firing had ceased. This time, however, rather than send them back to their old base and to be better able to respond to any future attack, the general transferred the Tennesseans to Brooke's Station, on the north side of Potomac Creek where the railroad bridge crossed the waterway six miles from Aquia and seven miles from Feredreicksburg. From there lateral movements could be easily made "to cross the coasts and forward movements to cover the batteries with great facility." Virginia's Governor Letcher, who believed the engagement had served no other function than to waste precious ammunition and to expose the condition and strength of the batteries to the enemy, reprimanded Ruggles for allowing forces under his command to respond to the attack at all.[19]

Though only one rebel battery had in fact been temporarily silenced, the others remained intact. The contest, which had resulted neither in gain nor loss for either side, had served little purpose other than to provide field experience for rebel gunners and naval artillerists, and for Ward a test of his innovative gun carriages. The commander, of course, lauded his men. "I can not speak in too high terms of the officers and men," he wrote, "whose coolness and activity under great exposure are beyond praise. As the former are all acting, having volunteered from civil life, none but myself being of the Regular Navy, I beg leave to ask for them a favorable consideration by the Government." [20]

Nor were the Confederates shy in noting the service of their own defenders. Notwithstanding his reprimand, Ruggles, though not a witness to the action, was quick to offer praise. "The conduct," he wrote, "of the troops in the batteries – that of Captain Walker, with his 6-pounder rifle guns, having been brought early into the action – is represented as having been admirable, including the covering and protecting force on the field." [21]

For his part, Ward was delighted with the performance of his gun mounts. "Both the guns are on carriages of the new construction, devised by myself," he informed Secretary Welles with obvious pleasure, "and answered admirably, working with such ease that the crews came out of action wholly unfatigued. In the extreme sweep of 140° which these carriages have, together with their ease and rapidity of movement, enabling the vessel to constantly change position, yet keep up accurate fire, which impaired the enemy's range and direction – he firing always with rifled cannon – is to be materially attributed our escape without loss of life or damage to the vessels or machinery . . . The men say they are as free from fatigue as when they entered action." [22]

The success of the gun carriage design was lauded in the Washington press as "a good thing for the service," but the commander's sagacity, considering the very limited naval protection available in the region, was something else. The *National Republican* mildly scolded him by noting that "we trust Captain Ward will henceforth keep his flagship . . . out of further danger, unless in cases where the expected results will justify the exposure." [23]

The engagement had in truth proved two things. In his report to Secretary Welles, Ward expressed doubts that it was possible to reduce the rebel batteries on the heights. The enemy was proving to be an amorphous foe who easily moved about. Moreover, he felt the batteries weren't really that important as they were both remote from the ship channel and the river itself, and commanded only the railroad terminus. Owing to the fact that *Resolute* was armed with only a small smoothbore gun, he had been forced to forbid either her or *Anacostia* from coming closely under enemy fire to which they could not reply "with even an approximate effect." He requested both be supplied with the additional small rifled gun that had been originally requested the previous month.[24]

Whatever thoughts Ward may have felt regarding the limited value of the rebel batteries on the evening of May 31, however, would be all but forgotten by the following morning.

***

By the time the USS *Pawnee* had departed Washington on the evening of May 31 nothing more had been heard from the scene of combat. That night as the big warship warily steamed southward in the dark, she encountered Lieutenant Jared P. K. Mygatt's gunboat *Reliance*, which had been held back from participating in the fight during the day. Upon communicating with the little screw steamer, *Pawnee*'s commander, Stephen C. Rowan, was informed that Ward had retired to the south of Aquia. At 3 a.m., June 1 *Pawnee* steamed past the creek unobstructed and joined *Freeborn* three hours later. Rowan soon learned of Ward's latest plan, which, despite the acknowledged futility of a continued engagement, was quite simply a resumption of the previous day's fight. "At 9," he later reported after resupplying the flagship with ammunition, "I stood for Aquia Creek in company with the *Freeborn* for the purpose of attacking the batteries." 25

The reappearance of Union warships off Aquia several hours later was immediately communicated to Colonel Ruggles. The enemy, he was informed, had increased in numbers and strength to five steamers, accompanied by two transport ships with troops, one of which was of considerable size. They had appeared off the Aquia Creek batteries with the evident intention of attacking again. For the third time in as many days he embarked troops on a train. Soon after it had departed heavy firing was heard from the direction of the creek. Again deeply concerned, there being such a strong naval force present, that a landing may be in the offing, he immediately requested that headquarters dispatch more troops. "I am in want of at least 1,000 well disciplined volunteers as soon as it is possible to send them," he wrote just before departing for the front. "Twenty thousand musket caps are absolutely necessary for the use of troops with percussion arms." 26

Though as many as five vessels were in the area only two, *Thomas Freeborn* and *Pawnee*, would bear the brunt of battle as *Reliance* and *Anacostia* were both instructed not to go within firing range of the rebel guns (though the Confederates would later reported that *Anacostia* had also entered the engagement). At 11 a.m. the two main ships of the flotilla stood in towards the steamboat wharf on the creek in an attempt to approach the defenses at the railroad landing, dubbed Battery No. 1, or the Naval Battery, as near as the muddy, shoal water would permit before opening fire. As the warships closed in Rowan observed men scurrying about setting fire to the buildings at the end of the railroad wharf. Ashore, Battery No. 1 revealed numerous embrasures and was now armed with at least eight guns. Among them was one directed by Lieutenant Robertson that had been moved down from the Walker Battery, and under the direct personal command of Captain Lynch. The battery itself had been closed and its three remaining guns held in reserve along with Colonel Bate's unit, Walker's Legion, to prevent any Union landing attempt. As before, when approximately two miles from their destination, the approaching warships were greeted by rebel fire from two rifled cannon and a heavy gun supposed to be a 68-pounder.27

This time Union firepower was substantially greater than before owing to the eight 9-inch Dahlgrens and two 12-pounders aboard *Pawnee*, as well as *Thomas Freeborn*'s pair of heavy 32's. *Freeborn*, being of lighter draft, cautiously led the way while *Pawnee* kept just outside of her starboard quarter to avoid grounding. It was

11:30 a.m. when at a range of 2,000 yards, Captain Rowan opened fire but with little effect owing to distance. Carefully, he maneuvered behind Ward to push his own ship further in, until actually touching the mud bottom 1,700 yards from his target. "Finding my 15-second shell fell short with all the elevation the ports admitted of," recalled Rowan, "I ranged ahead of the *Freeborn* and edged in as near as I could, feeling the way with the lead till I got within range of the forts with the 15-second shell, when we opened a heavy fire." There, he began to liberally shower the enemy batteries and railroad facilities with both shot and shell in a veritable scroll of flame.[28]

Ashore, Captain Lynch had mistakenly observed during the May 31 engagement that the Union warships had been employing the cluster of buildings at the extremity of the railroad wharf as a line of sight upon his nearest battery. Upon learning of the return of the flotilla, he immediately acted to prevent its further use. "I had all the furniture, etc., together with the weather boarding conveyed to the rear of the battery," he later reported to Richmond, "and in the course of the forenoon set fire to and blew up the platform and outer edge of the bridge." Ironically Ward attributed its destruction by the rebels to a belief that it formed an *impediment* to their own aim![29]

In the meantime Commander Rowan did his best to maintain *Pawnee*'s position as long as possible but owing to wind and tide the ship fell off despite all efforts to hold her steady. It soon became necessary to round out into the river and approach once again on the same tack. This time, having brought his ship in to the northwest of *Freeborn* and nearer than the first approach – as close as could safely be done with but two feet of water to spare – he again opened a terrible fire from five of his 9-inch guns. The broadsides were devastating, and the big warship's sides appeared "often a sheet of flame owing to the rapidity of her discharges." [30]

Thrice the batteries were silenced. Men could be seen running from their guns when the fire was hottest, much to the glee of Union gunners, but resumed their own shooting whenever the naval ordnance fell silent. From time to time some of the Tennessee men carefully ventured forth from their shelters to better view the fight only to be driven back by Union fire. Houses near the rebel works were destroyed. *Pawnee*'s shells relentlessly pounded the southern edge of the railroad bridge, which was already afire. Soon the end of the wharf and the adjacent large passenger and freight depot were consumed. By late afternoon only charred piles of the pier remained to mark its former position. The Richmond, Fredericksburg and Potomac Railroad Company later estimated the loss at $11,200.[31]

The most noticeable effect of *Pawnee*'s fire, it was reported back in Washington, "was from the explosion of a shell in an angle of one of the enemy's batteries, with tremendous effect, driving out the defenders from their position of the works." [32]

Though horrific, the bombardment was not enough. "We knocked the depot to pieces, and dashed the earth about the ears of the men in the battery, but the rifled guns were too well protected to be injured at such a distance, and we have not men enough for a boat attack." But the damage was growing as houses in the Confederate rear were much "knocked about," and the railroad track torn up in three or four places.[33]

And still the battle continued though the firing from the shore was scarcely as spirited as even the day before. Aboard *Thomas Freeborn*, owing to the close proximity of the combatants, the "shot flew round among the men with great liveliness. The officers remark upon the peculiar 'whiz-z-z' made by the rifled cannon shots fired by the enemy." The Confederates' rifled guns were well served and, it was later reported in Washington, nearly "every shot was a good line shot, but they generally flew high, missing the hull and cutting us aloft." It was not so with *Pawnee*. Her size alone made for a far more promising target and thus the most easily hit. The ship was soon the recipient of numerous wounds both below and aloft. Yet the wall of fire from her own guns seldom halted.[34]

Captain Lynch, not knowing how long the fight would continue or if his ammunition could be replenished, later defended his rationing of return fire. "Our sand banks not being en barbette," he said, "we could only fire as the enemy came within range through the embrasures. This, added to the long distance at which he kept, and the necessity of occasionally repairing damages to the breastwork, combined with my desire to save ammunition, constrained me to withhold fire except when something like a fair shot presented." [35]

The subdued rebel fire now encouraged *Anacostia* to enter the fray with her single gun, which was said to have done good work firing without intermission. The fee was several hits by rebel guns, though none caused much damage.[36]

For the Union gunners, it was reported, the "practice was excellent. The men are well drilled, and seemed to regard the action as a frolic, laughing at the sharp whistling of the rifled shot that flew about us, and damning the 'secessers' cordially for getting into such an inaccessible place." [37]

About this time Colonel Ruggles arrived for a third time from Feredreicksburg, having entrained there at 11:00 a.m. after receiving the first report of the impending attack.[38]

***

As morning turned into early afternoon the heat of the day increased substantially. Unlike the day before, those sailors who were managing the burning hot iron guns began to grow fatigued. Ward's gun carriages performed with less effectiveness and more difficulty than the previous day when the pivoting arrangement of the after gun gave out in the last hour of the action and it became necessary for the weapon to be placed on traditional trucks. The recoil from the remounted gun, unhappily, "became severely racking to the vessel; the gun was served slower and with less accuracy, and with greater increased awkwardness as well as fatigue to the men." [39]

By 3:30 p.m. the rebel return fire, now from but one lone gun, was all but halted after which only two or three projectiles were thrown from the shore "by a few individuals seen stealthily now and then to emerge from concealment and hastily load and fire a single shot." It appeared from the deck of *Freeborn* that the bulk of the enemy gunners and infantry had left a half hour earlier, and groups of from two to twenty men "were observed from time to time taking to their heels along the beach with a speed and bottom truly commendable for its prudence and highly amusing to the seamen." For Ward, after a five hour long duel, it did "not seem advisable to permit so feeble a fire to wear out my men, therefore discontinued the

97

engagement." Ammunition was running short, and most if not all of the shells fused for long range had been expended. By 4:30 p.m. the guns on both sides fell silent.[40]

From the flotilla's vantage point it was impossible to tell what the enemy's casualties were, although it was believed they must have suffered. In fact the opposite was true. Both Lynch and Ruggles reported that no one had been hurt and no serious damage had been done to the batteries "thanks to a kind Providence, who seems to smile benignly upon our cause." [41]

As for the flotilla, notable damage had been incurred. Many if not most of the shots fired by the rebels were from rifled cannon and were so effective, it was said, that they passed through "a thin vessel like a dose of salts." Several of the hundred or more projectiles that had fallen near and aboard *Freeborn*, including elongated iron shot four inches in diameter and eight inches in length that were picked up on her deck after the battle, were but a small portion of the 1,000 shots discharged at the flotilla during the fight. Half a dozen shots had been put clear through the flagship – two through her larboard paddle box, which cut stout oak timbers clean off. Three more shots that struck home caused the ship to leak badly. The port wheel was crippled when a projectile careened off the wrought iron shaft that, Ward noted, would have otherwise been shattered if made of another material, "a point considered by me in selecting the vessel for purchase." It was surmised that with the engine being entirely exposed, had either of these shots struck the machinery the ship would have been crippled. Had the boiler or steam chest been hit, many on board would have been scalded or killed.[42]

Pawnee was hit nine times with rifled shot, four of which struck her hull. One had passed through the bulwarks, tore up the deck and was glanced on board by one of the iron straps. Of the shots that hit the ship above the hull, one passed through the maintopsail yard, another shattered the mizzenmast head and topmast, and another passed through the smokestack. The colors were also cut away. Fortunately, though Rowan and one of the men were slightly wounded by splinters, no lives were lost or serious injuries incurred. The enemy (though Ward may have felt otherwise) had paid their compliments particularly to the *Pawnee*, firing almost all their shot at her.[43]

Throughout the fight, Ward declared, both *Anacostia* and *Reliance* had been held in reserve and were not permitted to come under the enemy's fire, "their support having been necessary to embolden those engaged by giving them confidence that if disabled in the machinery, assistance was at hand to drag them out."[44] *Anacostia*, however, which carried a detachment of the 71st New York Regiment aboard, managed to fire a few shots from her 32-pounder simply "for the sake of having a hand in the action." [45]

By Captain Lynch's count *Pawnee* had fired no less than 392 times at the Confederate defenses, the greater portion being rifled shells. *Freeborn*, he estimated, had tossed 207. Ward claimed he had fired upwards of 200 shot and shell, requiring 1,700 pounds of powder, a rate of slightly over one a minute. In all, by Confederate estimates, a total of 599 shot and shell had been thrown at the battery.[46]

The commanding officers of both sides again had nothing but praise for their own men. Yet, the consequences of the three days of fighting, which had resulted in little more than a standoff with no significant losses on either side, were transparent.

Victory had eluded both sides yet neither had suffered defeat. Though the rebel batteries had been temporarily silenced they would soon be back in service; and the effects of their big guns were painfully obvious to Ward and Rowan, although the commander chose to downplay the negative side. Ashore, the rebels had failed to realize that the flotilla had been too crippled to renew the fight. By 5 p.m. they were already hard at work repairing the badly injured Naval Battery and building a new one suitable for mounting two heavy Columbiads that were expected to soon reach the Potomac and to be garrisoned by elements of the Caroline Grays. Two rifle companies of Walker's Legion were soon in position at the tip of Brent's Point on the northern side of Aquia with Captain Walker's big guns.

The speed with which the Confederates had restored and improved their defenses after the battle to meet the next expected onslaught was remarkable, but for those defenders who welcomed the next round, there was only disappointment. By Sunday morning, the day after the battle, the defenses had been in such a state of advancement, boasted one officer, that they "would have sunk their ships in an hour had they returned [to] their positions." The Confederates were in fact quite assured that they would be capable, with a few additional batteries, to meet any future attack and prevent a landing. Colonel William B. Bate, though anticipating nothing more than skirmishes, boldly proclaimed "We will sink their ships in another effort if they come in range." By June 15 a dozen big guns were in position at several locales. Soon afterwards a Confederate Navy deserter named John Dowling, who swam six miles across the Potomac to Maryland Point to escape, reported that there were three thousand rebel troops encamped behind the hills surrounding Aquia. A unit of forty-two men at the depot defended the naval battery. A second battery was now at Brent's Point and a third on a hill about a mile behind the landing. Soon it was learned, much to the navy's relief, that one of its primary concerns, the Confederate gunboat *George Page*, which was locked in the creek, was still neither manned nor armed.[47]

The contest had again, in many ways, served as little more than a gunnery exercise by both sides. Yet it also showed the vulnerability of fixed point shore positions against a very determined and mobile naval force while simultaneously exhibiting the hazard to wooden shipping on open waters from well placed and managed land batteries. And as the first land-sea engagement of the war, the lessons learned by both sides would not be forgotten.

Though Ward was unable to accurately assess the damage inflicted upon the rebels, he was now certain that nothing short of a major landing could ever dislodge them. [48]

8

THE CORDON OF OBSERVATION
". . . our boys are hiding their toy boats . . ."

Anacostia was the first of the squadron to reach Washington, bringing word to the Navy Department of the Battle of Aquia Creek and its outcome the same evening that the final engagement ended. The following morning *Freeborn* also arrived to begin undergoing substantial repairs and to refill her magazines. *Pawnee*, though slightly wounded, as one Confederate officer bitterly noted, "still coils about our shore like a wounded viper." *Reliance* would also remain off Aquia until *Freeborn* was able to return to station.[1] When the latest intelligence regarding the fight was circulated, the media quickly made its own appraisal of the enemy batteries. "They can only be dislodged," declared the Washington *Evening Star*, "by landing a party of men and attacking the battery in the rear." [2] It was an assessment about as far from possibility as an immediate march on Richmond.

The Battle of Aquia Creek left both sides smarting but intact, though Commander Ward, whose apparent eagerness to prove the capacity of his little flotilla, had only been re-energized by the fight and was eager to return downriver. But the damage to *Freeborn's* wheel and the need for significant repairs elsewhere, he informed Dahlgren early on June 3, would detain his ship at the Navy Yard for at least a week. He suggested that *Pawnee* be left to occupy the cruising ground off the creek until he might relieve her as she was the only warship powerful enough to contend with the CSS *George Page*, should she be armed and attempt to fight. Secretary Welles immediately approved and ordered the powerful man of war to remain on station. Commander Rowan would have to make do with his own repairs in the field until relieved.[3]

It was, Ward believed, imperative that *Pawnee* rather than one of the smaller flotilla vessels remain on station primarily to preclude any attempt by *George Page* to run, even though unarmed. If perchance mounting a gun or two the rebel steamer was able to escape into the open Potomac, river traffic could be severely disrupted. Even worse, if she should fall upon one of the lesser naval vessels by surprise and attempt a boarding on some moonless or foggy night, a tactical advantage might be gained just long enough to give the Confederates an opportunity to cross in force into Charles County. The consequences could be potentially disastrous. It was thus crucial that the big guns of *Pawnee* remain on station to counterbalance the threat.

Fortunately *Pawnee* and *Reliance* were not left alone to defend their position. About 9 p.m. on the evening of June 3 they were temporarily joined by two steamers with a third vessel in tow. This caused Colonel Ruggles, the senior rebel field commander in the area, while making observations from the highlands of Aquia, to express concern regarding the intention of the Federals. He had earlier stated his belief that a strong battery should be erected on the Virginia shore eight miles north of Aquia at a narrows on the river called Evansport, nearly opposite Budd's Ferry on the Maryland side, from which he feared a Union landing attempt might be made. It was his intention, he informed headquarters in Fredericksburg, to move an Arkansas regiment then stationed at Camp Jackson to the Potomac coast near a small waterway called Chopawamsic Creek, feeding into the river below Quantico Creek, as soon as the unit was in a condition to march. He begged that a battery of 24-pounder howitzers be sent up to the Chopawamsic and another unmounted battery of 6-pounders, then in Fredericksburg, be dispatched to reinforce Aquia where he had been fabricating gun carriages for them.[4]

Justifying the proposed battery at Evansport as "important in connection with the position at Manassas Junction, as well as the avenues of approach from the Potomac to this town," Ruggles requested that a competent engineer be sent without delay. His mission would be to examine the vicinity of the proposed battery site and make recommendations.[5]

The colonel was also quite concerned about Mathias Point, adjacent to another vulnerable choke point fifteen miles downriver and to the east of Aquia. The point, he knew, commanded a strategic narrows of the river to the east of the Nanjemoy Creek outlet on the Maryland side, and directly opposite the entrance to the Port Tobacco River. Both waterways were becoming primary conduits for the smuggling of men and contraband goods from Southern Maryland. Neither side had as yet occupied the brushy Mathias landscape, though both were well aware of its importance. Moreover, Ruggles was deeply suspicious of the range of patrols *Pawnee* had been cruising, primarily between Aquia and Nanjemoy Neck. He conjectured that it might be a prelude to a possible landing attempt at the point and had once before casually suggested to his superiors that the site be occupied. Now having apparently learned of Ward's reconnaissance of the point just before the recent battle at Aquia, he was almost certain of Federal intentions.

"The movements of the enemy indicate," he informed headquarters, "that an attempt will soon be made in force to land at or in the vicinity of Mathias Point in a brief period of time. I respectfully recommend that that point be covered by a good regiment of infantry, with a good battery of field guns, until measures are taken to establish a good and sufficient battery at that point to command the channel, for the establishment of which I respectfully renew my former recommendation." [6]

Ruggles's proposal had come none too soon for the Federals were indeed interested in Mathias Point. Though it was impossible for him to have known, one of the two steamers that had just come down river on the evening of June 3 was *Resolute*, which had been placed at the temporary disposal of Captain William R. Palmer of the U.S. Coast Survey. Together with sixteen armed men, Palmer had been sent to conduct a complete reconnaissance and mapping of Lower Cedar Point, Maryland, as well as Mathias and White House Points, Virginia. His objective was also to determine the precise width and depth of the river, the height and topographic features of the banks, and if the enemy had undertaken works on any of them. Having transferred to *Pawnee* on June 5 accompanied by two assistants, two officers and twenty men, Palmer landed without opposition at Lower Cedar Point, and on the following day at Mathias Point. White House Point was visited on his return trip on June 7. All sites were found to be thickly wooded and to have commanding elevated positions suitable for batteries. At each site a sketch map was made to accompany his final report.[7]

Mathias Point was in fact now but one of a number of rebel contraband transit points from Maryland into Virginia of which Secretary Welles was becoming increasingly aware. Yet it seemed from all quarters every incoming piece of intelligence brought with it bad news. Though still unsubstantiated, he was informed that the rebels had commenced secretly throwing up earthworks between Aquia Creek and Chopawamsic. Then less than a week after the battle, he was told that vessels were clearing from Baltimore bound for the St. Mary's River laden with provisions and stores intended for the Confederacy. Upon arrival they waited for the first favorable opportunity to cross the Potomac and enter Coan River through the alleged barrier of sunken boats to discharge their contraband lading and sometimes men bound for the Confederate Army. Two vessels had already been reported to have recently discharged such cargoes. The information was immediately provided to Commander Ward to consider appropriate countermeasures. Then on June 8 Dahlgren reported to the Secretary that *Pawnee* was lying at anchor three miles below Aquia, off Maryland Point where Rowan suspected that rebel communications had also just been opened with the Virginia shore. The commander had good reason to be concerned.

About June 3, during a brief reconnaissance of the coast of Nanjemoy Neck, Rowan had discovered ten hogsheads of bacon (upwards of 10,000 pounds), six barrels of whiskey, three casks of sugar, and two sacks of coffee in a fish house at Thomas Point Landing, in Charles County, opposite Aquia. He already suspected the loyalty of the owner though he had no proof of his secessionist affiliations. Fearing the goods were intended for the enemy he ordered that his boats keep a strict watch on the landing at night. Two weeks later, thanks to his vigilance, the goods were still there when he dispatched Lieutenant Lowry to reexamine the premises. The owner of the fish house, G. W. Carpenter, who was charged with holding the goods, when asked why they were still there replied simply that "the owners have not sent for them." Rowan's suspicions were not assuaged.[8]

In Ward's absence Rowan had already taken additional action elsewhere as well and ordered Acting Master William Budd in *Resolute* to investigate rebel activities along the lower Potomac shores of Southern Maryland. Thus on the morning of June 6 the diminutive screw steamer departed from her anchorage off Aquia on a short reconnaissance.

The imprints of invisible secessionists were everywhere. While making his first stop at Blackistone Island Lighthouse off the mouth of St. Clement's Bay, Budd was informed by the keeper, Joseph L. McWilliams, that he had received a letter threatening him with personal violence and the building with destruction unless the light was immediately extinguished. The white brick tower rising through the keeper's two-story brick house was barely ten years old, but was already a fixture for bay and river mariners and critical to navigational safety. Further inquiry revealed that the probable authors and senders of the threatening note included a man named Blackwell, living on the Virginia shore immediately opposite the lighthouse, and two others, both prominent men of St. Mary's, "Benjamin Gwinn Harris of Ellenborough and Mr. Key of Tudor Hall" in the Breton Bay area, three or four miles east of the lighthouse in St. Mary's County. The keeper ignored the warning and calmly requested that Budd provide him with arms and ammunition to defend himself and the Federal property under his charge.[9]

"Cutting off a Confederate dispatch-galley on the Potomac, near Freestone Point (1861)."
The Illustrated London News [London], New York Public Library, New York.

Pressing on toward Breton Bay, Budd's discoveries soon revealed that supplies and men were constantly passing from the bay to the Virginia shore. Leaving an officer and a boat crew to keep watch on all vessels in that vicinity, he then proceeded downriver to the Piney Point Lighthouse, a squat, round brick tower at the tip of the Piney Point peninsula; completed in September 1836, it was a much older structure than Blackistone but just as important to navigation. After a peek into the St. Mary's River *Resolute* crossed the Potomac to Hog Island near the outlet of Coan River while in search of possible rebel batteries before turning her prow back toward the Maryland shore.

On Saturday, June 8, while revisiting Breton Bay, Budd later reported that he had encountered the Virginia pungy schooner *Somerset* at the Leonardtown wharf. Upon seeing the approach of the warship, the pungy's crew rapidly vacated their boat and disappeared ashore, which immediately raised the officer's suspicions. The vessel, it was surmised, had apparently been employed there for some time in carrying men and provisions from the town to Virginia. Unable to spare any of his own men for a prize crew and considering the vessel valueless, being without cargo and in very poor condition, he towed the capture close to the Virginia shore and set her ablaze that same evening, burning her to the water's edge. Then, informed that there was a battery at Ragged Point, opposite Piney Point, he cautiously approached that shore the next morning to investigate and fired three or four rounds from his bow gun. There was neither response nor visual indications of any works. Though two vessels were observed in Currioman Bay near the outlet of Nomini Creek, he was obliged to terminate the reconnaissance owing to the sudden illness of his one and only engineer.

The following morning, while en route back to Washington and just five miles above Aquia Creek, another suspicious schooner was spotted. Master's Mate John T. Fuller was immediately dispatched with a boat crew of four men to board the vessel and investigate. She proved to be the *William Sampson,* a schooner "well known" for carrying provisions to the Confederate shore. The boat was found to be in bad condition, without cargo, and abandoned by her owner and men; the latter watched helplessly from the nearby shore as Fuller put her to the torch.[10]

Budd's reconnaissance had been extremely productive, even if distressing. "From reliable information and my observation," he informed Rowan, "I am positive that large quantities of supplies and numbers of men are constantly passing the Potomac at Breton's Bay and St. Mary's. Vessels are loaded with provisions in Baltimore and dispatched without clearances or manifests, some from St. Mary's, others from Breton's Bay, and many when boarded state that their cargoes are for farmers along the Maryland shore of the river." There had been more provisions landed in St. Mary's within the last month, he stated, than the inhabitants of that vicinity would require for three years. "One schooner after anchoring in the harbor crossed over to Yeocomico [Virginia], twice discharged her cargo there, and is now in Baltimore loading for the third trip." [11]

On June 9, having learned of Budd's findings, Commander Rowan, assuming field command in Ward's absence, immediately dispatched *Reliance* to establish a temporary blockade of the Potomac between the St. Mary's and Wicomico Rivers and the Virginia shore. Lieutenant Mygatt was to provide the Blackistone lighthouse keeper with six muskets and some ammunition promised by Budd. Two days later the commander dispatched additional instructions for Mygatt to expand his blockade of the Virginia side of the river to include the range between Hog Island and Currioman Bay. He was also to visit the station keepers at the Point Lookout Lighthouse and at Blackistone to obtain as much new information as possible. And lastly, he was instructed to be "as guarded as the nature and object of your service will admit not to interfere with the people of the Maryland shore." [12]

Not surprisingly, the visits of the Potomac Flotilla vessels were noted with subdued indignation in the pages of the *St. Mary's Beacon* several days after Mygatt's arrival. "For the past few days a close watch has been kept by the Washington Government, upon the movements of our people in this vicinity," the paper reported. "A flotilla of schooners and steam tugs has been stationed in Britton's [*sic*] Bay, and the Potomac, for several miles above and below the mouth of the Bay, has been subjected to the strictest military espionage. All the Bay crafts upon the Potomac and in the Bay, coming within range of the 'blockading squadron,' have been boarded, searched and, so far as heard from, released." [13]

Though the local waters seemed infested with Yankees, and a Virginia pungy had been hauled off from the town wharf and destroyed, Leonardtown itself had not been occupied. "Our town," noted the editor in clearly coded but defiant terms, "has not as yet been honored (?) with a visit from these faithful vigilants, but our boys are hiding their toy boats and some, we learn, have even had the prudence to conceal their marbles that they may not be mistaken for grapeshot, and seized as contraband of war." [14]

The increasing flow of goods, arms, and men from Maryland to Virginia was now of enormous concern to Federal military and naval officials whose limited forces were hard pressed to even assess the true extent of the burgeoning contraband operations, much less halt it. As the alarm traveled northward it seemed to be reaching monumental proportions.

One newspaper echoed the general anxiety of Unionists over the situation: "Persons who reached the city this evening from Montgomery County, Md.," reported the *New York Daily Tribune*, "represent that vehicles of every description, laden with arms, ammunition, and provisions from Baltimore, are passing over the turnpikes leading through that county, during the entire night, on their way to Virginia. We are also credibly informed that contraband goods are being almost daily shipped down the Chesapeake, from Baltimore, to the mouth of the Patuxent River, and up the stream to Upper Marlboro, thence to the Potomac shore, where they are put on board scows and flatboats and taken across to the rebels." [15]

Commander Ward had little choice but to request that the additional naval support, the three schooners promised him at the outset as part of his squadron, be sent to plug the holes in the porous riverine border between Maryland and Virginia. Hamstrung by the extremely limited resources at hand, on June 11, while still at the Washington Navy Yard, he requested that three light draft schooners, *Bailey*, *Howell Cobb* and *Dana*, be requisitioned from the U.S. Coast Survey. A master's mate and six enlisted men armed with muskets were to be assigned to each to expand the "proposed cordon of observation." He intended to anchor or cruise under canvas one of the vessels in the vicinity of St. Mary's, another in the waters off Port Tobacco, and the third at whatever point she might be needed. The following day he enlarged his request and asked that two more Coast Survey vessels, then in New York, be sent to help cover every significant fixed point on the river, leaving his light steamers free to move about as circumstances dictated.[16]

Welles demurred, regarding the request for schooners, each crewed by half a dozen men armed with only muskets, which he considered entirely unsafe to occupy any position along the hostile Potomac shores, as they might be too easily overcome. But Ward eventually got them anyway.[17]

There was, of course, still the problem of Aquia. Ward was less concerned now about rebel batteries erected along the shores there than he was of the possibility of *George Page* emerging from the creek, perhaps newly armed and with several hundred rebels aboard. Besides *Pawnee*, which was not yet officially under his command, the only vessels in his squadron even remotely capable of opposing her was *Freeborn*; owing to her low sides she would likely fair badly in any enemy boarding attempt. Though he had contemplated a raid into the creek to destroy *Page*, the truth was that the enemy gunboat had by then been hauled a considerable distance upstream and was so heavily guarded that it made any cutting out operation a complete impossibility. Moreover, there were reports that on Maryland Point, opposite Aquia and Potomac Creeks, the rebels were gathering supplies to be carried across the river the moment *Pawnee* was removed from the scene. He deemed it particularly unwise to leave that coastline unwatched. It was thus necessary, he suggested to

Welles, to permanently assign either *Pawnee* or *Pocahontas* to a station between Aquia and the opposite shore and to continue to field rowboats at night to keep watch on the Maryland wharves and creeks. Rowan had in fact already been monitoring with small boats the shores of Maryland Point, and in particular the ferry landing at Thomas Point; but the Secretary had not been so informed. Welles immediately approved of the plan assuming it had been Ward's all along.[18]

With every new piece of intelligence, the need for more vessels and men was increasingly amplified. On June 5 William Thomas Valiant, Deputy Collector at the Customs House in Baltimore, informed Treasury Secretary Salmon P. Chase that there was undoubted evidence that a large quantity of goods was being shipped from the city aboard the schooner *Mount Vernon* (not to be confused with the Federal steamship of the same name). The vessel was ostensibly intended for a landing in St. Mary's, but her lading was really intended for Virginia. The goods were to be offloaded at a site called Tall Pine, then hauled by wagons across the county to the Potomac to the neighborhood of Swan Point, a distance of twelve or fifteen miles. From there they were to be carried three miles across the Potomac to the vicinity of Rossier Creek, where a wagon road to Fredericksburg intersected. "It would be well to have a Government vessel in the neighborhood of said locality for the next two or three nights," Valiant recommended, "as no doubt such vigilance would detect the parties in this illicit trade and the seizure more than repay the Government expense and trouble." [19]

Investigating and proving which craft were hauling contraband amidst the many merchant and fishing vessels plying the Potomac was easier said than done. When the USS *Anacostia* pressed down the river bound for Hampton Roads in early June, she would stop and investigate no fewer than thirteen vessels. Only one, the *Ben Vandiver*, ostensibly en route from Baltimore for Washington with a cargo of hay and corn, drew any suspicions whatsoever but could not be proved to be in the service of rebels. When good intelligence came in from a bona fide source such as the Baltimore Customs Officer, the delay in getting it to where it mattered was more than frustrating. A full week would pass before Collector Valiant's tip was received by Secretary Welles and then passed on to Commander Ward, by which time it was already too late to take action.

It was unquestionably difficult for Ward to digest and act upon all of the intelligence forwarded to him from the Navy Department regarding rebel contraband operations. Soon after receiving word of the *Mount Vernon* voyage he was informed of yet another smuggling scheme utilizing the steamer *St. Nicholas*, a well known passenger and freight hauler belonging to the Baltimore and Washington Steam Packet Company. The sidewheeler, which before the war visited both Maryland and Virgiinia shores, now only ran between Baltimore and Washington, with regular stops for passengers at Point Lookout to service the "celebrated Bathing Place" there. The ship usually left the Patapsco bound for the capital on Friday afternoons at 4 o'clock; the return voyage was every Tuesday morning at 6 o'clock, making well advertised landings on the Maryland side of the Potomac each way. There had been a report that the steamer recently had been brought to by a shot from a warship on the Potomac, almost certainly (from later evidence) *Pawnee*. She was compelled to lay by during the night, eventually assuring the warship's commander that she was in fact a peaceful steamer, and was thus permitted to resume her trip. The delay had not gone unobserved by rebel coastwatchers who incorrectly assumed she was supplying the man of war. Then on June 15 information from "a reliable source" also revealed that the ship was to be engaged in conveying and disposing of contraband articles to parties in Virginia, particularly clothes for the use of Confederate soldiers. "The plan of communication between Baltimore and Richmond," the Navy Department had learned, "is for the steamer to land at a small port on the Maryland side nearly opposite Aquia Creek [presumably at Thomas Point Landing], where a depot has been established. Small boats are ready to carry over the passengers, merchandise, and mails during the night." Thus, Secretary Welles instructed Ward to search the vessel and if the charges were true seize her. Ward replied that he had already given the *St. Nicholas* such an overhauling "as will render her circumspect," but vowed that on her next trip he would again search her thoroughly. Yet before such a search could be carried out, events of a far different nature would intervene.[20]

***

Despite the spirited efforts to make repairs to *Freeborn*, it was nearly two weeks after the Battle of Aquia Creek before Commander Ward was able to return to cruising the Potomac. His orders to Rowan on June 13, basically reiterating what that officer had already been doing – to maintain a strict watch on the Southern Maryland shore and intercept all intercourse with Virginia in precisely the manner he had been following for weeks – seemed redundant. The only thing new was that a six man flotilla schooner was to be placed on permanent guard between Port Tobacco and Nanjemoy. *Reliance* was to cruise about under slow steam at night when and where violations of the blockade were most anticipated. Another schooner, expected at any moment, was to be assigned as part of the cordon of observation at or near Budd's Ferry below Mattawoman Creek, in Charles County. The site had just been reported, although not verified, as a depot of supplies for rebel forces being ferried across at night by small boats under muffled oars. That popular line of enemy communications was considered too important to leave unwatched. Until the schooner arrived, however, a small guard launch was to be towed up by *Reliance* every night to the site and brought down every morning to the *Pawnee*.

"The boats at Budd's Ferry," Ward instructed Rowan, "must cease to ply, otherwise they must be seized and sent to Washington, leaving the owners to find a remedy there against the Government. In my absence, while perfecting arrangements for a more complete blockade of the lower Potomac, you will be pleased to carry out this order in respect to Budd's Ferry as thoroughly as your means will possibly allow."

Rowan was further directed to look after all the flotilla schooners stationed above Cedar Point. The schooners, each of which were armed with muskets but no cannon, were ordered as a precautionary measure to lie in a state of preparation for scuttling, with arms and ammunition ready to be thrown overboard "so that in the event of being overpowered by numbers the capture could add neither trophy nor strength to the rebel forces." But of equal importance, if he was convinced beyond a doubt that a depot of supplies, arms, and ammunition or provisions destined for

107

Virginia existed on the Maryland shore within ready reach, "waiting only the opportunity to elude you and be carried over," Rowan was authorized to seize and hold such property to await final judgment on the confiscation by Ward himself.[21]

Ward's concerns regarding the danger of a rebel boarding were prescient. On the night of June 14 a New Jersey schooner named *Christiana Keen*, while running opposite Lower Cedar Point not far from the abandoned lightboat station, stranded a half mile from the Virginia shore off Upper Machodoc Creek near "Barnsfield," the home of Dr. Abram Barnes Hooe, on Mathias Point. Hooe was proprietor of Hooe's Ferry on the eastern side of Mathias Neck, and an avowed secessionist "very active in his efforts against the Government." The vessel ran aground in four and a half feet of water where the river was two miles wide and the narrow channel lay near the Maryland shore. Though buoys had replaced the recently burned lightboat, Confederates thought to be operating from Mathias Point had removed them only two or three days before. Yet the master of the unfortunate schooner, it was later charged, had "unnecessarily exposed himself to this disaster by sailing at night when the navigation is very intricate and keeping to windward on the Virginia shore, when the channel lay on the other shore, the wind being entirely fair." Within a short time of grounding a party of thirty or forty gray uniformed Confederates had boarded the schooner and set her afire.

"Confederates trapping a boat's crew of the Potomac fleet (1861)." The hazards of small boat operations were frequently encountered by Union boat crews and landing parties throughout the war. *The Illustrated London News*, New York Public Library, New York.

From intelligence brought up from Coan River, Ward deduced that the soldiers had been dispatched from that place to protect Mathias Point against such visits as the Federals had recently conducted. He quickly circulated a public notice to prevent unnecessary alarm and to counsel mariners sailing in the area to anchor only where government armed vessels were operating, to proceed only in the company of other vessels, and to be armed with muskets to defend themselves. Then, just two days later, the propeller steamer *Josephine* was pelted with musket balls as she passed the point but instantly quelled the firing with a shell from a small gun she carried for protection.[22]

Though Ward could not have known it, the rebels that had attacked the *Christiana Keen* actually belonged to a regiment of cavalry called the Farmer's Fork Grays from Richmond County, one of the first to be detailed to Mathias Point as a consequence of Colonel Ruggles' recommendation of June 4. Arriving at the point just six days later they would soon be joined by Colonel John M. Brockenbrough's 40th Virginia Volunteers.[23]

Their arrival was timely, for the attack upon *Christiana Keen* would not go long without a reprisal.

***

Commander Rowan must have felt a bit like the little Dutch boy trying to simultaneously plug the great holes in the leaking dikes with all of his fingers and toes to prevent the flood from sweeping over his homeland. Keeping all of his available small boats rowing about every night, reconnoitering for enemy craft passing to and from the Maryland shore, was both wearisome and frustrating, but occasionally rewarded with success.

One typical operation, the likes of which would be repeated frequently by the Union blockaders, was both modest in scope and in achievement but helped bolster the spirits of all involved. On the evening of June 17 Rowan ordered Lieutenant James C. Chaplin, his second in command, to proceed with sixteen men in the ship's first cutter under tow of *Reliance* to Cockpit Point above the entrance to Quantico Creek, where rebel activity had been observed and from which communication with the Maryland shore at Budd's Ferry was frequent. Sheltered by the dark of night, the reconnaissance party landed and found five boats used for bringing men and provisions from Maryland. All of the craft were brought back to *Reliance* and destroyed. Skirting the shore as he proceeded cautiously southward in the dark, Chaplin saw little to arouse further suspicion until he arrived at Evansport a half mile below his former stop. Here he dispatched six sailors under Master's Mate Bogert to reconnoiter. Ten minutes later Bogert returned and reported that he and his men had come upon an enemy picket of mounted troops and driven them away.

Concerned about being discovered by the rebels, who would undoubtedly return in force while he was exposed on the open river, Chaplin withdrew and proceeded farther down stream to Scott's Landing. There he discovered four more boats hauled up on the shore under a fishing shed. Then, while a detachment of his men were engaged in hauling the vessels down to the water's edge, he and the remainder discovered a nearby dwelling house and began to inspect the premises. As the sailors gained the rear of the building they encountered three surprised Confederate troopers who immediately took off at a gallop. Forewarned of the

109

enemy's presence the landing party returned again to *Reliance* with their diminutive prizes in tow. The little steamer then turned her prow northward and returned to the waters off Evansport. In the early dawn light the raiders observed a large number of armed men running along the shore, unquestionably searching for the sailors who had driven in their pickets and stolen their boats. Suddenly, as the little tug came about once again, she was subjected to a fusillade of musket fire from behind some bushes. The firing was promptly silenced by canister shot from her howitzer. Much fatigued by their forays into enemy territory, with no loss and nine enemy boats captured or burned, Chaplin and his weary raiders returned to the mother ship. It was, after all, just another night of blockading on the Potomac.[24]

Still intelligence continued to filter in pertaining to potential Confederate support in Southern Maryland, especially in Charles County. Reports began to emanate from Port Tobacco regarding the assemblage of arms and men in both the town and nearby countryside. In response a U.S. Army detachment 150 strong, consisting of Company I, an artillery unit, and Company F, an infantry unit, belonging to the 71st New York Regiment, was dispatched aboard *Mount Vernon* at 9 a.m., June 17 to secure them. At the same time *Freeborn* had entered the Port Tobacco River, presumably to assist. One of the army's primary objectives was to conduct a surprise visit on Captain Samuel Cox, in whose possession it was believed the Charles County militia arms belonging to the State of Maryland were held. In so doing the army was engaging a man later destined to play a significant role in the final dramatic chapter of the war. "It seems," noted one subsequent press report, "that Port Tobacco has been headquarters for Maryland secession recruits, and when ten to twenty would arrive there and enlist they were boated across the river to Virginia."

For many years Samuel Cox had been a moving force in Charles County politics and society. Born November 22, 1819, as a youth he attended the Charlotte Hall Military Academy and in 1849 acquired his Rich Hill estate, including a two story home on 900 acres, as a gift. As early as 1845, being a slave owner concerned about possible slave insurrection and the problem of "restless negroes," he had been appointed to the Committee of Vigilance representing the First School District. Cox had once brutally killed one of his own slaves for insubordination. Thereafter he became politically active and served as delegate and secretary from Allen's Fresh to several county Whig conventions. In 1853 he was elected to the Maryland House of Delegates. As a prominent figure in country judicial and military affairs he was appointed by the Governor of Maryland to be Justice of Magistrates and a Justice of the Peace for the Second Election District, and later as the captain of Company I, 1st Regulars, Maryland Militia. Cox was equally engaged in county social affairs such as serving in executive positions for the Charles County Agricultural Society and chairing community action committees intent on improvements to the county road system, wharves, depots and steam navigation. Known as a prize winning horse breeder and onetime president of the county Jockey Club he regularly hired out his stallions bearing names such as Grey Medock, Knight of Malta, Wild Mountain Buck, and Arrago as studs at his mill or his Rich Hill farm, at neighboring farms and plantations, and at other locations throughout the county. An ardent states' righter, Cox's first loyalty was to Maryland, but only as a southern state. In

September 1860 he had switched his political allegiance and was a leading organizer in the county for the Constitutional Unionist presidential ticket of Bell and Everett. Following Lincoln's election he had been vocal among county leaders calling for a sovereign state convention with powers that the publisher of the *Port Tobacco Times*, Elijah Wells, called revolutionary and designed to overthrow the government.[25]

That Samuel Cox, now reputedly one of the leading secessionists in Charles County, would draw Federal attention came as no surprise. That he was prepared for a visit from the Yankees seems apparent from the events that soon transpired.

When *Mount Vernon* arrived at Chapel Point on the shores of the Port Tobacco River the two companies aboard disembarked without incident and marched but a short distance to Rich Hill. Perhaps not unexpectedly, considering that Maryland secessionist coast watchers could monitor every move the navy made on the Potomac, and despite its every effort to conduct operations with "secrecy and expeditiousness," the detachment found no arms in his possession. Worse, they discovered that he bore a captain's commission in the regular state militia authorized by Governor Hicks himself. With no hard evidence to justify an arrest, the unwelcome visitors departed, though "the belief among the soldiers was that the man was a secession recruiting officer, the commission referred to saved him from arrest." After taking a survey of the country thereabouts the New Yorkers soon returned to their ship and steamed back to Washington where they arrived late on the afternoon of June 18. A frustrated Dahlgren simply attributed the failure to the probability that the arms had already been removed to Virginia. The operation had proved a complete failure. Moreover, the local blacks, the one source of information that had been counted upon for assistance in locating the reported arsenal, proved of little help. They were, perhaps understandably, "afraid to give information as to the place of concealment" in the presence of their owners for they knew that once the soldiers had departed they would be subject to severe punishment. And it was well known that Cox had once whipped to death one of his own slaves for a far less indiscretion.[26]

In the meantime Commander Rowan, though lacking proof that the stockpile of goods at the Carpenter fish house on Maryland Point was intended for shipment to Virginia, finally decided to take action, but not before seeking permission from Welles, which was immediately granted. "Having determined in my own mind," he reported on June 18, "that this provision was not intended for consumption in Maryland, partly from the length of time it was allowed to remain in store, and partly from a firm conviction that Carpenter holds intercourse with the enemy and has been in Virginia the last two weeks, from whence he returned the night before last, crossing the river in a small boat near Nanjemoy Creek . . . I seized the provisions in Carpenter's fish house and put them on board a wood schooner that happened to be loading here." The tug *Reliance* was insructed to tow the schooner to the Navy Yard and to deliver the provisions, all but three barrels of whiskey and another of sugar, to the commandant of the yard.[27]

***

The assignment of schooners to Ward's tiny flotilla quickly began to prove their worth, not only in terms of interdicting vessels attempting to run the blockade but also as logistical support. By taking coal onboard from government and other transports as they passed upriver, each schooner kept a supply equal to forty or fifty tons of coal and was thus able to serve as a floating depot for the active steam powered vessels of the fleet. The action thus extended the range and duration of time for patrolling by reducing the number of trips to the Washington Navy Yard for refueling.

The stationing of schooners along the river at key points where "the secession feeling is largely demonstrative" – *Bailey*, under Acting Master's Mate James Gary, at St. Mary's; *Cobb* at Breton Bay to cut off traffic between Leonardtown and Virginia; and *Dana*, under Acting Master's Mate Robert B. Ely, at Nanjemoy and Port Tobacco – was beginning to prove of value. *Bailey* had been among the first deployed and was assigned by Ward to her cruising grounds on June 14. About the same time he ordered Acting Master Budd in *Resolute* to reconnoiter Smith Point, Virginia, at the mouth of the Potomac, and then to join him on the Yeocomico River, a tributary of the Potomac, the next day at noon. While en route from Smith's Point the following morning Budd spotted and captured two fishing vessels and brought their crews in for interrogation. "I extracted from them," Ward later reported, "the information that the suspected schooner *Mount Vernon* has not made a successful trip, at least directly to Coan River, but the schooner *Buena Vista* [William Fallon master] had. I therefore issued orders that said schooner should be seized whenever and wherever found and detained for my adjudication." Two days later the schooner in question was captured by *Bailey* and sent to the Navy Yard under escort of *Resolute*. *Buena Vista's* lading, shipped by G. R. H. Leffler of Baltimore and purported to be five barrels of whiskey, proved upon inspection to be barrels filled with pistols. About the same time *Dana*, while watching the Port Tobacco River and the Nanjemoy coast, seized a small sloop called *H. Day* "under suspicious circumstances." The sloop was appropriated by Ward and assigned to her captor as a tender to further enlarge the blockaders' cruising capacity. The commander was delighted for he considered the captures to be "the first fruit of the arrangement by which the schooners of this flotilla are stationed." [28]

The apparent validation of Ward's strategy of using sailing vessels to interdict small craft operating from Maryland to the Coan and Yeocomico notwithstanding, the commander was quick to point out the necessity of assigning another steamer to watch the whole breadth of the lower Potomac between the two Virginia tributaries. Just such was a ship called *Leslie*, then at the Navy Yard, which was armed with a rifled howitzer. "To anchor a sailing vessel off either of these rivers," the commander informed Welles, "might be hazardous, both on account of the weather and liability to attack." But with two additional schooners, which he had requested earlier, he boldly declared without hesitation that he could stop all illicit traffic on the river. [29]

In the meantime the War Department agonized over maintaining the lines of communication, especially with its toeholds in Virginia and lower Maryland. By mid-June the government began to consider the proposition of immediately establishing submarine telegraphic communication between Point Lookout and Fort Monroe, and ordered a guard placed at the former "to protect that station." At the same time the Navy Department continued to be concerned about the erection of rebel batteries at strategic choke points on the Potomac. Most important to the navy were the channel narrows on the Potomac dominated by White House Bluff and at Hooe's Landing on Mathias Point. Both of these positions, if controlled by the Confederates, might effectively cut off Washington from waterborne communication and supply. As had been the case since April White House Bluff, near the old Belvoir plantation estate, and closest to Washington, had been of prime concern; orders to keep an eye on the site had been issued by the department with some frequency. Commandant Dahlgren, who fretted continuously over the danger, was finally moved to recommend a plan to Secretary Welles.

White House Bluff would be best "guaranteed" by Union occupation, but the operation would require more force than could be spared. Moreover, because of the unfavorable lay of the land and its close proximity to the secessionist army, which had been moving steadily into the area, securing it could be costly. "Resort must be had," he said, "therefore, to a counter battery on the opposite shore, distant 1,700 to 2,000 yards, and some heavy pieces afloat to enfilade the principal front. Even with these it would be impossible to free the bluff entirely from batteries, so that the cover of the night would have to be used in passing."

As for Mathias Point, its geographic location was equally dangerous if the Confederates fortified the site. Because the channel was so narrow it was impossible for vessels to keep farther than 1,400 yards at any one place from the point, and would expose them to considerable chance of damage during a daylight transit. Yet the distance to the nearest opposite bank was deemed too great to preclude silencing batteries on Mathias from works erected on the Maryland shore. If the rebels occupied the point in force and were allowed to remain, water passage might be undertaken only at night; without navigational markers, that too could be extremely hazardous.

"The best plan," said Dahlgren, "is to seize and hold the point at once, which, from the nature of the ground, would not be difficult nor require a large force. Its extreme margin presents firm ground of no great extent, separated from the remainder by a swamp which can no doubt be made impassable by some field works and artillery, supported by five or six companies of good troops, and the guns of a few vessels near the edge of the channel. I would recommend a reconnaissance by proper officers to this end, and if their opinion, to be carried out without delay." [30]

Acting upon orders from Welles, Dahlgren ordered yet another reconnaissance of White House Bluff where local informants related that rebels had actually been on the site discussing the probability of a battery being erected there. On that same day it was also reported that rebels had occupied a village not far from the bluff. A sloop, known to have conveyed armed men from Maryland to the Virginia shores and quite probably the same arms that had been secreted at or near Port Tobacco, was subsequently seized by the steamer *Mount Vernon* and sent to the Navy Yard.[31]

But it was Mathias Neck that was of the most concern. As the rebel destruction of *Christiana Keen* had proved, Mathias Point was where the greatest danger to waterborne communications and shipping on the Potomac was thought to lie. It could no longer be ignored.

9

MATHIAS POINT

"...every man must die on his thwart."

There seemed little question in Commander Ward's mind that something had to be done about Mathias Point. If the danger of the Confederate presence there as exhibited by the *Christiana Keen* incident wasn't enough, the repeated firing on other passing ships from a range of only 500 to 600 yards was alarming. Even *Thomas Freeborn* had once been struck by several volleys. From Port Tobacco reports were now filtering in to Washington that the rebels were silently at work planting batteries on the point a short distance across the river. Passing vessels had observed clusters of men lurking among the bushes. One report even stated that a long strip, apparently of cloth, had been stretched along the beach, possibly as a blind to conceal work going on behind it. The commander attempted to place the threat on a more factual footing. "It is the alarm more than the material damage produced by the firing," he suggested to Welles, "which is injurious and ought to be abated." [1]

That the threat was causing some growing panic, however, was a reality. While lying on station off Lower Cedar Point Ward had been informed by vessels coming up from Cape Henry that they had been advised to await convoy protection in Hampton Roads before attempting to sail for Washington. He was incensed at the advisory, which he deemed needless and wrong, and requested that the Navy Department correct it. "No convoy is necessary," he counseled Welles, "except that which three or four vessels together will afford one another, and for this purpose they should assemble at Blakistone Island lighthouse, where there is a man of war schooner for protection." [2]

Immediate action of some sort seemed a necessity. Ward considered free navigation of the Potomac as his personal responsibility. He thus resolved that the best practical course would be to denude Mathias Point of its jungle-like ground-cover which concealed the enemy and whatever works they had or were likely to have under construction. By June 23 he had already informally requested from Dahlgren the aid of 200 troops and the proper tools to do the job, undoubtedly presuming that the military would be willing to provide the necessary assistance. Dahlgren and Welles took the request to the top, General Winfield Scott himself. Scott's enthusiasm for the project was at first electric. "A battalion!" he declared with gusto. "He shall have two!" Then after pausing a moment to reflect, the old warrior reconsidered. Undismayed, Dahlgren next addressed the request to General Joseph Mansfield, Commander of the Department of Washington. Mansfield demurred but called for a conference the next morning, June 24. [3]

The meeting was brief. In attendance were Dahlgren, Mansfield, Major John G. Barnard, Captains Daniel P. Woodbury and William Palmer of the Topographical Engineer Corps. The army men were as one in their opposition to the plan, suspecting that a significant Confederate force might already be in place at the point. Before any landing of consequence might be made, it would first be necessary to dispatch a reconnaissance team to assess the situation. Woodbury and Palmer were assigned the task.[4]

There was to be no delay in determining the status of Mathias Point. *Pawnee* was assigned the mission, though both the ship and her men were already exhausted. After nearly a month of continuous night and day patrolling between Indian Head, Maryland, and Aquia, daily boarding and searching of vessels, and occasionally destroying enemy smuggling boats plying between the Maryland and Virginia shores, duty aboard was being stretched to the limit. "It is beginning to tell rather keenly on the men," noted one commentator, "who, from drinking the river water and living on salt junk during the hot weather (they have had no fresh meat nor vegetables for four weeks), are suffering a good deal with sickness." [5]

Despite the condition of her crew, at 2 a.m., June 25 *Pawnee* surreptitiously departed her station off Aquia Creek and proceeded directly for Mathias Point. She was accompanied by the steamboat *James Guy*, which had brought the two engineers down from Washington immediately after the conference.[6]

At 5 a.m. Rowan dispatched an escort of forty sailors and marines in two boats under the charge of Lieutenant Chaplin and Master Blue and placed them under the command of Captain Woodbury. As the two ships approached the point a rebel force of one, perhaps two companies, was observed and promptly sent scrambling by a few well placed shells from *Pawnee*. Upon landing, the scouting party was sent out and soon encountered a small group of rebels led by two mounted men. "Our men charged upon them vigorously," it was later reported. "The cavaliers dismounted, and took to the bushes with their men, leaving behind their horses in the hands of the sailors." The engineers and their escorts continued to explore and soon discovered an empty rebel campsite in a meadow beyond the heavy underbrush a mile inland, and made an estimate of their strength based upon the camp's size. The Confederates were momentarily held in check by an occasional shell that forced them to keep their distance even as the landing party completed its reconnaissance.

On the party's return to the ship Rowan was informed that they had observed the enemy camp in the meadow below the hilltop home of a "notorious secessionist" named Grimes. Rowan promptly hauled *Pawnee* inside the dangerous shoal line and using 15-second shells dispersed the camp and set fire to something behind the hill. In fact, the bombardment narrowly missed killing a number of Confederates when one shell passed through the Grimes house in which thirty of the Farmer's Fork Grays had been billeted though only one man was inside at the time. When it blew up outside near a spring where twenty-five men were mustering following the departure of the Union sailors, only one soldier was slightly injured. Rowan later reported that during the reconnaissance some thirty shells were fired to hold the enemy in check, a force estimated by the engineers at 600 men of whom 100 or more were believed to be mounted troops.

While the investigation was still underway Rowan ordered Lieutenant Chaplin to bring off or destroy a boat that had been observed lying on the beach. Chaplin, Master Blue, Midshipman Snell and Engineer Trilley, with sixty men under the command of Woodbury and Palmer, were now set ashore. When the lieutenant reached the site he found a slave belonging to Dr. Hooe standing beside it, apparently eager to exchange information for his freedom. When brought aboard *Pawnee* he provided the commander with the disturbing news that 200 troops were usually kept patrolling the beach while the remainder of the soldiers were ensconced in camps thereabouts. He reported that the Sparta Grays, Captain Judson Sidner, and the Potomac Rifles, Captain Fleet W. Cox, under the overall command of Major Robert Mayo, had occupied the camp that had been shelled. One of the captured horses, he informed his interrogators with some amusement, had been the major's personal roan.

Having found no battery, but an enemy camp nearby where as many as 500 soldiers had been billeted, the reconnaissance party returned to their boats at 8 p.m. without incident. The sailors swam the two horses out to the ship and hoisted them aboard, "greatly delighted with their pets," which they dubbed "Rowan" and "Pawnee." Both were presented to the two army engineers "in the hope that they may do good service against their former masters," and sent aboard *James Guy* to the Navy Yard as prizes of war.[8]

The reconnaissance expedition to Mathias Point having discovered no batteries soon reconfirmed General Mansfield's decision against sending 200 troops to assist Commander Ward. This was in the face of fears noted by some northern newspapers that batteries at Mathias Point would almost certainly prohibit the free navigation of the river and still be impervious to attack except from the rear. "Mathias Point," declared one publication in an article later republished in the Richmond press, "is the most important strategic position on the river, commanding it even more effectually than the White House shore. The channel hugs the Virginia shore, and vessels of the lightest draft must necessarily pass within four or five hundred yards of the point. A battery once in position there would be extremely difficult to dislodge. The Union men here [Port Tobacco] are anxious to see the place looked after." [9]

Mansfield's decision was definitely not what Ward wanted to hear for it seemed only a matter of time before the rebels at Mathias Point would be reinforced with artillery. He now deemed it imperative that the navy alone would have to beat the rebel army to the punch. Soon after *Pawnee* returned to her station and Rowan's report was made, Ward decided to act independently of the military. But not until another enemy activity had first been put to bed.

***

Not long after the *Pawnee* reconnaissance a second landing was undertaken on the peninsula, though one partially motivated by a desire for revenge as much as an effort to help dismantle the Maryland-Virginia communications system. It was also apparently undertaken as an independent operation without direct orders from on high.

The recent burning of *Christiana Keen* and the rebels who had been responsible had not been forgotten by those charged with protecting the shipping on the Potomac. Reprisal must have seemed to Acting Master William Budd, commander of *Resolute*, a natural response. Precisely how and when he was able to secure information regarding the target of his attack is unknown. It is certain that he managed to identify the perpetrators, unmask a major Southern Maryland-Virginia contraband network, and temporarily cripple part of its local infrastructure in a retaliatory action eleven days after *Keen*'s destruction.

Budd learned, perhaps from local black informants, that Dr. Hooe had been very active in efforts against the U.S. Government from his estate on Mathias Point

Neck. It seemed he had been part of an elaborate system for harboring and forwarding men and supplies from Maryland to the rebels in Virginia. The Maryland side of the operation was managed by Major Roderick G. Watson of Clifton Plantation near Pope's Creek in Charles County. Watson was a wealthy planter who regularly received contraband supplies and mail from the north and forwarded them to Hooe using his own boats and slaves. Watson's estate bounded that of Thomas A. Jones, his nearest neighbor and friend. His residence was a large, commanding two-story frame house situated on a bluff nearly 100 feet above the water with upper story windows clearly visible from across the river. A respected leader in the county, Watson had succeeded Samuel Cox as president of the Jockey Club and was active in every component of county life. Upon his death, on November 8, 1861 he left behind several children, two of whom continued services for the Confederacy. His son Roderick D. Watson had been engaged during the summer of 1861 in arranging for the transport of Confederate mail across the Potomac, and in 1864 would be suspected of serving as a rebel agent in New York. Daughter Mary worked with Jones keeping watch for Union gunboats on the Potomac and signaled the Virginia shore on the approach of enemy naval vessels by managing the shades in the Watson home. The supplies and men would cross the river, presumably to Hooe's Ferry Landing when the passage was unguarded, and rendezvous at Hooe's house. The good doctor, it was also learned, had turned over part of his estate to be used as a barracks. Accommodations to host as many as twenty-five rebel soldiers had also been put up in the plantation schoolhouse and outbuildings. "He has a number of mounted troopers quartered in and lying about his premises," Budd later reported, "who were there for the purpose of protecting boats which got across from Maryland with men, &c." A number of them had occasionally taken pot shots from Hooe's place at *Resolute* and other vessels of the flotilla. But worse, it had been Hooe himself who had sent for the mounted troops when the *Keen* ran aground within a quarter mile of his home and requested them to burn her.[10] Budd, the Confederates later charged, had resolved to personally punish the physician.[11]

On the evening of June 24 *Resolute* made a surprise descent upon the Hooe plantation. Fortunately for the Federals there had been few enemy troops at the doctor's "extensive dwelling house," and those that did emerge were dispersed with a few rounds from the warship's bow gun. In a lightning assault Budd and his small force of sailors landed and entered the house wherein they discovered "several trunks . . . packed up ready for removal, and . . . several indications of a recent stampede." Some of the fugitives, it was deduced, were females. The house itself "was very richly furnished, and contained a valuable library, all of which fell a prey to the flames." Budd took only one prisoner, a young male slave and personal body servant belonging to Dr. Hooe, who stated that the family had left the house during a cannonade from *Freeborn* the previous evening. They had returned at 10 p.m. and spent the entire night in packing up and then departed in haste taking with them some of their effects in a number of wagons. Then they saw *Resolute* coming in. He reported that Dr. Hooe himself had been wounded by one of the shots from the rifled cannon. Before the rebels could return in force Budd fired the premises, including the main dwelling, "one of the most delightful on the banks of the Potomac," and five other buildings that were destroyed in their entirety. Nothing

117

was left but the brick chimneys. For days afterwards smoke could still be seen ascending from the smoldering ruins. [12]

During his brief visit Budd also learned that an enemy agent and spy named John M. Goldsmith had recently crossed from the plantation into Maryland and was already en route to Baltimore to purchase revolvers for the rebels. The agent, a small man with black hair and a moustache, "quick in action and speech" and strong in voice, was a cavalry officer in the Confederate Army and had left his dragoon uniform at the manor house while he traveled through Maryland disguised as a civilian. He had been to Baltimore at least twice on similar missions and, Budd surmised, had probably already returned to the city for the third time.[13]

When the raid was reported at Confederate headquarters in Fredericksburg it was immediately viewed as another Federal effort to determine if a battery was being erected at Mathias Point, and ignited some debate about the best manner of obstructing Federal navigation of the Potomac. Brigadier General Theophilus H. Holmes, an 1829 graduate of West Point, now commanding at Fredericksburg, believed Evansport, as Ruggles had suggested, was far better suited than Mathias Point for a battery. "There is very little difference in the distance of the channel from the shore," he informed Assistant Adjutant General George Deas, "and large guns will command either. From Evansport there is a good road to Fredericksburg, which would turn the position, and a good road to Manassas, turning that position; whereas from Mathias Point it would require a long land travel to any vulnerable point." He vowed that, if Richmond thought it worth the expense, with just two 32-pounder rifled guns or a pair of 8-inch Columbiads he could stop navigation on the river. Though he could not have foretold it, other events were to delay such actions for months.[14]

***

Two days after Budd's destruction of Hooe's plantation, Commander Ward prepared for a much more comprehensive effort to prevent the enemy from threatening closure of the Potomac at Mathias Point. He would physically occupy the point just beyond the bordering wetland, remove all ground cover in the area and then erect his own battery to preempt Confederate control there. The enemy blockade of the Potomac, he determined, must be prevented at all costs, even without the assistance of the army.

The commander's first move was to assemble adequate small craft for a landing and enough tools and equipment to erect the battery and earthworks. He requested Rowan supply two of his own boats, kedges and all other expeditionary outfits "as prescribed in the ordnance regulations" including a howitzer or two, replete with their crews. All were to be armed with muskets, ammunition, bayonets or cutlasses, and provisions for three or four days. Under command of Lieutenant Chaplin they were to be sent to rendezvous with *Freeborn* and *Dana* at Nanjemoy Creek. The boats were to carry "spirits of turpentine in a can, all the shovels and all the coal bags you have, except twelve retained to handle coal with; all the oakum you have, not exceeding one bale in quantity; a quantity of old canvas, all you can possibly spare, and your gunner's dark lantern. Send also every ax and hatchet you have, except the cook's." [15]

Having received Ward's orders about sundown on June 26, Rowan immediately dispatched the smallboat party as requested. Though Ward kept his plans to himself, Rowan correctly assumed the flotilla commander, "judging from the nature of the order he gave me to furnish him with such equipments as were necessary to cut down trees on the point and burn them," was intent on an amphibious landing and occupation of Mathias Point.[16]

Chaplin set off at 9 p.m. with two cutters and twenty-three men. With the cutters and a large open boat laden with the equipment all under tow of *Reliance*, he arrived at the appointed rendezvous only to find an empty stream. The following morning, June 27, he proceeded toward Mathias Point and found *Freeborn*, *Resolute* and *Dana* lying off the rebel encampment several miles below and immediately reported to Commander Ward for duty. Though the rebels ashore feared a landing on the beach near their camp, Ward now pressed on toward his primary destination. Upon her arrival off Mathias Point, *Freeborn* anchored broadside on and opposite a wooden house. To the left of the building was a gentle slope leading to the top of a tableland, and to the left of that a marshy ravine called Jotank Swamp. Beyond the ravine still farther to the left, lay a dense thicket of pines, running a considerable distance along the high bank to the extremity of the point. *Reliance* soon anchored a little lower down than *Freeborn*. A hawser was made fast onboard, connecting her with the flagship. *Dana* was anchored farther out. Once there Chaplin watched as the flagship commenced firing shot, shell and grape from both of her guns to clear the woods of any possible enemy units near the selected landing site. The commander's goal was to burn and destroy the woods and underbrush that afforded the enemy cover on the point. But first he would erect a breastwork in the pines near the end of the point to protect his men when later engaged in the clearing operation.[17]

With Ward personally taking the lead of thirty-four seamen (eleven sailors from *Freeborn* having been added to Chaplin's force), and assisted by Master's Mate John Kellogg, the landing was effected at 1 p.m. though not without opposition by forward pickets from the 40th Virginia Volunteers encamped three miles away. "The table land was soon gained," one of Ward's men later reported, "when the rebel pickets opened fire on our men, which the latter returned." On seeing this, a boat with nine men and a coxswain aboard, under command of Kellogg, immediately put off from the *Freeborn*. On grounding, the two other boats put off, Captain Ward telling the master's mate to cover the retreat of the other boats, which he did. When the enemy failed to show himself, the men lay on their oars between the *Freeborn* and the shore. Meanwhile, Captain Ward prepared to reboard the *Freeborn* to superintend the working of the guns to cover the second landing, which was soon effected by all three boats. Soon the acclivity had been surmounted, and pickets thrown out to the right, considerably beyond the wooden building, and to the left beyond Jotank Swamp. The former was composed of the *Freeborn* men; the latter from those of the *Pawnee*.[18]

Chaplin's men were now ordered to move out as skirmishers. All was quiet as they pressed slowly through the bush. Suddenly, when about 300 yards from their boats, firing broke out as they collided with rebel pickets who immediately took flight. Propelled by a rush of adrenaline the sailors set off in pursuit discharging their weapons as they ran, but halted after proceeding but a short distance. In an instant the chase was suddenly thrown into reverse when the lieutenant spotted an estimated four to five hundred Confederates charging toward him over the brow of a hill. Upon learning of the enemy's approach the commander immediately ordered his men back to their boats and to lay off shore while he returned again to *Freeborn* to fire her guns into the brush surrounding the landing site. The cannonade would continue without letup for hours.[19]

From the right of the wooden building, looking from the river, a view of the rebel encampment about three miles off was obtained where men could be seen moving to and fro. Some of them were on horseback, and one man was seen galloping down the road leading to the camp. To this point *Freeborn*'s shots were soon directed, guided by information furnished from the shore by Kellogg.[20]

Freeborn's big 32-pounders discharged round after round, driving the enemy from the field with raking fire for another quarter of an hour, and then turning upon the encampment. The shooting was intense but inflicted no casualties though there were close calls. Captain Fleet W. Cox of the Potomac Rifles, 40th Virginia, who had left Southern Maryland to join the Confederate Army, had emerged intact when a shell landed near him but miraculously failed to explode. At 4 p.m. the firing finally stopped. The enemy had been cleared from the field.[21]

When it appeared safe Chaplin and his men were again ordered to land. They were to begin construction of a sandbag breastwork and burn the brush on the point, while four men were sent out as pickets. Burning the wet, green wood and brush was difficult for those assigned, though most of the sailors under Chaplin's command and some from *Freeborn* were engaged in filling the coal bags with dirt and building the works. The erection of the battery was begun at the summit of the tableland at the top of the acclivity just above the landing site. The ground, with a strong fence running across, was well chosen. An embankment and a ditch already protected the site and formed a ready made defense under cover of which the construction detail might check the advance of the enemy when the works were completed and armed. Only one weak spot, forming an angle of forty-five degrees with the fence, was left exposed; and it was at this spot that the sandbags were soon being laid as fast as they could be filled. By late afternoon, about 5 p.m. as the construction neared completion and a large quantity of tree branches was being placed to camouflage it, *Freeborn* again commenced firing into the woods and on the rebel encampment upriver. With measured precision her bow gun delivered round shot after shot while the aft gun tossed deadly five-second shells. "Ward stood on the gallows frame," one sailor later reported, "directing the fire, which was excellent. Several of the shot and shell were distinctly seen to strike the white house, belonging to Mr. Grimes, at some distance above the wooden building, in which was ascertained that rebel troops were concentrated." [22]

Suddenly it was observed from the deck of the flagship that a number of *Freeborn*'s men were seen running in the direction of the Grimes house and were soon concealed from view. They were quickly met by firing from the building, which was promptly returned by the sailors. Then above the din, the voice of Kellogg was distinctly heard shouting "Rescue," and more men were seen engaged in the attack. Soon they all returned and Kellogg reported that all the rebels had been cleared out. In the meantime *Freeborn* had ceased firing so as not to hit her own men, but on their reappearance Ward ordered the forward gun trained "sharp forward, as it had been trained sharp aft all along." [23]

Now Ward sounded the whistle, at the same time hailing the shore. "All hands on board." Chaplin observed the signal to return and began to send the tools to the boats, leaving seven or eight men to cover the almost completed structure, composed of approximately 200 hand-filled sandbags. They would return the next day and finish the job. Or so they thought. Then came havoc.[24]

***

Ward was unaware of the actual strength of the rebel forces ashore or of the location of their other camp sites in the vicinity of Mathias Point, only that there were several hundred men in the area as evidenced from the charge earlier in the day. Yet he was confident the guns of *Freeborn*, *Reliance* and *Resolute* would be enough to hold them at bay while the breastwork was completed. In truth the situation was far worse than he imagined.

"Engagement between the Gunboat Flotilla, Freeborn and Reliance, under the command of Captain James H. Ward . . . at Mathias Point." Naval Historical and Heritage Command, Washington, D.C.

Although Ward could not identify the unit, it would later be ascertained that the Confederate troops belonged to Brockenbrough's 40th *Virginia Volunteers* and others from camps within but a few miles of the point. What he also didn't know was that the alarm had been sounded and reinforcements, consisting of a cavalry and three more infantry units from the camp at Brooke's Station commanded by Major Robert D. Mayo, had already been set in motion about 3 p.m. Mayo, a resident of the area, believing he was better acquainted with the topography of the

121

point than any other officer in the district, had determined to take matters into his own hands without awaiting orders. The major moved his command through the woods via a shorter path then being employed by either Brockenbrough or Ruggles, both of whom were by now also marching to the scene with reinforcements from even farther away.[25]

Having learned from the pickets that they thought the Federals were erecting a battery in the pines on the end of the point, Mayo took ten skirmishers from the Sparta Grays, and after halting the rest of his forces, pressed forward into the bushes to ascertain the correctness of the intelligence. Progressing some distance into the pines, and on the immediate brink of the river's edge, he could see a steamer and another vessel about 300 to 400 yards from the shore. He quickly determined that his skirmish party was too small to properly reconnoiter the ravines and bushes. Returning to his command, he promptly deployed a cavalry unit dismounted as skirmishers, leaving the rest of his troops in reserve. Quietly and swiftly the rebels swept through the bushes on the point but were still unable to get a clear view of the enemy until they encountered the Jotank Swamp, which separated them from the landing party. The approach was dangerously governed in its entirety by the guns of the Federal warships.[26]

Nevertheless, Mayo's troopers managed to close without discovery to within 250 yards of Chaplin and his men. Then, from concealed positions, they immediately opened a blistering fire from the thicket on the left bank of Jotank Creek, first upon *Freeborn* and then upon the sailors ashore. Despite a "perfect hail of musketry" from what he believed to be several hundred men, Chaplin calmly ordered the shore party to retire to their boats while he remained on the beach counting heads as they passed to insure all had made it safely away. "The boats," Mayo later reported, "returned our fire two or three times, and then all of their men, except two or three who had fallen overboard, lay down in their boats and it was some time before they could get their oarsmen to pull the boats from the shore." [27]

For a short time Chaplin was disturbed that the heavy guns of *Freeborn* had not opened up sooner to cover his retreat, but now he had little time to think of anything more than saving his men. He watched helplessly as the two cutters in which he had landed were rapidly filled with sailors, shoved off, and then began to drift aimlessly from the shore without oarsmen willing to expose themselves to the intense enemy gunfire. Yet they were relatively safe now though not everyone had managed to board. Some had been forced to swim. One man had not made it to the landing site in time and was unable to swim, but Chaplin considered it simply too dangerous to call back a boat to rescue himself and the lone straggler. There were but three choices now. Surrender, die, or take bodily to the river. With musket balls pelting the water all around them, the brave lieutenant took the sailor upon his shoulders, musket and all, and set out to swim for both their lives.[28]

Now the guns of *Freeborn* opened with some fury upon the Confederates, but only briefly. In the meantime having reached one of the cutters, Chaplin discovered the craft riddled by lead musket balls, her flagstaff shot away, and nineteen bullet holes in the flag. Though he had suffered not a scratch it had been a close call as evidenced by a bullet hole through his cap delivered by the very first shot of the enemy. Worse, several of his men had been seriously injured. Ordinary seaman John

Best had been hit in his right hand and right forearm; a third shot had fractured both bones of the left leg. Another seaman named John Waters was hit in the chest. The captain of *Pawnee*'s maintop, John Williams, while lying off in one of the boats, tried to rally the men as they cowered below the gunnels unwilling to expose themselves, by shouting out "that every man must die on his thwart soon than leave a man behind." For his trouble he had taken a bullet in the right thigh. Though severely wounded, reported one crewman, he heroically "retained charge of his boat, and when the staff was shot away held the stump in his hand with the flag till we got alongside the *Freeborn*." [29]

Once aboard the flagship Chaplin immediately discovered why there had been no covering fire for his retreat until he was on the beach. When the enemy opened fire, Ward had descended from the gallows frame and seized a rifle and commenced return firing at the enemy, as did the ship's pilot and others. In but an instant, when Yeoman Gunner George McKenny who had been manning one of the ship's guns, was hit in the thigh after firing but a few shots, the captain ran down to the forecastle deck and began to personally direct the ship's bow gun after first ordering it to be loaded with a round shot. Having just sighted the piece and being just about to withdraw to give the word to fire, he was struck in the abdomen by a musketball, which passed through his liver and other vital organs. Falling into the arms of Harry Churchill, the boatswain's mate, he stammered, "Churchill, I am killed." With one arm holding the commander, Churchill pulled the firing lanyard with the other, throwing the shot into the midst of the enemy. [30]

In a fury, George Couch, captain of the aft gun, shouted, "Boys, let us have our revenge." The gun was then pointed true and its five-seconds shell reportedly burst right in the midst of a cluster of rebels, followed by another and then two rounds of grape. The bow gun fired the same until the ship's doctor forbade the disturbance of the commander's last moments. The firing stopped. [31]

Barely alive, Ward was unable to give orders. Landsman William McChenny had also been badly wounded in the thigh and in the confusion that followed, Master's Mate Samuel Perry Lee, Ward's second in command aboard, shouted "Slip the cable and start her." Soon *Freeborn* and all the boats were out of the range of the enemy's deadly rifles and muskets as the ship steamed upriver to pick up two boats, which could not otherwise come near to her without exposing themselves to the rebels ashore. [32]

Upon the urging of surgeon Dr. J. W. Moore, *Freeborn* was ordered to return to *Pawnee*, then lying off Aquia. About 9 p.m., after the flagship pulled alongside *Pawnee*, her own surgeon, who had been sent on board of her in the morning, boarded *Freeborn* accompanied by Frederick Ward, the commander's second son. Though Dr. Moore had already pronounced the wound mortal, the commander and the five wounded sailors were transferred for speedier transit back to Washington to secure immediate treatment. But it was already too late. As *Pawnee* raised anchor and abandoned her station to return to the city, one observer recorded that the man some called the best educated officer in the United States Navy, was first laid upon the quarterdeck, but then moved to a more convenient position.

As the move was underway, Ward quitely queried: "Why remove me? I am quite comfortable."

Lee asked if he could do anything for him.

"Raise my head a little higher," replied the captain in a whisper.

Pointing to the pit of his stomach, he said to Dr. Moore, "Dr., the wound is here." Three-quarters of an hour later, with his son beside him, James H. Ward expired after a few gasps. A most profound grief pervaded the whole of the officers and crew of the *Freeborn*.[33] The founder and commander of the U.S. Potomac Flotilla, had become the first U.S. naval officer to die in action in the Civil War.[34]

As for Chaplin and his men, in Rowan's later estimation they had "escaped utter destruction by a miracle," making good their retreat against overwhelming odds without leaving the enemy a trophy other than a few sand bags and some axes.[35]

For the first time in more than a month *Pawnee* abandoned her station. "In consequence of the want of ordinary comforts in the *Freeborn* for wounded men," Rowan later reported in excusing his departure from his critical blockade rather than sending one of the other flotilla vessels, "I brought the two wounded men belonging to that vessel, with those two of this ship, with the remains of the late commander J. H. Ward, to the navy yard, Washington." [36]

Pawnee arrived at the Navy Yard at 9:30 a.m., June 28. What followed was a series of processionals that honored the U.S. Navy's first fallen officer and hero of the war. On the ship's arrival, forty men of the 71st Regiment were ordered out to escort the body to the Engine House, which was wholly draped in mourning cloth, followed by officers of *Pawnee* and the Navy Yard, and the boat crews who had participated in the engagement. All marched to a solemn dirge played by the 71st Regiment Band. Funeral services were held in the Engine House where the commander's remains lay in state wrapped in an American ensign. On the afternoon of Monday, June 29, accompanied by officers and seamen who were around him when he fell, the commander's body was placed aboard a train for New York City where it arrived at midnight, June 30. Immediately upon arrival the corpse was placed in a coffin and escorted to the New York Navy Yard to lay in state aboard the USS *North Carolina*, Ward's former command, covered by an awning draped in American flags. At the head of the pall, which lay upon the poop deck, was a large red cross and the colors draped with decorations and lights "according to the rituals of the Roman Catholic faith," of which Ward was a member. Across the lid of the open coffin was laid a cross of laurel, camellias and immortelles. There would be no religious services aboard the old warship, but in Catholic chapels across New York City and Brooklyn prayers were said for the soul of the deceased. Soon after the officers and employees of the Navy Yard, as well as many civilian mourners, passed the body in silence. The coffin was then closed and carried in procession to a steamer waiting at the dock to transport it to Hartford, Connecticut for burial.[37]

***

Commander Ward's mission to capture and hold a remote but strategically important point of land on the Virginia side of the Potomac River had been a humiliating failure. Virginia papers such as the *Fredericksburg News* and the Richmond *Daily Dispatch* lauded the affair as a great Confederate victory. There were claims that between six and nine Yankees had been killed, twelve or fourteen drowned, and from fifteen to twenty forced to take to the woods "where they were dodging about like scared partridges" with troopers "still hunting them like wild turkeys." Though there had actually been but one dead and a few wounded on the Union side, the rebels had miraculously suffered no losses in the first combat seen by many. They had soon fully occupied the disputed point and its nearly completed breastworks with fifteen companies of volunteers.[38]

The defensive victory was to cause considerable division among the Confederate command as to what should come next. Major Mayo, whose unit had marched to the point from Brooke Station, was adamant as to what he believed should be done. "I have never realized until yesterday," he informed Ruggles, "how absolutely necessary artillery is at this point. With a single smoothbore 12-pounder I could have sunk the steamer and vessel without exposing my men more than they were." [39] General Holmes sent along his own comments with Ruggles's report of the affair to General Robert E. Lee. He informed the new senior commander in Virginia that he had just dispatched Walker's battery, then at Aquia, to reinforce the units at Mathias Point. "This force I think sufficient to prevent a landing for the purpose of holding the point. If it be your design to erect a battery there to command the river, I think instructions to that effect should be given immediately and another regiment ordered to report to me for its defense after construction." [40]

Lee thought otherwise. The force at Mathias Point, too far from the main Confederate camp, was deemed insufficient to repel any truly large scale amphibious assault backed by the guns of the U.S. Navy. Indeed, as one historian put it, Lee came to regard the point "as somewhat of a nuisance." Its commanding position notwithstanding, he believed that it was no more important than any other point on the Potomac had troops never been stationed there. Yet if the troops were withdrawn the Federals would almost certainly reoccupy it. Better to just keep the few soldiers already there out of sight and cause no provocative action that might stir up another hornet's nest, thereby allaying Yankee apprehensions, and encouraging a belief that he had no intention of erecting fortifications on the point.[41]

Then just as suddenly as all eyes had turned towards the scrap at Mathias Point, they were captured by another even more daring enterprise conducted by a gruff old Baltimorean and a sagacious young soldier of fortune from one of St. Mary's County's most notable families.

125

10

MADAME LA FORCE
"A ruse de guerre."

Of the many citizens of Southern Maryland who chose to take up service in the Confederate cause perhaps none was more flamboyant or daring than Richard Thomas of Mattapany-Sewell plantation, a scion of St. Mary's County aristocracy. The great Thomas family estate was superbly situated overlooking the entrance of the Patuxent. Its centerpiece was a long and stately manor house that reflected the epitome of that small but influential circle of Southern Maryland's landed gentry in which he had been raised. He was the son of the late Richard Thomas, Sr., who had presided for years as speaker in the Maryland House of Delegates, nephew of James Thomas, an ex-governor of the state and eldest of three brothers who would fight for the South. Richard, Jr. had engaged in a life of adventure with which few could compare.[1]

Born on October 23, 1833, Richard Thomas had attended the Charlotte Hall Academy as a youth, and later the Maryland Military and Naval Academy on the Tred Avon River in Oxford, Maryland. He was accepted at the age of sixteen to attend West Point. Though excelling in physical and field training, his academics were poor, and he resigned from the academy on October 21, 1851. Eager to see the world, he began his career as a government surveyor in California and other western territories and then traveled to the Far East where he campaigned as a soldier of fortune against a plague of Chinese river piracy. Not long afterwards he found himself in Europe employed in Garibaldi's fight for Italian independence against the Hapsburg Empire. During the campaigns on the Italian peninsula he adopted as his *nom de guerre*, the adventurously exotic surname "Zarvona," which he later legally attached to his own by Confederate government authority. Thereafter, at least in the South, he was referred to as Richard T. Zarvona. While living for a spell in Paris he learned to converse in fluent French, a talent he would eventually put to use in his later adventures on the Chesapeake.[2]

The brewing possibilities of Civil War in the United States must unquestionably have been one of the attractions that brought twenty-seven-year-old Richard Thomas "Zarvona" home to St. Mary's County. Whatever the cause, his decision to volunteer along with his brothers George and James William for service to the Confederacy was almost certainly motivated by the time of the riots in Baltimore. The arrival of Federal troops on his native Maryland soil and the Virginia Convention's passage on April 17, 1861 for an ordinance of secession cemented his resolution in place. Brother John would become a sergeant in Company H of the 1st Maryland Regiment in General Robert E. Lee's Army of Northern Virginia and serve as a recruiter for the Confederate Maryland Line. Brother George would become a captain and acting adjutant for the 2nd Maryland Regiment and would be twice seriously wounded, first at Gettysburg and then at Cold Harbor. But Richard's destiny was to take him down a substantially different trail. In May 1861, already an acknowledged veteran of combat in Europe and Asia, he readily assumed the acting captaincy of a company in the St. Mary's Light Infantry, busying himself with raising provisions, uniforms and money for his unit. Believing that he was likely to find more immediate action and glory across the Potomac, he traveled to Richmond to offer his service to Virginia. His arrival in that city could not have come at a more propitious moment.[3]

From the very onset of hostilities in the Chesapeake Tidewater, beginning with the destruction and abandonment of the U.S. facilities and shipping, including ten mostly aged warships and 1,198 heavy cannon, at the Gosport Navy Yard in Portsmouth, Virginia, Federal naval forces had been severely crippled. Yet they were still a force to be reckoned with. Moreover the Navy Department had been working feverishly to beef up the fledgling Potomac Flotilla by purchasing, converting and arming numerous ferryboats, tugs, schooners, passenger and freight boats, and other vessels into makeshift warships to patrol the strategic rivers and tributaries of the Tidewater.

When Richard Thomas arrived in Richmond to offer his service to Governor Letcher and to form an independent unit called the Maryland Zouaves, a most convoluted but inventive plot was already in the making to capture *Pawnee*, the most powerful ship in the Tidewater, and turn her into a rebel raider. There is some dispute regarding the origins of the plan. What is known is that in April 1861 Major Thomas H. Williamson of the Virginia Army Engineers and Confederate States Navy Lieutenant Hunter H. Lewis, a graduate of the U.S. Naval Academy, had visited the strategic Aquia Creek region of the Potomac. Their mission had been to examine the topography and make recommendations for battery sites to protect the creek entrance and railroad approach to Fredericksburg, as well as others locations that might facilitate a rebel blockade of the river and the isolation of Washington, D.C.[4]

In early June Lewis had occasion to observe the 413-ton sidewheel steamboat *St. Nicholas*, a well known regular on the Baltimore to Washington run that made frequent stops to pick up or offload passengers and freight on the Potomac.[5] What intrigued the lieutenant was that the steamer had also apparently been allowed to draw near *Pawnee* to deliver supplies. But more importantly, she had been permitted to do so without being challenged during her approach and then allowed to stand by her for some time after. Or so it had been incorrectly assumed from his observation.[6]

The actual genesis of the plan, which was attributed by some to Lewis and by many others to the more colorful and dashing Thomas, was most certainly the product of a far older and more seasoned ex-U.S. Navy captain named George Nicholas Hollins. Born in 1799 in Baltimore, Hollins was a crusty 46-year naval veteran who, during his long sea career, had served under Stephen Decatur. He had once been a prisoner of war in Bermuda, fought in the Barbary Wars, and was last serving as skipper of the USS *Susquehanna* at Naples when the Southern rebellion began. It had not taken long, however, for him to determine where his allegiance lay when the war broke out. Like many other naval officers the old captain resigned his commission in the first week of June. On the 18th he traveled from Baltimore to the Patuxent aboard the steamer *Mary Washington* as the next to final leg of his journey to Richmond to join the Confederate Navy. After disembarking at Millstone Landing, he later claimed, he had visited the plantation "of Mr. S., where I suggested the idea (which originated entirely with myself), of seizing the *St. Nicholas* . . . manning her with volunteers, and then to take the *Pawnee*, a United States steamer commanded by Yankee Ward, and which was a great annoyance to the boats on the Potomac." [7]

While exploring with his host the possibility of launching the scheme from Southern Maryland, he was pointedly informed that because of the many Union men in the region it would most certainly be discovered before it could be executed. Hollins was not dissuaded. The captain resolved to make his way to Virginia in an open boat rowed by four blacks, probably crossing near the well used contraband route from Popes Creek to Hooe's Ferry. Upon his arrival in Virginia he made a call upon Dr. Hooe at his home near the ferry only a few days before the destruction of the plantation by the U.S. Navy. It was 1 a.m. in the morning when the old man arrived at the doomed estate.[8]

"This gentleman," Hollins later wrote of Hooe, "was a perfect stranger to me, but he received me kindly, entertained me handsomely, he and his charming family so soon to be rendered houseless and homeless by the incendiary act of the vandal Captain Budd, of the United States gunboat [*Resolute*]." Whether or not Hollins informed the doctor of his plan is unknown. Whatever the case Hooe chartered a buggy that same day and drove his guest the twenty miles to Fredericksburg, where they arrived about 6 p.m. The following morning the captain boarded a train for Richmond. Upon his arrival he proceeded immediately to the Navy Department and introduced himself to Secretary of the Navy Stephen R. Mallory and was immediately awarded a commission as captain in the Confederate States Navy. Upon receiving his papers he next visited the Bureau of Details where he met many of his old friends including Samuel Barron, Robert F. R. Lewis, Charles F. M. Spotswood, and the internationally famed oceanographer Matthew Fontaine Maury. All had also resigned from the U.S. Navy and were destined for significant roles with rebel forces afloat.[9] They would soon be joined by many other notable veterans includeing such experienced Maryland naval officers as Franklin Buchanan of Dorchester County, Raphael Semmes of Charles County and French Forrest of St. Mary's County, who would enter Confederate naval service and earn great notoriety for their exploits.

Hollins and his old colleagues were soon deeply engrossed in discussion during which the captain revealed his plan for the capture of *St. Nicholas*. The response was far from supportive. "I was told," he later wrote, "that the Secretary, Mr. Mallory, would not agree to the plan, but that the governor would. I walked into Mr. Mallory's room and asked his permission. He granted it, and I at once went straight to the governor's. When I made my proposition, Governor Letcher, without a moment's hesitation, acceded to the proposal and gave me a draft for $1,000 to send North for arms and men, etc." [10]

The plan he presented was a long shot by any standard. Traveling in disguise, the captain and a party of others would board *St. Nicholas* at various points along her route and overpower the crew by surprise after the ship's regular stop at Point Lookout. As soon as she was taken they would proceed upriver to *Pawnee's* cruising grounds, come alongside and capture the unsuspecting Yankee man of war by *ruse de guerre*. With the big warship in Confederate hands they might destroy or chase off the smaller vessels of the U.S. Navy's tiny Potomac Flotilla. At the very least they could then reopen a section of the river between Quantico and Occoquan Creek, Virginia, to trade and reestablish safe direct communications with friends and supporters in Southern Maryland.

USS *Pawnee* during the Civil War. Naval Historical and Heritage Command, Washington, D.C.

Governor Letcher, who had also just met Richard Thomas, immediately introduced the young adventurer to Hollins as a man who could be trusted to go North and purchase the necessary arms and transact other business as needed. The old veteran, who was to be given overall command of the *St. Nicholas* expedition, must have seen something in the dashing young man that made him agree to the partnership.[11]

The governor then called upon Navy Secretary Mallory to furnish pistols, ammunition and cutlasses for the expeditionaries. He also requested Secretary of War Walker to order the Confederate commander at Fredericksburg, General Holmes, to provide 500 soldiers from Bate's 2nd Tennessee Regiment then stationed there. They were to march down the Northern Neck to the Coan where they would rendezvous with Lieutenant Lewis to support the operation once *St. Nicholas* had been taken. There Lewis would take over from Hollins and with the Tennessee men aboard lead the expedition against *Pawnee*. Thus by giving each of the three a key role in the operation, Letcher had wisely removed any bones of contention for honors should success be achieved.[12]

Despite efforts to maintain secrecy it was not long before rumors were spreading about Fredericksburg concerning a covert expedition that was forming. By Friday morning, June 28 it had become the talk of the town; men gathered on many street corners conversing excitedly about the subject. Some suspicion was drawn to Thomas, now dressed in a dashing Zouave uniform, and with his head closely shaved. "He was evidently affecting a character very adverse to his true one," noted one observer, and some citizens of the town even suspected him of being a spy.[13]

Hollins and Thomas promptly left Fredericksburg bound for Point Lookout, Maryland that same afternoon. While en route the captain serendipitously encountered his two sons, George, Jr. and Fred Hollins, who were on their way to Richmond to join the Confederate Army. He readily enlisted them in the scheme as members, the very first, of Thomas's newly forming unit, the Maryland Zouaves. The four men slipped across the Potomac undetected by Federal patrol boats and reached the Maryland shore safely. Hollins and his sons found sanctuary at a friend's home where they remained through the next day until sundown. On the ship's return trip from Washington, Thomas boarded the Baltimore bound *St. Nicholas* at the Point Lookout wharf en route to secure the necessary arms in the city and, no doubt, to thoroughly assess the ship's layout while underway. Before parting with the Zouave, Hollins signed the $1,000 draft over to him to purchase the arms, to help recruit as many men as he could, and pay for their return down the bay in *St. Nicholas* on her next trip to Washington. In the meantime the captain himself would seek to raise a number of volunteers in St. Mary's. Their rendezvous would be at Point Lookout.[14]

It was apparently soon after Thomas's arrival at Baltimore that he paid a visit to the office of Severn Teackle Wallis, one of the leading secessionists in the Maryland State Legislature. Wearing a wig covering his shaved head he was totally unrecognizable to the legislator, whom he apparently knew. After taking a seat in front of Wallis and another individual he began to converse: "Well," he said, undoubtedly with some amusement, "if neither of you know me I think I am safe," and then removed his wig. He was then immediately recognized even as he informed them that they would soon hear from him again.[15] It is altogether possible that it was through Wallis's aid that the one time soldier-of-fortune was able to procure the arms he had come to Baltimore to secure.

The boldness of the plot notwithstanding, the Confederates faced many unforeseen circumstances that had already begun to dim their chances of success. On June 27, the same day as the Mathias Point affair, General Holmes informed Secretary of War Walker of an objection that he did not wish to hear: "I have respectfully to say that I did not feel justified in ordering volunteer troops on an expedition so fraught with ruinous consequences if it failed, and the success of which required that so many contingencies should be effectually accomplished. I referred the matter to the colonels of the regiments and they declined to volunteer their men." Walker agreed.[16]

An appeal for help in persuading the secretary came from Hollins's old friend, Captain Matthew Fontaine Maury, one of the most respected officers in the infant Confederate Navy. Walker was finally convinced and fired back a direct order to Holmes. The following morning the general, too, submitted – in part. It is uncertain whether or not the events at Mathias Point influenced his judgment. Nevertheless he finally agreed to dispatch 400 men under Colonel William B. Bate to assist Lewis, but with a caveat: the colonel and his men, a force that he personally considered "unnecessarily strong," were to take no part in the expedition on the water. He justified his directive by stating, "that an indispensable requisite to success would be the absolute concealment of 300 or 400 men on a comparatively small steamer, and those men untrained volunteers." Indeed, he concluded, that was only one of several problems with the whole scheme in which any success "would be miraculous." [17]

The men would be sent. Coercing them to participate would be something else.

***

When President Lincoln formally extended the blockade of Southern states to include Virginia and North Carolina on April 27, the need to control the Potomac River dividing line between the Union and the Confederacy had become a strategic imperative, as demonstrated by the fights at Aquia Creek and Mathias Point. The river would become the northernmost extension of General Scott's Anaconda Plan, the blockade of the Confederacy by sea. It would, in essence, become for more than the next four years the "Anaconda's Tail." A sizeable naval force, beyond the mosquito fleet Commander Ward had set in motion, was deemed necessary to insure its success in accordance with the president's directive. Though on May 1 the Navy Department had formally established the Potomac Flotilla as a component of the Atlantic Blockading Squadron, it would soon afterwards receive independent squadron status. Captain James Harmon Ward was replaced, upon the arrival of his remains at Washington, by Commander Thomas T. Craven, then on court martial duty in New York. Craven would not officially set off to take command until July 9.[18]

Well before the Hollins-Thomas expedition was fully underway the U.S. Navy Department had already received intelligence suggesting that *St. Nicholas* might be carrying contraband articles intended for Virginia. Instructions had been sent to Commander Ward to stop and search the freighter, which he had already done once, but would do again as necessary. Though Ward was now gone, it was unlikely that the steamboat would have been allowed to approach *Pawnee* as she had done earlier, or any other Federal warship for that matter, in the nonchalant manner that the Confederates perceived had happened earlier. However, neither Hollins nor Thomas could have known that. Thus, based upon a questionable premise and motivated by unadulterated sagacity, they proceeded as planned. In Baltimore Thomas was able to recruit with little difficulty twenty-five young men for his Maryland Zouave unit.[19]

Finally the moment of truth had arrived. Late in the afternoon of Friday, June 28, just one day after the Mathias Point fight and Ward's death, well over fifty passengers boarded *St. Nicholas* at Baltimore. The ship was already laden with a considerable amount of freight and consignment goods for the citizens of St. Mary's and Charles counties, all of which were to be offloaded with passengers at various Potomac landings. Cargo for Washington, Alexandria, and Georgetown, D.C., her final stop, had also been taken on. Among the passengers would be added sixteen laborers who would board in twos and threes en route to Southern Maryland to work in the tobacco harvest. Or so they claimed. None, however, had apparently bothered to read the day's news regarding Ward's death—or of the removal from her station of *Pawnee*, the objective of their expedition!

At 4 p.m., just as *St. Nicholas* prepared to depart, a very respectable, heavily veiled and rather masculine looking lady, Madame la Force, an "elderly" *modiste*, came aboard accompanied by a bearded man said to be her brother. Speaking broken English with a strong French accent she brought with her several "high, large, trunks such as milliners use." For Captain Jacob Kirwin, the steamer's skipper, everything seemed normal. "There was nothing in the movement of the passengers," remarked one observer soon afterwards, "to excite any suspicion of the daring act that was contemplated." As the lines were cast off, the rather dark complexioned lady was engaged in conversing in fluent French with various officials onboard as well as one of the men who had embarked at Point Lookout, all the while tossing her fan about "like a Spanish dancer" in a most feminine and seductive display. Her motions seemed to some so coquettish and scandalous "that all the other women on the boat were in a terrible state over it." No one noticed her most distinctive mannish features.[20]

Shortly after 10 p.m., welcomed by the beacon of the Point Lookout Lighthouse, *St. Nicholas* was nearing the wharf on the long, sandy spear that separated the entrance to the Potomac River from the Chesapeake. Here, about midnight, more passengers boarded. Among the new arrivals was a quiet, dignified, elderly looking bearded gentleman, along with between seven and twelve other men. The old man soon took station on the deck in the rear of the ladies' saloon ostensibly to observe the weather and enjoy the cool evening breeze. He quietly noticed the French woman, who appeared greatly concerned about the projected arrival time of the boat at Washington and soon afterwards excused herself from the music and frivolity in the saloon to retire to her stateroom. "As it was very warm in the berths," a few male passengers decided to spend the night in the arms of deck chairs. They would thus become unsuspecting witnesses to a most dramatic scene that was about to occur.[21]

About 1 a.m., as *St. Nicholas* cleared the wharf and began to skim effortlessly along on the dark Potomac waters, a handful of passengers continued to lounge about the deck, while most others had already retired for the night. In the distance the steamer *Diamond State* passed unnoticed in the darkness. Suddenly two of the passengers who had been lying in deckchairs observed a stalwart looking man "climbing over the railing of the deck." He was armed with a revolver and cutlass and dressed in stunning red flared trousers and a blue coat and cap – the uniform of Thomas's newly formed Maryland Zouaves. One of the passengers at first assumed he had come from a government boat and was boarding *St. Nicholas* "for the purpose of enquiry." [22]

For a brief moment the elderly gentlemen who had embarked at Point Lookout whispered to the man in uniform to "hold himself in readiness," and then in an instant both had rushed below. There, in Madame la Force's room, already crowded with the "laborers," they quickly opened the millinery trunks in which were stashed Colt pistols, carbines, cutlasses, Bowie knives and ammunition: all were soon distributed to the men who had come aboard at Baltimore and to those who had boarded with the elderly gentleman at Point Lookout. The old man took a Sharps rifle and a pair of pistols and upon his given signal all the men, twenty-five in number, spread throughout the ship. In an instant the old man was entering the wheelhouse. Putting a hand gently on the ship captain's shoulder he informed him that *St. Nicholas* had just been captured and must immediately steer for Coan River.[23]

In less than two minutes from the appearance of the Zouave the ship was stopped dead in the water. Captain Kirwin, apparently stalling or simply terrified, declined to follow the old man's orders, saying he was no pilot, indicating that he could not bring his ship into that river. The old man, Captain Hollins of course, responded with a threat that could not be ignored. "I told him I knew he was a pilot and that if he did not pilot me over I would set fire to the *St. Nicholas* and land all my men in his boats . . . I was determined she would not fall into the hands of the enemy." Kirwin immediately acquiesced but being so nervous that he could not handle the wheel turned the assignment over to one of his crew who could.[24]

In the meantime, a passenger who had observed the Zouave climbing over the railing grew curious about the proceedings underway and went below to investigate. To his astonishment he saw "about fifteen men, armed with carbines, revolvers and Bowie knives standing in battle array and in full possession of the boat!" Without wasting a moment, Captain Hollins had taken command of the ship, ordered lights doused, and passengers and crew to go below deck. At Kinsale, on the Coan River, the ship would be stripped of all unnecessary cargo, and the civilian passengers released ashore. All would eventually be permitted to return to Baltimore on their own if they wished. Kirwin and his fourteen-man crew would be held as prisoners, at least until the ship was out of danger. At Coan River *St. Nicholas* was to also take on board Lieutenant Lewis with part of the crew of the CSS *Patrick Henry*, then in the James River, and a third of the 125 officers and men of Colonel Bate's 2nd Tennessee Volunteers to assist in the capture of *Pawnee*. En route, Captain Kirwin, still stunned, was blithely informed by Thomas that *St. Nicholas* would soon be engaged in a "privateering" expedition, during which they would sail up the Potomac with the United States flag waving at the masthead to deceive their intended prey.[25]

For the next several hours, while they quietly awaited the appearance of the Tennesseans who had departed Fredericksburg on Friday morning and would not arrive until Saturday morning, Hollins and Thomas maintained order with a gentle glove. One witness later reported: "Throughout the whole night not a single act of rudeness was perpetrated, all the passengers being treated with the greatest civility. The commander told the ladies that they were in the hands of Southern gentlemen, and would be treated as his own sisters. Whatever opinions may be entertained of the capture itself, no one who was present on that eventful night can say aught but in praise of the gentlemanly deportment of all concerned."[26]

It seemed that phase one of the Lewis-Hollins plans had fallen flawlessly into place. Phase two was destined to a somewhat different outcome than anticipated — and, for the Confederates, in a most unexpected way.

***

On June 27, even as Hollins, Thomas, and Lewis were attending to the final details of their respective roles in the capture of *St. Nicholas*, the removal of the principal objective of the expedition, the USS *Pawnee*, which had been engaged to carry the body of Commander Ward to the Washington Navy Yard, was unknown to them. *Pawnee* and the rest of the squadron had remained at anchor at the yard so that their crews could attend services. There simply were no warships for the Confederates to capture as the blockade had been temporarily abandoned.[27]

133

Ironically, the loss of a brave U.S. naval officer had possibly saved *Pawnee* by removing her to a locale where capture would be impossible, none of which was known to the leaders of the expedition though everything else had proceeded as planned. At 4:30 a.m., an hour after arriving in the Coan, Lewis and a party of Confederate Navy sailors and thirty or forty men of the 2nd Tennessee Volunteers who had just marched in from Fredericksburg, boarded *St. Nicholas*. The Tennessee men appeared to one of the passengers, a Southern sympathizer, to be well armed with rifles and Bowie knives, and "anxious to meet the Federal troops to test the accuracy of their rifles and the virtue of their steel." They had marched twenty miles through a driving rain and mud the night before and were reportedly "spiling" for a fight. Then moments later while casually reading a Baltimore morning newspaper found aboard *St. Nicholas*, Hollins was stunned to learn of the death of Commander Ward and the removal of *Pawnee* to Washington. Of necessity, the well laid plan to capture the great warship was immediately abandoned.[28]

Hollins was well aware that news of the *St. Nicholas* capture would soon be spread throughout the Chesapeake Tidewater, and a pursuit was almost certain to materialize. Lingering about on the Potomac in an unarmed ship could be hazardous. A man of decision, he quickly resolved to take the prize down the bay and into the friendly waters of the Rappahannock River. From there she might be brought upriver to Fredericksburg and converted into a Confederate man of war. But first he attended to the few actual passengers aboard, all of whom were quickly landed along with any goods they had brought aboard with them. Those who wished to return to Baltimore on their own were given permission to do so. "Few," he later noted, "returned, as nearly all were on their way South, and although it was Sunday the ladies amused themselves by making Confederate flags out of the Yankee flags I had captured." [29]

The run down the bay was not without some unexpected bonuses. As the steamer left the Potomac and rounded Smith's Point on the Virginia shore, three vessels were soon spotted and captured in quick succession by boarding. The first was a fine brig called *Monticello*, laden with a cargo of 3,500 bags of coffee bound from Rio de Janeiro for Baltimore. Hollins ordered the brig's crew to board *St. Nicholas*, leaving only the captain and his wife on the ship with Lieutenant Robert D. Minor, CSN, in command to bring her up to Feredreicksburg. "The coffee," Hollins later took some delight in noting, "was a great treat to our 'boys in gray,' who were already beginning to endure some of the many privations that made them in later days 'truly an army of martyrs.'" [30]

An hour later *St. Nicholas* came upon the schooner *Mary Pierce* from Boston, carrying 200 tons of ice and bound for Washington. An officer and prize crew were placed aboard and she, too, was dispatched to Fredericksburg. "The ice," it was reported, "got there in time, for the wounded and sick in the hospitals were suffering for want of it." [31]

Later both Hollins and the skipper of *Mary Pierce* would coincidentally be attending the sale of the ice at Fredericksburg. The price of the commodity was apparently high enough to excite the Yankee whose subsequent proposal to Hollins astonished even that hardened old naval officer. Upon "seeing the fine prices paid for the ice," Hollins wrote afterwards, "he came to me and proposed that he should go to Boston, get another vessel loaded with ice, bring her down and let me know precisely when to meet him that I might capture him, take the vessel to Fredericksburg, sell the ice and divide the proceeds. Would anyone but a Yankee have been guilty of such rascality? He had a splendid flag of a 74 [gun man of war], an ensign that he had borrowed from the [Boston] navy yard, to hoist on the occasion of [Stephen A.] Douglas's death, but of that same ensign a goodly number of secession flags were made." [32]

Last, and perhaps most important, to fall prey to the rebels was the brig *Margaret*, Captain Edward Case. She had been hauling 270 tons of coal and was taken just in time to replenish the big steamer's dwindling supplies. Indeed, as Hollins later reported, the last capture was "a most fortunate prize, as I was on my last bucket of coal in the *St. Nicholas*." [33]

With their three prizes in company, Hollins and Thomas steamed up the Rappahannock to Fredericksburg. Their reception was one of royal welcome and military honors with Governor Letcher himself praising the expeditionaries, and in particular the colorful Zarvona and his Zouaves, none of whom but their leader having as yet his own uniform.[34]

"The French Lady and Brother Jonathan." The two scenes depict Richard Thomas "Zarvona" disguised as a flirting French woman who makes off with an entire ship. "Jonathan," depicted as a flummoxed Yankee, in astonishment says, "Wheres my boat. I do believe that Franch Ladys got it." *Harper's Weekly*, Prints and Photographs Division, Library of Congress, Washington, D.C.

It did not take long for Federal naval forces to learn of the *St. Nicholas* capture. The first suspicions of a possible rebel seizure were reported by the *Diamond State* upon her arrival in Washington late on the night of June 29. Having passed *St. Nicholas* as she was under steam making for Kinsale, Virginia, not her normal port of call, was suspicious enough. But when her lights were extinguished and *Diamond State* lost sight of her in the darkness fears were "seriously entertained that she has been seized by the rebels." On June 30 Acting Lieutenant Mygatt, commander of the USS *Reliance*, was en route down the Potomac when a boat was observed

135

apparently trying to cross to Virginia. The vessel was immediately stopped and the two men aboard interrogated. One of the men claimed he had been paid five dollars in paper money to take some men from Virginia to the Maryland shore. They were heading for Baltimore. Mygatt also learned in some detail from the prisoners about the seizure of *St. Nicholas* by a party of men "who went on board in women's clothes at the point," and of their flight into the Coan and then the Rappahannock. He immediately informed Lieutenant Reigert Lowry, the new commander of *Thomas Freeborn*. Upon consulting with his fellow commander, Mygatt recommended, "that the best plan is for me to go right to the [Hampton] Roads and inform Flag Officer [Silas] Stringham, as there is a chance of the steamer's doing much mischief." [35]

Reliance returned to Washington where Mygatt reported on the steamer's capture to Commandant Dahlgren on the afternoon of July 1. Dahlgren immediately informed Secretary Welles, who soon after received an even more comprehensive account from Charles Worthington, agent for the Baltimore and Washington Steam Packet Company. The following day the secretary received troubling intelligence that the "the *St. Nicholas* affair was a trap set to catch the *Pawnee*" and that there "may be other enterprises of the same character on foot and it would be well to be on the lookout for them." [36]

The warning was indeed prescient.

11

UNEARNED CONSEQUENCES

"A rendezvous for law breakers"

St. Nicholas arrived at Fredericksburg about 6:30 p.m. on the evening of June 30, and tied up at the Baltimore and Washington line steamboat wharf, which had been vacant since the start of the war. A crowd immediately began to gather. At first dubious about her identity, many were curious to know the circumstances under which she came, that is until the whole story was revealed. "Our citizens," remarked one ebullient eyewitness to the scene, "were thrown into quite a furor of excitement." [1]

Though the seizure of *St. Nicholas* was subsequently lauded throughout Virginia, not everyone was quite so thrilled. To the Federals, not surprisingly, the event was considered nothing less than outright piracy. But one Marylander, quite probably from St. Mary's County who was serving in a Confederate volunteer unit in Richmond, expressed his personal discontent regarding the capture to the editors of one of that city's newspapers, the *Daily Dispatch*, for other reasons. "The recent seizure of the steamer *St. Nicholas*," he wrote,

"whilst plying between the District of Columbia andBaltimore, and engaged in freighting agricultural products, &c., for the farners of Maryand, may be considered or contested as a belligerent right; but against the seizure, confiscation, or detention of the goods and groceries, farming utensils, and other property of the true and loyal citizens of St. Mary's and adjoining counties, I wish to protest. St. Mary's has been termed the South Carolina of Maryland, and at the late Congressional election gave only 73 Union votes against 1,043 majority for the Secession candidate. No county in the State has furnished more recruits for the Confederate army; and whilst they have left their families, homes, and property unprotected, and crossed the Potomac at great personal risk, as well as expense, to enlist in defence of the South, they have a right to demand at least an exemption at home from hostile acts and annoyances on the part of the South. Between the upper and nether millstones they may be ground to powder. An Exile." [2]

On July 2 Governor Letcher formally and retroactively commissioned Richard Thomas Zarvona "Colonel of the Active Volunteer forces of the State" as of July 1, 1861. The young man was sworn in as such by Richmond Mayor Joseph Mayo. Hollins, the actual commander of the expedition, all but ignored by the media, was promoted to commodore and moved on to become a Flag Officer in the Confederate States Navy charged with the defense of the Mississippi and Louisiana coast. Neither *St. Nicholas* nor her cargo would ever see Maryland again. She would soon be purchased for the Confederate Navy. Renamed *Rappahannock* and armed with a single gun, she would secure several more prizes before being destroyed to prevent capture in 1862 while locked in the Rappahannock.[3]

Though he had failed in achieving his main objective, the sagacious young Richard Thomas Zarvona was delighted by the ease with which the seizure of *St. Nicholas* had been carried out, regardless of the failure to capture *Pawnee*. Feted in

Richmond as a hero with gala balls held to honor all the bold expeditionaries, the colorful Zouave commander in particular, he had become an overnight hero. In one such event, to the delight of all, he appeared dressed in the garb of the lady milliner from Paris who had fooled everyone. At the annual Fourth of July celebration in Richmond Zarvona and his Zouaves paraded through the city streets. The newly minted colonel was described as "picturesque" in his red and blue Zouave uniform replete with white gaiters, red cap with gold tassel, and a light, elegant sword. Little public notice was taken of old Hollins, the Baltimorean who had orchestrated the affair, managed the bloodless seizure of the three prizes, and brought *St. Nicholas* and the three captures safely into the Rappahannock. Arriving on Capitol Square as a band played the "Marseillaise" in honor of "the French Lady," the Zouaves fired a twelve round salute. Eleven were for the Confederate States of America and one for their native Maryland, which all believed would soon join with them. As a guest in the executive mansion, young Zarvona had become in a matter of days the focus of incredible popular adulation. Undoubtedly filled with more than a little hubris and with the blessing of Governor Letcher, he quickly resolved to replicate as soon as possible the scheme that had rendered him so much instant fame and glory. To facilitate his operations he was duly authorized "to pass at will, *free*, over the roads and rivers of the Commonwealth upon his own certificate, and upon like certificate pass his men and baggage. All officers, civil and military, will respect him and give him such facilities as he may require, in their power to afford." He was also given a letter of credit on a Baltimore firm, declaring that the check to him for $1,000 would be duly honored by Messrs. R. H. Maury & Co. of Richmond.[4]

This time Federal authorities were far more watchful. From intelligence gleaned from informants on both shores of the Potomac, though somewhat mangled, word of the Zouave's next enterprise soon reached U.S. Army headquarters in Baltimore. Lieutenant Lowry in *Freeborn* was perhaps the first to discover a scent of the rebel raider when he paid a visit to Point Lookout and interviewed the female lighthouse keeper, Pamela Edwards. The keeper informed the officer that on Sunday, July 7, a pungy had landed the crew of *St. Nicholas*. One among the party she recognized as Zarvona by a scar on his face. "She also stated that from the conversation she overheard she inferred that they had some plan to intercept and capture the steamer *George Weems*." Another report came in from the USS *Pocahontas*, which sent an account of a pungy schooner that had sailed from Coan River and landed the crewmen of the three vessels captured by *St. Nicholas* at Point Lookout, from which they walked twenty miles overland to Millstone Landing. At Millstone they had taken passage to Baltimore aboard *Mary Washington*. More importantly the pungy was said to be proceeding up the bay with between eighteen and thirty well armed men. Among them, the "notorious Thomas went up in disguise, the idea of him and the armed party . . . is to capture the next steamer from Baltimore, which will be the *George Weems*."[5]

The intelligence proved only partially correct. Zarvona had indeed gained permission from Letcher for another expedition, although the governor may have done so in the belief that the colonel was going to New York to secure weapons and seize a vessel there to raid the Atlantic shipping lanes. An alternative scheme, however, was actually adopted: the plan called for the Zouave and a handful of his to proceed from Coan River across the Potomac in the colonel's privately owned schooner *Georgiana*, evading the Union blockade, land in St. Mary's County, and make their way overland to Millstone Landing. Adopting civilian camouflage, and unarmed to elude further suspicion or detection by search, they would then board *Mary Washington* on her regular run to Baltimore. Once in the city the Zouave would procure arms and replicate his first success. What the now famous Richard Thomas Zarvona, no longer wearing women's garb, had not counted upon was being recognized.[6]

***

In Baltimore Federal suspicion of key members of the city's law enforcement operations had been growing ever since the occupation began. Finally at 3 p.m., June 27 the city's police chief, George P. Kane, was arrested and incarcerated at Fort McHenry for his role in the bridge burnings. Later in the day Colonel John Reese Kenly, 1st Regiment, Maryland Volunteers, a veteran of the Mexican War and later a Baltimore attorney, was placed in command of the city police force, which was soon replaced by 400 soldiers. In but an instant on July 1 the powers of city police commissioners Charles D. Hinks, Charles Howard, William H. Gatchell and John W. Davis were summarily abolished, and all were arrested with the exception of Mayor Brown (whose day would soon be upon him). Their offense, it was claimed, was that they had attempted to dissuade members of the police force from carrying out their duties. The politician-turned-soldier, General Nathaniel P. Banks, had replaced General Cadwalader on June 11. He was particularly aggressive in his opinions of citizens with avowed secessionist sympathies. He thus ordered that all the city police commissioners be held without being charged for a specific offense or crime, other than that they had refused to recognize the general's appointees. None were given a trial. Provost marshals of the U.S. Army, authorized by the War Department, would soon administer all police operations and arrests in Baltimore and eventually throughout the state. The same day as the police commissioner arrests, large detachments of Federal troops took up key positions in the city in the event of riot. Inspection of Kane's police headquarters revealed a large quantity of arms and munitions, including eight cannon, 332 muskets, rifles, pistols and ammunition.[7]

Baltimore was now in a state of virtual lockdown. The new commanders of the city, despite total military control, were nevertheless becoming increasingly suspicious of every unusual movement or actions amidst the inhabitants. Even the most minor incidents were immediately addressed as either another Zarvona conspiracy or a possible spinoff. On July 4 the authorities were even unnerved by a suspicious character in a small boat observed circling about the steamboat *Columbia* at Fardy's Shipyard below Federal Hill.

Then in the very early morning hours of Monday, July 8 Colonel Kenly, the newly appointed Provost Marshal of Baltimore, received disturbing news: certain suspicious parties had chartered omnibuses to travel to the steamer landing at the hamlet of Fair Haven in southern Anne Arundel County. The colonel was deeply concerned that the now famous Zouave was about to arrive or was already there in disguise and ready to launch his next attack. Though sketchy at best, subsequent intelligence reported that Zarvona and seven companions had recently disembarked

139

"Anne Arundel County." Simon J. Martinet, Baltimore, 1861, Geography and Map Division, Library of Congress, Washington, D.C.

at the diminutive Anne Arundel fishing village from a schooner that had allegedly brought them down the Rappahannock and then up the bay. After delivering him and his men to the village for transit by steamboat to Baltimore, it was reported, the schooner had retired to the mouth of the Potomac to await his return, presumably in command of another captured vessel. Whatever the actual truth was Kenly also had some reason to believe that a number of persons in Baltimore were in collusion with the Zouave and that several others had left the city earlier in the day bound for North Point at the mouth of the Patapsco River. There he presumed they were to provide the schooner with an armed crew for further operations. He quickly resolved to attempt her capture and hopefully Zarvona as well. Fortunately, for the time being at least, word of the government's knowledge of the rebel's possible whereabouts had yet to spread to any of the landings on the Patuxent or along the western shore of the Chesapeake as far north as Fair Haven. Kenly wished to keep it that way and orders were immediately issued, it was later reported in Richmond, "to stop all bay steamers that usually start at an early hour to prevent any possibility of information being given that might defeat the purpose of the expedition." [8]

As all speed was imperative, the colonel immediately dispatched a pair of loyal Baltimore police officers, Lieutenant Thomas H. Carmichael and John Horner, and a squad of trustworthy privates on board a tug bound for Fair Haven. Upon arrival, to mask the true objective of the expedition, they arrested a "vacationing" barber from Baltimore named Neale Green on the charge of participating in the April 19 assault on the 6th Massachusetts regiment. But Zarvona, the actual focus of the expedition, was nowhere in sight, or so it appeared, as neither officer had the slightest knowledge of what the Zouave colonel looked like. Having seemingly failed in their intended mission the police, with Green in tow, boarded *Mary Washington* at Fair Haven for the return trip to Baltimore.[9]

The expedition to capture Zarvona appeared to be yet another Union disappointment. Then immediately before departure, Carmichael became engaged in a conversation with several of the more loquacious passengers. As fate interceded, one among them had been the pilot of *Monticello*, who had been released by the Confederates and was then making his way to Baltimore. From the pilot the lieutenant quickly discovered that Captain Kirwin and two of his officers from *St. Nicholas*, having likewise been released by their captors, were also aboard en route back to the city. The lieutenant was assured now that if anyone could identify Zarvona and the men who had taken their ship, it was the officers of *St. Nicholas*. Undoubtedly to his delight and perhaps concern, he then learned that the Zouave colonel and at least seven or eight of his men were also aboard, bound for Baltimore to carry out another expedition. But were they armed, and would they fight if cornered?[10]

It is quite probable that Carmichael and Horner had already made a quick assessment of the 160-foot-long vessel upon which they and their intended prey were traveling. The ladies' cabins, comprised of twenty-two berths, were situated below the main aft deck; and another six were beneath the forward deck, each with its own dresser and bed. Topside were cabin areas with six rooms on both sides aft with two berths in each, and a tier of three berths forward with the steering house. On the main deck aft was the ladies' and gentlemen's dining saloon, forty feet in length, replete with closets, water closet (toilet), washroom, and doors leading into the ladies' cabin. Forward of the dining saloon were the paddlewheel houses, six small rooms on both sides, each six feet square. There were of course other more utilitarian rooms on the same deck, mostly men's rooms, a pantry and a kitchen furnished with shelves. The engine room was discretely cased in on the main and promenade decks. Between decks the companion way was elegantly skylighted. All of the decks and awnings over the promenade were stanchioned. During good weather, many passengers congregated on the promenade or lounged on seats arranged along the aft rail. Though the overall area of the vessel was small, it would take many hours to search if Zarvona should attempt to hide, and even more difficult to patrol with the small squad of policemen at hand to prevent any escape attempt over the side. Of greater concern was the prospect of armed resistance and innocent bloodshed among the passengers. The two police officers thus resolved to reach Baltimore before making a move.[11]

On the evening of July 8 *Mary Washington* steamed into the Patapsco River and approached the city. Quietly instructed by Carmichael, Captain Weems ordered that she make directly for the dock at Fort McHenry instead of the company wharf on the Baltimore waterfront. As the ship neared the fort, Carmichael and Homer were standing in the ladies' saloon on the quarterdeck. Suddenly and without warning Zarvona himself appeared. Apparently unaware he was facing two law enforcement officers, he demanded to know by whose authority the steamer was being diverted. When Carmichael informed him it was by order of Provost Marshal Kenly, the Zouave drew a pistol and gathered his men around him. The two police officers drew their own weapons, undoubtedly backed up by their own men, whereupon a scuffle and then absolute pandemonium ensued. As terrified women screamed, running about in utter panic, several male passengers moved between the two adversaries in an effort to restore calm. Soon afterwards Richard Thomas Zarvona and at least three of his men were in custody. Or so it would seem. [12]

Upon docking, Carmichael and Horner notified General Banks, commanding the Department of Annapolis from his headquarters at the fort, that a party of the *St. Nicholas* conspirators was onboard. Banks immediately ordered a company of infantry to board the ship. Three of the conspirators were quickly arrested. Incredibly the elusive Zouave chieftain was not among them. Somehow, much to Carmichael's embarrassment, the daring rebel raider from St. Mary's had managed to simply disappear. For an hour and a half, as an aggregate of now almost twenty prisoners and additional suspects were being rounded up and landed at the fort, an intensive search of the ship for the notorious rebel colonel was conducted. Some assumed he had jumped into the Patapsco, but others vouched that he would have been observed. It seemed that the audacious Confederate had simply vanished into the ether.

Having scoured the entire ship for hours with no results, the unquestionably flustered authorities finally allowed her to depart from the fort. Then just as she began to pull away from the dock, Zarvona's location was betrayed at the last minute by some frightened women passengers: he was hiding in a lady's cabin, "secreted in a bureau" by several of the more Southern "afflicted" female passengers. Dragged from his confined concealment, rumpled and covered in perspiration "as though he was emerging from a Turkish bath," the colorful bald "pirate" with a scar on his face succumbed without a fight. The bottoms of several drawers, it was soon discovered, had been removed to provide him adequate hiding space. Almost as soon as he was pulled from his hideaway he attempted to pass his commission to a passenger named Edward Johnson, a physician, who was arrested on the spot, but later discharged "upon explanation." When the arresting officer identified Zarvona as a little more than a "West Point student" and hauled him off to a cell, the Zouave was no longer the boisterous, defiant rebel of just a few days earlier but simply another thoroughly disconsolate prisoner. Found among the confiscated affects was his commission as a colonel in the Virginia volunteer forces. The commission having been dated several days after *St. Nicholas*'s capture, he was thus charged not only with the crime of treason, but also piracy as he lacked any official status at the time of the ship's seizure. He was immediately incarcerated at Fort McHenry. Six months later he was transferred to Fort Lafayette, New York, considered by many as one of the worst prison camps in the Union.[13]

Many years later it would come to light that Richard Thomas Zarvona had been recognized from the moment he stepped aboard *Mary Washington*. At Millstone Landing, young James Russell Gourley, an acolyte to Captain Weems, would recall in his own seniority that he had spotted the colonel instantly, having known him personally. He had even warned him not to come aboard, fearing he might be recognized and arrested, but to no avail. Some historians have suggested that Gourley may have even been among the men who had joined him aboard *St. Nicholas* at Baltimore. Whatever the case Zarvona had rejected the warning, much to his later regret, with a confidant but scornful laugh.[14]

***

When news of the *St. Nicholas* seizure first reached Baltimore, it arrived amidst a flurry of reported spinoff conspiracy plots beginning to deluge Federal authorities. One of those plans, to "capture one or more of the steamers which ply between the city of Baltimore and the Patuxent River," surfaced only ten days after the now famous "French lady" episode, and was allegedly formulated by a city resident, a "man of notoriously bad character" named James C. Hurry. Discovery of the Hurry scheme was immediately reported "by a reliable source" to General Banks, and was just as quickly forwarded to George R. Dodge, the new Baltimore Marshal of Police. Owing to the *St. Nicholas* episode the capture of Zarvona and the alleged Hurry scheme, Federal authorities were understandably nervous. Dodge was instructed to stop all steamers plying between the city and the Patuxent until further orders were issued.[15]

In the meantime Navy Secretary Gideon Welles, as yet unaware of Zarvona's capture, circulated a memorandum on the threat possibility "for the capture during the present week of one of the steamboats plying between Baltimore and the Patuxent River, either by putting his men on board the boat at Baltimore or at Millstone Landing, on that river." He further elucidated the significance of the latter site: "This Millstone Landing or point," he emphasized, "is a position from whence more smuggling of men and provisions is carried on than any other place on the Chesapeake waters. Small vessels are constantly plying between that position and the Rappahannock and Cone [*sic*] Rivers, chiefly to the latter, where a Tennessee regiment is posted." [16]

Commander Benjamin M. Dove, skipper of *Pocahontas*, upon arriving off Point Lookout about July 8 on routine patrol, learned for the first time what Baltimore already knew – that a pungy schooner had come over from Coan River and landed the crews of the three vessels captured by *St. Nicholas*, who proceeded to Millstone

Landing to board *Mary Washington* for Baltimore. Dove debated his next action, whether to send a force on board a tender stationed in the neighborhood with a howitzer, or to personally proceed to the mouth of the Patuxent. That evening, at 7 p.m., Dove brough his ship up to the river, where he discovered a Bremen bark at anchor. From information provided by the bark, he was able to confirm that the crewmen of the *St. Nicholas*'s prize vessels had indeed arrived at Millstone Landing and already departed for Baltimore. The "piratical pungy" *Georgiana*, upon which he still believed the now notorious Zarvona "went up in disguise," was nowhere to be seen, although the vessel's description as a high decked schooner, with green bottom and red stripes, had been circulated. His report, the latest regarding the pungy, sent Baltimore military authorities into yet another fit of paranoia, even though Zarvona was already in Federal hands. Were other raiders, part of the Zouave's unit, still hovering about preparing to strike? The Navy Department was taking no chances. On July 9 the navy dispatched Lieutenant Commander Lowry in *Thomas Freeborn*, accompanied by *Resolute*, to cruise between Point Lookout and the mouth of the Patuxent. His orders were to look for "a suspected piratical party in a small vessel intended to capture the *George Weems*," even though his own ship had been scheduled for some necessary repairs at the Washington Navy Yard.[17]

Word of the capture of the dashing Zouave had yet to reach the other ships of the Potomac Flotilla then on patrol, and it was still believed that the pungy's objective was to capture the next Patuxent bound steamer from Baltimore, the sidewheeler *George Weems*. With a rebel schooner still loose on the bay anything was possible. Dove beseeched his superior to allow him to remain on station between Point Lookout and the Patuxent as the "pungy is too powerful for any of the tenders and the presence of one of the larger [Federal] steamers is very necessary." [18]

For the next several days the Patuxent would see repeated visits by Federal warships that had joined the search for *Georgiana*. Not long after *Pocahontas* had departed, the gunboat *Penguin*, John W. Livingston commanding, a 389-ton screw ferry commissioned and armed at the New York Navy Yard little more than a week earlier, poked her bow into the river. It was deemed by the ship's pilot to be an insidious "rendezvous for law breakers." On July 10 *Thomas Freeborn* joined her while reportedly in pursuit of a Confederate officer named Alexander who had just crossed over from Virginia. *Freeborn* proceeded as far upstream as Cuckhold Creek before returning empty handed to the mouth of the waterway. Though *Penguin* soon departed, after stopping *George Weems*, which had just come down from Baltimore on her normal run and was bound up the river with passengers, Lowry determined to await the next steamer from Baltimore and warn her of the danger. Not long after *Penguin* disappeared around Cedar Point (not to be confused with either Cedar Point on the Potomac), *George Weems* came down on her return trip to Baltimore. Lowry ordered her hove to again, and the thirty-seven passengers aboard were inspected. The lieutenant's suspicions were aroused as the "women did not hesitate to insult by sneering remarks and cries of three cheers for Jeff Davis." But without contraband aboard he could do nothing. The steamer's skipper, after again being duly warned of the danger, vouched for all of his passengers, mostly farmers, all of whom he knew personally. He was eventually permitted to resume his voyage homeward. Soon afterwards *Thomas Freeborn* also departed, but not before Livingston made one final recommendation: "I beg leave to suggest that all steamers running from Baltimore should have a guard of United States soldiers on board." [19]

***

Although Zarvona had been captured, the actions taken at Baltimore by the U.S. Army in response to the threats implicit in the purported Hurry plot were swift but continued to be clouded by conflicting information. There appeared to be no plan to meet the threat head on, nor was there coordination between the army and the navy. At 6 a.m. on the morning of Wednesday, July 10, a body of troops appeared at the Light Street wharf where the steamboat *Chester*, a spanking new 194-ton sidewheeler, was building a head of steam and boarding passengers bound for Chestertown on the Eastern Shore. The passengers were ordered by the soldiers to disembark and the ship was commandered. An hour later her lines were tossed, and she was ordered to cross the harbor to Fort McHenry where she was armed with a pair of brass 12-pounders, and boarded by forty men each from the Massachusetts and Pennsylvania Volunteers, an artillery company, and a squad of police personally commanded by Provost Marshal Kenly. Almost simutaneously, another body of troops appeared at the lower end of O'Donnell's Wharf and took possession of both *George Weems* and *Mary Washington*; the latter of which was now believed to have been engaged by the rebels to deliver two heavy guns to Zarvona before his capture. The former was briefly released, and about 10 a.m. "permitted to go on her route" and promptly set off. She would soon be recalled. General Banks notified both Mason and Theodore Weems that their vessels would not be permitted to make any more trips to the Patuxent River until further notice. Moreover, no other boats would be allowed to leave for the Potomac at least for the time being. *George Weems* and *Mary Washington* were formally "charged with giving aid and comfort to the enemy by landing supplies of men and munitions in St. Mary's, which are transported across the county to the Potomac and then boated over to Virginia at night." The object of the government, it was publicly stated, was "to stop this route of travel and traffic, as it is impossible to guard the whole line of the river." [20]

"It was declared," the Baltimore press reported soon after the ships had been boarded, "that the object of the seizure [of *Chester*] was for an expedition to the Patuxent and Potomac rivers, in search of a schooner in which, it is said, Colonel Richard Thomas traveled between Maryland and Virginia. The schooner was supposed to be awaiting his return, and an effort will be made to capture her and those on board. It was rumored that the schooner was lying in the mouth of the Potomac, and to prevent the possibility of getting information to her, the steamers of the Patuxent river route were seized." [21]

Some reckoned the probability of success to be slim. Captain Weems of the *Mary Washington* thought the schooner in question had returned to Virginia, "where, it is not probable she will be found by the *Chester*, as the shores of the Rappahannock are supplied with efficient [Confederate artillery] batteries." [22] Nevertheless *Chester* had soon set out upon her quest, followed immediately afterwards by several more vessels dispatched on the same mission.

145

Aside from the arrest and inprisonment, on extremely questionable grounds and without a warrant, of an unfortunate elderly skipper named Hagelin in the Patuxent and the confiscation of his stranded schooner, the expedition proved a total failure.

And the paranoia persisted.

12

BLOCKADE
"I shall command the Potomac."

For Southern Maryland the situation had suddenly grown dire. Steamer traffic halted by order of General Banks, particularly to the Patuxent, was not likely to be resumed for at least a month or more. The region's ability to communicate or conduct regular business with Baltimore, the primary destination point for the tobacco trade as well as the source of much of its domestic goods, had been drastically affected. The editor of the *St. Mary's Beacon* for one had been obliged to publish on half sheets owing to a lack of paper that was normally supplied from the city. Yet Federal authorities already felt as if an encroaching sea of rebellion was closing in upon Washington, even as thousands of Union troops arrived in the city every week. At the same time the northern press was crying out to put the rebels in their place, especially with the impending move of the capital of the Confederacy from Montgomery, Alabama to Richmond, Virginia. "Forward to Richmond! Forward to Richmond!" shouted the headlines of the *New York Tribune* on July 4. "The Rebel Congress must not be allowed to meet there on the 20th of July! By that date the place must be held by the National Army!" [1] But it was in Washington's own backyard, populated by a melange of secessionists of varied political complexions, that paranoia and suspicion was to prove the driving force of Federal action. The arrests of countless individuals, ranging from actual agents of the Confederacy to individuals suspected of being even mildly sympathetic to the Southern cause was to become a daily occurrence.

Reports of rebel activities in Southern Maryland proliferated. On July 7 tensions regarding secessionists on both sides of the river were raised when two large casks were observed floating down the river and passing within 200 yards of *Pawnee*, then lying on station off Aquia Creek. At the time *Resolute* was in the act of getting underway to proceed down the river on a special assignment. Commander Rowan instructed Acting Master Budd to secure the mysterious casks and bring them alongside of his vessel. Then, as Budd began to tow them under the stern of his ship, he received a second directive to "be careful, that they may be explosive machines acting upon concussion or friction," and to tow them to the flotilla schooner on station at Nanjemoy. Unfortunately, while the recovery was underway one of the casks filled and sank, but an examination and drawing was made of the other upon reaching Nanjemoy. The device proved to be a floating mine, or torpedo, the first to be encountered during the war – but definitely not the last. "The evident intention of the design of the machine," Rowan informed Secretary Welles soon afterwards, "was to drop it down with the tide, and at a suitable distance to set fire to matches, and when it had swung across the [ship's] cable with one of the machines close under each bow, to explode in due time and so destroy the ship." The concept was not new. Such a weapon had in fact been designed by Robert Fulton before the War of 1812 and was even deployed in the Chesapeake against British men of war. But Rowan was dismissive of it. "The idea was a wicked one," he said before sending the surviving device to Dahlgren for further examination, "but the execution was clumsy." No such ridicule would be forth-coming when both floating and electric mines began to take their toll of Union shipping later in the war. 2

"Infernal machines discovered in the Potomac [near Aquia] Creek by the flotilla, July 7, 1861." Alfred R. Waud Collection, No. 1040, Prints and Photographs Division, Library of Congress, Washington, D.C.

Distrust of the citizens of Southern Maryland, who were assumed by most northerners to be secessionists, spies, and blockade runners, was contagious among the Union military and naval commands. Not surprisingly the region's few small urban centers such as Leonardtown, Bryantown, Benedict, Prince Frederick and others were certain to draw the untender attentions of Federal troops sent to search out reported enemies of the state. Few of these modest towns and villages would be visited quite as often as Port Tobacco.

As the seat of Charles County government, Port Tobacco had since the 17th century been one of the key urban, social, political, commercial and judicial centers of Southern Maryland. Once a thriving riverport, by the onset of the Civil War it had already been cut off for years from major direct water access for shipping. Owing to the silting up at the headwaters of the Port Tobacco River, upon which in 1668 it had been officially established as Charles Town, the town had been moved downstream only to be closed off again by sediment accretion. Yet it still maintained a notable contact with the outside world by steamer traffic that called regularly at nearby Chapel Point and by smaller, shallow draft watercraft at the town's extremity at Warehouse Point. Thanks to the only newspaper published in the county, *The Port Tobacco Times and Charles County Advertiser*, founded by Elijah Wells, Jr. and George W. Hodges in the spring of 1844, the town had a voice and influence far beyond its middling size, even though erudition was not mandatory for success in the rural agrarian society. Indeed the county could boast of only thirty-two school teachers and the same number of school houses. At the outset of the war the student population numbered just 866 children and the annual county education budget was barely $7500. The venerable county courthouse, which had been in place in one form or another since 1731, was situated opposite the newspaper building and flanked by Christ Church, the town's ancient religious center. Behind the church was ensconced, perhaps symbolically, the county jailhouse. In 1861 the jail was a two story brick building with a slate roof "surrounded with a balustrade, giving it for so small a building, quite an impressive appearance," with two small cells per floor overseen by Sheriff John D. Covell.

By the late 1850s the town was flourishing perhaps better than any other in Southern Maryland, with professionals and tradesmen of all kinds occupying stores, offices and shops along its well laid out streets. Grocers, bakers, wheelwrights, undertakers, doctors, well diggers, barbers, mule sellers, tailors, milliners, carriage makers, lawyers, dressmakers, fishermen, stencilers, house and sign painters, dry-goods salesmen, hoteliers, cobblers, hatters, blacksmiths, saddle and harness makers, jewelers and clock makers, restaurateurs, and even a photographer conducted their daily business at a pleasant pace. Since 1848 Port Tobacco had enjoyed regular mail service as well as stage and overland public transportation. Intellectual stimulation was evidenced in the town's literary debating society, and until the onset of the war, by spirited political gatherings, debates and oyster roasts held by both Democrats and Whigs. The annual county fairs, organized in town by the Charles County Agricultural Society, were the highlight of every year, seconded only by seasonal or national holiday celebrations replete with orations, festivities and dinners. Nearly all of the leading county residents took part in activity organizing, serving as judges, or entering in livestock, produce and handicraft competitions, which brought them into regular contact. A "Grand Annual Party" was usually convened at the Indian King Hotel in February "so as not to interfere with the observance of Lent" and was "attended by the beauty and chivalry of the lower counties." Independence Day festivities were usually convened at Zachariah V. Posey's Planters and Farmers Hotel, a place in which professor E. H. Harrison had established a school for dancing and waltzing "For Ladies, Misses and Masters Tuesday and Friday 2-5 p.m.; for Gentlemen, Tuesday and Friday, 7-10 p.m." [3]

County professional and public service organizations were nothing new to the town. In the spring of 1860 the Medical and Chirugical Society of Charles County was formed at Port Tobacco and during the last week of May met at the court house to elect its first officers, Dr. Francis R. Wills, president, Dr. Stouten W. Dent, vice president *pro tem*, and Dr. B. A. Jamison, secretary *pro tem*. Among the first undertakings of the society was the standardization of medical fees.[4]

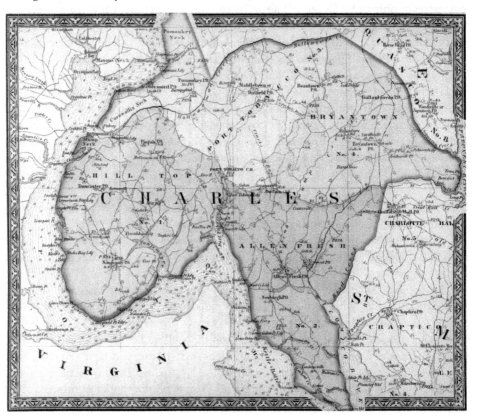

"Charles County." Simon J. Martinet, Baltimore, 1861, Geography and Map Division, Library of Congress, Washington, D.C. Washington, D.C.

Religion played a major role in community activities and connectness. Many residents were Catholics who attended St. Mary's Church near Bryantown or nearby St. Ignatius at Chapel Point, which were leadings centers of community contact. When the venerable old church was in need of a new organ, a grand concert was held at the county courthouse to raise the necessary funds. The concert was duly promoted in the *Port Tobacco Times*: "Mrs. Cecelia Young of the Clifton family, renowned native vocalist, will lead affair. Refreshments in the new upper rooms of the Court House. Tickets are on sale at different stores in Port Tobacco as well as Mr. Dillahay's in Chapel Point." Net proceeds amounted to $225, and the church got its organ.[5]

But that was all behind it now as the very soul of Port Tobacco's gentility was to become intricately entwined with, and its sons participants in the wider war rapidly engulfing the Potomac basin, as were all who inhabited or visited the towns, villages and hamlets along its shores.

Typical of the unwelcome attentions heaped upon Port Tobacco were several expeditions launched to arrest purported rebel agents almost immediately after the conclusion of the Zarvona affair. The first of these forays began at 5 p.m., July 11, 1861, when *James Guy*, Lieutenant Fred Prichard, USN, commanding, departed the Navy Yard with Company H of the 71st Regiment and Captain Nathan Darling, Chief of the Capitol Police, aboard. The objective of the expedition was the arrest of one James Taliaferro (also referred to as G. T. Taliaferro), formerly a Treasury Department clerk, "a noted Secessionist" and an alleged Confederate spy. While "in possession of papers of great importance," he had hurriedly left the city that same morning by stagecoach bound for Port Tobacco and from there to Virginia that same evening.[6]

Three and a half hours later, seeking assistance, *Guy* pulled alongside of the recently arrived gunboat *Pocahontas*, then lying off Aquia Creek. Having left the Navy Yard in such haste Captain Darling, being of the opinion that there was not a sufficient force aboard his ship in case of armed resistance in the own, quickly tendered a request for additional manpower from the warship's crew. Commander Dove immediately loaned him a ship's howitzer and launch, a crew armed with Sharps rifles to operate and man them, and a dozen U.S. Marines.[7]

By late evening, the expeditionaries had reached their destination but not without difficulty. Upon arrival at Chapel Point two and a half mile south of Port Tobacco, *Guy* was unable to locate the wharf "owing to the darkness of the night, added to the gloom of the surroundings, the banks being thickly studded with trees whosoever hanging branches lent a darker shade to the night." After unsuccessfully feeling around for some time in search of the wharf, one Edward Dunn, a marine sergeant from *Pocahontas*, jumped overboard followed by three of his men and by swimming succeeded in locating the landing place. Once ashore at Chapel Point they found a signal lantern posted near the water and believed to be used to communicate with the Virginia shore. After awaking the owner of the house at the landing, they "compelled" him to remove the light and then marched forthwith, just twenty-five strong, into Port Tobacco proper where they arrived about midnight. Obliged to exercise great caution and to prevent an alarm being given, they quickly arrested everyone they encountered including two blacks. One of the negro captives immediately told them that there were 150 secessionist dragoons in the town. Nevertheless, they silently pressed on in the darkness and with the prisoner's aid they found the hotel wherein they believed Taliaferro to be ensconced while he awaited word to cross the river.

Though the record is quiet regarding in which of the three hotels in town the suspect was located, it was quite likely the Brawner House operated by James Alexander Brawner. The hotel, erected ca. 1845 as the Burroughs Hotel, later known as the Union Hotel and then as Brawner House, was to soon become a noted gathering place for Confederate sympathizers, spies, and operatives.[8]

Quietly, the building was surrounded. The landlord was immediately aroused, but denied any knowledge of the ex-clerk's whereabouts. The Yankees were not to be put off. "They immediately proceeded on their own hook," it was later reported, "and finding by the register that Taliaferro was the occupant of No. 6, went to his room, and awoke him." [9]

There was no resistance. A Colt revolver was found on the suspect and seized. Taliaferro's reaction to his arrest is not recorded but as both he and his personal baggage were taken into custody, the latter with its contents as evidence of secessionist activities, he must have been a most unhappy fellow for his trunk contained a large number of letters written "to prominent secessionists" in Virginia and $1,700 in gold. Though the bluecoated visitors conducted themselves with civility, it was reported soon afterwards by the editor of the town newspaper that upon their return to Chapel Point they had purloined yard goods and sundries. They had also debased themselves with foul language and whiskey acquired from a merchant there named Francis Dillahay, all in a most uncivil manner. Nevertheless, now at a safe distance from the town they released all of their prisoners except Taliaferro.[10]

It appeared at the outset that the prize of the expeditionaries had been a rich one. One letter found in the trunk was particularly galling to loyal Unionists who would soon be made aware of its contents by the Washington newspapers. "My daily prayer to God," it read, "is, that the Confederates may prevail. I am tired of living under this Government, and my prayer is that God's blessing will rest upon the *cause*." Inflammatory perhaps but not grounds for arrest – yet! More importantly, the *National Republican*, an ardent Unionist paper in the capital, reported the letters "seem to indicate that he [Taliaferro] has heretofore sent quite a lot of information to Virginia, and some of them implicate a prominent banker of this city in the secession scheme." Upon his arrival in Washington the prisoner was taken before a District Justice of the Peace, Thomas C. Donn, and the evidence along with the pistol transmitted directly to General Mansfield. The general immediately ordered the captive jailed on charges of conveying information to the enemy. There was to be no civil trial or public hearing. The general acted as both judge and jury.[11]

Though the seized papers incriminated several prominent citizens of Washington with the Southern cause, a review of the case by Justice Donn apparently determined that the evidence against the prisoner was not sufficient enough to incarcerate him for treason despite the general's ruling. Donn's opinion, having dealt with such cases in the recent past, apparently carried weight with Mansfield. Upon the justice's recommendation and "at the request of many persons, and in view of his feeble health," Taliaferro was released from jail on July 26 upon taking an oath of allegiance.[12]

The utility of Port Tobacco as an important transit station from Maryland to the Confederacy was, by the midsummer of 1861, quite well known to both sides.

Confederates employed it frequently in spite of recurrent Union patrols. In mid-August J. H. Lindenberger, Secretary of the San Francisco Democratic Executive Committee, was one such traveler who had selected the town as his jump off point to Virginia regardless of the danger. Having traveled from California to Maryland with dispatches from the pro-secessionist California Constitutional Association intended for the Confederate Congress at Richmond, his mission had been an important one regarding support for the South in his home state. At 2 a.m. Sunday, August 12, after his arrival in Port Tobacco was somehow made known to the government, undoubtedly by an informant, he was arrested. The arrest was carried out under orders from the U.S. State Department by a squad of soldiers detailed from one of the flotilla boats stationed off Chapel Point. Brought to Washington, his baggage was thoroughly searched and turned over to Justice Donn. Lindenberger was then to await arraignment on the charge of treason and "thrown into a crowded jail, surrounded . . . by men who are mostly respectable and generally clean by nature, but who, from their close confinement and impurity surrounding them, are covered by filth and vermin." [13]

The transit of secessionists, sympathizers and operatives such as Taliaferro from Washington, along the many viable routes still open through Southern Maryland to Virginia, was becoming commonplace, and was not without comment in the city's Unionist press.

"Almost every day" read one typical headline "we hear of parties of known secession proclivities emigrating to Dixie. An individual, we hear, who was coerced into secession sentiments by having been removed from an assistant messengership in one of the Departments, recently, has made preparations to leave this morning for the 'land of cotton.' It is said that persons are continually leaving by way of Port Tobacco, crossing the Potomac at that point, if the coast is clear, but if not, proceeding down until they see that all is clear, and then crossing." [14]

Until all routes and departure points for both men and arms along the Southern Maryland shoreline could be continually monitored by both land and sea, there appeared to be no stopping those who keenly wished to head south. An air of veiled defiance continued to manifest itself throughout the countryside, and Federal efforts to stem the flow of men and arms, short of actual occupation, drew only scorn from Southern Marylanders. "It has been reported to high or headquarters," noted the *St. Mary's Beacon* in one cynical editorial,

> "by 'loyal citizens,' of course, that a great many arms are concealed in this county, which are to be used, when occasion offers, against the enemy, when Maryland shall enjoy her own again, the enemy aforesaid, being in the apprehension of these informers, the Government of the United States and its supporters in Maryland. Now, though there are none that are aware of 'concealed,' there certainly are arms in this county and, moreover, there are quite a number of men who know how to use them, but as these arms have been honestly and legally come by and are held for no purpose of disloyalty or treachery to the Government under which we live, we intend to hold on to them as long as we are able. They have been furnished by the State of Maryland, and are held in conformity and obedience to her laws, and are regarded as

necessary for the safety and protection of our wives and children. We are entitled to hold them, and we mean to do it—if we can." [15]

***

As June turned to July the heat of summer was no longer the topic of conversation in Southern Maryland as it usually was at that time of year. All talk was of the war. The growing strength of the Union forces, particularly those within the newly created Department of Northeast Virginia in and around Alexandria, commanded since May 28 by Brigadier General Irvin McDowell, was mustering for an invasion into rebel territory. It was to be the thrust that many Unionists hoped would end the rebellion once and for all. [16]

Yet the forces of the rebel hero who had evinced the surrender of Fort Sumter, General Pierre Gustave Tourtant Beauregard, had been appointed on May 31 to command the "Alexandria Line." On June 2 he assumed charge of all forces in Northern Virginia and raised expectations of secessionists throughout the South. Ever since the first shot was fired against Sumter, the Confederate cry had been for the capture of Washington.

"From the mountain tops and valleys to the shores of the seas," declared a most vindictive *Richmond Examiner*, "there is but one wild shout of fierce resolve to capture Washington City at all and every human hazard. The filthy cage of unclean birds must and will assuredly be purified by fire . . . Our people can take it – they will take it – and Scott the arch traitor, and Lincoln the Beast, combined, cannot prevent it . . . Great cleansing and purification are needed and will be given to that festering sink of iniquity, that wallow of Lincoln and Scott – the desecrated City of Washington." [17]

One who had led the charge toward secession, the Virginia firebrand Edmund Ruffin, had declared in 1860 that the City of Washington would soon become the "seat of federal government for the South." Some happily forecast that the world would be turned upside down. It now seemed to many that the world, as predicted, *was indeed* about to be turned on its head. [18]

On July 21, 1861, having been forewarned of the Federal advance by a spy in Washington, Mrs. Rose Greenhow, the poorly trained Confederate Army under Beauregard utterly defeated the Union Army of poorly trained ninety-day men under McDowell at the Battle of Manassas, also known as the Battle of Bull Run. A long war, which most Unionists had only days before believed would be over in a few months, was now guaranteed. The Potomac River, separating the shores of Southern Maryland from Virginia, was destined to become a veritable no-man's land dividing North and South for the next four years. Now more than ever Federal control of the river and its shores was imperative to prevent a possible rebel invasion of or insurrection in Southern Maryland and capture, or at the very least blockade, of the capital city of the United States of America.

***

Thomas T. Craven, the new commander of the Potomac Flotilla, was determined to increase pressure on what was believed to be multiple hotbeds of secessionist sympathizers along the waterways of lower Maryland. It was soon apparent to most in the southern counties that Federal visitation was to become an unwelcome but regular event all along the shores of the river. Closure of steamer traffic to St. Mary's following the Zarvona affair, which was causing considerable economic and social discord in that county, would be among the first problems Craven would be obliged to address. On July 21 a petition signed by thirty of the county's most prominent citizens representing St. Inigoes and Point Lookout was submitted to him requesting the resumption of steamboat services from Baltimore to towns and landings along the Potomac River reliant upon the traffic. Craven acceded to the request, undoubtedly with some misgivings, and service by the Weems Line and others were soon resumed.[19]

Craven's first major foray into St. Mary's County came on July 31, only ten days after the disaster at Manassas had so severely scorched national pride, when his newly designated flagship *Yankee*, accompanied by *Thomas Freeborn* and *Reliance*, arrived off Leonardtown. By midsummer when *Yankee* first joined the flotilla, the squadron had already grown to a hodgepodge of nine mostly small vessels including *Freeborn*, *Pawnee*, *Pocahontas*, *Reliance*, *Dana*, *Bailey*, *Chaplin*, *Howell Cobb*, and *Release* (formerly *Ice Boat*). More were coming.[20] And there was work aplenty for all.

Craven had learned "from reliable information" on the eve of the Battle of Manassas that recently arrived light ordnance, about forty stands of arms, and other military stores had been secreted in Leonardtown and were awaiting carriage to Virginia. The small arms were supposed to have belonged to the State of Maryland but had not been turned in as required by an earlier proclamation issued by Governor Hicks. Where the artillery had come from was anyone's guess. Eager to act, the commander requested that Secretary Welles dispatch the provost marshal or one of his deputies with the necessary search warrant. Yet, as timely action seemed imperative, *Freeborn* and *Reliance* were sent into Breton Bay without a marshal (undoubtedly owing to the chaos in Washington following the great battle in Virginia). A landing party consisting of fifty sailors and a dozen U.S. Marines belonging to the USS *Pocahontas* who were attached to the expedition, all under Lieutenant Commander Robert H. Wyman and bearing the appropriate warrants, were dispatched to conduct the search.[21]

Upon reaching the town Wyman inquired on the whereabouts of the sheriff, but upon being informed he was away settled for the chief magistrate. He quickly informed the magistrate that the object of his mission was to search for two pieces of field artillery and a number of muskets reportedly concealed in the county courthouse and that he wished to proceed "legally and formally in the prosecution of his search." He then presented his orders and a search warrant to the magistrate and the Maryland State's Attorney for St. Mary's County. Of course both vigorously denied knowledge of the existence of either artillery or muskets in either the town or the county, other than some rifles in the hands of the regularly organized company of Maryland militia legally armed and officered by the state government. Accompanied by the Clerk of the County Commissioners, the landing party nevertheless proceeded to search the courthouse, but found little more than a quantity of cartridge boxes and belt straps. All were the property of the state and had been deposited by the captain of the militia. The town officials eagerly sought to assure the naval officer that the arms still held by the company would only be used for self-protection and to guard against domestic trouble such as a slave insurrection. Wyman reluctantly ordered the cartridge boxes and belts restored, and then returned in frustration to his ship. The expedition into Leonardtown, "a rank secession hole," as the Washington *Evening Star* called it, had ended in failure and a belief by some that Marylanders had easily outfoxed the Yankees. Yet the only outright indication of secessionist sympathy came when a man mounted on a horse, later claimed by locals to be under the influence of alcohol rode up in front of the courthouse while it was being searched and issued several loud cheers for Jeff Davis before riding off.[22]

Craven's distrust of the statements of the town and county's leaders was manifest. He resolved to leave the tenders *Dana* and *Cobb* stationed off the mouth of Breton Bay with orders to cruise day and night to intercept any vessels carrying contraband articles.[23] Breton Bay was, however, but a small component of what he viewed as a bifurcated mission. While one half of his task, inherited from the late Commander Ward, was to maintain free navigation of the Potomac the second part, severing communication lines and contraband traffic between Southern Maryland and Virginia, was proving to be the most difficult.

Efforts to shut down rebel contraband shipping and receiving depots could often be hazardous. On August 10, when Acting Master Budd set out aboard *Resolute* to destroy one such depot and began probing in the mouth of Machodoc Creek, he was greeted with a fusillade of musket fire from the shore. The site was one at which men and myriad goods were landed after being shipped from Herring Creek in St. Mary's County. Despite the opposition, Budd's landing party destroyed the premises and captured a large boat that had crossed the previous evening from the Maryland shore. A party of Maryland secessionists was still in the area but quickly disappeared as the Yankee sailors gave chase. The expedition bore one more disturbing piece of intelligence when brought in by a party of contraband blacks. "The foreman of the contrabands," Budd reported, "who is a remarkably intelligent negro, informs me that an expedition is organized in Machodoc to capture any of the schooners that are anchored or becalmed in that vicinity." [24]

The following day the Maryland side of the smuggling operation was further exposed when another contraband boarded *Yankee* and informed Craven that "there was at Herring Creek one Maddox, an Irishman, who has been quite active in procuring supplies of men, munitions of war, clothing, etc., for the rebels, and that he has sent many boat loads of them to Virginia." As recently as five days earlier, on Tuesday, August 6, he had sent eight wagons and sixteen horses to Maryland Point in Charles County for transshipment. One wagon was loaded with uniforms. On that same day eight men from Baltimore also crossed.

Maddox, the informant further revealed, was in league with Dr. Charles Combs of Great Mills who was employing an old outbuilding as a barrack for the reception of volunteers for the Confederate Army. Maddox and Combs regularly employed their own slaves, horses, and wagons to transport the new recruits to a number of landings at night, awaiting an opportunity to cross when the Union cruisers were out of sight. Others involved in the smuggling cabal included a pair of siblings named Hughes and a man named Johnson who also harbored recruits. Another named Bell, who moved from place to place, was also engaged. At that very moment, the informant said, there were smugglers' boats fresh from Virginia still lying in Herring

Creek. Moreover, Johnson was currently hiding in his home the owners of the vessels as well as a "minister" from Virginia sent over as a spy.

Craven acted immediately by sending out an eight-man party to seize the vessels. The cutting out party returned the next day with three boats in hand. "From all I can see and learn of the people of Maryland," concluded the commander, "I am convinced that along the shores of the Potomac there is not one in twenty who is true to the Union, and I think there are many hundreds of them thoroughly organized into companies, perhaps regiments, and prepared to act against the Government at any moment." [25]

Complicating Craven's task was the U.S. Government's continued obsession with the threat of potential river closure from batteries at Mathias Point despite the Confederate decision to simply hold but not fortify the site. Soon after the previous month's engagement, *Reliance* had been ordered to take station off the point from sunrise to sunset. Continuous rumors circulated in Washington and anonymous telegrams and letters were sent to the president and Navy Secretary warning of the secret construction of gun emplacements on the site. Reports coming in from black informants were that a picket was maintained on the point, although they had never actually been seen in the daytime "but have several times been heard talking and laughing." Though existence of a battery was as yet unproven the Federals would continue with their fixation on Mathias Point for months, just as they would with the seemingly endless flow of contraband goods.[26]

The Confederates, in fact, had other ideas. By July 22, just after the Manassas fight, Generals Beauregard, Johnston and Holmes had agreed to the expediency of erecting a work capable of resisting a *coup de main* at Evansport, opposite Budd's Ferry. Holmes was assigned the task of constructing the battery at the strategic narrows well upriver from Aquia. It was to be armed with five guns captured at the Norfolk Navy Yard, a 30-pounder, two small Parrott rifles, and two 12-pounder howitzers. But other events and views interceded after the Battle of Manassas including the Confederates' general contempt for Union arms and leadership. For reasons unknown Holmes failed to begin construction on the battery following the fight; nearly a month after it had been agreed that one was needed, the work had still not started.[27]

Confederate General Joseph Johnston, once the Quartermaster General of the U.S. Army, had little concern regarding Mathias Point. But he was nonplussed that the right flank of his own army was still exposed by an unprotected Potomac shoreline, vulnerable to enfilade by both land and water, all of which he felt a battery at Evansport would help correct. His interest, indeed, was not in conducting an invasion of Southern Maryland as feared by many Unionists, but of a possible Federal landing somewhere on his own flank. "We think it of great importance," he informed President Davis on August 19, "that its effect [the proposed battery] would be to prevent the turning that position on its right by the enemy." He would, he stated, build the works with his own men if necessary and demanded that the guns which General Holmes still retained at Fredericksburg must be forwarded to the site, "and for the thorough command of the Potomac three or four of the large rifles, which it is understood have been made in Richmond, should be added." A detachment from Fredericksburg to man them would also be most welcomed.

Moreover, he suggested in a blatant exposure of his discontent with Holmes, that the Potomac frontier would be better managed under one command, namely his own, rather than two.[28]

Davis was in accord having as early as August 1 been under the belief that Holmes was going to build a battery near the mouth of the Chopawamsic, "where it is reported the channel can be commanded so as to cut off that line of the enemy's communication with their arsenals and main depots of troops." Coming so soon after the Manassas engagement, it was also his belief that the measure would no doubt "lead to an attack, and hence the preference for a position between his [Holmes's] column and yours [Johnston] rather than one lower down the river, as that on Mathias Point." [29]

On August 22, three days after Johnston informed Davis of the necessity of the Evansport works, Holmes received a direct order to proceed with construction. Johnston was to provide a competent engineer. Besides the guns initially proposed for the site, Holmes was informed, the Tredegar Iron Works in Richmond had been instructed to send a rifled Columbiad for the same battery.[30]

But with both sides fearing an amphibious attack by the other (which neither could yet actually mount with any prospect of success) and focused on re-building and reinforcing themselves after the bloody Battle of Manassas, the result was little more than stalemate.

In the meantime, Federal warships obliged to patrol the Potomac were growing increasingly wary. Lieutenant Commander Wyman, while in actual command of *Yankee* during an absence by Craven, was perhaps representative of the lot as he kept a keen eye on rebel efforts to collect small craft that could conceivably be used for crossing into Southern Maryland. "At Potomac Creek, just below Aquia," he reported on August 9, "they have a camp with four field pieces below the creek, and above the creek there is every appearance of a heavy battery, although it has not been fired to our knowledge. At Aquia it has been reported that they have taken over flatboats and scows from the Rappahannock. The steamer *Page* is there ready for service when she can get out." He strongly suspected something more was afoot. For the last several days very few persons had seen observed on the creek. The flags of the batteries had been hauled down, and at several other points on the river where their troops were stationed. It was his opinion that the enemy was busy collecting boats of every kind. Was an invasion in the offing? He fervently recommended that the boats be destroyed.[31]

Secretary Welles remained absolutely convinced that the rebels were only intent on erecting shore batteries at key points to interrupt communication, with Mathias Point still being his central concern. On August 20 Welles requested Secretary of War Cameron to take immediate measures to occupy, fortify and entrench the site that he deemed a "place as absolutely essential to the unobstructed navigation of the Potomac." A single regiment and two steamers, he believed, could still take and hold it. "I understand that troops will be sent to the Lower Maryland counties," he said with some prescience, "to keep the peace and prevent batteries from being erected on the left bank. This is a timely and wise precaution, but it is equally necessary that we should take possession of Mathias Point." [32]

Worrisome as it was for Welles, for Secretary Cameron Mathias Point was but a secondary concern. The main Confederate Army lay with its lines centered at Fairfax Court House barely sixteen miles from Washington. On July 22 Major General George Brinton McClellan was summoned to assume command of the Division of the Potomac to replace Major General McDowell, the same day the House of Representatives passed a resolution specifically stating that the war was being waged "To defend and maintain the supremacy of the Constitution and to preserve the Union." Three days later the Senate passed the resolution with the addition that the war was not intended to interfere with established institutions such as slavery. When McClellan formally took charge on April 27, the Union Army surrounding Washington was desperately struggling to rebuild itself while protecting the capital. There was little time or resources to attend to the occupation of such a remote location as Mathias Point. The youthful McClellan, known to his adoring followers as "Little Mac" and credited with a minor Union victory in far western Virginia, seemed the perfect choice to rebuild an army. Yet nothing was done regarding the rebel presence on the Virginia shore, which seemed, much to the chagrin of the Navy Department, to be ever expanding. Land-sea skirmishes were soon to become a regular occurrence.[33]

***

While reconnoitering in the vicinity of Marlborough Point three miles below Aquia Creek on August 23, Acting Lieutenant Mygatt in *Reliance* observed a large encampment of the 30th Virginia Infantry on the bluff overlooking the south shore of Potomac Creek, the same noted by Lieutenant Commander Wyman two weeks earlier. A possible second encampment was also sighted on the hills near the outlet of Chopawamsic Creek. Commander Dove of *Pocahontas*, now acting senior officer in the area, was at once informed and all available vessels in the immediate vicinity, including *Resolute, Penguin,* and the recently arrived *Jacob Bell,* were dispatched to investigate.[34]

The 229-ton tug *Jacob Bell* was another of those vessels purchased under duress at New York and armed with but a single 32-pounder smooth bore. Lieutenant Edward P. McCrea, the warship's commander, was eager to join the reconnaissance operation and offered to go in first to determine the strength of the enemy. In company with *Resolute* and *Relief,* which had belatedly joined the group, he proceeded to the creek. As Wyman had earlier noted, the waterway was well guarded by no less than two batteries of long-range rifled guns on opposite sides of the entrance. Though *Resolute,* which drew too much water to enter, was unable to accompany him, McCrea nevertheless boldly pressed on alone. Slowly working his way into just nine feet of water he closed with the encampment on the south shore and threw two shells over it to test the range. The reaction was instantaneous as rebels scurried to muster under their colors. Suddenly four enemy pieces to the left of the camp, dubbed Smith's Battery by the defenders, returned fire from the southernmost point of the creek. Shooting rapidly, the rebel gun crews began to close in on the erstwhile tug whose own single gun proved unable to reach the battery. McCrea had little choice but retreat even as a reinforcement, the bark-rigged *Relief,* Lieutenant Thomas Pattison, arrived on the scene.[35]

159

The rebel defenses proved no less a contest for *Relief*'s own eight heavy 9-inch rifled Dahlgrens. Nevertheless, Pattison opened at 4:45 p.m. as he passed a retreating *Jacob Bell* and, firing with great accuracy, silenced the Smith Battery after forty-five minutes of battle. He was now able to turn his full attention to the enemy ordnance on the north shore at Marlborough Point, a rifled siege gun dubbed by the Confederates "Betty Holmes" and another rifled gun detailed from the Walker Battery on Aquia, which he later reported "was playing upon me with vigor." The rebel fire seemed well directed as two shots whizzed close over the hurricane deck and six or seven more burst under the bow, though doing no injury to vessel or crew. As the contest continued, Lieutenant Mygatt came onboard to assist just as Pattison received a signal from his commanding officer, Lieutenant Commander Dove, to leave the fight. "Being thoroughly acquainted with the river," the lieutenant later reported, "he [Mygatt] piloted me into safe water, and then at my request took command of our enormous rifled gun and fought it during the action with skill and judgment." By 6 p.m. the skirmish was over without a resolution on either side.[36]

***

Protecting navigation and communications from closure and successfully interdicting rebel contraband on the Potomac were not the only challenges the U.S. military was obliged to address in Southern Maryland. With approximately forty-five of its 110-mile length being navigable for vessels of several hundred tons, the Patuxent River had become another important component of the rebel network of communications and illicit trade from the north. As the dog days of summer continued it had also become a significant weak point for Union planners as the Federal naval capacity was already severely taxed on the Potomac. Welles was not shy in attempting to secure waterborne support wherever he could, even if it meant seeking help from the military. Believing that the Union Army had already commandeered or otherwise secured several U.S. revenue cutters and a number of privately owned vessels at Baltimore, he was of the opinion that they might be better suited for use in blockading the Patuxent than patrolling the Patapsco. Major General Dix, headquartered in that city, in fact had at his disposal only two ex-revenue cutters, named *Forward* and *Hope*. The former was in terrible condition and was to be hauled for repairs while the latter had been a private yacht offered "for gratuitous service" but had also been deemed entirely unfit for duty.

On August 15 Dix received orders to again stop until further instructed all boats operating between Baltimore and St. Mary's and the neighboring counties of Maryland and Virginia, a directive more easily given than executed. Three days later he was allowed to permit a single steamboat to make just one trip down to bring away families who had been stranded in St. Mary's by the former order. The general was in a quandary. The Secretary of the Treasury had promised him four armed steamers of three or four hundred tons which he considered indispensable for traffic control. Not only were rebel smugglers using the Chesapeake and its tributaries as an open highway between Southern Maryland and Virginia, but they were also carrying on the same with growing Confederate forces on the Eastern Shore, expanding their network all the way to the Delaware line. With armed steamers, however, he believed he might maintain control the entire commerce of the Chesapeake north of the Potomac. With the U.S. Navy obliged to focus upon the Potomac and lower bay, there seemed no alternative. "My opinion" he said, "is that nothing short of it will suffice to break up the illicit commercial intercourse carried on between the Eastern Shore of Maryland with Virginia through the Patuxent and Potomac." But two decrepit revenue cutters simply would not be suitable for the task. In the end, nothing was done even as more holes in the blockade on both rivers continued to appear. There simply were not enough vessels to go around.[37]

In the face of the escalating difficulties in controlling the waterways, the consequences of the Zarvona affair continued to reverberate down the Chesapeake, affecting the lives and fortunes of many individuals, as well as whole communities in Southern Maryland. Though lauded by Union loyalists, General Dix's reactions to some reported plots in Baltimore, now seemingly a daily occurrence, were deemed by Southern sympathizers as overkill. Even they too ocassionally became the foci of interservice rivalry between the Union Army and Navy.

One such plot aimed at the capture of another steamboat was discovered when an advertisement appeared in the Baltimore papers promoting a pleasure excursion to Point Lookout on Wednesday, August 21. The excursionists were to board the 306-ton steamer *Hugh Jenkins*, a vessel which had only a month or so before been chartered by the U.S. Quartermaster's Department for an expedition to Easton, Maryland to round up a cache of rebel arms. It was now to be the one selected vessel permitted to bring up a number of ladies who had been vacationing at the point and to take others down.[38]

The true objective of the trip was soon deemed by General Dix to be something far more sinister and at the very least required military protection to prevent any possible mishap. Accordingly, the general notified the "getters up of the excursion" that the boat would not be permitted to leave the city unless accompanied by a guard from the 5th New York Volunteers. After considerable delay the charter parties finally consented to the general's "proposal." In the meantime a substantial number of persons had gathered at the wharf to embark aboard the steamer, but upon learning that troops would also be boarding refused to go. Thus only twenty-five excursionists and seven police officers under Lieutenant Carmichael had boarded when the boat set off. The ship stopped briefly at Fort McHenry to take onboard thirty-four soldiers under the command of Captain H. Duryea and then proceeded on her voyage.[39]

Little of interest took place en route down until a "passenger named McElwee expressed himself rather freely relative to the topics of the day, and made a boast that he would kill Captain (Griffin) of the boat before landing at Point Lookout." In an instant McElwee was placed under observation by a file of New York Zouaves and his movements closely watched until the boat landed at her destination.[40]

The ship's arrival at Point Lookout at 8:15 p.m. proved a surprise to all parties involved. McElwee was sent ashore with the passengers and nothing more was heard of him. But the visit by the police and bluecoats yielded more than a few shocks. "Considerable surprise was manifested at the Point," one newspaper later reported, "when the boat arrived, as it was understood that the boat, instead of being filled with federal soldiers, would bring down several hundred recruits for the

Southern army, and that the boat would be sold to the Confederates. The chagrin of the Secessionists, when they discovered how they had been out-generaled, was amusing in the extreme. They denounced our police as being intermeddlers in a business which did not concern them, and expressed themselves in so many other shapes that the poor fellows will not recover from the disappointment in a long time."

Then it was revealed to Carmichael by a black informant that during the day no fewer than 300 rebels had been awaiting the ship's arrival, but upon learning that a large federal force was aboard, they had promptly quitted the place aboard some schooners and returned to the Virginia shore. "The programme appeared to be, that when the boat landed at Point Lookout she was to be seized, provided with cannon, and be dispatched on a privateering expedition." [41]

That evening *Hugh Jenkins* anchored in the stream until 8 a.m. the next morning when she touched shore and took on passengers for Baltimore, unaware that she was under the watchful eye of two Potomac Flotilla schooners. Captain Duryea's commentary regarding the locals was anything but positive. "The sentiment of the people of Point Lookout is intensely Southern," he declared, "and I was informed by slaves who came on board to sell fruit that their masters offered every facility to the rebels in the ways of information and passing to and from the loyal States. Our anchorage was in the Potomac River, opposite Coan River. Vessels were passing in and out close under the Virginia shore at all times with perfect freedom, there being no blockading vessel at the mouth of the Potomac, and I saw none while we were at Point Lookout, or during our trip." [42]

When Secretary Welles informed Craven of the report, which had apparently been endorsed by General McClellan, "implying that the officers of the flotilla are neglect in the performance of their duties," the commander was furious. He informed the secretary in no uncertain terms that he had been informed by the two acting masters of the schooners that they had been in the vicinity upon *Jenkins* arrival at Point Lookout and had maintained a surveillance over her and all other movement in the region until her departure. "I can only attribute the misstatement of Captain Duryea's to his ignorance of nautical affairs, and, therefore, incapacity to distinguish a national cruiser from a wood barge." [43]

Unfortunately, the events that were beginning to overwhelm both the few citizens of Southern Maryland loyal to the Union and the larger majority who yearned for their state to join the rebel cause were proving a bitter foretaste of days to come. For her part in the apparent plot *Hugh Jenkins* was "sold" to the U.S. Quartermaster's Department nine days later and would not see civilian service again until the close of the war.[44]

***

Despite their rivalry the Union Army and Navy somehow managed to work together, though with difficulty. Intelligence forwarded from the army to the Navy Department in late August almost demanded immediate action on the part of the already overtaxed Potomac Flotilla. On August 24 Assistant Secretary of the Navy Gustavus V. Fox dispatched word to Captain Craven regarding Confederate military and contraband operations at no less than a half dozen locations on the Potomac and Patuxent. Moreover, the latest word was that there were now at least 2,500 rebels lodged two miles in the rear of Mathias Point. Though no batteries had yet been observed, some underbrush had been cleared, and the potential danger there seemed apparent. At Leonardtown in a reprise of an earlier report, two pieces of heavy ordnance were again reportedly being concealed in the back cellar of the St. Mary's County courthouse. Two hundred marines and sailors under the command of Major Reynolds, USMC, and Acting Master Budd were promptly landed from the steamers *Freeborn*, *Baltimore* and *Resolute*, entered the town, searched for hours and found nothing.[45]

Elsewhere twenty-three cases of muskets were reported at Spencer's Wharf on the Patuxent, apparently awaiting transport. There was now also a regular messenger service reported to be running between Maryland and Virginia. The operations were purportedly being conducted by Randolph Walton of Leonardtown and Thomas M. Maddox of St. Inigoes, on the St. Mary's River. Maddox and his brother Joe, it was alleged, were also engaged in furnishing supplies bound for Virginia. Worse, both Pope's Creek and Port Tobacco were now believed to be *the* principal rebel depots in Maryland, and possibly as muster stations for troops should an armed incursion actually be undertaken. The porous nature of the blockade became even more evident when reports that no fewer than eight suspicious oyster pungies had run unchallenged into Lower Machodoc Creek near Ragged Point, Virginia. Noting the intelligence to be "of so much importance as to require your particular attention," Fox immediately ordered Craven to call upon the commandant of the Marine Corps for a force of marines, not to exceed 200 in number, to assist "in your examinations" of the aforementioned trouble spots.[46]

Even the City of Washington, though now heavily garrisoned, was not exempt from potential rebel movements on the waters. On the same evening Fox informed Craven of the activities in Southern Maryland, Dahlgren had been obliged under a verbal directive from the assistant secretary to dispatch four steamers to secure all small craft along the city waterfront. The expedition returned to the Navy Yard at 3 a.m. with twenty-eight small boats. The following morning, additional boats lying in Tiber Creek in the heart of the city, which extended all the way to the foot of the Capitol Building, were rounded up as well.[47]

Such orders seemed less than important when even more disturbing intelligence came in predicting the impending action that everyone in Washington feared. An intercepted message dated August 13, quoted a statement purported to have been made by Confederate President Jefferson Davis himself less than a month after the rebel victory at Manassas: it recommended that Confederate agents restrain themselves from causing dissension in Maryland for the time being, for "in ten days, I shall command the Potomac and cross between Mathias Point and Aquia Creek into Charles County and St. Mary's counties (they are all friends there) and march upon Annapolis. Then, having two of the approaches to Washington in possession, let Baltimore rise and burn the bridges." The capital city, thus cut off by an end run and surrounded by secessionist states, could then be easily captured. The intercepted message was provided, according to Craven, by an "unquestionable source" who had also reported that a communications link between Maryland and the Confederacy was still being maintained by a line up the Patuxent, across Charles

County, "and then in open boat from Port Tobacco to the Virginia shore, after patrol boats had passed." [48]

Jefferson Davis, President of the Confederate
States of America. Prints and Photographs
Division, Library of Congress, Washington, D.C.

General McClellan had already received certain intelligence that seemed to verify the threat. On August 11, just two days before the dated message had been sent, the general dispatched a worrying note to Secretary Welles. "I have today received urgent information," he wrote, "which convinces me that it is more than probable that the enemy will within a very short time attempt to throw a respectable force from the mouth of Aquia Creek into Maryland. Such a movement on the part of the enemy, in connection with others probably designed, would place Washington in grave jeopardy. I most earnestly urge the strongest possible naval force be at once concentrated near the mouth of Aquia Creek, and the most vigilant watch be maintained day and night, so as to render such passage of the river absolutely impossible." [49]

McClellan recommended that the USS *Minnesota* and other vessels "available" at Hampton Roads be immediately ordered up and that a great quantity of coal be sent sufficient enough to support several weeks of uninterrupted naval patrols on the river. He also suggested that at least one strong vessel be kept at Alexandria and that a substantial naval force be posted on the Potomac without delay. "If the Navy Department will render it absolutely impossible for the enemy to cross the Potomac below Washington," he concluded "the safety of the Capitol will be greatly increased." [50]

Yet nothing happened.

Reinforcing the threat, on August 30 the Confederate government passed an Act authorizing the establishment of formal recruiting stations for volunteers for the states of Maryland, Missouri, and Delaware. Two posts were suggested for recruits from Maryland after they made it into Virginia, one at or near Fredericksburg, for those who crossed the river at or near Mathias Point, and the other at Winchester, for those who traversed the upper reaches of the Potomac. "The commanding officers at these points," reported Samuel Cooper, the Adjutant and Inspector General of the Confederate Army, on September 6 "will be instructed to make suitable arrangements at each to carry out the provisions of the law in respect to clothing and rations to recruits until they shall be duly organized into companies. Other places of assembly may hereafter suggest themselves according to circumstances and the success which may attend the recruiting." [51]

Something had to be done. On August 17, four days after the Davis message was made public, Secretary of War Cameron dispatched an urgent order to Pennsylvania, New York, Connecticut, Massachusetts, Vermont, Rhode Island, New Hampshire, Maine and Michigan to rush their volunteers to Washington as quickly as possible. The capital was in peril for the Confederates, as one northern paper put it, "were slowly moving their forces in the line of the Potomac, with a view of entering Maryland and supporting the revolutionary spirit there, with ultimate designs on Washington." [52]

Fear of an invasion of Southern Maryland now seemed to be the topic on everyone's lips. "All the talk about a direct attack on Washington," noted one correspondent, "are mere feints to cover Davis' real purpose, which is the closing of the lower Potomac and throwing a strong army across the river into [St.] Mary and Charles counties, both of which are secession. This done, they mean to march on Annapolis, counting on a formidable rising of the Maryland secessionists for the investment of Washington." [53]

The day after Cameron's urgent plea for help, journalists in Washington, sending their reports home, fanned the flames of panic even more. "An attack on Washington is looked for by many of the best informed officers," reported a stringer for the *New York Tribune* in an article that was picked up and reprinted in numerous northern papers. The rebels had reportedly advanced their lines and were in force within a short distance of the river, gathering their means of transportation across. "They have large encampments this side of Fairfax, but probably the bulk of the advanced corps is on the upper Potomac . . . Reconnaissance and close observations indicate that the rebels are closing in on our lines. The city is full of secession rumors today. We have various accounts of the rapid and near approach of from 170,000 to 200,000 rebels under Beauregard, Lee, Johnston and Jeff. Davis, but all agree that they are coming immediately down on Washington. Our military gentlemen don't seem to be alarmed." [54]

In the meantime the pesky problem of contraband traffic and Marylanders heading through the southern counties to join the burgeoning rebel army seemed to grow with each passing day. When a seizure of teams and wagons bearing a heavy load of Baltimore goods bound for Richmond was made near Annapolis Junction on August 18, along with a number of letters to Confederate officers and a $4,975 draft intended to pay for the merchandise, it was considered an important interception.[55] Yet as talk of an invasion, and the flood of goods, arms and men continued to stream south, it seemed a very slight victory indeed.

13

CAREFUL INQUIRY
"Make some observations for the Government."

Colonel Andrew Porter of the 16th U.S. Infantry had perhaps not expected his appointment by General McClellan as Provost Martial of Washington, D.C. not long after the Union defeat at Manassas. Having commanded a brigade of the Second Division during the fight, he and his men had suffered heavy losses and had been forced to retire rather ingloriously with the rest of the army afterwards. The importance of his difficult new assignment, to maintain law and order in a city and Federal District with a population that had declined within a year from more than 75,000 to approximately 70,000, could not be understated. Many residents were strong slave-owning secessionist supporters, even activists, while others were Unionist advocates, abolitionists, and free blacks. On August 1 news of his temporary appointment to the post of provost martial was published in the *National Intelligencer* along with a not-so-subtle command that he "will be obeyed and respected accordingly." [1]

Porter's job was destined to be monumental, as Confederate spies, sympathizers, and contraband runners abounded in both the District of Columbia and in adjoining Southern Maryland. He was fortunate to have as his right hand an aggressive intelligence officer just appointed by General McClellan as head of the U.S. Army's new secret service corps. The new chief operated under the assumed military rank of major and such various undercover identities as E. J. Allen, J. H. Hutcheson, or simply "Plum." His real name was Allan Pinkerton. A Scottish immigrant deemed by McClellan as both trustworthy and extremely efficient, Pinkerton was also considered by some as a self-serving, ruthless egocentric. But to the general, who was himself recently appointed commander of the Military Division of the Potomac, the Scotsman would be *the* most essential arm of army intelligence of all. [2]

Son of a Glasgow police sergeant and a social activist in his native land, Allan Pinkerton had come to America in 1842. He had quickly become a prominent abolitionist in Illinois and gained notoriety as Chicago's first ever police detective who in 1850 left the force and founded his own agency. Along the way, by solving a train robbery case for the Illinois Central Railroad, he had come in contact with McClellan who had served before the war as chief engineer and vice president of the line. He was also known to Abraham Lincoln who had represented the railroad as an attorney. Neither man had forgotten the Scotsman's skillful investigative capacities. He had been responsible for infiltrating the dangerous Baltimore underworld of "Plug Uglies" and "Bullies" and helped foil an assassination attempt on the President Elect while Lincoln was en route by train to his inauguration. Pinkerton's pioneering form of espionage, developed during his earlier career in the Chicago police force and based on surveillance and undercover work by a capable corps of "operatives" and spies, would become legendary. He was incredibly adroit at gathering and piecing together seemingly disparate fragments of data acquired by his agents from captured letters, informants and occasionally lips loosened by alcohol or seduction, to form a profile of his suspect before conducting an arrest. Now as head of the U.S. Army's own clandestine service, forerunner of the U.S. Secret Service, he would employ his skills on a scale never before undertaken in America. Much of his early attention in the war would be focused on casting a wide net of operatives from Washington to the shores of Southern Maryland, and even to the very halls of the infant Confederate government in Richmond. Typically each of his agents gained access to the enemy's plans and motions by "assuming a role" as secessionist or rebel sympathizer. Some, it was claimed, were even able to penetrate the very core of the rebel government and army. Not surprisingly one of his earliest objectives as head of the service was uprooting the rebel contraband operations in Southern Maryland.

Despite the heavy armed presence of the military, Baltimore remained the fountain from which contraband goods continued to flow southward, a traffic that the army struggled to interdict with only poor to moderate success. With the reopening of limited steamer traffic to the Patuxent a strict watch was being maintained on all outgoing vessels, and searches were common. For the Weems Line, which had recently been permitted to resume reduced operations between Baltimore and the river landings, the consequences proved devastating.

On August 16 just as *George Weems* (the only Weems liner permitted to sail) was preparing to depart from her city wharf with a considerable number of passengers, she was boarded and searched by Lieutenant Carmichael and a contingent of police officers. Upon discovery of contraband articles the lieutenant ordered the passengers to disembark with baggage. The ship was immediately forbidden by General Dix to proceed. Now it was not only *Mary Washington* that was prohibited from service but the entirety of the Weems liners. Other steamer traffic, sans passengers, might be permitted to take up the slack but only for the explicit purpose of allowing Southern Marylanders to send their produce to Baltimore markets. The suspensions, perhaps owing to the political connections of the Weems family, would once again prove only temporary. On January 6, 1862 *Mary Washington* would be briefly chartered by the U.S. Army and soon afterwards, in a world where connections were more meaningful than ever, returned again to her regular operations for the Weems Line. [3]

Pinkerton's intrigue with the seemingly open secessionist highway through Southern Maryland to Virginia was born on August 23, a week after the *George Weems* incident, and following his appointment as head of the Union Army's intelligence operations. On that date General Porter presented him with a curious letter from a loyal informant that had been forwarded by the secretary of state. A minister, the Reverand Dr. J. Van Santwood had sent the document the same day to Seward who had immediately forwarded it to Porter. Van Santwood wrote that an unnamed lady in Georgetown, D.C., identifyig herself only "A friend to her country," had sent an anonymous letter to General McClellan informing him of certain secessionist activities in that town. But upon the minister's advice that the busy general was unlikely to pay attention to an unnamed source, she had asked him to forward it to the secretary.

Notwithstanding the circuitous route the letter took, the informant accused a man named Rudolph Watkins living in Georgetown of making it his business for months past to convey secessionists from the town to his uncle George Dent's home on the banks of the Potomac in Charles County. From the Dent safe house they were ferried across to Virginia to make their way to Aquia Creek and thence to Richmond. The total trip took only two days. The Dent family, whose ancestors had been among the earliest settlers in the county during the 17th century, was well known throughout the region, and George Dent was among the most respected of all by his peers. Significantly the informant noted Watkins's own father George was still an official in the Navy Department, even though he and his wife were regarded as outright secessionists by their closest neighbors. [4]

Another letter sent to Postmaster General Montgomery Blair by one A. Atkins and immediately forwarded to Pinkerton was dated three days after he had received the Van Santwood document, further implicating Dent in secessionist activities. The informant hoped the report would encourage Blair to "cut off all this clandestine communication now so generally carried on from Lower Marlboro across and by secessionists all along the line." He reported that mail was routinely carried every night from the post office in Port Tobacco directly across the Potomac to King George County, Virginia, and from there to rebel army headquarters. The in- formant's own wife had been requested to dispatch letters via Dr. Stowten W. Dent to Port Tobacco so that it could be sent across. [5]

Dr. Dent, who was born in 1803, was a colorful character deemed by Thomas A. Jones to be one of the two most active Confederate agents in Southern Maryland, the other being Thomas H. Harbin. The latter, a native of the county who served as postmaster of the Bryantown Post Office, was also a courirer and spy who, it was said, reported directly to Jefferson Davis. Dent had two sons in the Confederate Army and lived near Centerville, a small village not far from central Charles County. As a practicing physician he made his professional rounds on horseback. In winter he invariably wore high boots and an overcoat, a garment provided with numerous and capacious pockets that reached down below his knees. In the summer he was cloaked in a linen duster also well provided with pockets. Jones later recalled: "The number of letters and papers he could conceal in his pockets and boot legs was astonishing. Some one in the neighborhood of Pope's Creek was always sick. Scarcely a day passed that some member of the Watson family or mine did not *need* Dr. Dent. He came and went unquestioned and unsuspected. He carried the mail as far as Port Tobacco, ten miles from my home, to Bryantown, a village in the eastern part of the county fifteen miles from Pope's Creek, and even as far as Charlotte Hall in St. Mary's County, fully twenty miles off. From these points the mail would be handed over to another agent who would convey it on toward its final destination." [6]

On various occasions Dr. Dent entrusted the mail to a ten-year-old son named Warren, as energetic, discreet and intelligent a lad as any agent in the Confederate service, according to Jones, to whom the most important materials were often safely entrusted. After all, what Yankee would suspect a mere child! [7]

Jones frequently worked with other rebel agents who came and went at Pope's Creek. One was a Canadian named Williams who carried the mail from the Con- federacy clear through to Canada. Mail matter, including Northern newspapers going South when it came via the regular United States mail route early in the war, was always addressed to Jones. He saw to it that the newspapers reached Richmond within twenty-four hours after publication. But the majority of mail going South was usually delivered through a number of messengers. [8]

One such individual was a prominent gentleman of Prince George's County, who served actively as one of the Confederacy's Southern Maryland mail agents. He masked his motions by gardening, "and, as he lived but a short distance from Washington City, would drive his wagon into town and get a load of manure, in which he would hide the matter destined for the South, and bring it safely out." But it was Jones who conveyed every packet going north or south via his boat at Pope's Creek. Sometimes he gave his neighbor and accomplice, Miss Mary Watson, mail to hold on to until it could be forwarded. Generally, however, he kept it hidden in a small, dark closet upstairs in his house. "This closet had a door just large enough to admit a man's head and shoulders. It was necessary to stoop down to see into it and with your head in the door you would have to turn over on your back to be able to see directly over your head; and right there was where I hid the Confederate mail. And though the house was frequently searched while the mail was in it, nothing was ever discovered." [9]

Decades years later, Jones would recall with candor: "I trusted no one that it was not absolutely necessary to trust." [10]

***

Pinkerton did his best to understand the complexity of the rebel contraband and mail operations. One clue was suggested by a statement provided by the Reverend J. H. Ryand of Washington. Ryand reported to the detective that he had been in communication with one of the few residents of the Port Tobacco district who could be trusted, the Reverend Lemuel Wilmer. Wilmer had served as the Episcopal minister of Christ Church, the town's most venerable place of worship, since 1822 and rector of Port Tobacco Parish. Though his brother William had been president of William and Mary College in Virginia and one of his uncles was the Episcopal bishop of Alabama and Louisiana, Wilmer was a "gentleman, known far and near, as a staunch and loyal Unionist." As would later be proved, he was perhaps the only man in that town to be trusted. Wilmer had informed Ryand that there was a constant communication being kept between Port Tobacco and Virginia. He also informed him of the names of the chief secessionists in the town, all members of some of the county's leading families, Mitchell, Stone, Brent, Posey and Middleton. At Pope's Creek, Maryland the principal agents (both of whom would later be engaged in operations of the "Secret Line") were George Dent and Thomas A. Jones. [11]

For Pinkerton the files on Dent and his neighbor Jones were soon growing by the day. Both had entered with zeal into the Confederate cause and were major rebel assets in Southern Maryland in the transport of men and goods across the river. "Scarcely a night passed," Jones would later write in his memoirs, "that I did not take or send some one to Virginia. I have frequently crossed the river – which is not more than two miles wide from Pope's Creek – twice in a night, and sometimes oftener." [12]

On September 1 one John Atwell, during a questioning at Pinkerton's City Guard office at the provost marshal's headquarters in Washington, related information he had observed during a visit he made to Pope's Creek about August 17

170

apparently with his wife to see her brother. He had returned to Washington alone and soon afterwards received a letter from his mate stating "that there were and had been a great many persons going over into Virginia at that place to Persimmon Point, directly opposite," on Mathias Point Neck. With the narrows between Jones's estate at Pope's Creek and the tip of Persimmon Point being just over a mile and a half wide, it was quite clear why the crossing had been so popular among southbound secessionists. Their landings, Pinkerton realized, were made at a spot where sailors from the USS *Pawnee* had been shot at ten days earlier while putting ashore "to see about a small boat then loaded lying at the shore." During his interview Atwell then produced another letter. This one was received from his wife the previous day and informed him that a body of Union troops had come in just the week before. They had, it was noted, just taken possession of a boat belonging to Jones that was purportedly used to ferry men across to Virginia. The effort had been in vain as "he [Jones] bought another on Monday and was taking passengers over night and day, keeping the boat on the Virginia side to keep the Northerners from getting it." [13]

While Pinkerton continued to gather information it was business as usual at Pope's Creek. From testimony later provided by a twenty-six-year-old runaway slave named William Hill it was revealed to Union officials that his late master, one James Grimes of Mathias Point Neck, was regularly engaged with Jones in transporting men across the river. He was, of equal importance, serving as the middle man for travelers between their landing site near his house and Richmond by providing lodging and transport. Pinkerton soon learned Grimes was also a man deeply interested in military matters as much as his farming business, which had been substantial, and proudly called himself a "shore guard."

The intelligence was considerable. Grimes's farm was about a mile below the purported rebel battery at Mathias Point and a little above Jones's place across the Potomac in Maryland but within viewing distance. Both maintained rowboats to ferry men across the river though Jones and his slaves did the principal part of the work. Although he never ferried horses or wagons across, Jones was both reliable and regular and primarily served the traffic from Baltimore. A steady flow of passengers, mostly traveling south, crossed from the Maryland side nearly every day or night, confirming Atwell's information, and always found conveyances waiting at Grimes' to take them into the country. Whenever Jones had passengers to ferry over during the night, he placed a light in his upper windows to signal across the river for Grimes to bring wagons down out of the hinterland to his farm. Whenever persons on the Virginia side wanted the boat to come over they gave a signal by a light at Grimes' house during the night and by hoisting a white flag in the daytime. Wary of Federal warships, Jones had hidden his boat in a gut on the Maryland side though Union soldiers had twice taken it away only to have another take its place. When a boat was unavailable he would employ one belonging to his neighbor George Dent who was also engaged in running men and goods primarily from Georgetown and Washington to the Virginia shore. Dent had suffered the confiscations of boats as well but somehow had also miraculously managed to have them restored. [14]

While Pinkerton was rapidly enlarging his files on the Pope's Creek operations, the navy was also securing information from its own sources. On September 6 a sergeant of the guard keeping watch over the steamboat *Alexandria* passed on intelligence to then Acting Secretary of the Navy Fox "that numbers of persons are crossing the Potomac from Maryland to Virginia nightly at Pope's Creek. They use punts or low ducking boats, by which a person is enabled to pass within a short distance of a sentinel without being observed." The intelligence was passed on to Commander Craven for possible action. [15]

That the Potomac Flotilla was already well aware of the myriad secessionist activities all along the Maryland shore, including the Pope's Creek area, was without question. Its ability, however, to attend to each and every one was impossible. Although relatively free navigation was still possible on the river, nothing went unnoticed by a rapidly developing system of rebel coast watchers on the Maryland shores. In early September when the steamer *Philadelphia* was making her way up the Potomac she readily observed that "the Marylanders sent up a rapid succession of signals to notify their Virginia neighbors of the steamer's approach."

One officer of the flotilla, in justifying the interdiction of suspicious vessels on the river, reported: "From Piney Point to Fort Washington there is a regularly established line of signals on the Maryland shore of the Potomac. A steamer cannot move at night but she is telegraphed by signal lights at every three to five miles of the river, which signals are answered on the Virginia shore. There has not been a vessel or boat taken from the Maryland shore where there has not been an abundance of evidence that they have been employed in unlawful commerce." [16]

The rebel coast watchers operating along the Potomac frontier of Southern Maryland proved as elusive as fireflies. But Confederate recruiters operating ashore were doing so under increasing danger of capture. On the evening of September 6 a party of thirty U.S. Marines from *Reliance*, under the command of Lieutenant Mygatt, quietly put in near Herring Creek in St. Mary's. At midnight they surrounded a house in which Joseph H. Maddox, Thomas H. Maddox (who was believed to be a Confederate officer), and one Joseph H. Wilson of Baltimore were surprised and arrested for recruiting men for the rebel army. [17]

In the meantime Pinkerton's network of agents was being cast far and wide. It was but a matter of time before the Dent-Jones-Grimes cabal was proven beyond a shdow of doubt to be a cancer that needed to be removed. The scope of their operations was astonishing. One Pinkerton operative who had been assigned to keep watch on Rudolph Watkins in Georgetown learned that the suspect had apparently bragged to a young lady that he had recently transported no less than fifty persons down to Charles County. They were then conveyed into Virginia, he said proudly, by his uncle George Dent. Having discovered the suspect's interest in the fair sex, the operative secured the services of a lady, possibly the same one with whom Watkins had earlier spoken, to call on him again. This time she carried a poison pill, a letter, which she requested be forwarded to Virginia via Dent. She gave Watkins twenty-five cents to send the letter, upon which he promised that his uncle would get it over to Grimes on Mathias Point Neck and from there to its destination. [18]

On September 14 when William Hill, who had earlier escaped from Grimes while ferrying secessionists across the Potomac, was brought in to Pinkerton for questioning, he informed the detective in great detail of the Pope's Creek operation.

It was all that was needed to close a key portal to the South. The Scotsman quietly prepared his plan to put an end to it all. After informing General Porter he secured orders to send a detachment of cavalry accompanied by one of his own operatives to arrest Jones and Dent. John Atwell was sent along as well quite possibly to identify the suspects when taken. A second operative was dispatched separately to Port Tobacco from which place he was to make his way to Mathias Point to "make some observations for the Government," and almost certainly to ascertain the whereabouts of James Grimes. [19]

Under the command of Lieutenant W. M. Wilson a small unit belonging to the 4th U.S. Cavalry was immediately dispatched to Port Tobacco. Not surprisingly their arrival on or about September 16 caused an immediate stir of excitement among the local inhabitants, though they were by now no strangers to visits by Federal soldiers. Only three days earlier when a pair of Union cavalrymen, escorting a reporter named F. W. Walker from the New York *Express*, who was also a volunteer officer, arrested a secessionist near the town, the operation immediately went afoul. The prisoner, who was found with "very valuable information" on him, had been previously arrested but escaped and had been prowling around the neighborhood when recaptured and taken to a house nearby. Then, when the soldiers were called away for a few moments to attend to their horses, leaving Walker alone with the prisoner, savagery was released. Walker had been busily engaged near the door in recording notes from his recent conversations, unaware of the prisoner's advance. Suddenly the prisoner drew a large knife, thrusting the deadly instrument into the reporter's bowels. In an instant Walker collapsed, screaming "Murder!" as he fell. The assailant lurched from the building to escape, when one of the guards discovered him and discharged his pistol, but without effect. Within seconds the killer had disappeared. [20]

Though an all out search was launched the escapee remained at large. The following day a detachment of the same cavalry arrested "three secessionist spies near Port Tobacco" and found in their possession topographic maps of the immediate countryside. [21] Thus when Lieutenant Wilson arrived upon the scene, the town was still in something of a community state of unrest.

It was not long before Wilson's mission was discovered perhaps, from a casual comment dropped by a trooper or by one among his men quietly sympathetic to the Southern cause. What is certain is that before their departure, word was en route to Pope's Creek to warn Dent and Jones. Unnoticed by the towns folk was the quiet arrival of Pinkerton's undercover agent who was intent on reaching Mathias Point. The agent's disguise was unquestionably superb as a pair of seces- sionists named Turner and Cole, who made known to him their own mutual in- tentions of crossing over to Virginia, immediately befriended him. They decided to make it a threesome, thus lending even more credibility to the stranger. [22]

Late that evening Wilson and his men departed the town. As soon as they were out of sight, despite the late hour, the townspeople adjourned to several meetings convened in local taverns and stores, some of which were observed by Pinkerton's Mathias-bound agent. Once the troopers were gone, he later reported, the residents, "throwing off all restraint talked over their opinions so freely that I could easily see that Union men were almost unknown in that locality." [23]

It was 2 a.m. on the stormy evening of September 17 when Wilson's cavalrymen arrived at Pope's Creek and quietly surrounded the home of Thomas A. Jones. Expecting to capture the suspect by surprise as they entered, they were in turn startled to discover that their quarry, apparently forewarned of their approach, had reportedly fled to Virginia only three hours earlier. Undoubtedly disgusted that the rebel had eluded him, Wilson nevertheless searched the house, seized all correspondence and other documents he could find, and then before leaving smashed to bits a boat found lying at the landing nearby, entirely unaware of the travails his quarry was at that moment undergoing. [24]

Jones was then actually engaged in his second crossing attempt of the evening with passengers bound for the Confederacy. His first try had begun hours earlier, at 7 p.m., with a boatload of ten or twelve men and women bound for Virginia. He had two oarsmen in the vessel, one of which was a trusted slave named Henry Woodland. Soon after his departure from the creek, the wind began to increase, and by the time the party had made it a third of the way across, "it was blowing such a gale that I not only saw it would be impossible to proceed, but became considerably alarmed for our safety." Fortunately the passengers were ignorant of their danger and remained quiet even as Jones watched for an opportunity to make shore – any shore – safely. Suddenly the boat rose on a swell, giving the oarsmen an opportunity to bring her about without capsizing and put back to the Maryland side. [25]

"I took the interrupted travelers up to my house," Jones recalled. "On reaching there I learned that another party of four or five had been there during my absence looking for some one to put them across, and, finding I was not at home, had gone up to Major Watson's." [26]

There were three schooners that had anchored in the cove opposite Jones's house, undoubtedly seeking shelter from the storm. The ferryman immediately determined to secure one of them by force if necessary in order to transfer the whole party to the opposite shore. Jones walked briskly over to Major Watson's house and explained to yet another party assembling there hoping to also make a crossing, and asked which of the young men present would go with him and assist in making the capture. Several men readily agreed, and together they set out for the creek.

"When we reached there," Jones later wrote, "we found another crowd, of a dozen or more, eager to get to Virginia. My party being joined by several volunteers, we got the rowboat out of the creek and boarded one of the vessels." The captain proved to be a timid man and begged not to be forced to do what would be sure to get him into trouble with the government. Jones, having some sympathy, told him he would try the captain of one of the other vessels, but if he was unable to make satisfactory arrangements he "would return and compel him to put us over." [27]

The captain of the next vessel they boarded was a man of an altogether different stamp who, Jones surmised, would have put up a fight had he not been out-numbered. After some argument the captain was obliged to give in. The rest of the party was soon aboard, and the schooner set sail for the Virginia shore. "No sooner were we well under way than the wind, that had been blowing such a gale that a small boat could not cross, died out, and it was sunrise before we succeeded in reaching the other side. Before landing we made up a purse for the captain, which he received with better grace than he had submitted to our coercion."[28]

By refusing to succumb to the weather and delay the crossing, Jones had unwittingly escaped almost certain capture!

***

As soon as they finished searching the Jones property the Federal troopers proceeded on to the nearby Dent farm, hoping upon hope the proprietor there had not yet been warned. The farmhouse, as at Jones's, was quickly surrounded and in the gray predawn light a demand for admittance was made. After some delay and "amidst the loud remonstrances of the family," the premises was searched. Unfortunately for the Yankees it was immediately discovered that Dent, too, was nowhere to be found. Upon interrogation of the servants and others, Wilson readily ascertained the man he came to arrest had departed for Virginia about 11 p.m. the previous night, accompanied by his son, George Dent, Jr., with possibly as many as twenty to twenty-five others. While gathering up all the correspondence he could find he also learned that Dent's home had served as nothing less than "the grand depot for the arrival and departure of goods and men for the rebel army." [29]

While Wilson was busy at Dent's, interrogating family and servants and searching for correspondence, weapons, and other evidence of the clandestine activities there, the Pinkerton agent who had stayed behind at Jones's continued his own investigation. Upon questioning one of the slaves he learned some of the finer details of the operation there. "The negro," he later reported, "said that Jones had some signals whereby he knew when any one wanted to go over the river; that when Jones who was then on the Virginia side would see those signals he would come over with his boat." Pressing on to Dent's the operative reconfirmed from the servants that both Dent and Jones "had been in the habit of carrying over the river all persons that wanted to go as well as goods, provisions, &c." Though Dent used some signals the servants did not understand, unlike Jones he never made them during the night (as they could be spotted by patrolling boats). Moreover, almost as if he were running a regular stage line, the boats he kept on the Virginia shore arrived at precisely 8 p.m. each evening to take over whatever or whomever was to go. He also reconfirmed that when they had received word of Wilson's impending arrival, Dent and his son had gone over to Virginia with more than a score of others, but not before telling their womenfolk to raise a white cloth to let them know when it was safe to return. [30]

Even as Wilson and Pinkerton's agent did their best to pick through the Jones and Dent farms for additional evidence regarding the transport operation, the undercover operative sent to Port Tobacco was doing his best to get over to Mathias Point. He had convinced his two new secessionist companions, Cole and Turner, as well as others in the town of his Southern loyalty and the sincerity of his need to get to Virginia. Soon he found "all that were present seemed willing to do all in their power to aid us." About this time it was learned in the town that Dent and Jones had escaped and that the regular crossing from Pope's Creek had been, at least for the time being, effectively broken up. [31]

Pinkerton's agent, in his efforts to find a way over to Mathias Point, was in a quandary as the closure of the ferry now prevented him from crossing. Fortunately he happened to discover by "careful inquiry" that one John Shackleford, the highly respected Constable of Charles County since 1858, had hidden a trunk filled with carbine rifles. The constable was unaware of the Wilson raids and was at that moment at Chapel Point, four miles below the town, preparing to proceed on to Pope's Creek and to cross to Virginia that same evening. Having learned that Shackleford was to have his baggage sent to him from the town, the agent seized the opportunity and volunteered to take it to him if he could cross in company, however the passage might be made. A suitable conveyance was hired, but when the agent arrived at Chapel Point he discovered that Shackleford and a small party with him had already departed for Dent's just a half hour earlier. Knowing that the constable and his men would have to return when they discovered that the crossing had been shut down, he waited at the only store on the point. The establishment, he discovered, was owned by Francis Dilllahay, an avowed secessionist who had for some months been trying to sell off his entire stock at cost to go south. [32]

When Shackleford finally returned he learned that before Wilson's troopers had arrived at Pope's Creek, sixty men, not two dozen, had managed to cross just before the cavalry had reached Dent's. After some persuasion and the payment of an "exorbitant price," Pinkerton's agent and the rest of the southbound company were able to hire the boat in which Shackleford had just returned to go to Mathias Point. The eight-mile journey took an hour and a half. [33]

Landing with the secessionists, the Yankee agent with Cole in company proceeded on their own until they approached a nearby house, "boldly making considerable noise in order to attract the attention of the pickets" they expected to be in the area. Though the house was empty they soon learned from a black woman that it was one of two that belonged to the Grimes clan, and that the second was another mile and a half below the nearest picket, right on the point. Returning to the boat they rowed down to the second house, situated near a ravine leading to the water, and found several rebel pickets lazily lounging about.

"We were very near landing," the agent later reported, "before they discovered us, and they were constantly surprised at our coming under the circumstances . . . This place is the principal landing for the Marylanders, and two boats are kept here for crossing the river. They are hidden by being drawn up on the beach within the spiles [*sic* piles] driven across the mouth of the ravine." Grimes was nowhere to be found. [34]

It was soon discovered that the Wilson raids had only a very minor impact on the ferry operations at Pope's Creek. When the agent, his mission completed, was permitted to return to the Maryland side soon afterwards, he was ferried back to Maryland by none other than George Dent's son, George Jr. Before he departed, still maintaining his Southern persona, he was entrusted with letters from one Captain Winey to be delivered to his wife and brother-in-law in Baltimore. After parting company with the captain, the agent immediately read the missives by which he learned that not just a few but many Baltimoreans had been making their way to Mathias Point "by way of the Patuxent and Benedict and thence across the country to the Potomac . . . Some ladies, wives of officers, have reached Virginia via Benedict and Mathias Point within the past week." [35]

On the face of it, it seemed that not only had Jones and Dent made their escape, but also a critical portal to the south was still quite open.

***

Though the Wilson raid on Pope's Creek had failed in its primary mission it had produced a substantial cache of documents incriminating many Marylanders sympathetic to or outright supporting the secessionists. Five letters taken at Jones's home before they could be hidden away were of particular interest to Pinkerton. One was from H. Rives Pollard, of the *Richmond Examiner*, requesting Jones to forward copies of the Baltimore *Sun* by persons making their way into Virginia. Not only did the newspaper provide the latest news from the north it was as yet uncensored and carried critical details of the latest Union appointments, troop strengths and movements. Another was from a young salesman named George F. Harbin at Meyerber's Store in Washington, who gloated at the Confederate victory at Manassas, while noting that he "expects from rumors to soon be living under another president. He thinks that Lincoln is pretty nearly played out and that one more victory in favor of the South will knock down the house." A second communication from Harbin stated: "He hopes and sincerely believes that the day is not far distant when the people of the North will condemn Abe's cruel acts and hurl him from power." Given that the mere utterances of anti-government opinions were becoming sufficient cause for individuals to be incarcerated, Harbin's sentiments would not go unpunished. He was soon afterwards arrested and taken to the 13th Street Prison in Washington "to await further developments and for the purpose of preventing further treasonable communication in a certain direction." [36] Another letter was from one S. B. Zimmerman requesting Jones to have his tobacco carried to Baltimore for sale to allow him to go south and join the rebel army. Still another was from an E. L. Rogers, which disclosed the fact that chloroform undoubtedly intended for the rebel army's medical needs was being smuggled across to Grimes's via Pope's Creek in jugs marked "Neat's Foot Oil." [37]

The documents seized at Dent's farm were even more incriminating. One of these suggested possible connections between at least one Baltimore banker and Confederate financial interests. The document in question was a letter of introduction from R. J. Brent of Baltimore, dated July 20, stating that Brent's friends, Messrs. Carson and Armistead, also of that city, were going to be in Dent's neighborhood on business. Brent had requested that Dent provide them with "every facility and attention as they are gentlemen of character." On the surface the request seemed innocent enough as there was nothing to suggest either man had any rebel connections. Yet being not only obsessively suspicious but also keenly observant, Pinkerton noted that from the letterhead on the document it appeared that Carson was a banker, and surmised, "it is not unlikely that the business of himself and companion in Dent's neighborhood had some connection with Southern financial matters." [38] Why else would a Baltimore banker be visiting the rural tobacco lands of Charles County at the very gateway to the South?

Two other letters, far more revealing, directly implicated Dent as an agent of the Confederacy on the payroll of Colonel Daniel Ruggles, regional commander of the Provisional Army of Virginia. One of these was apparently written by an agent working for Ruggles and intended to be forwarded by Dent; it was addressed to a Dr. Wivill with instructions for him to connect with the "courier line" that was to be immediately established the next day between James Grimes's house at Mathias

Point and the colonel's headquarters at Brooke's Station. The agent had separately noted to Dent regarding the instructions: "Please keep on the *qui vive* and at all expense[s] incurred shall be made satisfactory to you or any other person rendering service. Please so inform our friends and also Doctor Wivill. General Ruggles who knows of my authority has stated herein to the same effect as I represent." The note was personally indorsed and signed thus by Ruggles: "The bearer of this is authorized to certify bills to be paid at Richmond. All communications should be forwarded rapidly." [39]

Clearly, Pinkerton ascertained, Dent was without question an important paid agent of the Confederacy and a significant link in the rebel's rapidly developing north-south communications system and must be apprehended as soon as possible.

***

Even as the move against the Pope's Creek-Mathias Point operations were underway, Pinkerton's agent in Georgetown, using the name William Stephens, was personally closing in on Rudolph Watkins, the western end of Dent's underground railway for rebels. The agent began by masquerading as a secessionist fresh from the South who had come across at Pope's Creek on September 12 and arrived in Georgetown on a clandestine mission for the Confederate government. He quickly worked his way into Watkins's confidence during a face-to-face meeting. The latter was completely taken in and considered the agent to be "of the right stripe," and was soon proudly confiding in him since "he was as good a Southern man as there was in the country." Watkins spoke glowingly of being on the best of terms with Dent, Jones and Grimes. He declared that he wished for nothing more than to go south to join the Confederate Army, as did his cousin George Dent, Jr., and even had his uniform ready. Fulfillment of his wish seemed unlikely as "the old man," quite possibly his uncle, apparently finding him more useful in his present role, would not permit it. [40]

Having learned of the Wilson raid from the agent it must have appeared at first to Watkins that his job as interlocutor for southbound secessionists was over. But Stephens continued to gently press him for information on others seeking assistance or any connections he might have with men capable of helping him cross. The agent then learned that the route from Pope's Creek to Mathias Point had been used by at least one U.S. Army officer who, just before the Battle of Manassas, had resigned his commission and crossed over to join the rebel forces. Had there been others like him? Then, pressing his own purported need to cross back to Virginia to complete government business, he talked Watkins into composing a letter of introduction to one Joe W. Bowman living on Pope's Creek. Would he advise Stephens, who carried important papers on government business, and needed to cross? [41]

For Pinkerton the letter of introduction from Watkins was all the evidence that was needed to arrest him. On the night of September 23 a squad of soldiers from the provost general's guard in Georgetown, accompanied by a number of Pinkerton agents, descended upon the suspect's residence and arrested both Rudolph and his father George S. Watkins. [42]

Found among their papers were a number of letters incriminating themselves and additional rebel sympathizers and activists. Some, such as a note from George Dent's daughter Eleanor to George Watkins, informed him that her father was "perfectly charmed" by news of the "Grand Army" defeat at Manassas. Another dated June 13 was from Rudolph to his father while the former was apparently visiting at Pope's Creek, stating "that his Uncle George is very busy conveying persons to Virginia, and that it is really astonishing how many cross from Maryland to the other side of the river." A third document dated June 8 and written by one Harris Forbes to Rudolph's stepbrother H. Aston Ramsay, opened up yet newer avenues for investigation by Pinkerton as it mentioned Forbes' role in transporting recruits bound for the rebel capital. [43]

The search for the enemies within would continue unabated for the next four years.

As for the Pope's Creek secessionists the dragnet was deployed, and at least one of the three men operating the transport, courier and communications system would soon be snared, as would many others. Indeed a veritable deluge of secessionists, suspect secessionists and secessionist sympathizers as well as bystanders and other innocents in the wrong place at the wrong time would soon inundate the jail cells of the capital city of America. And for the inhabitants of Southern Maryland the nightmare was just beginning.

14

CROSS-BOWS AND POP GUNS
"Maryland is part of the sunny South and shall be free."

Richmond born James Dabney McCabe, Jr. was not yet twenty years old when news of the seizure of *St. Nicholas* by the dashing young Zouave from St. Mary's County, Maryland, Richard Thomas Zarvona, was heralded throughout the Virginia Tidewater. Son of James D. McCabe, a noted Episcopal clergyman and editor, James Jr.'s upbringing was firmly rooted in religion and literature. He was nevertheless destined for a vocation other than the ministry, as his father's had been. It is uncertain what promulgated the young man's enrollment before the war in the esteemed Virginia Military Institute. What is clear is that upon his departure he chose a career as a short story writer, poet, author and editor that at first seemed anything but martial in nature. Yet his love of the South, the military, and the great Confederate leaders of the day knew no bounds. It would influence him, his books and other works throughout his life. He would occasionally sign off on some of his earliest writings employing such pen names as "An Ex-Cadet" and "A Southerner."

It is equally uncertain how young McCabe first engaged the Honorable Severn Teackle Wallis of Baltimore, a respected attorney, elected member to the Maryland House of Delegates, and an outspoken advocate for state secession. As an 1832 graduate of St. Mary's College in Baltimore, Wallis had studied law with such notables as William Wirt, later Attorney General of the United States, and others. He shared with McCabe a similar taste for literature and history, particularly Spanish, and like the young Virginian began to contribute articles on historical and literary criticism as well as poetry to numerous journals. It has been surmised by some that he was an acquaintance of another young Baltimore writer, Edgar Allen Poe as well as his colleague John Pendleton Kennedy. At the age of twenty-seven Wallis was elected to a position as corresponding member of the Royal Academy of History of Madrid, and three years later was chosen as a fellow of the Royal Society of Northern Antiquities of Copenhagen. Soon afterwards he visited Europe and later served as a U.S. Government investigative agent in Spain.[1]

By 1859, as the national drift towards Civil War accelerated, Wallis's political affiliations, which began as a supporter of the Whig Party in Maryland, soon shifted to the American Nativist, or Know-Nothing Party. With substantial boldness he began to air his Southern sentiments in such pro-secessionist newspapers as the *Baltimore Daily Exchange* and others. Elected in 1861 as a "States Rights candidate" to the Maryland State Legislature, the same body that was ultimately moved by Governor Hicks from Annapolis to Frederick, his strong voice of opposition to the Federal "doctrine of military necessity" resounded throughout Southern Maryland and Virginia. As chairman of the House of Delegates' Committee on Federal Relations he had become the darling of secessionists and states' rights advocates by guiding the legislature in its initially strong stand against Federal actions.[2]

The resolutions he had introduced declared that "the war waged by the United States upon the people of the Confederate States" was unconstitutional, repugnant to civilization and sound policy, and subversive of free institutions. A protest was entered against the war on the part of Maryland, declaring that she would take no part directly or indirectly in its prosecution. An assertion was made that the State desired only the peaceful and immediate recognition of the independence of the seceded states. The "present military occupation of the State of Maryland" was protested against as unconstitutional, oppressive, and illegal. The final resolutions contended that because of existing circumstances it was unexpected to call a "Sovereign Convention" without delay, or to take any measures for the immediate arming and organization of the militia; he proposed the adjournment of the legislature to a day to be named. The report was adopted - yeas 40, nays 11 - and the resolutions made the order of the day.

Then on Friday, May 10, 1861 the Maryland House of Delegates by a vote of 42 to 12 adopted the resolutions reported by Wallis, imploring President Lincoln to cease prosecuting the war against the South. The legislature had agreed to adjourn to the 4th of June, so as to be ready to take advantage of any circumstances that favored the secession of their state. Wallis's leadership had thus inspired countless Southerners with hope that Maryland might yet join the Confederacy.[3]

It was thus not entirely surprising that young James Dabney McCabe, Jr. saw fit to include Wallis as the Baltimore anchor in a scheme that he labeled "A plan for the effectual organization of a military force in the State of Maryland to cooperate with the Army of the Confederate States against the U.S. troops," designed specifically "for the liberation of the State." It would, indeed, appear that he viewed the delegate as a leader of the secessionist movement in Maryland, a man who would be able to steer the government at the right moment into the arms of the Confederacy. On July 6, 1861 McCabe dispatched two lengthy letters, both in secret cipher, one to Confederate Secretary of War Walker and the other to Maryland State Delegate Wallis, with the plan attached to each communiqué.[4]

"My object in presenting these papers to you," he informed Walker, "is to ascertain the views of the War Department with regard to the proposed plan, and to request that, if it is possible, the letter and plan for Mr. Wallis may be sent to him as soon as possible. All correspondence may, if you desire it, pass through the Department, where it can be inspected. I will here state that if the plan succeeds, the moment the troops commence active service they will be prepared to enter the Confederate Army." [5]

"The great advantage of this plan," he informed Wallis in a separate coded letter, "is that when Maryland does turn upon her oppressors she will have a regularly organized force, and not a mere rabble without organization." [6]

McCabe proposed that a significant force be assembled in secrecy to assist the Confederate States "in their operations in Maryland" and to cooperate with it as the President of the Confederacy directed. "The organization is to be carried to perfection," he further proposed, by appointing certain trustworthy persons in Maryland as officers, and authorizing them to enlist men to be held in readiness to concentrate at such points as designated. The troops were to be armed with any weapons that were convenient to them. Shotguns, rifles, pistols, anything that might be "calculated to convey destruction to the enemy," would be used to advantage. "In the country it may be possible to organize companies of cavalry, and it is desirable that as many may be formed as possible."

He also recommended that the state be organized as a single division under a major general and divided into three brigades, each commanded by a brigadier general. Each brigade would consist of five regiments and each regiment of ten companies. The organization formed under this plan would simply be be referred to as the "Maryland." [7]

The 1st Brigade was to be comprised of units organized from secessionists in north, central and western parts of Maryland, specifically from Baltimore City and Baltimore, Harford, Frederick, Washington, and Carroll counties. The 2nd Brigade would be formed from Howard, Anne Arundel, Prince George's, Calvert, Charles, and St. Mary's counties in Southern Maryland. The 3rd Brigade, all from the Eastern Shore, was to be made up from supporters in Cecil, Kent, Queen Anne's, Talbot, Dorchester, Worcester, Somerset, and Caroline counties

The regimental breakdown for the 2nd Brigade, all the counties along the Severn, South, Patuxent and Potomac drainages of Southern Maryland, was thus: "Second Brigade-First Regiment, to be formed in Anne Arundel and Howard Counties; Second Regiment, to be formed in Anne Arundel and Prince George's Counties; Third Regiment, to be formed in Calvert and Prince George's Counties; Fourth Regiment, to be formed in Calvert and Charles Counties; Fifth Regiment, to be formed in Charles and Saint Mary's Counties." [8]

It was imperative, he noted, that the "utmost vigilance is to be observed in carrying out these arrangements, as the disclosure or discovery of one circumstance might lead to the ruin of the entire scheme." For the entire 1st Brigade each regiment was to be assigned a rendezvous point but would be obliged to remain dormant "until ordered to appear publicly." The capture of Baltimore was to be the objective. For the 3rd Brigade units on the Eastern Shore the rendezvous locations would be in Chestertown, Centreville, Easton, and Cambridge. For the 2nd Brigade units encompassing Southern Maryland, the 1st Regiment was to rendezvous in Baltimore to reinforce the 1st Brigade. The 2nd and 3rd Regiments would converge on Pig Point on the Patuxent River. The 4th Regiment would assemble at Hunting-town in Calvert County, and the 5th Regiment would gather quietly in Washington, D.C. When all was ready "for the defence of Maryland and the South," they would strike. "Having met at their different places of rendezvous it will be absolutely necessary to concentrate the brigades at some point." [9]

The 1st Brigade being in Baltimore, there would be no necessity for immediate action. With the 2nd Brigade the 1st Regiment would rendezvous in Baltimore. Within twelve hours after the appointed time the 5th Regiment of the 2nd Brigade, from Charles and St. Mary's, would cross the Patuxent and march with all speed upon Huntingtown, where it would rendezvous with the 4th Regiment, from Charles and Calvert. A delay of six hours would be allowed here to afford the men an opportunity to rest themselves, after which both regiments would push on for Pig Point, in Calvert County, where they would be joined by the 2nd and 3rd Regiments, from Anne Arundel and Prince George's. The four regiments thus formed would then press on with the utmost speed for Baltimore, to cooperate with the 1st Brigade. As the utmost caution and vigilance must be observed along the route, the troops must be unencumbered with baggage, each one being supplied with four days' provisions, cooked or uncooked, as the general commanding thought best.

Within twelve hours after rallying, the 3rd Brigade, the 4th and 5th Regiments would march to Easton, where, after a delay of six hours, join the 3rd Regiment, and march at once for Centreville. After a delay of six hours for rest, upon being joined by the 2nd Regiment, they would proceed to Chestertown and link up with the 1st Regiment. At this point it would be up to the brigadier general commanding as to whether it be more expedient to cross the bay and push on for Baltimore, or to march on by forced marches through Cecil County, and cross the bay near the mouth of the Susquehanna, and then to press on for Baltimore.

A key to the alphabet in cipher would be furnished to colonels of regiments, who might at their discretion furnish it to captains of companies, but to none others. To maintain contact with Richmond, post riders would be kept in readiness to carry communications to a transit point on the Maryland shore of the Potomac, opposite Aquia Creek. "Orders coming from headquarters shall possess supreme authority." [10]

Almost as an afterthought he suggested to Wallis that it might be a better plan if the men entered Baltimore two or three weeks earlier, and were secreted therein and held in readiness until the call for action was issued. All would be required to enter the Confederate Army. The young writer closed with an offer to Wallis "to serve you here in any manner." [11]

Precisely how young McCabe's grand plan for the Confederate overthrow of Maryland would have fared had it been initiated in the tumultuous summer of 1861 is uncertain. In truth, his bold if somewhat naive scheme was both sired by and symptomatic of the upwelling of the militaristic spirits sweeping the South, and certainly by no small amount of his own hubris and ambition. It was undoubtedly representative of the thoughts on the minds of many, including Jefferson Davis, in those heady days of the war's beginnings. That it gained traction in some corners of the Confederate government was possible, particularly after the resounding victory at Manassas, and as many thousands of Marylanders continued to find their way to the Virginia side of the Potomac River to join the rebel army. Yet successful implementation of the scheme was highly improbable following the Union occupation of Annapolis, Baltimore, and Washington, and the May 24 capture of Alexandria, Virginia. That its objectives, if not its specifics were eventually made known to Federal authorities, however, is clear. Indeed, the fear of just such an organized insurrection as envisioned by McCabe almost certainly influenced the ultimate Federal decision to occupy the lower counties of Maryland in the early fall. Its discovery, coming on the heels of Jefferson Davis's threat to invade via Southern Maryland and the beginning of the rebel army's buildup opposite Budd's Ferry, was unquestionably disturbing. As Marylanders continued to send men and supplies South, Federal authorities had many reasons, among them the intercepted McCabe cipher, to believe that an insurrection or invasion of the state was at hand.

By early August rebel activity on the Virginia side of the Potomac was, of course, becoming increasingly menacing. The establishment of the rebel lines as far north as Fairfax Court House, as well as earthworks and batteries being erected or planned along key choke points on the river had many in the U.S. War Department believing an invasion was indeed impending. The gathering of an armada of scows and flatboats in Aquia Creek under the protection of the CSS *George Page* (formally renamed *City of Richmond* by the Confederate Navy but generally referred to as *Page*) only reinforced such concerns. A very limited demonstration by *Pocahontas* against the rebel steamer on July 9 had accomplished nothing. Moreover, on August 8 President Davis had signed acts of the Confederate Provisional Congress granting commissions to persons in Maryland, Delaware, Kentucky and Missouri to raise volunteers.[12]

Marylanders along the lower Potomac were perceived by many in the U.S. Army and Navy, including Commander Craven of the Potomac Flotilla, to be almost as hostile, if not more so, than the rebels lining Virginia's Potomac River frontier. "From all I can see and learn of the people of Maryland," Craven wrote, "I am convinced that along the shores of the Potomac there is not one in twenty who is true to the Union, and I sometimes think there are many hundreds of them thoroughly organized into companies, perhaps regiments, and prepared to act against the Government at any moment." [13]

But what was to be done about it?

General McClellan's estimates regarding the needs for the protection of the capital, Annapolis, and Southern Maryland, and for promulgating the war against the rebels, were stunning. More than 200,000 men would be required, of which 35,000 and forty heavy guns would be needed for the protection of Washington alone. Ten thousand more men and a dozen heavy pieces of artillery would be necessary to secure Baltimore and Annapolis. Another 8,000 men and twenty-four guns would be essential to protect Southern Maryland against an invasion, incursions or in-surrection in that quarter.[14] Soon after assuming command, the general informed Navy Secretary Welles: "I have, today, received additional information which con-vinces me that the enemy will, within a very short time, attempt to throw a respect-able force from the mouth of Aquia Creek into Maryland." The attack would likely be preceded by the erection of batteries at Mathias and White House Points. The enemy's efforts, he believed, would place Washington in great jeopardy. He urged that the strongest possible naval force to be at once concentrated at the mouth of Aquia Creek and that a vigilant watch be maintained to make a passage across the river impossible.[15]

The following day, the Navy Department received a copy of Jefferson Davis's stunning message addressed to pro-Confederate supporters in Southern Maryland.[16]

The effect of the "invasion scare" was significant. Governor Thomas Hicks was almost certain that rebels would soon be landing on Maryland's shores, especially when myriad schemes such as McCabe's began to surface. He begged the Secretary of War to take immediate action by to repel the expected attack by land and water. "Do not think me scared," he said, "I only wish to head off the rebels." [17]

Numerous Unionists in Maryland echoed the governor's fear of invasion. Many rebels were just as ardently in support of one. Captain Fleet Cox of the Potomac Rifles, from his campsite near Mathias Point, wrote to his sweetheart "Miss Mollie" across the river in Port Tobacco that he was looking forward to the day when 50,000 Virginians and Georgians were finally standing on Maryland soil "to prove to the Yankees that Maryland is part of the sunny South and shall be free." As for himself, he was anxious to drill his men before her in the town after they crossed the river.[18]

By the beginning of September, the Confederate blockade of the Potomac by strong batteries along its shores was nearing reality though not where Federal military authorities expected. The *Richmond Examiner* was boasting manfully that before too many hours had passed no fewer than ten batteries would be ready for immediate use.[19] The closure of the river seemed to some to be inevitable and the invasion of Maryland, many Unionists feared, would not be far behind. Measures had to be taken even as the tripwire that set things in motion was being laid.

***

On Sunday, September 8 General McClellan received intelligence that two companies of rebel troops "and other small portions" of the enemy were observed that same morning marching from Calvert County toward Upper Marlboro. The enemy line of march was reported to extend along the Patuxent as far south as Lower Marlboro. The message was electrifying. Perhaps the insurrection that was to go arm in arm with the feared invasion was already underway! If there were two companies, might they not be the spearhead of an even larger force gathering beyond the lines of the Baltimore-Annapolis-Washington triangle? After the Federal drubbing at Manassas McClellan wanted answers and instructed Brigadier General Joseph Hooker to investigate.

An 1837 West Point graduate and a veteran of both the Seminole War and the Mexican-American War, Hooker had left the army to engage in farming and later political pursuits only to be appointed brigadier general by President Lincoln on Match 17, 1861. His selection, it was rumored, was "being accredited to the State of California." In contrast, several notables of his West Point class, Jubal Early, Arnold Elzy and Clifford Pendleton would serve in the Confederate Army. An efficient and capable officer, Hooker at once issued orders through Assistant Adjutant General Joseph Dickinson to Colonel Robert Cowdin. The colonel was commander of the 1st Massachusetts Volunteers, all veterans of Manassas and now ensconced at Camp Union near Bladensburg. He was to proceed by the most direct route to Upper Marlboro, the venerable county seat of Prince George's. Upon arrival he was to dispatch scouting parties southward toward Lower Marlboro, on the Calvert County side of the Patuxent, and find out what was actually going on.[20]

In addition to his own regiment Cowdin was promised two companies of cavalry, 130 mounted troopers, that were to be placed under his direct command and issued five days' rations, forty rounds of ammunition per man, and a dozen axes and spades. He was authorized to take with him just five or six supply wagons while his men were to carry with them only their overcoats and blankets. "Let their loads be light," Dickinson instructed, "so as not to embarrass your progress." [21]

The colonel was ordered to report on his movements twice a day. Anything and everything of importance regarding the enemy, or supplies intended for his use, were to be immediately sent to headquarters. "You will use your cavalry freely, and collect all the information possible about the enemy's movement, and will also hold your force in hand and not permit them to commit depredations upon the citizens."[22] Maintaining at least tolerable relations with the residents of Southern

185

Maryland, which lay on the important but as yet unprotected southern flank of the Baltimore-Annapolis-Washington axis, was critical.

Major General Joseph Hooker (left) and General Daniel Sickles (right). Prints and Photographs Division, Library of Congress, Washington, D.C.

A second expedition under the command of Lieutenant Colonel William Dwight, Jr., from General Daniel Sickles' New York Excelsior Brigade, was to be sent to rendezvous with the Massachusetts Volunteers at Upper Marlboro. Sickles was a most controversial figure from New York, a Tammany Hall stalwart, former Secretary of the U.S. Legation in London, New York State Senator and later a Representative in Congress. He had gained national attention in 1859 by shooting and killing his wife's lover, Philip Barton Key, son of Francis Scott Key, in the very shadow of the White House. None other than Edwin M. Stanton, who was destined to become Lincoln's Secretary of State and later Secretary of War, had mounted his remarkable legal defense and secured his acquittal. Now as a newly minted brigadier general of the 5,000-man Excelsior Brigade, which had personally cost him $180,000 to recruit and equip, he was detailing one of the first noteworthy moves of his military career.

Dwight's unit was separately instructed by Sickles, apparently without direct collaboration with Hooker, to also proceed on a reconnaissance mission down the west side of the Patuxent Valley, "moving with circumspection and with the utmost vigilance to detect the presence, in whatever force he [the enemy] may be, and destroying, dispersing, and capturing such of the enemy as you may be able to encounter successfully." He was also directed to "lose no precaution to keep open a line of communication with the base of operations and with the detachment from Hooker's brigade." In order that there be no accidents when the two units formed a junction at Upper Marlboro, Cowdin was issued a specific directive to exercise "great care to prevent your scouts from firing on Sickles' brigade." [23]

Dwight's advanced troopers, five companies strong, commanded by Lieutenant Colonel Henry L. Potter and accompanied by eight cavalrymen, were the first to arrive at Upper Marlboro. They encamped in the town on the open sloping grounds in the rear of the county courthouse. Even before the Massachusetts Volunteers finally arrived, Potter had sent out his own scouts. These had fanned out westward into Prince George's towards Alexander Ferry at the site of old Fox's Landing on the Potomac opposite Alexandria, and on the Calvert County side southwards toward Lower Marlboro. The scouts soon reported that there was "nothing to warrant the belief that any bodies of armed men exist in this country, if at all on this side the river." [24]

About 6:30 p.m., September 9 the Massachusetts Volunteers, sans the cavalry promised them, were obliged to make camp in the woods on the outskirts of Upper Marlboro, the better spot having already been taken up by Dwight's infantry. There were no accidents. Communications between the two commanders, who had never met although encamped in the same immediate vicinity, were conducted by courier and would soon become a serious problem.[25]

Immediately after his arrival Cowdin informed Hooker that from "my own convictions, upon investigation, and from consultation with Lieutenant Colonel Potter, of the other detachment, I am satisfied that no companies of rebel troops are in this vicinity or have been for some time." He had no doubt, however, that troops had been raised here for the Confederate Army and that the sympathies of the people were unquestionably with the enemy.[26]

The cavalry detachments assigned to Cowdin, commanded by Captain William H. Hamblin, finally arrived at 1:00 p.m., September 10. The colonel had already spent much of the day "trying to gain such information as may aid me in future operations" by interviewing the leading officials of Upper Marlboro. He quickly discovered that they had been expecting a visit by Union troops for some time and "were not disappointed in seeing us come," a sentiment certainly of questionably validity. The last time a whole army had come through town was in 1814, and they were bound the other way, intent on burning Washington. Some of the inhabitants sympathetic to the rebel cause no doubt silently wished the Confederacy would soon follow suit.[27]

The following morning Colonel Potter's detachment was scheduled to set off on a seven mile march northward to cross the Patuxent via the nearest bridge over the river at Queen Anne's Town, and then southward to Lower Marlboro "covering the ground that had not already been explored" earlier by Dwight's cavalry scouts. Cowdin would also move across the river with his main force, presumably like Potter at Queen Anne's, and also march southward toward Lower Marlboro. With his 1,500 men having arrived at Upper Marlboro first, Dwight informed Cowdin that he would rendezvous with him again at Lower Marlboro (presumably by ferry from White's Landing on the Prince George's side of the river). But then having received orders to the contrary he noted that he was to move southward "by an easy march" to Benedict, a decrepit village that had seen better days, and to arrive there on the west side of the waterway by September 13. A schooner, for which he had arranged, would drop down the river in tandem with both expeditions to provide communications between them as they proceeded. Incorrectly assuming he was in command of the entire operation, Dwight informed Cowdin that couriers should be dispatched to the schooner four times a day to keep each commander informed of the progress and findings of the other.[28]

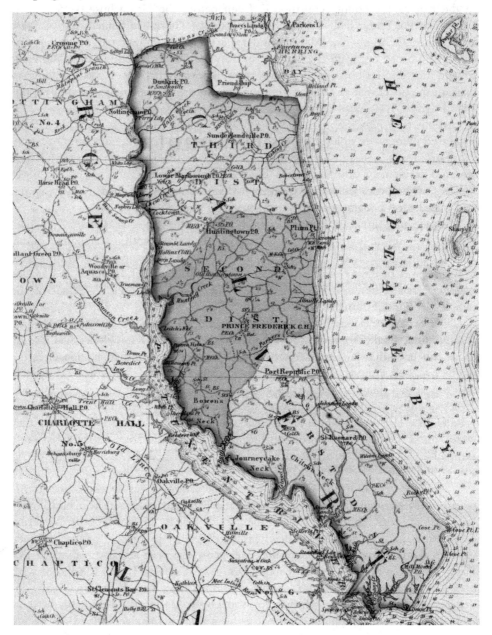

"Calvert County." Simon J. Martinet, Baltimore, 1861. Geography and Map Division, Library of Congress, Washington, D.C.

"If you meet any considerable force of the enemy," he wrote to his fellow commander, "I can easily throw you reenforcements, and you can cross to me at any moment I deem it necessary, if it should be necessary before you reach Prince Fredericktown. I move very slowly and carefully, and, as I hear there are cavalry of the enemy on your side, it will be necessary that you should do the same." Dwight's orders were that upon arrival at Benedict he was to veer southwest to Port Tobacco, the reported hotbed of Confederate contraband smuggling and transport of rebel volunteers into Virginia, "with a view [to] its capture and occupation." [29]

After proceeding five or six miles on his march and finding everything quiet Cowdin determined it unnecessary to go any farther and resolved to return to Upper Marlboro. En route he encountered a lieutenant from Dwight's regiment bearing orders to the colonel that he was to form a communication junction with the New Yorker at Lower Marlboro where, he was informed, it was believed a company of Confederate cavalry had been stationed. Still fully assuming he was in overall command Dwight instructed that each house in the town "known to contain a member will have to be searched." The message also informed Cowdin that he was then to proceed as far as Prince Frederick, and added, "I hope to see you in my vicinity, near Port Tobacco, by Saturday noon." [30]

Having received no specific orders from Hooker to proceed to either Prince Frederick or Port Tobacco, Cowdin, who was then at Smithville [modern Dunkirk], dispatched his own courier, Lieutenant William L. Candler, to Dwight: "I propose to proceed back from this place to a point which will enable me to march either north or south, where I shall await instructions from General Hooker." Then without directly challenging his fellow commander on the other side of the river, he simply informed him: "My present instructions will allow me to advance no farther than Lower Marlborough." [31]

Upon meeting with Dwight, Candler was examined at length about the Massachusetts colonel's orders. The colonel then showed him his own instructions from Sickles and noted that he had already marked out a route of march for Cowdin: "From Lower Marlborough to Huntington [Huntingtown], from Huntington to [Prince] Fredericktown [*sic*], from Fredericktown to Mackall's Ferry; hence to cross the river, and form a junction at Benedict with Colonel Dwight's force, which will proceed to that point direct; thence, by different routs, to Port Tobacco." The lieutenant was further informed that Dwight would be sending another courier to Cowdin at 2:00 p.m.[32]

At precisely the appointed time a messenger arrived in the New Englander's camp to inform him that Dwight was awaiting him on the other side of the river and "would receive me or any other person I might wish to send." Cowdin was perplexed since he had no instructions to place himself under Dwight's command. He promptly informed his superiors at Camp Union in Bladensburg of the situation. By 4:00 p.m. the Massachusetts Volunteers were on the march back toward Upper Marlboro.[33]

The next morning, September 13, Cowdin's dispatch having reached Camp Union, confirmation of his actions in following only the orders from General Hooker were sent back to him. "From the spirit of . . . [McClellan's] instructions from headquarters of the Army of the Potomac," the colonel was informed, "he is of the opinion that it was not contemplated that you should extend your reconnaissance farther to the south than Lower Marlborough; nor can be at this time, unless you should be in possession of information which you have failed to communicate, which [I] presume is not the case." As for Dwight, it was concluded that his instructions warranted him in covering a much larger field of operations than was intended for Cowdin's command. Thus, unless an appearance of the enemy to challenge Dwight's force was made, it would not be necessary to link forces. He was also advised not to take part in Dwight's operations, but to maintain an open line of communication between the two forces and be eady to provide support if necessary.[34]

That evening countermanding orders instructing Cowdin to turn around and march to Prince Frederick and then St. Leonard's were received from Hooker and forwarded to the colonel. His new mission was now to "gain all the information possible regarding the designs and movements of the enemy, capturing such organized parties as you may meet with, and taking all the arms and munitions of war you may fall in with." He was specifically instructed to prohibit his troops from committing depredations "upon citizens who attend to their own legitimate business and do not afford aid to the enemy, even if they are secessionists." Upon completion of the operation he was to return to Lower Marlboro, where supplies had been forwarded to him, to await further orders. And finally he was informed, undoubtedly much to his delight, that "it is presumed that you are senior officer to Colonel Dwight," who had just been ordered to proceed from Benedict to Port Tobacco.[35]

Colonel Robert Cowdin (left) and Colonel William Dwight (right). Prints and Photographs Division, Library of Congress, Washington, D.C.

If Cowdin was flustered by the seemingly fickle state of the high command he said nothing. Though he had already begun to experience disciplinary problems with the cavalry units assigned to him, he did his best to manage. On the evening of September 13 a detachment "of Zouaves and Dragoons" conducted an unauthorized raid near Upper Marlboro and arrested suspected Confederate sympathizers, among them being George B. Stewart and Richard W. Marriott, scions of two leading local families. At midnight, without benefit of a warrant, the soldiers broke down Marriott's front door, entered his wife's bedchamber and forced her to accompany them in her nightgown throughout the house, unlocking every door and closet for inspection as they proceeded. Upon discovery of a wine cellar they helped themselves to its contents for the next hour and a half. Afterwards, undoubtedly being somewhat inebriated, they awakened the house slaves in their cabins and forced them to slaughter a cow and cook a portion of it for them. Before departing at daybreak they confiscated two horses from the stable as well as all the bacon, lard and groceries they could carry, while conducting additional depredations against the general farm property and crops growing in the field.[36] The heavy handed usage of Marriott and his wife, it is safe to say, contributed little to the amicable public relations hoped for by the senior U.S. military command.

***

The Federal march through Calvert County, into what most of Cowdin's New England volunteers deemed enemy country and as foreign to them as China, where the black slave population exceeded in numbers that of their masters, may have triggered some troubling memories. It was not unlike the recent trek they had made into the Virginia countryside toward Manassas Junction to engage the enemy in what most incorrectly assumed would be the first and last major battle of the war.

"The roads in this part of the country," wrote Warren Cudworth, the regimental chaplain, while passing through Calvert, "were wholly unwalled and unfenced passways right through the centre of plantations. The plantations themselves were divided from each other by fences, and the passways closed by large gates swinging entirely across the road. Every mile or so, in traveling over the country, one of the gates would be encountered; and the occupant of a carriage would have to get in and out twenty times or more in the course of a day's ride." [37]

As the soldiers marched on they could see that the plantations varied substantially in both size and appearance. Some were "thrifty, well kept, and evidently profitable," while others appeared barren, desolate, and forsaken. In the fields they could see wheat, rye, oats, and corn growing, although tobacco seemed to occupy the greatest portion of the landscape. "Huge barns," the chaplain later recalled, "appeared on nearly every plantation for drying and storing the weed; and large quantities seemed to be on hand, waiting probably for a rise in price. Stock was abundant, especially pigs; and the colored people were more numerous than the white." [38]

By September 16 Cowdin had reached Lower Marlboro and established a temporary camp on the outskirts of the diminutive river town. Unhappily much of his ammunition had been spoiled on the march by getting wet, and he would soon be in need of another five days' rations that would all have to be sent from Camp Union. Moreover his cavalry units had been reduced from 130 to ninety men for no apparent reason. Some of his mounted force, he was informed by their commanders, had been sent as messengers and never returned. But the mass desertion of forty men was unacceptable. The "conduct of the whole force during their connection with me," he angrily informed headquarters "has been anything but satisfactory." Nevertheless he resolved to move both the Massachusetts Volunteers and the remainder of the adjunct cavalry units to Prince Frederick that same day with the expectation that he would be able to complete the reconnaissance and return to Lower Marlboro by September 20.[39]

191

The routes of the first major Federal military incursions into Southern Maryland, September 1861. The operations were specifically conducted to discover and destroy Confederate units believed to be operating in Calvert and Charles County.

The march to Prince Frederick was far less onerous than expected. Colonel Dwight, still anticipating that the Massachusetts troops would be crossing the river to join him at Benedict for the trek to Port Tobacco, had provided the use of a commandeered steamboat to ferry them across. Cowdin, however, employed the vessel to move his troops downriver, presumably to Mackall's Ferry at Hallowing Point, from which place the march to the county seat would be substantially shorter.[40]

The several days of delay in reaching Prince Frederick proved troubling for both the colonel and his superiors. Arriving in the town that same evening Cowdin, whose troops equaled nearly twenty percent of the population of the entire county, quickly discovered that the intelligence about Confederate units being formed there had indeed been correct. Two full companies of Calvert County men, one infantry and one cavalry, had been mustered and marched off before his arrival. He had already sent out scouts during the day prior to reaching the town and would send out more that same evening. It was now imperative that he immediately dispatch a strong detachment of cavalry as far as St. Leonard's in an attempt to flush out the rebels before they could somehow escape across the Patuxent or the Chesapeake.[41]

That the New Englanders were now deep in enemy territory was self evident. Yet Chaplain Cudworth chose to document the army's arrival in the county seat pragmatically. It was, he noted. little more than a "post village of about six hundred inhabitants . . . forty-six miles from Annapolis, and contains, besides several stores, a court house, jail, and church. It had been in open revolt against the authority of the United States, was the headquarters of a force of cavalry and infantry for the rebel army, and had allowed the stars and bars to float above the Court House in place of the true flag." That rebel colors had been raised over a government building was not only considered scandalous, it was, by military decree distributed earlier in the month, treasonous. By an order of General John A. Dix issued on September 4 the display of secessionist flags, badges, song sheets, photographs, neckties, infants' stockings or any other emblem of the Confederacy was to be strictly prohibited. Violators of the order would be subject to arrest by the provost marshal and imprisonment.[42]

As soon as the bloodless occupation of Prince Frederick was achieved, two Union prisoners were released from the town jail, and the rebel jailer was himself incarcerated therein. An immediate search was launched to locate the rebel flag that had flown over the courthouse. It was soon learned that the inhabitants had buried it in a field upon notice of the army's approach. Cowdin assigned a full company to search for the enemy colors by thrusting their ramrods into the soil anywhere it appeared to be freshly disturbed. As the hunt for the flag was underway other troopers combed the town for arms and provisions that might be intended for the Confederate Army. Within a short time nearly a wagonload of small arms and uniforms were found buried, hidden in closets, cellars, or in haystacks. Two boxes of contraband were found hidden in graves purportedly said to have been dug for Calvert County soldiers killed at the Battle of Manassas. Eventually the flag itself was discovered.[43]

It was soon learned that Colonel Levin Skinner, commander of the county militia and owner of "The Reserve" outside of Prince Frederick, had been responsible for Confederate Army recruitment in the county. He had organized the two known rebel units, if not more, for which Cowdin was searching. When warned that the approaching Federal troops were after him Skinner immediately escaped and went into hiding. When a detachment of soldiers appeared at The Reserve no one would reveal his whereabouts.[44]

The arrival of the detachment had not been the first time Federal troops had visited the Skinner estate. In May, shortly after Beauregard's capture of Fort Sumter, a small unit of U.S. cavalry on a rare patrol in the county rode up to The Reserve. Mrs. Skinner and her children, standing on the veranda of the house, met them with calm dignity. Struck by the beauty of little five-year-old Anne Skinner, the captain of the unit politely asked her name. Stamping her foot, she replied haughtily, "Anne Beauregard Skinner, sir." [45]

This time, the visit would not be as civil. When the troopers were unable to elicit any information about Colonel Skinner's whereabouts, his plantation overseer, an Irish immigrant, was reportedly hung by his thumbs from the limb of a great swamp maple. He refused to comply to the troopers' demands for information and was eventually cut down. A short time afterwards he was en route back to his native land.[46]

Another apparent target of interest was Augusts R. Sollers, a forty-seven-year-old former member of the U.S. House of Representatives (1841-1843, 1853-1855), delegate to the State Constitutional Convention of 1851, and *de facto* political leader of the county. According to Federal authorities he refused to acquiesce quietly to the military. His own twenty-four-year-old son, Major Somervell Sollers, was already serving in the Confederate Army. It was later reported, according to the ex-congressman, that he had forced his son to go south and join the rebel army and was himself an ardent secessionist. He claimed that from the first day of Cowdin's arrival in Calvert he had been a refugee from Union capture, driven from his home, family and business, and obliged to live in the woods. "They visited my house the night of their arrival and searched for me," he later informed Secretary Seward, "they placed a guard of 150 around it; they killed my hogs, sheep, poultry and wantonly shot the best horse on the farm." Somehow, he managed to elude his hunters, but not for long.[47]

During the search of the town it was discovered that a local pro-slavery newspaper was being published that instilled rage even in Chaplin Cudworth's heart. He described one issue of the paper as being filled with outrageous lies, warning the local blacks that the Union troops would do them harm. Another issue condemned the U.S. Government for dispatching "a large body of armed men to take from an inoffensive community a few crossbows and pop guns . . . It was plain enough where the editor's sympathies lay, and that he only spoke out what his patrons inwardly approved, but had the art or good sense to conceal." [48]

"The majority of the citizens," Cowdin informed General Hooker, "are opposed to the Government, and many fled the town at my approach, as has been the case in many other secession places. The professed object of the two companies organized is home protection, in case of Negro insurrection. I shall thoroughly investigate the matter, with the view of ascertaining the true state of affairs." [49]

Not everyone in the county was sympathetic to the Confederacy. Calvert was also inhabited by a number of non-militant Quakers, most of whom in the northern sector paid their pious obligations at the Quaker Meeting House on West River in Anne Arundel. The majority were opposed to slavery and the war in general and hostile to both the Union and Confederate militaries in particular.[50]

Over the next few days many citizens who had taken flight began to filter back into town. Chaplain Cudworth suggested that the "principal inhabitants" had departed prior to the arrival of the army "feeling guilty, no doubt, and fearing what might be the consequences of their misdeeds." Yet within "a day or two, some of them began to return, seeming astonished and delighted to find that their habitations had not been destroyed nor their friends molested." [51]

At Prince Frederick Cowdin proceeded to send strong detachments to fan out across lower Calvert County in search of the elusive Confederate infantry and cavalry home guard. No place was excluded from investigation. Plum Point, Parker's Creek, Mackall's Ferry, Buzzards Creek, Battle Creek, Saint Leonard's, Fishing Creek, Huntingtown, Port Republic, Buena Vista, Point Patience, Cove Point, and Drum Point were all visited, but the rebel troopers had seemingly vanished into the ether. [52]

Even as some of Cowdin's soldiers scoured the county, those remaining in town were frequently paraded to the accompaniment of the regimental band, which became popular with the townsfolk who flocked to watch the drills and listen to the music. As there were still some local Unionists about, Chaplin Cudworth also noted, they were intentionally serenaded by the band and invited to visit the camp. [53]

Finally at 6 p.m., September 19, having considered his expedition to Prince Frederick completed, Colonel Cowdin departed the town with his men. Seven hours later they arrived at Lower Marlboro where they would encamp for at least a week. Satisfied with his success, the colonel informed Hooker that he had been unable to find any trace of contraband trade, and believed that if it existed on the Calvert County side of the Patuxent it must be on a very small scale. "There is no doubt," he stated with certainty, "that the march of the regiment through this part of the country has had a good effect, and has broken or paralyzed all military organizations in this vicinity, and I am of the opinion that there will be no new organizations created, the leaders having fled and a large majority of the members having expressed their determination not to oppose the Government." [54]

But the Confederates now proved to have been operating in the county had not been cornered, nor had a single rebel soldier been killed or captured.

The expedition, with the exception of an acidental drowning, had been bloodless. It had not been without other mishaps, however, particularly as they related to the cavalry. Back at Camp Union rumors had already reached Hooker regarding "irregularities" committed by Cowdin's command. The colonel did his best to repudiate them, claiming that he was aware that complaints had been made but that most were simply exaggerated. He assured his superior that all of the cases brought to his notice had been investigated and the appropriate parties punished. "I believe that some of the cavalry," he confessed, possibly referring to the Marriott incident, "while on detached duty, have been chiefly the cause of these complaints, it being almost impossible to control them. Numbers of them have been intoxicated and unfit to perform their duty. I have hesitated to make this report, it having been my endeavor, since their connection with my command, to make them conduct themselves as soldiers." [55]

In any event he was confident that his mission had achieved its objective. The Confederate troops were gone, quite probably having escaped from the county by boats or quietly returned to their homes, and the local secessionist population had been cowed into submission. As for contraband smuggling, he assured his superiors it simply wasn't a problem. "I am also of the opinion," he concluded, "that the object of the expedition has been accomplished as far as lies in my power, and that there is no further necessity of a large body of troops remaining in this vicinity." [56]

Colonel Dwight's march from Benedict to Port Tobacco and then north to Piscataway had also been largely without incident, though it was later reported, "the population on his line of march were generally in communication with the enemy." [57] Frequent visitation to Port Tobacco by Union troops had been ongoing almost from the beginning of the war, and measures taken against some residents believed to be supportive of the Confederacy had become increasingly prevalent, even before Dwight's passage through town. In late September Elijah Wells, most recently captain of the Smallwood Rifles and well known publisher of the *Port Tobacco Times*, was one such who was arrested on the grounds of having published or advocated secessionist philosophy. As a result rumors quickly spread that the newspaper office had been seized and its press and type carried off by the military.

Sometime before September 26, though perplexed by his ordeal, Wells was released for lack of evidence. Resuming publication, he quickly informed his readers that his office and equipment had been left intact and that he and the paper had emerged without "even a hair singed or the smell of fire about us," though it was certain that there would be Federal scrutiny of every word published thereafter. Then on September 27 the army "requested" the use of the printing press and type to publish its own newspaper for the benefit of Union troops in the nearby encampments. Wells had little choice but to comply. Printers from the 74th New York were quickly engaged and set to work. Within but a short time, the first edition of the *Excelsior Edition of the Port Tobacco Times* was being circulted among the troops.[58]

The only significant variant in the operations of Colonel Dwight's arm of the expedition occurred when a detached company of fifty men under one Captain Burgess was sent to Leonardtown and then Chaptico, and several very important arrests by the detachment were made while at Piscataway.

Burgess and his men had traveled light, without baggage wagons, and arrived at the St. Mary's County seat on Friday, September 26 on an undisclosed mission undoubtedly linked to bringing in contraband smugglers. Taking up quarters in the courthouse the company promptly established a perimeter around the building but within the limits of the yard. The following day they were reinforced by an additional nine soldiers, bringing their total to sixty men. The occupation proved entirely docile. "The bearing of the officers was polite and courteous," remarked the editor of the *St. Mary's Beacon* in apparent surprise, "and the men conducted themselves in a very quiet and orderly manner. No arrests were made in the town or neighborhood, nor were any depredations committed upon the rights or property of any one . . . They expressed themselves as entertaining friendly feelings towards the citizens of Maryland, and declared it to be their purpose to molest no one, which declaration, we are happy to say, they strictly adhered to . . . They left, on Sunday morning last, for Chaptico, and are probably, ere this, at their headquarters in Port Tobacco, where we learn, quite a large force is stationed." Before departing Captain Burgess settled up with the citizens for provisions furnished him, and spoke in complimentary terms regarding the treatment he received at their hands. "Unless the reports that have reached here of the outrages committed, elsewhere," noted the *Beacon* editor, "by detachments of Sickles' brigade are exaggerated or unfounded, our citizens have good cause to be pleased with the result of the late visit, and should certainly think well of the conduct of Capt. Burgess and his entire command."[59]

The arrests by Dwight while at Piscataway proved more substantial than Burgess's visit to Leonardtown and were of considerable importance, namely the unexpected capture of the elusive Thomas A. Jones on Sunday, September 21. Jones had been found along with another man, one Samuel G. Acton, hiding in the bushes near Piscataway. He had only recently visited Richmond, presumably on Confederate business, and claimed that he was on his way to Washington. Acton identified himself as an unemployed pipe fitter en route from the Confederate capital, where he had formerly worked, bound for Anne Arundel County to see his family. The two men were immediately taken into custody and sent to the Washington Provost Marshal's headquarters. On October 4 Colonel Randolph B.

Marcy issued orders for their formal arrest and confinement in the 13th Street Prison. A week later Dwight and his men were ordered to break camp and make their way to Good Hope on the outskirts of the District of Columbia.[60]

Cowdin's 1st Massachusetts Volunteers would linger in the neighborhoods of Lower and Upper Marlboro for the next two weeks, interviewing local slaves and occasionally uncovering hidden contraband. By October 7 the regiment had returned in its entirety to Camp Union.[61] And with that the first Union invasion of the Patuxent Valley was ended with a reported mission accomplished. The only known result, it would appear, being that three or four Calvert County men had departed quite swiftly for Virginia "preferring a home in Richmond to quarters at Fort Lafayette" prison.[62] But the United States Army was far from finished with its activities along the quiet flowing river.

Sickles had not confined his expeditionary outreach to Calvert, Charles and St. Mary's. As September neared an end, he had also detached two companies of the 3rd New York Regiment on a fast patrol of Anne Arundel County without incident. However, upon their return the two units had occasion to stop on the outskirts of Bladensburg in Prince George's County at the estate of Washington Beall. There they were reportedly treated in a hospitable manner but responded in what was deemed by some as an illegal act. "They repaid his [Beall's] kindness," noted one newspaper, "by carrying off with them three of his best slaves. Mr. George W. Duvall, one of the newly appointed patrolmen for the county, saw them and tried to reclaim them, but they escaped from him, and he was laughed at by the soldiers. He succeeded, however, in arresting one of the 'contrabands' who was following the command and would not tell his master's name. He was lodged in jail." [63]

In an effort to subvert the secessionist movement among Maryland's leadership, and in coordination with the invasion of Southern Maryland, the Lincoln Administration quickly and methodically moved to sever the many heads of the Confederate hydra in the state. On September 11 Secretary of War Cameron dispatched a most draconian order to Generals Banks, then at Darnestown, Maryland near Frederick, and Dix in Baltimore: "The passage of any act of secession by the legislature of Maryland must be prevented. If necessary, all or any part of the members must be arrested. Exercise your own judgment as to the time and manner, but do the work efficiently." [64] Banks was to round up those suspected of rebel support or sympathies at and about Frederick, and Dix, who recommended that the sweep not be mounted until the following night, would arrest those in Baltimore. "No effort or precaution will be spared to carry your order into execution promptly and effectually," declared Dix. Those captured in Baltimore were to be immediately placed aboard a steamer and kept in close custody, *in communicado*, and taken to Fort Monroe for retransfer to an undesignated place of incarceration.[65]

On September 12, the same day Cowdin had arrived at Smithville, Dix issued an order from his headquarters at Fort McHenry to Provost Marshal George R. Dodge for the arrest of all allegedly disloyal members of the Maryland State Legislature, who had been scheduled to reconvene on September 17 in Frederick. He was also to arrest leading Baltimoreans believed to be devout secessionist and traitors to the nation. A similar command was issued by Banks in Frederick. In

Baltimore the operations were undertaken swiftly and efficiently under the direction of Allan Pinkerton.

"Hacks containing two police officers halted in front of the dwellings of those arrested," historian John Thomas Scharf, a former Maryland Confederate soldier, wrote more than a decade later. "The doorbell was rung, and the sought for party was informed that his presence was required at Fort McHenry. When the news of the arrests of the parties became known in the city, it created great excitement, and many declared that a most flagrant outrage had been committed." The arrestees were duly imprisoned at the fort without charges being filed and then later moved to Fort Lafayette. The sweeps in both Baltimore and Frederick netted dozens of prominent Marylanders including: U.S. Congressman Henry May; state senators Ross Winans (again), Dr. Andrew A. Lynch, and Henry M. Warfield; T. Parkin Scott, Henry M. Morfit, Dr. J. Hanson Thomas, Charles H. Pitts, William G. Harrison and Laurence Sangston, all members of the Maryland House of Delegates from Baltimore; Robert Denison and Leonard G. Quilan, members of the House from Baltimore County; Milton Y. Kidd, chief clerk of the House (later released in the last stages of consumption), and Thomas H. Moore, his assistant; William Kilgour, clerk of the Senate and L. P. Carmack, his assistant; Assembly members from various counties, including William E. Salmon of Frederick, Elbridge O. Kilbourne, Thomas J. Claggett, Richard C. McCubbin of Annapolis; George W. Landing, Dr. Bernard Mills of Carroll County; William R. Miller of Cecil County; Philip F. Raisin, Andrew Kessler of Frederick, president of the House of Delegates; Josiah H. Gordon, James W. Maxwell, Clark J. Durant of St. Mary's County; John J. Heckart and J. Laurence Jones of Talbot County; Mayor of Baltimore George W. Brown; Frank Key Howard, editor of the *Baltimore Daily Exchange*, Thomas W. Hall, editor of *The South*, and Elihu Riley, editor of the *Annapolis Republican* and printer for the House of Delegates. Soon the dragnet was extended throughout the state in an effort to sweep up lesser noteworthy citizens believed to be recruiting for the Confederacy or planning to join the rebel forces. Among the many notables arrested was the House of Delegates Member from Baltimore, the firebrand Severn Teackle Wallis, James Dabney McCabe, Jr.'s correspondent in the daring plan to overthrow Maryland.[66] It would seem that the youthful Virginian's grandiose scheme for the "liberation" of his neighboring southern state had come to naught. Not surprisingly, what was left of the Maryland Legislature decided not to reconvene at Frederick.

Three days after the roundups and the closure of the legislature, Goveror Hicks wrote to General Banks: "We see the good fruit already produced by these arrests. We can no longer mince matters with these desperate people." [67]

The sweeping apprehension and imprisonment of some of the state's most prominent pro-secession citizens and politicians, and the increasing presence of Federal spies in Confederate territory did not go unnoticed by the Davis Administration in Richmond. Saddened by the latest roundup and hoping that the Confederate Army might be able to do something constructive regarding secessionist refugees from Maryland, Acting Secretary of War Judah P. Benjamin dispatched an open-ended directive to General Holmes at Aquia Creek on September 20. "In the present condition of Maryland," he wrote, "the Government feels a deep solicitude in behalf of the unfortunate citizens who are cut off from all hope of escaping from the tyranny exercised over them. I do not desire to make any special order in relation to the mode of securing you against the abuse of such facilities as can be afforded for crossing the Potomac, but it is necessary that some means of passage for our friends be kept open if at all possible." [68]

Benjamin suggested to Holmes that one or more officers be selected to manage the point at which boats making their way from Maryland were landed in Virginia. But security was paramount. The general was advised that he must "by proper police regulations guard yourself against spies while affording means of passage for the inhabitants who are seeking refuge with us, as well as for the recruits who desire to join our service. I leave the mode of securing the safety of your command against the intrusion of spies to your discretion, and content myself with requesting that you open the communication at the earliest possible moment in such manner as you may think best." [69]

"I do not see," Holmes responded two days later, "how it is possible for me to aid the fugitive patriots in escaping from Maryland. They excite my liveliest sympathy, and, I have given orders that the troops in the neighborhood of Mathias Point shall extend to them every facility should an opportunity occur." However, every caution was advised in regards to possible spies making the crossing, as he noted that all persons coming from Maryland were permitted to land, "but very few, and those under the pass of the War Department, are permitted to return or visit Maryland." [70]

The great Federal sweep, unfortunately for secessionists in Maryland, would be but the first in an ongoing campaign that would not be completed until the war was over. From the Confederate perspective there seemed nothing that anyone could do about it.

A FINE PLATFORM
"Looking over into Maryland as the promised land."

Major General George B. McClellan had accomplished many things for his new Army of the Potomac, most notably by installing a high degree of military organization and greatly improving the general morale, training and performance of his troops. Though personally adored by his men, and many citizens and politicians alike, he had less than amicable rapport with his superiors. His relations with elderly Lieutenant General Winfield Scott regarding overall strategy for promulgating the war, and the radical Republicans of Congress relative to his pro-slavery views were hostile at best. He favored instead a military confrontation with the enemy in the grand Napoleonic style while rejecting Scott's plan for a total blockade of the South as unproductive. Despite Lincoln's hearty endorsement of the blockade, the increasing tensions amidst the high command was rapidly becoming palpable. "Genl Scott is the great obstacle," McClellan wrote to his wife Ellen, "he will not comprehend the danger & is either a traitor, or an incompetent. I have to fight my way against him." [1] His opinions of the president were even more troubling.

Throughout the summer of 1861 Lincoln ignored the growing animosity between the young general and his aged superior as he watched the army grow and improve with every passing day. It was a quite visible conversion of what had only a few months earlier been a mélange of volunteers and hundred-day men into a great army that could not be denied. It was a triumph that Lincoln deeply admired. Yet the respect for McClellan's accomplishment was not reciprocated. The general considered the president as little more than a country bumpkin. Lincoln wisely ignored the blatant insolence and contempt the officer publicly and privately held for him and patiently watched as he continued performing his organizational magic.

Believing the army must now be expanded to no less than 273,000 men with a field artillery of no fewer than 600 guns, McClellan proposed to defeat the enemy in a single campaign. He kept to himself the strategy for his great offensive though he made known that the method of war he hoped to conduct would be fought on an open field of battle. It would thus have little major impact upon the civilian population. Moreover it must not jeopardize the institution of slavery, which he considered constitutionally valid and entitled to Federal protection. "I will not fight for the abolitionists," he once vowed to his wife. It was an opinion that early on aroused opposition from many Republicans. But the army continued to grow, and for the time being there could be few complaints.[2]

McClellan assumed full command of the newly organized Department of the Army of the Potomac on August 20. That he was a master military executive was an accepted fact – with one exception: he repeatedly miscalculated the strength of the enemy, sometimes by as much as three to four times their actual numbers, often to justify his own ongoing troop buildup. As early as August 8 he declared a state of emergency for the capital while acting under the belief that rebel forces facing him numbered over 100,00 men when the reality was that they had managed to muster barely 35,000 at the Battle of Manassas only a few weeks earlier. By August 19, two days after the formal creation of the Army of the Potomac, he estimated the Confederate forces on his front to number 150,000 men when in truth the enemy never exceeded 60,000. By September McClellan's troop strength had increased to 122,000. But for the general it was never enough for the grand offensive that Lincoln hoped might end the war.[3]

McClellan seemed to have little direct concern regarding the U.S. Navy's roll in defending the Potomac frontier, the Chesapeake Tidewater, or in the interdiction of contraband and rebels heading south. As his troop strength reached immense proportions he no longer seemed concerned about the threat of a Confederate incursion into Southern Maryland, despite the announced intentions of Jefferson Davis. If an attack were to come it would be against Washington, and the utility of naval forces would be useful only as an amphibious corollary to his great master strategy, which he revealed to no one. The navy, it seemed, was secondary to any of his operations except as logistical support. The Potomac Flotilla, made up primarily of steam tugs, schooners, cutters, and a small number of ferry boats armed with but a few guns, muskets, pistols, pikes and sabers, and all poorly manned, were already stretched to the limit and could be of little use. Thus when naval assistance was needed he was certain that he could do just as well with soldiers as sailors.

On September 19 McClellan proposed a scheme to Secretary of War Cameron to field a brigade of five regiments of New England men to form his own amphibious strike force "for the general service, but particularly adapted to coast service," which had thus far been the navy's role. The officers and men would have to be "sufficiently conversant" with boat handling, and capable of managing steamers, sailing vessels, launches, barges, surfboats, floating batteries, and so forth. He proposed purchasing or chartering for the command an adequate number of propeller ships or tugboats for the transportation of men and supplies, with sufficient timber protection for the machinery. The vessels would have a corps of experienced officers from the merchant marine. They would be manned by details from the brigade with a naval officer attached to the staff of the brigade commander. Flank companies of each regiment would be armed with Dahlgren "boat guns" and carbines with waterproof cartridges, and uniformed and equipped as the Rhode Island regiments were. Launches and floating batteries with timber parapets, all suitably fitted to conduct amphibious landings, would bring the entire brigade into action. The whole would be under McClellan's own organizational management and incorporated as part of the Army of the Potomac. The objective of this force, to be organized as other land forces were, he informed the secretary, was to be employed for operations on the Chesapeake and Potomac and would enable amphibious landings where necessary. Operating in conjunction with naval forces, it might also be deployed against points on the Atlantic Coast. The disbursement for the vessels and troops would be made by the appropriate departments of the U.S. Army upon requisition of the division commander. It was McClellan's belief that such a force could be organized in just thirty days, "and by no means the least of the advantages of this proposition is the fact that it will call into the service a class of men who would not otherwise enter the Army. "

"You will readily perceive," he concluded "that the object of this force is to follow up, along the coast and up the inlets and rivers, the movements of the main army when it advances." [4]

Who needed the Navy? Or so he must have thought.

Within weeks the concept would soon begin actual development and eventual implementation, though on a far more massive scale than even McClellan had considered, through the offices of one of his junior commanders, Brigadier General Amrose E. Burnside. The objective, however, was not to be within the confines of the Chesapeake Tidewater but a major amphibious expedition to the North Carolina coast in January 1862.

In the meantime, however, there were more immediate concerns along the Potomac frontier. On September 25 the USS *Jacob Bell* and *Seminole*, both stationed off Indian Head and Stump Neck Creek to prevent the possible crossing of Confederate forces, were forced to retire after exchanging fire with a hitherto hidden rebel battery at Freestone Point manned by the 1st Texas Infantry. It appeared that a key rebel link in closing the river to maritime traffic was already a *fait accompli*. The flotilla was now suddenly segmented and would have to run at risk past the battery if the river were to stay open. The rebels, at least for the moment, could now pass into Southern Maryland at will. [5]

***

On Friday, September 26 Brigadier General Daniel Sickles accompanied by a squad of Indiana cavalry determined to examine in person the progress of the reported rebel battery being erected at Freestone Point. He believed that by observing how close to the shore the channel ran at Cockpit and Hallowing Points and other places on the Virginia side, and where no batteries had as yet been discovered, that the enemy was principally interested in a line of defense and not seriously intent on menacing the navigation of the Potomac. Though he was fired upon by rebel artillery he saw no threat. "The considerable bodies of troops encamped near the batteries at Aquia Creek, Occoquan, Freestone and Mathias Points," he suggested to his superiors, "corroborate this suggestion." It was an observation that went counter to the hitherto accepted fears of many in both the War and Navy Departments.

From his first arrival on the scene, Sickles was more interested in aggressive offense than defense. In anticipating possible future amphibious operations against Virginia from the Southern Maryland shores Sickles further suggested that a very large force could be conveniently and secretly put on board transports from either Budd's Ferry or Chapman's Point. If it were thought advisable to effect a landing lower down the river, menacing Fredericksburg and the enemy's line of communications, Pope's Creek and Lower Cedar Point, on the Maryland side, and the line from Roder's Creek to Monroe Creek, on the opposite shore, would deserve consideration, in view of the facilities afforded by an accessible open country for an advance. [6]

Having been instructed by General McClellan to examine the defensive topographic features of upper Charles County, particularly from a hamlet called Hill Top, Sickles reported: that it was a commanding position, overlooking an extensive valley to the southeast, unbroken almost to the bank of the Potomac. The valley was about a thousand yards in width, and proceeding onward's towards Budd's Ferry and the Chicamuxen there was another range of hills nearly as high as Hill Top, which sloped gradually towards the river. The country was generally wooded, with occasional openings of cultivated land. Unfortunately, the roads were bad, and often passed through defiles. "An advancing force could be impeded and harassed at every step," he concluded, "and for artillery the roads would present many serious inconveniences." [7]

"General Sickles and Staff in a reconnoitering expedition along the banks of the Potomac." Alfred R. Waud Collection, No. 1040, Prints and Photographs Division, Library of Congress, Washington, D.C.

In other words, the region would make a fine platform from which to launch offensive action but was equally adequate for defense should an incursion from Virginia be attempted. He believed, however, that a rebel invasion of Maryland would be ludicrous.

Whatever General McClellan may have felt about possible rebel sorties into Southern Maryland, he was assiduous in seeking out the latest intelligence regarding the enemy's strong points. He was particularly interested in rebel positions along Virginia's Potomac shoreline when reports of the erection of battery sites began to arrive. Apparently not eager to rely upon intelligence provided by the Navy Department, but willing to employ some of their other services, he determined to assign the task to John G. Barnard, newly appointed Chief Engineer of the U.S. Army. Forty-six-years of age, second in his class at West Point, with additional degrees from the University of Alabama and Yale, and twenty-eight years military service, he had been a perfect choice for the job. As a leading authority on American coastal defense he had authored several publications that garnered him the highest esteem in the scientific and engineering communities leading to his role as one of the incorporators of the National Academy of Sciences. On September 27 Barnard was instructed to assess all known and potential enemy battery sites on the Virginia shore extending from Whitestone Point on Gunston Cove to Mathias Point in King George County and covering a nearly forty-mile stretch of the river. After boarding the USS *Yankee* Barnard set off down the Potomac accompanied by a knowledge-able former rebel informant named Sherburne.[8]

Under the guiding hand of Lieutenant Commander Wyman, whose knowledge of the shoreline terrain proved invaluable, the general identified nine significant sites. These included: the 100-foot-tall bluff at Whitestone Point from which enemy guns, should such be mounted, could easily rake the entire width of the channel; Hallowing Point opposite Pomonkey Creek in Maryland, which was protected by a wide shoal but could possibly be circumvented by vessels owing to the width of the river there; Freestone Point, where a battery of five cannon, including possibly two 30-pounder rifled guns, with several pieces placed far to the rear on a higher elevation for unknown purposes, might challenge passage but could be evaded; Cockpit Point, a mile and half from Stump Neck, Maryland, situated on a fifty to sixty-foot wooded elevation fronted by a sand spit, which could also be evaded; and Shipping Point and nearby Evansport, which lay between Quantico and Chopawamsic creeks, "on a plateau generally cleared and on the termination of a peninsula, lying in front of wooden rising hills." [9]

After passing Chopawamsic, Barnard readily observed that the river widen-ed, and the shores receded too far from the channel to offer favorable locations for batteries. The extant batteries at Aquia and Potomac Creeks were of no danger to shipping in the main river channel and were deemed "evidently defensive." But it was at Mathias Point, the general noted candidly,

> "the one of the whole river (except perhaps Whitestone) where the navigation could be most effectually closed. The favorable location for batteries is the northern extremity, comprising an area of no great extent, and thickly covered with young pines. Why has not this point been before occupied by hostile batteries? Simply, I believe, because it would require a good many guns and a good many men to protect those guns at a remote point, where the men and guns would be lost for any other purpose than this subordinate one of inter-rupting our navigation." [10]

The enemy, he believed, would not risk a battery here without either a strong fieldwork for 1,000 men or a large field force in the vicinity. He assured his superiors that a fieldwork had not been built, and the evidence suggested that there were no batteries there. The best way to prevent their construction would be to cut or burn off the pinewood. A regiment, protected by the navy, might accomplish such an endeavor in hours. If the timber could be burned standing, an operation on a small scale might well do the business. In the same manner the construction of batteries on Whitestone Point could also be prevented.

The possible erection of works at High Point overlooking Occoquan Bay, at Cockpit Point, and along the Virginia shoreline as far down as Chopawamsic could not be stopped by either Federal naval action or counter-batteries. Construction of works on certain points elsewhere might be prevented, but along here the rebels would be able to erect as many batteries as they wished. Favorable circumstances, though not to be anticipated nor made the basis of any calculations, he observed, might justify and render a successful attack upon and capture of a particular battery. However to suppose that all might be captured to prevent the navigation of the Potomac from being molested "is very much the same as to suppose that the hostile army in our own front can prevent us building and maintaining field works to protect Arlington and Alexandria by capturing them one and all as fast as they are built. As long as the enemy is master of the other shore he can build and maintain as many batteries as he chooses." [11]

Though the batteries might not be taken, Barnard suggested, at the very least they could be counter-battered. With superior batteries established on Stump Neck and at Budd's Ferry Point, the enemy could be so assailed on all points so as to cause him to abandon his efforts. Such an undertaking would be costly in both men and munitions. It would require the erection of several strong field works which might have to be changed from time to time as the rebels altered their own positions. No less than ten to twenty heavy guns would be needed on the shores of Indian Head and another fifty distributed along sites ranging from Stump Neck southward to the Maryland shores opposite Evansport. Should the enemy attempt to establish works at Whitestone Point and Mathias Point, counter batteries might also be erected on the Maryland shores opposite them. The terrain just north of Cedar Point and the bluff north of Pope's Creek might provide "good employment" for batteries to counter works on Mathias Neck.[12]

In summation of his findings Barnard made one final recommendation regarding the construction of counter batteries: "I would wait," he wrote, "until the disposition and ability of the enemy seriously to molest the navigation is more fully developed before commencing." [13]

The wait would not be long, for while McClellan proceeded with planning, training and enlargement of his army while procrastinating in taking the offensive, the Confederates on the Virginia side of the Potomac continued to fortify, even as they gazed longingly towards the opposite shore. The rescue of Maryland, some truly believed, could end the war. "My command," wrote one Texas officer rather wistfully, "are looking over into Maryland as the promised land." [14]

VARMITS

". . . to do battle with the Dixie boys."

Affairs on the Potomac seemed to Commander Thomas T. Craven to grow more perplexing with every passing day, for he knew that whatever happened on the Virginia shore was certain to eventually influence events on the Maryland side. It was especially troubling when an account provided by one of Allan Pinkerton's men was forwarded to him in mid-October from McClellan's chief of staff, Brigadier General Randolph B. Marcy. The secret agent had initially begun his intelligence gathering sojourn into enemy territory at Millstone Landing on the Patuxent, from which he had proceeded to Herring Creek, a short distance west of Piney Point on the Potomac. There he had hired a negro to carry him over to Ragged Point on the Virginia shore. Finding the point empty he pressed westward toward Machodoc Creek where he encountered rebel guards. His cover story was that he was delivering letters to Confederate soldiers from Maryland – and had the letters to back it up. At Machodoc he was informed by a local farmer that an oyster schooner had loaded at or near Newcastle, Delaware and entered the Chesapeake through the Chesapeake and Delaware Canal. The vessel had recently come into the creek and delivered 200 kegs of gunpowder and 5,000 miniball cartridges. Much to his chagrin he also learned that at least one or more such smuggling vessels sailed into the creek every week to deliver such banned munitions.[1]

The agent pressed on to Mathias Point where he met a rebel soldier who conducted him to a Captain Edelin, possibly Charles C. Edelin of the 1st Maryland, CSA, where he presented five letters for delivery to Richmond. With little apparent difficulty he gained the captain's confidence and soon learned from him that there were currently two regiments stationed near the point. One regiment was from Virginia and the another was composed of companies from Charles, St. Mary's, and Calvert counties in Maryland. Three other Virginia regiments that had been stationed there had just been transferred to Freestone Point on the Potomac, barely twenty miles below Washington. At Mathias Point the soldiers were stationed about 400 yards to the rear of the point, with the officers quartered in a substantial house on a large hill, also in the rear. Significantly he discovered that there was still no battery there as many Union planners believed, just two 8-pounders mounted on four wheels. "They would have larger," he noted in his report, "and would erect a battery at the point, but the land in the rear of the point is swampy and they can not get larger cannon there. They commenced making a battery there, but abandoned making it." He was further informed: "that they wanted the Government to believe that there was a battery there, so as to prevent our troops landing there to go to Fredericksburg." [2]

The agent continued to successfully extract intelligence from the loose-lipped rebel officer. He soon discovered that no fewer than 10,000 men were stationed between Mathias Point and Aquia Creek, and small batteries of one or two guns hidden by brush had been erected "on nearly every point of the Potomac." There were strong earthen works at Aquia and others planned below Mount Vernon. Of equal importance he observed that three rebel agents separately crossed from Maryland to Mathias Neck every week. Agents from Washington and Baltimore also arrived once a week to provide the commander of the troops on the point, one Colonel Burgess, with the latest from the Yankee capital. Rebel intelligence gathering was buttressed by the reception of the Washington newspapers every other night. Their signaling system was quite simple. "When they want to go over to the point," he noted in concluding his report, "a small red lantern is hoisted in a cluster of trees between Port Tobacco and Pope's Creek." [3]

It was quite clear that the U.S. Army's efforts in early September to close the rebel Pope's Creek corridor to Virginia had been a total failure. But more importantly the shifting of so many troops towards Freestone Point, just downriver from Washington, suggested that something significant was in the offing.

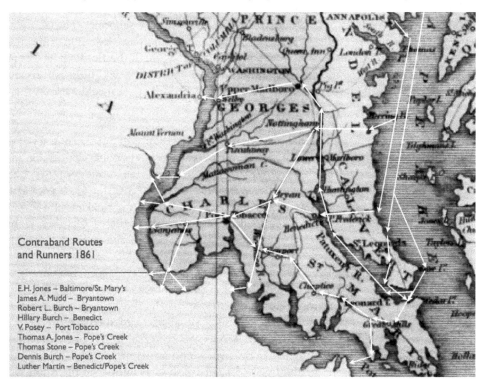

Confederate contraband routes through Southern Maryland in 1861.

The intelligence report could not have come at a more unwelcome moment for Commander Craven. Indeed his problems were only beginning as the Navy Department was already obliged to stretch its manpower and resources far more thinly than anticipated. To maintain the coastal blockade from the Chesapeake to the Gulf Coast the department was now forced to strip the Potomac Flotilla of several of its largest, most powerful vessels for duty elsewhere. When he learned that five ships ostensibly intended for service on the river, the USS *Seminole*, *Pocahontas*, *Pawnee*, *R. B. Forbes* and *Penguin* were being transferred to Admiral Samuel F. Du Pont's South Atlantic Blockading Squadron, he was without question disturbed. [4] His protests to the Navy Department went unheeded. Moreover, with few small launches available, landings would now be doubly difficult. Firepower to contend with the growing danger of enemy shore batteries would be almost nonexistent. Spreading what forces he had, now divided into two small divisions along the navigable entirety of the Maryland-Virginia border, was bound to invite an increase in contraband operations and improve the enemy's capacity to blockade river traffic altogether.[5]

As if to accentuate the danger Craven had also just received a disturbing report from the commander of the USS *Jacob Bell*, Lieutenant Edward P. McCrea: on his recent return from a reconnaissance mission to Aquia Creek he had definitely observed a battery being erected at Shipping Point, opposite Budd's Ferry. Several big guns had already been mounted. If true, rebel contention for control of the water access to Washington was becoming a strong possibility. Then word arrived of a firefight at Mathias Point. The contest had been between a unit of rebel infantry armed with two field guns and the little flotilla schooner *Howell Cobb*, Acting Master's Mate Andrew J. Frank, and the steamer *Island Belle*. This time the contest was over a grounded schooner on the point. Though the flotilla boats were eventually able to force the rebels to run down the shore "like wild turkeys through the bushes," it was clear that river passage was becoming more dangerous than ever.[6]

***

Concerns regarding potential raids or even an invasion into Southern Maryland, were now being fueled by repeated reports of enemy boats concealed along the Virginia shore. Worse was the intimidating threat if not the motion of the CSS *George Page*. As Confederate strength continued to grow and invasion fears escalated there were individual aggressive initiatives carried out by a few bold naval officers. One such operation was undertaken in the early morning hours of October 11 by Lieutenant Abraham D. Harrell, commander of the USS *Union*, a large, ungainly hermaphrodite brig-rigged steamer purchased for the navy in May at New York.[7]

Being informed of a large schooner lying in Quantico Creek and "knowing also that a large number of troops were collected at that point with the view of crossing the Potomac," Harrell determined, without orders, that he must destroy the ship as soon as feasible. It was 2 a.m. when he and a small party of men set off in two launches and the captain's gig and pulled across the Potomac in the pitch darkness. One of his launches was commanded by a midshipman named William F. Stewart accompanied by the master of the USS *Rescue*, Edward L. Haines. The the other was commanded by Acting Master Amos P. Foster of the USS *Resolute*. Accompanying Harrell in his gig was Lewis Penn, *Union's* pilot. Surgeon William R. Bonsall was brought along in the event of a bloody welcome.[8]

The entrance to Quantico Creek being very narrow, it was with some difficulty that the navy raiders were able to locate it in the dark. Quietly they followed the crooked channel west and then northward within pistol shot of either shore until they discovered the dark silhouette of the schooner looming up before them. "She was close to the shore in charge of a sentry," reported Harrell some hours later. Spotting the approach of the three boats the sentry immediately fled to alarm the camp, leaving the schooner unprotected. The raiders quickly boarded and discovered her fitted with a new suit of sails and all the furniture complete in the cabin.

The sails and furniture were quickly gathered together. Within a few minutes, about 3 a.m., Foster applied a match to the cabin of the doomed vessel, "producing a beautiful conflagration." In an instant an alarm rocket was fired into the night sky. A report of artillery echoed down the river as Harrell and his men rowed furiously towards the mouth of the creek, their positions now clearly exposed by the light from the burning ship. As the sailors scurried along the enemy "commenced a rapid fire from both banks of that narrow and tortuous stream and kept it up, inter-mingled with opprobrious epithets, until we were beyond their range," though not without random fire being returned from the boats. Upon reaching the safety of the Potomac the intrepid expeditionaries were greeted with three rousing cheers from two warships lying off Budd's Ferry. It had been a close call and without casualties for it was soon discovered that their boats and clothing were liberally perforated with bullet holes.[9]

"Birdseye View of the Burning a Confederate schooner in Quantico or Dumfries Creek, Potomac River, on the Night of October 11th, 1861, by Lieutenant A. D. Harrell, and a Detachment from the Potomac Flotilla." *Frank Leslie's Illustrated Newspaper*, New York Public Library, New York.

The brave demonstration by Harrell and his men changed little. If the commander of the Potomac Flotilla was concerned about the situation on the waterway dividing North and South, General George B. McClellan apparently was not. On October 14 Secretary Welles, having received a copy of Lieutenant Harrell's report and notation that "a large number of troops were collected at that point with the view of crossing the Potomac River," informed Craven of the troubling news.[10] "The commanding general of the Army of the Potomac," the secretary wrote, "considers the possibility or probability of the enemy crossing so remote that the Department suggests that you visit, as your judgment dictates, the whole length of the Potomac." [11]

It was perhaps well that McClellan's statement, one that totally reversed his previous opinion, was not widely circulated for within a matter of days he would be proven entirely wrong.

"Flotilla of the Potomac River" (detail). Arthur Lumley, artist. Sketch for *Frank Leslie's Illustrated Newspaper*, New York Public Library

***

On the same day that the commander of the Army of the Potomac sought to dismiss any concern about a Confederate river crossing, Dahlgren telegraphed more disturbing news to the Navy Department. One of his steamers had just returned from below and reported parties of rebels hard at work along the Potomac shore from Evansport to Shipping Point. He blithely noted the proximity of their works to the river channel that passed close to the shore. "As our vessels go down," he noted with some understatement, "a few rounds of shell and grape would disturb their operation." [12]

That the rebels were building batteries all along the Potomac now seemed obvious. The sheer extent of their work was rapidly becoming more than a troublesome threat. By now in the Aquia Creek area alone, at least two nine-gun batteries concealed by a pine forest had been erected. Venturing too close to shore was no longer an option.[13] The strengths of the works now being thrown up on a five-mile stretch between Chopawamsic and Quantico creeks, and even as high as Freestone Point, were still apparently works in progress, though not for long.

On the morning of October 15 the two second-class steam-screw sloops of war *Pocahontas* and *Seminole,* having worked up heads of steam, set off on their voyage to Hampton Roads to join the South Atlantic Blockading Squadron. At 9:40 a.m. *Pocahontas* passed Commander Craven, then ensconced in the Potomac Flotilla's latest flagship *Harriet Lane,* which lay at anchor off Occoquan Bay undergoing engine repairs. The commander may have watched somewhat enviously from the deck of his flagship as the men of war passed by him bound for the open seas. Then as the two ships began to push by Freestone Point just south of Occoquan, they observed a large body of men, possibly of battalion strength, marching northward, and at Cockpit Point another of the same size. At 10:30 a.m. as *Pocahontas*, being ahead of *Seminole*, was slowly steaming between Shipping Point and Evansport, she observed the enemy gathered in large numbers along the riverbank energetically cutting and clearing away trees in front of the just completed batteries. Though not attacked, the warship commenced firing upon the rebels but ceased after eight or ten shots. The effect was the same as throwing rocks at a hornet's nest. Commander Gillis later quipped, "*Pocahontas* stirred up the party with a gun or two as she steamed down ahead of us, which the batteries did not reply. She continued on, leaving us to do battle with the Dixie boys." [14]

It was now *Seminole*'s turn to steam by the rebel works but, unlike *Pocahontas*, with no intention of picking a fight. Getting his ship to Hampton Roads intact was Commander Gillis's mission, not an engagement with the enemy on the Potomac. Yet by 10:45 a.m. as the ship "was passing majestically slow by Evansport," three newly completed batteries suddenly opened a vigorous fire of shot and shell upon her. At least ten big guns, several of which were rifled and of heavy caliber, were mounted in the earthworks, two being directly on the bank of the river and the third some 400 yards inland. Gillis ordered an immediate response with *Seminole*'s pivot gun and two 32-pounders which opened with effect. For the next twenty minutes while in range, the contest between ship and shore continued unabated. With resolve, however, the commander kept his charge steadily on course as it was "a matter of more importance to take our vessel to her place of destination uninjured." [15]

"Perilous position of the U.S. Steam Sloop *Seminole*, while under a terrific fire from three batteries at Evansport shipping point, Potomac river, Oct. 15, 1861-10 o'clock A.M." Louis Sands, artist. Prints and Photographs Division, Library of Congress, Washington, D.C.

By the time *Seminole* was out of range she had fired twenty shot, and her shells "were seen to fall in and around their works." The Confederates threw between thirty and thirty-five well directed shots, as if to formally announce the river was no longer open to uncontested passage. Though Gillis passed off the damage as slight, the shooting of the "varmints," as he called the rebels, had in fact been quite well placed. One of their shot had crippled the mizzenmast fifteen feet below crosstrees, and cut away starboard after the mizzen shroud, another carried away mainstays near the masthead. Still another passed through the rail near the pivot gun. One shot strking amidships passed through both hammock nettings and rail, covering the deck with splinters. A heavy shell burst close under the starboard bow. The ship's waist boat was shot through and through when a rifled shot struck obliquely. Worse, the starboard fore rigging was torn away, and there were also some injuries inboard. [16]

The following day both *Seminole*, somewhat the worse for wear, and *Pocahontas* reached Hampton Roads intact. But the danger to Union control of the Potomac River was now clearly defined. Vessels passing either way would now be subject to almost point blank shooting from the rebel batteries erected at numerous points along a strategic five mile stretch of the river.

"Rebel Battery at Budd's Ferry, Va., Potomac River, February 1862." Library of Congress, Washington, D.C.

The first to realize the gravity of the situation was Craven. "So long as that battery stands at Shipping Point and Evansport," he warned Secretary Welles after the skirmish, "the navigation of the Potomac will be effectually closed. To attempt to reduce it with the vessels under my command would be vanity. Had our army occupied the points opposite, as I suggested in two previous communications, this insult would not have been perpetrated." [17]

Craven's opinion had an immediate impact upon the secretary. Departure of *Pawnee*, filled with troops, *Mount Vernon* and two tugs, which were also bound for Hampton Roads to join the South Atlantic Squadron, was temporarily delayed. But when *Pawnee* and the other vessels finally sailed they too were fired upon, albeit with less damage being inflicted. Fortunately, as Craven had warned Commander Wyman to simply run by the batteries and not stop to return fire, the injuries had been noticeable but limited. No one, happily, had been killed or hurt though the ship had been crowded with marines.[18]

With cool dispatch Dahlgren, who was not as sanguine as Craven, resolved to try the batteries during the night when darkness might shield ships from discovery. He thus dispatched three tugs and a steamer to explore the enemy's capacity for night shooting. Two of the tugs passed unnoticed and returned towing two loaded vessels from downstream. Though fired on neither was hit. The steamer refused to hazard the passage, however, and the third tug collided with a propeller ship in the dark. The enemy it seemed had been well prepared for such a test. "Lights are shown on the Maryland side," Dahlgren reported soon afterwards, "to give notice of our vessels coming." He recommended the lights be seized after small parties of troops were distributed near the locality of the signals to both observe and check communications by boats between the two shores. He also suggested that *Anacostia*, sometimes employed as a convoy for inbound vessels, be plated with iron for protection against battery fire.[19]

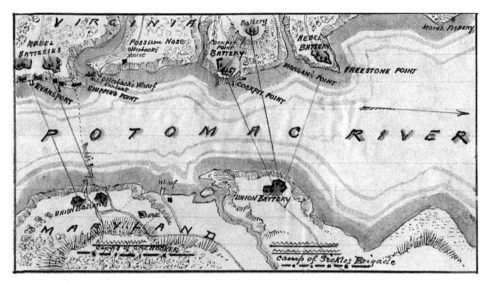

Union and Confederate battery positions on the Potomac River, 1861. U.S. Topographical Engineers. Geography and Map Division, Library of Congress, Washington, D.C.

Craven was now more alarmed than ever and immediately made his concerns known. "It shows," he informed Welles, "that the fire from the rebel batteries was much more effective than I at first supposed it to be . . . Considering the improvement of their gun practice I would respectfully suggest that until the enemy's batteries be silenced or removed that there shall be no more transportation of Government stores upon the river." But the situation continued to escalate.[20]

***

Acting Master Thomas M. Cash of the gunboat *Yankee* may have had some trepidation regarding the task assigned to him on October 17 by Lieutenant Thomas H. Eastman, the newly appointed commander of the ship. His mission was to proceed with four men down the Potomac in the ship's gig to seize a boat bearing three men observed crossing to the Maryland shore from Shipping Point. It seemed simple enough – just another interdiction of contraband runners. Yet upon reaching the mouth of Chicamuxen Creek he observed not a simple trio but a body of men collected near their landing site on the southern lip of the little waterway. Fearing the party to be superior in number to his own he communicated with a friendly schooner lying in the creek that was undoubtedly awaiting the shelter of night to pass the enemy batteries on the opposite shore. From her captain he discovered that several boats had crossed from Virginia since the opening of the Shipping Point battery. Believing that the enemy may have actually landed a small force he wisely deemed it inadvisable to go ashore. From the schooner captain he also learned of the locations of no fewer than nine battery sites ranging along a stretch from Chopawamsic Creek northward to Possum Nose, near Cockpit Point. Informed that the enemy's firing, at least at one point, reached far inland on the Maryland shore, he was undoubtedly stunned when handed a 30-pound Parrot gun shell fired from Shipping Point. The shell had been recovered from in front of the Richard B. Posey house at Budd's Ferry.

"Yankee Flotilla off Evansport." Arthur Lumley, artist. Sketch for *Frank Leslie's Illustrated Newspaper*. New York Public Library, New York.

The Posey plantation, nearly a thousand acres in extent, was one of the larger farms in the county, and "Big Dick" Posey was one of the more imposing characters on the Potomac. The ten room Posey house, replete with a reception hall and a porch running the length of the building but facing away from the river, was situated on a slight rise about a mile back from the ferry. It was already suspected of serving as a signal center for the rebels on the opposite side of the river, and Posey himself was thought to be in the service of the Confederacy. "It is believed," wrote one army officer, ". . . he communicates intelligence to the enemy by means of mirrors and candles from his windows, the women of the house taking an active part in these proceedings. It is very certain the rebels know all that we are doing. If heavy guns are to be brought to the ferry, that house should be closed or the inmates sent away." [21]

Posey was a respected farmer in Charles County, famed for his award winning Irish potatoes and oats, and active participation in community affairs. He was also a familiar face in Southern Maryland political circles. From at least 1845 on he had served as a delegate to the Charles County Whig Convention from Hill Top, and later from the First Election District. Each year, like many in the county, he performed his civic duty on grand and petit juries at the courthouse in Port Tobacco. And every year, like most reputable farmers, he served on various awards committees at the annual County Agricultural Fair and as a frequent participant, often winning awards for his horses and farm products. When the shad were running in the Potomac, he harvested the fish for sale at Lacy and Smith's store in Port Tobacco. But unlike most citizens in the county, as a slave owner and ardent supporter of the presidential candidacy of Constitutional Unionist John Bell of Nashville, Tennessee, one of the original founders of the Whig Party, he had apparently been torn between taking sides at the outset of the war. Though initially known to some as a Union man, but suspected by others as one who supported secession, by the fall of 1861 his loyalties had apparently been decided.[22]

When yet another battery was discovered and the full revelation of the enemy's deadly field of fire was ascertained, Commander Craven deemed it imperative that all vessels bound downriver be detained and so informed the commandant of the Navy Yard.[23] Dahlgren responded immediately the next morning by forwarding news of the peril to Welles. The secretary informed General McClellan "that the navigation of the Potomac River is becoming daily and almost hourly dangerous." He strongly recommended that the stationing of thousands of enemy troops and the erection of batteries on the Virginia shore "imperatively requires the action of the Army, unless communication by the river is to be abandoned, which on many accounts would be unfortunate and almost disastrous." [24]

Despite his earlier disavowal of any threat in that quarter McClellan responded instantly. An advance party of 800 infantry and 130 cavalry from the 3rd New York Regiment, Excelsior Brigade, Colonel Nelson Taylor commanding, accompanied by one of the general's own staff officers, Major William O. Stevens, and several topographical engineers were immediately dispatched. Their orders were to examine the countryside thoroughly and to ascertain whether or not it was necessary to erect heavy batteries for the protection of navigation and communication. Their major destination was to be the endangered Budd's Ferry site. By 2:00 p.m., October 18 Taylor was already on the march.[25]

***

The dawn of Saturday, October 19 on the Potomac arrived with a dense fog that obscured all visibility from either shore of the river. It proved to be but a short blanket of opportunity for Union vessels to run past the rebel shore batteries without being observed, and an early decision was determined to make the attempt. Thus, about 10 a.m. the USS *Resolute* took under tow two Washington bound schooners then lying off the Maryland shore well below Quantico. The two vessels, *Lady Ann*, laden with coal, and *Fairfax*, a Philadelphia-owned boat laden with hay, 150 barrels of cement, an assorted cargo of furniture and even a piano, all valued at $15,000 were to be taken quietly under tow by the little tug. *Fairfax* was connected by a line to the aft port of *Resolute* and *Lady Ann* by another line to the aft starboard, or Maryland side.

An hour after starting upriver, as the trio approached Budd's Point, the rebel batteries, perhaps alerted by the sound of *Resolute's* engines, opened a devastating fire just as the fog began to clear. A 12-pounder shot or shell fragment smashed through a pane of glass in the gunboat's pilot house, passing within inches of the helmsman's face and exiting the starboard window. Splinters of glass became thousands of shrapnel shards striking another seaman in the face. A 32-pound shot smashed through the aft awning of the steamer breaking the ridge pole within a few inches of a crewman and then deflecting diagonally through the corner of the trunk cabin. Another whizzed through the forward awning, passing through the sampson post of *Lady Ann* to the starboard of the gunboat, completely shattering it and carrying away the windlass gear.[26]

The schooner was pummeled mercilessly as shots struck in rapid succession. First her bowsprit was hit, then another struck her cutwater and, glancing, carried away her handrail. A third punched under the jib boom carrying away the foretop sail stay. Another tore away her mainmast shrouds, grazing the mast itself. Another carried away the corner of her quarter house and passed out through her bulwarks.[27]

The worst was reserved for *Fairfax*, the closest to the Virginia shore, while shielding somewhat the other two vessels from angled fire. An almost continuous rain of shot and shell literally rocked the schooner with at least twenty direct hits. Several shells exploded in her hold. "They were," remarked one witness, "sensibly felt by all on deck, the sensation being like lifting the vessel out of the water, and the shock was communicated to the *Resolute* and the other schooner." A number of projectiles went right through six-foot-thick trusses of hay mounted as a protective shield to absorb solid shot. One shot struck the pipe from a seaman's mouth without harming him in the least. Within minutes the fire had become so intense that the captain was obliged to order abandon ship, with his crew leaving all of their belongings behind. Suddenly *Resolute* was jarred by an abrupt jerk, breaking the hawse line connecting her to *Fairfax*. The Confederates, it seemed to everyone's amazement, had somehow secretly conveyed a chain connected to buoys and floats across the Potomac to the Maryland side of the river to obstruct marine traffic within range of the batteries.[28]

As *Fairfax*, now injured but afloat without crew and succumbing to the ebb tide, drifted towards the Virginia shore, Acting Master Foster prepared to lower a boat and send off a party to burn her to prevent capture. With shot and shell falling all about, however, he thought better of it, especially when a barge containing about thirty men, accompanied by a row boat, was observed putting off from the battery to tow the injured schooner to Quantico. It was later suggested that had he done so "the *Resolute* would have inevitably sunk, and the schooner off her starboard side either sunk with her or captured . . . Besides, he was apprehensive of getting his propeller entangled with the chain across [the] river." There was little alternative but to proceed on to Washington and report in.[29]

When Foster presented his account to Craven that evening, the commander of the Potomac Flotilla was livid. He immediately dispatched the officer to report directly to Secretary Welles, along with his own note of distress. "The necessary abandonment of a schooner laden with hay, and which has fallen into the hands of the rebels, has so mortified me that I can add nothing but my regrets that the attempt to pass the batteries was made this morning." [30]

As night descended yet another thick fog began to shroud the Potomac. This time it would mask a movement that was to evoke panic in certain quarters and set the stage for nothing less than the Union occupation of Southern Maryland for the duration of the war.

***

No one heard or saw the 500 Confederate soldiers, masked by the dense evening fog, as they paddled and sailed in fishing boats and scows the mile and a half from Quantico Creek across the Potomac River to Budd's Ferry. Arriving safely and without discovery the soldiers, conducting a reconnaissance in force, proceeded unopposed to the Posey residence not far from their landing site. Here they convened a conference with the leading secessionists of the neighborhood, including Posey himself, to inquire into the readiness of Maryland to receive a major rebel incursion. "They were told," it was later reported, "that all was ready for them in that part of the State; they then returned with the understanding that they would be in Maryland immediately." One of their first acts, it was also learned, would be to fortify Maryland Point as a bridgehead, undoubtedly a precursor to the main crossing from Aquia Creek. The return of the 500 to the Virginia side, it appeared, was equally unopposed by the unwary Potomac Flotilla in the area. [31]

Word of the unchallenged crossing into Maryland, possibly provided by an escaped slave, by nearly half a Confederate regiment first reached Lieutenant Harrell, then on blockade duty near Aquia. An alert was immediately dispatched to Craven who was undoubtedly anxious but not surprised. Not one to shrink from a task, Harrell resolved to proceed to and keep watch upon the ferry landing as long as possible and to destroy key buildings if another crossing in force was undertaken, even though his ship was desperately in need of long-denied repairs. He also vowed to keep the rebels, if at all possible, from landing on Maryland Point. Almost certainly his building targets included Posey's house, which might be used a headquarters or muster area for invading forces. It was a mission fraught with difficulties as the rebels now had complete command of the river between Chopawamsic and Cockpit Point, replete with batteries able to sweep from shore to shore. It was a tactical and firepower superiority that Harrell felt might compel him, if tested, to drop farther down. Adding to the difficulty was that he had only a two-day supply of provisions left onboard his ship. He begged for instructions "should the Maryland shore become fortified, which most assuredly will be the case in a few days unless the enemy is checked." After sending a messenger on the morning of October 20 to inform his superior of the discovery, he resolved to permit no shipping to pass until orders to the contrary were received or help arrived. [32]

Upon receipt of Harrell's distressing news Craven immediately sent off an officer from *E. H. Herbert*, a hired vessel in flotilla service, to reconnoiter the entrance of Chicamuxen Creek and another to Washington without delay. Acting Master's Mate Charles Bentrick had already heard the beating of drums the night before somewhere on the Mattawoman a few miles to the north, and upon receiving orders from Craven, personally went ashore at daybreak near the entrance of the little waterway. Proceeding on foot over fences and through cornfields and pinewoods for two miles he was astonished to hear the sudden report of musketry across the creek. Had the enemy already landed? Then after observing U.S. Army baggage wagons in the distance, a feeling of relief must have swept over him. "I fired a rifle several times and hoisted a white flag," he reported, "which soon attracted the attention of Colonel Taylor of the New York Third 'Excelsior.' A scow at hand paddled across the creek and I was introduced to the officers." [33]

The U.S. Army was indeed at hand, and not a moment too soon.

Taylor was at first leery of Bentrick, suspicious that he might be a rebel spy until the sailing master produced a document to support his identity. Thereafter the two officers immediately expressed their willingness to cooperate in every way possible, Bentrick on behalf of Commander Craven and Taylor on behalf of the War Department. The colonel's unit had arrived at Budd's Ferry about midnight October 21, not long after the rebel departure, and camped a mile south of Posey's house. Bentrick informed him of the commander's wish to see Posey and other members of the rebel cabal in the area, including Thomas Mason and a Mr. Runyean, arrested for entertaining "secessionist sentiments," although the colonel demurred and ignored the request. Had he known of Posey's hosting rebel troops he might have done otherwise. Nevertheless within another week the farmer was taken into Federal custody and it was also strongly advised that his son-in-law, one Linton, a paint foreman at the Capitol, also be taken up. By the end of October Posey and his associate Thomas Mason had been arrested and sent to Washington for incarceration. [34]

Now the news arriving in the capital from the Potomac was growing increasingly darker by the hour. One of the topographical engineers traveling with Taylor reported that some men encountered on the New Yorker's march towards Budd's Ferry informed him "the rebels in very small parties are in the habit of visiting this side every night. Others say (and those here) that they have been here but once, when they destroyed a vessel in the creek near by. People here are said to be generally secessionists, but they say nothing." The batteries at Shipping Point and vicinity had by now begun to fire at every small vessel attempting passage. They also commenced bombarding the opposite shore where the U.S. Army engineers were surveying the land and plotting the precise locations of the rebel guns. [35]

The Confederate blockade was rapidly taking effect. When a boat having successfully passed the batteries on the 20th reached the city, it was reported that some forty vessels were still waiting on the lower Potomac for a convoy ship to escort them past the line of enemy guns, but that there were no armed steamers available. The Navy Department publicly denied the report, and a very irritated Secretary Welles somehow maintained his composure when assailed by the press.

Given the circumstances it was now absolutely necessary to throw off kilter any rebel amphibious operations that might be in the works. Welles thus ordered Craven to conduct a shelling of the enemy batteries with whatever long range guns he had and force the rebels to expend as much of their ammunition – known to be in short supply – as possible. The order at first could not be followed as the range of many of the Confederate guns far exceeded those of the flotilla. To attack seemed suicidal. At the very least the commander was also ordered to "take prompt and severe measures with any parties on the Maryland shore who shall have made signals to the Virginia side." [36]

"In view of the evident preparations of the rebels for crossing the river" Craven responded, well aware that the enemy's guns had far greater range than his own, he "respectfully" recommended that it was an imperative necessity to increase the strength of the flotilla. The addition of at least five or six more vessels to the force assigned to blockade Aquia Creek, and an equal number to his own division above the rebel batteries would be necessary. They could not reduce the enemy by bombardment without suffering potentially serious loss, but given enough vessels they might prevent a crossing. The request, of course, given the scarcity of any kind of navy fighting boats in the region, was impossible to fulfill. [37]

As if to accentuate the negative, almost as soon as he had received the secretary's orders, Craven was handed another urgent message from Harrell, then lying off Aquia Creek in company with the gunboats *Satellite* and *Reliance*. This time it was to report that yet another powerful rebel battery, eighteen guns strong, had actually been erected on Mathias Point. A skirmish there between the rebels and *Thomas Freeborn*, *Island Belle*, and *Rescue* had already taken place forcing two of the vessels to retire below the point.

"Potomac River, Sept. 31st, 1861", detail showing the Potomac Flotilla gunboat *Satellite*. Alfred R. Waud Collection, No. 1040, Prints and Photographs Division, Library of Congress.

Harrell and the rest of the division off Aquia, with a line of rebel batteries both above and below them, were now in a most untenable position. "You will perceive," he informed Craven, "that I am placed between two fires. I await your orders." In view of his being entirely cut off he requested and received permission to drop downriver, passing Mathias under cover of darkness, to Lower Cedar Point. Now with *Harriet Lane*, *Yankee*, *Resolute*, *Reliance*, the converted ferryboat *Wyandank* and others confined to the waters well north of Shipping Point, at least twenty-five miles of the river between there and Mathias Point from shore to shore was for the first time under total Confederate control.[38]

Dahlgren maintained a level head about the crisis. "It does not seem advisable," he opined to Welles, "to permit the river to be closed without some effort, for the railroad [to Washington] is not infallible, but is liable to interruption from severe storms, particularly in the approaching season. Moreover, the disposition of the hostile batteries is such as not only to separate our flotilla, but to exclude its action from 25 or 30 miles of the river and leave this extent open to their one steamer and other facilities by water for communication with the Maryland shores and supply their forces along the bank, when by land this would be tedious and uncertain." [39]

In a matter of just a few days, it seemed, the impossible had happened. "The Potomac is now so far obstructed," Dahlgren wrote, "that it is no longer used by the army for the transportation of supplies, and the sole dependence for that purpose and for the supplies of the inhabitants of this city is limited to the railroads alone." Daily consumption of provisions by McClellan's Army of the Potomac, including feed for horses, was approximately 700 tons a day. Then there were the city's now nearly 70,000 residents to provide for. The capacity stated for the railroad, operating at peak efficiency, was between 1,500 and 1,600 tons, which it would seem was sufficient to meet the daily needs of both the military and civilian population. But all was not as it seemed. When the commandant queried Colonel Daniel Henry Rucker of the Quartermaster Department regarding hay supplies, he was informed that there was scarcely more than a single day's provender for the horses available, though up to that time both railroad and river had been open for all manner of supplies. Unfortunately shortages in all areas were likewise now threatening.[40]

Upon considering the logistical nightmare that loomed and digesting the devastating news of the new Mathias Point battery and all that it meant, Secretary Welles immediately informed the Secretary of War: "Efficient and thorough measures ought not longer to be delayed in sending detachments below to check and crush the proceedings." But even then fresh observations regarding the motions of the Confederates suggestive of an impending amphibious assault into Maryland continued to fuel another near panic in the capital. Early the next day Colonel Taylor informed Commander Craven, in the wake of the navy's abandonment of the central Potomac, that *George Page* had finally emerged from Aquia Creek. The rebel warship appeared briefly off Budd's Ferry and then brazenly anchored across the river under the guns of the Shipping Point battery. The situation was deemed even more critical than just twenty-four hours earlier. Confederate naval control of the central Potomac, enforced by the big guns ashore, had now become a reality. Charles County, Maryland, the underbelly of the Union front line, was now entirely vulnerable to attack. Whether or not the Confederates were capable of mounting such an operation was anyone's guess.[41]

The rebel command of a great swath of the navigable Potomac River was immediately noted and reported in the local press: "The accounts from the lower Potomac say that the Confederates at Quantico are unloading the schooner *Fairfax*, recently captured; that the schooner *Mary Virginia* [*Lady Ann*], of Washington, loaded with wood, has been taken by the Confederates; that the upper [U.S. Navy] fleet was laying at Indian Head; that the Confederates have a fishing boat anchored under Cockpit Point, mounted with two small guns; also, the schooner *Blossom*, mounted with two guns, lays in Aquia Creek." [42]

"The rebel steamer 'Page' now lying at Aquia Creek. Sketch by Lieutenant Osbon [*sic* Osborn]." *Harper's Weekly*, October 5, 1861. Naval Historical and Heritage Command, Washington, D.C.

As these and other observations were taken as a clear indication, at least by some officials, of rebel preparations for an invasion of the Maryland shore, and as Taylor had no artillery to combat such an event, the colonel felt obliged to retire to a safer encampment on the Washington road near the Mattawoman. The site was dubbed Camp Hooker. He immediately requested that Craven provide naval protection against a landing on the shores of Cornwallis Neck on the northern side of the creek, which he felt most likely to become the site of the next incursion. Army topographical engineer Robert S. Williamson summed up the seriousness of the situation.

Williamson reported that the arrival of *George Page* afforded the rebels the means of landing troops and artillery across the river at Cornwallis Neck or even higher up. If large rebel forces were sent across above Mattawoman Creek, or even Stump Neck, the detachment at Budd's Ferry might be be entirely cut off. Thus Colonel Taylor decided to move near Mattawoman. In the mean time a strong cavalry outpost was to remain at the ferry site to keep watch on the rebels while, Williamson continue his own work of "ascertaining the width of the river, &c., as if the command were to remain here, unless interrupted by the enemy crossing." [43]

Though inaccurate, the random and irregular bombardment of the troops that remained at the landing, which had commenced soon after Taylor's arrival, had nevertheless proved deadly in unexpected ways. On Tuesday, October 22, "whilst some of the soldiers attached to the regiment stationed at Budd's Ferry were examining a bombshell which had been thrown across the river by the Confederate battery on the opposite side, an explosion took place, caused by efforts to get out the powder. The damage was considerable, some nine or ten men were wounded, one of whom has since died, and two others likely to die. The tents and surroundings, it is said, were pretty demolished." [44]

Craven was by now completely dejected and frustrated with the "utter uselessness of the Potomac Flotilla for the further protection of the river." Fearful of an assault on the Maryland shore, he recommended that all the guns of the fleet as well as the powerful USS *Pensacola*, then at the Navy Yard, be landed at Mattawoman Creek and mounted upon Stump Neck opposite Cockpit Point. Then, with the aid of a competent officer to assist him and whatever siege mortars might be available, "we might, by concentrating our fire upon one battery at a time, be enabled to drive the enemy from his position." Anything and everything must be done to preemptively stem an assault for which no one was ready. As for the mélange of armed tugs, ferryboats and schooners that now composed the flotilla, he believed they were no longer of any use. His command of the now bifurcated squadron, he stated in a fit of utter depression, would be of no further benefit. "I respectfully request," he wrote to Welles on October 23, "to be detached from the command and appointed to some seagoing vessel." As if to again accentuate the negative he dispatched another express at 3:30 p.m. informing the secretary that he had only moments before learned that the gunboat *George Page* had just crossed the river, apparently with a deck load of troops on board. Then minutes later he shot off another message: the *Page* was below Stump Neck actually shelling Taylor's soldiers on the Maryland shore.[45]

The demonstrations of the enemy had indeed been intimidating, but the forceful and unexpected Federal response was far more than even the rebels had foreseen. At 11 p.m., that same night Dahlgren informed Craven that the Secretary of the Navy "desires me to inform you forthwith that General Hooker will proceed at daylight with a division of 8,000 men and eighteen guns to cooperate with you." Their objective was to do whatever was necessary to assist the flotilla commander in repelling an enemy invasion. The general was expected to reach the vicinity of Budd's Ferry by the afternoon of October 25. A strong Union Army crossing of the upper Potomac near Leesburg, Virginia, on the far right flank of the Federal lines, and a repulse of a Confederate counterattack there had successfully drawn enemy attentions, though only briefly, from the river theater south of Washington. [46] The reprieve had come, it appeared, in the very nick of time.

Yet one thing could no longer be ignored. A Confederate artillery blockade of the Potomac River was now firmly in place. Federal elections throughout the Union were looming large and secessionist disruptions throughout the State of Maryland were anticipated. The very real possibility of invasion of or insurrection in its southernmost counties was now uppermost in everyone's mind – except perhaps General George B. Mclellan.

A FRIENDLY COMMAND
"I am anxious to have a killing majority rolled up against secession."

For the Union the war had progressed from bad to worse, and following the major disaster at Manassas in July there had been but few minor military victories. Organizationally, however, the Union Army was finally moving forward. On August 17 the military Departments of Washington and Northeastern Virginia were united into one, and included the Valley of the Shenandoah, as well as the whole of Maryland and Delaware. It was now officially designated the Department of the Potomac. Under the command of McClellan the Army of the Potomac had grown to 192,000 by early December, far less than the general wanted but still out-numbering Confederates in the Northern Virginia theater by a staggering margin. It was, in truth, deemed to be the largest single army unit the modern world had ever seen. Moreover its commander had initiated the development of what would be seen as a nearly impregnable ring of fortified defenses encircling Washington, built almost from scratch by his chief engineer, the incredibly competent John G. Barnard. When completed, this vast defensive wall, including rifle pits and communications lines, would tie together forty-eight major forts and strong points, armed with 480 great guns manned by over 7,200 artillerists. In so doing the nation's capital had become the most heavily fortified city in the world.[1]

Though Union Army morale had improved, a siege mentality, enhanced by the rebel's newly instituted artillery blockade of the Potomac below Washington, still prevailed in Maryland. This was especially true in the city of Baltimore and in the southern counties. Throughout the Chesapeake, a few U.S. Navy warships and tugboats-cum-gunboats maintained a difficult watch on the bay and its many tributaries. Strongly armed pickets now patrolled roads and turnpikes throughout the upper Tidewater region. And with every passing day, Federal troops continued to mass in Washington and Annapolis, even as huge encampments began to spill over into Charles, Prince George's and Montgomery counties. Later an immense training and prisoner of war exchange dubbed Camp Parole was erected outside of Annapolis at a former railroad watering station. Several large hospitals sprung up almost overnight in and near the Maryland capital and around Baltimore. Advantageously positioned supply depots were organized from the Susquehanna to the Potomac. Yet in many regions, particularly in the extremities of Southern Maryland and on the Eastern Shore, considered to be of far less strategic import-ance than other fronts, Union control remained tenuous. Confederate sympathizers still covertly and successfully continued to maintain their own underground com-munications and supply lines connecting secessionist supporters in the North and South; men intent on joining the Confederate Army still eluded the struggling Federal naval blockade in small boats, canoes, and sloops to cross the lower Potomac on moonless or stormy nights. Crossings, it was repeatedly reported, were still being made almost every evening from the mouth of Breton Bay and the St. Mary's River on the Western Shore and on the Pocomoke and Nanticoke rivers on the Eastern Shore.[2]

Union naval raids by the flotilla and U.S. Army patrols began to accelerate from the several new camps being established along the shores of Charles County specifically to arrest suspected secessionists along the Southern Maryland coast. Yet the rebel artillery blockade at key choke points on the Potomac and the Union fear of – and secessionist hopes for – invasion were on everyone's lips. Now anyone and everyone in Southern Maryland who breathed a word of sympathy for secession had become subject to arrest. In late September one such Navy landing party came ashore in St. Mary's County and arrested J. Edwin Coad, Captain of the Clifton Guards, "a resident of the [Clifton] Factory district, and a distinguished and wealthy citizen of our county." 3

Soon afterward, on October 5 a small detachment under the command of one Lafayette C. Baker was dispatched to investigate the scope of the rebel communications operations in Southern Maryland. Carried aboard one of the Potomac Flotilla steamers, he and his men landed near the headwaters of the St. Mary's River in the heart of St. Mary's County. Baker was well aware that he was operating in hostile territory and had little trust in the loyalties of Marylanders in general. "The counties of St. Mary, Charles, and Prince George," he observed, "bounded on the north by the Patuxent River, and on the south by the Potomac, offer striking facilities for the purposes of the smuggler, the spy, and the rebel emissary. Its population, controlled and overawed by a few men of wealth, is identical in feeling and sympathy with the neighboring people of Eastern Virginia. There is scarcely a family in the whole district that has not a representative in the ranks of the rebel army scarcely a dwelling that does not offer refuge and protection to the smuggler, the spy, or the rebel recruit. In its villages, every country store has become a depot for supplying Virginia with food, clothing, and arms. It is in possession of a code of signals, under supervision of an officer of the rebel signal corps, and the people everywhere, with the exception of the blacks and a few timid Union men, are as much the worshipers of secession and the enemies of our Government as are their fathers, sons, and brothers, who fight the battles of treason under Lee or Beauregard." 4

Baker's primary mission was to investigate and stunt the rebel underground mail system in the region, which was a key asset to rebel intelligence gathering. His first objective was Great Mills Store in the same Clifton Factory District, about six miles from the Potomac, where he encamped. Two days later he and his detachment visited the post office and confiscated all the U.S. mail therein. Upon examination they discovered that a large number of letters, approximately a quarter of those seized, were addressed to parties in Virginia and other parts of the South, as well as letters from Virginia addressed to parties in Baltimore, Washington, Philadelphia and elsewhere. "I think, however, the postmaster is a loyal citizen," Baker later wrote, "but has been very negligent in his duties. Not desiring to incur the hatred of the secession community in which he resided, he has allowed letters to be received at his office from the rebel States, addressed to well known traitors, without reporting the same to the proper authorities." The postmaster in question, John S. Travers, was nevertheless arrested and hauled off to the flotilla without being informed why. He was charged with carrying the mails to and from the post office into enemy territory. The arrest of Travers was of particular significance for it now made the U.S. Mail system itself suspect.[5]

Baker informed the Secretary of State that he possessed positive information that an extensive rebel correspondence was being carried on through the region's U.S. Postal Service and recommended that the offices at both Leonardtown and Ridge Road be immediately seized. Fear wrought by the latest Union presence in the county was palpable. At the same time, from a base recently established by the 5th New York Regiment at Middletown on Cobb Neck, between the Wicomico River and the Potomac, and another by the 1st New York Regiment near Port Tobacco, troops were soon fanning out and arresting suspects upon even the slightest indication of support or sympathy for secessionists or their activities.[6]

Overshadowing all was the matter of the Confederate batteries on the Potomac. When the first portion of two brigades under generals Hooker, a career Army officer, and Sickles, a politician turned soldier, set out to reinforce the endangered shores of Charles County, mutual disdain between the two commanders threatened to injure the expedition in unforeseen ways. During the march toward the Mattawoman Hooker found much to complain about Sickles's Excelsior Brigade, which, unauthorized, had taken over use of many of the ambulances sent along on the mission. "During the march from Good Hope," Hooker complained in disgust, "I found them overloaded with [Sickles'] lazy soldiers, officers, and women's trunks and knapsacks to such an extent as to lead me to fear that if they reached camp at all, it would be with crippled horses and broken down ambulances." He had repeatedly ordered the men out of them, some of whom would heed him while others would not. Frustrated that with such an undisciplined crowd, with no assistance from a single officer of the command, he abandoned all efforts at discipline until reaching camp. However, when the troops finally reached their destination he ordered the ambulances to be put in depot under Surgeon Luther V. Bell who was to report on their condition.

The First Brigade had but one ambulance to a regiment to accompany them. The Second Brigade had undertaken a march of twenty-eight miles. "Had the march been double that distance," Hooker noted with some anger, "I question if I should have had one serviceable ambulance among them remaining . . . Among the troops, as you doubtless know, there is a feeling of destructiveness towards everything belonging to the Government, and I must say that I never saw it more expressed than during my late command, as you will be informed in due time. In some regiments there appears to be a total absence of anything like authority. The officers are on the same footing with the men, and I have yet to receive the first report from any officer of the outrages and depredations committed by their men . . . General Sickles calls this 'field service'; so was his camp at Good Hope just as much." [7]

The actions of the Excelsior's 2nd Regiment, it was later noted in the New York press, was in fact so irregular in marching that when the column arrived at Piscataway, barely two hundred out of eight hundred men were at their post. All along the route depredations of almost every description were committed. Fences were wantonly destroyed, poultry, pigs, sheep and cattle were killed without the consent of their owners, and either carried away or left where they were shot. After arriving at Piscataway similar assaults upon private property were committed.

Hooker was outraged, and adamant that there was no reasonable excuse for the widespread damage that had been inflicted and blamed the officers of the regiments. Some regiments were worse than others. The only reported exception was Colonel Nelson Taylor's 3rd Regiment, but other units of the brigade, their officers as well as privates, were reported as having utterly disgraced themselves. "They have forgotten to conduct themselves in accordance with that gentlemanly bearing, dignity and obedience which should be characteristic of the true soldier." The commander of one unit, Colonel George B. Hall, was placed under arrest for the "bad marching and subsequent reprehensible conduct of his men." [8]

Upon arriving at Mattawoman Hooker immediately ordered the ambulance train to be employed only for the movement of the sick and injured and placed within his own personal field of vision. Sickles protested strongly, to which Hooker testily replied: "In my official intercourse with veteran politicians suddenly raised to high military rank, I have found it necessary to observe their correspondence with especial circumspection." [9]

And so it was that rivalry and discord would attend the Union occupation of Southern Maryland. With a force of three brigades – Hooker's headquarters brigade composed of the 5th, 6th, and 7th New Jersey Volunteers and 2nd New Hampshire regiments; the 2nd Regiment, 1st Massachusetts Artillery and 11th Massachusetts; and the 1st, 2nd, 3rd, 4th and 5th New York Volunteers, all deemed the Excelsior Brigade – competition between the various leaders of state and individual units would prove troublesome indeed.

"Guard Mount in the Camp of the 1st Mass. Vol. Opposite the rebel position on the Potomac near Budd's Ferry (ca. October 22-28, 1861)." Alfred R. Waud Collection, No. 1040, Prints and Photographs Division, Library of Congress, Washington, D.C.

***

As the fall elections for congressional, state, and local representatives approached, Governor Hicks, by now an ardent supporter of the Union, grew increasingly nervous over the strength of rebel sympathizers in the state. He was particularly concerned about the influence they might assert at the polls in Southern Maryland. He and other state officials, as well as military authorities, were determined that only citizens loyal to the Union should be accorded the right to vote. In Maryland Republicans who favored continuing the war now called themselves the

226

Union Party, while those of the Democratic Party, sympathizers of the Southern cause, supporters of slavery, and the supremacy of states' rights over federal authority, organized themselves as the State's Righters or Peace Party. [10]

Governor Hicks was anxious that his own protégé, Augustus Williamson Bradford of Harford County, the unanimous Union Party candidate, defeat the main opposition candidate for governor, Benjamin Chew Howard of the the Peace Party. It mattered little that Bradford's son was serving in the Confederate Army. The U.S. Army was no less anxious for a positive turnout. On October 7 General Dix wrote to General McClellan requesting steamboats or tugs drawing no more than five feet of water to be used to go up the inlets and bays on the Eastern Shore to break up political meetings held in "hostility" to the country. As the elections drew near he was solicited by delegations from some 6,000 loyal Marylanders embodied in regiments and corps raised in the state, half of whom were posted in Baltimore, to not be removed from their voting districts as they wished to show their voting strength at the polls. Some even feared that there might be a danger of losing the state if the military vote was not included. Moreover, he told McClellan on October 25: "I think it very important for our future quietude that the Union ticket should not merely be carried, but that it should have an overwhelming majority. I earnestly hope, therefore, that the Government will make all practicable arrangements to enable the voters in the Maryland corps to attend the polls in the districts in which they reside on the 6th of November next."[11]

The governor followed by enlarging the request. "You will excuse me, I am sure," he wrote on October 26 from Annapolis to General Nathaniel P. Banks, then military department commander, "for suggesting the importance of looking closely to Maryland until our election is over 6th November. The Confederates will endeavor to offset something by which to operate on our election . . . that I am anxious to have a killing majority rolled up against secession . . . Will it be possible to have Col. Kenly's regiment [1st Maryland Volunteers] near Baltimore temporarily to save their vote? I hope so." [12]

The request to temporarily relocate loyal Maryland troops near their own voting districts to insure the Unionist majority at the ballot box was not ignored. On October 29 General Marcy, of the Army of the Potomac, informed General Banks that "the Major General commanding [McClellan] direct that you send detachment[s] of sufficient numbers of men to the different points in your vicinity where elections are to be held." All "disillusionists" known to have returned from Virginia recently and show themselves at the polls were to be arrested and held in confinement until after the election.[13]

General Hooker was in the midst of establishing Camp Baker, his base of operation near Chicamuxen. But in anticipation of McClellan's directive he had already given orders to four companies of newly arrived Indiana cavalry to hold themselves in readiness to march to various points in Southern Maryland at which polls were to open on November 6. Their mission was "to preserve quiet and good order, and to suppress any attempt at coercion or intimidation on the part of the secession leaders." Such a force, he believed, in connection with regiments recently stationed in Charles County, would be sufficient to accomplish such an objective. "The population is sparse at best, but at the present time no doubt but that a majority of the young men of the country are with the rebel troops and those remaining are filled with terror. They have no arms and no heart for resistance, however much they may desire it." [14]

Hooker overlooked no activities or individuals considered capable of asserting a secessionist influence on the elections. His troops were now stationed at Pomonkey and Hill Top, where a corps of artillery was also posted, and Port Tobacco, where Colonel Chares K. Graham's 5th New York Regiment and the 74th New York Infantry, belonging to Sickle's command, were encamped on the Mulberry Grove estate of Dr. Robert Ferguson. He considered these quite sufficient "to preserve quiet and good order, and to suppress any attempt at coercion or intimidation on the part of the secession leaders." When the general learned that a "noisy resident" of Port Tobacco named Peregrine "Perry" Davis, a tavern keeper and reputed secessionist candidate for the state legislature, had been stumping the district and "filling the heads of listeners with his secession heresies," orders were sent out for his immediate arrest. Judge William M. Merrick, whose secessionist proclivities were well known, was also placed under military guard. When another report came in that a "secession barbecue" was to be given at the White Horse Tavern a full company of Indiana cavalry was sent to attend. [15]

Then, at Hooker's new headquarters, intelligence was received regarding possible concealed weapons at Charlotte Hall in St. Mary's County that might be used to upset polling. Another cavalry detachment was immediately dispatched. Nothing was found although the search was extended far beyond the original target area. Other companies were sent to Allen's Fresh, Piscataway, Leonardtown, Trappe and Pleasant Hill to "guard" the polling stations and to remain there until the polls closed. Though the company ordered to Leonardtown "did not reach their destination in time to be present while the polls were open, in consequence of having been lost," Hooker noted that they "did good service in making rapid and orderly marches through the settled districts of the Peninsula." [16]

Similar orders went out throughout the state. Strong military forces were allocated to monitor all the polling stations, especially in the southern counties, the Eastern Shore, and Baltimore.

Ignoring the Union occupation troops and his recent arrest by Federal authorities, Elijah Wells maintained a dark sense of humor regarding the latest occupation through the use of a form of double entendre or code that was understood by all. Beneath a most provocative headline, "The Enemy's Approach," in the *Port Tobacco Times* on October 24, which could not fail to arouse Federal ire, he had written: "The *Bed Bug Season* is now in hand and every family and every owner of a bed should at once provide themselves with a bottle of '*Bed Bug Poison.*' It never fails as prepared, wholesale and retail by Apothecaries' Hall, Port Tobacco, Md., Corner fronting the Court House." [17]

***

As the day of decision approached hostility towards the growing presence of Federal troops, seen by most as occupation forces rather than protectors, was subdued but ever present along the fertile shores of the Patuxent and Potomac valleys. At Upper Marlboro soldiers belonging to Brigadier General Silas Casey's division had only recently replaced Cowdin and Dwight's units and established headquarters in the town to maintain the peace, especially during the upcoming elections.

Despite the Union military presence in Prince George's and along sectors of the Potomac shores of Southern Maryland the unrest was palpable, even as the movement of men bound south continued without letup. One glaring incident exemplified the situation in mid-October when the schooner *George Emily* was seized in the Patuxent by a force of 200 men, many of them from Baltimore and surrounding counties. They compelled the vessel's commander, one Captain Shreve, to carry them to St. Mary's, from which they intended to proceed down to Point Lookout and from there make their way to Virginia to join the Confederate Army. [18]

"The condition of things on the Eastern shore and the Patuxent peninsular counties in this State are deplorable," reported one Baltimore correspondent,

"Persecutions of the Union men are the order of the day, especially in St. Mary's, Calvert and Charles counties. Gen. Sickles has done much good in that quarter, but it would take 10,000 men to bring the mad people thereabout to their senses. Out of 1,300 votes in St. Mary's, there are not more than 100 Unionists, and they are daily peeled and scorched by the enemies of the republic. Many of the more wealthy class of rebels have left for Dixie. Nothing will cure the tendency to violence in those parts of the State but the speedy washing out of existence of the rebel army South of the Potomac by McClellan." [19]

But the elections were paramount. In Baltimore, General Dix issued a proclamation directing the arrest of all persons in rebellion against the United States who might return to the city and appear at the polls. He called "on all good and loyal citizens to support the judges of election, the United States Marshal and his deputies, and the Provost Marshal of Baltimore, and the police, in their efforts to secure a free and fair expression of the voice of the people of Maryland, and, at the same time, to prevent the ballot boxes from being polluted by treasonable votes." [20]

General Casey, commander of a division of troops ensconced at Camp Union near Bladensburg, was among the numerous officers who had received the same disquieting intelligence regarding potential infiltration of the polls by rebels, and the same instructions as General Banks. From sources in Virginia it was learned that certain persons who had been under arms in the rebel cause were returning home with the intention of taking part in the elections in Maryland. More importantly for the southern counties of the Western Shore it was also reported "that other individuals, residents in Maryland, who have been in sympathy and have given secret aid to the enemy, have concerted with the aforesaid individuals to obstruct the freedom of the coming election and control the votes in favor of their revolutionary scheme." [21]

Casey's orders from Washington were communicated without delay to brigadier generals Oliver Otis Howard and George Sykes, commanders of the First and Second Brigades of the division. They were ordered to begin their march deep into Prince George's on Saturday, November 2 with no fewer than eight regiments and several detachments of cavalry to oversee the elections. Like Cowdin and Dwight, Howard and Sykes were directed to cover the peninsulas on both sides of the Patuxent Valley from the Chesapeake to the Potomac.

Howard was relayed his written instructions through Captain Henry Warren Smith, Assistant Adjutant General. Soon afterwards he met with his immediate superior, General Marcy, and was given "such verbal instructions as would facilitate the execution" of his written orders. Marcy advised him to establish headquarters in Lower Marlboro rather than Upper Marlboro, undoubtedly owing to its central location on the Calvert County peninsula. He was also directed to maintain communications with General Sykes, who would be proceeding south on the opposite side of the river.[22]

Howard moved quickly, first to his camp at Bladensburg to order a full three regiments belonging to the First Brigade to prepare to march immediately. At 9 a.m. the following morning, November 3, he also ordered a troop of cavalry to proceed on the expedition. Another infantry unit, the 36th Pennsylvania, Colonel James Miller commanding, stationed at the time at Good Hope not far from Riverdale, Maryland, was also directed to move in time to rendezvous with the remainder of his forces at Upper Marlboro before pressing on into Calvert County.[23]

Upon arrival in Upper Marlboro Howard promptly informed his officers of their objectives. They were to remain in the town to "secure free and independent action at the polls. " Anyone who spoken oppenly of treason was to be arrested and held until the next day. Anyone arrested and found to have secretly bore arms againts Union forces were to be kept as prisoners. Discipline was paramount. "You will," he concluded, "preserve the strictest order in your own command, not allowing the slightest depredation. You must hold your officers individually responsible, as I do you, for the sobriety and good behavior of their respective commands. Remember that yours is a friendly command in a friendly country." [24]

On Sunday morning road damage caused by torrential rains the previous day somewhat retarded the march from Bladensburg. For the most part Howard's troops were green, lacked an experienced quartermaster or commissary, and were obliged to proceed over bad roads made almost impassable by the downpour, which had precipitated exceedingly high waters at river crossings. It was immediately found to be all but impossible to ford the Eastern Branch at the start of the march, and the army was obliged to take a circuitous route across a railroad bridge and pass back into Bladensburg by a narrow plank pathway only wide enough to permit men to march single file. Not until midday were the three regiments, the 7th Rhode Island, 5th New Hampshire, 45th Pennsylvania, and the cavalry able to clear Bladensburg and close ranks. Nevertheless under the direction of a guide the march continued on to Centerville until sunset where they found General Sykes' four regiments already bivouacked. Soon afterwards they were joined by Colonel Miller's 36th Pennsylvania. The march was even more difficult for the cavalry. Colonel Thomas Welch, commander of the unit, would later report that the brigade quartermaster had neglected to turn over to him oats that Howard had purchased at Upper Marlboro, and his horses suffered badly as a consequence. Even worse, foraging as they progressed was especially difficult as "there is scarcely any hay after crossing the Patuxent." [25]

The following day, Howard detached Miller's regiment along with two companies of the 5th New Hampshire and thirty stout cavalrymen under Major Samuel Wetherell to establish a headquarters at Upper Marlboro. The colonel was also instructed to send two companies to Nottingham on the Patuxent and its immediate vicinity in Prince George's. Another was to move westward to Piscataway, and a fourth north to the village of Queen Anne's Town "with permission to make such other distribution of his force as he should deem necessary to carry out the instructions I gave him." With these voting stations and his rear and flank thus secured, Howard proceeded on toward Lower Marlboro, a march of twenty-seven miles, with the rest of his command. [26]

Upon arrival near his destination Howard quickly established headquarters in one of the venerable old landmarks of the county, Patuxent Manor, the estate of the Honorable Thomas F. Grahame, a former Maryland State Senator. [27] On the morning of Tuesday, November 5, while retaining eight companies of the New Hampshire men under Colonel Edward E. Cross at headquarters, the general detached Major Wetherell with one hundred of his own troopers and fifty picked men from the 45th Pennsylvania to St. Leonard's. The balance of the Pennsylvania men under Colonel Welch were dispatched to occupy Prince Frederick. The Rhode Islanders under Colonel Isaac P. Rodman were sent to establish a camp on the outskirts of Lower Marlboro. All received instructions to monitor the polling stations in each of the towns in concert with federal marshals dispatched by Major General Dix for that purpose.[28]

The only commander who varied from his specific instructions was Miller at Upper Marlboro. "I told him to consult with gentlemen in the district," Howard would later report, "as to the best distribution of his force, and as to the best means of preventing an obstruction of the polls by badly disposed men. This he did, and, as will be seen by his report, he caused the oath of allegiance to be administered at two of his precincts. He assures me that at one precinct the deputy marshal sent by Major General Dix's authority caused the same oath to be administered to every voter." [29]

On election day the feared hostilities in Southern Maryland were minimal, undoubtedly owing to the blue clad soldiers standing guard with fixed bayonets at each precinct station. The presumption of fairness was all but trumped by the orderly but unquestionably intimidating presence of armed might. Prominently displayed at every station were printed copies of a proclamation authorized and signed by the commander of the military district requesting all persons to report anyone who had engaged in hostile acts against the United States or who had assisted those already in arms against the nation. All citizens so accused would be obliged to swear an oath of allegiance before voting. Howard, only recently promoted to brigadier general, was a Maine man, a graduate of Bowdoin College and West Point and known to some as "the Christian general" for trying to base his policy decisions on his deep religious convictions.[30] It was thus perhaps not surprising that he had welcomed the warm reception provided by the few Unionists in Calvert County, but pointedly downplayed the few miscreants who had the temerity, some would say foolhardiness, to demonstrate against the military presence. But they were there and offered a welcomed boost to morale.

In Prince Frederick Augustus R. Sollers, who had been sought by Cowdin two months earlier, was arrested but refused to acquiesce quietly to the military. The former congressman was reportedly anything but civil. "He used the most violent and treasonable language," Howard reported, "drew a large knife, and cut to the right and left. He was secured and brought in by Colonel Welch to Lower Marlborough, where he was taken so ill with gout that I could not bring him, but left him on his parole to report at Washington as soon as he is able to move." [31] Ordered to show himself to General Casey, he quickly claimed he had been wronged and requested General Dix to investigate his case.

Sometime later, in a direct appeal to Secretary Seward, Sollers claimed that Howard had been informed, possibly by Colonel Welch, that he and others had formed a plan to "take the polls on the day of the election" and prevent the Union men from voting. The charge, he said, was a pure fabrication. He vigorously claimed that he had taken no part in the election, and never attended a public meeting or expressed an opinion on the issues. As for his son, he had attempted to dissuade the young man from going south and had, he claimed, finally denounced him and refused to have any further contact. [32]

Four more men from old line Calvert County families, Mervin B. Hance, Walter Hellen, William D. Williams, and John Broome, were also charged with treasonable language and carrying weapons at Prince Frederick. They too were promptly arrested and brought to Lower Marlboro where Howard released them "under oath of fealty and that they had not borne arms against our forces." Elsewhere at Lower Marlboro, Colonel Rodman also made several arrests, all being drunk and disorderly men, but subsequently released them. At the St. Leonard's polling station "all went off very quietly without any arrest." [33]

At Port Tobacco the secessionist candidate for the legislature, "Perry" Davis, having been arrested, was brought to General Hooker "for making treasonable speeches during the canvass." However, he made them while running for office in a secessionist district, he assured the general, in which case his election was likely, but once in office he vowed that he would vote against any ordinance for secession if an opportunity presented itself. Hooker deemed it "politic" to release him. "Besides," he noted slyly, "the election was over." [34]

By Thursday morning, November 7 all of Howard's detached forces were ordered to be withdrawn and were soon assembled outside of Lower Marlboro at the Grahame estate for the march back to Upper Marlboro. Four days later the general was able to report on the conclusion of a successful expedition into Calvert County.[35]

General Sykes's operations to prohibit any unforeseen disturbances on the west side of the Patuxent drainage were also generally without incident. Having departed Washington on November 3 with the 5th, 6th, 7th, and 8th New Jersey Volunteers, he was bound for Charlotte Hall. After briefly crossing paths with Howard's force at Centerville, he arrived at his destination at 7 a.m. on November 5 and established camp with the 5th and 6th Regiments under colonels Samuel H. Starr and David Hatfield. Colonel Joseph W. Revere's regiment, the 7th, was detached to occupy Chaptico on the Potomac, approximately ten miles distant. A unit of cavalry under Major Myron H. Beaumont and Captain James E. Harrison, detached from Edward L. Halsted's 40th New York, was dispatched to Oakville near the Patuxent, and twelve miles distant. The 8th New Jersey, under Colonel Adolphus J. Johnson, was sent to Bryantown, eight miles north of Charlotte Hall.[36]

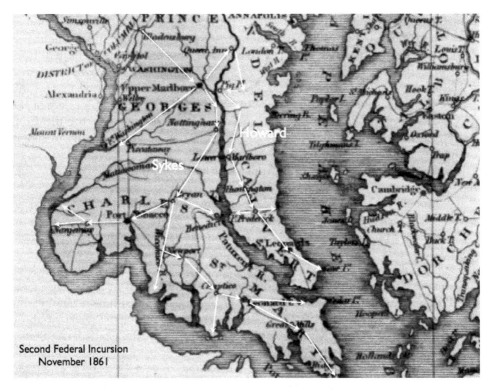

Second Federal Incursion
November 1861

Union incursions into Southern Maryland under Howard and Sykes during the fall of 1861 insured a pro-Unionist outcome of the statewide elections, which Democrats hailed as democracy at the point of bayonets.

As with Howard's operation, the march over roads in terrible condition had been difficult for Sykes's infantry. Yet the brigade behaved better than expected and made good time. Their efforts were not in vain as the elections went on without incident.[37] "The villages in possession of the troops," Sykes later reported, "were election precincts, and on the following day the polls were opened and the elections held without trouble or disturbance. The troops were not permitted to interfere, and the votes registered differed by a very small fraction from the number usually cast. It is believed that not a single inhabitant of that region, soldier or citizen, returned from the Virginia side of the river on the day of the election." [38]

The only incident of note, overseen there by elements of the 36th Pennsylvania, occurred at Nottingham on Election Day. There one M. J. Koldenback was arrested and charged for using treasonable language "and having hurrahed for Jeff. Davis and d....d of Lincoln." For his troubles, he was hauled off to the 13th Street Prison in Washington but later transferred to the Old Capitol Prison, opposite the U.S. Capitol. Not until December 28 was his release ordered by the Secretary of State.[39]

The outcome might easily have gone differently. Before his arrival, Sykes later reported, wild rumors regarding his mission had been circulated throughout the region, inciting alarm amidst the general population. He was informed by various "gentlemen of standing" that had his soldiers been the first to arrive in the area instead of Colonel Dwight's two months earlier, "the feeling towards the Union would have been greatly strengthened." Unfortunately, owing to the confiscation of slaves and horses and the destruction of private property by an unnamed commander under Dwight, many citizens had been completely alienated from whatever affections for the Union they may have had. Others, "who otherwise would have remained home," were driven across the Potomac. Complaints regarding the September incursion were universal. Yet the demeanor and propriety of the New Jersey soldiers quickly put fears (if not a general sympathy for the Confederacy) to rest, at least superficially, and "kindness and a general desire to supply our wants continued during our stay." [40]

In Baltimore the process was anything but pacific, as the Baltimore *Sun* would report:

"Throughout the city, as soon as the polls were opened, the federal police began to make arrests, and continued until all the police stations were filled to repletion. The charges upon which they were arrested were disorderly conduct, holding treasonable tickets near polls, using treasonable language, and attempting to pollute the ballot box by offering to vote treasonable (democratic) tickets, while a few were discharged with having been concerned in the affray of the 19th of April last, and others with having subsequent to that time taken up arms to prevent the passage of Federal troops through the city. Several of those arrested were charged with having been in the army of the Confederate States, and returned to the city for the purpose of participating in the election. In several instances candidates for magistrates and constables were arrested and sent to the police station, and some others were arrested because they declined to take the oath of allegiance to the Federal government. After the authorities commenced making arrests about noon, the polls were generally deserted by the voters of the opposite party, and little voting was done on the democratic side. There was some little wrangling, but no fighting of a serious nature. The parties arrested were mostly released last night, the charges against them not being sustained at their examination." [41]

When the election tally was counted, of the nearly 95,000 registered voters in Maryland, Bradford polled 57,502 votes to Howard's 26,700. He carried all but three Southern Maryland counties, Charles, Calvert and St. Mary's, and Talbot County on the Eastern Shore, where he lost by a single vote. In Baltimore, the most densely populated region in the state, out of 40,000 voters barely 10,000 were permitted to register. Approximately 60,000 Maryland voters, mostly supporters of the opposition estimated one ardent secessionist, had been disenfranchised or intimidated by Union troops stationed at the polls. There were strong protests from the Peace Party and charges that Maryland troops in the U.S. Army, then in the field, were given voting privileges, as were non-Maryland soldiers and sailors stationed in the region. The pretense offered was that they had been in the state long enough to qualify them as state residents.

The requirement that the loyalty oath be administered, as one Annapolitan publisher put it, "whose chief objuration was that the elector had no sympathy for the South or secession" was despised by many. "When these failed to prevent the obnoxious elector from voting, questions, yet more effectual in searching the conscience of the voter, were put until the desired disenfranchisement was accomplished." One incident in Annapolis drew particular attention, when soldiers guarding the Naval Academy grounds were "inspired" that they had the right to vote, and "on being placed on their *voir dire*, two hundred enlisted soldiers of the federal government, non-residents of the State, swore that they had come into the State of Maryland thirteen months previous with the intention of making it their residence." One of the judges of elections in the city received their votes without question.[42]

Countercharges by the Union Army did little to pacify the general population. In the end, though voters at polling stations along the Patuxent and Potomac corridors were unquestionably numerically much smaller than in Baltimore and Annapolis, the results were the same. Augustus Williamson Bradford of Baltimore, an avowed Unionist, along with a General Assembly now populated by a majority of that same party, were swept into power.[43]

Marylanders serving in the Confederate Army at Centreville, Virginia, unable to return home to vote, were determined to have a little mocking fun at the expense of their home state, and resolved to hold an election of their own. "They did so," it was later reported, "going through all the forms of an 'excited contest,' showing 'how things are done in Baltimore,' and electing 'electors favorable to Jeff. Davis as President of the Southern Confederacy.'" [44]

Though the election had been secured with a heavy hand for the Unionists, Southern Maryland was another issue. The Union Army had arrived but this time they would not be leaving. Soon many thousands of men belonging to General Joseph Hooker's troops would occupy the entirety of the Potomac shoreline from Mattawoman Creek to Port Tobacco and then down to Point Lookout with the army's flanks on either side protected by the Potomac Flotilla. The consequences for many white Southern Marylanders would be social and economic devastation.

Despite the opposition of Southern Marylanders, whose many sons had gone off to join the Confederate Army and whose slaves would soon be fleeing in droves, the die had been cast. A resultant decrease in agricultural production, economic decline and the specter of poverty suddenly began to loom large. The *Port Tobacco Times* perhaps best vocalized the white population's protests most diplomatically, without attempting to display any secessionist sentiments, though ignoring recent history. The State of Maryland, noted editor Elijah Wells, "has cast her vote for the Union and Government by the largest majority ever known to this State . . . Charles County then stands before the Government and the world this day as a loyal county. Charles County has ever been loyal; to challenge a disloyal act to be laid at her door – and what is her condition? As a loyal county and State, obedient to the recognized law, faithful to the Constitution, the citizens of this State have a right, an undisputed right to the protection of person and property." [45]

Yet with perhaps as many as 10,000 Union soldiers stationed upon the region's soil in camps extending from Mattawoman to Liverpool Point and beyond, the situation had become desperate. "These troops are here 'For our protection' we are told: 'to protect us from the Rebels,' and yet, in fact, we are exposed to more danger, to more losses and damage or at least as much as if these very Rebels were here. Our farmers are deprived of their provender to such an extent that their cattle must die. Our citizens are deprived of homes almost; and fences, farms, and fields fall prey to the ruthless hands of those very friends who come here to protect us." For Southern Marylanders the worst problem of all concerned the slaves. "Our negroes, – ah, this is the point, – our negroes – are taken from us time and again, with no remuneration and the threats of violence if we seek to recover them." [46]

For thousands of men, women and children of color who had been living in bondage, however, their first glimpse of possible freedom had already begun to show through.

STATIC WARFARE
"The random shooting of the enemy."

"I have found a man by the name of Anderson," reported Captain Robert Williamson of the Topographical Engineers, based near Mattawoman Creek a few days before the elections, "who knows every road and lane about here, and the name and character of each inhabitant . . . He says the rebels knew of our arrival near Budd's Ferry on the day we reached there. He says also it is the intention of the rebels to go from Richmond to the mouth of Aquia Creek by railroad, and then cross over to Smith's Point. This is to be done in a week or two. Mr. Anderson learned this yesterday from a friend who lives 3 miles below Budd's Ferry, and who has a brother in the rebel camp opposite. The two brothers are in constant communication." [1]

It was a disconcerting piece of intelligence but quite similar to many other tidbits of news filtering across to the Maryland side of the Potomac as the crisp, frosty harbingers of fall were setting in.

The blockade of the river, with the Potomac Flotilla now cut in half by rebel batteries controlling the waters from Shipping to Mathias points, was usually one of the major topics of the day in Washington. In Union-held Alexandria an erie silence reigned undisturbed at the city wharves south of King Street. There a handful of coasting craft and pungies were laid up in ordinary waiting the reopening of the river. From time to time an occasional boat might drop alongside a wharf, having been permitted to pass the Confederate works on the river.[2] One such vessel was the Potomac trading schooner *Constitution*, laden with wood, furniture and potatoes, which arrived from Mattawoman at Fowle's Wharf on the night of October 25. As she neared the rebel batteries she had been boarded by men from *George Page*. When an officer came on board, examined her papers, and learned that she was bound to Alexandria from Charles County, known to be secessionist in its temperament, she was freely permitted to proceed without further disturbance.[3]

Such occurrences were rare. For the most part the only signs of life in the vicinity were provided by the occasional passing stroller, a few sedentary fishermen, and sailors aboard the U.S. Brig *Perry* lying quietly in the distance. The only notable activities on the waterfront were the hourly arrivals of steamers from Washington at the King Street wharves. North of that avenue, the U.S. storehouses and the soldiers and employees about them were the only thing preventing the somber appearance of universal desolation. At the foot of Princess Street the USS *Pensacola* sat dark and quiet at her anchorage. Even at the coal wharf at the northern end of the waterfront, usually the busiest place of all, activity had all but died out since the closure of the river.[4] Nevertheless, the Union military presence on both sides of the Potomac was always evident, especially after dusk. Every night from any elevation or tall building in town the campfires of the U.S. forces occupying all the heights in the neighborhood could be seen burning brightly.[5]

Regardless of the ominous intelligence on a possible Confederate invasion of Southern Maryland, Captain Williamson, as befitting an engineer, was pragmatic about the danger. Upon receiving a confidential letter from General Marcy concerning the threat posed by *George Page* and the necessity of sinking her by a battery on the Maryland side, the engineer dismissed both the possibility of a rebel crossing or the significance of the gunboat in such an endeavor. "Our Army occupying this part of Maryland, there is little chance of the enemy attempting to cross the river. The *Page* is not of much importance to either party. The river is effectually closed by batteries from Mathias Point to where our fleet lies. The object of [Union] batteries must be to open the river and destroy the enemy's works." [6]

General Hooker was in agreement with the captain and of the wide ranging ignorance of what exactly was going on along the Virginia shore. While taking the opportunity of reporting on three new rebel batteries opening up on an incoming steamer on October 28, he blithely commented: "While the firing was going on, masses of infantry in the woods behind the batteries were descried from their glittering bayonets – in what numbers I have no means of determining. In this regard the opposite side of the river remains a sealed book to me. I have not been able to find any one able or willing to furnish me with any satisfactory information as to the number of the rebel force opposed to me. On one fact, however, I am most confident, and it is this: that they expect an assault more than they do of delivering one." [7]

The very fact that the enemy was erecting so many batteries indicated to him that they were acting defensively and not about to take the offense. Yet signs to the contrary kept appearing. When a rebel boat bearing a white flag was seen making for the Charles County coast, a party of ten or twelve sharpshooters proceeded down to the bank of the river to provide them with a bloody welcome. Nevertheless the boat stood on her course until within a thousand yards of the Maryland shore, where her men threw overboard a barrel, removed the flag, and retired as rapidly as they could pull. After reaching the Virginia side of the river the flag was flaunted by one of the crew over the battery at Shipping Point. The barrel remained apparently anchored in place. Whether it was thrown over to mark out the channel, serve as a range marker, or was one of the Confederate's new "infernal machines," or floating mines, was an enigma. Commander Craven nervously informed Captain Williamson, among other matters, that the enemy had three depots of boats in the vicinity opposite Budd's Ferry, containing not less than 100 small vessels in each, all manufactured at Fredericksburg and specifically designed for traversing the Potomac. Hooker expressed his belief "that the enemy doubtless intends to slip up the river with them instead of crossing it." [8]

By October 27 a number of field artillery pieces had arrived and were encamped behind the Posey house, including eight 10-pounder Parrott guns that Hooker had been instructed to use against *George Page*. The warship had, unfortunately for the Federals, taken refuge some distance up Quantico Creek. "She is up the river," Hooker reported, "and owing to a bend in it and the high banks make her perfectly safe from any fire we may deliver either on land or water. Indeed, the tops of the smoke pipes cannot be seen from an elevated position behind this bank. The tops of most of the schooners lying with her are scarcely perceptible." Ignoring occasional firing from the rebels across the river, by October 30 work was begun on erecting substantial earthworks and a riverfront battery seventy yards north of the Posey house.[9]

The ground upon which the fort was built under Williamson's direction was deemed favorable and could be approached under cover. It was positioned on an angle of the enemy's main work at Evansport between the guns, which were planted to range upstream and those to fire downstream. It was also directly across the river from *Page*'s anchorage in Quantico Creek. "We could see about three-fourths of the length of her smokepipe and the greater part of her walking beam," noted the general. "Her hull is entirely concealed from view; near to her, but higher up the stream, are two schooners, indicating that the stream is not navigable much above that point. " It was possible the steamer might be able to move a little higher up or down the river, but in neither case would it improve her anchorage. In any event, owing to the terrain, she was as concealed as she could be and presented but a very small target to strike at though possible. Thus the general instructed that construction on a battery to begin immediately, if for nothing more than to shelter the men and guns. "Even if it should not be wanted against the *Page* at her present anchorage, it may some time be of service when she leaves it, if she ever does.Hooker's activities immediately triggered grave concerns amidst the Confederate high command that a Federal offensive was about to begin. While the Union general was contemplating the best position for his own works, General Holmes was writing to Confederate Secretary of War Benjamin that an army spy sent across the river reported that no fewer than 15,000 soldiers and eighty pieces of artillery were being mustered "and the batteries are to be attacked as soon as their vessels can be prepared." [11]

"The ten-pounder battery gun (Federalist) at Budd's Ferry, lower Potomac, opposite the Confederate batteries on the Virginia shore (1861)." *The Illustrated London News* [London]. New York Public Library, New York.

The observation was not without some foundation as Hooker was anxious to take the offensive. Even as battery construction at Budd's Ferry was underway, which was to be connected to Washington by a telegraph line, he broached a proposal to his superiors in Washington for just such an action.

Directly above the main work of the enemy at Quantico was high ground on the edge of the river that he believed could be readily taken. In just one night, with the necessary supply of entrenching tools, it could be put in a condition of defense against three times his own force, which would then command the enemy batteries. With field artillery, he believed he might compel the enemy to abandon their guns the first day he opened fire on them. With these means at his disposal and the assistance of the navy and a number of scows, his command could be transferred to the Virginia side of the river very quickly on any given night to establish a strong foothold. "I can see no other speedy and successful mode of opening the navigation of the Potomac and keeping it open," he informed Adjutant General Seth Williams. "General I am aware of the presence of large bodies of troops in the neighborhood, but they need not know until the next morning, when it will be too late. If my command is insufficient, which I do not believe, sufficient force is close at hand, with water communication, to place the result beyond peradventure. I write of this with great confidence, for the reason that I feel no doubt of its absolute and complete success." [12]

It was a scheme that McClellan, for once, did not outright disapprove. But it was one as impracticable, given the resources at hand, the mobility of the enemy, and ignorance of the enemy positions and strength behind the lines, as any that had hitherto been broached.[13]

∗∗∗

The Budd's Ferry battery of at least two of its 10-pounder Parrott guns opened with stunning surprise on the afternoon of October 31, and much to the chagrin of the crew of *George Page* forced the gunboat to retire nearly two miles up the creek. Hooker had no delusions about sinking the ship at a distance, especially with the small caliber guns at his disposal and soon ordered the firing halted. But it was good practice, and something the rebels, who returned fire erratically and at long intervals, seemed unable to master. "The random shooting of the enemy," he noted regarding the few vessels that now successfully dared to challenge the rebel blockade, "renders it an adventure of comparative safety. My observation is that they are as likely to be struck by lightning as by the rebel shot." [14]

By the onset of November, the rapid increase of Federal troops along the shores of the Potomac in Charles and St. Mary's County, both for defensive purposes and to quell any opposition to the elections, had by some estimates in the press expanded to as many as 30,000 men.[15] Though the numbers were quite inflated, they were in truth enough to deflect for the first time Confederate dreams of an invasion of Southern Maryland, even though rebel reinforcements also seemed to be swelling by the hour. Moreover there was an accelerating Union roundup of local Confederate supporters including Richard Posey's family, Lemuel Hannon, recent widower and father of three small children, the Linton clan, and others suspected of collaborating with the Confederates across the river. Rebel intelligence sources in Maryland were suddenly in jeopardy, especially in the critical Budd's Ferry sector.[16]

By the end of the first week of November, when the rushed Union defenses on the Maryland shores of the Middle Potomac, which had finally been more or less completed, as were those of the enemy on the opposite side, a form of static warfare ensued. Occasionally shots were fired at vessels running the blockade or against the Federals on the Maryland side. A regular system of signals by lights were put in operation every night upon the Virginia shore, and *George Page* remained safely ensconced well up Quantico Creek beside the schooners *Fairfax* and *Mary Virginia*, formerly *Lady Ann*.[17] But little else of notice transpired. Throughout much of pastoral Maryland surrounding the capital city, however, the once tranquil country-side had been replaced by another of martial order. One observer would describe the scene in terms that left little to the imagination.

"The approach to Washington by rail just now presents a very picturesque, but, to a patriot, a mournful sight. All through Maryland the bridges on the railways are guarded by little camps. And as the noise of the train is heard, the men rush out of the tents to the line awaiting their shower of newspapers which is let fall by the passengers, and every drop of which is the object of a friendly scramble. As the train draws nearer to the capital, these camps increase in number and size, till the white canvas frosts every knoll, and gleams through every woodland and glade now coloring with the glorious tint of the autumnal foliage. Monster trains are passed, and the soldiers inside rend the air with yells and shrill cheers. The fields are filled with dark lines of infantry at drill; heavy trucks, laden with guns and munitions of war, block up the sidings, and look sulkily out of their secluded shunting places. On the undulating ground, from which all traces of forest and grove are fast vanishing, are visible immense packs of horses; commissariat camps, long lines of white tilted wagons, cities of mules, and columns of dust seam the sky, and mark the march or evolutions of armed men. Strains of music are heard as the unfinished dome of the Capitol and the spires of the city rise in view, and long stretching lines of tents wind in and out as if encompassing the place in their arms till they fade away in the distance. The air pulsates with the flash of arms in the sunlight, and now and then the booming of guns." [18]

***

With the onset of the autumnal cold and rainy season, a multitude of illnesses began to assail soldiers on both sides. An outbreak of smallpox aboard the USS *Harriet Lane*, at first attributed to escaped slaves brought aboard from Virginia, caused an immediate scare. Sickness was also prevalent in the Washington city jail where no fewer than 194 prisoners were incarcerated, mostly those arrested on charges of supporting the Confederacy in some way or another. General Hooker soon found it imperative to order the establishment of brigade hospitals at various points along his lines. If suitable local accommodations were not available, he intended to have log houses built for the purpose. To shield his troops from the storms of the coming winter he instructed that encampments be erected along the edge of forests to blunt the wind and snow.[19]

From his base at Camp Baker the general was pleased to report on November 8 that the First Brigade of his division had erected its hospitals. But there were, unfortunately, disciplinary problems. The Second Brigade had been gradually concentrating in the vicinity of Sandy Point, about three and half miles south of Budd's Ferry, and just above the northern lip of Mallow's Bay. He stated the reason assigned for such a disposition: "that discipline is so lax in some of the regiments of that brigade that it is necessary for me to see them oftener than I have heretofore been able to do, and, further, the roads are becoming so muddy that it is necessary for me to reduce the hauling as much as practicable to spare the teams." [20] Though more than thirty of thirty-five miles of telegraph line had finally been successfully run from Washington to his base at Camp Baker on the Mattawoman, it was the growing lack of discipline that bothered him the most.[21]

Drunkenness among the soldiers stationed along the Potomac had become one of the most serious problems. On December 5 it was reported that some twenty to thirty soldiers "from the upper camps found their way to Port Tobacco . . . obtained full supply of the 'juice' . . . became rather boisterous and exceedingly annoying to the citizens." A week later, in an effort to stem the problem, Hooker issued General Order No. 12 forbidding the use of alcohol. The core of the problem, it seemed at first, was based at Sandy Point where the too free availability of liquor, in violation of General Order No. 12, was comonplace. An example had to be set. Second Lieutenant George F. Young of the New York Excelsior Brigade, was thus arrested for "Conduct Unbecoming an Officer and a Gentleman." It was soon disclosed that his wife had been selling whiskey from the home of George H. Waters, a resident on the point. Mrs. Young, it was discovered, was employing the Water's house as "a kind of Sutlers Store for the sale of whiskey" to both officers and enlisted men, which caused "great rioting and disorder in the encampment." The business was shut down and Lieutenant Young resigned his commission rather than face charges. But depredations by drunken soldiers continued. With no fewer than forty-one ordinaries and traders licensed to sell liquor in the county in 1860, the abuse of alcohol by the troops should have come as no surprise to Federal authorities. But it did. Near the end of January 1862 one Philip Wedding, a "poor but worthy citizen of Nanjemoy," had his house burned to the ground by a band of drunken soldiers. When he attempted to save his property the assailants beat him senseless in a most brutal manner. Although a squad of cavalry soon arrested the perpetrators the event only served to widen the division between the occupied and the occupiers. The editor of the *Port Tobacco Times* beseeched the citizens of Charles County to refrain from selling liquor to the soldiers. Hooker ordered a captain of the 6th New Jersey Regiment stationed in Port Tobacco to "prevent the selling of alcohol to soldiers" from at least six liquor outlets in the town. But it was a futile undertaking.[22]

The presence of so many troops on lands along the Potomac that many considered to belong to secessionist families could not fail to cause friction and often the destruction of property. One typical case was that of Walter A. Haislip, a resident of Plum Point on Mattawoman Creek, whose property had been employed as a military landing and depot for army stores and occupied by the aides of General Hooker from November 17, 1861 onward into June 1862. In the process Haislip claimed to have suffered every panel of fencing destroyed as well as all of the flowers and shrubs on his premises. His houses were rendered "untenable" and his fishing outfit obliterated as was his 300-foot wharf.[23]

***

Hooker was now convinced that there would be no Confederate invasion of Southern Maryland. Despite the considerable activity in rebel battery construction it appeared that the enemy's forces had been substantially reduced within a matter of days and were indeed in a defensive mode. "They appear to be apprehensive of our crossing the river," he wrote on November 8. "For two nights in succession we have heard the long roll about midnight. Last night it was occasioned by the seizure of some boats along the shore of the Potomac by the First Regiment Massachusetts Volunteers, and the removal of them to the Mattawoman Creek, where they should be used in discharging the steamer." [24]

Hooker's troops were now spread from the Mattawoman down to Sandy Point. Soon to be extended as far southward as Port Tobacco, the line would provide a direct communications link with the lower arm of the Potomac Flotilla. The First Brigade was busily engaged in preparing winter quarters at Camp Baker and about Budd's Ferry. The Second was preparing quarters for the season farther down between Sandy Point and Liverpool Point. Yet the biggest problem in digging in was logistics, the day-to-day difficulties in keeping thousands of men fed, housed and warm for the winter. Though the rail lines between Washington, Baltimore and Annapolis were guarded by three full regiments, it was still no simple matter of getting provisions and other equipage to Hooker's forces, distended along the Southern Maryland shore for nearly ten miles, over the very few extant roads, all of which were in extremely poor condition even in good weather.[25]

On November 5 the USS *Stepping Stones*, the first Federal warship to run the blockade since it began, arrived at Washington with a load of escaped slaves, followed soon afterwards by the USS *Yankee*.[26] But the dangerous challenges to maritime traffic were ever present. Almost daily reconnaissance reports on the ever strengthening line of rebel defenses, batteries, rifle pits, and campsites now filtered into army headquarters, though not all of them were from expeditions approved of by the high command or expected. For the first time since October 21, when Lieutenant Harrell informed Craven of an eighteen-gun battery on Mathias Point, someone in authority decided to verify and test the actual strength of the works.

Colonel Charles Kinnard Graham, commander of the 5th Regiment, Excelsior Brigade, having been ensconced with his unit at Camp Fenton near Port Tobacco, was not a man to sit still. Born in the Ninth Ward of New York City, he had served as a midshipman in the navy during the Mexican War after which he had resigned to pursue a career in engineering. In 1857 he was engaged as a civil engineer at the New York Navy Yard, but upon the outbreak of the war, along with 400 other yard employees, had joined the Excelsior Brigade being formed by Daniel Sickles and was promptly appointed colonel.[27]

Soon after Graham's arrival at Camp Fenton, he had dispatched a number of men from Company I under Captain Arthur Wilkinson to seize several boats on the Port Tobacco River and man them with picked men from the company. The boating parties were immediately employed in reconnoitering the Potomac shore and neighboring creeks and in maintaining "a general surveillance over the move-

243

ments and actions of the secession sympathizers on this shore." Unlike the rivalry emerging between the army and navy elsewhere, Lieutenant Commander Samuel Magaw of *Thomas Freeborn*, and Acting Master Arnold Harris of *Island Belle* frequently assisted Wilkinson. Graham was not one given to lead from behind and vigorously participated onboard the steamers in several of their sorties. Significantly, his impressions gleaned from the findings were in direct opposition to what Lieutenant Harrell had said in his report that resulted in the bifurcation of the Potomac Flotilla.[28]

"I became convinced," Graham reported later, "that there were no batteries at Mathias Point sufficient to oppose the landing of troops. The commanders of the gunboats above named agreed with me in this opinion, and also as to the desirability of a thorough inspection of this point. They very kindly placed their vessels at my disposal for such a purpose." The colonel was about to launch an expedition without seeking permission from Hooker, or even informing him of his intentions.[29]

Sunday evening, November 10 was the time agreed upon for a landing on the point. Unfortunately Commander Magaw was prevented from assisting by Craven. Perhaps it was the commander's concern for the embarrassment it might have caused the service should no battery be found, or even induced by his own inimical regard for the Army. Nevertheless, Acting Master William T. Street of the U.S. cutter *Dana* immediately volunteered himself and his vessel to fill Magaw's place. Without seeking permission from Craven, *Island Belle*, under Acting Master Arnold Harris, with *Dana* in tow ran up Port Tobacco River to Chapel Point where Graham and 400 picked New Yorkers embarked in silence and good order. Then, arriving at Mathias Point without incident, the expeditionaries were landed under the direction of Harris and Street with the goal being to conduct a thorough reconnaissance of the point for several miles around. Master Harris was the first to land, and accompanied by a squad of skirmishers pushed forward and took possession of Custis Grimes's house, another belonging to Benjamin Grimes, and a third occupied by H. Mercer, a tenant. They discovered the Custis Grimes house "so perforated and injured by shells and bombs thrown from the Potomac Flotilla during the last few months that it was entirely untenable," and had not been occupied for some time. All were incinerated along with several barns and stacks of hay. A quarter of a mile from the shore they suddenly came upon a trio of enemy pickets. One of the surprised rebels immediately raised his musket and was about to fire when Harris shot him dead with his revolver. The other two pickets took to their heels. After securing the dead man's musket and the horses of all, the main body of Graham's command, with the colonel in the lead accompanied by his quartermaster, a lieutenant, and John McMillan, master's mate of *Island Belle*, proceeded to conduct a thorough inspection of the point for some four miles. Only two more pickets were encountered, one of whom was wounded in a brief firefight.[30]

"We discovered a few rifle pits and a battery partially masked, but upon which no guns had been mounted," Graham later reported. Beyond that no batteries or troops were to be found except a party of perhaps twenty Confederate cavalry who retreated precipitously as the New Yorkers advanced. Graham soon learned that there was a rebel camp at Hampstead some nine miles away, consisting in part of three pieces of artillery. Acting Master Street offered his howitzer and crew to assist in an attack on the camp, but the colonel deemed it far too risky. In the meantime a large quantity of forage and grain was burned, and more houses belonging to the enemy were captured. Several attempts were made to incinerate the woods on the point but, owing to dampness and the season, met with only limited success. Nevertheless the only earthworks on the point had been unmasked and found harmless. Finally, the sweep down Mathias Neck produced two more unexpected but positive prizes. At an estate named "Liberty," the private residence of Martha C. Stuart, the raiders discovered and captured the elusive George Dent, his son George, Jr., both armed and carrying papers of importance, and another secessionist named McNally, "under circumstances which leave no doubt of their complicity with treason." It was later reported in Fredericksburg that two ladies from Alexandria named Snowden had also been in the house but had managed to escape into the woods, though wearing little more than their nightclothes.[31]

After having completed their reconnaissance the New Yorkers finally withdrew to the beach, reembarked on the gunboats in good order, and reached Camp Fenton at 1 p.m. without loss. They were followed by at least eighty-one runaway slaves, men, women and children, some of whom came on board the gunboats, but a majority in a large launch that they had obtained by unknown means. Fifty of the men would be retained by General Sickles and employed as laborers, while the women and children would be sent on to Baltimore.[32] A few would volunteer their services as spies.

"The successful expedition by so small a force, and upon so important a point," Graham crowed, "cannot fail to have inspired the enemy with fear for the large portion of unprotected coast along the Potomac, and will not fail, I think, to cause them to scatter their forces along the exposed points, and thus prevent them concentrating a large force at any one position." His jubilation was not unanimous as he had conducted the operation without first securing approval from Hooker. For his initiative he was instructed to place himself under arrest and to remain so until excused by General McClellan.[33]

The results of Graham's foray could not long be ignored. Mathias Point was no longer deemed a strategic hazard to navigation, if in fact it had ever been such. Harrell's arm of the flotilla was now able to move upstream in safety and come to anchor off Smith's Point opposite Aquia Creek though the main blockade from Chopawamsic north was still in place. Graham's reconnaissance in force proved to be of significant importance along other lines as well, for it was the first of innumerable successful amphibious incursions into Virginia's lower Potomac frontier to be launched over the coming years from Federal bases in Southern Maryland. The raid had explicitly exhibited for the first time in the Maryland Tidewater the value of the still all too rare cooperation between the Union Army and Navy and the importance of maintaining naval domination of the Potomac. With control of the waters it was now clearly possible to conduct surprise raids and incursions from Southern Maryland against any points along the complex coast of the Northern Neck of Virginia and beyond. They would soon be able to project the Union spear into the weakly defended heart of the rebel hinterland as far south as the Rappahannock and Piankatank rivers. Now as Graham's raid had so clearly demonstrated, Southern

Maryland had become of major value as a potential launching pad for an invasion of Virginia.

Notwithstanding disproving the common wisdom, or perhaps because of it, Colonel Graham's report was not well received by Hooker, who had neither given his approval of the expedition nor was even informed of it until it was completed. "As it appears to have no unfortunate consequence so far as I have learned, I shall not censure him, but in future no operations will be projected without my sanction," he wrote with a touch of acid, "otherwise my command may be dishonored before I know it." [34] That Graham had temporarily provided him with a set of eyes behind enemy lines, an asset for which the general had yearned, seemed to matter little.

Another set of eyes, however, was already on the way – eyes that stood little chance of suffering loss or embarrassing the general in any way.

YOU ARE OF VALUE NOW
"Intelligence on the lightning's wings."

They must have seemed an ungainly looking pair as the two vessels departed the Washington Navy Yard early on the morning of Sunday, November 10. One was a little sidewheel gunboat called *Coeur de Lion*, a name perhaps more befitting a mighty man of war than the lighthouse tender she had once been. The other being towed by the steamer was an eight-year-old coal barge once called *Rotary*. Originally purchased by the navy in August for $150 for service at the yard, she had recently been refitted by Commander Dahlgren for a very special purpose at the express instruction of Secretary Welles – to help provide the eyes behind enemy lines that General Hooker so ardently craved.[1]

The U.S.S. *Coeur de Lion* of the United States Potomac Flotilla. Naval History and Heritage Command, Washington, D.C.

Renamed *George Washington Parke Custis* by the navy, the barge was anything but attractive. She had an overall length of 122 feet, a 14½-foot beam and a 5½ foot depth in hold. Rounded on both ends and of a somewhat oblong shape, she was of a very shallow draft, with a carrying capacity of seventy-five tons in two and a half feet of water, which was capable of being increased in deep water to 120 tons. With no engines, she was entirely dependent for propulsion upon another light draft powered vessel, tug or small steamer. In waters too shoal for towing she could be propelled by large oars or even pushed along with heavy poles into positions of advantage that might otherwise prove inaccessible.

Top: "Prof. T. S. C. Lowe, Civil war balloonist." Bottom: The *George Washington Parke Custis*, the first naval vessel in history purposely adapted for deploying a manned reconnaissance balloon. On November 11, 1861 the aeronaut Thaddeus Lowe's conducted his first seaborne launch from the deck of *Custis* in the airship *Constitution*. Prints and Photographs Division, Library of Congress, Washington, D.C.

Her new mission was to serve under the direction of one of America's most celebrated pioneers in the infant field of aeronautics, Thaddeus S. C. Lowe, showman, promoter, self-proclaimed professor of chemistry and aeronaut extraordinaire. Under Lowe's direction the superstructure of *Custis* had been remodeled by naval shipwrights to suit the requirements of her new service – balloon boat for the new Aeronautics Corps of the United States Army, of which Lowe was now in charge. Their destination was the mouth of Mattawoman Creek, from which Lowe proposed to observe the disposition of Confederate forces on the Virginia shore some three miles away from his mammoth balloon *Constitution* while tethered to *Custis*, but floating well above her.

The *Custis* hull was surfaced with a single flat deck, which provided a substantial horizontal platform for the inflation and ascension of Lowe's balloon. A small deckhouse on the stern had been erected as a headquarters for the aeronaut and his assistants. Moreover the shallow draft and considerable hold area made the vessel admirably suited to balloon operations by furnishing ample space for the stowage and transportation of iron turnings, acid, and other materials and equipment necessary for his portable gas-producing equipment. Owing to her accompanying tow ship she was provided with a swift means of communication and transportation between potential balloon stations all along the Potomac. It had been a long and torturous journey to get to this point where history was to be made, and Thaddeus Lowe may well have perused his exciting past as the two boats moved slowly down the Potomac towards the blockade.[2]

A native of Jefferson Mills, New Hampshire, poorly educated, and largely self-taught, Lowe had from early in his youth been the beneficiary of an unquenchable thirst for learning and discovery. At the age of eighteen he attended a lecture and aerial demonstration on the phenomena of lighter than air gases, specifically hydrogen, rendered by one "Professor" Reginald Dinkelhoff in a traveling balloon show. He became an assistant pilot for the showman's popular balloon rides. Two years later he bought out the show and began to bill himself, though having no actual college education, with the grandiose title of "Thaddeus Sobieski Constantine Lowe, Professor of Chemistry." Within a few years he had become one of the foremost builders, showman and promoters of ballooning in America. As a leading advocate of the potentials of trans-Atlantic flight, he constructed one of the largest balloons in history to that time, a mammoth affair 103 feet in diameter, weighing $2\frac{1}{4}$ tons and capable of lifting twenty tons. On the advice of publishing mogul Horace Greeley he dubbed the balloon *Great Western*, to rival the maiden voyage of the famed steamship *Great Eastern* in 1860. Though the initial test flight of the giant "air ship" from Philadelphia to New Jersey had been a success, his first attempt to cross the Atlantic ended in failure.

Lowe was not deterred. Just two days after Virginia seceded from the Union and on the day of Lincoln's declaration of a blockade of the South, at the suggestion of Secretary Joseph Henry of the Smithsonian Institute he set off from Cincinnati, Ohio, on a test flight in the balloon *Enterprise* bound for the Eastern Seaboard. Regrettably, the flight landed in Unionville, North Carolina where he was arrested as a Federal spy after making a trip of 900 miles. Fortunately able to identify himself as a man of science, he was released and sent home to Ohio. It would probably have been well for the Confederacy had they held him: soon after his return he received a summons to Washington from Secretary of the Treasury Salmon P. Chase to test his airship's "adaption to the great work in which we were engaged." The government, it seemed, needed both him and his balloon. As early as 1794 balloons had been successfully deployed on military reconnaissance missions by the French at the Battle of Fleuros and as recently as 1859 at the Battle of Solferino during the revolution in Italy. And if it was good enough for the Europeans, some planners thought, it most certainly could be of equal utility to the U.S. Army! [3]

Lowe was not the only aeronaut to come to Washington. Noted balloonist John LaMountain had also appeared, as did John Wise, and the brothers Ezra and James Allen, to compete for federal contracts and development of a military aeronautics corps. What they did not have was Lowe's promotional acumen and uncanny capacity to adapt to any situation. He was prepared to inflate his aircraft from public utility coal gas mains, hydrogen field generators, or jury rigged barrels of sulfuric acid and metal shell casings. His greatest contribution to aeronautics technology, which would later set him apart, was a portable and reliable hydrogen gas generator, or "gasometer" as it was called in the press, of his own design. The unit permitted his balloons to accompany the army wherever necessary and be inflated in the field in a very short time. Moreover, his new fawn colored seventy-five-foot tall, thirty-eight-foot diameter balloon was constructed, unlike those of his rivals, of double folds of extremely fine Chinese silk called Pongee, coated with four layers of varnish to prevent leakage and to withstand the wear and tear of campaign conditions. When fully deployed with ropes and passenger car, the *Enterprise* presented a most imposing sight to see, 100 feet tall and fully capable of ascending 1,000 feet or more into the atmosphere and remaining inflated for several days.[4]

***

On the afternoon of June 9, 1861 the first of Lowe's rivals appeared in Washington. James Allen was thus the earliest off the mark to demonstrate his own balloon, "a large oiled one," thirty-five feet in diameter and seventy-five feet in height from the car to the top. A former principal in the firm of Allen & Hunt but now a member of the Rhode Island Marine Artillery, Allen was an experienced aeronaut and rumored by some to have already been appointed aeronautical engineer by the government and charged with "taking observations of the enemies camps, movements, &c." The balloon was inflated from a public city gas main at the corner of Massachusetts Avenue and 3rd Street in the presence of a crowd attracted by the unusual sight. Once filled, it was promptly moved to the camp of a Rhode Island regiment near Glenwood, where it was then sent up to a considerable height. Soon afterwards it was prematurely announced in the press, based upon another rumor, that one Major Meyer, an army signal officer, was to have the super-intendence of the balloon as well as all other apparatus of the kind employed by the army.[5]

Lowe was not dismayed by the camp gossip though he would soon learn that the U.S. military was already beginning to play the competitors off against each other for Army contracts. Yet, the New Hampshire balloonist had his own contacts in very high places that might help offset the competition. On June 6 Secretary of War Cameron requested Lowe's patron, Professor Joseph Henry, to examine the aeronaut's apparatus and make scientific observations and assessments on his flights. On June 11 Henry, who had his own interests in the scientific potentials of balloon flight, introduced Lowe to the President of the United States. The aeronaut then began to field his balloon at personal expense to provide the Smithsonian's chief executive with all the scientific "rehearsals" he desired, taking the balloon up under many adverse conditions. Over the next few days numerous ascensions would be made from the grounds of the Smithsonian, the lawn of the White House, and in other environs of Washington, to satisfy the distinguished scientist as to its practical and military value. But it was the president that Lowe first needed to impress and Henry made it possible.[6]

Lowe's pivotal demonstration for President Abraham Lincoln, which was to be conducted on June 17, would be unlike any other hitherto attempted. For the first time a direct telegraphic connection from a soaring balloon to the earth would be tested, and not to just any convenient site on terra firma but directly to the White House. The flight, as extraordinary as it was, barely made the newspapers. "ARMY BALLOONING," read one small headline in the story lead.

"Prof. Lowe made his first experimental ascension on Tuesday, from the Armory grounds [now the National Air and Space Museum]. Messrs. Burns, of the [American] Telegraph Company, and Robinson, the operator [of the telegraph], accompanied him. The latter had charge of the aerial end of an exceedingly small Helix wire, insulated with green silk, and connected with the regular lines. An operator below repeated the message from the air after it had been transmitted through a mile of this helix wire. The White House, the War Department, Alexandria, and the Philadelphia office were communicated with."

From 450 feet above the earth in the airship *Enterprise*, the first message ever telegraphed from a balloon was sent to the Chief Executive of the United States. Though mundane in actual content, its importance to the new field of aerial military reconnaissance was monumental.

"*To the President of the United States:*

SIR:—This point of observation commands an area nearly fifty miles in diameter. The city, with its girdle of encampments, presents a superb scene. I take great pleasure in sending you this first dispatch ever telegraphed from an aerial station, and in acknowledging my indebtedness to your encouragement for the opportunity of demonstrating the availability of the science of aeronautics in the military service of the country.

Yours respectfully,

T.S.C. LOWE"[7]

The message was clear. Now, with the aid of a telescope, the use of the balloon might enable the commander of a military force to thoroughly inspect the interior lines of the rebels opposed to him, "and to know instantly any movements of troops of the enemy; and that, too, without the slightest danger to those making the observation and transmitting the required intelligence on the lightning's wings." Lincoln was impressed and immediately sent for the aeronaut. He insisted Lowe spend the night in the White House to discuss his plans.

"The President was intensely interested in my outline of the proposed Aeronautic Corps," the balloonist later recalled fondly. After the departure of the chief executive's secretaries and assistants the two men discussed the possibilities of the service and the details of its potential operations well into the night. Lincoln was especially interested in Lowe's plan for directing artillery fire on an enemy that the gunners themselves could not see. The president's quiet delight in the concept served only to enliven Lowe's spirits even more. "I [was] almost too excited to sleep, so enthused was I at the prospect of being directed to form a new branch of the military service. After breakfast the following morning, the President directed his Secretary to give me a letter of introduction to Lieutenant General Scott stating the object of my visit, and that the plans proposed had the President's endorsement." [8]

The meeting with Scott, at that time still senior commander of the U.S. Army, did not go well. It was clear from the beginning that the crusty old general, totally immersed in old school warfare, had no interest in either an aeronautics corps or Lowe.[9]

Nevertheless the aeronaut wisely continued his aerial feats for other important military commanders and men of influence. Two days after the demonstration for the president, now putting to good use his years of experience as a showman, he began his publicity campaign. "Considerable curiosity was excited this morning," it was noted in the evening newspapers, "by the ascension of Prof. Lowe's balloon from the grounds of the President's House. The Professor spent some time in taking up his friends and others fond of aerial rides, who enjoyed a fine view of the surrounding encampments." [10]

The flights helped spur the interest of both the public and the army. Indeed, the next day Lowe and his balloon were ordered aloft at 4 p.m. from the lawn of the White House to make his first actual military observations of the enemy across the Potomac in Fairfax, Virginia. A light northerly wind prevailed and the balloon, with a rope and telegraphic wire attached, floated gently across the river, attaining a substantial altitude. The country beyond Federal lines seemed to be dotted with the enemy's troops, and at several points they appeared in considerable numbers. Far on the horizon to the westward, could be seen a large body of soldiers believed to be a portion of the enemy moving down from the direction of Harpers Ferry. Several dispatches were sent to the military command during the flight. Soon after his descent Lowe personally reported his findings to the War Department. The following day Secretary Henry made his final and very positive report on the Lowe balloon to Secretary of War Cameron.[11]

Lowe refilled *Enterprise* from a Washington Gas Company main on the afternoon of June 22, 1861. After receiving a telegram from Captain Amiel Weeks Whipple of the Topographical Engineers directing him to bring the apparatus to Arlington, he moved the balloon, fully inflated, across the Long Bridge to meet the officer at Arlington House, Robert E. Lee's late residence. He immediately set off and with the assistance of a detachment from the 8th New York Infantry arrived there a few hours later. That evening Lowe made his first ascent from Virginia soil. By 4 a.m. the next morning the aeronaut and his balloon were on the road again, this time to an observation point at Falls Church suggested by General McDowell, who had learned that some 20,000 Confederates were massing between Fairfax Court House and Manassas, Virginia. Following a short ascent at Baileys Crossroads to determine whether or not rebel pickets were blocking the route, the party proceeded to its next destination. A series of aerial reconnaissance voyages, ascending as high as 1,000 feet, were made over the next two days. Topographical engineers and other officers who accompanied the aeronaut on several flights made sketch maps of enemy positions. All were impressed. Discussions were soon convened with officials about contracting for the construction of a dedicated military aircraft, of which the balloonist heartily approved.[12]

The balloon reconnaissance expedition into Virginia proved of immediate tactical value to the army. Upon Lowe's arrival in Falls Church and first observation aloft he "discovered scattering camps in the vicinity of Fairfax Court House – one of about twenty tents," against which a company of Union cavalry and several more of Connecticut infantry were sent. Then with his balloon fully inflated and amidst a violent storm, he managed to bring himself and aircraft safely back to Fort Corcoran. The fort had been erected in May 1861 on Arlington Heights as one of several works constructed to secure the Virginia end of the Potomac Aqueduct Bridge in Barnard's ring of fortifications.[13]

Even with endorsements from some prominent members of the military and the Smithsonian, Lowe learned to his dismay on June 27 that the contract for a military balloon was probably to be awarded to another competitor. The rival was John Wise, whom he considered little more than just another balloonist who possessed neither "the least idea of the requirements of military ballooning nor the gift of invention which later made it possible for me to achieve success." [14] To add insult to injury he was also informed that he "might be employed" to operate Wise's balloon. "I replied," he later informed Secretary of State Edwin M. Stanton, "that I would not be willing to expose my life and reputation by using so delicate a machine, where the utmost care in construction was required, which should be made by a person in whom I had no confidence." [15]

In the meantime Lowe persevered, having his balloon revarnished and repaired on the grounds of the Smithsonian and then, knowing full well the value of good publicity, taking members of the press on ascents.[16]

One such aerial excursion received inordinate attention in the pages of the *Evening Star*, one of the leading newspapers in the capital. Under the headline "Taking a Risk," one journalist, thoroughly animated by the experience, was struck by the wonder of it all. "Yesterday afternoon," he wrote,

"Prof. Lowe was exercising his balloon in the clouds for the benefit of those who were solicitous of an aerial trip, and were willing to pay their proportion of the gas bill. The fare was not high considering the expense of an inflation, and all who went up, we believe, held that they fully got their money's worth. It was our good fortune to participate in one of these trips. We liked it, rather, and vote for the 'air line' above all other modes of travel. Up we slid 500 or 1,000 feet into the evening sky, with so placid a motion that our vehicle seemed stationary and the earth sinking away from us. It was wonderful to see the people beneath, dwarf in proportions to squat Lilliputian figures, and it was odd to hear their voices 'simmer down' from the coarse huzzah to the faintest bee-like hum. Thus we began to notice the extreme beauty of the basin in which Washington lies, as seen from commanding points about that city. Just beneath us were the graceful sinuosities of the Smithsonian drives and walks, and [Andrew Jackson] Downing's admirable plan of these grounds was seen for the first time as a comprehensive whole. Then there was the checkerwork and radii of our city's system of streets all unfolded, with horses and vehicles creeping along insect like. Elsewhere the stately Potomac was seen stretching far into the distance southward till attenuated to a silvery thread. On the Virginia shore the white tents of the encampments stood out in minute dotted relief from the background of verdant foliage-draped hills. To the East of North could be seen bright flashes and puffs of smoke, showing where the Rhode Island boys were practicing their batteries. At this time an open umbrella, dropped from the balloon, sailed down parachute fashion, taking its time to reach the earth; and soon after we made our descent in the same tranquil frame of mind. On stepping out the sensation was something like getting down from skates after some tall sport on the ice – terra firma seemed decidedly flat and commonplace to the tread. Yes, we vote for the 'airline' and want no better conductor through the blue etherial than Prof. Lowe." [17]

While Lowe wooed the press and continued to charm the public his rivals were vexed with failures. When James Allen was called upon to conduct a reconnaissance of a rebel position near Washington, his first attempt to inflate his balloon on July 14 failed owing to the malfunction of his primitive gas generator and an inexperienced crew of assistants. Then, while the half-filled balloon was being towed back to army headquarters at Falls Church assisted by a crew of New York Zouaves, control was lost when a gust of wind caused it to crash into a telegraph pole. "There was a puff of gas," noted one observer, a lieutenant named Henry Abbott, "and our work was ended." And so were Allen's chances of becoming "Chief Aeronaut" of the U.S. Army.[18]

But the status of Wise was still unknown, and as forces for the coming great Battle of Manassas began to gather Lowe found his balloon again in demand. "I was suddenly required by Captain Whipple to fill my balloon and transport it into the interior of Virginia," he recalled. Though the balloon in question was not specifically intended for military deployment, he concluded to do the best he could and accordingly set about making the necessary preparations for the voyage. But difficulties immediately ensued. When all of the preparation had been completed, he discovered that Captain Whipple had been called away on other duties before being able to procure handlers, means for inflation, and transportation to bring his airship to the front. After seeking the advice of friends, Lowe concluded to inflate the balloon and procure men for its transportation on his own account, never doubting that his services would be properly appreciated. Then, to his great chagrin he was informed by the director of the local gas company that another balloon had just arrived, this one belonging to John Wise, and was to be deployed instead of his own. Undoubtedly miffed, he immediately removed his balloon from the inflating pipes, to which they had just been attached, and ceased all further work.

When news of the fight arrived it wasn't good. On Sunday morning, July 21, Lowe was informed that the Wise balloon had proved a total failure durig the battle. Urged on by "several patriotic individuals, and hoping still to render some service to the army at Centreville or Manassas," he immediately set about to inflate and transport his airship, and by evening, with the aid of Colonel William F. Small of the 26th Pennsylvania Volunteers, who furnished him with twenty soldiers from his command to assist, he was en route to Virginia.[19]

Unfortunately, upon arriving at Falls Church, Lowe was informed of the retreat then underway of General McDowell and his army from Manassas. At 4:30 p.m., July 22, amidst a driving wind and rain, he began his own retreat toward Arlington. By 8 p.m., with his airship still fully inflated, he had managed to reach Fort Corcoran, a distance of twenty miles, in spite of the storm. With frightening rumors of a Confederate march on Washington circulating at an accelerating rate, he made another ascent on July 24 and, to the relief of everyone, disproved them all.[20]

Lowe was excited when informed that the Bureau of Topographical Engineers had formally decided to adapt the balloon for military purposes despite the noninterest of General Scott. Then, when word again arrived that the enemy was marching on Washington (which proved erroneous) he made another ascent. This time he went aloft in an untethered free flight that provided an excellent view of the Confederate positions between Manassas and Fairfax. Unfortunately, to avoid a fusillade of gunfire by Union troops who supposed his airship to be a rebel balloon, he was forced to land in a grove of trees on or near the venerable Gunston Hall plantation, once home to the great Revolutionary War patriot George Mason, but behind enemy lines. The site was two and a half miles from the forwardmost Federal lines. In an amazing rescue effort, both he and his balloon were saved by his devoted wife, the beautiful former Parisian actress Leontine Augustine Gaschon. Disguised as an old hag, she had boldly driven a covered wagon through rebel pickets to find him before the enemy could. With the aid of the 31st New York Volunteers, all were returned battered but intact to Washington.[21]

The following day Lowe was again summoned to the White House to spend another evening with Lincoln. As the president was fully conversant on the subject, the aeronaut immediately suspected that Secretary Henry of the Smithsonian had already related to him of the difficulties with the army. With the military seemingly playing all of the balloonists off against each other and General Scott's view that the creation of an Army Department of Aeronautics was a total waste of time and money, the situation seemed intractable. Stragglers were still coming into Washington from the Federal catastrophe at Manassas; Lincoln was convinced "that had General MacDowell [*sic*] had the information that only observations from a balloon could give, the result might have been different."

They were seated at an old table in Lincoln's work room when the president said: "Professor I wish you would confer with General Scott again at once," and took out a card and wrote something on it to be presented to the army commander in person. But when Lowe visited the general he was again rebuffed and denied an audience, not once but four times. Upon reporting on the snub to the president, the aeronaut would later write, "he looked at me a moment, laughed, arose and seizing his tall silk hat bade me 'come on.' He proposed to find out what was the matter with Scott."

Upon reaching Army headquarters both men were met by the guard who turned out as the sentry called briskly "The President of the United States." An orderly saluted and within seconds they were in the presence of the old general, who was entirely startled by their unexpected appearance.

"General," said the President, "this is my friend Professor Lowe, who is organizing an Aeronautic Corps for the Army, and is to be its Chief. I wish you would facilitate his work in every way, and give him a letter to Captain Dahlgren, Commandant of the Navy Yard, and one to Captain Meigs, with instructions for them to give him all the necessary things to equip his branch of the service on land and water."

Thaddeus Sobieski Constantine Lowe, Professor of Chemistry, now had a new title: Chief of the Corps of Aeronautics of the United States Army.[22]

By August 2 Lowe had secured a contract to construct the first of a squadron of military balloons and set out for Philadelphia to begin production. By August 28 it was being reported that he had completed *Union*, a 25,000 cubic foot aerostat, his first aircraft designed specifically for military service, which was to be inflated at the Columbian Armory near the Smithsonian before reporting to Fort Corcoran.[23]

Aware that it would be impossible to have telegraphic connections on every reconnaissance, Lowe resorted to a simple but reliable scheme dubbed "The Paper Express" for passing information from sky to earth. "He has it so arranged as to take up an army officer," it was reported, "who will make the observations, and write out all the details on paper. The paper will be rolled up into a ball, a bullet tied to it, and fastened to a ring. It will be rund [*sic*] down a cord to be stretched from the balloon to the ground. The telegraph wire can also be used, but it renders it necessary to have a third person up to operate the instrument, and the paper express can be used with sufficient rapidity." [24]

Enterprise commenced with her first mission from the grounds of Arlington House on August 29 as the first official aircraft of the U.S. Army. She would make no fewer than twenty-three flights over the next thirty-four days, occasionally with rebel troops firing both shot and shell in futile attempts to down her. "The machinery of Mr. Lowe's ascension," reported the *New York Daily Tribune*, "consists of 1,000 feet of rope, a pulley made fast to a tree, a down pulling power of thirty men, and a guard of riflemen scouting the woods near his operations." [25]

The value of the balloon as a reconnaissance tool was finally being recognized by the army high command. On September 5 Lowe conducted an ascension from Fort Corcoran with generals McDowell and Fitz John Porter. Two days later another flight lasting two hours was made with none other than General McClellan himself. Many other generals such as John H. Martindale, William F. Smith, and Samuel P. Heintzelman would follow. As a result of McClellan's observation of the enemy lines a successful one mile advance of Federal pickets against forward rebel positions was made the following morning. On September 9 Brigadier General Porter would inform the aeronaut: "You are of value now." [26]

***

As he listened to the steady, rhythmical thumping of *Coeur de Lion's* paddles striking the water, while studiously watching the shores of Maryland and Virginia pass slowly by, Thaddeus Lowe may have considered the flight with General McClellan another turning point in his career. By mid-September the aeronaut had established his first formal military balloon camp adjacent to Fort Corcoran, from which he had been able to track almost hourly the position and motions of the enemy. "The establishment of a camp," it was noted in the press, "with all the necessary paraphernalia for conducting these reconnaissances, has heretofore been unheard of. General McClellan, McDowell, Brigadier General Porter and others of our officers, have availed themselves of the facilities thus afforded for perfecting plans of defense and attack, and they have now placed the balloon at the head of all the appliances of the Engineer Corps." [27]

When necessary, *Enterprise* was brought over the Long Bridge into Washington by way of Fourteenth Street, and taken to the gasometer in the First Ward where she was reinflated. She was then taken back to her base by way of Bridge Street, Georgetown, and the Alexandria Aqueduct. The whole operation, managed by Lowe's assistants, with Lowe in the car at all times "looking out for the safety of his charge," was efficient and impressive in the eyes of the military command.[28] For the first time the resilient aeronaut had conclusively established that the air reconnaissance service, when capably managed, could be reliable and continuous in the field.

Lowe was tireless. Somehow amidst seemingly endless ascensions he was able to finally submit his plan for the construction of a regular Balloon Corps. In completed form the plan called for four balloons, two of 20,000 cubic foot capacity and two 30,000 cubic foot models. Portable gas generators of his own design would allow field operations without need of a formal supply center. General Porter immediately forwarded Lowe's recommendations to McClellan.[29]

The aeronaut's services were now in demand as never before. When McClellan received a request from General Smith soon after reading Porter's recommendation that Lowe be permanently attached to his division, he acted quickly. Now, yet another revolutionary, never-before-tried use for aerial reconnaissance was about to begin.[30]

At 8:30 a.m., September 24 Smith intended to bombard Confederate earthworks in Falls Church and Munson's Hill from his batteries at Fort Corcoran and wished to have his artillery fire directed from Lowe's balloon. It would be the first aerial directed bombardment of an unseen enemy in history. The location of each shell explosion was to be telegraphed by flag signals to determine which shot fell short, overshot, or veered to right or left. "If we fire to the right of Falls Church, let a white flag be raised in the balloon; if to the left, let it be lowered; if over, let it be stationary; if under, let it be waved occasionally." The demoralizing effect of the subsequent well directed bombardment was devastating to the Confederate psyche. Without the ability to respond in kind or to destroy with ground fire the craft from which the attack was directed, the rebel command was more than dismayed.[31]

The success of the operation was apparent. General Beauregard was obliged to issue orders to camouflage earthworks and take other hitherto unnecessary measures to counter balloon observations and artillery spotting aided by telegraphic communications, flags, and the "Paper Express."[32] On the day following the attack Lowe was authorized to build the four balloons for which he had submitted plans, varying from thirty-one to thirty-five feet in diameter at the widest part, and including the cords and basket, about one hundred feet from top to bottom. He would also build portable gas generators for each. He quickly engaged approximately twenty persons, mostly women, in the construction and sewing program at

Philadelphia. Soon afterwards, much to the ultimate consternation of the Confederacy, another two smaller balloons were added to the order. In the meantime he also engaged in building a reliable corps of experienced balloonists, including William Paullin and Ebenezer Seaver, as well as ground support personnel for upcoming operations.[33]

By November, after a short time in Philadelphia to oversee the construction of the first squadron of the United States Army's infant Aeronautics Corps, Lowe was back in Washington with five balloons. These were to be distributed as follows: one with the Potomac Flotilla, three along the Federal lines in Northern Virginia, and one to be anchored in the river aboard the *Custis* at Mattawoman, to make reconnaissance flights and monitor the movements of the rebels on the Virginia shore. For the management of the five balloons, sixteen wagons, eighty-five horses and 600 men, exclusive of those on the boat, were to be employed. Lowe, with one of his balloons, would personally join General Joseph Hooker's command on the Potomac.[34]

***

Coeur de Lion, with the *G. W. P. Custis* under tow, skimmed down close to the Southern Maryland shore off Cornwallis Neck on the approach to Mattawoman Creek. The Confederate forts either built or under construction at Freestone Point and Cockpit Point were clearly discernable. For Thaddeus Lowe, accompanied by assistant aeronaut William Paullin and crew, and aided by a detachment of the 72nd New York Infantry, the test to come would be of singular importance. Only once before had a reconnaissance balloon flight been launched from a military vessel, and that was by John LaMountain, one of Lowe's early rivals. LaMountain's balloon deployment had been fielded from the little Union tugboat *Fanny* at Hampton Roads on August 3 to observe rebel batteries at Sewell's Point, Virginia. Lowe's flight, however, would be the first from a vessel specifically adapted for the purpose of fielding aircraft, which many historians would later claim constituted America's first true aircraft carrier.[35]

Tensions were undoubtedly taut on the Mattawoman as Lowe and his crew prepared on that same afternoon, Monday, November 11, for their first ascension from a dedicated vessel afloat, this time in the new balloon *Constitution*. Between 9 and 11 o'clock that same morning the rebel batteries on the opposite shore were in active operation as usual. When three schooners passed up river under a six-knot breeze, thirty-seven heavy guns were discharged to dispute their passage, though without effect. "They do fire wretchedly," General Hooker wrote that same evening with some derision. "Whether it is owing to the projectile or to the guns I am not informed. Several of the pieces are rifled, but they seem to throw more *wildly*, if possible, than the smooth bores. From what was witnessed today and on previous occasions, I am forced to the conclusion that the rebel batteries in this vicinity should not be a terror to any one." [36] He would later be quoted in the *Evening Star* as deriding the blockade itself, stating "that any vessel of any size may now conveniently run the blockade of the Potomac, the chances being fifty to one that they will not be hit, and five hundred to one that if hit no material damage will be done." [37]

Hooker's views regarding the poor rebel firing were probably of small consolation to Lowe, who was to ascend from *Custis*, at anchor in Mattawoman Creek, at 8 p.m. that same evening. The rebel firepower for all of its shortcomings was indeed enormous, and any single lucky shot could easily bring down his balloon. This time he would be accompanied not only by Paullin but by General Daniel Sickles who would ascend with him to an altitude of 1,000 feet.[38]

That evening the view of the Virginia shore, which was liberally sprinkled with the lights of thousands of enemy campfires, was stunning. The balloon was wafted almost directly over some of the rebel camps, which presented evidence of the strong enemy presence behind the waterfront. His observations showed campfires of the Confederates along the rear of their coastal line of batteries for ten or twelve miles in the direction of Manassas, as far as Dumfries and on the Occoquan, indicating the enemy in force in that vicinity as well. Here finally were the eyes for which General Hooker had cried and the ability to see beyond the menacing batteries that had all but closed the Potomac to traffic and threatened the shores of Southern Maryland. Now the spread and depth of rebel defenses, roads, camps, and artillery that backed up the river blockade could be seen for the first time. Lowe, as usual, was relatively restrained in his recall of the evening, noting simply, "We had a fine view of the enemy camp fires during the evening and saw the rebels constructing batteries at Freestone Point." [39]

The following day the aeronaut made several more ascents, but Hooker who seemed to have been less than impressed with his new set of eyes, deemed the Mattawoman station too far removed from the enemy's works to be of any value. He resolved to move the airship to a post near Posey's house at Budd's Ferry, three miles downriver and near his own headquarters on November 13. As the enemy appeared to be busily engaged during the day in the establishment of new batteries in the vicinity of Widewater, across from Sandy Point, the general also planned to expand the balloon's operational range to a locality still farther south. His picket line already reached Liverpool Point, with regular patrols being sent down as far as Maryland Point at the southern tip of Charles County. In the meantime McClellan ordered Lowe to deploy three other balloons to various theaters of strategic importance, even as the aeronaut returned briefly to Washington leaving Paullin in charge.[40]

The move to keep watch on the latest possible battery development farther down the Virginia side of the Potomac was not without justification. With the blockade endangering Hooker's direct river supply line to Washington, the general decided to establish a landing facility at Liverpool Point, a mile south of Sandy Point, to which supplies could be hauled around by water in transports from Annapolis. He thus ordered a number of privately owned scows to be confiscated and hauled up to Liverpool Point for use as lighters. He also requested that signal rockets be forwarded to his pickets at Sandy Point, "that I may, in case the *Page* should attempt to escape at night, convey the information to the flotilla below." [41]

In the meantime Lowe's flights from Southern Maryland shores were causing no end to confusion and concern among the Confederate command on the opposite side of the river. "Those balloon ascensions," said General Beauregard with some frustration, "indicate either offensive or defensive movements, most probably the former." But he could never be certain. The balloon ascensions on

November 12, 13 and 14, conducted in Lowe's absence by Paullin, were revealing. They readily disclosed strong enemy batteries at Shipping Point and at various locales along the river for a full four miles to the south, though an accurate count was impossible as some had been masked. Moreover, Confederate campsites extended in an almost continuous line parallel to the shoreline.[42]

The value of balloon reconnaissance flights was soon proven, though Hooker gave scant acknowledgment to the aeronaut or his aircraft. Nor did he apparently bother to venture skyward as had his fellow generals and senior commander, McClellan. Yet in one report on the disposition of rebel forces can be seen the handiwork of the balloonist without whom the data gathering would have been impossible, but to whom little notice was given. "The main body of the enemy's forces visible," reported Hooker,

"are stationed in rear of the batteries between Quantico and Chopawamsic Creeks. Two regiments appear to be posted near each other on the banks of the Quantico, and one regiment about one-third of a mile to the south of them. In rear of the former, in the valley extending towards Dumfries, are a long line of encampments, and a valley making off from that at Quantico at nearly right angles in a southerly direction is also occupied with camps. To the observer on this side of the Potomac all hills covered with forests but conceal a line of smoke rising above them. Farther to the south other camps can be seen at intervals of a mile or more. On the north of Quantico Creek, and behind a bold hill, is another camp of infantry, cavalry, and a field battery; all of these showed themselves the day we had the contest for the schooner. . . It is within a week that the rebels have established the camp at its base farthest from the Potomac . . . Nearly in rear of Cockpit Point is another infantry encampment." [43]

As his services were now in great demand it seemed inevitable that Thaddeus Lowe would eventually be summoned back to Washington for reassignment. With winter coming on and the Potomac blockade in a seemingly stagnate standoff, the aeronaut would soon be deployed elsewhere, leaving behind Ebenezer Seaver in command of one of his balloons for continued service under General Hooker.[44]

The invasion of Southern Maryland now seemed no longer likely and the effects of the blockade not quite so frightening. Hooker was now more than positive in his view of the situation. "The rebels will certainly abandon their purpose of claiming the navigation of the Potomac by means of the batteries now in position ere long," he wrote on November 22. "They must see that it is labor in vain. Of late the large number of vessels have passed and repassed at night, and no effort has been made to check them. Thus far their labor has been equally fruitless during the day." [45]

Though Thaddeus Lowe had been reassigned, he would provide a continuing stream of valuable information during the coming months of war in other theaters. One of his much vaunted balloons, under Paullin's and later Ebenezer Seaver's management, would continue to serve the Union Army along the shores of Southern Maryland. The operations were, as always, not without hazard no matter who was managing the craft. On November 30, while Seaver was engaged in a dangerous reconnaissance from Budd's Ferry, the screw of a shell fired by a Confederate battery across the river struck the car of the balloon, fortunately without causing damage.

Nevertheless observations continued and a draftsman was sent up to draw a map of the enemy's position. Six days later it was formally announced that an "Army balloon corps" had been officially formed. On December 8 Colonel Small of the 26th Pennsylvania, made an ascent to 700 feet with Paullin to observe Confederate positions on and adjacent to Quantico Creek. He may have done so with some trepidation for only the day before, an ascent had generated a stunning reaction from the rebels resulting in a general fire fight between Union and Confederate batteries. From his camp at Quantico, E. O. Perry of the 1st Texas Regiment, recorded: "The Yankees hoisted a balloon this evening just across the river. Our batteries commenced throwing bombs at it when quite a cannonading took place between our batteries and the Yankee batteries. What the result was I know not." [46]

Lowe would inform Washington that same day: "Colonel Small while up with the balloon made a very fine map of the enemy's works and surrounding country, a copy of which is being prepared, and will be forwarded to headquarters." The panoramic map, detailing the Virginia landscape, enemy batteries, troop positions, and topographic features from Chopawamsic Creek to Freestone Point, a distance of seven miles, was an incredible example of just how a manned aerial vessel could be employed for intelligence purposes. Small's close estimate of enemy troop strength of 12,000 men was made by comparing the smoke from campfires and the number of enemy tents with those of Hooker's own forces.

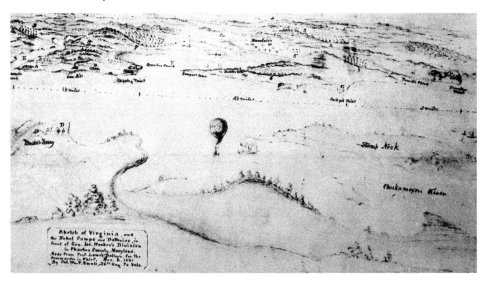

"Map drawn December 8, 1861 by Colonel William F. Small, 26th Pennsylvania Infantry, from the balloon, Constitution, showing Confederate batteries, camps, and terrain from Chopawamsic Creek to Freestone Point." National Archives, Washington, D.C.

On December 11 it was announced in the Alexandria press: "Eight ascensions have been made by Prof. Lowe's balloon, near Budd's Ferry, and opposite the Confederate batteries. A topographical engineer is engaged in making a fine map of their fortifications, showing every point in detail. Another balloon was placed on board a canal boat, and dispatched to the Upper Potomac, where balloon recon-naissance will be made about Leesburg, and that vicinity." So it would continue until March 1862, on both the upper and middle river, when the rebel blockade would finally be lifted. The only significant revision of the enemy defenses between Christmas and February had been the addition of another battery on the outlet of Timber Branch, to bear on Union positions on Stump Neck on the opposite side of the river. From time to time Confederates could not resist taking shots at the great airship with its portrait of George Washngton painted on its side looking down upon them. But for all their shooting it appeared that the rebels could do little more than make light of the airship that had revealed their every move to Union planners too timid to act. [47]

One rebel prisoner named Asa Hartz, incarcerated in a Washington jail, but still hoping against hope for the Confederate seizure of the city, could do little more than make jest. "Jeff Davis is expected here every moment," he wrote. "Lincoln has got Lowe's balloon all ready, with that Herring Patent safe attached to it. The first Confederate bayonet that shows itself in Alexandria will be the signal to cut the ropes, and old Abe will swing off into space. Mrs. Lincoln has gone to Utah, and Seward has not been seen today . . ." [48]

20

DESERVING OF NOTICE
"The postmaster assures me that he is a good Union man."

The winter of 1861-62 was an unusual one for wild fowl on the Chesapeake Bay, or so said those who regularly traversed its waters. Compared to previous years the number of game birds was uncommonly small, notwithstanding an abnormal abundance on the Susquehanna River. The reason, it was claimed, seemed simple: "Heretofore the lower Potomac has been a great feeding place for wild fowl, but the discharge of heavy ordnance has driven them almost entirely away." [1] The frequent cannonading of big guns had been enervating not only for birds but also for folks obliged to live and work on Southern Maryland's shores and waters. Yet most of the shooting by largely untrained gunners on both sides had usually been without effect – but not always.

On the evening of November 15 during a spirited artillery exchange across the river, the first casualty of the long standoff occurred when a private in the 1st Arkansas Regiment manning the Evansport battery was mortally wounded in the abdomen by an exploding shell fired from the Maryland shore.[2] More upsetting than anything, at least to the white citizenry on the Maryland side of the river, were the visits by Union cavalry and flotilla landing parties. They were always in search of contraband, spies, secessionist sympathizers and blockade runners, where anyone and everyone was suspect and liable to arrest. For the bluecoats patrolling both land and water such missions had become just another unpleasantness to accompany the winter's first snow.

And then there was the *George Page*, whose very existence consistently kept Union naval forces on the alert, diverting resources that might have been better deployed elsewhere. Fear and rumors of a sortie by the little warship were easily melded in the minds of both naval and commercial mariners alike. When on Friday, November 29, the schooner *Delaware* reached Washington, having run the rebel blockade, her skipper reported "certain proceedings" of the Confederate gunboat the night before that excited grave concern. At the time there were four vessels opposite the rebel batteries waiting to run the blockade to Washington. The night was black, and he had not actually seen anything, though he was certain the gunboat had emerged from her anchorage and captured two schooners in the darkness. One of the vessels, with a white bottom, was supposed to be the coal laden *John Francis* of Baltimore. The other was hauling lumber for the government. Both were thought to have been carried into Quantico Creek by the *Page*. Though *Delaware*'s captain relied totally upon "what was heard" in making his assumptions of the episode, his statement was backed by a Captain Mister of the oyster sloop *Broom*. Mister claimed to have just managed to escape the rebel that same night. It was a newsworthy story of questionable veracity, but one that managed to elevate even higher fears of the lone rebel gunboat.[3]

There were some positives for the Northerners. McClellan's army continued to grow and improve in both size and discipline even as it was in the process of being cantoned in winter quarters. Under the careful superintendence of the chief army engineer, John G. Barnard, the fortifications around Washington had also expanded almost overnight to what was being heralded by some as the greatest defense works in the western world. By the beginning of December no fewer than four dozen strong forts encircled the city. Though connected by intricate lines of rifle pits, gun emplacements, roads and other features, and constructed at a cost of $344,053.46, they were still unfinished, and the general was obliged to lobby Congress for another $150,000 to complete them. And he would get it, for the city it seemed was finally emerging from the dark cocoon of paranoia that had once all but paralyzed its very heart.[4]

Perhaps in an effort to help dispel public fears, First Lady Mary Todd Lincoln, accompanied by Commandant Dahlgren and John Hay, the president's personal secretary, made an early excursion down the Potomac aboard the steamer *Mount Washington*. The trip was conducted as far as Stump Neck, just above the entrance to Chicamuxen Creek, in defiance of rebel batteries. By late afternoon the ship had returned to Washington without incident. That evening Hay joined the president to visit the home of General McClellan, an officer some now truly believed to be endowed with a Napoleonic ego who had famously, at every opportunity for months, personally snubbed the chief executive of the United States. For Lincoln it was indeed an effort to engage the man he had chosen to replace General Scott as commander of all the armies of the nation to discover the reason for his failure to engage the enemy. Lincoln and Hay sat for some time awaiting his arrival. Then upon his return home, the general retired without speaking to either of his visitors.[5]

Lincoln's problems and patience with McClellan notwithstanding, the war was escalating across the land at a maddening rate. The irritating problem of what to do about Southern Maryland was also growing. The most exasperating issue that needed to be dealt with was the expanding rebel communications and support network that had spread vein-like through the five southern counties to Baltimore, the Eastern Shore and beyond.

For rebels in both Virginia and Maryland intelligence gathering by agents hidden in the highest echelon of the Federal Government, as well from the most obvious and public of sources was everything. At the end of November 1861 for example, the new Confederate Secretary of War, Judah P. Benjamin, had directed General Holmes in Fredericksburg to make arrangements for having Northern newspapers regularly delivered to him. The circuitous delivery route was through Southern Maryland and across the Potomac to one Captain Richard Lee Tuberville Beale, 9th Virginia Cavalry, at Camp Lee, near the hamlet of Hague in lower Westmoreland County. Packages of uncensored newspapers, usually bloated with the latest Federal military data, staff promotions, troop strength and movements, were sent to Hague every Tuesday and Thursday by special courier. From Camp Lee they were to be carried to Carter's Wharf on the Rappahannock by an express rider provided by Holmes. There they were received by one J. J. Grindall or one of his assistants for direct delivery to the Secretary of War in Richmond.[6]

The appointed agent chosen by the Secretary of State and the Postmaster General to try to put an end to the Confederate mail service was Colonel Lafayette C. Baker who was already familiar with the territory. In his memoirs Baker would later write of just how serious the situation had become.

"It was a surprising fact during the first six or eight months after the war began, that the result of every Cabinet meeting at Washington was reported in Richmond within twenty-four hours after it was held. The secret was, that every postmaster in Lower Maryland, comprising the counties of St. Charles, St. George [*sic* Prince George's], and St. Mary's, with three exceptions, were disloyal. It had been taken for granted that the State was true to the Government, while rebel emissaries were constantly conveying information from Washington to the post offices along the Potomac, from which it was transmitted to Fredericksburg by blockade runners and spies, and thence telegraphed to Richmond." [7]

The engagement of numerous Southern Maryland agents in the intelligence network, a virtually amorphous rebel underground, was a given. Many of them would suffer the consequences for their allegiance to the Confederacy, and Baker would lead the punitive effort with a reconnaissance to investigate specific conduits of enemy communications. On November 20, acting under orders o f the Secretary of State, he initiated an offensive plan. Accordingly one hundred men from the 3rd Indiana Cavalry at Budd's Ferry, commanded by Captain Daniel B. Keister and Lieutenant Charles Lemon, were detached from Hooker's Brigade. They were to report to the newly designated agent for the purpose of arresting "parties suspected of rendering aid to Virginia rebels, to discover the channel through which contraband correspondence was being carried on, and if necessary, to take into custody any persons found in arms against the United States Government." If deemed essential, they were to permanently occupy the lower counties of Maryland to break up the rebel communications system.[8]

From Budd's Ferry Baker marched briskly to Port Tobacco, Colonel Graham's regimental hedquarters, where he found the inhabitants complaining bitterly "at their alleged ill treatment and depredations committed by the soldiers" under the colonel's command. Closer inquiry revealed that the townsmen had in fact been the first aggressors. "There are residing at this place," Baker informed the secretary, "but four or five Union men the balance either being sympathizers with secessionists, or open and avowed aiders and abettors of treason. The postmaster at this place is secretly doing all in his power to further the interests of the Confederacy." [9]

At Port Tobacco numerous and repeated complaints, reinforced by charges made by the few Union men residing in the vicinity, had been forwarded to Baker by government detectives concerning the loyalty of the town postmaster. Upon investigation he soon discovered that on three different occasions the postmaster had received packages of letters, postmarked at Baltimore, which were forwarded to Virginia. The postal run, however, was not simply one way. On or about October 10 a Confederate spy delivered 140 letters, which he carried from Virginia with the full knowledge and consent of the postmaster who had also been advising young men in the neighborhood to cross the river and join the Confederate Army.[10]

A visit to Allen's Fresh, eight miles from Port Tobacco, revealed only two Union men in the village. The postmaster there, Baker discovered, seldom if ever attended personally to the duties of the office but left the business in the hands of a young boy of twelve or fourteen years old. In the post office the colonel discovered five letters [he later claimed nine] addressed to fictitious names. Upon opening them he discovered that they contained sealed letters addressed to well known secession-ists in Virginia. "The postmaster," Baker reported, "was one of those who assisted and contributed to organize and equip Confederate soldiers now in Virginia." [11]

At the Newport Post Office, a few miles from Allen's Fresh, he found a package of thirty-four letters [he later claimed fifty-two], postmarked "Newport P.O., Maryland," all ready to be forwarded to different localities in the North including Baltimore. All were written in Virginia. One person had dropped all of them into the office. "The postmaster is a first class rebel. In my opinion, this office could be discontinued." [12]

Investigations at three small post offices, Charlotte Hall, Oakville and St. Inigoes, yielded little of note. At Charlotte Hall, managed by Postmaster F. D. Browne, only one contraband letter was found. "The postmaster assures me that he is a good Union man," Baker later reported, "and is doing all he can to assist and forward the interests of the Government. I think him a highly intelligent gentleman, but hardly sound." At Oakville he found the post office under George W. Buckler "located in a thrifty, settled community, and is but of little importance; being some distance from the Potomac, has less facilities than other offices for conducting contraband mail matter. I consider the postmaster a loyal, good, and reliable man." St. Inigoes, where little of anything was mailed, was considered of no importance at all.[13]

At the village of Chaptico, a place Baker estimated to be of only two to three hundred inhabitants, there were but four loyalists as all who dared to avow Union sentiments had been threatened with hanging and the destruction of their property by rebel supporters. Though the town had been visited several times by Union troops, he quickly learned that a regular communication with Virginia had been carried on there for months. His surprise visit quickly confirmed as much. Upon arrival in town he immediately proceeded to the post office where he found James Cooke, the postmaster, and the rest of his family, with the exception of a bright little girl twelve years of age, sick in bed. When the officer rapped upon the door the girl raised the window and said: "Father told me I must not let any of the Yankee soldiers in."

"I am not a Yankee soldier," Baker replied, "but an agent of the Post Office Department."

Having thus allayed the girl's concern, Baker was admitted and asked where the office was kept. The girl pointed to a box of pigeonholes for letters. Upon examin-ation the officer discovered a rough pine box with an iron hasp and a United States mail lock. The box was partitioned through the center with a hole for letters in each side. Over one part was inscribed "Southern Letters" and the other "Northern Letters."

"What is this box for?" Baker asked the child.

Innocently pointing to the inscriptions, the child answered: "Why, the letters put in that hole (the Southern) go to Richmond; and those in the other go to Wash-ington."

The postmaster, who was in bed but overhearing the conversation, spoke out excitedly from another room. "No, that ain't so; why do you tell the gentleman such a story?"

"I guess the girl tells the truth," replied the officer.

The box was promptly confiscated and taken to Washington. Upon examination it was found to contain letters from rebels on their way to the Confederacy, as well as those "whose hearts, if not their faces, were toward rebeldom." [14]

"The postmaster here," Baker informed Secretary Seward, "openly declares himself a traitor. I should have placed him under arrest, but found him confined in his bed with chills and fever, besides having a large family depending on him for their daily support."

The postmaster had very superior facilities, he observed, for conducting a large contraband business, "which he has not failed to improve to a greater extent than any other officer in Lower Maryland. Indeed, he openly boasts that he holds two appointments as postmaster one from Washington, and one from Richmond." A large number of contraband letters were found in his office. Baker described Postmaster Cooke as a habitual drunkard who neglected the duties of the Postal Service. He had repeatedly failed to lock the mailbag, having often left the key in the bag, and sometimes simply refused to open the mail at all. "From the importance of this office," the colonel concluded, "it could hardly be discontinued without a positive injury to a large number of good and loyal citizens."

Despite the anti-Union stance of most of the citizens of Chaptico, some of them were still ready to do business with their uninvited guests. The 3rd Indiana cavalrymen, Baker later recalled, being principally Germans who were "addicted, of course, to the use of intoxicating drinks," were ordered to encamp apart from places where liquors were sold. When the colonel first entered the town with his orderly to notify all vendors of strong drink to close their bars, and under no circumstances to sell to the soldiers under his command, all seemed quite in order.

That same evening while passing one of the drinking establishments Baker found it full of troops "having a jolly old time" with the proprietor. He immediately stepped in and angrily demanded of the host: "Did I not give you an order not to sell liquor to my men?"

"Why, Colonel," said the proprietor innocently, "these ain't no soldiers; they are officers. They have got swords on."

The colonel was amused at what he deemed to be ignorance, as the proprietor had confused officers, who generally wore swords, with lowly cavalrymen who also wore swords. The proprietor was sure that he was honored with men quite above common soldiering. Or so he said.

From Chaptico Baker and his cavalry pressed on to Leonardtown, which he deemed long "the residence of aristocratic families" and the largest and by far the most prosperous village in Southern Maryland. Arriving within two miles of the town at the onset of evening, the colonel and his detachment encamped in a grove of pines. With a captain, sergeant, and two orderlies he rode ahead into the village and found the people had already heard of their approach. The collision between the Federals and "the principal men of the place" was unfriendly. The town leaders protested, "in the most violent manner against Yankee troops disturbing their peace" and declared that they were simply "State rights people, who only wished to be let alone." Baker later reported that they made threats of personal violence if his soldiers were brought into the town, though he sought to cool the heated tension of the moment with a fallback on the use of force only if necessary. "I am here under orders of the Secretary of War, on a peaceful investigation, and not as charged, to steal your slaves, to burn your houses and barns, or to molest the inhabitants. I have money to pay for forage and rations if you will sell them," he said calmly, but then added, "if not, I shall take them." [15]

At this point, James Downs, publisher of the *St. Mary's Beacon*, who had apparently been among the town leaders that met Baker upon his arrival, "became boisterous in his condemnation of the Government and its officers." Quietly, the colonel ordered a guard placed around the printing office. He then instructed one of his officers, an Ohio man with some experience as an editor, to write an article for the paper, in which Downs was made to "recant his secession heresy and declare for the Union, advising all his subscribers to do the same." The compositors were then compelled to set it up, and the pressmen reluctantly struck off the paper. The subscription book was consulted, and to each name a copy of the paper was mailed. "The excitement and indignation which followed the distribution of the suddenly loyal sheet," Baker later wrote with some amusement, "and the discovery of the serious joke, made one of the most ludicrous incidents in my official experience." [16] It is safe to say that the town's people were not amused.

Baker's main mission, to examine the Leonardtown Post Office for secessionist-related activity, of course was already colored by his impression of the town itself. "I do not consider it safe to say that there is one Union man in the town or vicinity," he reported, "although many declare themselves State Rights Men, which is but a milder term for secessionists. At this place has been enlisted, equipped, and conveyed to Virginia, a very large number of men for the Confederate Army. But very few hesitate to declare openly their secession sentiments." He attributed the disparity, almost wholly, to the publication of the *St. Mary's Beacon*, a "bitter and uncompromising secession paper." In the town post office he dscovered a large number of letters going to and coming from Virginia. Though the postmaster, William J. Yates, declared himself to be a good Union man Baker later claimed to have obtained the undeniable proof of his disloyalty to the government and sympathy with the rebels. As a sconsequence, it was his opinion that Leonardtown be at once placed under martial law, and a provost marshal appointed, "in order that the few Union men residing there may have some kind of protection against these traitors." [17]

The surprise visit to the Leonardtown Post Office yielded a half bushel of letters to and from Richmond though Yates denied any knowledge of the authors of the contraband letters or of the parties to whom they were bound. In self defense, he described himself as a States Rights man. To Baker, despite his own misgivings regarding the town's postmaster, it was clear that "the citizens generally speak in the highest terms of him, and, so far as I can judge, the office was well managed. Everything seems to be conducted with a great deal of system and regularity. As no better man could be induced to take the office, I should think a change not advisable at present." [18]

From Leonardtown the Union postal raiders pressed on a dozen miles to Great Mills, in the very heart of St. Mary's County, a site that Baker had visited only the month before. He reported but few inhabitants residing directly on the road, the major portion of the county's population being mostly on the Potomac and Patuxent rivers.[19]

The fruits of the raid, the confiscated contraband letters, were no doubt of some value, but it was the paucity of loyal citizenry in Southern Maryland that was most discomforting. "I have found it exceedingly difficult to find good, reliable, loyal men, who would accept the appointment of postmaster," Baker informed the Postmaster General of the United States. Many who were competent were unwilling to devote the necessary time required to perform the duties of the office. He had, however, obtained the names and consent of some loyal citizens willing to accept appointment to a number of the offices he had mentioned in his report. It was, he believed, a matter of the greatest importance to the government that "our post masters should be loyal and true to the Union, particularly when their offices can by any possibility be used in any manner as a medium to convey information to the Confederate States. To discontinue altogether our mail facilities in Lower Maryland, at present time, would result in a great inconvenience and injury to the few loyal people residing in that section, as well as our military forces, which, at my suggestion, have been stationed along the Potomac, to break up the contraband trade so successfully carried on during the past summer." [20]

It was Bakers's opinion that Millstone Landing, four miles from Great Mills and eight miles from Redmond's Landing near the head of St. Mary's River, was now the most important rebel communications center in all of Southern Maryland owing to the renewed daily steamboat communication with Baltimore. The roads to those two places, unlike in the rest of the lower Maryland counties, were deemed "most excellent" in all seasons. Moreover, they lay in the heart of regional rebeldom wherein only four or five inhabitants had been Union men, as "most of those who have declared themselves as such have either been driven from the county, or dare not avow themselves in favor of the Government." A number of the known local residents held commissions in the Confederate Army, he stated with some exasperation, but it was exceedingly difficult to arrest them. The approach of any considerable number of troops "is a signal for these cheats to leave their houses, or secrete themselves, and it can only be accomplished by the most shrewd and well laid plans." [21]

Learning of an organization known as the Lower Maryland Vigilance Committee, Baker resolved to run down as many of its members as possible, but noted that actually making an arrest was difficult if not almost impossible as "the county is wild and unsettled." A complete set of signals had been established among the inhabitants, he later reported, and notice of his arrival had been given throughout the entire countryside, making it necessary to move about only at night.[22] Nevertheless, by using threats to coerce the natives to reveal the whereabouts of certain individuals he managed to root out four key personnel: E. W. Sissell, E. H. Jones [also given as June], Dr. William M. Abell and B. L. Hayden.

Sissell was a Confederate spy indicted by a Baltimore grand jury for engaging in the notorious Pratt Street Riot, but made his escape into Virginia. Up to the time of his arrest he had kept out of the way. Memorandums of importance were found in his possession.

Jones was a native countian who resided at what was known as the Old Factory [Clifton Factory] in St. Mary's, and had been engaged in merchandising, farming, and other endeavors for his livelihood. As an ardent secessionist he had been charged with intimidating Unionists in the county to leave or else. When the April 1861 upheavals in Baltimore were about to spew forth, he had traveled to the city and was there during the riots. On his return he brought no less than four hundred stands of arms, which were afterwards sent to Virginia. During most of the summer and fall he had employed his own wagons for hauling incoming Northern Neck contraband goods, usually farm poducts, from the Potomac to the Patuxent. His home had served as headquarters for rebel spies passing to and from the Confederacy, and he had personally been engaged in enlisting, equipping, and forwarding a large number of men for the South.

Dr. William M. Abell was one of Jones's neighbors who assisted in all of his operations and had openly defied the government. As Secretary of the Vigilance Committee, his hatred of the Union bordered on rabid. After his capture and arrest, he vowed to Baker in no uncertain terms, "that he would yet kill a Yankee for every day that he was imprisoned by the Government."

Baker's prize catch was B. L. Hayden, who he believed would prove of the greatest importance to the government. Hayden was well known and somewhat famous for the murder of a neighbor, Philip H. Burroughs, during a dispute in the spring of 1858, and for his acquittal in court in December of that same year. He resided at Millstone Landing and allowed a hotel he operated there to serve as a rendezvous for all the secessionists in the county. He also owned property in Medley Neck adjacent to an estate owned by Joseph H. Maddox, a prosperous merchant in Leonardtown, and an avowed secessionist and blockade runner. At Hayden's home were convened all of their meetings and deliberations. Moreover, he kept two teams of wagons constantly running from the landing to the Potomac River and back, carrying whatever needed to be moved for the Confederate cause. Only the night before his arrest he had spirited away to Virginia three hundred Colt revolvers in two large boxes. The boxes had earlier been buried in a patch of sand about two hundred yards from his house. When interrogated, Hayden's wife, undoubtedly with tears in her eyes, said that she had frequently tried to dissuade her husband from his nefarious activities but he had repeatedly ignored her advice, "and told her that he was determined to make money in some way." Incriminating letters of the strongest secessionist character as well as Confederate envelopes, stamps, and circulars were found in his possession. Baker considered Hayden to be "the master spirit, and the worst man in the county." [23]

All four men were promptly carted off to Washington under a cavalry guard, charged with espionage for the Confederacy and then taken to Fort McHenry. Their captures received little public attention and may have even generated a few more arrests, but for the most part went unnoticed except by the indignant editor of the *St. Mary's Beacon* and the families of those taken into custody.[24] Such incidents were by now quite common and caused little more than a stir of pious indignation among the silent rebels of the lower counties. Yet, the illegal mails and smuggling would continue to flow between North and South with regularity until the end of the war. And contraband could be delivered in numerous disguises.

On one typical occasion, when the steamer *George Weems*, bound for St. Mary's with over 120 passengers, was boarded by the police at the foot of the Frederick Street dock in Baltimore she was thoroughly searched. Though hidden behind the back of a sofa in the ship's saloon, a half bushel of letters was found addressed to parties in St. Mary's County was discovered, none were addressed to parties in Virginia or were of an otherwise suspicious nature. It was all quite legal. Nor were any goods of a "contraband character" identified amidst the freight. The ship was eventually allowed to sail again but only after the Weems brothers posted a bond and agreed not to carry contraband upon pain of confiscation. Thus after the cursory inspection, it was at first assumed that the vessel was clean. The passengers were another matter.

"A Female Rebel in Baltimore, An Everyday Scene." Note the great hooped skirt, with defiant rebel flag motif, which proved excellent for concealing contraband goods. *Harper's Weekly*, New York Public Library, New York.

"There was . . . quite a curious garment found," it was later reported, on the person of an extremely attractive young lady named Milburn. The woman wore a balmoral skirt "into which was ingeniously quilted a large quantity of the finest sewing silk" of different colors, much prized in the Confederacy where such luxuries were scarce. The contraband items, worth $200, weighed twenty-five pounds and included a large quantity of pins, needles, and other items as well. The skirt worn by Miss Milburn, specially designed for smuggling and weighing thirty-five pounds when fully laden with contraband, had exceptionally strong bands for the shoulders, allowing the wearer to carry the unusually heavy load. At first refusing to give her name, she denied that the goods were bound for the "Southern market." Then upon the person of her young brother was found thirty pounds of quinine sewed up in the linings of a "contrivance resembling an undershirt." And finally, two muslin bags, "so constructed as to be worn by a lady, and filled with stockings, needles, pins, thread and numerous other articles, were found in the yawl boat of the steamer." The bags, it was said, had evidently been placed there in a hurry by the owner, as the strings upon them were broken, indicating that the wearer 'sluffed' them as speedily as possible.

The articles were seized by the police, the young lady and her brother taken into custody, and *George Weems* hauled to Fort McHenry for detention to await the military's decision about its future, which was now in grave jeopardy. "The residents of St. Mary's, and other counties, and Capt. Weems, are very active in preventing contraband articles from being conveyed by the steamer *Weems*," assured one Baltimore newspaper that had itself been repeatedly accused of pro-Southern sympathies, "for should the boats be withdrawn by orders from the Government, the citizens of the counties would severely feel the loss of communication with the city." [25] For unknown reasons the ship was soon after restored to its owners. The Weems brothers, who had yet to be proven complicit in the smuggling operations of their passengers, were able to almost immediately return their vessel to service.

That St. Mary's had become a center of a "vast extensive trade with Virginia," was by now an established fact.[26] And though try as it might, often with substantial success to its credit, the Potomac Flotilla was nonetheless unable to plug all the holes in the 100 miles long sieve that was the lower Potomac frontier. General Hooker, who was no strong admirer of the navy, believed the U.S. Army could do better though he was the first to admit that he knew he could not succeed entirely. But he was resolved to try.

On December 6 Hooker dispatched a detachment from the 3rd Indiana Cavalry under Captain George H. Chapman to take post at Millstone Landing on the Patuxent River. From there they were to conduct patrols radiating in all directions and at all times. The captain was instructed to visit all places "deserving of notice" lying between Point Lookout and Port Tobacco. His primary mission was to intercept all contraband trade and correspondence, arrest all concerned in the operations, as well as "all traitors," an open ended code meaning anyone he deemed suspect for whatever reasons, and send them under guard to camp. Hooker preferred cavalry to infantry for such work "for they move with more celerity, and can do more service than three times the number on foot. They can encounter no resistance in this part of Maryland they cannot overcome, and by moving rapidly they inspire more fear than can a column of infantry." [27]

Three additional companies of cavalry were also soon operating between Port Tobacco and the mouth of the Patuxent, but supplying them over the poor Southern Maryland thoroughfares was quickly proving to be a logistical nightmare.

Thus Hooker instructed Captain Chapman to make his requisitions for provisions "on the heads of those departments in Baltimore" and to send them directly from the city to Millstone Landing by steamer. The arrangement, he correctly determined, would save sixty miles of land transportation "over horrible roads." [28]

The establishment of a cavalry base at Millstone Landing soon paid off. Little more than a week after arriving there, Chapman was able to inform the general of a major capture. While on patrol near Spencer's Landing, just seven miles north of their base, a detachment of his men had seized the 40-ton Baltimore blockade running sloop *Victory*. The crew had succeeded in making their escape at the first appearance of the troopers, but the prize they left would have been quite valuable to the rebels had it run the blockade. "I found on board," Chapman informed Hooker with apparent satisfaction,

> "86,250 percussion caps, 43 pounds flax thread, 87 dozen fancy brass buttons, 2 boxes of needles, 1 sack of gum shellac, a box of carpenter's tools, 1 carpet sack and contents, consisting of wearing apparently and some silver forks, spoons, &c., marked J.C.M. and McC., a trunk and its contents, mainly clothing, and $25,328.17 in promissory notes, payable to Hamilton Easter & Co., of Baltimore, on parties throughout the Southern States, directed to Mr. James H. Weedon, 9 Pearl street, Richmond, Va., care Messrs. J. B. Ferguson & Co., with letters of instruction accompanying. I have brought the sloop to this landing. I very much regret that my men did not catch those on board. I will make such disposition of the sloop and things on board as you may direct. The caps are suitable for Colt's revolvers, I believe. I regret that my men are not so armed." [29]

General Hooker was delighted and resolved to request an officer of the flotilla to man the prize and bring her and her cargo up the Potomac to Liverpool Point. Upon arrival the freight could be forwarded by a land route directly to Washington and avoid the rebel blockade batteries farther up river. If the sloop was found suitable she might be retained for service on the Potomac in the general's quartermaster's department.[30]

With Spencer's Landing, which was one of the very few commercial wharfage facilities on the Patuxent still operative, now suddenly coming under the watchful eyes of government patrols and inspectors, the impact upon some businesses was soon apparent. One concern that was effected was the *St. Mary's Beacon*. On January 2, 1862 the newspaper's editor, James S. Downs, attributed a recent long lapse in publishing to Federal meddling at the landing: "We have been prevented from publishing the *Beacon* for the past two weeks in consequence of the detention of a portion of our printing materials at Spencer's Wharf, the government agent there detaining them on the supposition, we suppose, that they were contraband of war and destined for Dixie. – They have now been delivered to us and we are again in motion." [31]

As the roads of Southern Maryland were in such dreadful condition, Hooker considered it of great importance to send out only the smallest possible forces necessary, owing to the difficulty in supplying them. Yet he was determined to close as many holes in the Potomac sieve as possible. Another cavalry company was assigned picket duty between Smith's Point in Charles County and Port Tobacco.

His main forces were now concentrated between the Mattawoman and Smith's Point, while cavalry units patrolled from there south and eastward. He now had a continuous line of pickets and patrol units operating along the shores of the Potomac all the way to its entrance at Point Lookout and from there northward to the mouth of the Patuxent. "They may not be able to cut off all intercourse across the Potomac; this I cannot expect," he assured his superior, "but they will arrest some, and defeat the plans of many." [32]

Southern Maryland, hotbed of secessionist sympathy and contraband trade, was now an occupied land.

21

APPLE PIE ORDER
"We are still floundering about in the mud."

Monday, December 9, 1861, 9:30 a.m. was, as usual, cold at the water's edge on Mattawoman Creek. Lieutenant Commander Wyman, who had assumed command of the Potomac Flotilla aboard the flagship *Harriet Lane* only eight days earlier, had just learned of rebel activity at Freestone Point. Enemy pickets, three camp wagons and a mounted officer had been spotted moving down the road south of the point and then halting by some buildings near the fishing landing. Suspecting the rebels were bringing a field battery to the point, he immediately commanded *Jacob Bell* and *Anacostia* to shell the buildings. Ordering his own ship in as close as the shoal water would safely admit to provide protection for the two smaller vessels, the lieutenant watched intently as the bombardment of the buildings and hill commenced. Soon after the enemy had been pushed back, Lieutenant Commander McCrea with a few men belonging to *Jacob Bell* landed uncontested and set fire to four houses containing sutler's stores, flour and myriad other items. Eighteen hours later all had finally burned to the ground. Only one building remained. It belonged to Samuel Cropley of Washington and still contained his entire outfit of commercial fishing gear, seine lines, rope, barrels, salt vats and other equipment valued at several thousand dollars. Soon after the raid, Cropley, who had for years leased the landing and operated a fishery from there, beseeched the Navy Department to protect his property but in vain.[1]

Such was how a typical winter's day now began and ended along Southern Maryland's frontier with the Confederacy.

***

As cold weather set in, pneumonia, bronchitis and other contagious illnesses were beginning to take their toll on the residents of the winter encampments on both sides of the Potomac. Nevertheless, activities on the Confederate shore, as well as those of sympathetic secessionists, spies, agents, and blockade runners on the Southern Maryland side, were conducted as always. And as McClellan's army matured, rebel defense works and winter quarters on the Potomac continued to be erected, all under daily observation (weather permitting) of Lowe's balloons. Troops on the Maryland side had also begun construction of their own somewhat more considerable quarters. At General Sickles' main base, Camp Stiles near Budd's Ferry, a substantial military village was being built much to the delight of the nearly thousand men who would pass the season there.[2] As the first heavy winter snows of the new year of 1862 came on, those ensconced in the cantonment, especially the officers, were likely to pass the time in some comfort as suggested by a report from one of the soldiers in residence:

"The village of Fredonia (which is to be the name of the place which we are building) is going up finely, nearly half of [the] houses being already done. Col. Small's house is as fine a log cabin as can be seen in the county for the size, while Major Berry's is just such a one for comfort as he would have. The privates' houses number sixty and can accommodate sixteen men each. Each

275

company has one house for its commissioned officers, and one house for its commissary sergeant, to keep the company's stores in. Then there are to be the adjutant's house, the quartermaster's house, and a number of others for launderesses, servants, cooks, teamsters, &c. The streets are laid out at right angles, and forty feet wide." [3]

"Camp of the 8th New Jersey Volunteers near Mattawoman Creek, Charles County, Maryland." Arthur Lumley, artist. Prints and Photographs Division, Library of Congress, Washington, D.C.

Even during the winter blows and ice flows on the river, Confederate efforts to move goods and recruits from the Maryland side to Virginia continued without letup. As always ingenuity was often required to counter the roving Union blockaders. One such endeavor designed to get a rebel steam powered vessel into service on the river was revealed to the Federals by sources initially deemed questionable. The effort was first noted by a report from five runaway slaves picked up by the flotilla schooner *Bailey*, Captain James L. Gray commanding. The refugees stated that on the night of December 7 a small wooden steamer sheathed with sheet iron and armed with a small howitzer and 100 muskets had been hauled overland on wheels from the Rappahannock to Lower Machodoc Creek. It was, they said, to be employed in carrying goods across the Potomac and possibly even to capture the flotilla cutter *Dana*. Though the veracity of the account may have been in question, Lieutenant Commander Wyman was obliged to take counter measures with vessels he could ill afford to spare.[4]

The arrival of the unnamed steamer on Lower Machodoc, commanded by a captain from Maryland, was soon causing as much commotion among the rebels as it was concern for Wyman. Richard R. T. Beale, who had just been promoted to major in the Confederate Army and appointed Provost Marshal of Westmoreland

and Northumberland counties, had apparently not been informed of the vessel or its mission until after its appearance on the creek and complained to Secretary of War Benjamin of the recruitment officers who preceded her. He had, it seemed, inherited command of a district filled with problems of loyalty. There was already discontent in the Northern Neck stemming from the removal of so many home guard volunteers to the Aquia District, which was augmented by a persistent rumor that the region was to be abandoned by the military. Even more disturbing was that the poorer non-slave owning citizenry had begun to doubt the Confederate cause itself.

For some time intelligence from the lower Northern Neck had been reaching General Holmes in Fredericksburg indicating that the pressure from the Federal blockade on cross-river smuggling had resulted in the absence of such necessaries as salt, coffee, and other items normally acquired through commerce with Southern Maryland. There was also the issue of the heavy stress on the women and children of the region "incident to the absence of the men on militia and volunteer duty," which was beginning "to tell to the prejudice of our cause among the non-slave-holders." The general had strong doubts that the Federals had any intention of assaulting the battery complex opposite Budd's Ferry. He thus seriously considered transferring Brockenbrough's "very excellent regiment" from Evansport, where it had recently been stationed, back to its home territory on the Northern Neck, and disbanding the local militia there.[5]

What most bothered Major Beale was the recruiters siphoning away what manhood there was left in the region, as well as the reduced traffic flow between Southern Maryland and the Northern Neck. Of equal concern was the unwillingness of the lower caste of citizens, most of whom owned no slaves, to volunteer for service. After consulting with Colonel George E. Pickett, commander of the adjacent Rappahannock District, he informed Secretary Benjamin: "There [*sic*] gentlemen, with the full endorsement of the Government, captain's commissions, are here recruiting, and claiming the right to run boats to Maryland. Any man who crosses [the Potomac] is taken in, and may go back as a hand on board the boat, and for aught I know any deserter from Sickles' brigade may come, get any desired information, and go back." He cited a letter from the secretary himself to a colonel in King George County, sent in September, which authorized the recuiters be furnished every facility to recruit. The recruiters claimed the right to send any one to Baltimore to do this. "Are they under my control or not? I cannot discharge my duty as provost marshal to the people here as my judgment directs if they have full discretion in this matter. I have permitted them to use boats, under the impression your order was imperative upon me." He questioned his jurisdiction over the steamboat recently deployed from Machodoc and her freedom to pass freely? If she was allowed to do so, he declared, "I hazard little in saying that all communication with the Maryland shore will be cut off in a few days and our creeks will be blockaded by tugs . . . I have forbidden the Maryland captain's boat to cross for the present because of misconduct and by request from friends in Maryland . . . The desertions so far about equal the recruits." [6]

Five days later Secretary Benjamin responded to Beale's complaint. Noting that at the time authority was given to "the several Maryland captains to recruit for our service," the condition of affairs on the opposite shore of the Potomac was very different from the present state of things, "and there was a strong desire to enable our friends on the other side to cross and join us." Ample time, he noted, had been given for that purpose, but now Beale was to be permitted to use his own discretion in the matter, albeit with a proviso. The secretary succinctly ordered that as full "facilities" had already been given to help Marylanders across the river, it was no longer of "advantage to our service to continue the recruiting of Marylanders on the Lower Potomac." [7] The official campaign to enlist them in the Confederate military at government expense was at an end. It was now simply too dangerous.

There were of course other issues. Colonel Pickett, a West Point graduate, had little confidence in the militia system of Virginia, and like Beale was equally concerned regarding the "contamination" of disloyalty among the lower class citizenry. "A greater portion of our loyal men, the chivalry and high toned gentlemen of the country," he noted to his superiors, "have volunteered, and are far from their homes. There is a strong element among those who are left either to be non-combatants or to fall back under the old flag . . . We have to fear them most. All during a war like this must suffer, but for the good of the general service it will not do to yield to those persons who have refused to volunteer, while the proprietors of the country are actually in the field, and who plead poverty and would join the enemy should an occasion occur." He suggested to Holmes that the militia of Westmoreland and Northumberland counties be organized and relieved by other troops, "they being ordered away from the dangerous ground and placed under the immediate supervision of some one able to govern them." [8]

To the Union forces arrayed along the Potomac the problem of what seemed to be the ever expanding complex of rebel batteries on the Virginia shore was still foremost in their minds. On December 12 it was learned that a battery of six rifled fieldpieces supported by a full rebel regiment had been established to the westward of Boyd's Hole, opposite Hooker's picket stations on Maryland Point, and near the estate of Colonel John Tayloe. The guns were planted on the riverbank during the day and removed at night. The battery, which was opened on December 17, was under the command of Captain John R. Cook and manned by soldiers from Stafford County. It was, however, not armed with just field guns as first reported but two heavy cannon. Passing vessels were now obliged to haul perilously close to the Maryland shore, though the enemy's range reached well inside the shoreline. On December 30 news of the battery's first victim, reportedly sunk two miles distance from the gun, was reported in the *National Republican*. "The schooner which was sunk by the rebels a few days ago is understood to be the 'Three Sisters,' loaded with wood destined for this city. She was not, however, sunk by what is known as rebel river batteries, but by fluid artillery, drawn to the Virginia shore by the enemy at a point far below their fixed batteries on the Potomac. The place where the schooner was sunk is known as 'Boyd's Hole.'" [9]

Other works were also in progress. "At Potomac Creek," one report stated, "some work is going on, sounding at night like the beating of boiler iron." A third new battery was under construction on a neck of land at Chopawamsic Creek, and more guns were being added to the southern face of the Shipping Point battery. The latter had supposedly even exploded a shell over Sandy Point, two and a quarter miles to the southeastward.[10]

Wyman's problems with blockade runners seemed never ending, particularly those operating from the St. Mary's County shore, especially now in and about Piney Point. More often than not the best intelligence regarding their smuggling operations came from the local black population. Some runners, however, often employed their most trusted slaves to assist them in their activities. In mid-December, for example, one smuggling operation was briefly disrupted near the point through the assistance of John Hanson, a slave belonging to one of the many members of the Abell family. Hanson reported the location of a pair of boats on nearby Flood Creek. One belonged to Thomas W. Gough, a prominent citizen of St. Mary's and a secessionist who had once served as county commissioner. Gough often used his personal servant, William Dims, to smuggle goods on dark nights to the Virginia side. He also used his own team of horses to haul the goods from Leonardtown. The other belonged to a man named Mattingly.

Responding to the new intelligence, Acting Master's Mate William T. Street, commander of *Dana*, set off with four of his own men and four from *Bailey* and located the two boats. Their oars had been hidden in the woods and the oarlocks muffled with sheepskin. Soon afterwards another black named William Lawrence provided even more information regarding a veritable smuggling cabal that included both Gough and Mattingly as well as six other men, John Blackiston, Jr., N. Ford, a Mr. Phinick, a Mr. Dills, George Simms, sergeant in the Leonardtown Home Guard, and his brother. The informant also reported that five blacks, John Gordon, Wat Barnes, John Bradmar, Ned Downs, and Ned Owens, had been employed by their masters to ferry goods to Virginia only a few nights earlier.[11]

Soon afterwards it was learned at the Navy Department from a Captain Shore of the Philadelphia canal steamer *Chamberlin*, which was employed by the U.S. Army to provision troops in Charles County, that in coming up the Potomac he had seen a distress flag raised above the Piney Point Lighthouse. Assuming possible trouble he went ashore and entered the building. There he met the distraught acting lighthouse keeper, Mrs. Robert Marshall, who beseeched him to report to the navy on smuggling activities nearby and of imminent danger to the lighthouse. Every evening at midnight, said Mrs. Marshall, five or six boatloads of rebels crossed the river to Ragged Point laden with provisions and other contraband. Excitedly she reported that there was at that moment $10,000 worth of goods, ammunition, clothing and the like hidden in the woods just above the lighthouse waiting to be carried over to the rebel shore. Every day men came to badger her for information and to inquire if there were any Union cutters about. There was also, she learned in a verification of the story rendered by the escaped slaves picked up by *Bailey*, a small rebel steamer in the creek just above Ragged Point that had been hauled overland from Fredericksburg. But even more disconcerting was when the blockade runners told her in no uncertain terms that "she had better keep away as they intended to destroy the light house." [12]

Wyman ordered an immediate canvas of the coastline between Point Lookout and Piney Point but reported "nothing of a suspicious nature was found." Nor did it seem that there was evidence of the rebel steamer. Timing, it appeared, was everything, and the rebel coast watch system was very efficient. There were of course the now usual rumors of enemy troops massing for a crossing, this time from

Currioman Bay, opposite Blackistone Island, but nothing could be proved. Some intelligence, however, seemed to confirm what many already knew. "From what information I can gather," Wyman informed Secretary Welles, "I am led to believe that the greater part (if not all) of the goods, etc., carried into Virginia are brought from Baltimore to the Patuxent." From there it was but a short hop to the Potomac.[13]

***

One of the most difficult problems of maintaining a naval blockade on the navigable 100-mile length of the Potomac, much being subject to significant blockage by enemy batteries, were the logistics inherent in keeping the flotilla manned, provisioned, fueled, and operational in the field. Owing to the defection of a massive number of naval officers and men to the Confederate side at the beginning of the war, naval manpower was often inadequate to meet the emergency. Logistical support was not just an army concern. Keeping the few small flotilla vessels supplied was a perplexing problem at best. Providing adequate coal for steamers, which were kept on constant patrol on the lower river far from base occasionally for weeks on end, required strong measures. Sometimes outright seizure of supplies from commercial shipping had been necessary. As more flotilla vessels began to come on line and the range and missions of the fleet expanded, its operations were now becoming far more than a logistical difficulty. Keeping those same vessels in repair, with the only convenient regional facilities being at the Navy Yard, would prove a continuing challenge never fully met until the end of the war. Establishing a forward coaling or repair facility farther down the river posed an obvious solution. The concern, however, was that if such was erected it would have to be in the heart of territory that was ardently secessionist in sympathy, replete with all the inherent dangers.

Wyman did his best with the resources at hand. On December 20 he suggested to the Navy Department that sending provisions, clothing and such from Washington for the use of the flotilla downriver was now simply too dangerous. Any supply ship would be obliged to run the gauntlet of rebel batteries and hazards posed by the frequent freezing of the river above Mattawoman. Why not station one of the unarmed flotilla schooners off Liverpool Point to serve as a store ship? Supplies could be brought around from Baltimore more safely and economically, and communications capabilities could be maintained easily.[14]

Protecting his own weakly armed and manned schooners as well as the commercial transports chartered to the Army from enemy shelling or boarding attempts, especially in the vicinity of the enemy batteries, was still an ongoing concern. On Christmas Day the Navy Department was queried about the situation by Caleb S. Wright of Philadelphia, manager of the only commercial line maintaining a link between Washington and points on the middle Potomac. Wright was the owner of the supply steamers *Volunteer* and *Reindeer*, the former of which had been chartered to the Army, but was managed by him. The vessel was a new 37-ton sternwheel boat built in Easton, Pennsylvania. As she drew only eighteen inches of water she was perfect for use in the shoals of the Potomac's innumerable tributaries. For nearly a month beginning about November 27 both boats had been running daily from the foot of Eleventh Street on the Washington waterfront, to Rum Point

280

on Mattawoman Creek, servicing the military's needs. Wright's boats first came under fire soon after beginning service on the river. On December 15 a rebel battery had attacked *Volunteer* five miles west of Mathias Point where twenty-seven shots were thrown at her, two of which struck. The new run from Washington to Mattawoman, however, had suddenly become far too perilous to hazard. Owing to a possible rebel battery being erected at Hallowing Point, Wright called the stretch just a few miles below Mount Vernon "the most dangerous point on the river." If the government would land 1,000 troops there, he declared, he would gladly ferry them across. Otherwise he might have to shut down service.[15] His request was ignored,

To guard against enemy boats coming out of creeks near their batteries and attacking any craft daring enough to pass within their reach, Wyman requested the Navy Yard supply a light launch with gun and crew. As he had no steamers suitable for that shallow waterway, the vessel was to take to station in the Chicamuxen. She could be placed out of range of the enemy guns but might be moved out at night, when most vessels usually attempted the run past, to protect them from being boarded. Dahlgren responded that there would be no problem in providing the launch and gun, but "there are so few seamen left in the yard that a pressing emergency can hardly be met to man a gun." [16]

It was often left to individual commanders to deal with the enemy batteries as best they could. The captain of the U.S. Steam Sloop of War *Pensacola*, which had been ordered to Hampton Roads, requested two hay-filled army scows, seventy-five to a hundred feet in length, be lashed alongside of his ship to protect her machinery from penetration by enemy shellfire when going down the river. The request was immediately forwarded to Montgomery C. Meigs, Quartermaster General of the U.S. Army. The appeal was apparently not met, as *Pensacola* was obliged to steam for her destination about 5 a.m., January 12, 1862 without protective cover. She had been waiting days for the river ice to break up and sailed only with the assistance of Wyman's schooners bearing colored lights to show the way. Though the rebels, who had long been awaiting her appearance, were able to fire fifteen to twenty shot at her in the dimness of early morning, all were without effect and she arrived safely and intact at her destination two days later.[17]

The breakout of *Pensacola* did not sit well with the Confederates, as General Hooker soon noted. "Later in the day," he reported to headquarters, "the rebels were very active with their heavy guns, and blazed away at almost every object that presented itself, whether within range of their guns or not. To me it seemed like an ebullition of anger on the escape of the *Pensacola*, for they had evidently made unusual preparation to receive her. Their accumulation of ammunition was afterward expended on objects of little or no importance and without result." The general thought it worth noting that during his presence on the river the enemy had used the batteries more than 5,000 times, and with one exception, "not a vessel has been damaged in navigating the river nor the skin of a person broken on our shore," which was, of course, not precisely true.[18]

The navy was frequently under pressure from the U.S. Army to be more aggressive. When General Hooker feared a nighttime sally from Quantico Creek by *George Page* to assail army transports, he requested that the flotilla position vessels above, below and near the mouth of the creek but expressed little faith in the navy. He scoffed with some disdain that it was something "they can do with impunity *any night* when the moon is not shining." Wyman was obliged to challenge the discrediting remark by reminding Assistant Secretary Fox that his boats kept an incessant lookout for the rebel steamer, and adding that his unarmed schooners were often obliged to tow the army transports past the batteries as they could not manage it themselves.[19]

That Wyman was, in fact, never anything less than aggressive, given the situation, paucity of warships and lack of manpower, may be dismissed by the flotilla's first engagement of the New Year. After carefully examining the somewhat hidden enemy works on Cockpit Point, but wishing to learn more to see if they might be enfiladed, he ordered *Anacostia* and *Yankee* to stand inside to the northward of the point and throw their shells into the battery. The cannonade proved successful as *Anacostia's* bombshells, fired with admirable precision, were planted in the heart of the enemy's works. The only artillery firing in response was a reported giant 80-pounder and a 12-pounder, both rifled guns. The former managed to heave a shell through the port bow of *Yankee*, which lodged in a berth of the starboard side slightly wounding a crewman. Almost immediately after the big gun had disgorged its fourth shot, 9-inch and 6-inch shells from *Anacostia* exploded simultaneously above the piece, dismounting it, and forcing the abandonment of the works. The attack managed only to generate a more impregnable defense, for soon after the skirmish the works were reoccupied and the great gun was remounted. The battery was increased in strength to five guns, with several of them moved to the northern face of the works. A breastwork for yet another battery was also thrown up to make the northern face impenetrable to naval assault. [20] It mattered little, for far greater movements would soon to be underway and render such powerful defenses useless.

***

On January 3, 1862 General McClellan consulted with General Hooker regarding the best points and facilities, in particular at Port Tobacco, for embarkation of troops for pending and future operations. Hooker later reported: "The wharf at the town is 50 feet long, with 9 feet water at high tide. Three miles below the town, on the bay, troops can step from the shore on to vessels drawing not over 5 or 6 feet water. The town is 32 miles from Washington, with better roads than those leading to my camp." There were other options as well. Hooker had already started construction of a 300-foot L-shaped wharf at Rum Point on the Mattawoman. The structure was wide enough at the outer extremity, where there was six feet of water depth for vessel reception, for a four-horse wagon to turn around without difficulty. It would be quite suitable for boarding troops for amphibious operations. Almost all of the piles had been driven in and capped by January 11. On the following day the pile driver was scheduled to drop down to Liverpool Point, where elements of Sickle's Brigade were engaged in building winter quarters, to begin work on a second

"Government depot and landing at Rum Point, Mattawoman Creek, Md." *Official and illustrated war record, embracing nearly one thousand pictorial sketches by the most distinguished American artists of battles by land and sea*, Marcus J. Wright, ed. (Washington, 1899).

wharf sixty feet long and with six feet of water at high tide. This site would also be quite suitable for the departure of troops in proposed amphibious operations against Aquia Creek. "These two wharves," the general declared without hesitation, "are indispensable." [21]

The work on the winter cantonment at Liverpool Point, dubbed Camp Magaw, was begun about January 14. Within two weeks a veritable village of log cabins and tent sites replete with chimneys was almost finished, but not without notice by the enemy across the Potomac. "They are built on the bank of the river," wrote Private Felix Brannigan of Sickles' New York Excelsior Brigade on January 20,

"and directly opposite a Confederate battery which was not discovered until yesterday when it opened upon us, and kept up a heavy firing all the afternoon. The shells did us no damage as they either fell short or had too much elevation. For this we may thank our curtain of pine, which screened us from view. From the extensive preparation made at the point I suppose they are going to make it the commisaariat depot for the lower Army of the Potomac. Taking in connection with our building winter quarters, I think this means a stay for us at the Point all winter . . . The health of our regiment, and particularly our company, is excellent. Typhoid has almost disappeared. The weather is quite miled [*sic*], but we have frequent rains, so the consequence is mud – around, about, below, wherever you turn, the eternal mud has a permanent habitation. We, however, derive one benefit from it, that is, exemption from drill, it being an impossibility now as the mud is over our shoe tops all over the parade." [22]

***

Though the Potomac frontier between Southern Maryland and the Confederacy continued to be a significant focus of the Union's military attentions on the Eastern

Seaboard, it was certainly not the only one. In late October 1861 not long after General McClellan had suggested forming a U.S. Army amphibious force for coastal operations in the Chesapeake, he met with Brigadier General Ambrose E. Burnside, one of his officers, who mirrored the concept. "I mentioned to him a plan for the formation of a coast division," recalled the junior officer, "to which I had given some thought. After giving him a somewhat detailed account of the plan he asked me to put it in writing as soon as possible. The next day it was presented to him, and it met his approval. He laid it before the Secretary of War, by whom it was also approved." [23]

The features of the plan were not unlike those of McClellan's only larger in scope and strategic reach. The plan called for assembling up to 15,000 men from states mainly bordering on the Atlantic seacoast of the North, primarily mechanics and individuals familiar with the coasting trade. These would be engaged to fit out a fleet of light steamers, sailing ships, and barges suitable to transport the division, guns and supplies for rapid deployment along the rebel coast. The force would have to be strong enough to maintain a foothold on the enemy shore, penetrate the interior, and threaten his lines of communication.[24]

Following approval of the plan Burnside was dispatched to New York to begin fitting out the fleet. On October 23 orders were issued establishing his headquarters at Annapolis for the concentration of the troops, destined for the greatest amphibious operation of the war to that time. "Troops arrived from time to time at Annapolis, and all went well in the camp, which was established on beautiful grounds just outside the town," at St. John's College, on the campus of the U.S. Naval Academy, and amidst the gentle slopes of the hills and the oak groves along the rail line to Annapolis Junction. Soon, as railroad passengers passed, the trains were cheered by thousands of volunteers from Massachusetts, Connecticut, Pennsylvania and New York. In November a grand review was conducted under the watchful eyes of General Burnside, Governor Hicks, Governor John A. Andrew of Massachusetts and myriad spectators. It was immediately evident to Confederate agents that a great expedition was in the offing.[25]

Yet, nothing was easy. There was considerable difficulty in procuring light draft vessels as the navy had already called so many into service to facilitate the blockade of coastal and inland rivers ranging from the Potomac to the Texas coast. Not until December 12 was Burnside able to inform McClellan that sufficient transportation and armaments had been secured, but later noted sourly: "It was a motly fleet." Almost all of the Hudson River barges and propeller vessels from New York, coasting vessels, a few large passenger steamboats, tugs and ferries taken into service had required substantial refits, strengthenings, and other work. Coal and water vessels had to be chartered at Baltimore and all were ordered to rendezvous at Fort Monroe. But the core of the fleet, the transports, were ordered to Annapolis Harbor to take on the assembled troops, "at which point, after most mortifying and vexatious delays, they all arrived by the 4th of January, 1862." In all no fewer than sixteen transports, four schooners, and five floating batteries had assembled within sight of the waterfront. Embarkation of the troops, facilitated by a newly built wharf at the academy, began the next day. Following the January 8 inauguration ceremonies of the recently elected Governor of Maryland, Augustus W. Bradford, in which Burnside's officers and musicians participated, the expedition was finally able to depart. Their destination, after being joined by additional transports and warships in Hampton Roads, was to be Hatteras Inlet, North Carolina, where they were to rendezvous with a fleet of U.S. Navy warships. The expedition would culminate in the February 8 Battle of Roanoke Island, one of the first major Union victories of the war, and the occupation of strategic points of the North Carolina coast.[26]

***

Back on the Potomac, General Hooker anticipated a crossriver offensive against the rebels as part of an even larger operation being planned by McClellan. He thus queried Lieutenant Wyman on the precise number and strength of the Potomac Flotilla, which could be used in support of such an action. Wyman replied on January 24, 1862 that his force now consisted, temporarily as it turned out, of just eleven steamers scattered from Hallowing Point to Point Lookout. They carried a total of only twenty-four guns ranging in size from 8-inch shell guns to a single rifled 50-pounder. All were light and extremely vulnerable vessels, two of which were formerly ferryboats, drawing from four and a half to eight feet of water. Their total carrying capacity could accommodate no more than 1,000 men, 600 of whom would have to be transported aboard the ferryboats. "I am of opinion that were it desired to cross the river," he informed the general, "the vessels, with the exception of the ferryboats, could render better service in towing launches, barges, &c., loaded with troops, than by taking them on their decks." [27]

That little of the operational motions on the Union side of the river escaped rebel spies was evident with every passing day. It was reported in mid-January by a *New York Times* correspondent at Budd's Ferry in an article picked up by the national press "that the rebels not only derisively cry out our countersign of the night previous, but acquaint us what is to be the countersign of the ensuing night. They boast of having traveled along our entire division lines, and ascertained our exact locality, the numbers and nature of our armament by means of our countersign." [28] Yet work went on despite the enemy's intelligence gathering, poor weather, the rebel artillery blockade, impassable roads, and other significant logistical difficulties. Planning for a major offensive against the Confederate Army appeared to finally be commencing in earnest.

On January 27, 1862 General Hooker submitted a revised plan of attack to destroy the line of rebel batteries on the Potomac. The offensive, he proposed, would commence on the Union left with a single brigade to frontally assault the Aquia Creek gun emplacements with two columns of a regiment each. The amphibious attack would be launched from Liverpool Point, to which he could move his forces by inland route without being observed and embark without exposing his objective. The following day another landing at or near Powell or Neabsco Creek would be made by as much of his remaining division as he could move across the Potomac. This force would advance on the Colchester Road and attack the rear of the batteries disputing passage on the Occoquan. The door for a crossing by another division under General Samuel P. Heintzelman would thereby be opened. The result of the landings would be the destruction of the batteries before the rebels could parry the blow. The attack, he told McClellan, would inspire confidence among the men in his own division, deprive the enemy of a portion of their depot supplies, threaten their strategic communication line with Richmond, and force their relocation to protect their central depots inland. "The primary object in delivering an attack on my immediate front," he noted confidently, "I consider should be to destroy the batteries in order to give us the free use of the river and not to give battle; for there are other fields equally accessible, affording greater advantage." [29]

McClellan, who had other ideas that he kept to himself, personally opposed Hooker's plan as well as the president's desire for an immediate and general move toward Manassas. Nevertheless he let Hooker and others believe some action of sorts was in the offing, though weeks would pass without note. Finally, on February 17 a flotilla of barges, ostensibly for moving troops, was sent downriver from the capital, followed by thirty canal boats once employed on both the C&O and Alexandria canals until the onset of the war. Six howitzers were moved to Budd's Ferry for use in a landing by storming parties, with three hundred men assigned from New Jersey regiments to deploy and man them.[30]

The wharf construction projects, particularly at Liverpool Point, had of course not gone unnoticed by the Confederates. Undoubtedly anticipating the meaning of the wharf building as a prelude to an amphibious assault on the Virginia shore, the rebel command ordered even more new defensive works. On February 18 Hooker was informed that about 250 rebels had been breaking ground directly opposite Liverpool Point. There was some consolation in that the river was over three miles across at that location, and if the work was intended for establishing a battery it could do little harm to navigation. "If they cannot strike vessels distant 1 mile, they are not to be apprehended at more than three times that distance." But no one was prepared to say precisely what was going on. One of Lowe's balloons was up that same morning. The atmosphere being thick and remaining foggy into the evening, aerial observations proved unsatisfactory. Moreover, recently fallen snow now obscured the outlines of the enemy camps behind. The rebel actions could only be considered as defensive. Serious concerns about the works were soon dropped.[31]

At Camp Magaw on Liverpool Point, Private Felix Brannigan noted in a February 19 letter home: "There is a pontoon bridge coming down from Washington, and several barges to transport us to the Virginia side as soon as the weather permits. There are about 25,000 men to cross. So look out for a fight as soon as the roads become 'travelable.'" But the weather was not helping as the incessant rains, snow and deep muds had made movement out of the question. "It will be impossible to move artillery or baggage anywhere at present," he said. But there was some good news! "Notwithstanding the rain pouring down there is little sickness in camp." [32]

Hooker's plans for an amphibious assault, as a component of what everyone believed would be McClellan's offensive, were now more centered on the works opposite Chicamuxen and Budd's Ferry. "I now have the means, with the aid of the flotilla, of landing three brigades of my division on the rebel shore and of demolishing the batteries regularly," he informed headquarters. He proposed to begin with an attack on Cockpit Point, followed by a march down the river, and a crossing of the Quantico by boats. With six Dahlgren howitzers from high ground on the north side of Quantico, he assured, he could drive the rebels from the batteries at Shipping Point in just two hours. The guns and ammunition needed could be procured from the flotilla. Together with a Whitworth gun recently arrived, he was certain he could break up the camps supporting the enemy batteries, and place *George Page* in a most untenable position. "The free navigation of the river," he decided, "will give us immense advantage over the rebels, particularly so long as the roads remain in their present condition, and the destruction of the batteries will in no way expose future intentions of the Major General in the conduct of the war." [33]

By late February it seemed the Army of the Potomac was finally getting ready for the first time in seven months to move out from Washington, Alexandria and the Maryland shore to drive the rebels from Northern Virginia. A muster of Hooker's Division strength in Southern Maryland taken earlier in the month counted a total of eighteen field artillery pieces, 12,845 men in three brigades, Sickles', Cowdin's and Samuel H. Starr's, of which 387 officers and 10,415 men were present for duty. It was a small but critical component of McClellan's army, which now totaled 222,018 officers and men, sixty-nine pieces of heavy artillery, and 465 pieces of field artillery. Expectations were running high.[34]

As preparations for the offensive intensified, there were of course the usual "constant drill and discipline, the brightening of arms and polishing of buttons, and the exasperating fussiness on the part of company and regimental officers during inspection." But other signs were afoot as well. There was abnormally greater activity upon the Potomac in front of the Union campsites, as steam tugs pulled great sailing ships, barges and craft of every kind here and there. Morale was high in spite of atrocious weather and Confederate batteries on the opposite shore conducting sporadic bombardments.[35] During an inspection and review by General Sickles at Camp Magaw on February 28, all regiments of the Excelsior Brigade were deemed "in apple pie order" though the troops had "the distinguished *honor* of serving as a target for a Long Tom rifled howitzer in a Confederate battery opposite for the short space of three hours." Almost every shot fell on the drill field. One of the shells fell amidst a squad of twenty men, but thanks to the soft mud sank too deep to injure anyone, "only covering with a handsome *rough-casting* of that staple production of Liverpool Point on its explosion." [36]

With pressure building from his officers and from President Lincoln to move directly against the Confederate Army and then on to Richmond, McClellan chose to cancel the cross river assault. Depite appeals for action from Hooker and general disapproval from others, he remained adamant. Yet preparations continued as before regardless of bad weather.

On March 3 Private Brannigan, writing from Camp Magaw, described conditions in a letter to his loved ones back home:

"We are still floundering about in the mud, it is now pitch dark the wind is blowing a hurricane and lashing old Potomac's banks to an assault on the crumbling banks. I can hear the breakers dashing on the shore as I write. The wind comes in fierce gusts thro' the tall pines, bringing torrents of rain and spray down on our devoted shanties. The wind comes howling down the chimney in clouds of smoke, soot and ashes, the tears are in my eyes, and there is a perfect pandemonium, the boys singing and shouting 'Oh! Why did I go for a sojer.' The roof in sympathy with me sheds numerous tears from innumerable eyelet holes in its canvas back, which is now getting such a ducking. On such occasions as these we all go as noisy and jolly as possible, and if you ever want to see people who look as if they didn't care what corn is sold at by the bushel just look upon us at such times as these. The fact of the matter is, we're all 'spillin for a fight,' and don't know what to do with ourselves." [37]

Transports fully laden with soldiers, horses, hay and munitions began, slowly at first, to sweep down and across the river on March 7, 1862. Every possible water conveyance, from canal boats commandeered from the C&O and Alexandria Canal systems to enormous three decked steamboats, all pressed into service at McClellan's direction, were on the move. The long awaited advance against the Confederates by both land and water had finally begun. Not surprisingly, the move was well anticipated by the numerically inferior rebels who had already begun to retreat towards a new line on the Rappahannock. Yet in Washington McClellan remained adamant despite a now overwhelming clamor for his dismissal.

Finally, demoralized by the recent death of his son Willie and agitated by McClellan's arrogance, President Lincoln called the general for a meeting at 7:30 a.m., March 8. The conference did not go well at all. The general's condescending sense of superiority over his commander in chief was displayed as never before. The president's patience with his senior commander and his case of "the slows" had finally been exhausted. He immediately issued General War Order No. 3 calling for no alteration of the U.S. Army's base of operations, and explicit instructions for the army and navy to cooperate in a direct move to free the water route from Washington to the Chesapeake Bay from enemy batteries and other obstructions. Furthermore, he directed that no more than two corps of the Army of the Potomac be allowed to establish a new base of operations until the rebel batteries had been captured.[38]

Action was immediate. The onset of the Union offensive was intense both on the waters of the Potomac and all along the Federal lines on the landward Virginia side. The first reports to reach the public were sketchy at best. On the afternoon of March 8 the first news trickled out regarding the Union push. At 4 a.m. the steamers *Freeborn*, *Satellite*, *Island Belle*, and *Resolute* had opened fire on the line of rebel batteries extending from opposite Liverpool Point to Boget's Hill, including three at Aquia Creek. A number of shells had been thrown, but with what effect could not be ascertained in the prevailing darkness. The rebels had returned fire, but without striking any of the vessels. Between 10 and 11 a.m. the heavy cannonading could be heard from as far downriver as Blackstone Island. It was soon being reported that *Island Belle* and the *Satellite* had bombarded the railroad depot on Aquia Creek, and train cars filled with rebel troops were constantly arriving from Fredericksburg. The depot had been riddled with shot and shell. The enemy had returned the fire from several batteries and though their shot "fell thickly around the vessels . . . not one of them took effect." [39]

The troops at Aquia Creek were constantly receiving reinforcements. At the first bombardment the rebels beat the long roll in expectation of a landing, but as matters turned out they were more frightened than hurt. "Early this morning the steamer *Stepping Stones* ran past all the rebel batteries without eliciting a shot. About 9 o'clock the batteries at Cockpit Point and Shipping Point opened fire on Prof.

Lowe's balloon when in the air near Budd's Ferry. The fire was returned from the Maryland shore. The balloon was not hit." [40]

At 1 p.m. March 9 Wyman reported to Secretary Welles that both the Cockpit Point and Shipping Point batteries had been shelled for an hour without reply. Large fires were observed at both the latter and Evansport fortifications making it apparent that the rebels were destroying their material there. Frequent explosions provided evidence that the enemy's ammunition depots were being blown up as well. The gunboat *George Page*, lying in Quantico Creek, was burned and annihilated in a devastating explosion at her wharf. Hooker was soon delighted to report that all of the guns in the Cockpit Point battery had been left mounted on their carriages and were in good condition, except for a few that had been spiked. However, the enemy had made a mostly successful effort to burn the carriages of most of the guns at Shipping Point, though a large English rifled 98-pounder was left on its carriage uninjured. Most of the magazines had been blown up and great quantities of clothing and subsistence stores destroyed.

"I have sent 1,000 men across the river," Hooker reported with obvious glee, "to tumble the ordnance over the bluff banks on which the greater part of their batteries stand, in order that they may be more easily removed to such points as may hereafter be determined on. It is reported that the rebels took little or nothing with them in their retreat. Their roads appear to have been worse than ours, and their teams utterly worthless, from overwork and little or no feed." [41]

The unexpectedly hasty abandonment of the rebel works on the Potomac had provided Hooker with the opportunity he had long been hoping for, namely to conduct an amphibious sortie across the Potomac against the enemy batteries at Cockpit Point and Evansport. It was, however, not on the grand scale or the role for which he had been pressing for weeks. Early on March 9 he received orders to seize the "first favorable moment that presents itself" to destroy the batteries without incurring risk to his command. Even as Wyman's men were already addressing the rebel ordnance left in the fortifications overlooking the river, Hooker was belatedly ordering Colonel Starr to dispatch 500 men of his own New Jersey brigade to proceed onboard a barge anchored at Rum Point on Mattawoman Creek to undertake the mission at sunrise the following morning. They were to be towed by a navy tug to the Virginia shore to haul off the guns from the river banks tossed down by the Potomac flotillamen or left in the batteries. The detachment was to be provided with axes, spades and picks to cut away the parapets of the forts if necessary. Unfortunately, interservice communication failed, and Starr's men were still aboard the barge two days later awaiting a tug to tow them across.[42] The amphibious assault had fizzled, though McClellan's central landward thrust from the north seemed unstoppable.

At Centreville General Joseph E. Johnston had already ordered his heavily outnumbered and outgunned troops to retire toward the Rappahannock from their positions at Evansport, Dumfries, the Occoquan and Manassas, all of which had been held for nearly nine months, to establish a new line of defense. Within two days the rebels had reached Rappahannock Station, wearied by the trek through ice and cold, and thick Virginia mud, but intact. When the Federal juggernaut finally reached Centreville and occupied the abandoned enemy camps they found only deserted huts and fortifications defended by fake cannon, dubbed "Quaker guns." All about them the astonished bluecoats found destruction, wrecked railroad tracks, burning supplies and installations. The rebel army, still a major force in being however, had deftly managed to slip intact from McClellan's grasp.

But now, for the first time in months, the Potomac River was entirely open to navigation. Washington was once again deemed secure. The threat of invasion or even incursions into Southern Maryland also seemed to be at an end.

Then troubling news was laid upon the president's desk. On the day before the Federal offensive began, two navy warships in Hampton Roads, the frigate *Congress* and sloop of war *Cumberland*, had been totally destroyed, and the steam screw frigate *Minnesota* driven aground. It had all been the work of the monster rebel ironclad warship CSS *Virginia*, ex-USS *Merrimac*, former pride of the U.S. Navy. In Washington there was immediate consternation that the great ironclad's next target would be the capital city. Notwithstanding the diminutive wooden boats of the Potomac Flotilla, some feared that there was little in the way to prevent it. Then on March 9, even as Federal troops were pressing into Northern Virginia, a monumental battle between the revolutionary Union ironclad *Monitor* and CSS *Virginia*, though ending in a standoff, altered the history of naval warfare forever after. It also introduced yet another threat to the capital of the United States of America.

AN ACT

". . . the theatre of these outrages . . ."

Within hours of the appearance of the CSS *Virginia* and the destruction wrought upon the American fleet in Hampton Roads on March 8, 1862, waves of dread were communicated almost instantly via telegraph from the Chesapeake Tidewater as far north as New York City and then across the nation. Even as General McClellan's grand Army of the Potomac was pressing the Confederates from their position in Northern Virginia, the Navy Department was struggling to patch together a defensive posture should the seemingly unbeatable rebel behemoth steam up the bay and into the Potomac to attack Washington.

By the late afternoon of March 9 Commandant Dahlgren had already proposed and prepared emergency measures for guarding the river. Eight canal boats provided by the Quartermaster's Department had been loaded with stone and were being readied for scuttling in the channel dowriver to block the rebel ironclad from ascending. Another eight vessels were to be ready for sinking by that same evening. Instructions had been sent to the Potomac Flotilla directing that the last eight barges were to be sunk as a backup at some choke point where the channel had the least depth of water. An 11-inch gun and a 50-pounder were being moved to Giesboro Point where platforms were being rushed to completion for a battery of even heavier guns. Shot was being hurriedly cast at the Washington Navy Yard for both of them, and it was expected that a full supply would be ready by the following day. "If there should be any use at all for a battery on Giesboro," Dahlgren suggested to Secretary Welles, "there ought to be twenty of the heaviest cannon; shot of 170 pounds at 50 and 100 yards will be apt to do something." And finally, Dahlgren ordered a "smart steamer" to be sent to the mouth of the Potomac to watch for the expected appearance of the dreaded ironclad.[1]

In the meantime Secretary Cameron was busily visiting all of the critical defensive positions on the river, and readily authorized Dahlgren to draw on any of the regiments or forts around Washington for men, guns and munitions that he might need. He also authorized the Navy Yard commandant to seize any or all of the private steamers plying the river under Army charters to be sent around for whatever use was deemed necessary.[2]

It must have been with some trepidation that Captain Edward P. McCrea received his orders late on March 8 to depart from the Navy Yard, immediately proceed to Point Lookout with *Jacob Bell*, and watch for the ironclad's approach. He was indeed well aware that his 141-foot wooden sidewheel steamer, armed with but a single 8-inch Dahlgren smooth bore and a standard 32-pounder, would unquestionably end up as kindling should she encounter the great warship in a fight.[3] But that was not his mission. To give early warning of the enemy's expected arrival was his only objective. For *Jacob Bell*'s undoubtedly nervous crew it is likely that almost every vessel seen from a distance was not scrutinized with complete objectivity. Early on the morning of March 10 McCrea put in at Point Lookout to send an urgent telegraph to headquarters: "From appearances the *Merrimack*

[*Virginia*] is off the point." The message was received by Lieutenant Foxhall A. Parker, Executive Officer at the Navy Yard, and immediately conveyed to Secretary Welles.[4]

Fortunately the sighting had been in error. Word soon reached the Navy Department from Fort Monroe regarding the actual events in Hampton Roads, namely the arrival of *Monitor* and her historic engagement with *Virginia*, which somewhat alleviated the immediate tension. At 10 p.m., March 9 Secretary Welles learned that *Virginia* had retired from the scene of battle. Then even as McCrea, unaware of the actual events, was reporting sighting the phantom rebel off Point Lookout the next morning, Dahlgren was already suspending the deployment of guns and other defensive measures for Washington.[5]

Within days of the monumental engagement between ironclads at Hampton Roads serious concerns regarding the defense of the capital against a possible enemy naval incursion began to garner the attention of Federal military planners. *George Page* had been little more than a nuisance, a minor threat compared to that of a heavily armed ironclad warship. Washington had already been encircled by fortifications, but the water approach was still vulnerable to the newly born menace. The navy, no longer focusing upon a blockade by rebel batteries but upon a potential naval attack by water, was now forced to rethink its defensive posture on the Potomac. Again the sinking of obstructions in several key shallow passages was considered as was strengthening the waterway's ship defenses. A major warship at Hampton Roads, the great old frigate *Brandywine*, was ordered up as a reinforcement but only after Wyman had taken soundings of the ever-shifting bottom at its most dangerous points. He informed Secretary Welles of his findings and opinions regarding the river's defense on March 19, and in particular those pertaining to the dangerous Kettle Bottom Shoals off Mathias Point Neck.

"Doubts have arisen in my mind," he wrote, "regarding the practicability of blocking the channel at the Kettle Bottoms. I have had it sounded, as also the channel in the narrowest point at Nanjemoy, both of which are wider and have much more water than the chart gives (which throughout is incorrect). I now think that Smith's Point [in Charles County] and Mattawoman Muds are the best point for blocking, and that the frigates had better come up to Smith's Point and the barges which are at present at Kettle Bottoms removed to that point." [6]

On March 25 Welles informed Wyman that *Brandywine*, which was needed elsewhere, would not be coming into the Potomac after all. Ignoring the lieutenant's doubts regarding obstructing the channel, the secretary was adamant. If sunken vessels and obstructions wouldn't do the trick, try something else. "Nets and hawsers," he determined, "stretched across the narrowest part of the channel will foul the *Merrimack*'s propeller." Wyman was at once authorized to prepare such for obstructing her progress.[7]

The precaution fortunately proved unnecessary. Less than two months later, on May 11, the terror of the Chesapeake, the CSS *Virginia*, while attempting to retire up the James River during the Confederate evacuation of Norfolk, was accidentally run aground and blown up to prevent capture. Regardless of the early anxiety worn by Federal authorities, the threat temporarily subsided as the theater of war quickly began to shift elsewhere. It seemed to many, however, that other ironclads might soon be built by the enemy and sent against Washington. Such a threat would require the implementation of more definite measures than nets and obstructions to defend the capital.

Soon plans were underway to erect two massive river defenses. The first was dubbed Battery Rogers, a half mile below the city wharves at Alexandria. The second was Fort Foote, erected on the Potomac shores of Prince George's County on Rozier's Bluff eight miles below Washington. The former was situated on an elevation twenty-eight feet above high water with parapets twenty-five feet thick. It was to be armed with five giant ship-killing 200-pounder Parrott guns and one 15-inch Rodman. The great Rodman weighing in at 49,000 pounds, was capable of firing 300-pound cannonballs three miles down the river, and required fifty pounds of powder to make a shot at a twenty-five degree elevation. General Barnard later wrote that the battery "was arranged to throw its principal fire upon any vessel attempting to pass up the river at a range of 600 yards, that being the distance to mid-channel, half a mile. It also commanded, with an enfilading fire, the entire river channel, from shore to shore." Battery Rogers was completed in 1863.[8]

Fort Foote, designed by Barnard and finally begun in 1863, was even more substantial in size, with a perimeter of 472 yards, and provided with massive firepower. It was armed with four 200-pounder rifled Parrotts, two giant 15-inch Rodmans, and six 30-inch Parrott guns mounted *en barbette*. Platforms for eleven additional guns were incorporated in the construction should more artillery be needed. Construction of the works, described as a "model" fortification by army engineers, would be ongoing from 1863 to the end of the war, and was a most laborious undertaking indeed. Owing to the extremely poor condition of roads, the artillery, among the largest guns built during the Civil War, had to be transported from the Washington Arsenal by boat, and moved up the bluffs from the river shore by 300 to 400 soldiers. The concussion generated by firing at targets in the river obliged witnesses to stand on the tips of their toes and open their mouths to minimize the effects of the blast. In 1864 Barnard would describe the fort as "a powerful enclosed work and the most elaborate in its internal arrangements of all the defenses of Washington." [9]

Barnard's successor, Colonel Barton S. Alexander, concerned about the possibility of an entire rebel flotilla penetrating the Potomac, advocated additional defenses, primarily obstructions in the river itself. The main impediment would be a massive chain 400-feet in length. Dubbed the "Alexandrine Chain," this great linked barrier was to run across the river from the waterfront slightly south of Fort Foote and be held in place by twenty-three great anchors. The $300,000 project was designed to detain an enemy fleet for an hour or more in a position that would expose it to the murderous fire of the fort above.[10]

First garrisoned by 180 men of Company I, 2nd U.S. Artillery, and Company G, 3rd U.S. Artillery, Fort Foote would, during its construction, welcome many important dignitaries such as President Lincoln and his cabinet, who were awed by the works and the stupendous size of the guns. On August 20, 1863, the president and a party of notables including now Secretary of War Stanton, Quartermaster General Meigs, Barnard and others personally toured the fortifications and dined on local peaches, crackers and cheese before returning to Washington aboard the steamer

General Hooker. Yet not everyone was delighted by the works. Gideon Welles for one, while acknowledging the defenses to be strong, believed them to be a terrible waste of money and manpower. As the navy's reliance on wooden men of war was shifting almost overnight to propeller-driven ships of iron, so did its belief that the Potomac's defense must rely upon ironclads and torpedoes. "In going over the works," he later wrote, "a melancholy feeling came over me that there should have been so much waste, for the fort is not wanted, and it will never fire a hostile gun." [11] And it never did.

***

As a result of the March 9, 1862 offensive the route south as far as Aquia now appeared open to unopposed Federal invasion, perhaps as far as Fredericksburg. Yet McClellan had been unwilling to pursue the enemy as Lincoln hoped. The general had other plans after undertaking what essentially proved to be an offensive exercise in massive force. In truth he wasn't quite sure where Johnston's army was, nor apparently cared to pursue. In the meantime Hooker's and Sickle's troops in Southern Maryland patiently awaited orders to cross the Potomac from Liverpool Point for a landing at Aquia Creek, the far left flank of the Union invasion of Northern Virginia. Lincoln was exasperated. Two days later, on March 11, he removed "Little Mac" as General-in-Chief of the Federal Armies though he would retain his command of the Army of the Potomac.

Precisely where was the enemy? McClellan was soon obliged to send down to Hooker to see if something could be done to obtain trustworthy information. Hooker in turn handed the mission to Sickles, who had continued to prepare for a move against Aquia and had since 1861 been aggressively employing black fugitives knowledgeable with the countryside and now regularly deployed them in reconnaissance operations.

One of the most notable and briefly famous of Sickle's black spies was James Lawson, an escaped slave from the Taylor plantation near Hempstead, Virginia, opposite Maryland Point. Having left his wife and children he had fled to the Potomac where he was taken aboard *Thomas Freeborn* and enlisted. His valuable knowledge of the landscape on the Virginia shore was immediately apparent soon after his arrival. Captain Samuel Magaw was impressed with the new recruit's quiet intelligence and courage and soon decided to dispatch him on "a scouting tour through the rebel fortifications, more to test his reliability than anything else." Pressure for a Union strike against Confederate forces had been mounting and reliable data gathering on rebel positions and strength was imperative. Balloon observations were one thing but hands-on was deemed far more superior by most. Such an assignment for a white scout was dangerous enough. For a black spy there was the assurance of torture and certain execution if captured. Nevertheless Lawson faithfully carried out the mission without fanfare, which duly impressed the captain even more. In the late fall of 1861 Magaw resolved to utilize his new agent as often as necessary.[12]

Shortly after returning from his first foray into enemy territory, Lawson again alighted at night on the Virginia shore, this time at White House Landing below Mount Vernon. Somehow evading enemy patrols, he managed to penetrate several miles into the interior until his advance was abruptly stopped short by fire from rebel pickets and posted sentries. There was no alternative but to beat a hasty retreat to the Potomac where he was brought off safely by Magaw's own gig, though under intense enemy musketry.

Having earned the trust and admiration of Magaw and all aboard *Freeborn*, Lawson's next mission was to be even more precarious than his last and far more personal. Having left his family behind when he escaped from the Taylor plantation, his longing for his wife and four children by now knew no bounds. Finally, one cold January day in 1862, he approached the captain and requested permission to be landed on the Virginia shore that same evening to rescue his family.

"Why, Jim," said Captain Magaw, "how will you be able to pass the pickets?"

"I want to try, captain," said the former slave quietly. "I think I can get 'em over safely."

"Well, you have my permission," said the officer, well aware that Lawson was daring the impossible. He promptly ordered one of the flotilla gunboats to land his prized spy "on whatever part of the shore Jim designated, and return for him the following evening."

When the gunboat arrived at the appointed rendezvous site, Lawson, his wife and children were there to meet it. Transported across the Potomac to Liverpool Point, they were given a log house to live in by Colonel Graham, immediately behind his own new quarters. It was soon learned that the intrepid black spy had literally run a gauntlet of sentries unharmed, never taking to the roads and always keeping to the woods, "every footpath of which, and almost every tree, he knew from his boyhood up."

At Liverpool Point Lawson's reunion with his family was short lived, for his fame and fearlessness had by then reached the highest levels of the Union command. A few weeks after his family's escape he was dispatched on another critical reconnaissance and again returned unscathed with more valuable intelligence. This time he was highly complimented by Generals Hooker and Sickles as well as officers of the Potomac Flotilla. Now, though he could not have known it, his most dangerous assignments of all loomed before him.[13]

Soon after the Confederate withdrawal toward Fredericksburg on March 9, the Union high command again sought Lawson's services. Hooker was almost entirely dependent on his black spies in the area and information provided by refugee slaves, but Lawson was the best.[14]

This time both Sickles and Magaw personally selected him. On or about the evening of Saturday, March 9, even as the rebel army was in full retreat, he was summoned to Colonel Graham's quarters on Liverpool Point. As he entered shortly after 9 p.m. he saw awaiting him three men, Sickles, the colonel, and a reporter from the *New York Times*.

Sickles got right to the point.

"Jim," he said, "I want you to go over to Virginia tonight and find out what forces they have at Aquia Creek and Fredericksburg. If you want any men to accompany you, pick them out."

"I know *two* men that would like to go," answered the black man, well aware that the assignment was tantamount to a suicide mission.

"Well get them," replied the general, "and be back as soon as possible."

No more words were exchanged as Lawson turned toward the door, and within minutes was en route to the contraband camp where more than 130 blacks who had come across from Mathias Point with Colonel Graham on his last raid were ensconced. In short order he had returned with two "very intelligent looking" men.

"Are you all ready?" inquired the general.

"All ready, Sir," responded the trio as if one.

"Well, here, Jim," said Sickles, unbuckling his belt and holster, "you take my pistol and, if you are successful, I will give you $100."

All six men in the room were well aware that success was likely to be an elusive mistress, but the three black spies displayed no sign of fear.

Bidding the three white men goodbye the black trio immediately started off to board the gunboat *Satellite*, Captain Amos P. Foster, which already had a head of steam raised. The trip from the army wharf at Liverpool Point across the river to the landing site a little below the rebel batteries on Potomac Creek, masked by the midnight darkness, was short and without incident. The reconnaissance team had less than a few hours to accomplish their mission and return by daybreak to the appointed pick up site with whatever information they could assemble.

The expedition proved more difficult than even Lawson had anticipated owing to the great distance his team was obliged to travel on foot into the interior. Sunday came and went, but the three spies were nowhere to be seen from the deck of *Satellite*, which was awaiting a signal light to announce their position in the predawn darkness. The following morning the gunboat returned again to the station off the appointed pickup site. Still no signal. Then as dawn broke, Captain Foster observed a mounted picket guard on patrol near the beach, and almost in the same instant spotted Lawson in a woods to the left of the cavalrymen, sighting his pistol on the unwary rebels.

The captain instantly ordered his gig manned and rowed toward shore, undoubtedly as a distraction. Slowly the mounted rebels moved along the beach intent on intercepting the boat, still unaware of the recon team in the woods. A shot from *Satellite*'s gun, however, soon sent the horsemen scurrying. As the boat came ashore, Lawson, one of his colleagues, and two additional black fugitive he had gathered up while en route, boarded. The other colleague, a man named Cornelius, who had left Liverpool Point with him, was nowhere to be seen.[15]

The *New York Times* reporter later detailed Cornelius's end while the party made its way towards the shore through the rebel infested countryside.

"He had been challenged by a picket when some distance in advance of Jim, and the negro, instead of answering the summons, fired the contents of Sickle's revolver at the picket. It was an unfortunate occurrence, for at that time the entire picket guard rushed out of a small house near the spot, and fired the contents of their muskets at Jim's companion, killing him instantly. Jim and the other three hid themselves in a hollow, near a fence, and after the pickets gave up pursuit, crept through the woods to the shore. From the close proximity of the pickets, Jim could not display a light which was the signal for Foster to send a boat." [16]

Upon hearing Lawson's tale Foster immediately determined to revenge the black volunteer's death. Steaming his gunboat dangerously parallel to the shore he sighted his guns upon a barn behind which the rebel cavalry was hiding. He fired two shells, one of which went straight through the structure, killing four of the enemy and seven of their horses. "Well, Jim," he said solemnly, "I've avenged the death of poor Cornelius." [17]

The specifics of the information gleaned by Lawson can be seen in the communications from Robert Wyman, commander of the flotilla, to Secretary Welles immediately after the spy's return: "I have received information through our spies, landed the night before last, that there are about forty regiments of the enemy at Fredericksburg; that they are still in force at Aquia, but making all preparations to leave. The enemy expect to make a determined stand at Fredericksburg. They are working fast on their gunboats. The *St. Nicholas* [now *CSS Rappahannock*] and *Virginia* are moving from Lowry's Point to Feredreicksburg; there is a battery at the former place. Mr Henry Lewis has charge of the battery and bats." [18]

Lawson's bold enterprises as a Union spy did not go unrecognized. Soon after the ex-slave's safe return to Liverpool Point, General Hooker transmitted to the War Department an account of the daring reconnaissance mission to Fredericksburg in the very heart of enemy territory, "and united with the army and navy stationed on the left wing of the Potomac, in the hope that the Government will present Jim with a fitting recompense for his gallant service." Indeed, for a brief moment in time, James Lawson, dubbed "Potomac Jim" by the *New York Times*, was celebrated as a negro who deserved more honor than that accorded to the famed black Haitian revolutionary Toussaint L'Ouverture.[19]

The subsequent spy missions of Lawson and his colleagues have not been documented as such, but it seems likely that their services were continually engaged. By March 12 Hooker had learned from his spies that the rebels were finally evacuating Aquia and possibly fortifying Fredericksburg where at least 17,000 troops were assembling. But of equal importance, it was discovered that the rail lines from Manassas were still operational and the key bridges over the creek and elsewhere were still intact. If an advance were to be made, the bridges would have to be taken. But what forces were there to protect them? "My negro spies are not in," he had assured McClellan's adjutant, "but this information is reliable." And it was, for soon more intelligence arrived.[20]

"One of my negro spies," he wrote only hours later, "reports that he went to the Rappahannock; saw large bodies of troops yesterday below Fredericksburg, on the Caroline [County] side of the river. Troops, he says, are concentrating there in good numbers. Intrenchments are being thrown up on the racecourse – a place, it is said, artillery commands the approach for a great distance; vicinity a level plain. The bridges about Fredericksburg are standing. The rebels expect a battle there. The prominent citizens there have their goods packed, ready for a move. This can be relied on." [21]

The disposition of the rebel army, detailed by spies such as Lawson and his colleagues, had provided the Union Army with critical data that would have otherwise been difficult if not impossible to acquire. It also produced opportunities. One such opening was acted upon when it was learned that a rebel cavalry force of about 180 men was still stationed nearly opposite Camp Magaw and three miles back from the Potomac. The site was believed to be the enemy headquarters from which pickets were sent out in the direction of Dumfries to monitor the Union lines.

On March 16 General Sickles was undoubtedly delighted to receive direct orders to destroy or capture this force. He was instructed to immediately detach five companies to attack and eliminate the enemy pickets that same night. The preparations and execution were to be undertaken in the utmost secrecy. "An excellent guide, a negro, whose home is in that vicinity, can conduct the command to the point without observation. He will be sent to report to you today." It is not known if the guide was Lawson though it seems likely. The general was instructed to place "an intelligent and discrete officer" in charge of the operation, though it appears that he may have chosen to personally take command. A tug was to be obtained from Lieutenant Commander Magaw, as well as a scow and barge to carry the troops and transport them back, upon completion of the expedition, along with any captured horses. If none were available the expedition was to be deferred. [22]

The mission was delayed for the next two weeks undoubtedly owing to the deployment of all available vessels to facilitate McClellan's expedition to Hampton Roads and the beginning of his ill-fated Peninsula Campaign. Nevertheless on or about April 1 Sickles selected 1,000 men, 200 from each of his five regiments who, in light marching order with nothing but arms and ammunition and cooked rations for two days, were transported and escorted by the Navy from Liverpool Point to Shipping Point. Their primary objective was to test the force and positions of the rebels to the south. The Excelsiors landed on the Virginia shore a little after daybreak, and by 7 or 8 a.m. they had commenced an audacious, unmolested advance into the interior toward Fredericksburg. Sending out scouts in every direction they rapidly proceeded to within a short distance of Potomac Creek. When but a few miles from Stafford Courthouse they encountered videts of a regiment of rebel cavalry thrown out to meet them "in consequence of information furnished by negroes, who had been sent forward to spread the report that Sickle's command was of the Army of the Potomac." The general ordered an immediate advance at double quick time.[23]

Now was seen the spectacle of a compete subversion of military rules. Instead of cavalry charging infantry, infantry accosted cavalry, drawn up in line of battle and eager to assault and stampede the latter. The rebel horsemen quickly fell back in confusion upon two regiments of North Carolina infantry and some artillery to defend the Potomac Creek Bridge. Panic stricken and not knowing the strength of the Federals, both horse and foot streamed back through Stafford Courthouse to Fredericksburg where Beauregard had massed his troops. All in their camps was captured or destroyed. The bridge was seized and occupied without resistance, and the Yankees advanced to a hill overlooking Stafford Courthouse beyond which lay more camps of the rebels. Here Sickles halted, bivouacked, threw out his pickets, detached a provost guard to protect the village and fed his troops on captured supplies from the enemy encampment. A New York City clock was taken from Stafford Courthouse and brought back as a prize of war by one of the brigade.

While the Excelsiors were enjoying the halt of two hours, Sickles was gathering information about the enemy and sent scouts to the river to communicate with the gunboats. These he had expected to follow on his flank down the Potomac and cover him if pushed by superior enemy numbers. To his undoubted dismay, nothing could be seen or heard of the gunboats. It was later discovered that the warship had dropped down the river only eight or ten miles – as far as Commander Magaw believed it possible for Sickles to march – and then returned to Shipping Point, where it was supposed he would find the raiders ensconced.

In a private letter the general recalled his next move: "I at once decided to return by the same road I took in the advance, thinking the enemy would suspect I might seek safety from pursuit in detours and crossroads. My guess was a good one, for while I took the more direct route the enemy wasted time in looking for me everywhere, and so I got back to the place of embarkation – Shipping Point – at daylight of the following morning, having marched 40 miles in 24 hours, defeated a force of double my numbers supported by artillery, and gaining full information of the position and numbers and disposition of the enemy." [24]

The Excelsiors left Stafford Courthouse about dusk and reached the banks of the Potomac toward daylight, where the navy was lying to cover the re-embarkation. The next morning, while they were waiting to embark and secure approximately forty captured horses, the rebels launched a series of brief attacks upon the stragglers. "On this occasion a Gatling gun (then known as coffee-mill guns) was brought into play, and proved effective at a range of 1,500 yards. Thus was the first time this species of artillery was used against any enemy." When the Federals initially landed they dragged it along by hand, but soon tiring of this experiment they impressed horses, improvised harness, and moved it along expeditiously and serviceably as it proved. In the face of the enemy the Excelsiors built a raft to ferry over the captured animals and in the course of the day arrived safely at Liverpool Point.[25]

The reconnaissance in force, which would not have been possible without the information supplied by Lawson and the cadre of black spies employed by Hooker and Sickles, was a minor but unmitigated success. A number of saddles were emptied among the rebel cavalry in the skirmishing, and considerable stores were captured, used or otherwise destroyed. General McDowell's subsequent advance on Fredericksburg and the occupation of that town were doubtless based on the information received on his trip from Liverpool Point to Washington in company with General Sickles soon after the foray into enemy territory, Sickles having been relieved from his command immediately upon his return from the ably conducted expedition from Southern Maryland. For this reconnaissance Sickles received but few words of acknowledgment, for greater enterprises and battles were already underway elsewhere.

Owing in part to intelligence gathered by Lawson and others like him, Fredericksburg was surrendered to the forces of General McDowell on Saturday, April 19, 1862. The gunboat *St. Nicholas*, captured by the daring exploit of Hollins and Zarvona less than a year earlier, and the schooner *Virginia* along with forty private schooners were destroyed by the retreating rebels. Strategic bridges were burned along with critical corn and grain stocks. Now on the peninsula between the James and York rivers farther to the south, the Union Army was again on the march. It seemed that the long anticipated Federal advance to end the war was finally underway.

***

It was on March 17 that General McClellan, though diminished in rank, nevertheless began embarking his legions in an armada of transports at Alexandria bound for Fort Monroe. Leaving behind 2,000 men for the defense of Washington and 35,000 for the Shenandoah Valley, his own force of 135,000 was bound for the peninsula lying between the James and York rivers. The first division, the III Army Corps under General Charles Smith Hamilton, sailed without opposition under escort of *Anacostia, Freeborn,* and *Island Belle.* The second division, which sailed several days later, was shepherded by *Satellite, Coeur de Lion* and *Island Belle,* with the third division under General Fitz John Porter following soon afterwards. On April 1 McClellan embarked with his headquarters staff aboard the steamer *Commodore.* His general intention was to conduct a grand endrun against Richmond that would soon be known as the Peninsular Campaign. Though the campaign was doomed to fail, the operational move would ultimately result in the capture of the historic port of Yorktown, the rebel abandonment of Norfolk, and the destruction of the rebel ironclad *Virgina.* Owing to McClellan's goal of maintaining a substantial numerical superiority over the enemy, many of Hooker's troops then in Southern Maryland were soon ordered to muster with the rest of the Army of the Potomac at Fort Monroe in Hampton Roads.

The departure of a major component of the occupation forces in Southern Maryland was not without misfortune for the inhabitants. Purportedly outrageous actions by the U.S. Army as they passed down the Potomac in transports were reported by the *St. Mary's Beacon* to have occurred in, among other places, the St. Inigoes District of St. Mary's County. "We have been informed," it was stated,

> "that a detachment of Federal soldiers, some fifteen hundred in number, connected with General Hooker's brigade, heretofore stationed in Charles county, while *en route* for Fort Monroe, landed last week in the lower section of our county and greatly distinguished themselves by robbing and plundering the hen roosts and pantries of our people in that section and by the commission of other acts of violence of a still more shameful and atrocious character. We have not been informed of the name of the regiment or detachment which committed these outrages or under which command it was acting at the time. We have been promised a full and impartial account of the achievements of these gallant defenders of the Constitution and Laws during their stay in St. Inigoes District, which we expect to present to our readers next issue. We learn, with pleasure, that, during the stay of these marauders, the small squad of Indiana cavalry which is stationed in that district, exerted itself manfully to protect our citizens, and in one or two instances with signal effect. We prefer not to give this week any particulars in regard to the number and character of the outrages said to have been committed, because our information at present is chiefly of a second hand character and may be modified somewhat by subsequent accounts." [26]

One of the inhabitants who reportedly suffered from the looting was Father Basil Pacciarini, a Jesuit priest of the Roman Catholic Church who had arrived in Southern Maryland in 1860 to become Superior of the venerable St. Inigoes Church. He had at first found the inhabitants of his parish to be "happy and affluent," but with the outbreak of war his labors in tending to his flock had intensified tenfold. A simple man of character known for his great tact in dealing with all men and women, both black and white, the good Father would, during his long career, bring many converts into the faith. It apparently mattered little to the soldiers who invaded his house at St. Inigoes Manor off the St. Mary's River who were unknowingly replicating the ravages of British invaders during the War of 1812. Nor was the symbolism of the invasion lost on the editor of the *St. Mary's Beacon*. Referring to the landing of Lord Baltimore's first settlers in 1634, the editor noted that "the theatre of these outrages" was "the consecrated spot where was first proclaimed on this continent by the Maryland Pilgrims the doctrine of civil and religious freedom." [27]

Though the charges were never verified and were soon forgotten, Pacciarini's true faith was not impugned as he repaid the purported outrage with unrestrained character by establishing a temporary chapel on Johnsons Island [on the approximate site of modern Star of the Sea Catholic Church, Solomons Island] in Calvert County, near the entrance to the Patuxent, for the spiritual needs of the occupying troops.

***

The ill treatment of Southern Marylanders by Union troops notwithstanding, for Washington and the adjacent Maryland countryside it seemed the crisis that had cast its long shadow over the region since April 1861 had been resolved. No longer was the rebel blockade of the Potomac a problem. Nor were Confederate incursions into Southern Maryland a threat. Now President Lincoln could finally turn his attention to an issue that he had long championed, the emancipation of slaves in the District of Columbia. It was a move that without question would elicit the hostility and anxiety of white Southern Marylanders, especially those who lived on the outskirts of the city, and slave owners with a vested interest in their human property. But the president was resolute.

For Lincoln, who had been attempting to steer a middle road toward gradual emancipation, it was to be an important step though one with which he would not be entirely comfortable. As early as December 21, 1848, while still a congressman from Illinois, he had opposed a plan introduced by Representative Daniel Gott of New York to abolish the institution in the nation's capital as too immediate and unacceptable to Southerners. The bill failed and Lincoln prepared an alternative plan calling for gradual abolition in the District, with compensation paid to slave owners willing to manumit their living property for a price. Lacking support, the measure died aborning.[28]

Yet abolitionist sentiment in Congress was now running high. Many residents, however, were apprehensive that emancipation of slavery in the city would provoke unanticipated consequences. In December the Washington *Evening Star* defined the fears held by some that such an act might set off a chain reaction. If "revolutionary changes be made in the local law of the District, for buncombe at the North instead of a free negro population of perhaps 14,000, in the current anomalous condition of the country the District of Columbia cannot fail to become at once the harbor for at least 50,000 negroes, practically freed as an incident of the war. With such a population, without especial restraining laws, Washington will be rendered almost uninhabitable to the white man." [29]

Nevertheless that same month Henry Wilson, the junior Senator from Massachusetts, sponsored another bill, drafted and promoted by Colonel Marshall Key, a judge advocate on the staff of General McClellan, calling for the total abolition of slavery in Washington, D.C. In the face of substantial opposition from slaveholding legislators, aldermen and city residents, the bill passed the Senate on April 3, 1862 by a vote of twenty-nine in favor to fourteen opposed. Eight days later the House of Representatives also approved the bill despite certain wishes of the president, who wanted the measure to include a proviso making the emancipation effective only after a positive vote from the citizens of the District. He had also hoped that the measure would postpone implementation until a certain amount of time after the bill was signed. But it was not to be. On April 16 Lincoln finally placed his signature on the document, which was formally titled "An Act for the release of certain persons held to service or labor in the District of Columbia." [30]

The emancipation plan that freed 3,185 men, women and children still enslaved in the District relied on a three-person Emancipation Commission to distribute $1,000,000 in allotted funding to pay $300 in compensation to every slaveholder for each individual legally owned slave. An additional $100,000 was authorized to pay up to $100 to each former slave if he or she would agree to emigrate to colonize in a foreign country such as Haiti or Liberia. In order to receive compensation slaveholders were required to provide written evidence of their ownership of each individual freed as well as swear allegiance to the Union. Although most of the petitioners who submitted for compensation were white, a few black freemen also filed, many of them having once purchased their family members away from their own onetime owners but still legally deemed as slaves. In the end almost all of the million dollars appropriated in the act was spent.[31]

In a limited effort to improve the situation, on Saturday, July 12, 1862 Congress passed an addendum to the original act, permitting people once held in bondage whose former owners had failed to file claims for compensation to do so. Additionally the District of Columbia "Supplemental Emancipation Act" permitted blacks to testify to the veracity of others' claims in a court of law. Prior to the addendum the admissibility of testimony provided by African Americans had usually been challenged. Thus it was also a new and elevating development for those who had fought for impartiality of treatment under the law.

There were of course problems for both the newly emancipated as well as freemen in the District. The older fugitive slave laws still applied to those who had run away from their owners in Maryland and Virginia to reach what many believed would be salvation in the city. Such fugitives were still subject to the Fugitive Slave Act of 1850 under the tenants of the Supreme Court's Dred Scott Dcision of 1857, which it was now argued by some applied only to States while others included the Federal District, and that slaves that had fled there could be retrieved by their owners. It would cause unending difficulties as waves of refugee blacks, especially from Southern Maryland, began to flow into Washington believing that they would be free as well. Not until the Maryland laws were finally repealed in 1864 by a new State Constitution would their hopes be finally realized.[32]

The immediate reaction in some quarters of Maryland was, as expected, quite miserable. "Up to the time when the administration identified itself fully with the Abolitionists, by destroying slavery in the District of Columbia," noted one publication, "the loyal men in the Border States were hopeful of a speedy suppression of the rebellion, the preservation of the Union and returning peace and prosperity, but since then, they are without hope and know not where to look for succor. They have nothing to cheer them – nothing to hope for – nothing to look forward to with joy, since abolitionism has forced the administration to falsify its pledges and drive them from its support by invading their rights. A dark and gloomy future is now before them and they are in the depths of despondency." [33]

As word of emancipation in the District, as predicted, rapidly spread among the slaves of Southern Maryland, many chanced an escape and sprint to the capital city hoping to find sanctuary. In St. Mary's County alone, within less than a month after passage of the bill, no fewer than twenty slaves had fled to Washington seeking freedom, the vanguard of many to come. Four slave owners who had lost them, Thomas Davidson, James Inglehart, Fayette Ball and William Mackall, traveled to the city to reclaim their property under the still active provisions of the law. A deputy provost marshal, however, informed them that he did not think the Fugitive Slave Law had any application in the Federal District, and the question would have to be decided by the president.[34]

Soon the initial trickle of runaways turned into a stampede as slaves desperate for freedom began to attempt escape singly, in small groups, and even en masse from several plantations in Southern Maryland. During a single week in June in Charles County it was reported that more than forty blacks had run off from their homes in Nanjemoy, thirty-seven fled from the plantation of William H. Mitchell and five more from the farm of Samuel Adams. Even more disturbing to the white population, as publisher Elijah Wells noted: "These stampedes are becoming common." [35]

Despite the small steps towards freedom in the District of Columbia, the impact upon the black population of Southern Maryland was not without dire consequences. As Colonel Lafayette Baker, now Provost Marshal for the District, would write in impassioned terms to President Lincoln: "The colored people, slave and free, of this District and the adjoining counties of Maryland, are daily subjected to a more ferocious despotism, and more flagrant and shameless outrages, than were ever before tolerated by any Government claiming to be either wise or humane." As was well known, slaves were by then almost hourly making attempts to escape from their masters and flee to the city.

Desperate slave owners in Maryland, whose plantations were rapidly being abandoned as a result of the now constant exodus of their chattel, were no longer relying on the protection of their own laws and legally constituted authorities. Many began to form into armed bands for the purpose of pursuing and recapturing their property. Frequently now parties of slaves, men, women, and children were hotly pursued within the bounds of the District of Columbia, some being brutally beaten, fiercely assailed or shot down in the process. Others who had been retrieved were locked up in local Southern Maryland jails or in private homes where they were harshly punished or tortured. One returned slave, incarcerated in the Prince

George's County Jail in Upper Marlboro, had been blinded after capture by a charge of shot fired directly int his face by his enraged owner.

In another instance two black girls were found wounded in the garret of a private house in a neighborhood of Washington after having been mercilessly beaten by three white men. The girls were left chained up in utter darkness and left to die, with their backs blistered by masses of festering wounds. One of their captors had used a raw chain to inflict the blows. Many retrieved slaves were quietly conveyed in gangs, bound together in shackles, across the lower Potomac to the protecting arms of the Confederacy for later retrieval by their owners when the war ended. Any further escape attempts were rewarded from the barrel of a gun. The pursuit and capture of runaways entering the District of Columbia had become a bloody affair. Baker reported that by the end of September 1863 no less than forty slaves had been killed in such encounters. The dead bodies of escapees were regularly found lying in the woods on the perimeter of the city.

"Lafayette Curry Baker, 1826-1868, Brig. Gen. and Chief, National Police."
Prints and Photographs Division, Library of Congress, Washington, D.C.

Even the status of free blacks was in jeopardy as some city officials charged with addressing owner's rights under the Fugitive Slave Law looked the other way when they were abused. The colonel cited one incident, less than a month earlier, in which an armed band of Maryland slave owners surrounded the house of a free negro woman not three miles from the Capitol, broke open the door, presented loaded pistols to the heads of the frightened residents and, "after exercising all their powers of abuse and insult, took away by violence three free negroes."

Baker was sorely aggrieved over the inhumanity of it all and begged the president to allow him to take action. "It can not be that such atrocities will be longer permitted," he later wrote, "and that men, whose every sympathy is with slavery, and its legitimate offspring, treason, shall be longer suffered to visit upon the poor slave the hatred they feel to freedom and the Union. I respectfully ask for such instructions as shall enable me effectually to protect the now helpless victims of the slave masters vengeance, and the perjured oaths of their friends, official and otherwise, in this city and District." [36]

When he could, often bending the law, Baker did his best to correct abuses though some would say he frequently did so in the interest of self promotion and advancement. In one such instance, when slave chasers who through perjury obtained the proper papers to carry a freeborn mulatto girl off to a "pretend" owner, the colonel took personal charge of the case. "By a military order I compelled the woman stealer to restore to her friends the captive robbed of her rights in the name of law. The tinge of African hue alone made the outrage a trivial incident to all but the grateful and, I might add, graceful young lady." [37]

On another occasion when returning from an expedition into Southern Maryland, Baker met a farmer with a wagon load of slaves, consisting of a man and woman, their two small children, and a sister, within a mile of the state line. All were under the charge of a constable and a force of armed citizens. The slaves, all bound hand and foot and thrown upon the straw in an old country wagon, were on their way back to bondage.

Though exhausted from the expedition, the colonel was nerved to action "by indignation too intense for expression" and demanded to see the slave owner's papers. The claimant produced a parchment bearing the seal of Commissioner Cox in the District. "He flourished the precious document before me," Baker later wrote, "and directed my attention to the great seal of the United States."

Carefully and with deliberation the colonel perused the text and noted that it bore the name of only four slaves, while the cartload included five. When he pointed out the discrepancy, "the chivalrous and confident owner to the apparently unimportant circumstance" replied: "We don't count that baby," pointing to a three-moth-old infant cradled in the arms of its mother.

"The mother," who was leaning against the side of the cart with her feet tied together "was a slave, and the child was born in bondage," declared the officer. "You claim the mother, and of course the child is kidnapped; and as you profess to be a law-abiding citizen, and are violating the statute, I arrest the entire company."

Surrounded by his armed friends and the constable, the slave owner heatedly protested and threatened resistance. "Take the baby," he shouted. "What in hell do we want of the baby? We want grown people."

The mother began to weep. One of Baker's men was deeply touched and, turning to the colonel with a pleading tone, inquired if he should separate the mother and child.

The display of a dozen Colt revolvers by the colonel and his men quickly satisfied his excited friend that he was in earnest in expressing his own interpretation of the law. Springing onto the wagon, Baker cut the ropes with a saber and freed the slaves. He then directed the horses drawing the cart to be turned toward the capital. The owner and driver protested and with an oath shouted: "Let the niggers walk to Washington."

"No," responded Baker. "You brought them here, and must carry them back."

Stunned by their sudden change of fortune the slaves dropped as one to their knees. The patriarch of the family, with uplifted hands, exclaimed "Bless God." The mother added "God bless Colonel Baker."

The slaves were brought to the colonel's headquarters in Washington and immediately set at liberty. But the affair was not quite over. According to Baker's own sometimes inflated memoirs, the next day a delegation of slave owners called upon President Lincoln to protest against the colonel's "arbitrary act" and produced the document the colonel had examined. Within hours, the officer was summoned before the president.

"Baker," said the chief executive slowly, directing the officer's attention toward the document, "a serious charge, is preferred against you. What do you know about the case?"

Baker recited the events, giving prominence to the number of the slaves and the infant "supernumerary" that had not been included in the document.

"Well, Baker," said Lincoln somewhat jocosely, "I guess the baby saves you," and dismissed the whole affair, leaving the escaped slaves at large in their newfound freedom.[38]

***

Despite such tragic byproducts of emancipation in the District of Columbia, the momentum towards freedom for all slaves seemed to be underway at last. On the same day as passage of the Supplemental Emancipation Act Lincoln appealed to Border States congressmen to support an even bolder move towards compensated emancipation of slaves. Lengthy and bitter congressional debate followed. Soon a bill dubbed the Second Confiscation and Militia Act, though formally addressed as "An Act to suppress insurrection, to punish treason and rebellion, to seize and confiscate the property of rebels, and for other purposes," was hanging in the balance. Supported by the extreme abolitionist and radical forces in Congress, the proposed legislation called for the emancipation of all slaves belonging to those who aided or supported the rebellion. It also addressed those serving in Confederate military or naval service as soon as they came under Union control. The bill called for the confiscation of many forms of property including human, and provided the president with the authority to employ blacks for the suppression of the revolt. The proposed act also gave him the power to provide for the colonization of some tropical country outside the limits of the United States by such persons "of the African race" freed by the provisions of the act who were willing to emigrate. Finally it authorized the president to pardon and offer amnesty to those rebels he deter-

306

mined to be fit. Ignoring his own opposition to certain provisions, and after weighing the possibility of vetoing the bill, Lincoln signed it on July 17, 1862. Two days afterwards slavery was abolished in all U.S. territories, with the exception of slave Border States.[39]

Five days later on Tuesday, July 22, during what his cabinet believed would be a typical meeting, President Abraham Lincoln stunned his confidants and advisers. In a moment that would shake the nation to its core he read the first draft of a decree that he had been working on quite independent of consultation with anyone but his own conscience. It was to be called the Emancipation Proclamation.

"The first reading of the Emancipation Proclamation before the cabinet." Painted by Francis Bicknell Carpenter; engraved by A.H. Ritchie. This print shows a reenactment of Abraham Lincoln signing the Emancipation Proclamation on July 22, 1862, painted by Carpenter at the White House in 1864. Depicted, from left to right are: Edwin M. Stanton, Secretary of War, Salmon P. Chase, Secretary of the Treasury, President Abraham Lincoln, Gideon Welles, Secretary of the Navy, Caleb B. Smith, Secretary of the Interior, William H. Seward, Secretary of State, Montgomery Blair, Postmaster General, and Edward Bates, Attorney General. Prints and Photographs Division, Library of Congress, Washington, D.C.

THE MERE LOVE OF GAIN

"The crossing from Maryland to Virginia has almost entirely ceased."

With the onset of the summer of 1862 it had appeared that southbound crossings along the Potomac frontier had not diminished at all but actually intensified. In early May Federal authorities renewed efforts to counter the problem of smuggling from the Maryland shores. Curfews were ordered for villages such as Chaptico, off the Wicomico River, considered hotbeds of rebel support. Patrols ashore were stepped up.[1]

By mid-summer Federal spies and local informants who had silently remained loyal to the Union now began to provide increasingly better intelligence regarding neighbors engaged in cross river smuggling. Hubs of rebel support such as Leonardtown became the subject of more frequent surprise military visits. Still, bacon, coffee, sugar, whisky, and other articles were regularly carried to Virginia, and corn and wheat brought back in exchange.[2] Yet owing to the southward shift of the axis of war, necessitating the withdrawal and often reassignment of some of the flotilla vessels to other areas, the enforcement capacity of the Union's Potomac blockade was severely stressed. The flotilla's size was now reduced to four steamers, *Anacostia, Thomas Freeborn, Reliance, Resolute,* and a handful of small schooners and cutters. However, its mission was expanded to include not only the Potomac but also the Rappahannock River and all the shoreline between.[3]

With the naval blockade net so thinly spread, Southern Marylanders were quick to take advantage. They soon expanded blockade running with renewed energy, albeit with smaller watercraft, namely rowboats and small bay canoes. Whenever reports of a successful interception or closure of a supply or communication route was made, word flooded in almost immediately of old ones being reopened or new ones established.

At the end of July the latest Provost Marshal of Washington, Major William E. Doster of the 4th Pennsylvania Cavalry, actively succeeded in ferreting out and breaking up two rebel routes. One was for mail and the other for spies, between Richmond and Washington, by way of Alexandria and Fredericksburg. [4] The second route had been employed for aiding deserters from the U.S. Army and sending them north via Upper Marlboro, Fair Haven and Baltimore. Along the latter route rebel supporters had sent through two agents posing as deserters from the 86th New York Regiment "who fancied they would make a tour of observation among Maryland 'secesh.'" Somehow Doster was able to break up the operation and numerous arrests were made including a lawyer, a wealthy farmer from Upper Marlboro, a merchant from Colesville in Montgomery County, a female Confederate mail carrier in Alexandria, a spy near Leesburg, Virginia, and others.[5]

Yet for every plug in the levee massive new holes continued to appear. On July 30 the new commandant of the Navy Yard, Andrew A. Harwood, informed Secretary Welles of disturbing intelligence provided by a government river pilot named George Bailey. Harwood, a forty-four-year veteran of naval service, had hitherto been Chief of the Bureau of Ordnance and Hydrography. He had replaced the younger Dahlgren, who was promoted to head that same agency, and then soon afterwards to admiral and commander of the South Atlantic Blockading Squadron. Contraband boats were now running at all hours of the night from St. George's Island as far upriver as Washington. Laden with provisions and bound for Virginia, even more were putting out from Leonardtown and other locales along isolated shores. At one point a pilot reported that he had seen at least fifty boats at one time. Anything and everything, including even surgical instruments were flowing across with apparent ease. Harwood was aghast, especially when he also learned that a regular business appeared to have been established and carried on at all times, over a span ranging from the mouth of the Potomac to Maryland Point. "I do not doubt that there is a regular mail communication between Baltimore and the rebel lines through the channel indicated, which may and ought to be promptly stopped." [6]

The Confederates' ability to smuggle contraband and pass intelligence southward could not be underestimated. One keen observer noted in his diary a description of how some secret messages were sent by boat: "They would be put in a tin case, enveloped in lead. This was tied to a string and suffered to drop over the side of the vessel. In case of danger, the string was cut or broken at the last moment." [7]

The problem of detection was monumental since only two of the flotilla steamers were stationed on the Rappahannock and at Fredericksburg, and the other two on the Potomac.[8] All needed repairs. The Confederate blockade runners from Maryland, moreover, were constantly inventing newer ruses to mislead the Yankees. One of those deceptions began to unravel about August 1 when Acting Master James L. Plunkett of *Freeborn* seized the schooner *Mail* six miles up Coan River. Plunkett later reported the six-man crew had been using every exertion to unload the vessel before he arrived. "After firing several shots at them they desisted and retired to the woods. I then ran alongside and took the schooner in tow, and proceeded down the river without any molestation. I found on board the schooner about 75 bags of salt, a large quantity of wheat and groceries, together with some whisky, and 1 box of musket balls." There was nothing unique about the prize, but the authority under which it was operating was something else. The owner, when captured, claimed he was trading in Virginia under authority of the U.S. Treasury Department. After an inquiry at Treasury, an undoubtedly embarrassed official ordered the vessel released. It seemed the boat had been carrying a pass to trade on the shores of Confederate Virginia. Or so it was believed. No one bothered to inquire why such a pass had been issued or if it was even authentic.[9]

The incident was quickly forgotten but within a few weeks would soon reappear in a different and more distressing form.

In the meantime, regardless of setbacks, improved intelligence by spies and informers were often able to produce substantial results, thought constant vigilance and inspections often paid off just as well. On Saturday morning August 2 the Weems Line steamers *Mary Washington*, inward bound from the Patuxent to Baltimore, and *George Weems*, outward bound from Baltimore to the Patuxent, were both stopped for the usual inspections. William Wilkins Glenn, proprietor of the Baltimore *Exchange* newspaper, had been among the many jailed duirng the September 17, 1861 roundup of suspected secessionists who were later released. Now he was a passenger aboard *George Weems* and related to his diary the proceedings regarding the arrests on the steamers: "About six o'clock as we neared North Point, the *Mary Washington* hove in sight. An officer hailed us from the deck, the boat bore down upon us, the two ran alongside of one another and a company of soldiers preceded by half a dozen detectives came quickly aboard. The *Mary Washington* then proceeded on her way. All the gang ways of the *George Weems* were immediately taken possession of & guarded. The men passengers were ordered back to the upper cabin, the women to the lower one." [10]

Taken to Fort McHenry, Glenn, like others aboard, doggedly refused to take the oath of allegiance. A few, who had been resolute in their Southern sympathies only an hour before, "became suddenly quite loyal, some wanted to know what the oath was, some man wanted to consult his wife first." Those who refused the oath were taken ashore under guard and marched through a crowd of hooting, jeering soldiers into the garrison. Most, including Glenn, were eventually released.[11]

There were exceptions. At least seven of those arrested were men from St. Mary's County. The Reverend George K. Williams was a well known minister. George R. Garner, a resident of Chaptico, had been one of the original leaseholders in William Cost Johnson's Point Lookout development scheme in 1861. He would later become postmaster of the Chaptico Post Office, a founder of the Chaptico Joint Stock Wharf and Transportation Company, and in 1891 a delegate to the Maryland State Legislature. The elderly William H. Burroughs had been a veteran of the War of 1812. But there were two men who were of particular interest to Federal authorities: B. L. Hayden was taken as a spy. He had been a principal in the Lower Maryland Vigilance Committee engaged in contraband operations and was earlier arrested in late 1861 by Colonel Baker. Incarcerated in Fort Lafayette but later released, he had immediately returned to his old ways. Dr. James Waring was perhaps the most prominent of the lot, having served, among other positions, on the Board of Commissioners for the St. Mary's Female Academy. More significantly, he was a leader of the April 23, 1861 county assembly in Leonardtown that had endorsed the secession of other southern states and provided financial support for the pro-Confederacy militia in the county. Others such as M. B. Chunn and Henry Adams were simply residents caught up in the web of war and happenstance. Only one of the seven, George Garner, would be released "unconditionally." [12]

Mary Washington had not escaped completely for when she was stopped, twenty-five of her passengers were taken off, conducted to the fort, and all their luggage seized and searched. While rummaging through the baggage, seven hundred dollars in Confederate bonds were discovered and confiscated. After hours of investigation the passengers were allowed to reboard, but only after swearing an oath of allegiance. Those who expressed a willingness to do so were allowed to proceed. Those who declined were taken back to the fort and arrested.[13]

For the Federal authorities, the almost regular seizures of contraband on the Weems Line steamers had by now become far too frequent to ignore. This time *Mary Washington* would not be returned to her owners. Less than two weeks later, on August 13, 1862, *George Weems* was also seized by order of Major General John E. Wool, who in June had replaced General Dix as commander of the Middle Department in Baltimore. The ship was taken while in the Patuxent River by a detachment of the 37th New York, which had come down onboard the steam tug

Tempest. The Weems liner was at the time bound for Baltimore laden with a cargo of tobacco and grain from the lower counties of Maryland. She also carried nineteen passengers, five of whom were females. Captain Theodore Weems and the white portion of his crew were arrested and sent aboard *Tempest* to Baltimore under the charge of a squad of Baltimore police. Though the arrestees were released at the provost marshal's office, the ship was commandeered and would not be returned to the owners for the remainder of the war. "This seizure," the Washington press noted, "breaks up the line as all the steamers are now in custody. The *Mary Washington* having been seized previously. The former is in Baltimore, and the latter here." All were charged with being engaged in the contraband trade. On August 14 *George Weems* was officially removed from public service and chartered for use by the U.S. Army.[14]

Undoubtedly cursing their bad luck with Federal authorities, the Weems Line owners might also have expended some less than acceptable language on those whom they had secretly supported, for the loss of their third steamer, *Planter*. About the same time as the seizure of *Mary Washington*, it was erroneously (or perhaps for propaganda purposes) reported in Richmond, that approximately 100 Virginia-bound Marylanders, had captured the ship. They had been intent, it was stated, on proceeding from Baltimore to the Patuxent River when they "encountered the steamer *Planter* lying at her wharf, and soon mastered the parties in charge of her, raised steam and set off across the Potomac, in the direction of the Virginia shore. Running the vessel quite up to land, they disembarked and fired her, and set out for Richmond, reaching here without interruption. These refugees report a large number of others on the way here. It is probable that the most of them will enter the army." Fortunately for the Weems Line, *Planter* was not destroyed but simply "chartered," willfully or otherwise, by the Quartermaster's Department and engaged periodically through 1865. By the end of the war she would be back in full operation for her old masters.[15]

***

Some believed that the paltry number of captures signaled the blockade was finally having an effect. To others it seemed to indicate that the rebels were simply better able to avoid the Federals than ever before. As one sage observer would later note: "These fellows are too sharp to be caught by the gunboats or revenue cutters, as they know them all and keep out of their way." [16]

On August 10 in his monthly report on the disposition of the flotilla, Commander Magaw was able to note that the squadron was widely dispersed with *Anacostia* at Fredericksburg, *Resolute* cruising the Rappahannock, and only *Freeborn*, *Reliance*, and a handful of schooners and cutters able to monitor the Potomac. Nevertheless, sixteen white and nine black men had been arrested in the vicinity of Leonardtown, charged with "engaging in improper communication and traffic between Maryland and Virginia," and turned over to the provost marshal in Washington. Along with the arrestees, three large boats had been seized; they carried 203 bushels of wheat, ten sacks of salt, 30,000 cigars, twenty-eight ounces of quinine, twelve ounces of morphine, four pounds of opium, percussion caps, and a quantity of tea, coffee, and medicines. It wasn't much, but it seemed to the commander to indicate the blockade was actually starting to make some new inroads on smuggling operations. It was a conclusion that was soon strongly reputed.[17]

By mid-August a survey of the middle and lower Potomac by the USS *Corwin*, Lieutenant Thomas S. Phelps commanding, reported an actual surge in rebel crossings from Southern Maryland. Phelps stated with some dismay that articles of almost every description from wheat, corn, and fruits, to Virginia currency were being carried by flatboats and small fishing schooners principally at night but often by daylight. The boats were frequently manned entirely by blacks and their cargoes were being exchanged at a discount of from forty to fifty per cent. Nomini, Pope's, Bridge, Mattox, Upper Machodoc and Rosier creeks were the most prominent places where the goods were landed in Virginia. These quickly found their way to the Rappahannock and York rivers, to Richmond and beyond. "Nearly all the grain bound to the Maryland shore," the lieutenant noted, "is exchanged for articles to be sent South." All boats and schooners bound to the Virginia shore, he concluded, "may be considered as being engaged in trading or carrying mails or passengers." Although the principal range of smuggling from Maryland's lower Potomac coast now extended from the St. Mary's River to Swan Point, it appeared to Phelps that the most important depots were still Leonardtown and in the Wicomico River Valley, with the latter location now providing the larger amount of traffic. One Charles Clement Spalding of Chaptico was identified as the primary furnisher in the Wicomico.[18]

Not all charges were strong enough to be proven. Spalding, for instance, was arrested in his home soon afterwards, and his entire stock of goods, worth at least $20,000, was seized and conveyed to Washington. Tried by a military commission in the capital upon charges of illicit intercourse and trade with the South, he was honorably acquitted in January 1864.[19]

Phelps also learned of rebel deceptions in conducting the smuggling: "A Virginian or other person, owning or commanding a small schooner or sloop, takes the oath of allegiance to the United States, clears from Alexandria or Georgetown for Baltimore, Md., and from thence back; but before leaving the former place procures from the military governor of the district permission to touch at certain creeks in Virginia to carry away grain which he happens to own." From the testimony of their neighbors, Phelps learned, such individuals were "loyal" to both governments. The grain was either purchased from rebels or owned wholly by them, but in removing it they often transported rebels with it to Baltimore, undoubtedly for the purpose of intelligence gathering.[20]

Harwood was immediately disturbed by what appeared to be the muscular resurgence of rebel smuggling activity along the Southern Maryland shoreline, as well as that of Virginia extending now as far south as the York River. It was also upsetting that permission purported as being granted by the Federal military governor of the district was being given to certain individuals to "touch at certain creeks" on the rebel coast. First noticed two weeks earlier, when supposed authority had been granted by the Treasury Department to land goods in Virginia in the *Mail* incident, it was now evident that something was not right. An immediate query by Secretary Welles sent to Brigadier General James S. Wadsworth, commander of the district, was answered with an assurance that no such permits had been granted.[21]

"I feel convinced," the commander informed Welles, "that the mere love of gain induces many persons on the border to 'blow hot and cold' in the matter of allegiance, and therefore feel anxious that the authorities who are empowered to grant passes should be made aware that not only contraband goods, but spies, have free circulation by these means." It was soon determined that the rebels had simply been producing forged documents. Worse, no one had bothered to double check. "It seems," Harwood informed Magaw on August 18, "that permits were shown by some of the vessels said to be from General Wadsworth and you will put the officers under your command on their guard against forgeries, and give them each a written order that there must be an entire interdiction of all traffic until the blockade is raised." [22]

Magaw was now ordered to expand his blockade, including night patrols, from the Potomac southward to the York, with special attention being paid to Pope's Creek and a small tributary above it on the Maryland side, as well as the Virginia coast opposite Cobb's Point. "If you have any of the ordinary bateaux or flat-bottomed boats with sliding keels in your possession," Harwood added, "or can get hold of any, by putting an armed crew properly disguised in the rough dress of the country on board of them and visiting these localities at night, you will be able to capture a number of these traders." [23]

Commander Magaw was nevertheless limited in his authority even when the enemy was captured red handed. The War Department, it seemed, had just been allocated jurisdictional supremacy over the Navy Department when it came to arrests. Harwood informed the commander that the navy could no longer relegate to his officers the power to take into custody any citizen of Maryland or Virginia suspected of disloyalty. The commander was instead ordered to "discreetly and diligently" obtain sufficient evidence against them, and permit the arrest to be made by the military. The reduced authority only served to further hamper the navy and frustrate those in the field obliged to maintain the blockade.[24]

By the time the long awaited launches for night patrols finally arrived, a newly authorized and highly controversial Federal military draft in Maryland was in full swing. On March 3, 1863, with the Union having suffered staggering casualties in major engagements such as the Shiloh fight, the Seven Days Battle, Second Manassas, Antietam and Fredericksburg, and consequently a shortage of men in military service, President Lincoln had signed the Conscription Act. For the first time in history, the government had instituted a military draft on a national scale. On April 16, 1862 the Confederacy, also desperately short of troops, had already begun their own draft, which was equally unpopular. The Enrollment Act assigned a quota for each congressional district that mandated all male citizens between the ages of twenty and forty-five be enrolled. Resistance to conscription was virulent in many places such as New York City, where bloody riots erupted in opposition. It was, however, perhaps nowhere as reviled as in Southern Maryland. Many Marylanders whose affections for the Confederacy had not been strong enough to oblige them go south, now decided to leave, though conscription in the Confederacy was also in force, reasoning that if they were going to be obliged to fight, then it would be for the side they favored. A virtual swarm of Marylanders, desperately trying to cross the river, now began to challenge the Potomac Flotilla as never before. Magaw was thus compelled to inform his superior that "traffic between Maryland and Virginia is much diminished, but large numbers of men from Charles and St. Mary's counties, I learn, have crossed to escape drafting." He thanked Harwood for the launches, *Nos. 1* and *2*, but noted with some air of cynicism regarding his own limited manpower that "without men and officers they are useless." The flotilla was already stretched as thin as possible.[25]

Despite Magaw's assurances that the blockade had suddenly begun to reduce the illicit traffic between Southern Maryland and the Confederacy, on August 26, only three days after the commander's report, Harwood informed him of a major smuggling operation that needed to be stopped. He instructed Magaw to first conduct an investigation, but not to communicate information more than necessary to his officers. The extensive enterprise, he was told, was being run by a man known only as Sable who crossed over twice a week from Presley's Creek, a few miles below the mouth of Coan River, to Smith's Creek between Point Lookout and the St. Mary's River. Only a fortnight before in a small sloop he had transported, unquestionably in several transits, nearly 200 persons, a larger number being Maryland recruits bound for the Confederacy. His main vessel was a Chesapeake log canoe capable of carrying fifty or more people. The boat was described as having "a white bottom, dark gunwales, two leg of mutton sails, foresail bright and new, mainsail not more than half as large as the fore, of dark color, mildewed and old." Sable was usually disguised as a fisherman and assisted by a crew of three.[26]

The smuggler's main depot on the Maryland side was in Smith Creek "up a long, unfrequented cove," at Edward S. Abell's landing. From the landing the smugglers crossed westward a short distance to St. Inigoes Creek. There they were reportedly supplied from a store maintained by Robert F. Taylor, the St. Inigoes postmaster since 1859, and James C. Bean, the former postmaster, a sergeant in the St. Inigoes Dragoons in 1860 and the current St. Mary's County tax collector. Both, noted Harwood, were "spoke of as rank rebels." [27]

"If, therefore, you come in contact with them," Magaw was warned, "be upon your guard, as they may mislead you and will no doubt profess loyalty. Do not let them know you suspect them." The distance from St. Inigoes to Abell's was short and the smugglers put out only at favorable moments. En route out they were obliged to pass by the tax collector's office, and though he was not yet accused of being a traitor, it was said he much feared Sable. For security's sake, Harwood suggested that Magaw inform his own officers of only what was necessary. In concluding, he recommend that the commander "proceed cautiously with this wary rogue." [28]

Once satisfied with whatever additional intelligence he might glean regarding the smuggling operation, Magaw was to be joined by the USS *Wyandank*, a former New York sidewheel ferryboat, Acting Master John McGowan commanding. He was to "be provided with enough men to fit out a boat expedition," which Harwood noted, "if managed quietly and the boats crew disguised, I think will result in the capture of the smugglers and some at least of his gang . . . You will, however, use your own discretion, as, being upon the spot, you have better opportunity of knowing what to do and how to do it." [29]

Magaw maintained a steady watch on the entrance to Smith's Creek for more than a week without observing any suspicious activity. On September 4 he reported back to Harwood, perhaps a bit prematurely: "The crossing from Maryland to Virginia has almost entirely ceased. Although cruising in night boats, we have not succeeded in catching any parties." Then in the predawn gray of September 6 a large white log canoe answering Harwood's description of the Sable boat was seized with two men aboard in the mouth of the creek. The two captives, Thomas Richardson and William Allen, professed that they were oystering, which Magaw deemed highly improbable "from the fact that they were without [oyster] tongs." The commander fully believed they were on their return trip to Virginia. Though Magaw lacked authority to arrest the two men, they were nevertheless promptly charged with having transported ammunition and recruits for the enemy.[30]

Such minor successes notwithstanding, Magaw's latest intelligence sources suggested that Confederate support of operations between Baltimore and St. Mary's were still ongoing, in spite of his recent opinions that the trade was diminished. Even as Sable's boat was being hauled away, he reported that one Richard Colton of the St. Clement's Bay area, whose son was already serving in Virginia, was preparing to make a trip to Baltimore for the purpose of purchasing arms and supplies for the rebel army. Colton had once served as postmaster of the St. Clements Post Office and later as a St. Mary's County commissioner. With Federal authorities believing his loyalty to the Union was solid, he was authorized, after passage of the Federal Conscription Act, to serve as an enrolling officer for his district. Like others in St. Mary's quietly sympathetic to the South, he had declined. Now, perhaps inspired by recent Confederate victories in driving General McClellan's army from the Peninsula, defeating General John Pope at the Second Battle of Manassas, and with General Lee aggressively on the move, he was showing his true colors. As Magaw observed, all of the "inhabitants of this county are very bitter and exulting over what they call our late reverses. You will see in Mr. McGowan's report that one of his boats was fired on last night from the Maryland shore. I recommend a land force; say two companies, to cooperate with the steamers. I have sent word to certain parties that I would hold their farms responsible if any of my officers or men were killed or wounded by shots fired there from." [31]

Such threats failed to halt traffic either to or from Southern Maryland, but for those who dared cross and were caught the treatment could be coarse or even brutal. For women, the brief age of chivalry was at an end. In his diary William Wilkins Glenn, commented just how short. "I recollect on one occasion," he wrote,

"a young lady, who was a governess in a private family in St. Mary's County, crossed over from Virginia to return to her home. She was seen by the Commander of the Gunboat who overhauled the boat, putting something in her bosom. The boat was hailed and hauled alongside. The officer ordered her on deck. She replied that he might have civility to hang over a companion way. This was done and she came on deck. The officer immediately seized her and thrust his hands in her bosom for the papers he said were concealed there. He did not ask for them. He then said that he did not believe she was a woman at all. She replied that 'she thought his own indecent act had already convinced him of that.' His answer was 'that he had known many a man with as large breasts as she had' and in spite of her entreaties took her down into the cabin for further examination. The brute was afterwards killed." [32]

***

Change and more challenge along the Southern Maryland shores of the Potomac were in the wind. On September 2, 1862 Secretary Welles officially expanded the Potomac Flotilla's area of operation to extend as far south as Virginia's Piankatank River, although the region had often been visited by individual gunboats. Flag Officer Louis Goldsborough was relieved of command at Hampton Roads and Rear Admiral Samuel Phillips Lee was assigned to take charge of the North Atlantic Blockading Squadron. At the same time, the aging and sometimes dithering Harwood, Commandant of the Washington Navy Yard, was appointed to head the Board of Examiners and serve as Secretary of the Light House Board. A fiery and controversial commander of the James River Flotilla, Commodore Charles Wilkes, was placed in command of the Potomac Flotilla, whose numbers had now increased to six steamers and a few more schooners, cutters and small boats. The new commander promptly issued strict new instructions on how the blockade was to be conducted and enforced. Owing to the depredations of two successful Confederate sea raiders, the CSS *Alabama*, commanded by Captain Raphael Semmes of Charles County, and *Florida*, which had been terrorizing U.S. commerce on the high seas, Commodore Wilkes was reassigned. His mission was to take charge of a seven ship flying squadron specifically designated to seek out and capture the raiders. A week later on September 9, Secretary Welles ordered command of the flotilla again be turned over to Harwood.[33]

***

Notwithstanding the far more publicized and stirring events on the ocean and in the many theaters of war ashore, Federal efforts proceeded as always to maintain control and policing operations along the Potomac frontier. In mid-November 1862 reports were received of a Confederate visit to St. George's Island. Acting Master Thomas Nelson Provost, now commander of *Anacostia*, was ordered to investigate and make captures as necessary. A number of prisoners were taken, one of whom had been a former pilot of Provost's own vessel who had been discharged for cowardice.

As Harwood was confident that rebel activity on the lower river was now requiring even more constant vigilence, a forward Federal naval supply depot or coaling station was soon authorized. For the first time it was deemed necessary to erect a permanent naval station in the heart of the Southern Maryland waterfront, at either Piney Point Wharf or Plowden's Wharf on the banks of the Wicomico. Harwood was allowed to use his discretion as to precisely where. Finally a decision was made. On October 5 the government rented the wharf at the entrance of the Wicomico from Edmund P. Plowden for $140 a year for use as a midpoint landing and supply depot for the flotilla.[34]

Unfortunately for the Union, the possible reoccupation of Manassas by rebel forces and a concern about renewed hostilities along the river's edge had already ignited a plethora of demands for more action, many being simply absurd. One such was from Lewis McKenzie, Mayor of Alexandria, who was of the strong opinion that trees along the entirety of the 110-mile long tidal Potomac shoreline must be cut down "sufficiently far back to prevent the building of batteries or the planting of fieldpieces to fire on vessels." [35]

Southern Marylanders with Confederate sympathies had little say, as even the slightest challenge to Union military rule could easily end in arrest. In December 1862 Major General Robert C. Schenck, a former Ohio attorney and Whig congressman, replaced the somewhat dictatorial General John E. Wool, then commander of the Maryland Department. Schenck appointed Lieutenant Colonel William S. Fish as his provost marshal. Even more zealous in defining every aspect of society in terms of Union loyalty, Fish's harsh actions infuriated many. A religious congregation was ordered to display a large American flag at their gatherings; the sale of Southern-leaning ballads on broadsheets was made illegal; a bank president was arrested for tipping his hat to rebel prisoners. But in April when the colonel ordered that women "found guilty of disloyal practices" be banished beyond Federal lines, the ire of the editor of the *St. Mary's Beacon*, James Downs, was aroused to a fever pitch. The brutal war was one thing, but the assault on womanhood was something else. Noting that the charges were filed against three women thus accused for no other reason than "a higher grade of offense than is in frequent commission in every section of the State, where a southern sympathy or element exists." [36] On April 2, 1863 Downs published an editorial entitled "The War Upon Women," which would have unexpected consequences.

"Our first revolution gave to history its score of women patriots, and the Frenchmen still remembers with a commendable pride the names of Charlotte Corday and Madame Roland. The advent of these Maryland women at Richmond will not be without its influence upon the heart. Driven from their homes and families by the unrelenting hand of a fanatic and a ruffian, they will be welcomed to the South with outbursts of generous sympathy, and their wrongs will become identified with the great cause in which her sons are battling . . . Will not the husband strike for the partner of his bosom, and lay the infant from his arms, that his rifle may be grasped? Will not the brother doft the civilian's garb, that the grim paraphernalia of war may be donned? And who, we ask, dare question the justness of this conduct? Is Mr. Lincoln a man? And has he a wife and children and, yet, will sanction this conduct from Gen. Schenck? If so, he does not deserve to be ruler over free men, nor is he entitled to either obedience or respect from any Christianized or civilized people." [37]

For his efforts, James Downs was taken into military custody at Leonardtown having published the editorial now "considered by the Government as treasonable." He was initially imprisoned at Point Lookout but soon after transferred to a cell in Balimore. For the next five months St. Mary's County was without a newspaper. On October 1, 1863 the first edition of the *Beacon*'s replacement, the *St. Mary's Gazette*, appeared under the management of a new publisher, Walter Thompson, as simply "a news anda dvertising sheet" until the *Beacon* might be restored to "the good graces of the Government." [38]

It never was.

***

In Port Tobacco, across the street from the office of the *Port Tobacco Times*, sat the judicial center of Charles County, the county court house. There was perhaps some unofficial symbolism inherent in its position, for right beside the court house lay the venerable Christ Church, religious center of the town. The rector of Christ Church, the Reverend Lemuel Wilmer, was perhaps unique in the community, for he was believed to be a Unionist whose loyalty never wavered despite the intimidating sympathies of his now substantially diminished congregation. Though Wilmer and his son, Dr. William R. Wilmer, had been threatened with censure, ostracism and worse by some of their neighbors, they never swerved from their purported fidelity toward the Union. The reverend even maintained an unfurled American flag in his church during services, which were frequently attended by the Federal troops encamped nearby.

On April 26 General Joseph Hooker's Army of the Potomac finally began to move against Richmond by crossing the fords of the upper Rappahannock. The grand Army of the Potomac, 70,000 strong, was again on the march. Four days later, not long after the arrest of James Downs, Hooker, began to set up camp in the Wilderness of Virginia at a place called Chancellorsville, confident of success in a coming contest against General Lee. On that day President Lincoln proclaimed a national "day of humiliation" and Reverend Wilmer held a special service to commemorate the event. Not surprisingly, the service was widely boycotted by the citizens of Port Tobacco, with barely a dozen of his old congregation in attendance. Soon, however, "a goodly number of soldiers" began to enter through the back door, and rapidly filled the pews. As the soldiers were filing in, the rector suddenly noticed to his horror that the flag had been furled, possibly in protest by a civilian congregant. But when the soldiers were being seated, he "observed the motion of the hand of the commanding officer, and the staff placed horizontally and a beautiful flag unfurled." He would later write: "I had nothing to do with it directly or indirectly. I knew then that bedlam would be let loose." For several minutes he watched as civilians and soldiers stared at each other in an icy, silent standoff. Recovering his composure, the rector proceeded with the service and then his sermon on the disasterous condition of the country, concluding "that it was on account of sin that we were thus visited . . . that we should beseech the Lord to the cause in his own hands." [39]

At the end of the sermon, Wilmer's daughter Becky and son William began to play the organ. The music was soon joined by the stirring voices of the soldiers and then the entire congregation, which reverberated throughout the church. The service ended in peace as congregants and soldiers alike left quietly. "My heart glowed," the rector later informed Bishop William Rollinson Whittington of the Episcopal Arch Diocese, "I lost sight of flag, circumstances, everything." [40]

REFLECTION OF THE HIGH BLUFFS

". . . not one letter or paper was ever lost."

Though the war had moved south by the Spring of 1862 and Southern Maryland now lay some distance from the main theater of combat, many of its citizens did not relent in providing whatever aid possible to the Confederacy. Lines of communication and supply of both men and materiel had been stretched and often ruptured by Potomac Flotilla cruisers and U.S. Army cavalry patrols that roamed throughout the lower Patuxent-Potomac drainage region, yet some nevertheless remained open.

Colonel Baker's efforts to shut down the Confederate mail service in Southern Maryland by intercepting correspondence at the various post offices had been, from his own viewpoint, productive. It would, however, soon be completely countered by the unswerving loyalty of one of Charles County's most ardent secessionists, a man destined to serve as the principal cog in the delivery service itself.

Thomas A. Jones of Pope's Creek had been languishing in a Washington jail since late September 1861 after his capture by Colonel Dwight's men at Piscataway. First interred in the 13th Street Prison, he had been moved to the darker chambers of the Old Capitol Prison at 1st and A Streets on Capitol Hill. There he, like many others, submitted declarations of his innocence as well as requests to numerous Federal officials for release to attend to his ailing wife and family.[1]

It had been a period of unquestionable suffering in the dank penitentiary, but also one of considerable significance. During his imprisonment, Jones would later recall, he made the acquaintance of several prominent "and very interesting ladies and gentlemen who were fellow prisoners with me." Among them was Rose Greenhow of Washington, a young and exceedingly handsome widow that Jones was much taken with. "She was tall and symmetrical in figure, with fine black eyes and dark hair," he would later recall. "Her little daughter, Rosie, an attractive child about twelve years of age, was with her in the prison." [2]

Among the other inmates of note incarcerated with Jones were the Honorable Benjamin G. Harris of St. Mary's County, ex-member of Congress from the Fifth Congressional District of Maryland, Captain George Thomas of Alexandria, Virginia, a Confederate officer, and his old friend and neighbor George Dent and son George, Jr.

It was indeed a substantial assemblage of Confederate spies, agents and activists with whom Jones became associated during his inprisonment. No doubt they were a source of continued inspiration during his darkest days. Rose O'Neal Greenhow had contributed substantially to the Confederate victory at the Battle of Manassas through her intelligence gathering and secret communications with General Beauregard. She was deemed one of the Confederacy's principal agents in Washington. After her release, she was dispatched by the Confederate Government to England on a diplomatic mission, but upon her return was drowned while attempting to land on the coast of North Carolina. Her daughter, who was with her, was saved. He also met with two other widowed ladies, both agents in the Confederate service. One of them was Mrs. C. V. Baxley of Baltimore, an enthusiastic secessionist and spy. The other was Mrs. Augusta Heath Morris (alias Afa Hewitt and Mrs. Mason), a French émigré married to an American, who had also served as a spy and courier for the Confederate Army.[3]

In March 1862, following the strategic Confederate retreat to the Rappahannock, Congress ordered a "general jail delivery" release of rebel sympathizers and others housed in Federal lockups in Washington. Both Jones and the Dents were among the prisoners set free.

Upon his return to Pope's Creek Jones was saddened to learn that his dear friend and neighbor, Major Watson, had died. Soon afterwards his own wife, "whose health had been broken through care during my absence," was also taken from him. A bereaved and saddened man, he resolved to resume the life that he had enjoyed before the war as a simple farmer and fisherman. But it would not be for long.[4]

In the spring of 1862, soon after returning to his farm following six months of incarceration, Jones was visited by Benjamin Grimes whose house was now lying in partial ruins on Mathias Neck just opposite his own. Grimes informed him that he had been sent by Major William Norris, a native of Baltimore County and now the Chief of the Confederate Signal Corps. Jones was well acquainted with Norris, who had visited him shortly before his own arrest and had spent a night at his house. The following morning they had walked together along the bluff overlooking the Potomac. "He was struck," recalled Jones, "with the extensive waterview from that point, and remarked to me: 'What a place this would be for a signal station!'" [5]

Now Grimes was there to carry an offer from Norris on behalf of the Confederacy: would Jones accept the position of Chief Confederate Signal Agent north of the Potomac?

At first Jones refused and told Grimes that his first duty was to his children, an obligation that would not permit him to take the risk of imprisonment that such operations would involve. His wife was gone, and he had already suffered immeasurably in a Federal penitentiary. Grimes was unrelenting and pleaded that Norris had said "that it was of the utmost importance to the Confederacy that it should have communication with points north of the Potomac, and that nowhere on the river was there a better location for a signal station than the bluffs near Pope's Creek, or a more suitable place for putting the mail across the river than off my shore."

Finally, after careful deliberation Jones agreed to accept but only if he was given control of the ferry operation and all of the agents in Maryland. Moreover, he must be allowed to have a voice in the management on the other side of the river as well.[6]

Grimes informed Major Norris, who soon visited and held an interview with the prospective chief signal agent. Jones readily agreed to the terms.

The mission, of course, required the greatest of caution and perpetual vigilance. The river was filled day and night with gunboats patrolling up and down. An armed patrol guarded the shore and it seemed the Federal Government had a spy upon nearly every river farm in Southern Maryland, especially those at the better crossing points. There was a detachment of troops stationed at Pope's Creek and another commanded by a Captain Groff on Major Watson's place barely three hundred yards from Jones' own house. Their headquarter was at Ludlow's Ferry, the next significant crossing place below Watson's.[7]

Still the Pope's Creek crossing, through skill and observation, would remain the major passage route until the close of the conflict. On the opposite shore a signal camp had been established in the low, swampy grounds behind the Grimes house and placed under the command of Lieutenant Charles Caywood, CSA. Now the boats used in the mail service were kept on the Virginia side for security. Experience and observation served the new Confederate signal agent well. As he later wrote,

"I had noticed that a little before sunset the reflection of the high bluffs near Pope's Creek extended out into the Potomac till it nearly met the shadow cast by the Virginia woods, and therefore, at that time of evening it was very difficult to observe as small an object floating on the river as a rowboat. The pickets did not go on duty until after sunset. It was therefore arranged that if the coast was clear the boat from Grimes' should come across just before sunset, deposit the packets from Richmond in the fork of a dead tree lying on my shore, and take back the packet from the North found there. Unless for some especial reason, I would not be on the beach when the boat arrived." [8]

If it was not safe for the boat to cross, a black signal was hung in a certain high dormer window of Major Watson's house. The person who attended to the signal was Miss Mary Watson, a pretty young woman in her early twenties. Jones, a man of twice her age, was impressed and possibly even enamored by what he considered to be the epitome of Southern womanhood. "She had a mass of black hair, dark eyes shaded by long lashes that made them appear even darker, and heavy black brows," he wrote. "Her carriage was erect, and figure slender, which made her appear a little above the average height. She loved the Confederacy with an ardor so intense that I believe, for its sake, she would have made almost any sacrifice. I know that I owe, in a great measure, the successful management of the Confederate mail to her ceaseless vigilance and untiring zeal." [9]

A routine was soon established. Every morning the Yankee pickets went off duty. Sometime during the day Jones would go down to the shore and retrieve the packet left there the evening before. Items going north, such as letters and small packages, were then transferred to a post office, though seldom at Allen's Fresh about three miles distant and the nearest one to the Jones farm for fear of exciting suspicion. They would instead be sent by a trusted agent to be posted at different places some distance off. Especially important matter was never sent by the mail but always entrusted to an agent.[10] Soon a regular and reliable mail line extending from Richmond to Canada was established that would not be broken or closed until the end of the war.

"From the time I accepted the position of chief signal agent . . . til the close of the war," the onetime ferrymaster would note with pride more than thirty years later, "there was scarcely an evening that the boat did not make its trip across the river; and not one letter or paper was ever lost." [11]

***

The first weeks of August 1862 had been a troubling month for the Union as the war continued to expand in scope and complexity. McClellan's Army of the Potomac lay ensconced at Harrison's Landing on the James River as the nation watched, wondering what was to come after two previous months of successful Confederate resistance and victories. Another force, the Union Army of Virginia under General John Pope, appeared to be preparing for an offensive that many hoped would set things right by forcing Lee to oppose two armies at once. In the west, the cigar chomping Ulysses S. Grant was laying down plans for an offensive in Mississippi despite failures by the Union Navy north and south of the rebel stronghold at Vicksburg to make much headway against it. In Tennessee a rebel effort under General Braxton Bragg to retake Southern territory was about to begin. And throughout the North the subject of emancipation becoming a component of the war itself was talk of the day. Yet in Southern Maryland some residents attempted to proceed with their lives as if the war had never begun.

T. M. Harvey was owner of several thousand acres of land known as the Piney Point Property in St. Mary's County. He maintained an assortment of vacation cottages by the water and leased the buildings to a congenial entrepreneur named Marshall, who managed them for the summer trade. Harvey had once been challenged by William Cost Johnson's grand Point Lookout vacation emporium. Now he was attempting to make a renewed go of it "catering again for the health and pleasure seeking community" of Washington. Old and new adherents seeking to escape the oppressive summer heat and illnesses of the capital city were once more flocking to take in the healthy airs and waters of the lower Potomac despite the war. It seemed to matter little that just across the river lay enemy territory, that Piney Point frequently hosted smugglers, spies and secessionists of all sorts, or that the Federal occupation of Southern Maryland had only surficially quelled the rebel spirit of the region. The vacationers, mostly well-to-do Washingtonians, often came by military chartered boats, which for reasons never fully explained were occasionally allowed to also carry private citizens.

The government charter steamer *Keyport*, which made a once a week round trip, had brought them down. There were also quite a number of Washington businessmen, some of whom had proposed to stop while others expressed a "design to enjoy a sniff of the salt water air and return by Keyport tomorrow night." There was also a "gay sprinkling of smart uniforms" from the gunboats *Reliance*, *Freeborn*, and others of the Potomac Flotilla that were occasionally allowed to tie up over night "whereby the good looking young officers are enabled to take part in the nightly hops at the Point." If everything went well, Harvey proposed to erect a fine hotel after the war and otherwise improve the property "to make it a first class watering place, such as Washingtonians will be glad to have here." He also proposed "to give the ground and offer other inducements to parties desiring to build cottages of their own here." The only thing that seemed to be lacking was "a tri-weekly or daily boat communication with Washington, a desideratum not perhaps attainable this war year." [12]

For most vacationers the war seemed very far away indeed. That is until a hot summer night when a military tragedy of hitherto unprecedented proportion in Potomac history occurred within site of the Piney Point waterfront.

322

"We left Newport News on Tuesday, the 12th inst.," recalled Lieutenant Colonel Charles Scott, of the 6th New Hampshire Regiment in General Burnside's army, "with 254 soldiers, four officers, three ladies and one child. At Fortress Monroe we took on 17 men, making 279 souls." [13] They had boarded the 409-ton steamer *West Point*, J. E. G. Doyle commanding, chartered by the Army three weeks earlier on June 20. She was a relatively new boat built in 1860 at Keyport, New Jersey, first home ported at New York, and typical of the carriers the military was now engaging for service in the Virginia theater of war.[14]

It was not an unusual departure other than that the majority of soldiers aboard were convalescents being sent from the front to Washington to be hospitalized.[15] One of the women making the trip was the colonel's wife, who had been visiting with him during the campaign and was no doubt pleased to be returning to a less dangerous environment.

The voyage up the Chesapeake had been uneventful as was the entry into the Potomac on Wednesday evening, August 13. About 8 p.m., *West Point* was steering for Ragged Point to obtain soundings about twenty five miles from the river's entrance and "about five miles above Lower Machodic [*sic*], about west to south across the channel," when a single whistle blow was heard two points off the starboard bow. Doyle immediately answered with a signal for the oncoming ship to keep to his starboard. Though all of his own lights were reportedly burning at the time, the only one the stranger could see was green.[16]

The large, dark oncoming vessel was the 1,017-ton steamship *George Peabody*, built in Baltimore in 1857, operating under Army charter since October 26, 1861, and a veteran of the Roanoke Island Expedition in February 1862. According to later testimony of her pilot, William F. Kerwin, which was corroborated by an Army captain named Travers on deck at the time, the steamer had left Aquia Creek at 4 p.m. the same day with troops bound for Fort Monroe. She had been proceeding past Ragged Point, steering east by south, when she spotted *West Point* off her port bow. Aboard *West Point*, Captain Doyle, seeing the far larger *Peabody* bearing down on him, immediately stopped the engine and backed the boat, but it was already too late.[17]

"I gave one blow of our steam whistle," said Kerwin, "which was answered in return by the steamer *West Point*. When the steamer neared I ported our wheel. The pilot or whoever had charge of the steamer *West Point* starboarded his wheel and struck our bows on the port side, forward of our water wheel, at five minutes past eight o'clock p.m." Going at full speed, *Peabody's* port guard and paddle box instantly stove, taking with it about ten feet of *West Point's* bow. All aboard the small steamer were immediately startled by the shock, and no doubt a few convalescents berthed in the bow compartments were instantly killed.[18]

Captain Doyle immediately hailed *Peabody* to stand by but she quickly passed, carried by her own momentum and still under full steam. Aware that his ship was in a sinking condition Doyle ordered the pilot to beach the boat immediately.[19] For reasons never fully explained the pilot instantly turned his ship toward the Maryland shore rather than the much closer beach at Ragged Point. Perhaps it was fear of capture by Confederates or just blind panic that guided his decision. Whatever the cause, however, it proved fatal. Within ten minutes of the collision and before reaching the nearshore above Piney Point, *West Point* sank in four fathoms of water, taking with her scores of helpless sick and wounded soldiers.[20]

Criticisms of the pilot's decision would soon be abundant in the Washington press: "The *West Point* lays about a mile from the Maryland shore, a long distance from the ordinary track of vessels going up and down, and it is evident that on striking the *George Peabody* and finding herself in a sinking condition she ran for the Maryland shore, miscalculating the distance. Had she run for the Virginia shore, she could have been beached apparently without difficulty and all lives saved." [21]

Doyle was quick to defend his actions. "I did everything to avoid the collision," he said, "and used my utmost exertions to save all I could. The entire number missing is seventy-three, of whom a portion may be saved, as a number were picked up by small boats and schooners in the vicinity." Some claimed that it was the brief period during which *West Point* remained afloat after striking and the consternation which prevailed that had prevented the efforts to save all from being as successful as could be desired. Both Doyle and Lieutenant Colonel Scott were the last to leave the vessel. Nevertheless, what could and should have been done was contentious. *Peabody* suffered her side stove in but "being a new and staunch boat" had not been materially injured. Though only momentarily disabled, she could render no assistance except with her small boats. *West Point* began to quickly take on water owing to the great damage to her bow, and it was ascertained that she would sink in less than a few minutes. Assistance from passing vessels traversing the disaster scene was substantial. The chartered Army propeller transport steamer *John Farron* had been passing, and with the guidance of two quartermaster captains named Biggs and Hall was immediately able to render service in saving many of the unfortunates. The flotilla gunboat *Reliance* and an unidentified bark that came up soon afterwards also rendered critical aid. Through the combined efforts of all at least 203 persons were rescued. Apparently picked up by small boats later, six more were also eventually accounted for. All that could be seen of the ill-fated steamer was her smokestack, masts, "and some wrenched up plankings on her deck" protruding from the water.[22]

First reports reaching Washington stated that upwards of eighty passengers, soldiers and convalescents had drowned, a number soon revised downward to seventy-three, and finally seventy. Only one crewman, fireman John Russell, had perished.[23]

Laden with rescued soldiers and passengers, *George Peabody* limped back to Aquia Creek where she arrived at 2:25 p.m. on August 14. Lieutenant Colonel Scott, charged with getting what remained of his convalescents and wounded troops to Washington, was among them. But not his wife.[24]

For the many vacationers who had come down to T. M. Harvey's at Piney Point to escape the heat and humidity of the capital, the sight that met them on the morning of August 14 must have been disturbing. Between them and Ragged Point, one observer wrote, could be seen "the smoke stacks of the sunken steamer West Point emerging from the water, a melancholy sight, indeed . . . The scene of this terrible tragedy is likely to be ghost haunted (if ghosts walk in these matter-of-fact days) for all coming time, as it is near by where the Federal boat's crew were decoyed ashore and murdered by the Confederates, and also where the gallant Captain Ward met his bloody death." [25]

For more than a week many articles from the wreck floated ashore on the Maryland side of the river. On August 21 it was learned that the body of a lady, supposed to have been a passenger, had drifted ashore on the Virginia side of the Potomac. The body was promptly taken charge of and temporarily interred "to await the action of friends." Upon the corpse was found a gold watch, which was taken into custody by the sheriff of Westmoreland County. The deceased proved to be Mrs. Scott.[26] By September 3 more than thirty bodies had washed ashore. Some were buried on the Virginia side at a place called the Glebe, eighty-five miles below Washington.[27]

The commanders of both *West Point* and *George Peabody* were immediately arrested upon their return to Washington. Soon afterwards an investigation was begun and a hearing set to determine "which of the commanders of these boats blame is to be attached." [28] On August 29, two weeks after the disaster, the findings of the investigation were aired before the Supervising Inspector of Steamboats for the Baltimore District. Following the decision of the inspector, a further present-ation of the case was aired before the District Court. [29]

It mattered little to Southern Marylanders whose attention had been im-mediately redirected to events elsewhere what the verdict of the court was and who was responsible for the tragedy. On August 30, the day following the case being aired before the supervising inspector, the Second Battle of Manassas was fought and little notice was given to the court's ruling. There were more important things to occupy Yankee minds. Manassas had been another Confederate victory. And once more a rebel army was ensconced near Washington D.C. and Southern Mary-land secessionists again took hope.

***

The *West Point* disaster did little to alter the ongoing difficulties faced by Union authorities on the Potomac frontier. The problems caused by the Maryland-Virginia cross-river mail service and rebel contraband operations were soon to be magnified by the need to counter small boat attacks on commercial shipping by guerrillas or irregulars operating out of the Northern Neck. One such attack was a demonstrable example of just how difficult protection of shipping could be.

On the night of October 7, 1862 Acting Master Thomas Poynton Ives, new commander of the USS *Yankee*, had brought his ship to anchor off Pope's Creek. All seemed quiet until a few minutes after midnight when a report came in that an unidentified vessel was seen on fire some distance down the river. Ives immediately aroused his crew and in short order the gunboat was underway to provide assistance. About mid-channel off Bluff Point near the Kettle Bottom Shoals they discovered a hay-laden schooner fully ablaze, a fierce candle in the darkness. As they drew closer Ives could see that the fire was already approaching the heel of the bowsprit. No one appeared to be aboard though the schooner's small boat, which had only a short time before been hanging from the davits, was still loosely attached but now in the water. For the next two hours *Yankee* continued to circle the blazing vessel, helpless to do anything but secure its half burned small boat and four singed oars.

From two schooners that were anchored nearby Ives soon learned that they too had seen the fire well before it had reached the doomed vessel's mainmast, but upon sending their own boats out found no one aboard. A single boat was observed leaving the schooner and pulling for the Virginia shore. "They say," Ives reported, "that the forecastle had every evidence of having been recently inhabited, and one captain says that one of his men found a lamp (unlighted) on the windlass, and also a tin can, containing two or three pounds of powder, which he threw overboard." He had little doubt that the schooner and its crew had been captured by rebels and then set ablaze, eventually burning to the water's edge. When word of the loss reached the Washington press two days afterwards there was no mention of a rebel attack or capture of crew, which would have aroused public concern. It was instead insinuated that the crew had been burned up by an accidental fire.[30]

Two weeks later the full story was disclosed to the navy. Captain Jarvis Smith and his six-man crew belonging to the unfortunate schooner had indeed survived and been captured. Upon their eventual release from Richmond's notorious Libby Prison, they were able to tell their story. Their vessel, they related, was the *Frances Elmore* and a party of Confederates calling themselves "Partisan Rangers," all well armed with cutlasses and pistols, had boarded her from a small boat. After gaining the deck of the *Elmore* and overpowering the crew, it was subsequently reported, "they secured them all in the boat, and, cutting open a bale of hay in the cabin, threw tar balls saturated in spirits of turpentine among it, and then applied the torch. They then left, taking the persons with them." A former U.S. Navy officer commanded the raiders. The officer in question was Lieutenant John Taylor Wood, an 1853 graduate of the Annapolis Naval Academy and, until the onset of war, a gunnery instructor there who later would serve aboard the feared CSS *Virginia*.[31] Wood was also, by way of pedigree, grandson of former President of the United States Zachary Taylor, and a nephew, aide-de-camp and confidant of Jefferson Davis.

Wood's tale was one of both incredible bravery and initiative. With the fall of Norfolk and the destruction of *Virginia* in May 1862, the lieutenant had retired up the James River along with what remained of the Confederate Navy. Not satisfied with inaction, he had, unlike the rest of his comrades in Richmond quickly turned his attention from the seemingly impregnable Union blockade at Hampton Roads to target rich opportunities elsewhere. It was thus that he proposed to the Confederate command a daring scheme to initiate a series of raids against vulnerable Yankee targets and Union shipping, where least expected, from the safe shores of the Northern Neck, the Rappahannock and Piankatank Rivers. With the approval of his superiors and the assistance of his second officer, Lieutenant Francis "Frank" L. Hoge, Wood handpicked a small crew from the Confederate school ship *Patrick Henry*, anchored off Richmond. Armed with cutlasses, French revolvers, shotguns, and muskets the daring raiders set out on October 1. Relying only upon stealth, surprise and mobility, they carried with them four small boats that had been saved from the late ironclad *Virginia*. Secrecy was paramount. Only at the last moment before departure was his crew informed of their destination. They then learned that they were to proceed to Mathews County on the Piankatank, and link up with one William E. Hudgins, an acting master in the Confederate Navy and a knowledgeable resident of the area. Hudgins, who managed his own group, which called itself "The

Arabs of Mathews County," would provide whatever assistance was needed. Another local named Peter Smith was to serve as pilot.[32]

John Taylor Wood, ca. 1867, was one of the most accomplished Confederate seaborne guerrilla raiders of the Civil War. *Confederate Military History; a Library of Confederate States History written by Distinguished Men of the South*, Clement A. Evans, ed. (Atlanta, Ga.: Confederate Publishing Co., 1899).

The success of Wood, Hoge and Hudgins and their team of raiders against *Frances Elmore* would, unfortunately for the Union, be repeated time and again. Less than three weeks after *Elmore*'s destruction the raiders would capture the 1,400-ton merchantman *Alleghanian* and burn her south of the Rappahannock. On August 23, 1863 in an audacious night boarding attack upon the Potomac Flotilla gunboats *Satellite* and *Reliance* as they lay anchored at Butler's Hole in the Rappahannock, both ships would be taken after hand to hand combat with their crews. *Satellite* would then be employed to capture three Union merchantmen, the schooners *Golden Rod*, *Two Brothers* and *Coquette*, all of which would soon be destroyed to prevent recapture, as would be the two gunboats. In February 1864 in another enterprising expedition, Wood would lead a small boat raid in the Neuse River, North Carolina, to capture and destroy the USS *Underwriter*. In August 1864 he would be awarded command of the CSS *Tallahassee* to successfully run the Union blockade at Wilmington, North

Carolina, and conduct another short but brilliant foray against Union shipping on the open ocean. The cruise of *Tallahassee* would trigger a massive search and the diversion of substantial forces from the Atlantic Blockading Squadron from their main mission. Before the war was over John Taylor Wood would account for the loss of thirty-four Union ships and commercial vessels.[33]

But the destruction of *Frances Elmore* was, sadly for the Union blockaders on the Potomac, just another unfortunate event in what seemed to be a growing problem in maintaining control of the long dividing line between Southern Maryland and the Virginia shore. It would not be the last of such affairs, and far larger defeats were in the offing elsewhere. One of the most incredibly bloody Union debacles of the war, the Battle of Fredericksburg, between the Army of the Potomac under Ambrose Burnside and the Army of Northern Virginia under Robert E. Lee, was to be fought on December 13, 1862. Of 114,000 Union troops engaged versus 72,500 Confederates, Federal losses numbered 12,653 killed, wounded and missing compared to 5,309 Confederate casualties. It had been a stunning Yankee defeat followed by a retreat from the field of battle. Not surprisingly, little public attention was given to the seemingly lesser problems of blockading along the Potomac frontier, the Anaconda's Tail.[34]

***

The geography of the great estuary system of the Chesapeake Bay and its scores of major and minor tributaries had caused no end of problems for Rear Admiral Samuel P. Lee, commander of the North Atlantic Blockading Fleet. "It is," he blithely informed Secretary Welles on January 19, 1863, "impossible to maintain inviolate the blockade of a coast so extensive and so indented with navigable waters as the western shore of the Chesapeake." Recurrent efforts were required to destroy the boats, canoes and myriad other watercraft employed by the rebels in illicit trade. Actions both ashore and on the water were unremitting as interceptions of rebel contraband, raids and ambushes continued without letup. During the winter, even as a mighty flotilla of ironclads and other warships were gathering in Hampton Roads for a spring offensive against Savannah and Charleston, a combined army-navy penetration of the York and Pamunkey rivers was undertaken. A Potomac Flotilla raid led by Acting Master Thomas J. Linnerkin in the USS *Currituck* on the Oscar Yerby salt works in Dividing Creek, somewhat north of the Rappahannock, deprived Richmond of a much a needed resource hard to replace. But the pace of war in Virginia was unrelenting, and the raid was but a small foretaste of many more to come.[35]

25

NOTHING LESS THAN ROBBERY
". . . the greatest raid of the war."

The constant string of defeats had failed to depress all of the Union's military leaders, some of who were increasingly aware that the war was to become one of much longer duration than either side had considered. One of these was Quartermaster General Montgomery C. Meigs. His opinion was that ultimate victory would hinge not only upon success in the field, but upon endurance, numbers and supply. But most significantly, it would also depend upon the basic ability to deny the enemy, through the occupation of his most productive territory, the resources, namely men, money, food and materiel, necessary to keep his own army in the field. Such occupation, if handled correctly, might readily divert those same resources from the enemy to the Union cause.

By the onset of 1863 Meigs had begun to address his views in terms of readily feasible targets. On the evening of January 11 he sat in his headquarters engrossed in studying maps of the Virginia theater of war, as he had done on so many nights, and in particular those of the little addressed Northern Neck Peninsula between the Potomac and Rappahannock. That the region was susceptible to incursions by the navy had already been proven. As early as April 1862 gunboats from the Potomac Flotilla had intercepted and captured no fewer than eight rebel blockade runners on the Rappahannock River, including the steamer *Eureka,* and schooners *Monterey, Lookout, Sarah Ann, Sydney Jones, Reindeer, Falcon,* and *Seaflower.* Many more would follow. Meigs was convinced the region was ripe for picking. Thus on January 12 he wrote to General Burnside relating his idea for "the relief of our Treasury which, I thought, might be gained by foraging in the country between the Potomac and Rappahannock, and below Fredericksburg." [1]

"In looking at the map last night, and thinking how little rebel territory we had really repossessed and made available for our own use, I was impressed with the fact that in this peninsula, commanded at its narrowest part by your army, and whose whole coast is under command of our fleet, there are over 800 square miles of territory. These lowlands of Virginia are, I believe, generally fertile, and pretty well settled and cultivated. Now, here is a territory of greater extent than provinces for the possession of which European nations have waged long wars. Is it not worth while to occupy it, to deprive the rebels of its resources, in produce, in taxes, in conscripts, in recruits, in information? Could not a small column have restored the authority of the Union over this land; enabled the Government to give effect to its conflation and sequestration acts; cut off from the rebels valuable supplies, and draw from loyal owners by payment, and from rebels by seizure, and receipts payable after the war, on proof of loyal conduct from their date, large supplies of grain, of forage, of tobacco, of cattle, of horses, for the support of our army." [2]

To send a column through the region, fortifying principal points of communication such as court houses and crossroads, and taking physical possession of the countryside would prove that the U.S. Government was still strong. At the same time it would revive loyalists who had acquiesced to the enemy and drive out those who were supporters of the Confederacy. If the region were occupied by perhaps 10,000 men, and the necessary animals and livestock needed to keep them a viable force in being, it would also generate "an important economy" for the inhabitants as well as major forage for the army.[3]

That there were resources aplenty and ripe for the taking was apparent even to Confederates. "That peninsula," noted one prescient Virginian, "is especially well stocked with grain & other products, because of the want of means for two years to get to markets. Many farmers had sold no crop for two years. I suppose now that all will go to plundering & destroying enemy, as there is no possibility of our defending that region, almost surrounded by broad waters, from the enemy commanding the water, & having every naval ability, of which we are totally destitute." [4]

Meigs noted that there were landings on both the Potomac and Rappahannock from which products and produce of the peninsula had been shipped before the war, especially for trade with Southern Maryland. Could not these same landings be put back into use to ship the plunder of Union foraging parties? Able bodied blacks, just freed by Lincoln's Emancipation Proclamation, would "gladly assist in the work." Much was to be gained by cutting off the resources of the Confederacy in King George, Lancaster, Northumberland, Richmond and Westmoreland counties, "all of which," he pointed out to Burnside, "are at your mercy." According to the 1860 census these counties contained a total of 34,391 persons (15,318 whites and 19,073 blacks). He reasoned that more than one half, namely the blacks, were therefore loyal and "looks for delivery and protection of our government." If Stafford County, which was already occupied by Federal troops and contained 4,922 whites and 3,633 blacks, were added the population of the six counties therefore numbered about 43,000 with an average density of forty-three persons per square mile.[5]

Employing the Northern Neck as rich, easily tapped, lightly defended foraging grounds for the Union Army seemed a must. "The war," Meigs concluded, "appears to me to be gradually assuming the aspect of a long one, to be settled by exhaustion, and every pressure we can put upon a rebel is so much toward the end." [6]

The quartermaster general's concept, thought not credited to him, met with belated adoption by the War Department. After the defeat at Fredericksburg, the replacement of General Burnside as commander of the Army of the Potomac, an officer who had little interest in the Northern Neck, by General Hooker, who did, seemed to be one motivating factor. Thus the peninsula was soon to become the target of myriad foraging and disruption raids by both the U.S. Army and Navy, operating initially out of occupied stations on the Potomac and Aquia Creek, Virginia, and later from Southern Maryland. They would continue until the end of the war.

Little less than a month later General Hooker set to putting Meigs' concept into practice. Justification for the first major foray into the Northern Neck since 1861, however, was provided by the Confederacy itself when advertisements fell into Union hands announcing a formal military conscription to be held at Westmoreland Court House on February 10, 11 and 13.[7] Hooker resolved to send a force by water to nip the affair in the bud, and at the same time "seize such supplies as they might find, and all persons and papers connected therewith." Also to be targeted was the hitherto untouched town of Heathsville, at the headwaters of Coan River, in Northumberland County, believed to be a key depot for supplies for the enemy and where mail from Baltimore to the South was regularly received and forwarded.[8]

Queries were immediately dispatched by Major General Daniel Butterfield at the War Department to Commander Samuel Magaw of the Potomac Flotilla, and then stationed with a small gunboat squadron off Aquia Creek. Could he provide the necessary navigational intelligence for the army transports, though the navy itself or its knowledgeable and seasoned pilots would not be employed? "Do you know the Heathsville Landing?" Butterfield asked. "How far from Heathsville? What depth of water? Can you give me by telegraph a list of all landings between that and Belle Plain where steamers could land, and depth of water? Indicate them by Coast Survey maps." [9]

The "invasion" of the Northern Neck was to be a concerted three-pronged all-Army affair, with an overland strike by Union cavalry, and separate amphibious landings, using chartered civilian transports, at Mattox Creek and Coan River. The cavalry operation, which came in two separate waves were touted simply as scouting forays. They were to be conducted by the 8th Illinois Cavalry under the command of Major William D. Medill and a second by a Captain Caleb Moore with detachments from the 8th New York Cavalry. Their purported mission was to be "breaking up the ferries, and capturing cavalry reported to be in the section." The landing at Mattox Creek was to be conducted by 350 men of 7th Indiana Volunteers under Colonel James Gavin. The expedition against Heathsville was to be carried out by 236 men of the 2nd Wisconsin Volunteers under Lieutenant Colonel Edward S. Bragg, and 250 men of the 6th Wisconsin Volunteers commanded by Colonel Lucius Fairchild. It would appear that the Mattox Creek and cavalry operations were actually intended, though having discrete missions unto themselves, as diversions to distract attention from the most important expeditionary target, Heathsville. "It is important that none of the citizens should know of the movement," Major General John F. Reynolds instructed Brigadier General Alfred Pleasonton, commander of the Cavalry Division, I Army Corps. "Will you please notify your cavalry of this in such a manner as to avoid it being made public, and if you have no direct instructions in the matter, would like a regiment of cavalry sent down as far as Westmoreland Court House to cover the embarkation of such property as may be brought in at Nomini Bay." [10]

The first operation off the mark was Medill's 8th Illinois, which, unopposed, reached Westmoreland Court House from their forward base at Edge Hill at 10 a.m., February 10, the morning of the second advertised day of conscription. To his dismay the major learned that he was already too late, "the meeting that I was sent to preside having been transacted the principal portion of the business on Monday, and was, therefore, ready to adjourn." The conscription board had managed to escape with all their papers. The only captures made were two conscripts, a few horses, a quantity of smuggled tobacco, sugar, and coffee, some saltpeter, and nearly fifty barrels of a "villainous whiskey." The conscripts were immediately paroled, the whiskey and saltpeter destroyed, and the remainder of the plunder divided among Medill's men.[11]

That evening the 8th Illinois camped near the courthouse. The following morning, having information that Colonel Brockenbrough of the 40th Virginia was then fifteen miles away in the town of Warsaw, county seat of Richmond County, the cavalry promptly set off to take him. Upon their arrival, though two infantrymen from the 40th were made prisoners, they discovered their prey had already "taken his departure." [12]

The visit was not without some rewards. Inside one building called "Fleetwood Academy" was found an orderly book containing the names of persons subject to Confederate conscription. In the post office was discovered "in full blast" a plethora of letters and papers. In perhaps a symbolic gesture, (the postmaster, William E. Callahan, having fled into the woods along with the proprietor of the town hotel), Medill destroyed the mailbags that once belonged to the U.S. Postal Service, "and suspended the office in the name of the United States."[13] Having failed in his pri- mary mission, the major and his men returned to Westmoreland Court House where they bivouacked for the evening, and then set off for their base at Edge Hill the following morning.

The scouting expedition had produced little in the way of prize goods except for a pair of horses, some mail, and a few documents. It did, however, provide intelligence that would be of later value. Medill found that there were "a great many good Union families in those counties, who gladly furnish information when approached properly." As for the general population, "healthy men [were] few and far between, there having been four drafts made upon the horses and men previous to this one." The roads were good and forage was to be had in sufficient quantity for a large force of cavalry, but horses were scarce. There was "a very large trade in contraband goods of every description carried on between Maryland and Virginia, the principal depot being at a place called Union [Wharf], in Richmond County, and the principal port of entry at a place called, in Lloyd's military map, the Hague, on the Potomac shore." Yet the enemy's actual military presence in the region was minimal, with perhaps no more than 500 Confederate soldiers present, most of whom were deserters or home on furlough. From time to time between twenty and thirty cavalry, which were deemed "partisan rangers" or "guerrillas," might cross the Rappahannock to round up deserters and stragglers. But that was all.[14]

Captain Moore's foray into the Northern Neck with two squadrons of the 8th New York Cavalry began on February 13 from Belle Plain, about the time Medill's troopers were returning to Edge Hill. On verbal instructions from Assistant Adjutant General Lieutenant Colonel Charles Kingsbury, I Army Corps, Captain Craig D. Wadsworth, Aide de Camp to General Reynolds, accompanied Moore at the direction of the general undoubtedly to see first hand the foraging prospects of the region.[15]

Upon reaching Westmoreland Court House about midnight, Wadsworth's observation somewhat mirrored those of Medill's. He quickly learned that mail was received from Richmond every Tuesday and Friday evening at Warsaw Court House, and that the town was a major rendezvous point for smugglers. The follow-ing evening, about dusk, the New Yorkers arrived at Warsaw and immediately confirmed his findings. A Marylander returning from Hague in a sulky, accompanied by two other citizens who had crossed the Potomac on February 1, was immediately arrested. "They brought with them three wagon loads of goods, which they took to Richmond. He has also been in the habit of carrying the mail between the two rivers" and had with him at the time of his arrest "several hundred yards of dress stuff."

At Warsaw the Yankees intercepted the Richmond mail, which had just arrived from across the Rappahannock that afternoon, the carrier being unaware of the temporary occupation of the town. A search of several houses and a hotel employed as a contraband depot was carried out though everything of importance had already been removed by the rebels several days earlier.

Wadsworth's intelligence gathering proved even more informative than Medill's. He soon learned that there was a regular line between Warsaw and Hague, and that a large amount of contraband goods, undoubtedly from Maryland, had been brought through during the previous month. The rebels employed two large boats and several small ones at the ferry crossing the Rappahannock to the riverport of Tappahannock, which was about three miles from Warsaw. The ferry, a large vessel, was capable of bringing over sixteen horses at a time, and there was a brigade of rebel cavalry stationed in Essex County opposite Richmond and Westmoreland. "The enemy," he discovered, "are in the habit of sending small parties of cavalry across two or three times a week to patrol the counties. They are granting a great many furloughs, and there are a large number of soldiers home on the Neck."

The New Yorkers departed Warsaw on February 14 riding northwest toward Hague. Their arrival at the hamlet was totally unexpected by the residents. Three rebel soldiers belonging to the 9th Virginia Cavalry and 40th Virginia Volunteers, at home on furlough, and one Confederate Signal Corpsman, on duty "watching the Potomac River," were taken prisoner. That afternoon was spent searching houses in the town and surrounding county in the vicinity of Lower Machodoc Creek where large quantities of contraband were frequently landed and sent forward to Warsaw. Only the night before one Dr. Samuel E. Spaulding (or Spalding), a resident of Leonardtown in St. Mary's, considered the largest and wealthiest trader on the creek, had come across without any hindrance from Union patrols on the Maryland side or by the Potomac Flotilla. It was soon clear that the Northern Neck was serving as a veritable breadbasket for rebeldom south of the Rappahannock, and providing convenient transit stations for contraband trade with Maryland. To Wadsworth's dismay, it was also evident that a great deal of stock, bacon and grain had already been sent southward across the Rappahannock from the upper counties. "There is still a large quantity on hand, especially bacon and grain," as little had as yet been sent from the lower counties.[16]

Having completed their mission, Moore and Wadsworth departed Hague, arrived at Millersville on February 15, and returned the following day to camp at Belle Plain. Their take had been only seventeen horses and one mule but much new intelligence. Of particular interest was word that in less than a week, on the 20th and 21st, another Confederate Army conscription was to be held at Warsaw Court House.[17]

That damage inflicted during the raid was perhaps more than the two Union officers claimed is probable. One family that had suffered from the incursions had been the Willoughby Newtons at "Linden," near Hague. Recounting the raids one family member wrote in a letter: "There had been rumours of Yankees for some days, and this morning they came in good earnest. They took our carriages, and two others . . . as many of our sugar cured hams as they wanted . . . many prisoners and all the horses they could find in the neighborhood . . . we now see many campfires, and what we suppose to be a picket fire between here and the rectory . . . The 8th New York is the regiment with which we are cursed. The officers are polite, but are determined to steal everything they fancy." [18]

Three days later the same writer reported of having met with many neighbors on February 16 and compared losses noting that the Yankees had finally taken their departure the previous morning. A vessel brought up the creek to carry off the plunder was loaded not only with goods and livestock but also with Negroes. "We feel very anxious about our friends between the Rappahannock and Potomac, both rivers filled with belligerent vessels."[19] Newton claimed he had personally lost five horses, and forty-five hams from his store of bacon, but "got of[f] cheaply compared to many of his countrymen, who were stripped of almost all stores of food, horses, & even their stock of bacon burnt, when not carried off." [20]

***

The second prong of the Union raid on the Northern Neck, was to be conducted by Colonel Gavin's 7th Indiana Volunteers. The colonel's instructions, written on the morning of February 12 by General Reynolds, were succinct though he was provided with little more than a sketch map of the Northern Neck to govern his directions. His extremely loose orders were to embark his troops at Belle Plain, proceed to "some landing near Mattox Creek" to conduct a foraging operation, re-move contrabands, and address rebel forces as required. The troops were to proceed from Mattox, intercepting rebel mail along the way, and rendezvous with his transport at "some landing at Nomini Creek." Reynolds also suggested that a foray might be considered towards Leedstown, a reputed transportation link across the Rappahannock connecting Westmoreland and Essex counties. "If you can learn of anything at Leedstown which will make that place worth while visiting, you can do so; you might possibly find a mail there." His final instructions, given that the mis-sion was to plunder the inhabitants, appears from a modern perspective somewhat hypocritical. "You will enforce the strictest discipline, and extract from all a strict compliance with orders upon the march, and summarily punish any unauthorized plundering, it being understood that everything taken is for the use of the Govern-ment. Anything more than this is nothing less than robbery." [21]

Gavin's expedition was far less successful than even the middling Union cavalry incursions had been. He and his soldiers had boarded the steamer *Edwin Lewis* on the evening of February 12 and arrived at Mattox Creek the following morning at daylight. Unfortunately planning for the operation had been minimal. With the only wharf or landing suitable to offload troops lying two miles from the mouth of the little waterway, the 178-ton ship, which drew five feet of water, was unable to proceed as the only channel that could be found was four feet in depth. Moreover, as "the channel is intricate, and can only be followed by an experienced pilot," even if it could be penetrated, the pilot who had been provided by the quartermaster knew nothing of the landings or how to get to them. As no lighters or small boats had been provided for the expedition to offload the troops for a beach landing or to bring off forage, the entire day was spent in an exasperating search for the elusive channel. At 3 p.m. the transport became stranded, and for the next five hours struggled to escape. Finally, about 8 p.m., with a rising tide, the ship was refloated.[22]

Frustrated, Gavin ordered *Lewis*'s captain to proceed to Nomini Bay where they arrived in the dark, dropped hook and wisely awaited the morning. Here, too, the pilot was "entirely unacquainted" with the intricate entrance to either Currioman or Nomini bays. As with the day before the 14th was spent taking soundings and trying to find a channel. This time, Gavin put ashore, presumably in *Lewis*'s gig. Much to his chagrin, he found that Confederates had burned the wharf on Currioman Bay, and he could not locate one on Nomini. Thus, after consulting with Major William H. Sterling of Hooker's staff, who had come along as an observer, and deeming it impossible to land his troops at either place to accomplish expedition objectives, Gavin ordered the ship to return to Belle Plain.[23]

The information gained was minimal. There were only "a few contrabands in this section of country, and they are generally old and valueless. The valuable slaves have nearly all been sent south. The country is rich and productive." The mission had been an abject failure owing to lack of an adequate pilot and suitable landing craft.[24]

***

The expedition to Heathsville under Fairchild and Bragg, like Gavin's operation, was undertaken with less than sufficient forethought, as speed and surprise were considered paramount. Fairchild, who was to have senior command, was also issued only a sketch map of the Northern Neck and instructions on the same day he was to depart from Lower Belle Plain, February 12. He was to embark before evening and expected to arrive at his destination by morning. Once in Heathsville he was to take possession of whatever supplies were there and intercept the mail. All confiscated goods, contrabands, and prisoners were to be loaded aboard the ship in Coan River and sent to the landing in Nomini Bay. (It was never mentioned that the army river pilots did not know the location of the landing). He was then to march overland to the Nomini, gathering up as he went all the forage he could, rebel soldiers on parole, contrabands, and other material, while also "seizing for this purpose such transportation as you may find in the country." Field decisions as to the directions he wished to move his command were left to him to be made on the spot, and as with Gavin, he was to "summarily punish any unauthorized plundering." [25]

At 3 p.m. the amphibious expedition to Heathsville, 488 strong, departed Pratt's Landing, near Lower Belle Plain, aboard the 283-ton Army charter steamer *Alice C. Price*. Arriving the following morning at 10 a.m. the raiders landed unopposed, and pressed on to Heathsville but not before destroying three small blockade runners in the Coan and sinking two more in nearby Cod Creek. Fairchild was eager to prevent word of his approach from reaching the town and thus arrested and detained anyone encountered along the line of march. The town was taken without opposition though not by complete surprise. Having learned of the cavalry incursions into Westmoreland, the Confederate commissioners for conscription, who were to have met in the town, had fled on the evening of February 12. It proved, unfortunately for the raiders, an utter disappointment.[26]

335

From all of the intelligence that Fairchild could acquire, it seemed that Heathsville, near the headwaters of the Coan, though a prosperous town, was not what Union planners had anticipated. "I am convinced there is no depot of supplies in that neighborhood," the colonel informed his superiors, "none were found." What mail that could be confiscated was forwarded to headquarters. Seventy contrabands and a sizeable number of horses and mules had been taken, forty-three in all, along with 10,000 pounds of bacon, one box of shoes, a bale or two of cotton, two anchors, a cable chain, a wagon, and two sets of harnesses. It was learned, however, that a number of pungies or scows were employed at certain points in the Rappahannock to ferry goods across the waterway to and from the Northern Neck. But Heathsville was not the grand depot most had expected. Several arrests were made, one being a blockade runner from Coan River named James Smith, and another man named Dowling, leader of a party that had taken captive eight men who had been stranded near Cod Creek with two coal barges a few months earlier. Hoping to link up with Gavin's expedition in either Nomini Bay or Mattox Creek, Fairchild and Bragg embarked their men, booty, and the contraband negroes aboard *Price* on the evening of the 14th. Failing to find him there, they returned to Belle Plain the following evening and disembarked at 5 p.m.[27]

Though the expedition had been only moderately successful, like the other three exploratory incursions into the Northern Neck, it had confirmed what the War Department wanted to hear. "Forage," the colonel reported, "can be had in large quantities in the neighborhood of Heathsville, if gathered in from the plantations round about." There were valuable resources to be had if the military only made a concerted effort to take it.[28]

General Hooker, now in command of the Army of the Potomac, then massed and preparing for a new offensive against Lee, was moved to gain even more intelligence regarding the Northern Neck and to sever, if possible, the reported rebel ferry operations on the Rappahannock. Immediately after Fairchild's return to Belle Plain, he requested Commander Magaw to seize not only the vessels reported on, but also "all that are capable of carrying supplies or men across the Rappahannock, in the vicinity of Heathsville or above." It was, in fact, about the only aggressive action feasible. With a deep snowfall plaguing all movement on the ground, the only motions possible were upon the waters.[29]

Lieutenant Commander Magaw acted as quickly as he could. With the gunboats *Thomas Freeborn* and *Dragon* he cautiously pressed up the Rappahannock. By Friday, February 20, the two warships had passed the town of Tappahannock, and pushed upriver another six miles without finding either pungies or scows. The presence, so far inland, of Union warships was quickly forwarded to General Lee's cavalry headquarters and an immediate response was initiated. Brigadier General William H. F. Lee dispatched Lieutenant C. E. Ford of the Stuart Horse Artillery with a Napoleon and a Blakely field gun to Ware's Point, just below Tappahannock and an abandoned defense works called Fort Lowry to await the downriver passage of the Yankee gunboats. At 2 p.m. Saturday the two warships were spotted steaming down. "Lieutenant Ford, his men and guns being concealed," the general later reported of the ambush, "took them completely by surprise. For fifteen or twenty minutes he poured a deadly fire, damaging both boats, as well as could be ascertained, considerably. They showed very little disposition to fight, but ran by as quickly as they could, firing as they passed, but doing no damage. Our range was three-quarters of a mile." [30]

Magaw's official view of the reconnaissance and the skirmish that followed was reported to Commodore Andrew Harwood three days later. Harwood had relieved Wyman of command of the Potomac Flotilla in June 1862. Though no boats were found, the rebels were observed to be in considerable force on the river as far down as Urbanna, and General W. H. F. Lee was personally present at Occupacia Creek, ten miles west of Tappahannock when the gunboats passed the town the first time. As for the brief fight, Magaw was not impressed by the Confederates' efforts. "One of the enemy's guns ceased firing after our tenth shot. The *Freeborn* was struck twice, but none of the crew injured. One of the shot damaged some woodwork which we can not repair ourselves, and when I get through with the work here I will come to the yard for a day or two." [31]

Within a few days of Magaw's departure from the Rappahannock, the navy at least was convinced that owing to the occupation of the peninsula by Union troops, which was in fact only temporary, the contraband trade had for the moment been checked. But nothing lasts forever, and the likelihood of a resumption of activity by smugglers was probable. "A sharp eye must be kept," Harwood warned, "on the sutlers by the boarding officers for liquor smuggled in cans under guise of milk, etc." [32]

***

With the Army of the Potomac relatively inactive, General Wadsworth was eager to take advantage of the lull in fighting, and the Northern Neck offered intriguing potential. Indeed, immediately upon Fairchild's return from the Heathsville raid, the general expressed to his staff his anxiousness to get up another expedition "to bring in the grain and bacon, of which there is represented to be considerable quantities scattered through the lower counties." All that was needed, he believed, was to find a pilot who could be relied upon. Within short order he had found a negro who claimed to be competent enough to take a ship into the Nomini — if only the weather would cooperate! But it refused. [33]

Not until late March 1863 would another expedition be readied to pay an unwelcome visit to the Northern Neck. In selecting Colonel Fairchild and his 2nd Wisconsin Volunteers to carry out the raid, Wadsworth hoped their prior experience in the region would prove more rewarding than their last visit. Thus, at 4 p.m., March 25 the colonel, twenty-six officers, 241 infantrymen, and a squad of twenty cavalrymen set off from Belle Plain Landing aboard the steamer *W. W. Frasier*, this time bound for Westmoreland County. [34]

Frasier steamed down the Potomac throughout the evening before coming to anchor at daylight approximately sixty miles below Belle Plain. Fairchild immediately disembarked his cavalry to reconnoiter. Three hours later he landed his troops and marched three and a half miles to Lower Machodoc Creek. For the next two days, until the morning of March 28, the 2nd Wisconsin would seize and load upon transports sent down to the creek "such articles of subsistence and forage as could be easily gathered" from the immediate region. [35] The soldiers methodically foraged from small local farms and plantations alike. The plunder loaded aboard the transports was perhaps not as substantial as hoped but nevertheless productive: fifteen horses and mules, 3,000 bushels of corn, 300 pounds of bacon, 230 bushels of wheat, twenty-five bushels of oats, fifteen bushels of beans, three pairs of harnesses, three anchors, and one chain cable taken from a rebel schooner found in the creek, which after being dismantled was burned. Also brought along were thirty contrabands, a rebel deserter named Everett accompanied by his wife and child, another lady and child, and a refugee bound for the north, all from Richmond County.[36]

Having stripped the area of as much as could be found, on the morning of March 28, Fairchild and his men reboarded *Frasier* and returned to Belle Plain. They left behind the cavalry and twenty-three volunteer infantrymen under Captain James D. Wood to make their way back overland to Belle Plain, capturing whatever else of use they might find along the way. Wood and his men arrived in camp on the 29th bringing with them an additional forty-eight confiscated horses and mules acquired on their march.[37]

The operation had proceeded without mishap or loss. General Wadsworth's delight with the end results, which only seemed to validate his wish to occupy the Northern Neck, was clear. Nor did he have any compunction regarding the impact the raid had on the local citizenry. "I think the report confirms the opinion I have hitherto expressed," he stated unequivocally, "to the expediency of occupying the Neck with sufficient force of infantry and cavalry to intercept contraband trade, the supplies furnished to the enemy, and receive supplies for our own army. These supplies are taken from wealthy farmers, undisguised rebels, and who are only anxious to send their crops to the enemy." [38]

It seemed clear that an occupation force on the Northern Neck would "give facility to deserters from the enemy and intercept his means from procuring information" from within Union lines. Moreover, what Wadsworth construed to be the wealthiest region, the territory surrounding the Yeocomico, which bordered both Westmoreland and Northumberland counties, and included the thriving little riverport of Kinsale, had yet to be touched. The general practically begged for troops from his division, which was fully supplied with horses and mules, to be sent on another raid, this time to the Yeocomico. There would be a raid, but not on the target Wadsworth had wanted.[39]

Three weeks later the Union Army would mount another thrust into the Northern Neck, this time through the heart of King George County with the 24th Michigan Volunteers and the 14th New York Volunteers. With three days provisions in their haversacks and a number of breakdown boats, the expeditionaries departed on foot from Belle Plain at 1:30 p.m., April 22 under the command of Colonel Henry A. Morrow. Their destination was the strategic Rappahannock River ferry crossing between Port Conway, a speck of a community of five or six whitewashed houses, and the more substantial town of Port Royal. By 10:30 p.m. the raiders had arrived at the former and bivouacked in the rear of the village. At 3:00 a.m. on the 23rd the regiments were roused and under arms to march into the little hamlet "to set up boats and cross the river to Port Royal." Nature refused to cooperate, and a heavy rain combined with "the ignorance of the men as to the manner of constructing the boats," delayed the passage for hours. By 6 a.m., however, thirteen boats laden with troops were finally able to cross without opposition. Upon landing, parties were dispatched through the town of Port Royal. A wagon train was promptly surprised, captured and destroyed, several prisoners taken and the mail confiscated. By 9 p.m. the boats had returned to Port Conway. The hard spring downpour that had fallen throughout the entire operation had never ceased. At 11 a.m., April 24 the well-soaked soldiers commenced their march back to Belle Plain via muddy roads that were nearly impassable. They arrived at 7:30 p.m. footsore, caked in grime, and tired. But the lightning strike had been a success and without loss.[40]

Not until May 17 was another raid able to be mounted down the peninsula, "on that section of debatable ground lying between the Rappahannock and Potomac Rivers" southeast of Fredericksburg. This time, perhaps motivated as much by a thirst for revenge for recent Federal defeats as well as direct action against the elusive guerillas and smugglers of the region, "the former having caused our cavalry pickets no little annoyance in one way or another," the results would be stunning.[41]

The expedition would be multifaceted, employing fast moving cavalry, amphibious landings, and extensive overland movements by Union infantry. The 8th Illinois Cavalry, commanded by an aggressive colonel named David R. Clendenin, would conduct the initial surprise overland thrust deep into Westmoreland County and beyond. Their principal objective was, as before, to destroy enemy supplies and boats, capture horses and mules, bring off all the contrabands encountered, and wreck as much havoc possible upon the rebel hinterlan.

A second and much smaller amphibious raid commanded by Captain George E. Thompson, Company E, 3rd Indiana Cavalry, was to embark at Aquia Creek aboard the steamers *Manhattan* and *Tallaca* on the evening of May 20. Thompson was accompanied by General Pleasonton's aide-de-camp, a young, aggressive lieutenant named George Armstrong Custer. The raiders' mission, as per their unwritten instructions, appears to have been to penetrate as far as Urbanna via a circuitous route to capture and bring off unnamed parties, presumably ranking Confederate and partisan officers, intelligence personnel, or political officials.[42]

A third penetration of the countryside, commanded by Colonel Morrow with a force of 1,200 men belonging to the 24th Michigan, 2nd and 6th Wisconsin and 19th Indiana, was to be launched on the morning of May 21. Their objective was "to clear the Peninsula of any rebel troops which might have crossed the Rappahannock for the purpose of intercepting the Eighth Illinois Cavalry." [43]

Thompson's expedition with but a squad of twenty cavalrymen would cover far more ground than projected for even Clendenin's regiment. Having left Aquia Creek late on May 20 aboard the two assigned transports, the Indiana men did not reach their offloading site at Moon's Landing, near the mouth of the Wicomico in Northumberland County, until the morning of May 22. The passage had been far slower than anticipated owing to several unfortunate groundings of the transports, with the loss of time throwing off schedule what was to have been a surgical operation deep in hostile territory. Nevertheless, after landing at 11:30 a.m. Thompson and his men immediately galloped towards Heathsville, from which place they pivoted south on the road to Lancaster Court House and then on to

Chowning's Ferry on the lower Rappahannock, covering an estimated thirty-seven miles during their march.[44]

That night the troopers bivouacked at the ferry landing on the Rappahannock in the heart of hostile country. The following morning, they found two boats that were so leaky they required repairs to be made before they could set out on a four-mile row across the river. While in passage, Thompson espied a boat with four men who, upon seeing the bluecoats and their horses, immediately sought to escape. The Yankees gave chase. Upon reaching the shore, most of the pursued, believed to be a portion of the party the troops had been sent to kidnap, disappeared. Only one man, his wife and four children, who claimed to be refugees from Richmond were captured, having with them $130 in Confederate cash.[45]

At 11:00 a.m. the pounding of horses hooves and the clatter of metal and swords was heard as Thompson's raiders rode into Urbanna, taking the town by complete surprise. Their arrival, however, was a day too late. Though all efforts at secrecy and "proper steps" had been take to surprise his intended targets unawares, the captain's mission had failed. "Owing to the grounding of transports and their slow passage down the Potomac, and the distance which we were forced to travel," he later reported, "I found myself too late to be successful, the travelers having left Urbanna the day before we arrived." Though the secret primary objective of the raid had been subverted, Thompson nevertheless did as much damage as possible, destroying every boat he could find, and burning a bridge leading south, presumably over Urbanna Creek. Fifteen horses (two of which had been personally taken by Lieutenant Custer), a rebel artillery officer, and several men claiming to be enemy deserters and refugees from Richmond were also made captives and brought in for later interrogation.

After reboarding the transports, presumably at Urbanna, Thompson and his raiders returned to Aquia Creek, arriving there at midnight, May 23, and disembarking the following morning, ending another failed Unin mission.[46]

Unlike Thompson's fast and daring raid deep within enemy territory, Colonel Morrow's expedition, which departed on May 21 on a march overland from its base on Aquia Creek, was far more ponderous in that it involved more than 1,200 men. Their objective was to insure the safe extraction of Clendenin's regimental raiding force, which was to penetrate to the furthest reaches of the peninsula. The first leg of Thompson's march was to terminate at King George Court House near a strategic intersection on the Northern Neck. Two miles beyond the courthouse lay the crossroads, with one fork leading to Port Conway, and another to Oak Grove by way of Millville and Mattox Creek. A third, known as the Ridge Road, led to Westmoreland Court House by way of Oak Grove.[47]

After stopping for dinner at King George Court House on the afternoon of May 21, Morrow pressed on toward Millville, leaving a detachment of 160 men of the 6th Wisconsin to guard the fork. It was an unseasonably warm day, and before reaching their destination at dark, many men had given out from sheer exhaustion and the heat. There would be no respite, however, for the following morning the soldiers were aroused early and again on the march by daybreak for the eight-mile trek to Mattox Creek. Upon arrival at 8 a.m. they discovered the bridge across the creek in ruins, having been totally destroyed by the rebels four days earlier. All means of communication between the opposite banks, except by canoe, had been cut off. "Work of destruction is complete," noted the distraught colonel, "and except for a few half burned timbers no timber on hand to reconnect bridge."

At low tide the waterway was approximately fifty feet wide at the Mattox Creek Bridge, and was only approachable by a causeway 200 yards long through a low, marshy swamp that at high tide was entirely submerged. A work party was immediately set to repair the crossing, which in but a few hours had been completed enough to permit the passage of cavalry and infantry.

While the bridge was being repaired, Morrow was informed that an enemy force was assembled just a few miles to the south, near the little Rappahannock hamlet of Leesville. The colonel determined to immediately move to meet them. Leaving a small detachment behind to finish and guard the bridge he set off with his troops to engage the rebels, though taking "the necessary precaution to scour the country on either side of the road, to be sure that the enemy did not get in our rear or fall upon us in ambush." Having marched a total of sixteen miles during the day while encountering little more than a few horsemen but no rebel force of size, the raiders reached their destination a little before sunset. Where, Morrow must have wondered, were the reported and illusive Confederates?

That evening the bluecoats bivouacked behind a skirt of woods and out of sight a thousand yards distance from the hamlet of Port Micon, on the opposite side of the Rappahannock. Morrow established picket lines at the water's edge above and below Leesville to prevent enemy communication with the opposite bank. A detachment of mounted troops was dispatched as far downriver as Leedstown, two miles to the east of Leesville. He soon learned that the rebels had two boats of considerable size at Port Micon and quickly determined to destroy them. The following morning, May 23, having located an old boat on the north shore of the river, he dispatched ten men with instructions to burn or otherwise destroy the enemy craft across the river. "The attempt was made with every prospect of success, but failed," undoubtedly owing to the presence of a hitherto undetected Confederate cavalry squadron doing picket duty on the opposite shore. A volley of fire promptly caused the enemy to withdraw behind a slight rise of ground a quarter mile behind Port Micon. Though the withdrawal had the effect of removing rebel pickets, infantry and cavalry from closely watching the Yankee motions, Morrow now deemed a crossing in force to be too risky. Even with possible enemy stores in the hamlet, he chose not to hazard a landing, believing he needed a boat capable of carrying at least twenty or more men before he might have any chance for success.[48]

With his primary mission being to intercept any Confederate forces that might impede the safe retirement of the 8th Illinois from the peninsula, at 7 a.m. on the morning of May 23 Morrow feinted a move downriver towards Leedstown. As soon as he was out of sight of the enemy, he turned his march towards Oak Grove, "thinking it likely I should intercept any rebels there might be in that section, who would probably be seeking to make their way to the river." As his forces were in the process of turning, two men in Confederate uniforms were spotted making for the water. A detachment led by Private Aaron F. Bickford, Company H, 1st Maine Cavalry, an orderly at I Corps headquarters, was immediately sent off in pursuit. Within short order Bickford had returned with a prisoner, one Lieutenant Colonel

John Critcher, 15th Virginia Cavalry. The capture earned Bickford a commendation from Morrow and a prize prisoner of war for the Union. Then it was on to Oak Grove, which was entered a little after noon.[49]

"Oak Grove is a place of little importance," noted Morrow, "except that it is at the intersection of several of the principal roads of the Northern Neck. These roads lead to King George Court House, Mattox Creek, Westmoreland Courthouse, Leedstown, and Port Conway." Though he had met no resistance from the enemy supposed to be in the area, he also had no intelligence on the disposition or whereabouts of the 8th Illinois Cavalry that he had been sent to protect. It was thus deemed necessary to dispatch a squadron of cavalry from the 19th Indiana to Westmoreland Court House, through which Clendenin and his men would likely pass, while Morrow remained at Oak Grove until he "could get definite information in relation to the probable whereabouts of the Eighth Illinois Cavalry." That evening, Lieutenant Colonel William W. Dudley, in command of the 19th Indiana, dispatched the unsettling message that three regiments of rebel cavalry and one regiment of infantry were now in the vicinity.[50]

Undoubtedly expecting trouble, and leaving a detachment behind at Oak Grove, Morrow marched his troops to Rappahannock Creek, a mile outside of town, early on the morning of May 24. The crossing there was such, he estimated, that a hundred men might hold a thousand at bay unless there was a better route to be had. Here, he opined, two or three companies might defy several regiments of cavalry. It was a most defensible location indeed, which could be easily held. But where was Clendenin? "This, if any place, was the point where the rebels would make a stand," he decided, "and here I concluded to leave my infantry under Colonel Samuel J. Williams, Nineteenth Indiana, while I pressed on toward Heathsville in Northumberland County, with the Eighth New York Cavalry." He had to find Clendenin.

Then it happened.

"All the preparations were made, and an advance had actually started," Morrow reported five days later, "when the Eighth Illinois Cavalry, with an immense train of wagons, carts, horses, mules, and contrabands, came up accompanied by my scouts." [51]

The Clendenin arm of the operation, a monumentally destructive sweep through the fields and farms of the entire Northern Neck, proved to be by far the most successful of all. He had set out from the main camp of the Army of the Potomac on May 17 with 500 men and just four days' rations. His avowed mission was "for the purpose of inflicting summary punishment upon these citizen marauders," meaning the guerillas, smugglers and Confederate supporters of the region. Upon reaching King George Court House he had divided his command into three columns, each taking a public turnpike road and marching the entire length of the neck, capturing and destroying rebel property without limit. "Every nook along the banks of the two rivers," it was later reported "was explored for smugglers' boats and goods, which, when found, were destroyed. One hundred sloops, yawls, ferryboats, etc., were burned, with all their contents, consisting of salt, oil, whiskey, leather, stationery, wool cards, percussion caps, boots, shoes, clothing and many other articles of especial value to the rebels. About 20,000 pounds of bacon and a large quantity of flour were also destroyed." [52]

At Leed's Ferry it was ascertained that the ferryboat, said to have been employed for smuggling purposes, was on the south bank of the Rappahannock, and it was especially desirable that it should be destroyed. Accordingly, a few of the Illinois troopers were dressed in captured rebel uniforms and escorted a few of their companions as if they were prisoners. The ruse worked, and the ferryboat was brought across, captured along with a few Confederate guards, and destroyed.[53]

Upon returning, the line of march was joined by hundreds of black slaves, "in squads of from five to 20," belonging to plantations along the way. By the end of the expedition a total of 810 men, women and children had joined the "emancipating column," bringing with them all their belongings as well as horses, mules, carts, and clothing, "some of which did not legitimately belong to them, but which they had confiscated from rebel masters under the 'sequestration act.'" It was thus discovered that there were still many "good and loyal citizens in this section of the country," no doubt among the poorer inhabitants who had neither slaves nor property to lose, who rendered considerable assistance to the troops.

One of the most important accomplishments of the raid was the acquisition of 500 horses and mules, which were acknowledged to be far superior to those purchased by the Federal Government for cavalry service. Upon termination of the operation one correspondent to the *New York Tribune* noted somewhat acidly: "It may be mentioned here that the most serviceable horses the cavalry have had during the past year have been those captured from the enemy. One company that I know has, out of 50 horses, 35 which were formerly in the Confederate service, and this company has not had a horse condemned in six months. The reason for this is, the rebels press into service the best horses to be found within their lines, while our Government buys the poorest horses to be had for a very limited price." [54]

Weary but ebullient, the troopers of the 8th Illinois arrived safely in camp on the night of May 28 leading a "ludicrous procession . . . of cavalry, negroes, captured horses, mules, carts, wagons, oxen, rebel soldiers, trotting sulkies, top carriages, etc." Among the parade were scores of prisoners, some of them guerrillas, several officers and a few smugglers. Upwards of $5,000 in Confederate currency and a trove of rebel securities had also been brought off.[55]

Of the many hundreds of freed slaves, 300 were assigned to duty as laborers at a wage of ten dollars per month per man plus rations. Most of those remaining were old men, and the wives, children or mothers of the fit men. To feed this large number of contrabands, as well as his own men, Clendenin "made heavy levies upon the granaries of the Secesh" by taking possession of their grist mills and turning his soldiers into temporary millers to produce an abundant supply of meal and flour.

At the same time it was ascertained that some of the wealthiest citizens of the Northern Neck were among those engaged in the business of smuggling or "contributing" in some way to the Confederacy, and were destined to pay heavily for their secessionist sympathies. As their slaves had left them, "it was thought but just that the soldiers should take their rations. So these Illinois emancipators fared sumptuously during their trip." [56]

343

General Hooker's Chief of Staff, Major General Daniel Butterfield, would later crow about the damage inflicted by the Illinois men: fifty boats destroyed, breaking up the contraband trade "as effectually as possible," $30,000 worth of contraband goods intercepted and destroyed while in transit; more than 800 black contrabands, approximately five percent of the peninsula's slave population and workforce, freed and escorted to Union lines; a quantity of mules captured; and between forty and fifty rebels, including two officers, taken prisoner. Damage done to the enemy, primarily the destruction of supplies, was placed at an astonishing $1,000,000.[57] General Pleasonton declared that considering the force engaged and the results obtained, "this is the greatest raid of the war." [58]

***

The May 1863 operations on the Northern Neck, though complicated, had finally met with the very success that Quartermaster General Meigs had predicted five months earlier. Relying upon its naval control of both the Potomac frontier and lower Rappahannock, the Union had been able to deploy its forces when and wherever it wished. Opposition had been hardly extant and the romp through the rich, unprotected territory had given Northerners a few positive nods after the wrenching defeats at Fredericksburg and Chancellorsville among others. In most cases the Federal troops had performed well. In a little over five days, Morrow's infantry had marched over 130 miles in unseasonably warm weather that left some prostrate. Clendenin's cavalry had conducted a textbook raid in enemy territory that rivaled even some of the fabled horsemen of the Confederacy. Despite some mismanagement and bumbling about the operations had indeed cut into rebel support.

Yet the invasion would have its negative effects, as Colonel Morrow so cogently observed. Though the country was full of reports of the presence of rebel troops on the peninsula, he noted, "I now have no reason to believe that any considerable force was at any one place on this side of the Rappahannock." The enemy had no doubt put reports in circulation, he theorized, "to deter us from sending our cavalry down the Neck into the wealthy and flourishing country embraced in the counties of Westmoreland, Richmond, Northumberland, and Lancaster, which is abundantly supplied with corn and wheat." [59]

There was indeed a large, acknowledged contraband trade still being carried on between the peninsula and Maryland. "Blockade running and dealing in contraband articles have become professions," the colonel observed, and the best way to stop it, he believed, was to occupy the vicinity of Heathsville with troops. Moreover, a gunboat on the Rappahannock might find gainful employment in assisting to make the blockade more effective by installing a great uneasiness in the enemy.[60]

Yet it was, as in Southern Maryland, the hearts and minds of the inhabitants, primarily those who were the more impoverished, non-slave owning folk, that would have to be dealt with to wean them from the Southern cause. Morrow was perhaps alone in his observations regarding the effects of the Clendenin raid upon the white population of the Northern Neck. He was certainly not as complimentary as either Butterfield or Pleasonton, neither of which had personally visited the region. "Everywhere I found a majority of the people bitterly opposed to the Government," he wrote, "which they charged with sending among them cavalry to rob and plunder them. In several instances I was assured by intelligent men and women that the wholesale plunder and pillage of our cavalry had done more to weaken the affection of the people for the Government than all other causes combined, and, in fact, the cavalry have left the inhabitants very little cause to respect them as men and soldiers. They have robbed and plundered all that came in their way."

Morrow charged that the Union raiders, "pretending to be representatives of our Government," had stripped helpless women and children of their last horse, and in many instance of their last article of food, and then grossly insulted them for complaining. It was his opinion that the commander of the Army of the Potomac was aware of "the utter want of every principle of true soldiers which characterizes the intercourse between the cavalry and the inhabitants of the Northern Neck." The people, he declared, were actually anxious to renew their commercial intercourse with Maryland. He thus had taken action to apply for passes for some who were willing to bind themselves under oath not to aid in any manner the enemy to visit Baltimore to purchase necessary articles of food and clothing. Some of the applications in writing were forwarded with the colonel's report "for the consideration of the proper department." [61]

Morrow's efforts proved entirely in vain. The renewal of commercial intercourse between the Northern Neck and Maryland, the plundering and ill treatment of the citizenry, and the general Federal disposition towards all areas of rebeldom or those sympathetic to the Confederacy, justified or not, would not be altered in the least. Indeed, aggressive plundering incursions into the Northern Neck, though temporarily halted after the May raids, would eventually be resumed. This time the attacks would be launched from the shores of St. Mary's County, as the war along the Anaconda's Tail progressed in an increasingly vicious cycle of plunder, chaos and misery.

26

FOR THE BENEFIT OF THE SICK AND WOUNDED
"Truly they are ministering angels."

The first few years of war had not been kind to William H. Allen, the Baltimore entrepreneur who had assumed the mortgage on the late William Cost Johnson's luxurious Point Lookout resort. Steamer traffic to the point was frequently halted by the military; the Zarvona scandal was still lingering in everyone's memory; and Federal patrols and arrests throughout Southern Maryland were on the rise. The all but empty resort seriously threatened to cast Allen into a financial abyss.

The owner of Point Lookout, however, was no less a visionary than Johnson had been when it came to property – especially unoccupied property in the right location. He, like anyone else who read the papers, was also well aware of the rising cost in human lives and suffering the war was causing. By the late spring of 1862 recent military engagements at Front Royal, New Bridge and elsewhere posed new challenges to the medical arm of the U.S. military. At the beginning of the war, there were only thirty surgeons in the army (a number that would eventually rise to 11,000 by the end of the conflict). The escalating demand for medical facilities and personnel, however, was unceasing. The battles at Mechanicsville, Hanover Court House, Winchester, and Seven Pines, Virginia, had taken a ghastly toll on Union troops. At Seven Pines alone, out of 42,000 Federals engaged, casualties were numbered at 790 killed, 3,594 wounded, and 647 missing. Medical facilities in Washington, Baltimore, New York, Philadelphia and other cities were stressed to the limit to handle the sick and wounded. Governor Andrew Gregg Curtin of Pennsylvania suggested that the casualties of each state's units be removed to hospitals in their respective states; and an order to that effect was issued. The concept was quickly countered in favor of breaking up the hospitals in New York and Philadelphia and other cities and "to establish, in lieu thereof, hospitals within the limits of the several military departments." [1] Why not, Allen considered, offer to rent or lease to the army the already extant but empty hotel, cottages and other facilities at Point Lookout for military hospital purposes?

And he did!

Surgeon General William Alexander Hammond immediately saw great merit in the proposal, and dispatched a medical officer to the point on an inspection visit to ascertain the possibilities. Upon receiving a favorable report, Hammond requested permission from Quartermaster General Meigs on June 5, 1862 to rent the buildings and grounds at Point Lookout. "It is estimated," he wrote, "that they will accommodate from 1,300 to 1,500 men besides ample room for quarters, storehouses, dispensary, kitchens, etc." [2]

On July 4, having been selected as a viable hospital site, Point Lookout was taken over by the military and the erection of a hospital unlike any other in the nation was ordered. The proposal was approved and five days later Assistant Quartermaster Captain L. C. Edwards arrived to immediately begin construction of a dining room, laundry, warehouses, stables and other support facilities to enhance the already extant infrastructure. A week later plans and specifications for the large, radical hospital design were received by Meigs and forwarded at once to the captain to proceed with construction.

Edwards received his orders along with the architectural plans on July 19 and must have gazed with incredulity at the revolutionary layout of the main hospital building. The structure was designed like a wheel, with fifteen spokes 175 feet in length and twenty-five feet in width. Every spoke was fitted with thirty-two windows to admit the fresh sea air in warm seasons, with each spoke serving as a ward reserved for a particular illness or injury. A sixteenth building spoke, 175 feet by fifty feet and two stories in height, was to be employed as headquarters for the medical staff, and storage for linens and other hospital stores. All were connected on the inside of the circle by a ring corridor that was eight feet in width and 100 feet in circumference. At the center of the hub was an elevated 10,000 gallon water reservoir with hose for fire protection, encompassed by a small circling corridor, into which ran at 90-degree angles four crossing passageways that joined the hub to the ring. In the angle of the circular interior space formed by these corridors were four buildings, each seventy-five by twenty-five feet, to serve as a chapel, a "half- diet" kitchen, a library and reading room, and a knapsack or baggage room. Tucked into the two spokes nearest the lighthouse, but not connected, was an immense T-shaped dining hall. On the Potomac side of the hospital was a small covered wharf for the reception of craft shuttling supplies in from Baltimore. All of the structures were elevated several feet above the ground by pilings in the event of extremely high tides or storms. It was soon being over optimistically reported that the whole complex would be capable of administering from four to five thousand patients at a time. Besides the main hospital building there were also the hundred or so cottages, the Pavilion Hotel and miscellaneous outbuildings constructed before the hospital. They were to be put in order and used for medical purposes, staff housing, and so forth.[3]

Eventually a steam laundry capable of washing 10,000 pieces of clothing daily, and a steam saw for cutting all the firewood used by the hospital would also be added. By February 1863 it was expected the facility could handle at capacity 2,500 patients, a medical staff of thirteen physicians, and 250 stewards, nurses and other employees, all under the supervision of the chief medical officer. Religious services were to be provided by the Reverend John Alden Spooner, USA.[4]

"The appearance presented by the Hammond Hospital," noted one observer when the complex was almost completed in early 1863,

"whilst approaching it from the river, is very striking, and one could almost fancy himself on the 'Great Father of Waters,' and approaching one of those Western towns which seems to have sprung up by magic . . . The hospital buildings reach into the bay on one side and the Potomac on the other, insuring full share of whatever breeze may be stirring. Indeed, during the most severe heat of summer the buildings are so constructed that a constant draught of fresh air is wafted through every ward, while the facilities for bathing, fishing, and all physical amusements, such as would interest invalids, are unsurpassed." [5]

Another observer wrote that its location was both healthy and idyllic for the same reason that William Cost Johnson had chosen it as the site for his much ballyhooed resort. Not only did it have the fresh breezes from the Chesapeake and

Potomac, but it also had the advantage of fine groves of pines, "whose grateful shade is always a pleasant relief from the scorching rays of the August sun. No more pleasant scenery could be found along any river, than that which abounds on the shores of the Potomac, and scattered along in such profuse variety." [6]

Hammond Hospital was a revolutionary design and concept generated by the benefits of the massive pioneering medical triage practice accorded the wounded after the April 1862 slaughter called the Battle of Shiloh. The clash had produced more than 25,000 casualties and threatened to overwhelm Union surgeons during and after the fight. For the first time, on a great scale, the wounded had been treated according to the type and seriousness of their wounds in areas designated for the particular injury so that expertise in each could be more efficiently and speedily addressed. Now it was to be put to use in a fixed care facility for the first time, with a tent city to serve as auxiliary wards to take up overloads. And with McClellan's long awaited Peninsula Campaign finally underway, it was certain that all the facilities would be quickly filled.

Soon the tidal wave of sick and wounded began to arrive by steamer even before the great hospital was completed. Ironically, the first load of patients consisted of both Confederate prisoners and Federal soldiers who had been engaged during the campaign. On the afternoon of July 24, 1862 the 780-ton sidewheeler *John Brooks*, which had been chartered by the U.S. Army in March, arrived at Fort Monroe with 222 wounded Federals and a number of injured rebel prisoners. There she was to take on coal before setting off the next morning for Point Lookout "where her patients will be landed and placed in new hospitals fitted up for their reception." [7] By mid-August, it was reported that Point Lookout was still in the process of "being rapidly fitted up for Hospital purposes, and already there are a goodly number of large Hospital tents erected there for that purpose, and boats are daily being relieved here of their invalid passengers." [8]

All was not perfect, of course, for there were a great number of difficulties to be overcome. On August 17 for example, when the Army chartered steamer *State of Maine* arrived at the point and began to unload 350 sick and wounded Union soldiers, the main wharf, originally built for the resort, collapsed. Fortunately there was no loss of life, but a new wharf, 280 feet by eighteen feet, had to be constructed. The structure was later lengthened to 310 feet when the point was also designated a supply depot for the Army of the Potomac.[9]

Wharf or no wharf, the arrivals of wounded was unrelenting. The same day as the collapse, the steamer *Knickerbocker*, chartered for the army in March, arrived from Harrison's Landing on the James River. The vessel had only recently been turned over to the Sanitary Commission for use as a hospital ship and now carried 541 more patients, including eighty officers, who had been evacuated two days earlier during the retirement of McClellan's forces from the James. Thus in a single day nearly 900 patients had been delivered for medical treatment and recuperation.[10]

The respite from the fighting for at least 1,300 patients lodged at Point Lookout, now being generally called "Hammond Hospital," after Surgeon General Hammond, was duly noted in the Northern press, as was the excellent staff charged with day to day care. Here, it was noted, even shell-shocked soldiers might convalesce where a "few weeks' rest and quiet will enable them to join their commands." The head army physician in command of the hospital, Dr. Anthony Hager, and his surgeons were noted as "assiduous in their attentions." The nursing staff was headed by a Mrs. Gibbons of New York City, who was described as "a most excellent lady" who faithfully performed her duty, ably supported by a staff of lady nurses.

"Truly," it was said, "they are ministering angels." [11]

***

The city of Washington and its environs was, by one measure, a natural hospital center for the Union Army owing of its proximity to both the Virginia and later Maryland theaters of war. Yet it was seriously handicapped in that it had always been considered an unhealthy place, chiefly because of the large open canal that extended across the city and into which substantial sewage was dumped. The city was once known as "Swampoodle" for the marshy lands upon which much of it was built, where standing pools still remained and in which legions of anopheles mosquitoes bred. The capital of the United States of America, especially in mid-summer, was downright insufferable. Not surprisingly malaria and intestinal diseases flourished. Moreover, by the end of 1861 the city had only 2,000 general hospital beds to serve the incredible onslaught of sick and wounded, many of whom departed either sicker than when they arrived or dead.

The substantial slaughter suffered during the Peninsular Campaign was the beginning of the first truly great flood of casualties to fill the region's hospitals. Then in Virginia on August 26, 1862 the Second Battle of Manassas commenced and concluded four days later with the stunning victory of Generals Robert E. Lee and Thomas "Stonewall" Jackson over Union General John Pope. The number of Federal casualties was astonishing. Of the 75,000 northerners engaged there were 1,724 dead, 8,372 wounded, and 5,958 missing, or more than twenty-one percent of the total. The wounded immediately taxed the already overfilled hospital facilities between the District of Columbia and New York. In Washington, Alexandria and vicinity more than fifty places were already housing thousands of wounded, and even churches were converted to hospitals almost overnight. On September 10, 500 sick and wounded were transferred to New York, more than 100 to Philadelphia, and another 400 to Point Lookout, which was already filled. It wasn't enough. A week later there were still 13,769 patients in emergency facilities spread just between Washington and Alexandria. At one point even the halls of the U.S. Pension Office were converted into a hospital, with cots spread among the exhibitions, as was the Georgetown jail, and the House and Senate in the Capitol.[12]

The deluge of casualties continued unabated as the first Confederate invasion of Western Maryland followed in mid-September. Two great fights, the Battle of South Mountain, with 2,325 Federal dead, wounded and missing, and Antietam, one of the bloodiest engagements of the war, where Union losses included 2,010 killed, 9,416 wounded, and 1,043 missing, flushed a flood of wounded combatants into hospital facilities throughout the North.[13] A total of 56,050 cases were treated in Washington alone by the end of 1862.

Despite the often heroic efforts to meet the crisis, public outrage at the inability of the government to manage the many thousands of wounded, and the resultant diminished quality of care was soon echoed throughout the Union. In Philadelphia large numbers of letters were received at military headquarters from all over Pennsylvania, bitterly complaining of bad treatment of soldiers in hospitals in Washington, Annapolis, Philadelphia, Chester, Providence and Point Lookout. All claimed neglect in supervising the duties of surgeons in charge on the part of the Medical Bureau at Washington. "It is very evident," noted one editorial, "that the Medical Bureau is unable properly to meet the present exigency and people must agitate the question of proper treatment of our sick and wounded soldiers until the President himself directs better arrangements to be made by the United States Surgeon General." [14]

The problem was compounded by prisoners of war in equally difficult situations, many being paroled Union soldiers arriving from the battlefield who were desperately sick or wounded. In July 1862 the first round of parolees arrived in Annapolis and were lodged on the green at St. John's College, which had been commandeered by the government. By the end of August there were some 2,000 men, many of them desperate medical cases, waiting there to be either mustered out or formally exchanged and permitted to return to their units. Lacking tents and often obliged to sleep on the ground with no bedding, some became surly and caused general havoc among the local population, plundering and occasionally attacking the citizenry. By September their numbers had swollen to 3,000 and the situation was approaching a crisis level. The government responded by erecting a virtual prison called Camp Parole several miles from the edge of Annapolis. On September 24 the exchanged prisoners of war, many of them in horrendous physical condition, arrived from Confederate prison camps aboard a steamer. The hospital facility on the academy grounds was designated by the Medical Department at Annapolis as U.S. General Hospital Division 1. The buildings at St. John's College, quickly customized to facilitate the special needs of extreme medical conditions among the worst cases, was eventually designated U.S. General Hospital Division 2. Up to 600 cases could be housed in the St. John's barracks and tents. New arrivals of exchanged men and parolees landing at the Naval Academy wharf were marched to the Severn and obliged to discard their clothing and wash before being given new attire and fed. From there they were admitted to the academy facilities, the St. John's Hospital, or the barracks on St. John's Green. After a few days most were sent to Camp Parole. Occasionally, sick and debilitated prisoners were sent from the hospital to the camp simply to make room for the next round of incoming men. By November between seven and eight thousand men were ensconced in a tent city at Parole, all adequately fed and clothed but lacking heat or suitable sanitary facilities.[15]

At Point Lookout the expansion and improvements on the Hammond Hospital and the new wharf proceeded slowly well into fall. By mid-October it was expected that seventeen new hospital buildings would be added to the extant accommodations to reach the facility's target capacity of 2,500 patients. Interestingly, William Allen, who was leasing the land to the government, had also secured the contract for carpentry work; a Mr. Carrolto had charge of plastering and a Mr. Bump was the project roofer, all from Baltimore. It was understood that as soon as the first buildings were completed, they were to be duplicated. Within a short time, though little notice was taken of it owning to its isolated situation, the Hammond

General Hospital complex would be claimed as one of the largest institutions of its kind in the country.[16]

In mid-November 1862 the firm of C. Greer & Co., engaged in the enterprise of publishing, as noted in its masthead, a "neat little" newspaper "For the Benefit of the Sick and Wounded in Hammond General Hospital." It was the second newspaper to be published in St. Mary's County during the war.

In his salutary first column the editor of the sheet, dubbed the *Hammond Gazette*, wrote: "Point Lookout is rapidly assuming the proportions of a considerable town; the population a month ago was something over eighteen hundred; within a few weeks it will be increased to over three thousand. Previous to the war it was the fashionable resort of the chivalry of Eastern Virginia, and Southern and Western Maryland; but within a very brief period a large town has suddenly been produced, peopled with cripples, demure looking doctors, sedate matrons, reserved Sisters of Charity, and intelligent contrabands." [17]

Over the next year and a half the newspaper, one of nineteen hospital newspapers issued during the Civil War, would publish numerous articles, military themed poems, columns of war news, and regular features such as "Congressional," "Telegrams From the Army of the Potomac," "Highly Important from Washington," local interest stories, and special items on holidays. Within three months, much to the delight of the patients, the *Hammond Gazette* would be published twice weekly.[18]

By February 1863 the hospital could boast of a theater "conducted in a very excellent manner by the patients, who furnish scenery, dresses, actors and audiences, and exhibit considerable skill in its management, and a proper appreciation of these efforts to amuse and interest them." A regular post office was established, which provided a great morale boost for the convalescent, and it was said, "to see the poor fellows pile out in strings of two or three hundred, all anxious to hear from 'the dear one's at home,' is a sight well worth witnessing." By the spring of 1863 regular scheduled stops were being made at Point Lookout by the passenger steamer *Keyport*, Captain E. A. Ryther, which had commenced operations between Baltimore and Washington, thus permitting visitation to hospital patients. In November, a second steamer, *W. W. Wildin*, Captain Riggins, was authorized to open regular runs from the foot of Barre Street, Baltimore to Alexandria and Washington, with regular stops at landings on the Potomac, including Point Lookout. All passengers were required to secure permits from the office of Major General Samuel P. Heintzelman. Freight had to be prepaid, and custom house permits were required for shipping. A small military guard commanded by Major John Carter Brown, with several companies dubbed the "Lost Children," was stationed on the point to protect the facility from rebel raiders and to help interdict the ever active blockade runners.[19]

But it was the overall comfort of the patients that was the most unique thing about Hammond Hospital. "We have enough to eat and everything comfortable, and good care in the hospital," wrote one wounded soldier from Company C, 5th New Hampshire Regiment, to his folks at home.[20]

Not everything was perfect, for in hospitals where pain and suffering might be eased but not always disposed of, patients sometimes died. And in death there was always poignancy. When one patient succumbed, he left only his *Bible*. On the flyleaf of the Holy Book he had written: "If I die on the field or in hospital in the name of humanity write home." To this was signed his full name and address. A lock of his hair was cut off and laid on the leaf in the *Bible*, and this sad relic was the message sent to his family to inform them of his demise.[21]

Patient suicides were not uncommon, especially among those who suffered from battlefield trauma, debilitating wounds and amputations, or believed they had been entirely forgotten. One such case was that of William Turner of Company H, 23rd Pennsylvania Volunteers, who took his own life by drowning. "He was evidently insane," the surgeons reported, "superintended by a fear that his family might suffer for the necessaries of life—he not having received any pay for the last six months. A paymaster should visit here immediately." [22]

***

The sick and wounded continued to arrive at the Hammond Hospital in substantial numbers well into the third year of warfare. Many had first been transported from various battlefields to frequently overloaded Washington, Alexandria or Baltimore facilities before being finally transferred to Point Lookout. In late November 1862, for instance, approximately 500 sick soldiers were sent down at one time aboard the steamer *Daniel Webster* to Hammond Hospital from several facilities in Alexandria.[23]

Then in mid-December, with the monumental Battle of Fredericksburg looming, it was said that Union General Ambrose E. Burnside, anticipating very heavy casualties, telegraphed Surgeon General Hammond on December 11 to have 15,000 beds immediately prepared for the reception of wounded. Unfortunately, it was estimated, there were only 5,000 vacant beds in the Washington hospitals, 2,000 in Philadelphia, 2,500 in New York, 1,000 at Baltimore, and an estimated 1,000 at Point Lookout. The general was not far off the mark. Of the 114,000 Federal troops engaged, the Army of the Potomac suffered 12,653 casualties, of which 1,284 were were killed, 1,769 captured or missing, and 9,600 wounded, in one of the greatest Union defeats of the war. General Robert E. Lee, Burnside's opponent, later commented: "It was a great slaughter pen . . . they might as well have tried to take Hell." [24]

On the morning of December 17 three steamers arrived at the Washington waterfront from Aquia Creek carrying as many as 2,000 wounded and a number of corpses of men who had died en route. More were already on the way. That same day a great many of the casualties were immediately rerouted to Point Lookout.[25]

***

By the spring of 1863, though the great bulk of construction at Point Lookout had been completed, there was still work to be done, especially as it related to the interment of the dead. On May 8 Surgeon General Hammond complained to Quartermaster General Meigs of the work that lay ahead, especially regarding proper burial sites in the cemetery, a mile and a quarter away. "As the utmost capacity of this hospital may be required at any moment, I request its completion may be expedited as much as possible . . . the graveyard is without fence or protection, the graves only marked through the kindness of friends or wardmasters; not a single properly marked head board has been put up by the Quarter Master." [26]

Though hundreds of patients had died at the point, it was nothing compared to what lay ahead. On July 1, just 120 miles to the north in the rolling, pastoral farmlands of southern Pennsylvania, near a small town called Gettysburg, a titanic battle had just begun that would define the course of American history. It would also alter Point Lookout, once a place of recreation and respite, and then a place for care and healing, into a veritable hellhole of suffering and death for thousands of prisoners of war. Many of them were Southern Marylanders who would pay the ultimate price for their allegiance to the Confederate States of America.

CAMP HOFFMAN
"It was root, pig, or die."

When the first figures came in on Union and Confederate casualties suffered at Gettysburg, Pennsylvania, during the epic struggle that began on that pivotal morning in early July, it was apparent to all that the cost, in human terms, would be appalling for both sides. As 85,000 troops belonging to the Army of the Potomac, under newly appointed Major General George Gordon Meade, marshaled to counter the Army of Northern Virginia's invasion of the North with Lee's nearly 65,000 Confederates, the fight was certain to be long and bloody. Culminating at midday July 3, the brave but hopeless assault known to history as Pickett's Charge brought the war to a defining crescendo.

"Men fire into each other's faces, not five feet apart," recalled one eyewitness to the climactic clash. "There are bayonet thrusts, sabre strokes, pistol shots . . . men going down on their hands and knees, spinning round like tops, throwing out their arms, gulping up blood, falling; legless, armless, headless. There are ghastly heaps of dead men." [1]

Now all that remained following the uncontested retreat of Lee's defeated army was the body count, which was numbing. When all was finally tabulated, Federal losses numbered 3,155 dead, 14,529 wounded and 5,365 missing. Confederate losses were equally appalling. Among the enormous number of rebel prisoners taken at the Battle of Gettysburg, the medical inspector from the U.S. Surgeon General's office initially estimated that 8,000 to 10,000 were wounded and the dead at least in the thousands. A final tally placed Confederate losses at 2,592 killed, 12,709 wounded and 5,150 missing. Many of the nonambulatory casualties had been left on the field of battle by the retiring rebel army.[2] The toll immediately taxed the stretched Federal capacity for management of injured and the already large prisoner of war population throughout the North. Just where both the whole and the injured prisoners were now to be incarcerated, housed, fed and taken care of posed an immediae crisis for the War Department.

Soon after the battle Acting Surgeon General Joseph R. Smith immediately began to search for facilities capable of taking on the burden of managing the Confederate wounded. After consulting with the Commissary General of Prisoners, Colonel William Hoffman, and learning of the enormous numbers involved he first telegraphed the medical director at New York City and instructed that a hospital at Davids Island be prepared to receive them. He then contacted the officer in charge of transportation at Gettysburg to send all rebel wounded to that hospital. The army medical director at Philadelphia was also ordered to prepare the hospital at Chester, Pennsylvania, "for the exclusive use of the rebel wounded." But it would not be enough, and there were many additional issues that compounded the difficulty in finding adequate care facilities. Immediately afterwards he received a direct order from Secretary Stanton "to keep separate as far as possible the rebel wounded from those of our army," and that the former be sent under proper guard to Point Lookout.[3]

The only problem with Stanton's directive was that many of the current count of 1,400 beds at Hammond Hospital were still occupied by Union soldiers, and there were far more rebel wounded than they could possibly handle. It was thus decided that the Federals at Point Lookout be transferred to Baltimore to make room for the rebel casualties, a move with which some in the War Department were uncomfortable. Brigadier General Edward R. S. Canby, for one, wrote on July 11 to Major General Schenck at his headquarters in Baltimore: "I beg leave to make two suggestions, one that it might be best to send the rebels as far as practicable to hospitals north of this point, unless it is thought that Northern copperheads [pro-Confederates] will sympathize with and pet them too much; the other that rebel officers have a bad influence on their men, many of the latter of whom are penitent when they are permitted to be, and they ought therefore to be separated both in prisons and hospitals." [4] Both suggestions were ignored, at least initially.

Following the Gettysburg Campaign it fell to Quartermaster General Meigs to provide an adequate place to house the tremendous influx of captives, both whole and wounded. He soon came to focus upon the hospital facilities on the remote Point Lookout Peninsula. It was, he decided, an ideal location not just for wounded rebels, but also for a new prisoner of war camp to which steamers could transport the captives en masse and where medical facilities already existed. Meigs issued orders for Chief Quartermaster General Daniel Henry Rucker on July 20 to formally establish a depot at Point Lookout suitable for up to 10,000 prisoners. "Old tents should be sent from those in depot and necessary camp and garrison equipage, lumber to erect kitchens and store houses, and large cast-iron boilers for cooking. The labor will be performed by the prisoners themselves, but preliminary arrangements should be made by this department . . . Lumber should be obtained by requisition from Baltimore." [5]

Meigs recommended Dr. Augustus M. Clark, an army surgeon who had already conducted a preliminary visit to the point, to prepare the plans and a cost estimate. Anxious to get underway, he declared that even "the slightest sketch will enable us to begin the work on a system and increase it as may be necessary." [6] To facilitate better administrative procedures under Army General Order No. 226, St. Mary's County was detached on July 23 from the Middle Department and the direct authority of General Schenck, and formed into a separate military district under the command of Brigadier General Gilman Marston of New Hampshire.[7]

Marston, an austere looking man with a high forehead and a perpetual scowl, was a graduate of Dartmouth College and Harvard who had served in the New Hampshire Legislature and as a Republican member of the U.S. Congress. He had his baptism of fire at the First Battle of Manassas, where he was wounded. Then, in December 1861, while sitting in his tent at Budd's Ferry, he was accidentally shot by a man cleaning his gun in the next tent. The ball struck him in the hip, glanced off the bone and exited from his abdomen. Somehow he survived. While commanding the 2nd New Hampshire Volunteers, he had healed enough to fight in the Peninsula Campaign, Second Manassas, and at the Battle of Fredericksburg. Afterwards while assigned to the defenses of Washington, he returned to his seat in Congress, albeit only briefly. Now, appointed to the command of the St. Mary's District and Point

Lookout, he was about to take on an assignment unlike any in which he had hitherto been engaged.

On the same day that General Order 226 was issued Secretary of War Stanton, accompanied by the new General in Chief of the U.S. Army, Henry Wagner Halleck, and Major General E. A. Hitchcock, Commissioner for Exchange of Prisoners, set out on a personal inspection of Point Lookout. "This location has been chosen," it was quickly pointed out, "not only on account of the salubriousness and convenience for the receipt and transportation of prisoners, but also on account of its isolation and the opportunity of reaching it [by water] without carrying the prisoners through communities where demonstrations of sympathy might be made by rebel sympathizers." [8]

Simultaneous to the inspection of the point, General Marston was ordered to proceed there at once with 300 men to actually begin building the prison camp. He was informed that the Quartermaster's Department had already placed orders for tents, cooking apparatus, lumber for the erection of kitchens and other construction necessities. The facility was to be laid out to accommodate 10,000 prisoners. He was also to make requisition from the Quartermaster's Department for twenty horses and equipment for mounting patrols and scouts to relieve the company of Maryland cavalry that had been posted there earlier.[9]

Though considered isolated enough to be secure by land, the possibility of water access by the enemy or as an escape route for prisoners was not overlooked. On July 31 Secretary Welles dispatched orders to Commander Harwood to "direct a sufficient naval force to be always in close vicinity and in communication with the senior Army officer at this point." [10]

Marston arrived at Point Lookout on August 2 accompanied by his staff and two units of New Hampshire Volunteers, the 3rd and 12th Regiments, and set to work immediately. Two weeks after receiving his instructions he informed Colonel Hoffman that he was ready to start taking delivery of prisoners of war although the camp was far from finished. Arrangements for the mess houses and other facilities had yet to be completed. Nevertheless, the general declared "prisoners can be taken care of here with perfect ease and safety." He expected the initial 1,000 to be sent immediately. On August 8 Hoffman initiated the first transfers to the point, 500 soldiers being held in the Old Capitol Prison in Washington. Another requisition for 800 prisoners being held in Baltimore under General Schenck's authority was made soon after.[11] Delays in sending the first loads of rebels down from both cities, however, tested the logistics requirements that the new prison had created. By mid- month not a single prisoner had arrived at the point.[12]

Finally, on the afternoon of August 15, 425 Confederates captured at Gettysburg and confined in jail at Baltimore, were shipped to Point Lookout. Nearly 600 more men would be dispatched soon afterward. A third shipment of another 600 or so arrived on August 21, increasing the number to nearly 1,700 men. The following day, the fourth shipment of 263 rebels being held in the Old Capitol Prison were sent down by steamboat." [13]

The deluge of new prisoners had begun. Though large numbers of rebels finally began to arrive in late August, no containment area or pen had yet been erected within which to confine them. Reliance was upon guards with bayonets fixed and rifles at the ready to watch the unwalled portions of the prisoners' campsites. Not surprisingly several escape attempts were made during this period, some successful and others resulting in the loss of life.[14]

Though officially designated as Camp Hoffman, named after the Commissary of Prisoners, the site was generally called Point Lookout even in official dispatches. It was a name that most Confederates would soon come to equate with suffering, starvation and death.[15]

***

Despite logistical and maintenance problems, construction work on the prison camp at Point Lookout progressed rapidly under the direction of Acting Quartermaster Captain Nelson Plato, especially in the building of a number of large cook and mess houses, and the digging of sixteen wells. "The prisoners are all quartered by themselves on the bay shore, one mile north of the lighthouse," reported one of the Union guards, painting a most rosy picture of the site and the ongoing operations,

> "on a level piece of land, with everything to make them comfortable; and owing to their proximity to the water are enabled to enjoy the luxury of salt water bathing, which is admitted to be very conducive to their health. The 2d [*sic* 3rd] and 12th New Hampshire regiments are quartered opposite, about a quarter of a mile from the rebel camp, on the Potomac river shore, and are placed very nicely. They also have a good time of it fishing, crabbing and bathing.
>
> Owing to the large quantity of commissary and quartermaster stores required, we have regular steam communication between this point and your city [Baltimore] every other day in the shape of the steamer *Trumpeter*, by which we have the morning paper and a mail.
>
> Our hospital, the 'Hammond,' is in a flourishing condition, under the direction of Surgeon Anthony Heger. We have had some 1,100 [Union] patients here; but the number was somewhat reduced yesterday by some 400 going off to their regiments, home and into the Invalid Corps. In the large circle everything looks beautiful, as all of the fronts of the wards are embellished with flower gardens in full bloom, the handiwork of the convalescents." [16]

On August 30 General Hitchcock conducted an inspection of the prison camp and informed Secretary Stanton of his findings. There were by then 800 sick and wounded Union soldiers in the hospital, and about 1,800 rebel prisoners encamped on the Chesapeake side near the point. A guard of 400 Union troops was ensconced on the Potomac side opposite the rebel camp. "I found everything apparently in excellent order," the general reported, "guards well posted with every appearance of vigilance and security." He also noted that General Marston wanted his cavalry increased to 100 men. If thus provided, the district commander believed they would do much toward preserving order in the surrounding countryside and suppressing blockade running, which was still excessive regardless of the occupation forces. He also complained that there were only two gunboats at the point, one with about forty men and the other "not half manned," and neither having steam power. One had no engine at all and the other had a wholly disabled one. The Potomac Flotilla seemed to be seldom in evidence, Hitchcock implied, by noting that he had seen only three gunboats on the entire stretch of river between Alexandria and the

357

point.[17] He was, in fact, apparently unaware that the squadron's service was by then distended as far south as the Rappahannock and no longer limited to just patrolling the Potomac.

Keeping the prison camp facilities supplied was an ongoing labor for Captain Plato. Calls for sealed proposals for the delivery of such basic necessities as wood, required for both construction and fuel, were becoming commonplace in the Washington papers. Military manpower at the point was often limited. General Marston was obliged to make do by employing inmates for such jobs as clerking in his office and preparing rolls of prisoners received or transferred.[18]

General Gilman Marston. Civil War Photographs Collection, Prints and Photographs Division, Library of Congress, Washington, D.C.

Nevertheless, progress on the construction work, in which prisoners were by now forced to provide much of the manual labor, continued unabated but not without controversy. Word had reached Richmond early on that inmates were compelled to perform all kinds of work and were mercilessly punished if they refused. On September 5 Confederate Agent of Exchange Robert Ould's protest against the use of forced labor and other goings on at several prison camps including Point Lookout were published in a northern newspaper. Born in Georgetown, D. C. in 1820, Ould was a handsome, urbane and ambitious man who had been a lawyer of some fame before the war and had once garnered national headlines as the prosecuting attorney against Daniel Sickles in the notorious Philip Barton Key murder case.

The accounts he now furnished were troubling: "I saw a man a few days ago who had received brutal punishment for refusing to work. Our officers and citizens are often compelled to do regularly the most disgusting and filthy labor, such as cleaning prison ships, privies, &c. A ball and chain for them is a common thing. I have also received complaints as to the quantity and quality of provisions furnished our men. It is a very common thing to take away their money and never return it; in some instances they take away good money and return counterfeit." [19]

Ould's superior, General John H. Winder, immediately wrote to Colonel Abdel Delos Streight of the U.S. Army to complain of the treatment. A wall of silence met the protest. Yet it is of some note that only a few days later on September 12, the U.S. Christian Commission requested that Hoffman grant permission for that agency to dispatch a minister of the gospel to "labor" among the inmates at Point Lookout. The request was worded in such a way as to intimate that the minister, should he be granted access, would seek to bring prisoners over to the U.S. Government. It took nearly a month for the request to be considered. When permission was finally granted on October 9 Hoffman advised Marston that clergymen would be authorized to visit, but only at specified times. He also warned: "There must, of course, be no doubt about the unqualified loyalty of the clergymen admitted, and their visits must be for religious purposes only, and not to engage in political discussion." Among those permitted to call was Father Basil Pacciarini from St. Inigoes who was allowed to visit once a week, and who undoubtedly provided the last sacrament to many inmates.[20]

In the meantime Point Lookout's remarkable hospital and burgeoning prisoner of war camp had somehow assumed a strange new celebrity status that invited visits by both well meaning officialdom and curiosity seekers alike, eager to see actual rebels in the flesh. In mid-September, when the Honorable Joseph A. Gilmore, Governor of New Hampshire, arrived in Washington on matters of state, it was decided that an excursion down the Potomac by steamer to visit the point was in order. After all, it was reasoned, the commander and troops on duty at the camp were all veterans from New Hampshire who had been in many of the important battles fought by the Army of the Potomac. It was thus deemed quite natural for such a distinguished official, accompanied by members of the Thirty-sixth and Thirty-Seventh Congress (in which General Marston had served from the First Congressional District of New Hampshire) to pay respects to their countrymen. Logistics and facilitation for the trip were "politely" furnished by the government.

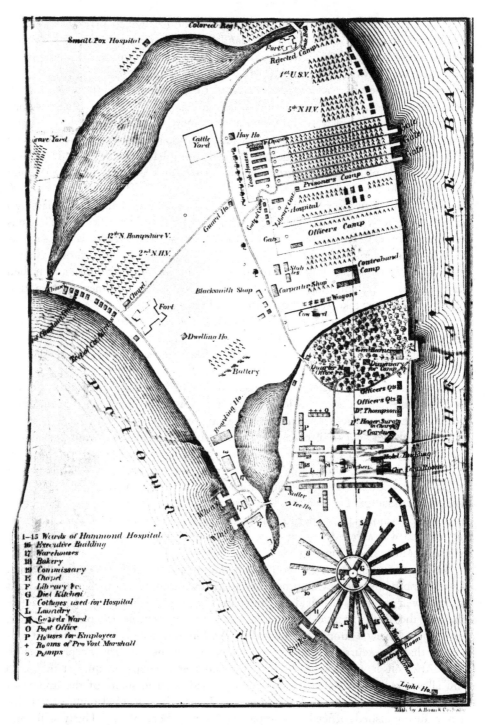

Hospital & Military Prison at Point Lookout. By Rev. A.B. Cross, U.S. Christian Committee.
New York Public Library.

With something of a holiday air about the excursion, the party arrived at the point about 5 p.m. on September 20. The next five hours were occupied by the governor in reviewing and addressing the troops, in examining the new rebel prisoners' camp and quarters, "in partaking of the generous hospitality of Gen. Marston, and in snuffing the refreshing salt sea breeze of the broad bay of the Chesapeake" before reembarking for the return trip to the "city of magnificent distances." [21]

Much less an august visit was launched at 9 a.m., the day after Gilmore's return, when another outing set off. This time it was a subscription pleasure jaunt aboard the Washington and Alexandria Steamboat Company sidewheeler *Thomas Collyer*, Captain Samuel Gedney commanding. The excursion party was considered a select one consisting, with few exceptions of well-to-do citizens of Washington, their wives, sons, daughters, and sweethearts. These expeditionaries were seventy-five strong, the majority belonging to the female sex. The committee entrusted with the arrangements included several prominent Washingtonians and others: Messrs. Samuel R. Sylvester, a noted city apothecary and commissioner of elections; one T. F. McNeir; City Ward 7 Alderman Thomas E. Lloyd; Colonel W. T. Dennis, agent in Washington for Indiana troops stationed in the city; and John Van Riswick, president of the Washington and Alexandria Steamboat Company. The passage on the trip down "was replete with the most exhilarating enjoyment," one participant later reported.

"Music, of the sweetest character, and mirth the most innocent beguiled away the hours as the boat sped her way down the beautiful Potomac. Arriving at Piney Point about sundown, the party after supper joined in the 'mazes of the giddy dance,' continuing this health giving pastime until the night encroached upon the domain . . . The ladies were provided with inviting couches in the hotel, while the gentlemen, or at least the unmarried and those who had left their wives at home, wooed the god of sleep from the soft sides of wooden substances. We doubt not that the luckless 'old bach's,' if any were present, resolved, when they awoke in the morning with aching bones, to become husbands as soon as possible." [22]

On a Wednesday morning the party, which included the popular Ward Hill Lamon of Illinois, a longtime intimate of the president, who had appointed him as United States Marshal for the District of Columbia, proceeded to Point Lookout. Several hours were spent in visiting the "immense Government hospitals and quarters there." It was impossible to ignore the great prison and guard facilities nearby. With so many women in the party, it was also less than surprising that nothing exceeded the hospitable treatment the excursionists received, "the officers vieing [*sic*] in their courtesies" to all, while only several hundred yards away languished thousands of filthy, poorly garbed, sick and dying prisoners of war. Before departure, a fresh supply of oysters was taken aboard *Collyer*. "These same oysters afforded us one of the most amusing episodes. Many a painful hand will bear testimony to the vigorous efforts of the gentlemen to place 'a dozen raw' at the disposal of a fair one." As the steamer slowly pulled away from the wharf, the boating party gave three rousing cheers to the Union soldiers ashore. Then, as the "crack little steamer" sailed northward, leaving the grim, ever growing prison behind, songs and felicitous speeches were sounded as the merriment continued late into the evening. The party reached Washington about midnight September 25, "all highly delighted and refreshed and wishing the early return of such a gay and festive affair." [23]

And still the deluge of prisoners of war poured into Point Lookout. Not all were soldiers of the Confederate Army. Soon private citizens arrested on suspicion of secessionist loyalties or activities, as well as numerous local blockade runners that had been apprehended, added to the growing population. In mid-September no fewer than a dozen runners, captured with $30,000 in property still in their possession, were sent to the prison. By the end of the month more than 4,000 souls, both military and civilian, had been incarcerated. And still they came. For many it seemed that there were but three possibilities of ever returning home: escape; swearing allegiance to the United States and praying for release; or parole in a formal prisoner exchange.[24]

The problem of prisoner exchanges had been manifest since the beginning of the war. Then it had been considered that the Confederacy and its supporters were in nothing less than a state of rebellion against the constituted authority of the U.S. Government and thereby had no foundation for existence under the law. The rebel leaders and all who endorsed and supported them were engaged in treasonable activities and were subject, if captured, to the punishment deserved of traitors as the law prescribed. However, retaliation against captives taken by the South was a realty that could not be ignored. Adding further problems to any exchange was the fear by Union authorities that any formal agreement with the South regarding prisoner exchange would constitute "de facto" recognition of the Confederacy as a belligerent sovereign power. Not until June 1862 were Federal and Confederate authorities forced to begin negotiations due to the large number of prisoners held by both sides. On July 22, 1862 an agreement governing exchanges, dubbed the Dix-Hill Cartel, was finally reached by Major General John A. Dix, for the Union, and Major General Daniel Harvey Hill, for the Confederacy. Diplomatically the Preamble to the agreement sidestepped the question of recognition by not naming the Confederate States: "The undersigned having been commissioned by the authorities they respectively represent to make arrangements for a general exchange of prisoners of war have agreed to the following articles." Thereafter seven articles and three supplementary articles addressed such issues as the scale and equivalent values of prisoners by rank, civilian and militia prisoners, paroles, and conditions of release, though no address was made to their uniform treatment.[25] Despite major subsequent disagreements on both side until the end of the war, at least a door had been opened through which each side would pass from time to time.

***

When the first discussions were held concerning the possibility of an exchange of Confederates at Point Lookout, Old Capitol Prison in Washington, and Fort Delaware in return for Federals incarcerated in Richmond, many obstacles were presented. Forward motion was nevertheless soon underway. On September 18 five hundred invalid rebels at Point Lookout, paroled for the purpose of exchange, were placed under the charge of Captain Michael Egan, Company E, 20th Regiment, Veteran Reserve Corps, and boarded the steamer *Dictator*. A guard of fifty Union soldiers, one commissioned officer, two surgeons, and one hospital steward accompanied them. Forty-six Union convalescents returning to their regiments at City Point as nurses were engaged to tend the sick prisoners while en route. By the time they arrived at Fort Monroe four of the parolees had already died on board. At 11 a.m. the following day *Dictator* proceeded on to Bermuda Hundred to await the transfer. By the morning of September 20 four more parolees had died. The bodies of the deceased were transferred to the post surgeon at City Point, while the remaining 492 were placed aboard the flag of truce boat *New York* for transport to Richmond. The forty-six Union convalescents were assigned to the provost marshal at City Point as nursing staff in the field hospital. On September 21 Captain Egan and his men returned to Point Lookout aboard the steamer *Silver Star*.[26]

It had been a textbook delivery and awaited only reciprocity from the rebels. Hoffman was eager to proceed and queried Marston on future undertakings. The general replied with a hint of sarcasm: "There is a large number here who do not desire to be exchanged. Some wish to take the oath of allegiance, and some are willing to enter the naval and a few the military service of the United States. Others, if allowed to take the oath of allegiance, would, I have no doubt, soon find their way into the rebel army." [27]

In late October 530 more prisoners held in the Old Capitol Prison in Washington were sent down to the point to await exchange. Others had already been streaming in from Fort Delaware, though not without problems, the worst of which was the appearance of a highly contagious disease among them. On October 26 Marston complained that with every lot of rebels sent down from the fort many were infected with smallpox. Some twenty-six cases had arrived with the last group alone. The introduction of the disease into a camp of thousands required immediate attention. But that wasn't all. Many new arrivals and some of those already in the camp were also suffering from scurvy, a result of vitamin deficiencies that would only be compounded at the point. Unfortunately, the War Department had forbidden friends of inmates from sending food that might have helped alleviate the problem. Members of a prisoner's immediate family were prohibited from sending anything but clothing. No luxuries or gifts of any sort provided by Southern sympathizers and intended for the general benefit of inmates would be permitted. To counter scurvy, Marston issued orders that prisoners be allowed to purchase vegetables from sutlers allowed in camp.[28]

Reports of cruelty towards the prisoners at Point Lookout and in other Federal military prisons were perhaps not unexpected considering charges of the same levied against Union soldiers in Confederate pens. Judging from the journals of those incarcerated and accounts from those who had been exchanged or escaped, many charges were not without foundation. Nevertheless, there were moments of kindness, though usually cancelled out by enmities. In the early winter when a batch of half-clothed men arrived at the point, one Union surgeon, observing a cold and shivering rebel lacking trousers, went to his personal quarters to fetch a pair of his own for the man and asked permission from the guard to present them. The lieutenant in charge replied: "No, sir; the clothes he has on are a d—d sight better than he deserves." [29]

On another occasion a Union steward in the hospital lost some money. One of the Confederate surgeons, being found outside of his quarters when it was missed, was instantly accused of having stolen it. The surgeon was immediately thrust into the stocks where he was kept until he fainted. He was then thrown into what was known as the "middle room," a place used for the confinement of "cutthroats and thieves of the Yankee army, whose crimes are base enough to require punishment in Yankee eyes." Here he was kept until the day before being exchanged, "when he was turned out nearly naked, not having clothes enough upon his person to cover his nakedness." In Richmond he reported his treatment, the account of which soon made it into the rebel press.[30]

As commander of not only Camp Hoffman but also the entire St. Mary's Military District, Marston was frequently required to address other problems within his command area, which sometimes diverted his attention from camp duties. The latest flood of Marylanders to Virginia, driven in part by efforts to avoid the Federal military draft as much as their pro-secessionist ideology, seemed almost unstoppable. In late August one unnamed military correspondent at the Hammond Hospital summarized the situation quite adequately: "Upon reliable authority," he informed the Washington press, "I am authorized to say that nightly, and even by day, men are passing from this and adjoining counties in droves. These renegades and traitors to the old flag head for Virginia, under the delusion that they will not be drafted upon their arrival there, but be received as refugees. Of course this sudden exodus to rebellion is to escape being drafted in Maryland. I trust that the Government will see to it immediately." [31]

But the flood continued without letup.

On October 21 in the midst of the latest prisoner exchange, Marston was obliged to dispatch troops to interdict the exodus. A detachment of 106 troopers from the 2nd and 5th U.S. Cavalry, under the command of Lieutenant John Mix were dispatched in yet another effort to stem rebel underground operations in the county and the ongoing flights to Virginia. The lieutenant was instructed to proceed by way of Three Notch Road to Leonardtown where he was to establish headquarters. His mission was specifically to focus upon "suppressing contraband trade and all disloyal practices, arresting deserters and escaped prisoners, and preserving the public peace." Small detachments were to be sent to Charlotte Hall, Chaptico, the mouth of the Patuxent River, and other points deemed necessary. He was to arrest all blockade runners, seize their goods and send them to Point Lookout. And finally, well aware of the hostilities that existed between the citizenry and Union "occupiers," Marston instructed: "I desire that you will be particularly careful that no depredations are committed by any of your men under your command upon the property of any person whatever." [32]

***

Despite General Marston's reports that all was well at Point Lookout, a surprise visit to the camp by the U.S. Sanitary Commission strongly suggested otherwise. The subsequent firestorm resulting from the visit threatened to severely impugn, if not halt, further prisoner exchanges. The inspection was conducted by one Colonel William F. Swalm on November 9-10. The colonel's report, sent immediately to Dr.

John H. Douglas, Associate Secretary of the commission, was a scathing review guaranteed to arouse the anger of Marston and embarrass the U.S. Army.[33]

Swalm reported that the size of the camp, which had swelled to over 8,000 prisoners, was 1,000 feet square, of about sixteen acres in overall area (actually twenty-three acres). The entire camp was surrounded by a board fence twelve feet high (rebel sources claimed fourteen and fifteen feet). "Just below the top," wrote one prisoner, "was built a platform about three feet wide, and on this platform the guards walked to and fro with their guns on their shoulders" From their vantage point they could overlook the whole camp as the grounds were perfectly level. Ten feet from the parapet wall was a trench designated the "dead line," across which prisoners were forbidden to stray. The price for such error, intentional or not, was frequently a bullet.[34]

The prison hospital was erected in the southern part of the camp hundreds of yards from the Hammond facility. It was comprised of eighteen hospital tents, arranged in pairs end on end and placed in two rows with a broad street between them, with a cooking and dining tent on the eastern end facing the street. In the tents were a hundred or fewer patients, five or six to a unit, lying on raised mattresses, with a single blanket per man. Only one tent had a board floor, the remainder had dirt floors upon which lay the mattresses of the patients. Among the eight enlisted men assigned to take care of the sick were six graduates of medical schools in New York, New Orleans and Cincinnati, the other two having been medical students at the University of Pennsylvania. Swalm reported that the attention they provided their sick comrades, aside from giving them food and medicine, was negligible especially as it related to sanitation. The patients were dirty, their "faces and hands apparently strangers to soap and water and hair seemingly uncombed for weeks." [35]

No effort was given to separating the sick by disease: wounded, erysipelas (a skin infection occurring on the face and legs) and fever patients lay side by side in the same tent. Among those wounded were two who had been shot while trying to escape. Two of their comrades had been killed during the same attempt. All were living in filthy conditions, with no stoves for heat, and chronic diarrhea being the most prevalent disease among them. The mortality rate in the prison hospital was zero, for on an average day twenty to thirty of the most seriously ill were transferred to the Hammond Hospital to die, when it was usually already too late for treatment. Those sick that had no recourse other than to suffer without care in their own quarters immediately filled the vacant berths in the camp hospital. "The dispensary," Swalm wrote, "is a poor apology for one, having little or nothing but a few empty bottles . . . Here also was shown a want of discipline and cleanliness; everything covered with dust, and what few articles they had were exposed to air and placed indiscriminately along the counter and in the most perfect confusion." The only good thing about the dispensary was that the books were well kept.[36]

Though hospital rations were adequate in both quality and quantity, food preparation was something else. Cooking was done by inmates, though there was a want of cooking utensils, and a lack of tin cups, knives and forks. Patients were thus obliged to eat with unwashed fingers and hands. The large cook stove for the hospital was sufficient, but both stove and cooking tent were dirty, as was the tent in which the nurses and attendants ate.[37]

The U.S. Army surgeon in charge of the prison hospital, Dr. Sylvanus Bunton, was accused of being quite slack in his duty though he was now aided by two recently arrived assistant surgeons, doctors Russell and Walton, who were quite active. Of Bunton, the inspector wrote: "There is a lack of system and want of discipline, neither of which . . . do I think he is possessed of." [38]

As for the condition of the main prisoner quarters, he found the inmates crowded in tents around a few coals. Some had good blankets thrown across their shoulders while many others had only a piece of carpet, a gum blanket, or oil cloth normally used for tablecloths. Some had nothing. "Men of all ages and classes, descriptions and hues," he reported,

> "with various colored clothing, [were] all huddled together, forming a motley crew, which to be appreciated must be seen, and what the pen fails to describe the imagination must depict . . . They are ragged and dirty and very thinly clad; that is, the very great majority. Occasionally you will find one the fortunate possessor of an overcoat, either a citizen's or the light blue ones used by our infantry, and those serving for as coverings for the rags beneath. Others, again, are well supplied as regards underclothing, especially those who are from Baltimore, being sent to them by friends. But the great mass are in pitiable condition, destitute of nearly everything, which, with their filthy condition, makes them really objects of commiseration. Some are without shirts, or what were once shirts are now hanging in shreds from their shoulders. In others the entire back or front will be gone, while again in some you will see a futile attempt at patching. Their clothing is of all kinds and hues – the gray, butternut, the red of our zouaves and the light and dark blue of our infantry, all in a dilapidated condition." [39]

Living conditions were in some ways better than those of the hospital quarters. They had good tents with both fireplaces and chimneys. These had been the product of the industry of the inmates as they were manufactured from bricks made from the local clay, which they dug from the earth and baked in the sun. Nevertheless, ventilation was a problem and the tents were usually filled with smoke. A great many of the tents had been erected over old sinks that, after being filled with excrement and other waste, were lightly covered over. "The interior of the tents are in keeping with the inmates, filthy; pieces of cracker, meat, ashes, &c., strewn around the tent, and in which they lie." In most tents, lacking furniture such as stools, men were obliged to sit on the naked ground, adding to personal filth. Yet many of the inmates, Swalm stated bluntly, "seem to abhor soap and water," both of which were available in abundance.[40]

Keeping fires burning was undertaken with difficulty in that prisoners had to find their own firewood, sometimes driftwood that had floated ashore, but mostly brought in by work parties. The work parties, which were also employed in white-washing buildings or emptying supply boats, were not permitted to cut down timber, but were obliged to dig out stumps with their hands from already cut trees. It was never enough. As the general population increased many prisoners were obliged to make do with a single blanket for every three or even more men, while others had none. All suffered severely from the cold.[41]

Swalm reported that prisoners complained they didn't get enough to eat and only half their ration of meat was being provided. Meals were prepared in the camp kitchens by inmate cooks and served in six wooden dining halls (of which five were in use). Each hall was 160 feet in length and thirty feet in width, and located in the northwest corner of their camp known as the "bull pen." The bull pen was a noxious place where scurvy, diarrhea, and "itch" was prevalent. The daily diet was limited but, he felt, adequate: three ounces of salt pork or four ounces of beef (served only at dinner), ten ounces of hardtack (served at breakfast and supper), and a pint of coffee were the principal day's rations, with soup and soft bread served once a week, potatoes and beans every five days. The dining rooms contained several great tables, and in each 1,529 men were fed, 500 or more at a time. The kitchen arrangements were deemed "very good," with each containing five fifty or sixty gallon cauldrons.[42]

Men who were sick but obliged to remain in their quarters and unable to consume the regular rations were allowed three ounces of vinegar, five potatoes, a gill of rice, and a gill of molasses per day. Each was obliged to cook his own meals.[43]

Swalm found the hospital grounds had not been policed for some time. "Filth is gradually accumulating, and the sinks are not at all thought of, requiring a little exertion to walk to them. They void their excrement in the most convenient place to them, regardless of the comfort of others." Sinks were horrible and entirely neglected, and night boxes filled with excrement were often not removed during the day. Though sinks over the water had been built, the inmates paid little attention to them unless they should be in close proximity when nature called. Instead, holes dug around tents for clay used in brick making served the same purpose. And they were everywhere, though some inmates chose to ignore all such disposal areas when they relieved themselves. Camp drainage was terrible, especially at high tides and during storms when many dirt floors in the tent city were inundated. Drainage ditches dug throughout the camp were constantly filled with water and were employed as places to deposit waste and offal. It was, Swalm noted, a perfect mystery to him why there wasn't even more sickness in camp. "God knows they have enough, for they live, eat, and sleep in their own filth." He blamed the military authorities for the bad conditions and recommended among other things that more medicine and clothing be provided. Though the inmates refused to attend to their own unsanitary conditions, he blamed the prison commander for failing to appoint someone to take charge of the situation.[44]

While in the midst of Swalm's inspection, an additional 1,300 prisoners arrived in camp on November 10. With so many men confined to such a small area, indolence and petty crime were rife. "A great many are employing their time," the inspector noted,

"in making bricks and have now a great quantity on hand. Others employ themselves in making rings, chains, seals, &c., from bone and gratta percha, and notwithstanding the complaint that they do not get enough to eat, you will find them on the main street, which they call The Change, gambling for both money and rations. They have games at cards, keno, sweat cloth, &c. Also on this street

367

they do their trading, hardtack for tobacco and tobacco for hardtack. It is here that you will find them in crowds, sitting or kneeling in the dirt, eagerly watching the games, and see them rise dissatisfied at having lost their day's rations, and while thus engaged they are unmindful of the cold." [45]

The inspector also visited the Hammond Hospital, its wards now largely occupied by the rebel sick, with its kitchen, half kitchen and dining rooms tended by nine Catholic Sisters of Charity. Of the 1,277 patients only 493 were Union soldiers, mostly convalescents; the remaining 784 were rebels, suffering primarily from chronic diarrhea. There were seventy beds in each ward, allowing 900 cubic feet per bed, totaling 1,050 beds in the main wards, as well as 350 beds in the convalescent wards and the wards for erysipelas and hospital gangrene. That conditions even here were less than acceptable was reflected in the death rate among the Confederate inmate population. Between October 4 and November 30, no fewer than seventy-nine North Carolinians died while in the superior facilities of the Hammond Hospital. That the overall mortality rate was on the rise throughout was perhaps not unexpected given the change of season. Most of the rebels that died had diarrhea but succumbed to pneumonia, which had been masked by their extremely weak condition when first brought in. From March to September, when the bulk of patients had been Union soldiers (with a peak number of 1,330 and an average of 1,100), only twenty-eight deaths were reported, mostly from typhoid fever, diarrhea, and pneumonia. In a single week before Swalm's visit, of the 1,208 sick in the hospital, there had been forty-six deaths, and the mortality rate was on the increase. Otherwise, the hospital itself and its management were given a very high rating.[46]

The introduction of smallpox from Fort Delaware had obliged the authorities on September 30 to also erect an isolated smallpox hospital a quarter mile north of the prison camp on a narrow strip of land amidst a stand of pine bushes. The facility was under the direction of Dr. W. Broadbent, assistant surgeon. In the two weeks after its opening and Swalm's visit, 133 patients had been brought in, of which thirty-three had died. The sick were housed in wedge tents, three to a tent, and lying on a bed of straw spread on the naked ground, with a blanket and a half to a man. Their rations were the same as in the prison hospital with the exception of a serving of bean soup or coffee each day, and on occasion some soft bread. Most of the smallpox patients were also suffering from scurvy and scabies and were in a horrid condition. Nevertheless, Swalm reported, patients there were more comfortable than those in the encampment, and most did not want to go back. Though medicines and cathartics were in short supply, he declared they were "getting along as well as they could expect." [47]

Marston received a copy of the Swalm report from Fred N. Knapp, Associate Secretary of the Sanitary Commission, on November 26 along with a request that a further inspection be permitted. Infuriated with the findings, the general immediately denied permission. "I beg to say," he replied the following day, while attempting to be civil, "that medical inspectors of the army make frequent inspections of the camps referred to, and it is therefore not thought necessary to impose this labor on the Sanitary Commission." [48]

When sending off a copy of the Swalm report to Hoffman on the same day, he admitted to some shortcomings but vigorously denied others. "I do not know by what authority the inspection was made," he recorded,

"but we may take advantage of the information it gives to correct some omissions which it points out and some errors which I think the inspector has fallen into. From the report it appears that there is a great want of clothing among many of the prisoners. Though it is the desire of the War Department to provide as little clothing for them as possible, it does not wish them to be left in the very destitute condition which this report represents. I beg to call your attention to this subject, and if, in your judgment, the clothing is needed please have the necessary estimates prepared and sent in. There is an abundance of inferior clothing on hand, and the department would prefer to issue it rather than it should be contributed by sympathizers. The amount of the ration which the report gives I am sure is erroneous in every particular, and I would be glad to set the Sanitary Commission right in this particular. The various matters which are mentioned in reference to police, the condition of the sinks, &c., are worthy of attention." [49]

Stung by the Sanitary Commission report, Marston conducted his own inquiry and ordered an accounting from the camp's commissary sergeant, J. H. Wilkinson, on daily food allowances, and complaints regarding the cooks and sanitation. Wilkinson reported on December 1 that there had indeed been a reduction of bread, 13.7 to 13.3 ounces, and meat, 8.7 ounces to 8.1 ounces per day, between October and November (an amount far in excess of the three to four ounces reported on by Swalm). Bean or some other soup was served every third day, a pint of coffee twice a day except on soup days, and all vegetables and molasses allowed by Army regulations were drawn and issued. Rice was seldom served, as it was generally unpopular among the inmates. There were no restrictions on the amount of soap issued, only so far as to prevent waste.

The sergeant bitterly noted: "I ever [*sic* never] knew a time during my service when Federal troops got so constant a supply of vegetables as has been issued to the prisoners here . . . If complaints have been made to you of the inefficiency on the part of the cooks, I would respectfully suggest that these complaints have come from persons desirous to get in the cook rooms. The cold weather coming on renders this position desirable. I would remark that there are prisoners here whose only disposition is to eat and sleep."

He concluded his report by defensively stating that it was his firm conviction that the physical condition of the prisoners was far better than when they arrived at the camp.[50]

Having waited for Wilkinson's report, which was now in hand, Marston sent a sharp and insulting personal rebuttal to Swalm. "Of the report I have to remark that one more disingenuous and false could not well have been made . . . It is surprising that the commission should employ agents so stupid and dishonest as the author of this report." [51]

Citing Wilkinson's investigation, he declared charges of prisoners on half rations "erroneous in every particular." The statement that guards had killed two prisoners, he said, was simply untrue. His denials continued. Every bed in the hospital tents was supplied with two blankets. There was a laundry for cleansing the clothing of sick men, and the hospital was abundantly supplied with washbasins, towels, and soap. Two or three nurses were assigned to every ward, one of which was always present therein day and night. The prison surgeon had all the table furniture he desired, and for the use of the sick he was supplied with farina, cornstarch, meal, soft crackers, fruit, beef extract, wine, jelly, and cordials, though he admitted that at one time there had been considerable delay in filling out requisitions for medicines. That only one blanket was allotted to every three men was also denied, and if such was indeed the case with some, he declared it was because the blanket had been sold or gambled away. As for lack of clothing, he said, frequent inspections were made and coats, pants, shirts, shoes, and blankets were issued "as health and decency required." The sinks for use by day were outside the encampment and on walkways erected over the waters of the bay, which carried away the excrement. Boxes were provided for use at night, which at reveille were removed to the bay and washed. The camp was policed every day. "The drainage is not good," he admitted, "and will not be until some genius equally as brilliant as the author of this report in question discovers a method of causing water to flow as readily from a level surface not much elevated above the surrounding seas."

In concluding his rebuttal with a sweeping denial of the Swalm report, Marston declared: "The prisoners are treated as prisoners of war ought to be by a civilized people, and they and their friends are content." They were provided with shelter, clothing, and wholesome food sufficient to insure vigorous health. They had an abundance of fresh water and daily access to the waters of the bay. "That they are a dirty lousy set is true enough, but having afforded them every facility for cleanliness the duty of the Government in this regards as respects the well men is accomplished . . . Now, colonel, come and inspect the camp yourself or send some one, a soldier or army surgeon, who knows what camp life is and who has sufficient ability to apprehend the facts and integrity enough to state them." [52]

On the same day that Marston dispatched his rebuttal to Swalm, Hoffman passed on an order from the Secretary of War that he "prohibit all trade with sutlers by prisoners of war." Now the prisoners could not even purchase vegetables or any other necessity and were obliged, like it or not, to rely almost entirely upon the U.S. Army. [53]

The military did its best to suppress publication of the Swalm report, but it was impossible to prevent word of the conditions at Point Lookout from getting out. By the end of December nearly 9,000 prisoners had been crowded within the confines of the great wood-walled pen. News of the conditions within had even reached the Confederate capital, from which Robert Ould wrote to Hoffman to inquire if smallpox was raging among the inmates, but worse, if reports were true that the prisoners were being confined in company with men of color, former slaves. [54]

Soon the military was being pelted with requests for authorization to provide aid to the inmates. Many folks in St. Mary's County began writing to the *St. Mary's Beacon* importuning the public for donations for the rebels "in rags" at the point. One respondent, the Reverend Dr. Richard Fuller of Baltimore, citing Secretary Chase, General Schenck and a U.S. Senator from New York as references to his loyalty, employed a merchant to prepare a box of flannel shirts, drawers, socks and cheap hats valued at $125. Some of the inmates, he informed Hoffman, were "relations or sons of old Christian friends . . . As the persons are in want and the point very bleak, some of them wounded and others diseased, I beg you to confer a favor of honoring this with your immediate attention." [55] But such charity was routinely ignored, unless from an inmate's family, and even then many items never made it to their destination owing to thievery among the Union soldiers whose duty it was to inspect them.

From as far away as Montreal a noted physician, Dr. Montrose A. Pallen, a Confederate medical officer sent to Canada to investigate conditions of prisoners held at Johnson Island in Lake Erie, wrote General Hitchcock requesting permission to visit Richmond on a flag of truce boat. It was his intention to secure Confederate funds for supplies for the prisoners, not only at Point Lookout, but also in other Union prisons where inmates were also in desperate conditions. He cited as personal references to his trustworthiness numerous men of importance including generals Ulysses S. Grant and William Tecumseh Sherman. "Many of these men," he wrote concerning the inmates, "are without the necessary clothing even to hide their nakedness, and during the late cold weather several absolutely froze to death at Point Lookout, where they are living in tents, and more than half of the nearly 9,000 and more there confined have not even a single blanket for covering or bedding and sleep on the bare ground, which you well know is certainly productive of an immense amount of disease and suffering." [56]

By December 15, still smarting from the Swalm report, Marston sent another angry letter to the Sanitary Commission, this time to Secretary Knapp. "Your inspector has strangely been led into many errors in his report," he charged, "and their publication cannot but do much harm to our cause by exciting the friendly sympathies of the people for those who seem to be treated with unnecessary harshness and neglect, and by giving the rebel authorities an apparent excuse for the cruel treatment which they have heaped upon those of our people who have been so unfortunate as to fall into their hands." [57]

But still the blizzard of charges of mistreatment continued, not the least of which were from the Confederates. Two days after Marston's letter to Knapp, the *Daily Dispatch* in Richmond ran a scathing account of prison life at Point Lookout. One Robert Craddock, who once served as an orderly to Jefferson Davis and later with the Richmond city detective force, provided the damning report. Captured during the bloody Peninsula Campaign and sent to Point Lookout, he had somehow escaped and made it back to Richmond with a full description of camp life.

The approximately 9,000 prisoners uncomfortably housed in tents during the winter were constricted to say the least. Three thousand were in the 650 small common "A" tents, five men to a tent; the remainder, 6,000, were in 330 Wall & Sibley or French bell tents, with fourteen to sixteen to a tent (the numbers were exaggerated in the Confederate press to suggest as many as ninety inmates forced into a tent). The tents, were crowded too closely together with few being more than two feet apart, and were laid off in camp form, one hundred men to a company, and ten companies to a street or division. There were now nine division streets, each sixty feet wide, running east and west. (In truth, the prison was the only one of its kind in the Union, as all others housed their inmates in barracks). On one side of the enclosure were the mess houses, where 500 men ate at a time, with each house feeding 1,500 men. The daily provisions consisted of four ounces of damaged pork or beef, and ten small crackers, "and a pint of wash, called by the Yankees coffee." Rice or Irish potatoes were occasionally substituted for bread, and about once a fortnight half a loaf of soft bread and one spoonful of molasses was provided. About twice a week bean soup was served in lieu of coffee. [58]

"Each day a detail of five men from each company is made to go for wood," Craddock reported, "and as the guard will not let them go beyond the creek, they have to dig up stumps and roots in an open piece of new ground, without an axe, unless they steal one. With as much wood as would last comfortably for half an hour they must shiver over for four nights; and this is all the wood allowed them." Many of the prisoners had no blankets, and nothing but the cold damp ground to sleep on. Indeed, on one occasion, being generally poorly clad and emaciated, they had orders to appear in front of their quarters with their knapsacks and blankets, and then marched to the beach to pass in review by the provost marshal, four or five abreast, as fast as possible. One in every five who had no blanket was told to stand aside, and was given a cover. Many had already given up all hope, "and will of course die. " [59]

The prison hospital was laid out on two sides of a wide street with the kitchen or mess tent at one end. Each ward had two small wall tents joined at the ends and holding fourteen beds. The sick were as well attended as possible by the Confederate surgeons and nurses, but there had been weeks at a time when no medicine at all was on hand. Now three to four men died there per day. For those whose cases appeared hopeless, most were sent to the Hammond Hospital, outside of the enclosure, "and this is the last seen of them." As soon as a patient died he was taken out on a stretcher. Once a day a two-horse wagon came in and bodies "were laid in like so much cord wood," unconfined, taken out and buried in long trenches seven feet wide and three feet deep with bodies laid across the trench side by side and covered with earth. Their sheets were changed and another sick patient brought in and placed in the "still warm" bed of the deceased. The separate smallpox hospital, situated on a small creek outside of the main guard, averaged six to eight cases per day, with about half that number dying.[60]

Death arrived not only through sickness and disease, but also sometimes from sudden gunfire during escape attempts, for violations of the deadline, or simply from malice of the guards, none of which were uncommon events. "The guard shoot the men without halting them," Craddock said. "On one occasion five of them bribed the sentinel to allow them to escape, and after letting them pass he called the guard, and two of the men were shot after they surrendered. A young man, named McLeary, was shot through the head, exposing the brain, and then through the body, by a man who was called an officer. Another one of the men was shot down and kicked about after surrendering. – These men were made to walk about half a mile in that condition." [61]

Hitchcock was now under pressure to quell the mounting storm lest it adversely affect future prisoner exchanges. On December 19 he directed Hoffman to order the commanding officers, including Marston, of the four major Union prison camps in the North to report on the Pallen charges. Hoffman ordered another survey of conditions at Point Lookout, this time to be conducted by Augustus M. Clark, the Surgeon and Acting Medical Inspector of Prisoners of War who had originally scutinized the site prior to its designation as an official depot. The investigation was carried out on December 17-18, and its findings were reported back to the colonel on December 22.[62]

Clark's report was detailed though some of the information was obviously provided to him rather than acquired through his own personal observations. Many conditions were still bad, even after Marston had improved upon a few in the month since the Sanitary Commission inspection. At the Hammond Hospital Dr. Heger's staff now consisted of one assistant surgeon, U.S. Army, one assistant surgeon, U.S. Volunteers, eleven acting assistant surgeons, and four hospital stewards. There were 787 rebels and 293 Union patients under Heger's care. Clark declared that "there is no fault to be found" with the hospital with minor exceptions. Although the water supply was sufficient, it was deemed "not very good" owing to shallow surface wells that were contaminated by unsanitary camp conditions. One prisoner recorded that the water "was brackish to the taste. The only water we had was from pumps scattered about over the camp . . . the pumps were always surrounded by a thirsty crowd of from 40 to 50 prisoners, each with his tin cup, trying to wedge his way in, that he might quench his thirst." Chronic diarrhea, dysentery, and general scorbutic taint were still the prevalent illnesses. More worrisome was the disparity between death rates at the hospital. In November alone 145 Confederates had died, a mortality rate of 13.98 per cent, while only a single Union man had expired.[63]

The prison camp was another story. Of the 8,764 prisoners confined therein, 1,196 were sick. Three large sinks had been built out over the water on the bay side for daily use but were deemed lacking in number; "for night use large boxes are provided to be emptied in the morning; these are insufficient and are not properly attended to; in many places excrement was found in the division streets." The excrement was simply thrown into the bay or removed by high tides.[64]

"Each tent," Clark stated, "has a shallow ditch around it leading into a ditch running along the side of the street. These main ditches are not kept clean, nor are their outlets well designed or properly attended to . . . Many tents are built up at the sides and some are floored with material obtained from cracker boxes; many are floored with gravel packed hard. No tents are excavated, a few had been but are now removed." The packed gravel, dubbed "Sea Feathers," was gathered by the inmates for their beds. As for the streets, they were in the process of being leveled and covered with the same coarse gravel, of which there was a natural abundance.[65]

No wood for fuel, as Craddock noted earlier, had yet been directly issued to prisoners. Some inmates, he acknowledged, were sent out in squads into woods to dig and cut up stumps, and "in this way they procure an abundant supply, and in many of the tents they have piled away stores of it." He noted that in several tents he had observed heaps of wood containing at least half a cord, taking up room that might have been more advantageously occupied by inmates.[66]

Clark reported that the food was acceptable and rations of meat, vegetables (costing the government $4,000 a week) and biscuits, now served in six mess rooms accommodating 500 men at a time, was quite sufficient. There were nine cook houses, six of which were in use, each containing five 40-gallon cauldrons capable of producing 9,600 pints of soup per day. As for the cleanliness of the inmates and their clothing, he reported them "dirty, as usual in similar camps; apparently no laundry regulations." Most of the clothes they wore were their own, although some had been donated and others came from condemned Federal stocks, and were, with the exception of overcoats and underclothing, deemed "apparently sufficient." Their bedding and blankets, some of which had been brought by the prisoners themselves, but most supplied by the army quartermaster, were also considered very foul but adequate. The overall condition of the inmates, who were noted as "indolent, but willing to work if ordered," and whose only duties were policing the camp and hunting for fuel, and whose few recreations were making bricks and gambling for rations, clothing, wood, and other items, were declared to be as "good as is usual or to be expected in similar camps." [67]

By the time of Clark's investigation the prison hospital had increased in size from eighteen tents to forty-two. Thirty were for the sick, three for quarantined patients until able to be sent immediately to the smallpox hospital, and nine for miscellaneous uses. These were arranged in three wards on either side of a fifty-foot-wide street, each with a stove in the center, and ventilation provided by tent doors and slits in the walls that could be kept open as needed. A dead house was situated a hundred yards from the hospital. With few exceptions, Clark stated, patients were now on iron bedsteads, exceptions being well-built wooden bunks. "The men look clean and comfortable; the clothing is clean and in good order, and the surgeons in charge complains that until very recently it has been impossible to obtain a sufficient supply of underclothing." [68]

Now under the overall charge of Surgeon James H. Thompson, U.S. Volunteers, the current hospital staff included two acting assistant surgeons, and a dozen Confederate physicians, who performed their duties "with alacrity and skill." Nine of the medical personnel were assigned to duties in the camp, one to each division, two were employed in the hospital (most certainly including Thompson), and one was a dentist. Inmates were engaged as hospital stewards under the direction of a chief steward. [69]

The illnesses, not unexpectedly, were the same as before. Smallpox cases, which appeared to Clark to be on the decline, were still generally confined to the isolated contagious hospital unit northwest of the prison camp. The facility was now guarded by sentries and entirely shut off by a barricade running across a narrow neck of land leading to it. The patients there were finally housed in eight Sibley tents and thirty-five common tents. This facility remained under the charge of the "utterly incompetent" Dr. Bunton of the 2nd New Hampshire, and seconded by an acting assistant surgeon and nine Confederate acting medical officers. The camp, which Clark personally inspected with Surgeon Heger, was in terrible shape, overcrowded, unventilated, and in desperate need of a cleaning. "The books," he noted regarding the records for the smallpox hospital, "are almost illegible, and the following is all I could glean from them: Average daily sick since December 1, 165; total deaths since December 1, 43; number of cases December 17, 168; number of deaths December 17." [70]

Yet the main tent city medical facility in the prison camp, declared Clark, was now well kept, adequately provided with medical supplies and surgical instruments, and now with 217 patients housed, had a capacity of 225. Though he was lax in pointing it out, overcrowding was already an ongoing problem. Some 380 sick had thus to be simply confined to their own quarters. The statistics regarding recoveries and mortality from diseases and wounds, perhaps more than any other data private or official, suggested the true condition of the prisoners. In November, the total number of reported sick engaged by the hospital was 2,900, of which thirty-five had died, or a mortality rate of 1.2 percent. But with the arrival of the winter cold, the average number of daily sick since December 1 was 666, and the death rate had risen to 2.5 percent.[71]

Clark's two-day inspection of the Point Lookout prison camp at first glance seemed thorough. He was indeed critical of certain issues such as the poor drainage, which could not be remedied even with the best engineering, and some that could, such as the crowding of tents, poor sinks and night box policing. Yet, time and again many of his statistics cited in the report simply did not add up. At least some were almost certainly provided to him by hospital and prison staff perhaps more interested in looking good on paper than in actuality. Inmates were far less positive in their daily assessments of conditions, as indicated by entries in their journals, and accounts passed on to their comrades back in Richmond via escapees or prisoners fortunate enough to be exchanged.[72]

But it was prison life itself that brought out the best and worst in many who often had to compete for the very necessities of survival. The first thing many new arrivals saw upon landing at Point Lookout in late 1863 was a pile of coffins which were now on occasion being used for dead Confederates. The second was a large and ominous circular sign over the main gate to the compound saying "Prison Camp." Private C. W. Jones, Company H, 24th Virginia Cavalry, captured in an engagement at Charles City Court House, Virginia, was among many "Johnnies" determined to "scuffle" to stay alive and later write about it. "It was amusing to see the ingenuity of the prisoners," he said years later.

"Every conceivable trick was resorted to in order to make buckle and tongue meet. It was 'root, pig, or die,' and that was the then general term with the prisoners was 'a possum eyed time.' The various occupations, the scheming, the tricking, the hustling for grub, the flanking and pointing to the goal for hardtack and pickled pork, and trading for rations, were the issues, which required no oratory or preaching. My strong forte was molasses taffy and corn mush, with black strap syrup. Whenever I could collect enough of the material together I could fry flap jacks so thin you could read through them, and dilute the molasses so that it would run on a board. My price for a palatable dish was five hardtacks and a chew of tobacco . . . Every type of humanity was exhibited in all the different phases of a prisoner's life in this assembly. A variety of proceedings was carried on – the pious praying, the wicked fighting, the tradesman tricking an' the thieves stealing; all kinds of gaming, from trick cards, keno, lotto, to dice and dumbells." [73]

Whatever the truth of prison conditions had been, it was all going to change soon and not for the better. Crowding and the mortality rate would increase dramatically as the arrival of thousands more captured rebel soldiers, civilian sympathizers, collaborators, spies and blockade runners would make Camp Hoffman, one of the largest prisoner of war camps in the Union, a veritable city unto itself. At the same time, a new regime under the direction of the Confederacy's most hated man in the Union Army, Major General Benjamin F. Butler, was about to take command of the regional prisoner exchange program. His administration would directly influence the lives of tens of thousands of soldiers who had fought for the Conederacy, the supremacy of States' Rights, the continuance of the institution of slavery and, indeed, their own way of life.

And there was some irony, perhaps, that even as Butler was taking charge, just a little over forty miles to the north of Point Lookout, near the diminutive river hamlet of Benedict, located in the heart of Southern Maryland, more than 5,000 men of color, most of them former slaves, would be trained as Union men of war.

28

FOREVER THEREAFTER FREE
"Slavery and martial law in a free country are altogether incompatible."

When in the early days of the Civil War patriotic fervor was at its peak in the North, and thousands of men stepped forward to volunteer for what they believed would be a short conflict, the concept of arming African Americans was not taken seriously. Indeed, in 1861 when free men of color in New York City rented a hall to voluntarily practice military drilling, the chief of police ordered the meetings discontinued. When black men in Boston met to offer their services to the Union on April 23, they too were all but ignored. Not everyone, however, was willing to overlook the potential for black service. On May 24 General Butler, then in command at Fort Monroe, declared that fugitive slaves who had reached the sanctuary of the Union defenses, since they had once been the chattel property of men now in rebellion against the United States, were to be declared "contraband of war" and could be put to work.[1] Thereafter, most black refugees from slavery were referred to in the North as "contrabands." The war, of course, evolved into more than the anticipated three-month lark foreseen by many, and as casualty rates soared, a more sober assessment of the military manpower needs of the nation began to take hold. Soon there was a marked decrease in the enlistment of white volunteers and the formidable enormity of the task ahead imposed a new realization regarding the employment of both blacks for military service, as well as the needs for a national conscription law and military bounties. Not unexpectedly, the concept of arming men of color met considerable opposition in many civilian and military corners of the North. The issue would soon have a profound effect upon both the free black and slave population of Maryland, and particularly throughout Southern Maryland. The process would prove to be both convoluted and torturous.[2]

The navy was first off the mark. On September 20, 1861 Navy Secretary Welles formally authorized the recruitment of fugitive blacks for U.S. naval service, when deemed useful. "The Department," he ordered, "finds it necessary to adopt a regulation with respect to the large and increasing number of persons of color, commonly know as contraband, now subsisted at the navy yard and on board ships of war . . . You are therefore authorized, when their service can be made useful to enlist for the naval service, under the same forms and regulations as apply to other enlistments. They will be allowed, however, no higher rating than 'boys' [apprentices, the lowest rank in the navy], at a compensation of $10 per month and one ration a day." [3]

A little over three weeks later, on October 14, Secretary Cameron authorized General Thomas West Sherman to engage, if needed in his campaign against coastal South Carolina, escaped slaves as Union soldiers, thereby recognizing the conversion of fugitives into contraband. It was Cameron's view that slaves should be emancipated and armed, and on December 1 recommended the action to the president, who disagreed. When Cameron issued the annual report for the War Department, Lincoln, who was desperate to maintain the loyalty of the remaining Border States with established systems of slavery, summarily ordered the deletion of passages advocating both emancipation and the employment of ex-slaves for military labor or service as soldiers.[4]

Lincoln began to advocate a program of gradual emancipation as early as March 6, 1862 by proposing a resolution providing for monetary aid to any state that abolished slavery, "to compensate for the inconveniences, public and private, produced by such a change of system." On April 10 Congress passed the resolution, and then adopted a provisional article of war forbidding any members of the U.S. army or navy from returning to their owners fugitive slaves that had come in.[5] Six days later Lincoln signed the act freeing all slaves in the District of Columbia. Yet the manpower demands of war proved to be all consuming.

Some senior commanders in the army saw the passage of the resolution as a permit to conduct their own emancipation program, while others had already taken measures into their own hands. Major General David Hunter, a Virginia-born Unionist and now military commander of the Department of the South (South Carolina, Georgia, and Florida), was one of those who was quite eager to utilize men of color in military service. In January 1862 he had already begun enlisting blacks, though without official approval. In March, soon after Lincoln's proposal appeared, he began to issue certificates of emancipation to slaves that had been employed by the Confederacy.[6] After the Confederate surrender of Fort Pulaski, Georgia on April 11, only a day after the Congressional resolution had passed, and without the approval of the U.S. War Department, Hunter began enlisting "fugitive refugees" from occupied districts of South Carolina into a black Union regiment, the 1st South Carolina (African Descent) Volunteers. Perhaps inspired by the recent acts of Congress and the emancipation of slaves in the District of Columbia, he followed soon after with an even more controversial action, again without official approval: on May 9, 1862 in General Order No. 11, he unilaterally authorized the emancipation of all slaves in states comprising the Department of the South.[7]

Ten days later, stating that Hunter had exceeded his authority, Lincoln declared the orders null and void, reserving for himself the power to free slaves. Though the regiment was ordered disbanded, the general's actions had already ignited a firestorm. When word of General Order No. 11 reached Washington, Congressman Charles A. Wickliffe of Kentucky introduced a resolution in the House of Representatives calling for Secretary Cameron to provide information concerning the arming of fugitive slaves and by what authority it was undertaken. The War Department referred the resolution to Hunter, who on June 23 replied in a defiant, sarcastic manner and concluded: "The experiment of arming the blacks, so far as I have made it, has been a complete and even marvellous success. They are sober, docile, attentive, and enthusiastic; displaying great natural capacities for acquiring the duties of the soldier. . . I would say it is my hope, – there appearing no possibility of other reinforcements owing to the exigencies of the Campaign in the Peninsula, – to have organized by the end of next Fall, and to be able to present to the Government, from forty eight to fifty thousand of these hardy and devoted soldiers." [8]

In Southern Maryland the affair was, of course, met with utter dismay. "Evidently the abolitionist element has at length gained complete ascendancy in Congress," wrote the editor of the *St. Mary's Beacon*, "in the various Departments of the Government and at the North." [9] The editor's comments were not without foundation.

While abolitionist Republicans in Congress were vigorously encouraged by the general's actions, in the Border States pro-slavery politicians such as Wickliffe and fellow Kentuckian Robert Mallory were not. Mallory described the uproar in Congress following the reading of the order as follows: "The scene was one of which I think this House should forever be ashamed . . . A spectator in the gallery would have supposed we were witnessing here the performance of a buffoon or of a low farce actor upon the stage . . . The reading was received with loud applause and boisterous manifestations of approbation by the Republican members of the House . . . It was a scene, in my opinion, disgraceful to the American Congress." [10]

Notwithstanding his concerns that premature emancipation in the South might drive some slave holding Unionists in Border States and elsewhere to support the Confederacy, the national mood, and especially within the U.S. Army, was quickly moving ever more strongly against the institution of slavery. Moreover, the President and Congress had already enacted several laws to severely restrict the institution, beginning with the First Confiscation Act. Signed on August 6, 1861, the legislation freed slaves employed or used by rebels in arms or labor against the United States, by confiscating them as "property" that had been utilized for the purposes of insurrection. Then, on July 17, 1862 Congress approved the Scond Confiscation Act that effectively freed all slaves in former rebel territory who fell within areas of Union control. The complimenting legislation known as the Militia Act, authorized Lincoln to receive in Federal service "for the purpose of construct-ing entrenchments, or performing camp service, or any other labor, or any military or naval service for which they may be found competent, persons of African descent." Any such individual would be provided one ration per day and ten dollars a month, with three dollars deducted for clothing. His mother, wife and children would also be declared free. Those seeking refuge in Union Army camps were to be welcomed, given protection against recapture, and put to work. The act forbade military personnel from surrendering fugitive slaves to disloyal owners. Congress also passed a law declaring that no slave escaping from one state into another would be returned except for a felony, or unless he still belonged to a loyal owner. The act also freed the slaves who crossed into Union territory in flight from disloyal owners. Some, ignoring the status of slavery in Border States, began to interpret the legislation as a virtual act of emancipation.[11]

Soon afterwards on July 30, 1862 General John W. Phelps, commanding at Carrollton, Louisiana, proposed raising three regiments "of Africans." He made a requisition to General Butler, then commanding at New Orleans, for arms, clothing, and provisions for the black units. Cognizant of the limits to the Confiscation Acts, which did not specifically extend to recruiting blacks for military duty, Butler refused. He instructed Phelps to only utilize the "contrabands" as laborers to build fortifications, which was acceptable under the Second Confiscation Act, instead of training them as combatants. Incensed, Phelps refused, stating in no uncertain terms: "I am not willing to become the mere slave driver you propose, having no qualifications in that way." Whereupon he immediately resigned his commission and returned home.[12]

Notwithstanding the row with Phelps but mindful of the Second Confiscation Act, Butler proceeded on his own authority to issue orders less than a month later on August 22, 1862. These sanctioned the formation of free voluntary black military units from the 1st, 2nd, and 3rd Louisiana Native Guards, or Corps d'Afrique. These men, he said, in reference to the 1815 Battle of New Orleans, were now authorized "to defend the Flag of their native country, as their fathers did under Jackson at Chalmette, against Packenham and his myrmidons, carrying the black flag of 'beauty and booty.'" This time the president allowed the action to stand, and three days afterwards his newly appointed Secretary of War, Edwin M. Stanton, formerly the Secretary of State, approved the enlistment of men of color in the United States Army. For the secretary charged with the organization and deployment of the largest army in American history to that time, weeding out the unfit and unwilling in its officer corps was just one of many difficult tasks. Contracting for the massive accoutrements needed for a military to wage the monumental conflict that still lay ahead was but one more.

Secretary of War Edwin M. Stanton. Brady National Photographic Art Gallery (Washington, D.C.). Prints and Photographic Division, Library of Congress, Washington, D.C.

On August 28 by special order, Stanton authorized General Rufus Saxton, Hunter's successor, to arm, equip and receive up to 5,000 black volunteers for military duty. The first regiment organized under this order, authorized by Congress on August 25, was the 1st South Carolina Volunteers (afterward the 33rd U.S. Colored Troops).[13]

In the face of pressure from all sides for and against incorporating blacks in regular military service, some professed that the matter could not be adequately resolved until the larger issues of general emancipation itself were addressed. Yet once he had determined to meet the problem head on, the president determined that he would still be obliged to await the proper moment, such as a major battlefield success, before taking action. Finally on September 22, 1862, following the Union victory at the Battle of Antietam in Western Maryland, he issued a preliminary public announcement, which was released to the press the following day. The statement was startling: a proclamation would be made on January 1, 1863 regarding the emancipation of slaves if the war continued. Only two days later he suspended the writ of *habeas corpus* throughout the nation. The crucial turning point had been reached. The terrible bloodletting in the eastern theater of war had prompted a substantial revision of strategy that now fully embraced the concept of total warfare and mandatory conscription. To fill the incredible losses incurred and expected, the emancipation of an enormous black manpower pool would become a key component of future military policy.

On the appointed day, justifying his action as a war measure within the constitutional powers of the president as commander in chief, Lincoln formally issued the Emancipation Proclamation, declaring all slaves in states or parts of states (with designated exceptions) then in rebellion against the United States and still in Confederate control "be thereforward and forever free." Those forty-eight counties of Virginia that became West Virginia, seven others in Virginia under Union control (Berkeley, Accomac, Northampton, Elizabeth City, York, Princess Anne, and Norfolk, including the cities of Norfolk and Portsmouth), all of Tennessee, and six parishes in Louisiana, were exempted. Freedom could now also be legally obtained by state action or by the Thirteenth Amendment in these areas and in the slave states of Maryland, Delaware, Kentucky, and Missouri that had not formally seceded, the latter four being excluded from inclusion in the act for fear of sending them into rebellion. As slavery in the District of Columbia had already been unilaterally abolished, it was not addressed. The effect was to have an almost immediate influence on Southern Maryland slave holders, farmers and merchants alike, whose fates and fortunes would rest on the tidal wave of Federal and State actions that most feared was likely to follow despite the declared exclusions.

***

The president had made public for the first time in the Emancipation Proclamation that the freeing of slaves and their sharing in the national emergency was a "necessary war measure," and it was considered as such by liberal newspapers in the North. The *New York Times*, for one, was quick to support the proclamation on grounds of military necessity rather than purely abolitionist sentiment.

"The proclamation is simply a weapon of warfare – perfectly legitimate and perfectly proper. From the very moment when the slaveholding aristocracy raised the barrier of rebellion against the Government, it has been perfectly competent for the Government to resort to emancipation as a means of crushing their hostility. We had just as much right to free their slaves, as we have to take their horses, to seize their ships or destroy their lives. It was ridiculous and absurd to say that we might wage war against them. – that we should bombard their towns, kill their troops, confiscate their goods, occupy their lands, forfeit their cattle, their crops, and everything else they possess. – but that we could not strip them of their slaves. What gave them such supreme sanctity to this specific form of property or labor?" [14]

The war to suppress the great rebellion had now become more than a struggle for the preservation of the Union as stated by Congress in 1861. It was now rapidly becoming a war to end the very institution of slavery itself. Soon after the formal issuance of the proclamation, owing to the enormous manpower needs of the war effort, the U.S. Senate passed the Federal Conspcription Act on February 16, 1863. The bill was rounded out by the full Congress on February 25 and signed by Lincoln six days later, permitting him to draft able bodied citizens into the military. It was the first such large scale mandatory Federal conscription in American history. The Act was roundly condemned in the Border States, by Democrats in New York and Ohio who pressed for a negotiated peace, by pro-Southern "Copperheads" opposing the draft, and especially in "loyal" Maryland where the Emancipation Proclamation did not apply to the tens of thousands of slaves in bondage but was considered a forecast of what was to come. Not surprisingly, it was but a short time before the New England states, heartland of abolitionist sentiments, took the initial steps toward positive action.

The first official federally recognized movement towards employing free black men as soldiers and sailors within the tenants of the proclamation came less than three weeks after its issuance. On January 20, 1863 Massachusetts Governor John Albion Andrew became the first state executive authorized to enlist men of color in separate volunteer organizations. But the mechanism for organized recruitment by the Federal Government would have to wait. Not until March would Stanton accelerate recruitment by ordering Adjutant General Lorenzo Thomas to enlist blacks for military service in the Southwest. In the meantime a bill was introduced in Congress to provide $10,000,000 to facilitate emancipation in Maryland and was reported on February 23, only to die aborning. Finally, on May 22, 1863 the War Department centralized control of black military enlistment when it formally established the Bureau of Colored Troops. The bureau's mission was simply to relegate and supervise the enlistment of black soldiers and selection of white officers to command them. The recruitment program had finally begun in earnest.[15]

The effect of the Emancipation Proclamation on the Union military was almost immediate in Southern Maryland, and complaints rolled in regarding the first Yankee raids to free slaves. On February 4, 1863 four residents of the Port Tobacco district, F. Churchill Burgess, James W. Neale, George P. Jenkins, and Peregrine Davis, wrote to Governor Bradford of one such raid. Only two days earlier, they reported, a Union officer arrived by steamboat at Chapel Point, near the town, and spent the night there. He left the next morning with fifteen or more slaves belonging to citizens of Charles County. On her way up the waterway the steamer had stopped opposite the farm of the Messrs. Ware and sent a boat ashore, which "undoubtedly was done to notify their slaves of being at Chapel Point, as six of them absconded that night, and were seen to leave next morning in the boat." Other farmers living in the same vicinity also lost their property that same night, but not to the extent of Burgess, Neale, et al. "These slaves far from being prevented, were openly invited and received aboard the boat," and their departures were witnessed by citizens who were present.[16]

But it wasn't, the residents claimed, just the occasional raiders that were causing the greatest problems among the blacks in Charles County; it was the Union occupation troops. It was vigorously charged that they tended to "demoralize the slave population in our midst, by enticing, harboring, and otherwise tampering with them." Moreover they subjected the local farmers to continual depredations by confiscating stocks and even the farms themselves. Three companies of Federal troops were now cantoned at Chapel Point, two of which had been earlier stationed at Poolesville, Maryland. Two of the companies had been sent there, it was reported, after having become so "exceedingly annoying and troublesome" at their former cantonment that the Secretary of War had removed them to remote Chapel Point as punishment.[17] Not surprisingly, the cumulative effect upon the local slave population was of course unacceptable to white residents.

Even as the bureau was being instituted, the organization of the first all black regular U.S. Army unit, the 1st Regiment, U.S. Colored Troops, had already been initiated two days earlier on May 19 in the District of Columbia. It was under Colonel Kenly, the former Provost Marshal of Baltimore, and Captain John C. McConnell, but was not formally authorized until May 27. Many of the first recruits for the unit were drawn from free men of color in the city, as well as Baltimore, Howard, and Frederick counties. Soon afterwards a board for the examination of potential officers of black troops, all of whom were to be white, was organized under the direction of Major General Silas Casey. A decade after the war, the general recalled his service: "The Board for the Examination of candidates for officers in colored regiments, of which I was President, was appointed in May, 1863, and continued its duties about two years. This movement was, at first, very unpopular with a portion of the people of the country, as also with a large portion of the army. I, although doubting at first with regard to the expediency of operating in large bodies with this species of force, determined, that so far as I was concerned, it should have a fair trial." [18]

Casey instituted a system for the examination of officer candidates, he later stated, that "did not allow influence, favor or affection to interfere with the enforcement of its provisions." Before the war was over, the board would examine nearly three thousand candidates, seventeen hundred of whom were recommended for commissions in various grades, from colonel on down. From his experience connected with receiving and organizing nearly 300,000 white soldiers in the City of Washington and as commander of a division in the Peninsula Campaign, the general was effusive in his praise of the officer corps that the board would select. "I have no hesitation in saying that the officers of the colored regiments, *who passed the Board*, as a body were superior to them [the officers of white regiments], physically, mentally and morally." [19]

The establishment of a white officer corps to command black Union troops was not without its hazards for those officers who might be captured. In response to the Emancipation Proclamation, and not long after the War Department's recruitment program for blacks had begun, an angered Confederate Congress passed a retaliatory act, one section of which read: "That every white person, being a commissioned officer, or acting as such, who, during the present war, shall command negroes or mulattoes in arms against the Confederate States, or who shall arm, train, organize or prepare negroes or mulattoes for military service against the Confederate States, or who shall voluntarily aid negroes or mulattoes in any military enterprise, attack, or conflict in such service, shall be deemed as inciting servile insurrection, and shall, if captured, be put to death, or be otherwise punished at the discretion of the Court." [20]

The act also provided that all black or mulatto soldiers captured must be turned over to the State in which they were taken prisoner, to be dealt with according to the laws of said State: in most of the Confederacy that meant a return to slavery and, almost certainly, punishment or even death. No black prisoners were to be exchanged.[21]

In a General Order issued on July 30, 1863 Abraham Lincoln responded with vehemence. "It is," he directed, "therefore ordered that, for every soldier of the United States killed in violation of the laws of war, a rebel soldier shall be executed; and for every one enslaved by the enemy or sold into slavery, a rebel soldier shall be placed at hard labor on public works, and continued at such labor until the other shall be released and receive the treatment due to a prisoner of war." [22]

***

The impact upon most white Marylanders of the new recruitment policy by the War Department and the establishment of the Bureau of Colored Troops was as contentious as in any of the Border States that had remained loyal to the Union. Almost as soon as it was created the board directed a native Marylander, Colonel William Birney, son of ardent abolitionist and politician James G. Birney, to conduct the recruitment program for free blacks in his home state. The assignment was not to be easy. As Birney would later write: "Going into the colored troops was personally a sacrifice to me. My friends generally were surprised and grieved at it. But I had gone into the army to aid in abolishing slavery; I thought the national interest demanded the use in the army of a vast neglected physical force; I had confidence that, by entire devotion to the work, a most efficient body of troops could be put into the field, and I hoped that the opposition and prejudice of officers high in rank might be so far moderated as to give to the colored troops a fair chance of distinction in the field." [23]

Birney's difficulties were substantial, both politically and logistically. "Recruiting slaves in Maryland, a loyal State, was done," as he would later recall, "at first without the knowledge and always without the approbation of President Lincoln. I did it with the knowledge and tolerance of Secretary Stanton but without his official sanction, he having distinctly informed me that I did it on my own responsibility. At Baltimore, I was stopped several weeks by the order of the President and was not allowed to resume except under strict limitations of an order intended to protect loyal slave owners." [24]

Brevet Major General William Birney. Prints and Photographs Division, Library of Congress, Washington, D.C.

That Birney was ardent about his new assignment is without question. Almost as soon as he received orders to begin organizing he established temporary head-quarters on Camden Street between Sharp and Hanover in Baltimore, and later at Druid Hill, soon to be dubbed Birney Barracks. His first move was to descend upon Camlin's (or Campbell's) "negro jail," situated on Pratt Street, accompanied by a guard of troops. He informed the clerk in the office that he had official orders from Major General Schenck "to take in charge any colored persons who might be in that so called prison." When the keys were handed over and the cell doors opened, Birney found fifty-six shackled inmates, about half of whom were female, from various sections of the state, sent by their owners "to Mr. Campbell's place for safe keeping." Birney asked the men emerging "whether they would enlist or not as now you are free," but added rather forcefully that "we expect you to enlist." And not suprisingly they did. "Sixteen of the men were shackled together by couples, by the ankles, by heavy irons, and one had his legs chained together by ingeniously contrived locks connected by chains suspended to his waist. I sent for a blacksmith and had the shackles and chains removed." The sixteen slaves enlisted immediately. Soon afterwards, military guards were placed around the Wilson and Hines pens on Camden Street and the Donovan pens on the corner of Eutaw and Camden to prevent slaves therein from being removed, as it was expected more releases would be forthcoming.[25]

Though the slaves from the Pratt Street pens became the foundation of the first black regiment Birney would establish, the 7th U.S. Colored Troops, it was a move certainly met by expected obstructions from the pen owners and many in the

Baltimore establishment. Yet Birney's eventual mission farther afield in the Maryland countryside was bound to be far thornier. Many small white farmers who did not own or could ill afford to own slaves, but were dependent upon the labor of free blacks, soon also rose in protest. By 1860 free men of color already numbered 83,942 in the state. The farmers argued that if their free black labor force was recruited or drafted into military service, they would be obliged to hire slave labor from the 13,783 slave owners who now owned more than 87,000 slaves, at damaging if not ruinous rates. Still, even with resentment growing, some influential officials such as Congressman Henry W. Davis, former State Senator Henry H. Goldsborough, commandant of the drafted militia, and Baltimore's Circuit Judge Hugh L. Bond were soon suggesting that the War Department begin enlisting not only free blacks but slaves as well, with or without compensation to the owners.[26]

Although by mid-summer 1863 the War Department had yet to issue specific orders to enlist Maryland slaves, some recruiters under Birney's command had already begun to take the initiative on their own. The result was increased resistance from both small farmers and slaveholders. When John P. Creager, one of the colonel's agents, began enticing slaves away from their masters in Frederick, slave owners there, after conferring with authorities in Annapolis, secured his arrest in August. The arrest set off yet another firestorm. Since Creager was a citizen of Maryland and punishable under state law, the War Department immediately refused to come to his legal aid. In Congress, Senator Reverdy Johnson quickly came to the defense of the state's slave owners in a heated debate on the Senate floor, and protested the unfairness of recruiting slaves without providing compensation. Former Governor Thomas Hicks voiced the considerable apprehension that Maryland farmers had regarding black recruitment, especially during harvesting and planting seasons when they were most needed.[27]

Hicks dispatched a letter to Lincoln on September 4 to express his anxiety over black troops in general. It was his strong desire that the president stop the deployment of armed negro soldiers and that they only be used if the rebels fielded their own blacks as troops. Later in the month, as congressional elections were approaching, he grew even more concerned that the "Negro question" might politically embarrass the Lincoln Administration at the polls. And he was not entirely wrong.

As the Federal military grip tightened over Maryland following the Battle of Gettysburg, the U.S. Army moved to further control the potentially serious erosion of loyalist support. In Baltimore authorities closed down no fewer than three major newspapers that were not supportive of the government's objectives: the *National Republican*, the *Daily Gazette*, and the *Evening Transcript*. [28] In the September elections under the "guidance" of the military, candidates belonging to the Unconditional Union Party were overwhelmingly elected over Governor Augustus W. Bradford's conservative Union Party and the pro-slavery Democratic Party.[29] The governor stood in vehement opposition to the radical agenda of the Unconditional Unionists, which supported the immediate emancipation of all slaves and the enlistment of blacks in the military. Though he was himself a slave owner, he fervently believed that slavery was the primary cause of the war. As an institution it was all but dead, and he wished to see an end to it, but an end that must come on its own and slowly over time.[30]

Bradford refused to surrender his belief in a gradually stepped emancipation and pressed both Lincoln and Stanton to discontinue the recruitment of slaves. In an effort to mollify the disgruntled governor they declared that no decision to enlist slaves had been made and no authorization to do so had officially been given, which was true. On his own Bradford moved to halt the "illegal" recruitment of slaves and to prohibit the quartering of legally enlisted free black troops in Maryland, even as Federal agents continued, without authorization, to enroll slaves for military service.

As a result of the governor's entreaties and the unrest caused by quartering black soldiers in the state, as well as his own fear of losing the fealty of loyal slave owners, on October 1, 1863 Lincoln ordered the suspension of the recruitment of all negro troops in Maryland. In doing so, he found himself in an even deeper quandary than before. The U.S. Army, having suffered enormous losses during the campaigns of the previous six months, was in critical need of new recruits, and the manpower pool among blacks in Border States was enormous. Nevertheless, it was clear to all that such recruitment in Maryland would only serve to exacerbate the already fragile peace between much of the citizenry and government. Thus, immediately before the suspension was formally ordered, Lincoln instructed the Secretary of War to meet with Governor Bradford in an attempt to negotiate a settlement. The conference proved productive, and the governor agreed that free blacks in the state could be recruited, and slaves could be enlisted but only with the permission of their owners. Slaves might also be enlisted even without their owners' consent, "if it were necessary for the purposes of the Government," but with the proviso that the owners received monetary compensation. Stanton, who was convinced that drafting blacks in Maryland was imperative, reported to the president on the same day as the suspension went into effect: "There is therefore, in my judgement, a military necessity, in the State of Maryland . . . for enlisting into the forces all persons capable of bearing arms on the union side without regard to color, and whether they be free or not." [31]

The president readily approved the secretary's recommendations, but was careful to elucidate the provisions: "To recruiting of slaves of loyal owners without consent, objection, unless the necessity is urgent. To conducting offensively, while recruiting, and to carrying away slaves not suitable for recruits, objection."

General Order No. 329, which now allowed slaves to enlist with their master's permission, had officially opened Pandora's Box.

***

While Lincoln, Stanton, Bradford, and the pro- and anti-black enlistment parties agonized and debated over the issue of recruitment in Maryland, the organization of various regiments of colored troops proceeded as if the issue had already been resolved. The 4th Regiment, USCT, had slowly been formed between July 15 and September 1, 1863, when it was completed. It was followed by the establishment of the 7th Regiment, USCT, of which companies A, B and C, 299 men strong, under the command of Lieutenants Andrew Coast and Eben White, were mustered into service at the Birney Barrack in Baltimore on September 26. Officers of the and 4th Regiments USCT had enlisted most of those enrolled. In overall command of enlistment was Colonel Birney himself. He was joined in October by Lieutenant Colonel Llewellyn F. Haskell of New Jersey, who would eventually take personal charge of the organizational end of the newly formed 7th Regiment.[32]

The speed with which Stanton set into motion the managerial and regulatory means to facilitate the recruitment program was exhibited on October 3, just two days after Lincoln first suspended and then reinstated the project. On that date the War Department issued General Order No. 829, which established regulations for the recruitment of free blacks and slaves in Maryland, Tennessee, and Missouri. The chief of the newly formed Bureau of Colored Troops, acting under these orders, was authorized to erect recruiting stations throughout Maryland where free men of color and slaves, with their masters' consent, could be enlisted. If county draft quotas were not met within thirty days, and deeming it "necessary for the purposes of the Government" as agreed to by Governor Bradford, the Bureau also authorized the enlistment of slaves without their owner's approval. In compliance with Bradford's wishes all loyal Maryland slave owners whose slaves were taken without consent would upon formally filing a deed of manumission be allowed compensation for each slave recruited. Upon the enlistment of a slave, his owner would receive a description of the enlistee and certificate of enrollment. To insure that owners who were unaware of the enlistment of their slaves were compensated, muster rolls and recruitment lists were to be made public.[33]

There was a definite caveat for slave owners not inclined to support the Federal Government, as well as the reward for those owners interested in parting company with their chattel property: "No claims," the order read, "will be received or entertained from any person who is or has been engaged in rebellion against the Government of the United States, or who in any way has given aid, or shall give aid, or comfort to the enemies of the Government; and all claimants shall take with their claims an oath of allegiance to the Government of the United States." It added, however, that any citizen of Maryland "who shall offer his or her slave for enlistment into the military service shall, if such slave be accepted, receive from the recruiting officer a certificate thereof, with a descriptive list of such slave, and become entitled to compensation for the service or labor of said slave, not to exceed the sum of $300, upon filing with the above board a valid deed of manumission and release, and making satisfactory proof of title, and any slave so enlisting shall be forever thereafter free." [34]

For several weeks after the issuance of General Order No. 829 the War Department refrained from any public announcement regarding that specifics of the recruitment program to prevent organized opposition before implementation. The tardiness in making the announcement must also be attributed to Governor Bradford's appeal that it be delayed to permit further discussion and more time for the dissipation of the public's adverse sentiments on the issue. Secretary Stanton thus deferred a public statement until the end of October.[35]

In the meantime, without awaiting the formal establishment of a compensation board, the U.S. Army had already begun moving forward with outfitting and arming the men who constituted the new 7th Regiment. By October 8 the first six companies of the unit had been formed at Baltimore and on the 18th four of them, Companies A, B, C, and D, received uniforms and arms. Daily drilling began in earnest, four hours and a quarter for the men, and an hour's drill each morning and an hour in the evening for recitation for their officers.[36]

Circulars addressing the management of the program were issued by the Adjutant General's Office, Bureau for Organization of Colored Troops, and were quite specific in scope. If any slave owner should lay claim to any enlistees who were inducted into military service, his claim was to be adjudicated by a board appointed by the president at regular sessions to be convened at Baltimore. Rolls and recruitment lists were to be furnished to the board for public information and exhibited on demand to any person claiming that his or her slave had been enlisted without consent of their owners. It was reiterated that all claims were to be presented within ten days of filing. Colonel William Birney, 2nd U.S. Colored Troops, having recently been appointed as recruiting and mustering officer for the State of Maryland, was instructed to furnish official copies of all muster-in rolls for the information and guidance of the board.[37]

On October 26 Secretary Stanton appointed three men, Hugh L. Bond, Thomas Timmons, and L. E. Straughn, to award compensation to slave owners. The Board would grant a claim of $100 to owners of slaves at the time of enlistment for men who served more than three years and less than five years, $200 for more than five years and less than ten, and $300 for slaves owing more than ten years service or life.[38] Such remuneration, it was argued, did not sit well with slave owners who had paid substantially more for their property. Nevertheless, on October 30 the War Department officially ordered the recruitment of blacks in Maryland, Missouri and Tennessee with owners being compensated for the loss.[39]

To promulgate the filling out of the 7th Regiment and other future black units, nineteen major recruitment stations were to be established in Maryland, three of which were to be on the shores of the Patuxent: at Forrest's Wharf in St. Mary's County, Benedict in Charles County, and Lower Marlboro in Calvert County. It was not going to be an easy task, especially in the very heart of Southern Maryland.

29

HOMICIDES ON PUNCTILIO
"A neighborhood of rabid secessionists."

For many slave owners in Southern Maryland the establishment of recruiting stations for soldiers of color appeared to be nothing less than a blatant, provocative effort to entice their slaves from their masters by making them rebellious and inclined to run away. Many believed the program nothing less than a Yankee scheme designed to outright punish and humiliate the white population of the region for their way of life.[1]

Such concerns mattered little to the military. As soon as he received orders from General Schenck, Colonel Birney moved to find a site "for a camp of instruction and rendezvous for colored troops." A large recruiting squad was quickly dispatched by steamboat into the lower Patuxent Valley. One recruiting officer and several black soldiers were soon ensconced at each of six locations on the river: Millstone Landing, Spencer's Landing and Forest Grove in St. Mary's, St. Leonard's and Duke's Landings in Calvert, and Benedict in Charles. All were under special instructions from the general to maintain good discipline and to harm no one.[2]

The recruitment effort, not surprisingly, was destined to meet resistance from the day it began. The tip of the spear, a recruitment team of twenty officers and men sent to Benedict, was destined to encounter the most vocal and deadly opposition. They were placed under the command of a pair of young white Massachusetts-born officers, Lieutenant Charles H. C. Brown, of Company A, and Lieutenant Eben White of Company B, 7th USCT. On the morning of Monday, October 19, 1863 they departed Baltimore aboard the 111-ton sidewheeler *John Tracy*, which had been under charter by the Quartermaster Department for the last four months. Late that same afternoon White and his men landed at Benedict wharf and immediately commenced moving to a shelter with the rations and tools needed to begin work on erecting a camp. The remainder of the day was spent by the troops cleaning weapons and making their temporary situation as comfortable as possible. Guards were posted, and the first night at Benedict was spent without incident.[3]

Colonel Birney had determined that a key to the recruitment effort was the erection of a formal training base at some place near the two initial recruiting sites on the Patuxent, at Millstone Landing or Benedict, for easier access to Baltimore by steamer. Town Creek on the St. Mary's shore, just inside the entrance of the Patuxent and well south of Benedict, was selected as a temporary headquarters for the recruitment program. Captain Lewis Ledyard Weld, Company B of the 7th Regiment, was placed in command and soon landed with his men, presumably on Town Point, the most defensible location on the creek, and began establishing a base camp.[4]

There is no record of White's reception in Benedict, but subsequent events indicate that news of the army's arrival and its specific mission spread with incredible rapidity among both whites and blacks throughout the lower Patuxent region. Unfortunately for all, the beginning of the recruiting service by the officers of the 7th Regiment was destined to be marked by a sad event that would resonate all the way to the White House. Yet Tuesday morning October 20 began without a hint of the tragedy that lay ahead. The guard was called, and Lieutenant White went into Benedict proper and talked with "a good many" of the residents.[5]

The arrival of the small contingent of uniformed black Union troops from Baltimore, who were dubbed "stealers" by the local populace at the landings along the river, immediately instigated outrage among the white inhabitants of the Patuxent Valley. A delegation of angry citizens, later reported in the *New York Times* as a "Committee of wealthy slave owners," applied to a former congressman to assist in securing an interview with President Lincoln. They immediately set off for Washington to protest against sending black soldiers into Southern Maryland to enlist slaves from their plantations.[6]

Even as the delegation of irate Marylanders was setting off for the capital events on the river were already turning nasty. Apparently while seeking information in town, Lieutenant White determined upon his first recruitment call. Colonel John Henry Sothoron, the fifty-five-year-old patrician master of a large plantation called "The Plains," a little under a mile south of the town and lying directly on the river, "had two negroes tied up in his house, to prevent their enlisting." White was apparently unaware that Sothoron was in Benedict that same morning. Upon leaning of the lieutenant's intentions to free and enlist at least the two tied blacks, the colonel publicly vowed to kill him if he should set foot on his farm. About 3 p.m. the young officer, perhaps eager to prove his mettle, set off from the Benedict wharf with another officer and two black privates from Company B, John W. Bantum and Benjamin Black. From there they proceeded in a small boat across the mouth of the little creek south of the town and went ashore at the landing near Sothoron's plantation. Anticipating possible trouble, White ordered his two soldiers to cap their weapons and then walked up the bank toward a number of slaves, both men and women, working in the fields. The lieutenant was perhaps not unaware of the magnitude of the endeavor upon which he had embarked, but appeared at ease and intent on maintaining control.[7]

"When we had come within fifteen rods of them," Private Bantum later testified, "the lieutenant told us to halt, and he went on to them [the slaves] and talked with them. He then went off toward the house and called us to come up to him. We joined him at once. I was on the right side of him and Black on the left. When we got to the house he sent Black to the back, and I went up to the porch with him. Colonel Sothoron and a young man, said to be his son, were standing in the porch." [8]

According to Sothoron's own account it was clear that the soldiers were on a recruiting expedition, "bent on kidnapping darkies to serve as substitutes," and the old politician, with his twenty-one-year-old son Webster standing beside him, had no intention of complying with the lieutenant's mission.[9]

John Henry Sothoron was not simply a gentleman farmer: he was one of the wealthiest, most influential planters in all of Southern Maryland, and an ardent pro-slavery old fashioned Whig. His plantation was almost 1,200 acres in extent. His slave population between 1850 and 1860 had grown from seventy-two to eighty-eight men, women, and children, all housed in fourteen separate buildings.[10] The plantation, though sizeable, was once known as "Orphans Gift." It was all that remained of a 10,000-acre patent called "Chelsey Hill," awarded to a once infamous character named Peregrine Jowles during the mid-17th century. The manor house itself was formidable, with thinly stucco-covered brick walls twenty inches thick, a uniquely recessed porch, and massive chimneys that still bore evidence of damage incurred by British cannonballs fired during the War of 1812.[11]

Politically, Sothoron was a major leader in antebellum St. Mary's County as well as in state government, having served three terms in the Maryland House of Delegates beginning in 1831 and in the Maryland State Senate from 1852 to 1856.[12] On April 23, 1861, at the great public meeting convened in Leonardtown to form a committee of public safety to show support for southern secessionist states, Sothoron was elected vice president of the organization. He had visited Richmond often after hostilities commenced, and his home was known as a welcome center for neighborhood residents who had become officers in the rebel army. In October of the same year, soon after Cowdin's and Dwight's provocative incursions along the shores of the Patuxent ended, he had traveled to Richmond. From there he had sent a letter of recommendation to Judah P. Benjamin, the Confederate Secretary of War, seeking a commission for his son S. P. Webster Sothoron as lieutenant in the Confederate Army. The youth, he noted proudly, had been a former military student at Charlotte Hall Academy and was serving with distinction as a private in Captain William H. Murray's company of the 1st Maryland Regiment, CSA. Another son, Marshall Lyles Sothoron also served in the Maryland Line of the Confederate Army.[13]

The actual events that evolved thereafter will perhaps never fully be known, for two differing accounts would eventually surface. According to Sothoron's own re-collections, later recorded by an acquaintance, Lieutenant White and two black soldiers came up from the landing to the plantation where a number of slaves were laboring in the adjacent fields, "and without further ado laid hands upon some forty of them, and was carrying them off to the stealer. Upon this Colonel Sothern [*sic*], seizing his double barrelled fowling piece, which was loaded, and followed by his son, who was armed with a brace of pistols, sallied out to protect his servants and his property, and on reaching the party called to his negroes to return to him. Reassured by the appearance of their master, they immediately did so, and in spite of the threats and menaces of the officer refused to proceed any further with him."[14]

Union accounts, including the subsequent government investigation of the affair, differed substantially and indicated that White had first encountered Sothoron and his son at the house. They were armed with a double barreled shotgun and two pistols.

"Is this Mr. Sothoron," asked the lieutenant as he approached the two men on the porch.

"Yes, that's my name," replied Sothoron.

"I heard that you have some servants tied up."

"Yes, sir. I have them tied."

Without mincing words the lieutenant stated calmly, "I want them."

The confrontation could no longer be avoided as both soldier and slave owner steeled themselves for what was to come.

"You can't get 'em," challenged Sothoron.

"Well, sir, you know the law."

"Yes, sir," the planter said defiantly. "I know it."

It was immediately obvious that Sothoron had no intention of offering any compliance whatsoever, whereupon White turned and called Bantum and Black to go with him to the side of the house. "We started right down the fence to the barn," Bantum later stated, about 150 yards from the house. "There we met a young colored man. The lieutenant told him to come on, then, and go with him. We went on farther and found another colored man piling up tobacco. Lieutenant White asked him to come on and go with him, when the boy looked behind him and saw his master coming and stopped."

Though White wasn't intimidated by Sothoron and his son, the slave was.

"Come on, my friend, and go with me," White prodded.

Watching the approach of his master, the boy responded in fear, "I'm afraid my master will shoot me."

"Never mind about that," said White encouragingly. "Come with me."

The slave was not the only one who was nervous. Private Bantum, looking behind him, also saw the two plantation men, father and son, coming down with guns in their hands. "Lieutenant, let's shoot 'em," begged the soldier.

Recalling his orders to do no harm, White stared into the private's face, still hoping for a peaceful resolution, and said, "Oh, no. Don't shoot them," and proceeded on a few steps more.

But there was no going back. From behind the three soldiers, Sothoron shouted towards one of the old slaves in the field. "Tell all them niggers to come to me, every one of them." He roared to another, "Tell that nigger woman to come to me." Then he ordered the old man to "catch hold" of White.

"My man," said the lieutenant to the old slave, "don't you touch me." [15]

The inevitable altercation between the two sides exploded, with the infuriated Sothorons, father and son, hurling invectives and death threats at White, calling him a "damned nigger stealing son of a bitch."

The officer immediately stopped in his tracks, turned, and with the two black soldiers by his side walked back towards the slaves. "Mr. Sothoron," he said, "I am attending to my business, as I was sent to do."

Fuming, the now enraged planter retorted. "Business?" he shouted. "Hell and damnation! I know right from wrong as well as you do."

At that moment young Webster Sothoron jumped out in front of White and waved a revolver in his face. "Don't talk to me about business, you damned son of a bitch," he screamed, then stepped even closer shouting more epithets, and spit in the officer's face.

"How dare you bring your men on my premises with their guns half cocked," Sothoron shouted, even as his son was belching up another threat.

"God damn you, I've a mind to blow you down," screamed Webster, fingering his piece.

The three soldiers jumped back as White grabbed Webster's gun by the muzzle and then ordered Bantum to cock his piece. "If I die, I'll die fighting," shouted the lieutenant.

Staring straight at Bantum, John Sothoron cried out, "Don't you cock that piece," even as Webster Sothoron repeated his threat. "God damn you," he screamed again, "I have a mind to blow you down."

"You might get yourself in trouble by it," responded the lieutenant. At that same moment both Sothorons fired, one at the head, the other at the breast. The colonel's ball struck White in the left chest near the shoulder while Webster's, though aimed at the head, struck near the same place.[16]

Sothoron's account differed substantially from the later testimony of Private Bantum, and stated that "the lieutenant, furious at his disappointment, seized a musket from one of his men, and, pointing it at young Sothern [*sic*], pulled the trigger. Fortunately the cap exploded without discharging the piece; the lieutenant then rushed at Mr Sothern with fixed bayonet, which was within an inch of his son's breast when Colonel Sothern fired and shot the ruffian dead." [17]

The officer crumpled to the ground, badly wounded, perhaps mortally. In an instant Private Black, the now unarmed guard from whom White had taken the musket, turned and ran for his life. Private Bantum managed to get off a shot at the elder Sothoron, which barely grazed his cheek, and then knowing "there was no use in staying there," turned to join his fleeing companion. As the soldier pivoted, the colonel fired back, striking him in the back of the head with buckshot, tearing off his cap, but causing only superficial wounds.[18]

Glancing over his shoulder as he pressed down the bank towards the creek, Bantum was horrified to hear two more discharges. "As I ran I looked back, and saw Lieutenant White lying on the ground and the young man beating him over the head with the butt of his gun." He was most certainly even more stunned when he reached the river where the boat had been only to find that Private Black had already boarded and, with the white officer who had been left behind, was pushing off for the Benedict side of the creek. Providentially, they returned for him.[19]

Together they made their way back to the town. As soon as Bantum changed his blood-soaked coat for his blouse, the two privates reported the whole affair to Captain D. K. Leary of the steamer *Cecil*, which had just arrived at the village wharf from Town Creek. Within a short time the captain, with his engineer James Black, two crewmen and five black soldiers, went ashore on Sothoron's property, landing about 6:30 p.m.[20]

After tying up, Leary and his men headed for the field where the altercation had turned deadly to recover the lieutenant's corpse. According to the *Record of the Seventh Regiment, U.S. Colored Troops,* "They found the dead body of poor White in the field where he had fallen, which, upon examination, showed that he had been twice shot after he fell, and his head badly beaten, as if with gun stocks." John and Webster Sothoron and other members of the family had already lit out for Richmond, first crossing a stream behind their home and then escaping in a carriage provided by a neighbor named Thomas. Before leaving, in an effort to deny the Yankees whatever he could of his property, the colonel released the two slaves bound up in his house and told them to run away.[21]

Cecil immediately pressed down river to Town Creek with White's body on a stretcher, where Leary presented the facts of the tragedy, as far as could be ascertained, to Captain Weld. The captain immediately ordered an officer to escort the body aboard *Cecil* to Baltimore, and to report in full to Colonel Birney, who was still in the city preparing to depart. Another officer and a guide were ordered to start off at once on horseback for St. Mary's County army headquarters at Point Lookout to warn the commander of the cavalry post there, as well as any gunboats in the region, that the Sothorons were endeavoring to escape through his lines to Virginia.[22]

The following day, still unaware of the events that had transpired, the delegation of Southern Marylanders intent on protesting the establishment of recruitment stations on their lands met with President Lincoln. Caught off guard, having been kept in the dark by Secretary Stanton and knowing nothing of the order to establish such stations on the Patuxent, the president handled the situation as well as could be expected.

He asserted, it was later reported, "that he did not know by what authority the force in question had been sent there, and accordingly he directed Mr. [Peter H.] Watson [Acting Secretary of War] in the absence of Mr. Stanton, then on a visit to the army, to communicate with Gen. Schenck upon that point. He then added . . . that he thought that Negroes might be recruited in Maryland by consent of masters, as they had been in the Army of the Cumberland, but he did not wish to effect the object in any rude or ungentlemanly manner."

The president said he had promised Governor Bradford, Senator Reverdy Johnson, and others that the enlistment of blacks should not take place under ninety days. He thought he would order the withdrawal of the black troops now upon the Patuxent. "However," he noted sternly, "so far as sending negro soldiers was concerned, that might be modified and white soldiers sent. But so far as the negroes were concerned, Government must have all the slaves in Maryland and the Border States for military purposes." He was, nevertheless, deeply upset when informed of the murder of White, because it clearly represented the scorching animosity held towards his policy in Maryland.[23] And though he said nothing of it, being left in the dark by Secretary Stanton regarding the recruitment issue undoubtedly troubled him.

Disquieted by the meeting, Lincoln dispatched a query to General Schenck, then in Baltimore. "A delegation is here," he wrote, "saying that our armed colored troops are at many, if not all, the landings on the Patuxent River, and by their presence with arms in their hands are frightening quiet people, and producing great confusion. Have they been sent there by any order; and if so, for what reason?" [24]

Precisely four hours later Schenck responded to Lincoln's query. "The delegation from Saint Mary's County," stated the general, "have grossly misrepresented matters." He acknowledged that he had ordered Birney to look for a site "for a camp of instruction and rendezvous for colored troops" He had taken with him a recruiting squad, who were stationed, each with one officer, at Millstone, Spencer's, Saint Leonards, Duke's, Forest Grove, and Benedict Landings, on the Patuxent. All were under special instructions, good discipline, and had harmed no one. The only violence has been the murder of Lieutenant White, a white man. The only danger of confusion, the general concluded, "must be from the citizens, not the soldiers . . . Colonel Birney himself visited all the landings, talked with the citizens, and the only apprehension they expressed was that their slaves might leave them. It is a neighborhood of rabid secessionists. I beg that the President will not intervene, and thus embolden them." [25]

The president did not intervene.

As Lieutenant White's body was being conveyed to Baltimore, where it was briefly to be placed in a vault to await the action of his friends, news of the tragic events at The Plains began to filter out, first through the Baltimore *Sun* and the *New York Times* [26]

On the day after the killing, the affair gained momentum in the national press and simultaneously garnered considerable indignation among Southern Maryland planters. Lincoln ordered Schenck to Washington for further explanation. "The fact of one of our officers being killed on the Patuxent," he noted rather icily in the communication, "is a specimen of what I would avoid. It seems to me we could send white men to recruit better than to send negroes, and thus inaugurate homicides on punctilio." [27]

General Schenck informed the president that he would come the next day, but in the meantime had learned that Sothoron himself had been recruiting for the Confederate Army. Perhaps to distract from any accusations against him for failing to inform the Executive Office regarding the Maryland recruitment effort, he declared that he had already been planning to arrest the planter when he learned of White's death. Many years later it was suggested "that he may have been covering over some activity he, others above him, or subordinates had been involved in." [28]

Whatever the general's personal reasons may have been, it fell to Colonel Birney to inform the ill-fated lieutenant's father of the loss of his son. On October 22 he provided the elder White with a complete account of the tragedy, and informed him that the body had been taken to the Loudon Park Cemetery, on the Frederick Town Road, three or four miles from Baltimore. The colonel himself would look after the deceased's effects for the next few days. In concluding, he offered his sincere condolences. "Did I not feel that the expressed sympathy of a stranger could not be cold and possibly unwelcome at such a time I would endeavor to express the deep sympathy I feel for the Lieutenants bereaved family." [29]

Some Federal officials deemed the escape of the Sothorons inexcusable. It seemed apparent to all that both John and his son Webster had fled across the Potomac to Virginia, followed by his wife and other female members of the family. It was also assumed that the large and valuable "estate they have thus abandoned to the United States" would soon be used in some way to indemnify Lieutenant White's family for their loss. On November 12 the Washington *National Intelligencer*, citing an article in the *Richmond Examiner* of October 28, confirmed that Sothoron and son had indeed arrived in Richmond where they found succor and support among friends.[30] Rumors of the colonel's return to Maryland, however, were running hot and soon gained traction. On the evening of November 30 an expedition was finally mounted to look for the killer who, it was reported, was concealed in a house some miles distant from Benedict.

The party was personally led by Colonel Birney, Colonel James R. Shaw, Lieutenant Colonel Haskell, Major Eldelmiro Mayer, Lieutenants Joseph E. Lockwood and George R. Sherman, and a number of officers of the newly formed 9th Regiment, USCT, making about twenty men in all. Taking the main road leading northward, the party rode some twenty-five miles, bringing it to the vicinity of Upper Marlboro. On the way they searched several houses and captured a parcel of rebel mail and the man carrying it, but failed to find the Sothorons. The party returned to Benedict at 7 a.m. the next day, having ridden nearly sixty miles in twelve hours.[31]

On the evening of December 6 Major Mayer and another party set out on the same errand. This time they pressed up the river by steamer, "landed on the left bank, and then rode fifteen miles, but failed, as in the other case, to find the murderer." The party became separated, and Major Mayer and three others did not return until some time after the rest had arrived in camp.[32]

The search for Sothoron would never be consummated successfully during the war. "We afterwards heard of his arrival in Richmond," recorded one member of the 7th Regiment, "where he was received as a hero. After the close of hostilities he returned home and surrendered himself to the civil authorities and went through the farce of a trial. All the witnesses to the murder being either dead or still in the service elsewhere, an acquittal followed." [33]

***

Within days of the death of Lieutenant Eben White, the deluge feared most by the slaveholders of Southern Maryland would begin – the erection of a major military training camp for freed slaves on the very shores of the Patuxent River, in the heart of one of the largest slave-holding regions of the state. On October 22, the day after White's death, Companies C and D of the 7th Regiment joined Colonel Birney's men on Town Creek. But by the time they arrived the colonel had changed his mind, having decided to move to a location just to the west of Benedict on a road leading to Bryantown, possibly to insure pacification of the region following the episode at The Plains. The following day the two companies were moved down to the historic little riverport, and on the 24th the few remaining troops at Town Creek were also brought up. Much to the chagrin and dismay of the locals, work on the training camp began in earnest, as did the aggressive recruitment of thousands of free blacks and slaves of Southern Maryland.

30

THEY LOOK LIKE MEN OF WAR

"Give them a chance, stop calling them 'niggers,' and call them soldiers."

The murder of Lieutenant Eben White and the escape of Colonel John Henry Sothoron had sent ripples of anger through the Washington military establishment. It also intensified hostilities against the Federal administration from the citizens of Southern Maryland. Yet the successful introduction of black troops into the United States Army, already begun in Maryland during the summer of 1863, was a fact that few could now ignore. White officers mostly from northern states would command all of the recruits. Those enlistees destined for military training in the Patuxent Valley, just a few miles from the great prisoner of war pen at Point Lookout, would be recruited almost entirely from Southern Maryland and the lower counties of the Eastern Shore of Maryland and Virginia. The exuberance that most blacks demonstrated, both freemen and slaves, regarding their newly gained rights to enlist and fight for their freedom was manifest. One among them undoubtedly expressed the view of most when his prayer was published in the *Baltimore Daily Gazette* on October 23, 1863: "Great Doctor ob doctors, King ob Kings and God ob battles help us to be well. Help us to be able to fight wid de union sojers de battles for de Union. Help us to fight for de country – fight for our own homes and our own free children and our children's children."

Still, many expressed doubts regarding the successful recruitment of men of color, and if they did enlist would they fight? The fiery black abolitionist Frederick Douglas was not among them. "Do you ask me whether black men will freely enlist in the service of the country?" he asked rhetorically. "I tell you that depends upon the white men of the country. The Government must assure them of protection as soldiers, and give them a fair chance of winning distinction and glory in common with other soldiers . . . I know the colored men of the North; I know the colored men of the South. They are ready to rally under the stars and stripes at the first tap of the drum. Give them a chance, stop calling them 'niggers,' and call them soldiers . . . Stop telling them they can't fight, and tell them they can fight and shall fight, and they will fight, and fight with vengeance. Give them a chance." [1]

One of the first black units formed in the state, the 4th Infantry Regiment, USCT, was mustered at Baltimore on July 15. By September the unit had completed training and was already being deployed to the Virginia theater of war. The arrival on the Patuxent of the still to be fully formed 7th Regiment, the unit designated to establish the training camp near the town of Benedict, could not have been more inauspicious. [2]

Nevertheless, the momentum that had already been set in motion could not easily be altered. And the quiet little town that had witnessed one hostile invasion during the War of 1812 was about to witness another of a far different sort. As one of the officers would later write, "The spot chosen was something less than a mile from the river and from the village of Benedict, – if a collection of a dozen tumble down buildings deserves the name – and was, to all appearances, well suited to the purposes, the ground rising gradually from the bank of the river to the camp." Unfortunately, the selection of the site, as events afterwards would prove, though convenient to steamboat access and to the nearby village of Bryantown via an adjacent dirt road, had been an ill chosen one from a sanitation point of view.[3]

Unofficially dubbed Camp Stanton after Lincoln's Secretary of War, Edwin M. Stanton, the site was to be established on the Patuxent just to the northwest of Benedict and would become the largest training base for black troops in the state. Its actual erection was begun by the handful of newly recruited soldiers of the 7th Regiment landed at the town's steamboat wharf on October 19. They were soon joined by an additional small cadre of recruits and placed under the command of Lieutenant Colonel Haskell.[4] A portion of the 7th began construction of a stockade, bunks, officers' quarters, cookhouses, kitchens, and eventually a hospital. Others put up sleeping quarters for enlisted men, almost certainly a few Sibley pattern tents, which would soon be replaced by the "A" or common camp tent used throughout the Army. Each tent site was to be warmed by a chimney "made of sticks laid up cob house fashion, and treated to a coating of the same material, and surmounted by a barrel." Despite the care taken in chimney construction, few if any of the enlisted men's tiny habitations would ever be considered comfortable, for after every heavy rain the chimneys had to be replastered. Work at camp maintenance was ongoing and often dismal as the fall and then winter weather made the muddy labor difficult. Men hauled earth for the grading of narrow streets, paths and avenues. Trees had to be cut and used for corduroy roads as well as for supports to prevent the sagging of tents. Ditches were dug around the tents for drainage to insure dryness.[5]

It is of note that notwithstanding the eventual size of the program to establish the camp near Benedict, the operation was initially conducted as quietly as possible. The objective was undoubtedly to delay the inevitable negative reaction of the populace once actual recruitment got underway as well as to forestall political opposition. Word of the undertaking was even withheld from other major military units in the area. At Point Lookout on October 21 General Marston, who had not been informed of the black recruitment effort, ordered an investigation. "It is reported," he informed one of his staff, Lieutenant John Mix, "that some persons are now engaged near the mouth of the Patuxent and above there in enlisting into the military service slaves and free persons of color without proper authority from the War department. You will enquire into the matter and if you find such to be the case you will cause them immediately to desist and to leave this military district forthwith if they are not residents therein." [6] The result of Lieutenant Mix's foray is not recorded, but may have been for General Marston the cause for some degree of irritation at not having been informed of the nearby training and recruitment program. But it soon mattered little.

***

The presence of so many Federal troops in Southern Maryland and the government's willingness to offer succor and safety to runaway slaves who managed to reach a military encampment or a Potomac Flotilla blockader had nurtured hopes of freedom in many a black man's breast. And many now made the attempt to flee from bondage. By late October, as Union Army recruiters were beginning to fan out across the region, the difficulties for plantation owners to hold onto their labor

399

force, was increasing by the day. "Negroe Stampedes," that is mass escapes by large groups of slaves, were becoming disturbingly common. On October 22 the *St. Mary's Beacon* reported on the crisis:

"Our losses, here, can no longer be counted by ones and twos, but by hundreds. It is no longer the isolated and occasional case of shirking the reciprocal obligation that the slave is under to his master, but has become the wholesale mediated and organized business of this branch of the population. On Saturday night last, about fifty negro men left their homes in this vicinity and have not since been heard from. Since then, we daily hear of others that are missing from various sections of the county, and the tenure to this species of property has become so insecure as to render it entirely valueless. Whether or not the Government connives at this certain destruction of our interests, or the statements of Mr. Reverdy Johnson and others to the contrary are correct, we know not; but we know this, – these negroes find shelter and protection somewhere, and the laws of the State are powerless to reach them . . . Since the above was in type, we learn, that from 50 to 100 slaves, belonging to citizens on the Patuxent side of the Factory District, have left their masters during the past two days." [7]

***

Well before construction to erect a training camp on the Patuxent was begun in earnest, a major recruiting foray to Somerset County on the Eastern Shore was underway. On the morning of Tuesday, October 20 army recruiters aboard the steamer *General Meigs*, "long looked for by the darkies" declared the *Somerset Herald*, arrived in the Wicomico River, "for the purpose of taking off the *patriotic negroes* from our county." Word of the ship's arrival spread rapidly and many blacks "left work, family, and wardrobes to get on board." Fully laden with willing recruits, the ship departed that same evening for the Patuxent. Two days later, she was back to take aboard eighty more men. The rush was overwhelming and a great many wishing to embark had to be turned away including "a great number of boys too young to endure the fatigues of war." For those who could not be immediately boarded owing to crowding and could not be identified by their owners (for later remuneration), the recruiters issued receipts. Six slaves belonging to the Honorable John W. Crisfield and nearly all of those belonging to the Honorable Edward Long, both major figures in the region, had departed on the same boat. On Saturday, October 24 *General Meigs* returned for a third visit. By October 27 at least 140 slaves of the Eastern Shore had left the neighborhood to join the Union Army. [8]

On October 28 Companies E and F of the 7th arrived by steamer from the Birney Barracks in Baltimore. To flesh out the regiment it was necessary to fill the four remaining companies that were to be organized, G, H, I, and K. It was thus imperative that the recruitment campaign be immediately instituted. Even as work on the camp was started on a slight decline of the rolling hills overlooking the river, planning was begun for the next round of recruitment to fill out the ranks of the regiment. Several more units were scheduled for establishment, and training at Camp Stanton was quickly put in motion. Construction of log huts was soon begun to replace tents for winter quarters. [9]

Thus on October 30, less than two weeks after The Plains incident and two days after the last four companies had arrived from Baltimore, the next major recruitment foray was launched. In the early morning chill a party of six officers, five from the 7th Regiment, one detailed from the 1st Regiment, USCT, and a small detachment of soldiers, including a brass band, all personally led by Colonel Birney, formed in line and marched the short distance to the Benedict waterfront to board the steamboats *Balloon* and *John Tracy* bound for the Eastern Shore. They would land the following day at Snow Hill, much to the dismay of the inhabitants, where they marched through the streets with fixed bayonets.

The operation to fill out the 7th and other regiments soon to be formed on the banks of the Patuxent was complex. Officers and small bodies of black soldiers were to be put ashore on the Eastern Shore at numerous points: on the Pocomoke River, at Shelltown, Rehoboth, Newtown, Shad Landing and Snow Hill. Four days later the officers were to rendezvous at Newtown where the new recruits were to be placed aboard *John Tracy* for transport back to Camp Stanton. The initial operation came off efficiently if not seamlessly, and seventy recruits were taken onboard, though not without some emotional incidents.[10]

One such occurred when *Balloon* first arrived at the mouth of the Pocomoke. As one officer later reported: "Accompanied by Lieut. Brown and with a boat's crew, we pulled up the river to the plantation of a Mrs. D., a noted rebel sympathizer. We were met, as we expected, with the most violent abuse from the fair proprietoress [*sic*], which was redoubled when three of her best slaves, each of whom had probably been worth a couple of thousand dollars in antebellum days, took their bundles and marched off to the boat. We bade the lady farewell, and pushed off amid the shouts and screams of a score of negro women and children, and the tears and execrations of the widow." [11]

The next stage was considered a bit more hazardous as the officers were ordered to take five horses that had been pressed into service at Shelltown and proceed down the peninsula into Accomac and Northampton counties, into the very heart of Eastern Shore Virginia. There, no fewer than eleven recruiting stations were to be set up and manned by a small reinforcement of seven additional officers, both commissioned and noncommissioned, and men from Camp Stanton. Stations were soon operating at towns and hamlets such as Drummondville, Eastville, New Church, Chesconessex, Modest Town, Messengo, Cherrystone, Franktown, Capeville, Pungoteague, and Belle.[12]

The recruiters faced a daunting challenge amidst the seemingly docile but unwelcoming white inhabitants. The slave population, especially in Eastern Shore Virginia and the southern counties of the Western Shore of Maryland, were apparently eager to abandon their masters. Confrontations abounded. Slaveholders, Colonel Birney would later report on subsequent campaigns, often alleged that recruiters *compelled* blacks to enlist, occasionally threatening to have them shot if they refused. The colonel denied such charges, stating that the free will of each potential enlistee was always sought beforehand. They had often rejected appeals from slave owners "to take by force their slaves, whom they could not make work, and wished to put into service." When an owner alleged that his slave had been pressed, the colonel claimed that he always queried the recruit if it was his wish to return to the plantation, which was always refused![13] The truth, perhaps, lay somewhere in between.

Sometimes the work of the recruiter could be heartbreaking. On one occasion an officer visited a large plantation near Capeville, Virginia. Calling upon the elderly proprietor, he ordered that he bring in his slaves. The plantation owner complied without a word. When the slaves appeared and were asked if they wished to enlist, their positive response came as no surprise. They were soon formed into ranks by the guard accompanying the officer. As the new recruits started away the elderly proprietor turned to the officer and, with tears in his eyes, said: "Will you take them all? Here I am, an old man; I cannot work; my crops are ungathered; my negroes have all enlisted or run away, and what am I to do?" Another officer was called upon by a gentleman with this question, "You have taken all my able-bodied men for soldiers, the others have runaway, and only the women and children are left; – what do you propose to do with them?" There were no answers.[14]

Occasionally the mission could become precarious. At Princess Anne, Maryland another officer, Lieutenant Charles G. Teeple, having incurred the displeasure of some of the residents and the wrath of the editor of a newspaper published in the town, found himself and the U.S. Government roundly castigated. Taking the law into his own hands, Teeple quietly visited the newspaper office and unilaterally suspended its publication. Within days a brother of the editor, who happened to be an officer of the 1st Eastern Shore Volunteers, met with the lieutenant and demanded personal satisfaction on behalf of his sibling. "This demand," it was later reported, "was made in the presence of the Provost Marshal, an officer of his own regiment, who at once interfered and the matter dropped. It afterward transpired that this officer [the editor's brother] was at the time absent from his command without leave, and he was afterward dismissed [from] the service." [15]

Despite such impediments, within two weeks, as one of the officers on the expedition later recalled, "the country had been pretty thoroughly drained of recruits, some 500 having been sent to Benedict. This number included several hundred that had been enlisted by Col. Nelson, and taken possession of by Col. Birney." [16]

The induction of the troops, originally recruited by Nelson for another unit, into the 7th Regiment was not undertaken without some difficulty. The operation was in essence an illegal raid by recruiters of one military commander, Colonel Birney, upon the already recruited manpower of another, Colonel Nelson. Birney regularly issued verbal instructions rather than written: and like many senior recruiting officers he was not immune to the prospects of stealing recruits from other units to flesh out his own. The hijacking of Nelson's recruits was an example worth reviewing. The event occurred, as one officer of the 7th Regiment who was directly involved would later write, during a foray to Pungoteague:

"To illustrate the unreasonable orders Gen. Birney was sometimes in the habit of giving to officers engaged under him on recruiting service, the writer well remembers being placed by him, at Pungoteague, Va., in charge of some 200 recruits he had forcibly taken from an officer recruiting under Col. Nelson's orders, and receiving from him (Gen. Birney) the most positive orders under no circumstances to allow Col. Nelson to get possession of them, – Col.

Nelson's steamer was hourly expected – and that I should be held personally responsible that they were put on board his own steamer, and this when I had neither men nor muskets to enforce the order. Fortunately (for myself) Gen. Birney's steamer arrived first and the men were safely put on board. Some days later, Lieut. Brown, who was then in charge of the same station, had a squad of recruits taken from him by Col. Nelson, in retaliation." [17]

Upon their arrival at Camp Stanton inductees found a less than hospitable welcome awaiting them. The camp was far from complete and lacked proper housing and clothing for the recruits. They were nevertheless subjected to the standard army medical exams, assigned whatever quarters where available, and immediately commenced their new lives as military trainees. For most, days would be filled with the monotony of camp life, drilling, instruction and a form of regimentation that was wholly new to them.[18]

***

Near the end of October an incident erupted in Prince George's County that threatened to inflame the smoldering hostilities of the slaveholders along the Patuxent Valley against the enlistment efforts of recruiters from Camp Stanton. A number of prominent merchants and planters in the Upper Marlboro district had become, like those of Charles, St. Mary's and Calvert counties, infuriated about the potential sway free black soldiers would have on the local slave population. They protested loudly to Senator Reverdy Johnson, who had once served as Attorney General under President Tyler but also as an attorney defending slave owners in the famous Dred Scott case. Johnson informed his constituents that he had been promised that all the black troops would be removed from the area. On October 28 a committee of eight prominent members of the community sent a communiqué to Johnson informing him of alleged depredations by the black troops.

The committee, led by Thomas Hodgkin, and including Thomas Clagett, Jr., Shelby Clark, R. H. Lasscer (Sasscer?), C. C. Mapson, William B. Hill, J. F. Lee, and Samuel H. Berry, expressed dismay that none had been withdrawn as promised. "The promise made to you," they wrote, "has not been kept. They [the Union recruiters] are still harassing us, plundering us, abducting our negroes. So far from being withdrawn from the field or their raid upon us is much extended: now all the way up the Patuxent." They claimed that only the day before, a steamboat filled with black soldiers came up to Hill's Landing, the head of navigation on the river, but the slaves in the fields refused to go off with them, despite threats from the recruiters. It was expected the soldiers would soon return and carry them off by force. In concluding their plea the committee begged Johnson's urgent intervention.[19]

When finally called to task for the actions of his recruiters and troops, Birney responded to the charges with restrained ferocity, declaring the authors to be "reckless in their statements." It had, he said, indeed been his intention to send recruiters up the Patuxent to sites above Camp Stanton but had never done so.[20] The steamboat allegedly filled with black troops had, in fact, carried only three soldiers and a single white officer placed on board to prevent slaveholders from burning the boat. "The object of the trip," he said, "was to observe the landings, with a view to future recruiting under order No. 329 and to give the regular pilot of the boat the advantage of the instruction of the Patuxent river pilot who

403

accompanied him." He denied any harassing, plundering or abducting by his men. As for the alleged threat to return and "carry them off by force," he declared to be nothing more than "the coinage" of Messrs. Hodgkin and associates.[21]

Birney's anger over the charges, but more precisely against the slaveholders of the Western Shore of Maryland in general, whom he called "more unscrupulous than the same class elsewhere," was evident in his scathing rebuttal. He reminded his superiors that two slaveholders had already killed one of his lieutenants while others had helped the murderers escape, and nearly all had deemed the act quite justifiable. Indeed there were now even strong suspicions that four of the camp's black soldiers who had died suddenly after unexplained convulsions had actually been poisoned "by the emissaries of these men." [22]

The proximity of Camp Stanton to the The Plains plantation, where the murder of a Union officer had cast a dark shadow over the beginnings of the recruitment program only weeks earlier, was bound to be a sore point for both sides of the issue. It was perhaps not surprising that foragers from Camp Stanton had targeted the farm not only for recruits but also for provisions and other necessities. After all, they must have reasoned, Sothoron was a murdering secessionist who had escaped and as such his property was thus open for confiscation. Sothoron's wife and family who had earlier fled had returned, but it made no difference. The farm was constantly being assailed for its bounty. On November 19 the Reverend James W. Hoskins, rector of the venerable ninety-five-year-old All Faith Episcopal Parish in St. Mary's County, beseeched Bishop William R. Whittingham to employ his influence to halt the military's indiscretions. The Sothoron family, he wrote, "are besieged in their dwelling by negro soldiers, who are eating up their substance, and soon what little they have in their storeroom will be consumed, when they must suffer and perhaps be turned out of doors to meet the approaching winter without provision, except such as they may find in the pity of those neighbors who feel for them, and are willing to share with them. I ask again why should they be thus punished? They are guilty of no rebellion against the Government. They have done nothing to merit such treatment . . . have the negro soldiers removed from the Plains, and let the family enjoy what little is left." [23]

But it was not to be

***

The influx from the Eastern Shore of the new recruits at Camp Stanton on November 12 for the first time allowed a formal parade muster of the 7th Regiment, USCT, Maryland Volunteers. As Birney would later write, men of the same physical height were placed in companies of men of like size "giving to the regiment that handsome appearance which brought strangers from great distances to see it on drill." [24] Four days later, even as another unit, the 9th Regiment, USCT, Maryland Volunteers was being formed and mustered from some of the latest inductees, soon under the command of Lieutenant Colonel Samuel Armstrong, a second recruitment expedition was launched. At that time Colonel James Shaw, Jr. replaced Colonel Haskell (who had been promoted in October) as commander of the 7th Regiment. Birney's initial impression of Shaw, who had personally presented his commission to him, was favorable. It would over time sour as the senior commander later described him as "a neat, softly spoken little gentleman, who had never

404

smelt powder and whose experience and skill as a jeweler could not be put to use in the army." [25] However when Major Henry Z. Hayner, General Schenk's aide de camp, and recently superintendent of the recruiting service for all troops of color in Maryland arrived from Baltimore to serve as Birney's regimental officer, it was determined that he would oversee the overall operation.

The arrival of the additions to the base command was accompanied by new orders for further recruitment operations. On the same day, five officers, two sergeants and a party of soldiers promptly set off on another expedition for the Eastern Shore aboard the steamers *Tracy* and *Balloon*. After touching at several stations on the Pocomoke, the recruiters were eventually landed at Salisbury and White Haven on the Eastern Shore Wicomico, and at other points in Somerset County, Maryland. In the meantime one of the officers left behind on the last expedition at Shelltown was moved to Potato Neck and from there to Princess Anne where he took station.[26]

On the evening of November 28, after more than two weeks of recruitment on the lower Maryland Eastern Shore, the recruiters again returned to Benedict with more enlistees in company. But there was to be no letup in the enlistment campaign. The following morning, four officers, Lieutenants Thompson, Mack, Cheney, and Califf, and two sergeants, Yeaton and Swift, again departed from the Patuxent aboard the steamers *Balloon* and *Cecil*. Having depleted most of the lower Eastern Shore of as many black recruits as possible, a new destination was determined upon. This time the sweep would be into the fertile oystering grounds at the mouth of the Patuxent River between Cedar Point and Drum Point, and farther down the bay in Tangier Sound. And this time their targets would be the great fleets of oyster boats, manned by both whites and blacks, that had begun their seasonal working of the bountiful waters of the Chesapeake. Although the recruitment pickings were not as productive as the descent upon the lower Eastern Shore had been, by December 9 the steamers had returned with more than 130 additional enlistees plucked from an estimated twenty-five vessels or more.[27]

There would be no rest. Almost immediately upon landing at the Benedict wharf, the recruiters from the 7th Regiment were ordered back. This time they sailed to the upper Maryland Easter Shore to establish stations at Cambridge, Easton, Oxford, Kent Island, Queenstown, Chestertown, and Cecilton. About the middle of December some respite was finally allowed when officers of the 9th relieved those of the 7th. By the end of the month the aggregate head count of officers and troops of the 7th and 9th regiments and the skeleton of the 19th Regiment assigned to Camp Stanton numbered 2,330 enlisted men and fifty-nine officers. On January 5, 1864 *Balloon* arrived on the Eastern Shore with the relief recruiters and began to pick up the various detachments and their most recent enlistees for transport back to Benedict, where they arrived three days later. Three officers, Lieutenants Warren, Teeple and Brown, who had been recruiting in the upper counties of Cecil, Kent and Chester, had already begun a march with their recruits via Elkton and from there by rail to Baltimore, where they found *Balloon* awaiting their arrival. On January 16, 1864, accompanied by their latest batch of enlistees, the recruiters again set ashore at Benedict. By the end of the month the collective head count had increased by another 630 enlisted men and twenty-one additional officers.[28]

The officers of the 7th Regiment, having filled the last half of their own unit and nearly all of the newly formed 9th, now satisfied themselves that their mission had been accomplished, and that a brief rest was awaiting them. They were grievously mistaken.[29]

***

As fall turned into cheerless winter, the inevitable dirty weather soon set in. Frequent heavy rain and then snow turned the campgrounds and drill field at Camp Stanton into muddy quagmires, even as the first recruits for the 19th Regiment were being officially mustered into service on December 15.[30] The camp byways were nearly impassable, and the avenues between officers and enlisted men's quarters required continuous labor to maintain clear paths. Unsanitary conditions at the campsite were unquestionably of great concern, and the onset of extremely cold weather began to extract a heavy toll as bronchitis, pneumonia and other communicable respiratory sicknesses arrived. The building of the camp itself had been a most difficult task for the material employed in the construction of stockade, bunks, kitchens, and all of the other necessities of a military facility, had to be brought from a distance. Moreover, the time allocated for work was comparatively minimal as exercise and drilling occupied most of the day. Both training and recruitment nevertheless continued unabated, while *esprit de corps* grew almost daily. Indeed, the first battle hymn of black soldiers recorded during the Civil War, originated among the men of the 9th Regiment.[31] As Colonel Armstrong would later write:

"While recruiting and drilling the 9th Regiment, U.S. Colored troops at Benedict, Maryland, in the winter of 1863-64, the men gathered around the campfire would sing by the hour the melodies of the plantation slave life that they had just left – not always very melodious; but late one evening I was startled by a magnificent chorus from nearly a thousand black soldiers, that called me from my tent to listen to its most inspiring strains, and I caught the following words which I call the 'Negro Battle Hymn.'" [32]

Not long afterwards, the music, a mixture of the martial and spiritual that stirred the souls of free men of all colors, would be set down and forever after known as *They Look Like Men of War.*

"Hark I listen to the trumpeters, They call for volunteers,
Their horses, white their armor bright, With courage bold they stand,
It sets my heart quite in a flame, A soldier thus to be,
They look like men, they look like men, They look like men of war.

On Zion's bright and flow'ry mount, Behold the officers.
Enlisting soldiers for their King, To march to Canaan's land,
I will enlist, gird on my arms, And fight for liberty,
All armed and dressed in uniform, They look like men of war.

We want no cowards in our band,
That will their colors fly;

We call for valiant hearted men,
Who're not afraid to die.
They look like men, they look like men, They look like men of war.

To see our armies on parade,
How martial they appear.
All armed and dressed in uniform,
They look like men of war.
They look like men, they look like men, They look like men of war.

They follow their great General,
The Great Eternal Lamb,
His garment stained in His own blood,
King Jesus is his name.
They look like men, they look like men, They look like men of war.

The trumpets sound, the armies shout,
They drive the host of Hell,
How dreadful is our God to adore
The great Immanuel.
They look like men, they look like men, They look like men of war." [33]

Although the daily regimen for the three regiments at Camp Stanton was by now well established, recruitment efforts were still necessary to replace losses caused by sickness and disease and to flesh out each unit. On January 28, 1864, having recently been promoted to the rank of brigadier general, Birney issued orders that yet another unit, the 30th Regiment, USCT, was to be raised and trained at Camp Stanton. Twenty officers belonging to the 9th and 19th Regiments and five belonging to the 7th were to be detailed to recruit throughout Southern Maryland between Benedict and the Potomac to fill the new unit. Among the locations selected for recruitment stations for the latter were Port Tobacco, Lower Cedar Point, Pleasant Hill, Charlotte Hall, and Chaptico in Charles and St. Mary's counties.[34]

The already high tensions existing between the Union troops in Southern Maryland and the inhabitants were frequently exacerbated by both sides. Senior officers of both the army and navy were obliged to spend a substantial amount of time mending social fences. One typical incident occurred during the night at the home of Mr. and Mrs. James Raley, an impoverished couple living three miles from the river. A complaint was filed with Acting Master Street, now temporary commander of the flotilla gunboat *Jacob Bell*, then lying in the Patuxent. Raley stated that late on the evening of November 24 he was awakened by a naval officer and four men, two of whom were black. The officer told him that he had been informed that there was a rebel flag in the house, the possession of which was strictly against the law, and he had come to search for it.

"After overhauling and tearing some of his wife's and children's clothes without finding anything," the befuddled resident reported, "the officer asked for all the written papers about the house." After seeing them, the officer informed Raley that there was some $17,000 worth of goods marked on them, and that he would be back the next day at noon to arrest him. The sailors then left, taking about a pound of shot and three ounces of powder that Raley had in the house, and "would have taken his gun, but one of the men persuaded him not to." The house, Raley further claimed, was visited twice afterwards during the night, and the party said they had also searched six other houses on the road.[35]

Acting Master Street immediately ordered one of his officers, Acting Ensign George E. McConnell, to visit Raley and conduct an investigation. The ensign's report was short and succinct. "I found Mr. Raley to be a very poor and ignorant man, not knowing how to read or write, and living in great wretchedness. I apologized to him for the conduct of the officer, and returned the papers, shot, and powder as you directed." [36]

Regardless of such public relations problems, often caused by overzealous officers and the military's efforts to correct them, such confrontations would continue. Undoubtedly because of such hostilities, the experience of the recruiters acquired in their forays to the Eastern Shore proved of little value in Southern Maryland. The officers of the 7th Regiment obtained very few black recruits. Within two weeks the stations were broken up and the officers returned to Benedict, thus ending the enlisting service for the recruiters of the regiment. The officers from the 9th and 19th apparently met with far more success as they soon began to fill the ranks of the newly authorized 30th Regiment.[37]

In late January and early February 1864 the new regiment, commanded by Colonel Delavan Bates, was methodically assembled at Camp Stanton from men enlisted in the fields of Charles and St. Mary's counties and on the Eastern Shore. The methodology adopted for the more bountiful recruiting was not unlike that employed by the 7th. The process began by selecting specific points in the region, then occupying the most suitable public buildings, dwellings, warehouses, and even vacant barns if necessary to serve as rendezvous points. From these stations, small detachments consisting of a noncommissioned officer and up to a dozen men under the charge of a regular or noncommissioned officer, were deployed. These were dispatched into the surrounding countryside within a twenty or thirty mile radius to systematically visit each plantation or farm therein.[38]

Travel was usually conducted on foot, although horses were soon being con-fiscated and pressed into service when possible. When a station was established, the first available team of horses or oxen were usually confiscated, either directly from a stable or picked upon a highway, for the purpose of transport-ing new recruits, rations, and equipage. "Sometimes a horse was taken at one place," wrote one officer, "a harness at another, while a third party supplied the vehicle and all without the customary formality of 'by your leave, sir.' When the distances were great the first team taken was sent back after ten or fifteen miles travel, and the baggage transferred to the first suitable vehicle met upon the road; and so on to the end of the journey." [39] One recruiting officer described typical operations by his unit in Charles County. "In these journeys through the country . . . Recruits were taken wherever found, and as their earthly possession usually consisted of but what they wore upon their backs, they required no time to settle their affairs. The laborer in the field would throw down his in the field would throw down his hoe or quit his plow and march away with the guard, leaving his late owner looking after him in speechless amazement." On one occasion the officer met a planter on the road who was followed by two of his slaves, each driving a loaded wagon. The usual questions were asked and the willing slaves immediately joined the recruiting party, leaving their teams and late master standing in the highway. On another occasion a slave with a horse and wagon was encountered on the road, and "having expressed his desire to 'list,' he turned his horse's head toward home, which was nearby, and marched away in the opposite direction." [40]

***

The position of a recruiting officer was by no means a pleasant sinecure. It was indeed one that was attended with hardships, annoyances and difficulties without number. Moving about from place to place in very unfriendly territory, often on minimal rations, and always on foot without transportation save what could be pressed into service, the recruiter was usually obliged to sleep in barns, outhouses, or public buildings, wherever shelter could be found. He was then required to meet people who were everywhere opposed to his mission and held him in contempt. To have been a white officer of colored troops was in itself sufficient to be ostracized, often by one's own fellow officers. When it became necessary to take black slaves from the local white population, dislike readily turned to rage and absolute hatred. "There were," as one officer wrote, "of course, exceptions, and doubtless every officer engaged on this disagreeable duty can bear testimony to receiving at times a hospitality as generous as it was unexpected, even from people whom duty compelled them to despoil. But this was always from 'union men,' for it must be confessed that a large proportion of the property holders on both the eastern and western shores of the Chesapeake were as deeply in sympathy with the rebellion as their brethren over the Virginia border." [41]

For many of the recruiters perhaps the most disconcerting feature of their mission, as already noted, was that Birney rarely provided written orders, preferring to rely upon verbal directives. Recruiting officers were often instructed to open recruiting stations, and then to raid the countryside to carry off slaves in full view of their owners. They might press horses for the use of themselves and their men, and teams and vehicles for transportation without reimbursement to owners. They could and did confiscate forage as necessary, occupy buildings without permission, and appropriate fuel when needed. For all such acts – always at the expense of the white population – recruitment was deemed as full justification. When an aggrieved individual or slave owner who had suffered the loss of property or slaves demanded who had authorized their actions, the officers could only show their commissions and recite the verbal instructions given to them by their superior. Fortunately for the recruiters, that had all changed when Major Hayner eventually took command of the recruiting service, and explicit orders were issued in writing. It would, however, never relieve the overall tensions between the military and civilian populace in Southern Maryland. [42]

Other difficulties were related to funding. Though there were generally adequate funds "in the hands of the Superintendent, or obtainable by him, for the Government was not in those days parsimonious in any matter that pertained to the recruiting of its armies," officers were often dispatched on expeditions that could occupy weeks and required hundreds of miles of travel, with never more than ten dollars to defray expenses. And even then, as one officer noted, "this was considered as a sort of personal loan and had to be repaid." [43]

Sometimes information regarding the actual lay of the land, roads, towns and plantations therein was less than accurate and caused problems for recruiters. Maps were a luxury. On one occasion an officer from Camp Stanton was ordered to take station in a town a few miles distance from Port Tobacco on the Potomac. The unfortunate officer allocated to the task, after two days of fruitless search, eventually discovered that the assigned town had, in truth, been little more than a post office two decades earlier. When finally located, it was found to be but a single deserted, uninhabitable house, and not another building lying within five miles of the place. [44]

Local informants, often quite rare, were considered essential to recruitment. After opening a station the normal procedure was to secure confidential information on slave owners in the area, usually provided by a friendly black from the vicinity or, less frequently, a loyal supporter of the Union. The slave owner who "had sworn to shoot the first recruiting officer who put foot upon his plantation" was usually the first one visited. Though the reception was often less than cordial, it never reached open opposition or violence as had been the case at The Plains. [45]

The difficulties of recruitment continued to oblige Birney to repeatedly defend the actions and methodologies employed by his recruiters against charges by slave owners. Nevertheless, allegations continued to crop up. William B. Hill, a prominent farm owner on the Patuxent on the outskirts of Upper Marlboro, complained to General Henry Halleck of black recruiters coming ashore at his private landing on the river. They took possession, he claimed, of one of his houses, in which they were soon quartered, "having been roaming over my plantation, intruding into my barns, into my servants quarters, and into my kitchen." They were sometimes accompanied by a white man at the landing, who represents that he is their commanding officer, & that his name is Thorburn." The officer, Hill charged most vigorously, informed him that he had orders to "send negroes upon every plantation to persuade the farm negroes to enlist; and afterwards to go himself upon the plantation." [46]

Birney countered the charge by claiming that the house had been loaned to Lieutenant Thorburn by a man who had been leasing it, and that "no outrages whatever" had been committed upon the residents of any of the dwellings. [47]

Unfortunately for Birney, frequent difficulties with the slaveholders of Southern Maryland would continue to dog him and the recruiters based at Camp Stanton for months.

***

While recruitment continued, military training and construction of the camp itself went on unimpeded except by the weather. The recruits were drilled two hours a day, instructed in the use of the manual of arms, and in loading and firing weapons for another hour. They policed their quarters and stood for inspection therein by a first sergeant each morning. Every enlisted man was required to perform guard duty and participate in skirmish practice. Daily instruction was also given in the construction of breastworks and parapets. In whatever time was left they carried on work on the camp itself.[48]

The conversion of former slaves into soldiers was not entirely without the vestigial shadow of their former employment. In addition to the training and other military duties, the new enlistees also acted as valets, cooks and laundrymen for the all white officer corps. The skills and jobs in which many had been employed during their lives as either plantation slaves or freemen artificers were often put to use. One soldier, Peter Butler, Company I, 7th Regiment, was ordered to manage a sailing vessel, a trade in which he was quite familiar during his earlier servitude. Many would provide services not only as soldiers but as pilots on sailing vessels, hospital attendants and stewards, nurses, butchers, blacksmith, mechanics, teamsters, carterers and haycutters.[49]

Regimental colors were brought out for the first time at a dress parade on December 6, 1863, and a color sergeant and color guard for each regiment was selected. In the 7th Regiment, Colonel Shaw took the opportunity to assemble all the noncommissioned officers of the unit together to tell them of the dangers ahead as well as the honors to be had in the positions to be filled, and then called for volunteers. Almost to a man, nearly everyone stepped forward, and a selection was made from among those volunteering. The choice was without a doubt difficult. Three days later arms were issued to the last four companies in the regiment. Finally on December 19, to the relief of the troops, the construction work at Camp Stanton was deemed completed.[50]

Although the government was providing the basic necessities of uniforms, shoes, and arms, other needs of the men, primarily small articles of personal comfort and books for instruction, had not been forthcoming. About the same time as the dress parade, Colonel Shaw moved to address the problem by writing a letter to the Reverend Augustus Woodbury in his hometown of Providence, Rhode Island. Having quite probably been a friend of the minister before the war, the colonel pleaded for his assistance on behalf of his troops. "Our men," he wrote, "are much in need of warm mittens, towels, material for mending clothes, and of books suitable for their instruction. They have not, like our [regular white] volunteers, a State to care for their wants; they have no friends at home able to send them such articles; they have no bounty to enable them to buy them themselves, and the Government pays them but seven dollars per month." [51]

The letter had the desired effect. Reverend Woodbury not only read it from the pulpit to his congregation but also had it published in the *Providence Journal* along with a letter of his own asking for contributions. The charitable donations raised by the citizens of Rhode Island for the 7th Regiment arrived at Camp Stanton on January 18, 1864, though not without some delay caused by ice in the Chesapeake and damage to the boats employed in bringing them. As soon as they were delivered, the colonel brought to his quarters all the boxes, containing 500 volumes of books, 855 towels, 238 bags furnished with thread, needles and pins, buttons, mittens, gloves, socks, and handkerchiefs. Included was cash for the purchase of additional articles and various other necessities. All of the contents of the boxes were soon distributed to his men. The next day Shaw dispatched a letter of thanks to the minister along with a report of the receipts and expenditures, which Wood-bury soon published in the same newspaper.

"Dear Sir . . . I wish that you and other kind friends, who so promptly responded to the call, could have been here and have seen the happy faces of the men as I handed them the various articles, and told them that their friends in Rhode Island had bought and made them; I think it would have repaid you for your kindness.

I have distributed the school books as equally as possible amongst the companies, giving the larger ones to those that could read.

'Give me a spelling book,' says one, 'and me,' 'and me,' said others, with eager, anxious faces that showed their interest and desire to learn.

Two months ago I don't think fifty men in the regiment knew the alphabet — now, with what assistance they have received from their officers and from each other, three-fourths of the men at least have learned it, and many can already read fairly.

The other books I have taken to my quarters, and propose to use as a circulating library amongst the men.

I gave to nearly every man a towel, and to each squint one of the little bags.

The gloves to the men in each company that had the cleanest arms and equipments. The mittens and stockings I retain to give as I see men that need them, and the bandages I sent to the surgeon.

More timely gifts, and better selected ones, could not have been made. Please thank those that contributed so liberally, both of means and labor, and tell them how much good it has done and will do.

I should prefer to have you retain the amount now in your hands until such time as it can be most useful to my men.

Very truly yours,
JAMES SHAW, JR.
Colonel Commanding." [52]

Soon after the arrival of the boxes from Rhode Island, Birney, who had been absent in Washington, returned to Camp Stanton bringing with him news that the 7th Regiment was to be deployed by or soon after January 15, though its destination was uncertain. Soon rumors began to circulate that the whole unit was to be sent to Texas. It was also formally announced that the colonel had been pro-moted to the rank of brigadier general while at Washington, upon which the officers of the camp called upon him in a body and offered congratulations.[53]

***

As the winter slowly progressed the organization of the four regiments continued with unvarnished energy. At times the duties of the officers seemed, as one of the 7th Regiment later wrote, to be "increased a hundred fold with colored troops, where the men had not only to learn their strictly military duties, but had to be instructed and looked after like so many children; ignorant not only in the simplest branches of education, but with their moral and social ideas all awry. The officers labored faithfully, and in their efforts they were met by a desire, even more eager, on the part of their men to learn. That these mutual efforts were successful the subsequent career of the regiment clearly showed." [54]

Though training was proceeding well, adversities were ever present, not the least of which was the prevalence of sickness and disease. An outbreak of measles had laid low many recruits in November, and by January congestive ailments had made "sad havoc in the command." The nearby home of Peter C. Henderson in Benedict was requisitioned by the Army to serve as a field hospital. As the measles took on epidemic form and the death toll mounted, a military cemetery was created in the open fields behind the house. One officer attributed the substantial number of illnesses to a variety of causes: "to the radical change in the habits of life of the men; to the exposure they were subjected to during the building of camp, and to the unhealthy location." The measles epidemic apparently did, however, influence the anticipated movement of the 7th Regiment, which was delayed until the contagion had played out.[55]

On January 16, even with the outbreak of the campwide sickness, a benchmark of sorts had been reached. The recruiting phase of Camp Stanton's history was finally over when a steamer arrived at Benedict bringing with it the last officers who had been recruiting on the Eastern Shore. For the first time all of the officers and men of the four regiments were together at one time. It was an auspicious moment, for on that same day the U.S. Army paymaster arrived in camp and paid the men their first wages as soldiers in the United States Army. It was for many the first wages they would receive as free men and for most the first money they were able to call their own. Though the amount was small, just seven dollars per month, all the government would allow, and far below that of a white soldier's pay, to most of the troops the sum must have seemed handsome indeed.[56]

Nearly a month more would pass as the four regiments at Camp Stanton continued to hone their skills, marching, drilling, and training. Finally, on February 13 their orders arrived. The 7th Regiment was instructed to hold itself in readiness. As soon as adequate water transportation could be brought the unit was to proceed to Hilton Head, South Carolina. Then came the long wait, which seemed interminable as one by one the four regiments began to depart for their allotted destinations, with the 7th, which had been the first to arrive, being the last to go. [57]

"During the following two weeks," recorded one officer, "we looked from day to day for the arrival of the steamers, and had begun to think that these orders had likewise been countermanded, when, early on the morning of the 3d of March, we were awakened by the singing of the Ninth marching past our camp on their way to Benedict, to embark on the steamer *United States*, lying a short distance down the river. Soon after orders came for companies A, C and I, of the 7th, with Lieut. Col. Haskell, to join the Ninth." [58]

Early the next morning the remaining seven companies of the 7th Regiment marched out. Orders had been issued that the camp, which had taken nearly three months to build, was to be destroyed. Nothing was to be left that might be scavenged by the locals. Thus when the last troops finally departed, little remained but "the smoking and burning ruins of Camp Stanton." Then the last soldiers of the 7th Regiment boarded the steamer *Cecil*, from which they would be transferred to the steamer *Daniel Webster*. At 3 p.m. General Birney and his personal staff,

413

accompanied by the regimental field and staff officers and the final contingent of the small army they had created, over 5,000 officers and men strong, set off down the Patuxent. As the last transport cleared the shoals off Cedar Point at the southern entrance of the river and steamed south many of the new soldiers aboard must have contemplated their futures as well as their past lives. Some may have mourned the loss of the 210 comrades who had enlisted with them but perished from disease and sickness at Camp Stanton during the harsh winter training. For many more, well over a thousand men who would never return, it would be the last time they would ever see Maryland. By daylight the following morning *Webster* was at anchor off Fort Monroe. And for all of the black soldiers aboard, each a liberated man now about to set out to fight for the United States of America, freedom and equality, it was to be a new beginning.[59]

Unfortunately, the 19th Regiment, especially a newly mounted unit attached to it known as the Purnell Cavalry, which was first assigned to take up post near Millersville, Maryland to continue recruiting, conducted itself with little discipline. While under the command of Lieutenant Colonel Joseph G. Perkins, a portion of the regiment, it was later reported to President Lincoln by Brigadier General Erastus B. Tyler, passed through Anne Arundel County on March 17 and 18, 1864. The unit was soon purported to have engaged in committing "a great many depredations without any provocation" at a warehouse at Taylorsville, at the terminus of the South River Ferry. The warehouse was filled with grain and other commodities intended for transfer to Baltimore. The troops, the general stated, "were permitted to pour the grain out of the bags and use the bags to take away other things that were stolen by them." A young local resident protested to an officer that the soldiers were killing his chickens, and was promptly thrown into the river for his troubles. Crossing the ferry to the other side of the river, the regiment encamped "on a poor widow's place who hardly has a support for herself, and took without compensation, nearly all of her pigs; her tobacco was taken or destroyed, and her fodder fed to the horses." Fires were built in her barn. When the regiment finally arrived at Millersville, their conduct of inflicting havoc continued unabated. "The Union men of the Co[unty]," the general concluded, "are greatly insinced [*sic*], and for their sakes, I hope the Government will not delay in making a through investigation into the matter." [60]

Whatever transgressions of the 19th Regiment had been, it would appear that neither Colonel Perkins nor his men would suffer the consequence as they continued to recruit in both Anne Arundel and Prince George's counties. Sometimes force was obligatory. Only ten days after the purported outrages committed on the South River Perkins descended on the Prince George's County Jail in Upper Marlboro on a recruiting foray where he discovered a sizeable number of black prisoners had been incarcerated. The jail was situated to the rear and one side of the county courthouse. The lower part of the jail was divided into two rooms, each ten feet square. In the front room he discovered a dozen black women and their children confined there, many since the beginning of the war, by order of their masters "for safe keeping" while their owners were off fighting for the rebel army. Undoubtedly suspecting that what might follow would cause a disturbance, Perkins ordered a guard posted in the courtyard.

As he entered the back room he discovered, much to his horror, eight able-bodied male slaves, chained by both legs to one large post in the center of the room. They were chains like ordinary cast chains, but "each manacle had been put on hot and riveted down with a hammer and anvil." One of the prisoners, Perkins was told, belonged to the now notorious John H. Sothoron and had been there for two years "just because his master thought he would run away if he had the chance."

"The filth and stench was so utterly inhuman," Perkins reported to Colonel Samuel M. Bowman, who had been newly assigned command of black recruitment in Maryland, "that I had but little time to discriminate, although I was informed; and since then even in the communications referred to above; I have no reason to think that any of them were confined for any greater offence than either trying to escape or assisting others to do so. I at once sent for a blacksmith, and told him to cut the chains of these men, saying I will not have any man enlisted into the Military Service of the United States with *irons* on."

Though challenged by a Mr. Clark (possibly Upper Marlboro attorney Shelby Clark), who claimed to be the provost marshal, though bearing no insignia of rank, Perkins proceeded to free the male prisoners for enlistment in the military. Lacking jurisdiction over the women and children, he was sadly obliged to leave them in the horrid bondage into which they had been born.[61]

31

HEWERS OF WOOD AND DRAWERS OF WATER
". . . they caught a Rat and cooked him and eat it."

For Sergeant Bartlett Yancey Malone, Company H, 6th North Carolina, CSA, it had seemed the war was over when he was captured along with thirty-one others of his unit during a spirited action near Warrenton, Virginia on November 8, 1863. Yet he was now faced with a new struggle, this time perhaps even more challenging: to survive as a prisoner of war. Transported by train from Warrenton Junction to Washington, and from there by the Federal transport steamer *John Brooks* to Point Lookout, Malone was immediately struck by the harshness of his new environment. The first thing that stunned him were the rations, five crackers and a cup of so called coffee for breakfast and a small piece of meat, two crackers, three potatoes and a cup of soup for dinner. There was no supper. If he wanted more, he would have to pay a Yankee "greenback" dollar on the open street market in the camp for eight crackers and a chew of tobacco. Housed in a tent with fifteen others, he struggled to keep warm by a pitiful fire fueled by "one shoulder turn of pine brush" every other day. Soon after his arrival he was further shocked when for no apparent reason one of the inmates was shot in the head and killed by a Yankee guard while at the prison yard wall.[1]

The November killing of an inmate by sentries had not been the first nor would it be the last to occur within the timber walls of Camp Hoffman. Hitherto the sentries had been armed only with muskets. As the prison population continued to expand, Federal concerns about possible insurrection in the camps, not just at Point Lookout but in all of the prisoner of war facilities in Union territory, was growing exponentially. In one effort to counter the danger the Commissary General of Prisons, Colonel William Hoffman, recommended to Secretary Stanton on November 27 that 400 revolvers and 25,000 rounds of ammunition be sent to the point. It would, he said, add greatly to the firepower of the guards there and in the other camps as well if they could be provided such sidearms. "A sentinel on post with his musket," he noted, "can only give one shot in case of an attack upon him, but if armed with a revolver it gives him the strength of two or three men without such arms." The request was immediately approved and filled. Unfortunately one of the unanticipated effects was that it would also facilitate an almost immediate rise in the shootings of unarmed inmates.[2]

Indeed on December 16, following the distribution of the pistols, a large unplanned, almost extemporaneous incident occurred that was officially reported as a mass escape attempt. The deadly event proved the utility of the weapon far sooner than anticipated when "a large body of prisoners made a rush for liberty, the gunboats having been removed from in front of the prison." A Union officer repeatedly fired his newly acquired weapon into a crowd of inmates pressing around the main prison gate and wounded five men, one of whom soon died. In the confusion at least two inmates belonging to the Maryland Line, Jacob N. Davis and George Klotworthy, managed to escape to Richmond to report the event.[3]

Another account in the Southern press, quoting from the *Bible*, Joshua 9:21, gave a slightly different rendering of the affair:

"The prisoners are 'the hewers of wood and drawers of water' for the whole prison post. On one occasion the prisoners detailed for wood pressed too closely upon the gateway before it was opened. A brute, named Sides, with the title of captain prefixed, who was outside, ordered them to 'fall back,' but not being obeyed in a moment, he drew a five-shooter and discharged each of the five barrels through the aperture into the crowd gathered at the gate, shooting one through the head, another through the arm, and a third in the leg. No more notice was taken of the bloody occurrence by the authorities in charge than if Sides had fired into a flock of birds!" [4]

That any breakout attempts might be met with such brutality and increased firepower by the guards was a possibility that had to be anticipated by all those daring enough to try. On one such occasion six prisoners willing to hazard death contrived an escape plan and proceeded to dig a tunnel, commencing in the concealment of their little cracker box shanty. The shallow tunnel, despite the high water table, was run under the enclosure and out the side of a slight ledge at the shore of the Chesapeake. Though the distance was short, the labor was intense, and several anxious weeks passed before the light of freedom broke in at the water's edge. At length, everything was ready and a night was fixed upon. When they emerged from the tunnel, a sentinel whom they had bribed with a gold watch and seventy-five dollars in "greenbacks" to look the other way directed them. He advised them to keep along the water's edge until they reached a high embankment where they might conceal themselves. As they approached the designated place, they were unaware that a dozen cavalrymen, revolvers in hand, were lying in ambush. The escapees discovered them in just enough time to turn back but were immediately pursued. With flight now out of the question and mounted troopers bearing down on them, the Confederates cried out: "We have been betrayed! We surrender." Nevertheless, their pursuers, "intent on their murder, and not their recapture," rushed up and fired upon them with their revolvers. Four out of the six were severely wounded. One was shot through the lung, liver and bowels; another, a cousin of General John Hunt Morgan, CSA, had his head slashed by a cavalry saber and scalped by a ball. Two were mortally wounded, and were in the hospital dying when their companions last heard of them.[5]

Frequently flight attempts were simply spontaneous or opportunistic. Prisoners were sometimes allowed to go outside of the enclosure to bathe on the Potomac beach side. As one prisoner named Luther Hopkins later noted in his recollections of internment, if an empty barrel or box happened to be floating by, "a prisoner in bathing would watch his opportunity, slip his head under the barrel or box, and then as the tide drifted up the river, would follow it, keeping as near the shore as necessary until he got beyond the reach of the guard, and then take to the woods." On one occasion two Confederate officers convalescing in the Hammond Hospital simply left their beds, wandered out into the Chesapeake up to their necks and walked by the sentinels patrolling the shore. Both were eventually caught and placed in close confinement. Another attempt was made by an inmate named Anderson who sought to repair a leaky old derelict boat at the wharf by crawling out during

417

the night to put in plugs. But to no avail. Punishment for such failed escape attempts was often cruel. "Those who were caught at it, " Hopkins recalled, "were strung up to a pole by the thumbs, with the tips of their toes just touching the ground. Sometimes the men would faint, and had to be cut down." [6]

The message was clear for all those Confederates who had arrived at Point Lookout like Sergeant Bartlett Yancey Malone, who would never dare to hazard escape: the only reasonable hope of relief was still exchange, parole or death.

Then, another choice was offered.

***

On December 8, 1863 President Lincoln issued a Proclamation of Amnesty and Reconstruction. The decree offered pardons and restoration of property other than slaves to Confederates who swore allegiance to the Union and agreed to accept emancipation. It proposed a plan by which loyal voters of a seceded state could begin to apply for readmission to the Union. It also pardoned those prisoners of war who directly "or by implication" participated in the existing rebellion if they swore the same oath. There were exceptions, namely men who would not be pardoned, which included members of the Confederate government, high ranking military officers, U.S. Army and Navy officers who had resigned their commission to join the rebel military and those who treated both blacks and whites in Confederate custody "otherwise than lawfully as prisoners of war." Moreover if one tenth of the citizenry in any seceded state that voted in the election of 1860 so desired, and were willing to take the oath, a state government would be recognized by the Union with the proviso that slavery would be barred. It was not only Lincoln's first step toward ultimate reconstruction but would, he hoped, serve as an instrument of redemption among many thousands of rebel prisoners of war, especially those drafted into Confederate service and not eager to return to the fighting.[7] More importantly, it might provide a means of increasing the manpower of both the U.S. Army and Navy from the hoped for pool of prisoners willing to take the oath and enter Federal service. And finally, it might better facilitate prisoner exchange and the reduction of the rapidly increasing prisoner of war population itself.

The original concept of recruiting from the prisoner of war population had been floated as early as July 1862 when Secretary Stanton had written to Robert Murray, the U.S. Marshal in New York City, "to visit and hold communication with the persons now held as prisoners of war at New York for the purpose of ascertaining whether any and how many of them are willing to enter the military service of the United States, and make a report to this Department." About the same time General Butler, then in command at New Orleans, much to the chagrin of the Confederate Army, had actively begun successful recruitment among rebel prisoners of war taken at the fall of the city.[8]

Although there had been some disagreement by Stanton on the recruitment issue, by mid-December there was a substantial possibility of a large scale prisoner exchange in the works. It was championed by Butler, whose success was now serving as a poster child for the concept. Yet there were still to be obstacles. On December 17 Lincoln submitted to Congress a plan organized by the Freedmen's Aid Society for the establishment of a Federal Bureau of Emancipation to provide

418

aid to freed people of color. It was a measure guaranteed to inflame Southern ire even farther than extant levels of hatred for the Union, and was certain to inflict obstructions to general exchange efforts.[9]

Five days later on December 22, the St. Mary's District was included in the Department of Virginia and North Carolina, which had recently been placed under Butler's charge. The general who had just been transferred from the command of the Department of the Gulf, which included occupied New Orleans, Louisiana, now replaced General Solomon Meredith as "special agent for the exchange of prisoners of war at City Point." Brigadier General Edward W. Hinks, a thirty-three-year-old former newspaper printer and politician-turned-soldier from Bucksport, Pennsylvania was slated to eventually replace Marston as commander of the St. Mary's District and at Point Lookout.[10]

Now in overall charge of the Virginia and North Carolina Department but also of the nearly 10,000 prisoners at Camp Hoffman, Butler began by proposing a major exchange of six to eight hundred rebels for a like amount of Union soldiers, man for man, including both black and white troops. Almost immediately rumors surfaced that those USCT soldiers taken prisoner by the Confederates would be ignored. "On the contrary," the Union press retorted, "most stringent orders have recently been issued, under which the rebel authorities are to be held to a strict accountability with regard to colored prisoners." At the outset, however, the prisoner swap seemed to be off to a positive start. But the exchange of black Union soldiers for white rebels, now strongly rejected by Southern officialdom, would prove to be a sticking point. Sadly the intransigence of the rebel government over race would produce significant and even more unpleasant consequences for the inmates at Point Lookout. In the meantime, on December 21 a flag of truce boat reported to be bearing 1,000 rebel prisoners (though the actual number was half that) departed Point Lookout for City Point.[11]

For those left behind, the thought of escape undoubtedly still weighed heavily on many minds, especially those who considered swearing an oath to the Union anathema. Even as the great prisoner exchange was getting underway and news of the amnesty offer began to circulate, a most disturbing account of a possible Confederate rescue of the inmates at Point Lookout was winding its way through the Federal bureaucracy in Washington. Interestingly, the plot appeared to have been an offshoot of another successful Confederate seizure of a Yankee ship at sea. The vessel in question was the steamer *Chesapeake*, belonging to the New York and Portland Line. The ship had been taken on December 7 off Cape Cod, Massachusetts while en route from New York City to Portland, Maine by a party of seventeen Confederates led by John C. Braine. Disguised as passengers, the rebels had boarded carrying only small sidearms purchased at New York. Braine had successfully seized the ship, but only after killing the second engineer in a brief exchange of gunfire. Within a short time the navy had dispatched a veritable swarm of warships from Philadelphia northward to canvas the North Atlantic coast for the captured vessel. On December 17 the USS *Ella & Annie* recaptured the unfortunate steamer in the neutral harbor of Sambro, Nova Scotia, but not before Braine and most of his men disappeared. Unlike the *St. Nicholas* episode, the rebel leader and his men had cleverly eluded their pursuers and would later reappear to conduct a similar attack off Southern Maryland.[12]

The *Chesapeake* affair, which was a story soon on everyone's lips, though ultimately unsuccessful, nevertheless served to inspire similar efforts elsewhere including an alleged conspiracy in which the rescue of Point Lookout's prisoners of war figured prominently. News of the rescue plot first surfaced publicly in a Philadelphia newspaper "stating that a gentleman while traveling in the [railroad] cars from New York to Philadelphia, had for his companion on the seat of the car a garrulous Celtic female, slightly intoxicated." The gentleman had at the time been engaged in a discussion with a friend in another seat regarding the capture of *Chesapeake*. The woman soon joined the conversation and "remarked something to the effect that if the Government was not careful something of the kind would originate in the port of Philadelphia." With lips apparently loosened by alcohol she then quite matter-of-factly remarked that a vessel was at that moment fitting out and ostensibly starting for California, but would soon be subjected to the same fate as *Chesapeake*. Upon his arrival in Philadelphia the gentleman dutifully reported the exchange to the authorities. A search for the ship was immediately instituted. Soon an identical vessel described by the woman, about to depart for California, was found and detained.

The plan, it was reported, was that "Rebel emissaries" were to seize the steamer at Philadelphia or some other port in a manner similar to that by which the *Chesapeake* was taken. She was then to be run down to Point Lookout in company with one or two armed schooners, which, it was also stated, were fitted out in some of the creeks of the bay. Upon arrival at the point they would attack the guards, and the prisoners would rise *en masse* and make their escape. A veritable army would then be set free behind Yankee lines and in the heart of pro-Confederate Southern Maryland.

Ironically, rumors of some form of effort to free the prisoners were also circulating among the Maryland units in Lee's Army of Northern Virginia, then in winter quarters at Hanover Junction, Virginia. For days the soldiers of the Maryland Line were abuzz with an all pervasive story that they were about to be sent across the Potomac to their home state to release thousands of inmates. Though it created a mild sensation, as with most such camp tales, no one including the officers could confirm its veracity or pinpoint its origin.[13]

Although actual proof of the intended attack was not forthcoming, precautionary measures had to be taken. The prisoners at Point Lookout denied all knowledge of the affair. It was also stated in the northern press, perhaps not so believably, "that many of them who are very comfortably quartered would not join in an insurrection, even if an armed force of rebels made their appearance." [14] Nevertheless, a battery of Rhode Island light artillery was dispatched just in case. By December 24 an additional 500 men had been sent to reinforce the 2nd New Hampshire, bringing their strength to over 1,000 men. The U.S. Army gunboat *General Jessup*, a 150-ton sidewheel tug captured from the Confederates, was also sent to reinforce the Potomac Flotilla's defense of the water approach to the point. The increased precautions to counter the purported plot, real or imagined, failed to deter the escape of one inmate who had feigned death and was carried from the prison in a coffin.[15]

***

Christmas Eve was clear, cool, and for Bartlett Malone just another dull day with a growling stomach. He was but one among the now more than 11,000 men incarcerated at Point Lookout. If there was any vestigial component of Christmas spirit about the encampment left, it was thoroughly dashed by the Federal's policy of no gifts, which seemed to all just another example of Yankee cruelty. It was later reported in Richmond, "that about Christmas a number of families of that county [St. Mary's], who have friends and relatives in the hands of the enemy, fixed up boxes of clothing and provisions with which to cheer the prison life of their loved ones. These boxes were permitted to be sent, but never to reach or benefit those for whom they were designed. After arriving at Point Lookout they were robbed of their contents, and the empty boxes handed around among our poor boys, to aggrav[a]te their loss and make it seem greater to their cold limbs and hungry stomachs." [16]

Point Lookout, Md. View of Hammond General Hospital & U.S. government depot for prisoners of war (ca. March 2, 1864). George Everett, publisher. Geography and Map Division, Library of Congress.

The only deflection from the dreary repetition of prison life was when General Butler rode through the camp with Secretary Stanton purportedly on an inspection. The general's visit to Point Lookout was, in fact, no mere cursory inspection tour. He was now avidly interested in the prospect of turning rebel inmates, disenchanted with the Confederacy or simply seeking relief from their current situation, into Union men. His declared main objectives were two fold: to investigate the possibility of a revolt or insurrection among the prisoners stemming

421

from the recent rumors from Philadelphia; and to secure testimony from the prisoners themselves regarding their rations and condition. If there were to be any more prisoner of war exchanges, which he hoped to soon engineer, it would be imperative that he knew the status of the inmates falling within his jurisdiction. But it was the president's amnesty program and its corollary, the possibility of recruitment of prisoners into the Union cause, that was also uppermost in his mind.

Thus, even as Bartlett Malone was scribbling in his journal on the coolness of the weather, the general was summoning six rebel inmates. W. A. T. Oliver, R. M. Brooks, J. D. Palmer, W. T. Johnson, C. P. Morring, and Thomas Otis, all sergeants of the cookhouses, to be personally quizzed on conditions in the prison.

Having instructed General Marston to leave the room, Butler addressed the assembled inmates as one. "The command of this district being put under my charge I want to know exactly, from each of you, how the prisoners are treated, and as I can't examine them all I have taken you as representative men, who know the most about it. I want to know the facts. You may state them to me without fear, favor, or affection, and that you may not feel embarrassed at all by General Marston [as he] has withdrawn, and if you have any desire, any of you, I will ask Sergeant Wilkinson [acting commissary sergeant] to withdraw also." [17]

Then commenced a long face to face interview regarding everything from quality and quantity of food, number of men being fed daily, adequacy of clothing, supplies and housing and the use of obligatory and volunteer labor details, to the major complaints among the inmates. With Sergeant Oliver serving as spokesperson for all six Confederates it appeared that the food was satisfactory, but shortages in clothing and blankets were an ongoing complaint. Whether or not the six inmates were informing the general of the actual conditions or telling him what he wanted to hear and report on is uncertain.

Whatever the facts may have been, Butler readily utilized the spokesmen's testimony in an attempt to assuage, during the next round of prisoner exchange negotiations, rebel charges of mistreatment at the point. "It will," he informed Secretary Stanton, "be observed that their statement is a complete answer to all slanders against the management of the prisoners." Moreover he was delighted with the strategic isolation of the prison site itself. "I am convinced that Point Lookout is one of the best situations and with sufficient capacity to retain and control all rebel prisoners that we have or are likely to have in our hands. It is entirely defensible, owing to its situation, with much less than the present force guarding it, against the attack of the whole of General Lee's army." [18]

Finally, having taken what he believed to be the sense of some in the prison population regarding their willingness to even join the U.S. Army to escape from the privations of prison life, he queried Stanton the day after Christmas on recruiting and enrolling such men in Federal service. "Is there any objection to my enlisting as many prisoners as may desire to do so after they know they can be exchanged either in the regular or volunteer force of the United States or that of any State?" [19]

The general's query was not lost on the secretary who may have already brought it up with the president. It had recently been rumored in Washington that both Secretary Stanton and Secretary Welles had been discreetly informed that a large portion of the rebels in Union hands, indeed as many as a third of them, were now "desirous of enlisting in the navy" and that General Marston had reported that he could on very short notice furnish 1,000 men ready to take the oath and enter naval service. The president was intrigued by the prospects. Now the head of the United States Government, unquestionably traveling incognito for security purposes, would see for himself.[20]

The origins of what was to be a secret visit by the President of the United States to Point Lookout had begun only a few days earlier. At that time Secretary Stanton, capitalizing on Lincoln's amnesty proclamation, issued a pivotal order to Colonel Hoffman and to the commanders of three prisoner of war depots, Camp Douglas, Fort Delaware and Point Lookout. They were specifically directed to turn over to officers designated by the Secretary of the Navy "such of the prisoners of war under their charge as will take the oath of allegiance and enlist in the Navy of the United States." [21]

On the day after Christmas Lincoln sent a brief query to Stanton which suggested that both had earlier consulted on a possible visit to Point Lookout to examine the prospects first hand. "Shall we go down the river tomorrow?" he asked. "And if so, at what hour shall we leave the wharf? and which wharf? Mrs. L. & Tad, perhaps would go. I am not at all urgent about it, & would not have you incur the least inconvenience for it. I merely mean now that if we go, the details better be fixed." [22]

Stanton's reply is unknown but it would appear that the president wisely chose to visit the camp the next day incognito, sheltered from the view of both prisoners and guards, as none of the inmate journals or memoirs, or official military communications mention his presence as most assuredly would have been the case had he been seen. The most descriptive account of the tour, documented in the memoirs of Private C. W. Jones, Company H, 24th Virginia Cavalry, mentions only Secretary Stanton and General Butler. "We were overjoyed on one occasion," recalled the former prisoner, "by a visit from General Butler and Secretary Stanton, thinking the object of their coming was the result of arrangements that might have been made between the Confederate government and the Union for an exchange of prisoners." The visitors, he noted, drove through the camp in a closed carriage, accompanied by a troop of cavalry, and traversed "every division from the First to the Tenth and last division in which were Irish soldier prisoners, among them a portion of the famous 'Louisiana Tigers' captured at Gettysburg, and just on the eve of their departure, our distinguished visitors were given a yell raised by the 'Tigers' that shook the whole point." [23]

Although no further evidence of the president's trip to Point Lookout is known, the *New York Tribune* of December 29 briefly reported on his return to Washington on the evening of December 28: "The President and Secretary of War returned tonight from a short visit to the encampment of Rebel prisoners at Point Lookout. It is understood that they satisfied themselves that not less than a thousand, or about a tenth of the whole number, are ready to enter the service of the United States." [24]

The secret meeting between Lincoln, Stanton and Butler at Point Lookout was apparently pivotal to the future of many inmates. Butler was quick to secure Stanton's support in writing and to offset any objection he might have "to my enlisting as many prisoners as may desire to do so after they know they can be exchanged either in the regular or volunteer forces of the United States or that of any State?" [25]

Both Lincoln and Stanton were indeed satisfied. There would be no objection to the general's proposal to induct prisoners of war into military service. On January 2, 1864 Lincoln informed Butler: "The Secretary of War and myself have concluded to discharge of the prisoners at Point Lookout the following classes: First. Those who will take the oath prescribed by the proclamation of December 8, and, by the consent of General Marston, will enlist in our service." [26]

In the meantime, other events were transpiring in Annapolis that would soon plant the seeds of further heated controversy throughout much of the state but most significantly in Southern Maryland and the Eastern Shore. On January 6, 1864 the Maryland State Legislature in its first order of business moved to fill a vacancy created by the recent death of U.S. Senator James Alfred Pierce. The position to serve out Pierce's term was readily filled by former governor Thomas Holliday Hicks. Yet far more importantly a bill was introduced at the recommendation of Governor Bradford calling for a state constitutional convention to be convened for the purpose of abolishing slavery in Maryland.[27]

***

On January 8, 1864 General Butler formally authorized General Marston to "enlist from the rebel prisoners under your command all those who may desire to enlist in the service of the United States either in the Army or Navy, and you will release all such as reside within our lines as in your judgment you may think proper and safe to do so upon taking, the oath of allegiance and the parole, as prescribed in General order No. 49." [28]

Soon copies of "Abe's amnesty proclamation" were being posted all over the prison camp "for the benefit of those who wish to swallow the pill," noted Charles Warren Hutt. Almost immediately, to his great consternation, a substantial number of prisoners were lining up to take the oath of allegiance.[29]

The president's amnesty decree and Butler's examination of conditions at Point Lookout were quickly lauded by the Unionist press, especially in the pages of the paper most hated by the South, Horace Greeley's *New York Tribune*. On New Years Eve the paper reported the following half-truth-half-propaganda piece, which was soon being republished as far away as the Hawaiian Islands:

"The *Tribune's* dispatch from Washington contains the following private advices from the lower counties of Maryland and the counties of Virginia on this side of the Rappahannock: The Amnesty Proclamation of the President has been received with very general satisfaction here, and the people think that the time for such a proclamation had arrived. It is believed that Gen. Butler has written a statement from six rebel sergeants confined at Point Lookout, affirming that the prisoners are well fed and cared for. It is also believed that a larger number than one thousand rebels would express a wish to take the oath, but for the inter-meddling of the more violent of their comrades. It is reported that a rebel called for three cheers for Gen. Butler, on the occasion of the General's recent visit to Point Lookout, and that the man was at once knocked down by others, who remembered Jeff. Davis's proclamation on that subject . . . There is great dissatisfaction among the rebels, and deserters who heard the President's pro-clamation with surprise, have hastened to come in. They declare that if the proclamation could be distributed freely among the rebel troops, thousands would at once enter our lines." [30]

The exchange program was not ignored, though moving forward only in fits and starts. Butler returned to Fort Monroe followed soon after by 502 prisoners from Point Lookout, "all serviceable men and substantially those longest in con-finement," to be exchanged for a like number of Federals. Along with a letter to the Confederate Commissioner of Exchange Robert Ould he also included a transcript of his interview with the six inmates.

Anticipating what he considered misrepresentations regarding conditions at the prison, as well as long standing charges by the rebel government against him person-ally as a war criminal, Butler sought to soften Ould's expected criticism: "I have made this examination and this statement to you in order that you may be able to satisfy the friends of the prisoners who may be disturbed by the unfounded reports of ill treatment and cruelty suffered by the prisoners at Point Lookout, in like manner as our people are excited by what I hope are like groundless stories of ill usage and starvation suffered by our soldiers in your hands." [31]

Though the general had taken special care to send home many of the severely wounded men captured at Gettysburg, he had also taken a pragmatic view of those exchanged. "Men without arms and legs and debilitated by sickness are certainly unfit to bear the necessary hardships incident to a condition of prisoners of war," he stated quite frankly, "besides, they encumber our hospitals." These men, he pro-posed, would be dispatched by a separate vessel, adequately provisioned, which could be sent straight through to Richmond.[32] In other words, as they were handi-capped and no longer of possible military use, they were now to become the burden and responsibility of the Confederacy rather than the Union.

The exchange of Confederate prisoners set off a storm of controversy in the South, not for their return but by the tales of their treatment while at Camp Hoffman and the humility of being guarded by black soldiers. "The prisoners who returned from Point Lookout on the last flag of truce," wrote one North Carolina newspaper, "all declare their intention to give their lives up before they will again test the humanity of a Yankee prisoner. The fare at Point Lookout is one degree removed from starvation. The guard there has recently been reinforced by the 36th U.S. 'colored infantry.' These negroes are reported by our men to be far more humane sentinels than their white brethren – not taking advantage of the prisoners by firing upon, before halting them, and are respectful in their answer to questions. Their officers, however, are a sort of brutes, and one of them celebrated his arrival at the Point by cutting one of the prisners over the head with his sabre for merely laughing at the "American citizens of African descent." [33]

Nothing went smoothly owing to events that had occurred during Butler's former military tenure as commander of the Department of the Gulf, to which he had been appointed on March 20, 1862, and to the issue of exchanging U.S. Colored Troops for white rebels, man for man.

Following Admiral David Farragut's capture of the city of New Orleans on April 25 of that year, mob rule had prevailed. On the following day one William B.

Mumford had torn down and destroyed the American flag from the U.S. Mint there and would soon be charged with treason by Federal authorities. Five days later Butler's reign over the city commenced with a heavy hand, beginning with his controversial Order 28 in which he declared that any woman of the city who verbally abused Union soldiers would be "held liable to be treated as a woman of the town plying her avocation." Southern sensitivities were enflamed by Butler's total lack of chivalry, but not as much as by his execution of Mumford on June 7 for his "treasonous" act. Considered a tyrant for his strong dictatorial rule over the city, the general was soon known throughout the South as "Beast Butler" and was perhaps the Confederacy's second most hated man in the United States.[34]

President Davis vainly sought redress from the U.S. military concerning Butler's act, but with negative results. Finally on December 23, 1863 he issued a lengthy proclamation declaring Butler to be a felon deserving of capital punishment who must be treated as an outlaw and common enemy of all mankind. Moreover the general was also charged with war crimes and repeated atrocities against non-combatants, including inviting U.S. soldiers "to insult and outrage the wives, the mothers, and the sisters of our citizens" and the imprisonment of women. Added to that were charges of plundering of the inhabitants, confiscation of property, forcing the Union oath of allegiance upon the citizenry of the Confederacy against their will, and extortion of plantation owners. But worst of all he was accused of driving slaves from the plantations of their masters, and exciting and arming them to rise in open insurrection against their owners. If captured he was to be hanged immediately. Furthermore, no commissioned officer of the United States taken captive was to be released on parole before an exchange until Butler had been so punished. It was, the rebel president claimed, "a war in its nature far exceeding in horrors the most merciless atrocities of the savages." [35]

Davis's proclamation was not limited to Butler. All commissioned officers serving under him were also declared robbers and criminals who were to be executed upon capture, though white private soldiers and noncommissioned officers who were taken would be treated "with kindness and humanity." All slaves captured in arms were to be dealt with according to the laws of their respective states. And finally all commissioned U.S. officers serving in company with armed slaves were to be treated as such, usually meaning execution.[36]

The consequence of the draconian proclamation was to oblige Commissioner Ould to inform the U.S. Commissioner of Exchange, General Hitchcock, that General Butler would not be recognized as an agent of exchange, even as the cartel steamer *New York* was en route to City Point with 500 more prisoners from Point Lookout. For all the prisoners concerned, on both sides, it appeared that things could only get worse. And so they did.[37]

***

As New Year's Day 1864 arrived at Camp Hoffman along with yet another influx of rebel prisoners, the morning air was unseasonably pleasant. Towards evening as dark clouds formed and rain showers began, the temperature plummeted and another hard freeze set in. With a ration of pine wood for heating limited to three pieces to a tent of sixteen men, many of whom were obliged to sleep on frozen ground upon retiring, to keep warm it was necessary to form a circle around the fire called "spooning". It wasn't enough. And as he had done for so long, Sergeant Bartlett Yancey Malone, Company H, 6th North Carolina, CSA, made another entry into his diary: "[It] was so coal [*sic* cold] that five of our men froze to death before morning. We all suffered a great deal with coal and hunger too [*sic* two] of our men was so hungry to day that they caught a Rat and cooked him and eat it." [38]

32

TRANSFUGES
"Was there ever such a thing as civilized warfare."

At the White House, soon after New Years Day 1864, President Lincoln met with Secretary Seward regarding the recent Proclamation of Amnesty as a means of relieving the growth of the prison population at Point Lookout. The specific issue at hand was how to address the order in which prisoners who had sworn the oath of allegiance were to be discharged. It was finally decided that, with the consent of General Marston, those inmates who had taken the oath and agreed to enlist in Federal military service would be the first discharged. Those whose homes lay within Union military lines, but had not enlisted, would be second in line for release.[1] The mechanics of determining who, if any, would be willing to swear allegiance would be left to General Butler and instituted by General Marston.

On January 9 from his headquarters at Fort Monroe, Butler dispatched instructions to Marston regarding the new format for swearing the oath and issuance of paroles for selected prisoners, all of which were to be provided in a special volume sent for that purpose. "You will adopt the form set forth in this book, and each signature [of prisoners swearing the oath] will be witnessed, causing the oath and parole to be read to each man, the questions to be propounded to these men alone and apart from any other rebel prisoners."

The questions were direct and clearly written:

"First. Do you desire to be sent South as a prisoner of war for exchange?

Second. Do you desire to take the oath and parole, to be sent north to work on public works, under penalty of death if found in the South before the end of the war?

Third. Do you desire to take the oath and

Fourth. Do you desire to take the oath of allegiance and go to your home within the lines of the U.S. Army, under penalty if found South beyond those lines during the war?"

Those who chose to enlist would be engaged for a period of three years upon the same terms as other soldiers of the U.S. Army.

Lieutenant Francis M. Norcross, 30th Massachusetts Volunteers, disabled and lame from wounds incurred during action at Port Hudson, Louisiana, volunteered to serve as recruiting officer.[2]

The complicated *modus operandi* of a large scale exchange having already been set in motion, unfortunately for all involved, still had one major obstacle: the Confederate refusal to exchange black prisoners of war. It was a decision that would quickly provoke a none too subtle response from General Butler, and one that would fiercely enrage his bitterest enemies.

There were other problems as well, especially regarding what to do about blockade runners and Confederate deserters who had been captured and sent to Point Lookout, of which there were a substantial number. As recently as November 1863 it had been learned that a large number of rebels, possibly deserters, had assembled on St. George's Island. Acting Volunteer Lieutenant Edward Hooker, the recently appointed commander of the Second Division of the Potomac Flotilla, who had discovered the enemy presence, immediately informed General Marston of the circumstance. Eighty-five soldiers were detailed under the command of Assistant Adjutant General Center H. Lawson to round up the intruders. Fifty soldiers embarked aboard the *Jacob Bell*, Acting Master Gerhard Schulze, and the rest on an army tug. On the afternoon of November 22 guard boats were positioned at the north end of the island to prevent the rebel party from escaping to the mainland. *Jacob Bell* was stationed at the south end to prevent their escape to Virginia. The troops were then landed and commenced a search of the island that lasted until the next morning. By 11 a.m. sixty-three persons had been rounded up, thirty-two of whom, presumably local residents, were discharged. The remainder, consisting of blockade runners and Confederate deserters, were immediately sent to Point Lookout and added to the general prison population. Blockade runners were generally civilians and not subject to military exchange. Deserters, if exchanged, would be subject to military execution by the rebel army. Not surprisingly, their status was to be one of long standing uncertainty, and one that neither side even attempted to address.[3]

***

Though the recruitment program seemed to be off to a good start, Marston would soon be obliged to utilize the forces at his command in an unexpectedly aggressive fashion, not against insurgent inmates in the prison, but against enemy forces across the Potomac. On January 6, a typically cloudy, cold day, during which nine men died in the prison hospital, the general received an unanticipated order.

Information had been received at Fort Monroe that a small force of rebel cavalry was roaming Westmoreland, Richmond, Northumberland and Lancaster Counties, Virginia, collecting conscripts, deserters, horses, mules, grain, and other "neat stock," and sending it to Richmond and the Confederate Army. It was thus that General Butler saw fit to order Marston to cross the river "with such force as you may deem necessary and as can be spared from the service, and with the aid of the gunboats at your command," effect a landing to capture or dispose of any hostile forces encountered. He was also directed to "seize and fetch away the negroes, livestock, tobacco, and grain of rebel owners, and also the boats used in carrying men and supplies across the Rappahannock." Any commodities, boats or property that could not be carried off was to be destroyed. "It is hoped," noted Butler in concluding his directive, "that large quantities of wood and cattle for the use of the prisoners [at Point Lookout] may be thus obtained." It would be the first major attack on the Northern Neck since the devastating raids of May 1863.[4]

On January 11 General Marston, the outgoing commander at Point Lookout, informed the new commader of the Potomac Flotilla, Commander Foxhall A. Parker, of the order and that he intended on carrying out an amphibious raid on the Northern Neck, between the Potomac and Rappahannock. It was to be his final major act as commander of the district. Parker, forty-one years of age, was a navy combat veteran of twenty-six years service who had assumed charge of the flotilla in December 1863. He was a rigid officer, son of a U.S. Navy commander, and author of several textbooks for the U.S. Naval Academy. As with many families divided by the war, his own son, Lieutenant William H. L. Parker, had ventured to sea at the age of fourteen, gone south to join the rebel cause, participated in the *Monitor-Virginia* fight in 1862, and had recently taken command as superintendent of the Confederate Navy "floating academy" school ship *Patrick Henry*. Commander Parker was not one who was particularly enamoured with cooperating with the army in such actions, unless on an equal command basis.

Although documentation of the attack plan has not been found, from subsequent events it seems clear that the War Department and the navy had already secretly agreed upon a two pronged incursion, one by land and the other by water. The land operation was to be carried out by cavalry, disembarking on one of the tributaries feeding into the Potomac and then moving swiftly across the peninsula from point to point. A seaborne incursion into the Rappahannock would serve as a diversionary demonstration to draw off whatever enemy forces were in the vicinity, and also provide the cavalry with an emergency escape if needed. Parker's flotilla was thus to conduct in concert with Marston a surprise diversionary landing at Union Wharf on the Rappahannock, deep in enemy territory, where it was believed there would be little more than home guard units to oppose them. Though there were approximately 3,000 Union troops, officers and men, occupying the St. Mary's District, Marston was to chiefly rely on seveal detachments from the guard force at the prison.[5]

Several flotilla vessels would be engaged to carry some of his troops from Point Lookout. Ships of the Second Division of the flotilla were engaged to facilitate the operation, including the gunboats *Yankee*, *Currituck*, *Anacostia*, *Tulip* and *Jacob Bell*, under division commander Acting Volunteer Lieutenant Edward Hooker. Hooker, with *Yankee* as his flagship, was ordered to use "every precaution against surprise" and was specifically directed by Commander Parker to prohibit all officers and sailors from going ashore. With naval manpower in short supply, the flotilla could ill afford any casualties. Moreover, to prevent word of the raid from leaking to the enemy, the movement had to be swift and immediate.[6]

The cold early morning hours of January 12, were perfect for embarkation, which at first went unobserved by inmates of the prison camp, where activities went on as always. Little notice was taken as the prisoners began their daily routines, trading for blankets, working at making trinkets to sell to the guards, or tending to their multitude of illnesses. When a prisoner named Silas Douglas was shot by one of the sentries, it was noted only by a seven word entry in one inmate's diary and little more.[7]

Within a short time the transport ships of the squadron had crossed the Potomac and entered the Yeocomico River. After pressing up the narrow passage to the little river port of Kinsale, they disembarked 100 troopers of the 5th Cavalry under the personal direction of General Marston. At Kinsale the general dispatched his soldiers towards the town of Warsaw, governmental seat of Richmond County, wherein a Confederate warehouse was reported. The balance of his mounted troops, thirty to fifty in number, and 300 infantry, remained onboard the flotilla, which was already bound for the Rappahannock.[8]

By 10 a.m., Hooker later reported, his gunboats had entered and then moved up the Rappahannock. Each vessel of the division was assigned to a station on the river as they proceeded. At 5 p.m., with *Currituck* in company, he reached Union Wharf, some distance below the town of Tappahannock, which served as both a major steamer landing and a ferryboat site on the middle river. Finding all quiet, he dispatched *Currituck* to an appointed station downriver while he remained at the ferry wharf.[9]

In the meantime, after an eleven mile ride without opposition, the cavalry dispatched to Warsaw reached their destination. The town was taken by surprise along with a rebel major and several soldiers. In the government warehouse they discovered a quantity of enemy stores consisting of pork, bacon and a stockpile of grain. Without interruption and with great celerity, the work of destruction was completed after which the troopers set off for a very brief rendezvous with the flotilla at Union Wharf. From there they proceeded down the river, crossed Farham's Creek, having traveled about sixty-two miles in a little over twelve hours of hard riding, and at 4 a.m., January 13, finally came to rest.[10]

Five hours later, as the morning broke hazy and cloudy, the cavalrymen were again underway southward, bound for the hamlet of Little Waltham where they skirmished with and promptly routed a small force of rebel cavalry. In the village they tarried only long enough to destroy several hundred bushels of grain and some valuables in the possession of the local military authorities before pressing on to Lancaster County Court House. At the courthouse the main body rested while a small detachment under a Lieutenant Dickenson was ordered on to the village of Kilmarnock, approximately ten miles away, to destroy an extensive tannery reported to be in the area. Upon arriving at the little village the raiders "gave to the torch a large stock of leather, hides, machinery, oil, &c." The descent on the town was not without some opposition provided by a small force belonging to the 9th Virginia Cavalry. Following a brief skirmish, in which one rebel private was severely wounded and captured, the raiders returned to Little Waltham and then pushed on toward the Corrotoman River.[11]

About the time Dickenson's cavalry was setting off toward Little Waltham, Hooker's naval force, anchored at and near Union Wharf, observed a large number of men on the south bank of the Rappahannock some distance above the anchorage. Having just been reinforced by *Commodore Read*, which had been on blockade duty on the river, and assuming the unidentified force to be the enemy, Hooker immediately proceeded up as far as Totouskey Creek, nearly opposite the rebels. He soon discerned a number of men, several on horseback preparing to cross the river, in five large boats, three of which were drawn on wheels towards the river by long teams of horses and cattle attached. Owing to the shallowness of the water, he was unable to bring his ship near, though three shots from one of the her rifled guns quickly dispersed the enemy. Observing Parker's orders forbidding the landing of any seamen, and deeming it imprudent to send out a landing party to destroy the rebel boats that had been left behind, he decided to retire farther downriver.[12]

About noon a white flag was spotted on the northern shoreline. It was soon learned that the Union cavalry was two or three miles inland and bound toward the Corrotoman River. Hooker then proceeded to communicate orders to each vessel of the squadron as he moved down, after which he again turned his own ship's prow upriver.

"During the night," he later reported, "the weather becoming thick, I found the *Currituck*, and anchoring that ship made the *Yankee* fast to her stern, and so remained until the fog lifted (about noon on Thursday), when I got underway and proceeded down the river, collecting the vessels as I advanced. At 7 o'clock p.m. I reached the mouth of the river, having had no direct communication with the land forces and no intimation of their position after the communication with the flag on shore. Having assigned night stations to the vessels, I proceeded with the *Yankee* to cruise Fleets Bay," [13]

Part of the squadron had been assigned anchorages at or near the Great Wicomico River, which unquestionably attracted the attentions of local rebels. About 10 p.m. Dickenson's cavalry, having bivouacked for the night, were aroused by the sound of distant firing and pressed on toward the Great Wicomico where direct communication with the fleet was finally established. The following morning, January 14, part of the squadron moved up the river to Rubetts where the troops began construction of a sixty-six-foot-long wharf to allow reboarding of the cavalry and livestock they had captured along the way. Though several of the vessels soon found themselves aground with the falling tide, the building project went on at full speed until evening. Finally the troopers began embarking, just as *Commodore Read* arrived from Fleets Bay to lead the line out of the river and bid farewell to the Northern Neck expedition. She took with her twenty-five prisoners, sixty horses, twenty mules, twenty-five head of cattle and 116 sheep, at the cost of one man killed. It had been a modest haul indeed for such a potentially dangerous operation.[14]

Though initial reports reaching Confederate headquarters stated that 5,000 Yankees had landed at Kinsale, they were quickly assumed to be exaggerations. It was soon noted, however, "there is no doubt that a considerable body have landed in the county, to destroy our means of subsistence in pursuance of their established policy." [15] The official Confederate military report, compiled by Captain John S. Braxton, Assistant Adjutant General to General Arnold Elzey, a brigade commander with the 1st Maryland Infantry, CSA, and a native of Somerset County, demeaned the raid as "a very small one, and I think indicates nothing of importance." [16]

The expedition returned to Point Lookout in the early morning hours of January 16, a cloudy but unusually warm day for the season. Though limited in prize goods and prisoners, it had again amply demonstrated just how vulnerable and helpless the Northern Neck was to amphibious operations launched from Southern Maryland.[17] And more were likely to be on the way. For some in the Union high command it appeared that, for all intensive purposes, the almost defenseless Northern Neck had been neutralized.

Upon returning to the Potomac River it was business as usual for the flotilla. *Commodore Read* and *Anacostia* were temporarily sent to guard Point Lookout, and *Jacob Bell* to patrol off Blackistone Island. Feeling some apprehension for the safety of a merchant fleet temporarily anchored off Piney Point, Commander Parker instructed the gunboats *Wyandank* and *Sophronia* to maintain station there. Soon afterwards the flotilla was shuffled again, always with the aim of preventing blockade running, as it relentlessly sought to tighten the garrote around Mathias Neck.[18]

***

On Monday, February 1, acting under the authority granted to him by the Federal Conscription Act on March 3, 1863, President Lincoln prepared for another nation draft, this time of 500,000 men, to be issued on March 10, 1864. The draftees were to serve for a period of three years or the duration of the rebellion. The concurrence of the draft, which was unpopular in many sections of the North, and the enlistment program among Confederate prisoners of war was not surprising. Its machinations in Southern Maryland quickly became one of the main topics of conversation. At Point Lookout the success of the enlistment program was already the subject of many rumors, all of which mutated from day to day. On February 5 a Union soldier on duty at the camp, Almon D. Jones, wrote to his sister, informing her of the latest scuttlebutt: "The rebes are interesting [*sic* enlisting] in to our army Four hundred has inlisted already and more will inlist as soon as these states come back in to the union." [19]

As word spread westward regarding the amnesty and enlistments at Point Lookout, the numbers said to be involved continued to grow almost exponentially by the mile. It was reported in Sandusky, Ohio on February 12 that 500 prisoners had enlisted and 3,000 were determined to take the benefit of the Amnesty Proclamation. Eight days later on the Pacific coast, word of the purported total of enlistments was said to have grown to 5,000 with an additional 500 seeking the amnesty provisions.[20]

The exaggerated numbers notwithstanding, the aggressive amnesty and enlistment program was, in fact, making considerable progress and relieving stress from overpopulation in all of the prisoner of war camps. By mid-February it was being officially stated that there were 3,000 Confederate officers and between 43,000 and 45,000 enlisted men incarcerated in Union camps around the nation, and Point Lookout was bearing a substantial portion of the burden. The reduction of inmates by any measure had become almost a necessity.[21]

The vetting process at Point Lookout for those inclined to seek amnesty or enlist with the Union Army or Navy was closely regimented, as historian Edwin Beitzell pointed out in his superlative history of Camp Hoffman. On March 1, 1864 Private Bartlett Yancey Malone, a prisoner taken less than six weeks earlier, lined up with the rest of his mates from Company H to be interviewed by a Union officer on the subject of his willingness to swear the oath of allegiance. He was unquestionably influenced by the countless traumas of his incarceration. He had already suffered from starvation and deprivation, witnessed five of his comrades freezing to death, and the shootings of six or more prisoners.[22]

"Our Company," he recorded, "was examined on the Oath question every man was taken in the House one at a time and examined: the questions asked me was this: Do you wish to take the Oath and join the U.S. Army or Navy: or work at government work or on Breastworks or Do you wish to take a Parole and go to your home if it be inside of our lines or do you wish to go South. I told I wished to go South: He then asked me my name County State & Regiment The 2d two thousand [paroled] Rebels left Point Lookout M. D. for Dixie." [23]

Nine days later, another 600 parolees were released to head home, followed by an additional great boatload the next day.[24]

Still the Confederates refused to release black Union soldiers in return. Butler now determined to respond in a retaliatory manner that was certain to further arouse rebel dander. In late February he dispatched the 26th North Carolina, an all black Union regiment, to Point Lookout. The unit had been formed almost entirely from freed slaves and was being sent to serve as guards over the white rebel prisoner population. The Northern abolitionist were delighted. "General Butler has put a regiment of North Carolina negroes over the rebel prisoners at Point Lookout," reported the *Xenia Sentinel* in Xenia, Ohio, in one typical report. "He says that if the Richmond authorities will not exchange negro prisoners, Southern prisoners will have the pleasure of being guarded by bayonets in negroes' hands." [25]

On February 25 when the black troops suddenly made their debut, the response from the prisoners was at first incredulity. "Was there ever such a thing as civilized warfare[?]" asked Private Charles Warren Hutt in utter disbelief. But then came the reality of their situation as some former slaves, now armed, from time to time began to extract revenge upon their late masters.[26]

"The negroes are not disrespectful to the Southern men," reported the *Richmond Enquirer*, "but lord it over their white brethren to their heart's content in the complete immunity of the Beast's protection." [27]

Captain Robert E. Park, one of the inmates belonging to the 12th Alabama Regiment, provided a far more jaundiced view of the consequences of the arrival of black guards. From a report provided by a fellow inmate, he wrote: "He says that several of the negro soldiers guarding them were once slaves of some of the prisoners, and have been recognized as such. Some of them are still respectful and call their young owners 'master,' and declare they were forced to enlist. A majority of them, however, inflated by their so called freedom, are very insolent and overbearing. They frequently fire into the midst of the prisoners, upon the slightest provocation." [28]

One negro sentinel, only a few days earlier, shot an extremely debilitated prisoner as he walked slowly away "from the foul sinks to his tent, simply because he did not and could not obey his interpretive order to 'move on faster dar.'" Instead of being court martialed and punished for the murder, the sentienl was seen a few days afterwards exulting in his promotion to a corporalcy, and posting a relief guard. Park was certain that the employment of former slaves to guard their late masters was specifically intended to insult and degrade the latter. "No generous heart," he noted, "could have ever devised or sanctioned such contemptible meanness and littleness." [29]

Though Butler's calculated measure served to greatly enhance his eminence in the pantheon of the Confederacy's most hated Union officials, it did not reduce his hopes for an ongoing program of large scale white prisoner exchange. By March he was anticipating a transfer of as many as several thousand prisoners a week, and regularly requested that inmates be sent to Point Lookout from many other prison camps in the North. "I wish you would send to me at Point Lookout what privates, prisoners of war, there at Fort Delaware, and other points," he wrote in one such request to the Commissary General of Prisoners in Washington, "so that we may not have to bring them, in case the exchange comes on, as I believe it will. If it does we shall want them at the rate of 2,000 per week . . .We can accommodate 20,000 as well as any other number at Point Lookout. We want them there time enough to have the four [amnesty] questions directed by the President put to each one of them." [30]

Transporting prisoners from one camp to another was dreadful indeed, not just for the guards, who were charged with preventing escapes, but also for the prisoners, who had no control over themselves or their belongings. When one load of inmates captured at Port Hudson, Louisiana, was transferred from the Federal compound on Johnson's Island in Lake Erie, "the trunks, valises, and other baggage of the . . . prisoners reached Point Lookout almost entirely rifled of their contents," with several trunks and valises totally missing.[31]

Though escapes occasionally occurred, by stealth or as a result of mishaps along the way such as an accidental train derailment, the delivery system was both efficient and for the most part humane. Some prisoners, however, primarily those whose notoriety had garnered repeated public attention, were treated with extra caution. When the dashing Kentucky Brigadier General John Hunt Morgan and an intrepid band of his cavalrymen conducted a foray into Ohio, the northernmost penetration by regular rebel forces during the war, they were taken on July 26, 1863 in the little town of Salineville. The foray brought to an end more than a year of Morgan's successful and devastating raids in Kentucky and Tennessee that had captivated the news media in both the North and South and provided no end of trouble for the Union military. Then in November, Morgan successfully carried out a daring escape from the Western Penitentiary near Pittsburg, Pennsylvania. Thus it was eventually decided to move his officers to the Columbus Penitentiary in Ohio, deemed a more secure location. When it was learned that the daring rebel was organizing another raid and possibly reprisals, Butler requested the Morgan men in hand in Ohio be transferred to Point Lookout, as a number of them had already been sent there as a security measure.[32] On March 18, 1864 one hundred and fifteen officers of "Morgan's Raiders" were placed in a "special train of cars" and dispatched to Point Lookout. One hundred and five arrived alive. Two days later one of the officers, a Captain L. M. Peyton, was shot dead by a Union sergeant named Edwin Young. After a formal trial, Young was acquitted. The Union press proceeded to justify the killing and as often the case got all of the details wrong. Though many inmates would be shot to death during the existence of Camp Hoffman, not a single charge of murder, besides the one mounted against Young, would ever be tried in a military court.[33]

Regardless of such dreadful events, by March 20 General Butler was able to inform Secretary Stanton that a full regiment of "repentant rebels whom a friend of mine called 'transfuges'" were recruited at Point Lookout. Most, he assured the Secretary, were "truly loyal, and I believe will make as efficient a regiment as those as in the service." He sought to organize and train such a unit for the spring campaigns as "one more regiment who will fight à l'outrance." All that was needed was the blessing of the War Department.[34]

Four days later Butler received the answer he had hoped. He was fully authorized to enlist and organize the regiment at Point Lookout to serve for three years or for the duration of the war. "The recruitment, musters, and organization must conform to the requirements of the mustering regulations of the Army. All appointments of officers will be made by the War Department, upon your recommendation. Arms and other supplies will be furnished by the proper supply department upon your requisition. " [35]

Butler assigned Major Charles Augustus Ropes Dimon, a native of Salem, Massachusetts, to handle the formal process of organizing regiments of rebel prisoners of war enlisting in the service of the United States.[36]

***

Not all inmates were willing to even consider amnesty, and some continued to contrive an escape, at the same time as their fellow prisoners were lining up for interviews. One bold attempt had apparently been weeks in preparation and was only discovered by guards at the eleventh hour, on February 14, during a surprise search of the camp. The inspection was draconian in the extreme, as the entire prison population was ordered to pack up and evacuate the camp under guard while the examination was underway. Private Charles Warren Hutt later remarked in his diary: "They [the guards] went into wholesale plunder." [37] Sergeant Bartlett Yancey Malone was more descriptive, noting that "they sirched and taken evry mans blanket that had more than one. And taken every little trick that the Rebels had. They found too [*sic* two] Boats that the Rebs had made." [38]

The discovery of the vessels was a surprise indeed. Several prisoners had somehow managed to procure or have smuggled in lumber with which they constructed two small boats. They had also somehow acquired a substantial stock of old guns, which were hidden in their quarters, probably by burial. The vessels had needed only some caulking to make them seaworthy enough to permit the planned flight of two score or more inmates.[39]

Word of the escape attempt was first carried to the Washington Navy Yard and then reported by the city press. "It appears," said the *Evening Star*, "that they had collected some 70 old muskets and a lot of stones, (a scarce article in that locality, and which must have been brought some distance,) which they probably designed using as weapons against any persons who should resist them." It was thought, however, that but a few prisoners were to attempt the escape unless more boats were to be built, as the two that had been found could carry less than fifty men.[40] Precisely how the lumber and muskets were acquired is unknown. The stones, which may have been smuggled into camp by wood cutting parties, were more likely to have been used as ballast than weapons. The consequences for the loss of goods confiscated during the search, especially blankets, was telling as it was so cold "a mans breath would freeze on his beard going from the Tent to the Cookhouse." For several days after the boat discovery heavy snow, laced with hail, brought considerable discomfort even to those with a blanket, and not a few men froze to death.[41]

General Butler arrived six days later, apparently without notice, to conduct another surprise inspection of the point. Perhaps it was the despicable conditions in the camp, amplified earlier by the Clark and Swalm reports, and once again by his own observations. Or perhaps it was the poor showing of captured goods, livestock, grains, prisoners and contrabands that had been gleaned from Marston's recent incursion into the Northern Neck. Whatever the cause, Marston's time as commander of the St. Mary's District was coming to an end: within a month, he

436

would be replaced in command. But prisoners would continue to die, even as smugglers would carry on their trade on the Potomac just a few miles away as always.

***

For General Hinks, who had finally assumed command at Camp Hoffman, the first order of business regarding his responsibilities was to attend to the distressing lack of hygiene in both the prison camp and military support facilities. Immediately after taking charge the general issued a series of new regulations for policing the point in an effort to improve sanitation conditions. Animal waste had become a problem that the general sought to control. Henceforth, no horses would "be picketed or permitted to be fastened in the wood" within 150 yards of the General Headquarters. The passage of all horses and other animals were to be limited to thoroughfares through the camp, which were to be delineated by the quartermaster. Moreover, the open spaces between the cottages used by the military and the rear of the General Headquarters building were to be thoroughly policed, and no teams of animals were to be permitted to pass thereon except by a passage near the woods. The rear of the cottages and all other buildings were to be "thoroughly cleaned of all litter and filth that has now accumulated, and refuse and offal will hereafter be thrown into barrels or boxes and daily removed." To improve sanitation conditions in the prison camp, mostly a problem of indiscriminately deposited human excrement, he ordered that all the trenches used as sinks, or primitive latrines, were to be filled and covered with clean gravel. "Proper sinks will be constructed over the water, at points to be indicated by the Inspecting Officer of this District, and no nuisance will be permitted elsewhere, either by day or night." [42] Other issues, however, were by then already taking precedence.

By early 1864 Commander Foxhall Parker seemed to be constantly upset by the divisions of command and authority regarding his jurisdictional control. Of great concern was a decision by the U.S. Treasury Department to permit the resumption of limited trade with supposedly neutralized sections of the Northern Neck. The Provost Marshal General of Maryland, James P. McPhail, disputed the order as nothing less than "the equivalent to raising the blockade." He was informed that arrangements had already been made to place a gunboat on the Great Wicomico in Northumberland County to superintend the disposition of trade goods. Uncertain that such actions were actually ongoing, on February 5 he wrote with some dismay to Parker to report of one such trading operation that was already underway. On Sunday, January 31 the schooner *Ann Hamilton* had departed Baltimore with a cargo, recorded at the customs house, consisting of groceries, dry goods, boots, shoes, hats, stationery and notions, valued at $8,000. One Samuel G. Miles, "a well known secesh merchant of this city," was the agent for the owners and would attend to the sales. McPhail was certain that these parties intended on bringing out tobacco, "which is known to be in large quantity in that section of country," though most of which had been sent over from Richmond to be forwarded at the first opportunity to Baltimore. As the Treasury Department's permits allowed only products produced in the Northern Neck, and the tobacco was not such, he recommended the schooner be seized as a prize. He also promised to keep the commander informed of any other vessels bound from Baltimore to the that same region.[43]

McPhail's recommendation for the seizure of *Ann Hamilton* had, in fact, come a day late. While proceeding south off Point Lookout the schooner was stopped on February 4 by the U.S. Revenue steamer *Hercules*. Captain Baker, the skipper of the steamer, acting on instructions from the Customs Collector of Baltimore, who also apparently had strong suspicions regarding the schooner, seized and detained her within sight of the Potomac Flotilla schooner *William Bacon*. As the vessel was taken within view of the flotilla blockader, Parker considered the capture as a joint prize. But warned by McPhail of her suspicious nature, he set out to investigate the incident before dispatching a request to Secretary Welles regarding the joint prize claim. He soon discovered that the schooner had sailed from Baltimore for the Great Wicomico, "having a pass to enter that river" from none other than Major General Butler and the Assistant Secretary of the Treasury. He was certain that as she carried such official documents that she would ultimately be released and returned to Baltimore rather than considered a prize of war. Knowing the region around the Great Wicomico to be in possession of rebel cavalry, he was at first stunned at the possibility of release. Upon close examination of the schooner's cargo, in addition to the items listed on the bill of lading, he also discovered fifty sacks of salt, four boxes of concentrated lye and $15,299.50 in Confederate currency that had not been listed. As such he was adamant that she must be considered a blockade runner, or at the very least a smuggler. Thus, before the vessel could be returned to Baltimore, he placed a prize crew aboard and sent her for adjudication to the district court at Washington. Unfortunately such events would become even more commonplace as the shading between areas considered pacified or neutralized became ever more indistinct.[44]

Compounding Parker's frustrations was rebel guerrilla activities on the Rappahannock. He was especially aggravated by the threat posed by enemy units, now estimated at between 800 and 1,000 men, ensconced on the narrow peninsula, which he later dubbed "a guerrilla haunt," separating the Rappahannock and Piankatank rivers. Lieutenant Commander Hooker, now in charge of the First Division of the Potomac Flotilla, strongly suspected the massing of that number of men in such a remote area suggested it was "related to a strong probability of disturbance" at Point Lookout, "and this may be something tending that way." No one, however, could be certain.[45]

By then, even more unsettling news was already on the way.

On February 9 Acting Master Schulze, commander of *Jacob Bell*, stationed off Blackistone Island, reported having received on board six refugees fleeing from Richmond, which was not a particularly unusual event. When questioned, what one of them had to report was something else, and it rapidly made its way up the chain of command.

The refugee in question was Joseph Leuty (or Lenty), an Englishman by birth and an iron moulder by trade, who had lived in the South for four years after emigrating from his homeland. For the last eight months he had been working in an artillery shop on Seventh Street in Richmond. What he had to say was indeed unnerving.

In the shop, Leuty reported, "they are now making a shell which looks exactly like a piece of coal, pieces of which were taken from a coal pile as patterns to imitate. I have made these shells myself. I believe these shells have power enough to burst any boiler. After they were thrown in a coal pile I could not tell the difference between them and coal myself." [46] The "coal torpedo," as it was called, was believed to have been placed in production in January, and its application was immediately obvious to all.

When Parker forwarded the intelligence to the Navy Department, it was not long before Rear Admiral Porter issued a general order and alarm regarding the new weapon. "The enemy have adopted new inventions to destroy human life and vessels," he wrote, "in the shape of torpedoes, and an article resembling coal, which is to be placed in our coal piles for the purpose of blowing the vessels up, or injuring them. Officers will have to be careful in overlooking coal barges. Guards will be placed over them at all times, and anyone found attempting to place any of these things amongst the coal will be shot on the spot." [47]

Parker did not have long to consider the consequences of rebel torpedoes. That would come soon enough. His next challenge would be to deal with a daring Confederate seaborne guerrilla raid at first, but incorrectly, believed to have been led by the redoubtable Colonel/Commander John Taylor Wood, CSN, with fifteen men who were proving to be a major thorn in the side of the U.S. Navy, especially in the Chesapeake Tidewater. The raiders had crossed the bay, captured and destroyed the Union telegraph station and surrounding warehouses at Cherrystone Point on Virginia's Eastern Shore, and surprised and seized two army steamers, *Aeolus* and *Titan*. On March 5 they recrossed the bay and escaped into the Piankatank before Yankee forces realized what had happened. The raiders simply disappeared without suffering capture or injury. Five of Parker's gunboats had, of course, set off in chase, and soon discovered *Titan* had been destroyed. Then, even more disturbing intelligence came in: a number of large boats were being prepared to conduct yet another foray from the Rappahannock. A reconnaissance of the river was immediately ordered, and on March 9, Commander Hooker reported, *Freeborn* and other vessels had penetrated the waterway as far up as a mile below the riverport of Urbanna and within sight of enemy pickets. No force of any consequence aside from twenty or thirty cavalrymen and a few infantry had been observed. It had been a humiliating episode for both the U.S. Army and Navy. General Butler requested Parker to keep a watch on the Rappahannock from ten miles below Urbanna to its mouth, which was promptly undertaken.[48]

It was now clear that the Northern Neck had not been neutralized after all.

Control of the Potomac and the shores opposite Southern Maryland was no longer simply a matter of intercepting and stopping supplies and men going south. Change of strategy was now an absolute necessity. On March 10, following his decisive victory at the Battle of Chattanooga, General Ulysses Simpson Grant was appointed commander in chief of the U.S. Army. He had already been busily planning for a major thrust against Richmond, as well as an offensive on all fronts of the war, including the "Breadbasket of the Confederacy," the Shenandoah Valley. It was to be a new policy of total war, dictating the destruction of not only the rebel armies but all agricultural and industrial resources.

Now diversionary activities, primarily plundering raids between the Potomac and Piankatank launched from Southern Maryland and elsewhere, would increase substantially as Grant's policy and advances began to take shape. Ironically, it was the bold Confederate partisan cavalry commander John Singleton Mosby who had early on defined the parameters of what the term "raid" actually entailed, and precisely what was expected of the raider. "A *raid*," he wrote, "is a predatory incursion, generally against the supplies and communications of an enemy. The object of a raid is to embarrass an enemy by striking a vulnerable point and destroying his subsistence."[49] He had become one of the most feared raiders in the Confederate cause. Yet the Union forays from Southern Maryland into the heartland of the Northern Neck and beyond would soon become as predatory as any in the rebel lexicon.

On March 17 a Federal expedition consisting of five transports, two U.S. Army gunboats and 4,000 men from Fort Monroe arrived on the Piankatank under General Charles K. Graham. However, it had departed by March 24 "without having derived any moral or material benefit," other than to temporarily worry the local Confederate command. Nevertheless, rebel usage of the inland waters from the Piankatank to the Potomac was now being largely impacted if not neutralized for the first time in the war.[50]

The flotilla had been growing in size, and the necessity for a more forward operating station on the Potomac than Plowden's Wharf was deemed necessary. Another coaling depot, better protected from the elements but providing a large, convenient anchorage, would soon be established a short distance up St. Inigoes Creek adjacent to stately Cross Manor, a Federal Period estate in the heart of St. Mary's County. The property was owned by Dr. Caleb M. Jones, a physician, local politician and one of the few Unionists in the region willing to rent a portion of his waterfront to the navy. The Jones manor house itself stood on a high bank overlooking the creek and river. About 100 yards to the northeast the bank sloped down to over an acre or more of flat, sandy land projecting into the creek, and adjacent to a substantial anchorage less than a mile from the little waterway's entrance into the St. Mary's River. The location was less than a dozen miles by water from Point Lookout, provided a copious refuge and mooring area for most of the Potomac Flotilla gunboat fleet, and was superbly situated as a forward naval coaling station.

Soon after the twenty-five dollar a month rental agreement was approved on March 28, 1864, as Jones's grandson John M. Ellicott recalled many years later, "a huge pair of timber wheels drawn by a team of oxen . . . brought, one by one, long, underslung pine logs and left them at the water's edge" on a low point of land well beyond the manor house. Here a sizeable wharf was soon erected. A boat landing jetty constructed from condemned cutters, whaleboats, and dinghies taken from the converted vessels of the fleet "laid like a barricade along the water's edge inside a wall of small piling and filled with sand to form a sort of small sea wall around the station." Within a short time a carpenter shop, blacksmith shop, powder magazine, coal bins, equipment store, telegraph office with connections direct to the Washington Navy Yard and Point Lookout, and other necessary structures had also been erected. Then came all descriptions of gunboats of the flotilla, most of which had been converted by the navy from shallow draft ferryboats, yachts, lighthouse tenders, sidewheeled steamers and tugs. One of the vessels assigned to a permanent mooring was the USS *Wyandank,* a former ferryboat, stripped of her boilers and engines, and anchored close to the shore in a cove up the creek to serve as a station ship. St. Inigoes Station thus quickly became the central downriver base from which most flotilla operations would be orchestrated for the remainder of the war, and from which coaling vessels such as the schooner *Mathew Vassar* and the steamer *Eureka* might sally forth to provide support as needed round-the-clock.[51]

For Jones's young grandson, the arrival of the U.S. Navy on his doorstep was a delight. He recalled:

"One day I accompanied my parents to an afternoon tea on board the *Don,* flag boat of Commander Foxhall A. Parker. As I recollect her she must have been a converted yacht, and I was fascinated by her spotless decks, her natty sailors, and her brass railings and guns, and by 'Commodore' Parker himself, who showed us around. Though only a commander, he was called commodore . . . because he commanded a flotilla . . . My delight was divided between the coming and goings of the gunboats, with their swanky uniformed officers, and the work going on in the buildings ashore . . . My greatest pal was the head blacksmith in charge of the blacksmith shop. His name was Thiers, and I spent hours watching him weld and shape the red hot iron, or listening to his stories during the noon hours. . . With the coming of the flotilla . . . the neighborhood teamed with officers and enlisted men, and social intercourse by ship's boats between home[s] near the water became frequent. A number of officers sought lodging for their families in the homes which could be so reached." [52]

By April the vessel force engaged in the blockade of the Potomac and Rappahannock had expanded almost exponentially in strength. It now began to dramatically impact the hitherto endless stream of blockade runners from Southern Maryland and irregular guerrilla activities in the Northern Neck and beyond. The force now numbered more than three times its original strength three years earlier, with Parker commanding a fleet of nineteen vessels, all armed and adapted for service in the shoals of the Tidewater. Numbers, however, were deceiving for at any given time as many as five ships of the fleet were ensconced at the Washington Navy Yard undergoing repairs for the incredibly hard duty demanded of them. Parker requested three more ships, which would bring his total force number up to twenty-two.[53]

The establishment of a coaling station and anchorage off the St. Mary's River had helped somewhat by permitting Union blockaders to stay at sea longer. But the navy's own ability to conduct operations ashore had been stymied owing to a lack of marines. It was Parker's belief that with a hundred U.S. Marines and a few field pieces, 'supported' by infantry in their rear, he could shut down the operations of what be believed were now only fifty to sixty enemy infantrymen and cavalrymen who seemed to reappear ghost like on the peninsulas between the Potomac, Rappahannock and Piankatank, and put an end to smuggling once and for all.[54]

***

Though Federal occupation, the blockade, and shortages of myriad goods and materials once commonly available before the war had drawn a pall over eveyday affairs in Southern Maryland, somehow life went on. Arrests had become commonplace as a region-wide black market, usually involving blockade runners, began to infect all manner of commerce and trade, frequently with sad consequences. In late 1863 one such incident was reported in the *Port Tobacco Times* when several arrests of citizens were made in the Nanjemoy District by government detectives on charges of selling goods to blockade runners. After being detailed to Washington for about a week, the arrestees were discharged for lack of evidence. Among those arrested were two merchants, Messrs. Wheeler and Rowe, whose store lay near the hamlet of Pisgah. "A military guard was placed at their store by the detective, which was replaced by another guard before the return of Messrs. W. & R. to their store. Upon going into the store the sum of $1,150 in money, and goods to the amount of $150, were missing, no part of which have been able to recover since." [55]

Somehow, commerce continued to go on. In Leonardtown, Scott & Nevitt's country store advertised its line of goods including "Cloths Caimers Vestings–Hats Caps–Ladies Goods of every variety and description. Dress Trimmings. Domestics. Notions Confectionaries–Cigars, and Smoking and Chewing Tobacco of choice quality. A large and complete assortment of Ready Made Clothing, in short every-thing except Groceries and Shoes, that is usually kept in a country Store." John and Theophilus Bray, continued to offer harness making and saddlery service and sold their products as always. Not far down the street J. Felix Morgan, carried on his dentistry practice. In April the town welcomed four new physicians, Doctors Richard P. Blackistone, Charles Massey Hammett, T. J. Stone and Charles Combs who had opened new practices therein. Youthful scholars could still apply to Miss Nannie F. Maddox to attend the White Hall Academy. Some competition was offered by Kate Camalier, who in February 1864 began advertising that she was taking on four new young ladies under her care in her "Select School for Young Ladies" to provide board and instruction in all the "usual branches taught in the best Female Academies – including French, Music, Drawing, Needle Work &c." [56]

A little over twenty-five miles southeast of Leonardtown, there was no such thing as normal at Point Lookout, only distress. Even the weather of early spring 1864, it seemed, had conspired to make the lives of the prisoners miserable. On April 5 Bartlett Yancey Malone recorded in his diary: "a very bad day it raind hard snowed and the wind blew the Bay was so high that it overflowed part of the Camp. Some men had to leave thir tents and move up to the Cook house." But it wasn't only the weather that was adding to everyone's distress; it was also some of the miscreants within the camp who had turned to preying upon their fellow soldiers, including Malone and his tentmates. "There was some men in camp," he recorded after the storm, "who had been going about of ni[gh]ts and cutting tents and sliping mens Knapsacks Hats Boots and Sumetimes, would get Some money They cut into ours and our money and cloathen all amounting to about one hundred dollars: One nite the Negros was on guard and caught them they was then plaised under gard and made ware a Barrel Shirt (and marched) up and down the Streets with large letters on them." On each barrel was written the words "Tent Cutters." There was no mention of how the general population treated the thieves upon their release.[57]

On the waters the military had finally permitted the veteran Weems Line steamer *Planter* to resume service. In January 1864 her published schedule called for her to leave Baltimore every Wednesday morning, calling at Fair Haven and Plum

Point and then proceeding to the Patuxent calling at the "usual Landings on the River" before arriving as Hills Landing, near Upper Marlboro. On Friday morning she would return downriver, making the usual stops. Her last call on the river was at Benedict, where she anchored overnight, and departed at 6 a.m. every Saturday morning for Baltimore. Passage to Fair Haven was one dollar, to Plum Point, a dollar fifty, and to Patuxent River a dollar fifty. Meals on board were extra.[58]

By the summer of 1864 the departure of so many men to join the Confederate Army, as well as many hundreds of slaves and black freemen being recruited into the Union Army, had caused an acute labor shortage for farmers throughout Southern Maryland. Many struggled simply to make ends meet. Typical of efforts to counter the crisis was a meeting of the farmers in St. Mary's County, convened in the Factory District on Saturday, June 18, "for the purpose of determining upon the wages to be given for hands during the tobacco harvest. They decided to give good cradlers $2.50 per day, and binders $1.50." The scarcity of labor in this section of the county, it was feared, would make bringing in and tending to the harvest extremely difficult for many families, and good hands were commanding higher wages than many farmers could pay. In some sections of the county it was said that good cradlers were being offered as much as an unheard of rate of three dollars and fifty cents per day.[59]

***

On or about Monday, April 11, 1864 the new commander of the St. Mary's District, General Edward W. Hinks, following in General Marston's footsteps, launched yet another raid into the Northern Neck of Virginia. This time it was against one of the major rebel smuggling centers, Lower Machodoc Creek "to break up blockading establishments." Three hundred men belonging to the newly arrived 36th Regiment, USCT under Colonel Alonzo Draper, sent up by General Butler from Fort Monroe, and fifty more U.S. Cavalry under Lieutenant Mix were embarked late on the evening of April 12 aboard the Army charter steamer *Long Branch*. From Commander Parker, Hinks was able to secure *Resolute*, *Teaser* and *Anacostia* of the Potomac Flotilla as covoy escorts, under the overall command of Lieutenant Commander Thomas H. Eastman of the USS *Yankee*. *Resolute*, with Eastman aboard as naval commander of the expedition, was to serve as flagship.[60]

At 5 a.m., April 13 the expeditionaries departed St. Mary's County and arrived at their destination three hours later. After communicating with General Hinks, Commander Eastman led the way into the anchorage on the creek to cover the infantry and cavalry landing. "Nothing was seen of the enemy," he later reported, "except a few cavalry, thirty or forty in number, on the right side of Machodoc, and they retired on the landing of four armed boats' crews from the *Teaser* and *Anacostia*, which vessels had joined me, according to orders." Unfortunately, *Long Branch*, which was towing two small boats carrying twelve soldiers, had come "unprovided with any means of landing," and Eastman was obliged to put the troops ashore, twenty at a time, in the flotilla's launches.[61]

Hinks effected his landing on the right bank of the creek. Had opposition been mounted, the operation might have ended in serious bloodshed, but none was encountered. Encouraged by his initial success, the general dispatched another boat expedition under Colonel Draper to search, presumably with cavalry, for contraband goods on the peninsula between the Lower Machodoc and Nomini Creek.[62]

Draper's search resulted in the seizure of 177 boxes of "superior Gravely tobacco, probably worth $40,000 U.S. currency," and the arrest of Joseph H. Maddox, who excitedly claimed to own the tobacco "and to be an emissary of the Federal Government." The claim, of course, was immediately repudiated when it was discovered that Maddox had been arrested once before as a blockade runner, along with his brother Tom and others, in September 1861 on Herring Creek in St. Mary's County. That he had been previously charged was perhaps not as surprising as how he had been released. Maddox freely claimed that "he paid Reverdy Johnson $1,000 to get him clear, which statement is confirmed by a declaration previously made by his brother, who resides in this [St. Mary's] county." [63]

The implication that a U.S. Senator from Southern Maryland had been bribed to secure the freedom of a secessionist blockade runner was disturbing in itself. The involvement of one so powerful and influential as Senator Johnson could only inject frustration as he was often hostile but pivotal to the implimentation of the Lincoln Administration's policies in Maryland, and was thus untouchable.

Nevertheless Maddox was sent as a prisoner to Point Lookout. Of the 177 boxes of tobacco captured, most were loaded aboard *Long Branch* for shipment to the Quartermaster's Department, with the exception of five boxes that Eastman placed aboard *Teaser* for his superior, Commander Parker, presumably as a gift. A subsequent reconnaissance of nearby Nomini and Currioman bays was undertaken but found nothing of importance.[64]

That evening Captain Lawrence, Hinks' assistant adjutant general, with 150 men of the 36th Regiment and Lieutenant Mix's troopers discovered the presence of a small body of approximately thirty rebel cavalry under one Captain John Murphy on the right bank of the Lower Machodoc, and immediately advanced to attack. The enemy under hot pursuit quickly fell back to a hill five or six miles from the landing site. Not deeming it profitable to be drawn too far from the creek and the flotilla's big guns, Hinks ordered the chase abandoned. During their march, however, they were fired upon from a barn belonging to the Honorable Willoughby Newton II, a representative in the Confederate legislature in Richmond and, with Edmund Ruffin, founder of the Virginia Agricultural Society. More sniping came from a house belonging to a rebel colonel named Laurence. Both buildings were burned to the ground. En route, the army had also taken up approximately fifty contraband blacks seeking freedom and the protection of Union arms.[65]

On the morning of April 14 Eastman detailed *Anacostia* to assist in transporting Hinks's force back to Point Lookout. The expedition had been without loss on either side, except for the capture of Maddox and his tobacco, the two burned buildings, and fifty liberated slaves. It had, in fact, served little more military purpose than perhaps a training exercise for more intrusive operations to come. For the Confederates, however, the first employment of black Union troops at Point Lookout and then on the Northern Neck posed some enigmatic questions. One observer of the Hinks raid suggested it might have some implications for the wider war, especially as forces under Grant prepared to move south, and other components of the Union Army were going to deploy even more black troops out of

Maryland. For many within the Confederate command, what the future held seemed anybody's guess.

As for Lieutenant Commander Eastman, the raid had indeed served as little more than a training mission. After sending *Anacostia* to Point Lookout with Hinks's men embarked, he took the opportunity on his way back to St. Mary's to conduct naval exercises with *Yankee, Teaser,* and *Fuchsia* "in forming line and column in accordance with the teachings of Parker's Squadron Tactics under Steam." Later he personally reported to Parker and stated, without hint of a sycophant's blush, "I was struck with the simplicity and ease with which a squadron may be maneuvered, and also am glad to be able to say that I have the honor to be the first officer of the U.S. Navy to record an experience in the use of the work . . . *Yankee, Fuchsia, Teaser, Resolute,* and *Anacostia* did all of their duties well and promptly, and especially with regard to the evolutions, the signals being answered quickly and not a single mistake being made." [66]

By 5 p.m., April 14, 1864 the last of the Potomac Flotilla squadron engaged in the raid on Lower Machodoc had returned unscathed.

The ease and lack of resistance which the raiders had encountered now tended to only whet Union appetites for more. In less than a month, a second incursion was mounted from the shores of Southern Maryland. This time the raid was justified by concerns regarding the deployment of the much feared "infernal machines" of the rebels, floating mines known as "torpedoes," in the blockaded river systems of the Rappahnnock and Piankatank.

And it came none too soon.

33

INFERNAL MACHINES
". . . a column of water sixty feet high."

Lieutenant Commander Charles A. Babcock, captain of the USS *Morse*, one of the many ferryboats purchased at New York and converted to warships, had been operating for months with substantial efficiency on the York River in Virginia. Among other attributes, he had acquired noteworthy experience in countering the machinations of the Confederate Torpedo Service, and appears to have done his best to keep tabs on the enemy's deployment of the "infernal machines" in the nearby theaters of war as well. In early May 1864 he learned of an effort by a party of rebels somewhere in the vicinity of Urbanna, Virginia, to place torpedoes in both the Rappahannock and Piankatank to blow up gunboats at rendezvous points employed by Union blockaders. Most notably, they intended to deploy torpedoes at Butler's Hole, an anchorage oft employed by Union warships within the immediate entrance to the Rappahannock, between Mosquito Point and Mill Creek. He immediately dispatched the intelligence to Commander Parker, which arrived on the afternoon of May 10. The disturbing news confirmed fears that the commander had held since early February when he received the first reports of Confederate coal torpedoes being manufactured in Richmond.[1]

Now Parker's own intelligence system had apparently provided him with just who might be involved in the scheme. "I think I know where the men who are engaged in this business live," he informed Gustavus Fox of the Navy Department the next day, "and if I can get army cooperation from Point Lookout will endeavor to capture them tonight." The foe, he had learned, was operating out of Mill Creek in Middlesex County, quite close to Butler's Hole. Yet since first learning of the rebels' expanding use of floating mines, he had begun preparing for just such threats by rigging "torpedo catchers" for all the vessels of the Potomac Flotilla, though most had yet to be outfitted. But a preemptive strike before the enemy might deploy the deadly mines at critical points was deemed far more expedient then the necessity of having to address countermeasures after the fact.[2]

That same afternoon Parker met with Lieutenant Hooker. He instructed him to proceed in *Yankee* to a point a little under five miles east of Tappahannock, and from "thence to communicate to me all the information he can procure about the torpedoes in the Rappahannock. [I] am quite sure he can get to Bowlers Rocks without injury."[3]

Hooker would have preferred to rely on U.S. Marines rather than colored troops and loudly made his opinions known. "The peninsula between the Rappahannock and Piankatank rivers is a guerrilla haunt," he reminded Assistant Secretary Fox, "which I would effectually break up had I 100 marines." His suggestion went nowhere. As he had none already assigned to him, and as the only such troops in the region were in Washington, approval for the deployment of marines had to come from the Navy Department. Fox quickly fired back a telegram: "Army cooperation must be obtained from Point Lookout at the discretion of the commanding officer there. No orders will be given at this time from the War Department. Marines from the barracks are clumsy, and would require several days to move them." [4]

Parker had little alternative but to request the assistance of Colonel Draper, who had in April replaced Hinks as commanding officer at Point Lookout. The colonel agreed but first had to secure approval from department headquarters. Upon receiving permission and instructions telegraphed from Fort Monroe, the colonel immediately mustered 300 infantrymen of the 36th Regiment, USCT, and fifteen cavalrymen, and resolved to personally take command of the land force. Without wasting a moment, he boarded the Army tug *Commodore Foote* and met with Lieutenant Commander Hooker as his flagship emerged from the new naval coaling station in St. Inigoes Creek. The colonel immediately informed him that he was ready to proceed on the raid proposed in the morning, and had already telegraphed Parker to that effect. "Believing that it would meet your approval," Hooker later informed his superior, "I at once proceeded to the wharf, and took on board troops" on the evening of May 11. Quickly and without incident the soldiers embarked aboard the transport steamer *Star* and the flotilla's First Division flagship *Yankee*, accompanied by a small squadron. Their primary mission: to destroy as many torpedoes as possible.[5]

Owing to the slowness of *Star*, the squadron failed to reach its destination as early as hoped. Not until 7 a.m., May 12, did the USS *Fuchsia*, now under the command of Acting Master William Tell Street, arrive off the entrance to Mill Creek, "near the torpedoes." Manning his small boats with sixteen seamen, Street rowed up along the edge of the creek to avoid possible enemy mines in the channel. He was closely followed by the troop laden *Star*. John Jay Jackson, *Fuchsia*'s pilot, who was well acquainted with the local waters and countryside, was selected to serve as guide for the whole expedition and would later be lauded for his "coolness and efficiency" in the promulgation of his mission. With care they succeeded in passing the farm of one R. C. Garland, where rebel pickets had been stationed to explode the electronic torpedoes on the Yankees' approach but had instead fled. Upon landing, the raiders immediately discovered conductor cables leading to two lines of torpedoes. Three more would later be discovered. Immediately afterwards Draper and his men, along with the ship's howitzer and twenty more sailors as support, were landed in safety. Garland was quickly apprehended and arrested. [6]

As soon as the troops were ashore, three torpedoes were exploded and two more raised. Apparently acting upon intelligence from Parker, Draper's force, including Street's detachment of seamen with the howitzer in tow, began a two-mile march inland to the home of one Henry Barrack, "an accomplice of the men who placed the torpedoes." It had previously been learned that at his estate no fewer than sixty rebel guerrillas or marines had recently been encamped, but had already disappeared.[7]

From the Barrack house the raiders divided forces and marched down two different roads leading towards Stingray Point, at the tip of the narrow peninsula formed by the Rappahannock and Piankatank. Street advanced with a detachment of 100 sailors and soldiers up the Saluda road to the Barrack gristmill in which was discovered a large quantity of corn and wheat. The gristmill, together with an adjoining sawmill and a quantity of lumber, were promptly put to the torch. With the remaining detachment of soldiers, Draper pressed ahead on a separate road to the farm of "the notorious" Dr. R. C. Taylor, near Fishing Creek, approximately three miles from the landing point. At Taylor's, a number of graineries containing 60,000 bushels of grain belonging to Bennett, Siff & Co. were also burned. "On throwing out pickets in the heavy woods, they discovered four torpedoes, two of them complete, also powder, tar, beeswax, lies, etc., for their manufacture." Within hours Street and his men had rendezvoused with Draper at the Taylor farm and rested.[8]

While the Yankee raiders were scouring the peninsula for any signs of the enemy and his torpedoes, Hooker's squadron was equally engaged. One boat from each ship of the squadron, *Yankee*, *Currituck*, and *Fuchisa*, under the command of Acting Master Lewis G. Cook, were dispatched to look for additional torpedoes. Several were discovered and exploded, "sending the water up in huge jets." Two more were recovered intact. The whole collection of units, each of which was deemed quite adequate to sink a ship, proved of great interest. "They were constructed of tin cases filled with powder, and were to have been exploded by percussion, a tarred string leading to the shore being arranged to set them off by. The amount of powder in them varied from thirty to sixty pounds." About noon the USS *Resolute* arrived with a launch, which was immediately dispatched to Cook. He was soon en route into the shallows of Mill Creek itself, wherein he discovered and destroyed thirty small boats and more grain. The raid, thus far unopposed, seemed as easy as plucking feathers from a dead chicken. But where was the enemy?[9]

***

Draper strongly suspected that some small armed parties of rebels, probably the same as had been engaged in deploying the torpedoes, had been effectively cut off and trapped between his own forces and Stingray Point, and resolved to take action against them. The advance began at 2 p.m., but had not proceeded more than two miles when a party of rebel cavalry was finally spotted ahead. Draper immediately extended a long line of skirmishers across the entire width of the peninsula between the Rappahannock and the Piankatank, a distance of approximately three miles, to block their escape. A reserve of infantry and cavalry, with the howitzer and sailors under Acting Ensign Joseph A. Havens, was left to guard the road. The maneuver was not without its difficulties. "The ground being covered in most places with thick woods and underbrush, and intersected with creeks and swamps, it was almost impossible to maintain an unbroken line." [10]

With each soldier approximately fifty feet from the next, methodically advancing in a rough line, the bluecoats cautiously pressed forward for another mile. Suddenly, five or six skirmishers on the right center of the line encountered a small cluster of rebels, believed to be marines and cavalry, concealed in a dense woods. Despite the fact that no officers were present, the men of the 36th attacked, though the numbers of their foe were still unknown. In an instant the forest resounded with a sustained exchange of gunfire. For the next twenty minutes the skirmishers were heavily engaged.

Bravery on both sides was much in evidence. An account of one Union soldier in particular stood out. David Berry, one of the wounded, had been shot through the bone of his right arm, which compelled him to drop his musket. In an instant, despite the pain, he picked up the gun with his left hand, followed the retreating rebels, and captured one and brought him in. Though Yankee numbers counted, the few rebels actually engaged fought hard against overwhelming odds. Then it was over and within short order it was reported that the entire rebel force was believed captured or killed. Acting Master Bennett G. Burley, CSN, noted as a "marine guerrilla," as well as a sergeant and corporal of cavalry were taken alive. Draper reported five rebels dead, including Acting Master John Maxwell, while Street noted ten killed and twenty captured at a cost of one soldier of the 36th killed, two seriously injured and another slightly. "The little affair was conducted wholly by the black men," it was later reported, "as no officers arrived until after the fight was over. The colored soldiers would have killed all the prisoners had they not been restrained by Sergeant Price, who is also colored." [11]

Both Burley, a Scotsman, and Maxwell were well known to Federal authorities as volunteers who had been engaged with Master John Yates Beall, CSN, a daring maritime guerrilla raider who had operated on the Virginia peninsula between Mobjack Bay and the Piankatank beginning in 1863. Documents found on Burley, including a letter of instructions from the Confederate Secretary of the Navy dated April 29, under which both officers acted, were incriminating indeed. "Gentlemen: Submarine telegraphic wire is much needed for the public service, and learning from your report the practicability of obtaining some from within the enemy's lines, you will proceed at once and endeavor to obtain it. You will exhibit this order confidentially when necessary to obtain assistance from our military authorities, and use every exertion to insure success. Yours, respectfully, S. R. Mallory, Secretary of the Navy." [12]

Another document addressed Burley's British protection and included a pass, authorized by the Confederate Secretary of War on March 30, 1864, to travel beyond the limits of the Confederate States. It appeared to Draper that the Scotsman was expected to act as a spy behind Union lines. It was also believed that he had been involved in the recent capture of the steamer *Titan* at Cherrystone, Virginia.[13]

Maxwell, formerly a U.S. Navy officer, was assumed dead, but was neither dead nor inoperative and somehow escaped. Only three months later, serving as a field agent for the Confederate Torpedo Sevice, he and a compatriot named R. K. Dillard would successfully penetrate Union lines to plant a clockwork torpedo containing twelve pounds of powder onboard a Federal transport at City Point, Virginia. The subsequent explosion set off a chain reaction that devastated the majority of the U.S. Army's storage facilities and even General Grant's headquarters. Both Maxwell and Dillard escaped.[14]

Though he could not have foreseen how much damage the escape of Maxwell would soon cause, Draper was delighted with the outcome of the skirmish. He immediately dispatched the papers found on Burley to Fort Monroe "to show the character and purpose of these parties."[15] At 5 p.m., after meeting no further resistance, the Federals arrived at Fishing Bay where they encamped for the night to await their transports.[16]

***

449

Having received word that the expedition was pushing forward toward the Piankatank, Lieutenant Hooker upped anchor in the Rappahannock and at 6 p.m. sailed for Fishing Bay, leaving behind the other vessels of the flotilla to take on fuel from a recently arrived coaling schooner. Within four hours he was nearing his destination and in communication with Draper's troops. He was quickly inform-ed of the raider's "brilliant success" and the capture of a quantity of powder and torpedoes.[17]

At daylight, May 13 the remainder of the squadron, including *Yankee*, *Fuchsia*, *Currituck* and *Jacob Bell* (having arrived during the night) had reached Fishing Bay. By 5:30 a.m. Draper's men were re-embarked aboard to begin the next stage of the raid. By 9 a.m. they were en route across the little embayment. Within the hour they had been landed on the south side of the Piankatank, and by 11:30 a.m. were en route toward the Matthews Court House, some three miles away The descent upon the county seat was again conducted without notable opposition. By 8 p.m. the raiders had returned to the landing site having destroyed "considerable property," captured a rebel sergeant and private, and brought off thirty-three head of cattle, twenty-two "serviceable" horses and mules and forage for the use of the newly established refugee farms on the Patuxent. "The object of the expedition being accomplished," Street reported, "we arrived at the landing at 7 p.m., but, being stormy and not being able to take onboard the horses and cattle, the force encamp-ed on shore for the night." [18]

At 4 a.m. the following morning, May 14, the tired expeditionaries began re-embarking for the short trip back to Point Lookout. By 11 a.m., delighted with their success, though against only negligible opposition, all were aboard. Draper's cavalry and black infantry and Street's naval contingent had thoroughly scoured the lower peninsula. Hooker's flotilla, with the boats from the *Yankee*, *Currituck*, and *Fuchsia*, had effectively swept the rivers and creeks for torpedoes. The main objective of the expedition, the capture of torpedoes, had been accomplished and several of the "infernal machines" were soon being dispatched aboard *Currituck* to Washington for study.[19]

Some of the captured torpedoes, however, were brought back to the St. Inigoes Naval Station for actual field testing. The examination was conducted by Lieutenant Commander Eastman and witnessed by many at the naval station and some of the residents of Cross Manor, incuding young John Ellicott. It was a dangerous operation personally handled in the creek by the commander himself.

"Having attached a sinking weight to the two handles, which are on the sides," Eastman later reported, "I pulled in a small boat into the channel, and then ran my line ashore, and after this was done I carefully rewired the tin cap and towed the torpedo in three fathoms. The boat was then pulled ashore, and the line pulled from about fifty yards back in the marshes, when, without any noise, a column of water sixty feet high and five feet in diameter was thrown up, and, covering the woods with sprays, fell, sending a circular wave, about one foot high, to the surrounding shores." [20]

The latest foray across the Potomac had been instructional. It mattered little that opposition had been negligible in a rural countryside that was by now both virtually defenseless and with few inhabitants. Yet it had demonstrably shown how the now notably improved working relationship between the U.S. Army and Navy could produce results. It would become an absolute necessity within the next few weeks and thereafter until the end of the war.

In the meantime, rebels from the Northern Neck were not long in extracting some retribution of sorts for the recent raid. On the night of May 19 a dozen Confederates led by John M. Goldsmith of Westmoreland County, a "known spy and trafficker in contraband," crossed the Potomac in a small boat and landed at Blackistone Island. There they destroyed the valuable lens and lamp of the lighthouse and escaped unopposed, taking with them fifteen to twenty-five gallons of oil belonging to the facility. The raiders had intended on carrying off Keeper Joseph L. McWilliams, but "through the entreaty of his family he was allowed to remain." Goldsmith had made several previous forays into Southern Maryland. The most recent attack had been to rob a store on the Maryland shore and then compel the owner to carry the plunder to Goldsmith's boat. Fortunately, the majestic brick lighthouse, built by John Donahoo in 1851, was unharmed, though the light had to now be maintained by a hand lamp. Word of the foray did not reach Commander Parker until May 21.[21]

In the few days following the raid into the Northern Neck, the flotilla had come under considerable stress to support now extensive Union Army operations not only on the Potomac, but on the James, and elsewhere. With navigational aids and stations once more threatened by rebel guerrillas from across the Northern Neck, Parker appealed to Colonel Draper to station a guard at Blackistone Island, at Piney Point, and onboard the lightship off Smith Point, at the mouth of the river. "I am of the opinion," said the man who only a short time earlier believed less than a hundred Confederates ranged on the Northern Neck, "that while there are so many rebel sympathizers in Maryland and on the eastern shore of Virginia none of the lighthouses there located are safe without a guard on shore to protect them." The colonel's protection would now be required at these sites, normally within the mission of the flotilla. But the fleet was already stretched to provide protection for Army transports operating on Aquia Creek, on the Rappahannock, and in convoying prisoners of war to Point Lookout and Fort Delaware from the battlefront on the James River.[22]

The stress, despite the flotilla's growth in numerical strength, was showing.

34

USE YOUR OWN JUDGMENT
". . . the rebels set up their customary yell . . .

By the winter of 1863, the problem of what to do with the many thousands of black refugees escaping to Union held territory or into the Northern states had posed a management and humanitarian crsis of hitherto unparalleled dimensions for government authorities. Ever since September 22 when President Lincoln released a preliminary announcement of his intent to issue the Emancipation Proclamation, the flight of slaves to freedom had increased almost exponentially by the day. The influx of escaped blacks, many relocated from combat zones by the military to so called contraband camps in safer locales, had at first swamped the government, which struggled to provide housing, clothing, food and medical assistance. A substantial camp had been erected at Point Lookout, replete with three large barracks buildings, adjacent to the military stables and a prison yard for Confederate officers. It was almost immediately filled and was soon overflowing. Those refugees who could, sought employment but fought to ward off sickness, sometimes starvation and death in the camps. Some had found menial jobs with the Union Army as laborers, teamsters, blacksmiths, carpenters, guides, and the like. Yet wages were minimal for those fortunate enough to find work, and there were continual disputes and clashes with officialdom. Both military and civil entities frequently viewed the refugees as lazy, profligate and unclean. Though critical assistance was rendered by Yankee missionaries and abolitionist support organizations, it never seemed enough.

One solution that gained prominence about this time, was to resettle refugees on government farms established on lands confiscated from property owners who had gone to fight for the Confederacy, such as large estates near Hampton and Norfolk, Virginia. In Maryland, however, only three major plantations, The Plains of Colonel John H. Sothoron, and the great Sand Gates and Cole's Creek agricultural tracts belonging to Joseph Forrest, were to be established, at first informally and then as recognized "government farms" for refugees. All were situated on the fertile banks of the Patuxent River in St. Mary's.

The move towards confiscation of the three plantations was not without support amidst Unionists, especially those New Englanders who had taken to heart the killing of Lieutenant White by the owner of The Plains. Indeed, a little under four months after the event, a petition from one O. S. Sterns and others of Newton, Massachusetts was submitted to the first session of the Thirty-Eighth Congress. The petition requested that the family of Lieutenant White be granted a portion of the estate that was already "liable to confiscation." Though it was reported that no fewer than 130 slaves had been removed from the property and sent to Norfolk to serve as laborers in the Union cause, the plantation itself was still intact and its lands left unworked and presumably deemed more useful in Federal hands than private ones.[1]

Joseph Forrest's case differed somewhat from Sothoron's, but his lands had also been vacated and were quite attractive. Before the war Forrest had been an active citizen and leader in St. Mary's County affairs and business. Having been among those who had signed on to William Cost Johnson's ill-fated development scheme, he had been an early lease holder at Point Lookout. He had also been one of five incorporators of the Clifton Manufacturing Company, Inc. along with Joseph Maddox, E. L. Spaulding, Thomas W. Gough, and Henry J. Carroll, all of whom would later be engaged in some form of service to the Confederacy. The company, which was offered up for sale on November 26, 1860, had proved a failure. It may have contributed to Forrest's financial difficulties soon afterwards.

The Sand Gates manor house, ca. 1894, by then referred to as Sandgate, was central to the great Sand Gates and Coles Creek estates belonging to Joseph Forrest and confiscated for use as refugee farms by the U.S. Government. Courtesy of Janet and William Brown, Pasadena, Md.

Forrest was not without military experience, having commanded the 4th Maryland Artillery, commonly called the "Chesapeake Battery," organized in 1861. When war broke out, he was appointed from his election district to serve on the notorious Leonardtown committee of April 23, 1861 to present resolutions authorizing county support and endorsement for the Confederacy. Like so many Southern Marylanders, he had fled to Virginia, abandoning his two large plantations. Sand Gates had been inherited from his father, the Register of Wills for St. Mary's County, and Cole's Creek had been the property of his wife, Henrietta Plowden, heiress to the considerable Fenwick estates. Combined, the properties contained 1,800 acres of the most arable land in the county. It has been surmised that although Forrest was a strong Southern sympathizer who may have had more substantial reasons for heading south: his property was heavily mortgaged to Benjamin G. Harris and others and several judgments had been entered against him. If he remained in St. Mary's and lost his few remaining slaves, he would become a penniless indigent. At the beginning of the war, he had crossed the Potomac accompanied by six slaves, and all of his livestock and farming equipment. Later he thought better of it and petitioned President Lincoln for a pardon for having "left a loyal district." The request was denied, and he joined the rebel army, serving as captain and recruiting officer for the Maryland Volunteers on the Northern Neck at Hague. He later moved to Louisiana and then to Texas where he continued in service to the Confederate Army.[2]

A group of "Contrabands." From an original stereograph. Prints and Photographs, Library of Congress, Washington, D.C.

The refugee population in Southern Maryland was exploding. From his headquarters in Baltimore Major General Lew Wallace, who had been appointed commander of the Middle Department and the VIII Army Corps on March 12, took a decidedly bold step to remedy the situation. In April 1864, he issued the following as General Order No. 33:

"Many citizens of this Department have gone voluntarily into the States in Rebellion against the United States, some to join the rebel army, and others to aid and encourage the rebellion by their presence and otherwise, who have left property in real estate, slaves, stocks of various description and other securities for money in this Department. And many citizens of the States in rebellion, who have participated in and encouraged that movement, have similar property within this Department. It is deemed important that such property should not be under the control of such persons, and liable to be used in whole or in part in the support of the rebellion, and against the interests of the United States. It is therefore hereby ordered that the proceed of all real estate, the hire of all slaves, the interest of all debts due from persons in this Department, the current interest on all private debts, the dividends and interest on all Stocks and Bonds of railroad Companies, and public corporations however declared and payable, which are the property of the persons above described, and are within this Department, shall be withheld by the persons authorized, and whose duty it is to pay over the same from such persons their representatives, agents and attorneys, howsoever confiscated; and that the sums shall be paid to Lieutenant Colonel Alexander Bliss, Quartermaster of this Department, or such other agent as the General Commanding may authorize and appoint from time to time. All persons having authority over such property will be held responsible for such sums as may be paid in violation of this order, and be otherwise punished by Military Commission.

The hire and proceed of the labor of such slaves as are in the counties of Maryland in this Department and belong to the persons above described, will in due proportion be set apart and reserved for the usage of such slaves, when they shall have been freed by the Constitutional Law of Maryland, as it is hoped they soon will be.

By command of Major General Wallace
SAMUEL BY. LAWRENCE
Assistant Adjutant General,
JAMES R. ROSS, A.D.C" [3]

In early May 1864 the estates of Joseph Forrest and John Sothoron were taken possession of by Major H. George Weymouth, Provost Martial of Point Lookout. The Plains, Sand Gates and Cole's Creek were very soon afterwards occupied by hundreds of black refugees desperately seeking to eek out an existence in a hostile countryside seething with anger. Keeping the establishments supplied and in working order would become a Herculean task, not only for those dwelling within, but for the Union Army charged with providing the tools and other necessities for the farms themselves. To do so, it was soon clear that the army need only look across the Potomac to the fertile farmlands of the lightly defended Northern Neck of Virginia.

***

On June 11, under the command of Colonel Draper, the third major raid against the Northern Neck set out from St. Mary's County. This time the mission objectives were not simply to destroy Confederate facilities and the region's ability to provision rebel troops. Unlike earlier forays, the objective was clearly defined: to proceed to Pope's Creek, Virginia, near the birthplace of George Washington, "for the purpose of procuring horses for the quartermaster's department, and farming implements, transportation, &c., for the contraband settlement on the Patuxent River." [4]

Four charter steamers, *Charleston*, *Favorite*, *Georgia*, and *Long Branch*, were to be employed by the Army to transport 475 men of the 36th Regiment stationed at

Point Lookout, and forty-nine troopers of the 2nd and 5th U.S. Cavalry, under the command of First Lieutenant Jeremiah C. Denny.[5]

Captain William H. Smith was to have command of the naval forces afloat on the Potomac, then assembling in the St. Mary's River. Acting Master Street, who was by now intimately familiar with the countryside of the Northern Neck, was given command of the naval landing party. He was specifically assigned to work with Colonel Draper, with whom he was ordered to cooperate "as your combined judgment dictates." On June 1 he was given instructions to be ready to move by sundown with the following ships and men, including one officer on each: *Fuchsia*, twenty men; *Anacostia*, thirty men; *Commodore Read*, twenty men; and *Sophronia*, thirty men. All were to have three days of cooked rations and fifty rounds of ammunition, and to be equipped for shore duty.[6]

Commander Hooker allowed Street wide latitude in his mission: "Use your judgment; burn grain and other things you think proper; take boats, etc., nets, seines, etc. I see lots of canoes below us. I think we had better clean them out. Be as expeditious as possible. [The] darkies, bring off, etc. You know what to do. Again, use your own judgment." [7]

As the troops boarded the transports at Point Lookout and then set off to rendezvous with the flotilla gunboats in the St. Mary's River, the inmates at Point Lookout took little note of the move. Indeed, the only event of significance reported in the journals of several prisoners was the arrival of between 500 and 900 more Confederates captured on the James. Not until June 12, when the raid was well underway, did word of the expedition even begin to circulate in the camp.[8]

As in every such undertaking unexpected events sometimes got in the way. When the four transports touched at the St. Mary's River to rendezvous with their escorts, the USS *Resolute*, which was not intended for the operation, accidentally collided with the steamer *Long Branch*, rendering it necessary to send her in for repairs. The troops onboard were transferred to *Georgia* and the expeditionaries, now totaling 628 men strong, finally set off.[9]

On the morning of June 12 the Union raiders put ashore unopposed at Pope's Creek in Westmoreland County, Virginia (not to be confused with Pope's Creek, Charles County, Maryland). As the troops and sailors were landing Hooker arrived and boarded *Commodore Read* to join the expedition. Once on shore the force was divided into two detachments, 500 infantrymen and fifty cavalrymen under Colonel Draper's command, and 100 sailors under Acting Master Street. Of these, three hundred of the 36th (Street reported 150 soldiers and twelve cavalry) under the command of Captain James P. Hart, were to march by a northerly course to Smith's Wharf on the Rappahannock and then on to the town of Warsaw.[10]

A second column consisting of Draper's remaining men and Street's sailors took the main road to Northumberland Court House in the town of Montross. From this column, Draper detached seventy-five men to canvas the road to Currioman on his left flank, and then to meet with the column at Montross. The column was then to press on to Warsaw to rendezvous with Hart's force on June 13. Detachments from both columns were to be thrown off at every crossroads leading to Warsaw "to collect horses and cattle and to drive all scattering parties of the enemy toward Wind Mill Point, where we hoped to meet and destroy them." At 11 a.m. the invaders departed on their independent lines of march.[11]

The infantry's trek through the countryside of the Northern Neck, preceded by a screen of cavalry, was without armed opposition as they conducted their raids on plantations, farmsteads and private homes. One of the most noted sufferers was Willoughby Newton whose Linden estate near Hague was particularly hard hit. When the raiders arrived, he lost "his farming implements, the negroes saying they would have farms in Maryland and would need them. They said when they came again they would take everything Mr. Newton had; that they had orders to come every week for a month or two, so as to get all the growing crop of wheat, &c. among other great sufferers was Mr. Brown, near the Hague. Everything but his home was destroyed . . . Mr. Ben English, after having everything destroyed, was stripped, tied up and given thirty-nine lashes with the cowhide." [12]

It was later reported in Richmond that among other persons who were the "object of particular spite" was Major Richard L. T. Beale. His family was abused, his corn, bacon and other provisions carried off, and his personal estate torn apart.[13]

Nothing, however, incited the wrath of white manhood on the Northern Neck more than the later charges of atrocities committed against their women by the black troops of the 36th Regiment. In a recounting of the purported events, presumably by an eyewitness of the Draper raid, published in the *Richmond Enquirer*, it was said to be "more horrible but only too true." It was stated, "twenty-five or thirty ladies were violated by this party of negroes." The narrator deemed it best not to give names of the victims, but declared that both black and white women were not "spared by these demons, who were encouraged by their white officers. It is surely not time to raise the black flag." Later in the report is was further stated: "On the route six negroes violated the person of Mrs. G eleven different times, she being the wife of a brave soldier of the Ninth Virginia cavalry, being also sick at the time, with an infant six weeks old at her breast. This is only one instance out of twenty others of a like outrage." There were heroines. A brave "Mrs. Dr. Belfield whipped five negroes from her room, thus heroically defending herself." But the Yankees were reported to be unrelenting, plundering "everybody of every thing in their line of march." [14] It is of note that the supposed atrocities against the women of the Northern Neck was never again mentioned, nor did they appear in any documentation, Union or Confederate, regarding the raid. But the propagandistic value of alleging black savagery and the rape of white womanhood, a formuatic racist trope common to the slave states before, during and after the war, was not lost on the populace.

In the meantime, about four miles from Montross, Street dispatched a small detachment to Nomini Bay to communicate with Captain Smith to inform him that a rendezvous would be made with the vessels of his squadron at Lower Machodoc Creek. There all the horses, cattle, farming implements and other materials captured thus far would be taken off. Accompanied by fifty sailors and cavalrymen, Street would proceed to the point while Draper marched on to Warsaw.

Street assigned acting Ensign Thomas Nelson and the other fifty sailors to continue with Draper on the understanding that both parties would rejoin the main force the following day after the war prizes had been loaded aboard the ships. At

457

9:30 p.m. Street's men reached Lower Machodoc, embarked their captured livestock and farm gear aboard, and encamped for the night.[15]

As Draper's cavalry screen approached their first destination and three of the advanced guard entered Montross, they were fired upon. The attackers were believed to belong to a rebel unit under John M. Goldsmith, who had recently conducted the raid on the Blackistone Island Lighthouse. Apparently aware that the cavalrymen were the advance of a larger force, the rebels judiciously "took to the woods and made good their escape." [16]

While establishing camp at Montross, Draper dispatched a company to hold the main crossroads at Durrettsville, nine miles above Warsaw. That evening, accompanied by a cavalry escort, he set off on a short ride southward to the banks of the Rappahannock opposite the town of Tappahannock. There he communicated with the blockading gunboats *Thomas Freeborn* and *Jacob Bell*.[17]

From the officers of the two warships Draper was delighted to learn that horses were to be found in abundance at Occupacia Creek and Layton's Wharf on the south side of the Rappahannock above Tappahannock. "Finding horses scarce and poor on the Northern Neck, between the Potomac and Rappahannock," he later reported, "I resolved to transfer the field of operations to the south bank" of the river.[18]

Accordingly that night, after instructing his men to march the next day to Durrettsville, Draper personally made the hard ride back to Machodoc Creek with a small body of cavalry. He informed Hooker of his intentions and requested that he convoy the transports around to Union Wharf on the Rappahannock. Arriving on the morning of the June 14, he met with Hooker and Street to present his plan. "This proposition met with the approval of Captain Hooker and myself," Street recorded, "from the fact that we could join him in a much shorter time than by marching across the land." Not all of the vessels could participate, as *Commodore Read* was short of coal and would have to return to base.[19]

The transports, already loaded with captured property, were immediately dispatched to offload at Point Lookout, return to the Rappahannock and then press upstream to Union Wharf. The booty rounded up was considerable: 150 head of cattle, thirty-three horses, twenty sheep, a large quantity of farming implements, fifty contrabands, and eight prisoners.[20]

Following the meeting with Hooker and Street, Draper returned to Durrettsville where he found the bulk of his troops concentrated. The following morning, June 15, they set off for Union Wharf where they were soon joined by the gunboats and transports. Unfortunately, they discovered the wharf in total ruins after Confederates had burned it to deny usage by the Federals.[21]

***

Though rebel forces were never far from the marauding Yankees, their negligible opposition had made some Union soldiers careless. Invalid and local home guard units had not been slow to form as Draper's troops passed. It was soon being dramatically reported in the Confederate capital that "the men of Richmond county, in their rear, had become aroused, and the cry of vengeance from ruined women and desolated hearthstones arose to the very heavens. Old men and boys, and even deserters and conscripts, with such arms as they could collect, with a few disabled soldiers who were at home, with Col. Brockenbrough at their head, marched down towards Union wharf, determined on revenge." [22]

Brockenbrough's small force was soon joined by another under the command of Lieutenant Colonel Meriwether Lewis of the 9th Virginia Cavalry. Lewis, who had been at his home in Lancaster on furlough, had gathered "such men as he could hastily collect." Most were old men and boys as well as a few of the Lancaster Cavalry who happened to be in the county, not more than thirty men in all. They assembled, armed with shotguns and whatever else was at hand, at a crossroads near the farms of the Pearson and Rockwell families, where "Colonels Brockenbrough and Lewis having made a skillful disposition of their small and badly armed commands, quietly awaited the charge of the enemy." When they arrived, the Richmond press later reported, they "found the infernal negroes at their devilish work, utterly destroying everything belonging to Messrs. Pearson & Rockwell, tying Mr. Rockwell up and cowhiding him." [23]

On the morning of June 16, while Draper's men began work on rebuilding the wharf, for unknown reasons three men were permitted by their commanding officer, "to leave the battalion and go to a house about a mile distant." The action was in direct violation of Colonel Draper's orders that no one be allowed to leave the column. Only one man returned to camp, reporting that rebel cavalry had killed one of his companions outright while the other had managed to crawl off into the woods, never to be heard from again.[24]

That afternoon gunfire was heard nearby. Draper and forty cavalrymen immediately set off to investigate. Emerging from the forest near Pearson's Farm about a mile from the wharf, they perceived a body of rebel cavalry a mile ahead of them at a fork in the road leading to the landing. The colonel dispatched three men ahead as a forward guard and then ordered a general advance. Soon the pickets returned and reported sighting the presence of 200 enemy cavalry approaching in a column, though subsequent information showed the force to be much smaller.[25]

"At a suitable distance" from the rebels Draper ordered a charge at the same moment the enemy opened fire. Personally leading the assault accompanied by his assistant adjutant general and a few faithful orderlies, the colonel was soon within sixty yards of the foe when he turned and saw his troopers, who had first set out in platoons at a double quick pace with guns leveled, lagging behind. "Close up," he shouted, whereupon the rebels set up their customary yell. The frightful noise, punctuated by the firing of shotguns, which could do no damage as they were out of range, did the trick. In an instant, Draper later reported, "my escort turned their horses' heads to the rear and ran for their lives." Within seconds the rebels were in hot pursuit.[26]

"I tried in vain to rally my men," the Yankee colonel noted in utter humiliation, "calling upon them a dozen times to halt and face the enemy. In this attempt I was seconded by Captain [Peleg H.] Gibbs, of the 4th Rhode Island Volunteers, my acting assistant adjutant general, and by a few men among the cavalry who repeated my orders to halt. I remained on the ground until my orderly and one other man had been captured by my side, and another dismounted man had had time to run to the rear, get over the fence, and escape." [27]

Draper had little choice but to join the flight into the woods where the enemy horsemen might not pursue. Colonel Lewis nevertheless ordered his cavalry to charge "which they did in most gallant style, killing four negroes and several others, and capturing two of the cavalry with their horses and equipments." Fortunately for the Federals, who had actually suffered no casualties, the rebels gave up the chase after only 200 to 300 yards before turning back, possibly believing they were being drawn into an ambush.[28]

From the edge of the woods Draper immediately sent back orders to his main body at the wharf for reinforcements. Under the command of Captain Joseph Hatlinger, whom Draper described as an inefficient officer, the reinforcements were tediously slow in coming up. But when they arrived the colonel posted half of the men at the edge of the forest. After dismounting his cavalry he took seventy-five troopers through the skirt of the wood hoping to get to the rear of the rebels "and cancel the account."

"From my base of operations at the point where the road from Union Wharf emerges from the woods," Draper reported, "I could see, as I thought, a complete circuit of woods, by which I could keep constantly under cover while marching to the enemy's rear. I found upon trial that the open plain made numerous bays into the woods, increasing the circuit to about seven miles of close thorny underbrush." [29]

Slowly, cautiously, the Federals pushed on, always hidden behind the edge of the forest. By dark they had moved to within 600 or 700 yards of the enemy's main camp, just as the rebels were lighting campfires and preparing to bivouac for the night. Suddenly, a percussion cap accidentally exploded amidst the advancing soldiers. In an instant the rebel camp was alive and in motion as its residents raced into the darkness, though not without some sharp skirmishing. Draper and his men soon emerged from the shadows in the rear of the campfires to find the site completely deserted. Eager to avenge the humiliating rout earlier in the day, he ordered pursuit, but after a fruitless mile-long chase in the dark, wisely returned to his main base at Union Wharf.[30]

Even as Draper had been engaged in jousting with the rebels, Hooker in *Commodore Read*, which had just returned, was en route up the Rappahannock with the transports. Arriving at Union Wharf about noon, unaware of the skirmishing going on in the countryside, he immediately began embarking Street's sailors onboard. He would not communicate with the shore again until the following morning.[31]

***

Colonel Draper was resolved "to wipe out the disgrace which the cavalry had brought upon the expedition" and moved to make one more attempt against the enemy on the morning of June 17. Leaving 300 men to load the transports, at 7 a.m. he marched with 200 men of the 36th Regiment and thirty-six cavalrymen to a point about 1,000 yards from the rebel position of the night before. Here he again found the enemy, this time in a force consisting of 150 men of the 9th Virginia Cavalry, and 450 infantry, mostly home guardsmen, the whole being under the command of Lieutenant Colonel Lewis.[32]

Within but a short time the Federals had arrived at the same fork where they had encountered the enemy the day before. Draper quickly posted his cavalry at the bend in the road, with fifty infantrymen concealed in the woods behind them "in such a position as to rake the road in case the cavalry should be repulsed." He instructed the infantry sergeant to charge whenever the bugler sounded the order. With the remaining 150 infantrymen he began to move quietly through the woods to a position within 500 yards of the rebel position. At the edge of the clearing with a ditch directly in front he formed a line of battle and posted twenty men in his rear as a reserve.[33]

At first unaware of the Federals' presence, the rebels had been working "like ants" to complete a wooden barricade across the road behind which their dismounted cavalry stood facing the Union horsemen. For tense minutes both sides prepared for a clash. The Confederates reserved their fire, "evidently expecting a combined charge from our infantry and cavalry, and intending to open upon us at short range." [34]

Moving about his men, Draper ordered them to fix their gunsights for 500 yards and directed the company commanders to pass along the line and see that every sight was properly raised. "Aim steadily," he instructed, "and fire at the bottom of the fence," behind which the rebels were ensconced.[35]

Riding out of the woods by the right flank of the battalion, he could better observe the effect of his men's first rounds. He then ordered the firing commenced by rank. A portion of his firepower, however, was reserved until he could determine the strength and intentions of the enemy, and ascertain whether he had any flanking force in the woods where his own men lay.[36]

"Our first volley had a marked effect," Draper reported afterwards, "evidently taking the enemy by surprise, as he expected a charge. At the first fire several of the enemy were seen to fall, and heard to scream. They immediately returned our fire, apparently every man for himself. We poured in our volleys in rapid succession, and soon threw the rebels into great confusion; at every discharge crowds of them took to the woods in their rear, and their officers could be distinctly heard shouting frantically for them to 'come out of the woods,' and cursing them for their cowardice."

Sensing the moment for a charge was at hand, Draper dispatched a mounted officer to show the cavalry where they could pass through the fence, and thus avoid the enemy's stockade in their attack. A sergeant, undoubtedly recalling the earlier debacle, sought the colonel's assurance that they would have infantry support on the flank. He need not have worried, for about the fifth volley from the line, the enemy disappeared. Draper immediately ordered another volley fired and sounded the charge for the cavalry, at the same time moving the infantry forward into the open field and forming an assaulting and supporting line. The cavalry advanced at a slow trot, and afterward at a walk, the infantry being obliged to halt for them to come up. The whole force then converged upon the rebel position en masse, which was found entirely abandoned.[37]

The Pearson's Farm skirmish was all over by 1 p.m. Draper quickly sent forward some cavalry to reconnoiter, but the rebels had vanished. It was soon reported that they were rallying and fortifying at nearby Farham Church. Several pools of blood were discovered at the fork, but all of the enemy dead and wounded had been carried off. First reports were that two had been killed, but a black woman reported that she saw four corpses, besides another covered up in a wagon, and that the "chief captain" had been wounded. The affair at Pearson's Farm had cost the Federals nary a scratch, "the rebels firing too high," with their shots in most cases passing over the head of Yankee cavalrymen. The Richmond press reporting on the affair sometime later erroneously claimed that Draper and four or five of his cavalrymen had been mortally wounded at the first meeting on June 16 and that rebel losses included only four wounded, two seriously, but none killed.[38]

After giving nine rousing cheers while standing on ground recently occupied by the rebels, the cavalry was recalled. With the infantry they marched back to Union Wharf where they assisted in embarking more captured property from the surrounding countryside.[39]

Draper had only praise for his black infantrymen. "The gallantry of the colored troops on this occasion could not be excelled. They were as steady under fire and as accurate in their movements as if they were on drill."[40]

The rebels had other ideas.

A little after dusk, about 6 p.m., as the bluecoats were still in the process of embarking, a long cloud of dust announced that the enemy, having reorganized, was on a road skirting the edge of the woods three-quarters of a mile from Union Wharf, presumably preparing for a night attack. The colonel immediately recalled those troops that had boarded ships and prepared for defense. Oddly, the rebels then remained stationary for some time, disappeared and then reappeared, as if their objectives were indeterminate. Again the Federals resumed embarking even as Draper informed Hooker of the direction in which the enemy had been observed. Within minutes *Commodore Read* prepared to fire her great 100-pounder Parrott and 9-inch Dahlgrens.[41]

"I at once opened upon them from this ship," Hooker later stated, "and soon the cloud of dust moving along the road showed that they had been dislodged. Guided by the dust I continued shelling them until they were out of range. As soon as it was dark we commenced embarking the troops, and nearly accomplished it when the enemy's cavalry made a dash at the wharf, but my crew being still at quarters, they were promptly met by a broadside from this ship and skedaddled in confusion."[42]

Embarkation was completed without further molestation. Two transports laden with cattle and other captured property, as well as four prisoners of war, were again dispatched to Point Lookout to unload, with orders for them to return as soon as practical. *Jacob Bell*, now low on coal, was ordered back to base to refuel and then to return as quickly as possible.[43]

Immediate departure for Draper and his main force was another matter. Soon after the transports were out of sight, word arrived that two rebel regiments, the 59th Virginia Infantry, numbering 680 men, and the 7th Virginia Cavalry, numbering 440, were in the area. They had reportedly crossed the Rappahannock the night before, three miles above Layton's Wharf opposite the village of Leedstown, and above the town of Tappahannock. Their mission, he observed, was "for the purpose of helping to chastise our party." He quickly resolved to meet the enemy again. As evening approached, Hooker's flotilla, with Draper's raiders onboard, was under full steam bound for Layton's Wharf. Acting Master Street, "from his intimate knowledge of the country" would serve as a guide. One vessel was left behind to guard the channel at Bowlers Rocks.[44]

***

The operation was growing in scope far beyond what had originally been planned. Union intelligence sources indicated that the Confederate force was divided, with as many as 500 of the rebel troops still on the south shore of the Rappahannock near or at Occupacia Creek, a few miles below Layton's. Draper's plan was to land at the wharf at daylight on June 18. "By this move," Hooker informed Commander Parker, "we hope to surprise and rout those on the south side of the river, and thus throwing those on the upper side off their guard, to be enabled to come back and whip them too." [45]

Since the army lacked field artillery to support a more intense operation than originally anticipated, Hooker proposed that the navy send several howitzers and 100 seamen "to help us along." Draper thought the big guns would impede his movements but accepted the services of the seamen. For his own part, having penetrated deep into enemy territory by water, Hooker dispatched a request to Parker for an additional gunboat or two be sent from St. Mary's to keep the waterway open in his rear.[46]

The landing at Layton's Wharf was unopposed. Draper quickly dispatched the cavalry three miles out along the Layton road, while he marched with the infantry to a hamlet called Lloyd's, seven or eight miles from his disembarkation point. Four miles from Layton's he came upon a large grist mill belonging to Robert M. T. Hunter. It had been turning out flour for the rebel army since the beginning of the war. The mill was soon left in ashes.[47]

Here Draper learned much to his surprise and delight that his weren't the only Federal troops in the area. But to his dismay he was also informed that a far larger enemy force than he had anticipated was also not far off.

"In this section," he noted in his final report of the operation, "we found an abundance of fine horses, mules, and beef cattle. At Lloyd's we received information from so many different sources that we were forced to believe it reliable, that General [Philip] Sheridan, after passing up the country on a raid with 8,000 men, had the night before passed through Newtown and crossed the Mattapony [River] at Dunkirk bridge, and that [Wade] Hampton's cavalry division was in full pursuit. Our informant stated that Hampton's pickets were within five miles of Lloyd's." [48]

Moreover, throughout the day, small parties of rebel cavalry were discovered watching Draper's every move. Not wishing to be suddenly surprised by a vastly superior force, he thus deemed it prudent to return to Layton's Wharf that evening and load the captured livestock aboard the flotilla. By 5 p.m. everything was afloat. By 4 a.m. June 19 the squadron was underway, and three hours later arrived off Tappahannock.[49]

Draper's troops were to begin a march overland to the same destination. Nothing went as planned, for the rebels were closer than anyone had anticipated. At Layton's Wharf the colonel posted infantry in line, and sent the cavalry out six miles on each road leading from the hamlet to collect horses and give notice of the approach of any large force of rebel troops before departure. It was soon discovered, however, that a strong body of hostiles lay between Layton's and Tappahannock. The army was again forced to travel by water.

***

Upon learning of the proceedings of the previous several days in Virginia, Commander Parker, from aboard his flagship *Ella* in the St. Mary's River and far from the scene of action, was entirely displeased with the navy's role in the operation. He was especially dismayed with the deployment of Street and his force of sailors ashore with Draper's infantry and cavalry and immediately dispatched new orders indicating his displeasure to Hooker:

> "This force Colonel Draper thought it proper to divide, sending a portion of it across the country from the Potomac to the Rappahannock, and advising that 'the rest be sent around by water,' by which division the naval commander whom I had selected was left on board the *Commodore Read*, while an officer [Street] in whom I had just expressed a want of confidence remained in command of the shore party. I can not now permit either seamen or howitzers to be landed on either bank of the Rappahannock, to engage in enterprises of which I know not the nature. You will therefore, immediately upon the receipt of this, notify Colonel Draper that you are ready with the gunboats under your command to render him all the assistance possible from the river, but that the land force must consist of soldiers alone. He can certainly get reinforcements from Point Lookout should he need them, as I have three gunboats stationed there at this time." [50]

But it was already too late. On the morning of June 19 the expedition was preparing to land at Tappahannock to resume "our labor" without, it was hoped, opposition. While lying off the town Hooker was soon joined by *Jacob Bell* and *Fuchsia*, which carried Commander Parker's letter. Two of the transports, being filled with cattle, horses, and other plunder from the countryside, were again sent to Point Lookout to unload. *Fuchsia* was dispatched to Bowler's Rocks. At the same time, Hooker sought to provide maximum naval artillery coverage for the forces ashore by placing *Jacob Bell* below the town, *Thomas Freeborn* above it, and his own *Commodore Read* directly in front.[51]

Having as yet to open Parker's instructions, or perhaps simply ignoring his order prohibiting the deployment of sailors ashore or providing mobile artillery support for the army, Hooker quickly assembled an impromptu fieldpiece. This was accomplished by simply lashing a boat carriage upon the axletree of a cart and mounting one of his own howitzers upon it. Twenty seamen were soon landed with the gun. Once ashore, it was learned that two regiments of rebel infantry foraging about had crossed the river the day before and marched to Union Wharf, arriving there about the same time as the Federals had departed.[52]

Finding the country above Tappahannock apparently devoid of an enemy presence, at least temporarily, the bluecoats at once went to work embarking all the cattle "which could be got near here at this wharf." Refugee slaves, not surprisingly, were now coming in by the hundreds, even as another rebel force began to assemble undetected nearby. They would soon make their presence known, obliging the Federal occupation of Tappahannock to be very short lived.[53]

464

Later in the afternoon of June 19 Draper's scouts were unexpectedly assailed and driven in as sharp picket line firing echoed through the surrounding countryside. At the same time a cloud of dust was seen coming down the road toward the town. Quickly the Yankee infantry prepared for battle. Expecting an attack at any minute as they mustered to arms, the black troops suddenly started to sing the melodious "John Brown," which to many former slaves had become an almost spiritual anthem.[54]

For ten long minutes they sang, their weapons at the ready and hearts pounding as they watched the dust cloud in the distance grow and listened as the sounds of gunfire echoed down upon them. With some relief it was soon learned that returning Union cavalry had raised the dust cloud. They had encountered a detachment of Hampton's Legion and had been driven in during a blistering skirmish. Hooker later reported that the Legion was 10,000 strong and was pressing Sheridan's forces before it. Whatever the actual facts were, it was clear that Draper's expeditionaries had little choice but to retreat as soon as their latest plunder and refugee contrabands had been taken aboard. But it would be close. Believing themselves to be outnumbered fifteen to one, there was no other choice. Their only hope of delaying the enemy long enough to complete their mission now lay in the guns of Hooker's squadron.[55]

The U.S. Navy did its job with gusto. As sunset approached, Hooker reported with some delight, the enemy detachment that was rapidly driving in upon the Union line from south of the town came within rage of *Jacob Bell*'s guns "and received such greeting that they soon left." [56]

That night and throughout most of June 20 the loading of captured livestock, farming implements and other goods rushed ahead without letup. There was no time for sleep or eating, only work. Space was soon at a premium as the two transports at hand were quickly filled to overcapacity and obliged to depart before day's end. There was now little alternative but to take the troops aboard the gunboats, which were quickly and dangerously overloaded until the emptied transports could return.

While still anchored off Tappahannock awaiting the return of the transports, Hooker, tired and worn from the ceaseless activity, was well satisfied with the success of the mission despite the necessity of abandoning the town. "I will make a report covering all the movements soon," he informed Parker, "but feel much more inclined to sleep than work at present. Officers and men have worked day and night and done their duty faithfully and promptly." [57]

Soon the squadron was underway.

As the overloaded guardships passed down the Rappahannock, boats were sent ashore at the Union Wharf, Urbanna, and Carter's Creek for information, undoubtedly regarding the location of the two enemy regiments that had threatened the expedition, but learned nothing. At the mouth of the river the flotilla encountered the two returning transports and offloaded the troops onto them for safe return to Southern Maryland.[58]

When the expedition reached Point Lookout early on the morning of June 21 it delivered 375 more head of cattle, 160 horses, nearly 200 sheep, and approximately 600 more black refugees, including sixty to seventy new recruits for the army and navy. It also delivered an incredibly full steamer load of plows, harrows, cultivators, wheat drills, corn shellers, harnesses, carts and carriages and other implements for the use of the government refugee farms on the Patuxent.[59] The very survival of the farms and the hundreds of black refugees ensconced thereon now depended upon the labors of men and women working, for the first time in their lives, in free enterprise and for themselves.

In Richmond, the expedition was touted as merely another example of Union brutality. "Let the people of the South" extolled the *Richmond Enquirer* regarding the alleged atrocities committed during the raid, "remember what it is to be the fate of our women if the Yankees succeed." [60] No one, however, Union or Confederate, could have been predicted the devastating storm of war that was soon to be heading their way.

35

EARLY TO RISE

"As the next best arrangement I can make."

The month of June 1864 began auspiciously enough when on the 7th the National Union Party convened at the Front Street Theater in Baltimore for its presidential convention. It came as no surprise when Abraham Lincoln was unanimously nominated on the first ballot. Perhaps a bit more surprising was the nomination of Andrew Johnson of Tennessee, a slave owner but a man Lincoln deemed vital to securing the support of Border State independents.

For prisoner of war Charles Warren Hutt at Camp Hoffman the month was much like those that had preceded it. From time to time, a letter or a copy of *Harpers Illustrated* from cousin Annie P. Hall in Horse Head, Maryland, or a few dollars from relatives elsewhere might arrive to briefly alleviate the boredom and personal poverty. But spells of continuing sickness and deep melancholia now plagued him. To address the ennui of prison life, like other inmates he occasionally traded for necessities or handmade trinkets that might be sent to loved ones in response to gifts sent to him. Some were actually delivered. Indeed for many of the prisoners without money, the manufacture of such items to send home or used as barter were also sold to guards or to Sanitary Commission agents who resold them at fairs in New York and other cities. Such handicraft had become a cottage industry in the camp and helped keep heart and soul together for many. One inmate made shell imitations of the Washington Monument in Baltimore, site of major secession rallies in the spring of 1861, for which he received twenty to thirty dollars in U.S. "greenbacks." Another specialized in miniature steam engines, while still others made fans and jewelry such as rings, charms, badges, necklaces, watch chains and other items from bones and shells.

Prisoners, who in their civilian lives had been mechanics and artisans, were the drivers of the prison economy. From blocks of wood or metal acquired by myriad means, "were manufactured a great many interesting little articles, small locomotives, wooden fans, rings from rubber buttons set with gold and silver, and sometimes gems. One ingenious fellow built a small distillery and made whiskey from potato rinds and whatever refuse he could pick up, and got drunk on the product . . . All about the camp were boards on which these articles were exposed for sale. A cracker would buy a chew of tobacco. The tobacco was cut up into chews and half chews." [1]

But hardship was universal, even for those privileged prisoners whose personal connections in the North made their sufferings somewhat less painful than most. Some relaxations of restrictions regarding gifting had made things easier for a few, especially for those Maryland Confederates who had relatives close by and were willing to lend assistance. For those whose families and friends lived in rebel territory, however, such luxuries were seldom to be enjoyed. Frequently fluctuating restrictions, for which no motives were provided, often made everyone miserable. Typical of one such seemingly unprovoked event came on June 4 when for some inexplicable reason coffee and sugar were eliminated from the daily mess. It was rumored that the coffee removal had been in retaliation for the elimination of coffee from Yankee inmates at the Confederate prisoner of war camp at Andersonville, Georgia. The following morning bacon was served for breakfast with vinegar, which was to be poured over the meat to prevent scurvy, and as a substitute for the coffee. On June 12, the day the camp learned of the latest raid on the Northern Neck, a depressed Hutt tersely reported to his diary on the event, noted the usual camp inspection by the guards, and little more. Had he known what was about to transpire that day, his spirits might have been elevated, for another Confederate invasion of Maryland was about to take root in the minds of several senior Confederate leaders. But unlike both the Antietam Campaign of 1862 and Gettysburg Campaign of 1863, which were intended to transfer the war into the heartland of the North, this incursion had as one of its main objectives nothing less than the rescue and release of the entire prisoner of war population at Point Lookout, and perhaps even the capture of Washington.[2]

***

It is uncertain when and where the concept for a military expedition to free the prisoners at Point Lookout was born. Rumors of such a plan had from time to time floated about in the Army of Northern Virginia only to be quietly buried beneath news of more dire events or battles. As one senior Confederate officer from Maryland would later recall: "During the winter quarters of the Maryland line, at Hanover Junction, 1863 and 1864, a rumor pervaded the camp that we were to be sent across the river and attack Point Lookout and release the prisoners there, some 30,000 of them, it was estimated. Where this story came from, I nor any of the staff ever knew, but it created a mild sensation in camp for a few days. Then Grant moved on the North Anna, and we were hurried around from pillar to post and the Point Lookout expedition died out of expectation." [3]

The recent Federal bloodbath at the Battle of Cold Harbor, May 31-June 12, eight miles from Richmond in which Lee had inflicted as many as 12,000 casualties on General Grant's army, had been a stunning Confederate victory and boost to rebel morale. But it had not relieved the reality of the growing stress on Lee's ragged, heavily outnumbered and outgunned army, whose ability to maneuver was already being steadily eroded. For the Union to maintain its unrelenting offensive in Virginia, and at the same time pressure on its other major fronts in Georgia, in the Shenandoah, along the Atlantic and Gulf coasts and in the Mississippi Valley, a great many more men and far more money would have to be raised. It was of small consolation to Lee who had little of either with which to defend Richmond.

There was one strategy at which the Confederate general was superbly adept at, and an approach that could perhaps save his army: a diversionary foray into the enemy's backyard that might at least temporarily remove pressure on his defenses and the capital of the Confederacy. The gestation period for the concept was not long in maturing. The earliest known indication that some in the Confederate cause were already considering such a measure, at least for the Virginia theater of war, first appeared in a covert correspondence in cipher from a rebel secret agent in Southern Maryland. The agent, identified only as "DARST," was apparently a colleague of the chief of the Confederate Signal Corps, William Norris, during the final days of the fight at Cold Harbor. "It is thought that Old Abe would call for at least 300,000

468

men and a loan of $500,000,000 between this and the 1st of July," the agent had written in discussing the Union manpower problem.

"Indeed, we are almost sure he will, judging from expressions of his Cabinet. We think it all important that a diversion should be made, either to capture or release our prisoners at Point Lookout or a raid upon Washington with a view to the destruction of the military supplies and public property, or both at the same time would certainly be better, if the necessary troops can be spared at this time. There is not a troop stationed in our county [St. Mary's?] or Prince George at this time. We therefore infer that the garrison at Point Lookout must be weak. There are a few soldiers stationed at Leonardtown, Lieutenant Denny's company. They sometimes send up four or five to Bryantown to hunt up deserters and rebel mail carriers." [4]

That the suggestion for a diversion into Maryland may have made its way up the chain of command or was more likely already being secretly considered by higher Confederate officialdom soon became apparent. Within three days of the DARST correspondence, what began as an expedition to defend the Confederate hub city of Lynchburg, Virginia against a Union force under Major General David Hunter, was eventually to morph into a diversionary invasion on the largely unprotected State of Maryland and a threat to Washington itself.

On June 12 a substantial Confederate force, the II Army Corps under the command of General Jubal A. Early was detached from the Army of Northern Virginia and left Richmond soon after. Early's assigned mission was complex, ambitious and with major strategic goals that would influence the next year of war. Acting under direct orders of General Lee, he was to take his three divisions of infantry and two artillery batteries, approximately 8,000 men strong, roughly a quarter of the Army of Northern Virginia, and move west to protect the major Confederate rail hub of Lynchburg and prevent a Union Army force under General David Hunter from destroying the junction. A battle weary force under former Vice President of the United States and Southern Democratic Party presidential candidate John C. Breckinridge of Kentucky, now a rebel general, defended the town. Afterwards if successful, he would join forces with Breckinridge to drive Hunter from the Shenandoah Valley. One of the benefits of the campaign, if all went well by mid-month, would be to lay open a route eastward through Maryland to threaten Washington, Baltimore and Pennsylvania. It was Lee's hope that General Grant would thus be either forced into another suicidal attack or send troops to defend the District of Columbia and Maryland, leaving the weakened Union Army in Virginia vulnerable. An expedition into Maryland might also replenish much needed military supplies, horses and livestock. His own ultimate objective, Early told his wife quite candidly, was nothing less than the relief of Richmond and to make "Yankeedom smart in a sore place." [5]

On June 16 Hunter's army of 16,600, while ravaging the Shenandoah Valley as part of Grant's policy of total war, began the investment of Lynchburg. But Early, traveling ahead of his troops, had already arrived in the town. The following day, the II Army Corps linked up with Breckinridge. For Hunter, it was immediately apparent that he would be unable to successfully attack the superior numbers of rebels holding the town and began his withdrawal northward on June 18. Early vigorously pursued, driving the Union forces toward the Kanawah Valley of West Virginia and leaving the Shenandoah again under Confederate control. For three days the rebels relentlessly tracked Hunter until successfully engaging him at and near the town of Salem and at Catawba Mountain, after which the chase was called off on June 21.[6]

While Early allowed his men a day of rest at Salem word of the potential rebel menace to the Shenandoah and its richest Union pearl, Harpers Ferry, did not go unnoticed in Washington. By mid-June, a visible uneasiness had already begun to sweep across the central counties of Maryland. In Baltimore myriad rumors flourished, contributing to a muted wave of anxiety. As a precautionary measure, General Schenck moved to prohibit the sale of arms and munitions except by military permit. All daily business was suspended. All shops, drinking saloons, manufacturing establishments and places of business with the exception of apothecary shops, were closed. Public buildings, Federal and municipal, were placed under heavy guard. Passes were required to leave the city. Just in case, the 11th Maryland Infantry was recruited and placed under the command of Colonel William T. Landstreet with an enlistment bonus of fifty dollars offered to those who would serve for 100 days. At nearby Camp Bradford the new volunteer regiment of citizen-soldiers was mustered into a vague semblance of military order on June 16 and sent to Camp Carroll for a brief training. From Camp Carroll these green expendables, never before tested in battle, were to be dispatched to Relay Station on the outskirts of the city for immediate transfer farther west if necessary to meet any incursions from the Shenandoah. On June 20 the Unionist Council voted $400,000 for defense of the city and a thousand negroes were commandeered by the Baltimore police to construct fortifications.[7]

In order to more effectually address a possible emergency, if the threat began to grow, the War Department also issued General Order No. 214 on June 21. It added "That portion of Maryland between the Patuxent, the Chesapeake Bay and the Potomac River, including the Prisoners' Camp at Point Lookout" to the Department of Washington.[8]

For Charles Warren Hutt, whose world was confined by four wooden prison walls, such events still meant little. On Friday, June 24, he reported to his diary: "Have been in the Chesapeake bathing . . . The camp is more unhealthy than usual, averaging from ten to fifteen [deaths] per day." The following morning it was simply more of the same with one exception. "Clear and warm," he wrote. "The weather is more oppressive than it has been any time this summer. All the Confederate officers here have left for Fort Delaware. Several prisoners arrived from Beauregard's army." [9]

Due to overcrowding, the deplorable living conditions in the camp were now reaching a critical stage. Surgeon James H. Thompson, U.S. Volunteers, who was now in charge of sanitation, was obliged to address the issue to the St. Mary's District high command. He first "respectfully" protested the reception of additional prisoners, as there were already "fully 14,000 within the camp, near 20,000 on the Point in all, including the U.S. Hammond General Hospital, with 1,300 wounded men, the contraband camp of indefinite numbers, the quartermaster's department, and troops of the garrison," as well as 250 horses and mules. His major concerns were with the limited area of the camp and surface within the stockade itself, and the insufficient quantity and injurious quality of the water from the camp wells, which was unfit for consumption and to which he attributed an increase of fatalities since mid-May. Though policing of the camp had improved over the past few months and was now deemed "excellent," he feared that overcrowding and "an epidemic will decimate not only the ranks of prisoners, but affect alike all the inhabitants of the Point." A month earlier he had requested the enlargement of the prison hospital, an application that was completely ignored. And now, there were no less than 200 men in camp that desperately needed to be in a hospital, but with no adequate facility in which to place them.[10]

Thompson's appeals were simple: permit no increase in the current prison population; purchase condensers capable of producing a sufficient quantity of clean, fresh water; reduce the allotment of salt pork and increase the issue of fresh vegetables to reduce scurvy; and immediately construct a hospital barrack for the accommodation of the additional hundreds of sick.[11]

This time his request was heard. Within forty-eight hours Colonel Draper responded that he had forwarded an application to the post quartermaster to purchase a condenser capable of producing 17,000 gallons of fresh water daily, and for sufficient materials to build the hospital addition that Thompson had asked for.[12] Then, for the first time, an effort was undertaken to reduce prisoner over-crowding by dispatching inmates to other newer or less crowded prison camps. Unfortunately, such humanitarian initiatives would soon be put in abeyance owing to the growing crisis not so far to the west, a crisis that threatened to engulf Camp Hoffman and the Hammond Hospital in their entireties.

***

On June 23 General Early, "Old Jube" or "Jubilee" as his men affectionately knew him, having combined forces with Breckinridge's army of veteran soldiers, and driven Hunter out of the Shenandoah, began marching north from Salem unopposed on the Valley Pike. Though severely afflicted with rheumatoid arthritis and barely able to mount his horse without help, at only forty-six years of age, Early maintained a gruff and profane exterior. But he had earned a reputation as a fighter at Fredericksburg, Gettysburg and Chancellorsville as well as having gained Lee's full trust. As it passed through the village of Lexington, the II Corps briefly diverted to file past the grave of General Thomas "Stonewall" Jackson, who had once been their corps commander. Three days later, after a hard march down the valley, they arrived at the picturesque little town of Staunton, Virginia. Here Early reorganized his command, gathered supplies, reduced his wagon train to increase mobility, and renamed the II Army Corps the Army of the Valley District. Though he could not have known it, the course of his campaign was about to change dramatically. Even as he and his men were taking a two-day respite in the town to allow for the reorganization of his army, a scheme for an amphibious operation to free the prisoners at Point Lookout was rapidly maturing in the fertile mind of General Robert E. Lee at Petersburg.

"Great benefit might be drawn from the release of our prisoners at Point Lookout," Lee pointed out to President Davis, "if it can be accomplished." First hinting at an attack launched from the Northern Neck, he suggested that the

471

number of troops employed in such an operation would necessarily have to be small, "as the whole would have to be transported secretly across the Potomac where it is very broad, the means of doing which must first be procured." A second coordinated assault from the landward side of the St. Mary's peninsula would have to be made to insure success. For the land attack he was willing to devote the whole body of his highly regarded veteran Marylanders, the 1st Maryland, all serving in the Army of Northern Virginia. Their inclusion would afford the operation a sufficient number of men "of excellent material and much experience."

The specifics of how the two operations, land and sea, were to be coordinated, or how a land force was to reach Point Lookout at all were never mentioned, suggesting that the overall strategy was still a work in progress. He was also at something of a loss as to where to find a proper leader for the overland operation, but quickly honed in on perhaps the best man available. As that officer was to command Maryland troops and operate upon Maryland soil, he deemed it important that whoever it was, he must be a Marylander. Unlike the Antietam Campaign of 1862, and the Gettysburg Campaign of the following year, in which Maryland was considered a friendly secessionist state waiting to be "liberated" by Confederate arms, it was now firmly under Union control and considered an enemy. But there were, he believed, still tens of thousands of Marylanders whose sympathy remained with the South, especially in Southern Maryland wherein lay the prison camp at Point Lookout. Thus it was only logical that the commander charged with the rescue operation on land be a Marylander.

Though the general had not quite decided upon a selection, there was one such officer who stood out. "Of those connected with this army I consider Col. Bradley T. Johnson the most suitable. He is bold and intelligent, ardent and true, and yet I am unable to say whether he possesses all the requisite qualities. Everything in an expedition of the kind would depend upon the leader." [13]

Bradley Johnson was to many who knew him just such a leader. A native of Frederick County, Maryland, he was a cerebral man with a high forehead, receding hairline and a narrow face liberally decorated with mustache and stylish goatee popular among Beauregard admirers. During his military career he was once described as "one of the handsomest men in the First Maryland." His relations were of some note as he was a grandnephew of Maryland's first elected governor, Thomas Johnson, of Calvert County. He was also a superbly educated man, a graduate of Princeton in 1849 who had completed his law degree at Harvard soon afterwards. Admitted to the bar in 1851, he had married well and as an attorney engaged in politics early on. In 1860 he had served as a delegate to the National Democratic Convention in Baltimore, and was among the majority delegation that withdrew to unite with the Southern wing of the party supporting Breckinridge for president. Soon after the Pratt Street Riot, he had organized and equipped a company of Frederick County volunteers for the secessionists' defense of Baltimore. He then marched his seventy mounted militiamen from Frederick City to answer Marshal Kane's call for assistance. And like many others, he had been obliged to flee to Virginia to join the Confederate cause before the Federal occupation and roundup of prominent secessionist supporters began. Believing that his strongest obligation was to fight under the flag of his own state, he was instrumental in forming the 1st Maryland, CSA, at Harpers Ferry in May 1861. A participant in numerous campaigns and battles, he had soon risen to the rank of colonel. After he almost single handedly put down a mutiny among the regiment, his unit had been the first to engage a loyal Maryland unit of the same strength, the 1st Regiment Maryland Volunteer Infantry, at the Battle of Front Royal on May 23, 1862. Other fights and adventures followed.

General Bradley T. Johnson, CSA. Prints and Photographs Division, Library of Congress, Washington, D.C.

His popularity among the citizenry was substantial. One biographer noted that following the First Battle of Winchester, May 25, 1862, just two days after the Front Royal fight: "having dismounted from his horse in an unguarded moment, [Johnson] was espied and singled out by an old lady of Amazonian proportions, just from the wash tub, who, wiping her hands and mouth on her apron as she approached, seized him around the neck with the hug of a bruin, and bestowed upon him half a dozen kisses that were heard by nearly every man in the command, and when at length she relaxed her hold the Colonel looked as if he had just come out a vapor bath." [14]

Why, it may be asked, was Lee willing to hazard such a thrust deep behind Federal lines? The potential risk to a key component of his army, penetrating a narrow, isolated, highly defensible peninsula with few roads, to rescue an army of weak, sick and wounded soldiers who were perhaps of questionable military value was enormous. The camp in which they were being held, surrounded on two of its three sides by water, was quite defensible and protected by an unknown number of Federal troops and the U.S. Navy, which was in total control of the waters of the Chesapeake Tidewater.

Part of the reason may be ascribed to the limited military intelligence available to Lee, the bulk of which was being provided by northern newspapers and agents in Southern Maryland. The general was given to understand that most of the Point Lookout garrison was composed of blacks. As a slave owner who believed negro troops were far inferior to white soldiers, he naturally also believed that such was a distinct advantage for the Confederates. "I should suppose that the commander of such troops" he wrote, "would be poor and feeble. A stubborn resistance, therefore, may not be reasonably expected." He appeared to be unaware that the St. Mary's District was no longer commanded by Hinks, but under the administration of Colonel Draper, an aggressive commander of substantial mettle.

But what of the amphibious arm of the operation?

What is known is that on or about July 1 President Davis met with Commander/Colonel John Taylor Wood of the Confederate States Navy, a man of proven abilities who was intimately familiar with the Chesapeake Tidewater and a genius at what would one day be called asymmetric warfare. Whether or not Wood presented his own plan for a seaborne operation to President Davis is unknown. What is certain is that Davis wrote to General Lee on July 2 to inform him of "the arrangements made to release the prisoners" at Point Lookout, deep behind Federal lines at the tip of the distant St. Mary's peninsula, indicating a scheme was already in development at that time. He believed the camp contained a ready made army of experienced soldiers, perhaps more than a full corps in strength. If liberated and ably led, they could assist in achieving something that had eluded Confederate arms throughout the war, namely the capture of Washington, D.C., capital of the United States of America.[15]

The parameters presented in President Davis's letter of the amphibious attack plan are unknown, as the document has disappeared. Yet from Lee's response the following day, it would appear that the concept had Davis's full approval, and the details of the operation were to be left to the general. That Wood should lead the seaborne expeditionaries seemed a given. "I think under the blessing of a merciful Providence," Lee wrote, "they will be successful & result in great good. If any human agency can insure success I think it will be accomplished by Col. Wood to whom I would be willing to trust the operations on land as well as sea." Davis may have suggested that the prisoners at Point Lookout be informed of the expedition in order that they might conduct a simultaneous uprising in the camp at the same time as Wood's arrival and capture of the Union guardships by surprise. If so, it was a point with which Lee strongly disagreed. In any event it would first be necessary, he intimated, for Wood to capture the small schooner gunboats believed to be guarding the point.[16]

"I think we cannot with safety attempt any communication with the prisoners," the general informed his president. "The first indication of relief must be borne to them by the guns of the captured gunboats – Neither in my opinion would it be safe to throw across the Potomac [from the Northern Neck] any party. Their advance to the river even would be dangerous. Their transit would certainly be discovered." Nevertheless, an amphibious operation entirely by sea seemed possible. But before it could be carried out, it would first be necessary for Wood to send a boat across the Chesapeake to Cherrystone, Virginia, to cut the telegraph wire to Old Point Comfort, severing communications with Grant's forces in Virginia. Then, if feasible, before the attack he was to cut the wire from Point Lookout to Washington. "If this can be done a great advantage will be gained." [17]

Lee was cognizant that it would be necessary, especially in light of Lincoln's recent granting of amnesty and the ongoing enlistment efforts among the prison population, that it would be most judicious to send along with Wood "some officer known to the prisoners, to organize inspire confidence & put them quickly in motion."[18] Unfortunately, the only officer Lee could recommend was General Robert Frederick Hoke, a North Carolina commander instrumental in the recent victory at Cold Harbor, and a man he could ill afford to spare.

"As the next best arrangement I can make," Lee informed the president, "I send today an officer to Gen Early to inform him that an effort will be made to release the prisoners about the 12 Inst: & if successful he will certainly know it through Northern sources. In that event, if circumstances will permit he must send down a brigade of Cav[alr]y with Genls Gordon & Lewis to command & lead around Washington the prisoners &c – I think this is all that can be done. The rest must be left up to the operators." [19]

During this preliminary stage of planning, Lee seems to have paid substantial attention to the surprise seaborne assault on Point Lookout. By taking along a company of Maryland artillerymen armed as infantry, as well as dismounted cavalry and regular infantry on the amphibious end of operations, Wood might rescue as many men as he could procure transportation to carry. "By throwing them suddenly on the beach with some concert of action among the prisoners, I think the guard might be overpowered, the prisoners liberated and organized, and marched immediately on the route to Washington." The artillery company sent with the expedition could operate guns captured at the point. Provisions and other necessities would have to be collected in the friendly Southern Maryland countryside as the army passed through. The dismounted cavalry and released prisoners could mount themselves on horses captured on the march and along with the infantry "would form a respectable force." Such a body of men, although they might not be able to take Washington without assistance, could march around the city and cross the upper Potomac where fordable. Lee thought it improbable that they could cross the river in a body at any point below Washington, unless perhaps at Alexandria. They would at the very least create a major threat wherever they appeared and would most certainly draw troops away from the Virginia theater of war. Anything was possible given the right set of conditions. The concept, he believed, was "worthy of consideration and can only be matured by reflection." But a decision had to be made soon, for timing and coordination were paramount.[20]

For Lee it was not a matter of if such an attempt could be made, but how soon it might be started. His planning evolved rapidly. With a success in the Shenandoah Valley, Early would be well positioned for an invasion of Maryland from the west to ultimately threaten both Washington and Baltimore, and actually send troops to assist in the taking of Point Lookout. If "all the troops in the control of the United States are being sent to Grant . . . little or no opposition could be made by those at Washington." The sooner a cohesive plan was put into execution on Early's end the better – but only if he deemed it practicable. Given the sympathies of Southern Marylanders towards the Confederacy, which they had continuously supported with men, money and supplies, it was altogether possible that additional aid might be raised. These silent rebels had been quietly waiting for such an opportunity to show their true colors. If Washington should actually be taken, and held for even a short while, the whole complexion of the war might be dramatically altered in favor of the South.[21]

The concept was bold indeed, but part of the prize, the thousands of Confederate prisoners at the point, was in truth of questionable immediate military value. At the end of June, the monthly count of inmates at Camp Hoffman indicated a total of 14,489 soldiers, blockade runners, spies, secessionist sympathizers, and even a few women confined in camp. Of those, an average of 626 were on any given day in sick quarters, another 520 bedridden in the hospital, unlikely to be capable of either travel or fighting. Though the officially reported count of daily deaths numbered between three and four, with a monthly total posted at 105, unofficially the mortality rate may have been as high as ten or fifteen a day as recorded in the diaries of several inmates. The total ambulatory population averaged 12,272, but most were half starved, poorly clothed and shod, and many were far from capable of making a forced march. Conducting full military operations against Washington, surrounded by a complex of defense works that made it the most heavily fortified city in the world, was even more problematic.[22]

Nevertheless, the original purpose and true utility of the proposed operation still lay in its diversionary capacity to distract Grant's offensive against Lee's army. The release or threat to liberate nearly 14,000 Confederates (though rebel estimates incorrectly placed the number at between 15,000 and 30,000) into Southern Maryland and menace or even capture Washington could not help but make heavy demands upon Grant. With the Union general still believing Lee's II Army Corps to still be at Richmond, it meant that speed and timing were essential. For the Confederates the moment could not have been better. Washington, Baltimore and even Annapolis were poorly defended. The great circle of fortifications surrounding the District of Columbia, though extensive, were weakly manned, and had been allowed to fall into a sorry state of disrepair.

Significantly, Point Lookout was at its weakest state since the opening of the prison camp. The devastating Federal losses at Cold Harbor had required immediate replacements of manpower, and one source of ready troops had been the garrison at the point. On June 28, as Early prepared to march from Staunton, the 4th Rhode Island, which had been guarding the inmates at the camp, was ordered to join General Butler in Virginia. Colonel Draper and the 36th Regiment, USCT, were also ordered to the front, leaving the prison very lightly guarded. The whole of Maryland, it seemed, was totally vulnerable to attack and ripe for disaster.[23]

Lee's plans were greeted by Early's full approbation. Having taken his superior's directives to heart, "Old Jube" informed him of his willingness "to turn down the valley and proceed according to your instructions to threaten Washington and if I find the opportunity – to take it." He would also, as instructed, sow further confusion among the Yankees by sending "a select body of the cavalry to cut the railroads between Washington and Harrisburg and Baltimore and Philadelphia while I am moving on Washington" and to "make an effort to release the prisoners at Point Lookout." [24]

In the meantime Bradley Johnson, Lee's ultimate choice for disabling the railroads and carrying out the landward attack on Point Lookout, was promoted in the field to the rank of brigadier general and given command of a cavalry brigade formerly commanded by General William E. "Grumble" Jones. The newly minted brigadier's mission in the coming campaign (of which he was still entirely unaware) would be difficult if not impossible under the best of conditions. He was not only to disrupt communications and rail lines and overwhelm the garrison at Point Lookout, but also to organize and arm the prisoners, then march to the vicinity of Washington and rejoin Early before the city. Incredibly, given the importance of the mission, there appears to have been no mention of actually coordinating the attack on the point with Wood's amphibious expedition as outlined in Lee's communication with Davis, only that a landing was to be made.[25]

In Washington the first solid indication to reach the city of serious danger from the west came on June 29 when B&O Railroad agents at Harpers Ferry telegraphed company President John W. Garrett at his headquarters at Camden Station, Baltimore. They reported that between 15,000 and 30,000 rebel troops were moving down the Shenandoah Valley. Garrett immediately passed on the information to Secretary Stanton. Though he was partially incorrect in noting that it was Generals Ewell and Breckinridge that were on the move, and entirely unaware that the former had been replaced by Early as head of the II Army Corps in May, he blithely stated: "I am satisfied the operations and design of the enemy in the Valley demand the greatest vigilance and attention." [26]

That same day, Jubal Early's cavalry struck the railroad and telegraph lines near Martinsburg. Now Washington had something to worry about.

36

HEAVEN GRANT IT
"I told General Early that horseflesh could not do it."

It had been sweltering hot and dry all across the Piedmont and Tidewater landscapes as the month of July approached, but it had also begun with some promise for the Union despite the Federal defeat at Cold Harbor. Grant's grand army now lay only several miles below Richmond near the diminutive riverport of Petersburg in the opening days of a long campaign and siege of Lee's veterans. In Georgia a massive legion under William Tecumseh Sherman was relentlessly driving a stubborn Confederate force under Joseph Johnston before it towards Atlanta. But all seemed quiet and relatively safe in the Middle Department, which extended from Baltimore westward to the Monocacy River just east of Frederick, all under the command of Major General Lew Wallace. Following the Gettysburg Campaign a year earlier, the department had become little more than a backwater of the war. Consequently only 265 officers and 6,027 men present for duty garrisoned it. Most were cantoned in and about Baltimore and Annapolis. The cities of Washington and Alexandria, however, were considered by many to be impervious. Sixty-eight enclosed forts with hudreds of cannon, ninety-three field gun battery positions with 404 emplacements encircled the cities. There were twenty miles of rifle trenches, three blockhouses connected by miles of military roads, telegraphic communication, headquarters buildings, camps, ordnance dumps, hospitals and support facilities crowded about. All were defended by a total of 950 heavy and thirty-nine field artillery pieces. As of June 30 a total of 38,906 officers and men, with 814 serviceable horses supported the defenses, at least on paper. Many, however, were convalescents, militia, provost marshal units and the like. Others, often weakened by their ordeals in rebel prisons, were marginal soldiers at best, and less than maneuverable or suitable for confronting hardened veterans of the Confederate Army. More than a third of the manpower was stationed at defense works on the Virginia side of the Potomac. Moreover, there were only a few artillery technicians among them needed to service the heavy guns of the defenses. And until Confederate forces appeared ready to roll in from the west, it seemed to many that the war's end was finally in sight. Congress had even begun to urge the president forward on a robust reconstruction agenda, albeit one in which he was not wholly in support. No one, least of all the prisoners at Point Lookout or their guards, many units of which were also comprised of invalid soldiers, had any portent of the ominous forces swiftly rushing in from the Shenandoah.[1]

***

"Several hundred prisoners arrived," Charles Warren Hutt recorded at Point Lookout on June 30. The following day more were brought in by steamer, all captured in front of Petersburg.[2] Indeed over the previous ten days, noted one newspaper correspondent writing from the prison camp, two thousand rebel prisoners had arrived, a large portion of which belonged to Beauregard's command captured during the fighting in Virginia. As was now common procedure, previous to their entering the camp, they had been closely examined. The provost marshal, who supposedly kept an exact account, so that when they departed their belongings might be returned, took all extra clothing, watches and money from them.

There were, of course, frequent efforts to circumvent confiscation, as it was well known that valuable items were commonly purloined by the guards and would never be returned. Some of the new arrivals, one reporter noted, "have gold and notes, hid under their hair; some sewed up under the lining of their clothing; some in the bottom of their socks; others think they have safely secured their specie in the lining of their boot tops, but the vigilant eye of Lieutenant Phillips and his corps of detectives soon show its existence, and the gold comes forth. One knapsack lately examined, contained two full suits of female apparel and some baby clothing, and when the same was brought to light, it caused some merriment among his comrades, who had quite a laugh at his expense. The clothes came quite handy, and were immediately sent to the female prisoners confined at the camp hospital." [3]

To Hutt it seemed just business as usual, that is until July 2 when a "new regiment of Negroes called the 2nd. Mass. Cavalry" replaced the units sent to the front. At the same time, the first of what would eventually number thousands of inmates were sent north to a new Union prisoner of war depot at Elmira, New York. The move was the first step to relieve the overcrowding situation, although it would appear to the Confederate Government to be for reasons not so mundane.[4]

Though Hutt could not have known it, John W. Garrett's word of a possible threat was finally being circulated in Washington. Then even as new prisoners were disembarking from steamers at Point Lookout, on June 30 Early's army in the Shenandoah had reached New Market, Virginia, less than a hundred miles to the west of Washington. Two days later his advanced column, driving north, had made Winchester, approximately sixty miles northwest of the capital and only forty miles from Harpers Ferry.[5]

Suddenly the menace was growing more frightening by the hour. Reports of a cavalry fight at Winchester and of further Confederate advances began to filter in. Forward elements of Early's army were driving back outpost guards belonging to Major General Franz Sigel's garrison at Harpers Ferry. The following day Garrett learned that Federal forces in Leedstown had been attacked. Martinsburg, West Virginia, just west of Harpers Ferry, was being abandoned. At 9:15 a.m., July 4 Secretary Stanton received confirmation from Garrett of the powerful forces marching up the Shenandoah and for the first time actually threatening Western Maryland.[6]

Garrett was deeply concerned that B&O property, locomotives, cars, warehousing and other facilities, especially at the railroad's central hub at Harpers Ferry, now well fortified but lightly manned, were most certainly primary targets for destruction by rebel forces. Worse, an invasion of Maryland seemed to be in the immediate offing. He personally met with General Wallace in Baltimore to seek Federal military support. The general was well aware of the railroad's vital importance to the Union's strategic access and control, or at least presence, in Western Maryland and the upper Shenandoah. But with extremely limited troop strength at his disposal, he was at first obliged to demur. Yet, the threat was now real.

By July 5 the emergent danger not only to Western Maryland but to both Washington and Baltimore made it clear that Wallace's choice of action and use of the few troops in hand required the Wisdom of Solomon. He could defend Baltimore, the fourth largest city in the United States, one of the greatest maritime centers in the nation, and surrender fifty miles of Maryland to the enemy, leaving the backdoor to the nation's capital open to attack. Or he could attempt a stand on the Monocacy River at the western boundary of the Middle Department to hold the enemy until reinforcements might arrive. Hunter was somewhere to the west (though no one knew quite where), but Grant was only a little over a hundred miles to the south and possessed substantial water transport to move men quickly to Baltimore, Annapolis or Washington. He made his choice decisively and began an immediate shift of the meager forces in hand via the B&O Railroad toward Monocacy Junction and Frederick.[7]

Harpers Ferry was well beyond Wallace's military jurisdiction. The best that he could do was to send a regiment of 100-day volunteers to protect the strategically important railroad span crossing the river at Monocacy Junction. This critical point was several miles southeast of Frederick, on the very westernmost border of his geographic authority. At 4:30 p.m. that same day Garrett provided two engines and thirty-five troop cars for moving a thousand men to delay the oncoming flood.[8] About midnight, having received little guidance from Washington and without orders to do so, Wallace quietly slipped aboard a B&O locomotive at Camden Station bound for the Monocacy to personally confront the dire threat of enemy invasion.

Even as Wallace was en route west, Commander John Taylor Wood and a small party of officers were on their way from Richmond to Stony Creek Depot "28 miles by the road they have to march where they will take the [railroad] cars to Weldon," and from there to the seaport of Wilmington, North Carolina. Upon their arrival at Wilmington, Major General William Henry Chase Whiting, commander of the District of Cape Fear, would meet them. The general was to "provide them with two 20 pd Parrotts if possible & to furnish every other facility in his power to expedite their movements." The Wilmington end of the operation was to be coordinated with General George Washington Custis Lee. "I have gone over all the points of the expedition with Cols: Wood & Lee," the commander in chief reported hopefully to President Davis, "& we can now only trust to their energy & judgment & the blessing of a merciful Providence." If all went well, the expedition would sail on Saturday, July 9 and arrive for the attack on Point Lookout on July 12. "Every thing I think has been done that can be; & we have good ground to hope for the success of the enterprise." [9]

***

With the now very strong probability of a crossing by the rebel army onto Western Maryland soil, Secretary of War Stanton ordered a new commander, Brigadier General James Barnes, to Point Lookout to replace Colonel Draper. When he received his orders from Major General Christopher Columbus Augur on July 3, Barnes, who had most recently commanded the First Division of the V Army Corps, was comfortably ensconced in Washington at Willard's Hotel on Pennsylvania Avenue. General Augur's directives were quite concise: "The Secretary thinks you had better go down to Point Lookout at once. You had better get a tug. He is a little anxious concerning the prisoners there, in reference to the movement of the rebels near Harper's Ferry." Almost as an afterthought he added: "Report to me by telegraph every evening." [10]

Stanton's anxiety was by now well founded, for even as Augur was setting pen to paper, Robert E. Lee was writing a confidential dispatch to President Davis informing him again of one of the principal objectives of the new Maryland campaign, and reiterating a specific target date: "An effort will be made to release (the prisoners) about the 12 Inst." Now the clock was ticking.[11]

The invasion was indeed a gamble against the odds for Early, but especially for Johnson's brigade. The unit had only a month earlier numbered 5,600 men while under General Jones, but had been seriously reduced by the loss of 1,600 men killed or captured at the recent Battle of Piedmont. To improve the game, Johnson was given permission on July 3 to attach the crack 1st Maryland Cavalry under Captain Warner G. Welsh to his unit and was formally ordered to join Early's army, which was then moving towards Harpers Ferry. The advance had been only lightly opposed with mostly skirmishing at points along the way. The few Union forces lying before it barely managed to escape across the Potomac into Maryland at Shepherdstown. But Johnson, still unaware of his upcoming assignment, had little idea of what trials lay before him.[12]

"Parole Camp, Annapolis, Md. (ca. May 5, 1865)." Prints and Photographs Division, Library of Congress, Washington, D.C.

By now news of the threat from the west was causing uproar in Baltimore and Annapolis; even Washington was alarmed over what appeared to be an impending invasion. In Annapolis, Colonel Adrian Root of the 94th New York Volunteers, who had taken charge at Camp Parole a year earlier and additional duties and command of the Annapolis District of the Middle Department in April 1864, learned of the threat on July 3. Immediate mobilization of the few forces available to him was deemed imperative. The capital of Maryland, he knew, must be defended, but was overruled by higher authority. Instead, upon receiving orders from department headquarters in Baltimore he was directed to hold six companies of

Ohio militia and Company I, 1st Eastern Shore Maryland Volunteers in readiness for service in the field elsewhere. To protect the capital city of the state he was to be left with little more than a handful of troublesome troops at Camp Parole and convalescents in the hospitals of Annapolis.[13]

***

Independence Day was clear, beautiful and very warm throughout the Maryland Tidewater. In Washington the first session of the Thirty-Eighth Congress was adjourning. The adjournment unfortunately arrived in the midst of growing discord over what would become the policy of postwar reconstruction over states that had seceded. Moreover, there was the question of who was to administer it, the Executive or Legislative Branch of the government? Called the Wade-Davis Bill, authored by Senate Majority Leader Benjamin Wade of Ohio and Representative Henry Winter Davis of Maryland, the proposed legislation addressed for the first time the mode of reorganization of a seceded state when the war was over. It stipulated that such action would only be initiated after a majority of white male citizens had sworn the oath of allegiance, separating political sheep from goats, and adopted and approved a constitution agreeable to both the president and the U.S. Congress. There was a caveat: those individuals who had willfully borne arms for the South or held a state or national office in the Confederacy, whether they had sworn their allegiance to the Union or not, would be ineligible to vote or serve as a delegate to any state's constitutional convention. The bill also called for the total emancipation of human chattel in all slave states, but through the actions of Congress rather than a constitutional amendment convention or by presidential proclamation. It detailed certain other restrictions on office holding and the cancellation of all Confederate debts. As Lincoln saw it, certain provisions of the bill would make reconstruction for any Southern state difficult if not impossible. Even worse, it might lead to control by the radical arm of the Republican Party, which seemed hell-bent on punishment rather than reconciliation, and would only exacerbate hostility and promote further opposition in the South, or even guerrilla warfare. But more importantly, it would in effect allow Congress rather than the Chief Executive to control the restoration of the former Confederate states and the terms of their re-entry into the Union.

The president took some consolation in several recently enacted pieces of legislation, including the Equalization Bill passed on June 15, granting black soldiers equal pay to that of whites, and the repeal of the Fugitive Slave Law, which he had signed on June 28. Now he resolved, much to the great chagrin and frustration of many members of the U.S. Congress, to simply pocket veto the Wade-Davis legislation.

Lincoln spent the morning in the President's Room of the White House not only addressing the controversial Wade-Davis act, but also in signing other legislation, such as a bill establishing the office of Commissioner of Immigration, and another repealing certain exemption classes of the Enrollment Act. He conferred with several legislators, most notably Senator Zachariah Chandler of Michigan and Congressman Isaac Newton Arnold of Illinois, on such domestic matters as other recently proposed bills and postal issues. A meeting with his newly appointed

Secretary of the Treasury, William P. Fessenden, was also in order. And for a brief moment, for a very weary president, the war seemed far away.[14]

At Point Lookout, as Lincoln deliberated on political affairs of the moment in Washington and more prisoners were being shipped off to Elmira, New York, the focus of thousands of remaining inmates was on the water. There they could see the gunboats of the Potomac Flotilla lying off the point, fully rigged and decked out to celebrate the eighty-eighth birthday of the United States. Even they were taken aback by the festive scene. "The 4th day of July," recorded Bartlett Yancey Malone, "was a beautyfull day And the Yanks had thur Vesels Rigged off with flags and they had about 34 flags on each Gun Boat about 12 O'clock they fierd Saluts boath from thir land Batry and Gun Boats." [15]

Far to the west, an Independence Day event of a substantially more dire nature was underway. General Sigel's forces, outnumbered by Early's army, had retired to strong Union fortifications on Maryland Heights across the Potomac from Harpers Ferry. The move was a significantly tactical one as the heights controlled the critically important bridge crossing the river, which had also been purposely disabled, thereby denying the Confederate Army a straight route into Western Maryland. If Early now chose to directly bypass the heights, an inferior force could easily assail him, thereby causing additional delay. Nevertheless, small parties of thirsty and hungry rebels were soon looting the saloons and stores of Harpers Ferry, which had been stocked for the holiday. Sigel's move, which now forced Early to find another passage across the Potomac, had most importantly imposed what would prove to be the critical loss of a full day or more that would be hard to make up in the assault of Maryland.

But "Old Jube" was not about to be denied the third and final invasion of the state that could substantially alter the very course of war.

***

It is something of a mystery as to how, on the very day of Early's advance, news of the rebel offensive seemed to have spread across Maryland at light speed. Unquestionably aware that something was afoot on state soil, even before definitive word of the Confederate motions arrived, General Augur, who was obliged to maintain a static defense of the capital from his Department of Washington headquarters, was taking no chances. On July 5 he immediately instructed Colonel William Gamble, commander of the Camp Stoneman cavalry depot at Giesboro Point on the southeastern outskirts of the District of Columbia, to dispatch a lieutenant and ten men to the vicinity of Upper Marlboro. They were to remain there for a few days to watch the roads leading down the peninsula toward Point Lookout. Only "as many days' rations of subsistence and oats as they can carry on their horses" were to be brought along. Their main mission was to watch for "anything like small bodies of cavalry" going down that way and to report back daily. The balance of their company was to be sent to Port Tobacco to protect the telegraph line between Washington and the town. From Port Tobacco the party was then to proceed in the direction of Point Lookout for the same purpose as before and also to report daily.[16]

Somehow by the evening of that same day, word of the invasion had even reached the general prison population at Point Lookout. "We hear," noted one

483

hopeful inmate in his diary entry that same day, "that Ewell [Early] is in Frederick City Maryland, heaven grant it." [17]

***

After days of receiving conflicting intelligence from both Confederate deserters and his own officers, General Grant, with his army heavily engaged before Petersburg, was still uncertain of the enemy's objectives far to the north. Major General Henry Halleck, his own chief of staff, refused to believe that Washington, Baltimore, or Harpers Ferry might be in jeopardy at all. It was a view that significantly influenced Grant's delay in taking action. As a precaution, however, all available transport vessels were dispatched to Fort Monroe just in case. Finally, at 11:30 p.m., July 5, a rapid movement of troops to Maryland was ordered.[18]

Convinced by mounting evidence that Harpers Ferry was most certainly in danger of capture, Grant acted despite Halleck's skepticism that an incursion in force was actually about to begin in Maryland. The intelligence that tipped the scales appears to have come from General George G. Meade at City Point, who provided confirmation from two rebel deserters regarding the enemy motions. "They state it to be correctly reported at Richmond and in Petersburg that Early, in command of two divisions of Ewell's corps, with Breckinridge's command and other forces, was making an invasion of Maryland with a view of capturing Washington, supposed to be defenseless." Grant immediately ordered Meade to send one infantry division to the capital, but to be followed "if necessary" by the rest of a full corps, though he could ill afford to send even one off. Selection of which troops would be dispatched was left to Halleck. For the moment at least, Grant was of the opinion that Federal forces believed to still be in the Shenandoah Valley could readily defend Harpers Ferry if attacked. He was as yet unaware that the valley had been virtually swept clean by the rebels. Unfortunately, he was also unaware that the first troops selected by Halleck dispatched to the capital consisted of just 2,496 sick and invalid men from the 3rd Cavalry Division Corps, mostly without arms, all of whom were deemed expendable and of no use in the Virginia theater.[19]

For Lincoln it was to be another sleepless night in the White House. At 1 a.m., July 6, he received an urgent telegram direct from John W. Garrett. His reaction can only be imagined. The railroad mogul informed him of the stunning developments in the west. Confederate troops under General Early, after taking Martinsburg and Harpers Ferry, it was reported for the first time, were actually advancing toward Baltimore and Washington. Now there was not a moment to waste.

At the president's immediate direction, Secretary Stanton was fully alerted and telegraphed Pennsylvania Governor Andrew Curtin and New York Governor Horatio Seymour to request 12,000 militia or volunteers be sent from each of their states to serve for one hundred days in the defense of the capital.[20] It seemed to matter little that such a large force could hardly be raised and organized, much less armed, trained and then sent to the rescue on such short notice. The request revealed, for the first time, the actual level of desperation under which the admin- istration was operating. It must have seemed to Lincoln like the worst days of April 1861 all over again!

About the time the president was digesting the horrific news in those predawn hours at the White House, General Barnes was disembarking at Point Lookout from

484

the steamer that had brought him down from Washington. Still unaware of the dramatic events in Western Maryland, his first mission later that morning was to inspect the prison camp, hospital and the several commands on the point. In the evening he was serenaded by the bands of the 5th Massachusetts Regiment and the 10th and 20th Regiments of the Veteran Reserve Corps, invalids all. They comprised the skeleton force of 3,615 officers and men and just seven field pieces now guarding the entire St. Mary's peninsula.[21]

***

The July 5 rebel crossing into Maryland at Boeteler's Ferry near Shepherdstown, West Virginia, ten miles downstream from Harpers Ferry, had found Federal authorities taken quite by surprise and most certainly unprepared. It would soon prove costly for the North as rebel cavalry under Brigadier General John D. Imboden began to wreck B&O railroad bridges and culverts as far west as Cumberland. Major General John Gordon assailed the Chesapeake and Ohio Aqueduct over Antietam Creek, destroyed several canal barges full of coal, and demolished the Antietam Iron Works. That same day Confederate cavalry under Brigadier General John McCausland, a graduate and later professor at the Virginia Military Institute, was ordered to seize Hagerstown, ten miles north of Sharpsburg, Maryland. He was to hold it for ransom in retribution for depredations caused by Hunter in the Shenandoah. McCausland quickly detached a small unit under Lieutenant George M. E. Shearer of the 1st Maryland Cavalry toward the town. The unit briskly skirmished with a small force of Federals before being driven back. The following day, as Early completed the crossing with the remainder of his army, McCausland, leading some 1,200 cavalrymen and a battery of artillery, easily took the town of 6,500 residents. He then demanded and received, upon threat of total destruction, a ransom payment of $20,000 in U.S. dollars, 1,500 pairs of shoes and boots, suits, hats and shirts, and 1,900 pairs of drawers. Though the cash payment was arranged through James D. Roman, President of the Hagerstown Bank, it was impossible to gather all the clothing required, obliging McCausland and the town elders to negotiate a secret compensatory agreement before the soldiers departed.[22]

Within the next two days, several columns of rebels advanced ever deeper into the heart of Maryland, marching through placid villages and towns such as Sharpsburg, Keedysville, Boonsborough, Rohersville, and Burkittsville, engaging in repeated skirmishes against inferior numbers as they went. A wave of refugees, both white and black, fled before them.

***

As the menace now seemed to be growing exponentially by the hour, General Augur informed General Halleck that one regiment of heavy artillery must immediately be sent to Washington "to be distributed among the 100-day militia in the forts, as the latter are not sufficiently instructed in the use of heavy artillery." In Annapolis Colonel Root received orders at 5:30 p.m., July 6, to send his militia by rail to the Monocacy with three days rations and 100 rounds of ammunition to support Wallace.[23] The following morning six companies of Ohio Volunteers from Camp Parole departed for the new front. That same afternoon, more reinforcements, this time wholly able and armed men from Grant's army, were also underway. At 11:30 p.m. the night before, the general had finally ordered the 3rd

485

Division, VI Army Corps under Brigadier General James B. Ricketts, to Locust Point, Baltimore, for transfer west via the B&O. Within three and a half hours the division, twelve regiments, approximately 4,400 men strong, had begun the march to City Point. There they would embark aboard the fast transports *Columbia, Thomas Powell, Jersey Blue,* and *Sylvan Shore* to carry them to Baltimore. At noon the next day, the first of the transports arrived at its destination. The rest were not far behind.[24]

"J. A. Early CSA" (left), and Major General Lew Wallace (right) . Civil War Photographs Collection, Prints and Photographs Division, Library of Congress, Washington, D.C.

At 8 p.m. that same evening far to the west, five companies of the 8th Illinois Cavalry Regiment, 230 strong, under Lieutenant Colonel David R. Clendenin (the same commander who had conducted the successful May 1863 raid through the Northern Neck), were the first Federal troops to finally reach Frederick upon orders of General Wallace. They had been sent out two days before from Camp Relief in Washington via Muddy Branch to Point of Rocks on the upper Potomac to investigate disruptions of telegraph lines between Harpers Ferry and Washington. They had fought a series of skirmishes there and at Noland's Ferry to prevent a crossing by rebel cavalry units of the 43rd Virginia Battalion under Lieutenant Colonel John S. Mosby. But their real fight was just beginning.[25]

By now, like a violent summer thunderstorm, the Confederates were rolling in fast from the west. At 12:50 p.m., July 7, Halleck received an urgent telegram from Wallace, who had already arrived on the Monocacy, informing him that the Confederate Army was now at hand. That morning, Clendenin's cavalry had been driven back by a far superior force of rebel infantry, cavalry and artillery approaching from the vicinity of Middletown, barely seven miles west of Frederick, which had already been looted of stores and horses and ransomed for $5,000. Soon afterwards, he was engaged in a five-hour firefight that would only temporarily stall the rebel advance. Bad news was followed by worse when Halleck informed the general that the hoped for Union reinforcements from Hunter was now out of the question. But there was some light, if not from Washington. From Garrett, Wallace learned that Ricketts' reinforcements were en route. It was not as many men as desired, but enough to at least help make a stand.[26]

At 9:42 p.m. General Halleck belatedly instructed Wallace to send the troops coming in at Locust Point to the Monocacy or Point of Rocks, sites menaced by the rebel army. He was also tardily instructed: "In the operations now in progress you will not restrict yourself to departmental lines." [27]

Soon a mélange of Federal units from the Virginia theater of war had arrived at Baltimore, infantrymen, cavalrymen and artillerymen with homes in Ohio, New York, Illinois, New Jersey, Pennsylvania, Vermont, and Maryland. Immediately upon arrival they were boarding cars at Locust Point following those already en route to the distant but strategic railroad bridge over a meandering river of which most had never heard.

***

Secretary Stanton did his best to keep everyone that needed to know apprised of the situation, including the few commanders in charge of Southern Maryland. As protective fortifications for the prison camp at Point Lookout were minimal, General Barnes placed extra pickets at strategic points, and his entire command was ordered, "to be ready to move at a moment's notice." On July 7 the secretary dispatched several telegrams to the general repeatedly advising him to be vigilant, "as the enemy is now operating in Maryland in large force." He also informed him that the navy was to provide additional gunboats in numbers deemed adequate for protection. Barnes immediately convened a meeting with the commanders of the steamers *William H. Brown* and *Currituck*, both guardships assigned to the point. The specifics for additional flotilla support were quickly arranged. Again the navy and army somehow, remarkably, managed to work together. Navy Secretary Welles dispatched explicit orders to Commander Parker: "Take additional precautions relative to covering the camp of prisoners at Point Lookout and its approaches by your gunboats." Soon an additional warship was en route down to the point and then another. Within hours *Resolute* and *Fuchsia* had joined *Brown* and *Currituck* for guard duty.[28]

As the Yankees were doing their best to prepare for the enemy at the gate, additional streams of intelligence regarding rebel intentions were starting to flow in to the Union command. At 10 p.m. General Butler, in the field near his head-quarters at Bermuda Hundred in Virginia, sent off a most disturbing message to one of Grant's adjutants: "A rebel deserter reports that it is part of Early's plan to attack Point Lookout and release the prisoners, amusing us meanwhile at Martinsburg." Not fully taken in by the account, the general added skeptically, "This is sent for what it is worth." The adjutant immediately forwarded the intelligence to Washington.[29]

By July 8 Wallace, who had established his headquarters at Monocacy Junction, visited Frederick and briefly aroused the hopes of residents, albeit for naught. Early's army was on the outskirts of the town, having driven off the small force of Federals before it, with every indication that the thrust against Washington would be successful.

The invasion was proving bittersweet for some of the Maryland Confederates. General Johnson, a born native of Frederick County, was among them, especially when the fighting was closing in on his hometown, family and friends. Anxious to lead the attack, he was prohibited by his senior commander, Major General Robert Ransom, who declared him overly enthusiastic.

Though he was not permitted to assail the town directly, his artillery did. He would later learn of its effects: "I had had the Baltimore Light Artillery on the Hagerstown pike by the limekiln, and had been firing on some infantry in Reich's orchard, nearer the town. One of the shells went whizzing by the cupola of the courthouse, filled with women, some of whom were my old friends, and one shell struck my own house, on the division line, between my house and Dr. George Johnson, my cousin's . . . Another shell struck the Presbyterian church." [30]

Wallace and all the Federal forces in the area were now obliged to fall back to the Monocacy to hold the strategic crossings at and about Monocacy Junction. Not long afterwards a ransom of $200,000 was demanded by the rebel army and received from the city of Frederick, even as Confederates scoured the countryside farms for "money, meat, chickens, cattle, sheep & anything that came their way." That same evening, Johnson received an order from Early to report to him at his headquarters in John Hagan's Tavern near Middletown, three miles west of Frederick. He had just received a confidential letter from General Lee carried by his staff officer, his own son, Captain Robert E. Lee, Jr., who had arrived at 8 p.m. from Petersburg. The written instructions he carried, though somewhat vague, were of the utmost importance. Indeed, they were of such significance that the captain had been instructed by his father to commit them to memory. If he found himself in danger of capture, he informed his hosts, he was to destroy the document to prevent discovery of the critical orders contained therein. [31]

General Johnson was perhaps a bit taken aback at the demanding scope of the instructions, particularly as they related to his own operations. He and his cavalry were to be detached from Early's army and sent eastward to destroy all bridges and telegraph wires north and east of Baltimore, then circle back around the city and sever communications between Baltimore and Washington. They would be obliged to ride over 300 miles in three and a half days through the heart of Union territory. On the evening of July 12 they were to participate in a coordinated attack on Point Lookout with Commander John Taylor Wood, whose ships would be launched out of Wilmington, North Carolina, more than 350 miles to the south by sea, and with whom Johnson would have no prior contact. The orders were demanding in the extreme. "I told General Early that horseflesh could not do it," Johnson later he recalled in later years, "but I would do whatever man and horse could do."

Early's own mission was even more monumental in scope, being nothing less than assailing Washington itself. With the Union capital in peril, it was Lee's hope that the Potomac Flotilla protecting the prison camp would be recalled to defend the city and Wood might approach Point Lookout without naval opposition. Expecting to find between 15,000 and 30,000 prisoners eager for release, Johnson was to take command of them, march to Bladensburg, and there rendezvous with Early. With this combined rebel force, between 30,000 and 45,000 strong, the undefended capital of the United States could be easily carried and communications established across the Potomac with Virginia. Grant would have no choice but to abandon, or at the very least lessen his stranglehold on Petersburg and the threat to Richmond and return to retake Washington.[32]

It was a gamble at best, but one with remarkably high stakes. Wood would first have to elude the U.S. Navy blockaders off Wilmington, enter and pass up the Chesapeake undetected, and count that Lee was correct about the recall of the Potomac Flotilla to Washington. Early would have to reach the District of Columbia intact and without delay menace the city, the most heavily fortified metropolis in the world. Johnson's men and horses would have to survive an incredible ride of over eighty-four hours without stopping, to free an entire army and change the course of the war and history. And it all depended on secrecy, an almost fluid commodity difficult to control under the best of circumstances.

***

On the morning of July 8, even as the Confederates were pressing the Yankees before Frederick, Benjamin Butler's warning of a possible attack on Point Lookout was being forwarded by General Augur to Barnes: "General Butler telegraphs that a rebel deserter reports that Early intends, among other things, to attack Point Lookout and release the prisoners there. Be on your guard, therefore. Notify the gunboats and keep some of your cavalry well out." [33]

"Brig. General James Barnes and Staff, Point Lookout Civil War Prison Camp." New York Public Library.

The warning changed everything. Though he could not have known it, Lee's hopes for a withdrawal of the Potomac Flotilla gunboats protecting the prison camp quickly proved to be the first of many flaws in his bold plan. At Secretary Stanton's request, instead of removing ships for the defense of the capital, Secretary Welles had ordered the seaborne approach to Point Lookout secured from attack. Gunboats were already at the point, and soon others, even more powerful and numerous, would be on the way.[34] Barnes doubled up on security with the few troops and naval craft already at his disposal. "All the command [is] ready at a moment's notice all night," he informed Stanton, "and will be kept so." [35]

Everything that could be done had been done. "All quiet here," Barnes informed Augur soon afterwards. There was, however, one problem. "Two hundred and fifty prisoners of war left here this p.m. for New York by Colonel Hoffman's order; extra precaution taken." Unfortunately, the "precaution" required by the colonel consisted of 341 guards to be detached from the already weakened Point Lookout defenses and transferred to Elmira to accompany the prisoners, which left the camp even more dangerously depleted of manpower than ever.[36]

And not very far to the west, as the gathering storm was about to strike on the Monocacy, anything now seemed possible. For the Confederacy the capture of Washington and the freeing of the prisoners at Point Lookout seemed now within reach. Then, at 7:25 p.m. an urgent telegram was received by Lee concerning Wood's amphibious operations, which were scheduled to get underway the following day. "The expedition is spoken of all through the army, information having been brought from Richmond." The hitherto secret plan to attack Point Lookout by water was no longer secret at all. "I will," Lee informed Davis bluntly, "inform the leaders and let them judge." [37]

37

BAD HUMOR
"I will shoot any man that touches that flag."

General Lew Wallace's stand against the overwhelming numbers of General Jubal Early's army came to be known as the Battle of Monocacy. It was a contest that some historians would later deem a small but significant engagement of the Civil War. Begun early on the hot, cloudless morning of July 9, the fight would see the deployment of a patchwork of defenders hurriedly assembled from numerous sources. They were sent directly into harm's way at Monocacy Junction, just southeast of Frederick. Wallace's force was small. With approximately 4,400 to 5,000 New Jersey, New York, Pennsylvania and Vermont veterans under Ricketts' VI Army Corps, 2,500 men of the VIII Army Corps, mostly green and untrained hundred day Maryland and Ohio militiamen, four small cavalry units, one field gun battery and some unattached howitzers, Wallace intended to make a desperate gamble to buy time. The site of the clash of arms was to be on the banks of the gently flowing Monocacy River, amidst farmlands the general lyrically and perhaps somewhat ironically compared to a western prairie replete with fields "golden with wheat just ready for the reaper." [1]

The battle had opened between 8:00 and 9:00 a.m. After intense and very bloody fighting, it was all but over eight hours later. Having suffered a loss of between 1,294 and 1,968 in killed, wounded and missing, including 600 captured, versus approximately 900 rebel casualties, Wallace's little army was in tatters. He immediately began a retreat from the field eastward toward Ellicott's Mills (modern Ellicott City). Word of the defeat was first dispatched to John Garrett, who was to provide the critical rail connection for the army's escape. "I did as I promised," Wallace reported. "Held the bridge [at Monocacy Junction] to the last. They overwhelmed me with numbers. My troops fought splendidly. Losses fearful. Send me cars enough to Ellicott's Mills to take up my retreating columns. Don't fail me." His message to General Halleck was equally terse. "I fought the enemy at Frederick Junction from 9 a.m. till 5 p.m., when they overwhelmed me with numbers. I am retreating with a footsore, battered, and half demoralized column. Force of the enemy at least 20,000. They do not seem to be pursuing." And as if to assert the importance of the event, he warned: "You will have to use every exertion to save Baltimore and Washington." [2]

What was left of the Union Army fell back from Monocacy Junction to Urbanna, then northeast to Monrovia. Soon afterward they reached the Baltimore Pike near Ridgeville to begin the twenty-mile trek to Ellicott Mills and then via train at Relay to Baltimore. The long day purchased by the Union's sacrifice in blood, however, would soon prove crucial to the preservation of the capital city of the United States.

***

Even as the fight on the Monocacy was unfolding, hundreds of miles to the south John Taylor Wood was engaged in his own struggle to launch the amphibious arm of the expedition to free the thousands of prisoners at Point Lookout. He had been accompanied on the trip from Richmond by a battalion of marines under the command of Brigadier General G. W C. Lee, and a number of sailors belonging to the Confederate States Navy, 800 men in all. Upon his arrival at Wilmington, he found two fast, armed blockade runners awaiting him, both having been specifically commandeered for his use. But there had been a problem in securing the arms intended for the prisoners upon their being set free. Nevertheless, he proceeded to divide his forces evenly between the two ships, with two detachments per vessel, and then set to rounding up the required weaponry. By July 9 he had managed to secure several field pieces but only 2,000 muskets with which to equip and organize 13,000 liberated prisoners. Surprise and audacity, he knew, would again have to compensate for the deficiency in guns and manpower.[3]

Unfortunately for Wood, the mantle of secrecy had already, somehow, been lifted.

***

Throughout the bloodletting on the Monocacy, General Bradley Johnson's brigade had been assigned a position north of Early's main force. His unit consisted of 1,500 men from 8th, 21st and 36th Virginia Cavalry regiments, the 22nd and 34th Virginia Cavalry battalions, the 1st Maryland Cavalry Regiment, and the 2nd Maryland Cavalry Battalion, along with a battery of horse artillery belonging to the Baltimore Light Artillery. Their mission was to guard the army's left flank commanded by General Robert Rodes. As soon as Johnson, who had taken station at Worman's Mill, believed the battle was well in hand, he began to execute his next orders by moving the brigade down Old Liberty Road. It would be the first step of what can only be regarded as an epic ride.[4]

Striking out eastward, Johnson quickly passed through the hamlets of Liberty and Uniontown, where he secured boots, shoes and clothing from reluctant shopkeepers in return for Confederate script. Before departing, he burned a railroad station and a bridge. Soon after arriving at New Windsor, the next town on the route, he detailed another native Marylander, Major Harry Gilmor, and twenty handpicked troopers to destroy the telegraph lines near Westminster. Following a brief skirmish at Westminster with a 150-man unit of the surprised Union cavalry garrison there, Gilmor received orders by courier to levy 1,500 shoes, boots and suits from the town before Johnson's main force arrived. Because the mayor was unable to convene the town council before the full brigade's arrival, a sympathetic Gilmor was able to persuade the general to forego putting Westminster to the torch. Instead, the Confederates focused their energies in gutting a local B&O branch line.[5]

By 8 a.m. on the morning of Sunday, July 10, Major Harry Gilmor and his 2nd Maryland Calvary, serving as a screen before the army, had reached Reisterstown. General Johnson was not far behind. The general would later recall with some fondness the welcome he received as he passed through the town when "a man come to my horse at the head of the column and threw his arms around the horse's neck and fairly cried, 'Ain't I got it on Jake. He always said they'd never come, and I said they would come, and here they are sure enough.' And that fellow hugged my horse and cried and sobbed all through the village." As they pressed south and entered Randallstown, another man rushed out in a state of excitement. His wife had just given birth to a baby boy they had named "Brad Johnson," which enormously elated the general. Twenty-five years later he noted: "I owe that baby a silver cup to the present day." [6]

Johnson again rejoined Gilmor at Cockeysville where "we struck [at] the church hour, and I fear we rather broke up the meeting. We were greater attractions than the preachers." Here the morning was spent destroying one turnpike bridge, two railroad crossings as well as "a lot of cars." Now, with his whole force less than fourteen miles north of Baltimore, the general detached Gilmor on a special mission. The major was to proceed eastward with 135 men of his own unit and the 1st Maryland Cavalry Regiment to destroy the Gunpowder River Bridge of the Philadelphia, Wilmington and Baltimore Railroad. His route was briefly altered when he and several officers headed a few miles south to visit "Glen Ellen," his own family estate in Towsontown, on the banks of Loch Raven. Later that evening, refreshed and revived by his family, which he had not seen in two years, he headed northeast through the hamlet of Timonium, over the York Road and Philadelphia Pike towards his main target.[7]

***

John R. Kenly, now a brigadier general operating from the headquarters of the VIII Army Corps in Baltimore, was alarmed. When news of the Wallace defeat reached the city on the evening of July 9, a public near panic ensued. Liquor stores were closed at 8 p.m.[8] City officials appointed by Mayor John L. Chapman wired the president requesting reinforcements. They were assured that all available troops were being deployed to protect everyone, and that the latest reports suggested the enemy was moving against Washington, not Baltimore. The reply was not comforting and to some it seemed that confusion and alarm were becoming all pervasive in the highest government circles, the major exception being President Lincoln himself. To one group of terrified Baltimoreans appointed by the mayor to confer with him on needed assistance, he simply suggested calm. "Let us be vigilant but keep cool. I hope neither Baltimore nor Washington will be taken." [9]

At daybreak the following morning, July 10, definite intelligence regarding the enemy's approach arrived in Baltimore. Bells sounded the alarm throughout the city. "I have the honor to report," Kenly informed the assistant adjutant general, "that a scout returned with the information that at about 8 a.m. this morning a body of rebel cavalry, said to number 1,600 men, under command of Johnson and Gilmor, passed through Reisterstown, and it was reported that they were moving to destroy the bridges of the Northern Central Railroad, and also the bridges on the Philadelphia and Baltimore Railroad." Governor Bradford and Mayor Chapman issued a joint proclamation addressing the peril to the city as real and called for immediate assistance from the public to man all extant fortifications and help construct new ones. Halleck placed Brevet Brigadier General William W. Morris in command of all Baltimore defense construction. General Henry Hayes Lockwood, a former professor at West Point, was appointed commander of all loyal civilian Union League militia called out by the mayor and all fortifications east of Jones Falls. General Kenly was placed in command of all fortifications west of Jones Falls. Major General Edward O. C. Ord was to replace General Wallace as commander of the VIII Army Corps and all military operations and movements in the Middle District. "I would give more for him [Ord] as a commander in the field than most of the generals in Maryland," Grant informed Halleck in justification for the appointment. Wallace, who had gambled all to delay the enemy's advance, was consigned to remain in charge of "administration" in the district.

Now the enormous pro-secessionist demonstrations of only a few years earlier seemed a distant memory as the citizen call-up was enthusiastically met with a patriotism that seemed contagious. Lockwood immediately issued instructions for the city's streets to be barricaded, with labor for the work raised by the mayor, and the necessary construction materials furnished by the Quartermaster's Department. Countless numbers of city residents of all colors were soon turning out to form military units and build defenses. The response among the free black population, which formed their own militia companies and contributed to the construction of fortifications and logistical support, was substantial. Within two days Baltimore's home defense force numbered 3,000 militiamen, 500 blacks, 200 sailors, and a miscellaneous body of armed citizens. General Ricketts' division, bloodied, ragged and worn from the defeat at the Monocacy, reduced to only 2,488 weary soldiers, were also readied. One hundred thousand dollars was appropriated by the city to build defense works. Barricades were erected at key points to obstruct enemy cavalry charges into the city, even as the contents of warehouses were emptied and transferred to ships in the harbor made ready for quick departure if necessary. "The banks and insurance companies have all deposited their valuables on board of a steamer chartered for the purpose, and ready to leave at a moment's notice . . . Arrangements have also been made to remove the archives of the State from Annapolis." Records and documents belonging to the provost marshal and the paymaster general's offices, the U.S. Customs Office and post office were also placed aboard a steamer for safety.[10]

In Annapolis the threat had become visceral when reports began to circulate, prematurely as it proved, that the invaders had seized the railroad between Baltimore and Washington. The town was already abuzz and on the edge of panic when the bell atop city hall summoned the citizens to a general meeting that evening. With the Maryland Constitutional Convention, ongoing ever since its first meeting in the city on April 27 to formulate a new state constitution, the arrival of the enemy at the gate was troubling indeed. State Comptroller of the Treasury Henry H. Goldsborough of Talbot County, president of the convention, and Dr. Washington G. Tuck called for volunteers to protect the city. "The soldiers stationed there, with about a thousand citizens, the Union men volunteering and the traitors being forced by the military authorities – went to work throwing up earth- works on Monday night for the defense of the place." Goldsborough picked up a shovel and joined in the labor. A delegate from Cecil County, not content with the preparations, was said to have actually girded himself with a suit of armor "and made ready to take a hand in the threatening conflict." In the harbor, a gunboat was readied for combat, even as a handful of citizens were being sent out to reconnoiter, and a "heavy picket guard" patrolled the outskirts of town. Everyone spent a sleepless night. On July 11 martial law was proclaimed.[11]

***

The alarm was now general throughout the region. Not the least to be surprised by the rapid turn of events was Foxhall A. Parker who was on leave at his home,

"Relay House," a few hundred yards from Relay Station near Baltimore. He learned of the invasion from retreating troops from the Monocacy and soon after received an urgent dispatch from Secretary Welles.

"I came out to my home late last night," he reported, "and to my astonishment this morning find that our army is falling back upon Baltimore. I have received your dispatch and will obey immediately. Before receiving the dispatch I telegraphed to Captain Eastman, at the Washington navy yard, to send a gunboat to Baltimore, whither I intended to drive, as I feared railroad communication between this and Washington may be cut off. I also telegraphed to Captain Eastman to have the whole flotilla ready to act as circumstances may require. What shall I do now? Go to Baltimore, or come to Washington in the first train?" [12]

Welles replied quickly, ordering Parker to Washington but countermanding the order to send a gunboat to Baltimore. He was more deeply concerned about maintaining protection of the strategic bridge and ferry crossings over the waterways north and east of that city, particularly on the Gunpowder and Bush rivers, ever since news of the rebel invasion first materialized. Fortunately, plans to dispatch two light gunboats for their defense were readily unfurled. Now he ordered Lieutenant Commander Eastman to dispatch not two but three ships from the Potomac Flotilla to the endangered area. *Currituck* was instructed to proceed to defend the Havre de Grace crossing over the Susquehanna. *Fuchsia* was ordered to the Bush River to protect the Bush River Bridge, while *Resolute* was sent to protect the Gunpowder crossing, all strategic points of access for reinforcements coming by land from the north. He also ordered the great steam frigate *Minnesota* and four gunboats from Hampton Roads to proceed immediately to the Potomac to further reinforce the defenses at Point Lookout.[13]

***

After receiving a complete briefing on Sunday afternoon regarding Wallace's defeat at Monocacy Junction, an anxious President Lincoln telegraphed General Grant. He recommended that he leave a holding force at Petersburg and come to Washington with the rest of his army to contend with Early, but left the final decision to the general. "This is what I think . . . and is not an order," clearly deferring to his senior commander in whom he had the utmost faith and confidence.[14]

Grant responded by informing the president that he had already sent 6,000 veteran soldiers to Washington, including one division of the XIX Army Corps, which would be in the city by the following night, and a second, the VI Army Corps, soon afterwards. This force, under Major General Horatio Wright, he felt, together with the forces already in the city, would be able to contend with Early. He also believed, erroneously as it turned out, that General Hunter would soon join Wright to successfully help turn back the rebels. If Hunter, who had been summoned from the west, made his appearance, the enemy's escape route would be entirely closed off. Grant was now convinced that it was Lee's goal to use Early's invasion to relieve the pressure on Petersburg. It was relief he was not about to provide, and so informed the president: "I think on reflection it would have a bad effect for me to leave here." General Halleck would have to cope with the by now weary invaders until the reinforcements arrived. Lincoln resignedly accepted his top commander's decision. By 10 a.m. the first of Wright's corps was boarding sixteen transports bound for Washington. Though there would be fighting ahead, and no one could have foreseen it, Grant's decision would soon define the high water mark of Early's offensive even before his main attack on Washington had begun.[15]

***

By now Early's main force, preceded by McCausland's cavalry brigade, was progressing from Monocacy Junction southward along the Georgetown Pike, traversing a countryside of divided loyalties through the towns of Urbanna, Hyattstown, Clarksburg, and up Parr's Ridge to the village of Gaithersburg. At Gerrardsville, three miles northwest of Rockville, McCausland encountered approximately 500 men of the 16th Pennsylvania Cavalry under Major William H. Fry and elements of the 8th Illinois Cavalry that had been sent out to reconnoiter. After several hours of fighting, beginning at the Summit Hill farm of John DeSellum, the Yankees were driven back to a line a mile south of Rockville, a town noted for its strong secessionist element. Then, under fire from an artillery battery, they were forced into retreat again. By 4 p.m. McCausland had pushed to within two miles of Tennallytown, D.C., a popular Union training ground at the beginning of the war. The approach, however, was guarded by strong defense works, the largest being Fort Reno, situated on an elevation of 429 feet, the highest point in the District of Columbia, and mounting twenty-seven guns, including a 100-pound Parrott rifled cannon. Caution prevailed and the decision was made to retire for the night towards Rockville, leaving a small force at the edge of the District. He would be back for another try in the morning.[16]

***

Well to the north, Federal efforts to deploy scratch detachments for the defense of the strategic railroad bridges and junctions were undertaken with difficulty at Bush River, Gunpowder River, and the crossings on the Susquehanna at Conowingo. Thirty-two men under Lieutenant Robert Price of Company F, 135th Ohio National Guard, had been dispatched to the Gunpowder, and soon after were reinforced by fifty-five more from the just formed 7th Delaware Infantry under Captain Thomas Hugh Stirling. Another scratch force of sailors and marines along with a naval battery and a unit of Pennsylvania artillery under Major Henry B. Judd were sent to the Susquehanna crossings.

Neither Gilmor nor his weary Confederate troopers were about to be deterred. After leaving "Glen Ellen" they had headed east toward the Gunpowder. Riding hard, the raiders quickly passed through Timonium, over York Road and the Philadelphia Pike. Without opposition along the Bel Air and Harford roads, they cut telegraph lines belonging to the American Telegraph Company, the Independent Line, and the People's Line. Critical wire communications to the north from both Washington and Baltimore were now severed.[17]

While on the Harford Turnpike the rebels stopped briefly at Dampman's Hotel, eight miles from Bel Air, and then passed through Long Green Valley. Another short stop was made in the valley at the farm of Joshua Price, whose son was one of Gilmor's party, and then the riders pressed on again. Soon after crossing the Bel Air Road, thirteen miles from Baltimore, they came upon the farm of Ishmael Day, a sixty-five-year-old farmer "well known in the county and city for his loyalty." Over the gate to his farm Day had raised an American flag, which drew a party of

496

Confederates who demanded it be taken down. The defiant old man refused. "Gentlemen," he warned the invaders, "you may take my horses and cattle, or burn my house to the ground, but I will shoot any man that touches that flag." On that, a rebel named Fields approached to remove the flag. Without hesitation the farmer shot him in the face and chest, mortally wounding him. Day immediately fled before the rebels could apprehend him, eventually making his way to the safety of Baltimore. In retaliation the raiders burned his house, barn and outbuildings.[18]

It was still dark when Gilmor's raiders crossed the Gunpowder Turnpike Bridge, some distance north of the railroad bridge, instead of heading straight for it, to evade Union defense forces at the crossing. Leaving the turnpike on the east side of the river, they then headed south for the B&O line at Magnolia Station, approximately a mile east and above the railroad bridge. About 4:30 a.m., July 11 in the predawn gray, they took the station by complete surprise, quietly, and without difficulty or knowledge of the nearby Yankees. The scratch force of fewer than ninety men of the 7th Delaware and Ohio National Guardsmen that maintained watch over the western approach to the bridge (from which direction the attack was expected) heard nothing. The armed transport steamer *Juniata*, which lay several hundred yards to the south, remained motionless. Believing the bridge to be protected by the armed gunboat, which had rendered a direct approach to the bridge "impracticable," the rebels settled down, silently awaiting the arrival of the first train. Five hours later, about 9:30 a.m., the 8:40 a.m. Baltimore to Philadelphia train with a dozen passenger cars was brought to a halt after crossing the bridge by a volley of gunfire from the rebel cavalry. In an instant Gilmor's Confederates had "dashed up to the cars, presenting their pistols, and yelling like savages. Some dismounted, entered the cars, and commenced robbing the passengers, which, however, was soon forbidden; private property and persons were protected, and a strict search made for officers of the army and navy, the mails, and other public property." Among the passengers were some acquainted with many of the raiders, all Marylanders, "and after the work of destruction was well nigh over, there was considerable gallantry, exhibited by both gentlemen and ladies, with the Rebel officers. Mementoes, in the shape of Southern buttons, were quite liberally distributed to the eternal disgrace of the truculent recipients." [19]

Among the passengers in the first car, dressed in civilian clothing, was Major General William B. Franklin, USA. The general, wounded in a recent battle and en route home to recuperate, managed for some time to escape discovery until, it was later reported, a lady passenger of Southern sympathies betrayed him. The general and at least three officers of his staff were immediately taken prisoner and placed in the custody of Captain Nicholas Owings, a Baltimore County native. Under a picked guard Franklin was put aboard a confiscated buggy, "the only indignity offered him being by a private soldier, who exchanged hats with the general." His pistol and book were delivered to Gilmor who issued orders that only the money of the officers should be confiscated. Citizens were to be protected.[20]

After all the Union officers captured with Franklin and male passengers were taken care of, the ladies in the first passenger car were transferred to the rear car and the rest of the train set on fire. It was later reported that some of the women had brought with them bottles of wine and other liquors, which were offered "their

Confederate friends." While the cars were burning, the women were allowed to vacate the last car to retrieve their personal belongings that had been removed from the baggage car. The vacated car was then burned as well, the smoke alerting for the first time the Union guards on the other side of the river and only minutes before the arrival of the next train.

It had been less than a half hour after the first capture had been made when the sound of the arrival of the next train, the Washington to New York express, which had left Baltimore between 9:30 and 9:45 a.m., was heard. Inexplicably, a later press report noted, notwithstanding "the dense smoke from the burning cars, and a frame building, the conductor ran the train within one hundred yards of the burning cars. This seems unaccountable, as the smoke must have been seen for miles, and especially in crossing the Gunpowder, Magnolia Station being but a short distance off." The captured train was a prize indeed, and consisted of two baggage and nine express cars.[21]

Harry Gilmor's Raid on Magnolia Station. Prints and Photographs Division, Library of Congress.

When the train came to a halt, some of the passengers, the fireman and conductor attempted to escape, but were brought to by several shots. The fireman was later reported killed, but there were no other casualties. This time there were a greater number of lady travelers than men on the train, but all were treated the same as those on the first train. Soon all passengers were taken off. A decision was made to set the cars afire, and then push them backwards onto the downgrade where gravity would take hold and press them to the center of the bridge to destroy it as well.[22]

With the blazing train rolling down towards them, a small party of the 159th Ohio led by Captain Stirling rushed onto the bridge and managed to detach and save two cars before the whole line took fire. They were, however, no match for rebel sharpshooters on the east bank. Moreover, *Juniata*, Ensign William J. Herring commanding, lying just 300 yards downriver, was unable to muster enough power to provide any fire support for the defenders, and proved useless. General Wallace later stated that the ship simply had no steam up. It was also later erroneously reported: "A guard of twenty men at the bridge were gobbled up." Soon the bridge drawspan was in flames but only partially consumed before the locomotive and all but the two cars uncoupled by the defenders fell into the Gunpowder. Within minutes the whole bridge was aflame; a single train engine and six cars that had been on the siding, which the rebels had retained for their own transport to the Bush River Bridge, were now unnecessary. Thus, before departing Magnolia Station, Gilmor oversaw the destruction of all railroad property, including the cars and engine on the siding.

Gilmor's retreat would be to retrace his route to the north and then over the Gunpowder Turnpike Bridge, which would also be burned after crossing. The station building and water tank at Magnolia were spared as the former was occupied by the mother and sisters of Mr. Lytle, the station master, and the latter because burning it would have jeopardized the dwelling and deprived the women passengers of the train of water. Nor was the railroad track injured. The passengers and Union military officers that had been aboard the two trains, most of whom were paroled on the spot, now found themselves stranded on the peninsula between the Gunpowder and Bush rivers. Soon after the raiders departed, their last act was to descend upon the nearby estate of Major General George Cadwalader and carry off some thirty horses.[23]

With telegraph lines having been cut, the rebels had been able to maintain a certain level of surprise. Yet Baltimore would soon learn of the attack. George Owen, a line repairman for the American Telegraph Company, had been en route toward Magnolia when at Harewood, on the south shore of the Gunpowder, "he was an eye witness to the destruction of the bridge and train." When briefly captured he had overheard the rebels stating they were going to Havre de Grace to destroy the ferry and any vessels there, as well as "all the road from that point to Stemmer's run." Somehow he had escaped or, more likely, been released by the rebels. Observing smoke arising from the direction of the Bush River Bridge, he was certain that site had also been destroyed. By means of a handcar he was able to work his way back to the city, arriving at 9 p.m. that same night, and informed the company agent of the disaster. He also reported 1,000 to 1,500 rebels had taken the trains, not the 135 who had actually conducted the raid, which of course only instigated more fears "that a number of the mills, factories, and foundries around the city will be destroyed tonight." [24]

It could have been worse. One early report of the incident at Magnolia Station claimed that a great amount of money, $178,000 in cash shipped by the Adams Express Company in an agency car on the 9:30 train from Baltimore, might have also fallen into rebel hands. Much to the relief of Adams Express clients, it was soon learned "that the company took the precaution to transmit on the previous night their freights instead of yesterday morning, and that they had no car with the captured train." [25]

Late that evening Harry Gilmor's uncle William Gilmor and a colleague named G. B. Hoffman, emboldened by word of the attack on the Gunpowder, attempted to leave Baltimore to join the raiders. Federal pickets arrested both while passing into Baltimore County and immediately returned them to the city for incarceration.

A thorough search of Gilmor's house on the corner of Park and Franklin Streets resulted in the recovery of 500 muskets and 700 rounds of ball cartridge.[26]

***

Acting Master William Tell Street, commander of the USS *Fuchsia*, had perhaps not expected the urgent message he received on the morning of July 10 while lying off Point Lookout. The order directed him to immediately proceed to Bush River to protect the strategic railroad bridge from an expected attack by Confederate raiders. The little warship made good time and arrived off the mouth of the river at 7 a.m. the following morning. Not having a pilot acquainted with the waterway, the ship grounded twice before coming to anchor: a boat was sent on shore in search of one. Fortunately, aided by a passing schooner, Street found the channel and with a favorable tide succeeded in crossing the bar. By noon he had moored 150 yards from the bridge where he spied a body of bluecoats, twenty strong, coming toward him in a small boat, having been driven off by rebel cavalry. *Fuchsia*'s arrival had been timely indeed.

"They reported the enemy on both sides of the river," Street later informed Commander Parker, "and that the telegraph operator had just left his station. Shortly after cavalry were seen on the hill (right bank), when I opened fire upon them, causing them to fall back beyond our range. Had we been fifteen minutes later I have no doubt they would have had the bridge on fire. The soldiers were again landed and pickets thrown out, and during the afternoon were twice driven in, but the enemy would not advance from under cover of the woods or within range. Finding they could not approach the bridge, we were not annoyed by them after 7 p.m." [27]

***

Commander Parker, with the Potomac Flotilla already stretched thin, was desperate to provide as much naval assistance available to protect the bridges above and east of Baltimore. At 9:30 a.m., even as *Fuchsia* was attempting entry into Bush River, he wired a request to Assistant Secretary of the Navy Fox to have the coast steamer *Bibb*, then at wharfside at the Washington Navy Yard, armed and readied to proceed to the Gunpowder Bridge as soon as feasible. *Currituck* had already been sent to protect the ferry at Havre de Grace and would be in place by 1:40 p.m. By 7:30 p.m. *Bibb* had been armed and was already underway.[28]

It was all, however, just a bit too late. Gilmor, who now intended on riding straight through Baltimore, had learned at the last minute that the streets were barricaded. After sending off General Franklin and the rest of the prisoners to Reisterstown under a small guard commanded by Captain Owings, he quickly redirected his route to Towsontown. Though he and his men were absolutely fatigued they were able to ambush and drive off a party of seventy-five Union mounted volunteers sent to capture them. Making his way west to Owings Mills via the Reisterstown Road he finally came upon Captain Owings and his party, all fast asleep by the roadside after nearly three days in the saddle. General Franklin and the rest of the prisoners had escaped and sought sanctuary in a house outside of Baltimore. Gilmor dispatched a detail to scour the countryside for him. Obliged to elude horsemen sent out from the city, the rebel detail searched in vain until giving up at 5 p.m. that evening. The general would remain in hiding until rescued by a patrol of the 8th Illinois Cavalry on the evening of July 13. The capture of Gilmor and his raiders was by now out of the question. By the afternoon of July 12 the daring Confederates had departed Pikesville and lodged in Randallstown until the following morning when they again took to the saddle to hopefully rendezvous with Early.[29]

Though work to repair the cut telegraph lines and the Gunpowder Bridge was almost immediately begun, and little actual damage had been suffered to property or persons in the countryside (with the exception of the loss of a few train cars and locomotives), the Gilmor raid had been remarkable. With but a handful of men, he had thrown the entire countryside north of Baltimore as well as parts of Delaware and Pennsylvania into a state of panic and confusion as the numerical threat was magnified tenfold with each telling.[30]

***

For his own part, General Johnson had pressed on, sweeping around the north of Baltimore "appearing simultaneously on so many different roads at intervals from 6 to 10 miles, that many different columns were reported as advancing at once." General Ord had even written General Halleck late in the evening of July 12: "Have party out in pursuit of raiders who are reported all over the country in force from 5,000 to 7,000." A portion of Johnson's morning was spent disrupting the railroad from Baltimore to Westminster and cutting telegraph lines. Soon the brigade took up a line of march south towards Owings Mills, arriving about midday at the "Hayfield" farm of the now famous John Merryman. Here the general spent a pleasant Sunday afternoon and lunch apparently not too eager to maintain the regimen needed to get him to Point Lookout on time. At Hayfield he found "the charming society, the lovely girls, the luxuriant verdure" of the place most inviting, which may have been responsible for unnecessarily delaying his stay for a few hours before pressing on.

Johnson's brief visit, however, was not all devoted to socializing. Before setting out again he dispatched a trusted friend and officer, Colonel John C. Clarke, into Baltimore to gather intelligence on the city's defenses as well as those of Washington. Then at sunset, he arrived at "The Caves," the estate of John N. Carroll a dozen miles northwest of Baltimore, where he and his staff were to dine. While there he was informed by a number of his Maryland cavalrymen that the home of Governor Bradford lay nearby, though barely five miles from Baltimore. His informants eagerly followed with requests for permission to burn it. Johnson justified the mission as a reprisal for General Hunter's annihilation of the home of Virginia Governor John Letcher at Lexington, Virginia, and the Virginia Military Institute a month earlier. A ten man detail commanded by Lieutenant Henry Blacki-stone of the 1st Maryland Cavalry was assigned to carry out the deed. Then, after dinner, he called briefly on the priests of St. Charles College, "where the fathers were much pleased with the 'Boy General.'" [31]

Early the following morning Blackistone set off for the Bradford residence, where Mrs. Bradford was roused from her bed about 9 a.m. even as the first floor was being set afire. Confederate accounts claimed that the governor's wife was informed that she would be permitted to save some clothes and a few valuables, personal belongings and furniture with the aid of neighbors and a few rebel soldiers.

501

Johnson, attempting to put a chivalrous face on the incident, maintained the men he had sent were gentlemen. "They behaved with the greatest courtesy to the ladies of the house, helped them move their clothes and things and pianos out. A quantity of gold found was given to one of the young ladies on her assurances that it was her property." Mrs. Bradford's postwar depositions regarding damages stated quite the obverse. She remarked unequivocally that she had been awakened by soldiers piling up furniture downstairs and by rebels pounding on her bedroom door. She and her family escaped with little more than some clothing as the house was completely incinerated. Fortunately, the governor had left for the city the previous day.[32]

About midnight, July 10 two couriers who had been posted by Johnson to remain at Hayfield arrived with a critical dispatch sent by Clarke, who had somehow managed to enter Baltimore undetected. The news was all bad. The Union's XIX Army Corps, all the way from New Orleans by steamers, and part of the VI Corps of Grant's army were at Locust Point preparing to entrain for the relief of Washington. Though the report was only partially true, as the XIX Corps was actually bound for Washington via the Potomac and not Baltimore, Johnson quickly resolved to strike the B&O first at Woodstock and later stations on the main line between Baltimore and Washington to retard the reported Union reinforcements from reaching the capital. Unaware that the two corps were en route to their destination via the Potomac and not the Patapsco, he immediately dispatched an officer and escort south to warn Early of the situation.[33]

Now well aware that Early's motions on the outskirts of Washington had been compromised, as were his own, Johnson nevertheless resumed his march the following morning, though in a more leisurely fashion than before. The planned evening assault on Point Lookout on July 12 was looking less and less probable, as consideration now had to be given to marching conditions through the heart of enemy territory in horrific heat with weary troops and worn down horses. Some prominent historians have contended that the general had by now already determined that meeting his deadline, much less successfully assailing Point Lookout itself, was impossible.[34] Indeed, while awaiting the return of Lieutenant Blackistone's troopers from their mission at Bradford's country house, his men were permitted a rare respite from their onerous trek with a most unusual breakfast. The meal was unlike any they had ever consumed before.

While Blackistone was busy as an incendiary and Gilmor was riding hard to the east, Johnson had resumed his southerly march the morning of July 11. Just beyond Owing's Mills his men encountered and captured three wagons bound for the Baltimore markets laden with freezers full of ice cream from nearby Painter's Mill Farm. The Confederates, who by now were out of rations, immediately confiscated the frozen cargo. Using any implements available, including their hats, to scoop what some soldiers christened as "frozen mush" or "frozen vitals," the freezer contents, which came in three flavors, lemon, vanilla and raspberry, were quickly distributed among the sweating horsemen. The ice cream was consumed while they rode along. Some of the "wild mountaineers" from southwestern Virginia, who had never before seen or eaten such a confection, thought the frosty dairy product to be a type of beer too cold to drink and stuffed it into their canteens for later consumption after it melted. All were obliged to "eat with their hands out of their old rough, hats." One hungry soldier from Tazwell County, Virginia gobbled a mouthful, "then clapped his hands to both sides of his head and jumped up and down . . . It hurt so bad he forgot to spit it out." [35]

Now Johnson's brigade pressed across Howard County, traversing the B&O north of Woodstock, a few miles west of Ellicott's Mills, cutting telegraph lines and tearing up railroad track as they went. At Doughoregan Manor the general again took a brief detour to dine with the owner, John Lee Carroll. By 9 p.m., having ridden on a southwesterly course, the army bivouacked for a few short hours at the little mill town of Tridelphia on the Patuxent River border between Howard and Montgomery counties. The night was exceptionally warm and the troops passed a most restless and short-lived evening. When warned of a Federal cavalry unit bivouacked at the village of Brookville five miles to the south, the men were immediately aroused, saddled up and moved out, but found only an empty camp.[36]

At 2:00 a.m., July 12 Johnson's troopers continued on. By dawn they were making their way towards the town of Laurel with the intention of crossing and cutting the B&O tracks between Bladensburg and Baltimore. At Spencerville, eight miles west of Laurel on the Sandy Springs Road, they encountered several Yankee pickets who were easily driven off. Warned by his scouts that "a respectable force" of Union troops had been posted at Laurel Junction, he decided to pivot closer to the capital to destroy the rails at the village of Beltsville five or six miles southwest of Laurel. It had been an unnecessary move since the guards at both Laurel and Annapolis Junction had been ordered to fall back before the rebel advance. Nevertheless, the work of destruction continued.

As the rebels neared Beltsville between noon and 1 p.m., a dozen miles from Washington, the daily 10 a.m. train from Baltimore was but a mile from the village when a number of men working on the tracks came running towards it giving the alarm. The rebel cavalry "in some force" was approaching. Following a delay of about fifteen minutes, however, and after sending someone ahead to investigate, it was discovered the horsemen were actually Union scouts. The train continued on unimpeded, unaware of how close it came to being captured, for the enemy was immediately behind them.[37]

In Washington, about 1 p.m., it was learned that the telegraph wires between the capital and Baltimore had been cut. This time the rebels were clearly observed by railroad workmen leaving Bladensburg who had set off in a ballast engine. The enemy's dust cloud could be seen even as they departed Beltsville, which was followed by the sounds of gunfire. Upon their arrival at the village the rebels discovered little more than a construction train and another work crew that had failed to escape. Without delay they set to address their familiar incendiary agenda. It was first reported that twenty gondolas and ballast cars (though later counts stated three passenger, two dining, and two house cars as well as one small four wheel car), and other miscellaneous railroad property were set afire. Eight telegraph poles with more than a dozen lines were destroyed, severing all direct communication between the North and Grant's headquarters at City Point, Virginia. Smoke from the conflagration could be seen from Bladensburg and Fort Lincoln six miles to the south.

That afternoon George S. Koontz, the chief agent for the B&O, ordered an engine and one car prepared to go out and conduct a reconnaissance along the rail line to ascertain the condition of the road. At 3:00 p.m., just as the agent was about to depart, an urgent message was received from the secretary of war that no train was to be permitted to run to Baltimore, and that it was "advisable" to retain all rolling stock within the city. It was then that a torrent of refugees, many of them blacks, began to flood in from Prince George's County. Soon it was being reported in one Washington newspaper: "The roads leading to this city are filled with contrabands making their way here. They represent the country between Beltsville and Bladensburg as filled with rebel cavalry." It was later stated that a detachment from the 5th Michigan Cavalry, presumably the Union scouts seen earlier by the workmen at Beltsville, had been surrounded by rebel forces and were forced to cut their way through to escape. Several were missing.[38]

***

Word of John Taylor Wood's expedition had already been circulated as early as July 9, at least in the Richmond-Petersburg area. The first evidence of such appeared in a letter sent by John Tyler, Jr., son of former President John Tyler, to Major General Sterling Price in far off Arkansas. The letter not only informed the general of the latest news regarding the Maryland campaign but a somewhat inaccurate version of the scheme to attack Point Lookout. "The plan is that he [Early] shall seize Baltimore and hold it with his infantry while his cavalry proceed to Point Lookout to liberate our prisoners there concentrated to the extent of near 30,000. In the meantime Captain Wood, of the Navy, proceed from Wilmington with 5 gun-boats and 20,000 stand of arms for the same point by water. If successful in thus liberating and arming our imprisoned soldiers, Washington will be assaulted and no doubt carried. This I regard as decidedly the most brilliant idea of the war." [39] If someone like Tyler, who had no need to know, was apprised of the plan, then surely others knew as well.

In the meantime Wood had gone to work at Wilmington meticulously organizing the amphibious operation he was to command. By the evening of July 9 the battalion of 800 marines and sailors were being taken onboard two commandeered blockade runners, *Let-her-B* and *Florie*. Wood wired his uncle, President Davis, that all was now in readiness. "Will try and get out tonight," he reported. "Am badly off for officers, but hope for the best." Having outfitted the expedition as adequately as he could in the short time allotted, he made ready to sail down to the inlet of the Cape Fear River to await the evening tide and then, sheltered from the view of the Federal blockading fleet by the darkness of night, put out to sea.[40]

***

Despite what appeared to be a security breach, Robert E. Lee was in a positive mood regarding the Early expedition, especially after reading the July 8 edition of the *New York Herald*, which he forwarded to President Davis on July 10. The invasion of Maryland was already having a chilling effect on the New York stock market where gold had closed at more than a startling $266 an ounce and the cost of provisions and other commodities were rapidly rising. "You will see the people in the U.S. are mystified about our forces on the Potomac—The expedition will have the effect I think at least of teaching them they must keep some of their troops at home & that they cannot denude their frontier with impunity—It seems also to have put them in bad temper as well as bad humor." [41]

President Davis was not so positive. The security breach was real. Moreover, in the pages of the newspaper sent to him by the general, it was reported that most of the prisoners at Point Lookout had already been sent to Elmira, New York, and the remainder were being transferred as rapidly as possible, which seemed to negate the objective of the mission. Were the Yankees already aware of Wood's operation and removing the prisoners to avoid their being rescued? [42] Convinced now that the top secret expedition was already in jeopardy, he fired off two telegrams to Wood, one quoting the *New York Herald* article on the removal of prisoners and the second indicating that it was now his belief "the attempt would be fruitless." A third telegram was dispatched to General G. W. C. Lee informing him of the same. "If you have no other information," he stated candidly, "I advise abandonment of the project." [43]

The following morning Davis dispatched yet another telegram to Wood: "The object and destination of the expedition have somehow become so generally known that I fear your operations will meet unexpected obstacles. General R. E. Lee has communicated with you and left your action to your discretion. I suggest calm consideration and full comparison of views with General G. W. C. Lee and others with whom you may choose to advise." In other words, it was still Wood's call.[44]

At the mouth of the Cape Fear River, beneath the guns of the great sandy walls of Fort Fisher, Wood's naval expedition awaited the tide and word that Early was closing against Washington. It was then that he received Davis's last telegram. And it was then that the seaborne assault on Point Lookout was cancelled. The following day the commander belatedly received the news from the President of the Confederacy that the Point Lookout prisoners were already being transferred to Elmira. The objective of the expedition was now moot. Wood may have quietly congratulated himself that he had not set off to attack an empty hen's nest.[45]

It was, unfortunately for the rebel campaign in Maryland, impossible to inform either Early or Johnson of the cancellation.

At Point Lookout General Barnes was able to report on the following morning: "All quiet. Five gunboats on duty last night." [46]

38

THE HOTTEST DAY

"Military riffraff, invalids, veteran reserves, and every government employee."

Jubal Early's army, having endured a forced march from the Monocacy through the oppressive heat of a Maryland summer, found little relief from the temperature on the night of July 10 as it encamped on the outskirts of the town of Rockville. The following day would be even worse, but the general was determined to meet his appointed schedule.

By 3:30 a.m. July 11 the main elements of the Confederate Army began their march from Rockville towards Washington. The advance was screened by Brigadier General John Imboden's cavalry brigade, followed by four divisions of infantry led by Major Generals Robert Rodes, Stephen D. Ramseur, John B. Gordon, and John C. Breckinridge. Lieutenant Colonel J. Floyd King's battalion of artillery brought up the rear. The route east from Rockville followed the old Union Road (modern Viers Mill Road), which at Leesburgh (modern Wheaton) became Seventh Street Road (modern Georgia Avenue) into the District. It bypassed several notable estates and farms including "Silver Spring," the manorial home of Francis Preston Blair, just beyond the northern rim of the District of Columbia. Nearby lay "Falkland," the manse of his son, Postmaster General Montgomery Blair.[1]

About the same time McCausland's cavalry had split off on a separate route, down Rockville Pike towards Tennallytown and the District. A portion of his command was detached at the hamlet of Montrose, where the Georgetown Road veered off. Again Fry's 16th Pennsylvania Cavalry clashed with him on the highway. And as on the previous day, as the fighting intensified, the Yankees were forced back through the village of Bethesda. Late in the morning Colonel Charles R. Lowell took command of the Union cavalry, slowly retreating to within two miles of Tennallytown, just within the District where another defensive skirmish line was hurriedly formed. The morning's 90° heat made the sporadic combat insufferable on both sides. It would continue throughout the day, a hardship difficult to surmount. One footsore North Carolina infantryman marching with Early deemed it the "hottest day we have experienced." Soon men began to fall out of the line of march, parched and exhausted by the heat. Two prisoners collapsed and died of heatstroke. Nevertheless, urged on by Early's repeated entreaties, the offensive continued.[2]

After a hard ride of twenty miles, the first of Imboden's cavalry arrived at 9 a.m. outside of Fort Stevens, the northernmost defense work in the ring of fortifications encircling Washington. Leading the advance General Early appeared to make his first assessment of the Union defenses, which he initially deemed "feebly manned." However, while awaiting the arrival of Rodes's division he was able to query a local planter on the nature and strength of the fortifications. "Nothing but earthworks," replied the farmer, who then slyly added that 20,000 men defended them. Though somewhat chastened by the estimate, the general coolly replied, "we would not mind that."[3]

The Confederates were all in a state of absolute fatigue from the long and arduous march in the sweltering heat. "The men [are] completely exhausted," Early acknowledged, "and not in a condition to make an attack." But the challenge was tantalizing. "[I can] plainly see the dome of the Capitol," wrote one hopeful Alabama infantry officer. It was as close to actually entering Washington as any rebel force had been since the summer of 1861.[4]

Early must have questioned whether his weary army was strong enough to seize the capital of the United States. He would later write in his memoirs: "My force, when I arrived in front of the fortifications of Washington, on the 11th of July 1864, was 8,000 muskets, three small battalions of artillery, with about forty field pieces, of which the largest was 12-pounder Napoleons, and about 2,000 badly mounted and equipped cavalry, of which a large portion had been detached to cut the railroads leading from Baltimore north."

The morning temperature had by then reached 94° and was still rising. Clouds of choking dust churned up by troops still coming in only added to the misery of the march, but also provided ample notice of their approach.[5]

Before the Confederates lay a daunting complex of works. Fort Stevens, named after fallen Union hero Major General Ingalls Stevens, was soon to become the epicenter of battle. It was an imposing work situated on high ground overlooking several miles of countryside. The fort was armed with nineteen big guns ranging from 24-pounder seacoast cannon, siege guns and cohorn mortars to howitzers and Parrott guns, though manned by largely green, untested artillerists. Making matters even more disturbing for the rebels, the first arrivals were greeted by a barrage of artillery fire, which passed well overhead and burst far to their rear. Though the aim was poor the message was clear. Guarding the far left of the city and west of Rockville Pike were five great forts, Sumner, Mansfield, Simmons, Gaines and Bayard, as well as five major battery sites. From the Union left, east of Rockville Pike to the far right in Prince George's County, eleven major forts, Reno, Kearney, De Russy, Stevens, Slocum, Totten, Slemmer, Bunker Hill, Saratoga, Thayer, and Lincoln were equally imposing. Thirteen major battery sites connected by a complex of rifle pits shouldered these. Fort Reno dominated the Rockville Pike approach to Tennallytown, Georgetown and the city, and mounted a signal tower that notified defenders of the enemy's every move. Fort Stevens guarded the Seventh Street Road access from the north. Saratoga lay nearly astride the Bladensburg Road approach from the east. Fort Thayer protected a section of the B&O Railroad, and Fort Lincoln overlooked the town of Bladensburg on the far right.

It would appear that the defenses seemed impenetrable. They were, however, unbeknownst to Early, questionably manned by weak and numerically inferior components of the Veteran Reserve Corps, formerly know as the Invalid Corps, and Ohio National Guard. Only a mélange of Maine and Wisconsin infantry and New York artillery units of untested capacity supported these. Major General Alexander McCook of Ohio had established his field command headquarters for the city's defenses in the Mooreland Tavern at Brightwood, a short distance south of Fort Stevens. His assemblages of defenders were thinly stretched in a four-mile arc from Fort Reno on the west to Fort Totten on the east, near the Military Asylum, or Soldier's Home. Here the Lincoln family shared a summer cottage. At Totten a signal station and direct telegraphic link to the War Department in the city center provided instant communication of activities in the area to the high command. Yet either flank of the overall defense line was still vulnerable. The general's first estimate of the rebel force immediately in front of the city above Fort Stevens was placed at fifteen to twenty thousand men.[6]

The situation in the capital, amidst both Unionists and closeted supporters of the South, was one of excitement and urgency. Rebel sympathizers, it was noted in one District newspaper, "were jubilant in this city with the idea that Washington was soon to be in Confederate possession, and showed their faith in it, some of them to the extent of going out to assist the rebels in its capture." [7]

For refugees attempting to escape the rebel onslaught, there was little consolation for their situation exhibited by nervous city defenders. "The farmers in the vicinity [of Seventh Street Road] lost the most of their stock, owing, as they say, to our pickets refusing to let the drivers pass through the lines without a permit. The farmers had taken the precaution to drive their stock towards the city as the rebels advanced, but, not being allowed to enter, fell into the hands of the enemy." [8]

Nevertheless, Federal authorities were now doing their best to meet the emergency head on. The Secretary of War, in an effort to muster into service and arm every available source of manpower, directed that all civilian clerks, orderlies, messengers, "military riffraff, invalids, veteran reserves, and every government employee who could carry a weapon," were to be called upon to defend his country. Quartermaster General Meigs, who would soon field perhaps the most interesting lot of *ad hoc* defenders to be summoned, enthusiastically engaged the order. He thus assumed command of the so called "Emergency Division," a unit initially formed under Major General McCook. He was to take over the northernmost defense line, from Fort Totten to Fort De Russy, which included Fort Stevens. The evening before, Colonel Elias M. Greene, General Augur's quartermaster, had by sheer surprise raised a regiment of 950 employees of his department. "Each one was awakened from sleep about 1 o'clock in the morning and furnished with a musket and equipments before his eyes were fairly opened." A "special inspection" was made in the city hospitals to ascertain which invalids and wounded soldiers had "recovered their strength sufficiently to take the field, and about *thirty five hundred* of them were ordered to duty." Though the overall numbers of invalids raised may have been somewhat inflated, from one facility alone, Campbell Hospital, at least 250 men were in service by July 11. It appeared that anyone who could walk and carry a weapon was called to emergency duty. Within short order even the clerks of the Adjutant General's Office were drilling in Lafayette Square in front of the White House, fully armed and equipped.[9]

Preparations for defensive measures to meet the expected onslaught of the rebel army were hurriedly undertaken. Numerous houses on either side of the Seventh Street Road in front of both Fort Stevens and Fort Totten were destroyed to prevent occupation by enemy sharpshooters. Among the houses laid waste were those belonging to Richard Butts, William Bell, John H. McChesney, Robert McChesney, Abner Shoemaker, then occupied by one David Danlay, and another occupied by the family of the late William M. Morrison. "Time," it was initially reported, "was allowed the owners of these to remove furniture, and the road leading to this city was lined with wagons conveying it to a place of safety." Other reports, however, suggested that some families were summarily turned out and their homes plundered by straggling Union soldiers coming into the city lines. In many locales chaos seemed to reign supreme.[10]

Even as Early was arriving before Fort Stevens, President Lincoln had set off about 9 a.m. towards Tennallytown on an inspection, where skirmishing on the Rockville Pike had already commenced at an early hour. Assistant Adjutant General James Hardie and a mounted escort accompanied him. Though the historical record is vague regarding the president's precise itinerary, it is probable that he then visited Fort Stevens. According to numerous but varied accounts he came under fire, exposing himself briefly before being pulled down by a soldier, believed to be Private John D. Bedient of the 150th Ohio National Guard. Frederick Seward, son of the Secretary of State, would write some years later that Secretary Seward, Secretary Welles, Mrs. Lincoln, General Wright and he accompanied the president to the fort. If such was indeed the case, it was likely to soon become part of an even more provocative legend in American history.[11]

***

E. J. Turton had not expected to find himself in the center of a major military confrontation when he had signed a contract with Postmaster General Blair to remodel his Falkland estate, just off the Seventh Street Road. The house lay about an eighth of a mile from the well known manse of Blair's esteemed father, Francis Preston Blair. The elder Blair had once been in the pubic eye as editor of *The Globe*, an influential newspaper during the Andrew Jackson Administration. He had also owned a townhouse, frequented by many illustrious personages and politicians of the day, directly across the street from the White House. Even before building his country estate just outside of the District line and beside a sparkling spring he discovered by accident in 1842, he had been a member of Jackson's "kitchen cabinet." Blair had dubbed his new home "Silver Spring," which became well known for its visitation before the war by the great men of means and power. There was some irony in that Francis Preston Blair was related through Kentucky kin to John C. Breckinridge, a friend he had frequently entertained at Silver Spring. Now Breckinridge was a rebel general, a traitor intent on the destruction of the city and government in which he once served as Vice President and the Constitution he had once sworn to uphold and defend.[12]

About 11 a.m., while working at Falkland, Turton was taken by surprise by six Confederate soldiers, undoubtedly belonging to Imboden's advanced guard, "who dropped down upon him as if from the skies." They immediately inquired as to whether or not the house belonged to Postmaster General Blair. Upon learning that it did the leader of the group exclaimed matter-of-factly to the others: "This house must go up." The rebels promptly began breaking down doors and "despoiling" everything they touched. Blair's great library and papers were scattered in every direction and anything deemed of use or value was carried off as spoils of war. Their next stop was to be Silver Spring, a mile and a half north of Fort Stevens. Turton was taken along as a prisoner and then carried to another farm where rebel troops appeared to be gathering in force.[13]

Early's line of infantry and artillery following in the path of Imboden's advance continued to arrive throughout the morning by the Seventh Street Road and spread out to the right and left in a wide skirmish line. First to arrive was Rode's division,

509

which rested near Falkland, then Ramseur's, which stacked its arms on the outskirts of Fort Stevens about 2 p.m. Gordon's division assembled near Silver Spring about 4 p.m. Then after a grueling seven hour forced march from Rockville, Breckinridge's tired warriors finally came up even as units under Brigadier Generals John Echols and Gabriel Wharton marshaled near the Thomas Batchelder farm, just to the east of Silver Spring. With them were 576 Union prisoners taken at the Battle of Monocacy. All were held at the John Wilson farm near Silver Spring.[14]

It was fortuitous that Postmaster General Blair had removed himself and his family to the city well before the arrival of the Confederate Army. Such had not been the case with his father, the venerable master of Silver Spring, who had refused to abandon the premises. When the first rebel party entered the house in the morning they found the elder Blair serenely reading his morning paper. They forcefully compelled him to leave the building "saying they wanted it for their sharpshooters." The nearby Carberry estate was occupied for the same purpose.[15]

General Breckinridge's arrival at Silver Spring about 6 p.m. luckily came just in time to save it from total destruction though by then the house had been thoroughly ransacked. All of its drawers, bureaus, and writing cases had been forced open and their contents thrown about the building. The elder Blair's silverware and other valuables were carried off as war booty. Pictures were sliced from their frames. The wine cellar was divested of its contents, undoubtedly to the delight of the hot, weary and thirsty men who had been marching and fighting for more than a month. His private papers, including correspondence with notables such as Andrew Jackson, Henry Clay and other men of importance, as well as his silver plate were fortunately transferred to the John Wilson residence, along with a personal note to him from General Breckinridge, and thus escaped destruction. One particularly important prize, however, proved to be more than simple booty: a county by county map of the State of Maryland. The map was gently removed and placed in the hands of a noted rebel cartographer, Major Jedediah Hotchkiss. "This map was carefully borne away, and for many hours afterwards a corps of Rebel draughtsmen (occupying the house of Thomas Gettings, at the third toll gate) were busily employed over it making sketches and copies." The Silver Spring estate was spared destruction and a guard placed over the house and grounds as Breckinridge fortunately chose to make his former friend's home his headquarters thereby saving it from total destruction. The house itself would also serve as a hospital to which Confederate wounded could be brought and temporarily treated.[16]

***

At 11 a.m. Imboden's cavalry dismounted and moved forward to begin the first skirmish attack of the day. They had soon driven back Federal pickets of the 150th Ohio National Guard's Company K, then stationed near Silver Spring and the farm of the Clagett family. The Clagett farm lay to the west of the Blair estate and extended from the perimeter of Union fortifications northward to the northern boundary stone of the District of Columbia. "Subsequently," it was later noted, "the rebels appeared in Carberry's woods, (high ground,) on Rock Creek, between Clagett's place and Fort De Russy. They showed themselves here in squads of fifteen and twenty, but a well aimed fire of shells from Forts Stevens and De Russy caused them to get speedily under cover, and afterwards they showed more caution in exposing themselves to view." [17]

First reports reaching the city were disturbing, noting that at least 15,000 of the enemy were already in the vicinity of Silver Spring and "that rebel pickets are stationed in Blair's, Clark's and Brown's woods." [18] Later intelligence inflated rebel strength to as many as 30,000 men assembled at the Wilson farm, to which Turton had been brought for questioning by General Gordon. Whatever their principal assemblage area may have been, within two hours the rebel skirmish line had successfully pressed to within an alarming 150 yards of the walls of Fort Stevens and fifty yards to its right.[19]

The Confederates were well protected in the adjacent woods from which their skirmishers had emerged to the north of the fort, cautiously creeping along the ground and independently firing from behind tree cover. Within such close proximity to the fort their sharpshooters were soon able to pick off or wound several Yankee artillerists, quickly downing two and successfully stopping artillery fire for twenty minutes. "The rebels used no artillery," noted one journalist on the scene, "but their movements indicated that they were endeavoring to plant a battery to bear on Fort Stevens, (lately known as Fort Massachusetts,) and in order to frustrate their designs the fort threw shells occasionally amongst them." [20]

The advance of the rebel skirmish line was disconcerting but soon met with stout resistance from the 25th New York Cavalry, all dismounted, the 2nd Regiment of District of Columbia Volunteers, and cavalrymen from Camp Stoneman. Backed by artillery fire from the forts the reinforced defenders were able to drive the rebels back after another half hour of fighting. By 1:30 p.m. a new Union skirmish line had been established well forward of the fort.[21]

At 3 p.m. another regular rebel line of battle was formed, this time by Rode's division, stretching across farms, orchards, and countryside, and backed by artillery. Aggressively the line pressed forward again, this time to within 400 yards of Fort Stevens. What they had not expected, however, was a new body of fresh reinforcements, all hardened veterans that had arrived just hours before by ships from Richmond and New Orleans at what can only be termed the very pivotal moment of combat.[22]

About noon, at Washington's Sixth Street Wharf, the first contingent of the battle scarred Second Division of the VI Army Corps had disembarked from the steamboat *Essex* and four others that had raced from Grant's army at City Point. Six hundred more men, all belonging to the XIX Army Corps from New Orleans, arrived aboard the steamer *Crescent.* Soon others would also tie up at wharfside and disgorge many more. President Lincoln was personally on hand, as were crowds of enthusiastic citizens of the city, to greet the new reinforcements, veterans originally heralding from Pennsylvania, New York and Rhode Island. The XIX Corps was immediately ordered to march down the Bladensburg Road towards Fort Saratoga to reinforce the several poorly manned defense works threatened by General Johnson's forces to the northeast and east of the city. Major General Quincy Gillmore, a New Yorker in command of a detachment of the XIX Corps, would soon be assigned to the defenses along the northeast perimeter of works from Fort Lincoln to Fort Totten, including Fort Saratoga. Major General Wright's VI Corps, approximately 10,000 strong, was ordered to the western city defenses near Chain Bridge, but the directive was countermanded when Early's forces began to seriously threaten Fort Stevens. The VI Corps was soon on the march again. Within hours Wright had reported at Crystal Spring, a half-mile south of the fort. His troops camped at the crossing of Fourteenth Street and Piney Branch Road. Upon arrival at Fort Stevens about 4 p.m., eager to test his mettle against the Confederates, the general requested permission to immediately attack and remove the enemy threat for good. Augur demurred, preferring to first stabilize his forward skirmish line.[23]

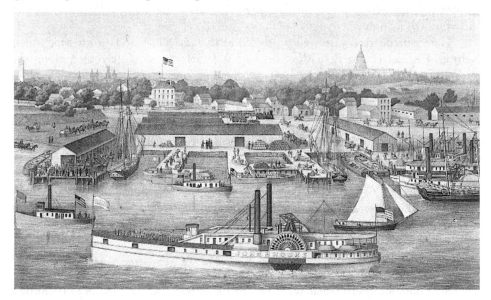

"Birds eye view of Sixth Street wharf, Washington, D.C. published by Chas. Mangus, 12 Frankfort St., New York, & 520 7th Street, Washington, D.C., c1863." Print shows the busy wharves in southwest Washington, DC, where wounded soldiers often arrived. In the foreground, the paddle steamboat *John Brooks* filled with Union soldiers in the foreground, soldiers standing on dock at left, and the Mount Vernon Hotel (the Thomas Law House) flying the American flag. In the background are the unfinished Washington Monument (left), the Smithsonian Institution, and the U.S. Capitol, portrayed as if the dome, which was then under construction, were completed (right). Prints and Photographs Division, Library of Congress, Washington, D.C.

That the defenders were now highly motivated to engage the enemy was suggested by the actions of the 5th Wisconsin and the 6th Maine, of the First Division, VI Corps: their enlistment time in service had expired but they "patriotically agreed to remain on duty, so long as there was any danger to Washington." Thus as Rodes's skirmishers pressed forward they were met by a vigorous Union counterattack ordered up by General Frank Wheaton, commander of the First Brigade, Second Division, VI Corps, to recover the line held in the afternoon. Again the rebels were aggressively pushed back, this time by the 98th and 138th Pennsylvania regiments who were soon joined by the 93rd Pennsylvania and 62nd New York, veterans all.[24]

Now a wide defensive skirmish line was established from Battery Snead, a quarter mile west of Fort De Russy, along the battlefront just above Fort Stevens and then eastward to Fort Slocum, a distance of more than two miles in overall length. Between the rebel and Union fronts lay the no man's land that would henceforth constitute the field of battle.[25]

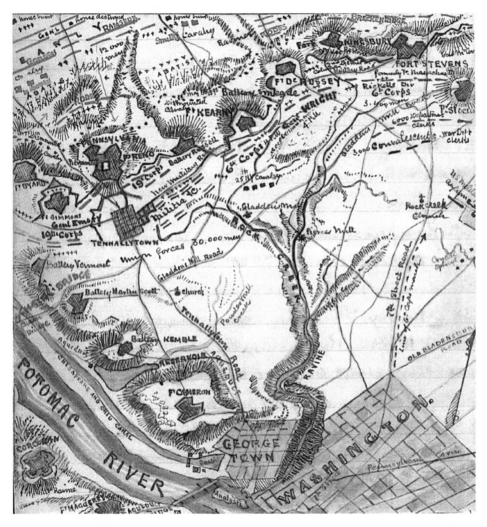

"Plan of the Rebel Attack on Washington, D.C. 11th and 12th July, 1864. Copy of Official Plan Made in the Office of Col. Alexander, U.S.A. Chief Engineer of the Defenses of Washington by R. K, Sneden Topog Engs, USA, Sept 1864." Geography and Map Division, Library of Congress, Washington, D.C.

Soon shells from Union guns at Forts De Russy, Slocum and Totten joined the fray with those of Fort Stevens. One was seen to explode "amidst a group of rebels as it fell, doing great execution," forcing the unit to repeatedly move from the nearby farms and a few stately private homes that had been occupied north of the Yankee defenses.[26] An hour after the latest round of fighting began a single artillery shot from Fort Stevens smashed into the Carberry House (also known as the Lay House), on the west side of the Seventh Street Road and half a mile north of the fort. The shot succeeded in driving rebel troops clustered within to disperse in confusion. Soon no fewer than ten private homes and farms were destroyed or damaged during the ensuing bombardments.[27]

Greatly annoyed by the Union artillery fire, General Gordon quickly dispatched a battery of Confederate Parrot guns to the front. One rebel veteran, Isaac G. Bradwell of the 31st Georgia Infantry, later reported that one gunnery unit "unlimbered in front of the brigade out in the open field in full view of the Yanks about four hundred yards away, and replied, knocking up the red dirt around the muzzles of the big fellows in the fort, while the enemy continued to aim at the moon and stars."[28] It made little difference as the engagement proceeded in staccato fashion with neither side gaining an advantage.

Artillery from Fort De Russy, a mile west of Fort Stevens, provided significant support by shelling rebel forces as their columns advanced down Seventh Street Road. Shells from the fort twice struck the outbuildings of the John Wilson farm a half-mile north of Silver Spring. Again the enemy was forced to move from place to place. When rebel skirmishers established a position in and around another house a mile north of the fort, a brutal rain of shells soon set it afire, forcing the skirmishers to briefly retire towards the Wilson farm. Once more the rebels advanced, this time to the west of Fort Stevens, and concentrated their attentions on a ravine of Rock Creek. To counter the move three companies of the 9th Regiment, Veteran Reserve Corps, and one company each from the 1st and 6th regiments, were ordered to form a skirmish line on the summit of an adjacent ridge. When in position, they opened a crippling fire reinforced by artillery from De Russy. Again the rebel advance was repulsed. With deliberate but undoubtedly cautious resolve the bluecoats deployed from their defensive position, vigorously counter-attacked, and advanced their skirmish line 1,500 yards.[29]

About 5 p.m. the Confederates tried once more to advance, and again the Union skirmish line was pressed back towards Fort Stevens and the Piney Branch Road. Wright's request to enter the fray was now heard, but only partially, when McCook moved to relieve pressure on the forward line. Five hundred men of the First Brigade, Second Division, VI Corps, including the 98th, 102nd, and 139th Pennsylvania Infantry, were sent forward to relieve seven companies of the 9th Regiment, Veteran Reserve Corps, the 2nd Regiment of District of Columbia Volunteers, and the 25th New York Cavalry who had been on the front all day. An infantry and cavalry charge about 6:30 p.m., just as evening began to fall, was preceded by another artillery bombardment on the Carberry and Rives (or Reeves) houses. It had the effect of once more driving the enemy back some distance with the loss of two killed and fourteen wounded. A half hour later more infantry moved to the front of the fort to solidify the line while cavalry was deployed to the right.[30] By 7:00 p.m., after hours of seesaw fighting along the skirmish line above Fort Stevens, the positions of both sides were finally reinforced and stabilized for the night 800 yard north of the fort.

The battle had many witnesses who were not engaged, but not before the heat had dissipated somewhat, for it had been a record setting day in many ways. At 1 p.m. the thermometer had registered a deadly 112° F in the sun and 88° F in the shade at the office of Franklin & Company Opticians, at 214 Pennsylvania Avenue, obliging most citizens to remain indoors.[31] However, the *Evening Star* later reported on the public's desire to watch the carnage from as close as possible. "Early in the evening thousands of persons could be seen passing out Seventh street by every conceivable means of conveyance, while the road was literally lined with pedestrians. The hills, trees and fences within sight of Fort Stevens were covered with human beings, quite a number of who were ladies. Quietly seated in carriages, at a commanding point, was Secretary Seward, viewing the progress of affairs." The heat nevertheless had soon overcome many soldiers and citizens alike.[32]

Union troops departing from Fort Stevens, 1864. Prints and Photographs Division, Library of Congress, Washington, D.C.

At day's end anxiety regarding a major assault by the Confederate Army was general. "If the rebel force now in this vicinity design attacking Washington," the evening newspapers predicted, "we shall doubtless hear the thunder of guns about 3 o'clock tomorrow morning; the hour of the twenty-four always selected at this season of the year for an attempt upon fortifications by sudden assault, or to get in between fortifications by suddenly overpowering the defenders of works connecting fortifications." [33]

Prognosis for an all out attack in the offing was one that could not be allayed. Indeed, soon after sunset and the sound of major skirmishing had muted General Early summoned a council of war at Silver Spring with Breckinridge, Gordon, Rodes, and Ramseur in attendance. Given the increasing opposition faced on the front and the universal physical exhaustion of his troops, he may well have had reservations regarding an assault. He was justifiably apprehensive of being able to do little more than throw Washington and Baltimore into an extreme state of alarm. The rescue of the prisoners at Point Lookout appeared now to be the least of his concerns. But there seemed no turning back. His army had come too far to quit now. It was thus determined that barring unforeseen circumstances a vigorous assault would be made, but it was obvious to all that it would have to await the morning. Soon after the meeting, however, an urgent express arrived that was about to change everything.[34]

The message in question was from General Johnson, sent the night before, reporting that two corps of Union troops had arrived in Baltimore from the Petersburg front and were on the way to Washington. The information wasn't entirely accurate, of course, though Early could not know it, since the reinforcements had already arrived not by way of Baltimore but by steamers at the Washington waterfront. He thus presumed the city was to receive even more and better troops than it already had. He now decided to delay the next morning's attack until he again personally inspected the defenses of the city. Whatever he decided, one thing now seemed clear: the attack on Point Lookout would have to be called off. He simply could not, at this stage, spare Johnson and his cavalry.

39

JUST TO SHOW YOU WHAT WE COULD DO
"Boldness is all that is wanted."

The stream of transports ascending the Potomac River, bearing reinforcements from Grant's base at City Point, was alarming to Confederate observers on the Virginia and Southern Maryland shorelines. Equally distressing was that the mail and intelligence filtering down the "Secret Line" had been stopped owing, ironically, to the success of the Johnson and Gilmor raids at destroying communications lines north of Baltimore. On July 12 one officer of the Confederate Signal Corps who regularly passed between the two shores hurriedly reported to Richmond regarding the increased marine traffic. "I crossed the river tonight for the mail, but got none. The agent [Thomas A. Jones] informed me that none came down . . . Yesterday and today thirty large steamers loaded with troops have gone up the Potomac River, and I think several passed up last night and tonight with troops also. The agent also informed me that full as many have gone up the bay to Baltimore." Most of the steamers, he added, were large ocean going vessels, all crowded with men.[1]

Ascent up the Potomac for the Washington bound transports was not without its hazards. Pilots and others navigating the waterway were finding considerable difficulty in making their way up owing to the repreated removal of navigational aids by the rebels. The displacement of others at critical locations further endangered Union pilotage on the river. The most recent removal of one key buoy at Lower Cedar Point, and another transferred to a position four miles from its original location, made ascension hazardous in the extreme. Though the river between the point and the opposite shoreline on lower east Mathias Point Neck was 4,000 yards in width, the curving and ever-migrating channel was barely 1,000 yards, with meandering ship killing shoals on either side. "There are," noted one observer on July 11, "one or more vessels ashore there constantly." [2]

Despite the hazards not only military reinforcements for Washington but also naval support for Point Lookout were en route. On July 12 the 11-gun steamer *R. R. Cuyler* appeared off the prison complex followed by the 10-gun *Massasoit*. The gunboat *Saco* also soon arrived from the Boston Navy Yard, as did the 20-gun frigate *Minnesota* from the North Atlantic Blockading Squadron and the 10-gun sidewheel steam schooner *Mackinaw*.[3]

Yet it was the seemingly unending flow of troops to the capital that was now of the most consequence, even as the snarled command structure for its defense was being modified. At 12:30 a.m., July 12 a revised chain of command was announced. General Gillmore was to have overall charge of the front between Forts Lincoln and Totten. Quartermaster General Meigs would command the central line between Totten and De Russy while Brigadier General Martin D. Hardin was to control the reach from Fort De Russy to Fort Sumner and the Potomac on the Union left. General Wright's corps would be held in reserve. Overall command of the northern defensive perimeter remained in the hands of General McCook who had held the line the day before.[4]

As in other military emergencies there was always the danger of overuse of liquor by the troops and the public leading to unending problems. And as in like situations during the war the military governor of the District of Washington, Colonel Moses N. Wisewell, issued Special Order No. 118 forbidding the sale of alcoholic drink in the city at any place on Seventh and Fourteenth Streets north of F Street. Confiscation and imprisonment awaited those who sought to evade or violate the order.[5] The order was immediately ignored.

***

As with the day before, the morning of Tuesday, July 12 arrived hot and muggy when General Early set out to inspect the Union lines against which his planned attack would have to be made. "As soon as it was light enough to see," he would write some years later, "I rode to the front and found the parapets lined with troops." [6] The defenses seemed stronger than the previous day, and his anxiety grew as he began to reconsider an all out assault. Even if an offensive charge were successful it would most certainly result in substantial losses that his weary and much diminished army could ill afford. It was even possible that the engagement might culminate in debilitating street-to-street fighting in the city itself, which would be impossible to hold even if captured, against the reported Union reinforcements coming down from Baltimore. There seemed only one realistic answer to the situation: try to maintain a demonstration along the front, keep the Federals guessing, and prepare for a strategic, staged withdrawal towards the upper Potomac.[7]

While Early reluctantly turned to planning for his army's retirement westward, Union reinforcements belonging to the Second and Third Brigades of the VI Army Corps had been arriving at the Sixth Street waterfront all through the night and into the morning hours. As soon as each company disembarked they were marched north through the city to join their comrades being held in reserve near Fort De Russy. This time the streets were devoid of all but the military as none of the city residents turned out to receive them. Having endured a suffocating voyage aboard the tightly packed transports, all of the troops were anxious to leave the ships and make their way towards the front. Upon arrival two Vermont regiments were quickly deployed to rifle pits between Forts Stevens and De Russy while others were sent to the forward skirmish lines. The remainder was kept with Wright's reserves.[8]

As during the fighting the day before, rebel sharpshooters occupying many of the homes and farms beyond the Union lines again opened the morning with a sputtering but deadly fire on the front at Fort Stevens. Confederate sharpshooters ensconced in the already battered Carberry, McChesney, Selden, Lay and Rives dwellings, barns and outbuildings on both sides of the Seventh Street Road, and hidden in the fields all around, laid down a galling fire. Shooters ensconced at the Noble farm on the left fork of Rock Creek Church did their best to pick off any defender foolish enough to expose himself in front of Fort Slocum. Others firing from buildings to the right and front of Fort De Russy quickly challenged the safety of McCook's and Hardin's soldiers.[9]

The sharp cracking sounds of gunfire by rebel sharpshooters and skirmishers would continue without letup, and was returned in kind from the forward Union skirmish line and rifle pits. By mid-afternoon casualties along McCook's front began to mount. Uncertainty regarding the enemy's intentions was prevalent. At Fort

Stevens Navy Secretary Welles was seen conferring with the Republican Senator from Ohio, Benjamin Wade, regarding what seemed to him to be an apparent paucity of Confederate strength and the presence of Union superiority in numbers. Was an all out assault actually coming? Hundreds of yards away behind the Confederate lines, where the bulk of Early's troops stood at the ready for whatever might come, planning was for evacuation not an advance. As George W. Nichols of the 61st Georgia wrote: "We lay around all day (the 12th) and skirmished, and pretended like we would charge the enemy's works till night." [10]

The Federal response was to employ their greatest battlefront asset, over-whelming artillery firepower, in a massive attempt to displace the rebel sharp-shooters from their protected shelters. Lieutenant John G. Frazee, commander of Fort Stevens, opened the bombardment with a salvo of three 30-pounder Parrott gun shells directed at the Carberry House 1,078 yards from the battery. Another salvo was aimed at the Rives house just 1,009 yards out. Soon a heavy fire was laid down upon rebel troop concentrations along the Seventh Street Road, centered 1,050 yards away, as well as on targets farther out including a carriage shop at 2,075 yards and a former U.S. Army campsite 1,950 yards from the fort. In the meantime the big guns of Fort Slocum had chimed in with fire directed at the Bramel family house 3,000 yards away and the Blair house 3,200 yards distance. Not to be left out, the cannons of Fort De Russy also joined the attack firing at any standing structures that might be employed as cover by rebel sharpshooters. By the end of the barrage Fort Stevens had thrown sixty-seven shot at enemy positions, Fort Slocum fifty-three, and Fort De Russy 109. It was later noted that whenever the shells "fell among the rebels they were seen to run in all directions. The main force of the rebels keep prudently in the woods, and only show themselves in any numbers when they relieve their skirmishers." [11]

Nevertheless, the bombardment failed to deter the enemy firing or men appear-ing from time to time in the open. For several hours a lone rebel officer mounted on a horse could be seen riding in and out of the woods fronting Fort Stevens, during which time he provided a perfect target for Union gunners. Yet all attempts to dismount him proved in vain. Elsewhere Union snipers were more effective. One sharpshooter from the 76th New York, which had been earlier cantoned at Camp Doubleday near Fort Stevens, had taken position in a tree and in short order successfully picked off six rebel soldiers.[12]

Though the shooting in the vicinity of Fort Stevens seemed to be the most intense, the fight continued to a lesser degree along other points of the Union line. "In front of Fort Slocum . . . the rebel skirmishers were not so active, but whenever they showed themselves in sufficient numbers, the Fort treated them to a shell dance."[13] And so it was all along the front, as the rebel firing continued unabated, with sharpshooters providing no end to bloody labor for Union medics and volunteer civilian physicians. When a Union cavalry lieutenant passing under the guns of Fort Stevens on the outside of the works was downed by a Confederate sniper, the officer died in a matter of minutes despite the on site surgery of Dr. W. J. C. Duhamel, medical director of the city jail. Hardened veterans not directly engaged in the fight seemed unaffected or concerned about what was going on. "Some were joking and laughing in groups, others were picking blackberries, taking the chances of a compliment from the tube of a rebel sharpshooter." [14]

Nothing, it seemed, was likely to stop or hinder the bloody Pyrrhic crossfire that continued to wound, maim and kill men on both sides. Then about 2 p.m. the heavens opened for the first time in well over a month with a heavy downpour of rain that suspended the fight. The guns were silenced but not for long. As soon as the brief but cooling deluge had stopped, firing was resumed and men continued to die. [15]

***

Since his brigade had left Frederick on July 9 General Bradley T. Johnson's order of march was for the right regiment to fall out at intervals and take the rear. "Marching in front," the general noted, "rest men and horses, in the rear [it] fatigues them." And it had been a fatiguing march indeed. Throughout he had religiously deployed flankers on either side of his main column. Not only were they to provide protection from surprise attack on the right and left, but they were also tasked with sending in all the horses they could get. The captured animals were dispatched to the rear of the column. When a man's steed gave out he simply fell out from the line and waited on the roadside until the rear and refreshed horses came up. Remounting a fresh horse he then turned his former ride onto the roadside and rejoined his command. The Confederate mounts, Johnson later complained, "were well bred horses from Southwest Virginia and far better than the overfed, fat, pudgy horses that we got [from Maryland], these last could not stand over 20 miles march." But they would have to do. [16]

As the skirmish lines were re-engaging all along the front above Fort Stevens, Johnson had pressed farther south from Beltsville towards Bladensburg and the eastern ring of fortifications. The B&O bridge over the Paint Branch, just east of the Maryland College of Agriculture (now the University of Maryland) and approximately two miles north of Bladensburg, was set ablaze. Inside the Union lines at Fort Lincoln overlooking Bladensburg, defenders could see smoke rising from the fire a few miles away. About 8 a.m. a detachment of rebel cavalrymen appeared at a point about three miles from the fort and a mile northwest of the town. A probe of 500 cavalrymen of the 16th Pennsylvania under Major Fry, most being dismounted veterans of the Army of the Potomac, was dispatched to investigate. The Confederates were prepared. Johnson readily deployed his troopers and a single field gun from the Baltimore Light Artillery to meet the Federals near the Paint Branch crossing. The firefight that followed was short, not more than half an hour in duration. Johnson's superior numbers and single piece of artillery had a telling effect. As the bluecoats were about to break he "let loose" two companies of the 1st Maryland Cavalry under Captains George W. Emack and William I. Rasin. Both men had scores to settle, especially Rasin who had once been imprisoned at Fort Warren for spying in Maryland. He had somehow escaped to Virginia and later, after forming his own company for the 1st Maryland, received a near fatal saber wound in a skirmish in the Shenandoah Valley. Johnson later recalled that "they went like a charge of canister," and his men reveled at watching the Yankees "skedaddle in fine style" as the fight was abruptly ended. Federal losses were reported at thirty-five missing. [17]

520

***

It was in the afternoon that President Lincoln and Secretary Stanton, escorted by a cavalry guard, again appeared at Fort Stevens after having visited a hospital in the rear of the fort. As they approached they were loudly challenged to show their passes by Sergeant Hiram Thompson of the 49th New York who was unaware of just who they were. As soon as they entered, the president, accompanied by General Wright, quickly mounted the parapets. Their stay was short as the big guns boomed and bullets zipped by. For a very brief moment the President of the United States stood upon the works of Fort Stevens fully exposed to enemy fire, momentarily watching the shelling of the Carberry House.[18] It was an event equaled by only one other Chief Executive, President James Madison, during the August 1814 Battle of Bladensburg, the last time Washington was under attack by an enemy army bent on its destruction. There was also great irony in that less than a mile away was a former Vice President, John C. Breckinridge, once sworn defender of the Constitution of the United States and now a sworn enemy of that same nation and its capital city. It is unknown whether the president was cognizant of that irony or was even aware that Breckinridge was present, for the events that followed came in rapid succession.

As Lincoln stood gazing out over the battlefield, his famous stove pipe hat announcing to all just who he was, a bullet suddenly slammed into Surgeon Cornelius V. A. Crawford of the 102nd Pennsylvania who was standing nearby. Accounts of what actually occurred in the succeeding moments are as varied and colorful in the telling as the many versions published or recorded by those present or who later claimed to be so, and perhaps confused or mixed with the events of the previous day. The most popular tale is that Captain (Brevet Lieutenant Colonel) Oliver Wendell Holmes shouted at the president "Get down you fool." Another is that a free black woman, "Aunt Betty" Thomas, once owner of the land upon which the fort was erected, shouted the president down from his perch, perhaps saving his life from a Confederate sharpshooter.[19] Whatever impression the incident may have made upon the chief executive, he did not refrain from his attempts to encourage the troops. It was noted in the *Evening Star* the day after that "President Lincoln and Mrs. Lincoln passed along the lines of the city defenses in a carriage last night, and were warmly greeted by the soldiers wherever they made their appearance amongst them." [20]

***

By mid-afternoon amidst McCook's forward skirmish line, held by 7,836 men, casualties had again begun to mount. Still, General Augur continued to move units about, plugging spots determined to be weaker than others, and jostling the organizational structure of his entire command. As word of Johnson's activities to the northeast and east of Washington began to filter in, Rear Admiral Louis Goldsborough, then overseeing operations at the Navy Yard, was ordered to reinforce Fort Lincoln and vicinity to seal off access to the city with 1,000 to 1,500 sailors from that direction. Great faith was placed in the sailors: "Our Navy Yard men are mostly versed in the use of arms, and will no doubt do themselves credit if brought under fire." [21] Major General Doubleday, who had earlier commanded citizen volunteers of Washington organized in bodies called Loyal Leagues, was given command of all fortifications beyond Anacostia on the east side of the capital. General Gillmore was charged with the command between the Anacostia and Fort Slemmer. Meigs would continue to hold the center from Fort Totten to Fort Kearney, while Hardin would hold the line on the far left from Fort Reno to the Potomac.[22]

Though few citizens of Washington failed to turn out to welcome the later reinforcements from Grant's army, many seemed eager to witness the fighting near Fort Stevens. "The road to the fort," it was reported, "was literally blockaded by pedestrians, horses and vehicles, about four o'clock p.m., guards having been posted on the hill near the first tollgate to prevent civilians from going nearer to the scene of conflict." Many were driven by rumors that there had been casualties among the 2nd District of Columbia Volunteers, causing considerable anxiety among those who had relatives and friends in the regiment.[23] Whatever the cause for the rush towards the front, those who had made the effort were not about to be disappointed for the most significant fight before the capital of the United States was about to start.

It is uncertain as to what the Union's driving motivation for the coming struggle may have been. It has been suggested by some notable historians that the close call on the president's life caused the senior military command to take more aggressive action. It is also possible that frustration over the morning's bombardment that had seemingly failed to dislodge the enemy was the determining factor. Undoubtedly General Wright's desire to simply clean out the rebel sharpshooters, a wish from which he had earlier been dissuaded, played a role in the decision to attack. For the task at hand he chose the Second Division of the VI Corps, temporarily under the command of Brigadier General Frank Wheaton. The just arrived Third Brigade of the division, consisting of fresh Maine, New York and Pennsylvania Volunteer regiments led by Colonel Daniel D. Bidwell, would lead the assault. Wheaton's own First Brigade of New Yorkers and Pennsylvanians would act as backups. The Third Brigade of the First Division, consisting of Maine, Massachusetts, Pennsylvania, New York, Rhode Island and Wisconsin units under Colonel Oliver Edwards, would be held in reserve in front of Fort Stevens. The fight would begin when a flag was raised to signal the big guns of Stevens and Totten to again rake the buildings sheltering rebel sharpshooters. After three salvos totaling thirty-six shots had been fired, Bidwell's brigade was to begin the ground offensive.[24]

As the late afternoon slipped towards twilight the preliminary bombardment began. "To dislodge the sharpshooters from the house a shell from Fort Stevens by the skillful gunners of the 6th Maine artillery was lodged in the cupola of the Carberry house, firing the building and sending the rebels skedaddling from its shelter like so many rats." Then, as the last shell was fired about 5 p.m., the Third Brigade, approximately 1,000 strong, poured from the main gate of Fort Stevens at double quick time with fixed bayonets. To get at the enemy, Bidwell's men were first obliged to fight their way across an open killing zone with little cover for protection to assail the wooded slope behind, from which seemingly invisible men fired their muskets with deadly accuracy. The heaviest opposition appeared to be concentrated between the Carberry and Rives properties, but slowly the offensive gained ground though at substantial cost. As the forward rebel line began to sag General Rodes quickly sought to slow the assault by sending in one or two brigades as reinforcements and opened a blistering fire with his own field artillery. A pitched battle was soon engaged in the vicinity later occupied by Walter Reed Army Medical Center, see-sawing back and forth as the evening progressed.

A spirited Confederate counter attack was launched against the Union forces concentrated on the Rives property, driving the 122nd New York Volunteers back. Though out of ammunition the veteran New Yorkers refused to acquiesce and launched a successful, if costly, countercharge with fixed bayonets to retake the farm. The heaviest fighting of the evening was between 5 and 7 p.m. Perceptibly now, as the rebels were pushed back little by little a mile and a half, the Union offensive began to slow. Then with the exception of an occasional outburst of gunfire, the fight ceased entirely three hours later. Though Confederate resistance had been considered strong, in truth only a small component of Early's army, a lone brigade consisting of four regiments of General Rodes' North Carolina troops, had held the last skirmish line against Bidwell's attack, even as their comrades were beginning the evacuation.[25]

"The operations near Washington--scene of the fight in front of Fort Stevens, July 12 & 13." Wood engraving from a sketch by E. F. Mullen. The illustration shows: soldiers behind low wooden barricades; the remains of a building burned to the ground; and the smoke from cannon fire in the background. *Frank Leslie's Illustrated Newspaper*, Prints and Photographs Division, Library of Congress, Washington, D.C.

The charge had been, in the eyes of Washingtonians reading about the battle the following day, a complete success. The rebels had been dislodged from their positions and pushed back beyond the Blair House. Yet the cost had been substantial. Though initial estimates of Union casualties had been placed at 300, Bidwell's brigade alone had suffered between 250 and 375 dead and wounded, nearly thirty-six percent of the men sent forward. One unit, the 49th New York Volunteers of the First Division, had suffered the loss of twenty-five men out of eighty-five deployed. The intensity of the fighting can, perhaps, best be gauged by the loss relative to men engaged – more than double the per capita loss ratio of Union troops at Antietam, Chancellorsville and Gettysburg. [26]

***

As evening set in, General Johnson, unaware of the intense fighting near Fort Stevens, had moved to the east, circumventing Bladensburg and riding towards the Western Branch, a tributary of the Patuxent River. He wished to pay a personal visit to an old friend, one Dr. John Fairfax, and to "to unsaddle and feed." While at the doctor's estate, about eight miles north of Upper Marlboro, he dispatched a messenger on a hard ride down to the St. Mary's peninsula "to let my friends know that we were coming and telling them to have their good horses by the side of the road and we'd exchange, leaving better ones than we took." The dispatch proved premature for it was soon after that he received a most critical message from General Early. The mission to Point Lookout, already behind schedule, had been cancelled, and he was to report to the general on the Seventh Street Road. The effort against Washington was also over even though no one in the capital city knew.[27]

***

By 10 p.m. a welcomed silence washed over the battlefield, but the Union Army was still alive with speculation as to the enemy's intentions. "The night was beautiful—a peaceful moonlight—and a large proportion of the population of the city was out to a late hour," noted one reporter, "waiting in anticipation that the rebels might make some demonstration in pursuance of their old tactics of night attacks." Many took note of what appeared to be signaling going on between the different stations at the Soldiers' Home, along Nineteenth Street and elsewhere within and adjacent to the city environs.[28]

Were the Confederates, as some began to speculate, about to retire from the scene of battle? Even when the fighting was heaviest, dense clouds of dust had been observed in the rear of the rebel skirmish line indicating that either they were leaving or that reinforcements were on the move to the front. From Union positions at Fort Bunker Hill on the right of Fort Stevens, the consensus of many military officials was that the rebels were retreating towards Rockville and Edward's Ferry on the upper Potomac "as the columns of dust seemed to be receding in a northwest direction." [29]

Much to the relief of many in Washington, the enemy had indeed begun their departure from Silver Spring, some perhaps almost as soon as Early had decided against an all out attack. "Their cavalry having accomplished their work as far as foraging was concerned, they commenced to retire," it was later observed, ". . . the wagons leaving early in the morning and the troops about four in the afternoon, excepting Grimes', Battle's, Old's and Cox's Brigades and a portion of Gen. Ransom's cavalry, who covered their retreat. They also state that in the attack on Tuesday night they lost considerably, and that their wounded were mostly taken away with them." Local residents near Silver Spring, however, stated that the retreat had begun around 7 p.m. July 12.[30]

About 11 p.m., as rebel infantry columns silently passed Falklands, Montgomery Blair's home, the lust for revenge was finally satiated as the flames from the burning estate began to illuminate the evening sky. The unfortunate Mr. Turton was finally released, having suffered no personal harm other than to have his clothing taken. Upon complaint to his former captors he was told: "We can't help it, you are where you can get plenty, we can't." [31]

The first Union reconnaissance in the early morning hours of July 13, two companies of infantry flanked by cavalry, confirmed what many had suspected: the rebels had disappeared from the front and were on the march west toward the Potomac. To the east of the city General Johnson had already begun his own move west, taking with him captured horses, cattle and other goods of necessity. As his forces were reported just "a short distance above the station at Bladensburg," a single parting shell was thrown towards the town, landing near the Union camp in the vicinity of Spa Spring in Bladensburg Park.[32] The rear guard of Johnson's cavalry would not pass by Blair House until 5 a.m. the following morning.

Soon afterwards Union cavalry units would report that the rebels had disappeared from the immediate front. Neither General Halleck nor Lincoln seemed disposed to give orders to pursue. Nevertheless, Colonel Charles Lowell, Jr. and approximately 750 men of the 2nd Massachusetts Cavalry had already begun pursuit of the enemy towards Rockville. About noon, after reaching the town, the colonel dispatched several companies under Lieutenant Colonel Casper Crowninshield towards Darnestown. They soon encountered the enemy rear guard, General Johnson's cavalry brigade, which had stopped to feed their horses near Rockville. Johnson dispatched a squad of the 1st Maryland Cavalry under Captain Wilson A. Nicholson and Lieutenant Thomas Green into the town to stall the main Union column. The bluecoats immediately dismounted and took up positions in a building, dispensing a maddening fire upon the rebels. A spirited engagement ensued. Soon they were joined by a detachment of Major Fry's Pennsylvania cavalry as the fight swayed back and forth. The horses of both Nicholas and Green were downed and both men wounded and taken prisoner. Learning of the captures, Johnson personally led a bold charge to repatriate his officers. The onslaught was fierce, forcing the bluecoats to retreat. One trooper of the 1st Maryland would later recall the event: "I remember well how we almost all of us dropped our bridles and with pistols in one hand and sabre in the other, and with our spurs into our horses' flanks, we followed them yelling like Indians, and as they seemed to be satisfied to get away from us, we concluded to let them go." Thereafter, the rebel army was allowed to retire without harassment.[33]

In the meantime, about 4:30 p.m., General Wright finally received orders to ready his troops for a general pursuit even as laborers had begun to improve the defense works of the city in the event the enemy returned. At 5:00 p.m. the general set off toward Rockville with 10,000 men, but deeming his force insufficient to continue the chase encamped at the village of Poolesville, recently abandoned by the rebels, as more Union reinforcements arrived at Washington. Wright's troops remained in Poolesville until July 16 when the pursuit was officially called off, and it was obvious to all that Early had escaped.[34]

The Confederate's withdrawal across the Potomac at a crossing called White's Ferry had been masterful. As one member of the 1st Maryland Cavalry would later record: "The Federals pressed on our rear guard, but our cavalry held them in check until dark and the Baltimore Light Artillery fired the last shot, as the First Maryland Cavalry were the last troops that crossed the Potomac on Early's withdrawal from Maryland in 1864." [35]

***

As territory around Washington just occupied by the invaders was being cautiously probed, the detritus of the fight appeared everywhere. Both Confederate and Union dead were found lying about the fields and woods and near several of the bombed or burnt out farms and estates. Some had been quickly buried. Most had not. In the fields between Fort Stevens and the Lay House at least ninety rebel bodies were discovered. One rebel was found buried so hastily by his comrades in their exit, that his feet were sticking out of the ground. A burial detail of black contra-bands was dispatched and hours later returned bearing trophies picked up during their labors.[36] Many rebel bodies were buried where they fell, though the largest concentration, seventeen men, were interred at Grace Episcopal Church in a "bivouac of the dead." No fewer than forty Union soldiers would be laid to rest at Battle Ground Cemetery. At Blair's Silver Spring, which had been entirely ransacked and its wine cellar despoiled, eleven Confederate officers and ninety men too severely wounded to be carried away by the retreating army were discovered lying about. In hospital tents beyond the third tollgate on the Seventh Street Road the retreating enemy had left sixty-three more of their wounded, including eleven officers, none being above the rank of captain. A surgeon, two assistant surgeons, twelve nurses (soldiers) and a chaplain had been left with them. All were soon placed under the care of Dr. W. E. Waters of Washington, the Army Hospital In-spector. The first group of forty was removed to Lincoln Hospital where Surgeon J. Cooper McKee treated them. The remainder were soon sent in as well and placed in wards by themselves, with visitation allowed only by special pass.[37]

***

The potential presence of enemy rear guard units in the area did little to stem the curiosity of civilians from the city eager to see the wreckage of the battlefield or to learn about friends and loved ones engaged in the fighting. In order to prevent citizens and others not connected with the army from passing to the front strong cavalry guards were stationed on the various roads leading north of the city. "This is a wise precautionary measure," noted one newspaper, "as the large number of persons flocking to the front tended to interfere with prompt military movements."[38] Such measures did little to obstruct those who were determined to evade the checkpoints. But finding liquid refreshment along the way during the stifling heat of day was something else! As one wag, filled with curiosity, later recalled:

"To go out 7th street road was the correct thing yesterday. Supposing you couldn't afford a horse – with flour at $25 per barrel – there were the street cars to the Boundary, thence on foot . . . At the boundary our progress was barred by a difficulty in getting lager. There was no getting to the front without lager and no lager to be had. There were bars in plenty, (7th street north is lined with them,) and lager in plenty, but 'not a drop to drink,' – military orders against it. The barkeepers looked sorry and we looked sorry . . . Then we saw some soldiers coming from the rear entrance of a restaurant wiping their mouths. We went in and came out wiping our mouth. Barkeepers there evidently hadn't heard the order." [39]

Passing Fort Stevens, the curiosity seeker was faced with the grim evidence of war in earnest. Gaunt chimney stacks stood amidst smoking ruins. To the right lay the gutted remains of a peach orchard just felled after the enemy was gone to open a better field of fire should he return. To the left, some distance away, could be seen a building set ablaze by the Confederates during their retirement. The fire had already spread through the underbrush and enveloped another dwelling house. It was yet smoldering. In the Lay House ruins a thin spiral of smoke twisted skyward from a clump of shrubbery. "It is difficult to realize," noted one observer, "that not 24 hours ago the rebels were hiding in this house with such impudent temerity directly under the guns of our fortifications."

Upon investigation it soon became clear what the previous hard day of fighting had really been about and how much closer the rebels had been to the defense line than at first believed.

"In fact they were yet nearer the fort, occupying positions behind knolls, bushes, and trees. Here it was that the veterans of the 6th corps, spreading themselves out in fan-form line of skirmishers, advanced with audacity gained from previous baptism in fire, across the open field, directly under the deadly rifle fire from those leafy coverts. On they advanced, sweeping past the Lay house on the right, and throwing up rifle pits at once, which they held through the night, and on the left pushing up to the white fence of the Lay house, or rather its blazing ruins, when the rebels sent two reinforcing brigades, pushing our skirmishers back on that side. It was a bit of display on their part of a bold front as at that very hour, 7 o'clock Tuesday night, the main portion of their force was stealing away towards the fords of the Potomac." [40]

The devastation of private homes, from both the Federal bombardments and during the rebel evacuation was extensive. At the home of Michael Bonnifant all furniture and personal effects were destroyed. Signs of revenge for earlier Union conflagrations in Confederate territory were common. In the Roach estate near the Seventh Street Road, the damage was overwhelming. Here were found books "which bore inscriptions from hands which had fingered the fly leaves." On the flyleaf of a book entitled *Father's Spiritual Conferences*, one of the enemy soldiers had inscribed: "On examination of this house you may form a faint idea of the sufferings of 50,000 Virginians. — A Rebel." In another book entitled *Francais en Egypte* was written, "In retaliation for 50,000 Virginia houses devastated in this manner." [41]

In a grove near the destroyed "Falkland" residence of Montgomery Blair, a book, the eighth volume of Lord Byron's collected works, was found tacked to a tree. On its flyleaf was a warning inscription composed and signed by "the worst rebel you ever saw" belonging to the 58th Virginia and dated near Washington, July 12, 1864: "Now, Uncle Abe, you had better be quiet the balance of your administration, as we only came near your town this time just to show you what we could do; but, if you go on in your mad career, we will come again soon, and then you had better stand from under." [42]

The news coming in from the countryside was equally disturbing. "In addition to their work of plunder and devastation," it was reported on July 14, "we hear that they have been forcing nearly every able bodied man they have been able to pick up in Maryland into their ranks, carrying them off with them." Reports from farmers suggested that rebel sympathizers were the principal sufferers of the enemy incursion. Not only were their houses and cattle taken by the raiders for "the good of the cause," but also many residents were pressed directly into Confederate service.[43] Rebel sympathizers in the city, once energized by the appearance of Early's army, now chose to downplay the whole affair speaking of the invaders as a mere raiding party. It was a claim that the press caustically rebutted, noting no less than two major generals and half a dozen brigadiers led "the raiding party"! [44]

On the morning of July 14, if there was any remaining question regarding the vulnerability of Washington by water, it was laid to rest with the arrival at the Navy Yard of further reinforcements, the gunboats *Pontiac, Mackinaw* and *Commodore Barney* and the ironclad *Atlanta*. At noon *Resolute* also turned into the Eastern Branch with flag officer Samuel P. Lee in his flagship not far behind.[45]

***

At Point Lookout distorted accounts of the attack on Washington had already begun to filter into the prison camp. On July 13 even as Early's army was retiring westward, Bartlett Malone was thrilled to report to his diary that "General Ewel [*sic*] was a fitting at Washington And that our Cavalry was [with]in 4 miles of this place." He also recorded that the Union guards at the prison were upset and had hurriedly sent out details at 2 a.m., run out their artillery in front of the blockhouse and placed it in a position of defense.[46] Charles Warren Hutt was as delighted as Malone. "The news from the Confederate arms everywhere is glorious. We hear that seven shells have been thrown in Washington City and that England and France have recognized us." [47]

Whatever buoyant effect the rumors may have engendered in the hearts of hopeful rebel inmates, it was not universal in camp. On July 14 the great old frigate *Minnesota* arrived off Point Lookout. Though she would soon be ordered to rejoin the North Atlantic Blockading Squadron, her appearance must have had a dismal effect upon the inmates. A double set of guards had been stationed upon the parapets of the camp. Strict order was maintained within as a heavy patrol enforced silence after "taps" at 8 p.m. All lights were to be doused and no talking allowed within the tents. Union reinforcements of a regiment of cavalry and a company of infantry had taken up positions outside the prison gate, and all of the troops on the point had rested on their arms. That same morning between 500 and 1,200 prisoners signed the Oath of Allegiance. All were allowed outside of the prison gates, undoubtedly much to the disgust of many of their comrades.[48]

By now rumors of the Confederate plan to free the prisoners at Point Lookout had belatedly taken root in Baltimore probably as a result of the capture of several of Johnson's troopers during their visit to the environs. The first to take notice was General Ord, in charge of the defense of that city, who promptly informed General Grant. Unaware that the entire mission had been called off, Grant opined to Halleck on the morning of July 15: "This can hardly be possible," he said, "in view of the narrow outlet through which they would have to go in passing Washington with them. I call attention to the rumor, however, that you may direct the proper steps, if such a thing should be possible. I think it well to notify the Navy Department of this, that they may prevent the possibility of an attempt to cross the Potomac in boats." [49]

Within days, belated news of Colonel Wood's plan to attack Point Lookout by sea with two armed vessels and 800 men had also reached the point via four refugees picked up by Acting Master James C. Tole. The intelligence was forwarded verbally to his senior, Commander Hooker, who began cruising farther out in the bay than usual, and then to Commander Parker. Lieutenant Moses S. Stuyvesant, commander of the recently arrived USS *Minnesota*, immediately informed Navy Secretary Welles and senior officers at Fort Monroe. Welles was confident that the naval forces already stationed at the point were sufficient to defeat any such attempt. Nevertheless, on July 18 he ordered Acting Rear Admiral Samuel P. Lee to guard the mouth of the Chesapeake both night and day with tugboats. The brig-rigged steam gunboat *Fort Jackson* was to maintain close signal range. Admiral Lee, in turn, fearing that the raiders might make an attack on the blockading fleet off Wilmington to escape, ordered greater vigilance than usual on that station. On July 19 he directed the USS *Santiago de Cuba*, *Monticello*, and *Cohasset* to the mouth of the Chesapeake Bay, which they were to guard until relieved by the *Fort Jackson*. Once relieved *Santiago de Cuba* and *Monticello* were to proceed directly to a station off New Inlet, North Carolina. The order went out, ironically, the day after the two commandeered blockade runners that were to be employed by Wood were returned to their captains.[50]

When the account of the purported threat to free 13,000 prisoners at Point Lookout by sea finally reached the Washington press, it was received with absolute disbelief. "This is a pretty story," noted the *National Republican*. "There is nothing like 13,000 prisoners at Point Lookout, and the idea of armed transports from Wilmington passing the gunboat fleet at Fortress Monroe on such an expedition is absurd." [51]

***

As the fallout from the third and final Confederate invasion of the North rapidly began to recede, one of the main Confederate objectives of that expedition, Point Lookout, was evolving almost by the day. On July 27, just two weeks after the last sounds of skirmishing at Washington had subsided, Colonel Hoffman, Commissary General of Prisoners, reported that there were just 11,430 prisoners of war. Some 3,050 had already been removed to Elmira, New York. Whether the estimate included three hundred of the inmates who were civilians, some of whom had been held there for as much as fifteen months without charges having been made against them, is unknown. A steamer was scheduled to leave the point that day with 850 more prisoners, and another, carrying about the same number, was to sail on July 29. A suitable steamer was to be available every other day thereafter, which was about as fast as the rolls and other preparations could be readied. "I propose to remove all 8,000 to Elmira," Hoffman informed Colonel James A. Hardie, Inspector General for the War Department, "which will leave at Point Lookout 6,000 to

7,000." The guard at the depot then consisted of two regiments of veteran reserves, one of 100-days' men and one black Massachusetts regiment. There were by then four warships at the point including the steam frigate *Minnesota*. The two necks of land that connected the point with the mainland were now each protected by a stockade and fieldworks, the latter to guard against attack from without and the former to meet any effort of the prisoners to liberate themselves from within. "With proper vigilance on the part of the troops stationed there," Hoffman now boldly declared, "and with the assistance of the gunboats no successful attack can be made on the depot." [52]

The security from assault was of small interest to most of the inmates who remained behind as many of their fellow prisoners were sent north to Elmira, first by steamboat and then transferred to rail. But in one sense they were the lucky ones. On July 15 a train filled with prisoners from Point Lookout bound for what was to be their new prison home in upstate New York collided with a coal train near Lackawanna, Pennsylvania. Over one hundred prisoners were killed outright or injured.[53]

40

A CONVENTION OF MARYLAND
"I wish all men to be free."

For many citizens of Southern Maryland the third Confederate invasion of their state had at first produced a sense of joyous euphoria followed by bitter disappointment. Most sympathizers of the Southern cause were no longer able to communicate their sentiments freely with anyone but trusted family members and friends lest they face arrest. The whole affair seemed more than just another setback. The resumption of the Maryland Constitutional Convention, which began on July 16, was to be even more disturbing. As the primary goal of the Union Party majority was the emancipation of all slaves within the state, the prospects for total economic and political disenfranchisement of a substantial portion of Southern Maryland society loomed large. Many believed it would result in nothing less than the total ruination of the white population of the southern counties and Eastern Shore.

As early as December 1862 an assemblage of citizens on the West River in Anne Arundel County had met with Governor Bradford to express their concerns regarding the effects on the state resonating from Lincoln's forthcoming Emancipation Proclamation. Was the governor going to issue an opposing proclamation for Maryland?

Bradford had demurred. The president's decree included only slaves in states and territories under rebel control. "If the slaves [in Maryland] at present believe that they are by law free on the first of January," he stated, "it is doubtful whether any sudden change of that conviction produced by Executive action would not of itself incline them to make arrangements during a Holiday for a general stampede as the only alternative method of effecting their freedom." [1]

Inexorably the motion towards emancipation in Maryland, spurred by Lincoln's general proclamation, had pressed forward. Unlike some states the mechanism legally permitting the action was already embedded in the state's constitutional laws. Specifically, the Constitution of 1851 had required the General Assembly to conduct a referendum after each census year to determine if voters wished to convene a constitutional convention to update and revise the laws of the State of Maryland. It was an opportunity Maryland abolitionists had seized upon with fervor. Thus throughout late 1863 and early 1864 Unionists in the legislature began to lay the groundwork for a state constitutional convention, the original date of 1861 having been delayed by the war emergency. On January 6, 1864, five days after Lincoln's momentous proclamation was formally issued, the newly elected Assembly was convened in Annapolis. Governor Bradford, in his annual address to that body, called for a convention to reframe the Maryland Constitution with a rigorousfocus on slavery. In less than a month the legislature had passed an enactment calling for a Maryland State Convention to form a new constitution specifically aimed at abolition without compensation. The subsequent election to select delegates for the convention was deemed by some a travesty of democracy, as voters were obliged to prove their loyalty by swearing an oath even as troops, bayonets gleaming, were on patrol at polling places. Only a small minority of eligible voters thought to favor emancipation were permitted to cast ballots. In Baltimore, with a voting population of over 40,000, barely 9,000 votes were cast. Not surprisingly the only clusters of outright opposition were centered in the lightly populated counties of Southern Maryland and the Eastern Shore, but to no avail.[2]

"Birdseye View of the City of Annapolis, 1864." E. Sachse, artist, Charles Magnus, publisher, E. Sachse, lithographer. Geography and Map Division, Library of Congress, Washington, D.C.

In mid-April Governor Bradford issued a formal proclamation to convene the convention. At noon, April 27, "being the appointed day for the meeting, in accordance with the Act of Assembly, in accordance with the Governor's Proclamation of April 14 of the Convention to Frame a New Constitution and Form of Government for the State was opened in the Chamber of the Maryland House of Delegates." [3] Henry H. Goldsborough of Talbot County, the Comptroller of the Treasury and a leading champion of abolition in the state, receiving the unanimous approval of Union Party members, was elected President with fifty-eight votes. In protest to what they believed would be a railroaded convention the minority Democratic Party delegates, all from Southern Maryland, Montgomery County, the Eastern Shore and one from Baltimore, declined to vote. Indeed, fourteen Democrats had failed to even take a seat in the proceedings, though all would eventually do so.[4]

Seventeen of Southern Maryland's most accomplished men, all of whom opposed emancipation, had been elected to stand for their counties wherein the Democratic Party held sway. Anne Arundel was represented by Oliver Miller, Spriggs Harwood, William B. Bond, and Eli J. Henkle; Prince George's by Daniel Clarke, Samuel H. Berry, Edward W. Belt, and Fendall Marbury; Calvert by James T. Briscoe, Dr. John Turner, and Charles S. Parran; Charles by Richard H. Edelen, Frederick Stone, and John W. Mitchell; and St. Mary's by Chapman Billingsley, George W. Morgan, and John F. Dent.[5]

Some of the Southern Maryland delegation such as James Briscoe, one of the wealthiest men in Calvert who had represented his county in the State Assembly before the war, could trace family lines back to Maryland's founders. Briscoe's ancestor had arrived in 1634 with Governor Leonard Calvert and the colonists aboard the *Ark* and *Dove*. Many of the delegation had served in elected positions in county and state governments, as school board commissioners, sheriffs, judges, and delegates to county, state and national political conventions. Some were attorneys at law, doctors, and vestrymen of their church. Chapman Billingsley and George W. Morgan of St. Mary's had served on the Board of Trustees for the St. Mary's Female Seminary. Spriggs Harwood of Anne Arundel, among his many other achievements, had been appointed State Treasurer in 1860 by Governor Hicks. John Dent of St. Mary's, regularly re-elected to the State Legislature, had once served as Speaker of the House of Delegates. Most had known or worked at some time or another with the others. Between 1847 and 1858 Richard Edelen, Frederick Stone, and John Mitchell had together been members of the Literary Debating Club of Port Tobacco. All were men of public note. And most were slave owners.[6]

A few of the Southern Maryland delegation had at the outset of the war made no secret of their sympathies. George Morgan had served as Quartermaster for the Smallwood Vigilants in 1861. Mitchell had acted as Secretary for the Mounted Volunteers of Charles County and instructed the unit in the use of arms. Billingsley had been a Vice President of the April 23, 1861 meeting in Leonardtown that had voted support for the Confederacy.[7] Somehow all had managed to steer clear of arrest, or at least extended incarceration.

The proceedings of the convention were conducted in the formal parliamentary manner that Maryland legislative proceedings had always been carried out, though the partisan divisions were always evident. The avowed goal of the majority Union Party from the very outset, the abolition of slavery in Maryland, was never far from the fray. On April 28, following the day's adjournment, the Union members of the Convention held a caucus and adopted the following resolution clearly defining their primary objective: "*Resolved*, That this Conference unanimously accept the policy of immediate emancipation without State compensation as the instruction of the late election, and we will, in this respect, faithfully represent the expressed will of the people of Maryland." [8] Thus began the final drive for abolition in Maryland, interrupted only by Early's invasion in early July when the assembly adjourned for a week.[9]

The convention was resumed on July 16. As might be expected, formal thanks were offered to the military and leaders who had blunted the recent rebel offensive in the state. Thanks were even "tendered to the old citizen and patriot of Baltimore county, Ishmael Day, for the heroic and gallant act in shooting down the traitor who dared to pull down the Country's Flag, which he had raised as an evidence of his loyalty and patriotism." The convention also took the opportunity for revenge against Confederate sympathizers by passing a resolution requesting the President of the United States and the commanders of the military department in which Maryland was included to "assess upon known sympathizers with the rebellion, resident in this State, the total amount of all losses and spoliations sustained by loyal citizens of the United States resident in this State, by reason of the recent rebel raid, to compensate loyal sufferers." [10]

Slowly but with measured sureness the convention moved forward with undisguised zeal. In Southern Maryland, however, particularly in St. Mary's and Charles counties where most residents considered the outcome almost unavoidable, newspaper editors made conscious decisions not to publish the daily proceedings as was being done elsewhere.

***

Not surprisingly, it was the war news that predominated public attention, and especially those events that were close to home. One such incident occurred on July 23 when the steamboat *Kingston*, which had run aground on Diamond Shoal Marshes between Smith Point and Windmill Point, Virginia not far from the mouth of the Potomac, had been captured and burned by Confederate guerillas.[11]

Undeterred by such events, convention delegates endlessly debated protocol, wording, and even punctuation. From time to time military intelligence, rumors and intrigues conspired to keep the authorities and citizens alike on edge. In early August General Halleck informed General Barnes: "It is reported that arms have been sent from Richmond to some points on the Potomac or bay for the use of prisoners at Point Lookout, and attempts will be made to smuggle them across. This matter should receive your careful attention." But nothing came of it.[12]

Rebel support, even within the occupied and patrolled boundaries of Southern Maryland, continued to be sustained. This was evidenced not only by the ongoing smuggling operations, but also on occasion by more lethal activities. One such incident occurred in August 1864 when Dr. Thomas H. Quinan, a U.S. Army surgeon and immigrant from Ireland, reported to General Barnes of blockade running activities in the county. The general took immediate action on August 16 by ordering Lieutenant George D. Odell of the 5th Massachusetts Colored Cavalry, charged with conducting mounted patrols in the district with but minimal forces at his command, to investigate the matter. The lieutenant promptly dispatched a sergeant named Winslow and six men with three days rations from Point Lookout to Millstone Landing. Leaving their horses at the landing they set out across the muddy Patuxent in a boat to visit Dr. Quinan "and from him learn how to proceed further." [13]

Possibly seeking to avoid any visible connection with the black troopers who were all on foot, Quinan referred them to the county provost marshal, a civilian, at Drum Point. The marshal suspiciously "retained them in that locality" until the early morning of August 22 by claiming that he was expecting a boat soon to take on board some slaves. The troopers resolved not to be delayed any further and took another vessel to carry them to Cove Point, eight miles to the north, where it is assumed they were to conduct their investigation.[14]

It was still early in the morning when they arrived at their destination. Upon landing part of the squad sat down on the beach to have breakfast while the remainder began to survey their surroundings. Suddenly, from a ravine a few rods away, three men clad in gray appeared and opened fire with carbine rifles. Summoned by the gunfire, Sergeant Winslow and the remainder of the troopers returned, even as a dozen or more men appeared from the ravine, all clad in gray and firing carbines.

"Come on, you Yankee sons of b___s," cried the attackers as they fired volley after volley.

Taken by complete surprise the cavalrymen returned fire but it was too late. Within minutes Winslow and two of his men had fallen wounded. There was little choice but to retreat as even more "bushwackers . . . decorated in gray uniforms and armed mostly with carbines" and greatly outnumbering the troopers, chased after them. As the retreat became a rout two of the Massachusetts men became separated and struck out for the government refugee farms on the other side of the Patuxent from which they might make their way to Leonardtown. The two soldiers arrived at the town at 1 a.m. on August 23. Lieutenant Odell and the rest of his squad were still at Millstone Landing with the horses when he learned of the firefight.

Details were sketchy. Yet the lieutenant had little choice but to send another two men across the river "to learn more of the affair" before reporting to General Barnes by telegram, while reinforcing his squad at the landing just in case. He would later excuse himself from having personally crossed by stating: "My men and horses cannot stand a long march at present, or I should have gone myself with a squad. I have but fifteen present for mounted duty." Instead, he respectfully recommended to the general that a gunboat be sent to Drum Point for a few days to intercept the purported blockade runners.[15]

By August 31 Winslow and the remainder of his ill-fortuned troopers had somehow made their way back to Leonardtown. In the meantime the incident had been reported, with substantial embroidery by editors, in both the Washington and Baltimore press and even in the *Hammond Gazette* at Point Lookout.

According to the *Hammond Gazette*, in a most colorful fiction, thirty rebel guerrillas near Chaptico had surprised Winslow and four soldiers belonging to the 20th Volunteer Reserve Corps. They were taken prisoners and carried to the Eastern Shore where they were paroled, though two of their original squad "coming on in their rear made their escape." [16]

Upon his return, though wounded, Winslow countered the false reports. The editor of the *St. Mary's Gazette* was incensed at the Federal media accounts. He noted with some derision that the event took place in Calvert County not St. Mary's. "We merely mean to state, that there are not now, and never have been any guerrillas in this country . . . It is more probable that they fell in with a band of 'contraband runners,' who also availed themselves of this method in making their escape. Guerrillas would hardly trouble themselves to take prisoners to the Eastern Shore of Virginia to release them, however plausible this may appear to the editor of the *Gazette*." [17] Moreover, the very notion that black troops would be so easily set free by rebels seemed preposterous especially when many such captives in other areas had been either murdered, severely "punished" for having served in the Union Army, or retained to be sold back into slavery.

In the end the incident was quickly forgotten as other events superceded it in importance, especially when counter measures against rebel activities seemed to the few loyal Unionists in Southern Maryland to be ineffective at best. Operations of the Confederate "Secret Line" in the lower counties of the state were among the most irritating, endlessly confounding both Union blockaders on the waters and patrols ashore. In a Sunday letter to Bishop William R. Whittington in Baltimore, the Reverend Lemuel Wilmer, the Union supporter and pastor of the Episcopal Church in Port Tobacco, could not hide his frustration with Federal efforts to stem the unceasing rebel smuggling and postal operations. He was particularly upset by the predominance of still strong, unvarnished rebel support in the region and that "the mails and stages instead of being in the hands of invalid soldiers still remain in the hands of those who thrive in contraband traffic. I go tomorrow, if Providence permits, to visit some troops lately arrived. For a considerable time the country has been left to riot in unfaithfulness. What infatuation! Could not fresh troops drill here, and at the same time crush out this immense contraband trade?" [18]

Still, despite the criticism and frustrations espoused by loyal Unionists, the Potomac Flotilla vigorously continued its efforts to impede rebel activities on the river, the Northern Neck, and between the Rappahannock and the Potomac. As often as not captures of blockade runners were rewarded with periodic successes.

On September 3 the USS *Primrose*, an ex-army tug now serving in the flotilla under the command of Acting Ensign Silas Owen, intercepted a small sloop with four men aboard near Ragged Point. One of those men was Philip F. Edelen, a private in the 1st Maryland Artillery, CSA, described as "a sharp, shrewd fellow, and is to all appearances a spy in the rebel service." The vessel had been carrying a small cargo including shoes, hats, laudanum, revolver percussion caps and gunpowder.[19]

Simple patrol duty was as hazardous as it had ever been and deadly exchanges were frequent. One such incident occurred on the night of September 16 when a withering fire from the shore suddenly ambushed a search party under the command of Acting Ensign Thomas Nelson, operating from one of *Currituck*'s boats while hunting blockade runners in the Yeocomico River. William King, captain of the hold, was instantly killed and George H. McNeil, landsman, was severely wounded. The fire was promptly returned from the boats, and it was reported a shell exploded in the midst of the shore party. And so it went.[20]

***

As the days and weeks slowly passed the Maryland Convention methodically began to address every aspect a reformed constitution might engender for a postwar Maryland. They included receiving petitions, arguing over finer wording of proposed articles, and always managing to subdue the opposition of the Democratic Party members from Southern Maryland and the Eastern Shore. There were three major changes to be addressed: the abolition of slavery; the declaration that United States Government was supreme over the Maryland State Government; and prohibiting the right to vote or hold political office to anyone who had shown sympathy or support for the South.[21]

One contentious issue that particularly rankled the Southern Maryland delegates related to a Unionist resolution permitting Maryland soldiers to vote in absentia in the ratification election for or against the proposed Constitution. "Any qualified voter of this state," read the final resolution,

> "absent from the county or city of his residence by reason of being in the military service of the United States so as not to be home at election to be held on the Tuesday next after the first Monday in the month of November 1864,

shall be entitled to vote as follows: 'A poll shall be opened in each Company of every Maryland Regiment in the service of the United States, or of this State, on the day appointed by the Convention for taking the vote on the new Constitution, or on some day not more than five days thereafter at the quarters of the commanding officer thereof, and voters of this State belonging to such Company who shall be within ten miles of such quarters on the day of the election, may vote at such poll.' (Polls open 8 am to 6 p.m.) The commissioned officers of the company shall act as judges." [22]

Opposition by the Democrats, led by Thomas Lansdale of Prince Georges, was visceral. On August 26 Lansdale and Delegate A. J. Crawford of Somerset County submitted a vigorous protest. Voting by soldiers could never be a free exercise, they argued, as it would enable officers who commanded them to control the votes, especially those "who feel and know the power of their officers, to make them suffer in various ways the penalty of disobedience to their wishes." To a soldier on duty the first great lesson taught was obedience to his commanding officer. Military necessity required a rigid exaction of this duty and allowed for neither discussion nor discretion. To fail in the smallest respect insured harsh treatment, even in cases where martial law prescribed no specific penalty. "It will not be doubted," they believed, "that the only safe approach to the favor of an officer is to gratify his wishes by voting his ticket." [23] Their votes, which could easily alter the outcome of the election, in the eyes of the protestors were neither acceptable nor legal.

There was also the matter that until a new Constitution was instituted, voting should be regulated under the procedures authorized by the existing Constitution of 1851, not by one that had yet to be adopted. "The present Constitution exists," charged Lansdale and Crawford, "until the new one is adopted. How then can the provisions of the present Constitution be violated, or interfered with, until the new one has an existence by the adoption of the people? The great purpose of the majority seems to be, to deprive those who form the constituency of the Convention of the privilege secured to them by the present Constitution of passing upon protest against the Report in the particulars mentioned." [24]

Notwithstanding opposition by Democrats, Southern sympathizers and opponents to radical Republicanism, Maryland soldiers, including those unable to cast a ballot in their own districts owing to their military dispositions, were authorized to vote by provisions in the yet-to-be-ratified Constitution. But the greatest upset to the opposition was Section 3, XXIV of the proposed Constitution, designed to deliver in just thirty-nine words a terminal blow to slavery in Maryland: "That hereafter, in this State, there shall be neither slavery nor involuntary servitude, except in punishment of crime, whereof the party shall be duly convicted; and all persons held to service or labor as slaves, are hereby declared free." Even the hope for compensation to slave owners for the loss of their property was assailed in Section 36 of the article, which stated: "The General Assembly shall pass no law, nor make any appropriation to compensate the masters or claimants of slaves emancipated from servitude by adoption of this Constitution." [25]

For Southern Maryland slave owners, the potential economic loss would be devastating not only to the region's labor force, but to the economy in general. The monetary loss of 4,600 or more slaves in Calvert County alone was estimated at more than three million dollars.[26]

For the opposition there seemed little to celebrate. The finished proposed document contained damning provisions designed to also emasculate anyone, particularly Southern Marylanders, who had endorsed the Confederacy either publicly or privately, which included several members of the Convention itself. There were provisions written in to prohibit anyone who served in the Confederate Army, who had aided the rebel cause or been a sympathizer, from voting or holding public office in the state. Other articles were designed to restrain freedom of the press and to broaden the scope of quartering the military in private homes under certain conditions. Anyone presenting himself at the polls on an election day would be required to swear an oath of allegiance to Maryland and the nation. The votes of any county failing to exact such an oath would be rejected.[27]

The opposition was neither slow in their protests nor in characterizing the convention as "wholesale robbery." There was, they pointed out, no provision for the care for or welfare of the former slave population, which would now be freed but thrown upon their own resources for the first time. It was almost certain that it would be their former masters who would have to assume the cost of feeding, housing, and clothing them to prevent them from starving, "until such time as they could become self supporting." [28]

Ignoring resistance from the opposition the convention proceeded to address the critical format for the statewide balloting. Finally, upon conclusion of nearly four and a half months of work, it came time to vote for or against adoption of the proposed Constitution to allow the public ratification process to begin. A total of fifty delegate votes were in the affirmative while twenty-one were opposed. Eleven of the seventeen Southern Maryland delegates voted in the negative, while six were either absent or recused themselves. On September 6 the Convention adjourned.[29]

It was then publicly announced that to ostensibly "ascertain the sense of the people for adoption or rejection of this Constitution, the Governor shall issue his proclamation within five days of the adjournment of the Convention, directed to Sheriff of city of Baltimore, and sheriffs of several counties commanding them to give notice in manner now prescribed by law, that election will be held in Baltimore on October 12, 1864, (8 a.m. to 5 p.m.) and in the counties on October 12 and 13 at usual places for holding elections." [30]

Procedures were defined. Once cast, all ballots were to be threaded onto a string to permit easy counting and recounting if necessary. The judges of election for Baltimore and all of the counties of Maryland were allowed to receive "the votes only of such electors as are qualified according to the provisions of this Constitution, who may offer to vote at such election." Each ballot was to be clearly marked "For the Constitution" or "Against the Constitution." [31] The judges were to administer "the oath of affirmation prescribed by this Constitution" to every voter before casting a ballot. The governor was authorized to exclude from the final tally "the votes of any county or city, the return judges of which shall fail to certify in the returns . . . that all persons who have voted have taken the oath prescribed to be taken, unless the Governor shall be satisfied such oath was actually administered, and that the failure to make the certificate has been from inadvertence or mistake."

But the most damning inclusion, at least to Southern Marylanders, was authorization of absentee voting by Maryland soldiers. To further aggravate opponents it was included that the governor was to delay announcing the final outcome for fifteen days after the last ballot had been cast "so as to allow the returns of the soldiers' vote to be made before the result of the whole vote is announced." [32]

Organized opposition to ratification was intense in Southern Maryland. On Tuesday, September 13, just a week after the articles of the proposed Constitution were made public, a mass meeting was convened at Prince Frederick in Calvert County to formally adopt resolutions opposing several very key tenants of the document. The gathering, a last ditch effort to secure Governor Bradford's intervention on the grounds of legal technicalities, was presided over by John Parran, scion of one of the foremost families of Southern Maryland. Another Parran, William J., served as secretary. Daniel R. Magruder, a former delegate to the State Legislature, 1858-1859, offered several resolutions designed to contest the protocol and legality of the election, all of which were unanimously adopted:

"*Resolved*, That we protest against the imposition of the illegal test oath prescribed by the Convention at the election which is to decide the question of the adoption or rejection of the proposed constitution, and we call upon the judges of election to disregard the said illegal mandate of the Convention.

Resolved, That we call upon his Excellency, the Governor, to interpose his executive power to enforce the obligation of the existing constitution and laws at the said election, and not to allow the said proposed constitution to go into effect or supersede the existing constitution until the same shall be legally and properly ratified by the free and unrestricted suffrages of the 'legal and qualified voters of the State.'

Resolved, That a committee of three be appointed by the chair to report to this meeting a memorial to the Governor, asking his aid in the premises, to be signed by the voters of the county, and that a committee be appointed to procure the said memorial to be signed by the voters and presented to the Governor."

The committee, Basil Duke Bond, Daniel Kent and Daniel R. Magruder, was then designated to prepare and report to the meeting a formal memorial for presentation to Governor Bradford. The report was unanimously adopted by the assembled. Magruder, William Parran and Octavius C. Harris were appointed to have the petition signed and delivered to the governor.[33]

The governor's response came on September 21. The challenge by memorialists was simply that the mode of conducting the ratification process was illegal because it was not being carried out within the parameters of the existing Constitution of 1851, which was still the governing law of Maryland until the people had approved the proposed Constitution. Thus such new components as the oath of allegiance and soldiers' voting from beyond their home districts were invalid because they did not exist in the current Constitution.

Governor Bradford's reply, that he would not interfere, was perhaps not unexpected. He declared that he had no authority to challenge or alter the Convention's end product. That was a judicial function. "I deem it altogether unnecessary to enter into any arguments as to the propriety or constitutionality of the act of the Convention to which you take exceptions," he informed Magruder in a letter dismissing the charges outright and widely circulated for publication a week before the balloting was to begin.[34]

Calvert County's pleas were not conducted without support. St. Mary's also protested the questionable circumstances of the vote of Marylanders by the absentee ballots of soldiers in the field. They too appealed to Governor Bradford to have that ratification declared invalid. Their protests would also be ignored and ultimately aborted by the Court of Appeals' rejection of the case.[35]

***

As the date of the election inched closer events of the war continued to send ripples onto the shores of Southern Maryland. Confederate activities along the Potomac, Piankatank and Rappahannock went on as always. Yet the navy continued to maintain the offensive with a series of almost continuous raids from Southern Maryland to keep rebel guerrillas off balance. One such expedition occurred on September 26 when the much worked flotilla gunboats *Fuchsia, Thomas Freeborn* and *Mercury* proceeded from their base in St. Inigoes Creek to Milford Haven, Virginia. Intelligence that the Confederates were preparing a number of boats to attack the blockading force at the mouth of the Piankatank River had generated the move. Leaving *Fuchsia* and *Freeborn* at Milford Haven, expedition leader Acting Master Street took armed boats under tow by *Mercury* and proceeded to Stutt's Creek. A force of forty sailors was landed three miles upstream under the command of Acting Master William A. Arthur and Acting Ensign Philip Sheridan at the farm of the "noted rebel" Lewis Hudgins, chief of the "Arabs of Mathews County." Four Confederate boats were destroyed, five were captured and a fishery demolished. The end product had been petty, but demoralizing if not crippling to the rebels. Though the Rappahannock was by now dominated by Union forces, navy warships and commerce vessels alike were still obliged to remain on alert for audacious Southern raiders who continued their surprise attacks.[36]

In one such incident, less than two weeks later on October 8 and only a few days before balloting in Maryland, rebel guerrillas struck in Wicomico Bay and captured the steam torpedo boat *Picket Boat No. 2*, Acting Ensign Andrew Stockholm commanding. The vessel was one of two acquired in New York by Lieutenant William Barker Cushing, USN, for a planned small boat expedition against the Confederate Navy ironclad *Albemarle*, lying in the Roanoke River, North Carolina, and was bound in company with *Picket Boat No. 1* to Fort Monroe. Unfortunately, while en route, mechanical troubles forced *No. 2* to stop in hostile territory for repairs. While these were in progress *No. 1* continued pressing on ahead. Suddenly, Stockholm and his men found themselves under attack by a body of guerillas. He later reported: "I immediately returned their fire, and fought them until I had expended my last cartridge; previous to which I slipped my cable, and trying to get out of the enemy's reach, grounded on a sand bar." Though the sailors succeeded in burning their vessel and destroying their supplies before being captured, Cushing was highly indignant at what he considered the unnecessary loss of one of his boats. He later wrote of the affair: "This was a great misfortune and I have never understood how so stupid a thing could have happened. I forget the name of the volunteer ensign to whose care it was intrusted, but am pleased to know that he was

540

taken prisoner. I trust that his bed was not down or his food that of princes while in rebel hands." [37]

***

For President Lincoln there was a great deal riding on the impending ratification vote in Maryland. It was well known that if Marylanders approved the proposed Constitution by popular vote, their's would become the first Border State to do so, leading the way for others to follow. To lose would mean political chaos in the state, provoking even more extremism from the Republican abolitionist right, and lending heart to the pro-slavery Democratic Party. With the coming national general election also looming large the very popular General George B. McClellan, a hero to many Marylanders for his stance against abolition, who was running on the Democratic ticket against the president, the very future of reconstruction after the war was an open question.

Lincoln did not waver. On October 3 Henry W. Hoffman, Chairman of the Unconditional Union Central Committee, wrote to the president inviting him to speak at a mass meeting in favor of the "Free Constitution" to be held at Monument Square, Baltimore on the evening of October 10. "In consequence of local dissensions and with a view to general harmony and cordial fraternization upon the new Constitution," he wrote, "the Committee have resolved to rely exclusively upon speakers from other States at this meeting. We are convinced that your presence on the occasion would insure its success both as to harmony and point of numbers and that its influence upon the vote to be taken on the following Wednesday would be to add hundreds and perhaps thousands of votes to the free State column. We therefore most cordially and earnestly invite your attendance" [38]

The president's response was immediate. He could not attend but would send a letter of support. On the evening of the rally his compelling missive was read before an assembled audience of thousands of cheering supporters.[39]

"A convention of Maryland has framed a new constitution for the State; a public meeting is called for this evening, at Baltimore, to aid in securing its ratification by the people; and you ask a word from me, for the occasion. I presume the only feature of the instrument, about which there is serious controversy, is that which provides for the extinction of slavery. It needs not to be a secret, and I presume it is no secret, that I wish success to this provision. I desire it on every consideration. I wish all men to be free. I wish the material prosperity of the already free which I feel sure the extinction of slavery would bring. I wish to see, in process of disappearing, that only thing which ever could bring this nation to civil war. I attempt no argument. Argument upon the question is already exhausted by the abler, better informed, and more immediately interested sons of Maryland herself. I only add that I shall be gratified exceedingly if the good people of the State shall, by their votes, ratify the new constitution.

Yours truly A. LINCOLN" [40]
***

The first official returns began to come in days after the polls had closed throughout Maryland. The initial reports seemed to indicate a majority against ratification in fifteen counties including all of Southern Maryland, but strong

541

support in Baltimore City, Frederick, Alleghany and Washington counties. Soon after, on October 20, updated returns from most of the state, with the exception of Queen Anne's, Dorchester, and Somerset counties, reported 20,408 for and 22,351 against ratification, though 1,524 soldiers' affirmative ballots gave the edge towards approval by 319 votes. The final tally was going to be breathtakingly close.[41]

By October 29 all of the officially sanctioned ballots were in and tallied. The legal vote for the Constitution was 27,541, and 29,536 against, showing a clear majority of 1,995 votes against. The controversial soldiers' vote, however, was first reported at 2,633 for and 263 against but later modified. Nevertheless, the new Constitution was approved by the slimmest margin of only 263 votes out of a total of 59,973 recorded. Only one-third of Maryland voters had gone to the polls. An unknown number had simply been turned away unwilling to swear the prescribed oath or acquiesce to the intimidating presence of the military. Not surprisingly of the 5,892 citizens who had voted in the five Southern Maryland counties, 5,293 had cast their ballots against and only 599 for ratification.[42]

On November 1 Governor Bradford issued a formal proclamation declaring the adoption of the new Constitution by the people of Maryland though not without considerable controversy even in some Unionist circles. "The declaration is made on the aggregate vote of the soldiers and people," declared the *Weekly National Intelligencer*, "so far as the latter were willing to cast their suffrages in view of the obnoxious test oath imposed by the Convention. This oath, it appears, whilst imposed upon the legal voters of the State, was not required of the soldiers, whose votes, given outside of the State or away from their respective places of residence, the Convention had no power to legalize." [43]

That same evening the metropolis of Baltimore, once a hotbed of Maryland rebellion but now the hub of Union control, celebrated. Sixty-five big guns at Fort McHenry roared their approval. Church bells rang out from every religious center in the city. In the harbor ships were festooned with flags, as were many buildings along the myriad city avenues. Black freemen, regarding the day as one of thanksgiving, filled the pews of their churches while newly emancipated slaves "took freedom in stride often remaining tactful and understanding before their former masters and rejoiced more appropriately among themselves." [44]

Not too far away in Southern Maryland a pall of almost universal sadness and defeat unlike any other experienced to date was cast over the white population. Their only hope, many believed, lay in the coming national presidential election wherein General McClellan, a Democrat popular among dissidents and anti-abolitionists, challenged the incumbent Republican President Abraham Lincoln. The failure to defeat the ratification of the new Maryland Constitution, for some Southern Marylanders, seemed to illustrate the need to support the Democratic candidate if there was to be even the slightest chance of returning to the old order. One wag, identifying himself in a Washington newspaper only as "Prince Georgian" wrote:

"The result of the recent election will, we trust, teach our people one lesson, viz: the ease with which they can assert their power in the state if they only have the manliness to make the assertion. In the late election no effort was made. A mere spontaneous and unorganized casting of ballots has, except for fraud and illegality, defeated the Constitution. As it is, our vote was thirty to forty thousand short. Although the Governor, regardless of law and right, may proclaim the Constitution accepted by virtue of the soldiers' votes, the moral victory and the *legal* triumph are unquestionably with the opponents. The result of the election struck terror to the hearts of the small and fanatical coterie that has labored so earnestly and incessantly for our ruin. It has demonstrated beyond all mischance, that Maryland is sure for McClellan and [George H.] Pendleton and the Democratic State ticket, if the people will only exhibit like energy. There is now no excuse for those who have formerly held back." [45]

Not all Southern Marylanders were of a like mind. For the newly emancipated blacks, over half of the region's population, there seemed a newfound experience of joy, hope and freedom. Jubilee, it seemed, had come at last. But first the war had to be won.

41

TULIP
". . . moistened with a tear of regret."

For many white Southern Marylanders, the fall of 1864 was seen as a watershed season. If the ratification of the new Maryland Constitution and the abolition of slavery in the state had not been disturbing enough, the potential re-election of Abraham Lincoln to the presidency and seating of a Republican/Unionist majority in Congress was maddening. For the first time in history, the armies of a major nation were going to be allowed to vote in a national election, and the outcome of the recent Maryland balloting in October had buoyed the administration's hopes for the president's return to office. Recent Union military successes in the Shenandoah, in Missouri, and the capture of Atlanta, Georgia, bode well for the Republican ticket. Yet in Southern Maryland, even Mother Nature seemed to be conspiring against the remaining plantations and farmsteads. On October 9, only a few days before the voting on the new Constitution was to begin, the region was stricken by a severe freeze. "Clear and very cold. It is indeed winter and no prospect of deliverance . . . It is the coldest day of the season," recorded Charles Warren Hutt.[1] St. Mary's County was hit particularly hard, as noted a few days later in the *St. Mary's Gazette*.

"On Sunday night last we were visited with a heavy frost in this locality, and the tobacco crop of this county has been badly damaged. Not more than one-fourth of the crop is supposed to have been housed at the time, and the loss will consequently be very severe. The crop for the present year is very small, but such is the scarcity of labor here our farmers were unable to save it from the frost. The aggregate loss in the county from Sunday night's frost is estimated at $50,000. This is but the beginning of the promised advantages of a free labor system, and we commend it to the attention of all who have the real interest of the State at heart." [2]

Now for the first time, white landlords and small farmers alike began their struggle to come to terms with the new social order. The abolition of slavery in Maryland and the necessary readjustment of labor practices on a scale hitherto unheard of in the region, was setting the world topsy-turvy.

While the southern counties were reeling from seemingly endless adversity, the Potomac Flotilla continued its ceaseless patrols between Washington and the Rappahannock, conducting raids and occasionally picking off unsuspecting blockade runners here and there. In mid-October rebel snipers operating from the shores of Fleets Point on the shores of the Great Wicomico, fired two volleys at several officers of the blockader *Commodore Read* who were fishing in the river. The attack did not go unanswered. On October 25 Commander Parker in the USS *Don*, accompanied by *Yankee*, landed a small force on the point and in reprisal burned to the ground three houses, barns and outbuildings. In the next two days Parker pressed up the Rappahannock to within a few miles of Port Royal, capturing five boats and burning four others. While on the river, the gunboats elicited frequent musket fire from the shore, which was always answered with the ships' big guns.[3]

While Parker was carrying out his petty reprisals and steaming about the Rappahannock, the flotilla schooner *Adolph Hugel,* Acting Master Sylvanus Nickerson, was aggressively rounding up vessels violating the blockade on the Potomac. *Hugel,* a veteran of Admiral Farragut's attack on Forts Jackson and St. Philip, Louisiana, and the Vicksburg Campaign, had become one of the more successful of the flotilla blockaders in the latter days of the war. On October 26, she captured the Baltimore schooner *Coquette,* Captain J. C. Deavers, with a crew of five and two passengers, in Wades Bay, just north of Smith's Point, Maryland. The vessel was charged with running boxes and bales of Lynchburg tobacco from the Virginia shore, and was carrying at the time of her capture $3,590.64 in gold, silver and paper currency.[4] Two days later off Alexandria, Nickerson seized the coasting sloop *James Landry,* commanded by a black captain named Franklin Perry. Though carrying six black passengers, all of whom were in Federal employ, the skipper confessed that his clearance had been made under false pretense. The vessel was seized for violation of blockade regulation.[5] *Hugel*'s last capture of note was the sloop *Zion,* taken on the morning of November 2. And so the game of hide and seek continued.[6]

The patrols of the Potomac Flotilla and the presence of Union troops in their midst, though stifling to many Southern Marylanders, failed to subvert the activities of some resolute supporters of the Confederacy. Resident rebel spies and agents of both sexes were still numerous, and often called upon to survive by their personal wiles even when surrounded by Yankee "occupiers." Union officers and troops were occasionally billeted at the substantial and venerable Rose Hill estate owned by the Floyd family, near Port Tobacco, though one of the family members, Robert Semmes Floyd, was serving in the Confederate Army. Nevertheless, Floyd's wife and beautiful sister Olivia were frequently obliged to entertain Yankee officers who were unaware of their host's allegiance to the rebel cause. Olivia, operating directly under the noses of her military guests, was in fact a rebel agent. Employing a wooden boat model made by her brother as a secret place for concealing money and papers, she was one of several critical links between Confederate secret agents in the North and command centers in the South.

One of Olivia's most trying episodes involved saving a handful of rebel soldiers operating out of Canada who had conducted a successful raid into Vermont. The foray had been an ambitious undertaking commanded by Lieutenant Bennet H. Young, CSA, with about twenty-five Confederate soldiers. Crossing the border into the United States they struck the town of St. Albans by complete surprise on October 19, 1864 and robbed three banks of $208,000. Within an hour, after a brief resistance by townsfolk in which one citizen was killed and another wounded, the raiders escaped back into Canada. Soon afterwards, however, the Canadian Provincial Government took Young and twelve of his men into custody. Outraged by what seemed to many to be little more than a case of robbery and murder, the United States Government demanded extradition so that they might be hung, unless they could prove that they were duly commissioned officers and soldiers of the Confederate Army. An underground message started south through the "Secret Line" requesting proof of their commissions from Confederate authorities. Olivia Floyd was the last link in the chain of rebel supporters who had hand carried the information from the North to Maryland. Hiding the note in the ball of a pair of brass andirons right by the fire and at the foot of one of her unexpected Union visitors, she cleverly eluded detection. The message made it through to Richmond, the commissions were produced, and the rebel raiders were saved from the gallows.[7]

***

On October 18 the ratification of the nominations of Abraham Lincoln and Andrew Johnson for the offices of President and Vice President of the United States by the Union Convention in Baltimore had been a foregone conclusion. Lincoln's ability to win the election in Maryland, however, was questionable as he was opposed by an unknown quantity of strong backing for his opponent General McClellan, particularly in Southern Maryland and the Eastern Shore. On ballot day the voter turnout was greater than the Constitutional election, yet the president carried the state by only 7,432 votes, with his strongest support in Baltimore. Rural Maryland went for McClellan. Nevertheless, the Union (or Republican) Party swept all of the key state offices. Thomas Swann, formerly of the Know Nothing Party and Mayor of Baltimore turned conservative Unionist, defeated Ezekiel F. Chambers for the governorship by a vote of 40,579 to 32,068. A surge in Democratic votes for other state offices, however, rivaled those of the Union Party, securing a slim majority in the State Senate, placed two candidates in the U.S. Congress, and set the stage for a Democratic resurgence in subsequent elections.[8]

Less than robust support for McClellan in some quarters, perhaps surprisingly, came from the troops quartered in Maryland. In the St. Mary's District, when by order of General Barnes the polls were opened for Iowa, Maine, Pennsylvania and Wisconsin troops, the vote was small as many soldiers who could travel were granted furloughs to go home. Of those who remained and cast ballots, 278 voted, with Lincoln winning by a majority of 116, though charges of irregularities were rife in some units.

"The vote for Wisconsin was taken in the 2d Battery of that State," reported one soldier of the 20th Pennsylvania Reserve Corps who noted that sixty-one of the seventy-four Wisconsin votes had been for McClellan. "No other Wisconsin men were allowed to cast their ballots at the polls established—the commanding officer of the battery saying, that if he allowed it his returns would not be considered legal. The officer wears the rank of Captain, and is a M'Clellan man. His patriotism and devotion to his country is about as strong as a keg of Lager beer. His men being filled with beer voted as their gallant Democratic Captain directed. This affair of driving men from the polls is about equal to their robbing the Union heroes graves of their names, to make votes for their party." [9]

There would be little recourse. Lincoln was re-elected by a national ballot of 2,330,552 popular votes to McClellan's 1,835,985, providing a plurality of 494,567, or more than fifty-five percent of total ballots cast. In the Electoral College, Lincoln and Johnson received 212 votes while McClellan and Pendleton received only twenty-one. Even in the military, Lincoln had triumphed, receiving 116,887 over McClellan's 33,748. Two days after the election, the general resigned from the U.S. Army. "For my country's sake," he wrote in disgust, "I deplore the result." [10] The Union disagreed.

On November 10 the ironclad *Roanoke*, another warship brought in to Point Lookout as a guardship soon after the Early raid, fired a 21-gun salute in honor of the re-election of Lincoln. The reverberations passed like a physical shock wave through the prison camp. The following eve, the sound of another blast was also heard. This time, it was the aftershock of a terrible tragedy.[11]

***

Captain William H. Smith, commander of the U.S. Navy gunboat *Tulip*, was anxious to get to Washington. He had been away too long and his loving wife Kathy was awaiting him there. Hailing from Philadelphia, he had been attached to the Potomac Flotilla for almost two years, and was a much esteemed officer. He had received orders from Commander Parker early on Friday, November 11 to bring his ship to the Washington Navy Yard from her anchorage off the St. Inigoes Naval Station "for the purpose of having her starboard boiler repaired, which was reported by Chief Engineer John E. Reilly to be in an unsafe condition." Impatient to see his wife, he telegraphed her to meet him at the yard on Monday morning. The ship would be undergoing at least ten days worth of repairs, during which the officers and crew might enjoy a much welcomed shore leave. Eager to be underway, Smith may have gently fingered the ring bearing her name as he dictated the message of his coming to the telegrapher in the station telegraph office. The weather was clear and pleasant, a perfect day for sailing. He had enjoyed midday dinner with Dr. Jones and family at Cross Manor, but could only think about getting to Washington, expressing with chagrin to his host about how he had been instructed not to use his ship's defective starboard boiler.[12] The voyage to Washington was not expected to be an exceptional one, though the threat posed by rebel snipers on the Virginia shore was always a possibility. Yet the expectation of a few days ashore in Washington with his wife was undoubtedly inviting indeed.

Tulip, unlike many other vessels in the flotilla that had served in their former lives as ferryboats, lighthouse tenders, tugs, and passenger vessels, was a purpose-built gunboat, though not initially intended for service in the U.S. Navy. The ship had originally been constructed in the winter of 1864 at New York as the *Chi Kiang* by master builder James C. Jewett under contract to "Mandarin" Henry G. Ward, an accredited American agent of the Chinese government. Daniel McCleod provided her engines.[13] She had been one of three that Ward had contracted to accompany a large purchase of arms and munitions, all intended for China's Ever-Victorious Army. The army was commanded by his brother, General Frederick Townsend Ward, a mercenary engaged in suppressing the Taiping Rebellion for the government of Tzu Hsi, a long conflict that had been underway since 1850. The other two vessels, *Dai Ching* and *Kiang Soo*, her sister ships, had followed a similar route and would also end up in the U.S. Navy.[14]

Tulip's acquisition by the Navy Department, like her two sisters, had largely been a consequence of Ward's own financial difficulties that followed the death of his brother before the ship's completion, and to no small extent by the Federal Government's concerns over selling arms to a foreign entity. Rear Admiral Hiram Paulding, then commandant of the New York Navy Yard, had purchased *Dai Ching* for the Atlantic Blockading Squadron on April 21, 1863. *Chi Kiang* and *Kiang Soo*

547

(changed to *Fuchsia* after acquisition) were obtained at a cost of $30,000 each for the Potomac Flotilla on June 22.[15]

With her name changed on June 4 from *Chi Kiang* to *Tulip*, the new gunboat formally entered the Navy rolls listed as a 183-ton 4th-class tug-rigged screw steamer, 97 feet 3 inches in length, 21 feet 9 inches abeam, 9 foot 6 inches depth in hold, with a draft of about 8 feet. Her original registry at the Port of New York under the name *Chi Kiang* noted that she had two decks, two masts for long distance deployment, a round stern and tuck. An eagle's head was chosen for her figurehead. Her hull was diagonally strapped to prevent hogging in rough waters. On September 30, 1864 she was armed with one 20-pdr. Parrott rifle, two 24-pdr. howitzers, and two heavy 12-pdr. smooth bores. A single horizontal direct acting compound engine with a short stroke and a short connecting rod provided her power. There were two cylinders, one high pressure and one low pressure. The horizontal engine had been intentionally chosen over the vertical type to keep the machinery below the water line, presumably to prevent danger from potential combat injury, although the vertical type engine took up less space. Moreover, the more fuel efficient compound engine, albeit less reliable and costly to maintain, was capable of producing twenty-three horsepower and generating a speed of up to eight knots, though the compound was more unreliable and costly to maintain. She carried two tubular boilers, occupying an estimated 230 to 276 square feet, both of which were bolted in the firebox. Her light hull and shallow draft would permit her to operate with impunity in the narrow passages and shoally rivers of the Tidewater. Overall, the *New York Times* pridefully declared, she had "all the modern appliances of warships." [16]

Tulip's unrelenting operations were, like most of the flotilla vessels, demanding upon both ship and crew. Her engines, like many in the fleet, were less than safe. Such flaws were deemed by Secretary Welles to be a product of poor workmanship caused by the government's need for quick production of machinery, which had often resulted in the use of faulty materials and consequently an inferior end product. Despite a reset of production standards in 1864, for vessels previously acquired such as *Tulip* it was already too late. The Navy Secretary had earlier placed operational accountability on every ship's engineers and senior officers. "From negligent use by engineers," as one historian has noted, "who often threw in grease, tar, pork or anything that would burn quick to raise steam pressure during pursuit of fast blockade runners . . . had a corrosive effect from residue on ship's machinery." Welles held engineers liable for the condition of a vessel's machinery and obliged them to submit daily reports to commanding officers, who were in turn instructed to address the problems as quickly as possible. But the needs of war quickly trumped such time consuming necessities as maintenance and violations of the order were often set aside or totally disregarded.[17]

The consequences for the Potomac Flotilla was that breakdowns had become so common during the 1863-1864 period that between a quarter to a third of the fleet was either out of service or unfit for duty at any given time. Like many flotilla vessels faced with constant duty and machinery designed for speed rather than quality, *Tulip* suffered from frequent breakdowns. Owing to the inadequate number of ships for the requisite duties, it had been necessary to keep as many operational for as long as possible. Such requirements resulted in limited maintenance that all but insured serious boiler and engine problems. In the harsh Tidewater environment the brackish and salty waters caused scaling in the boilers, which produced sluggish performance underway. Dirt and tallow clogged oil holes and condensers. Though plagued by breakdowns, major repairs, which could only be made at the Navy Yard, were frequently ignored owing to the continual need for ships on line.[18]

Tulip was no exception.

In September 1863, only weeks after joining several ships of the squadron at the mouth of the Rappahannock, the gunboat had returned to the Washington Navy Yard for major repairs, her engines deemed to be in a hazardous condition. By mid-October she was still undergoing work, having a larger steam drum added. Unfortunately, though no one could have known it, the practical but temporary repair only made the problems worse. The boiler's old shell, which was cut away to add the new appendage, only weakened the structure rather than enhancing it.[19]

Tulip was initially assigned to the First Division of the Potomac Flotilla, which patrolled between Blackistone Island and the Piankatank. By November 1863 she had been transferred to the Second Division, Station H, which kept watch on a twenty-five mile strip between Smith's Point, Virginia, on the southern lip of the Potomac's mouth, to the Piankatank and Rappahannock.[20]

By August 1864 the ship's engineers, Jeremiah Biddle and John T. Buckley, again declared Tulip's boilers unsafe. Leaks around the boiler drum were so dangerous, they declared, the vessel was unfit for service. They deemed her boilers so unseaworthy that both men refused to run the boat. For bringing the unwelcome problem to the attention of their superiors and their refusal to work aboard they were suspended for a time and assigned to subordinate positions. It saved their lives.[21]

Soon afterwards, on September 3, Third Assistant Engineers George H. Parks and Erastus Barry, driven by the same alarm as Biddle and Buckley, also complained of the extremely dangerous condition of the starboard boiler. *Tulip*'s Surgeon's Steward John S. Kennedy supported their concerns about the machinery, as well as disclosing the horrible working conditions in the engine room, a result of the extreme temperature. The steward noted that another third assistant engineer, William Miller, two second class firemen and other crewmen had already been hospitalized or were on the ship's sick list because of the intense heat, which reached as high as 130° to 136° F in the engine room. Steam leaks from the boiler only made conditions more insufferable.[22]

Now it was time to put things right.

***

It was 3 p.m. when *Tulip*, watched with keen interest by little John Ellicott from the upper portico of Cross Manor, left her anchorage in St. Inigoes. Having heard discussion at midday dinner regarding the danger posed by the ship's defective boiler and Captain Smith's stated intention to employ it despite the hazard, the youth had become extremely nervous and had to be put to bed early.

An hour after the ship's departure, she exited the St. Mary's River and started to round the southern tip of St. George's Island to enter the main channel of the Potomac. The slow crawl under one boiler was torturous for Captain Smith who,

549

some later said, was still concerned about rebel ambush from the Virginia shore and was eager to be fully underway on the open river. Hostilities along the Potomac frontier, however, were neither more nor less than they had been over the last few months. Only a few days earlier, the USS *Anacostia* had destroyed two rebel army wagons on Aquia Creek that were used to convoy blockaded goods to Fredericksburg. Two days later, on November 9, she had burned the Alexandria sloop *Buckskin* in Chopawamsic Creek. Rebels had captured the unfortunate sloop only ten days before while her crew was gathering wood along the creek's shore. At Point Lookout it was also business as usual as "a general wash up" was in progress, wood was being drawn in camp for the first time for the coming season, and news of Lincoln's majority in the recent election and Sherman's burning of Atlanta was on everyone's lips.[23]

For the fifty-eight officers and crewmen aboard *Tulip*, Ensign and Executive Officer Robert M. Wagstaff, Acting Master's Mates John Davis, Julian L. Reynolds, John Raffenburg, John Hammond, Senior Engineer George F. Parks, Third Assistant Engineer John Gordon, and Third Assistant Engineer Benjamin T. Teal, the prospect of leave in Washington must have been inviting. Yet Engineer Parks, who hailed from Brooklyn where he lived with his wife, three children and aged mother, and was in charge of the engines, must have still worried about the defective boiler. Gordon who hailed from Philadelphia where his family resided, may also have experienced some trepidation, but apparently said little.[24]

Captain Smith's orders regarding the voyage had been explicit, the most important of which was that *Tulip* was to proceed under steam only from her port boiler. Parks had been specifically instructed by the Navy Yard's Chief Fleet Engineer John Reilly not to get steam up in the starboard boiler under any circumstances. The ship would thus be obliged to proceed slowly upriver under only half power for safety. The captain, however, had other ideas. Once the gunboat had passed the guard boat *William Bacon*, Henry E. Ripley commanding, at the mouth of the St. Mary's, and was out of signal distance of the naval station, he ordered Parks to have a full head of steam worked up in the faulty boiler. The ship was to press ahead under full power. Whether or not Parks followed orders is unknown, but it appears from subsequent events that Gordon was the one who activated the defective boiler.[25] Smith's reasoning for ignoring the order, whether it was actually fear of rebel sharpshooters ashore somewhere along the route, or just his own fervent desire to see his wife as soon as possible, will never be known. Whatever it may have been, it was as flawed as the starboard boiler.

Several hours after entering the Potomac the captain and Executive Officer Wagstaff were standing on the bridge when Engineer Parks informed them that *Tulip* would have to make a two hour stop at Piney Point, which would be necessary for him to work up a head of steam in the damaged boiler.[26] Approval was immediate, and the pilot, one James Jackson, was instructed to set a course for the point without explanation being given. Casually, the pilot asked Acting Master's Mate John Davis, officer of the deck at the time, why they were heading for the point. "I told him I did not know," the officer later reported. "He then asked Senior Engineer George H. Parks, and he told him that they were going to get up steam on the other boiler." Just then, Assistant Engineer Gordon, then on watch, said to an undoubtedly surprised Parks that it was not necessary to stop, "that he had already steam on the other boiler." Wagstaff then reported to Smith what Gordon had said and the captain, happy to be fully underway, directed that no stop was necessary and to proceed up river.[27] Despite all of his concerns, it appeared that Parks had been circumvented. The ship was now steaming with both boilers operational.

Davis was relieved from his duty as officer of the deck at 6 p.m. and everything seemed in order, but only momentarily. Between 6:10 and 6:20 p.m., while standing on the forepart of the ship, he heard noise and sensed excitement and activity aft. Suddenly he saw "volumes of steam coming up the engine and fire room hatchways." Then came a strangled shout filled with urgency. "Haul your fire." It was Gordon. At that moment Parks, who had been sitting in the wardroom with Wagstaff, leaped up to the deck and rushed down into the engine room as Gordon cried out, "For God's sake, someone raise the safety-valve." Seeing the danger, Davis also started aft to assist. Then as he was coming abreast of the cabin companionway, it happened.[28]

The boiler explosion that tore the heart out of the USS *Tulip* as she was passing Ragged Point, Virginia, about fourteen miles west of the St. Mary's, was horrific. At the moment of disaster, Captain Smith, Pilot Jackson, Acting Master's Mate John Hammond, and Acting Master's Mate and Quartermaster John Raffenburg were standing on the bridge over the boilers "and must have been blown to atoms," as was the entire upper portion of the ship. All of the off duty officers had been assembled in the mess room, also located above the ship's boilers. Officers and crewmen alike, those that had not been torn apart by the blast, were cast in all directions. Engineer Reynolds "was thrown up into the air a great distance and fell into the water where he first became conscious of what had occurred," and then of the unbearable pain of a broken thigh. A few of the crew somehow escaped without serious injury after running immediately to the lower gig. But before they could get it down, the wreck of *Tulip* sank, carrying with her most of those still alive, as well as the dead and injured still on board. The only trace of Captain Smith was his hat, which was picked up later.[29]

The USS *Tulip* slipped beneath the brown Potomac waters within two to three minutes after the explosion, leaving the surface of the river littered with the detritus of catastrophe. Another account stated: "She was blown to pieces so completely that her hull disappeared below the surface in five minutes from the explosion." [30] Whatever the difference in minutes may have been, it mattered little to those few men who managed to cling to life against all odds.

Some officers and sailors, scalded and broken, seized whatever floating wreckage they could lay hands upon. A small number succeeded in keeping afloat for forty minutes to an hour, though most soon disappeared. By 7 p.m. only ten men were left to be picked up by the diminutive tugboat *Hudson*, Captain James Allen commanding, which finally appeared on the scene. They were believed to be all that had escaped from the ill-fated ship. It was reported many years later by John M. Ellicott, then in his seniority, but not verified, that the ship's purser, who is unidentified in the official reports, also survived, having been blown clear, by swimming ashore. The only two survivors escaping major injury were Ensign

Wagstaff, who suffered only a contusion to his right foot, and Master's Mate Davis.[31]

As soon as the remnants of *Tulip*'s men were hoisted aboard the tug, her crew immediately prepared coffee and refreshments for them, "and gave them the kindest attention." For more than an hour *Hudson* plowed vainly through the floating wreckage in the failing evening light, searching for more survivors and bodies. With eight of the critically injured in need of prompt medical attention, and the mantle of evening obscuring visibility, Captain Allen was obliged to call off the search and steam towards St. Inigoes. At 9:30 p.m. he encountered *William Bacon* at the entrance of the St. Mary's and was immediately permitted to proceed towards the naval station.[32]

Upon arrival at St. Inigoes at 11 p.m., the survivors were transferred to the USS *Wyandank*, then lying at anchor somewhat north of the station. Two local physicians, identified only as Doctors Tappington and Miles, were summoned by Acting Assistant Surgeon M. F. Delano to assist with the wounded until more substantial aid was secured.[33] James Tier, the station blacksmith, a carpenter by civilian trade, was enlisted to make crude splints to support fracture wounds that several of the injured had incurred. In the meantime Delano had sent a note via *Hudson* to Dr. Hager at the Hammond Hospital on Point Lookout urgently requesting that he dispatch a surgeon and medical supplies. The dispensary at St. Inigoes, it seemed, was completely empty of the needed stores to tend survivors scalded by the blast or suffering from major fractures.[34]

At 4 a.m., November 12, less than ten hours after the calamity, an assistant army surgeon named Westerlin arrived from Hammond Hospital with anesthetics, splints and cotton. By mid-afternoon the injured had been taken aboard the U.S. Army steamer *Northern Lights* and carried to the hospital. Early reports reaching Washington claimed that as many as sixty lives had been lost. One of the injured, a landsman named Burrell Fleet, suffering from dislocations, contusions, and scalding of his left arm and hand, would have to undergo a partial amputation of his foot. Masters Mate Julian Reynolds, and three others, 1st Class Boy Frank Snowden, and Landsmen Nelson Gaskins and James Watkins, suffered from severe contusions and fractures. Of the eight survivors, two or three were reported in a "hopeless condition" and not expected to live even before reaching Point Lookout. While en route, Fireman James Porter and Wardroom Cook Michael Holland died of severe burns. Word of the disaster spread about the prison compound with alacrity and no doubt became the talk of the day. The two uninjured survivors, Wagstaff and Davis, were sent to Washington aboard the USS *Ella* to report on the loss, arriving there on the morning of November 14.[35]

On the morning after the disaster, the youthfully inquisitive John Ellicott, curiosity perked by the activities on the waterfront of the station, wandered down to the modest assemblage of government buildings near the dock on St. Inigoes. When peeking into an equipment room, he saw *Tulip*'s purser sitting on a coil of rope, and immediately began to bombard him with questions. The paymaster, looking morose, dazed and pale, and undoubtedly still in shock, immediately walked down to the water's edge, evading his inquisitor, and "stood a long time gazing toward the Potomac." [36]

Commander Parker let no time escape before ordering an immediate search for the bodies of *Tulip*'s still missing complement. A list was drawn up of the injured and missing and Acting Ensign Philip Sheridan, commander the USS *Juniper*, a steam tug, was given the unpleasant assignment of finding them. Upon arrival off the site of the disaster, Sheridan sent out two boats and landed on the beach. There he found a trunk belonging to Julian Reynolds, a valise belonging to the pilot, a coat, a bag, several blue shirts and a number of officers' caps. Also recovered were two sponges, numerous soggy letters marked "U.S. steamer *Tulip*," large portions of her deck, ribs and knees, the top of her pilot house, and her first cutter, which had been entirely stove in. There were no bodies.[37]

Upon *Juniper*'s return and after a formal verification of the wreck remains was made, tribute was paid to *Tulip*'s dead by the officers and crew of the flotilla. Aboard the USS *Don*, flagship of the squadron, the ensign was lowered to halfmast and unfurled by a gentle northwest breeze.[38]

For weeks following the disaster, scorched, burned, and mangled bodies, bloated beyond recognition, began to wash ashore. Ultimately eight unidentified corpses were recovered, wrapped in burlap and buried along the lower bank of St. Inigoes Creek in a locust grove near *Wyandank's* berth. Young John Ellicott would later recall that there were "eight graves, two rows of four each," with no head markers.[39]

As if the loss of *Tulip* had not been enough, five days later on the night of Wednesday, November 15, a mile from Point Lookout, the USS *Dragon* collided with *Thomas Freeborn*, "knocking off the nose and arm of the latter, causing her to leak badly, three feet making in her hold in about seven minutes." By the use of pumps, however, the old battle-scarred veteran was kept afloat long enough to reach St. Inigoes Station where she was beached. It was estimated that her damages were so bad she would have to be sent to the Washington Navy Yard for extensive repairs.[40]

A harried Foxhall Parker returned to Washington in the flagship *Don* on the night of November 18, bringing with him the latest disturbing news from the lower Potomac, which was published, in the city press. "She [the USS *Don*] reports that the six survivors of the ill fated *Tulip*, who are in the hospital at Point Lookout, are doing well and it is probable that they will recover. There are also two others belonging to the unfortunate steamer, Master's Mate Davis, now on the *Wyandank*, and Ensign Wagstaff, now on the *Commodore Read*. Now and then pieces of the wreck and hats, &c., belonging to the officers and men of the *Tulip* are seen floating in the river, which causes the eye to become moistened with a tear of regret for the untimely loss of the brave officers and men of the boat." [41]

Nearly a month later, on December 13, a bloated and badly decomposed body washed ashore at St. George's Island. The remains were immediately interred there by an officer from *William Bacon* but not before identifying the corpse as that of Captain William Smith's by the ring still on his finger marked "Kate." It was the last thing forwarded to his widow in Washington.[42]

It was expected that a formal inquiry on the loss of *Tulip*, a normal procedure in normal times, would be undertaken. "Doubtless the [Navy] Department will order an investigation into the circumstances of her loss," it was suggested in the Washington press. But these were not normal times. The disaster, which might have been avoided, was a product of not simply poor maintenance, but the dire demands of the war and poor command decisions, which might beleaguer and embarrass an already stressed war effort. No investigation was forthcoming and within weeks, the tragedy was all but forgotten. After all, what did the lives of a few score sailors matter when thousands of men died every week on battlefields all over America? [43]

42

A MELODY FROM LANIER'S FLUTE
"O, how much I would like to be home."

The tragic loss of the USS *Tulip* was quickly eclipsed in the swirl of news of far greater events from the battlefronts of the great war, all of which vied for the public's attention. On November 16 General Sherman began his momentous march to the sea from the still burning ruins of Atlanta, Georgia. Nine days later, Confederate agents in New York failed in an attempt to set fire to ten hotels in an effort to raise support from pro-Confederate "Copperheads." On the Virginia front, Grant's unrelenting offensive continued to press Lee in a bloody war of attrition. Throughout the South, battles, skirmishes, and destruction continued without letup in an orgy of blood, fire and sword now called total war.

At Point Lookout affairs within and without went on as always, with prisoners arriving from disparate theaters of combat, while others were transferred elsewhere. Among them were eleven officers and half of the crew of the famously successful Confederate commerce raider *Florida*, taken on October 7 by the USS *Wachusett*, Napoleon Collins commanding. She was seized in the neutral waters of Bahia, Brazil, while her captain and half of her crew were ashore. The prisoners who had been aboard at the time of capture, arrived at the point on November 16 and soon piqued the interest if not the admiration of the inmates.[1] Though the rebel sailors would remain at the prison camp, their officers were quickly herded aboard the steamer *Daniel Webster* and sent to Washington. Their arrival in the capital under a strong guard of the 25th Regiment, Veteran Reserve Corps, Lieutenant M. S. Adams commanding, must have been a sight to the disconsolate prisoners in the Old Capitol Prison.

"These officers were all neatly dressed in new uniforms of Confederate gray cloth, and wore naval caps similar to those worn in the U.S. Navy," recorded the *Evening Star*.

"Nearly all of them wore 'chin whiskers', of the pattern worn by the pirate [Raphael] Semmes. They appear to be a harum-skarum set, and talked noisily among themselves while they were being conveyed from the 6th street wharf to the Provost Marshal's. All of them had gold watches, with large chains dangling from their vest pockets, and several displayed quite a profusion of jewelry, such as diamond pins, finger rings, &c., the proceeds of their piratical career. One of them carried under his arm a handsome mahogany writing desk, while several had huge meerschaum pipes, at which they puffed on their way. While on the pavement in front of the Provost Marshal's, awaiting admission to the office, an apple woman passed on the opposite side of the street, when they hailed her and bought the contents of her basket, paying for the same in greenbacks, and at the same time exposing to view handfuls of silver and gold." [2]

Their show of lucre did little to impress their captors, however, and after a temporary confinement in the Old Capitol, they were soon returned to Point Lookout. There they were to be held subject to instructions from the naval authorities and obliged to suffer along with the rest of the prison population.[3]

Blockade runners of both the local breed, captured while engaged on the waters of the Chesapeake Tidewater, and international runners taken while defying the South Atlantic and Gulf Blockading Squadrons, had become frequent arrivals at Point Lookout as the Confederacy collapsed. One recent capture had been twenty-two-year-old Sidney Lanier, scion of an aristocratic family from Macon, Georgia, a line steeped in Southern scholarly traditions with origins that extended back to 16th-century England. Sidney and his younger brother Clifford and sister Gertrude had been raised in an intellectual environment that had governed their formative years. During his early life Sidney, whose love of music had been described as hereditary, had become proficient in playing the flute, some said even before he could write, and later would master the violin piano, banjo and guitar.[4]

While in his teens Sidney was enrolled at the staunchly Presbyterian Oglethorpe University near Milledgeville, Georgia where he was deemed a superior student. There, under the superb tutelage of Professor James Wilson, his scholarship and mental attitude towards nature and life flourished as never before. Upon graduation at the top of his class in 1860, he was appointed as a tutor in the university, with the ultimate goal of pursuing further studies towards a PhD at the University of Heidelberg, Germany to qualify him for teaching and a professorship at an American university. All that had abruptly changed with the outbreak of the war.

Along with the majority of Oglethorpe's student and academic population, in April 1861 young Sidney enlisted in the Confederate Army. His brother Clifford also joined and drawn by their close sibling relationship, as well as mutual love of music and literature, they successfully managed to stay together in the same unit, the Macon Volunteers, 2nd Georgia Battalion, seeing action throughout, and especially around Richmond. In 1864, however, Sidney was assigned to duty as a signal officer aboard blockade runners, often in English bottoms running between the Bahamas and the coasts of Virginia or North Carolina.[5]

In early November 1864 Lanier was assigned to the English runner *Lucy*, which had made at least one previous successful voyage from Wilmington, North Carolina. Like many who dared the blockade, *Lucy*'s skipper had chosen to make the dash through the cordons of Yankee warships off the Cape Fear River when the weather was particularly bad. It was on Wednesday night, November 2, "when the sea was so rough no vessel could have maintained a close blockade of the bar," that the sleek runner made her quiet escape from Wilmington via New Inlet, bound for Nassau, New Providence Island. If she was successful, her cargo of 466 bales of cotton and twenty-five tons of tobacco would earn a lucrative reward on the European exchange. Owners, investors in the venture, and middlemen alike would glean a hefty profit.[6]

As *Lucy* sought to penetrate the outer ring of Union blockaders, it "was blowing a heavy gale of wind from the eastward," which may have contributed to the events that followed. About 9 a.m., just fourteen hours out of Wilmington, perhaps unable to make headway against the gale, she was sighted by the USS *Santiago de Cuba* and the chase was on. In a desperate effort to lighten ship, *Lucy*'s commander ordered her cargo thrown overboard, but to no effect. After two hours of pursuit, having tossed over only fifty-two bales of cotton, the blockade runner was brought to somewhat eastward of Charleston, South Carolina. Bringing the chase to was one thing, but physically taking possession in heavy weather was extremely dangerous. "We had difficulty in getting a prize crew on board without loss of life," the Yankee commander later reported. "I sought to obtain her log book and any other papers which might be on board of her, but I ascertained she had thrown them all overboard previous to capture." Nor could the disposed cotton be recovered.[7]

As the officers and crew of *Lucy*, mostly British nationals, prepared for their capture, they beseeched young Lanier to don one of their uniforms and pretend to be one of them. As had been done in many earlier cases, they knew they would eventually be released through the intervention of Her Majesty's government. Sidney refused, but managed to hide his flute and a twenty dollar gold piece in his Confederate uniform. Three weeks later on November 25, he was imprisoned at Point Lookout, somehow having successfully managed to smuggle his flute and gold into camp with him.[8] For the next five months, during which time he would contract a disease that would dog him throughout the remainder of his life, he somehow maintain his sanity with music.

***

As 1864 was drawing to a close, Confederate morale was eroding significantly throughout the Chesapeake Tidewater and Shenandoah Valley and desertion rates soared. On the morning of November 23, two days before Sidney Lanier had been incarcerated, five deserters from Major Harry Gilmor's 1st Maryland Cavalry arrived in Washington from Point Lookout, having crossed the Potomac from Virginia in a small boat. All were Baltimoreans who had traveled South at the beginning of the war, but had "become tired of the service." Upon interrogation they readily reported that their unit, which a week earlier had been operating in the Luray Valley of Virginia, was seriously depleted. It had become necessary to find replacements through transfers of Marylanders from other regiments. Cavalry units were among the most pressed, as government horses were becoming a rare commodity. "These deserters say that whenever a new recruit arrives," one account stated, "he is furnished with what they call a 'horse detail,' which authorizes him to procure a horse, in other words, steal one." Despite their claims to be deserters, at least one of the five, Thomas Cook, having been found within Union lines at Point Lookout, was promptly jailed at the Old Capitol Prison as a spy.[9]

From its main forward base on St. Inigoes, the Potomac Flotilla did its best to sustain unrelenting pressure with a string of punitive raids against the crumbling rebel infrastructure in the Northern Neck and beyond. By now, the flotilla had grown to twenty-four vessels, nineteen of which were either sidewheelers or propeller ships, mounting a total of seventy guns. Most were particularly adapted by now to the shallow, brown water warfare that was endemic to the Tidewater. On December 15, a cloudy, cold day, yet another typical expedition, this time under Acting Master William G. Morris, including USS *Coeur de Lion* and *Mercury,* seized and burned more than thirty boats massing on the Coan River, and drove off defending soldiers in a brief engagement.[10]

The inexorable force of Union arms on land and sea was telling as evidenced now by the increased frequency of flights of rebel deserters crossing the Potomac. On the evening of December 18 General Barnes received a message from Captain James Taylor, commanding at the St. Inigoes Naval Station. Taylor had been informed that the previous evening 150 armed Confederates had crossed the Potomac above Piney Point. Eight had been captured. The general immediately ordered the commander and his troops at Leonardtown "to be on their guard and to scour the country in pursuit of them," though the actual validity of the original intelligence source was uncertain. The following evening he received word from Leonardtown informing him that the rebels were in fact all deserters.[11]

For the prisoners at Point Lookout, the news that continued to filter in from the front seemed to be all bad. Two days after Christmas, Charles Warren Hutt would enter in his journal: "Cloudy and foggy. The weather is very disagreeable. We hear that Savannah has certainly fallen. Am feeling quite unwell. O, how much I would like to be home." [12]

Elsewhere in the camp, in the hated "Bull Pen" infirmary where sick prisoners usually went to die, Sidney Lanier, having contracted tuberculosis, lay convalescing but kept up his own and the spirits of others by playing haunting melodies on his beloved flute. One patient who was lying near his bed was particularly moved and resolved to meet him. The patient was John Bannister Tabb, descended from one of the oldest, wealthiest families in Virginia and he had much in common with the flutist. Despite the fact that he had been educated by a family tutor, he had been obliged to forego reading by the age of fourteen owing to poor eyesight and had turned to music. Though weak-sighted, at the onset of the war he had nevertheless enlisted in the Confederate Navy. At the time of his capture he had been engaged in carrying government dispatches to and from Bermuda on a British blockade runner.[13]

On June 5, 1864 while inbound to North Carolina, after two shots had crossed her bow, the steamer *Siren*, laden with a cargo including hoop iron and liquor, was captured off Beaufort harbor by the USS *Keystone State*, Commander Pierce Crosby. Tabb, though only nineteen years of age, having been entrusted with a batch of dispatches, soon found himself incarcerated and prostrate with fever in the Bull Pen at Point Lookout. As winter again descended with its arctic fury upon the Chesapeake Tidewater, he was drawn to the ethereal sound of Lanier's flute. Tabb's capture had been similar to Lanier's, which was no doubt common ground for their bonding. Soon, the two young men had become inseparable, friends for life linked by their love of music, literature, poetry and experience. Now occasionally joined by a Polish physician with a fine voice who sang arias, they passed the dismal days and weeks of confinement together. Tabb, who later became a renowned poet and Catholic priest, noted one historian, "carried in his memory a tune which Lanier had so often played on his flute in the prison camp. It was a sad, contemplative air. Years later, its haunting appeal never left him." Father Tabb taught the tune to one Edwin Litchfield Turnbull who preserved it by publishing it as 'A Melody from Lanier's Flute.' And in the meantime the seeds of Lanier's illustrious and acclaimed career as poet, author, lecturer and his first and only book, *Tiger Lilies*, were planted.[14]

***

Though the war was going badly for the South, Confederate intrigues in Southern Maryland continued, and the rebel spy apparatus became more refined than ever. On January 9, 1865, Secretary Welles notified Commander Parker of the latest intelligence received from R. J. Kimball, the U.S. Consular Agent in Toronto. Kimball's tale of how underground communications connecting that part of the world with the Confederacy was shocking. His information had been secured from a reliable "person who has seen the dispatches and has personal knowledge of the facts." [15]

Kimball's report on how the rebels in Toronto had maintained successful communications with Jefferson Davis and the authorities in Richmond was disturbing in the extreme.

"Having plenty of money at their command, they employ British subjects, who are provided with British passports and also with passports from Colonel ____ (probably Jacob Thompson), which are plainly written, name and date of issue, in fine silk, and are ingeniously secreted in the lining of the coat. They carry dispatches, which are made and carried in the same manner. These messengers wear metal buttons, upon the inside of which dispatches are most minutely photographed, not perceptible to the naked eye, but are easily read by the aid of a powerful lens. Letters are written but are closely interlined with imperceptible ink (as they term it) to which when a certain chemical is applied, is easily deciphered. The messenger arriving in Baltimore receives additional instructions from 'B____,' and proceeds to Washington; here he undergoes a thorough examination, is searched and permitted to pass. He takes a southeasterly direction to Port Tobacco, where he is sheltered by a widow, a 'Mrs. F[loyd],' and at dead of night crosses in an india rubber boat to the south side of the Potomac; thence he goes to Bowling Green, where his rebel passport is used to 'Guerrilla B____,' who hastens him on to Richmond. He returns by the same route. The last trip was made in fourteen days (December 14 to 28). Boxes are received from Port Tobacco marked 'Mineral specimens,' with dispatches secreted in the lining." [16]

Even worse news concerned a planned attack on the USS *Roanoke*, the 3,435-ton first class ironclad frigate stationed at Point Lookout as a guardship since the beginning of August. The intelligence was acquired during a January 4 raid on the Rappahannock under the direction of Acting Master James C. Tole of the USS *Don*, though the raid itself had resulted in little more than the capture of two torpedoes and two barrels of powder about six miles from the river's mouth. Though the prize haul had been minimal, the intelligence gained was disturbing. "I learn from various source," Commander Parker reported soon afterwards, "a torpedo expedition is being organized for an attack on this quarter." [17]

By January 6 further intelligence confirmed that the torpedo attack was to be made upon *Roanoke*, though her commander, Captain Augustus H. Kilty, who apparently learned on his own of the probable strike, had already begun preparations to fend it off even before receiving orders. Nevertheless, a directive was immediately dispatched that the big warship was to be "protected by means that will prevent a boat reaching the ship at night." Three days later Rear Admiral David D. Porter reaffirmed that a movement was indeed afoot to sink or blow up *Roanoke*. Porter had discovered the rebel torpedo boats were to be carried across the countryside to the Wicomico or other branches of the Potomac and then attack the big warship at night with their "infernal machines." Welles quickly dispatched additional orders to Kilty "to neglect no preparation or plan for preventing the insurgents from accomplishing their nefarious objects." He also instructed Commander Parker to have the flotilla keep close watch over the Wicomico and other tributaries of the Potomac.[18]

Captain Kilty's preparations had been substantial. He first had to obtain the necessary building supplies from ashore, most likely through the aid of General Barnes. Timbers were cut into the shape of spars, which were strongly secured to the deck of *Roanoke* and hung out over the sides of the ship, extending outward to a distance of twenty feet. From the tips of these extensions, which completely surrounded the vessel, a thick rope net was hung and kept steady by a heavy stream anchor chain running around the lower edge of the net under water. The great ship was thus completely enclosed by the net, which would, it was hoped, prohibit any torpedo boat from reaching the hull. *Roanoke*'s battery of great guns, were now manned day and night, with a strict watch being kept, to provide a wall of fire if necessary. In the meantime Parker had placed two vessels to guard the creeks opposite Point Lookout, and another to cruise between Smith's Point and the ironclad.[19]

Though his defenses seemed solid, Kilty was concerned about the ship itself, its machinery having suffered from overuse, and its galley and other facilities in shambles. Still the threat persisted. On January 26 Barnes relayed recent intelligence acquired from a refugee from Virginia that only seemed to reinforce the possibility of an attack. Perhaps owing to the ironclad's stout defenses, the rebel plan had been altered. It was soon learned that the assault was now not to be directly against *Roanoke*, but to destroy the weaker, more vulnerable vessels of the flotilla. The refugee, one James Brier, claimed he had crossed the Potomac with 500 other former Confederates, and surrendered to the Union commander at Leonardtown, Captain Francis F. Buckley. His report of rebel intentions against the flotilla was as disturbing as Porter's word of the planned attack on *Roanoke*.[20]

It seemed, claimed Brier, that the daring Confederate Army marauder, Colonel John Singleton Mosby, was preparing a raid with boats hauled overland from Richmond, against Yankee schooners and tugs operating in and about the St. Mary's River and on the Potomac. Under the command of an unnamed lieutenant colonel, between 400 and 500 rangers were to conduct the operation. Living in groups of threes and fours in local farmhouses of the Northern Neck, the enemy had cleverly dispersed his force to avoid detection. The largest number however, had assembled at the farm of Willoughby Newton, near Lower Machodoc Creek. Newton, who had from time to time apprised the Confederate War Department of Union activities at Point Lookout, was keeping the expeditionaries fed with a large quantity of pork from his own farm not far from Hague. Upon arrival of the boats from Richmond, all were to muster at four assembly locations: one company was to convene at Hague in Westmoreland County, another at Heathsville in Northumberland County, a third at Warsaw in Richmond County, and a fourth at Lancaster Court House in Lancaster County. Brier believed the expedition was to start from Port Jack Creek, a small waterway exiting into Currioman Bay, opposite Breton Bay. The alert, one of many that had been filtering in over recent weeks, was taken seriously. The USS *Fuchsia*, Acting Master Street, was ordered to stand by *Roanoke* until further ordered, "with just sufficient enough steam to go ahead at a moment's warning," and to be vigilant. Other vessels were to stand by on their stations, give up cruising and preserving their coal in the event they were needed.[21]

Brier's information, fortunately for the Union, proved false. Mosby had been seriously wounded on December 21 and neither he nor his raiders were anywhere in the vicinity.[22] But other rebel marauders were!

THEY INTEND DEPREDATIONS IN THE BAY
"We have holed the rat, but can't get at him."

By February 1865 the American Civil War was entering its final bloody chapter. The Army of Northern Virginia was now struggling desperately in the trenches at Petersburg, outside of the Confederate capital of Richmond, to hold its own against overwhelming numbers, arms, and the logistical superiority of the United States Army. Indeed, most of the Confederacy lay in smoldering ruins, its decimated troops reeling everywhere in defeat, its ports captured or closed, and its rivers and coastline sealed off by a mighty U.S. naval blockade. Munitions, weapons, food, clothing and every necessity of life were in critically short supply. At Petersburg besieged rebel forces suffering heavily from attrition and malnutrition somehow continued to hold out. Yet without supplies defeat was almost certain, if not from military attack than from starvation. With the Chesapeake Bay and its many tributaries firmly under control of the U.S. Navy, the last avenues of relief for much needed food and clothing had been cut off. This called for desperate measures by the Confederate high command.

***

In mid-February General Lee summoned Captain Thaddeus Fitzhugh of the 5th Virginia Cavalry for an "interview." The general wished to inquire whether the cavalryman thought it possible that an expedition might be mounted on the Chesapeake to capture a transport laden with supplies bound for General Grant's army. Fitzhugh, whose home was in Matthews County, Virginia, was no stranger to such operations. Only the year before, he had participated in the daring small boat raid on the Union communications center on the Eastern Shore at Cherrystone, Virginia. The strike had resulted in the capture of the station and two steamers. Though one of the vessels was ransomed, the other was employed on a devastating rampage behind Federal lines that resulted in the destruction of no less than four Union ships, and at virtually no loss or cost to the Confederacy. If such an operation was feasible then, Lee queried, might it not be possible to conduct another, and run the captured vessel or vessels into remote Virginia inlets on the Western Shore where they could be unloaded and brought overland to the army at Petersburg?[1]

The captain responded that he thought such a bold, unexpected action was indeed possible. In fact, as the general well knew, a number of such operations by John Taylor Wood and others had been conducted throughout the war on the broad expanses of the bay and its river systems with considerable success and embarrassment to the Federals. It was true that most had been carried out to destroy enemy shipping, and this would be a raid with a different objective, to secure provisions and supplies for the Army of Northern Virginia, but he believed it was eminently doable. Without hesitation, Fitzhugh volunteered to personally command the mission. Pleased, Lee instructed the captain to report to his commanding officer to secure a detail of thirty or forty men. Captain Sidney Smith Lee of the Confederate Navy would provide assistance as needed in the way of boats and nautical gear, though, like everything else, they were in very short supply. The gear would most likely have to be scavenged from the inert James River ironclad fleet lying near Drewry's Bluff.

Though the concept was approved early on, the most vulnerable targets, based upon the latest intelligence, would be plying between Baltimore and the Patuxent River. This area was now well behind the line of gunboats and ironclads now ringing Virginia's shores from the Potomac to the York. "I was directed by him," Fitzhugh later reported, "to go into Chesapeake Bay at or near the mouth of the Rappahannock in such boats as I could there secure and proceed up the bay to such point as in my judgment might promise the capture of the steamers *Highland Light* or *Harriet De Ford* at such point below Annapolis as a copy of the *Baltimore Gazette* informed us they stopped." [2]

The captain was instructed that if he was successful in capturing one of the designated steamers, he was to proceed down the bay, seize as many transports loaded with stores as he could, and "push them into certain inlets above the Rappahannock River." There he was to be met by two companies of the 43rd Virginia Cavalry, and a train of wagons belonging to the Quartermaster's Department. The goods aboard the transports would then be unloaded under guard of the cavalrymen, and carried across the Rappahannock at Boiulware's Ferry. From there they would follow an intricate circuitous route to the besieged Confederate Army at Petersburg and Richmond. [3]

That Fitzhugh's motions were not entirely secret is probable. On February 19, from aboard the USS *Commodore Read*, Commander Hooker reported from trustworthy sources "that Fitzhugh with his party from Mathews County have crossed the Rappahannock and transported their boats to the Potomac; how many they number I have not learned." Another report, of uncertain credibility, soon came in stating the 400 rebels had assembled on both Indian and Dimer's creeks on the Northern Neck, with fifteen large boats and a number of canoes intending depredations on the bay. If true, Hooker surmised, it was probable that Fitzhugh was among them. He immediately ordered the gunboat *Periwinkle* to patrol off Smith's Point. Within but a few days the little warship had brought in three blockade runners but not Fitzhugh. [4]

The intelligence had been spotty but was rooted in fact, for there were indeed other rebel units operating in the same area, but each with different objectives. On the same day Hooker reported on Fitzhugh, an account came in of a party of 154 rebel guerrillas with several small boats under the command of one Rice Airs being readied for a sortie into the Chesapeake from Smith's Point despite the presence of the blockaders. Airs was a most wanted man who had once led a raid on the Smith Point Lightship, capturing her commander. He had also been involved in the ambush shooting of Captain Thomas A. Dungan, USN, on the USS *Reliance* in September 1864. The arrival of Airs and his guerrillas had been discovered by a local resident, a Captain Goff, said to be a loyal Unionist. Goff had stated that Air's partisans had appeared on the evening of Monday, February 20, and their goal was a raid on Smith Island in the Chesapeake Bay. "The whole party is a most deseperate set of thieves, robbers, and murderers, who use the cloth of the rebel flag to cover their crimes," wrote Thomas Nelson, commander of the USS *Mercury*. "Their design on the island is to rob the stores, capture and bring back the numerous refugees and deserters who have gone there from Virginia, and probably to capture some steamer, with which they intend to attack the light vessel, and even surprise the blockading vessels." [5]

Commodore Parker immediately notified General Kenly, now in command of the Eastern Shore military at Salisbury, Maryland, of the expected raid on Smith Island. Soon afterwards, Kenly, whose available forces were quite small, received specific orders from Brevet Brigadier General William W. Morris in Baltimore, "to do the best he could with Smith's company of cavalry, and if he needed a company of infantry to call upon Colonel Samuel M. Bowman, at Wilmington, who has been directed to furnish him a company of regulars if he calls." The War Department also warned General Barnes at Point Lookout and instructed him to also keep a sharp watch. Soon word had spread, and many inhabitants of the islands of the central Chesapeake had also learned of the threat and were "much alarmed." [6]

For his own part, Parker reacted swiftly, having assumed that by the time he had been informed of the expected raid, Airs and his party had already left. Nine flotilla vessels then cruising the Chesapeake were instructed to intercept the guerrillas upon their return. By February 26, it was reported that the rebels had indeed crossed the bay, but no one seemed to know whether they had succeeded or failed. [7]

By March 1, from his semi-permanent station at Butler's Hole in the entrance to the Rappahannock, Commander Hooker was among the first to discern that the raid had in fact been aborted by the prompt action of the navy. "To day the citizens here report to me that the party which crossed have returned without landing, having become aware that the gunboats were there and the people aware of their intentions." [8] And for the moment, the purported threat of a foray by Thaddeus Fitzhugh was all but forgotten, as the Potomac Flotilla turned its attentions towards what it had learned to do best, striking the defenseless Northern Neck where rebel resistance was now essentially non-existent.

The now frequent Potomac Flotilla raids ranged in scope from single ship cutting out exercises to full blow squadron operations, with the Potomac theater being orchestrated from the St. Inigoes Naval Station, and the Rappahannock-Piankatank from the Butler's Hole anchorage. One typical strike began on the night of March 3, when a landing party under Acting Master Street put ashore from *Thomas Freeborn* on the north bank of the Piankatank, captured soldiers on leave from the 51st Virginia, and soon afterwards a blockade runner commanded by one William Smith.[9]

When the Provost Marshal of Charles County brought the navy's attention to an intelligence report regarding an intended rebel small boat attack on the Potomac, the flotilla command reacted immediately. Parker later reported that the craft was being readied for "the purpose of making a raid into Maryland" and was "a remarkably fine one, painted lead color, and capable of holding fifty men. It had been recently brought from Fredericksburg, and its rowlocks carefully muffled for night service. On March 5 in a little waterway called Passpantansy Creek, to the southeast of Potomac Creek, a landing party under Acting Ensign George E. McConnell from Parker's flagship *Don*, in a pre-emptive cutting out operation, destroyed the large boat after a brief but hot skirmish with a group of Mosby's raiders. Five boxes of tobacco were found near the boat, which Parker ordered distributed to the captors.[10]

The following day, Parker ordered Hooker to proceed with *Commodore Read*, *Yankee*, *Delaware*, and *Heliotrope* up the Rappahannock to conduct a raid into the hitherto heart of rebeldom near Fredericksburg. The operation was to be carried out in cooperation with a detachment under General Samuel H. Roberts, the army gunboat *Chamberlain*, and several troop transports. Only a few months earlier such a penetration would have been costly if not suicidal, but the Confederacy, all believed, was on its last legs. Yet, mindful of past experiences, he cautioned "you will be particularly careful in looking out for torpedoes; having all narrow channels and shoal places carefully swept by the small boats in advance of the flotilla. At points where torpedoes may be exploded from the shore, you will land flanking parties, and you are to shell as usual all heights." [11]

By March 7 the expedition had penetrated to within six miles below Fredericksburg. Unable to proceed farther with the squadron owing to a dangerous line of rebel obstructions preventing large ship passage, the expeditionaries successfully assailed the adjacent hamlet of Hamilton's Crossing. Commander Hooker and General Roberts personally pressed on in a small gig. They soon landed unopposed at the city's steamer wharf. There they found scattered detachments of Union troops coming in. Fredericksburg, the site of some of the worst bloodshed of the Civil War, had been abandoned and was temporarily occupied. The successful foray had resulted in the burning and destruction of a railroad bridge and depot, portions of track at and near Hamilton's Crossing, the cutting of telegraph lines and the removal of the telegraphic apparatus. Even more significantly, twenty-eight railroad cars, eighteen of which were loaded with tobacco, a Confederate Army wagon train and several small boats were also captured and burned. A "quantity of valuable information" was acquired along with thirty or forty prisoners and a number of mules. At 3:30 p.m. the troops were re-embarked, and within hours the squadron retired down river leaving the site of some of the most ferocious fighting of the war to its fate.[12]

Nearly a week later on March 13, Hooker again led another naval expedition up the Rappahannock to assist Army units in what was becoming a general mopping up operation on the Northern Neck Peninsula. The squadron consisted of Hooker's *Commodore Read*, *Morse*, Acting Master George W. Hyde, *Delaware*, Acting Master Joshua H. Elkridge and the army gunboat *Mosswood*. This time its major target was the town of Tappahannock, where a shore party from *Delaware* succeeded in capturing and destroying eight boats and a flatboat employed as a ferry. For a period of two hours a spirited exchange between the squadron and two rebel rifled field guns concealed in the woods nearby continued without letup. Then, close in gunfire from *Delaware* and *Morse* succeeded in destroying a bridge connecting the town and an empty Fort Lowry. When Confederate cavalry units appeared, Hooker later boasted, his squadrons successfully "emptied some of their saddles." [13]

The pressure upon the Northern Neck was unrelenting. While Hooker was concentrating on the Rappahannock, another expedition out of St. Inigoes was being prepared by Commander Eastman against one of the remaining rebel hotbeds of activity on the Potomac shoreline. Acting under verbal instructions from Commander Parker on March 15, Eastman departed the naval station the same day at 7 p.m. with the gunboats *Stepping Stones*, Acting Master Edmund A. Roderick, *Heliotrope*, Acting Ensign George T. Griffin, and *Resolute*, Acting Ensign William T. Gibson. Their objective was to scour Mattox Creek for rebel vessels and supplies, presumably to prevent their transfer to Lee's army.[14]

Eastman's squadron entered the narrow, shoaly and unmarked entrance of the creek at daylight on March 16. Almost immediately the gunboats ran aground. Unwilling to surrender the element of surprise, the commander at once landed armed parties of sailors and U.S. Marines while those who remained aboard worked to free the ships. The raiders quickly began searching every building encountered on one of the shores as they proceeded in small boats. About 2 p.m., Acting Ensign John J. Brice, Eastman's executive officer, was dispatched to the south side of the creek with forty men and immediately found himself opposed by some fifty rebel cavalry. Quickly he began to form his men for an expected attack, even as eight or ten of the enemy were driven off while attempting to envelop his left flank. About this time *Stepping Stones* was refloated and steamed into the creek. Suddenly, intimidated by the warship's five 12-pounders, the rebels disappeared into the adjacent woods as quickly as they had appeared. Brice now began to search more homes, but found little more than a few bales of cotton and a quantity of musket cartridges and caps.[15]

With evening approaching and *Heliotrope* still aground, Eastman decided to leave the creek and await the following morning to continue operations. Unfortunately, in departing, *Stepping Stones* once again grounded just about the time *Heliotrope* got off. Eastman's situation was now precarious should the rebels decide upon a concerted attack. Luckily, about 4 a.m., on the 17th *Heliotrope* entered the creek and was detailed to assist her sister, though rescue was going to be difficult. A stiff wind had been blowing, driving the stricken vessel ever harder aground. Eastman ordered *Stepping Stones*'s commander "to use every exertion to lighten his vessel," but it was going to be a struggle.[16]

With one gunboat protecting the other, Eastman now took the opportunity to renew the offensive operations ashore. At 8 a.m. he dispatched Acting Ensign William H. Summers, detached for the expedition from the USS *Wyandank*, with twenty sailors, all but two being black. In a launch armed with a single smooth bore howitzer they proceeded up the right branch of Mattox Creek. At the same time, Eastman would personally lead a force of seventy sailors and U.S. Marines along the shore itself. Within a few hours the main creek and the right branch had been cleared. Four enemy boats were found and destroyed.[17]

Concerned about *Stepping Stones*, Eastman briefly returned to the gunboat but sent Summers and his men in the launch into the left branch of Mattox Creek with orders to clear that waterway as well. This time the raiders would experience far more opposition than expected. As Summers entered the little feeder to the main creek he observed three schooners and a barge, apparently hidden to avoid detection. Almost as soon as he approached the vessels, a massive wall of musket fire from 300 to 400 rebel guns erupted simultaneously. His launch was suddenly and hopelessly exposed on the open waterway. Within a matter of moments the intense enemy fire had "cut away half of his oars, piercing the launch in many places, and cut the barrel off the musket which he was firing at the rebels." Fortunately, only one of the landsmen manning the boat, Robert Lee, was slightly wounded.[18]

The sailors fought back with fervor, though keeping sheltered as much as they could below the gunnels of the boat. Summers manned the howitzer, "gallantly" assisted by a boatswains mate named Mullen from *Don* and a brave black seaman named Aaron Anderson from *Wyandank*, who exposed himself repeatedly to defend the boat. Mullen lay on his back "while loading the howitzer and then firing carefully as to kill and wound many rebels." Unwilling to face the devastating fire from the howitzer, the rebels soon lost heart and retired from the scene. It was now time to destroy the three schooners and barge. The operation was accomplished with celerity under the admiring eyes of Commander Eastman who had just returned to the opposite side of the creek.[19]

By 5 p.m. the approach of evening found *Stepping Stones* still aground and the 400 rebels undoubtedly still in the area. Eastman resolved to defend the ship from the only approach an enemy attacker could take, through the property of one Mrs. E. A. Sutton. He decided to erect a small defense work on the Sutton estate, after the owner received the Yankees "kindly and loyally," as the commander later noted, "and gave me information which prevented about thirty of our men falling into an ambuscade which would have injured my force materially." [20]

To prepare for an attack he "ordered the cutting down of about ten small trees, and two sides of a fence, each about 100 feet long, for the purpose of constructing abates" and also ordering the destruction of a small shed which was in his field of fire. After dark, a reinforcement of twenty-two more sailors from the USS *Anacostia* arrived on the scene. A careful watch was maintained throughout a very long night for most of those ensconced behind the defense works as the much anticipated assault was at hand.[21]

At daybreak, March 18, Eastman's pickets were driven in, and his men, 134 sailors and fourteen marines, quickly formed to receive the enemy. If the previous day's estimate was correct, the Confederates were still at least 400 strong. From a distance they could be seen marching towards the defense in two columns. Everyone behind the works, no doubt, held his breath. Then, just as quickly as they had advanced they retired. As to why, Eastman noted, "I know not, unless they had hoped to surprise us, which they failed in doing." [22]

Soon *Stepping Stones* had been refloated, and the expedition returned to base. The commander was generous in the praise for his officers and men, who had incurred only two injuries during the whole affair, one of which had been from an accident. For his leadership in fending off an attack where he was outnumbered twenty to one, in an exposed launch, with only one slight casualty and still managing to sink four enemy watercraft, Commander Parker recommended to Secretary Welles recognition of Ensign William Summers for "conspicuous gallantry." Aaron Anderson, for his selfless courage under heavy enemy fire, would be awarded the Congressional Medal of Honor.[23]

Though individual ship landings would continue to be made along the shores of the Potomac, Eastman's raid into Mattox Creek would be the last appreciable major offensive naval foray of the war into the Northern Neck. But it would not be the last incursion. Nor had the rebels ceased in their own desperate efforts to survive and prevail.

***

It had taken more than a month's passage before Thaddeus Fitzhugh and his men were able to make their way through Union lines to reach Urbanna on the south shore of the Rappahannock. Now in three open boats rigged with sails and oars they pushed downstream to Windmill Point, somehow escaping detection by Union blockaders, and then from the entrance of the river northward hugging the Western Shore of the Chesapeake. It was on March 28 under cover of darkness, that Fitzhugh set out from the point with just twenty-nine soldiers, most being troopers from his own Company F, 5th Regiment, Virginia Cavalry, Payne's Brigade, with ten men to a boat, and reached the Potomac without incident before dawn. Owing to strong headwinds, the raiders were obliged to lie in the vicinity of Smith's Point, awaiting better weather until the night of April 2.[24] Not surprisingly, their progress had not gone undetected.

Union loyalists on the Northern Neck were few, but as the war had begun to turn against the Confederacy, the Federal intelligence network in the region, buoyed by the flotilla blockaders, had improved substantially. Thus, it was not extraordinary that Fitzhugh's passage down the Rappahannock had not gone entirely unobserved. What was astonishing was that he had made it at all. Barely two days after the rebel raiders had departed Windmill Point, Hooker sent an urgent message to Parker, albeit with outdated intelligence, regarding their motions.

"I have just received information," he informed the commander of the flotilla, "that Captain Fitzhugh, with quite a number of men and some boats, is at Robinson's Creek, just above Urbanna. It is said their intention is to make an attack on us, but I think it much more likely they intend depredations in the bay, or possibly the putting down of torpedoes. As I understand you are to be here in a few days, I shall not make any movement toward dislodging them until you come. In the meantime I will try to get more information." [25]

And once again, it seemed, Fitzhugh's raiders were not the only Confederates in the area on a surreptitious mission to harass the Federals behind their lines. Apparently operating independently of Lee's army, a small band of Confederate Navy seamen had also been dispatched on a similar mission, apparently unaware of the Fitzhugh expedition. The commander of the operation, Lieutenant John C. Braine, like Fitzhugh, was no stranger to behind the lines action and had already conducted several successful raids on Union merchant shipping, including the notorious capture of the steamship *Chesapeake* in December 1863.[26]

Those same raiders later appeared on September 29, 1864 in the warm waters of the Caribbean to inflict additional havoc on American shipping. On that occasion Braine's target had been the commercial steamship *Roanoke*, bound from Havana for New York. In an audacious plot hatched by himself, with the approval of Confederate Navy Secretary Mallory, it had been planned to board the steamer at New York and capture her en route before she entered the neutral waters of Spanish Cuba. Instead, Braine, then under a commission as Acting Master, organized and carried out the operation from Havana, and steered his captive for Bermuda. Unable to smuggle supplies onboard from the British owned island, and finding it

568

impossible to run the blockade of Southern ports, he burned the ship. The affair caused the Confederate government, then desperately seeking recognition and support from Spain and England, both concern and embarrassment. Though the British temporarily held the daring rebel raider in custody, it would not be for long.[27]

Now even as Captain Thaddeus Fitzhugh, CSA, was preparing his own strike behind Federal lines in Chesapeake Bay, Acting Master John C. Braine, CSN, had already turned his attentions to targets in almost the same area, the Patuxent River region of Southern Maryland. Neither officer, apparently, was aware of the other's mission.

Master John C. Braine, CSN, (left) and Captain Thaddeus Fitzhugh, CSA, in his seriority well after the Civil War, (right), were the last two successful Confederate sea raiders on the Chesapeake Bay. Prints and Photographs Division, Library of Congress, Washington, D.C.

Precisely how Braine organized his last daring expedition is uncertain. What is known is that on Friday, March 31, with a Lieutenant Murdock as his second and with twenty armed Confederates in company, he lay in the mouth of Patuxent River off Cedar Point in a yawl awaiting his next prey. The first likely vessel to come along was the 115-ton Baltimore-built schooner *St. Mary's*, Captain Howard, of St. Mary's County, with an assorted cargo of groceries, dry goods, provisions, and sundries, valued at $20,000. Representing "themselves at first to be Federal soldiers anxious to go to Point Lookout," and feigning that their own vessel was sinking and needing assistance, the raiders easily boarded and seized the unsuspecting merchantman without resistance. They "avowed themselves to be regularly employed in the rebel service and strict discipline was maintained." Although Captain Howard was allowed to retain his money and personal effects, the crew and passengers of the captured vessel were quickly relieved of their belongings and locked below deck. That night, Braine and Murdock put to sea in their new prize.[28]

By the end of the day, with a favorable wind behind them, *St. Mary's* was off Hog Island between the Yeocomico and Coan rivers, when she spotted the Federal charter steamer *J. B. Spafford*, bound from Wicomico for New York. *Spafford*, too, was readily captured but held only long enough to transfer the crew of *St. Mary's* and two of the passengers onboard before releasing her. However, three blacks that had also been aboard were retained as prisoners for later sale as slaves. Before leaving, in a most successful effort at planting misinformation to foil potential pursuers, Braine casually let it be known to the master of *Spafford* that he was bound for St. Marks, Florida. Then, like the crew and passengers of *St. Mary's*, those aboard *Spafford* were also relieved of their personal effects before being set free.[29]

Braine's ability to elude the many Federal warships on the Chesapeake and beyond proved to be absolutely masterful. "The *St. Mary's* was last seen by the released crew," it was reported to an undoubtedly irate Commander Parker three days after the *Spafford* seizure, "heading to the south, with the wind from the northward, on the night of the 1st instant, and they reported that there was a light in a southeasterly direction, which they supposed was a vessel the rebels had captured and set fire to." [30]

Within a short time, *St. Mary's* and her new Confederate crew had reached their actual destination and brought the vessel to anchor in the neutral waters of Jamaica. Before the American Consul on the island had learned of their arrival and could seek their arrest and extradition, the schooner was moved to the port of Anotta Bay on the north coast, and the rebels had already taken passage to Liverpool, England, aboard the steamship *St. Thomas*.[31]

Although Thaddeus Fitzhugh's raiders would soon cause even more dismay among Federal naval authorities, his mission and escape efforts would prove to be substantially more difficult than Braine's.

***

The several day time lag between Commander Hooker's receipt and dispatch of the intelligence regarding Fitzhugh and the actual disposition and motions of the Confederates would prove an embarrassing disaster for the Federals. On the night of April 2, even as Braine and his men were merrily making their way toward Jamaica, Fitzhugh's small party was again setting out in their boats. The wind and tide finally coincided favorably, though they were obliged to stay close to the shore to avoid discovery. That they had come this far without physical detection by Federal gunboat patrols was in itself something of a feat. Passing undetected by Point Lookout and through its naval screen bordered on miraculous. Shrouded by the mantle of darkness, the rebels sailed and rowed so close to the shore that they could clearly hear soldiers talking on the Point Lookout steamboat wharf.[32]

Under sails and oars they pressed on silently through the night, northward along the bay coast of St. Mary's County. Passing St. Jerome's and St. Clarence Creeks without incident, they soon commenced the long ten-mile haul along the low, dark and seemingly featureless shoreline to Cedar Point where they arrived at sunrise, and from which Braine had departed less than two days earlier. At the point Fitzhugh ordered the boats hidden in the cedar brakes, and allowed his men to rest during the day while he and one of his volunteers went in search of the latest intelligence. At a nearby hamlet they introduced themselves as deserters from General Grant's army attempting to get to Baltimore. The friendly citizens of St. Mary's undoubtedly easily discerned the true loyalties of the strangers. Fitzhugh quickly learned from them that the propeller steamer *Harriet De Ford*, Captain Albert H. League commanding, would soon be coming down the Patuxent from Upper Marlboro en route to Baltimore. *De Ford* was a new single masted and single prop vessel of 149 tons, "a beautiful little steamer" built in 1864 at Baltimore and valued at $50,000. Owned by Isaac and Thomas De Ford and others of Baltimore, she had been chartered by the U.S. Army to make regular runs between Baltimore and the black refugee farms on the Patuxent at The Plains, Sand Gates, and Coles Creek.[33]

De Ford seemed an opportune objective for capture, as the vessel would be laden with produce and other goods. But Fitzhugh also learned that there was a telegraph line between Upper Marlboro and Point Lookout. If by chance his boats *had* been spotted in passing the point, it would be dangerous to launch an ambush from Cedar Point on the steamer when she passed out of the river. As she would be making a scheduled stop at the village of Fair Haven, fourteen miles below Annapolis on the southern shores of Anne Arundel County, it might just be possible to waylay her at that place instead. He was also undoubtedly encouraged by knowing the repercussions such an attack so far behind Federal lines would have on Yankee morale.[34]

In the early afternoon and for some time thereafter, the tiny party of raiders was surprised to hear the dull but continuous rolling of heavy gunfire clearly resonating from the direction of Annapolis to the north and Washington to the northwest. All were at a loss to explain the mysterious cause since both positions were many miles from the battle lines. And as the cannon fire was more or less continuous, there seemed no logical explanation. They would soon, much to their substantial dismay, discover the cause.[35]

At dusk the Confederates finally launched their boats from Cedar Point, and with a fair wind and tide behind them, again started up the bay "as fast as our oars and sails would take us." At 4 a.m. they rounded Holland Point, the southern lip of Herring Bay, and rested. Ahead they could see the little embayment "dotted over with the lights from the mastheads of the numerous vessels at anchor." Selecting one of the largest, most isolated of the lot, an oyster pungy schooner, Fitzhugh quickly formulated a plan to quietly board and capture her for use as a temporary base of operations and to "secrete my men until time for action." [36]

Arousing his officers and men from their brief slumber, Fitzhugh quietly and efficiently proceeded to board and take possession of the pungy. As the vessel was only partially laden, there was adequate room below for her crew to be secured and for the raiders to hide. After feasting "on the fine oysters with which she was about one-third loaded," the rebel captain and his men moved to carry out the next phase of their plan. Soon after sunrise, with nineteen of his best soldiers dressed in the clothes of the captured watermen, Fitzhugh compelled the pungy skipper "to pilot them up the river." He then went ashore at the little fishing port of Fair Haven, leaving the prisoners under the charge of his second in command, a lieutenant, and a party of guards.[37]

Soon after landing, and undoubtedly to his delight, Fitzhugh learned that an even better target than *Harriet De Ford* was in the offing. He quickly revised his plans. The new objective was to be the well known sidewheel steamer *Highland Light*, one of the fastest boats on the Chesapeake. The 291-ton vessel, built in 1858 at Brooklyn, N.Y., unlike the newer *De Ford*, was already a famous fixture on the bay.

If she could be captured, and turned into a raider behind Union lines, it was certain to strike a most unpleasant note with Federal authorities and add some hope to Confederate supporters in Maryland who were desperate for any sign of a victory, no matter how small. Upon further inquiry, he learned that *Highland Light* would soon be making a landing at the steamer wharf on West River, which was just a few miles to the north by overland route.[38] It would be a race to meet her.

After securing a wagon and team of horses at Fair Haven, Fitzhugh later reported, "we started over, staging that we were wood choppers, who wished to go to the eastern shore of Maryland to procure work." Unhappily for the raiders, despite their alacrity, they arrived on the West River wharf "just in time to see the beautiful steamer majestically moving down the river, and out into the bay." [39]

Disappointed but undismayed, the raiders immediately turned about and returned to Fair Haven to await the arrival of *Harriet De Ford*. Within a sort time, a few minutes before 2:00 p.m., their unsuspecting target rounded Holland Point and was soon tying up at the landing on schedule to take on passengers and cargo. Though descibed in some accounts as a beautifuil ship, she was anything but dazzling to look at, with upper works painted a drab color and but a single mast standing in the event she was obliged to move under sail if her engine failed. The adoption of the propeller in lieu of the sidewheel or sternwheel propulsion system was relatively new, and shipping concerns in the Chesapeake were still hesitant to field screw driven steamers without backup sails.[40]

Still disguised as woodcutters, Fitzhugh and eight or ten of his men boarded the steamer as passengers. A pair of black crewmen recognized two of the men, but as both were apparently too intimidated to speak out, no one aboard was aroused.[41] Quietly the rebel captain began to position his men in strategic locations around the ship, from the engine room to the pilothouse, even as the vessel moved out into Herring Bay under a head of steam. Although armed with a brass pivot gun for protection, the ship appeared to be otherwise undefended. When about five miles from shore, finding everything in readiness, Fitzhugh later reported, "I went to the pilothouse, where the captain was, exposing my uniform and arms, and demanded the surrender of the boat in the name of the Confederate States. Seeing resistance useless, he ordered the surrender of the boat, and at a signal of the whistle my men quickly drew their pistols, to which was yielded the most perfect obedience." The rebels quickly threw off their disguises and revealed themselves to be regular Confederate soldiers "armed to the teeth." [42]

The capture was clean and bloodless, but provided some unwelcome surprises. The ship was laden with only about forty hogsheads of tobacco and a quantity of wheat, but hardly enough to feed an army. Even worse, when questioned by Fitzhugh about the mysterious cannonading the previous day, Captain League must have taken some cynical delight in his response. The firing, he told his captor, was "in honor to the capture of Petersburg and the fall of Richmond." The capital of the Confederacy had been abandoned and was in flames. Unquestionably stunned, Fitzhugh was now well aware that the Army of Northern Virginia, or what was left of it, would have to retreat and change its base to survive. Rendering the object of his expedition futile, there seemed "little choice but to hasten down the bay as fast as steam could take us, hoping to get back to Lee's army as best we could." But first, there was the matter of disposing of the many prisoners aboard.[43]

As soon as the ship was secured, Fitzhugh ordered her to come about and return to the wharf at Fair Haven. At the same time he signaled with *De Ford*'s whistle for the rest of his men and prisoners from the pungy to come onboard.[44] At the wharf all of the fifty-five white passengers and part of the ship's crew including the captain were landed in a small boat and granted "their parole of honor" with the stipulation that they not leave Fair Haven for four hours or spread word of the capture until the raiders could get safely down the bay. The ship's engineer and fireman were retained. The black crewmen and passengers, men, women, and children, approximately thirty in number, were kept as prisoners to later be sold as slaves.[45]

The escape proved a combination of luck and speed. By the morning of April 5, having hugged the Eastern Shore coast en route down under a full head of steam, *Harriet De Ford*, with three boats (two belonging to the steamer, and one in which they had originally set out) reached Dividing Creek, a few miles north of the Rappahannock, without incident. After securing a pilot to take them into the creek, they pushed up as far as they could into Dimer's [modern Dymer] Creek, a small waterway feeding into Fleets Bay, but not before running aground several times and being forced to throw some of the cargo overboard to get off.[46]

After proceeding as far as possible, Fitzhugh and his men began removing part of the ship's machinery and some of the more valuable cargo, with the aid of several local farmers, for transport to Lee's army. About 4 p.m., while the work of un-loading was still underway and some of the stores already ashore were being re-moved, a lookout spotted a squadron of seven Federal gunboats slowly ascending the creek at a "cautious gait," shelling both shores as they came.[47]

Fitzhugh knew little and undoubtedly cared less about how the Federals had learned of his sortie, only that discovery and pursuit was inevitable. That the raid had been a success was without question. "We started in three open boats," he later wrote, "going nearly 100 miles by water in three nights. Our captures, 2 vessels, 1 steamer, 1 cannon, 62 stand of small arms, and many other valuable stores, and 205 prisoners, including about 60 negroes. Our loss none." [48]

***

As *Harriet De Ford* was plowing southward, Captain League and the ship's mate were making their own way to Annapolis as quickly as possible where they arrived in the very early morning hours of April 5. The captain lost little time reporting to the Federal authorities regarding the capture of the ship, as well as the loss of $1,500, which had been in his possession. The news caught military authorities in the city, still reveling over the fall of Richmond, completely by surprise. The capture of *Harriet De Ford* and the seizures of *St. Mary's* and *J. B. Spafford* had the effect of a lightning strike. Reaction to the stunning intelligence was at first disbelief, but the news was quickly passed up the military chain of command. When the commander of the Annapolis District, Colonel Frederick D. Sewall, learned of the *De Ford* capture, he informed Lieutenant Colonel Joseph H. Taylor, Chief of Staff and Assistant Adjutant General to the army commander at Baltimore. Taylor also informed Commodore Thomas A. Dornin, the navy commander at Baltimore, who dispatched an urgent message to Secretary Welles informing him of the raid. "I have no small steamer to dispatch to look after them," he complained just before noon on April 5. "Could you not dispatch two light draught steamers, either from [the] Potomac Flotilla or Hampton Roads, to put a stop to this business?" [49]

Relations between the army and the navy, enhanced by the frequent inter-service rivalry, had often been difficult, and the crisis posed by the capture of *Harriet De Ford* was to prove no different. It was apparently with some reluctance and seemingly as an afterthought just before noon on April 5 that General Morris, at Middle Department Headquarters, Baltimore, informed Brigadier General Edward D. Townsend, Assistant Adjutant General at the War Department, that the "Navy have no steamers here to send in pursuit. Have telegraphed to Fort Monroe, as it is reported that the two steamers [*De Ford* and *Spafford*] went down the bay. If the Navy Department is informed *perhaps* Commander Parker can overtake them." [50] General Morris did not wait for the navy and moved to dispatch an army charter steamer, then at Fort McHenry, with troops. Orders were sent to the steamer's skipper, a Captain Vaughn and his second, a Lieutenant Smythe, "to turn over your command to the officer in charge of the steamer with troops on board from Fort McHenry. You will then accompany the united command and assist the officer in charge, giving him all the information about the bay and inlets you can, and do your utmost to overtake and recapture the captured steamers." The general also noted that an innocuous rumor was being circlated that Jefferson Davis, President of the Confederate States, was onboard the *De Ford*, making his escape from Richmond as General Grant's troops were closing in. It mattered little that the captured vessel was sailing south from Maryland, where it would have been impossible for Davis to have boarded. Nevertheless, he emphasized that "All rebels must be captured or otherwise disposed of." [51]

Assisted by Baltimore's chief of detectives, Vaughn set sail from Baltimore at 9 a.m. in a fast steam tug armed with a 24-pounder howitzer and manned by thirty handpicked men. Soon afterwards another steamer, having a hundred U.S. infantry- men and a squad of artillerymen with several pieces of heavy ordnance on board, was dispatched with orders "to the effect that if the tug was overtaken before recapturing the *Harriet Deford*, to take the force and howitzer from her and proceed to sea in search of the captured steamer." [52]

Warnings about the capture of *St. Mary's*, *J. B. Spafford* and *Harriet De Ford* were sent out as far afield as Wilmington, Delaware, where the commanding officer there, General Kenly, was informed: "Two steamers were captured last night by guerrillas in the vicinity of the Patuxent, Calvert County. They put out into the bay with large party of men on board. They may intend to land on the Eastern Shore. It may be some of the Davis party escaping. Instruct your cavalry to be vigilant." [53] For Kenly, the war had come full circle as events of the day must have evinced memories of the escapades of Zarvona and the capture of the steamer *St. Nicholas* almost four years earlier.

Since he had no vessels available in his district to take up the pursuit, Colonel F. D. Sewell, commanding at Baltimore, had already telegraphed Point Lookout and Fort Monroe informing them of the recent events. The commander at Fort Monroe, Colonel Edward T. Nichols, in turn dispatched the gunboat *Young America* to search for the raiders. He then telegraphed Rear Admiral David D. Porter, who was believed to be somewhere on the James below Richmond, and also, albeit belatedly, Commander Parker, then aboard his flagship *Don* at St. Inigoes.[54] Parker was also informed of the event by Colonel Taylor at Baltimore and by the Secretary of the Navy as well. In his communiqué Secretary Welles issued instructions "to use your best exertions to recapture the steamer or overtake the rebel party." The flotilla commander swept into action almost immediately. His first move was to order Captain James Tole, commanding the USS *Anacostia*, to steam down to the Great Wicomico River and warn all of the navy gunboats there of the Confederate actions and to instruct them to remain in place. He would bring his own ship down immediately.[55]

Parker's orders to Commander Hooker of the gunboat *Commodore Read*, his senior officer in the field presumed to be closest to the enemy raiders, left no question as to the action to be taken. "The transport *Harriet De Ford* has been captured in Chesapeake Bay by a party of rebels," he wrote. "You will therefore be particularly careful in overhauling all steamers and be prepared, to sink the *De Ford* should you fall in with her. Your station during the night and until further orders will be from the Rappahannock to Wolf Trap lightboat, and the following are the vessels of your command which you will dispose of as, in your judgment, you may think proper, viz: *Commodore Read, Yankee, [Jacob] Bell, Coeur de Lion.*" After providing a brief description of the *De Ford*, he added a note on the envelope: "Be particular that your vessels carry their running lights so that they may be taken for merchant vessels." [56]

To the commander of the gunboat *Don*, Thomas Eastman, he issued similar instructions, but ordered him to take immediate station to cover the bay between Point Lookout and Hooper Island. He was to also have at his disposal the gunboats *Currituck, Nansemond, Thomas Freeborn*, and *Mercury*. Then *Don*, with Parker aboard, set off at 1:20 p.m. from St. Inigoes in chase of the daring rebel raider. With a total of at least nine warships in hot pursuit there seemed little chance of Fitzhugh's escape.[57]

By the following morning, April 6, having neither heard nor seen anything more of *De Ford*, Parker concluded that she had to be lurking somewhere on the Eastern Shore or lower down on the Western Shore. Thus he instructed Eastman: "Send the [*William G.*] *Putnam* to Mobjack Bay, where she will probably find the *Western World*. Let them examine everything near that vicinity, and caution the captain of the *Putnam* to be very particular in allowing vessels to come near. During the day send your vessels out into the bay and overhaul everything passing, and at night take the same station as last night." [58]

Ironically, even as Parker was issuing instructions to Eastman, Commander Hooker's squadron, including *Thomas Freeborn*, which was already in the vicinity, was closing in on the prey. Having received his orders on the previous day, while cruising off the mouth of the Rappahannock and Piankatank rivers that night he had overhauled a number of suspect steamers and sailing vessels. At daybreak he communicated with the gunboat *Jacob Bell*, then in the entrance to the Rappahannock, and about 5 a.m. received on board from her two black men who had been picked up in a canoe. Both men, Simon Brown and James Hudson, had belonged to the crew of the *De Ford* but had escaped before being sent off to Kilmarnock, Virginia, with the three score blacks taken as prisoners, mostly contrabands, to be sold back into slavery. From the two men Commander Hooker quickly learned that the vessel for which he was searching had reportedly run up a waterway called Indian Creek, a mile or so south of the village of Kilmarnock. The inaccuracy of the information would prove critical to the Confederates' escape effort.[59]

Hooker was eager to pursue the rebels but was concerned that the quite shoally nature of the waterway would prohibit entry. He quickly fired off a message to Commander Parker: "We have holed the rat, but can't get at him; he is in Indian Creek. The *Coeur de Lion* and *Heliotrope* are coming here." [60]

Hooker did not have long to wait. Parker had quickly informed the commander that the gunboats *Mercury*, *Freeborn*, *Yankee*, and *Currituck* were already en route. But most importantly, he noted that *Coeur de Lion* and *Heliotrope* drew less water than *De Ford* and *Currituck* about the same.

"These vessels, with the *Freeborn*," he instructed, "will be enabled to go up the creek. Let them recapture or destroy the *Harriet De Ford* without a moment's delay. Be careful to preserve your whole blockade as usual. The *Harriet De Ford*, filled with men, may attempt to carry the gunboats by boarding; let them be prepared for this." As soon as the prey had been dealt with, he added, Hooker was to send the *Jacob Bell*, *Freeborn*, *Heliotrope*, *Coeur de Lion*, and *Stepping Stoness*, then also patrolling the area, back to St. Inigoes. About this same time, the commodore learned from *De Ford*'s engineer, who had also escaped from the rebels, that the vessel had been partially destroyed. Parker admonished Hooker: 'Be careful that you are not deceived with regard to their situation, and recapture or destroy her without delay . . . The engineer just made his escape from the vessel." [61]

Commodore Read entered Indian Creek accompanied by the remainder of his squadron by 10 a.m. and established a blockade while awaiting the arrival of the lighter draft gunboats. He was entirely unaware that the waterway was empty.[62] He was soon joined by *Heliotrope*, *Coeur de Lion*, and *Thomas Freeborn*. Upon arrival of *Coeur de Lion*, her commander, Captain Thomas Nelson, quickly informed Hooker that he could pilot in the squadron. By 11:30 *Commodore Read* and *Coeur de Lion* were cautiously steaming up the empty creek, shelling the woods on both sides of the waterway to abort any ambush that might be awaiting them. They had only proceeded a mile or so when Nelson's ship ran hard aground and was rescued by *Commodore Read* with some difficulty. Then, as the two ships struggled, *Heliotrope* arrived. Much to his delight, Hooker discovered that onboard was a pilot who well knew the channels of the winding creeks.[63]

"I therefore directed her to lead the way," Hooker later reported, "using the same signal with regard to depth of water that you instituted on a previous occasion on the Rappahannock River. In this manner I proceeded up the creek to as high a point as I could reach in this vessel, say about 5 miles, the light drafts going from 1 to 2 miles farther than I could carry the *Read*, all of us shelling woods and suspicious places. While there we took on board a number of contrabands, among them one of the crew of the captured steamer."

Soon after taking the escaped blacks aboard, Hooker was informed, much to his dismay and undoubtedly by the former black crewmen from *De Ford*, that the captured steamer wasn't in Indian Creek after all, but in Dimer's. Without wasting a minute, he ordered signals made for his squadron to return, and then directed *Freeborn* and *Coeur de Lion* to immediately proceed to the new destination. *Heliotrope* was detained to pilot the commander out of the unfamiliar waters of Indian Creek and into Dimer's, "a service which was most satisfactorily performed, her pilot carrying me to a higher point in each creek than any other gunboat of equal draft has ever before attained." [64]

Three hours later they were at the entrance to Dimer's (also noted as Diamond) Creek, which was promptly entered, their guns again firing at both shores to prevent ambush.[65]

With a creek of barely two miles length, discovery of the *De Ford* was now inevitable. Within minutes the gunboat squadron had located their quarry and observed a substantial number of men furiously engaged in wrecking and burning her. Immediately, the warships opened fire while at the same time dispatching a landing force in three armed boats. For a short spell the engagement was hot, but with the Confederates having already destroyed or carried off the most important cargo and machinery and most having already fled, the fight was soon over. Though boarded by men from the Yankee gunboats, it was quickly deemed impossible to staunch the flames of the burning ship, and she was soon incinerated to the water's edge. Nevertheless, the boilers on the wreck were bombarded by gunfire from *Freeborn* and the other vessels of the squadron until effectively destroyed beyond further use. Then having completed their mission, the Federals returned to the Rappahannock.[66]

The full impact of the Confederate capture and destruction of *Harriet De Ford*, however, was not completely played out. On the day following the affair on Dimer's Creek, Commander Parker was informed by the engineer of the unfortunate steamer that he had learned that other "parties were organizing for the purpose of capturing vessels on the bay, and that an attempt would be made to seize the *Highland Light*, a steamer running between West River and Baltimore." It is probable that the engineer had overheard or otherwise obtained a somewhat blurred account of Fitzhugh's effort to capture that vessel at West River in a much greater plot, though in light of recent events it was intelligence that could not be ignored. It is certain, however, that the scheme was immediately lent further credibility and magnified in the minds of Federal authorities when the plan was confirmed presumably by the two black crewmen that had escaped at Dimer's Creek. It was thus not surprising that Parker immediately informed Secretary Welles of the danger and of an even greater plot, the origins of which were never disclosed but would be quickly acted upon. "I am led to believe that an attempt will be made to burn the bridges over Gunpowder and Bush rivers, and to destroy the boat belonging to the railroad company at Havre de Grace." [67]

The war, it must have again appeared, was coming full circle from that day four years earlier when those same bridges had gone up in smoke. Welles replied immediately: "Rear Admiral Porter has been instructed to station three vessels outside the capes and send to you such light draft steamers as he can spare, not exceeding six. In view of the information gained it would seem prudent to dispatch a vessel to each of the points named, the Gunpowder [River], etc., to guard [against] the designs of the rebels." A copy of Parker's report was communicated to the Secretary of War, with a suggestion that it might do well to once again scour the Northern Neck by a military force.[68]

Compliance with the order and redeployment of a substantial portion of the U.S. Navy on the Chesapeake and in the Virginia theaters were quickly instituted. Then, on April 9, even as the naval forces were en route to begin cruising against further raids, at a modest courthouse in a hamlet called Appomattox, General Robert E. Lee met with his mortal adversary, General Ulysses S. Grant, to surrender the Army of Northern Virginia. The Civil War in the Chesapeake Tidewater, and soon after across the entire expanse of America, was over.

Now the nation would face yet one more devastating trauma as the last great tidal wave of the great rebellion finally subsided. And for the last time Southern Maryland and the Potomac frontier would be convulsed in one finaly orgy of tragedy and retribution.

44

HAIL TO THE CHIEF
"Now he belongs to the ages."

It had been eleven days since the fall of Richmond, and just ten since President Abraham Lincoln visited that city and sat in the Confederate State House behind the abandoned desk of Jefferson Davis, now a rebel fugitive on the run. Though mobbed by masses of newly freed slaves, the president had moved uncontested through the streets of the now rudderless Southern metropolis, the acrid smoke from still smoldering fires lit on April 3 by Lee's retreating rebel army still heavy in the air.

For many white citizens who had remained in the city, most of whom did not appear on the streets unless driven by curiosity, desperation or hunger, it had seemed the end of times. But for Unionists it had been a glorious triumph dearly earned after four years of conflict, ceaseless sacrifice and despair on an un-precedented scale. The following day, filled with hope for the future, the now jovial president returned to Washington aboard the steamboat *River Queen*.[1] Four days later, Lee and the Army of Northern Virginia laid down their arms at Appomattox Court House, and the world was forever changed.

On April 10, the day following Lee's surrender, Washington awoke to the booming of cannon. A carnival spirit, manifest by the euphoria of victory that would last for days, emerged with the sunrise as bands led a joyous population through the city streets. Groups sang "Rally 'Round the Flag" and "The Star Spangled Banner." At the Navy Yard, merry workers fired half a dozen howitzers celebrating the end of strife, death and destruction.

The nation rejoiced. The *New York Times* perhaps best expressed the enormous sense of national relief and triumph upon the conclusion of the long, exhausting, bestial conflict.

> "The history of blood – the four years of war, are brought to a close. The fratricidal slaughter is all over. The gigantic battles have all been fought. The last man, we trust, has been slain. The last shot has been fired. We have achieved too, that for which the war was begun – that for which our soldiers have so long and grandly fought, and that for which so many thousands of brave men have laid down their lives. We have achieved the great triumph, and we get with it the glorious Union. We get with it our country – a country now and forever rejoicing in Universal Freedom. The national courage and endurance have their full reward." [2]

From the second floor window of the Executive Mansion Lincoln appeared, humoring the masses with his famous *ad libs*. With a wry smile, he asked for the Quartermaster's regimental band to play *Dixie*, declaring it to be one of the best tunes he had ever heard. "Our adversaries over the way attempted to appropriate it," he declared with a smile, "but I insisted yesterday that we fairly captured it. I presented it to the Attorney General, and he gave it as his legal opinion that it is our lawful prize. I now request the band to favor me with its performance." The crowd roared its hearty endorsement even as the music began. When the tune was finished, a grand rendition of *Yankee Doodle* followed, and then three rousing cheers for General Grant and the troops. And with that the president withdrew.[3]

Abraham Lincoln. Alexander Gardner, photographer. Taken February 5, 1865, this photograph is believed to be the last made of the president during his life. Prints and Photographs Division, Library of Congress, Washington, D.C.

The following evening, April 11, with bands playing and banners flying, a torchlight parade marched to the carriageway of the White House. Again, Lincoln appeared. A few feet behind him, in the near darkness, stood his wife Mary and Elizabeth Keckley, the first lady's black dressmaker, watching in silence as the president addressed the adoring masses below. "What an easy matter would it be to kill the president as he stands there!" whispered Elizabeth to Mary with some concern. "He could be shot from the crowd." [4]

"Yes, yes," replied Mary sadly. "Mr. Lincoln's life is always exposed. No one knows what it is to live in constant dread of some fearful tragedy. The president has been warned so often that I tremble for him on every public occasion." She paused and then confessed darkly: "I have a presentment that he will meet with a sudden and violent end. I pray God to protect my beloved husband from the hands of the assassin." [5]

The president spoke with measured and deliberate grace, this time asking the nation to prepare for the difficult task of rebuilding the South and the nation. "We meet this evening, not in sorrow, but in gladness of heart." For a pregnant moment he hesitated and then resumed, announcing the preparation of a call for national thanksgiving, and generously acknowledged all those who deserved credit for victory. The speech soon morphed into an even more serious subject as he spoke of reconstruction and his wish that black people, and in particular those who had served in the military, be granted the vote. Universal suffrage and the right for men of color to cast their ballots in freedom were thus brought to the fore to a mostly, but not entirely, welcoming audience.

Standing in Lafayette Square watching the proceedings was a well dressed man, an actor by profession, and a dowdy looking young accomplice. Unlike those around him held spellbound by the president's words, the actor sneered at the notion of blacks voting. "That means nigger citizenship," he whispered to his colleague. "Now, by God, I'll put him through."

A moment passed as his anger grew. "Shoot him," he suddenly demanded of his companion. The accomplice refused. It would have been suicide to do so amidst such a huge crowd. Disgusted, the actor stomped off the grounds, vowing to no one in particular: "That is the last speech he will ever give." [6]

***

Good Friday, April 14, 1865, 10:35 p.m. Sergeant Silas T. Cobb of the 3rd Massachusetts Heavy Artillery must have watched the approaching horseman with interest as he stood by the guard station on the Navy Yard Bridge that traversed the Eastern Branch of the Potomac. As the rider neared at a fairly rapid pace then slowed, the soldier could discern in the moonlight that the bay horse was rather small sized, a white star on its forehead, "with a shining skin," that "looked as though he had just had a short burst – a short push – and seemed restive and uneasy, much more so than the rider." He estimated the horseman was about five foot eight inches tall, perhaps twenty-five years of age, and somewhat muscular. He was dapper and well attired, wearing a black felt slouch hat, black wool coat, black pants, and great knee high leather cavalry boots with spurs. Combined with a haughty carriage and demeanor, Cobb suspected the young rider enjoyed membership in some well to do family of the region. What he could not discern was that the man was masking a searing pain from an injury in his left leg near the ankle.[7]

The bridge over the Eastern Branch that Cobb was guarding was a major military crossing connecting Washington with Southern Maryland that had seen constant usage throughout the war. Military traffic that night had been light, but his instructions, as usual, had been quite clear. He was to permit absolutely no one other than military teams to cross after sunset. Stepping from the guardhouse he challenged the stranger.

"Who are you, sir?"

"My name is Booth," replied the rider.

"Where are you from?"

"From the city."

Cobb examined him closely then asked, "Where are you going?"

"I am going home," the rider responded haughtily, "down in Charles."

581

"You must live in some town," said the sergeant.

"I live close to Beantown, but do not live in the town."

Cobb, a New Englander, declared that he didn't know the place.

"Good God!" replied the rider in mock exasperation. "Then you never went down there."

The sergeant ignored the comment and asked why the rider was out and about at such a late hour. Didn't he know the bridge was closed at 9 p.m.? The stranger replied in feigned shock that he was unaware that the crossing was shut down and declared that he had departed Washington at a late hour so that the rising moon might light his way.[8]

Perhaps taken in by the rider's story, or maybe it was his clothing and commanding deportment that suggested some wealth and importance, the sergeant let him pass. In all, the conversation had lasted only three or four minutes before the horseman had crossed the bridge. Then, after turning once to see if he was followed, the man in black disappeared into the darkness, apparently making for the Prince George's County countryside.[9]

Five to ten minutes later, another rider on a medium sized roan approached the guard station, moving at a less hectic pace then his predecessor. Again Cobb stepped forward to challenge. Again he asked the horseman to identify himself. The man gave his name as Smith and said he was on his way home to White Plains, in Charles County. Why, Cobb demanded, was he out so late? The man replied with "an indelicate expression" that he had been "in bad company." The sergeant brought him up before the guardhouse door, so that the light shone more fully upon his face and on the horse.[10]

"You can't pass. It is after nine o'clock," said the soldier matter-of-factly. "It is against the rules."

"How long have these rules been out?" replied the rider.

"Some time. Ever since I have been here."

"I didn't know that before," said the rider in simulated ignorance.

"Why," questioned the sergeant, "weren't you out of the city before?"

"I couldn't very well," came the answer. "I stopped to see a woman on Capitol Hill and couldn't get off before." [11]

The New Englander perhaps smiled in acknowledgement and motioned him on, undoubtedly with a jaundiced eye. After all, wasn't the war over and everybody but him celebrating?

But the monumental blunder had been made. Within the space of ten minutes Sergeant Silas T. Cobb, ignoring direct orders, had permitted the passage of one of the most notorious assassins in American history and his accomplice to escape from the scene of one of the most heinous crimes of all times.

***

As the noted thespian John Wilkes Booth galloped across the Navy Yard Bridge, passed through the diminutive hamlet of Uniontown and then into the ink of night, he traveled over a route he had carefully traversed before. The last time had been in a rehearsal for what had proved to be a flawed scheme hatched to kidnap the President of the United States. The plan, which had largely gestated at the boardinghouse of one Mary Surratt on H Street, NW, and elsewhere amidst an

582

ever changing cabal of co-conspirators, had originally been to waylay the president's carriage at gunpoint, less than a month earlier, on March 17, St. Patrick's Day. Booth's scheme had called for Lincoln to be waylaid and taken captive while en route from the White House to Campbell Hospital, on 7th Street Road, near the Old Soldier's Home, where he was to attend a comedy performance of *Still Waters Run Deep* being held for the benefit of wounded soldiers. He was then to have been secretly carried via a route through Southern Maryland, across the Potomac and then to Richmond. The ultimate objective was to hold him as a hostage to facilitate a massive prisoner exchange or even recognition of the Confederacy. The plot had proved a debacle from the beginning as the president was, in fact, nowhere near the hospital at the time, but presenting a speech at the National Hotel, the very establishment wherein Booth was lodged.[12] Soon afterwards, the actor departed for New York to stew in frustration, but returned to Washington, this time with a far more ambitious and bloody objective.

Though only twenty-six-years old, as scion of one of the most prominent theatrical families in America, John Wilkes Booth had already achieved noteworthy fame as an actor at an early age. Born in Bel Air, Maryland in 1838, he was the son of the near legendary Shakespearean performer Junius Brutus Booth, Sr. and brother of Edwin and Junius Brutus Booth, Jr., both equally noted celebrities of the theater world with whom he had starred on stages from Boston, Massachusetts to Montgomery, Alabama. He had led a storied life since his stage debut in 1856. Once described as "a rare specimen of manly beauty," with an athletic, compact build "most gracefully formed," he was handsome to watch and enigmatic both on and off the stage. With "large dark eyes, dark brown hair" inclined to curl, and heavy dark eyebrows, he evoked a charisma that easily captivated all when he chose to do so. It was said even by his critics that "this young man possesses the charms of Adonis and almost the strength of Hercules . . . ninety-five men out of a hundred would be no match for him at fighting. He is a dead shot, a fine fencer, a thorough horseman, and a master of the dagger or bowie knife. His personal bravery has been unquestioned." Being a noted unsettled tenant of the great cities, theatrical districts, oyster bars and saloons along the Eastern Seaboard, he was frequently recognized and adored by the public since his astonishing rise to stardom, begun in earnest in Richmond about 1860. He was well known for his conspicuous passion for fashionable attire and beautiful women, but particularly for his belief in Southern honor, and especially the romance and drama of lost causes. His affinity for what he deemed to be the nobility of the "Old South" was varnished smooth and well known among his friends. As a sophisticated denizen of the urban world, however, finding his way now through a dark, rural countryside, injured, while possibly being pursued for his life, was well beyond his comfort zone. Now, more than ever, he needed help.[13]

As he plunged headlong into the night towards Sopher's Hill, in the rural Silver Hill district of Prince George's County, just across the state line, Booth hoped to successfully rendezvous with at least one of his gang members, David E. Herold, who was a loyal agent in his plot to bring chaos and retribution to the Union. There were others as well, all from the initial cabal of well over half a dozen major co-conspirators and confidants during various stages of planning for the kidnapping.

Now there were, besides Herold, only two others left, Lewis Payne and George Adzerodt, with whom he had collaborated for weeks.

Under Booth's leadership, they were an unlikely lot indeed. Herold was a twenty-two-year-old dropout from Georgetown College, employed as a clerk in a drugstore a block from the White House. From the very beginning of the war, it was surmised, he had also been active as a guide for blockade runners. Why Booth had chosen him, particularly as it related to his escape plans, was clear. "Herold, a young man of idled, vagabond habits," reported the *Evening Star* when his association with Booth was later made known, "was a good shot and a capital boatman, spending much of his time in gunning and fishing excursions in the lower counties of Maryland, acquiring in this way a thorough knowledge of the country, especially its bypaths, forests, swamps and creeks sought only by the hunter and fisher." [14]

Lewis Thornton Payne, who also went by the name of Lewis Powell, was a handsome, twenty-year-old, hard-edged ex-Confederate who had been wounded at Gettysburg and escaped from a Union prisoner of war camp. He was a broad shouldered man of great brute strength, whose brawn the actor had deemed more than adequate to consummate a key component of the latest plan. His physical appearance belied a most cruel and vicious personality. "The villain," as he was later described, "was about six feet in height, of medium sized round face, with light sandy hair, and whiskers and moustache, both light in color and in growth . . . He wore a slouched hat . . . a light colored overcoat, buttoned down closely to the throat with what seemed to be pearl buttons. His hands were soft and delicate look-ing, but he displayed wonderful muscular power." But most importantly, he was utterly devoted to Booth, who he always addressed as "Captain." His mission, assisted by Herold, was the murder of Secretary of State William H. Seward.[15]

The third and most recent member of the cell, George Adzerodt, was a surly looking, heavy drinking, often unshaven Prussian immigrant, a carriage maker and painter by trade, living with a widow and four children (the last of which was his) in Port Tobacco. Often deemed uncouth by some of Booth's associates, he was some-times disparagingly referred to as "Port Tobacco" George. For Booth, however, Adzerodt's saving grace was his knowledge of the roads and byways of Charles County and experience as a ferryman on the waters of the Potomac. And when not in his cups, he was usually pliable. His assigned mission had been to kill the new Vice President, Andrew Johnson.[16]

Booth had saved the most savory, dramatic, news making act of savagery for himself, the murder of President Abraham Lincoln, which had been undertaken less than two hours earlier at Ford's Theater. Yet, riding on through the dark, he was totally unaware of the present status of his three agents or of their successes or failures. Indeed, he was even uncertain of the success of his own attempt on the president's life. The event, as he most assuredly had hoped, had been high theater indeed. But had he completed the job?

It must have seemed to Booth hard to believe how rapidly events had unfolded since listening to the speech that had enraged him to a murderous pitch only a few nights earlier. To kill the President of the United States had become his sole objective, an obsession that could not be easily contained as he had searched for the right opening. That opportunity had revealed itself only two days later while visiting

Grover's Theater in the city, when he learned from the manager, Dwight Hess, that a card was being sent to invite Lincoln to a performance of *Aladdin or The Wonderful Lamp* on the evening of April 14.[17] Here, it seemed, had been the very break that he had been awaiting.

The next morning he had breakfasted as usual at the National Hotel, where he often resided while in Washington. Afterwards, he returned to his room and gathered clothes, riding boots and spurs, a Bowie knife, a one shot Derringer, keys, a velvet encased compass, a whistle, a date book, a pocketknife, a pencil, photographs of five of his most intimate female friends, and other small items. He then revisited Grover's Theater to reserve a box seat adjoining the president's, only to learn at the last minute that Lincoln had accepted an invitation to Ford's Theater instead. Undeterred, about noon he had walked to Ford's to pick up mail, which he routinely had delivered there as he was often out of the city. As chance would have it, theater owner James Ford had just drafted text for an advertisement in the city papers announcing the evening's performance with an emphasis, to stir up customers, that both Lincoln and Grant would be attending.[18]

That afternoon, while James Ford's brother Harry supervised a theater hand and carpenter named Edman "Ned" Spangler in the decorating, outfitting and enlarging of the presidential box by removing a partition between boxes Nos. 7 and 8, Booth set to work on his own mission. Owing to his celebrity status and familiarity with both staff and management at the theater he had easy access to all therein. Moreover, he had an intimate knowledge of the layout, the stairway, and the underground passage beneath the stage, hallways, doorways, boxes and alleyway access. It was here, he decided, that he would kill the president. He had just eight hours or so to prepare and there was much to do.[19]

To facilitate his escape, a bay mare was hired at the livery stable of James Pumphrey, which he arranged to pick up between 4:00 and 4:30 p.m. Later in the afternoon he returned to the theater, after Ford and Spangler completed work on the presidential box, and slipped in undetected. He cut a peephole in the box door, and secreted a wooden bar, part of a music stand made of pine, which he concealed near the carpet edge.[20]

His next stop was at the Kirkwood House Hotel on the northeast corner of Pennsylvania Avenue and 12th Street, where the new vice president resided, unguarded and exceedingly approachable. With the desk clerk he left a scribbled note to be placed in Johnson's room slot. "Don't want to disturb you: are you at home?" he had written and signed with his own name which he assumed, owing to his great celebrity, the vice president would recognize.[21]

Booth's next stop was at Mary Surratt's boardinghouse to reconnect with one of his closest allies, Mary's son John. He was soon to be informed by Mary that her son, long an agent for the Confederacy, had departed for New York on Confederate business. Still, Booth resolved that the visit would not be wasted. Apparently during the conversation, he learned that Mary would be riding out of the city that afternoon for a brief visit to her former home and inn that she had recently leased out in Prince George's. Seizing upon an opportunity, he informed her that he too would be departing the city that evening, and asked if she would deliver a modest package to the tavern, which he would pick up that same evening along with two carbines that John had hidden there for him a month or so earlier. She agreed. He then produced a small parcel, wrapped in newspaper and twine and asked her to tell her tenant innkeeper, John Lloyd, to get things ready for his visit.[22]

Later that afternoon, accompanied by one of her boarders, a clerk at the War Department named Lewis Weichmann, Mary Surratt left for Surrattsville by carriage. When they arrived, John Lloyd had not yet returned from Uniontown where he had gone to purchase food for the inn. Mary waited impatiently. When he finally appeared, partially intoxicated, and began unloading his cargo of oysters and fish near the woodyard, Mary quickly descended upon him.

"Talk about the devil," she declared in mock humor, "and his imps will appear."

The somewhat tipsy innkeeper responded: "I was not aware that I was a devil."

"Well, Mr. Lloyd, I want you to have those shooting irons ready. There will be parties here tonight who will call for them."

She then gingerly handed him a small package wrapped in newspaper. The evening callers, she explained, would be wanting this as well, and added that he should also give them a couple of bottles of whiskey. Having done everything Booth had asked, she waited while Lloyd fixed several broken spring bolts in her carriage and then, with Weichmann still in company, drove back to Washington.[23]

Soon after Mary's departure, as per her instructions, Lloyd carried the package upstairs, and unwrapped it to find a pair of binoculars. He then went into the room where, several weeks earlier, John Surratt had shown him how to conceal a pair of Spencer carbines between joists and ceiling in an unfinished upstairs compartment to avoid detection from Union searchers. Quickly he retrieved the weapons along with a box of cartridges and took them and the binoculars to his bedroom.[24]

***

It was about 8 p.m. when John Wilkes Booth convened his gang together for the last time at the Herndon House Hotel, near the U.S. Patent Office. Adzerodt would later recall that it was then that their leader revealed his stunning proposal "that we should kill the president." It would, the actor declared with theatrical timing, "be the greatest thing in the world." At 10 p.m., he proposed, they would inflict total chaos upon the Union by simultaneously murdering Lincoln, Johnson, and Seward and thereby help the Confederacy to continue the war. With good fortune he might even kill Grant, who, it was advertised would be seated at the performance as the president's guest.[25]

Unanimity of purpose at first seemed evident, that is until Adzerodt expressed serious doubts, and then declared he could not agree to the scheme. He simply refused to go along. Infuriated that his whole plan had been put in jeopardy at the eleventh hour, Booth attempted to threaten him by saying that he would accuse him of participation anyway and he would be hung even if he didn't go along. It didn't work, and the coarse carriage maker from Port Tobacco left to have a drink.[26]

Unbeknownst to either Adzerodt, Payne or Herold, their leader had already implicated all in a letter, contained in a sealed envelope, which had been entrusted to a fellow thespian and friend, John Matthews, to see that it was published the following day in a city newspaper. The letter, which was intended, in a mad, perverted act of hubris, to justify the killings, had included his associates' names and potentially doomed not only Adzerodt but also the entire group if published.[27]

***

When Abraham Lincoln and his wife were ushered into Ford's Theater at 8:30 p.m., a half hour after the play had begun, there had been no crowds to greet them or announcements of their belated appearance made to the audience. Yet, owing to the advertisements placed in the day's newspapers, some patrons had specifically come with hopes of catching a glimpse of the president while others, such as James P. Ferguson, had purchased tickets in hopes of seeing their military hero, Ulysses S. Grant and his wife. Somehow, before Lincoln and his actual company had reached the president's box, everyone – musicians, actors, stagehands and patrons alike – had been made aware of the great man's arrival. For a moment the play in progress was halted and, to the happy approval of all, the orchestra struck up "Hail to the Chief" as the president and his party entered the presidential box. The audience stood and cheered wildly. Abraham Lincoln, in perhaps one of the happiest moments of his life, with the war and all of its carnage and misery now behind him, looked down upon them, smiled and acknowledged their loving ovation with a modest bow, after which the show was resumed.[28] For a very few moments, the world seemed right again.

Among those in the theater audience, seated just forty feet from the president's box, was Dr. Charles Leale, a twenty-three-year-old surgeon who had graduated only six weeks earlier from Bellevue Hospital Medical College in New York City. Leale was now in charge of the Wounded Commissioned Officer's Ward at the Armory Square General Hospital, a mile from the White House. Like almost everyone else, Leale was unaware of Booth, who had arrived riding a rented horse, which he had led by the reins down an alley to a back door of the theater. There he had asked Ned Spangler, the carpenter and scene shifter who had done favors for him in the past, to hold the horse for ten to fifteen minutes, vigorously instructing him not to hitch the reins to anything. It was imperative. Yet, as soon as the actor had entered the theater, Spangler had turned over the assigned task to another theater employee, a peanut peddler named Joseph Burroughs, known fondly to both patrons and stagehands as "Peanuts John." [29]

Booth had been mindful of the time as he walked down a theater basement side passage into another alleyway leading to 10th Street. There was just enough leeway for a quick drink of whiskey and water in the Star Saloon, a watering hole where actors, stagehands, and theater patrons frequently assembled. About 10 p.m. he left the saloon and made his way back into Ford's Theater and with little trouble to the passage leading to a vestibule door and access to the president's box. He was unaware that in the audience a casual acquaintance, James Ferguson, who he had briefly encountered that same afternoon, had been watching the presidential box hoping for a glimpse of General Grant. What he saw at first meant little.

After a brief exchange of words with Lincoln's servant, Charles Forbes, who was sitting near the door, Booth had proceeded on, then "stopped two steps from the door, took off his hat, and holding it in his hand, leaned against the wall behind him." For half a minute he peered through the peephole that he had bored through the box door with a gimlet earlier in the day. Quietly, Ferguson observed, "he stepped down one step, put his hand on the door of the little corridor leading to the box, bent his knee against it" and entered.[30] What he could not see was Booth deftly placing the pine bar, which he had earlier secreted at the carpet's edge, between the door and the wall so that no one else could enter after him.

The play, starring the British born actress Laura Keene, was a comedy called *Our American Cousins*. It was a production that Booth knew well, and had been underway since 8 p.m. He had planned the precise moment of execution for when there was to be but a single actor on the stage, four scenes before the end of the show. The script called for the performer, Harry Hawk, to deliver the line "You sockdologizing old mantrap," a tritely humorous insult really, which Booth knew would send the audience into such uproarious laughter that it would drown out the sound of his gun.[31]

When Hawk spoke, Lincoln had been sitting comfortably in his favorite high back rocking chair, delivered to the box before his arrival. Then chaos reigned supreme as Booth closed in behind the president and fired a single shot. He knew in an instant that his pocket Derringer had placed the .44 caliber bullet directly in his victim's head, on the left side below the ear. It seemed likely, as the president collapsed forward, to have been a mortal strike, but he could not be certain. Harry Hawk's words were, in fact, the last Lincoln would ever hear, for at that precise moment the bullet had tunneled through his brain, coming to rest behind his right eye. In that instant the future of the United States of America had been irrevocably altered.

Executing a murder was one thing. Managing a successful escape from one was another. Indeed, Booth's flight would not be easy, though as dramatic as any great tragedian could have imagined. A guest couple in the box – he had hoped it was to be General and Mrs. Grant as prognosticated earlier in the theater advertisements, or even Secretary of War Stanton and his wife – turned out to be a mere army major named Henry Rathbone. The major's fiancé, his own stepsister Clara Harris, daughter of Senator Ira Harris of New York, had accompanied the officer, who worked in the War Department's Disbursement Office.[32]

As soon as the shot had been fired, Rathbone, who had been sitting on a sofa to the far right of the president, the first lady and Harris, had sprung upon Booth with a vengeance. In but a second, dropping the Derringer onto the floor, the assassin had pulled away and drawn his backup weapon, a razor sharp double edged Rio Grande Bowie camp knife. In the next instant, shouting "Freedom," he had thrown up his right arm and then brought the cutting edge of the weapon down hard upon his assailant. Fortunately, the blow was blocked at the last instant by the major's right arm. Though the slashing blade had just missed Rathbone's brachial artery in what would have proved a fatal cut, the wound was nevertheless deep and blood gushed forth in surges. Ignoring his injury, the major struggled to get a grip on the killer.[33]

Desperately seeking to disengage, Booth laid his left hand on the railing of the presidential box, and brought a leg over the side. The box was festooned on its front with a hanging portrait of George Washington and decorative bunting composed of United States regimental flags that had been brought over from the Treasury Department specifically to honor the president's visit. Despite his wound, Rathbone again grabbed for the escaping assailant, taking hold of his coattail and thereby causing him to become entangled, first in the portrait and then with a riding spur on his right heel in the bunting. As the audience became aware of the fight, Booth suddenly managed to free himself and land on the stage, albeit off balance, losing the spur in the process but still holding the knife in his right hand. "He crouched as he fell," one witness later recalled, "falling on one knee, and putting both hands to help himself to recover an erect position, which he did with the rapidity and easy agility of an athlete." A sharp pain raced up his left leg from the ankle but the adrenalin coursing through his brain, for the moment, had neutralized all senses but the will to survive.[34]

"Assassination of President Lincoln, at Ford's Theatre, Apl. 14th 1865." Published by H. H. Lloyd & Co., St. John St., New York (1865-1870?). Prints and Photographs Division, Library of Congress, Washington, D.C.

Somehow, now the focus of every eye in the theater, he managed to stand erect and take center stage for the last time in his career. This, he knew, would be the final and most memorable public appearance of his life, and he did not waste an instant of it. Pausing for a moment, drenched with Shakespearian gravitas, he raised high the doubled edged knife dripping with blood and roared out the Virginia state motto in a stentorian presentation: "Sic semper tyrannis!" meaning "thus always to tyrants." Then he shouted triumphantly: "The South is avenged!" [35]

As pure bedlam ensued and the assassin started across to the far side of the stage, passing behind Harry Hawk, he was heard to say, almost in a self con-gratulatory fashion, "I have done it." Orchestra conductor William Withers hur-riedly stepped aside to avoid being cut by the killer moving across the floor. In the initial seconds of pandemonium no attempt was made to stop the mad man hacking all about as if possessed. As the assailant ran past the many stagehands off stage, all were taken by complete surprise. One staff carpenter who briefly attempted to block his escape was driven back by the flashing instrument of death.[36]

From the president's box, Clara Harris screamed, "He has shot the president" even as a profusely bleeding Rathbone cried out in desperation above the din, "Will no one stop that man?"[37] At that moment, a member of the audience who immediately recognized the famed actor began to shout wildly, "He is John Wilkes Booth, and he has shot the president." Another theater patron, a six-foot-five man named Joseph Stewart, took up Rathbone's challenge and leaped from the first row of seats and across the orchestra pit on to the stage in a vain attempt to seize the killer as he dodged into the wing on his way to the back alleyway door.[38]

Barely steps ahead of Stewart, Booth reached the alley and slammed the door shut behind him, purchasing a few critical seconds of reprieve. Breathing hard, he shouted to Peanuts John: "Boy! Give me my horse!"[39] Scrambling frantically to escape, he was mounting the rented mare just as his pursuer burst from the alleyway door and reached for the reins. Booth swiveled the horse off in a tight circle to evade capture, but Stewart again made a grab. This time, with one spurred boot, the assassin kicked his horse hard, broke free of his antagonist's grasp and fled.[40]

Dashing through the dark alley, the assassin reached F Street in seconds and turned right, riding hard. Soon he was passing Herndon House and then approaching the U.S. Patent Office, site of Lincoln's second inaugural ball only a few weeks earlier. Looking off to his right he could see the merrymakers, soldiers and citizens alike, all along Pennsylvania Avenue, still raucously celebrating the end of the war. The city had remained illuminated and filled with euphoric jubilation for days, and was still entirely unaware of the treachery just conducted. Riding hard as he crossed the Capitol grounds, he may have recalled having stood quietly on the balcony of the Capitol on March 4, glumly gazing down upon Lincoln being sworn into his second term of office. "What an excellent chance I had, if I wished, to kill the president on Inauguration Day!" he had recently told confidants in New York. "I was on the stand, as close to him as I am to you." But that was all behind him now.[41] There was little time to think of what might have been as he pressed on for the Navy Yard Bridge.

As he approached the crossing it had been necessary to slow his pace to avoid suspicion, though the sweat on his steed could not be hidden. After talking his way past the bridge guard with little trouble, the first stage of a successful getaway had been completed. But getting to Richmond, his intended destination, or perhaps Mexico where a rebel army was said to be heading, would be far more hazardous.

***

Lewis Payne had been incredibly brutal in conducting his own assigned mission, which was to murder Secretary of State William H. Seward in his bed. Only a few days earlier the secretary had suffered from an unfortunate carriage accident that had totally incapacitated him, and consigned him to the care of his family, who tended his every bedside need. For Payne it had been a matter of tricking his way into the Seward home, late in the evening, by playing the role of messenger delivering a package of medicine from the secretary's personal physician, Dr. Tullio Verdi. He had cajoled his way past a nineteen-year-old house servant named William Bell and all the way up to the secretary's bedroom door with little difficulty. Outside, on the street below, Herold had patiently held his horse, a half blind nag purchased by Booth for the escape once the deed had been done.[42]

Payne's entry had been easy, but problems getting to Seward's bedside quickly ensued. Talking his way past Bell, he was next met at the top of the stairs and just outside the secretary's bedroom by Seward's son Frederick who demanded he turn over the package and depart. Drawn by the war of words that ensued, Frederick's sister Fanny, a tall, slender, brown haired woman of twenty who had been at her father's bedside, opened the bedroom door: "Fred," she said gingerly. "Fred. Father is awake now." Suddenly Payne confronted her and rudely pressed forward to peek into the room.[43]

"Is the secretary asleep?" he demanded.

Stunned by the stranger, and perhaps at a near loss for words, Fanny replied: "Almost."

Frederick intervened, slammed the door shut and faced the intruder. Again he challenged him, demanding that he depart immediately and leave the package behind. The stranger glowered, stuffed the package in his pocket, and turned towards the stairs as if to leave. Frederick also turned and headed back to his own bedroom. Then, in but a split second, the visitor had reversed course, leaped up the few stairs he had started down, and pulled a 36-caliber revolver from his pocket. The weapon was pointed only inches from Frederick's face when Payne pulled the trigger, but the gun misfired. For a naked second the two men glared at each other. In the next instant the ex-Confederate began to viciously pummel Seward's head with the pistol, blow after blow, driving him to the floor in an attack so violent that the weapon was broken to pieces.[44]

Terrified, William Bell leaped down the steps and into the street, screaming "Murder." Across the way, Herold, who had been waiting patiently on his own horse while holding the reins of his comrade's nag, panicked and galloped off into the night leaving the one-eyed steed behind. Within but a few seconds of the beating Frederick Seward lay senseless in a growing puddle of his own blood, his skull shattered. Payne now turned towards the bedroom door to finish the mission. He was unaware that the secretary had been assigned a guard, one Sergeant George Robinson, a veteran Maine volunteer who had been wounded, hospitalized, and upon recovery ordered to watch over the injured secretary.[45]

Having heard the commotion in the hall, Robinson opened the bedroom door to investigate and was met by a sudden blow from Payne's knife handle, which struck him in the forehead and drove him to the floor. Without delay his assailant pressed past him into the secretary's bedroom. Frantically, Fanny rushed to a window, screaming "Murder." Ignoring the young woman, the assailant prepared to stab the secretary in the face, dealing a tremendous blow, but missing the mark at the last instant. Just as Fanny screamed "Don't kill him!" her father awoke and struggled to raise himself.[46]

Payne lunged forward, now pinning his victim to the bed, striking twice with his foot-long knife on the left and right of Seward's face but missing the fatal mark as the victim struggled for his life. A third blow, aimed at the throat, also missed but dug deep through Seward's lower right cheek, exposing the jawbone. Blood poured into his mouth, choking and gagging him. Before another strike could be made, however, Robinson had regained his senses and grappled with the assassin. But it was not enough to stop the assault.[47]

Sleeping in a room nearby was another of the secretary's son's, Augustus Seward, suddenly roused by Fanny's screams. Dressed only in his nightshirt, he rushed into his father's darkened room, thinking the old man to be delirious, and mistaking Payne for Robinson trying to restrain him. He quickly discovered his error. Again Robinson, having by now been twice slashed to the bone in the shoulder, sought to restrain the assassin, this time aided by Augustus. As the three men wrestled from the bedroom into the hallway, the knife found new flesh, cutting Augustus five or six times in the head, forehead and forearm. With eyes ablaze as he placed Robinson in a chokehold, Payne suddenly shouted in a strangled voice, "I'm mad. I'm mad!" Then, in a bizarre act of clemency, rather than slit the New Englander's throat as he might easily have done, he punched him in the face and stood. With bloody knife in hand he raced down the stairs and into the street, slashing an unfortunate passerby named Emerick Hamsell in the back as he went.[48]

Finding himself abandoned by Herold, who was supposed to guide him from the city, Payne mounted his horse, threw down the knife and rode off, pursued as far as Vermont Avenue by young William Bell screaming "Murder" as he ran. Somehow, he knew he must make his way to a friendly safe house. It would be the only place he knew well, the boarding house run by his friend John Surratt's mother, Mary. But where was it?[49]

Though Payne's maniacal assault had been brutal it had fortunately failed. Though badly wounded, all of his victims, except the unfortunate Hamsell, had shown great courage in fending him off, and though seriously injured, would survive. Still bleeding profusely and in great pain, the brave Sergeant Robinson, ignoring his own acute wounds, gently lifted Seward into the bed from which he had fallen in a feeble effort to avoid the killer's blade. With great labor, spitting blood from his mouth, the secretary whispered: "I am not dead. Send for a doctor. Send for the police. Close the house." [50]

***

In Ford's Theater, confusion ruled as 1,500 patrons morphed from the panic filled auditorium into a surly, angry mob calling for the assassin's blood. Dr. Leale had been the first to actually respond to the dying president's plight and tend to his wound. Rathbone, still bleeding profusely, had removed the bar that Booth jammed in the doorway and admitted the young surgeon. Ignoring the major's plea to tend his wound, Leale went straight to the president's side, introduced himself to Mary, who was weeping over her husband's body, and deftly began his examination. "Oh Doctor, is he dead? Can he recover? Oh, Doctor, do what you can for him," Mary pleaded between sobs. "Can he recover? Will you take charge of him? Do what you can for him. Oh, my dear husband."

Discovering the hole behind the victim's left ear to be matted and clogged with hair and coagulating blood, the physician knew immediately that it had been a bullet wound to the brain and not a knife blow as he first suspected upon seeing the major's wound. With nimble fingertips he carefully opened the blood clotted bullet hole to remove pressure on the brain, and then cleared a passageway through his throat to allow him to breath. He then began to resuscitate the victim by pressing his chest, and with the aid of two men, who had just appeared on the scene, had his arms moved repeatedly like levers. Breathing directly into the president's mouth and nostrils he soon instigated a faint sign of life. Though slight, the president resumed breathing on his own even as Mary continued to sob uncontrollably. "My husband! My husband! My God, he is dead!" [51]

Two more physicians, Dr. Charles S. Taft and Dr. Albert F. A. King, soon appeared. Leale spared no words. "His wound is mortal," he declared slowly. "It is impossible for him to recover." But he was still technically alive. What should be done next? They could not let the President of the United States die on the bloody floor of a theater box. To move him far, perhaps to the White House as someone suggested, would surely kill him! He would definitely not survive the passage over the rutted, unpaved streets of the city. In any event, they would still have to move him through a mob of angry, confused and frightened citizens unsure if their president was alive or dead. But move him to a more secure and comfortable quarters they must.[52]

Just then, Laura Keene appeared, still in costume, having talked her way to the door, through the vestibule and into the box, while bearing a pitcher of water. She was undoubtedly well aware that she would be present at a major history making incident and, perhaps, remembered for her actions of a few minutes rather than for her entire acting career. With Leale's permission, she cradled the president's bleeding, oozing head in her lap, her dress to be forever after stained.[53]

Though no one knew where the president must be taken, Leale and others decided to make the move and gently lifted him. Twice Leale called out, "Guards clear the passage," which was rapidly executed. Soon, they were crossing 10th Street through a stunned and jostling crowd. Take him to the nearest house across the road, bellowed a soldier. No one answered the door. The adjacent house next door, belonging to one William Peterson, was then assailed. This time, someone opened the door. A boarder named Henry Safford raised a candle and shouted, "Bring him in here. Bring him in here." [54]

Ever so carefully, they carried the president down a dim hallway to the rear of the building, past two parlors, to a diminutive room rented to a boarder who was out celebrating the end of the war. The tall, lanky but surprisingly muscular body was laid with knees half bent on a walnut bed far too short for him, less than twenty minutes after the bullet had entered his head. The countdown to the end of Abraham Lincoln's mortality had now begun even as word of the evil deed of the famed actor began to radiate ever outward, block by block, and soon city to city, and state to state. The greatest manhunt in American history was about to begin.[55]

***

Among those in the audience at Ford's Theater that tragic evening had been Leonard J. Farwell, former Governor of Wisconsin, then Inspector of Inventions at the U.S. Patent Office, who knew Vice President Johnson well. Having been witness to the assassination and the escape of Booth, he immediately recalled an article he had seen in a December issue of the *Selma Dispatch*, a Confederate newspaper from Alabama. A subscriber offering a $1,000,000 reward for anyone who would assassinate Lincoln, Johnson and Seward had posted the article. Stunned by the possibility that such a conspiracy was already underway, he rushed from the theater and sped on foot the two blocks to the Kirkwood House, shouting at the clerks that the president had been assassinated and to guard the entrance. Then, pounding vigorously upon the vice president's door, he shouted: "Governor Johnson, if you are in this room, I must see you."

"Farwell, is that you?" came a voice from inside.

"Yes, let me in." [56]

Once admitted, Farwell quickly briefed the stunned Tennessean on the events, and then departed upon his orders to spy out the evolving situation. Unaware of what had already transpired at the Seward home he rushed out to inform the secretary of the danger.

In the meantime, Johnson left, without benefit of guard, to discover the status of Lincoln's condition. As he entered the tiny room of the Peterson House in which the president lay, he looked upon the dying man and departed. Though now in virtual command of the nation, he did nothing, unaware that he had been saved from death by sheer good luck and the inner fears of a heavy drinking immigrant.

***

It had not taken long for word to spread from the Seward residence about the attack on the Secretary of State. At the home of the Secretary of War at 13th and K Street, Edwin M. Stanton had been upstairs preparing for bed when Major Thomas Eckhert from the Military Telegraph Office, on 13th and F Street, erroneously informed him that his good friend Seward had been killed in an assassination attempt. Having just paid a visit to Seward only a short time before Payne's arrival, Stanton was at first in a state of disbelief. "Humbug" he shouted down the stairs. "I left him only an hour ago." He was unaware that he had missed Payne's visit, and perhaps injury or death, by only minutes. It was a quirk of fate that would have significant consequences. Soon confronted by others bearing the same news, he quickly dressed and set out to visit his esteemed comrade and colleague. At the Seward home, he rushed upstairs to the gory scene of mayhem, arriving about the same time as Secretary Welles, who had also been informed of the attack. Together they quickly discovered doctors attending to Seward's lacerated face even as Fanny, in something of a daze, wandered aimlessly about in her bloodstained dress. With a crushed skull, Frederick lay still and unconscious, while his brother Augustus and Sergeant Robinson sat wounded, patiently awaiting their turn with the doctors. Fortunately, Stanton learned, none of the wounds had been fatal, but the danger was all too apparent.[57]

Seeing that they could do little more at Seward's, Stanton and Welles took a carriage to Ford's Theater, where they knew Lincoln was to be attending a performance. As they proceeded down F Street, they began passing angry throngs of citizens and learned to their horror of the assassination attempt on the president. When they arrived at the theater, the street was mobbed by thousands of infuriated men and women, crying out for the execution of the assassin, and blocking passage of the carriage. There was no alternative but for two of the most powerful men in the United States Government to push through on foot.

Inside the Peterson House the scene was grim indeed. Mary Todd Lincoln, Clara Harris and Major Rathbone, whose bleeding had only been partially checked, had followed some distance behind Leale and the others when they crossed the street with the president's body. When they had entered the Peterson House, Mary was screaming hysterically, "Where is my husband? Where is my husband?" Rathbone fainted in the hallway from loss of blood and was taken by carriage to his residence five blocks away.[58]

In the dim, gaslit room to which the president had been taken, now crowded by several doctors, state and military officials and others, the atmosphere was thick with gloom. Leale ordered a window opened to clear the air, and then instructed everyone to leave as the doctors worked to remove the dying man's blood-soaked clothing. Quietly, he encouraged Mrs. Lincoln to wait in the parlor.[59]

Again Leale and the other doctors examine the president's body for signs of other wounds. Though his eyelids were filled with blood and his bodily extremities were growing cold, his breathing was regular but difficult and sporadically interrupted by sighs. All were signs of a shattering injury to the brain. It was clear the end was near though his condition was for the moment stable. Gently they covered his body with a sheet and blankets and laid a clean white napkin over the bloody pillow beneath his head. It was now time for Mary to see her husband off. Leale instructed an officer to fetch her from the parlor. "Love," she said tenderly, "live but for one moment to speak to me once to speak to our children." But it was not to be.[60]

Undoubtedly moved by Mary's sorrow, Leale quietly sent for the president's eldest son, Robert Todd Lincoln, who had been attending the performance intended for his father at Grover's Theater. He also sent for the Surgeon General, Joseph K. Barnes, the family physician for the Lincoln family, and their pastor, the Reverend Dr. Phineas T. Gurley.[61]

When Stanton and Welles arrived, after due solemnities were observed, it was clear that no one had addressed the greater potential danger that might be facing the nation. Stanton immediately took charge, converting the back parlor of the Peterson House into a field office. It was his belief that the assaults on Lincoln and Seward were part of plot to eliminate the key leaders of the United States and to reverse the Civil War, with a rebel army possibly even at that moment advancing on Washington.[62]

With the vice president having simply acquiesced from taking command of the situation, Stanton moved with cool, resolute and, some would say, ruthless determination to prevent the escape of the assassins and counter any insurrection or military attack that might be in the making. He quickly ordered military guards to be sent to the residences of Lincoln's cabinet members, the vice president, and the quartermaster general. All roads leading from the capital and Baltimore were to be blocked. Trains were to be prevented from departing from both cities. The first three early morning trains leaving Washington at 6:15 a.m. were permitted to proceed only after painstaking search by soldiers and detectives. All were stopped several times en route before reaching Baltimore. All vessels going down the Potomac were to be stopped and everyone aboard them was to be held until further notice. All suspicious persons attempting to leave the city were to be arrested, as were all individuals of dubious character in Alexandria, Baltimore and Washington. A telegram was dispatched to General Grant, ordering his return to the capital. Troops were ordered to turn out into streets. Guards were doubled at key points and the forts surrounding the city placed on alert with their guns to be manned and ready for any possible attack. The guards at and surrounding the Old Capitol Prison were reinforced. The mob of thousands of citizens milling on the streets around the theater and the Peterson House had to be cleared. Within hours, the city was soon placed on a lockdown unlike any other in its history.[63]

***

It was deadly still as John Wilkes Booth pushed on into the darkened countryside, now riding hard towards an appointed rendezvous spot to link up with his fellow conspirators. As he neared the location, he passed two horsemen, a half mile apart, both heading toward Washington. The riders, Polk Gardiner and George Doyle, were each asked if he had seen any horseman go by, to which they replied in the negative. Where was the road to Upper Marlboro? he asked Gardiner, and upon being informed rode on. Not a few minutes had passed before Gardiner saw another rider come up beside a band of teamsters and their ten covered wagons. The rider asked if they had seen anyone dash by. The teamsters replied in the affirmative and the lone traveler galloped on. To George Doyle, it had seemed that both horsemen had been riding their steeds to death to catch up with each other.[64]

Somehow, in that dark, bloodstained night, Booth and Herold miraculously met at their appointed rendezvous. Both undoubtedly issued sighs of relief, but there was little time to halt or talk, except to exchange the pertinent events of the last few hours. Where were the others? Booth queried. Lewis Payne had apparently succeeded, at least as far as the former drugstore clerk knew. After all, the intended victim had been lying helpless, convalescing in bed at his home. Herold's specific job had been to hold Payne's horse, a half blind steed Booth had purchased for him, while the ex-Confederate soldier was dispatching the secretary. But in the chaos that followed, when someone shouted "Murder" from the Seward home, both he and Payne had become separated. The former rebel, who knew little about getting around Washington by himself and had depended upon Herold to lead him out of the city, was apparently still trapped, wandering about somewhere therein.

What about George Adzerodt? He had been assigned to murder Vice President Johnson at his residence in the Kirkwood House. Hadn't Adzerodt registered as a guest at the hotel that morning as instructed by Booth, in room 126 to be precise, directly above the vice president's apartment, less than 125 feet away from him? All he had to do was to knock at the man's door – Johnson, like the president, having no bodyguard – and shoot or stab him to death. Had he succeeded? It was impossible to know.[65]

Yet, the fates of both Payne and Adzerodt and their successes or failures mattered little now to Booth as he and his follower pressed on, riding ahead of the news of the assassination attempts, news that they knew would soon envelop the nation. Both were well aware that it was only a matter of time before countless soldiers would be swarming across the landscape like angry hornets looking for them. It was imperative that they stay ahead of their pursuers if they were to reach safety.

Coming to a crossroads, with the right branch leading into the Piscataway District, and eventually to Port Tobacco, and the left branch through open countryside towards the hamlet of Surrattsville, the two riders veered toward the latter. It was imperative now that they reach their first "safe place," the Surratt House, thirteen miles southeast of Washington, to pick up firearms and other items specifically stockpiled earlier for their escape.

Calling Booth's first destination, a crossroads upon which Surratt's inn was ensconced, anything but a hamlet was certainly a misnomer. In 1861 only three private farms were located in the vicinity, one being the Surratt tavern-cum-farmhouse, which also served as the district post office. The property once belonged to the late John H. Surratt, Sr., and was now owned in absentia by his widow Mary. It was at the time an extremely rural region, with the Surratt Election District having a pre-war population of just 456 whites, forty-nine of whom owned all 640 slaves in the district. There were just twenty-four free blacks, and two foreign born residents. Real and personal property value for the entire district had been placed at only $481,425.[66]

The whole Surratt family had been staunchly secessionist in sympathy. In December 1861, John and Mary's son, John H. Surratt, Jr., a skeletal looking, light haired, pale-complexioned youth with sunken eyes and a prominent forehead, had dropped out of St. Charles College, a Catholic seminary some distance from Baltimore, to join the rebellion. He had become a reliable courier connecting the Confederate spy network in Washington with rebel boatmen on the Potomac. Shortly after the death of his father and the settling of the estate, his mother had come under a cloud of suspicion thanks to the loyalties of her husband and son. In December 1864 she moved the family to Washington to manage a boardinghouse at 604 H Street, NW, in the very heart of the Federal city, and safe from the constant Yankee patrols and searches that were so common just a few miles away in Prince George's County. The D.C. property, a gray painted building with seven bedrooms on three floors and in the attic, could sleep as many as ten people, and provided enough income for the Widow Surratt and her daughter Anna to survive on. She had maintained ownership of the tavern, however, which was rented to John Lloyd, an old man much prone to the bottle.[67] As for John, Jr., he had become one of Booth's early and most trusted confidants and one of the original conspirators in the kidnapping scheme, though he had disengaged when it came to murder. But John was no longer available, having been called away on secret Confederate business in New York and Canada, or so it was said.

The dull, rust colored tavern was difficult to spot in the dark of night and was, except to the weariest of travelers, not particularly inviting even during the day. The building was segmented into public and private sections, with a customer entrance being a side door leading directly to a bar and the post office inside. Booth and Herold, both being familiar with the place, cautiously rode up to the side entrance in the dark, though neither intended on staying long. Because of his injured leg, Booth remained in the saddle, leaving his colleague to dismount and fetch the guns and other items that were supposed to be awaiting them.

Having apparently been in something of an alcoholic induced sleep, Lloyd responded slowly to Herold's repeated knocks on the door but immediately recognized the visitor he knew to be a friend of young Surratt. The caller entered and wasted not a word: "Lloyd," he said sharply, "for God's sake, make haste and get those things." Having been instructed by the Widow Surratt earlier that day to have the arms and other items, concealed weeks before by son John, to be ready for just such a visit, he knew exactly what was required. With little delay, he produced the small package wrapped in twine, containing the set of binoculars, and the two loaded Spencer repeating carbines and ammunition he had removed from between the upstairs wallboards only a few hours earlier. Only one carbine, however, was taken as Booth, now hurting mightily from his injury, felt he could not comfortably carry it while riding. A bottle of whiskey was also produced, which Herold took to drink on horseback.[68]

Yet, now that there was distance between himself and Washington and feeling relatively safer, Booth could not refrain from bragging about his accomplishment.

"I will tell you some news, if you want to hear it," said the actor.

"I am not particular," replied Lloyd, who was perhaps eager for his visitors to leave and displayed only mild interest. "Use your own pleasure about telling it."

Well," said Booth as his partner was mounting up, "I am pretty certain that we have assassinated the President and Secretary Seward."

The visit had taken less than five minutes. The two visitors rode off toward yet another inconsequential crossroads called T.B. Junction. After having a few more drinks, an unimpressed Lloyd went to bed.[69]

***

Dr. Samuel A. Mudd. (left), Prints and Photographs Division, Library of Congress, Washington, D.C., and Mary Surratt (right), New York Public Library, New York..

The two-story farmhouse belonging to Dr. Samuel Mudd, approximately seventeen miles southeast of Surrattsville and but a few miles north of Bryantown, was a handsome structure, though the two riders who approached in the pre-dawn darkness had little interest in its appearances. Here, Booth knew, they could find temporary respite and medical treatment for his leg. After all, he was a close acquaintance of the doctor, who had been an integral component of the kidnapping plot, and he knew well of his Southern sympathies. He was a slave owner whose family members, at least some of them, had been deeply involved in the contraband trade and the Confederate mail service. But could he be trusted with news of the assassination? Booth had perhaps deliberately failed to tip off any of his colleagues in the kidnapping scheme to his assassination plot other than Adzerodt, Payne, and Herold and possibly, though never proven, Mary Surratt. Still, Mudd's farm was far enough from Washington that word of the murder had undoubtedly not yet reached it. Even if it had he knew that because of the doctor's political kinship, he would most assuredly provide him with some measure of assistance.

Because Booth could not easily dismount from his horse, Herold again acted as intermediary, and went to knock on the farmhouse door. The loud rapping soon summoned Mudd. "Who's there," demanded the physician in a subdued voice, hoping not to awaken his wife Frances and their four children. Not knowing who might be in the house or if it was being watched, Herold replied politely, or so he later testified, that they were a pair of strangers en route to Washington, one having suffered a broken leg when his horse had fallen in the dark. The doctor cautiously peered out a side window, observing two men under a cedar tree a short distance from the house, and then unlocked the door. Soon he was helping the injured man to painfully dismount. With the assassin leaning on his shoulder, they slowly made their way toward the house, followed by Herold.[70]

It was by now 5 a.m., April 15, as the three men entered. In the dim lamp-lit room, Mudd quickly recognized Booth, the man with whom he had conspired to kidnap the president, as he set to work tending to his visitor's injury. By then, the leg had swollen to such an extent that it was impossible to take off the riding boot. Carefully, the doctor cut the boot about the ankle and had soon removed it and the sock beneath to diagnose the wound. It was, he told the patient as he prepared a splint, a fractured tibia above the ankle joint. He said little or nothing about the pair of belted pistols he spotted hidden under Booth's coat.[71]

Would it be possible for them to rest a bit at the farm before moving on that evening? Booth queried. The doctor acquiesced. After all, how could he send off two tired, bedraggled men who had been riding throughout the night, one of whom was injured, and with whom he had been intimately involved in conspiracy only a month or so earlier, without granting them some respite? Quietly, Mudd offered them a room upstairs, showed them the way, and went back to bed.[72]

Back at Ford's Theater, someone mentioned that the assassin Booth and young John Surratt, a suspected Confederate agent, had been close friends. And wasn't the boarding house run by Surratt's mother just a few blocks away?

Across the street, as the predawn gray of April 15 began to lighten, Charles Leale closely monitored the president's increasingly labored breathing. Then, at precisely 7:22 and 10 seconds a.m. Abraham Lincoln, 16th President of the United States, slowly exhaled his last breath. "He is gone," whispered one of the doctors. "He is dead." For a moment all was hush. Solemnly, Stanton requested that Reverend Gurley offer a few words. "I will speak to God. Let us pray." And they bowed and prayed. For a moment a deep stillness enveloped all.[73]

"Now," said the Secretary of War, "he belongs to the ages." [74]

45

A MAN NAMED BOOTH

"The coast seems to be clear and the darkness favors us."

It was in the very early morning hours of April 15 that Lewis Weichmann heard a heavy knock on the front door of the Surratt boardinghouse on H Street. At the entrance he found himself confronted by a number of police detectives who announced they had come to search the building. After admitting them, he immediately knocked on Mary Surratt's bedroom door to inform her of the visitors. Aroused from sleep, and seemingly certain as to specifically why they had come, she instructed the tenant: "For God's sake! Let them come in. I expect the house to be searched." [1]

While Mary was dressing, the detectives began to question Weichmann on the whereabouts of Booth and Mary's son John. "John Wilkes Booth has shot the president," one officer informed him bluntly, "and John Surratt has assassinated the secretary of state." That was impossible, declared the apparently stunned boarder just as Mary entered the room. John was not there but in Canada, he stuttered, so how could he have done such a thing? Perhaps as if to confirm the veracity of his comments and at the same times shield him from suspicion, he gamely offered to help with the investigation. Then it was Mary's turn. Unlike Weichmann, she pleaded total ignorance, claiming to have absolutely no knowledge of her son's whereabouts. As for Booth, though she knew him well, she remained silent as to their relationship. For the moment satisfied with the inquiry, the detectives then proceeded to conduct a cursory search of the house and, after finding little of interest, departed.[2]

What may have been going through Mary's head as she quietly answered the detectives' questions and then stoically watched them ramble through each room of her home will never be known. It is likely she had been well prepared to mask the most recent events that might implicate her son or herself in any of Booth's plots. In truth, John Surratt was not in Canada but in Elmira, New York, well aware that the war was nearing a close and that he, revealed as a Confederate agent, would likely become a hunted man. Only three months earlier on January 24, while supposedly on Confederate business in Canada, he had taken the precaution to secure a passport under the name of John Watson, one of his aliases, which was authorized by Governor Lord Monck. The documents would later be used to facilitate his safe escape to the Papal State in Italy. But he had indeed been deeply involved with Booth, as both Mary and Weichmann well knew, though not in the actual murder of the president.[3]

Mary's relationship with Booth had at first been peripheral. Indeed, it had been only a few months earlier, on December 23, 1864, when her son and Weichmann had been walking towards the boardinghouse on H Street that Mary had just acquired, when they encountered Booth and Dr. Samuel Mudd. Their meeting on the avenue would prove pivotal. After introductions were made, the actor had invited all three men for drinks and confidential discussions at his apartment in the National Hotel, where he frequently resided when in town. It was then that John

Surratt and Samuel Mudd were recruited to join the actor in the plot to kidnap the president. As the conspiracy evolved, John had been assigned several missions. In preparation for the overland escape to the river, he was to hide the pair of carbines at the Surratt place in Prince George's County. Then he was to find a boat to be used for the escape across the Potomac, and soon secured one from a Richard Smoot who lived a few miles from Port Tobacco. Mudd's role was to return home to await instructions and to stockpile liquor and supplies sent to him by Booth. A week after Christmas at a meeting in the boardinghouse, John introduced George Adzerodt, an acquaintance of his, thus adding another member to the cabal. Soon the famed actor and his collaborators were regular callers at the Surratt house on H Street, and in the process had become close friends of both Mary and her daughter Anna, the latter of which immediately became infatuated with the handsome actor.[4] Now, that relationship had suddenly turned deadly.

***

While John Wilkes Booth and David Herold slumbered in temporary safety in an upstairs bedroom at the Mudd farm, at the direction of Secretary Stanton the U.S. Army had already begun to send out squadrons of cavalry and detectives to run down every lead they could on the rout of Lincoln's assassin. He was profoundly worried about the very safety of the government and the possibility of other plots that might be afoot.

The secretary moved with speed and deliberation while acting on still very slender intelligence regarding the assassin. Within hours a Federal dragnet was expanding precipitously in scope and in every direction. Concerns that the assassins may have actually crossed from Washington into Northern Virginia were being addressed even before the president had expired. At 4 a.m., as Lincoln lay abed in the Peterson House taking in every breath with difficulty, General Augur, at Stanton's direction, was already dispatching orders to forces surrounding the city and beyond. "The murderer of the president is undoubtedly J. Wilkes Booth, the actor," he informed General John P. Slough, the military governor at Alexandria. "The other party is a smooth faced man, quite stout. You had better have a squad of cavalry sent down toward the Occoquan to intercept anything crossing the river. The fishermen along the river should be notified and kept on the lookout." [5]

Within an hour and a half, Slough had ordered a tug down river to inform the watermen, and was already assembling troops to scour the countryside between Alexandria and the Occoquan. From their camp at Fairfax Court House, major elements of Colonel Clendenin's 8th Illinois Cavalry, were dispatched to scour Fairfax County. They were to make a detailed sweep from the Orange and Alexandria Railroad to the Potomac to the east, and as far as Brentsville, Gainsville, and Aldie and nearly to Leesburg to the west. Another 447 officers and men of the 16th New York Cavalry formed a skirmish line, commanded by Lieutenant Colonels John Nicholson and Lawrence Leahy, extending from the Potomac River to Fairfax Station. The line advanced simultaneously southward toward the outer ring of fortifications, examining every house and suspicious person encountered along the way. At Point Lookout General Barnes was informed of the assassination only hours after Lincoln's death, and was ordered to arrest "every person found moving in your district who cannot account for himself." [6] Within a few hours he was able to inform General Halleck that he had immediately communicated with the gunboats in the area, and the river and bay were already being closely watched. Moreover, he assured his superior that the St. Mary's District was being thoroughly patrolled by mounted men. Yet with now more than 22,000 prisoners to watch, and the prospect of insurrection or some unseen military conspiracy being in the works, his request for reinforcements was not to be taken lightly or ignored. It would, however, take three days before the call was finally addressed, and two regiments were ordered down from Baltimore.[7]

Early Saturday morning, as bells of mourning began to toll throughout the city, the first wave of soldiers was crossing the Eastern Branch, with others following in quick succession, "until Prince George's, Charles and St. Mary's counties were fully enveloped." That the assassin was headed into Southern Maryland was soon clear: a man who had identified himself to Sergeant Cobb as Booth at the Navy Yard Bridge had verified the fact. The quartermaster general of the department was called upon to furnish horses, but the demand was such that soon afterwards at headquarters not a single horse or wagon was to be found. The first and reasonably reliable information was obtained that same morning when a cavalry unit called upon John Lloyd at Surratt's tavern, but failed to secure a "definite statement," only that he had not seen the two fugitives pass. Upon a closer examination and search of the premises by others the next day, the old man finally revealed that the owner, the Widow Surratt, had been there late on Friday afternoon "and left word that two men would arrive during the night who were to be generously provided for. She also directed that two carbines suspended by a string between the plastering of a partition should be given them." The two men, now positively identified as Booth and Herold, had arrived as expected late that same night and, though taking only a single carbine, some ammunition and whiskey, had set off immediately for the "lower counties." [8]

One of the many patrol parties that were sent out had been the 13th New York Cavalry, commanded by Lieutenant David Dana, brother to Assistant Secretary of War Charles Dana. The unit would be directed to ride into Southern Maryland to establish a temporary headquarters at Bryantown. The town was dangerously close to the Mudd residence, but fortunately for the fugitives Dana, who had established his headquarters in a tavern, was at the outset busily preoccupied with pursuing what proved to be the first of many deviations. Though having leads regarding Mudd, he had failed to follow up thereby allowing the fugitives more time to escape.[9]

***

Herold's sleep had been brief and quite probably fitful as after only two hours abed, perhaps aroused by the smell of breakfast being prepared by Mrs. Mudd's servants, he had risen and walked down stairs. Soon the help had also prepared a breakfast for Booth as well, which was delivered to his bedside. After eating, both men shaved while Mudd had a set of crutches made for his injured guest from a pair of planks. When the actor finally appeared, it was noticed that he had shaved off his signature mustache. There was little time to waste, but continuing their journey on horseback, Herold may have complained, would of necessity be arduous and painfully slow owing to his friend's injury. Perhaps eager to have the two men off before they were found on his farm, Mudd offered to ride with the young man into Bryantown, less than five miles from the farmhouse on the excuse he needed some household supplies. There they could secure a buggy or some other carriage in which to carry Booth. Both were entirely unaware that Lieutenant Dana and his troops, among the first of many thousands that would be deployed in the hunt for Lincoln's killer, had already reached and occupied the town.[10]

"John Wilkes Booth," (left), by Silsbee, Case & Co., photographic artists, Boston, and "David E. Herold, a conspirator, manacled. Washington Navy Yard, D.C., 1865," (right). Prints and Photographs Division, Library of Congress, Washington, D.C.

Within but a short time, the two riders were approaching Bryantown when the former drugstore clerk suddenly reined in his horse. Were those mounted men in uniform ahead? Yankee cavalry? His demeanor changed instantly. They didn't need a carriage after all, he told Mudd, and Booth could still mount his horse if necessary despite the injury. He must return to his colleague quickly, he nervously declared. He used as a handy excuse that he and Booth were to set off to visit the home of the Reverend Lemuel Wilmer at Piney Church, five miles west of Zekiah Swamp. Or so Mudd later testified.[11]

Though he later claimed he was puzzled by Herold's sudden change of plans, Samuel Mudd continued on into Bryantown, supposedly to shop for supplies and purchase some calico, soda and matches for his spouse. While casually chatting with several friends, someone exclaimed that the president had been shot last night and had died this morning. The assassin's name, it was first said, was John H. Boyle, a guerrilla who had threatened Unionists in the area. Soon afterwards he was informed that both detectives and cavalry were combing the countryside for none other than John Wilkes Booth, the man lying injured in his own upstairs bedroom.[12]

Mudd somehow maintained his composure, though apparently only now discovering that he was personally complicit in directly facilitating the flight of the president's killer. Even if they escaped but were later caught alive, it would surely go hard for him. After all, he had also been engaged in the kidnapping plot, which was certain to be revealed. Returning directly home, he realized, could be hazardous as soldiers blocked the main exits from the town, and he might be followed. Soon after departing via a circuitous route to skirt the checkpoints, he briefly rode off the main road to visit a friend named Francis Ferrell supposedly to inquire about securing some rail timber. Ferrel was employed by a neighbor named Thomas Hardy, and upon the physician's approach, Ferrell stepped out from Hardy's house to greet the visitor. He seemed anxious to learn the latest news of the assassination. Who had committed the crime? he asked. Mudd responded matter-of-factly: "A man named Booth," and declared the murder to be "one of the most terrible calamities that could have befallen the country at this time." It would, he solemnly acknowledged, make it even worse for the nation than when the war was going on.[13]

The Bryantown Tavern, later known as Murray's Hotel, Bryantown, Maryland, was used by John Wilkes Booth as a meeting place with Dr. Samuel Mudd in late 1864 while planning the kidnapping of President Lincoln. After Lincoln's assassination it was employed by the U.S. Army as headquarters in the search for Booth in Charles County, and later to hold suspects such as Dr. Samuel Mudd and Samuel Cox before their transfer to prison in Washington. Cox was ultimately released. Brady-Handy Photograph Collection, Prints and Photographs Division, Library of Congress, Washington, D.C.

In the meantime, Herold had hurried back to the Mudd farm to inform Booth, who had returned to his bed, that Union cavalry was already in the neighborhood. It was by then about 3 p.m. Despite the danger, the actor decided to await the doctor's return to learn the latest news, undoubtedly praying that he had not been betrayed. Three hours later, a much distressed Mudd arrived with confirmation that Lincoln was indeed dead.

The doctor did not attempt to hide his anxiety now, especially with the knowledge that if his guests were captured he would be deemed complicit in the conspiracies. He knew they must leave at once, but readily agreed to facilitate their flight as best he could. If the cavalry or Federal detectives should visit him, he promised to tell them only that he had attended to a pair of strangers requiring medical assistance, and then to dispatch the Yankees off in the opposite direction.

But who could be trusted now that news of the crime had spread, with cavalry patrols likely to be roaming about everywhere, and quite probably a hefty reward having been or soon to be posted? It has been stated in certain histories of the events that soon ensued that Mudd gave Booth the names of two local rebel operatives, William Burtles and Captain Samuel Cox, who could be counted upon as dependable. To reach the Burtles' place, two miles to the south, it would be necessary to maintain a healthy distance from Bryantown as they traveled to avoid Union cavalry patrols. From Burtles' it was only a few more miles to the southwest to Captain Cox's home, from which they could find assistance to cross the Potomac into Virginia. Mudd also recommended a physician in the Northern Neck who could attend to Booth's leg if need be. However, from his own account of events, it would appear that he had, in fact, provided them only with instructions on how to reach Reverend Wilmer's private residence at Piney Church via a short cut that would take them clear of the Yankee patrols. After Herold had assisted in getting Booth on his horse, Mudd watched them set off about 7 p.m. with a sigh of relief just as the evening sun disappeared.[14]

It was not to be an easy ride, for unable to determine east from west after the sun had set, the two fugitives soon became disoriented and lost. Herold cautiously scouted ahead and shortly came upon Electus Thomas, a black employee of Mudd's father, Thomas's wife, and two other men. He quickly discovered they were crossing the farmlands of Henry L. Mudd. They were clearly way off course, but soon recovered their bearings.[15]

For nearly two hours they pressed south in the dark, always attempting to keep to the east of the great Zekiah Swamp. It was about 9 p.m. when they happened upon Oswald Swann near his modest home, about two and a half miles to the southeast of Bryantown. After some persuasion, Swann, part Piscataway Indian and part black, who knew the region well, agreed to guide them through the marshes and directly to Captain Cox's doorstep for the princely sum of five dollars.[16]

For several hours the trio mucked through the fen. Sometime between midnight and 4 a.m., Easter Sunday, they reached Rich Hill, Cox's farm. Nervous, Herold ominously warned the guide to remain silent or "you will not live long." [17]

Again Herold took the lead, dismounted, approached the house on foot, and knocked on the door, while Booth remained hidden under cover of a nearby tree. "Who's there?" came a voice from a second story window. Unsure whether or not he could trust the man inside, Herold replied only that there was a man here who needed help.[18] With a degree of caution, Cox opened the door and examined the young man before him. At that moment he also saw another dismounting with difficulty from his horse beneath a tree near the gate to his yard and then hobbling towards him. He could not see the halfbreed, who was intently watching the proceedings from the dark edge of the yard.

Booth now threw caution to the wind, placing his full faith in a man said to be one of the leading secessionists in Charles County. Though he had never met his visitor, in the moonlight Cox was able to make out the letters J.W.B. in an India ink tattoo on Booth's hand and after some further discussion agreed to let the two strangers in. He knew instantly who the men were as he had learned of Lincoln's murder from one of his former slaves only hours earlier. With unvarnished candor, as the two men stood apart from Swann so as not to be heard, he informed Cox that he had shot Lincoln and needed his help.[19]

For the next three to four hours Oswald Swann watched attentively from the darkness as the three men conferred inside the residence.[20] It will never be known what specifically was said that night within the house. From subsequent events, however, it would appear that despite certain trepidations, and his son looking on, Cox agreed to assist the two visitors after Booth revealed all. The captain undoubtedly proved to be a cornucopia of information, but informed his guests that there was now only one man who could get them safely across the Potomac to Virginia.

Cox was, perhaps like Mudd, eager for the pair of night visitors to leave his house as soon as possible before someone, perhaps one of his many former slaves still working for him, might see them and report to the authorities. It was simply too dangerous to let the two fugitives remain on the farm. They would, he strongly recommended, have to go into seclusion for a time in a densely wooded pine thicket a quarter mile from the road and a mile from Rich Hill, where they would be safe from discovery by any locals. Promising to secure someone of unquestionable loyalty to the South to help get them across the Potomac, he instructed them to remain concealed and to build no fires. They were to await the sound of a particular three note whistle as a signal, which was to be given by their rescuer as he approached. Only then should they reveal themselves. The only man he could trust to assist them was his own foster brother, the Confederate Signal Agent in Maryland, Thomas A. Jones.[21]

***

Unknown to Booth and Herold, the Federals had finally begun to determine in which general direction that they had fled, beginning with information provided by John Lloyd after further visits and intensive interrogation by investigators. It seemed probable that they had headed southeast and not directly south from Washington. By the evening of April 16, it was deemed necessary to extend the barriers to their escape to include not only the Potomac, but also the Chesapeake Bay.

At 8:30 p.m., General Meigs issued instructions to the chief quartermaster at Baltimore to send out army patrol steamers from the Department of Baltimore to watch the Western Shore of the bay as far south as Point Lookout.

"Let a vessel watch particularly the mouth of the Patuxent River. Put three or four armed men on each tug or other steamer. Let them keep out of sight, and admit on board any persons desiring to come off from shore. Detain all such persons, overhaul all small vessels or boats, and detain them until examined. The murderers of the President and secretary of State have, it is believed, gone southeast, and will perhaps escape by water to the Eastern Shore, or to board some vessel waiting for them, or some vessel going to sea. The Potomac will be patrolled by steamers from Washington. Report the sailing of each vessel and the orders given her. Let a suitable vessel cruise up and down the bay and keep up communication. The object is to catch the murderers if they attempt this way of escape." [22]

Within twenty-four hours no fewer than seven army vessels, mostly chartered steamers that had already seen extensive service, had been deployed to cover a cruising area extending from Fort McHenry to the mouth of the Patuxent. Each vessel was armed, and carried besides crew, a sergeant and ten men. Their instructions were to stop and detain any and all small vessels and boats encountered on the bay and all individuals aboard them until ordered otherwise.[23] From Alexandria, at least one old steam canal boat, known as *Black Diamond*, employed by the Quartermaster's Department off and on since 1862 and manned with fire fighting volunteers from the United States Steam Engine Company, was dispatched to assist the navy in patrolling the Potomac.

On April 17 Commander Parker was informed by Secretary Stanton, inaccurately as it was later discovered, that Booth had been traced to Upper Marlboro on the Patuxent "and that he would like that river and the coast of Maryland from Point Lookout to Baltimore very carefully guarded." For once the U.S. Army and Navy would be operating harmoniously. Parker promptly informed Commander Eastman to take charge of the duty assigned by Stanton with the USS *Don* and any other boats that could be spared from the Potomac. He also suggested that boats be ordered up from Norfolk to cruise the bay, and Commander Wyman was so directed. Parker then made a careful disposition of the vessels then under his command. Ten gunboats and an armed sloop were assigned to patrol from Mattawoman Creek to the mouth of the Potomac. The ironclad monitor *Chimo* was to be stationed at Point Lookout, while two gunboats cruised from the point due east to the Maryland Eastern Shore, a distance of six miles, "intercepting all vessels bound down the bay, and sending them to General Barnes to be overhauled and detained." Four fast boats were to cruise between Point Lookout and Annapolis, and seven more were to patrol the coast of Maryland from Point Lookout to York River. Two boats were assigned to patrol the York, and three more the Eastern Shore coast of Virginia from Cherrystone to Smith Island. One boat each was assigned to the Gunpowder River, Bush River, and Havre de Grace. All were ordered to act in concert and cooperate fully with the military authorities.[24]

Not only was their mission to intercept any waterborne traffic departing Maryland, they had also been authorized to seize or destroy all watercraft, large and small, that might be employed by the fugitives to escape. The operations of the gunboat *Cactus*, Acting Master John Evans, which entered the Patuxent hell bent on rounding up every vessel encountered, was one such example. About 4 p.m., April 23, *Cactus* steamed up into Mill Creek, behind Johnson Island in Calvert County, and confiscated every boat found along the shores of the natural harbor, mostly fishing canoes, belonging to both black and white watermen. [25]

***

It was early Monday morning at Rich Hill when, provided with food, Booth and Herold saddled up again, hoping upon hope to reach Virginia by evening with the assistance of the man recommended by Mudd. Neither were apparently certain about the captain's true allegiance, despite his apparent willingness to help, for as they rode off, Oswald Swann overheard Herold state disparagingly: "I thought Cox was a man of Southern feeling." Then as they headed from the farm, guided by Franklin Robey, Cox's overseer, Swann too disappeared ghost like into the darkness.[26]

Upon reaching the appointed thicket, David Herold dismounted and assisted his mentor off his horse. They were now on their own again, obliged to place their trust in a man they had just met, who was to provide assistance from another they had yet to meet. Before returning to the farm, Robey sternly repeated Cox's instructions for them to remain quiet. He reiterated his boss's promise to send help soon, after agreeing upon the signal whistle. Then he too vanished.[27] Having laid their blankets out, Booth and Herold could do little more now than wait and attempted to sleep.

Back at Rich Hill, Cox wasted little time. Almost as soon as his visitors had departed, he dispatched his adopted son, Samuel Cox, Jr., to Jones' farm, approximately four miles to the southwest of his own. It was now imperative to secure his foster brother's help. With the Confederacy in collapse, and few trustworthy folks available to continue the resistance or aid rebel fugitives to safety, there seemed little alternative. Perhaps wary that his son might be stopped and questioned by Yankee patrols, he instructed the boy to tell Jones to come immediately to Rich Hill to talk about seed corn. When the youth reached Huckleberry, Jones's farm, however, and inadvertently mentioned that some strangers had been at his house the previous night, his uncle quickly understood the invitation for what it was. Informed the evening before by two soldiers on patrol that Lincoln's assassin might be heading his way, he quickly surmised who the strangers must be. Nevertheless, he resolved to ride with Samuel Jr. to Rich Hill to find out for himself [28]

A few hours later, in an open clearing at Cox's farm where they might not be overheard, the conversation between the two men was terse. "Tom," said Cox, getting immediately to the point, "I had visitors about four o'clock this morning."

"Who were they, and what did they want?" queried Jones.

For a moment there was silence,

"They want to get across the river. Have you heard that Lincoln was killed Friday night?" [29]

Jones nodded, replying quietly that he had found out from the soldiers passing through the night before. For a moment there was complete silence between the two men. Once again, he must have reflected, he found himself in a most difficult position, but unlike those of earlier days. The money he had invested in now worthless Confederate bonds was gone. Having just visited Richmond to collect payment owed to him for three years of service as a signal agent, he had arrived just in time to discover the city abandoned by Lee's army, and to find his hopes for compensation for his dedicated labors bitterly crushed. He was broke. His wife was dead. The war was over. "Nothing now," he thought to himself, "could raise from the dust the trailing Stars and Bars." He knew that the whole of Southern Maryland was even then swarming with soldiers and detectives, "like bloodhounds on the trail, eager to avenge the murder of their beloved President and reap their reward." Now, he was being asked to put his life on the line again, without any payment whatsoever and for a cause and way of life that had been all but extinguished, to facilitate the escape of the assassin who had killed the President of the United States. Though in the South he might be looked upon as blameless, in the North he knew he would be judged a "vile aider and abettor of a wretched stained dark a crime as the recording angel ever wrote down in the eternal book of doom." [30]

"Tom, we must get these men who were here this morning across the river," declared Cox passionately. He then enlightened him about the meeting with Booth.

"Tom," he begged, "can't you put these men across?"

"Sam," Jones replied solemnly, "I will see what I can do, but the odds are against me. I must see these men; Where are they?" [31]

Cox gave him their location and the sound of the agreed upon three whistle signal after also informing him that they had already spent a night in the thicket awaiting rescue. "Take care how you approach them, Tom. They are fully armed and might shoot you through mistake." [32]

Jones departed soon after and made his way to the thicket. As he approached he observed a mare, apparently unattended, grazing in a small clearing. Possibly a stray, he told himself, and tied the animal to a tree. At the perimeter of the ticket he whistled the designated signal and waited. Suddenly he found himself confronting the muzzle of a Spencer carbine, cocked and ready.

"Who are you, and what do you want?" said David Herold.

"I come from Cox," replied Jones. "He told me I would find you here. I am a friend. You have nothing to fear from me."

"Follow me," said the rifleman, releasing his grip on his weapon ever so slightly as he turned back into the piney thicket.[33]

A short distance on, Cox found a pale, unshaven, crumpled looking man lying on the ground with pistol, knife, a crude crutch, and a blanket drawn partly across him. The man's dark clothes were stained and dirty, and his face bore signs of distress and pain. In a matter of minutes confidence was restored, and Booth informed Jones of the details of the assassination. The probability of escape was limited, but it seemed to matter little to the man on the ground. Referring to himself in the third person, as he often did for theatrical effect, the infamous actor vowed that "John Wilkes Booth will never be taken alive!" [34]

Nevertheless, the master of Huckleberry, ignoring Booth's dramatic display, laid out a plan that just might work, a plan that required patience and total reliance upon him. The two fugitives would have to stop running, remain hidden in the thicket and absolutely silent until he determined that the soldiers now canvassing the area had departed and conditions were right on the river for a nighttime crossing. "You must remain right here, however long," he told them, "and wait till I can see some way to get you out; and I do not believe I can get you away from here until this hue and cry is somewhat over. Meantime, I will see that you are fed." [35] There would be, he concluded, no medical assistance for Booth until after crossing, but there was little alternative.

Booth agreed, asking only that when Jones returned he bring copies of current Washington newspapers detailing the assassination. He was not just eager to read of his deed and what the world thought of him, but to see if the letter he had given his friend John Matthews justifying his actions had also been published.[36]

***

For Edwin Stanton, who was desperately attempting to plug all the holes of escape that Lincoln's murderer might possibly employ, reports coming from St. Mary's County had been especially disturbing but also hopeful. There had been a number of unverified sightings of Booth, but nothing had been pinned down. The most troubling related to a report that had reached military authorities well to the southeast in Leonardtown. At Point Lookout, General Barnes was informed in the early morning of April 15, while still unaware of the assassination, that a party of well armed Confederate soldiers, twenty-seven privates and three officers strong, had been spotted eighteen miles from the county seat. The specifics were foggy and their location was reported as somewhere between the village of Newport and Crookshank's Store near St. Inigoes. The sighting had reportedly been passed on to a Union scouting party sent out from Leonardtown on routine patrol. The only information available, however, that the rebels were headed in the direction of the Patuxent River, was questionable. The initial supposition offered by Captain Seneca G. Willauer, then commanding at Leonardtown, was that their objective was to capture a Chesapeake Bay steamer. After all, hadn't three vessels been captured by Confederate raiders on the bay only days earlier? "There is no doubt but that there are armed bands in the district," he reported. "I will be on the alert and do all I can with the forces at my disposal." A cavalry unit under Captain Francis F. Buckley was dispatched in the direction of the refugee farms on the Patuxent to investigate, even as Barnes was notifying General Augur in Washington of the purported incursion.[37]

Buckely arrived at the farms that same evening. His report of what allegedly followed was succinct. "I have overtaken about thirty-five men of Garland Smith's command, and captured one prisoner," he informed his superiors the following day. "Some very heavy skirmishing took place about 10 o'clock near Mechanicsville, in which I lost one man. I had to fall back in consequence of not having men enough." An urgent request was made to Willauer to send all the men he could spare to the refugee farms. Lieutenant Edward F. O'Brien of the Veteran Reserve Corps, then in charge of the farms but not present at the time, was also informed by Buckely of his alleged fight with Smith's men at the edge of the farms. All of the rebels were believed to belong to John S. Mosby's notorious raiders. O'Brien gathered as many men as possible and rushed to the rescue after telegraphing the Chief of the Bureau of Government Farms in Washington requesting additional reinforcements.[38]

On April 17, even as John Wilkes Booth and David Herold were meeting with Thomas Jones in their uncomfortable hiding place, Edwin Stanton was reading the first reports, passed on by Augur, of the elusive guerrilla band said to be roaming about in St. Mary's County. He had soon convinced himself that the group was somehow connected to the assassination, and quickly dispatched instructions to Barnes. "The murderers of the president and Secretary Seward are no doubt in the gang of rebels mentioned in your telegram. Have the Navy vessels scour the coast, and spare no effort to arrest and hold them. Put your whole force on the work as far as can be done with safety to your command." [39]

General Barnes, who had been apprised of the assassination almost immediately after sending his report to Augur late on April 15, may well have also suspected linkage between Booth and the mysterious guerrilla band even before Seward's instruction arrived, for he had already taken action. On the evening of the 17th he informed Augur "I have sent reinforcements of cavalry and infantry to Leonard-town today, and the greatest enthusiasm is manifest by all the men to overtake the band prowling in that district. They have not been able to find them today, but no place will be left unvisited. The gunboats are all on the alert, and the Patuxent and Potomac are closely watched. Extra pains will be taken on the river tonight." [40] He also relayed a dispatch from Stanton to the naval forces at Point Lookout and St. Inigoes alerting them to the guerrilla band and directing them to "scour the coast, and spare no effort to arrest and hold them." [41] All steamers bound down the bay were to be hailed and ordered to proceed to Point Lookout and remain there until further orders. A strict patrol between Point Lookout and the Patuxent was to be established, with the gunboat *Nansemond* being sent to the latter, while the USS *Thomas Freeborn, Delaware* and *Mystic* would patrol the bay in a line across from St. Mary's County. All vessels not already employed on duty at Hampton Roads were to be sent to further enhance the blockade of the Eastern Shore of Virginia and Maryland coast from Point Lookout to Baltimore.[42]

From XXII Corps headquarters in Washington General Halleck ordered a battalion of the 8th Illinois Cavalry under Major John M. Waite to canvas the St. Mary's countryside. One of Waite's companies was to strike out for Benedict on the Patuxent to follow up that waterway, and while they were there seize a blockade running schooner called *Lydia* reported to be in the river. A second was to be dispatched to scour the countryside down the Potomac, with particular focus on the Wicomico River and vicinity where they might apprehend a number of runners reportedly in the area and destroy their boats. A third, under the major's personal command, was to head for Leonardtown and assist an infantry detachment sent out from there to Allen's Fresh to also capture a blockade running schooner called *Breeze* said to be in the vicinity.[43]

Yet the most important objective of the mission was of course the capture of Booth. "There is in that vicinity of the county a band of guerillas," Waite was informed, "who are supposed to have collected for the purpose of assisting in the escape of the conspirators. The special object of your expedition will be to capture and destroy this band, to arrest all suspicious persons, allow no one to pass who cannot explain his business and status satisfactorily." Employing Leonardtown as his base of operations, he was authorized to search houses and make arrests at his own discretion and to cover the countryside, especially in the Patuxent region, where it was reported the rebels were headed.[44]

***

For Lewis Payne, the events following his attack on Secretary Seward and family had been challenging. He knew little of Washington and, without Herold's guidance had quickly become lost in the city. Somehow his half blind horse had gone astray, and he had wandered aimlessly about on foot still wearing his bloodstained coat, sleeping in trees at night. With a poster now circulating showing the faces of three men believed to have been involved in the assassination plot, John Wilkes Booth, David Herold and John Surratt, it was clear that it would only be a matter of time before he too was implicated. His only hope was to find the safety of the Widow Surratt's boarding house. Or so he thought.

Unfortunately for Payne, as the sweep for potential conspirators in Washington intensified on April 17, General Augur's attention had returned to the Surratt family, even though the initial visit by city detectives had turned up nothing. That evening, Major Henry Warren Smith, then on duty at the Freedmen's Bureau, while also serving as assistant adjutant general to Augur, received orders to visit Mary's H Street boardinghouse and "arrest her and any suspicious personages" he might find there. The linkage between Mary, Lloyd and Booth was damning. This time soldiers were dispatched, arriving just as the Surratt's were preparing for bed, to interrogate both Mary and her daughter Anna, after which they were to be arrested and transported by carriage to army headquarters.[45]

It was quite dark, bordering on 11 p.m., only minutes after the soldiers' arrival and entry into the boardinghouse when the guards stationed at the front door heard a knock and then the doorbell. Upon opening the door they were confronted by a powerful "villainous looking person" standing on the front steps armed with a pickaxe and dressed in a gray coat and black pantaloons. He was muddy and scruffy looking. "His boots were rather fine . . . had red tops to the legs. The pantaloons were tucked into the top of one of his boots, and the other leg was hanging round his feet. He had on his head a woolen sleeve, appearing like a nightcap . . . which he had pulled down over his head, letting the end hang down like a tassel." With little ceremony, he stepped inside and announced that he was there to see Mrs. Surratt and asked if he was at the correct address. After being informed that he was at the right place, he was immediately subjected to a fusillade of questions. Who was he? Why was he there so late in the evening? How old was he? What was his occupation? Where did he live?[46]

Though Lewis Payne could not have picked a more inappropriate moment to find the Surratt boarding house, now filled with Union soldiers, he somehow maintained his self-control. Claiming that the Widow Surratt had seen him working in the neighborhood and offered him a job digging out a ditch in the backyard, he declared that he was there to see what time she wanted him to start in the morning.[47]

Then came the inevitable confrontation when Mary appeared. "Do you know this man? And did you hire him to dig a ditch for you?" Mary was asked, as she stood face to face with Payne.

"Before God, sir, I do not know this man," she lied, "and I have never seen him and did not hire him to dig a gutter for me." [48]

Though armed with a dangerous looking pickax, Lewis Payne surrendered without a fight and identified himself. Within a few hours he was readily pointed out by Seward's young manservant, William H. Bell, as the mad fanatic who had assaulted the secretary, his sons and Sergeant Robinson.[49] At 5 a.m. April 18 the ex-Confederate soldier and loyal henchman to John Wilkes Booth was carried in chains onboard the ironclad *Saugus*, anchored in midstream off the Washington Navy Yard, and interred until further notice.[50] Onboard the warship, final confirmation of the identity of the would-be-assassin was made when Augustus Seward was brought face to face with him. Payne was made to repeat, "I'm mad! I'm mad!" and was instantly identified as the assailant.[51]

At the Surratt boarding house, Mary and Anna Surratt, Lewis Weichmann, and all of the boarders therein were arrested. This time a more thorough search of the house was undertaken, and ammunition and a photograph of Booth, concealed behind a picture frame belonging to Anna, as well as images of Jefferson Davis and several Confederate generals were discovered. Despite her dire predicament, Mary remained calm and in control of her wits during the intensive questioning that ensued at headquarters, revealing nothing that her interrogators didn't already know about her son, Payne, Adzerodt, and Booth.[52] Though soon afterwards sent to the Old Capitol Prison with her daughter, from which she would never return home again, Mary Surratt remained stoic and strong until the end.

By now the roundup of suspected conspirators was relentless, some having been little more involved than being at the wrong place at the wrong time. Others taken into custody in the roundup were acquaintances such as Ned Spangler, or men involved, knowingly or unknowingly in various stages of Booth's plotting such as Samuel Arnold and Michael O'Laughlen. Spangler was arrested at Ford's Theater for the crime of holding Booth's horse, though only for a moment, and for failing to inform which way the assassin had escaped. Both Arnold and O'Laughlen, ex-Confederate soldiers, had known Booth in their childhood and school years, and had been active participants in the scheme to kidnap the president, but not in the murder. The Fords and other theater employees were also rounded up as suspects in the plot, as was Harry Hawk. The theater itself was ordered closed, with a round-the-clock guard mounted to maintain it as a sterile crime scene. The noted photographer Matthew Brady was sent to produce a photographic record of its key components as it was at the time of the murder. The theater itself would eventually be confiscated by the government.[53]

A search of Adzerodt's room at Kirkwood House readily linked the carriage maker's roll in the plot to Booth, although he alone had refused to carry through on his assigned mission and simply walked away. It mattered little now. Soon, he too would be located, arrested and, like other suspects, taken in chains aboard the USS *Saugus*. There he readily confessed to his roll in both the plot to kidnap and later to kill the president, vice president and secretary of state, while directly incriminating both Samuel Mudd and Mary Surratt in the process. Soon after Adzerodt's capture, Stanton authorized a reward of $100,000 for the apprehension of the key assassin.[54]

***

Samuel Mudd, unaware of having been implicated by others, was anxious to dispel the inevitable suspicion he was certain Federal authorities might have about him as their net tightened. Yet he was determined not to betray the man with whom he had once been in league. Pre-emptive disinformation, he believed, was the best course of action. Thus he dispatched a cousin, George Mudd, to report to the cavalry in Bryantown on the late night arrival of two "strangers" seeking medical assistance at the doctor's residence. The messenger, for unknown reasons, delayed his visit to the town for more than a day. When he finally delivered the information to Lieutenant Dana, however, it was immediately ignored as being dated and inconsequential, as the officer was already preoccupied with following other leads, all of which were false. On April 18 Mudd was again visited by the U.S. Cavalry, this time two dozen riders under the command of Lieutenant Alexander Lovett with cousin George in tow.[55]

At the farm, both Samuel and his wife Sarah were questioned while the house, barn and outbuildings were searched in vain. The doctor seemed unnaturally edgy as he provided the lieutenant with a bare bones account of a visit by two men on horseback, one with a broken leg. He neither knew, he claimed, nor could provide anything but an imperfect description of either one. When asked which route the two men had set out upon when leaving, he pointed them off in the opposite direction from the one they had taken. Lovett was convinced the now visibly nervous physician had merely been presenting "a blind to throw us off track." He could prove nothing, but was convinced the doctor was somehow complicit. He was also certain that he would be coming back to make an arrest of importance.[56]

On April 21, when Lovett returned, Mudd's well rehearsed story rapidly began to crumble. Upon "discovery" of Booth's slit leather boot, which his wife Sarah claimed had been found under a bed while dusting the front bedroom, the doctor began to slowly reveal all, especially when inspection of the inside revealed the name "H. Lux, maker. 445 Broadway. J. Wilkes." That Booth had been there was now certain. Mudd's arrest was immediate.[57]

***

Tuesday morning, April 18. At Huckleberry, Thomas A. Jones conducted the morning farm chores after breakfast as always. If anyone was watching, he well knew from years of experience how to avoid suspicion. Federal soldiers had already visited his farm several times and searched his house, but he had remained calm. Now, he gathered up a bit of food, bread, butter, some ham, and a flask of coffee, which he stuffed in his coat pockets, along with a folded newspaper. At 10 a.m., carrying a bag of corn over one arm, which he could claim to any inquisitive soldier was intended for his hogs, which ran wild in the forest, he set off for the assassin's hideaway.[58]

Within a short time he was approaching the concealed encampment. A hundred yards from the thicket, he dismounted, tied his horse, whistled and, unlike his previous visit, was immediately welcomed. The hungry fugitives feasted, and Booth took delight at seeing his name in print, though dismayed that the letter he had given to his actor friend John Mathews to deliver to the *National Intelligencer* had not been published. Though he could not have known it, being frightened at the prospect of being implicated in the assassination plot, his friend had destroyed the document. To make matters worse his leg injury had degenerated from ugly to appalling, as was the pain. But there was still the business of the moment to attend to with Jones, and physical discomfort would have to be ignored to make rational decisions.[59]

Unfortunately, as the three men began to discuss escape options, the clopping of approaching horses and the clanking of metal sabers caused an instant halt to speech. For Jones, the sound of Union cavalry riding towards the thicket was all too familiar. Escape was impossible. With just two revolvers and a Spencer carbine for defense, there was no chance of winning in a fight. Their only hope was to stay low in the thicket, remain quiet, and pray for the best. Within several minutes the soldiers, all black troopers belonging to the 8th Illinois Cavalry, passed within 200 yards, but stayed on the road until they finally disappeared.[60]

"You see, my friend," said Jones, "we must wait."

"Yes," replied Booth with resignation, "I leave it all with you." [61]

With cavalry in the area there were considerations to be addressed other than just keeping out of sight, food and escape routes. Though Jones promised to return the next morning with another meal, he would not, he informed the fugitives, be bringing feed for the horses. Not only was it difficult to carry and likely to raise suspicions among Union patrollers, the horses themselves had become a liability as they were hungry, restive, often noisy, and might attract the soldiers.

"If we can hear those horses," Jones declared, pointing in the direction of the departing cavalrymen, "they can certainly the neighing of ours, which are uneasy from want of food and stabling." [62]

They would simply have to be put down. After Jones's departure, Herold led the two unfortunate animals into a quicksand pit in a nearby fen where he shot both and let their bodies sink from view. He then returned to the hiding place and would pass yet another uncomfortable night with Booth in the obscure pine thicket of lower Charles County.[63]

In the meantime, after again consulting with Cox, Jones resolved "the first night the neighborhood was clear of soldiers and detectives to get my charges to the river at Dent's Meadow and let them cross in the boat I kept for that purpose." [64] It was thus deemed necessary to visit Port Tobacco on Tuesday, a day usually reserved for public transactions in the county, to glean what information he could regarding the hunt for Lincoln's killer. The town, he knew, was often visited by Union troops from army camps long situated close to Chapel Point, Hill Top and other sites nearby. There was, he knew from experience, no better place to pick up the latest news and a drink than in the Brawner's Hotel bar. He did not have long to wait. While at the bar, he heard a Federal officer named Williams extend a reward of $100,000 "to anyone who will give me the information that will lead to Booth's capture."

"That is a large sum of money," said Jones in mock amazement, unwilling to take the bait, "and ought to get him if money can do it." [65]

Though talk of the reward was on everyone's lips, Jones was not tempted though it was obvious that with such a price on their heads escape by the two fugitives would now be more difficult than ever.

For days soldiers had been riding hither and yon about the countryside, visiting every house in the region, even penetrating the marshlands, but never the dense pines and thickets through which travel on horseback was difficult. Several more times the patrols visited Huckleberry, but learned nothing.[66]

***

The tension throughout the region was palpable, with thousands of troops and scores of ships actively or soon to be engaged in the massive manhunt, and the demand for revenge often blistering the fabric of reason and logic.[67] On the morning of April 15, after being formally notified of the president's death in a brief letter signed by members of the Cabinet, Attorney General James Speed informed Vice President Andrew Johnson: "The office of president has devolved under the Constitution upon you." At 11 a.m., little more than three and a half hours after Lincoln drew his last breath, Chief Justice Salmon Chase issued the oath of office to the new President of the United States in his room at Kirkwood House.[68] It was, however, Secretary Stanton who was to bear the brunt of the massive responsibilities of state. Several rebel armies, though in total disarray, were still operative in the field and had to be dealt with, as did Jefferson Davis who was still on the run. There was also the institution of Lincoln's plans for reconstruction that had to be attended to. And, of course, there was the search for the president's assassin and the possibility of a general conspiracy to overthrow the government to be addressed. He needed help, someone to take over the search for the killers and investigators to bring to ground other possible conspirators while he attended to the national crisis. Thus, request for assistance was dispatched to the New York City police for detectives. Less than five hours after the assassination Stanton had also summoned from New York Lieutenant Colonel Lafayette Baker, now head of the National Detective Police, which was attached to the War Department. "Come here immediately and see if you can find the murderers of the president." As one of the secretary's favorites, the colonel seemed just the man for the job and on April 16 arrived in the capital eager to take command of the chase.[69]

For the moment, however, there was also the very real and poignant issue of dealing with the late president's formal funeral.

On April 19, a clear and sunny day, tens of thousands of men, women and children watched and wept as Lincoln's coffin, wrapped in crepe and drawn by six splendid white horses, moved slowly down Pennsylvania Avenue from the White House to the U.S. Capitol, where the president's body would lie in state. There, in the center of the magnificent Capitol Rotunda, a select group of 600 mourners, including Supreme Court justices, Cabinet members, foreign diplomats, clergy, businessmen, civil and military leaders of the nation, its states and great cities, and others would attend a private service, surrounding the coffin. The following day, the public was to be admitted to have one last look at the man who had saved the Union and ended slavery. On the morning of April 21 the president's coffin would be removed from the Capitol, placed aboard a train and dispatched to Springfield, Illinois for final interment.

In the meantime, the hunt for the conspirators continued to expand. Even as the solemnities of Lincoln's funeral were taking place, investigators were preparing to search the residence of Asa Booth Clarke, John Wilkes Booth's sister, and seize anything remotely connected to the assassin. And in the Southern Maryland countryside, the search for Booth himself had intensified to a fever pitch.

***

Thomas A. Jones was a diligent but extremely patient man. To survive the always perilous role of Chief Confederate Signal Agent in Maryland, such attributes had been a necessity. Now his stoic perseverance in getting the two fugitives hiding in the nearby pine thickets down to the Potomac and off to Virginia was about to bear fruit.

One of Jones's most trusted helpers was Henry Woodland, an able net fisherman. Knowing he was reliable and loyal, Jones had pressed the former slave into service early on in the escape, though never mentioning what it was all about. His only directive was for the old man to carry on his fishing activities as normal, but at day's end to bring his boat in at Dent's Meadow, the narrow valley opening behind Huckleberry, a mile and a half north of Pope's Creek and in an uninhabited area a mile from the public road. There the diminutive waterway was shouldered and sheltered by wooded cliffs, which had served him so well over the previous years in his secret operations for the Confederacy. Here the boat could remain hidden from both land and water patrols until needed to ferry the two fugitives across the river. But Woodland had no inclination as to why he had been given the order. And it was well that Jones did not tell him for on one occasion the former slave was questioned and threatened by the Yankees to tell all he knew. But he knew nothing.[70]

Thomas A. Jones, (left) Chief Confederate Signal Agent in Maryland, who assisted John Wilkes Booth in his escape, and "Huckleberry," (right), Jones' residence near Pope's Creek, Maryland, from which he served the Confederacy for four years. Thomas A. Jones, *J. Wilkes Booth: An Account of His Journey in Southern Maryland after the Assassination of Abraham Lincoln, his Passage Across the Potomac, and his Death in Virginia* (Chicago: Laird & Lee, publishers, 1893).

Everything was readied for the most opportune moment when the bluecoats would be looking the other way. That moment arrived on Friday, April 21 when Jones rode into Allen's Fresh, where the great Zekiah Swamp ends and the Wicomico River begins, as he had done every day since Booth had been in hiding, to gather information regarding the ongoing search. While visiting Richard Colton's store, where a number of cavalrymen were drinking, he overheard the excited directives of one soldier, a Marylander from St. Mary's named John R. Walton, who had just entered. "Boys," said the breathless man, "I have news that they have been seen in St. Mary's." The information Jones knew referred to Booth and Herold and was, of course, totally incorrect, but it posed just the opportunity he had been waiting. He watched intently as the troopers quickly mounted their horses and rode off out of town towards the east and well away from their actual quarry.[71]

Jones immediately departed. There was not a second to lose. By the time he was nearing Booth's hideaway, it was already dark and a fog was starting to slink across the countryside. As usual, he approached cautiously, giving the signal whistle, and was soon met by Herold. Wracked by pain in his fractured leg and frustrated by his immobility, Booth was in a black and sour mood. His impatience to cross the river, recalled Jones, had become insufferable. But now the moment was at hand. "The coast seems to be clear and the darkness favors us," said Jones. "Let us make the attempt." [72]

The moment of escape was at hand, but before setting off the master of Huckleberry gave a few brief instructions. "I will get you some supper at my house," he whispered, "and send you off if I can. Now as we cannot see twenty yards before us, I will go ahead. We must not speak. When I get to the point where everything is clear from me to you, I will whistle so." Giving a simple whistling signal, he set out on foot, walking between fifty and sixty yards ahead of Booth who was riding Jones's horse and Herold who was on foot. Quietly they abandoned the pine thicket campsite. Reaching the public road and then passing several negro shacks in silence, they turned and headed for the farm. Finally arriving at their destination, they halted some fifty yards from the farmhouse.[73]

Jones walked briskly to the building, leaving his companions hidden in the darkness beneath two pear trees, and upon entering spoke briefly with Henry Woodland. Supper was waiting on the table, but he focused his attention on the old man. Was the boat in place in Dent's Meadow, he asked? Woodland replied in the affirmative. Without further adieu, he gathered enough food from the table for the two fugitives, though he ignored the coffee, for which Booth had begged. With so many black servants, former slaves, in the house it would simply not be safe as someone might become suspicious of their boss taking hot coffee with him at such a late hour.[74]

Within but a short time, Jones rejoined the two fugitives beneath the pear trees. Together they quietly set off for Dent's Meadow, less than a mile away. At a fence line, which the horse could not cross, Booth was obliged to dismount, and with Herold under one arm and Jones under the other, press slowly forward on foot. Upon arrival, Jones fetched the twelve-foot-long boat by wading into the shallows. Soon, both Booth and Herold were aboard, the former stationed in the stern with the steering oar and the latter in the oarsman's seat near the bow. Jones handed them their weapons, food, and Booth's crutch.[75]

Almost ceremonially, the master of Huckleberry handed Booth a candle from his coat pocket and advised him to conceal its glow during crossing. He then told him to take out his own compass, and instructed him in the course he must steer by in the dark. "Keep to that and it will bring you into Machodoc Creek. Mrs. Quesenberry lives near the mouth of this creek. If you tell her you came from me, I think she will take care of you."

Few words were spoken as Jones began to shove the boat into the waterway.

"Wait a minute," said Booth, who then handed his guide eighteen dollars in payment for the boat. Jones refused to accept only what he had paid for the vessel a year earlier in Baltimore. "God bless you, my dear friend for all you have done for me," said the murderer in all sincerity. "Goodbye, old fellow." [76]

46

IN THE BARN
"Prepare a stretcher for me."

Secretary Stanton was now certain that the fugitives were being harbored in the lower counties of Maryland. Even as Booth and Herold had been hiding in the pine thickets of Charles County, investigators and the military had been piecing the puzzle together from its many disparate parts. Dr. Mudd had finally been arrested, as had Surratt, Adzerodt and many others even remotely associated with Booth and his plot to kidnap or kill the president. Those in Southern Maryland who had assisted in any way, the secretary declared, would also be held accountable.

"The counties of Prince George's, Charles, and St. Mary's," he wrote, "have, during the whole war, been noted for hostility to the government and their protection to rebel blockade runners, rebel spies, and every species of public enemy. The murderers of the President harbored there before the murder, and Booth fled in that direction. If he escapes, it will be owing to rebel accomplices in that region. The military commander of the department will speedily take measures to bring these rebel sympathizers and accomplices in the murder to a sense of their criminal conduct. " [1]

The massive manhunt throughout St. Mary's County by Major Waite's cavalry had been tireless and ongoing since April 20th. It had been underway, searching in every direction without a break for forty eight hours, but nothing could be learned of the purported guerilla band. "Officers report the driest scouting," the major reported in frustration on the afternoon of the 22nd. "Have had five parties out today in as many different directions. Have heard from all except the one scouting up and down the Patuxent on this side. Have also sent party of eighty to scout Calvert County. They will cross at Benedict in steamers." [2]

Incredibly, Waite was astonished to learn that the reported fight between Buckley's cavalry and the alleged force of guerrillas "was all a humbug." It had never happened! As with a substantial portion of news filtering back to military headquarters in Washington and Baltimore during the frenzied search for Booth, the actual existence of an elusive guerrilla band in St. Mary's, was pure fiction based on little more than hearsay and tweaked by false reporting, for unknown reasons, by a U.S. Army officer in the field. Or had it been part of the conspiracy designed to siphon troops away from the assassin's actual hiding place? Whatever the answer was, the end product had indeed been to draw off almost all the Federal troops canvassing Charles County, a massive diversion of Federal resources that would allow the escape of the very criminals the U.S. Army and Navy had been sent out to apprehend. When Captain Buckley was finally questioned at Bryantown about the purported fight, he confessed that he had never even seen a rebel. Moreover, Captain Willauer, commander of the Leonardtown garrison, reported that one of the scouts Buckley claimed lost in the alleged skirmish had merely fallen from his horse and had just come in. "There may be now and then a rebel soldier in the county," Major Waite concluded with unvarnished frustration, "but there is no armed band." [3]

Nevertheless, the search had proceeded without letup as the latest shreds of intelligence continued to filter down to the searchers, altering their investigations in fits and starts. On the same day Waite learned that the rebel band never existed, he received a report from headquarters that redirected his search once again. "Booth fell near Bryantown and broke his leg," he was informed. "Is supposed to have gone toward the Wicomico River, probably with the view of getting down the stream and thence across the river. His accomplice, Herold, is with him." [4]

General Augur was taking no chances and informed Commander Parker. "There is reason to believe that Booth and his accomplice are in the swamps about Allen's Fresh, emptying into the Wicomico River. He is evidently trying to cross into Virginia. Have you the Potomac well guarded about there and above. Fearing he may have already crossed, I wish to send a force of cavalry to Nomini Bay. Can I land horses there or in that vicinity, and with how much water? Please inform me at once." [5]

Anxious and apparently without waiting for a reply, Augur ordered a battalion of 16th New York Cavalry under Colonel Nelson B. Sweitzer to embark aboard a Quartermaster's Department steamer and land on the Virginia shore as nearly opposite the Wicomico, "probably at or near Nomini River, as practicable." Once ashore, the colonel was ordered to use his troopers as he thought best to find the assassin and his accomplice.[6] By the time Parker's response was received that same evening, that there was no wharf in Nomini Bay, but there was a "good landing in Coan River with eight feet of water about fifteen miles below where cavalry can disembark very readily," the expedition was already well underway.[7]

Yet rumors, false leads and erroneous sightings of Booth at various locales in the county continued to proliferate and draw off even more searchers from Charles County. One such account reported from Leonardtown by steamer from Point Lookout to Washington, stated that "a person bearing the exact description of J. Wilkes Booth" had been spotted making preparations to cross the Potomac a short distance from the point on April 18. He had supposedly "engaged a colored man to ferry him across, but the boat being intercepted, he made a hasty return to the Maryland shore. The colored man was captured, however, and is now a prisoner at the Point." But nothing had actually been confirmed.[8]

Another account turned in to Waite on April 23 was equally frustrating. "Sergeant Bagley, of the mounted detachment stationed at Millstone Landing, informs me that J. Wilkes Booth was seen passing through Great Mills on foot about 9 o'clock this morning. He is dressed in women's attire. The sergeant and his men are in pursuit. I will send all the cavalry I have out immediately. Everything shall be done that can be done to secure him. The citizens recognized him as he was passing through." Again, the subject proved to be a red herring.[9]

***

John Wilkes Booth may have recalled with some comfort a line from Shakespeare's *Romeo and Juliet* as his boat moved silently from Dent's Marsh into the dark Potomac. "I have night's cloak to hide me from their sight." It was not the cloak that he was counting on, however, but a candle, pocket compass, and Jones' directions that he hoped would soon guide him to the Virginia shore and safety, just six miles away. Yet as Herold the oarsman and Booth the helmsman both proved a poor match for the devious river currents, but more significantly for Yankee patrol boats, the success of the voyage was anything but assured.

Only hours before the fugitives launched their fragile little boat into the dark Potomac, Navy Secretary Welles had issued orders to Lieutenant Commander Eastman to send out a steamer to locate and destroy all boats on both shores of the river. General Augur, too, had issued a directive to Commander Parker to maintain "a rigid and active blockade of all the Potomac" to prevent Booth's possible escape into Virginia," and to communicate the order to all tugs and other U.S. Army Quartermasters' boats that were now guarding the entirety of the waterway's navigable reaches. Patrols were to be ongoing day and night, even as the public was being informed that a reward of no less than $100,000 was being offered for the capture of the notorious tragedian now known to be crippled and moving about on crutches.[10]

Evading the ubiquitous river patrols would prove the next great challenge. Booth and Herold had been on the water but a short time when the ominous silhouette of a gunboat suddenly loomed out of the darkness, anchored some 300 yards away. Instantly startled, Herold stopped rowing, hoping upon hope they had not been seen or heard. Fortunately for the fugitives, the ship apparently failed to spot them in the shadows of night. Slowly but incessantly, as they were now driven by the current, their course was altered to the northwest instead of the southwest bearing they had been on, which would have assuredly resulted in capture. Now, locked in by a muscular spring tide, of which Jones had failed to inform them, they were soon rounding the northern tip of Mathias Point, moving rapidly in the opposite direction to the one that they had set out upon.[11]

Finally in the leaden gray dawn, Herold spotted the profile of a landmark he could recognize. It was Blossom Point at the mouth of Nanjemoy Creek, just four miles upriver from where they had started out, but in Maryland and not Virginia.[12] Yet all was perhaps not as bad as it seemed, for Herold had friends and acquaintances in the area.

It was morning when the boat put ashore at the mouth of the creek, and its two passengers slowly made their way towards a nearby estate called Indianhead, belonging to Peregrine "Perry" Davis, the once controversial Democratic Party delegate from the Second Election District arrested for dispensing pro-secessionist rhetoric in his campaign. He had also been, for the previous five or six years, Herold's close friend and hunting companion.[13]

Unfortunately for the fugitives, Davis was absent, but his son-in-law John Hughes, who farmed the tract, was at home. Given the alarm that had spread throughout Southern Maryland, the farmer refused to admit them into his house, though they were fed, provided with the latest news, and permitted to lodge in an old slave cabin for the night. Booth was crushed. With Federal troops racing about the countryside and gunboats patrolling the Potomac, the two men seemed temporarily paralyzed and unable to do more than hunker down and wait in the remote wetlands of Nanjemoy Creek. In the meantime, Hughes set off for Port Tobacco to consult with an attorney, since anyone even remotely associated with the two criminals was now likely to be arrested or worse for aiding and abetting murderers. His counsel informed him to relate all to the Federal authorities. Now,

Booth's window of opportunity for escape across the Potomac was rapidly closing. There could be no further delay despite the Yankee river patrols.[14]

For the next day, Booth lay in pain, agonizing over his situation. On the evening of April 22, as he worked up his courage once again to try a crossing into Virginia, he sat in the dark slave cabin near Nanjemoy Creek writing in his pocket diary:

"After being hunted like a dog through swamps, woods, and last night being chased by gun boats till I was forced to return wet, cold and starving, with every man's hand against me, I am here in despair. And why; For doing what Brutus was honored for. What made Tell a Hero . . . Tonight I will once more try the river with the intent to cross; though I have a greater desire and almost a mind to return to Washington and in a measure clear my name, which I feel I can do. I do not repent the blow I struck. I may before my God but not to man . . . To night I try to escape these blood hounds once more. Who, who can read his fate. God's will be done. I have too great a soul to die like a criminal. O may he, may he spare me that and let me die bravely." [15]

It was time to go. With little ceremony, the fugitives again set out upon the waters in the dusk of April 22. The crossing attempt would be as difficult as before, though now compounded by the breaking of an oar.[16] Hours passed as Herold rowed mile upon mile with considerable difficulty. Again they narrowly missed being discovered by a gunboat. The vessel later proved to be the USS *Jupiter*, Acting Ensign Philip Sheridan commanding, possibly the same warship they had eluded two nights earlier.[17] Finally, after traversing miles of black water and silhouetted shores, their destination was in sight. As they approached Machodoc, Booth was aghast to find it crowded with a number of small boats and deemed it too dangerous to enter. A rivulet called Gambo Creek, a half mile north of Machodoc seemed far safer, though a bit farther from the home of Elizabeth Rousby Quesenberry. But land they must.[18]

***

It is not known if John Wilkes Booth had ever heard the name Elizabeth Quesenberry before Thomas Jones had advised him that she would be of help, or that she had reputedly served the Confederacy as a spy. All that mattered was that her house, not far from the entrance to Machodoc Creek, be quickly located. To do so on foot, however, was now well beyond Booth's capabilities, even with his crutches. Thus, Herold was obliged to leave him alone on the creek and set off again by himself. When finally arriving at the Quesenberry home on the north bank of Machodoc, he found the mistress of the house at first suspicious and refusing to help. He declared that he and "his brother," an injured man who had broken his leg in a fall from his horse and was now resting back at the creek, were prisoners escaping from the Yankees. They were, he said, in need of a conveyance to move himself and his colleague south as quickly as possible. Mistress Quesenberry remained adamant. It was likely she was well aware who the visitors were and wanted them gone as soon as possible. Would she sell him a horse? Herold asked. She again declined and now ordered the two men to leave her property, but then mercifully offered them some food.[19]

Fortunately for Herold, there were at the time two of Elizabeth's colleagues, Joseph Baden of the Confederate Signal Corps and Thomas Harbin, Jones's brother-in-law, former postmaster at Bryantown, and later a top rebel spy, staying at her home as house guests. It was perhaps a most fortuitous coincidence, for Harbin personally knew John Wilkes Booth, having been early on engaged by him at Bryantown in the initial planning stages of the kidnap plot. They delivered the quick meal Elizabeth had prepared and offered to help.[20]

Securing a horse on the Northern Neck was far more difficult than simply renting one at a livery stable as it had been in Washington. The frequent Union raids in the region had made horses difficult to find. As Booth and Herold ate, Harbin and Baden volunteered to carry them to the home of one Richard Bryant, a mile away, where they might be able to secure horses. After dropping them off at Bryant's, but before riding off, they strongly suggested they seek out Dr. Richard H. Stuart, reputedly the wealthiest man in King George County and a loyal supporter of the Southern cause, at his estate of Cleydael, some eight miles from Bryant's. Now the two fugitives found themselves again on foot and stranded in front of the Bryant home.

As always, it was Herold who was obliged to approach the owner and plea for mounts to take both himself and "his brother," who had been thrown from his horse and suffered a broken leg, to Stuart's for treatment. The reception was not a wel- coming one. Why didn't they visit a doctor much closer? asked Bryant. Herold replied that Stuart had come recommended, and then stated his willingness to pay the farmer ten dollars to help him carry Booth to the doctor's home. Bryant agreed and soon the one man on one horse, accompanied by himself and John L. Cris- mond, one of his workmen, on a second, were off to pick up Booth, who was lying in an open field where he had been left by Harbin and Baden, and then headed off towards Dr. Stuart's estate.[21]

When the men arrived at Cleydael, Stuart, his wife, three daughters, son-in-law S. Turbeville Stuart and a guest, Major Robert Waterman Hunter, a Confederate officer recently belonging to the staff of General John B. Gordon, were just finishing up dinner. While Bryant waited outside, Herold again did the talking, declaring he and Booth were Confederates from Maryland in need of accommodations for the night. Dr. Samuel Mudd had, he said, recommended them. They also needed a carriage to get to Fredericksburg as they were hoping to join up with Colonel Mosby's men. Stuart was already suspicious of the two disheveled, grubby visitors and, though he did not directly reveal his concern, soon realized who they were as they fit the description being circulated of the fugitives involved in the Lincoln assassination. Blithely he said he had no accommodations for anybody and did not know Mudd, though he had heard of the family. Moreover, he wanted to know nothing more about Herold or his compatriot. If they were really hoping to join Mosby it was too late. He had already surrendered. As for transportation, he would not help, but recommended they visit a neighbor, William Lucas, a free black farmer who occasionally hired out his wagon if he wasn't busy.[22]

Eager to see the two fugitives gone, Stuart fed them quickly and then sternly ordered them to leave immediately once they were done. His resolve was made doubly clear when he stepped outside and told Bryant: "You must take these men away. I know nothing about the men. I cannot accommodate them. You will have to take them somewhere else." Returning to his table where Booth and Herold were still eating, he ordered them to depart at once. "The old man is waiting for you. He is anxious to be off. It is cold. He is not well and wants to get home." [23]

Desperate for a night's lodging, but more so for transportation in the morning, Booth and Herold followed Stuart's advice and soon were at the diminutive log cabin of William Lucas.

"Lucas?" one of them cried outside the cabin door. A dog began to bark

The elderly black farmer, awakened by an unfamiliar voice, was too apprehensive to open the door. His fear was that someone was intent on stealing his livestock or even something worse, until the voice mentioned the name of Bryant.

"We want to stay here tonight," said one of the two unkempt, dirty men when Lucas finally opened the door.

"You cannot," replied the old man, declaring that as he was colored he had no right "to take care of white people." His wife was sick and he had only one room in the house.

His callers persisted, lying that they were Confederate soldiers who had served for three years, and wasted little time with civility. They had been knocking about all evening, they said, and didn't intend to any longer. With that, they attempted to force their way in, declaring as they pushed forward, their intention of staying the night.

Lucas bravely resisted, and somehow remained adamant, at least until Booth revealed his two pistols and knife, raising the latter in a threatening manner.

"Old man, how do you like that?"

Terrified of knives but more so by the man in black bearing one, he replied "I do not like that at all."

Booth got right to the point as to why they had come. "We were sent here, old man. We understand you have good horses."

Lucas was now convinced that the visitors were indeed intent on stealing his team, as he had initially feared. They were not available, he replied, stating matter-of-factly they would be needed for his family working the fields the next morning.

Booth continued his intimidating offensive as the two fugitives now forcefully pushed their way into the house: "Well, Dave, we will not go any further [sic] but stay here and make the old man give us the horse in the morning."

For William Lucas and his wife, too frightened to sleep in their own home with the two armed white intruders, there seemed little choice but to spend the night on the open porch.[24]

***

Among the many vessels assigned by the Quartermaster's Department to patrol the Potomac to prevent Booth's escape was an antiquated 184-ton propeller driven barge called *Black Diamond*. She probably wasn't much to look at, her battered iron sheathed hull having been subjected to as many as two decades of loading and offloading coal in Pennsylvania and since late 1862 serving as a chartered freight hauler for the U.S. Army. From her base in Washington, she had seen constant duty in the Chesapeake Tidewater since her first charter, and had most recently been engaged in hauling freight from Alexandria and salt pork and beef from Washington to the Union Army base at City Point, Virginia. Then, following Secretary Stanton's mobilization of almost every military, naval and charter vessel afloat in the upper

Tidewater, she had taken on the most important and traumatic mission of her career.

With as many as 10,000 Union soldiers, sailors and even civilian resources deployed to find and capture John Wilkes Booth, the decision to send *Black Diamond* to reinforce the ships patrolling the lower Potomac had been made without objection. Fully manning the vessel, as with most regular army and navy personnel and shipping already deployed in the manhunt, had been a problem and there was an immediate call for volunteers. Within but a short time, a full complement of twenty firemen had been raised from the United States Steam Engine Company at Alexandria, which at the time had been administered by the Quartermaster's Department. The ship's commander, one Captain Meredith, was assigned to cruise the waters off Blackistone Island and to intercept and arrest anyone trying to cross the river to Virginia.

It is not known what brought the skipper of *Black Diamond* to anchor his ship on the night of Sunday, April 23 near the main channel of the Potomac, a mile off Blackistone Island, or why she had but a single light displayed. The night was clear but quite dark, there being no moon. A brisk wind was blowing. All was otherwise quiet – that is until about 12:30 a.m.

It is probable on that fatal evening that no one aboard *Black Diamond* saw the 400-ton army charter steamer *Massachusetts* or her running lights looming suddenly out of the darkness until it was too late.[25] Yet, in the instant of collision, with the big transport's bow crashing into the boiler area of the anchored ship, and collapsing in upon itself as she plowed forward, all aboard both vessels were awakened and thrown into instant chaos.

Aboard *Massachusetts* there were nearly 400 men belonging to the 3rd Regiment, Veterans Reserve Corps, former invalids all. The greater part having been recently exchanged prisoners of war released on parole from the Confederate hellhole called Andersonville, and now bound for Fort Monroe and from there to North Carolina as occupation troops. Many on deck who had not been thrown into the water upon impact, believing they were about to sink as their bow had been stove in, began to jump over her sides within seconds after impact in hopes of boarding the seemingly stable barge. Hundreds of men floundered about in the cold, dark Potomac waters, desperately grasping for anything afloat. Some began seizing planks torn loose from the two shredded ships but many more quickly disappeared. Captain Meredith, erroneously supposing that the only vessel that had sustained damage had been the transport steamer, quickly brought his own ship around to her aid, even as men struggled to board his own from the water. It proved a fatal mistake, for within three minutes *Black Diamond* herself suddenly disappeared, along with many soldiers who had made it aboard, as well as a number of her own twenty-man crew. Soon, only the silhouette of her smoke stack and pilot house were visible above the inky Potomac waters.

Though critically injured and struggling to stay afloat, *Massachusetts* remained at the site until daylight desperately attempting to recover the hundred or more men, alive and dead, floating about the wreck site. Later in the morning, the steamboat *Marion*, Captain Mott, happened upon the scene and relieved the crippled ship of a large portion of the soldiers aboard. Soon afterwards, another passing ship called

Warrior stopped to take off more survivors before *Massachusetts* made for Point Lookout where she landed the remainder of the troops still aboard.

When the search for victims was finally concluded in mid-May, it was determined that of the eighty-seven lives lost, mostly soldiers from Connecticut, Massachusetts and New York, only thirty-seven bodies had been recovered and taken to Point Lookout, presumably for burial. An additional four belonging to the citizen volunteers of the United States Steam Engine Company, were brought to Alexandria. Being among the sole casualties of the many thousands of men engaged in the hunt for John Wilkes Booth, they were interred with full civil and military honors from the fire company, the city, and the U.S. Government in the Soldiers Cemetery, now Alexandria National Cemetery.[26]

***

Early the next morning, Booth and Herold wasted little time in ordering their unwilling black host, William Lucas, to hitch up a pair of horses to his wagon. Perhaps timidly, assuming they were simply going to drive off with the rig and disappear, he asked if they were taking the horses without payment. Surprisingly, instead of confirming his fears, they asked how much it would cost to drive them to Port Conway, just ten miles away. Ten dollars in gold or twenty dollars in greenbacks, he answered. Despite some pushback from Booth, the price was agreed upon for the use of horses and carriage. The greenbacks were then counted out and handed to Mrs. Lucas. The old man's son Charlie would drive the rig, and the team would be returned when they reached their destination.[27]

Several hours later the wagon carrying the two fugitives reached the hamlet of Port Conway on the north shore of the Rappahannock River, directly opposite the town of Port Royal. Young Charlie Lucas, who was well acquainted with the little assemblage of houses, brought his rig to a halt at the home of William Rollins, a waterman and farmer. Rollins, who also managed the ferry, was at that moment busily engaged in preparing fishing nets in his back yard. Again Herold did all the talking, querying the waterman if they could find transportation to the Orange County Court House, not far from the Confederate rail hub of Gordonsville, or even better, could he take them there. As the courthouse was approximately fifty-five miles away, Rollins declined, noting that he never traveled that far. During the discussion, Herold again introduced Booth as his brother, lied that his leg had been injured during the recent siege of Petersburg, and that he needed a few days of rest somewhere. There was, Rollins suggested as he continued work on his nets, a hotel in the nearby town of Bowling Green, which was only fifteen miles away. The establishment, conveniently, was just two miles or so from the R.F.& P. Railroad depot from which they might entrain for Richmond. He could take them across the river if they wanted, but no farther, and it would cost ten cents, but they would have to wait a bit.[28]

Though the two strangers were clearly in a hurry, Rollins was not. The tide was rising and the waterman had to first set his nets. All were unaware that they were being observed by three mounted soldiers watching from the heights above Port Conway.

The soldiers were Lieutenant Mortimer B. Ruggles of the 43rd Virginia, Absalom R. Bainbridge and Willie Storke Jett. Now that the war was over, they were making their way southward from Fauquier County to Ashland, Virginia outside Richmond, to secure both the documentation that they had laid down arms in surrender and a certificate of parole. It proved to be a most fateful meeting when the three riders descended to the ferry landing.

Having readily taken note upon their approach that the horsemen were all wearing Confederate uniforms, Herold saw a golden opportunity for assistance. He immediately did his best to befriend them as they dismounted by casually asking what company they belonged to and what their destination was.

"We belong to Mosby's command," said Ruggles, with Jett curtly adding that their destination was a secret.[29]

Herold identified himself as David E. Boyd. Sticking to his now familiar response, he informed them that his brother had been wounded in the fight below Petersburg, and that they were heading south but had been stopped at the river as their wagoneer refused to go any farther.[30]

"I suppose you are raising a command to go South to Mexico," he said as they walked towards the waterfront. "I want you to let us go with you."

"I cannot go with any man that I don't know anything about," replied Jett, a former member of the 9th Virginia Cavalry, CSA, which had been stationed in Caroline County, and for a time fought with the famed Mosby's Rangers. "Who are you?"

Having sized up the three men in gray as true Confederates, Herold screwed up his courage, as by now he desperately needed help with Booth. "We are the assassinators of the President," he confessed. Then, pointing to the cripple in the wagon, he blurted out, "Yonder is J. Wilkes Booth, the man who killed the President."

The soldier stood stunned, as Herold repeated the statement to Lieutenant Ruggles, who was watering his horse nearby. At that moment Booth struggled to disembark from the wagon and with the aid of his crutch limped toward them. "I suppose you have been told who I am," he said sardonically, drawing one of his pistols for effect. Jett clearly saw the tattooed initials on the injured man's hand: "J.W.B." and there was no question as to his identity. "Yes," he continued, almost as if daring someone to challenge him, "I am John Wilkes Booth, and I am worth $175,000 to the man who captures me." [31]

Perhaps impressed with Booth's bravado and sympathetic to his cause or condition, Ruggles assured the man with the gun that they were not interested in the reward money and promptly offered to take him across the river. They would do what they could to help. He then gently assisted the cripple onto his own horse, while Herold informed Rollins that he would not be needed after all. "I have met with some friends," he cheerfully told the farmer, "and they say it is not worthwhile to hire a wagon to go to Bowling Green, as we can all go together." Soon the five men were crossing the Rappahannock aboard a wobbly flat scow manned by a black ferryman named Washington.[32]

Upon reaching the south shore of the river, they rode into Port Royal to find two or three days lodging for the fugitives. The first visit was to a known safe house, where they asked if the owner, Sarah Jane Peyton, would take in a wounded Confederate. But the war was over now and things were different. She at first agreed, but upon seeing Booth in person declined. Perhaps, she suggested, they might try Locust Hill, the farm of Richard H. Garrett, just two miles down the road toward Bowling Green. Herold demurred and tried across the street at the Catlitt residence, but the owner was out. Frustrated, it was decided to try the Locust Hill option.[33] After all, old man Garrett had been a loyal supporter of the South and his two eldest of nine children, John and William, both Confederate soldiers only several days earlier, had returned home from the war and were still in uniform.

It was Monday afternoon, April 24, when the three soldiers and two fugitives made their way to the 517-acre Garrett farm, though none of them personally knew the owner or his sons. Booth was in a foul mood during the ride and had informed Jett that he had no intention of being taken alive. "If they don't kill me," he declared to the man riding with him, "I'll kill myself." [34]

Riding up through the open gate at the Garrett farm, just a few hundred yards off the road to Bowling Green, Jett introduced himself under an alias, Captain Ira Scott, and Booth as Mr. James William Boyd, a Marylander injured by a shell during the evacuation of Petersburg and pursued by Yankee cavalry. "Here is a wounded Confederate soldier that we want you to take care of for a day or so," he said to the elder Garrett. "Will you do it?" It would be only for two days, he promised, while they went on "a little scout toward Richmond." The old man agreed, Booth shuffled into the house, and the soldiers, with Herold now in company, rode off toward Bowling Green.[35]

That evening John Wilkes Booth suppered with the Garretts. About twilight he sat on the their front porch smoking his pipe and talking pleasantly for a while with John Garrett, but never revealing his secret. Afterwards, he made his laborious way up to the ex-soldier's bedroom. There he would spend the night in the man's bed while John slept with his younger brother William, entirely unaware of the forces already closing in upon them.

* * *

Colonel Lafayette Baker, known for his espionage exploits behind enemy lines in Virginia as well as his early work in Southern Maryland, had arrived in Washington eager to latch on to any shred of a clue and exploit it as soon as possible. After all, there was an enormous reward offered and he was eager to make it his own. He would seize any and every opportunity possible, even if it meant cutting others out of the honors – and money. When word arrived by telegraph from Port Tobacco that several men had been sighted crossing the Potomac on the morning of Sunday, April 16, he was not slow to appropriate the lead acquired by others. Snatching up the communiqué, he hurried to headquarters, having incorrectly assumed the men who had made the alleged crossing were Booth and Herold.[36]

Baker lost little time in organizing an expedition. He pitched upon General Augur's office for a reliable commander to report to him immediately, as well as all the troops deemed necessary. The officer chosen proved to be Lieutenant Edward Doherty, twenty-five, who was to select a volunteer detachment of the 16th New York Cavalry for the mission. Doherty announced a call for volunteers; twenty-five were accepted, including two sergeants, seven corporals and sixteen privates. The colonel got right to the point by handing the lieutenant pictures of Booth, Herold and John Surratt and some circulars, of which the officer could only recognize one,

John Wilkes Booth. If perhaps surprised at having been selected to lead the special expedition to capture the assassin, he said nothing. He was to be accompanied by two of Baker's most reliable detectives, Luther Byron Baker, the colonel's own cousin, and Everton Conger, twenty-nine. Both were hardened combat veterans recently mustered out of the military. Luther Baker had once served as a army secret service agent and later a lieutenant in the District of Columbia Cavalry, while Conger had been a lieutenant colonel. Both were now detectives working for Lafayette Baker.[37]

Colonel Baker's instructions were brief. Indicating with a pen in his hand to a point on a map, he said: "I want you to go to Virginia and get Booth. I have information that Booth crossed the river there and that he landed about here." [38]

It was sunset, April 24, when the expeditionaries set out aboard the steamer *John S. Ide*, Captain Henry Wilson commanding, from the Sixth Street Wharf at the Washington waterfront. It was now ten days after the assassination, and Conger, the senior of the two detectives, and Doherty were not shy in motivating the cavalry detachment. Should they capture Booth, they were told, they would share in the reward money, now increased to $200,000, including the original War Department reward and additional monies offered by state and civil authorities. It was soon agreed upon that Conger would take charge. Four hours later, at 10 p.m., they disembarked at Belle Plain, eager for the hunt.[39]

From the landing site at Belle Plain they proceeded just a mile and half when Baker and Conger separated, the former splitting off with five cavalrymen towards the Rappahannock, and Conger and Doherty with the rest of the detachment riding on the main Fredericksburg road. Both would rendezvous at King George Court House. En route everyone encountered was stopped and asked if they had seen two men meeting Booth and Herold's description, one of whom was lame. Every home and farm they came upon along the way was visited and its residents asked the same question. Conger and Doherty, in civilian clothes, even claimed that on several occasions when deemed necessary to have passed themselves off as rebels on the run who had lost contact with one of their own, a man with an injured leg. All who were queried answered in the negative.[40]

The following day, April 25, their search would unwittingly prove far more productive than ever anticipated.

***

The Baker-Conger expedition was not the only effort to scour the Northern Neck in search of Lincoln's assassin, of course, since the Sweitzer mission with other units of the 16th New York Cavalry had been sent to search the territory between Coan River and Heathsville and the lower part of the peninsula. Though the initial foray results were disappointing, Sweitzer determined to head west and canvas the reach between the Coan and Potomac Creek "to arrest any suspicious person who have crossed the Potomac [River] from Maryland," a sweep expected to take three days.[41] To effectively do so, however, would require more men than he had on hand. On April 25 a substantial reinforcement from the 16th New York, under the command of Lieutenant Colonel John Nicholson, was ordered to board transports the following morning at the Sixth Street Wharf in Washington bound for Coan River to join Sweitzer. "Upon arriving at your destination," Nicholson was instructed,

> "you will scout the adjacent country thoroughly, directing your attention to the discovery of the parties concerned in the assassination of the President and Mr. Seward. You will understand that the energies of yourself and command are to be directed to this object and not to the prosecution of hostilities against the inhabitants. You will remain at the point above designated until joined by Colonel Sweitzer, who will then give you further instructions . . . you are further directed to take charge of all stores and supplies which may be landed at Coan River for your own or Colonel Sweitzer's command." [42]

***

It has always been uncertain as to why Herold had ridden off to Bowling Green with the three Confederate soldiers. Perhaps he was eager for some respite from attending to the every need and whim of his cantankerous, crippled colleague, or maybe it was simply to reconnoiter the countryside before pushing on. At Bowling Green Jett had hoped to reunite with his sweetheart, Izora Gouldman, daughter of the owner of the Star Hotel, where he had first met her while recuperating from a war wound. While stopping briefly at a wayside tavern called The Trap, they encountered Jesse Gouldman, Izora's brother. Jett could not restrain himself from bragging that among his companions was David Herold, one of the conspirators, who he was taking with him.

"My God, Jett," said Gouldman in horror as he took the soldier aside. "Why the whole country is swimming with Yankee cavalry, and the hotel is the first place they will search . . . If they find Herold then they will burn it down and hang every one of us." Jett reconsidered. Instead, he decided, Herold would have to accompany Bainbridge to the home of one Virginia Clarke, with whom they would stay the night while Jett and Ruggles continued on to Bowling Green. The following day Herold revisited Port Royal to spend the day and have dinner.[43]

The next day Herold pressed on to Bowling Green with Bainbridge and again linked up with Jett and Ruggles. Though his intent now appeared to be to keep moving, if possible toward Orange Court House and leave Booth to his own destiny, it was not to be. Word that a large Yankee cavalry unit was also headed that way changed things immediately. Did he want to go back the way he came? asked Bainbridge. "No," replied Herold in exasperation. "I am not anxious to do so, but the gentleman left there yesterday will be anxious for me to come back, and I am almost afraid to stay away from him." Thus it was that Herold, Bainbridge and Ruggles returned to Locust Hill, while Jett remained in the Star Hotel with young Izora Gouldman. It was a decision that all but sealed the former drug store clerk's fate.[44]

***

On Tuesday morning, after breakfast, John Garrett rode in to Port Royal to have boots repaired at the shop of a local shoemaker. While there he met a friend who mentioned that he had read in a Richmond newspaper that Lincoln had been killed and there was reportedly a $140,000 reward offered for the capture of the assassin. For Garrett, though rumors of the murder had been circulating about the countryside for several days, it was the first confirmation of the crime and report of a reward that he had heard.[45] That afternoon, having returned home, he mentioned the news at dinner. "I wish he would come this way," said John's brother William, "so that I might catch him and get this reward."

Booth, a master of nonchalance, responded with a question. "If he were to come out, would you inform against him?"

William declared a giggle that if Booth came this way he would be gobbled up.

"How much did you say had been offered?" asked Booth.

"$140,000," John replied.

"I would sooner suppose $500,000," said the actor, without the slightest display of concern.[46]

The conversation continued for a while longer, after which Booth adjourned to the porch and about 4:30 p.m. began jotting in his diary. Suddenly the sight of a pair of riders passing by the main gate on the Bowling Green Road interrupted his concentration. John Garrett instantly recognized them as two of the men that had brought Booth with them the day before. "There goes some of your party now," he said casually. Booth, however, suddenly became obviously distressed.

"You go get my pistols!" he shouted, as if in a sudden panic.

Garrett was startled over the house guest's sudden reaction. Why did he want the guns? he asked, perhaps fearful that a firefight might suddenly erupt in his front yard. Booth's abrupt reply, that he felt safe when armed, was less than convincing. Only when the riders disappeared, however, did Booth soon settle down, that is until he saw a lone man walking through the gate and up towards them from the road. The stranger proved to be David Herold, who had been brought along and dropped off by Bainbridge and Ruggles, both having continued on their way without stopping. The reunion of the two conspirators was taut as Booth, without a greeting, curtly asked his accomplice if he intended on staying.

"I would like to go home," said Herold. "I am sick and tired of this way of living."

John Garrett's suspicions regarding his guest was now further aroused, as much by Booth's sudden demand to be armed as by his display of nervousness at the appearance of the horseman. He grew even more wary when Herold approached and Booth introduced him as his cousin and asked if he could stay the night. As his father was away for the day on business, and much to Booth's upset, John Garrett did not accept his request. At that moment, all were surprised to see Bainbridge and Ruggles galloping back up the road and through the farm gate. Yankee cavalry, they shouted excitedly, were on the road from Port Royal. And with that they rode off into the woods with alacrity, warning two of the three men standing in front of the Garrett farmhouse, "Marylanders, you had better watch out."

Again Booth called for his pistols. This time, within seconds, John's brother appeared with the actor's gun belt and handguns, which were quickly buckled on as he limped across the yard towards the barn and for the woods beyond. Sheep-like, Herold followed behind. Suddenly Booth stopped and turned. Perhaps it was time to end it all and surrender. Or, maybe it was time to stand and fight.[47]

John Garrett was now more concerned than ever that the two visitors might embroil his family with problems they did not need. Why had they run towards the woods? Didn't they know the war was over? "If you have gotten into any difficulty," he said with some stridency, "you must leave at once, for I do not want you to bring any trouble upon my aged father."

Booth and Herold attempted to dispel Garrett's alarm, claiming they had only gotten into a little brush in Maryland, but they would certainly not get him into any trouble, and there most assuredly wasn't any danger. At that moment, Doherty's New Yorkers galloped past en route to Bowling Green obviously hell bent on some unknown mission.

"There goes the cavalry, now," said Garrett with some exasperation.

"Well, that is all," replied Herold.

Again Garrett demanded they leave at once. Herold responded with a question: was there any place in the area they could purchase a horse? There were few to be had, replied the former soldier, as most had already been stolen by both the Yankees and Confederates during the war. What about hiring transportation? Garrett direct- ed them to a black man named Freeman but said he had to be paid in specie. Herold replied he had no specie, only a ten dollar greenback.

Now more than anxious to have the two visitors leave, Garrett personally called upon the Freemans, where he learned that the Yankees had already paid a visit, asking if they had taken in any white men. Frustrated and even more alarmed than before, he returned home, now well aware that if he were to rid the farm of the unwanted guests, he would have to move them himself, which could be dangerous. This time he gingerly queried them as to when they expected to leave. They replied they would have to stay the night and leave in the morning.

After supper they adjourned to the front porch where both John and William again questioned Herold, who perhaps being a little intoxicated, spoke incoherently and mentioned he had served in the 30th Virginia Regiment under a Captain Robinson. Garrett, who was familiar with the regiment, knew there had been no such officer. Cornered in a lie, Herold backpedaled by claiming he had served there-in for just one week and had been wounded, so he might have been wrong.

Seeing through the visitors' lies, Garrett had had enough and, ignoring their loud protests and excuses, again ordered them to leave at once, but soon thought better of it. If they left on foot, he assumed they might very well return at night and steal his horses. He reconsidered. They would be allowed to stay only until morning, but they would have to bed down in the nearby shed and not in the house. With little choice, the visitors agreed.[48]

The shed in question was in fact a tobacco barn situated about 200 yards from the farmhouse. It was an open slated wooden structure forty-eight by fifty-foot in size, supported by heavy cedar posts. Inside it contained myriad farming and tobacco curing equipment, bushels of seed corn, fodder and hay, as well as some house furniture. The goods had been earlier stored for neighbors for protection from Union marauders, such as those who had been raiding to support the refugee farms on the Patuxent. Unlike most tobacco barns employed strictly for agricultural purposes, the Garrett shed had a door lock to protect the furniture from theft.[49]

John Wilkes Booth, limping with pain on his crutch, with carbine slung over his shoulder and his now reluctant compatriot walking slowly behind him, entered the barn and prepared a bed in the hay. Behind them John and William Garrett quietly closed the door and locked it. The brothers would spend the night in a nearby corncrib keeping watch to insure their now unwelcome guests did not escape to steal their horses. It was to be but a very short night for all.

***

Like many soldiers in wartime, Willie Jett had undoubtedly missed his lady friend, Izora Gouldman, while on duty far away and had long anticipated the moment of their reunion at her father's hotel in Bowling Green. Now having chosen to leave his fellow travelers to follow their own paths, he and Izora were finally together again. Their meeting, nonetheless, was to be brief, for only a few miles away Baker, Conger, Doherty, and the weary detachment of the 16th New York Cavalry, had finally reached Port Conway. Having satisfied their orders, they were preparing to return empty handed to Belle Plain when a fortunate encounter suddenly altered everything.

While standing briefly at the ferry landing, one of the detectives interviewed an employee of William Rollins, a black man named Dick Wilson. Then during what began as just another round of routine questioning, Wilson mentioned that strangers came through frequently. When shown photographs of Booth, Herold and Surratt, however, he replied much to the delight of the inquisitors that he had seen two of the men pictured. When the images were shown to Rollins, and the previous visit by Booth and Herold was readily confirmed, Baker realized the first solid lead in the hunt for Lincoln's killer was in hand. Though he had his hat pulled down when he last saw him, Rollins noted, the man on crutches was clearly John Wilkes Booth. The two fugitives' were making for the county court house, but beyond that he knew nothing. Why not talk to Willie Jett, he suggested, who was one of the three soldiers that had crossed the river with them? When Rollins' wife Bettie suggested that they might find Jett at the Star Hotel in Bowling Green where his girl friend lived, the pursuit took on new life.[50]

The ferry scow could only carry seven horses at a time across the Rappahannock, and had to first be brought back from the other side several times before the hunt for Willie Jett could get moving with Rollins leading the way. Unknowingly, on their ride to Bowling Green the New Yorkers would pass within 400 yards of the Garrett farm and the objective of the greatest manhunt in American history without knowing it. By 9 p.m. they had reached The Trap, which some considered to be a house of ill repute, and queried the young women therein regarding the passage of men, one of whom was on crutches. The sudden appearance of so many soldiers unnerved the women, but their concerns were eased when they were told the riders were in search of men who had sexually assaulted a young girl. Undoubtedly eager for the band of armed Yankees to be on their way, the women readily let drop that five men on three horses had passed, and all but one had eventually returned "for a drink." The detectives quickly assumed the exception had been the injured assassin who had probably been taken to Bowling Green.[51]

The next step, however, would be to find Jett.

It was between 11 p.m. and midnight when the soldiers arrived outside of Bowling Green, dismounted a half mile from the town, with only Conger remaining in the saddle. Leading their horses on foot, they noiselessly surrounded the large two-story hotel that stood on the main street and directly across from the county

633

court house. [52] Upon encountering a black man in the alley behind the hotel, Conger was directed to a back door where he waited in the dark for a signal that all the exits from the hotel were guarded. Finally, with everyone in place, he knocked on the door. Who was there? a woman's voice asked.

"Open the door or I will break it down," Conger ordered. Then with pistol drawn and Doherty beside him, he forced his way in to confront Julia Gouldman, Izora's mother, the proprietress whose husband was away on a fishing trip. Unquestionably frightened and as ordered, she led the night visitors to Jett's room, which was immediately stormed. "Is your name Jett?" Conger shouted at the man lying in bed. "Get up. I want you." Forced to dress quickly, the stunned Confederate was then hurried to the hotel parlor and, with Conger, Baker and Doherty circling him, interrogated with a pistol aimed at his temple.

"Where are the two men who came with you across the river?" demanded Conger.

"Can I see you alone?" asked Jett.

Conger agreed. After all the others had departed but himself and the Yankee detective, Jett spoke openly. "I know who you want, and I will tell you where they can be found," he said, but then demanded a guarantee that he would not be charged with aiding and abetting Booth's escape.

Conger agreed.

"They are on the road to Port Royal, about three miles this side of that."

"At whose house are they?"

"Mr. Garrett's. I will go there with you and show you where they are now, and you can get them." [53]

With Jett guiding the way but under threat of death if he led them into an ambush, the two-hour-long, twelve mile ride back to the Garrett farm in the dark, moonless night, was difficult for men who had been in the saddle for the better part of thirty-six hours. They were looking for a gate approximately four hundred yards from the road in the dark. Though once riding past the entrance, the objective was soon relocated.

"Show yourselves smart!" Conger ordered in a hushed command. "We are going to surround a house." [54]

Doherty cautioned his men to remain quiet until they heard his command. "They are in that house and we must take them. Shoot any person you see running away."[55] After ordering his men to draw their weapons and check that they were loaded, he paused for a moment, then commanded: "Open file to the right and left – Gallop!" [56]

Within seconds the split column was rushing to surround the farmhouse, with Baker and a number of horsemen covering the only three entrances to the building. Doherty ordered Corporal Herman Newgarten to surround the barn with six or seven men. Awakened by the clamor of horses, sabers and dogs barking, Richard Garrett came to his bedroom window.

By the time Conger, accompanied by Jett, had come around to the front porch door, he found Baker already dismounted and telling someone to strike a light, and then reporting that there was an old man inside. At that moment Richard Garrett, in his nightclothes, stepped barefoot onto the porch and was instantly assailed. "Where are those parties who were at your house last night?" Baker demanded. "Answer my questions or I'll blow your brains out."

The frightened old man stammered that they had been by earlier but had disappeared into the woods. Conger wanted to know where in the forest they had gone. Baker, however, refused to believe that a crippled man would go into the woods, even when Garrett declared that he had done so on crutches. Standing in the dark in little but his nightgown, the old man asked for his boots. Someone inside handed him his pants and footwear.

"I don't want a long story out of you," said Conger. "I just want to know where these men have gone." Garrett still seemed befuddled.

Obviously angered at the old man's apparent confusion or maybe clever obfuscation, Conger ordered one of the soldiers to bring him a rope. "I will put that man up to the top of one of those locust trees," he snarled. Perhaps the threat of hanging would stir his memory. "Will you show me where they are?"

At that moment, John Garrett, still in Confederate uniform and aroused from the corncrib in which he had been sleeping, came striding forth towards a sergeant and demanded to speak with the commanding officer, just in time to see his father being threatened with hanging. "Father," he said as he moved onto the porch, "you had better tell him, for they have a whole regiment of cavalry here." In an instant, Lieutenant Doherty seized him by the collar and sent the sergeant to his post. With force he roughly dragged the former rebel bodily from the porch, put a pistol to his head and demanded to know where the fugitives were hiding.[57]

"In the barn," exclaimed his prisoner.

Within but a minute several soldiers had completely surrounded the building. William Garrett was ordered to fetch the key to the lock on the door. Doherty shoved John toward the structure and ordered him to bring the two fugitives out. The ex-Confederate protested, declaring that they would surely shoot him if he went inside. It was now Baker's turn to intercede as he walked to the locked barn door, and gave the prisoner a choice: "They know you, and you can go in," he said, but if he refused, he would shoot him himself. Obey or die! [58]

By now, Booth had been aroused. Waking his compatriot, he quietly informed him that the barn was surrounded. Immediately frightened by the consequences, Herold suggested they surrender. "I will suffer death first," said the actor quietly, so as not to be heard outside. "Don't make any noise. Maybe they will go off, thinking we are not here." [59]

With candle now in hand, Baker instantly destroyed any hope Booth had of evading discovery as he shouted out, "You men had better come out of there. We know who you are."

From inside Booth's stentorian voice retorted. "Who are you?"

"Never mind who we are," said the detective. "We know who you are, and you had better come out and deliver yourselves up." [60]

Slowly the barn door was unlocked and opened. Reluctantly John Garrett stepped into the darkened room, anticipating a bullet to be fired in his direction at any second. "Gentlemen," he said, "the cavalry are after you. You are the ones. You had better give yourselves up."

There was movement in the shadows as one of the fugitives shifted uncomfortably. Then silence. Garrett repeated his advice. Suddenly Booth rose from the dark- ness, and John, without thinking, exclaimed that the barn was surrounded.

In a strident voice, Booth assailed his former host, ordering him to leave the building or be shot. "You have implicated me," he said acidly.[61] In an instant, as Booth reached behind his back, Garrett was convinced he was going for his gun.

At that moment Conger shouted an ultimatum from outside: "I want you to surrender. If you don't, I will burn the barn down in fifteen minutes." Doherty immediately disapproved of the move, opting to hold off until daylight, when the building could be stormed from all directions. One of his men, Sergeant Boston Corbett, a small, quiet but aggressive soldier, volunteered to go in by himself, but was denied.[62]

Booth demanded to know who was at the door, but Baker again refused to identify himself. Instead, the detective ordered the actor turn over his weapons to Garrett and surrender, and gave him ten minutes to decide. Though Booth remained adamant, Herold had by now begun to crumble. Yet again he implored his mentor to let him submit, but was angrily cut off. Afraid for his life, Garrett backed toward the door and begged Baker to let him out, which he did. Again the door was locked.

Now Booth stalled for time, pelting Baker with requests for alternatives. When he suggested that it would be easy to shoot his way out since the detective was standing outside the door with a lit candle, a target illuminated through the cracks in the siding, Baker retreated from the door and placed the light some distance away in the yard. Returning to the entrance, which was again dark, he reissued his ultimatum to the assassin: give up his arms or the barn would be set afire around him.

"Captain," Booth bellowed, "that's rather rough. I am nothing but a cripple. I have but one leg, and you ought to give one a fair chance fight."

Baker refused to negotiate and told him to consider his options.

"Well, you may prepare a stretcher for me," said the actor defiantly, as if reading from a script. "Throw open your door, draw up your men in line, and let's have a fair fight." [63]

Baker replied that he had not come to fight but to take prisoners. "This is no child's play," he said. "We are in earnest, and shall carry out our threats. We will give you just five minutes to consider the matter." [64] There was no response.

It was about 1:30 a.m. when Everton Conger instructed John Garrett to start piling pine twigs against the side of the barn. Booth readily detected the movement through the siding cracks. "You had better look out there," he warned. "Put no more brush there or someone will get hurt." With that, Garrett backed away, although Conger had by then also picked up some hay, which was twisted into a rope. While Booth was being diverted by Garrett, he had tucked the coiled grasses via a split in the barn siding into a stack of hay within. Now, without a moment's hesitation, he lit it.[65]

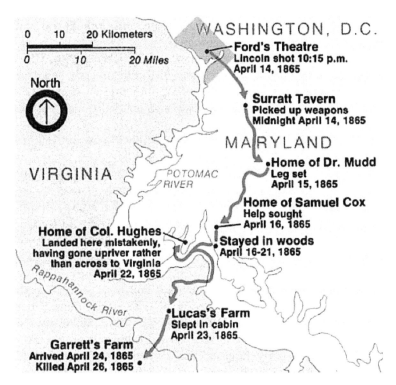

Plan of the escape route taken by John Wilkes Booth and David Herold from Washington, D.C. to the Garrett Farm, near Port Royal, April 14-26, 1865.

The flames, having soon transmitted to the haystack, began slowly at first to lick the barn siding. As the seconds passed and the fire grew, he could hear Booth and Herold arguing loudly. Herold was in a complete state of panic and declared that he was leaving. "I don't intend to be burnt alive," he screamed in absolute terror. [66] Angrily, Booth threatened to kill him if he moved, and then shouted in exasperation to the young man who had loyally followed him for months and cared for him in his last desperate days, "Go away from me you damned coward." [67] At that, Herold moved to the door, only to be yanked back. The crippled man held him for a moment and then whispered, "When you get out, don't tell them the arms I have." Then, releasing his grip, he shouted out to Baker, "Captain, there is a man in here who wants very much to surrender. He is innocent of any crime."

Released by his master, Herold immediately rushed to the door and started to pound upon it, crying out in fear and desperation as the flames began to leap about him, "Let me out! Let me out!" [68]

John Garrett, who was now standing beside Baker, urged him to allow the surrender, as there would be one less fugitive with which to deal.[69] Accepting Garrett's logic, Baker cautiously unfastened the door, though keeping the lock in the hasp in case of a trick, and instructed Herold to throw out his arms.

"I have no arms," screamed Herold.

"We know exactly what you've got," replied the detective.

637

"On the honor of a gentleman, he has no arms," chimed in Booth. "I own and have all the arms that are here, and he cannot get them." [70]

With Doherty and several soldiers providing cover with cocked pistols, Baker quickly opened the door, and instructed Herold to put his hands out, one at a time. In an instant, Doherty grabbed his wrists and yanked him outside, free of the burning building. The prisoner was quickly led away and tied to a nearby locust tree.[71]

John Wilkes Booth, the great tragedian and the most hunted man in America, was now alone, hopelessly trapped, but still resolute. Standing with one hand clutching the carbine he had picked up at the Surratt tavern seemingly ages ago, and the other holding a crutch, he was unaware of being watched by a few soldiers through cracks in the barn siding. As the flames spread to the rafters, blazing "almost like powder," Conger later recalled, Booth dropped his crutch and shuffled painfully forward, alternately "stooping and springing step by step towards the door, rifle in hand." Was he making his way towards the inevitable suicidal gunfight, or to finally surrender?[72]

Sergeant Boston Corbett watched keenly through a siding crack as the trapped fugitive hobbled on with deliberation, slowly raising his rifle as he moved, perhaps intent on exiting with a fusillade of gunfire. Taking his .44 Colt revolver in hand, even as Booth elevated his own weapon and pointed it towards the doorway, Corbett fired between the crack, aiming, he later claimed, for the shoulder. Instead, the bullet passed through his target's neck, smashing through vertebrae and spinal cord, and exiting on his right side above the clavicle. At that moment Baker opened the door, just in time to see Booth slump to the ground in a bent position, totally paralyzed.[73]

Having heard the shot, Conger ran from the other side of the barn as Baker rushed into the burning building where he found Booth lying on the floor, his carbine lying between his legs, but still tightly clutching a revolver. Doherty was right behind, and quickly retrieved the rifle and removed the knife from the assassin's belt. Conger entered only seconds later. "Is he dead?" he asked. "Did he shoot himself?"

"Where is he shot?" he asked as he lifted the flaccid body, and then spotted the bloody hole in the neck. But there was little time for answers.[74] With the barn burning around them, Conger and two soldiers began to pull the body towards the door while a cavalryman cradled Booth's head in his arms.[75]

Still alive but unable to speak, the man who murdered the President of the United States was dragged to a patch of grass thirty feet from the burning building. Baker sat beside him and gently rested the man's head on his knee. He could see now by the light of the fire that the man was trying to say something. He put his ear to Booth's lips. Though barely audible, he could make out the words.[76]

"Tell my mother I die for my country. I did what I thought to be best."

As the heat from the fire became more intense, the body was carried to the Garrett porch where Mrs. Garrett had laid out a mattress. There the dying man rallied somewhat but could still barely whisper. He called for water but couldn't swallow, even when turned on his side or face down.

"Kill me," he pleaded. "Kill me."

"No Booth, we don't want to kill you," said the detective gently. "We want you to get well."

For the next few hours, John Wilkes Booth, famed thespian, *bon vivant*, and man of the world, suffered with every movement as his heart quivered and his lips turned plum purple. His vital organs were rapidly shutting down as he began to slowly suffocate. Detective Baker sat by his side, tending his wound, occasionally relieved by others, as all awaited the inevitable.

A doctor at Port Royal had been sent for, but it would matter little.

Again Baker placed his ear to Booth's lips.

"Tell my mother – tell my mother that I did it for my country – that I die for my country."

The sun was coming up. Baker lifted the assassin's limp hands above his face to shield it from the rising sun, and then heard his last faint, dying words.

"Useless. Useless." [77]

EPILOGUE
"An now may God be with you all. Farewell."

The assassination of President Abraham Lincoln had alterably challenged both the country and the new president. Without prior warning Andrew Johnson had found himself burdened with the totally unexpected responsibilities of governing a country still bleeding from the horrors of civil war. The recent seven-week-long trial of the conspirators who had been engaged in the kidnapping plot, the murder of the president, the attempted murder of Secretary Seward, and the scheme to kill the vice president had been arduous and stressful.

Secretary of War Stanton's aggressive roundup of many scores of suspects, indeed almost everyone even remotely associated with or related to Booth and his henchmen, had begun even before the assassin's corpse was removed from the Garrett farm. The body, shrouded by a blanket, had first been transported to Belle Plain by horse and wagon. It was transferred soon after to the ironclad warship *Montauk* and taken to the Navy Yard. There it was identified, autopsied and secretly buried, albeit temporarily, in a storage room at the Old Arsenal Penitentiary.[1]

The arc of history had been brutally bent during those weeks as the arrests of suspects had continued almost to the beginning of the trial of the seven men and one woman deemed to be the key conspirators. The government's action had been swift if not totally effective. Most of the arrestees, including several who had actually been directly involved with Booth's escape, would be released for lack of evidence or witnesses. Nevertheless, the cries in the North for retribution and revenge had been deafening, and the fear of retaliation throughout the South had needed immediate address. The nation demanded action. Many sought only revenge.

Two weeks after the assassination, on May 1, Johnson ordered the formation of a military tribunal comprised of six battle-hardened U.S. Army generals and two colonels to try the accused. Major Generals David Hunter (presiding) and Lew Wallace, Brigadier Generals Robert Sanford Foster, Thomas Maley Harris, Albion P. Howe, Brevet Brigadier General James A. Ekin, Lieutenant Colonel David Ramsay Clendenin and Brevet Colonel Charles H. Thompkins had been selected to sit. Brigadier General Joseph Holt had been chosen to serve as Judge Advocate General leading the prosecution, assisted by Ohio Congressman John A. Bingham and Colonel Henry Lawrence Burnett as Special Judge Advocates. The eight defendants, David Herold, Lewis Payne, George Adzerodt, Mary Surratt, Samuel Mudd, Samuel Arnold, Michael O'Laughlen, and Edman Spangler, were permitted to have their own lawyers and call upon witnesses but were not allowed to testify themselves. On May 10 the court convened on the third floor of the Old Arsenal Penitentiary, albeit not without opposition.

Secretary Welles, believing the trial should be held in a civil court, had criticized the use of a military tribunal. Attorney General James Speed, however, quickly pointed out that martial law was still in force in the District of Columbia at the time of the crimes and that the defendants had acted as enemy combatants. The true nature of the conspiracy, to decapitate the leadership of the United States in time of war, could only be construed as military in nature and thus justified a military court.

Conviction required but a simple majority of the jury, and two-thirds was required for the death sentence. No appeal was to be granted except by the president.[2]

The lengthy trial, which had included extensive testimony from 366 witnesses, was finally concluded on June 30 with all of the defendants, as expected, found guilty. Herold, Payne, Adzerodt, and Surratt were condemned to death by hanging. Mudd, Arnold and O'Laughlen were sentenced to life imprisonment. Spangler was given six years. Though five jury members formally appealed by letter to Johnson recommending clemency for Mary Surratt, it was refused. The president would later deny having even seen the document.[3]

The Board which tried Lincoln conspirators. Portrait includes standing left to right: Brig. Gen. Thomas M. Harris, Maj. Gen. Lew Wallace, Maj. Gen. August V. Kautz, and Henry L. Burnett. Seated left to right: Lt. Col. David R. Clendenin, Col. C.H. Tompkins, Brig. Gen. Albion P. Howe, Brig. Gen. James Ekin, Maj. Gen. David Hunter, Brig. Gen. Robert S. Foster, John A. Bingham, and Brig. Gen. Joseph Holt. Prints and Photographs Division, Library of Congress, Washington, D.C.

It had been unseasonably warm on July 7, 1865 as final preparations were made for the execution of Herold, Payne, Adzerodt, and Surratt on the grounds of the Old Arsenal Penitentiary. At 11:25 a.m. an experiment testing the drops on the gallows was made with four conical Parrott cannonballs weighing one hundred pounds each. Two of these weights were placed upon each drop. The props were then knocked from under and the experiment with the northern drop was satisfactory, though there was a hitch with the southern drop. The experiment was repeated with the drops until they worked perfectly. Just south of the gallows stood an ominous looking pile of four boxes of rough, shoe-shaped board coffins for the convicts. All were unpainted and without identification of any kind. Finally, the prisoners were brought up, blindfolded with a hood over their heads, and a noose placed about their necks. At 1:26 p.m. the signal was given by a wave of the hand; the large blocks supporting the uprights were knocked out, the drops fell with a heavy slam, and the four bodies hung suspended. There was breathless silence for several minutes among the observers after the drop fall, but in a short time the crowd commenced to move about as usual. The bodies were allowed to hang suspended for twenty minutes, then examined and each pronounced dead. Ten minutes later they were cut down and placed in their respective coffins without ceremony.[4]

"Washington, D.C. Hanging hooded bodies of the four conspirators; crowd departing." Alexander Garner, photographer. Prints and Photographs Division, Library of Congress, Washington, D.C.

As for the remaining convicted conspirators, fate had other plans. Michael O'Laughlen was destined to die of yellow fever on September 23, 1867 while incarcerated in prison at Fort Jefferson, Florida. Mudd, Spangler and Arnold would fare better and be pardoned by the president in 1869. Mudd, released for his humanitarian aid while still a prisoner during an epidemic at Fort Jefferson, would return to his farm in Charles County to live out his days in silence regarding his role in the conspiracies. He would die of pneumonia on January 10, 1883. Ned Spangler went to work for John Ford for several years in Baltimore. He would eventually move to Charles County to live out his days on land that Dr. Mudd had given him. Samuel Arnold would live an unremarkable life until his own demise in 1906. John Surratt, finally captured in 1867, would eventually stand trial and be released after the jury failed to come to a verdict. He would soon after set out upon an ill-fated lecture tour, beginning in Rockville, Maryland, to tell the tale of his life as a Confederate agent and his role in the conspiracy to kidnap the president.[5]

***

Secretary of the Navy Gideon Welles had come to a crossroads in his own life perhaps as difficult as building the greatest navy the nation had ever seen. He was now obliged to dismantle it. With the war over, the demobilization of the military and naval forces of the United States had become a priority driven as much from economic necessity as a desire to see a symbolic end to the militarism that had governed national life since 1861. No longer was it necessary to patrol Southern Maryland with troops or the Potomac frontier with ships. For the Navy Department the reduction of the Potomac Flotilla as soon as possible had become one of the many cost saving necessities of the government. By April 1865 the flotilla had grown in size to include forty-four vessels, including ironclads, which were now simply no longer needed. Thus, barely more than three weeks after the surrender at Appomattox, Welles issued orders to Commander Parker governing the first stage of dismemberment.[6]

Two days later, on May 5, Parker dispatched twenty-three warships to Washington where most would be decommissioned and, when possible, placed up for sale. Among them were a number of battle-scarred veterans such as *Thomas Freeborn, Resolute, Coeur de Lion, Jacob Bell* and *Yankee*, ships that had been on line from the very beginning of the war. More would soon follow. By the end of the month only nine ships remained in service.[7]

Commander Foxhall A. Parker, USN. Naval Historical and Heritage Command, Washington, D.C.

On July 18, 1865 Parker received additional instructions ordering the final demise of the fleet. He was to first sell the wharf at St. Inigoes "for as much as you can, but not less than 33 per cent below its cost." In the event he could not sell it, he was to dismantle and remove it to the Washington Navy Yard. Then on July 31 he was to "lay up the Potomac Flotilla, with the exception of the *Don*, sending the vessels to the Washington navy yard." [8]

On that final day of service, Foxhall A. Parker dispatched his last message to the officers and men of the squadron that he had commanded for more than a year and a half.

"The war for the preservation of American liberty being at an end, the Potomac Flotilla, which took its rise with it and grew with its growth until it had become a fleet rather than a flotilla, this day happily ceases to exist.

In taking leave of those with whom I have been so long associated, my heart is filled with varied emotions – with sorrow at parting, gladness that our beloved country no longer has need of us, and pride . . . I can truly say 'the Potomac Flotilla has not been unmindful of the traditional honor and glory of the Navy.'

Your services, however eclipsed by the daring deeds of your more fortunate comrades in arms on other stations, have, equally with theirs, contributed to the suppression of the rebellion, and in discipline, in drill, and in the requirements in short of an organized force, I have not, in the course of a naval experience of twenty-eight years, served in a squadron which excelled the one which for the last nineteen months it has been my good fortune to command.

To those of you who are about to return to civil life I would like to say: Render the same cheerful obedience to the civil that you have rendered to naval law; cast your voices, as good citizens, regularly and quietly at the polls, so keeping your hearts 'with malice toward none, with charity for all,' that after each Presidential election, whether it be with or against you, you may be enabled to respond heartily to our old navy toast: 'The President of the United States, God bless him.'

And now may God be with you all. Farewell." [9]

It had, of course, not all been a naval war. A total of 46,638 Marylanders had served in the Union Army while more than 20,000 others had donned uniforms of the Confederacy.[10] Of those who served in the Union cause, 8,718 had been men of color, mostly former slaves, of which 5,398 had entered service and trained at Camp Stanton in Southern Maryland. The four black regiments trained on the banks of the Patuxent River, the 7th, 9th, 19th, and 30th USCT, soon proved their mettle in innumerable contests after leaving Maryland. The 7th, under the command of Colonel James Shaw, had first been sent to Virginia to participate in the defense of Portsmouth and Suffolk. Later transferred to Hilton Head, South Carolina, and then Jacksonville, Florida, the regiment found itself actively employed in the construction of fortifications. They were eventually engaged in several spirited skirmishes including two fights at Cedar Creek in May 1864, as well as being deployed as pickets and scouts. In July the men of the 7th, having been transferred north again to Hilton Head, participated in an epic seventeen-day march northward along the Edisto River while engaging in contnuous combat along the way. The unit subsequently returned to Florida where it took part in numerous raids against Confederates. It was again redeployed to Virginia in late 1864, this time to the James River where it was assigned to the Colored Brigade, Third Division, X Army Corps, and saw months of endless combat along the north bank of the waterway. From August 1864 to the spring of 1865 the 7th was actively engaged in the massive Federal effort leading to the evacuation of Petersburg and the surrender of the Army of Northern Virginia at Appomattox Courthouse. The unit, along with the 30th Regiment, was cited for its uniform good conduct and soldierly bearing at Appomattox. With the collapse of the Confederacy the regiment was destined to perform guard duty operations in Texas until October 14, 1866 when it was sent home to the Chesapeake and discharged at Baltimore on November 15. The 7th Regiment was credited with participation in no less than eleven major engagements as well as numerous skirmishes.

While still under the overall command of General Birney, the 9th Regiment had sailed directly for Hilton Head and saw frequent action in many heated skirmishes, particularly around Jane's Island. Later transferred to the Virginia theater of war, the men of the 9th were prominently engaged at the Battle of Fussel's Mill, in the siege of Petersburg, and in the courageous but unsuccessful assault on Fort Gilmer near Richmond on September 29, 1864. In April 1865 the regiment had the honor to be among the first Union military units to enter the late Confederate capital city of Richmond. On June 7 they sailed for Brazos Santiago, Texas to be employed in garrison duty at Brownsville and along the Rio Grande until October 1866. Embarking at New Orleans, the veterans of seven major engagements under the commands of Colonel Thomas Bagley and Lieutenant Colonels Samuel C. Armstrong and George M. Dennett finally returned to the Chesapeake and debarked at Baltimore where they mustered out on November 20.

The 19th Regiment, mostly made up of men from Southern Maryland and the Eastern Shore, would participate in bloody fighting from the Rapidan River to the James. After being transferred to the Army of the Potomac it saw almost continuous action in the Battle of the Wilderness, Spotsylvania, in the suicidal thrust at Cold Harbor, the Weldon Railroad fight, Cemetery Hill, the siege and capture of Petersburg, and finally Appomattox. Like the 9th Regiment, it was among the first Federal units to enter Richmond in early April 1865. And like their compatriots in both the 7th and 9th regiments, on June 6, 1865 the men of the 19th, veterans of eleven major engagements under the commands of Colonels Henry G. Thomas and Joseph G. Perkins, would embark for Texas to perform garrison duty at Brownsville and on the Rio Grand. The unit was mustered out of service on January 15, 1867.

The 30th saw its first action in Virginia with the Army of the Potomac during the savage Wilderness Campaign and would later be heavily engaged in the siege of Petersburg. Under the command of Colonel Delavan Bates the regiment participated in two major expeditions against the "Gibraltar of the Confederacy," Fort Fisher, North Carolina in December 1864 and January 1865, the subsequent capture of Wilmington, and the advance on and capture of Raleigh. On December 10, 1865 the 30th would be mustered out of service after having participated in four major engagements and numerous skirmishes.[11]

The men of color who had volunteered to serve in the six Maryland USCT regiments constituted over five percent of the 186,000 African-Americans who donned Union uniforms in the Civil War.[12] Of the original 5,398 officers and men who became an army on the banks of the muddy Patuxent, eight officers and 228 enlistees would be killed or mortally wounded in combat. Six officers and 998 enlistees would succumb to disease, accident, or execution after capture by the enemy. Thus a total of 1,226 men, or nearly twenty-eight percent of their original number, would perish as free men in the service to their country.[13] Twenty-five black soldiers and sailors would be awarded the Congressional Medal of Honor during the Civil War. Two from St. Mary's County, William H. Barnes, for his role at the Battle of Chaffin's Farm, and James H. Harris at the Battle of New Market Heights, Virginia, would be awarded for service and heroism above and beyond the call of duty. Some would later leave their own indelible marks on society. Sergeant John H. Murphy of the 30th Regiment, but one among them, would hold many menial jobs before becoming president and publisher of the Baltimore *Afro-American*. And when it was over many of those who survived would tell their children about how it all began as free men at Camp Stanton.[14]

On June 13, 1866 Congress passed the Fourteenth Amendment to the United States Constitution, granting citizenship to "all persons born or naturalized in the United States" and forbidding any state from depriving "any person of life, liberty, or property, without due process of law." The amendment was ratified by twenty-eight of thirty-seven states, and formally adopted July 9, 1866. Slavery in America had finally been outlawed though the vestige of human bondage, forced apprenticeship, still lingered. Finally the issue would reach the United States Supreme Court. On October 15, 1867 Chief Justice Salmon Chase ruled that under the 14th Amendment, generally referred to in the press as the Civil Rights Law, the binding of negro apprentices by the Orphans Court of Maryland was declared illegal. The following year, the ruling was confirmed in United States District Court, and the last gasp of legalized slavery in America would come to an end.[15]

***

Though the actual fires of battle, with the exception of the Early-Johnson campaign of 1864, had not swept across the fertile fields and forests of Southern Maryland, its effects had nevertheless been devastating. Yet they were hardly recognized in the grand scheme of reconstruction. Years would pass before the new order would take hold, though many of the old traditions and beliefs would remain. The racial scars left after centuries of black slavery would run deep and influence the slowly changing tapestry of society, politics and the economy of Southern Maryland for decades to come. For whites, the physical effects were equally apparent and difficult, albeit in disparate ways. In the ten-year period between 1860 and 1870 the Charles County population had declined from 16,517 to 15,751 residents living in just 2,512 dwelling. Only Dorchester, Prince George's and Queen Anne's counties had fewer occupied dwellings. Charles County, once one of the most agriculturally prominent counties in the state, could boast of only 501 operating farms, the fewest of any in Maryland. Barely a dozen very small industrial establishments were still functioning. Only Calvert County had fewer working industrial operations of any kind. In St. Mary's County, the black population would decline from 8,415 to 7,726, an 8.19 percent decrease, though an increase of whites from 6,798 to 7,218, or 6.18 percent, had somewhat blunted the manpower loss owing to a conscientious effort by county leaders to recruit white laborers from elsewhere. The combination of emancipation, the Union's military recruitment of blacks from the St. Mary's labor force, and the number of white men that had left to serve in the Confederate military, not surprisingly, had a particularly negative impact upon farm production. In 1865 a government agent reported that as a result of the paucity of labor in the county barely half of the arable land in St. Mary's had been cultivated during the preceding year. Consequently, economic distress prevailed.[16]

Bankruptcies and foreclosures throughout the lower Maryland counties and those of the Eastern Shore would become the order of the day. The threat of financial collapse for both individuals and institutions loomed large. Barely more than two years after Appomattox, in the single month of May in St. Mary's, eleven farms totaling well over 4,051 acres were placed up for trustee's sale, including one on which the venerable Clifton Factory was located. Five more, totaling 598 acres, included horses, oxen, cows, calves, hogs, tobacco, wheat machine, reaper, screw prize, wheat fan, and the wheat crops were soon to be placed on the market. Collection notices were also filed for fourteen tracts totaling 1,098 acres, which included seven of the cottages at Point Lookout. Thus a total of thirty tracts totaling 5,747 acres were up for grabs in but a single month.[17]

An editorial in the March 12, 1868 edition of the *St. Mary's Gazette* blamed the distressing situation on the same population that had hitherto provided the labor and insured economic stability, namely the former slaves.

"A gentleman who has had occasion recently to visit many sections of our county, drew in our presence the other day a melancholy contract between the condition of our people now and their condition some six years ago when his duties led him to intimate association with them. Then, the evidence of prosperity and comfort met him at every homestead he visited. The dwellings, outhouses, fencing, gates, stock, household and kitchen arrangements, the appearance and condition of the fields and gardens, all gave a token of a rapid and healthy progress. Now prosperity and comfort are the exception – not the rule. Many, who before the war were in easy if not independent circumstances, have been utterly ruined, and their homes have passed or are passing to the stranger – The great majority are still struggling on but struggling at great disadvantage. Many are still heavily in debt and the means and credit of all are very limited. The labor system of the county is hopelessly disorganized. The negro as a free laborer has been fairly tested and, with very few exceptions, has been found utterly unreliable. The native white labor of the county is grossly inadequate to the demands of agriculture and white immigration is yet to commence in this direction. Hence it is that contracted fields, dilapidated dwellings and perishing fences meet the traveler at almost every step. The chief study is to keep the wolf from the door and everything else is subordinated to this. Indeed it is impossible to visit any district in our once prosperous county without noticing that a terrible political and social revolution has passed over the section, ruining many and leaving the great mass of our community in a condition of pitiful prostration." [18]

***

Though the war was over, for the prisoners at Point Lookout it had continued to be a vexing time, even though there had been ongoing paroles, prisoner exchanges, and releases for those who swore the oath of allegiance. At the beginning of April the prison population had been officially reported at 7,825. An incredible surge of new prisoners totaling 12,285, however, resulting from the fighting at Petersburg and around Richmond, had increased the total to a staggering record high of 20,110 inmates. The number of rebels held at Camp Hoffman had suddenly grown to its greatest size of the war, equal to over fifty-three percent of Richmond's total 1860 population of 37,910. Of these, ten per cent of the inmates were sick or had died during the month, during which time only thirty-eight soldiers and 183 civilian prisoners had been released. By May the official count of inmates had been reported at 19,818, of which nearly eleven percent of the total, 2,124 souls, were either sick or had died.[19] An unofficial count of inmates reported on May 12 by the *Alexandria Gazette* placed the number of prisoners at 23,700.

The situation demanded immediate action to address the humanitarian crisis that during the war would have been largely ignored. A 1,312-ton steamboat called *New World*, originally rigged as a military hospital barge for service on the James River, which had been lying at anchor off Alexandria for many months, was called back into emergency service and dispatched to Point Lookout. Unfortunately, the ungainly 300-foot long, four-stories tall vessel ran aground on a mud flat off Smith's Inlet on May 10. Despite the best efforts of several rescue craft the ship's services would not be employed at the prison camp.[20]

It was, however, but a matter of time before most inmates knew they would be released on parole. In mid-May it was reported that all but two prisoners had expressed a wish to take the oath of allegiance. "As fast as they take the oath," it was said, "they will be sent to Richmond to go to their homes."[21] Sadly, the repatriation effort failed to move as rapidly as hoped, even as Union occupation troops were rapidly leaving most of the posts in Southern Maryland. Leonardtown, a central hub of Union control in St. Mary's County, was no exception. "The troops, which have so long been stationed in our village as a Police Guard," reported the *St. Mary's Gazette* on May 25, "took up their line of march for Washington on Sunday morning last, where, we learn, they will be mustered out of service in obedience to the recent retrenching orders of the Government, except at Point Lookout, we are not aware that any now remain in our county." Tragically the death rate at Camp Hoffman continued to climb to as many as thirty a day by mid-June.[22]

The slow release process was a consequence of logistical problems generated by the rapid demobilization of the army and navy as it was, as some later claimed, insensitivity towards the former enemy. It was, after all, the equivalent of moving the entire population of a small city, many of whom were dreadfully sick, injured, crippled or immobile. The release of prisoners was in great measure dictated by the availability of water transportation necessary to remove them from the Point Lookout Peninsula to Washington or to southern ports. From the capital the Chief Quartermaster of the Department of Washington was responsible for issuing transportation for released prisoners to their homes. By June it was being reported that thirty prisoners a day were reaching the city, a number equal to the daily death rate at the camp. Soon, however, the release of up to 150 prisoners or more per day was underway.[23]

By Monday, June 19 the prison population had been reduced to 9,000, though those who were arriving daily at Washington were still being described as generally sick and destitute. The removal process accelerated greatly with the paroling of 3,000 more prisoners within the next four days as an increasing number of steamers began to arrive to transport inmates directly to Richmond, Charleston, Savannah and other southern ports.[24] By June 29 the *New York Herald* reported, "Of the twenty-two thousand rebel prisoners recently at Point Lookout but two thousand now remain, and these are ordered to be immediately released, excepting about eight hundred sick. The entire camp will be closed within a few weeks."[25] On Sunday, July 3 the Commissary General of Prisoners received word "all prisoners below the rank of colonel heretofore held as prisoners of war in the different prison camps of the country have been released on parole, including the last squad at Point Lookout numbering about one hundred and fifty." [26]

By July 15, little more than a week after the execution of the Lincoln assassination conspirators, it was being announced that Point Lookout would thereafter cease to be of importance as a military post and would be discontinued as a military garrison. With the exception of a single company of the 24th Regiment, USCT, left to guard Federal property, all officers on duty there were to proceed to their respective homes and report by letter to the Adjutant General of the Army. [27] Soon after the announcement, a very feeble William Seward and his son, their wounds still mending from the would-be-assassin's assault on that terrible night in April, paid a visit to the now empty camp where so many men had died. "The Secretary of State," it was reported on July 21, "accompanied by his son, Mr. Frederick Seward, and wife, and Major Wilson, U.S.A., returned this morning from a trip to Point Lookout, much benefited by the excursion. The health of Mr. Frederick Seward is rapidly improving." [28]

If the excursion proved of healing benefit to the secretary and his son, the pall of death still hanging over Camp Hoffman could not be denied.

General Barnes' final tally of prisoners of war that passed through the gates of Camp Hoffman from August 1863 to June 1865 was placed at 52,264 rebels, not counting civilians confined for various acts deemed inimical to the Union. Confederates and others incarcerated at one time or another at Point Lookout accounted for 23.76 percent of the 220,000 total number of rebel prisoners in all prisoner of war camps in the Union. At least 3,435 deaths occurred among the inmates, or 6.57 percent of the total population, a figure compiled from official records a century later by historian Edwin W. Beitzell. There were unquestionably many hundreds, perhaps thousands more that went undocumented. With a reported per capita death rate among the highest in the Union, and the deviations from humane treatment too numerous to calculate still fresh in many a survivor's mind, it behooved Federal authorities to dismantle the camp as soon as possible.[29]

The prison experience was indelibly etched not only upon the earth but also upon the souls, minds and bodies of those who had been imprisoned there. Two years after Appomattox, former prisoner of war Sidney Lanier would publish his antiwar novel *Tiger Lillies*, a story not particularly well received but one that had evolved from his incarceration at Camp Hoffman. "To go into a prison of war is in all respects to be born over," he had written. "For of the men in all the prisons of the late war it might be said . . . they came in and went out naked. Into the prison at Point Lookout, Maryland, were born, at a certain time, of poor and probable honest parents, twelve thousand grown men." Through his myriad writings he struggled, as his life progressed, to reconcile the differences between North and South. Yet he also began engaging issues of national and racial identity that would contribute to the very distinctiveness of Southern culture for the next century, one rooted in the concept of the noble "Lost Cause" of a chivalric, defiant and unbowed South that survives to the present day.[30]

***

The reduction of Camp Hoffman was not without some opposition. A Chicago philanthropist named Delphine Baker proposed the extant facilities at Point Lookout would prove an excellent site for the establishment of a veteran's asylum, and managed to secure support from General Grant and others. But the effort was in vain. On December 29, 1865 Colonel Marshall I. Ludington, Chief Quartermaster, Department of Washington, announced a public auction of all Federal assets at the point to be held on January 18, 1866. To facilitate the sales it would be advertised that "A steamer will leave the Government wharves, south side of the basin, near Fardy's shipyard, Baltimore, Md., at 10 o'clock, on the morning of Wednesday, January 17, 1866, for the transportation of bidders to Point Lookout, and will be retained until the close of the sale to return the passengers to Baltimore. Meals will be furnished on the boat at the usual (steamboat) rates." An itemized list of every building or item to be sold was to include: the Hammond Hospital and all of the associated buildings and structures used to support the medical complex; all of the buildings in and associated with the Camp Hoffman prisoner of war camp, including the great wooden fence and walkway surrounding the grounds; and all of the buildings belonging to the Quartermaster's Department, as well as all of the miscellaneous buildings and structures, such as guardhouses, storehouses, barracks and wharves used by the military. All purchases would be paid for in cash and purchasers allowed twenty days to remove their property. A military guard was to remain on site to protect property for fifteen days after the sale.[31]

Once the site of William Cost Johnson's idyllic, short lived Eden, Point Lookout was soon a desolate, abandoned ruin. It had become a graveyard for thousands who had died in support of a way of life doomed by the dynamics of war and the painful evolution of social justice and human rights. Within but a short time little physical evidence of the Union hospital, military depot and Confederate prisoner of war camp remained. Only a number of eroding earthen defense works, a foundation here and there, the Pavilion Hotel, the lighthouse, and a few relics of the war were visible to the infrequent visitor. The Confederate gravesites were soon identifiable only by sunken earth. Even portions of the graves were assailed as shore erosion claimed many human remains that were washed indiscriminately into the Potomac and bay.

In the 1870s efforts were initiated at exhumation of many unfortunates whose remains had not yet been lost. Those bodies that could be recovered were interred in a single mass grave. In 1878 the State of Maryland erected a marble obelisk at the

650

burial site to memorialize those Confederates who had lost their lives at Camp Hoffman. In 1910-11 a taller obelisk bearing 3,389 known names, companies and regiments of the Confederate dead was built of granite carried down river by freight schooners. [32]

Not long after the close of the war real estate developers initiated efforts to revivify the point as a resort. Development was to be boosted by the construction of a railroad line and the creation of a subdivision of private cottages. A company called the St. Mary's and Point Lookout Land and Improvement Company was formed and followed somewhat along the concept lines of William Cost Johnson's grand scheme. Failure of the railroad, however, brought development plans to a halt. William A. Smith, one of the original property owners in the area, reopened the Pavilion Hotel for a brief time but tragically the building burned down in 1878. For nearly half a century, Point Lookout was all but forgotten. Then, in the 1920s, the opening of another grand hotel helped spur further plans for a resort subdivision.

This time the delivery of holiday seekers was to be by automobile. Though plots of land were sold, few cottages were constructed as vacation goers were increasingly drawn to Atlantic Coast beaches thanks to the construction of the Chesapeake Bay Bridge in 1952. By 1962, when the State of Maryland finally purchased 495 acres of the point for a state park, as much as fifty percent of the 1860 landscape had disappeared beneath the waters of the Chesapeake Bay and Potomac River.[33] It had been a losing battle for the hotel, which struggled to remain open through the 1970s, when it became economically impossible to continue operations. In 1990 the hotel was demolished by the Maryland Department of Natural Resources and a public fishing wharf erected near the site.

With the formal establishment of Point Lookout State Park, the scene of so much suffering just a century earlier had been resurrected and sanitized. Development of the site as a rustic state recreational facility, replete with beaches, campground, fishing pier, picnic grounds, and a small museum, allowed thousands of citizens, young and old, black, white, yellow and brown, freemen all, to finally commune in harmony. Once again the sunny, sandy peninsula had become, as it was in 1860, an "elegant and comfortable retreat for surf and still water bathing, with all the luxuries of Salt Water, Fish, Oysters, &c.; affording elegant and beautiful drives in the distance of fifteen miles, surrounding the peninsular, through a handsomely cultivated country." [34]

William Cost Johnson would have been pleased, I am sure.

NOTES

Abbreviation Key

AJII	Andrew Johnson Impeachment Investigation
CTPitman	Conspiracy Trial. *Assassination of President Abraham Lincoln*
CTPoore	Conspiracy Trial. *Conspiracy Trial for the Murder of President Abraham Lincoln*
CWNC	*Civil War Naval Chronology 1861-1865*
JST	*Trial of John H. Surratt*
LC	Library of Congress
MDA	Maryland State Archives
MHM	*Maryland Historical Magazine*
MHS	Maryland Historical Society
M 599	Investigation and Trial Papers Relating to the Assassination of President Lincoln
M 619	Letters received by Office of Adjutant General
NARA	National Archives and Record Administration
ORA	*War of the Rebellion: A Compilation of Official Records of the Union and Confederate Armies*
ORN	*Official Records of the Union and Confederate Navies in the War of the Rebellion*
RR	*Rebellion Record*

Prologue

1. "Hamnond Hospital," *Daily National Republican*, Second Edition, 14 February 1863.
2. Edwin W. Beitzell, *Point Lookout Prison Camp for Confederates* (Leonardtown, Md.: Privately Printed, 1972), 2; F. Ross Holland, *Maryland Lighthouses of the Chesapeake Bay* (Crownsville and Colton's Point, Maryland: 1997, Maryland Historical Trust Press and The Friends of St. Clement's Island Museum, Inc.), 20, 24-27.
3. "Hammond Hospital."
4. "William Cost Johnson," in *Biographical Directory of the United States Congress 1774-Present*, http://bioguide.congress.gov/biosearch/biosearch.asp, accessed June 11, 2013.
5. "The Ocean Steamers," *The Daily Dispatch*, 8 January 1857.
6. "Arrived at Alexandria," *Evening Star*, 16 June 1857.
7. Beitzell, 2; "Project for the Establishment of a Bathing Place at Point Lookout," *The Daily Exchange*, 25 February 1858.
8. "Project for the Establishment of a Bathing Place at Point Lookout."
9. Ibid.; *The Daily Dispatch*, 8 March 1859; "Cape Lookout," *The Daily Exchange*, 14 April 1859; "Returned," *Evening Star*, 12 September, 1859; Beitzell, 2.
10. "Cape Lookout."
11. *Evening Star*, 19 August 1859, 12 September 1859; Beitzell, 19.
12. *Evening Star*, 23 September 1859.
13. "Point Lookout," *Evening Star*, 24 May 1860.
14. "Sketches of Summer Travel," *Evening Star*, 25 August 1860.

1. Night Vigilants

1. David C. Holly, *Tidewater by Steamboat: A Saga of the Chesapeake* (Baltimore and London: The Johns Hopkins University Press, 1991), 216, 249.
2. Ibid., 231-232.
3. See overview of the Weems Line activities in William J. Kelley, "Baltimore Steamboats in the Civil War," *MHM*, Vol. 37, No. 1 (March 1942).
4. Holly, 64, 69.
5. R. Lee Van Horn, *Out of the Past: Prince Georgeans and Their Land*, (Riverdale, Md.: Prince George's County Historical Society, 1976), 347; James Wiggins's Narrative, in *Maryland Slave Narratives: A Folk History of Slavery in Maryland from interviews with Former Slaves. Typewritten records prepared by The Federal Writers; Project, 1936-1938.* (Bedford Mass.: Applewood Books, published in Cooperation with the Library of Congress, n.d.), 66.
6. Parson Rezin Williams' Narrative, in *Maryland Slave Narratives*, 69, 75.
7. Dennis Simms' Narrative, in *Maryland Slave Narratives*, 62.
8. *Port Tobacco Times, and Charles County Advertiser* [hereafter *Port Tobacco Times*], 7 August 1845, 14

August 1845, 19 February 1846, 18 August 1852, 11, 18 and 25 December 1856, 25 June and 6 August 1857; *St. Mary's Beacon,* 14 February 1861.

9. Harold R. Manakee, *Maryland in the Civil War* (Baltimore: Maryland Historical Society, 1961), 21; Ron Field, *The Confederate Army 1861-65: Missouri, Kentucky & Maryland* (Oxford, UK: Osprey Publishing, 2008), 33; *Port Tobacco Times,* 20 December 1860, 27 December 1861.

10. *Daily National Intelligencer,* 26 January 1861; Benjamin Franklin Cooling III and Walton H. Owen II, *Mr. Lincoln's Forts: A Guide to the Civil War Defenses of Washington* (Shippensburg, Pa: White Mane Publishing Company, 1988), 233.

11. Ibid.

12. *Daily National Intelligencer,* 2 February 1861; *St. Mary's Beacon,* 21 February 1861.

13. Isaac Toucey to John Harris, 5 January 1861, *ORA,* Ser. I, Vol. 4, 409; Franklin Buchanan to John A. Dahlgren, 8 January 1861, *ORN,* Ser. I, Vol. 4, 411; Dahlgren to Buchanan, 14 January 1861, *ORN,* Ser. I, Vol. 4, 411-412; Dahlgren to Buchanan, 23 January 1861, *ORN,* Ser. I, Vol. 4, 412.

14. *Daily National Republican,* 31 January 1861; St. Mary's Beacon, 9 January 1861, 14 February 1861; Edwin W. Beitzell, *Point Lookout Prison Camp for Confederates* (Leonardtown, Md.: Privately Printed, 1972), 9; Regina Combs Hammett, *History of St. Mary's County Maryland* (Ridge, Md.: Privately published, 1977), 107.

15. *Baltimore Sun,* 18 January 1861.

16. Ibid., 21 February 1861. At least five other units in Anne Arundel, already formed or soon to be formed, including the West River Guards, Patapsco Light Dragoons, Union Rifles, Severn Guards, and the States Rights Guards, were blatantly secessionist. Others, such as the Union Guard, South River Guards, and even the newly formed Magothy Home Guard cautiously refrained from outright displays of disaffection while waiting to see which way the pendulum would swing. Only one unit, the Chesapeake Home Guard, soon to be formed in August, declared loyalty to the Union. Daniel A. Hartzler, *A Band of Brothers: Photographic Epilogue to Marylanders in the Confederacy* (Westminster, Md.: Heritage Books 2008), 23.

17. *Baltimore Sun,* 18 January 1861.

18. Harry Wright Newman, "Anne Arundel During the War of Secession," in *Anna Arundel County, Maryland: A Bicentennial History 1649-1977,* James C. Bradford, ed. (Annapolis: Anne Arundel County and Annapolis Bicentennial Committee, 1977), 269.

19. The first comprehensive survey and assessment of Maryland's highway system, undertaken in 1898, thirty-three years after the close of the Civil War, indicated that a total of only 2,316 miles of roadways crisscrossed the five counties of Southern Maryland, all of which were dirt roads except 225 miles of gravel passageways and five of shell. Only 410 miles were deemed "main" roads, the remainder being less than rural pathways or trails. *Report on the Highways of Maryland.* [In Accordance with an Act Passed at The Session of the General Assembly of 1898, Laws of Maryland 1898, Chapter 454]. (Baltimore, The Johns Hopkins University Press, 1899), 216-217, 221, 228, 244-247.

2. Blood Hounds

1. George William Brown, *Baltimore and the 19th of April, 1861* (Baltimore: Johns Hopkins University, 1887, reprint 1982), 113-114.

2. John Tory Caton, "Baltimore," in *The Old Line State: A History of Maryland,* Morris L. Radoff, ed. (Annapolis: Publication No. 16, Hall of Records Commission, State of Maryland, 1971), 199, 201; Harry Wright Newman, *Maryland and the Confederacy* (Annapolis: Privately published, 1976), 15; Scott Sumter Sheads and Daniel Carroll Toomey, *Baltimore During the Civil War* (Linthicum, Md.: Toomey Press, 1997), vii; Nathanial A. Branch Miles, Monday M. Miles, and Ryan J. Quick, *Prince George's County and the Civil War: Life on the Border* (Charleston and London: History Press, 2013), 8; Harry Wright Newman, "Anne Arundel During the War of Secession," in *Anna Arundel County, Maryland: A Bicentennial History 1649-1977,* James C. Bradford, ed. (Annapolis: Anne Arundel County and Annapolis Bicentennial Committee, 1977), 269; John Lockwood and Charles Lockwood, *The Siege of Washington* (Oxford University Press, Inc.: New York, 2011), 53-54; Jane Wilson McWilliams, *Annapolis: City on the Severn* (Baltimore: The Johns Hopkins University Press, and Crownsville: The Maryland Historical Trust Press, 2011), 162. The population count for Annapolis did not include 403 people living on the grounds of the U.S. Naval Academy.

3. Drew Gilpin Faust, *Mothers of Invention: Women of the Slaveholding South in the American Civil War* (Chapel Hill: University of North Carolina Press, 1996), 32.

4. *We Live Here, Too: Slavery in Prince George's County, Maryland, 1860-1864* (Clinton, Md.: Surratt House Museum, Undated), 2; John P. McCarthy, *Oxon Hill Manor: The Archaeology and History of "A World They Made Together"* (St. Leonard, Md. and Crownsville, Md.: Jefferson Patterson Park Museum and Maryland Historical Trust, 2010), 3.

5. James V. Deane's Narrative, in *Maryland Slave Narratives*, 7, 8; Charles Coles' Narrative, in *Maryland Slave Narratives*, 4; Dennis Simms' Narrative, in *Maryland Slave Narratives*, 60; Page Harris' Narrative, in *Maryland Slave Narratives*, 23; Newman, "Anne Arundel During the War of Secession," 269.

6. Parson Rezin Williams' Narrative, in *Maryland Slave Narratives*, 73.

7. Page Harris's Narrative, 22.

8. Ibid.

9. Charles Coles' Narrative, 4; James V. Deane's Narrative, in *Maryland Slave Narratives*, 8; Parson Rezin Williams Narrative, 74.

10. Richard Macks's Narrative, in *Maryland Slave Narratives*, 51-52.

11. James Wiggins's Narrative, *Maryland Slave Narratives*, 66-67; Wright Newman, "Anne Arundel During the War of Secession," 269.

12. See Josiah Henson, *The Life of Josiah Henson, Formerly a Slave, Now an Inhabitant of Canada, as Narrated by Himself* (A. D. Phelps: Boston, 1849), and Harriet Beecher Stowe, *Uncle Tom's Cabin; or, Life Among the Lowly* (Boston: J. P. Jewett and Company, 1853; and Cleveland: Jewett, Proctor, and Worthington, 1853) for Henson's earliest comprehensive autobiography and subsequent fictional narrative derived from it.

13. Dennis Simms's Narrative, 61.

14. James V. Deane's Narrative, 7.

15. Dennis Simms's Narrative, 60-61.

16. Ibid.

17. Richard Macks's Narrative, 55.

18. Dennis Simms's Narrative, 61.

19. "Cases Under the Civil Rights Law, " *Evening Star*, 30 May 1866.

20. At least eight slaves are known to have been owned or hired by the Surratts over time. These included: Henry Hawkins, James Butler, Alfred Hawkins, Rachel Hawkins, Sally, Susan, George and Jeff. At least two, Sally and Susan, were rented between 1861 and 1864. *We Lived Here, Too*, 5.

21. Parson Rezin Williams, 76-77.

22. Richard Macks's Narrative, 51. The St. Mary's Female Institute, established in September 1857, was a private women's boarding school at which reading, writing, spelling, tables, geography, English, needlework, orthography, history (ancient and contemporary), and mythology were the principal courses taught. *Port Tobacco Times*, 10 September 1857, 9 September 1858.

23. Richard Macks's Narrative, 52-53.

24. Kenneth J. Winkle, *Lincoln's Citadel: The Civil War in Washington, D.C.* (New York and London, W.W. Norton & Company, 2013) 132; Richard Macks's Narrative, 54.

25. James V. Deane's Narrative, 9.

26. *Census of 1860: Population of the United States* (Washington, D.C.: Government Printing Office, 1864), 215; Miles, et al, 9, 19; R. Lee Van Horn, *Out of the Past: Prince Georgeans and Their Land*, (Riverdale, Md.: Prince George's County Historical Society, 1976), 349.

3. A Peculiar Position

1. *St. Mary's Beacon*, 18 April 1861.

2. Ibid.

3. *The Rebellion Record: A Diary of American Events*, Frank Moore, ed., 12 Vols. (New York, 1861-68: Putnam and Van Nostrand), 1:188; *New Orleans Picayune*, 18 April 1861; *Vicksburg Whig*, 20 April 1861.

4. See George William Brown, *Baltimore and the 19th of April, 1861* (Baltimore: Johns Hopkins University. 1887, reprint 1982) and John Lockwood and Charles Lockwood, *The Siege of Washington* (Oxford University Press, Inc.: New York, 2011) for the most comprehensive accounts of the Baltimore mob actions of April 18 and 19, 1861.

5. Proclamation of the Governor of Maryland, Baltimore, 18 April 1861, RR, Vol. 1, Part 2, Documents and Narratives, 76-77. On January 6, 1860, soon after the election of Lincoln, Hicks had stated in addressing the General Assembly: "The attacks of fanatical and misguided persons against

property in slaves, and the warfare carried on in those States which still retain the institution of slavery, were formally confined to a few; who were forced to content themselves with refusing assistance to, or placing obstacles in the way of, our citizens, who proceeded to those States, under the guarantees of the Constitution, to recover their property." Nathanial A. Branch Miles, Monday M. Miles, and Ryan J. Quick, *Prince George's County and the Civil War: Life on the Border* (Charleston and London: History Press, 2013), 65.

6. Proclamation of the Mayor of Baltimore, Mayor's Office, 77.

7. A Proclamation by the President of the United States of America, Washington, 19 April 1861, *RR*, Vol. 1, Part 2, Documents and Narratives, 78; *CWNC*, 1:12.

8. Winfield Scott, General Orders No. 3, Headquarters of the Army, Washington, 19 April 1861, *RR*, Vol. 1, Part 2, Documents and Narratives, 78.

9. *ORA*, Ser. I, Vol. 2, 7; Brown, 46-53; Robert E. Lee to Anne Marshall, 20 April 1861, in *The Wartime Papers of Robert E. Lee*, Clifford Dowdey, ed., and Louis H. Manarin, assoc. ed. (Boston: Bramhill House, 1961, reprinted New York: De Capo Press, 1987), 9-10; Daniel Carroll Toomey, *The Civil War in Maryland* (Toomey Press: Baltimore, 1983), 11; Phineas Camp Headley, *Massachusetts in the Rebellion: A Record of the Historical Position of the Commonwealth, and the Services of the Leading Statesmen, the Military, the Colleges, and the People, in the Civil War of 1861-65* (Boston: Walker, Fuller and Co., 1866), 113.

10. Brown, 46-53.

11. George William Brown to Abraham Lincoln, 19 April 1861, *RR*, Vol. 1, Part 2, Documents and Narratives, 78-79; Thomas H. Hicks and George William Brown to Abraham Lincoln, 19 April 1861, *RR*, Vol. 1, Part 2, Documents and Narratives, 79; Brown, 56-57.

12. Report of Office of the Board of Police Commissioners (Baltimore), *ORA*, Ser. I, Vol. 2, 10; Report of Mayor George Brown, 9 May 1861, *ORA*, Ser. I, Vol. 2, 13; Harold R. Manakee, *Maryland in the Civil War* (Baltimore: Maryland Historical Society, 1961), 38; J. Morris Harris, "A Reminiscence of the Troublous Times of April 1861," *Maryland Historical Society Fund Publication*, No. 31 (Baltimore: Maryland Historical Society, 1891), 21-25.

13. *RR*, Vol. 1, Part 1, Diary of Events, 35; Ron Field, *The Confederate Army 1861-65: Missouri, Kentucky & Maryland* (Oxford, UK: Osprey Publishing, 2008), 41.

14. Harris, 21-25; Brown, 74-75; Field, 35.

15. Brown, 60-65. Trimble would later become a major general in the CSA and lose a leg at Gettysburg.

16. *Richmond Examiner*, 23 April 1861.

17. Testimony of Captain Philip Reybold before the Angus Commission, Senate Document No. 215, 59th Cong., 2nd sess.: *Report of the Commissioners Appointed by the President to Examine and Report upon a Route for the Construction of a Free and Open Waterway to Connect the Waters of the Chesapeake and Delaware Bays* (Washington, D.C.: Government Printing Office, 1907), 44-45; Donald G. Shomette, *Ghost Fleet of Mallows Bay And Other Tales of the Lost Chesapeake* (Centreville, Md.: Tidewater Publishers, 1996), 4.

18. Jane Wilson McWilliams, *Annapolis: City on the Severn* (Baltimore: The Johns Hopkins University Press, and Crownsville: The Maryland Historical Trust Press, 2011), 167; Richard S. West, Jr., *Lincoln's Scapegoat General: A Life of Benjamin F. Butler, 1818-1893* (Boston: Houghton Mifflin, and Cambridge: Riverside Press, 1965), 42, 47, 51-54.

19. Newman, "Anne Arundel During the War of Secession," 270; Thomas Hicks to Commander of the Volunteers Troops on board the steamer, 21 April 1861, *ORA*, Ser. II, Vol. 586-587.

20. *Annapolis Gazette*, 28 April 1861.

21. *Daily National Intelligencer*, 24 and 26 April 1861; Departure of the New York Seventh Regiment, *RR*, Vol. 1, Part 2, Documents and Narratives, 80-81; Newman, "Anne Arundel During the War of Secession," 270; "New York Seventh Regiment, Our March to Washington," *Atlantic Monthly*, Vol. 7 (June 1861), 746-748; *ORA*, Ser. I, Vol. 2, 593, 589-590. Superintendent Blake had, since the fall of Fort Sumter, been planning for the evacuation of *Constitution* to save her from Southern sympathizers. The ship was to be sent to either Philadelphia or New York and any munitions on the Naval Academy grounds were to be destroyed as well. Jack Sweetman, *The U.S. Naval Academy: An Illustrated History*, 2nd ed., rev. by Thomas J. Cutler (Annapolis: Naval Institute Press, 1993) 59-60.

22. *ORA*, Ser. I, Vol. 2, 591.

23. Benjamin F. Butler, *Butler's Book: A Review of His Legal, Political, and Military Careers* (Boston, A. M. Thayer: 1892), 194-195, 201-202; "The Seventh Regiment—How It Got from New York to Washington," The Capitol, Washington, 27 April 1861, *RR*, Vol. 1, Part 2, Documents and

Narratives, 152; *Daily National Republican*, 25 April 1861; *Albany Journal*, 27 April 1861. See also "New York Seventh Regiment, Our March to Washington," 750, for another version of the Homans story.

24. Thomas H. Hicks to Benjamin F. Butler, 23 April 1861, RR, Vol. 1, Part 2, Documents and Narratives, 144; Carl N. Evertine, *General Assembly of Maryland 1850-1920* (Charlottesville, Va.: Michie Co., 1984), 100.

25. Benjamin F. Butler to Thomas H. Hicks, 23 April 1861, RR, Vol. 1, Part 2, Documents and Narratives, 144.

26. Toomey, 15; Thomas C. Gillmer, *Old Ironsides: The Rise, Decline, and Resurrection of the USS Constitution* (Camden, Me.: International Marine, 1993), 107.

27. Salmon P. Chase to Abraham Lincoln, 25 April 1861, Abraham Lincoln Papers, LC.

28. *New York Times*, 25 April 1861; E. B. Long and Barbara Long: *The Civil War Day by Day: An Almanac 1861-1865* (Garden City, N.Y.: Doubleday & Company, Inc., 1971), 64; RR, Vol. 1, Part 1, 38-39; *Daily National Intelligencer*, 23 April 1861.

29. "Latest from the Seat of War," *New York Times*, 27 April 1861.

30. *Annapolis Gazette*, 25 April 1861.

31. *ORA*, Ser. I, Vol. 2, 605-607; *Annapolis Gazette*, 1 May 1861.

32. Walker Lewis, *Without Fear or Favor: A Biography of Chief Justice Roger Brooke Taney* (Boston: Houghton Mifflin, 1965), 450-452.

33. An Embargo at Baltimore, RR, Vol. 1, Part 2, Documents and Narratives, 134; *Baltimore American*, 23 April 1861; *Baltimore Sun*, 23 April 1861; *The South*, 23 April 1861.

34. *Daily National Republican*, 25 April 1861.

35. George Lovic Pierce Radcliffe, *Governor Thomas H. Hicks of Maryland and the Civil War* (Baltimore: Johns Hopkins Press, 1901), 68-74; Manakee, 51; Harry Wright Newman, *Maryland and the Confederacy* (Annapolis: Privately published, 1976), 58-59; *New York Times*, 30 April 1861; *Daily National Republican*, 11 May 1861; *Annapolis Gazette*, 3 May 1861.

4. Your Honor and Your Chivalry

1. *St. Mary's Beacon*, 18 and 25 April 1861.

2. Ibid.

3. Ibid.; Regina Combs Hammett, *History of St. Mary's County Maryland* (Ridge, Md.: Privately published, 1977), 97, 99.

4. The committee was composed of Benjamin G. Harris, J. P. Dent, Thomas Martin, William Coad, Dr. J. W. Forrest and Joseph Forrest. *St. Mary's Beacon*, 25 April 1861.

5. *St. Mary's Beacon*, 25 April 1861.

6. Ibid.

7. Ibid.

8. Ibid.

9. Ibid.

10. Ibid.

11. Ibid., 9 May 1861; Harry Wright Newman, *Maryland and the Confederacy* (Annapolis: Privately published, 1976), 215.

12. *St. Mary's Beacon*, 24 March 1859, 12 January 1860, 16 February 1860, 26 April 1860, 31 May 1860, 13 December 1860, 21 February 1861.

13. Ibid., 3 January 1861.

14. Ibid., 7 March 1861. Dr. Randolph Jones would be among the few who struggled with his loyalties. On August 18, 1861 his neighbor Colonel William Coad would write: "You cannot find a Union man from Bretons Bay to Point Lookout, except Doctor Randolph Jones and some inhabitants of St. Georges Island." E. W. Beitzell, *Life on the Potomac* (Abell, Md.: Privately published, 1968), 40.

15. Ibid., 9 May 1861. Officers elected to command included: Captain, Walter Dent: 1st Lieut., John V. Posey; 2nd Lieut., Robert Alvey; 3rd Lieut., J. H. Mattingly; Orderly Sergeant, William H. Blair; Ensign, William Mattingly; Quarter Master, R. M. Shanks; Surgeon, Dr. C. M. Hammett.

16. *Baltimore Sun*, 29 March 1861. Ron Field, in *The Confederate Army 1861-65: Missouri, Kentucky & Maryland* (Oxford, UK: Osprey Publishing, 2008), 38, notes that Colonel Richard Thomas of St. Mary's County joined with George W. Alexander and William C. Walters to form two companies of Zouaves for the Confederate service in not only St. Mary's but in Calvert County. I have been unable to locate any confirmation of that claim for Calvert County.

17. *Port Tobacco Times*, 3 May, 21 June, 20 December 1860, 3 January 1861; Field, 34; Harry Wright Newman, "Anne Arundel During the War of Secession," *Anna Arundel County, Maryland: A Bicentennial History 1649-1977*, James C. Bradford, ed. (Annapolis: Anne Arundel County and Annapolis Bicentennial Committee, 1977), 269.

18. *Daily National Republican*, 3 May 1861; *The South*, 23 April 1861; John Lockwood and Charles Lockwood, *The Siege of Washington* (Oxford University Press, Inc.: New York, 2011), 219; Roger Thomas, "Southern Maryland," in *The Old Line State: A History of Maryland*, Morris L. Radoff, ed. (Annapolis: Publication No. 16, Hall of Records Commission, State of Maryland, 1971), 146. Hartzler attributes the unit's command to Oden Bowie, later to become Governor of Maryland, though Bowie's official biography does not mention it. Daniel A. Hartzler, *A Band of Brothers: Photographic Epilogue to Marylanders in the Confederacy* (Westminster, Md.: Heritage Books 2008), 28.

19. *St. Mary's Beacon*, 9 May 1861; *Port Tobacco Times*, 26 November 1857.

20. *St. Mary's Beacon*, 9 May 1861.

21. Ibid.

22. Ibid.

23. R. Lee Van Horn, *Out of the Past: Prince Georgeans and Their Land*, (Riverdale, Md.: Prince George's County Historical Society, 1976), 346.

24. *St. Mary's Beacon*, 9 May 1861.

25. *ORA*, Ser. I, Vol. 2, 607.

26. A Proclamation by the President of the United States, Washington, 3 May 1861, RR, Vol. 1, Part 2, Documents and Narratives, 185-186; Toomey, 16-18.

27. *New York Herald*, 5 May 1861.

28. Thomas H. Hicks to Benjamin Butler, 10 May 1861, *Executive Letter Book*, Maryland State Archives, reprint in *Maryland Voices of the Civil War*, Charles W. Mitchell, ed. (Baltimore: The Johns Hopkins University Press, 2007), 104.

29. *New York Daily Tribune*, 10 May 1861.

30. George W. Brown, *Baltimore and the 19th of April, 1861* (Johns Hopkins University: Baltimore, 1887, reprint in 1982), 37-38; John Thomas Scharf, *The Chronicles of Baltimore: being a Complete History of "Baltimore Town" and Baltimore City from the Earliest Period to the Present Time* (Baltimore: Turnbull Brothers, 1874), 613; Harold R. Manakee, *Maryland in the Civil War* (Baltimore: Maryland Historical Society, 1961), 53; E. B. Long and Barbara Long: *The Civil War Day by Day: An Almanac 1861-1865* (Garden City, N.Y.: Doubleday & Company, Inc., 1971), 74; Harry Wright Newman, *Maryland and the Confederacy*, 194.

31. "Affairs in Baltimore: Habeas Corpus Case," *New York Times*, 29 May 1861.

32. Inclosure No. 2, James Miltimore and William H. Abel, 27 May 1861, *ORA*, Ser. I, Vol. 2, 574-575; "Decision of Chief Justice Taney on the John Merriman Habeas Corpus Case," *New York Times*, 29 May 1861

33. *Daily National Intelligencer*, 4 June 1861; Bernard Schwartz, *A History of the Supreme Court* (New York: Oxford University Press, 1993), 127; Daniel M. Thomas to Sister, 27 May 1861, The Papers of Daniel M. Thomas, 1674-1938, MS 758, Maryland Historical Society, reprint in Mitchell, *Maryland Voices*, 122.

5. Slow Steam

1. *Port Tobacco Times*, 4 June 1857, 10 November 1857, 24 May 1860, 3 January 1861.

2. Statement of George W. Smith, of Bryantown, Charles County, Md., [Taken by] T. B. Robey, *ORA*, Ser. II, Vol. 2, Part 1, 868.

3. *Port Tobacco Times*, 10 December 857, 1 November 1860, 9 August 1860, 3 January 1861.

4. Statement of George W. Smith.

5. Thomas A. Jones, *J. Wilkes Booth: An Account of His Sojourn in Southern Maryland after the Assassination of Abraham Lincoln*, (Chicago: Laird & Lee Publishers, 1893), 12.

6. Zachariah V. Posey took over the Farmers and Planters Hotel in January 1858. The hotel hosted Independence Day festivities in the summer of the same year. Posey was among those who called for a sovereign convention to elect state delegates to the Maryland Legislature, an initiative the editor of the *Port Tobacco Times* considered treasonous. *Port Tobacco Times*, 7 January 1858, 24 June 1858, 17 January 1861.

7. Luther Martin was the consort of Ellen Martin, 25, who died in late December 1856 at Port

Tobacco. *Port Tobacco Times*, 25 December 1856.

8. Statement of George W. Smith; Edwin W. Beitzell, *Life on the Potomac* (Abell, Md.: Privately published, 1968), 38; John M. and Roberta J. Wearmouth, *Thomas A. Jones: Chief Agent of the Confederate Secret Service* (Port Tobacco, Md.: Stones Throw Publishing, 1995), 5; William A. Tidwell, "Charles County: Confederate Cauldron," *MHM*, Vol. 91, No. 1, Spring, 1996, 20; Jones, 11, 12.

9. *Port Tobacco Times*, 10 May 1855, 8 May 1856, 11 June 1857, 24 June 1858; Wearmouth, 5; Tidwell, 20-21.

10. *ORA*, Ser. II, Vol. Vol. 2, Part 1, 321.

11. Beitzell, 38; Tidwell, 22.

12. Ron Field, *The Confederate Army 1861-65: Missouri, Kentucky & Maryland* (Oxford, UK: Osprey Publishing, 2008), 39-41.

13. Gideon Welles to S. L. Breese, 15 April 1861, *ORN*, Ser. I, Vol. 4, 413; Welles to Breese, 19 April 1861, *ORN*, Ser. I, Vol. 4, 414; *ORN*, Ser. II, Vol. 1, 180.

14. John A. Dahlgren to Franklin Buchanan, 15 April 1861, *ORN*, Ser. I, Vol. 4, 413-414.

15. Franklin Buchanan to Gideon Welles, 19 April 1861, *ORN*, Ser. I, Vol. 4, 414.

16. Buchanan to Dahlgren, 22 April 1861, *ORN*, Ser. I, Vol. 4, 418.

17. Ibid.; *Daily National Intelligencer*, 1 June 1861; Eric Mills, *Chesapeake Bay in the Civil War* (Centreville, Md.: Tidewater Publishers, 1996), 32. On June 1, 1861 the *National Intelligencer* listed the following resignations from the Navy Department: 16 major officers, 31 commanders, 76 lieutenants, 11 surgeons, 10 assistant surgeons, 10 paymasters, 1 chaplain, 1 professor of mathematics (Alex. W. Lawrence), 6 masters, 5 Naval Academy midshipmen graduates, 106 acting midshipmen (including 22 from the U.S. Naval Academy), 2 gunners, 3 sailmakers, 1 Marine Corps general staff, 3 Marine Corps captains, 6 marine captains, 5 marine 2nd lieutenants, 4 chief engineers, 6 1st assistant engineers, 1 2nd assistant engineer, and 7 3rd assistant engineers. *Daily National Intelligencer*, 24 April and 1 June 1861.

18. Charles Stone, "A Dinner with General Scott in 1861," *Magazine of History*, Vol. 9, No. 6, (June 1884) 528-532; *Washington During War Time: A Series of Papers Showing the Military, Political, and Social Phases During 1861 to 1865*, Benjamin Marcus, coll. and ed. (Washington, D.C.: Washington City [Press of B. S. Adams], 1902), 20, 23; *Memoirs of Thaddeus S.C. Lowe, Chief of the Aeronautic Corps of the Army of the United States During the Civil War: My Balloons in Peace and War*, Michael Jaeger and Carol Lauritzen, eds. (Lewiston, N.Y.: Edwin Mellen Press, ca. 2004), 71.

19. Warren Lee Gross, "Going to the Front: Recollections of a Private – 1," *Battles and Leaders of the Civil War*, 4 Vols. (New York and London: Thomas Yoseloff, 1956), Vol. 1, 157-158.

20. Ibid., 16-17.

21. Ibid.

22. *Daily National Intelligencer*, 15, 17, 18, 22, 23 April 1861; John Lockwood and Charles Lockwood, *The Siege of Washington* (Oxford University Press, Inc.: New York, 2011), 94, 95, 101.

23 *ORN*, Ser. II, Vol. 1, 172.

24. Buchanan to Welles, 19 April 1861, *ORN*, Ser. I, Vol. 4, 414.

25. Gideon Welles to John Harris, 20 April 1861, *ORN*, Ser. I, Vol. 4, 415; Gideon Welles to T. S. Fillebrown, 20 April 1861 [1], *ORN*, Ser. I, Vol. 4, 415; Gideon Welles to T. S. Fillebrown, 20 April 1861 [2], *ORN*, Ser. I, Vol. 4, 415-416.

26. Gideon Welles to Franklin Buchanan, 21 April 1861, *ORN*, Ser. I, Vol. 4, 416-417; Franklin Buchanan to John A. Dahlgren, 22 April 1861, *ORN*, Ser. I, Vol. 4, 417. The Potomac Steamboat Company was later to receive compensation of $170,000 from the United States for the seizures. Mary Ann Wills, *The Confederate Blockade of Washington, D.C. 1861-1862* (Parsons, West Virginia: McClain Printing Company, 1975), 15.

27. John A. Dahlgren to Gideon Welles, 22 April 1861, *ORN*, Ser. I, Vol. 4, 418; John A. Dahlgren to Gideon Welles, 23 April 1861 [1], *ORN*, Ser. I, Vol. 4, 421-422; John A. Dahlgren to Gideon Welles, 23 April 1861 [2], *ORN*, Ser. I, Vol. 4, 423-424. Gideon Welles to Simon Cameron, 23 April 1861, [1] *ORN*, Ser. I, Vol. 4, 420; Gideon Welles to Simon Cameron, 23 April 1861 [2], *ORN*, Ser. I, Vol. 4, 421. *Keystone State* would be purchased from Ocean Steam Navigation Company on June 10, 1861 for $125,000. *ORN*, Ser. II, Vol., Vol. 1, 120.

28. "Captain Ward," *Daily National Republican*, 1 July 1861; Navy Department, Office of the Chief of Naval Operations, Naval History Division, *Dictionary of American Naval Fighting Ships*, 8 Vols. (Washington: U.S. Government Printing Office, 1968), Vol. 8, 918.

29. Gideon Welles to John A. Dahlgren, 22 April 1861, *ORN*, Ser. I, Vol. 4, 419; Wills, 15.

30. Gideon Welles to John A. Dahlgren, 23 April 1861, *ORN*, Ser. I, Vol. 4, 421-422; [Log of] U.S.S *Mount Vernon* [George Willmuth], 22 April 1861, [Enclosure in Dahlgren to Welles, 25 April 1861, 9 a.m.]; Fillebrown to Welles, 23 April 1861, *ORN*, Ser. I, Vol. 4, 422.

31. Dahlgren to Welles, 23 April 1861, *ORN*, Ser. I, Vol. 4, 421-422; [Log of] U.S.S *Mount Vernon*, 22 April 1861.

32. Ibid; John A. Dahlgren to Gideon Welles, 25 April 1861, *ORN*, Ser. I, Vol. 4, 426.

33. T. S. Fillebrown to Gideon Welles, 23 April 1861, *ORN*, Ser. I, Vol. 4, 422; Dahlgren to Welles, 25 April 1861.

34. Gideon Welles to John P. Gillis, 23 April 1861, *ORN*, Ser. I, Vol. 4, 423; Gideon Welles to Stephen C. Rowan, 23 April 1861, *ORN*, Ser. I, Vol. 4, 423; Gideon Welles to John P. Gillis, 24 April 1861, *ORN*, Ser. I, Vol. 4, 424-425; Frederick Tilp, *This Was Potomac River* (Alexandria, Va.: Published by author, 1978), 108.

35. Dahlgren to Welles, April 25, 1861, *ORN*, Ser. I, Vol.4, 427. Beitzell identified five of the men who participated in the destruction of the lightship, John Johnson, William and Alexander Campbell, Frank Clements, and Alfred Naley, as hailing from the Port Tobacco area. Beitzell, *Life on the Potomac*, 41.

36. Mills, 38.

37. Gideon Welles to John P. Gillis, 23 April 1861, *ORN*, Ser. I, Vol. 4, 423; Welles to Rowan, 23 April 1861.

38. Winfield Scott to Robert Patterson, 25 April 1861, *ORA*, Ser. I, Vol. 2, 601; *Evening Star*, 25 April 1861; *Daily National Republican*, 26 April 1861; Lockwood and Lockwood, 229.

39. John A. Dahlgren to Gideon Welles, 25 April 1861, *ORN*, Ser. I, Vol. 4, 426.

40. John P. Gillis to Gideon Welles, 26 April 1861, *ORN*, Ser. I, Vol. 4, 428.

41. Thomas Scott to Gideon, 26 April 1861, *ORN*, Ser. I, Vol. 4, 429.

42. "Treachery in the Navy Yard," *National Intelligencer*, 29 April 1861.

6. Escalation

1. *New Orleans Picayune*, 2 May 1861; "War Declared by the Congress of the Confederate States," *Daily National Republican*, 13 May 1861.

2. J. Glendy Sproston to John A. Dahlgren, 1 May 1861, *ORN*, Ser. I, Vol. 4, 441.

3. Ibid.

4. Ibid., 442.

5. John A. Dahlgren to T. S. Fillebrown, 2 May 1861, *ORN*, Ser. I, Vol. 4, 443; Thomas Scott Fillebrown to Gideon Welles, 3 May 1861, *ORN*, Ser. I, Vol. 4, 444; Thomas Scott Fillebrown to Gideon Welles, 5 May 1861, *ORN*, Ser. I, Vol. 4, 447.

6. John P. Gillis to Gideon Welles, 5 May 1861, *ORN*, Ser. I, Vol. 4, 447.

7. "Public Meeting," *St. Mary's Beacon*, 9 May 1861; *Port Tobacco Times*, 30 May 1861.

8. Simon Cameron to Winfield Scott, 6 May 1861, *ORA*, Ser. I, Vol. 2, 623.

9. "General Butler at Baltimore," *Daily National Republican*, 16 May 1861.

10. "Intercourse with Baltimore," *Daily National Republican*, 9 May 1861.

11. Schuyler Hamilton to Benjamin F. Butler, 11 May 1861, *ORA*, Ser. I, Vol. 633-634.

12. *Washington During War Time: A Series of Papers Showing the Military, Political, and Social Phases During 1861 to 1865*, Benjamin Marcus, coll. and ed. (Washington, D.C.: Washington City [Press of B. S. Adams], 1902), 24; "The Seventh Regiment Camp," *Daily National Republican*, 8 May 1861.

13. *Washington During War Time*, 24-25.

14. *Daily National Intelligencer*, May 4, 1861; "The New York Fire Zouaves," *Daily National Republican*, 3 May 1861.

15. "The New York Fire Zouaves."

16. Ibid.

17. "Review of the New Jersey Troops," *Daily National Republican*, 8 May 8, 1861.

18. "Parade and Targeting," *Daily National Republican*, 8 May 1861; "Music at the President's Grounds," *Daily National Republican*, 8 May 1861; Joseph K. F. Mansfield to Winfield Scott, 3 May 1861, *ORA*, Ser. I, Vol. 2, 619.

19. *Charleston Evening News* (Charleston, SC), 6 May 1861.

20. [General Cocke's Proclamation], *The Daily Dispatch*, 8 May 1861.

21. "Expedition Down the Chesapeake," *Daily National Republican*, 8 May 1861; "The Latest from Annapolis," *Daily National Republican*, 10 May 1861.

22. Benjamin F. Butler to Gideon Welles, 18 May 1861, *ORN*, Ser. I, Vol. 4, 468-469; Gideon Welles to Benjamin F. Butler, 20 May 1861, *ORN*, Ser. I, Vol. 4, 469; *Baltimore Sun*, 17 and 20 May 1861.

23. "Affairs at Annapolis—Picket Guard Fired Upon," *Daily National Republican*, 13 May 1861.

24. Robert Spear to Gideon Welles, 10 May 1861, *ORN*, Ser. I, Vol. 4, 453.

25. John A. Dahlgren to Navy Department, 11 May 1861, *ORN*, Ser. I, Vol. 4, 456 [letters 1 and 2]; Gideon Welles to John A. Dahlgren, 11 May 1861, *ORN*, Ser. I, Vol. 4, 456; John A. Dahlgren to Gideon Welles, 12 May 1861, *ORN*, Ser. I, Vol. 4, 457.

26. Samuel L. Breese to Gideon Welles, 1 May 1861, *ORN*, Ser. I, Vol. 4, 443; Samuel L. Breese to Gideon Welles, 12 May 1861, *ORN*, Ser. I, Vol. 4, 458.

27. "Kinds of Gunboats Wanted," *Scientific American*, New Series, 24, 14 December 1861, 379. Navy records state both *Reliance* and *Resolute* were 88 feet 2 inches in length and 17 feet abeam.. *ORN*, Ser. II, Vol. 1, 190, 191.

28. Samuel L. Breese to Gideon Welles, 17 May 1861, *ORN*, Ser. I, Vol. 4, 467; John A. Dahlgren to Navy Department, 20 May 1861, (telegram), *ORN*, Ser. I, Vol. 4, 471. Construction of the Aquia Creek defenses was assigned to William F. Lynch, a naval officer, and R. D. Thorburn, H. H. Wilkinson, and John Wilkinson, of the Virginia State forces. "Our Naval Squadrons," *The National Tribune*, 29 June 1892.

29. Abstract log of steamer *Mount Vernon*, 13, 15, 18 May 1861, *ORN*, Ser. I, Vol. 4, 470-471; John A. Dahlgren to Navy Department (telegram), *ORN*, Ser. I, Vol. 4, 469; Thomas Scott Fillebrown to Gideon Welles, 17 May 1861, *ORN*, Ser. I, Vol. 4, 466.

30. J. Glendy Sproston to John P. Gillis, 14 May 1861, *ORN*, Ser. I, Vol. 4, 462-463; John P. Gillis to Gideon Welles, 14 May 1861, 11:30 a.m., *ORN*, Ser. I, Vol. 4, 462.

31. "Freight Trains Through Baltimore," *Daily National Republican*, 13 May 1861; "From Annapolis," *Daily National Republican*, 16 May 1861.

32. "Military Movements, etc., at Annapolis," *Daily National Republican*, 13 May 1861.

33. John A. Dahlgren to Gideon Welles, 20 May 1861, *ORN*, Ser. I, Vol. 4, 471-472; John A. Dahlgren to Gideon Welles, 22 May 1861, *ORN*, Ser. I, Vol. 4, 476.

34. John P. Gills to Gideon Welles, 21 May 1861, *ORN*, Ser. I, Vol. 4, 472-473; John A. Dahlgren to Gideon Welles, 22 May 1861, *ORN*, Ser. I, Vol. 4, 475.

35. John A. Dahlgren to Gideon Welles, 22 May 1861, *ORN*, Ser. I, Vol. 4, 474.

36. James H. Ward to Gideon Welles, 22 May 1861, *ORN*, Ser. I, Vol. 4, 475.

37. James M. Barbour, *Alexandria in the Civil War* (Lynchburg, Va.: H. E. Howard, Inc., 1988), 12.

38. Donald G. Shomette, *Maritime Alexandria: The Rise and Fall of an American Entrepot* (Heritage Book, Inc.: Bowie, Md., 2003), 154-162.

39. It was loudly proclaimed after the Alexandria incident that the first blood of the Civil War had been spilled. Colonel Ellsworth, with the enormous press coverage that followed, had become the Union's first recognized martyr of the Civil War. Few noted or remembered until later the Union soldiers that died during the Pratt Street Riot several weeks earlier. There is also some irony that the last operation of Ellsworth's Zouaves before they departed for Alexandria was to close down a rebel smuggling operation on the very doorstep of Washington. "Col. Ellsworth having discovered that provisions were surreptitiously conveyed from Baltimore by water to Marlboro and thence across Maryland to the Alexander ferry," reported the *Daily National Republican* on May 24, "by which they were put in possession of the Secessionists, took one hundred Zouaves, night before last [May 22], and, marching down six or eight miles, blockaded all the roads in the vicinity. He found undoubted evidence of the regular transportation of supplies, and learned that the last wagonload was carried across early that morning. Yesterday morning, some of the inhabitants, attempted to start off, apparently to spread a warning, but they were prevented. The Colonel remained on this duty until he had made himself thoroughly acquainted with all the routes used for these purposes. Hereafter there will be no more aid and comfort furnished Alexandria in this manner." "Provisions for the Rebels Stopped," *Daily National Republican*, 24 May 1861.

7. A Sheet of Flame

1. "Fort Washington," *Daily National Republican*, 27 May 1861.

2. *Daily National Republican*, 28 May 1861; S. C. Rowan to Gideon Welles, June 12, 1861, *ORN*, Ser. I,

Vol. 4, 508. Commander Rowan states the warship was the USS *Resolute* but as that vessel was then elsewhere the vessel was more likely the USS *Reliance*.

3. *Evening Star* [quoting *Richmond Examiner*)], 4 June 1861; James H. Ward to Gideon Welles, 31 May 1861, *ORN*, Ser. I, Vol. 4, 490; Daniel Ruggles to R. S. Garnett, 30 May 1861, *ORN*, Ser. I, Vol. 4, 496.

4. Ward to Welles, May 31, 1861.

5. *Evening Star*, 4 June 1861; Ruggles to Garnett, 30 May 1861.

6. Ruggles to Garnett, 30 May 1861.

7. James H. Ward to Gideon Welles, May 31, 1861, *ORN*, Ser. I, Vol. 4, 491. Ward's visit was later lampooned in the northern press when it was stated: "Reported battery at Matthias Point proves to be a wood pile." *Freemont Daily Journal*, 3 June 1861.

8. *Evening Star*, 31 May 1861; *Daily National Republican*, 1 June 1861.

9. William F. Lynch to Samuel Barron, 2 June 1861, *ORN*, Ser. I, Vol. 4, 495. Ruggles, who was not present, stated that the fight began at about 10 a.m. Daniel Ruggles to R. S. Garnett, June 1, 1861, *ORN*, Ser. I, Vol. 4, 497.

10. *ORN*, Ser. II, Vol. 1:223; Ward to Welles, May 31, 1861, *ORN*, Ser. I, Vol. 4, 491; *Daily National Republican*, 3 June 1861.

11. *ORN*, Ser. II, Vol. 1, 34.

12. *Evening Star*, 1 June 1861; Ruggles to Garnett, 1 June 1861; M. W. McCluskey to L. P. Walker, 1 June 1861, *ORN*, Ser. I, Vol. 4, 501. The rebels initially identified the largest vessel in the squadron, *Thomas Freeborn*, as the USS *Crusader*. Lynch to Barron, 2 June 1861.

13. Ward to Welles, May 31, 1861, *ORN*, Ser. I, Vol. 4, 491; Lynch to Barron, 2 June 1861; McCluskey to Walker, 1 June 1861.

14. McCluskey to Walker, 1 June 1861; Lynch to Barron, 2 June 1861.

15. *Evening Star*, 1 June 1861; Ward to Welles, May 31, 1861, *ORN*, Ser. I, Vol. 4, 491.

16. *Evening Star*, 1 June 1861; *Daily National Republican*, 1 June 1861; McCluskey to Walker, 1 June 1861.

17. *Daily National Republican*, 3 June 1861. McCluskey states that the firing ceased at 3:30 p.m. Ruggles, who had yet to arrive, states the time as "about 1 p.m." McCluskey to Walker, 1 June 1861; Ruggles to Garnett, June 1, 1861.

18. Ward to Welles, May 31, 1861, *ORN*, Ser. I, Vol. 4, 490.

19. McCluskey to Walker, 1 June 1861; Ruggles to Garnett, June 1, 1861; Mary Ann Wills, *The Confederate Blockade of Washington, D.C. 1861-1862* (Parsons, West Virginia: McClain Printing Company, 1975), 26.

20. Ward to Welles, May 31, 1861.

21. Ruggles to Garnett, June 1, 1861.

22. Ward to Welles, May 31, 1861.

23. *Daily National Republican*, 3 June 1861.

24. Ward to Welles, May 31, 1861, *ORN*, Ser. I, Vol. 4, 491.

25. S. C. Rowan to Gideon Welles, 2 June 1861, *ORN*, Ser. I, Vol. 4, 492; Wills, 26.

26. Ruggles to Garnett, June 1, 1861.

27. *Evening Star*, 4 June 1861; Lynch to Barron, 2 June 1861; Ward to Welles, June 1, 1861, *ORN*, Ser. I, Vol. 4, 491; Rowan to Welles, 2 July 1861, *ORN*, Ser. I, Vol. 4, 493. The *Evening Star* of June 4, says two miles though the *Daily National Republican* of June 3, says 1,700 yards. Daniel Ruggles to R. S. Garnett, 2 June 1861, *ORN*, Ser. I, Vol. 4, 497-498. Ruggles, who was not there at the start of the fight, states incorrectly the engagement started at 9 a.m.

28. *Evening Star*, 4 June 1861; Rowan to Welles, 2 July 1861, *ORN*, Ser. I, Vol. 4, 492-493; James H. Ward to Gideon Welles, June 1, 1861, *ORN*, Ser. I, Vol. 4, 491.

29. Lynch to Barron, 2 June 1861; Ward to Welles, 1 June 1861.

30. Ward to Welles, 1 June 1861, *ORN*, Ser. I, Vol. 4, 492; *Evening Star*, 4 June 1861.

31. *Evening Star*, 4 June 1861; Rowan to Welles, 2 July 1861; Ward to Welles, 1 June 1861; Wills, 27.

32. *Daily National Republican*, 3 June 1861.

33. *Evening Star*, 4 June 1861; Lynch to Barron, 2 June 1861.

34. *Daily National Republican*, 3 June 1861; *Evening Star*, 4 June 1861; Ward to Welles, 1 June 1861, *ORN*, Ser.1, Vol. 4, 492.

35. Lynch to Barron, 2 June 1861; Wills, 27.

36. Ward to Welles, 1 June 1861, *ORN*, Ser. I, Vol. 4, 491; *Daily National Republican*, 3 June 1861.

37. *Evening Star*, 4 June 1861.

38. Ruggles to Garnett, 1 June 1861, *ORN*, Ser. I, Vol. 4, 497.

39. Ward to Welles, 1 June 1861, *ORN*, Ser. I, Vol. 4, 491; Lynch to Barron, 2 June 1861.

40. Ibid.; *Daily National Republican*, 3 June 1861; *Evening Star*, 4 June 1861. Rowan reported that he had expended all of his 10-second and 15-second shells and the entire thirty-eight rounds allotted for the rifled guns as well as 155 hollow shot. Rowan to Welles, 2 July 1861.

41. *Evening Star*, 4 June 1861; Ruggles to Garnett, June 2, 1861; Lynch to Barron, 2 June 1861.

42. *Daily National Republican*, 3 June 1861; Ward to Welles, 1 June 1861; *Evening Star*, 4 June 1861.

43. Rowan to Welles, 2 July 1861, *ORN*, Ser. I, Vol. 4, 493; *Daily National Republican*, 3 June 1861; *Evening Star*, 4 June 1861; Ruggles to Garnett, June 2, 1861.

44. Ward to Welles, 1 June 1861.

45. *Evening Star*, 4 June 1861.

46. Lynch to Barron, 2 June 1861; Ward to Welles, 1 June 1861. The *Daily National Republican* claimed 280 projectiles had been fired. Ruggles claimed that the battery returned only seventy-five projectiles, but this estimate may be assumed to have been made as a result of his late arrival on the field. *Daily National Republican*, 3 June 1861; Ruggles to Garnett, June 2, 1861.

47. W. B. Bates to L. P. Walker, 11 June 1861, *ORN*, Ser. I, Vol. 4, 500; S. C. Rowan to Gideon Welles, 21 June 1861, *ORN*, Ser. I, Vol. 4, 530.

48. Ward to Welles, 1 June 1861.

8. A Cordon of Observation

1. John A. Dahlgren to Navy Department, 2 June 1861, *ORN*, Ser. I, Vol. 4, 493; Mary Ann Wills, *The Confederate Blockade of Washington, D.C. 1861-1862* (Parsons, West Virginia: McClain Printing Company, 1975), 29; William F. Lynch to Samuel Barron, 2 June 1861, *ORN*, Ser. I, Vol. 4, 495-496; *Daily National Republican*, 3 June 1861; W. B. Bates to L. P. Walker, June 11, 1861, *ORN*, Ser. I, Vol. 4, 500.

2. *Evening Star*, 4 June 1861.

3. John A. Dahlgren to Navy Department, 3 June 1861, (telegram), *ORN*, Ser. I, Vol. 4, 503; Gideon Welles to John A. Dahlgren, 3 June 1861, *ORN*, Ser. I, Vol. 4, 503. Colonel Ruggles observed *Pawnee* on June 4 lying off the creek "repairing damages and communicating with various steamers and other vessels passing up and down the Potomac." Daniel Ruggles to R. S. Garnett, 4 June 1861, *ORN*, Ser. I, Vol. 4, 498-499.

4. Ruggles to Garnett, 4 June 1861.

5. Ibid.

6. Ibid.

7. W. R. Palmer to A. D. Bache, 8 June 1861, *ORN*, Ser. I, Vol. 4, 505-506; S. C. Rowan to Gideon Welles, 10 June 1861, *ORN*, Ser. I, Vol. 4, 506.

8. Gideon Welles to James H. Ward, 6 June 1861, *ORN*, Ser. I, Vol. 4, 505; Navy Yard [Washington, D.C.] to Navy Department, 8 June 1861 (telegram), *ORN*, Ser. I, Vol. 4, 506; S. C. Rowan to Gideon Welles, 17 June 1861, *ORN*, Ser. I, Vol. 4, 520-521.

9. William Budd to S. C. Rowan, 9 June 1861, *ORN*, Ser. I, Vol. 4, 507; F. Ross Holland, *Maryland Lighthouses of the Chesapeake Bay* (Crownsville, Md.: The Maryland Historical Trust Press and The Friends of the St. Clement's Island Museum, Inc., 1997), 20.

10. Budd to Rowan, 9 June 1861, *ORN*, Ser. I, Vol. 4, 507-508; *Daily National Intelligencer*, 13 June 1861. One of Budd's informants in Breton Bay may have been a Mr. Goff, agent for the steamer *St. Nicholas*, with whom he spoke regarding Captain Lynch's defense of Aquia during the recent engagements. James H. Ward to Gustavus V. Fox, 11 June 1861, *ORN*, Ser. I, Vol. 4, 494; *St. Mary's Beacon*, 13 June 1861.

11. Budd to Rowan, 9 June 1861, *ORN*, Ser. I, Vol. 4, 507.

12. S. C. Rowan to Gideon Welles, 10 June 1861, *ORN*, Ser. I, Vol. 4, 507; S. C. Rowan to J. P. K. Mygatt, 11 June 1861, 1p.m., *ORN*, Ser. I, Vol. 4, 510.

13. *St. Mary's Beacon*, 13 June 1861. It was reported incorrectly in the press on June 20 that Mygatt captured no fewer than eleven vessels endeavoring to supply the rebels, two of which were burned, four sunk, and five brought in as prizes. A survey of Federal records by the author does not bear out the story. *Daily Ohio Statesman*, 21 June 1861.

14. Ibid.

15. *New York Daily Tribune* (New York, N.Y.), 14 June 1861.

16. James H. Ward to Gideon Welles, 10 June 1861, *ORN*, Ser. I, Vol. 4, 508-509; James H. Ward to Gideon Welles, 12 June 1861, *ORN*, Ser. I, Vol. 4, 510.

17. Gideon Welles to James H. Ward, 15 June 1861, *ORN*, Ser. I, Vol. 4, 514.

18. James H. Ward to Gideon Welles, 10 June 1861, 1 p.m., *ORN*, Ser. I, Vol. 4, 509-510; S. C. Rowan to Gideon Welles, 12 June 1861, *ORN*, Ser. I, Vol. 4, 508; Gideon Welles to James H. Ward, 10 June 1861, *ORN*, Ser. I, Vol. 4, 509.

19. John A. Dahlgren to Gideon Welles, June 15, 1861, *ORN*, Ser. I, Vol. 4, 515; Gideon Welles to James H. Ward, 12 June 1861, *ORN*, Ser. I, Vol. 4, 511.

20. Gideon Welles to James H. Ward, 15 June 1861, *ORN*, Ser. I, Vol. 4, 514; James H. Ward to William Budd, 17 June 1861, *ORN*, Ser. I, Vol. 4, 519.

21. James H. Ward to S. C. Rowan, 13 June 1861, *ORN*, Ser. I, Vol. 4, 512-513; "Washington, June 18," *Daily Ohio Statesman*, 21 June 1861. Though the terminal points for Budd's Ferry were at Mrs. Budd's adjacent to Quantico Creek on the Virginia side of the Potomac, and the ferry wharf near the Posey house on the opposite side of the river, the name was popularly ascribed to the facility on the Maryland shore.

22. James H. Ward to Gideon Welles, 16 June 1861, *ORN*, Ser. I, Vol. 4, 516-517; William Budd to Gideon Welles, 25 June 1861, *ORN*, Ser. I, Vol. 4, 533-534; *Daily National Republican*, 18 June 1861.

23. Wills, 34.

24. S. C. Rowan to Gideon Welles, 19 June 1861, *ORN*, Ser. I, Vol. 4, 525.

25. *Port Tobacco Times*, 14 and 21 August 1845, 12 February 1846, 29 July 1847; 15 June and 3 August 1848; 17 July and 7 August 1850; 30 July 1851, 28; July and 11 November, 1853; 13 April and 21 September 1854; 11 December 1856; 14 April 1859; 3 May, 3 June, 27 September and 1 November 1860; 9 and 17 January 1861.

26. John A. Dahlgren to Navy Department., 18 June 1861, (telegram 1), *ORN*, Ser. I, Vol. 4, 523; John A. Dahlgren to Navy Department, 18 June 1861, (telegram 2). *ORN*, Ser. I, Vol. 4, 523; John A. Dahlgren to Gideon Welles, 20 June 1861, *ORN*, Ser. I, Vol. 4, 524; *Port Tobacco Times*, 20 June 1861; *Daily National Republican*, 19 June 1861.

27. Gideon Welles to James H. Ward, 18 June 1861, *ORN*, Ser. I, Vol. 4, 521; S. C. to Gideon Welles, 18 June 1861, *ORN*, Ser. I, Vol. 4, 522; S. C. Rowan to John A. Dahlgren, 19 June 1861, *ORN*, Ser. I, Vol. 4, 522; S. C. Rowan to J. P. K. Mygatt, 19 June 1861, *ORN*, Ser. I, Vol. 4, 522-523.

28. James H. Ward to Gideon Welles, 20 June 1861, *ORN*, Ser. I, Vol. 4, 526-527.

29. Ibid.

30. John A. Dahlgren to Gideon Welles, 20 June 1861 (1), *ORN*, Ser. I, Vol. 4, 528.

31. Ibid.; John A. Dahlgren to Gideon Welles, 20 June 1861, (2) *ORN*, Ser. I, Vol. 4, 524.

9. Mathias Point

1. James H. Ward to Gideon Welles, 24 June 1861, *ORN*, Ser. I, Vol. 4, 533; *The Daily Dispatch*, 27 June 1861.

2. Ward to Welles, 24 June 1861.

3. Ibid.; Mary Alice Wells, *The Confederate Blockade of Washington, D.C., 1861-1862* (Parson, West Virginia: McClain Printing Company, 1975), 35.

4. Wills, 35.

5. *Evening Star*, 27 June 1861.

6. S. C. Rowan to Gideon Welles, 25 June 1861, *ORN*, Ser. I, Vol. 4, 535. No record of a Federal charter for *James Guy*, built in 1856 Keyport, New Jersey, has been found. She has been confused by at least one authority with the steamer *James Gray*, for which U.S. Army charter records have been found. See *Merchant Steam Vessels of the United States 1780-1868*, William M. Lytle and Forrest R. Holdcamper, comp. (Staten Island, N.Y.: The Steamship Historical Society of America, Inc., 1975), 108, 270, and Charles Dana Gibson and E. Kay Gibson, *Dictionary of Transports and Combatant Vessels Steam and Sail Employed by the Union Army 1861-1868*, 2 Vols. (Camden, Me.: Ensign Press, 1995), Vol. 2, 172.

7. S. C. Rowan to Gideon Welles, 25 June 1861, *ORN*, Ser. I, Vol. 4, 535; *The Evening Star*, 27 June 1861; Wells 35.

8. Ibid.

9. Wills, 36; "The Enemy Planting Batteries at Point Mathias," *The Daily Dispatch*, 27 June 1861.

10. William Budd to Gideon Welles, 25 June 1861, *ORN*, Ser. I, Vol. 4, 533; "Contemptible Villiany" *The Daily Dispatch*, 1 July 1861; Thomas A. Jones, *J. Wilkes Booth: An Account of His Sojourn in Southern Maryland after the Assassination of Abraham Lincoln*, (Chicago: Laird & Lee Publishers, 1893), 12.; James O. Hall and David Winifred Giddy, *Come Retribution: Confederate Secret Service and the Assassination of Lincoln* (Oxford: University Press of Mississippi, 1988), 65.

11. "Contemptible Villiany."

12. Ibid.

13. William Budd to Gideon Welles, 25 June 1861, *ORN*, Ser. I, Vol. 4, 534.

14. Thomas H. Holmes to George Deas, 27 June 1861, *ORN*, Ser. I, Vol. 4, 535.

15. James H. Ward to S. C. Rowan, 26 June 1861, *ORN*, Ser. I, Vol. 4, 538.

16. S. C. Rowan to Gideon Welles, June 27, 1861, enclosed in Foxhall A. Parker to Gideon Welles, June 28, 1861, *ORN*, Ser. I, Vol. 4, 537.

17. J. C. Chaplin to S. C. Rowan, 28 June 1861, *ORN*, Ser. I, Vol. 4, 539-540; "Captain Ward," *Daily National Republican*, 1 July 1861; Daniel J. Ruggles to H. H. Walker, 27 June 1861, 9:30 p.m., *ORA*, Ser. I, Vol. 2, 136; "The Fight at Mathias Point: The Northern Account," *The Daily Dispatch*, 4 July 1861.

18. "The Fight at Mathias Point: The Northern Account."

19. J. W. Moore to Gideon Welles, 28 June 1861, *ORN*, Ser. I, Vol. 4, 541; J. C. Chaplin to S. C. Rowan, 28 June 1861, *ORN*, Ser. I, Vol. 4, 540; Robert M. Mayo to Daniel J. Ruggles, June 28, 1861 *ORA*, Ser. II, Vol. Vol. 2, 137.

20. "The Fight at Mathias Point: The Northern Account."

21. Chaplin to Rowan, 28 June 1861; Civil War letters of Fleet W. Cox, Company Commander, Fortieth Virginia Regiment, University of Virginia Library, Collection No. 4380, UVL, Charlottesville, Va., referenced in Wills, 39; The Confederates estimated more than fifty men were engaged in the construction project. Daniel J. Ruggles to H. H. Walker, 27 June 1861, 9:30 p.m. It was later debated whether or not Chaplin and his men had been summoned back to the ship to bring off guns intended for mounting in the breastworks. Although that seems unlikely given that only 200 sandbags had been filled and placed there is no documentation to that effect. *The Evening Star*, 28 June 1861.

22. "The Fight at Mathias Point: The Northern Account."

23. Ibid.

24. Ibid.

25. Mayo to Ruggles, 28 June 1861.

26. Ibid.; "Correspondence of the Richmond Dispatch," *The Daily Dispatch*, 4 July 1861.

27. Rowan to Welles, 27 June 1861; Mayo to Ruggles, 28 June 1861.

28. Ibid.; "The Fight at Mathias Point: The Northern Account."

29. Chaplin to Rowan, 28 June 1861; S. C. Rowan to Gideon Welles, 27 June 1861, enclosed in Foxhall A. Parker to Gideon Welles, 28 June 1861, *ORN*, Ser. I, Vol. 4, 537; F. M. Gunnell to S. C. Rowan, 27 June 1861, *ORN*, Ser. I, Vol. 4, 538; Mayo to Ruggles, 28 June 1861. Seaman John Waters was not mentioned as wounded in the final reports of the battle. He would linger on until finally succumbing to his wounds in early November. "Funeral of a Sailor," *New York Daily Tribune*, 5 November 1861.

30. "The Fight at Mathias Point: The Northern Account." Edwin W. Beitzell, in his *Life on the Potomac* (Abell, Md.: Privately published, 1968), 36, states that Ward was shot by a Confederate sharpshooter named Andrew Pitt of Caroline County, Virginia.

31. "The Fight at Mathias Point: The Northern Account."

32. Ibid.

33. Ibid.

34. Chaplin to Rowan, 28 June 1861; *Daily National Republican*, 1 July 1861; Rowan to Welles, 27 June 1861; Gunnell to Rowan, 27 June 1861. The official report of Acting Assistant Surgeon J. W. Moore of *Thomas Freeborn* stated that Ward "was struck by a musket ball from the enemy while sighting his forward gun. The ball entered at a point just above and a little to the right of the umbilicus and passed directly through the abdomen, escaping at a point opposite, about 2 inches to the right of the spinal column. He died from internal hemorrhage about an hour after being shot," about 6 p.m. Moore to Welles, 28 June 1861.

35. Rowan to Welles, 27 June 1861. The Confederates reported that they had captured "a considerable

number of axes and spades, a very large coil of heavy rope (evidently to draw heavy guns on shore), left by the enemy in his precipitate flight." Daniel J. Ruggles to H. H. Walker, 27 June 1861, 9:30 p.m.

36. John A. Dahlgren to Gideon Welles, 28 June 1861, *ORN*, Ser. I, Vol. 4, 545. Presumably wounded, Seaman John Waters would have been carried back by another vessel, as there is no mention of him in the reports.

37. "Another Engagement at Mathias Point," *The Evening Star*, 28 June 1861; *Daily Intelligencer* (Wheeling, Va.), 1 July 1861; "Obsequies of the Late Capt. Ward," *The Sun*, 2 July 1861.

38. *The Daily Dispatch*, July 1, 1861; Thomas H. Holmes to Robert E. Lee, 28 June 1861, *ORN*, Ser. I, Vol. 4, 542; Mayo to Ruggles, 28 June 1861; "Correspondence of the Richmond Dispatch."

39. Mayo to Ruggles, 28 June 1861.

40. Holmes to Lee, 28 June 1861.

41. Wills, 40-41.

10. Madame La Force

1. *Daily National Republican*, 10 July 1861; Scott Sumter Sheads and Daniel Carroll Toomey, *Baltimore During the Civil War* (Toomey Press: Linthicum, Md., 1997), 41; Mary Alice Wills, *The Confederate Blockade of Washington, D.C. 1861-1862* (McClain Printing Company: Parsons, W.Va., 1975), 51; Regina Combs Hammett, *History of St. Mary's County Maryland* (Ridge, Md.: Privately published, 1977), 115; David C. Holly, *Tidewater by Steamboat: A Saga of the Chesapeake* (Baltimore and London: The Johns Hopkins University Press, Published in Association with the Calvert Marine Museum, 1991), 70.

2. E. W. Beitzell, *Life on the Potomac* (Abell, Md.: Privately published, 1968), 39; Hammett, 115; Sheads and Toomey, 41; Holly, *Tidewater by Steamboat*, 70; Hammett. 116; Thomas, 97; David C. Holly, *Chesapeake Steamboats: Vanished Fleet*, (Centreville, Md.: Tidewater Publishers, 1994), 107; "St. Mary's Light Infantry Company A", *St. Mary's Beacon*, 9 May, 1861.

3. Hammett.,116; Thomas, 97; David C. Holly, *Chesapeake Steamboats: Vanished Fleet*, 107; "St. Mary's Light Infantry Company A."

4. Wills, 21-22.

5. *St. Nicholas* was built in 1845 at Brooklyn, N.Y., where she was first home ported. Sheads and Toomey, 40, state the vessel was 1,200 tons, which does not correspond to the accepted authority on steamboat specifications indicated in *Merchant Steam Vessels of the United States 1780-1868*, William M. Lytle and Forrest R. Holdcamper, comp. (Staten Island, N.Y.: The Steamship Historical Society of America, Inc., 1975), 192, which places her tonnage 413.

6. Beitzell, 38; Wills, 51.

7. Extracts from notes by Commander George N. Hollins, C.S. Navy, *ORN*, Ser. I, Vol. 4, 553. In the debate regarding the origins of the scheme Sheads and Toomey, 41, state that it was Thomas who devised the plan. Beitzell, 38, who takes the middle ground, states: "Lewis received little encouragement from his superiors in Richmond but he was joined by Captain George N. Hollins and Richard Thomas of Maryland, who were enthusiastic about the plan, and ultimately it was approved." Lewis stated that it was he who had conceived the plan but had returned to his post on the Rappahannock after being rebuffed by General Holmes, and was surprised by the visit from Hollins and Thomas, who informed him they were already en route to Point Lookout and Baltimore. He then returned to Fredericksburg and found Tennessee troops as well as some naval officers and men who had earlier embarked aboard the CSS *Virginia* for Monaskon on the Rappahannock, and marched overland to the Coan to await the arrival of *St. Nicholas*. Holly, *Tidewater by Steamboat*, 70. Hollins, *ORN*, Ser. I, Vol. 4, 553, stated unequivocally it was his idea. Thomas made no statement but readily accepted the accolades.

8. Ibid.

9. Ibid.

10. Ibid., 553-554.

11. Ibid. 554.

12. L. P. Walker to Thomas H. Holmes, 27 June 1861, *ORN*, Ser. I, Vol. 4, 551-552.

13. "Correspondence of the Richmond Dispatch," *Nashville Union and American* (Nashville, Tenn.), 6 July 1861.

14. Hollins Extracts, *ORN*, Ser. I, Vol. 4, 554.

15. William Watkins Glenn, *Between North and South: A Maryland Journalist Views the Civil War: The Narrative of William Wilkins Glenn, 1861-1869* (Rutherford, N.J.: Farleigh Dickinson University Press, 1976), 2 July 1861, 34-35.

16. Thomas H. Holmes to L. P. Walker, 27 June 1861, *ORN*, Ser. I, Vol. 4, 552.

17. Thomas H. Holmes to L. P. Walker, 28 June 1861, *ORN*, Ser. I, Vol. 4, 552-553; Holly, *Tidewater by Steamboat*, 69.

18. Wills, 16, 41; Gideon Welles to Thomas T. Craven, 28 June 1861 *ORN*, Ser. I, Vol. 4, 540.

19. Gideon Welles to James H. Ward, 15 June 1861, *ORN*, Ser. I, Vol. 4, 514; James H. Ward to William Budd, 15 June 1861, *ORN*, Ser. I, Vol. 4, 519. Hammett, 115, states that Thomas recruited only a dozen men. John Thomas Scharf, *The Chronicles of Baltimore: being a Complete History of "Baltimore Town" and Baltimore City from the Earliest Period to the Present Time* (Baltimore: Turnbull Brothers, 1874), 613, places the number at twenty-five.

20. *St. Mary's Beacon*, 4 July 1861; Charles Worthington to Gideon Welles, 1 July 1861, *ORN*, Ser. I, Vol. 4, 550; Hollins Extracts, *ORN*, Ser. I, Vol. 4, 554; "Capture of Prize Vessels," *The Western Democrat* (Charlotte, NC), 9 July 1861; Holly, *Vanished Fleet*, 113; Beitzell, 38; Eric Mills, *Chesapeake Bay in the Civil War* (Centreville, Md.: Tidewater Publishers, 1996), 59. An account of the French lady's physical features notes that she was "of quiet manners" rather than "coquettish" as later reports have her. "Daring Feat," *The Daily Exchange*, 2 July 1861.

21. *St. Mary's Beacon*, 4 July 1861; Hollins Extracts, *ORN*, Ser. I, Vol. 4, 554; "Capture of Prize Vessels"; Scharf, 613.

22. *St. Mary's Beacon*, 4 July 1861; Hollins Extracts, *ORN*, Ser. I, Vol. 4, 554. Worthington, in his report of the incident, states that the steamer *Diamond State* had observed *St. Nicholas* "leaving Point Lookout and heading under great speed" for the Virginia shore, most likely the port of Kinsale, "about 1 o'clock that morning," the most reliable time frame available for the event. Worthington to Welles, 1 July 1861, *ORN*, Ser. I, Vol. 4, 550-551.

23. *St. Mary's Beacon*, 4 July 1861; Hollins Extracts, *ORN*, Ser. I, Vol. 4, 554. George Watts, a member of the rebel group, stated there were a total of seventeen men including himself and Thomas in the Zouave unit on board. He did not include the twenty-seven Confederate Navy personnel and landsmen under Hollins. George Watts, "Last Survivor of a Gallant Band," in *Evening Sun* (Baltimore), 27 August 1910. *The Daily Exchange*, 2 July 1861, reports that the total number of rebels aboard was twenty-seven.

24. *St. Mary's Beacon*, 4 July 1861; Hollins Extracts, *ORN*, Ser. I, Vol. 4, 554. Hollins's report of the capture differs markedly with that given by George Watts, which was published nearly half a century later. Watts reported that Thomas and two men had entered the pilothouse where he confronted Kirwin. Watts, a former sailor in the U.S. Navy, and John Frazier, a Baltimore pilot, reportedly placed a pistol to the head of the black quartermaster at the wheel, which was promptly surrendered to Frazier. Some historians have accepted Watts's account, published in the *Evening Sun*, 27 August 1910, as the correct one. This author prefers to accept Hollins's official report in the absence of any report by Thomas and Watts's reminiscences, which were quite probably influenced by the passage of time.

25. *St. Mary's Beacon*, 4 July 1861; Sheads and Toomey, 41; Scharf, 613; Wills, 52; Toomey, 26; Beitzell, 38. One who witnessed their arrival at Fredericksburg claimed the crew consisted of twenty free blacks and nineteen whites, all of whom were to be sent to Richmond. "Correspondence of the Richmond Dispatch."

26. *St. Mary's Beacon*, 4 July 1861; "Capture of Prize Vessels."

27. Wills, 36-37, 39; Beitzell, 38.

28. *St. Mary's Beacon*, 4 July 1861; Hollins Extracts, *ORN*, Ser. I, Vol. 4, 554.

29. Ibid.

30. Ibid.

31. Hollins Extracts, *ORN*, Ser. I, Vol. 4, 554-555.

32. Ibid. 555. Stephen A. Douglas, the famed orator, politician, and presidential candidate who had opposed Abraham Lincoln in the 1860 election, died on 3 June 1861 after rallying support for the Union.

33. Ibid.

34. Hollins, Thomas and all those involved in the capture of the three vessels were entitled to a share of prize money resulting from the sale of the vessels and their cargo but the results were not as some

had hoped. *Monticello's* coffee sold well, but as "she was a Baltimore vessel and owned by a gentleman of that city, Government ascertained that the price of the coffee in Baltimore and paid Messrs. Spence and Reid 12 cents a pound, and sold it at 25 or 30 cents in Richmond." The vessel was returned to the owner. Historian Mary Alice Wills, in her excellent study on the blockade of Washington, writes that as the months wore on coffee became increasingly scarce within Virginia lines. Eugene O. Perry of the 1st Texas Regiment, camped in the town of Dumfries on the Potomac, wrote to his brother in November that it cost one dollar a pound and in December one dollar and twenty-five cents a pound. By January the supply had diminished so that Captain William P. Townsend of the 4th Texas Regiment complained to his wife that there was but "a scanty supply of coffee." Hollins Extracts, *ORN*, Ser. I, Vol. 4, 555; Wills, 54; *The Daily Exchange*, 2 July 1861.

35. "Reported Seizure of the St. Nicholas," *Daily National Republican*, 2 July 1861; J. P. K. Mygatt to R. B. Lowry, 20 June 11861, *ORN*, Ser. I, Vol. 4, 549-550.

36. John A. Dahlgren to Gideon Welles, 1 July 1861, *ORN*, Ser. I, Vol. 4, 550; Worthington to Welles, 1 July 1861, *ORN*, Ser. I, Vol. 4, 550-551; Samuel Hinks to Gideon Welles, 2 July 1861, *ORN*, Ser. I, Vol. 4, 551.

11. Unearned Consequences

1. "Correspondence of the Richmond Dispatch," *Nashville Union and American*, 6 July 1861.

2. *The Daily Dispatch*, 9 July 1861. *St. Nicholas* was first libeled in Confederate District Court, Richmond, on January 16, 1861 on a motion by James Cooke, J. F. Dent, R. P. Blackistone, E. J. Plowden, Martin Kidd, R. F. Shanks, Wm. H. Hammerman & Co., T. H. Fowle, R.C. Wainwright, J. H. Knott, J. F. Mattingly, and Leach, and Herbert, parties claiming to own certain goods found on board of said vessel when she was captured on the Potomac. After the claims had been filed the court ordered that the papers in the case be referred to William F. Watson, Commissioner of the Court, who directed the sale of the proceeds "of the several parcels of goods and merchandise belonging or claimed to belong to several said claimants, as having been sold at the sale made by the marshal under the order of sale heretofore mentioned; also how much each of the said parties was entitled to out of net proceeds of said sale." No claims were made to the sale of the vessel itself. *St. Nicholas* was purchased by and for the Confederate Navy for $45,000, renamed *Rappahannock*, armed with a single gun, and thereafter operated on the Rappahannock River taking several prizes. She was burned at Fredericksburg, Va. in April 1862 to prevent capture. *St. Mary's Beacon*, 23 January 1862; Extracts from notes by Commander George N. Hollins, C.S. Navy, *ORN*, Ser. I, Vol. 4, 555; *ORN* Ser. II, Vol. 1, 264.

3. David C. Holly, *Chesapeake Steamboats: Vanished Fleet*, (Centreville, Md.: Tidewater Publishers, 1994), 117-118.

4. Ibid., 117-118; Ron Field, *The Confederate Army 1861-65: Missouri, Kentucky & Maryland* (Oxford, UK: Osprey Publishing, 2008), 38.

5. Benjamin M. Dove to S. C. Rowan, 9 July 1861, *ORN*, Ser. I, Vol. 4, 569-570; Holly, *Chesapeake Steamboats*, 121; J. W. Livingston to Silas Stringham, 11 July 1861, *ORN*, Ser. I, Vol. 5, 785.

6. Holly, *Chesapeake Steamboats*, 119. Thomas's hubris regarding his objectives could not be discouraged even by those closely involved. The press in Richmond later noted that "the party on board the schooner [had] done their best to persuade Colonel Thomas not to come up to Baltimore, and some of them endeavored to hold him by force. Finding that he was determined to come, seven of his companions resolved to accompany him." *The Daily Dispatch*, 17 July 1861.

7. Harold R. Manakee, *Maryland in the Civil War* (Baltimore: Maryland Historical Society, 1961), 52-53; George W. Brown, *Baltimore and the 19th of April, 1861* (Johns Hopkins University: Baltimore, 1887), 98-99. Secretary Stanton created the Office of the Provost-Marshal General to superintend state provost-marshals in Border States such as Maryland and loyal states of the Union. Once charged with protecting the property of citizens, provost marshals were now accountable for controlling military bodies, enforcing discipline, pursuing and arresting deserters, spies and disloyal individuals, and escorting them to the appropriate military commander. Kathryn W. Lerch, "Prosecuting Citizens, Rebels, & Spies: The 8th New York Heavy Artillery in Maryland, 1862-1864, *MHM*, Vol. 94, No. 2 (Summer 1999), 135.

8. *Baltimore Sun*, 10 July 1861; "The St. Nicholas Piracy," *Daily National Republican*, 10 July 1861; *The Daily Dispatch*, 17 July 1861.

9. *Baltimore Sun*, 10 July 1861; David C. Holly, *Tidewater by Steamboat: A Saga of the Chesapeake* (Baltimore

and London: The Johns Hopkins University Press, Published in Association with the Calvert Marine Museum, 1991), 72. Green's name is also noted in a Washington newspaper as Cornelius Green. *Daily National Republican*, 10 July 1861.

10. *Baltimore Sun*, 10 July 1861; *Daily National Republican*, 10 July 1861.

11. Holly, *Tidewater by Steamboat*, 252.

12. *Baltimore Sun*, 10 July 1861; *Daily National Republican*, 10 July 1861. Holly, *Chesapeake Steamboats*, 122, relates that Thomas was captured while attempting to lower the steamer's quarter boat.

13. Ibid.; *ORA*, Ser. I, 2:738; Scott Sumter Sheads and Daniel Carroll Toomey, *Baltimore During the Civil War* (Toomey Press: Linthicum, Md., 1997), 41; *Baltimore Sun*, 9 July 1861; *Baltimore American*, 9, 10, and 13 July 1861; Charles A. Earp, "The Amazing Colonel Zarvona", *MHM*, Vol. 34, No. 4 (December 1939), 334-343; Holly, *Tidewater by Steamboat*, 73.

14. Holly, *Tidewater by Steamboat*, 73.

15. Robert Williams to George R. Dodge, 10 July 1861, *ORA*, Ser. I, Vol. 2, Part 1, 739; Gideon Welles to William H. Seward, 8 July 1861, *ORN*, Ser. I, Vol. 4, 569.

16. Memorandum, Gideon Welles to William H. Seward, 8 July 1861, *ORN*, Ser. II, Vol. Vol. 2, Part 1, 17.

17. Benjamin M. Dove to S. C. Rowan, 9 July 1861; S. C. Rowan to Gideon Welles, 9 July 1861, 1 o'clock, *ORN*, Ser. I, Vol. 4, 569; Livingston to Stringham, 11 July 1861; St. *Mary's Beacon*, 11 July 1861.

18. Dove to Rowan, 9 July 1861, *ORN*, Ser. I, Vol. 4, 470; Livingston to Stringham, 11 July 1861.

19. R. B. Lowry to S. C. Rowan, 10 July 1861, *ORN*, Ser. I, Vol. 4, 572; Livingston to Stringham, 11 July 1861; St. *Mary's Beacon*, 11 July 1861.

20. *Baltimore Sun*, 10 July 1861; *Merchant Steam Vessels of the United States 1780-1868*, William M. Lytle and Forrest R. Holdcamper, comp. (Staten Island, N.Y.: The Steamship Historical Society of America, Inc., 1975), 35; Livingston to Stringham, 11 July 1861; "The Pursuit of Richard Thomas," *Daily National Republican*, 11 and 12 July 1861; *The Daily Dispatch*, 17 July 1861; "Stopping of Steamers," *St. Mary's Beacon*, 11 July 1861; Livingston to Stringham, 11 July 1861, 5:785.

21. *Baltimore Sun*, 10 July 1861; *Daily National Republican*, 11 July 1861; *The Daily Dispatch*, 17 July 1861.

12. Blockade

1. *St. Mary's Beacon*, 11 and 18 July 1861; E. B. Long and Barbara Long: *The Civil War Day by Day: An Almanac 1861-1865* (Garden City, N.Y.: Doubleday & Company, Inc., 1971), 95.

2. S. C. Rowan to Gideon Welles, 9 [7] July 1861, *ORN*, Ser. I, Vol. 4, 566-567; William Budd to S. C. Rowan, 8 July 1861, *ORN*, Ser. I, Vol. 4, 567; Donald G. Shomette, "Infernal Machines: Submarine and Torpedo Warfare in the War of 1812," *Sea History*, No. 158 (Winter 2012-13), 18-22.

3. *Port Tobacco Times*, 11 February and 24 June 1858; 9 September 1858; 24 May 1860; 14 March and 21 November 1861. For a comprehensive overview of Port Tobacco's convoluted history, see Donald G. Shomette, *Lost Towns of Tidewater Maryland* (Centreville, Md.: Tidewater Publishers, 2000), 193-245.

4. *Port Tobacco Times*, 17 May 1860, 24 May 1860, 7 June 1860.

5. *Port Tobacco Times*, 3 and 17 May 1860.

6. John A. Dahlgren to Gideon Welles, 11 July 1861, (telegram), *ORN* Ser. I, Vol. 4, 573; *Daily National Republican*, 9 August 1861; John A. Dahlgren to Gideon Welles, 11 July 1861, *ORN*, Ser. I, Vol. 4, 574; Benjamin M. Dove to T. T. Craven, 12 July 1861, *ORN*, Ser. I, Vol. 4, 547.

7. Dove to Craven, 12 July 1861.

8. *Daily National Republican*, 9 August 1861; "The Expedition of the James Guy," *Evening Star*, 13 July 1861; *Port Tobacco Times*, 18 June 1886.

9. *Daily National Republican*, 9 August 1861.

10. Ibid.; *Port Tobacco Times*, 18 July 1861; "The Expedition of the James Guy."

11. *Daily National Republican*, 13 and 16 July 1861, 9 August 1861.

12. Ibid., 16 and 27 July 1861, 9 August 1861.

13. Ibid., 13 August 1861; *The Daily Exchange*, 13 August 1861.

14. *Daily National Republican*, 7 August 1861.

15. *St. Mary's Beacon*, 18 July 1861.

16. Long and Long, 95.

17. *Richmond Examiner*, 23 April 1861.

18. Edmund Ruffin, *Anticipation of the Future: To Serve as Lessons for the Present Time* (Richmond: J. W. Randolph, 1860), 298-299.

19. Signators to the petition included: A. J. Foxwell, Randolph Jones, C. M. Jones, James F. Ellicott, J. W. Forrest, J. Piett Forrest, William R. Smith, John A. Crane, William C. Bayne, Joseph T. Artis, John W. Bennett, Thomas J. Bennett, R. B. Crane, James B. Locker, O. N. Evans, Thomas J. Byrd, Joseph Milburn, J. E. Bruffey, W. Murphy, B. F. McKay, J. B. Courtney, H. M. Langley, J. H. Hopkins, John G. Lilburn, James K. Jones, Walter Langley, N. B. Langley, T. T. Drury, and James H. Miles. Edwin W. Beitzell, *Life on the Potomac River* (Abell, Md.: Privately published, 1968), 38-39.

20. Mary Alice Wills, *The Confederate Blockade of Washington, D.C., 1861-1862* (Parson, West Virginia: McClain Printing Company, 1975), 41; *ORN*, Ser. II, Vol. 1, 244.

21. Thomas T. Craven to Gideon Welles, 26 July 1861—11 p.m., *ORN*, Ser. I, Vol. 4, 598; Thomas T. Craven to Gideon Welles, Report, 1 August 1861, *ORN*, Ser. I, Vol. 4, 595.

22. *St. Mary's Beacon*, 8 August 1861; Craven to Welles, 1 August 1861.

23. Craven to Welles, 1 August 1861.

24. William Budd to Thomas T. Craven, [Enclosure], 10 August 1861, *ORN*, Ser. I, Vol. 4, 604.

25. Thomas T. Craven to Gideon Welles, 11 August 1861, *ORN*, Ser. I, Vol. 4, 603.

26. Wills, 41; R. H. Wyman, Memorandum, 9 August 1861, *ORA*, Ser. I, Vol. 5, 557.

27. Joseph E. Johnston to Jefferson Davis, 19 August 1861, *ORA*, Ser. I, Vol. 5, 797.

28. Ibid.

29. Jefferson Davis to Joseph E. Johnston, 1 August 1861, *ORA*, Ser. I, Vol. 5, 767.

30. S. Cooper to Thomas H. Holmes, 22 August 1861, *ORA*, Ser. I, Vol. 5, 802; S. Cooper to Joseph E. Johnston, 22 August 1861, *ORA*, Ser. I, Vol. 5, 801.

31. R. H. Wyman, Memorandum, 9 August 1861.

32. Gideon Welles to Simon Cameron, 20 August 1861, *ORA*, Ser. I, Vol. 5, 573.

33. Long and Long, 100, 101. The main lines drawn by the Confederate Army occupied a strong front running south from Flint Hill through Fairfax Court House, Fairfax Station and Sangster's Crossroads. The Union Army line was anchored with both flanks on the Potomac, on the north at Chain Bridge and on the south at Fort Lyon, near Alexandria. Bradley M. Gottfried, *The Maps of First Bull Run* (New York and California: Savas Beatie, 2009), 78.

34. J. P. K. Mygatt to J. W. Livingston, 24 August 1861, *ORN*, Ser. I, Vol. 4, 633.

35. *ORN*, Ser. II, Vol. 1, 111; Edward P. McCrea to Thomas T. Craven, 21 August 1861; R. M. Cary, to D. H. Maury, 23 August 1861, *ORN*, Ser. I, Vol. 4, 633-634.

36. T. Pattison to Thomas T. Craven, 23 August 1861, *ORN*, Ser. I, Vol. 4, 632-33. Mygatt reported that the rebels fired on *Ice Boat* from three different points. Mygatt to Livingston, 24 August 1861. R. M. Cary to D. H. Maury, 23 August 1861, *ORN*, Ser. I, Vol. 4, 634.

37. John A. Dix to Edward McK. Hudson, 21 August 21, 1861, *ORN*, Ser. I, Vol. 5, 577; E. D. Townsend to George B. McClellan, 22 August 1861, *ORA*, Ser. I, Vol. 5, 578.

38. "Expedition to Easton, Md.," *Cavalier & Telegraph*, 11 July 1861; *The Daily Exchange*, 22 August 1861.

39. *The Daily Exchange*, 22 August 1861; "General Dix Spoils a Secessionist Game," *Cincinnati Daily Press*, 30 August 1861; H. Duryea to J. E. Hamblin, 24 August 1861, *ORN*, Ser. I, Vol. 4, 657.

40. "General Dix Spoils a Secessionist Game."

41. Ibid.; Duryea to Hamblin, 24 August 1861.

42. Duryea to Hamblin, 24 August 1861, 657-658.

43. Thomas T. Craven to Gideon Welles, 5 September 1861, *ORN*, Ser. I, Vol. 4, 658.

44. *Merchant Steam Vessels of the United States 1780-1868*, William M. Lytle and Forrest R. Holdcamper, comp. (Staten Island, N.Y.: The Steamship Historical Society of America, Inc., 1975), 98.

45. *Baltimore Sun*, 24 August 1861.

46. Gustavus V. Fox to T. T. Craven, August 24, 1861, *ORN*, Ser. I, Vol. 4, 635.

47. John A. Dahlgren to Gideon Welles, 25 August 1861, *ORN*, Ser. I, Vol. 4, 636.

48. *ORN*, Ser. I, Vol. 4, 612.

49. George B. McClellan to Gideon Welles, 12 August 1861, reprinted in *The National Tribune*, 9 June 1892.

50. Ibid.

51. S. Cooper to E. Louis Lowe, 6 September 1861, *ORA*, Ser. 4, Vol. 1, 600.

52. "Washington News," *Cleveland Morning Leader*, 20 August 1861.

53. "From Washington," *Cleveland Morning Leader*, 20 August 1861.
54. "This Afternoon's Report," *Cleveland Morning Leader*, 20 August 1861.
55. "From Washington."

13. Careful Inquiry

1. Ezra J. Warner, *Generals in Blue: Lives of the Union Commanders* (Baton Rouge, La.: Louisiana State University Press, 1964), 377-378; *National Intelligencer*, 1 August 1861.
2. *ORA*, Ser. I, Vol. 5, 51-52; Kenneth J. Winkle, *Lincoln's Citadel: The Civil War in Washington, D.C.* (New York and London, W. W. Norton & Company, 2013), 98.
3. *Daily National Republican*, 20 August 1861; Charles Dana Gibson and E. Kay Gibson, *Dictionary of Transports and Combatant Vessels Steam and Sail Employed by the Union Army 1861-1868*, 2 Vols. (Camden, Me.: Ensign Press, 1995), Vol. 2, 319. On August 15 General Dix was ordered by General McClellan to close down the Weems Line. Permission was given three days later for a steamboat to make one trip to bring away families left behind. E. D. Townsend to George B. McClellan, 22 August 1861, *ORA*, Ser. I, Vol. 5, 578.
4. E. J. Allen to A. Porter, 26 October 1861, enclosed, *ORA*, Ser. II, Vol. 2, 866.
5. Ibid., Vol. 2, 861-862. Ryand mistakenly mentioned Tom Stone in the place of Thomas A. Jones.
6. Thomas A. Jones, *J. Wilkes Booth: An Account of His Sojourn in Southern Maryland after the Assassination of Abraham Lincoln*, (Chicago: Laird & Lee Publishers, 1893), 29-30.
7. Ibid., 30.
8. Ibid.
9. Ibid., 31-32.
10. Ibid. 32.
11. Allen to Porter, 26 October 1861, *ORA*, Ser. II, Vol. 2, 862; Jones, 56.
12. Jones, 13.
13. Ibid.
14. Ibid.
15. Gustavus V. Fox to Thomas T. Craven, September 6, 1861, *ORN*, Ser. I, Vol. 4, 663.
16. "The Secession Signals Down River," *The Evening Star*, 9 September 1861. By late 1862, and quite probably much earlier, signaling equipment for both sides of the Potomac was being provided by the Confederate Signal Corps. During the Fredericksburg Campaign of December 1862 Lieutenant James Carey of the Signal Corps was directed to proceed to King George and Westmoreland counties to establish stations. Though the corps had its own uniform style, Carey was captured while dressed in civilian clothing, placing him in an "unpleasant position" as a possible Confederate spy. It was believed by Union authorities that the Confederates were attempting to set up signal stations on both sides of the Potomac, already "having their spies within our lines." A. Pleasonton to Major-General Parker, 8 December 1862, (letters 1 and 2), *ORA*, Ser. I, Vol. 21, 841.
17. "Arrests in the County," *St. Mary's Beacon*, 12 September 1861. Joseph Maddox would be released on parole from Fort Warren on or about November 25, 1861. *The Local News*, 25 November 1861.
18. Allen to Porter, 26 October 1861, *ORA*, Ser. II, Vol. , Vol. 2, 866.
19. Ibid., *ORA*, Ser. II, Vol. 2, 862, 863.
20. "Murder of F. W. Walker, of the New York 'Express'", *Daily National Republican*, 16 September 1861.
21. Ibid.
22. Allen to Porter, 26 October 1861, *ORA*, Ser. II, Vol. 2, 863.
23. Ibid.
24. Ibid.; Jones, 13.
25. Jones, 13-14.
26. Ibid., 14.
27. Ibid., 15.
28. Ibid., 16.
29. Allen to Porter, 26 October 1861, *ORA*, Ser. II, Vol. 2, 863.
30. Ibid.
31. Ibid.
32. Ibid., 864.
33. Ibid.

34. Ibid.
35. Ibid.
36. Ibid., 865, 867.
37. Ibid., 865-866.
38. Ibid., 865.
39. Ibid.
40. Ibid., 863, 866.
41. Ibid., 867.
42. Ibid.
43. Ibid.

14. Cross-Bows and Pop Guns

1. *Appleton's Cyclopedia of American Biography*, James Grant Wilson and John Fisk, eds. (New York: D. Appleton and Company, 1889), Vol. 4, 338-339; *New York Daily Tribune*, 13 August 1846.
2. *Appleton's Cyclopedia*, Vol. 4, 338-339; J. Thomas Scharf, *The Chronicles of Baltimore: Being A Complete History of "Baltimore Town" and Baltimore City from the Earliest Times to the Present* (Baltimore: Turnbull Brothers, 1874), 611.
3. *Daily National Republican*, 11 and 13 May 1861.
4. *ORA*, Ser. I, Vol. 51, Part 2, 155.
5. Ibid.
6. Ibid., 157.
7. Ibid., 156-57.
8. Ibid., 156.
9. Ibid.
10. Ibid., 156-157.
11. Ibid., 157.
12. Memorandum, 9 August 1861, *ORA*, Ser. I, Vol. 5, 557; Gideon Welles to Simon Cameron, 20 August 1861, *ORA*, Ser. I, Vol. 5, 573; Mary Alice Wills, *The Confederate Blockade of Washington, D.C. 1861-1862* (Parsons, WV: 1975), 57; Benjamin M. Dove to S. C. Rowan, 9 July 1861, *ORN*, Ser. I, Vol. 4, 566-567; E. B. Long and Barbara Long, *The Civil War Day by Day: An Almanac 1861-1865* (Garden City, N.Y.: Doubleday & Company, Inc., 1971), 106.
13. Eric Mills, *Chesapeake Bay in the Civil War* (Centreville, Md.: Tidewater Publishers, 1996), 79; Wills, 57.
14. *ORA*, Ser. I, Vol. 5, 10.
15. Wills, 58.
16. Ibid.; Mills, 79.
17. Ibid.
18. Wills, 59.
19. *Richmond Examiner*, 9 September 1861.
20. Joseph Dickinson to Robert Cowdin, 8 September 1861, *ORA*, Ser. I, Vol. 5, Part 1, 589; *The Alleghanian*, 5 February 1863. Dickinson erroneously ordered Cowdin to send scouting parties "in the direction of Alexandria and Lower Marlborough," apparently ignorant of the fact that the former site was in Virginia, on the other side of the Potomac and not along the Patuxent. It has also been stated by one historian that the motivation for the Union movement was that Confederate were gathering supplies and recruits as well as posing a threat to the impending state elections. See Daniel Carroll Toomey, *The Civil War in Maryland* (Baltimore: The Toomey Press, 1983), 28. No such notice regarding elections is evident in either Cowdin's orders or any other record.
21. Dickinson to Cowdin, 8 September 1861.
22. Ibid., *ORA*, Ser. I, Vol. 5, Part 1, 590.
23. Ibid.; Robert Cowdin to Joseph Hooker, 12 September 1861 [attachment], *ORA*, Ser. I, Vol. 5, Part 1, 596; Dickinson to Cowdin, 8 September 1861.
24. Robert Cowdin to Joseph Hooker, 10 September 1861, *ORA*, Ser. I, Vol. 5, Part 1, 590.
25. Ibid. Cowdin's line of march most likely followed the same route the British employed on their retirement from Washington and Bladensburg in August 1814. See Simon J. Martinet, *Martinet's Map of Prince George's County Maryland* (Baltimore: Engraved and Printed by T.S. Wagner, 1861). In his account of Cowdin's motions, James Samuel Clark states that the Massachusetts troops camped in

an oak grove on the outskirts of Upper Marlboro. There is, unfortunately, no indication precisely where the camp was or any mention of an oak grove in official accounts. James Samuel Clark, "A Union Army Reconnaissance Into Calvert County," in *Historian* (Calvert County Historical Society: Dunkirk, Md., April 1986), 38.

26. Cowdin to Hooker, 10 September 1861.
27. Ibid., *ORA*, Ser. I, Vol. 5, Part 1, 591.
28. Ibid.
29. William Dwight, Jr. to Robert Cowdin, 11 September 1861, attached to Robert Cowdin to Joseph Hooker, 12 September 1861, *ORA*, Ser. I, Vol. 5, Part 1, 596.
30. Ibid.
31. Dwight to Cowdin, 11 September 1861, attached to Cowdin to Hooker, *ORA*, Ser. I, Vol. 5, Part 1, 595.
32. Ibid., 595-596.
33. Cowdin to Dwight, 12 September 1861, *ORA*, Ser. I, Vol. 5, Part 1, 597.
34. Joseph Dickinson to Robert Cowdin, 13 September 1861, Camp Union, *ORA*, Ser. I, Vol. 5, Part 1, 597.
35. Ibid.
36. *The Baltimore Daily Exchange*, 14 September 1861; Harry Wright Newman, *Maryland and the Confederacy* (Annapolis, Md.: Privately published, 1976), 220.
37. Warren H[andel] Cudworth, *History of the First Regiment (Massachusetts Infantry), from the 25th of May, 1861, to the 25th of May, 1864; including brief references to the operations of the Army of the Potomac* (Boston: Walker, Fuller & Co., 1866), 87.
38. Ibid. According to the 1860 census, the black population, including 4,609 slaves and 1,841 freemen, comprised nearly sixty-two percent of the total population of 10,477 persons living in Calvert County. *U.S. Census for 1860, Maryland;* Newman, 15.
39. Robert Cowdin to Joseph Hooker, 16 September 1861, *ORA*, Ser. I, Vol. 5, Part 1, 601.
40. Ibid., 602.
41. Joseph Dickinson to Robert Cowdin, 14 September 1861, *ORA*, Ser. I, Vol. 5, Part 1, 601.
42. Cudworth, 92; Harold R. Manakee, *Maryland in the Civil War* (Baltimore: Maryland Historical Society, 1961), 55; Scharf, 616.
43. Cudworth, 90, 92, 93.
44. Newman, 220-221.
45. Betty Worthington Briscoe, "Know Your County," *Calvert Independent* [nd], clipping, Calvert Historical Society, Prince Frederick, Md.; Newman, 221.
46. Newman, 220 221.
47. Ibid., 93-94. Augustus R. Sollers to Governor Seward (received 9 December [1861]), *ORA*, Ser. II, Vol. 1, 615.
48. The newspaper referred to would have been either the *St. Mary's Beacon, Port Tobacco Times,* or *Marlboro Gazette; The Planter's Advocate and Southern Maryland Advertiser* or the *Annapolis Gazette*, the only periodicals published in Southern Maryland. All but the *Annapolis Gazette* would eventually be taken over by the U.S. Army or operated under Federal censorship.
49. Robert Cowdin to Joseph Hooker, 20 September 1861, *ORA*, Ser. I, Vol. 5, Part 1, 605.
50. Newman, 220.
51. Cudworth, 92.
52. Cowdin to Hooker, 20 September 1861.
53. Cudworth, 93.
54. Cowdin to Hooker, 20 September 1861.
55. Cudworth, 93; Cowdin to Hooker, 20 September 1861.
56. Cowdin to Hooker, 20 September 1861.
57. Daniel E. Sickles to S. Williams, 30 September 1861, *ORA*, Ser. I, Vol. 5, 609-610.
58. *The Planter's Advocate and Southern Maryland Advertiser*, 9 October 1861.
59. "The Soldiers," *St. Mary's Beacon*, 3 October 1861.
60. *ORA*, Ser. II, Vol. 2, 858; E. J. Allen to A. Porter, 26 October 1861, enclosed, *ORA*, Ser. II, Vol. 2, 864; Thomas A. Jones, *J. Wilkes Booth: An Account of His Sojourn in Southern Maryland after the Assassination of Abraham Lincoln*, (Chicago: Laird & Lee Publishers, 1893), 20.
61. Toomey, 28.

62. *Marlboro Gazette*, 25 September 1861, reprinted in *St. Mary's Beacon*, 3 October 1861.

63. "Soldiers Running of Slaves," *St. Mary's Beacon*, 26 September 1861.

64. Simon Cameron to Nathaniel P. Banks, 11 September 1864, *ORA*, Ser I, Vol. 5, 193. Though the document has not been found, it is apparent from a reply message from Dix to Cameron that he too had received a similar order. John A. Dix to Simon Cameron, 11 September 1864, 11 p.m., *ORA*, Ser. I, Vol. 5, 193-194.

65. John A. Dix to John E. Wool, 13 September 1861, *ORA*, Ser. I, Vol. 5, 194.

66. Nathaniel P. Banks to R. B. Marcy, 20 September 1861, *ORA*, Ser. I, Vol. 5, 194-195; Allen Pinkerton to William H. Seward, *ORA*, Ser. I, Vol. 5, 195-196; Scharf, 617; Manakee, 55, 56.

67. Thomas H. Hicks to Nathaniel H. Banks, 20 September 1861, *ORA*, Ser. II, Vol. 1. 685.

68. Judah P. Benjamin to Thomas H. Holmes, 20 September 1861, *ORA*, Ser. I, Vol. 5, 866-867.

69. Ibid.

70. Thomas H. Holmes to Judah P. Benjamin, 22 September 1861, *ORA*, Ser. I, Vol. 5, 871-872.

Chapter 15: A Fine Platform

1. Russel H. Beatie, *The Army of the Potomac* (Cambridge, Ma.: De Capo Press, 2002), 471–472.

2. Stephen W. Sears, *George B. McClellan: The Young Napoleon* (New York: De Capo Press, 1988), 98–99, 116-117; James M. McPherson, *Tried by War: Abraham Lincoln as Commander in Chief*. New York: Penguin Press, 2008), 122.

3. Sears, 101–104, 110.

4. George B. McClellan to Simon Cameron, 6 September 1861, *ORA*, Ser. I, Vol. 5, 586-587.

5. John P. Gillis to Gideon Welles, 9 p.m., 25 September 1861, *ORN*, Ser. I, Vol. 4, 688-689; Edward P. McCrea to Thomas T. Craven, 25 September 1861, *ORN*, Ser. I, Vol. 4, 689; Louis T. Wigfall to Jefferson Davis, 25 September 1861, *ORN*, Ser. I, Vol. 4, 691. "Our Naval Squadrons," *The National Tribune*, 9 June 1892.

6. Daniel E. Sickles to S. Williams, 30 September 1861, *ORA*, Ser. I, Vol. 5, 609-610; *The Local News*, 1 November 1861.

7. Sickles to Williams, 30 September 1871, 610.

8. John G. Barnard to George B. McClellan, 28 September 1861, *ORA*, Ser. I, Vol. 5, 606; Benjamin Franklin Cooling III and Walton H. Owen II, *Mr. Lincoln's Forts: A Guide to the Civil War Defenses of Washington* (Shippensburg, Pa: White Mane Publishing Company, 1988), 235.

9. Barnard to McClellan, 28 September 1861, 606-607.

10. Ibid., 607.

11. Ibid., 608.

12. Ibid.

13. Ibid.

14. Louis T. Wigfall to Jefferson Davis, 27 September 1861, *ORA*, Ser. I, Vol. 5, 882.

Chapter 16: Varmits

1. Gideon Welles to Thomas T. Craven, 11 October 1861, *ORN*, Ser. I, Vol. 4, 712-713.

2. Ibid., 713.

3. Ibid.

4. Gideon Welles to John P. Gillis, P. Drayton, R. H. Wyman, and H. S. Newcomb, 12 October 1861, *ORN*, Ser. I, Vol. 4, 714-715; Gideon Welles to T. T. Craven, 12 October 1861, *ORN*, Ser. I, Vol. 4, 715.

5. Thomas T. Craven to Gideon Welles, 13 October 1861, *ORN*, Ser. I, Vol. 4, 716.

6. Ibid.; A. J. Frank to Thomas T. Craven, 12 October 1861, *ORN*, Ser. I, Vol. 4, 715-716.

7. *ORN*, Ser. I, Vol. 4, 725; *ORN*, Ser. II, Vol. 1, 229.

8. A. D. Harrell to T. T. Craven, 11 October 1861, *ORN*, Ser. I, Vol. 4, 709-710.

9. Ibid. The vessels that greeted Harrell's return at Budd's Ferry were most likely the USS *Valley City* and *E. B. Hale*. See E. P. McCrea to Thomas T. Craven, *ORN*, Ser. I, Vol. 4, 708-709.

10. Harrell to Craven, 11 October 1861, 709.

11. Gideon Welles to Thomas T. Craven, 14 October 1861, *ORN*, Ser. I, Vol. 4, 716.

12. John A. Dahlgren to Navy Department, 14 October 1861, *ORN*, Ser. I, Vol. 4, 716-717.

13. Stewart Van Vliet to Gustavus V. Fox, 14 October 1861, [Enclosure], *ORN*, Ser. I, Vol. 4, 717.

14. Thomas T. Craven to Gideon Welles, 15 October 1861, *ORN*, Ser. I, Vol. 4, 718; John P. Gillis to

Gideon Welles, 15 October 1861, *ORN*, Ser. I, Vol. 4, 718-719; John P. Gillis to Thomas T. Craven, 16 October 1861, *ORN*, Ser. I, Vol. 4, 719.

15. Craven to Welles 15 October 1861, 718; Gillis to Welles, 15 October 1861, 719.

16. Ibid.

17. Craven to Welles, 15 October 1861, 718.

18. John A. Dahlgren to Gideon Welles, 15 October 1861, *ORN*, Ser. I, Vol. 4, 721; John A. Dahlgren to Gideon Welles, *ORN*, Ser. I, Vol. 4, 722; Thomas T. Craven to Gideon Welles, 17 October 1861, *ORN*, Ser. I, Vol. 4, 722; R. H. Wyman to Thomas T. Craven, 16 October 1861, *ORN*, Ser. I, Vol. 4, 722-723.

19. John A. Dahlgren to Navy Department, 17 October 1861, *ORN*, Ser. I, Vol. 4, 723.

20. Thomas T. Craven to Gideon Welles, 17 October 1861, *ORN*, Ser. I, Vol. 4, 722.

21. T. H. Eastman to Thomas T. Craven, 17 October 1861, *ORN*, Ser. I, Vol. 4, 724; Thomas M. Cash to T. H. Eastman, 17 October 1861, *ORN*, Ser. I, Vol. 4, 725-726; R. S. Williamson to R. B. Marcy, October 27, 1861, *ORA*, Ser. I, Vol. 5, 629-630; *Port Tobacco Times*, 31 October 1861; Mary Alice Wills, *The Confederate Blockade of Washington, D.C. 1861-1862* (McClain Printing Company: Parsons, W.Va., 1975), 130.

22. The noteworthy points in Richard B. Posey's public life may be readily traced in multiple entries in volumes 1, 2 and 3 in Robert J. Wearmouth, *Abstracts from the Port Tobacco Times and Charles County Advertiser*, 4 vols., Bowie, Md.: Heritage Books, 1990-1996.

23. Thomas T. Craven to Gideon Welles, 18 October 1861, *ORN*, Ser. I, Vol. 4, 726.

24. Gideon Welles to George B. McClelland, 18 October 1861, *ORN*, Ser. I, Vol. 4, 726-727.

25. George B. McClellan to Gideon Welles, 18 October 1861, *ORN*, Ser. I, Vol. 4, 727; Charles Bentrick to Commodore Craven, 21 October 1861, *ORN*, Ser. I, Vol. 4, 729.

26. "The Firing Into Vessels by the Potomac Batteries," *The Local News*, 21 October 1861.

27. Ibid.

28. Ibid.

29. Ibid.

30. Thomas T. Craven to Gideon Welles, 19 October 1861, *ORN*, Ser. I, Vol. 4, 727.

31. A. D. Harrell to Thomas T. Craven, 19 October 1861, *ORN*, Ser. I, Vol. 4, 728. It is incorrectly noted in some accounts that *Fairfax* and a second schooner identified as *Mary Virginia* were taken during the rebel incursion on the night of October 19, 1861.

32. Ibid.; Thomas T. Craven to Gideon Welles, 20 October 1861, *ORN*, Ser. I, Vol. 4, 728.

33. Charles Bentrick to Thomas T. Craven, 21 October 1861, *ORN*, Ser. I, Vol. 4, 728-729.

34. Ibid., *ORN*, Ser. I, Vol. 4, 729; James L. Van Buren to John A. Dahlgren, 22 October 1861, (received 9 p.m.), *ORN*, Ser. I, Vol. 4, 732; Report of Nelson Taylor to Daniel E. Sickles, October 22, 1861, *ORA*, Ser. I, Vol. 5, 372; Report of Joseph Hooker to S. Williams, October 28, 1861, *ORA*, Ser. I, Vol. 5, 385.

35. Report of Robert S. Williamson to R. B. Marcy, 22 October 1861, *ORA*, Ser. I, Vol. 5, 375; Report of Nelson Taylor to Daniel E. Sickles, October 22, 1861, *ORA*, Ser. I, Vol. 5, 373.

36. Gideon Welles to T. T. Craven, 21 October 1861, *ORN*, Ser. I, Vol. 4, 729.

37. Thomas T. Craven to Gideon Welles, 21 October 1861, *ORN*, Ser. I, Vol. 4, 729-730.

38. A. D. Harrell to Thomas T. Craven, 21 October 1861, *ORN*, Ser. I, Vol. 4, 430-431; John A. Dahlgren to Gideon Welles, Simon Cameron, 22 October 1861, (telegram), *ORN*, Ser. I, Vol. 4, 731; Thomas T. Craven to Gideon Welles, 23 October 1861, *ORN*, Ser. I, Vol. 4, 732; *The Local News*, 26 October 1861.

39. John A. Dahlgren to Gideon Welles, 25 October 1861, *ORN*, Ser. I, Vol. 4, 735-736.

40. John A. Dahlgren to Gideon Welles, 25 October 1861, *ORN*, Ser. I, Vol. 4, 735.

41. Gideon Welles to Simon Cameron, 21 October 1861, *ORN*, Ser. I, Vol. 4, 730; Nelson Taylor to Thomas T. Craven, 23 October 1861, *ORN*, Ser. I, Vol. 4, 731.

42. *The Local News*, 25 October 1861.

43. Taylor to Craven, 23 October 1861; R. S. Williamson to S. Williams, October 23, 1861, ORA, Ser. I, Vol. 5, 62.

44. *The Local News*, 26 October 1861.

45. Thomas T. Craven to Gideon Welles, 23 October 1861 (1), *ORN*, Ser. I, Vol. 4, 733; Thomas T. Craven to Gideon Welles, 3:30 p.m., 23 October 1861 (2), *ORN*, Ser. I, Vol. 4, 733; Thomas T. Craven to Gideon Welles, 3:40 p.m., 23 October 1861 (3), *ORN*, Ser. I, Vol. 4, 733.

46. John A. Dahlgren to Thomas T. Craven, 11 p.m., 23 October 1861, *ORN*, Sec. 1, Vol. 4, 734; Gideon Welles Thomas T. Craven, 24 October 1861, *ORN*, Ser. I, Vol. 4, 734.

Chapter 17: A Friendly Command

1. General Orders, No. 15, E. D. Townsend, 17 August 1861, *ORA*, Ser. I, Vol. 5, 567; Stephen W. Sears, *George B. McClellan: The Young Napoleon* (New York: Da Capo Press, 1988), 111, 116; Carl Sandburg, *Storm Over the Land: A Profile of the Civil War*. (New York: Harcourt Brace and Company, 1942), 62. A September 29 return of General Holmes's rebel troops in the Department of Fredericksburg numbered 9,407 officers and men, and generals Johnston and Beauregards' forces were approximately equal in strengh. Abstract for Return of the Department of Fredericksburg, commanded by Brig. Gen. T. H. Holmes, for September 1861, *ORA*, Ser. I, Vol. 5, 884.
2. Harold R. Manakee, *Maryland in the Civil War* (Baltimore: Maryland Historical Society, 1961), 54-55; William W. Averell to Gideon Welles, 4 September 1861, *ORN*, Ser. I, Vol. 4, 662.
3. *St. Mary's Beacon*, 3 October 1861.
4. General L. C. Baker, *History of the United States Secret Service* (Philadelphia; Published by L. C. Baker, 1867), 255-256.
5. "Troops at the Great Mills," *St. Mary's Beacon*, October 10, 1861; "Arrests by the Military," Ibid.; L. C. Baker to Secretary of State, 10 October, 1861, *ORA*, Ser. II, Vol. 1, 600. Baker later mistakenly states the visit was made in September. L. C. Baker to Postmaster-General, 14 January 1863, Baker, 100.
6. Baker, 100.
7. Joseph Hooker to S. Williams, 1 November 1861, *ORA*, Ser. I, Vol. 5, 636-637.
8. *The Local News*, 5 November 1861.
9. Hooker to Williams, 1 November 1861, 637.
10. Manakee., 56.
11. John A. Dix to George B. McClellan, 7 October 1861, *ORA*, Ser. I, Vol. 5, 614-615; John A. Dix to George B. McClellan, October 25, 1861, *ORA*, Ser. I, Vol. 5, 629.
12. Thomas H. Hicks to Nathaniel P. Banks, 26 October 1861, in Harry Wright Newman, *Maryland and the Confederacy* (Annapolis, Md.: Privately published, 1976), 60.
13. Ibid.
14. Joseph Hooker to S. Williams, 3 November 1861, *ORA*, Ser. I, Vol. 5, 640.
15. Ibid.; *The Local News*, 5 November 1861. Hooker ordered secessionist candidate Davis's release about November 8 upon his swearing an oath of allegiance. "Besides," quipped the general, "the election was over." Joseph Hooker to S. Williams, 8 November 1861, *ORA*, Ser. I, Vol. 5, 646-47; *Port Tobacco Times*, 31 October 1861.
16. Joseph Hooker to S. Williams, 5 November 1861, *ORA*, Ser. I, Vol. 5, 642-643; Hooker to Williams, 8 November 1861, 646.
17. *Port Tobacco Times*, 24 October 1861.
18. *The Local News*, 25 October 1861.
19. *Daily National Republican*, 23 October 1861.
20. *The Local News*, 2 November 1861.
21. Oliver O. Howard to Commanding Officers of Regiments on Expedition to the Lower Counties of Maryland, 4 November 1861, *ORA*, Ser. I, Vol. 5, Part 1, 503.
22. Report of Brigadier General Oliver O. Howard, November 9, 1861, *ORA*, Ser. I, Vol. 5, Part 1, 385.
23. Ibid.
24. Howard to Commanding Officers, 4 November 1861.
25. Ibid.; Howard Report, *ORA*, Ser. I, Vol. 5, Part 1, 386, 387.
26. Howard Report, *ORA*, Ser. I, Vol. 5, Part 1, 385-86.
27. Howard reports that he established his headquarters "at the Honorable Mr. T. J. Graham's farm, some 2½ miles from the town," but is probably mistaken in the initials.
28. The instructions, also included in Howard's final report, have been lost. Howard Report, *ORA*, Ser. I, Vol. 5, Part 1, 386, 387.
29. Ibid.
30. Manakee, 56; David Thomson, "Oliver Otis Howard: Reassessing the Legacy of the 'Christian General,'" *Today's History* (September 2009), 273-298.

31. Charles Francis Stein, *A History of Calvert County, Maryland* (Baltimore; Published by the author in cooperation with the Calvert County Historical Society, 1976), 168, 316.

32. Howard Report, *ORA*, Ser. I, Vol. 5, Part 1, 386. Sollers reported to Washington and was charged "with having formed with others a plan to take the polls on the day of election and prevent Union men from voting." He was then sent as a prisoner to meet with General Dix at Baltimore where his case was examined and charges against him dropped upon his swearing the oath of allegiance to the Government of the United State. Sollers would die the following year but his son, a major in the Confederate Army, would survive the war and later serve as Clerk of the County. *ORA*, Ser. II, Vol. Vol. 2, Part 1, 316; Augustus R. Sollers to Governor Seward (received 9 December [1861]), *ORA*, Ser. II, Vol. 1, 615; Stein, 168, 316.

33. Howard Report, *ORA*, Ser. I, Vol. 5, Part 1, 386. William D. Williams had earlier been arrested and jailed in July at Prince Frederick for "gross violation of the criminal law," but was released in October when a grand jury failed to find a bill of indictment against him. *ORA*, Ser. II, Vol. 2, Part 1, 291.

34. Hooker to William, 8 November 1861, 646-647.

35. Ibid., 385-386.

36. Report of George Sykes, November 11, 1861, *ORA*, Ser. I, Vol. 5, Part 1, 387.

37. Ibid., 388.

38. Ibid., 387.

39. *ORA*, Ser. II, Vol. Vol. 2, Part 1, 316.

40. Ibid., 388.

41. *Baltimore Sun*, 6 November 1861, reprinted in *The Local News*, 7 November 1861.

42. Elihu S. Riley, *"The Ancient City." A History of Annapolis, in Maryland. 1649-1887* (Annapolis: Record Printing Office, 1887), 310.

43. Newman, 60-61; Manakee, 56.

44. *The Local News*, 13 December 1861.

45. *Port Tobacco Times*, 18 December 1861.

46. Ibid.

18. Static Warfare

1. Report of Robert S. Williamson to S. Williams, 25 October 1861, *ORA*, Ser. I, Vol. 5, 375-376.
2. "The Riverside of Alexandria," *The Local News*, 26 October 1861.
3. "Late Arrival from the Lower Potomac," *The Local News*, 26 October 1861.
4. "The Riverside of Alexandria."
5. *The Local News*, 26 October 1861.
6. R. S. Williamson to R. B. Marcy, 27 October 1861, *ORA*, Ser. I, Vol. 5, 629-630.
7. Report of Joseph Hooker to S. Williams, 28 October 1861, *ORA*, Ser. I, Vol. 5, 384.
8. Ibid.; *The Local News*, 1 November 1861.
9. Joseph Hooker to S. Williams, 29 October 1861, *ORA*, Ser. I, Vol. 5, 632; Joseph Hooker to S. Williams, 30 October 1861, *ORA*, Ser. I, Vol. 5, 633.
10. Hooker to Williams, 30 October 1861, 633-634.
11. Thomas H. Holmes to Judah P. Benjamin, 29 October 1861, *ORA*, Ser. I, Vol. 5, 928.
12. Hooker to Williams, 30 October 1861, *ORA*, Ser. I, Vol. 5, 633-634.
13. S. Williams to Joseph Hooker, 31 October 1861, *ORA*, Ser. I, Vol. 5, 635-636.
14. Joseph Hooker to S. Williams, 31 October 1861, *ORA*, Ser. I, Vol. 5, 635; Joseph Hooker to S. Williams, 1 November 1861, *ORA*, Ser. I, Vol. 5, 638.
15. *The Local News*, 1 November 1861
16. Ibid., 2 November 1861; Joseph Hooker to S. Williams, 4 November 1861, *ORA*, Ser. I, Vol. 5, 642; *Port Tobacco Times*, 4 April 1861. Richard Posey was released two weeks after his arrest, about August 16, 1861, after swearing the oath of allegiance. *The Local News*, 18 November 1861.
17. "General Hooper's [*sic* Hooker's] Preparations," "Rebel Signals," The Rebel Fortifications," "The Confederate Marine," *New York Daily Tribune*, 5 November 1861.
18. *The Local News*, 7 November 1861.
19. Ibid.; Joseph Hooker to S. Williams, 7 November 1861, *ORA*, Ser. I, Vol. 5, 645-646.
20. Joseph Hooker to S. Williams, 8 November 1861, *ORA*, Ser. I, Vol. 5, 646-647.
21. *The Local News*, 8 November 1861.

22. *Port Tobacco Times*, 24 May 1860, 5 December 1861, 23 January 1862; *Maryland Voices of the Civil War*, Charles W. Mitchell, ed. (Baltimore; The Johns Hopkins University Press, 2007), 166.

23. *Maryland Voices of the Civil War*, 171.

24. Joseph Hooker to S. Williams, November 8, 1861, *ORA*, Ser. I, Vol. 5, 646.

25. Ibid.; *The Local News*, 16 November 1861.

26. *The Local News*, 7 November 1861.

27. "Obituary: Daniel K. Graham," *New York Times*, 16 April 1889.

28. Charles K. Graham to Daniel E. Sickles, 11 November 1861, *ORA*, Ser. I, Vol. 5, 410.

29. Ibid.; Joseph Hooker to S. Williams, 12 November 1861 *ORA*, Ser. I, Vol. 5, 407.

30. Graham to Sickles, 11 November 1861, 410-411; *The Local News*, 19 November 1861.

31. Graham to Sickles, 11 November 1861, 410; *The Local News*, 20 November 1861.

32. Graham to Sickles, 11 November 1861; *The Local News*, 10 December 1861.

33. Ibid., 411; *The Local News*, 20 November 1861, 28 November 1861.

34. Hooker to Williams, 12 November 1861.

Chapter 19: You Are of Value Now

1. *ORN*, Ser. II, Vol. 1, 60; John A. Dahlgren to Joseph Smith, 12 August 1861, *CWNC*, 1:35; Thaddeus S. C. Lowe to Albert V. Colburn, 12 November 1861, *ORA*, Ser. III, Vol. 3, 265-266.

2. Dahlgren to Smith, 12 August 1861.

3. Thaddeus S. C. Lowe to Edwin M. Stanton, 26 May 1863, *ORA*, Ser. III, Vol. 3, 253.

4. *Daily National Republican*, 24 August 1861; *The Daily Dispatch*, October 21, 1861.

5. "War Signals," *Cleveland Morning Leader*, 13 June 1861.

6. Robert V. Bruce, *Lincoln and the Tools of War* (Indianapolis: Bobbs-Merrill [1956]), 85; Thaddeaus S. C. Lowe, *Memoirs of Thaddeus S. C. Lowe, Chief of the Aeronautic Corps of the Army of the United States During the Civil War: My Balloons in Peace and War*, Michael Jaeger and Carol Lauritzen, eds. (Lewiston, N.Y.: Edwin Mellen Press, c2004), 68.

7. "Army Ballooning," *The Daily Exchange*, 20 June 1861. *The New York Commercial Advertiser*, 19 June 1861 in an article "A Balloon Ascension," refers to Lowe's assistant as "General Burns."

8. *Memoirs of Thaddeus S. C. Lowe*, 68-70.

9. Ibid., 71.

10. "Balloon Ascension," *Evening Star*, 19 June 1861.

11. Joseph Henry to Simon Cameron, 21 June 1861, *ORA*, Ser. III, Vol. 3, 254-255; Thaddeus S. C. Lowe to Edwin M. Stanton, 26 May 1863, *ORA*, Ser. III, Vol. 3, 255; *Memoirs of Thaddeus S. C. Lowe*, 68-69, 77-81. "The Enemy's Forces in Fairfax County, How They look to a Man in the Air," *Daily National Republican*, 21 June 1861; Tom D. Crouch, *The Eagle Aloft: Two Centuries of the Balloon in America* (Washington, D.C.: Smithsonian Institution Press, 1983), 346-347.

12. Crouch, 348-352; Thaddeus S. C. Lowe to Major Bache, 29 July 1861, *ORA*, Ser. III, Vol. 3, 256.

13. *Memoirs of Thaddeus S. C. Lowe*, 80-81; *The Daily Exchange*, June 24, 1861; "From Alexandria," *Evening Star*, 25 June 1861.

14. *Memoirs of Thaddeus S. C. Lowe*, 78. 80-81.

15. Lowe to Stanton, 26 May 1863.

16. "The Balloon," *Daily National Republican*, 12 July 1861.

17. "Taking a Risk," *Evening Star*, 13 July 1861.

18. Crouch, 348-352.

19. Lowe to Bache, 256-257.

20. Ibid., 257.

21. Lowe to Stanton, 26 May 1863, 258; *Memoirs of Thaddeus S. C. Lowe*, 78.

22. *Memoirs of Thaddeus S. C. Lowe*, 74-75.

23. A. W. Whipple to Thaddeus S. C. Lowe, 2 August 1861, *ORN*, Ser. III, Vol. 3, 259; *ORA*, Ser. III, Vol. 3, 260; "A Mammoth Balloon," *Daily National Republican*, 7 August 1861; "Reconnoitering Balloon," *Daily National Republican*, 24 August 1861.

24. "Professor Lowe's Mammoth Balloon," *The Daily Exchange*, 29 August 1861; "Reconnaisances," *The Daily Exchange*, 31 August 1861.

25. "Fortifying Munson's Hill," *New York Daily Tribune*, 31 August 1861; "Narrow Escape of Prof. Lowe's Balloon," *Evening Star*, 2 September 1861.

26. "This afternoon," *New York Times*, September 5, 1861; "News of the Day," *New York Times*, 9

September 1861; F. J. Porter to Thaddeus S. C. Lowe, 11 September 1861, *ORA*, Ser. III, Vol. 3, 261; Crouch, 355.

27. "The Balloon Camp," *The Daily Exchange*, 11 September 1861.

28. "The Balloon," *Evening Star*, 11 September 1861.

29. Thaddeus S. C. Lowe to F. J. Porter, 16 September 1861, *ORA*, Ser III, Vol. 3, 262.

30. W. F. Smith to F. J. Porter, 3 September 1861, *ORN*, Ser. III, Vol. 3, 262.

31. J. F. McQuesten to Thaddeus S. C. Lowe, 24 September 1861, *ORA*, Ser. III, Vol. 3, 262-263; W. F. Smith to F. J. Porter, 24 September 1861, *ORA*, Ser. III, Vol. 3, 263.

32. Charles M. Evans, *The War of the Aeronauts: A History of Ballooning During the Civil War* (Mechanicsburg, Pa.: Stackpole Books, ca. 2002), 112-113. The Confederate command soon ordered false campfires to be lit and dummy artillery batteries erected, with black logs, or "Quaker Guns," serving as fake artillery pieces built to deceive aerial observers.

33. *Scientific American*, 16 November 1861; "Affairs in Philadelphia," *The Daily Dispatch*, 21 October 1861; Montgomery C. Meigs to Thaddeus S. C. Lowe, 25 September 1861, *ORA*, Ser. III, Vol. 3, 264; Crouch, 355-356, 358-359, 306-361.

34. "Prof. Lowe's Balloon," *Cincinnati Daily Press*, 12 November 1861; Lowe to Stanton, 265; Thaddeus S. C. Lowe to A. V. Colburn, 3 December 1861, *ORA*, Ser. III, Vol. 3, 26

35. *CWNC*, Vol. 1, 21; J. Gregory Dill, *Myth, Fact, and Navigators' Secrets: Incredible Tales of the Sea and Sailors* (Guildford, Ct.: The Lyons Press, 2006), 170; Mary Alice Wills, *The Confederate Blockade of Washington, D.C. 1861-1862* (McClain Printing Company: Parsons, W.Va., 1975), 327.

36. Lowe to Colburn, 3 December 1861, 268; Thaddeus S. C. Lowe to Joseph Hooker, 10 November 1861, *ORA*, Ser. III, Vol. 3, 265; Joseph Hooker to S. Williams, 11 November 1861, *ORA*, Ser. I, Vol. 5, 648-649.

37. *The Local News*, 20 November 1861.

38. Hooker to Williams, 11 November 1861, 649.

39. *Daily Ohio Statesman*, 14 November 1861; *The Local News*, 14 November 1861; Thaddeus S. C. Lowe to A. V. Colburn, 12 November 1861, Ser. III, Vol. 3, 266

40. Joseph Hooker to S. Williams, 12 November 1861, *ORA*, Ser. I, Vol. 5, 407-408; A. V. Colburn to Thaddeus S. C. Lowe, 16 November 1861, *ORA*, Ser. III, Vol. 3, 266.

41. Report of Joseph Hooker to S. Williams, 14 November 1861, *ORA*, Ser. I, Vol. 5, 421-422. A total of fourteen vessels were seized and put under the charge of pickets at Liverpool Point. Joseph Hooker to S. Williams, 16 November 1861, *ORA*, Ser. I, Vol. 5, 554.

42. P. G. T. Beauregard to W. H. C. Whiting, 13 November 1861, *ORA*, Ser. I, Vol. 5, 950; Wills, 130.

43. Hooker to Williams, 16 November 1861, 553-554.

44. *The Local News*, 22 November 1861; Joseph Hooker to S. Williams, 22 November 1861, *ORA*, Ser. I, Vol. 5, 663.

45. Hooker to Williams, 22 November 1861, 663.

46. Wills, 132.

47. *The Local News*, 3 December 1861, 6 December 1861, 11 December 1861; Lowe to Colburn, 10 December 1861, *ORA*, Ser. III, Vol. 3, 268; Wills, 132.

48. "Asa Hartz. He Is Taken Prisoner, and Sees Dispatches," *Orleans Independent Standard*, 22 November 1861.

20. Deserving of Notice

1. *The Local News*, 7 December 1861.

2. Ibid., 29 November 1861.

3. *The Local News*, 2 December 1861.

4. John G. Barnard to George B. McClellan, 6 December 1861, *ORA*, Ser. I, Vol. 5, 676.

5. *The Local News*, 29 November 1861; E. B. Long and Barbara Long: *The Civil War Day by Day: An Almanac 1861-1865* (Garden City, N.Y.: Doubleday & Company, Inc., 1971), 139.

6. John Withers to Thomas H. Holmes, 23 November 1861, *ORA*, Ser. I, Vol. 5, 967-968.

7. Lafayette C. Baker, *History of the United States Secret Service* (Philadelphia: Privately published, 1867), 102.

8. Lafayette C. Baker to William H. Seward, 27 November 1861, in Baker, *History*, 105.

9. Ibid.

10. Lafayette C. Baker to Postmaster General, 14 January 1863, in Baker, *History*, 99.

11 Ibid., 99-100; Lafayette C. Baker to William H. Seward, 27 November 1861, in Baker, *History*, 105.

12. Ibid.

13. Baker to Postmaster General, 14 January 1863, 100, 110.

14. Baker to Seward, 27 November 1861, in Baker, *History*, 105.

15. Ibid.

16. Baker to Postmaster General, 14 January 1863, in Baker, *History*, 100.

17. Baker to Seward, 27 November 1861, in Baker, *History*, 105.

18. Baker to Postmaster General, 14 January 1863, in Baker, *History*, 100.

19. Baker to Seward, 27 November 1861, in Baker, *History*, 105.

20. Baker to Postmaster General, 14 January 1863, in Baker, *History*, 110.

21. Baker to Seward, 27 November 1861, in Baker, *History*, 106.

22. Ibid., 108.

23. Ibid., 107-108; "Heavy Purchase," *St. Mary's Beacon*, 12 January 1860; "Shooting Recontre," *Port Tobacco Times*, 30 June 1858; "Death of Philip H. Burroughs," *St. Mary's Beacon*, 24 June 1858; "Acquittal," *Port Tobacco Times*, 9 January 1862.

24. *The Local News*, 26 November 1861; December 3, 1861.

25. *Daily National Republican*, 3 December 1861; "Seizure of Contraband," *St. Mary's Beacon*, 12 December 1861, reprinted from the *Baltimore Clipper*.

26. *The Local News*, 7 December 1861.

27. Joseph Hooker, to S. Williams, 6 December 1861, *ORA*, Ser. I, Vol. 5, 675.

28. Joseph Hooker to S. Williams, 17 December 1861, *ORA*, Ser. I, Vol. 5, 469.

29. Ibid.

30. Ibid.

31. "The Reason," *St. Mary's Beacon*, 2 January 1862.

32. Hooker to Williams, 6 December 1861, 675-676.

21. Apple Pie Order

1. R. H. Wyman to Gideon Welles, 9 December 1861, *ORN*, Ser. I, Vol. 5, 3; Samuel Cropley to Gideon Welles, 17 December 1861, *ORN*, Ser. I, Vol. 5, 10.

2. *The Local News*, 26 November 1861.

3. "A Military Village in Charles County," *St. Mary's Beacon*, 2 January 1862.

4. R. H. Wyman to Gideon Welles, 12 December 1861, *ORN*, Ser. I, Vol. 5, 4; William T. Street to R. H. Wyman, 11 December 1861, *ORN*, Ser. I, Vol. 5, 4-5; R. L. T. Beale to Judah. P. Benjamin, 10 December 1861, *ORA*, Ser. I, Vol. 5, 991.

5. Thomas H. Holmes to S. Cooper, 12 December 1861, *ORA*, Ser. I, Vol. 5, 93.

6. Beale to Benjamin, 10 December 1861, *ORA*, Ser. I, Vol. 5, 990-991.

7. Judah P. Benjamin to R. L. T., 15 December 1861, *ORA*, Ser. I, Vol. 5, 997.

8. George E. Pickett to D. H. Maury, 10 December 1861, *ORA*, Ser. I, Vol. 5, 991-992.

9. R. H. Wyman to Gideon Welles, 12 December 1861, *ORN*, Ser. I, Vol. 5, 4; Joseph Hooker to S. Williams, 13 December 1861, *ORA*, Ser. I, Vol. 5, 686; "River News," *Daily National Republican*, 30 December 1861; *The Daily Dispatch*, 26 June 1862.

10. R. H. Wyman to Gideon Welles, 12 December 1861, *ORN*, Ser. I, Vol. 5, 7-8; Reports of a battery at Boyd's Hole began to appear in early November but were dismissed after a reconnaissance sent by Hooker revealed only one small field piece, which was deemed not a threat. Hooker to Williams, 12 November 1861, *ORA*, Ser. I, Vol. 5, 407-408.

11. Street to Wyman, 11 December 1861, *ORN*, Ser. I, Vol. 5, 5; Regina Combs Hammett, *History of St. Mary's County Maryland* (Ridge, Md.: Privately published, 1977), 106, 429.

12. "The River," *The Local News*, 26 November 1861; Gideon Welles to R. H. Wyman, 16 December 1861, *ORN*, Ser. I, Vol. 5, 7.

13. Wyman to Welles, 12 December 1861; R. H. Wyman to Gustavus V. Fox, 20 December 1861, *ORN*, Ser. I, Vol. 5, 8.

14. R. H. Wyman to Gideon Welles, 20 December 1861, *ORN*, Ser. I, Vol. 5, 8-9.

15. *The Local News*, 27 November, 9 December 1861 and 17 December 1861; Caleb S. Wright to Gustavus V. Fox, 25 December 1861, *ORN*, Ser. I, Vol. 5, 11; *Burlington Free Press* (Burlington, Vt.), 7 December 1861; *Merchant Steam Vessels of the United States 1780-1868*, William M. Lytle and Forrest R. Holdcamper, comp. (Staten Island, N.Y.: The Steamship Historical Society of America, Inc., 1975),

223; Charles Dana Gibson and E. Kay Gibson, *Dictionary of Transports and Combatant Vessels Steam and Sail Employed by the Union Army 1861-1868*, 2 Vols. (Camden, Me.: Ensign Press, 1995), Vol. 2, 327.

16. R. H. Wyman to Gideon Welles, 27 December 1861, *ORN*, Ser. I, Vol. 5, 11; John A. Dahlgren [endorsement], 28 December 1861, *ORN*, Ser. I, Vol. 5, 11.

17. Henry W. Morris to Gideon Welles, 28 December 1861, *ORN*, Ser. I, Vol. 5, 11-12; Gustavus V. Fox to Montgomery C. Meigs, December 28, 1861, *ORN*, Ser. I, Vol. 5, 12; Henry W. to Gideon Welles, 12 January 1862, *ORN*, Ser. I, Vol. 5, 18; Henry W. Morris to Gideon Welles, 14 January 1862, *ORN*, Ser. I, Vol. 5, 18; *The Local News*, 11 January 1862; Joseph Hooker to S. Williams, 12 January 1862, *ORA*, Ser. I, Vol. 5, 698.

18. Hooker to Williams, 12 January 12, 1862.

19. Joseph Hooker to S. Williams, 23 December 1861, *ORN*, Ser. I, Vol. 5, 13; R. H. Wyman to Gideon Welles, 2 January 1862, *ORN*, Ser. I, Vol. 5, 14.

20. R. H. Wyman to Gideon Welles, 3 January 1862, *ORN*, Ser. I, Vol. 5, 15. It should be noted that the designation of an 80-pounder gun was probably in error as that particular caliber weapon was almost certainly not in the Confederate arsenal, if it ever even existed, but was nevertheless reported on as such by Wyman and has thus been cited.

21. Joseph Hooker to S. Williams, 11 January 1862, *ORA*, Ser. I, Vol. 5, 697.

22. Felix Brannigan [letter], 20 January 1862, Fellix Brannigan Papers, 1861-1863, LC.

23. Ambrose E. Burnside, "The Burnside Expedition," *Battles and Leaders of the Civil War*, I, (New Brunswick, New York, London: Thomas Yoseloff, 1956), 661.

24. Ibid.

25. Ibid.; *New York Times*, 17 November 1861; *Baltimore Sun*, 19 November and 24 December 1861

26. Jane Wilson McWilliams, *Annapolis: City on the Severn* (Baltimore: The Johns Hopkins University Press, and Crownsville: The Maryland Historical Trust Press, 2011), 175, *ORA*, Ser. I, Vol. 5, 1019; Burnside, 661; *CWNC*, 2:7, 11.

27. R. H. Wyman to Joseph Hooker, 24 January 1862, *ORA*, Ser. I, Vol. 5, 707.

28. *The Daily Green Mountain Freeman*, 24 January 1862.

29. Mary Alice Wills, *The Confederate Blockade of Washington, D.C. 1861-1862* (McClain Printing Company: Parsons, W.Va., 1975), 134.

30. Ibid., 140.

31. S. Williams to Joseph Hooker, 18 February 18, 1862, 8 PM, *ORA*, Ser. I, Vol. 5, 724.

32. Felix Brannigan [letter], 19 February 1862, Brannigan Papers, LC.

33. Joseph Hooker to S. Williams, 20 February 20, 1862, *ORA*, Ser. I, Vol. 5, 725.

34. Abstract from return of the Army of the Potomac . . . for the Month of February 1862. *ORA*, Ser. I, Vol. 5, 732.

35. Warren Lee Gross, "Going to the Front: Recollections of a Private," in *Battles and Leaders of the Civil War*, 4 Vols. (New York and London: Thomas Yoseloff, 1956), 1:159.

36. Felix Brannigan [letter], 3 March 1862, Brannigan Papers, LC.

37. Ibid.

38. Wills, 146.

39. "From Washington," *The Daily Green Mountain Freeman*, 8 March 1862.

40. Ibid.

41. R. H. Wyman to Gideon Welles, 9 March 1862, 1 p.m., *ORN*, Ser. I, Vol. 5, 23; R. H. Wyman to Gideon Welles, 9 March 1862, 4 p.m., *ORN*, Ser. I, Vol. 5, 23; Joseph Hooker to S. Williams, 10 March 1862, *ORA*, Ser. I, Vol. 5, 525.

42. Joseph Hooker to S. Williams, 28 February 1862, *ORA*, Ser. I, Vol. 5, 731; Report of R. B. Marcy to Joseph Hooker, 9 March 1862, *ORA*, Ser. I, Vol. 5, 524; Joseph Hooker to S. H. Starr, 9 March 1862, *ORA*, Ser. I, Vol. 5, 524-525; Joseph Hooker to S. Williams, 11 March 1862, *ORA*, Ser. I, Vol. 5, 526. Starr's brigade, a month earlier on February 13, numbered 3,723 men and consisted of the 5th, 6th, 7th and 8th New Jersey Volunteers. Charles S. Tripler to S. Williams, February 6, 1862, *ORA*, Ser. I, Vol. 5, 716.

Chapter 22: An Act

1. John A. Dahlgren to Gideon Welles, 9 October 1862 (received 9 p.m.), *ORN*, Ser. I, Vol. 5, 24.
2. Ibid.
3. *ORN*, Ser. II, Vol. 1, 111.

4. Foxhall A. Parker to Gideon Welles, 10 March 1862, *ORN*, Ser. I, Vol. 5, 24.

5. John A. Dahlgren to Gideon Welles, 10 March 1862, *ORN*, Ser. I, Vol. 5, 24.

6. R. H. Wyman to Gideon Welles, 19 March 1862, *ORN*, Ser. I, Vol. 5, 27.

7. Gideon Welles to R. H. Wyman, 25 March 1862, *ORN*, Ser. I, Vol. 5, 29.

8. Benjamin Franklin Cooling III and Walton H. Owen II, *Mr. Lincoln's Forts: A Guide to the Civil War Defenses of Washington* (Shippensburg, Pa: White Mane Publishing Company, 1988), 290.

9. Ibid., 225, 229, 231, 232.

10. Ibid., 232.

11. Ibid., 229, 232.

12. "A Rival of Toussaint L'Ouverture: The Adventure of 'Potomac Jim,'" *Daily National Republican*, 29 March 1862, reprinted from *New York Times*

13. Ibid.

14. Joseph Hooker to R. B. Marcy, March 13, 1862, *ORA*, Ser. I, Vol. 5, 743.744.

15. "A Rival of Toussaint L'Ouverture."

16. Ibid.

17. Ibid.

18. R. B. Wyman to Gideon Welles, 14 March 1862, *ORN*, Ser. I, Vol. 5, 26.

19. "A Rival of Toussaint L'Ouverture. "

20. Joseph Hooker to R. B. Marcy, 12 March 1862, *ORA*, Ser I, Vol. 5, 743-744.

21. Joseph Hooker to S. Williams, 14 March 1862, *ORA*, Ser. I, Vol. 5, 756.

22. Joseph Dickenson to D. E. Sickles, 16 March 1862, *ORA*, Ser. I, Vol. 5, 761.

23. See J. Watts de Peyster, "An Ideal Soldier, A tribute to Maj. Gen. Daniel E. Sickles," *National Tribune*, 19 July 1888, for a complete recounting of the April 1862 Sickles expedition into Virginia. The Sickles reconnaissance in force is only lightly referred to in Federal records, and its dependence upon data provided by John Lawson and his colleagues from their missions into the same territory is, owing to the lack of a written report, conjectural. That Lawson's information was instrumental in Sickles's decision to undertake the route he ultimately followed is, however, almost certain given the repeated trips into the interior made by the intrepid black spy, though only obliquely referred to by both Hooker and Sickles in their communications.

24. Peyster, "An Ideal Soldier."

25. Ibid.

26. "Outrage in St. Inigoes' District," *St. Mary's Beacon*, 17 April 1862; Beitzell, in his remarkable works *The Jesuit Missions of St. Mary's County, Maryland*, (Sponsored by the St. Mary's County Bicentennial Commission: Abell, Md., 1976), 219, and *Point Lookout Prison Camp for Confederates*, (Leonardtown, Md.: Privately Printed, 1972), 11, errs in giving the date of the *St. Mary's Beacon* article as 17 February, which has unfortunately been repeated by Regina Combs Hammett in *History of St. Mary's County, Maryland*, (Ridge, Md.: Privately published, 1977), 211.

27. "Outrage in St. Inigoes' District"; Beitzell, *The Jesuit Missions*, 219. The chapel is today the site of St. Mary's, Star of the West Church. Beitzell, 349, n. 42.

28. Don E. Fehrenbacher and Ward M. McAfee, *The Slaveholding Republic: An Account of the United States Government's Relations to Slavery* (New York: Oxford University Press, 2001), 81-82; Karl Reiner, *Remembering Fairfax County, Virginia* (Charleston, SC: The History Press, 2006), 57.

29. *The Washington Post* (undated), quoted in *The Local News*, 12 December 1861. 30. John William Burgess, *The Civil War and the Constitution, 1859-1865*, (New York: C. Scribner's Sons, 1901), 78; "Emancipation in the District," *New York Times*, 4 April 1862; "Abolition in the District of Columbia," *The New York Time*, 12 April 1862; "Emancipation in the District—Mr. Lincoln's Opinions," *The New York Times*, 15 April 1862; "Mr. Lincoln's Views on Slavery—His Course Towards the South," *The New York Times*, 5 November 1860; "Thirty-Seventh Congress—First Session," *Baltimore Sun*, 17 April 1862; "Important News from Washington. The Abolition of Slavery in the District of Columbia," *New York Times*, 17 April 1862. 31. Peter Zavodnyik, *The Rise of the Federal Colossus: The Growth of Federal Power from Lincoln to F.D.R.*

(Santa Barbara, Calif.: Praeger, [2011]), 15; Burgess, 82; *Slavery in the United States: A Social, Political, and Historical Encyclopedia*, Junius P. Rodriguez, ed. (Santa Barbara, Calif.: ABC-CLIO, [2007]), 275.

32. Zavodnyik, 15.

33. "Nothing to Cheer Them," *St. Mary's Beacon*, 15 May 1862, undated excerpt reprinted from the *Fredrick Union*.

34. "Absconding Slaves," *St. Mary's Beacon*, 20 May 1862.

35. *Port Tobacco Times*, 19 June 1862.

36. L. C. Baker, *History of the United States Secret Service* (Philadelphia; Published by L. C. Baker, 1867), 191-192.

37. Ibid., 233.

38. Ibid., 233, 234.

39. E. B. Long and Barbara Long: *The Civil War Day by Day: An Almanac 1861-1865* (Garden City, N.Y.: Doubleday & Company, Inc., 1971), 241.

23. The Mere Love of Gain

1. "The Curfew," *St. Mary's Beacon*, 15 May 1862.

2. Gideon Welles to Senior Officer Potomac Flotilla, 18 July 1862, *ORN*, Ser. I, Vol. 5, 51-52.

3. Gideon Welles to Andrew A. Harwood, 31 July 1862, *ORN*, Ser. I, Vol. 5, 54.

4. William E. Dosier was appointed Provost Marshal of Washington on March 29, 1862. *Daily National Intelligencer*, 29 March 1862.

5. "Important Arrest of Rebels," *Daily National Republican*, 31 July 1862.

6. Andrew Harwood to Gideon Welles, 30 July 1862, *ORN*, Ser. I, Vol. 5, 55-56.

7. William Watkins Glenn, *Between North and South: A Maryland Journalist Views the Civil War: The Narrative of William Wilkins Glenn, 1861-1869*, Bayley Ellen Marks and Mark Norton Schatz, eds. (Rutherford, N.J.: Farleigh Dickinson University Press, 1976), 58.

8. Gideon Welles to Andrew A. Harwood, 31 July 1862, *ORN*, Ser. I, Vol. 5, 54.

9. Samuel Magaw to Gideon Welles, [1] August 1862, *ORN*, Ser. I, Vol. 5, 55; James L. Plunkett to Samuel Magaw, 1 August 1862, *ORN*, Ser. I, Vol. 5, 55; Gideon Welles to Andrew A. Harwood, 7 August 1862, *ORN*, Ser. I, Vol. 5, 55.

10. Glenn, *Between North and South*, 68.

11. Ibid., 69.

12. "Wholesale Arrests, " *St. Mary's Beacon*, 7 August 1862; Regina Combs Hammett, *History of St. Mary's County Maryland* (Ridge, Md.: Privately published, 1977), 109, 122, 146, 147, 306, 448.

13. "The Patuxent Boats Stopped—Arrests," *Baltimore Sun*, 4 August 1862.

14. *Daily National Republican*, August 16, 1862; Charles Dana Gibson and E. Kay Gibson, *Dictionary of Transports and Combatant Vessels Steam and Sail Employed by the Union Army 1861-1868*, 2 Vols. (Camden, Me.: Ensign Press, 1995), Vol. 2, 132.

15. "Arrival of Marylanders," *Richmond Dispatch*, reprinted in *Memphis Daily Appeal*, 27 August 1862; Gibson and Gibson, Vol. 2, 257.

16. Stephen Shinn to Gideon Welles, 7 September 1862, *ORN*, Ser. I, Vol. 5, 86.

17. Samuel Magaw to Gideon Welles, 10 August 1862, *ORN*, Ser. I, Vol. 5, 58; Andrew A. Harwood to Gideon Welles, 11 August 1862 (received 9:10 p.m.), *ORN*, Ser. I, Vol. 5, 59; Samuel Magaw to Andrew A. Harwood, 11 August 1862, *ORN*, Ser. I, Vol. 5, 59.

18. Thomas S. Pheps to Andrew A. Harwood, 13 August 1862, *ORN*, Ser. I, Vol. 5, 60-61.

19. "Acquitted," *St. Mary's Gazette*, 28 January 1864.

20. Phelps to Harwood, 13 August 1862.

21. Gideon Welles to Andrew A. Harwood, 16 August 1862, *ORN*, Ser. I, Vol. 5, 62.

22. Andrew A. Harwood to Gideon Welles, 14 August 18162, *ORN*, Ser. I, Vol. 5, 60.

23. Andrew A. Harwood to Samuel Magaw, 14 August 1862, *ORN*, Ser. I, Vol. 5, 61-62.

24. Andrew A. Harwood to Samuel Magaw, 18 August 1862, *ORN*, Ser. I, Vol. 5, 63-64.

25. Samuel Magaw to Andrew A. Harwood, 23 August 1862, *ORN*, Ser. I, Vol. 5, 66.

26. Andrew A. Harwood to Samuel Magaw, 26 August 1862, *ORN*, Ser. I, Vol. 5, 70. The mid-19th century Chesapeake Bay log canoe, a direct descendent of the Native American dugout canoe, was usually built from three to nine trimmed logs bolted together and hewn out in hull-first form, then fitted with frames, centerboard, and rigging. The type was commonly engaged in commercial fishing and oystering, but during the Civil War was frequently employed in blockade running in the Tidewater. See M. V. Brewington, *Chesapeake Bay Log Canoes and Bugeyes* (Cambridge, Md.: Cornell Maritime Press, Inc., 1963) for a comprehensive history of the craft type.

27. Ibid; Hammett, 106, 176.

28. Harwood to Magaw, 26 August 1862, 69.

29. Ibid., 69-70.

30. Samuel Magaw to Andrew A. Harwood, 4 September 1862, *ORN*, Ser. I, Vol. 5, 78.

31. Samuel Magaw to Andrew A. Harwood, 6 September 1862, *ORN*, Ser. I, Vol. 5, 80; Andrew A. Harwood to Gideon Welles, 15 September 1862, *ORN*, Ser. I, Vol. 5, 85.

32. Glenn, 22 September 1862, 73.

33. Andrew A. Harwood to Charles Wilkes, 2 September 1862, *ORN*, Ser. I, Vol. 5, 76-77; Gustavus V. Fox to Charles Wilkes, 2 September 1862, *ORN*, Ser. I, Vol. 5, 77; General Instructions, Charles Wilkes, 5 September 1862, *ORN*, Ser. I, Vol. 5, 79; *ORN*, Ser 1, Vol. 5, 72, 82; Vol. 7, 695.

34. Samuel Magaw to Andrew A. Harwood, 4 September 1862, *ORN*, Ser. I, Vol. 5:78; Nelson Provost to E. P. McCrea, 17 November 1862, *ORN*, Ser. I, Vol. 5, 157; Gideon Welles to Andrew A. Harwood, 16 September 1862, *ORN*, Ser. I, Vol. 5, 87. 294.

35. Lewis McKenzie to Gideon Welles, 6 September 1862, *ORN* Ser. I, Vol. 5, 82-83.

36. Eric Mills, *Chesapeake Bay in the Civil War* (Centreville, MD; Tidewater Publishers, 1996), 199; "The War Upon Women," *St. Mary's Beacon*, 2 April 1863.

37. "The War Upon Women."

38. *St. Mary's Beacon*, 23 April 1863.

39. *In a Place called Ivy Springs . . . Near the Pines: The History of St. Paul's Episcopal Church, Piney Parish* (Waldorf, Md.: September 1992).

40. Ibid.

Chapter 24: Reflection of the High Bluffs

1. See Thomas A. Jones's memoirs, *J. Wilkes Booth: An Account of His Sojourn in Southern Maryland after the Assassination of Abraham Lincoln*, (Chicago: Laird & Lee Publishers, 1893), for a view of the Confederate contraband and mail operations in Southern Maryland from the viewpoint of one of its principal operatives.

2. Jones, 20-21.

3. See *ORA*, Ser. II, Vol. 2, 561-576, 1346, 1347, and 1348 for correspondence regarding the espionage activities of Greenhowe, Morris and Baxley.

4. Jones, 23.

5. Ibid.

6. Ibid., 24.

7. Captain Groff was succeeded in command of these men by Captains Boyle and Watkins.

8. Jones, 25, 26.

9. Ibid., 27.

10. Ibid., 28.

11. ibid., 23.

12. Ibid.

13. "Dreadful Disaster on the Potomac," *Evening Star*, 16 August 1862.

14. Charles Dana Gibson and E. Kay Gibson, *Dictionary of Transports and Combatant Vessels Steam and Sail Employed by the Union Army 1861-1868*, 2 Vols. (Camden, Me.: Ensign Press, 1995), Vol. 2, 344; *Merchant Steam Vessels of the United States 1780-1868*, William M. Lytle and Forrest R. Holdcamper, comp. (Staten Island, N.Y.: The Steamship Historical Society of America, Inc., 1975), 228,

15. "Dreadful Disaster on the Potomac".

16. Ibid.

17. Lytle and Forrest, 84; Gibson and Gibson, 130; "Dreadful Disaster on the Potomac"; "Frightful Calamity." *Evening Star*, 15 August 1862.

18. "Dreadful Disaster on the Potomac".

19. Ibid.

20. Ibid.

21. "Affairs Down River." Another report stated the wreck lay a mile and a half from the shore.

22. "Dreadful Disaster on the Potomac"; "Frightful Calamity." *Evening Star*, 15 August 1862. *John Farron*, also known as *John Faron*, a 251-ton steamer, built in 1856 at Williamsburg, N.Y. and first home ported at New York, was first chartered on March 5, 1862 and then sold to the War Department in 1863. She would continue in service until early 1865. Gibson and Gibson, 178; Lytle, 113.

23. "Frightful Calamity"; "Dreadful Disaster on the Potomac"; *Alexandria Gazette*, 30 August 1862; Lytle, 306, says seventy-six lives were lost but does not acknowledge his source.

24. "The Disaster at Ragged Point," *Evening Star*, 15 August 1862; "Dreadful Disaster on the Potomac."

25. "Affairs Down River".

26. *St. Mary's Beacon*, 21 August 1862; *Alexandria Gazette*, 28 August 1862.

27. *Alexandria Gazette*, 3 September 1862.

28. *St. Mary's Beacon*, 21 August 1862.

29. *Alexandria Gazette*, 28 August 1862. Unfortunately, the verdict of the court as to guilt is unknown as the records have yet to be uncovered.

30. Thomas Poynton Ives to Samuel Magaw, 8 October 1862, *ORN*, Ser. I, Vol. 5, 118; *Alexandria Gazette*, 10 October 1862.

31. Andrew Harwood to Samuel Magaw. 25 October 1862, *ORN*, Ser. I, Vol. 5, 119; "The Burning of a Vessel on the Potomac," *Alexandria Gazette*, 14 October 1862.

32. A. Ludlow Case to Thomas Turner, 9 November 1862, *ORN*, Ser. I, 140-141; Walter T. Jones to French Forrest, 17 November 1862, *ORN*, Ser. I, Vol. 5, 141.

33. For accounts of the depredations of Lieutenant John Taylor Wood see Gordon Singleton Royce, *John Taylor Wood: Sea Ghost of the Confederacy* (Athens, Ga.: University of Georgia Press, 1979).

34. E. B. Long and Barbara Long: *The Civil War Day by Day: An Almanac 1861-1865* (Garden City, N.Y.: Doubleday & Company, Inc., 1971), 296.

35. *ORN*, Ser. I, Vol. 8, 450-451; Vol. Ser. I, 5, 209-211.

25. Nothing Less Than Robbery

1. "Our Naval Squadrons," *The National Tribune*, 9 June 1892; Montgomery C. Meigs to Ambrose E. Burnside, 12 January 1863, *ORA* Ser. I, Vol. 21, 966.

2. Ibid.

3. Ibid.

4. Edmund Ruffin, *The Diary of Edmund Ruffin*, William K. Scarborough, ed., 2 Vols. (Baton Rouge: Louisiana State University Press, 1976), Vol. 2, 593.

5. Meigs to Burnside, 12 January 1863, *ORA*, Ser. I, Vol. 21, 966.

6. Ibid., *ORA*, Ser. I, Vol. 21, 967.

7. Daniel Butterfield to John F. Reynolds, 8 February 1863, *ORA*, Ser. I, Vol. 25, Part 2, 63.

8. Joseph Hooker to J. C. Kelton, 19 February 1863, *ORA*, Ser. I, Vol. 25, Part 2, 88.

9. Daniel Butterfield to Samuel Magaw, 10 February 1863, *ORA*, Ser. I, Vol. 25, Part 2, 63.

10. J. F. Reynolds to Alfred Pleasonton, 12 February 1863, *ORA*, Ser. 1, Vol. 51, Part 1, 987; "Expedition to Northern Neck," *Alexandria Gazette*, 2 April 1863.

11. W. D. Medill, to William Gambill, 13 February 1863, *ORA*, Ser. I, Vol. 25, Part 1, 12-13.

12. Ibid., 13.

13. Ibid., 12-13.

14. Ibid.

15. Craig W. Wadsworth to Charles Kingsbury, 17 February 1863, *ORA*, Ser. 1, Vol. 25, Part 1, 14; Reynolds to Pleasonton, 12 February 1863.

16. Wadsworth to Kingsbury, 17 February 1863, 14, 15.

17. Ibid., 15.

18. Blake T. Newton, "The White Brothers," *Northern Neck of Virginia Historical Magazine*, Vol. 12, 1982, 1105.

19. Newton, 1105-1106.

20. Ruffin, 593.

21. John F. Reynolds to James Gavin, 12 February 1863, *ORA*, Ser. I, Vol. 51, Part 1, 986-987. Whatever the specific mission objectives may have been regarding foraging, contrabands and Confederate troops, they appear to have been delivered verbally and are only alluded to in the written instructions. The map is missing.

22. James Gavin to Charles Kingsbury, 14 February 1863, *ORA*, Ser. 1, Vol. 25, Part 1, 15; *Merchant Steam Vessels of the United States 1780-1868*, William M. Lytle and Forrest R. Holdcamper, comp. (Staten Island, N.Y.: The Steamship Historical Society of America, Inc., 1975), 61. *Edwin Lewis*, built in 1845 in New York, was first chartered by the U.S. Army on March 5, 1862 and would be repeatedly employed through to the Carolina campaign of early 1865. Charles Dana Gibson and E. Kay Gibson, *Dictionary of Transports and Combatant Vessels Steam and Sail Employed by the Union Army*

1861-1868, 2 Vols. (Camden, Me.: Ensign Press, 1995), I, 97.

23. Gavin to Kingsbury, 14 February 1863, *ORA*, Ser. 1, Vol. 25, Part 1, 16.

24. Ibid.

25. John F. Reynolds to Lucius Fairfield, 12 February 1863, *ORA*, Ser. I, Vol. 51, Part 1, 986.

26. Lucius Fairchild to T. E. Ellsworth, 16 February 1863, *ORA*, Ser. 1, Vol. 25, Part 1, 17.

27. Ibid. A report that varied considerably with Fairchild's official inventory of captured goods appeared in the *Alexandria Gazette* stating that 300 pounds of bacon, 1,000 pounds of pork, 230 bushels of wheat, 3,000 bushels of corn, fifteen bushels of whole beans, and a large quantity of oats were taken. A report mentioning the pungies and/or scows on the Rappahannock was provided to General Hooker but has been lost. The inclusion of the information regarding such activities is derived from later reports provided by the Navy relating their reconnaissance mission up the river to destroy them. "Expedition to Northern Neck." See also Samuel Magaw to Daniel Butterfield, 24 February 1863, *ORN*, Ser. I, Vol. 5, 236.

28. Ibid.

29. Daniel Butterfield to Samuel Magaw, 15 February 11863, *ORN*, Ser. I, Vol. 5, 235-236.

30. Samuel Magaw to Joseph Hooker, 24 February 1863, *ORN*, Ser. I, Vol. 5, 236; W. H. F. Lee to Norman R. Fitzhugh, 23 February 1863, *ORA*, Ser. I, Vol. 25, Part 1, 20.

31. Samuel Magaw to Andrew A. Harwood, 25 February 1863, *ORN*, Ser. I, Vol. 5, 235.

32. Andrew A. Harwood to Samuel Magaw, 27 February 1863, *ORN*, Ser. I, Vol. 5, 236.

33. John F. Reynolds to Charles Kingsbury, 16 February 1863, *ORA* Ser. I, Vol. 25, Part 1, 18; James S. Wadsworth, [Endorsement] 16 February 1863, *ORA* Ser. I, Vol. 25, Part 1, 18.

34. Abstract from "Record of Events," Fourth Brigade, First Division, First Army Corps, Brig. Gen. Solomon Meredith, U.S. Army, commanding. *ORA*, Ser. 1, Vol. 25, Part 1, 73.

35. Ibid., 74.

36. Ibid., 73, 74.

37. Ibid., 73.

38. James S. Wadsworth to Charles Kingsbury, Jr., March 31, 1863, *ORA*, Ser. 1, Vol. 25, Part 2, 175.

39. Ibid.

40. "Record of Events," Fourth Brigade, First Division, First Army Corps, extract from First Brigade return for April 1863, *ORA*, Ser. I, Vol. 25, Part 1, 137; Itinerary of the First Army Corps, April 19-May 26, 1863, extract from returns for April and May, *ORA*, Ser. I, Vol. 25, Part 1, 256.

41. "The 8th Ill. Cav.; A Contemporaries Account of One of Its Battles in 1863," *The National Tribune*, 19 July 1906.

42. George H. Thompson to G. S. Taylor, 24 May 1863, *ORA*, Ser. I, Vol. 25, Part 1, 1116.

43. Henry W. Morrow to Charles Kingsbury, 29 May 1863, *ORA*, Ser. I, Vol. 25, Part 1, 1112-1113.

44. Thompson to Taylor, 24 May 1863.

45. Ibid.

46. Ibid.

47. Henry A. Morrow to Charles Kingsbury, 29 May 1863, *ORA*, Ser. I, Vol. 25, Part 1, 1112-1113.

48. Ibid.

49. Ibid., 1114.

50. Ibid.

51. Ibid., 1113.

52. "The 8th Ill. Cav."

53. Ibid.

54. Ibid.

55. Ibid.

56. Ibid.

57. Daniel Butterfield to Joseph Hooker, 26 May 1863, 10:45 a.m., *ORA,* Ser. I, Vol. 25, Part 1, 111-1112.

58. Alfred Pleasonton to Joseph Hooker, 26 May 1863, *ORA,* Ser. I, Vol. 25, Part 1, 1112.

59. Morrow to Kingsbury, 29 May 1863, 1114.

60. Ibid., 1115.

61. Ibid., 1112-1115.

26. For the Benefit of the Sick and Wounded

1. Kenneth J. Winkle, *Lincoln's Citadel: The Civil War in Washington, D.C.* (New York and London, W.W. Norton & Company, 201), 213; E. B. Long and Barbara Long: *The Civil War Day by Day: An Almanac 1861-1865* (Garden City, N.Y.: Doubleday & Company, Inc., 1971), 220; *Cleveland Morning Leader*, 21 July 1862. Winkle, 366, notes that sick and wounded soldiers who actually reached a general hospital had a ninety-two percent chance of surviving. Nevertheless, approximately 87,000 soldiers died while undergoing treatment in Union hospitals.
2. Edwin W. Beitzell, *Point Lookout Prison Camp for Confederates* (Leonardtown, Md.: Privately Printed, 1972), 19.
3. "Hammond Hospital," *Daily National Republican*, 14 February 1863; Beitzell, 19; "Hospital at Point Lookout," *Evening Star*, 25 July 1862. Surgeon A. M. Clark stated in September 1863 that the water tank was of 10,000 gallons capacity, not 20,000 as many writers have reported. A. M. Clark, Surgeon and Acting Medical Inspector Prisoners of War. Report of Inspection of the Hammond U.S. General Hospital at Point Lookout, Md., December 17, 1863. *ORA*, Ser. II, Vol. 6, 741.
4. "Hammond Hospital," *Daily National Republican*, 14 February 1863; Clark, Report of Inspection of the Hammond U.S. General Hospital, 741.
5. Ibid.
6. "Correspondence of the 'Journal,'" *Raftsman's Journal*, 27 August 1862.
7. "Fort Monroe," *Evening Star*, 26 July 1862; "Fort Monroe," *The Daily Green Mountain Freeman*, 28 July 1862; Charles Dana Gibson and E. Kay Gibson, comp., *Dictionary of Transports and Combatant Vessels Steam and Sail Employed by the Union Army 1861-1868* (Camden, Me: Ensign Press, 1995), 177.
8. "Correspondence of the 'Journal.'"
9. Beitzell, 20.
10. Gibson and Gibson, 190; "From Point Lookout," *Evening Star*, 21 August 1862.
11. "From Point Lookout"; "Point Lookout Hospital," *Daily National Republican*, 22 August 1862.
12. Long and Long, 266; "The Sick and Wounded," *Evening Star*, 11 September 1862; "Sick and Wounded Sent Away," *Daily National Republican*, 11 September 1862; "There are 13,769 patients," *Daily National Republican*, 17 September 1862.
13. Long and Long, 266-68.
14. "Complaints of Hospital Arrangements," *Daily Intelligencer* (Wheeling, Va. [W. Va.]), 8 October 1862.
15. Jane Wilson McWilliams, *Annapolis: City on the Severn* (Baltimore: The Johns Hopkins University Press, and Crownsville: The Maryland Historical Trust Press, 2011), 179-181; *Baltimore Sun*, 22 July, 10 and 25 September 1861; *ORA*, Ser. II, Vol. 4, 542, 691, Vol. 5, 39, 328-337, 614.
16. "From Point Lookout," *Evening Star*, 9 October 1862; "Hammond Hospital."
17. *The Alleghanian*, 27 November 1862; "Point Lookout Hospital," *Daily National Republican*, 22 November 1862.
18. *Hammond Gazette*, 23 December 1862; "Hammond Hospital."
19. "Hammond Hospital"; "Major John Carter Brown," *Daily National Republican*, February 16, 1863; "For Baltimore, Point Lookout, and Landings on the Potomac Rive," *Evening Star*, November 11, 1863.
20. *The Caledonian*, 20 February 1863.
21. "Hospital Incident," *The Grand Haven News* (Grand Haven Mich.), 6 May 1863.
22. "From Point Lookout," *Evening Star*, 9 October 1862.
23. "Sick Soldiers Sent Off," *Daily National Republican*, 25 November 1862; "Sick Soldiers," *Daily National Republican*, 26 November 1862.
24. "Preparations for the Sick and Wounded," *Daily National Republican*, 12 December 1862; Long and Long, 296.
25. "The Wounded," *Daily National Republican*, 18 December 1862; "Washington, Dec. 17," *The Nashville Daily Union*, 10 December 1862.
26. William A. Hammond to Montgomery C. Meigs, 28 August 1862, in Beitzell, 20.

Chapter 27: Camp Hoffman

1. E. B. Long and Barbara Long, *The Civil War Day by Day: An Almanac 1861-1865* (Garden City, N.Y.: Doubleday & Company, Inc., 1971), 377.
2. Ibid., 378.

3. Joseph R. Smith to Edwin M. Stanton, 10 July 1863, *ORA,* Ser. II, Vol. 6, 98.

4. Edward R. S. Canby to Robert C. Schenck, 11 July 1863, *ORA.* Ser. II, Vol. 6, 102; Robert C. Schenck to Edward R. S. Canby, 11 July 1873, *ORA,* Ser. II, Vol. 6, 102.

5. Edwin W. Beitzell, *Point Lookout Prison Camp for Confederates* (Leonardtown, Md.: Privately Printed, 1972), 20; Montgomery C. Meigs to D. H. Rucker, 20 July 1863, *ORA,* Ser. II, Vol. 6, 132; *The Daily Green Mountain Freeman,* 29 July 1863.

6. Meigs to Rucker, 20 July 1863, 132-133.

7. General Orders, No. 226, E. D. Townsend, 23 July 1863, *ORA,* Ser II, Vol. 6, 132, 140.

8. "Selection of a Camp for Rebel Prisoners," *The Portage County Democrat,* 29 July 1863.

9. Henry W. Halleck to Gilman Marston, 23 July 1863,141, *ORA,* Ser. II, Vol. 6, 141-142.

10. Welles to Harwood, 31 July 1863, *ORA,* Ser. I, Vol. 5, 313.

11. "From Point Lookout," *Evening Star,* August 24, 1863; William Hoffman to J. H. Martindale, 6 August 1863, *ORA,* Ser. II, Vol. 6, 183.

12. William Hoffman to Gilman Marston, 18 August 1863, *ORA,* Ser. II, Vol. 6, 214.

13. "Rebel Prisoners," *Evening Star,* August 22, 1863; "From Point Lookout," *Evening Star,* August 24, 1863.

14. Beitzell, 21.

15. Beitzell, 20, 183. See also George S. Bernard, *War Tails of Confederate Veterans* (Petersburg, Va.: Fenn and Owen, 1892), 77.

16. "From Point Lookout," *Evening Star,* August 24, 1863.

17. E. A. Hitchcock to Edwin M. Stanton, *ORA,* Ser. II, Vol. 6, 243.

18. "Proposal for Wood," *Evening Star,* September 4, 1863; William Hoffman to Christopher C. Augur, 10 September 1863, *ORA,* Ser. II, Vol. 6, 277.

19. Robert Ould to John H. Winder, 3 September 1863, *ORA,* Ser. II, Vol. 6, 268.

20. William Ballantyne and M. H. Miller to William Hoffman, 12 September 1863, *ORA,* Ser. II, Vol. 6, 284; William Hoffman to Gilman Marston, *ORA,* Ser. II, Vol. 6, 363; Edwin Warfield Beitzell, *The Jesuit Missions of St. Mary's County, Maryland* (Sponsored by the St. Mary's County Bicentennial Commission: Abell, Md., 1976), 218.

21. "A Distinguished Party of Officials," *Daily National Republican,* September 21, 1863.

22. "An Excursion to Point Lookout," *Daily National Republican,* September 25, 1863.

23. Ibid.

24. Washington, Sept. 16," *The Daily Green Mountain Freeman,* September 17, 1863; Beitzell, *Point Lookout,* 20.

25. George G. Lewis and John Mewha, *History of Prisoner of War Utilization by the United States Army 1776-1945* (Washington, D.C.: Department of the Army, June 1955), 27-30.

26. Michael Egan to C. H. Drew, 22 September 1863, *ORA,* Ser. II, Vol. 6, 859.

27. Gilman Marston to William Hoffman, 7 October 1863, *ORA,* Ser. II, Vol. 6, 256-257.

28. "Prisoners of War to be Sent for Exchange," *Daily National Republican,* 26 October 1863; Beitzell, *Point Lookout,* 21; *ORA,* Ser. II, Vol. 6. 422, 473; William Hoffman to Gilman Marston, 23 November 1863, *ORA,* Ser. II, Vol. 6, 554-555.

29. *The Western Democrat,* December 8, 1863.

30. Ibid.

31. "From Point Lookout. Fugitive Marylanders en Route to Virginia," *Evening Star,* August 21, 1862.

32. Gilman Marston to John Mix, 21 October 1863, *ORA,* Ser. I, Vol. 29, Part 2, 364.

33. W. F. Swalm to J. H. Douglas, 13 November 1863, *ORA,* Ser. II, Vol. 6, 575, 579.

34. Luther Hopkins, "Prison Life at Point Lookout," in Edwin W. Beitzell, *Point Lookout Prison Camp for Confederates,* 88; C. W. Jones, "In Prison at Point Lookout," in Beitzell, *Point Lookout Prison Camp for Confederates,* 91.

35. Swalm to Douglas, 13 November 1863, 579. Swalm reports that he had no complaints regarding the tents, of which there were seven types: (1) Hospital tents, which housed fifteen to eighteen men each; (2) wall tents, which housed ten to twelve; (3) shelter tents, which housed three; (4) Sibley tents, from thirteen to fourteen; (5) wedged tents, which were the majority and housed five each; (6) under hospital tents, which housed ten to thirteen; (7) and under wall-tent fly, which housed from thirty to eighty. Only a few shelter tents were excavated and boarded at the sides. In a few of the Sibley tents holes had been dug, fires built in them, and then covered at the top. Ibid., 577.

36. Ibid., 576.

37. Ibid.
38. Ibid, 577.
39. Ibid.
40. Ibid, 577-578
41. Ibid, 577; C. W. Jones, "In Prison at Point Lookout," 91.
42. Ibid, 578.
43. Ibid.
44. Ibid., 576, 577, 579.
45. Ibid., 578-579.
46. Ibid., 580; "Deaths of North Carolinians," *The Western Democrat*, December 29, 1863.
47. Swalm Report, 581.
48. William Hoffman to F. N. Knapp, 27 November 1863, *ORA*, Ser. II, Vol. 6, 586.
49. William Hoffman to Gilman Marston, 27 December 1863, *ORA*, Ser. II, Vol. 6, 585.
50. J. H. Wilkinson to Gilman Marston, to William Hoffman, 1 December 1863, *ORA*, Ser. II, Vol. 6, 45-46.
51. Gilman Marston to William Hoffman, 4 December 1863, *ORA*, Ser. II, Vol. 6, 644.
52. Ibid., 644-645; Beitzell, *Point Lookout*, 22.
53. *ORA*, Ser. II, Vol. 6, 625.
54. Montrose A. Pallen to Edwin M. Stanton, 14 December 1863, *ORA*, Ser. II, Vol. 6, 718; Robert Ould to S.A. Meredith, 3 December 1863, *ORA*, Ser. II, Vol. 6, 637.
55. Beitzell, *Point Lookout*, 22; Richard Fuller to William Hoffman, 5 December 1863, *ORA*, Ser. II, Vol. 6, 649. See *St. Mary's Gazette,* December 1863, for letters.
56. Pallen to Stanton, 14 December 1863.
57. William Hoffman to F. N. Knapp, 15 December 1863, *ORA*, Ser. II, Vol. 6, 705-706.
58. "Prison Life at Point Lookout," *The Daily Dispatch*, 17 December 1863.
59. Ibid.
60. Ibid.; Luther Hopkins, "Prison Life at Point Lookout," in Beitzell, 89.
61. "Prison Life at Point Lookout," *The Daily Dispatch*, 17 December 1863.
62. E. A. Hitchcock to William Hoffman, 19 December 1863, *ORA*, Ser. II, Vol. 6, 718.
63. Clark Report, *ORA*, Ser. II, Vol. 6, 741; Luther Hopkins, "Prison Life at Point Lookout," in Beitzell, 88.
64. Ibid., 743.
65. Ibid.,742; "Diary and Other accounts of Prison Life. The Diary of Bartlett Yancey Malone," in Edwin W. Beitzell, *Point Lookout Prison Camp for Confederates*, 56. Clark states that the regulations at the camp assigned sixteen men to a Sibley tents, two more than the norm, and five to common (wedge) tents, which housed 8,530 exclusive of those in the hospital.
66. Ibid.
67. Ibid.
68. Ibid., 744.
69. Ibid.
70. Ibid, 744-745.
71. Ibid., 742-743.
72. Beitzell, *Point Lookout*, 23; *ORA*, Ser. II, Vol. 6, 740. None of Clark's figures add up and none agree with those in the Official Summary, which shows for November 1863: Prisoners, 9,371, Died 119, Sick 886.
73. C. W. Jones, "In Prison at Point Lookout," 90.

28. Forever Thereafter Free

1. [Joseph M. Califf] *Record of the Services of the Seventh Regiment, U.S. Colored Troops from September, 1863, to November, 1866. By an Officer of the Regiment.* (Providence: R.I. Freeman & Co., Printers to the State, 1878. Reprinted 1971. Books for Libraries Press, Freeport, New York), 1; Dorothy Schneider and Carl J. Schneider, *An Eyewitness History: Slavery in America: From Colonial Times to the Civil War* (New York, N.Y.: Facts on File, Inc. 2000), 301, 329.
2. Ibid.; John W. Blassingame, "The Recruitment of Negro Troops in Maryland," *MHM*, Vol. 58, No. 1 (March 1963), 20-24.
3. Herbert Apitheker, "The Negro in the Union Navy," *Journal of Negro History*, Vol. 32 (1947), 175-176.

4. Schneider and Schneider, 301, 329.

5. Ibid., 329.

6. Ibid., 301.

7. Ira Berlin, *et al. Free at Last: A Documentary History of Slavery, Freedom, and the Civil War*, (New York: The New Press, 1992), 46-48. Hunter first declared all persons of color that had been held by rebel forces in involuntary service within Fort Pulaski and on Cockspur Island to be free in conformity with the law and "shall hereafter receive the fruits of their own labor." Harry Wright Newman, *Maryland and the Confederacy* (Annapolis, Md.: Privately published, 1976), 139.

8. *Record of the Services*, 1; Berlin, 56-59.

9. "Enrolling Negroes," *St. Mary's Beacon* 15 May 1862; Schneider and Schneider, 302.

10. Edward A. Miller, *Lincoln's Abolitionist General: The Biography of David Hunter*. (Columbia: University of South Carolina Press, 1997), 106.

11. Berlin, 11, 46-48, 59-60; Newman, 139; E. B. Long and Barbara Long, *The Civil War Day by Day: An Almanac 1861-1865* (Garden City, N.Y.: Doubleday & Company, Inc., 1971), 106, 241; Schneider and Schneider, 301.

12. *Record of the Services*, 3.

13. Ibid., 2-3; Schneider and Schneider, 302.

14. "The Emancipation Edict," *New York Times*, 12 September 1862.

15. *Record of the Services*, 2-3; Schneider and Schneider, 302; Blassingame, 21; Benjamin Quarles, *The Negro in the Civil War* (Boston: Little, Brown, 1969), 110-119; Benjamin P. Thomas and Harold M. Hyman, *Stanton, The Life and Times of Lincoln's Secretary of War* (New York: Knopf, 1962), 263; Edwin M. Stanton to Benjamin P. Thomas, 25 March 1863, Negroes in the Military Service of the United States, Vol. I, Part 1, 1138-1141. Adjutant General's Office (AGO), Record Group (RG) 94, NARA; General Orders, No. 143, 22 May 1863, *ORA*, Ser. III, Vol. 3, 215; Eleanor Jones Harvey, *The Civil War and American Art* (Washington, D.C.: Smithsonian American Art Museum, in association with Yale University Press, 2013), 267, n76; Newman, 139. Winkle argues that it was the fact that the Confederacy contained eighteen times as many potential African American soldiers as the Union, nine-tenths of them slaves, which figured as one of Lincoln's motives for issuing the Emancipation Proclamation. Kenneth J. Winkle, *Lincoln's Citadel: The Civil War in Washington, D.C.* (New York and London, W.W. Norton & Company, 2013), 328.

16. *Maryland Voices of the Civil War*, Charles W. Mitchell, ed. (Baltimore: The Johns Hopkins University Press, 2007), 400.

17. Ibid.

18. *Record of the Services*, 4; Harold R. Manakee, *Maryland in the Civil War* (Baltimore: Maryland Historical Society, 1961), 108-109.

19. *Record of the Services*, 5.

20. Ibid., 3.

21. Ibid., 4.

22. Ibid.

23. *General William Birney's Answer to Libels Clandestinely Circulated by James Shaw, Jr., Collector of the Port, Providence, R.I., with A Review of the Military Record of the Said James Shaw, Jr., Late Colonel of the Seventh U.S. Colored Troops* (Washington, D.C.: Stanley Snodgrass, Printer, 1878), 5.

24. Ibid., 6.

25. William Birney to Wm. H. Chesebrough, 24 July 1863, *Rebellion Record*, Vol. 7, Frank Moore, ed. (New York: 1864), 394-395; "Excitement Among the Colored People—Slave Prisons Visited by the Military Authorities," *Baltimore Sun*, 28 July 1863; Eric Mills, *Chesapeake Bay in the Civil War* (Centreville, MD; Tidewater Publishers, 1996), 205.

26. Blassingame, 21; Charles B. Clark, *Politics in Maryland During the Civil War* (Chestertown, Md.: 1952), 100; Charles B. Clark, *The Eastern Shore of Maryland and Virginia*, 3 Vols. (New York: Lewis Historical Publishing Company, Inc., 1950), Vol. 1, 514; *The Biographical Cyclopedia of Representative Men of Maryland and the District of Columbia* (Baltimore: National Biographical Publishing Co., ca. 1878), 476-477. U.S. Bureau of Census, *Negro Population 1790-1915* (U.S. Government Printing Office: Washington, 1918), 57.

27. Blassingame, 22; "Thomas H. Hicks," in *Dictionary of American Biography*, John H. Finley, ed., 21 vols. (New York: C. Scribner's Sons, 1931), Vol. 5, 8-9; J. Thomas Scharf, *History of Western Maryland*, 2 Vols. (Philadelphia: L. H. Everts, 1882), Vol. 1, 211-226; *Congressional Globe*, 1st Session, 38th

Congress, Part I, 225-227, 633-634.

28. Manakee, 58-59.

29. Blassingame, 22; Clark, *Politics in Maryland*, 99-114.

30. Blassingame, 22; Clark, *Politics in Maryland*, 65-72; Heinrich E. Buchholz, *Governors of Maryland: From the Revolution to the Year 1908* (Baltimore: Williams & Wilkins Company, 1908), 178-183.

31. Blassingame, 23; Edwin M. Stanton to Abraham Lincoln, 1 October 1863, *Collected Works of Abraham Lincoln*, Roy P. Basler, ed., 9 Vols. (New Brunswick, NJ: Rutgers University Press, 1953-1955), 6:491.

32. Manakee, 124; *Record of the Services*, 7.

33. Circular, No. 1. Adjutant General's Office, Bureau for Organized Colored Troops, War Department, Washington, D.C., October 1863, *ORA*, Ser. III, Vol. 3, Part 1, 938; Blassingame, 24; *Baltimore American and Commercial Advertiser*, 5 January 1864.

34. Circular, No. 1.

35. Blassingame, 24.

36. *Record of the Services*, 7; Agnes Kane Callum, *Colored Volunteers of Maryland [in the] Civil War, 7th Regiment U.S. Colored Troops* (Baltimore, Md.: Mullac, 1990) [Typescript], Calvert County Historical Society, Prince Frederick, Md. The remaining companies did not receive equipment until 9 December 1863.

37. Circular, No. 1.

38. Blassingame, 24-25; Le Grand Benedict to C. W. Foster, 10 October 1864, Letterbook of U.S. Colored Troops, Adjutant Generals Office, RG 94, I, 31-32, NARA.

39. Schneider and Schneider, 331.

29. Homicides on Punctilio

1. Harry Wright Newman, *Maryland and the Confederacy* (Annapolis, Md.: Privately published, 1976), 218.

2. Robert C. Schenck to Abraham Lincoln, 21 October 1863, *ORA*, Ser. I, Vol. 29, Part 2, 364.

3. Murder of Lieut. Eben White. Letter from the Chief Clerk of the War Department Giving Circumstances of the Murder of Lieut. Eben White by John H. and Webster Southron, House of Representatives, 43d Congress, 1st Session, Ex. Doc. No. 281, 3; [Joseph M. Califf] *Record of the Services of the Seventh Regiment, U.S. Colored Troops from September, 1863, to November, 1866. By an Officer of the Regiment.* (Providence: R. I. Freeman & Co., Printers to the State, 1878. Reprinted 1971. Books for Libraries Press, Freeport, New York), 7; *Merchant Steam Vessels of the United States 1780-1868*, William M. Lytle and Forrest R. Holdcamper, comp. (Staten Island, N.Y.: The Steamship Historical Society of America, Inc., 1975), 204; Charles Dana Gibson and E. Kay Gibson, comp., *Dictionary of Transports and Combat Vessels Steam and Sail Employed by the Union Army 1861-1862*, 52 (Camden, Me.: Ensign Press, 1995), 182; "An Account of the Homicide," *Weekly National Intelligencer*, 29 October 1863.

4. *Record of the Services*, 15.

5. Murder of Lieut. Eben White, 3; *Record of the Services*, 11.

6. Fitzgerald Ross, *Cities and Camps of the Confederate State*, Richard Barksdale Harwell, ed. (Urbana, Ill.: University of Illinois Press, 1958), 164; *New York Times*, 23 October 1863; Abraham Lincoln to Robert C. Schenck, 21 October 1863, 2:45 p.m., *ORA*, Ser. I, Vol. 29, Part 2, 363; "An Account of the Homicide."

7. Murder of Lieut. Eben White, 1, 3. Sothoron's name has been variously spelled as Southron, Sothern, and Southern. The author has used that which has commonly been ascribed and employed in state and county land and census records, except where used in quotes.

8. Ibid. 3.

9. Ross, 164-165.

10. Stephen D. Calhoun, "Col. John Henry Southron 1807-1893," *Chronicles of St. Mary's*, Vol. 40, Summer 1992, No. 2, 114. Another account states the estate was 1700 acres in extent. It was also reported that as many as 130 slaves had been left behind when Sothoron abandoned the plantation.

11. "The Plains: Another Landmark Destroyed," *Chronicles of St. Mary's*, Vol. 6, October 1958, No. 10, 242.

12. Murder of Lieut. Eben White, 2; Regina Combs Hammett, *History of St. Mary's County, Maryland* (Ridge, Md.: Privately published, 1977), 447, 449. Sothoron's obituary in the *St. Mary's Beacon*, 20 April 1893, states he once served as the President of the Maryland State Senate.

13. Calhoun, 115-116.

14. Ibid., 118-119; Ross, 164-165; "An Account of the Homicide."

15. Murder of Lieut. Eben White, 3; Calhoun, 181-90; *New York Times*, 23 October 1863; *Record of the Services*, 11-12; "An Account of the Homicide," *Weekly National Intelligencer.*

16. Murder of Lieut. Eben White, 3-4; "An Account of the Homicide"; *Record of the Services*, 11-12

17. Ross, 165.

18. Murder of Lieut. Eben White, 4. Another report by W. Winthrop, Brevet Colonel and Judge Advocate to the Secretary of War, issued on 6 August 1866, states that it was Webster Sothoron who shot Private Bantum, despite the private's own testimony to the contrary. Ibid., 5.

19. Ibid., 4; "An Account of the Homicide."

20. Ibid.; *New York Times*, October 23, 1863; *Record of the Services*, 11-12; "Enlisting of Slave Soldiers," *Daily National Republican*, 22 October 1863.

21. *Record of the Services*, 12; "Enlisting of Slave Soldiers." *Record of the Services* states that Leary conducted the recovery of Lieutenant White's body, but in Birney's notification of White's death to the lieutenant's father on October 22, he reports: "Capt Weld heard of this he immediately went for him but he [White] had been killed instantly." That White's face had been badly beaten "as if by gunstocks" was noted by Birney as only being "a little bruised on one side." In his colorful account of the events that transpired at The Plains on 20 October 1863, Calhoun offers a variant to the story of where White's body was found. He was, he stated, once told by his own grandfather, Duncan Dashiell Burroughs, a grandson of John Henry Sothoron: "My grandfather shot the Yankee Lieutenant and the two soldiers ran away. The Lieutenant's body was hidden under the porch of the house. I used the gun that he killed the Yankee with to hunt squirrels when I was young." He also suggested that the "fact that my grandfather . . . told me that Lt. White's body was hidden under the porch of the house indicates a desire for concealment of the shooting victim by the Southrons. It is possible that the boat carrying the other Union troops had left and the Southrons thought the shooting might not be reported by the two Black soldiers who ran away." Calhoun, 113, 116, 119.

22. Murder of Lieut. Eben White, 4.

23. *Collected Works of Abraham Lincoln,* Roy P. Basler, ed., 9 vols. (New Brunswick, NJ: Rutgers University Press, 1953-55), 6:529-530; *New York Times*, October 23, 1863; Blassingame, 27; *Baltimore Daily Gazette,* 22 and 24 October 1863.

24. Abraham Lincoln to Robert C. Schenck, Baltimore, 2:45 p.m., 21 October 1863, *ORA*, Ser. I, Vol. 29, Part 2, 363. It is unclear if Lincoln took immediate action himself over and above his query to Schenck for there is no specific record to indicate such. That some orders were issued to the commander of the St. Mary's District, General Gilman Marston, is probable. This is suggested by Marston's directive, issued from his headquarters at Point Lookout, to Lieutenant John Mix on 21 October. "It is reported," he wrote, not naming his source, "that some persons are now engaged near the mouth of the Patuxent and above there in enlisting into the military service slaves and free persons of color without proper authority from the War Department. You will inquire into the matter, and it you find such to be the case you will cause them immediately to desist and to leave this military district forthwith, if they are not residents therein." What is apparent is that the commander of the St. Mary's District had not been informed by the War Department of the move to establish a recruitment and training base at Benedict. Gilman Marston to John Mix, 21 October 1863, *ORA*, Ser. I, Vol. 29, Part 2, 364.

25. Robert C. Schenck to Abraham Lincoln, 21 October 1863, *ORA*, Ser. I, Vol. 29, Part 2, 364.

26. *New York Times*, 23 October 1863.

27. Calhoun, 118; Ira Berlin, *et al. Free at Last: A Documentary History of Slavery, Freedom, and the Civil War,* (New York: The New Press, 1992), 215.

28. Calhoun, 118.

29. Ibid., 119. The *Daily National Republican* of 22 October 1863, citing the *Baltimore American*, stated that White's body was prepared by Birney and placed aboard a steamer that left for Massachusetts at 5 p.m. that same day. "Enlisting of Slave Soldiers." The term "homicides on Punctilio" means, quite literally, murder as a fine point of accepted etiquette.

30. "Escape of the Murderers Sothoron," *Evening Star*, 27 October 1863; "Col. Sothoron in Richmond," *Weekly National Intelligencer*, 12 November 1863.

30. *Record of the Services*, 17.

31. Ibid.

32. Ibid., 12.

33. Ibid., 15.

30. The Look Like Men of War

1. Frederick Douglas, "The Proclamation and the Negro Army," An Address Delivered in New York, N.Y., February 6, 1863, in Kate Masur, "'A Rare Phenomenon of Philological Vegetation': The Word 'Contraband' and the Meanings of Emancipation," *Journal of American History*, Vol. 93, No. 4 (March 2007), 116.

2. Harold R. Manakee, *Maryland in the Civil War* (Baltimore: Maryland Historical Society, 1961), 124-25.

3. [Joseph M. Califf], *Record of the Services of the Seventh Regiment, U.S. Colored Troops from September, 1863, to November, 1866. By an Officer of the Regiment.* (Providence: R. I. Freeman & Co., Printers to the State, 1878. Reprinted 1971. Books for Libraries Press, Freeport, New York), 15.

4. Manakee, 125. Shaw assumed full command of the 7th Regiment on November 15, replacing Colonel Haskell who was placed as second in command but eventually took full command of the newly formed 9th Regiment.

5. *Record of the Services*, 15; Agnes Kane Callum, *Colored Volunteers of Maryland [in the] Civil War, 7th Regiment U.S. Colored Troops* (Baltimore, Md.: Mullac, 1990) [Typescript], Calvert County Historical Society, Prince Frederick, Md. See also John W. Blassingame, "The Recruitment of Negro Troops in Maryland," *MHM*, Vol. 58, No. 1 (March 1963), 20-29.

6. Gilman Marston to John Mix, 21 October 1863, *ORA*, Ser. I, Vol. 29, Part 2, 364; "The Negro in the Military Service of the United States, Ser. 390, Colored Troops Division, Records of the Adjutant General's Office, RG. 94, reprinted in *Maryland Voices of the Civil War*, Charles W. Mitchell, ed. (Baltimore; The Johns Hopkins University Press, 2007), 413.

7. "Negroe Stampede," *St. Mary's Beacon*, 22 October 1863.

8. "Slave Abductions in Maryland," *Weekly National Intelligencer*, 5 November 1863, reprint from *Somerset Herald*, 27 October 1863.

9. *Record of the Services*, 15, 16.

10. Ibid., 7.

11. Ibid., 12.

12. Ibid., 7-8. The officers assigned to the stations were: Drummondville (Maj. Edelmiro Mayer), Eastville, (Capt. Thomas McCarty), New Church (Lt. Thompson), Chesconessex (Lt. Joseph E. Lockwood), Modest Town (Lt. David S. Mack), Messengo (Lt. Charles G. Teeple), Cherrystone (Lt. Alpheus H. Cheney), Franktown (Lt. Andrew Coats), Capeville (Lt. Joseph M. Califf), Pungoteague (Lt. Charles H. C. Brown), New Church (Sgt. Harris), Onancock (Sgt. Yeaton), and Belle Haven (Sgt. Swift). The six officers that arrived on the first wave included: Thompson, Lockwood, Teeple, Cheney, Coats, and Califf. *Record of the Services*, 7-8. Lieutenant Thompson, Sergeants Harris, Yeaton, and Swift do not appear on the enlistment rolls.

13. Blassingame, 25; William Birney to the Adjutant General, 4 February 1864; *Appleton's Annual Cyclopedia*, 1864, Vol. 4, 496.

14. *Record of the Services*, 12.

15. Ibid., 13.

16. Ibid., 8. Two officers, lieutenants Thompson and Temple, had been left behind to continue recruiting at Newtown and Shelltown.

17. Ibid.

18. Callum; Blassingame, 20-29.

19. Ira Berlin, *et al. Free at Last: A Documentary History of Slavery, Freedom, and the Civil War*, (New York: The New Press, 1992), 213-214.

20. Ibid., 214.

21. Ibid.

22. Ibid.

23. J. W. Hoskins to [William R. Whittingham], 19 November 1861, MDA, reprinted in *Maryland Voices of the Civil War*, 415.

24. Manakee, 125; *General William Birney's Answer to Libels Clandestinely Circulated by James Shaw, Jr., Collector of the Port, Providence, R.I., with A Review of the Military Record of the Said James Shaw, Jr., Late Colonel of the Seventh U.S. Colored Troops* (Washington, D.C.: Stanley Snodgrass, Printer, 1878), 2.

25. *Record of the Services*, 8; *General William Birney's Answer*, 5.

26. *Record of the Services*, 8. Califf incorrectly stated that Hayner was in overall command, a point Birney contentiously sought to correct in his attack on Califf and Shaw in a libel case against them in 1878. *General William Birney's Answer*, 5-6.

27. Ibid.; Daniel Carroll Toomey, *The Civil War in Maryland* (Baltimore: Toomey Press, 1988), 95. Of the four officers participating in the recruitment foray as reported by Califf, only David S. Mack, Alpheus H. Cheney and Joseph M. Califf appear on the enlistment rolls of the 7th Regiment. No sergeants or other enlisted men named Yeaton or Swift appear.

28. *Record of the Services*, 8-9; Abstract from return of the Middle Department (Eighth Army Corps), Brig. Gen. Hen H. Lockwood, U.S. Army, commanding, for the month of December, 1863, *ORA*, Ser. I, Vol. 29, Part 2, 611, 612; Ibid., Ser. I, Vol. 33, 475. At the end of December the three units under Birney were commanded as follows: 7th Regiment, Colonel James Shaw, Jr.; 9th Regiment, Colonel Thomas Bayley; and 19th Regiment, Major Theodore H. Rockwood.

29. Ibid., 9.

30. Manakee, 126.

31. *Record of the Services*, 19; www.dnr.state.nd.us/publiclands/aapaxstanton.html, accessed December 10, 2011; Margaret Brown Klapthor and Paul Dennis Brown, *The History of Charles County, Maryland* (La Plata, Md.: Charles County Tercentenary, Inc., [nd]), 129.

32. Michael Gayhart Kent, *Mulatto: The Black History of Calvert County, Maryland* (Privately published: 2019), 15. For context see also *African-American Traditions in Song, Sermon, Tale, and Dance, 1600s-1920: An Annotated Bibliography of Literature, Collections, and Artworks*, Eileen Southern and Josephine Wright, comp. (New York: Greenwood Press, 1990).

33. Kent, 15.

34. *Record of the Services*, 9: C. W. Foster to William Birney, *ORA*, Ser. III, Vol. 4, Part 1, 125.

35. G. E. McConnell to William T. Street, 24 November 1862, *ORN*, Ser. I, Vol. 5, 167.

36. Ibid.

37. *Record of the Services*, 9.

38. Ibid., 10; Manakee, 126.

39. *Record of the Services*, 10.

40. Ibid.

41. Ibid., 9-10.

42. Ibid., 10.

43. Ibid.

44. Ibid., 13.

45. Ibid., 14.

46. William B. Hill to Henry W. Halleck, 3 February 1864, Ser. I05, Letters Received by General Grant, Headquarters in the Field, Records of the Headquarters of the Army, RG 108, NARA, also cited in *Maryland Voices of the Civil War*, 417.

47. Ibid.

48. Callum, 7, citing 7th Regiment USCT Circulars, Guard Reports, RG. 94, NARA.

49. Callum 7.

50. *Record of the Services*, 18, 19.

51. Ibid., 19.

52. Ibid. The accounting that the Reverend Woodbury provided for the money and goods raised for the use of the 7th Regiment was published as follows: *To the Editor of the Journal:*

I hereby offer my report of the receipts and expenditures for Col. Shaw's Seventh Regiment U.S. C. T.

Previously acknowledged, $218; since received from Jas. Tillinghast, $6; W. B. Dart, $3; A lady in East Greenwich, $2; total, $220. From ladies in East Greenwich, through Mrs. W. P. Green, 1 box containing 12 handkerchiefs, 6 needle books, 6 towels, 7 pair mittens; Edward Burr, 9 pair mittens; Thomas Brown, 25 towels; Friends, 11 pair socks, buttons, papers, books, etc.

I have expended for books, $69.94; for crash [cash?] for towels, gloves, needles, thread, buttons and other articles, and express as per bills in my hands, $143.10, leaving a balance of $15.06, which I hold subject to the order of Col. Shaw, agreeably to his request. I have sent to the regiment three cases, containing over 500 volumes of books, 855 towels, 238 bags furnished with needle books, thread, buttons and pins, mittens, gloves, socks, etc.

All these have been safely transmitted and gratefully received. I append Col. Shaw's letter of acknowledgment.

A. WOODBURY.

53. *Record of the Services*, 19.
54. Ibid.
55. Ibid., 20; Ralph E. Eshelman, Donald G. Shomette, and G. Howard Post, "Benedict, Maryland, Cultural Resource Survey and Context Study." Report prepared for the Charles County Department of Planning and Growth Management, July 2009, 13.
56. *Record of the Services*, 20.
57. Ibid.
58. Ibid.
59. Ibid.
60. E. B. Tyler to Abraham Lincoln, 20 March 1864, enclosing Thomas H. Watkins to E. B Tyler, President 297 (1864), Letters Received from the President, Executive Departments, and War Department Bureaus, RG 107, NARA. A notation by John Hay indicates that Lincoln referred the report to the Secretary of War. See *Maryland Voices of the Civil War*, 419-420..
61. Joseph Perkins to S. M. Bowman, 28 March 1864, reprinted in *Black Military Experience*, Ira Berlin, ed. (Cambridge University Press: Cambridge and New York, 1982), 218-219.

31. Hewers of Wood and Drawers of Water

1. "Diary and Other accounts of Prison Life. The Diary of Bartlett Yancey Malone," in Edwin W. Beitzell, *Point Lookout Prison Camp for Confederates* (Leonardtown, Md.: Privately Printed, 1972), 55-56.
2. W. Hoffman to Edwin M. Stanton, D.C., 27 November 1863, *ORA*, Ser II, Vol. 6, 584.
3. "Escape of Prisoners from Point Lookout," *The Western Democrat*, 29 December 1863; Malone Diary, 56. The Richmond *Daily Dispatch* report cited in the *Western Democrat*, claimed that over a hundred men escaped, but if such was the case it does not appear in either military dispatches or the Northern press. The author has been unable to locate the *Dispatch* report.
4. "The Treatment of Our Prisoners at Point Lookout," *Memphis Daily Appeal*, 4 January 1864.
5. Ibid. Beitzell relates a story that Virginians from across the Potomac were said to have brought hams for Father Pacciarini and his assistant, who traveled weekly to tend the spiritual needs of Catholic prisoners at Point Lookout, to give to their relatives. Following the reported escape of several prisoners after tunneling out with little digging tools concealed in the hams, the priests were forbidden to bring gifts. Edwin Warfield Beitzell, *The Jesuit Missions of St. Mary's County, Maryland* (Sponsored by the St. Mar's County Bicentennial Commission: Abell, Md., 1976), 218.
6. Luther Hopkins, "Prison Life At Point Lookout," in Beitzell, 88; "Prison Life at the North," *The Weekly Intelligencer*, 15 March 1864.
7. E. B Long and Barbara Long, *The Civil War Day by Day: An Almanac 1861-1865* (Garden City, N.Y.: Doubleday & Company, Inc., 1971), 444.
8. Edwin S. Stanton to Robert Murray, 10 July 1862, *ORA*, Ser. II, Vol. IV, 162-163; J. K. Duncan to J. G. Pickett, 12 May 1862, *ORA*, Ser I, Vol. 6, 535.
9. Long and Long., 447.
10. Beitzell, 23; "Washington, Dec. 21," *The Dollar Weekly Bulletin*, 24 December 1863. Hinks had been wounded at Antietam and was promoted by Lincoln to brigadier general on April 4, 1863.
11. "Gen. Butler's Plan for Exchange of Prisoners," *Daily Ohio Statesman*, 20 December 1863; "Army Potomac, Dec. 21," *Cleveland Morning Leader*, 23 December 1863.
12. *CWNC*, Vol. 3, 162-163.
13. "The Reported Attempt to Rescue the Rebel Prisoners at Point Lookout," *Evening Star*, 21 December 1863; "Plot to Rescue the Prisoners at Lookout," *Cleveland Morning Leader*, 22 December 1863; Bradley T. Johnson, "Riding a Raid in July, 1864," *The Leader* (Laurel, Md.), 26 December 1902, reprinted in Beitzell, *Point Lookout*, 50.
14. "The Reported Attempt . . . "; "Plot to Rescue the Prisoners at Lookout,"
15. R. S. Davis to C. A. Hickman, 22 December 1863, *ORA*, Ser, II, Vol. 6, 745; Benjamin F. Butler to Edwin M. Stanton, 27 December 1863, *ORA*, Ser. II, Vol. 6, 763; "Washington, Dec. 24," *The Daily Green Mountain Freeman*, Evening Edition, 25 December 1863.
16. "How Our Prisoners Are Treated," *The Western Democrat*, 9 February 1864.
17. "Butler Returns," *Dayton Daily Empire*, 26 December 1863; Conversations between Maj. Gen. B. F Butler and six Confederate prisoners, sergeants of the cook-houses at the prisoner's camp. Headquarters Saint Mary's District, Point Lookout, Md., 24 December 1863, *ORA*, Ser. II, Vol. 764-767.

18. Benjamin F. Butler to Edwin M. Stanton, 27 December 1863, *ORA*, Ser. II, Vol. 6, 763.
19. Benjamin F. Butler to Edwin M. Stanton, 27 December 1863 (received 11:20 a.m.), *ORA*, Ser. II, Vol. 6, 768.
20. "Gen. Butler's Plan for Exchange of Prisoners," *Daily Ohio Statesman*, 20 December 1863; "Washington, Dec. 24."
21. Edward R. S. Canby to William Hoffman, 21 December 1863, *ORA*, Ser. II, Vol. 6, 736.
22. Abraham Lincoln to Edwin M. Stanton, 26 December 1863, *Collected Works of Abraham Lincoln*, Roy P. Basler, ed., 9 vols. (New Brunswick, NJ: Rutgers University Press, 1953-1955), 7.
23 C. W. Jones, "In Prison At Point Lookout, " reprinted in Beitzell, *Point Lookout*, 93.
24. *New York Daily Tribune*, 29 December 1863.
25. Benjamin F. Butler to Stanton, 27 December 1863, *ORA*, Ser. II, Vol. 6, 768.
26. Abraham Lincoln to Benjamin F. Butler, 2 January 1864, *ORA*, Ser. II, Vol. 6, 808.
27. *The Old Line State: A History of Maryland*, Morris L. Radoff, ed. (Annapolis: Publication No. 16, Hall of Records Commission State of Maryland, 1971), 91; Daniel Carroll Toomey, *The Civil War in Maryland* (Baltimore: Toomey Press, 1976), 98.
28. Benjamin F. Butler to Gilman Marston, 8 January 1864, *ORA*, Ser. III, Vol. 4, 15.
29. "The Diary of Charles Warren Hutt, of Westmoreland County, Virginia (Kept While a Prisoner of War at Point Lookout, Maryland – 1864)," reprinted in Beitzell, *Point Lookout*, 66.
30. "The Amnesty Proclamation," *The Pacific Commercial Advertiser* (Honolulu, HI), 28 January 1864.
31. Benjamin F. Butler to Robert Ould, 25 December 1863, *ORA*, Ser. II, Vol. 6, 654-655.
32. Ibid, 655.
33. "Prison Life at the North," *The Weekly Intelligencer*, 15 March 1864.
34. Long and Long, 212, 223.
35. By the President of the Confederate States: A Proclamation, [23 December 1863], *ORA*, Ser. V, Vol. 15, 906-908.
36. Ibid.
37. Robert Ould to E. A. Hitchcock, 27 December 1863, *ORA*, Ser. II, Vol. 6, 768; "From Fort Monroe," 26 December 1863.
38. C. W. Jones, "In Prison at Point Lookout," 92; Malone Diary, 56.

32. Transfuges

1. Abraham Lincoln to Benjamin Butler, 2 January 1864, *ORA*, Ser. II, Vol. 6, 808.
2. Benjamin F. Butler to Gilman Marston, 9 January 1864, *ORA*, Ser. II, Vol. 6, 823; Special Orders, No. 11, Henry Johnston, 11 January 1864, *ORA*, Ser. II, Vol. 6, 826.
3. Andrew A. Harwood to Gideon Welles, 1 December 1863, *ORN*, Ser. I, Vol. 5, 375.
4. "Diary and Other Accounts of Prison Life. The Diary of Bartlett Yancey Malone," in Edwin W. Beitzell, *Point Lookout Prison Camp for Confederates* (Leonardtown, Md.: Privately Printed, 1972), 56; R. S. Davis to Gilman Marston, 6 January 1864, *ORA*, Ser. I, Vol. 33, 360.
5. Foxhall A. Parker to Edward Hooker, 11 January 1864, *ORN*, Ser. I, Vol. 5, 386; Abstract from return of the Department of Virginia and North Carolina, Maj. Gen. Benjamin F. Butler, U.S. Army, commanding, for the month of January, 1864, *ORA*, Ser. I, Vol. 33, 482. The units occupying the district consisted of: the 2nd New Hampshire, Col. Edward L. Baile; 5th New Hampshire, Lieut. Col. Richard E. Cross; 12th New Hampshire, Capt. John F. Langley; U.S. Cavalry (detachment), Lieut. John Mix; and 2nd Wisconsin Battery, Lieut. Carl Schultz. *ORA*, Ser. I, Vol. 33, 484.
6. Parker to Hooker, 11 January 1864.
7. "The Diary of Charles Warren Hutt of Westmoreland County, Virginia," in Beitzell, *Point Lookout*, 66.
8. Braxton erroneously states the landing was made at 4 p.m. and the landing force consisted of 100 cavalry and 100 infantry. The *Evening Star* states that Marston's force was composed of 300 infantry (which is consistent with later raid forces) and 130 cavalry and that the landing was made at an early hour, which it must have been for the flotilla to have reached the Rappahannock by 10 a.m. as Lieutenant Hooker reports. "Important from the Potomac," *Evening Star*, 19 January 1864.
9. Edward Hooker to Foxhall A. Parker, 16 January, *ORN*, Ser. I, Vol. 5, 388-389.
10. "Important from the Potomac."
11. Ibid.
12. Hooker to Parker, 16 January, *ORN*, Ser. I, Vol. 5, 389.

13. Ibid.

14. Ibid., 388-89; "Important from the Potomac." Among prisoners taken were W. W. Walker and James English of Westmoreland and a man by the name of Bush from Lancaster. Hutt Diary, 66.

15. "Movements of Yankees in Westmoreland and Elsewhere," *The Abingdon Virginian*, 22 January 1864.

16. James S. Braxton to Major-General Elzey, 18 January 1864, *ORA*, Ser. I, Vol. 33, 19.

17. Hutt Diary, 66.

18. Foxhall A. Parker to Edward Hooker, 14 January 1864, *ORA*, Ser. I, Vol. 5, 389; Foxhall A. Parker to Gerhard C. Schulze, 19 January 1864, *ORA*, Ser. I, Vol. 5, 390; Foxhall A. Parker to Edward Hooker, 20 January 1864, *ORA*, Ser. I, Vol. 5, 390; Foxhall A. Parker to Edward Hooker, 2 February 1864, *ORA*, Ser. I, Vol. 5, 91.

19. Almon D. Jones to Carrie E. Jones and Ella, 5 February 1864, MS 1860, MHS, reprinted in *Maryland Voices of the Civil War*, Charles W. Mitchell, ed. (Baltimore; The Johns Hopkins University Press, 2007), 193.

20. *The Wyandot*, 12 February 1864; *Washington Standard*, 20 February 1864.

21. *The Soldier's Journal*, 17 February 1864.

22. Beitzell, *Point Lookout*, 57.

23. Malone Diary, 57.

24. Ibid.

25. *The Xenia Sentinel*, March 8, 1864.

26. Hutt Diary, 69.

27. *Richmond Enquirer*, undated, reprinted in *The Western Democrat*, 15 March 1864.

28. Diary of Captain Robert E. Park, December 9, 1864, in Edwin Beitzell, *Point Lookout*, 99, reprinted from *Southern Historical Society Papers*, Vol. 1, No. 17, 232-233. Portions of Park's diary appear to have been written well after the actual dates recorded and often relied upon the comments of others.

29. Ibid.

30. Benjamin F. Butler to William Hoffman, 11 March 1864, *ORA*, Ser. II, Vol. 6, 1033-1034. An exchange rate had been agreed upon. One commissioned officer equaled five privates; a non-commissioned officer equaled two privates. William Hoffman to E. A. Hitchcock, 17 March 1864, *ORA*, Ser. II, Vol. 6, 1072.

31. William Hoffman to Gilman Marston, 8 March 1864, *ORA*, Ser. II, Vol. 6, 1026.

32. Benjamin F. Butler to Edwin M. Stanton, 18 March 1864, (1) *ORA*, Ser. II, Vol. 6, 1074; Edwin M. Stanton to Benjamin F. Butler, 18, March 1864, *ORA*, Ser. II, Vol. 6, 1074; Benjamin F. Butler to Edwin M. Stanton, 18 March 1864, (2) *ORA*, Ser. II, Vol. 6, 1074.

33. *The Nashville Daily Union* (Nashville, Tenn.), 5 April 1864; *The Wyandot Pioneer*, 1 April 1864; "Rebel Prisoner Shot," *The Jeffersonian*, 31 March 1864. For a comprehensive coverage of the trial see *ORA*, Ser. II, Vol. 6, 1097-1104, 1106, and Beitzell, *Point Lookout*, 27-37.

34. Benjamin F. Butler to Edwin M. Stanton, 20 March 1864, *ORA*, Ser. III, Vol. 4, 190-191. President Lincoln stopped enlistments in September 1864. Yet by February 27, 1865, 1,105 rebel prisoners from Point Lookout were enlisted for the 1st U.S. Volunteers, and 379 for the 2nd U.S. Volunteers. James B. Fry to Edwin M. Stanton, 27 February 1865, *ORA*, Ser. III, Vol. 4, 1203.

35. James B. Fry to Benjamin F. Butler, Va., 24 March 1864, *ORA*, Ser. II, Vol. 6, 1090.

36. *Memphis Daily Appeal*, 26 March 1864.

37. Hutt Diary, 68.

38. Malone Diary, 57.

39. "Attempt of Rebel Prisoners at Point Lookout to Escape," *Evening Star*, 17 February 1864.

40. Ibid.

41. Malone Diary, 57; Hutt Diary, 68.

42. *Hammond Gazette*, 13 April 1864.

43. J. L. McPhail to Foxhall A. Parker, 5 February 1864, *ORN*, Ser. I, Vol. 5, 391-392.

44. Foxhall A. Parker to Gideon Welles, *ORN*, Ser. I, Vol. 5, 392.

45. Foxhall A. Parker to Gustavus V. Fox, 11 May 1864, (telegram received at Washington 5:10 p.m.), *ORN*, Ser. I, Vol. 5, 420; Edward Hooker to Foxhall A. Parker, 18 February 1864, *ORN*, Ser. I, Vol. 5, 395.

46. G. C. Schulze to Foxhall A. Parker, 9 February 1864, *ORN*, Ser. I, Vol. 5, 395.

47. *CWNC*, Vol. 4, 16.

48. Ibid., Vol. 4, 29; Foxhall A. Parker to Gideon Welles, 10 p.m., 7 March 1864, *ORN*, Ser. I, Vol. 5, 401-402; Edward Hooker to Foxhall A. Parker, 8 March 1864, *ORN*, Ser. I, Vol. 5, 402; Edward Hooker to Foxhall A. Parker, 9 March 1864, *ORN*, Ser. I, Vol. 5, 403-404; Foxhall A. Parker to Gideon Welles, 11 March 1864 [1], *ORN*, Ser. I, Vol. 5, 404; Foxhall A. Parker to Gideon Welles, 11 March 1864 [2], *ORN*, Ser. I, Vol. 5, 405.

49. John S. Mosby, *The Memoirs of Colonel John S. Mosby*, Charles Welles Russell (Boston: Little, Brown, and Company, 1917), 230.

50. G. C. Schulze to Edward Hooker, 20 March 1864, *ORN*, Ser. I, Vol. 5, 405.

51. Edwin W. Beitzell, *Life on the Potomac River* (Abell, Md.: Privately Printed, 1968), 81; Frederick Tilp, *This Was Potomac River* (Alexandria, Va.: Published by author, 1978), 181; J. M. Ellicott, "A Child's Recollections of the Potomac Flotilla," *Chronicles of St. Mary's*, Vol. 10, No. 9 (September 1960), 293.

52. Ellicott, 293-294.

53. Foxhall A. Parker to Gideon Welles, 1 April 1864, *ORN*, Ser. I, Vol. 5, 408-409; Foxhall A. Parker to Gideon Welles 7 April 1864 [2], *ORN*, Ser. I, Vol. 5, 409.

54. Foxhall A. Parker to Gideon Welles, 1 April 1864, *ORN*, Ser. I, Vol. 5, 408-409; Foxhall A. Parker to Gideon Welles, 7 April 1864 [1], *ORN*, Ser. I, Vol. 5, 409.

55. *St. Mary's Gazette*, 15 December 1864, undated reprint from *Port Tobacco Times*.

56. *St. Mary's Gazette*, 26 May 1864.

57. Malone Diary, 58.

58. *St. Mary's Gazette*, 26 May 1864.

59. "Meeting of the Farmers in the Factory District," *St. Mary's Gazette*, 23 June 1864.

60. Foxhall A. Parker to Gideon Welles, 15 April 1864, *ORN*, Ser. I, Vol. 5, 410; T. H. Eastman to Foxhall A. Parker, 14 April 1864, *ORN*, Ser. I, Vol. 5, 410. V. Camalin to William Norris, 23 April 1864, *ORA*, Ser. I, Vol. 51, Part 2, 873.

61. T. H. Eastman to Foxhall A. Parker, 14 April 1864, *ORN*, Ser. I, Vol. 5, 410.

62. Edward W. Hinks to R. S. Davis, 15 April 1864, *ORA*, Ser. I, Vol. 33, 268-269.

63. Ibid.

64. T. H. Eastman to Foxhall A. Parker, 14 April 1864, *ORN*, Ser. I, Vol. 5, 410.

65. Edward W. Hinks to R. S. Davis, 15 April 1864, *ORA*, Ser. I, Vol. 33, 269; Camalin to Norris, 23 April 1864.

66. T. H. Eastman to Foxhall A. Parker, 14 April 1864, *ORN*, Ser. I, Vol. 5, 410. When reading the Eastman report one cannot escape the notion of a junior officer pandering to his superior.

33. Infernal Machines

1. Foxhall A. Parker to Gustavus V. Fox, 11 May 1864, (telegram received 5:10 p.m.), *ORN*, Ser. I, Vol. 5, 420; Foxhall A. Parker to Gideon Welles, 13 May 1864, *ORN*, Ser. I, 421-422; "A Brilliant Raid," *Evening Star*, 16 May 1864.

2. Parker to Fox, 11 May 1864.

3. Ibid.

4. Gustavus V. Fox to Foxhall A. Parker, 11 May 1864, (telegram), *ORN*, Ser. I, Vol. 5, 420.

5. Parker to Welles, 13 May 1864, 422; Alonzo G. Draper to R. S. Davis, 15 May 1864, *ORA*, Ser. I, 37, Part 1, 71; Foxhall A. Parker to Gustavus V. Fox, 12 May 1864, (telegram received 10:20 a.m.), *ORN*, Ser. I, Vol. 5, 421; Edward Hooker to Foxhall A. Parker, 14 May 1864, *ORN*, Ser. I, Vol. 5, 422. Parker and Street state fifteen cavalrymen were employed while Draper states thirteen.

6. William Tell Street to Edward Hooker, 14 May 1864, *ORN*, Ser. I, Vol. 5, 423; Edward Hooker to Foxhall A. Parker, 14 May 1864, *ORN*, Ser. I, Vol. 5, 422; *St. Mary's Gazette*, 19 May 1864.

7. Alonzo G. Draper to R. S. Davis, 15 May 1864, *ORA*, Ser. I, Vol. 37, Part 1, 72; William Tell Street to Edward Hooker, 14 May 1864, *ORN*, Ser. I, Vol. 5, 423-424.

8. William Tell Street to Edward Hooker, 14 May 1864, *ORN*, Ser. I, Vol. 5, 423-424; Alonzo G. Draper to R. S. Davis, 15 May 1864, *ORA*, Ser. I, 37, Part 1, 72; *St. Mary's Gazette*, 19 May 1864.

9. Edward Hooker to Foxhall A. Parker, 14 May 1864, *ORN*, Ser. I, Vol. 5, 422; "A Brilliant Raid."

10. Alonzo G. Draper to R. S. Davis, 15 May 1864, *ORA*, Ser. I, 37, Part 1, 72; William Tell Street to Edward Hooker, 14 May 1864, *ORN*, Ser. I, Vol. 5, 424.

11. "The Rappahannock Expedition," *Daily National Republican*, Second Edition, 17 May 1864; Draper to Davis, 15 May 1864; William Tell Street to Edward Hooker, 14 May 1864, *ORN*, Ser. I, Vol. 5, 424. Hooker, who was not on the scene, reported eight enemy killed and "some prisoners," at a cost

of one Federal killed, three severely wounded, and six or eight slightly wounded. Hooker to Parker, 14 May 1864, 423.

12. "The Rappahannock Expedition."

13. *CWNC*, Vol. 6, 308-9. Burley would eventually be released, and quickly rejoin John Yates Beall in an unsuccessful effort to capture the USS *Michigan* on Lake Erie in September 1864. *CWNC*, Vol. 6, 282.

14. Ibid., Vol. 4, 102.

15. Draper to Davis, 15 May 1864.

16. Street to Hooker, 14 May 1864.

17. Edward Hooker to Foxhall A. Parker, 14 May 1864, 422-423.

18. The landing was probably made at the tip of the Cricket Hill Peninsula, just opposite the western entrance of Milford Haven. Hooker to Parker, 14 May 1864, 423; Draper to Davis, 15 May 1864; Street to Hooker, 14 May 1864.

19. Foxhall A. Parker to Gideon Welles, 13 May 1864, *ORN*, Ser. I, 422; Street to Hooker, 14 May 1864; Draper to Davis, 15 May 1864; Hooker to Parker, 14 May 1864, 422-423.

20. J. M. Ellicott, "A Child's Recollections of the Potomac Flotilla," *Chronicles of St. Mary's*, Vol. 10, No. 9 (September 1960), 295.

21. Foxhall A. Parker to Gideon Welles, 21 May 1864, *ORN*, Ser. I, Vol. 5, 433; "Raid on a Light House," *Evening Star*, 24 May 1864.

22. Ibid., 434.

34. Use Your Judgment

1. "Congressional," *Evening Star*, 11 February 1864; "U.S. Congress," *Alexandria Gazette*, 12 February 1864; *Memphis Daily Appeal*, 12 February 1864.

2. Benjamin G. Harris to Oliver O. Howard, 1 September 1865, Freedmen's Bureau Records, in James H. Whyte, "The Activities of the Freedmen's Bureau in Southern Maryland, 1865-1870," *Chronicles of St. Mary's: Monthly Bulletin of the St. Mary's County Historical Society*, Vol. 7, No. 2 (February 1959), 285; Regina Combs Hammett, *History of St. Mary's County Maryland* (Ridge, Md.: Privately published, 1977), 114, 122, 128, 163; *St. Mary's Beacon*, 29 November 1860; Joseph Forrest to Judah P. Benjamin, 17 December 1861, *ORA*, Ser. I, Vol. 51, Part II, 413.

3. *St. Mary's Gazette*, 12 May 1864.

4. Alonzo G. Draper to R. S. Davis, 22 June 1864, *ORA*, Ser. I, Vol. 37, Part 1, 163.

5. Ibid. *Charleston* was a 233-ton sidewheeler, chartered November 16, 1863-November 11, 1865; *Favorite* was a 350-ton sidewheel steamer; *Georgia* was a 617-tons steamer chartered December 29, 1862 thru April 15, 1863 for the Army of Virginia; *Long Branch*, was a 276-ton steamer chartered three times between March 8, 1862 and September 8, 1865, and later renamed *James Christopher*. Charles Dana Gibson, and E. Kay Gibson, *Dictionary of Transports and Combatant Vessels Steam and Sail Employed by the Union Army 1861-1868*, 2 Vols. (Camden, Me.: Ensign Press, 1995), 56, 114, 133, 171.

6. T. H. Eastman to Alonzo Draper, 11 June 1864, (telegram) *ORN*, Ser. I, Vol. 5, 442; Thomas H. Eastman, to William Tell Street, [11 June 1864], *ORN*, Ser. I, Vol. 5, 442; William Tell Street to E. G. Mitchell, 11 June 1864, *ORN*, Ser. I, Vol. 5, 443.

7. Edward Hooker to William Tell Street, [June 11, 1861?], (telegram) *ORN*, Ser. I, Vol. 5, 443.

8. "Diary and Other accounts of Prison Life. The Diary of Bartlett Yancey Malone," in Edwin W. Beitzell, *Point Lookout Prison Camp for Confederates* (Leonardtown, Md.: Privately Printed, 1972), 58; "The Diary of Charles Warren Hutt, of Westmoreland County, Virginia (Kept While a Prisoner of War at Point Lookout, Maryland – 1864)," in Beitzell, *Point Lookout*, 73.

9. Draper to Davis, 22 June 1864, *ORA*, Ser. I, Vol. 37, Part 1, 163.

10. Ibid.; Edward Hooker to Foxhall A. Parker, 21 June 1864, *ORN*, Ser. I, Vol. 5, 447; William Tell Street to Foxhall A. Parker, 15 June 1864, *ORN*, Ser. I, Vol. 5, 443.

11. Ibid.

12. "Outrages of Butler' Negro Troops," *The Western Democrat*, 19 July 1864, reprinted from the *Richmond Enquirer*.

13. Ibid. Beale, who had been promoted to the rank of major, is incorrectly referred to as a captain.

14. Ibid. It is the author's opinion that the veracity of the charge, which was not indicated in any other documentation of the raid, is questionable at best and a frequently employed racial trope which deemed black soldiers to be rapists, murderers and other forms of defamers of Southern

womanhood and civility. It can probably be relegated to the substantial arena of Confederate race propaganda.

15. Street to Parker, 15 June 1864, *ORN*, Ser. I, Vol. 5, 443-444. Street refers to the creek only as Machodoc, but as Upper Machodoc was a far greater march, the author believes Lower Machodoc would have been the loading point.

16. Ibid., 443.

17. Draper to Davis, 22 June 1864; Street to Parker, 15 June 1864, 163.

18. Ibid.

19. Ibid.; Street to Parker, 15 June 1864, 444.

20. Street to Parker, 15 June 1864, 444.

21. Draper to Davis, 22 June 1864, 163-164.

22. "Outrages of Butler' Negro Troops."

23. Ibid.

24. Draper to Davis, 22 June 1864, 164.

25. Ibid.

26. Ibid.; "Outrages of Butler' Negro Troops."

27. Draper to Davis, 22 June 1864, 164.

28. Ibid.; "Outrages of Butler' Negro Troops."

29. Draper to Davis, 22 June 1864, 164.

30. Ibid., 164-165; Edward Hooker to Foxhall A. Parker, 17 June 1864, *ORN*, Ser. I, Vol. 5, 444.

31. Hooker to Parker, 17 June 1864.

32. Draper to Davis, 22 June 1864, 165; Hooker to Parker, 17 June 1864, 445.

33. Draper to Davis, 22 June 1864, 165.

34. Ibid.

35. Ibid.

36. Ibid.

37. Draper to Davis, 22 June 1864, 165-166.

38. Ibid.,166; "Outrages of Butler' Negro Troops."

39. Draper to Davis, 22 June 1864, 166.

40. Ibid.

41. Ibid.

42. Edward Hooker to Foxhall A. Parker, 21 June 1864 [1], *ORN*, Ser. I, Vol. 5, 446.

43. Draper to Davis, 22 June 1864, 166; Hooker to Parker, 17 June 1864, 444-445.

44. Ibid.

45. Hooker to Parker, 17 June 1864, 445.

46. Ibid.

47. Draper to Davis, 22 June 1864, 166.

48. Ibid.

49. Ibid.; Hooker to Parker, 21 June 1864, 447.

50. Foxhall A. Parker to Edward Hooker, 18 June 1864, *ORN*, Ser. I, Vol. 5, 445-446.

51. Hooker to Parker, 21 June 1864, 446-447.

52. Ibid., 446.

53. Ibid.

54. Draper to Davis, 22 June 1864, 166-167.

55. Ibid., 167; Hooker to Parker, 21 June 1864, 446-447.

56. Hooker to Parker, 21 June 1864, 447.

57. Ibid.

58. Draper to Davis, 22 June 1864, 167.

59. Ibid.; "Successful Raid on the Rebels," *Evening Star*, 23 June 1864; Hooker to Parker, 21 June 1864, 447. It was publicly reported in the *Evening Star* that the expedition had captured 200 horses and mules, 400 head of cattle, fifty sheep, and brought off 400 contrabands as well as "farming utensils to a large amount." Hooker states that the take included between 400 and 500 cattle and nearly 200 horses and as many sheep, but Draper's count seems more specific and is quite likely more accurate.

60. "Outrages of Butler' Negro Troops."

35. Early to Rise

1. Luther Hopkins, "Prison Life at Point Lookout," in Edwin W. Beitzell, *Point Lookout Prison Camp for Confederates* (Leonardtown, Md.: Privately Printed, 1972), 89.
2. "The Diary of Charles Warren Hutt, of Westmoreland County, Virginia (Kept While a Prisoner of War at Point Lookout, Maryland – 1864)," reprinted in Beitzell, *Point Lookout*, 75; "Prison Life at the North," *The Weekly Intelligencer*, 15 March 1864; Ross M. Kimmel and Michael P. Musick, *"I Am Busy Drawing Pictures" The Civil War Art and Letters of Private John Jacob Omenhausser, CSA* (Friends of the Maryland State Archives: Annapolis, Md., 2014), 52; C. W. Jones, "In Prison at Point Lookout," in Beitzell, *Point Lookout*, 92.
3. Bradley Johnson, "My Ride Around Baltimore In Eighteen Hundred and Sixty-Four," *Journal of the United States Cavalry Association*, Vol. 2 (Fort Leavenworth, Kansas, 1889), 252-253, reprinted in Beitzell, *Point Lookout*, 50.
4. DARST to William Norris, 9 June 1864, *ORA*, Ser. I, Vol. 51, Part 2, 1000-1001. That DARST may have been an operative in St. Mary's County is suggested by his obviously personal observations.
5. Brett W. Spaulding, *Last Chance for Victory: Jubal Early's 1864 Maryland Invasion* (Privately published: 2010), 144; Benjamin Franklin Cooling, *Jubal Early's Raid on Washington 1864* (Tuscaloosa: The University of Alabama Press, 1989), 16; Richard R. Duncan, "Maryland's Reaction to Early's Raid in 1864: A Summer of Bitterness," *MHM*, Vol. 64, Number 3 (Fall 1969), 248, 249.
6. E. B. Long. and Barbara Long: *The Civil War Day by Day: An Almanac 1861-1865* (Garden City, N.Y.: Doubleday & Company, Inc., 1971), 523, 524, 525, 526, 527.
7. Scott Sumter Sheads and Daniel Carroll Toomey, *Baltimore During the Civil War* (Linthicum, Md.: Toomey Press, 1997), 70; Harry Wright Newman, *Maryland and the Confederacy* (Annapolis: Privately published, 1976), 203.
8. *Evening Star*, 23 June 1864.
9. Hutt Diary, 76.
10. James H. Thompson to Richard F. Andrews, 23 June 1864, *ORA*, Ser. II, Vol. 7, 399-400.
11. Ibid., 400.
12. Alonzo G. Draper, 25 June 1864 [Endorsement], *ORA*, Ser. II, Vol. 7, 400.
13. Robert E. Lee to Jefferson Davis, 26 June 1864, *ORA*, Ser. I, Vol. 37, Part 1, 767-768.
14. Sheads and Toomey, 69; W. W. Goldsborough, *The Maryland Line in the Confederate Army* (Baltimore: Kelly, Piet & C., 1869), 45, 59.
15. Robert E. Lee to Jefferson Davis, 3 July 1864, *Lee's Dispatches: Unpublished Letters of General Robert E. Lee, C. S. A. to Jefferson Davis and the War Department of The Confederate States of America 1862-65*, Douglas Southall Freeman, ed., (New York and London: G. P. Putnam's Sons, 1915), No. 149, 269.
16. Ibid., 269-270.
17. Ibid. 270.
18. Ibid.
19. Ibid., 270-271.
20. Robert E. Lee to Jefferson Davis, 26 June 1864, *Lee's Dispatches*, No. 148, 768.
21. Ibid., 769.
22. Tabular statement of prisoners of war received, died, sick, &c., at Point Lookout, Md. From July 31, 1863, to November 30, 1864, inclusive, *ORA*, Ser. II, Vol. 7, 1243.
23. Hutt Diary, 28 June 1864, 76; "Point Lookout, Md.," *Evening Star*, 8 July 1864.
24. Spaulding, 144.
25. Bradley Johnson, "My Ride Around Baltimore," in Beitzell, *Point Lookout*, 50-52; Douglas Southall Freeman, *Lee's Lieutenants: A Study in Command*, 3 Vols. (New York: Simon and Shuster, 1998. Reprint from C. Scribner's Sons, New York, 1942-1944), 564; Sheads and Toomey, 73.
26. John W. Garrett to Edwin M. Stanton, 29 June 1864, *ORA*, Vol. 37, Ser. I, Part 1, 694-695.

36. Heaven Grant It

1. E. B. Long and Barbara Long: *The Civil War Day by Day: An Almanac 1861-1865* (Garden City, N.Y.: Doubleday & Company, Inc., 1971), 530, 531; Abstract from returns of the Middle Department (Eighth Army Corps), Maj. Gen. Lewis Wallace, U.S. Army, commanding, for the month of June, 1864, *ORA*, Ser 1, Vol. 37, Part 1, 704; Benjamin Franklin Cooling, *Jubal Early's Raid on Washington* (Tuscaloosa: The University of Alabama Press, 1989), 92; Abstract from returns of the Middle Department (Eighth Army Corps), Maj. Gen. Christopher C. Augur, U.S. Army, commanding, for

the month of June, 1864, *ORA*, Ser 1, Vol. 37, Part 1, 697.

2. "The Diary of Charles Warren Hutt, of Westmoreland County, Virginia (Kept While a Prisoner of War at Point Lookout, Maryland – 1864)," in Edwin W. Beitzell, *Point Lookout Prison Camp for Confederates* (Leonardtown, Md.: Privately printed, 1972), 76.

3. *Cleveland Morning Leader*, July 1, 1864.

4. Hutt Diary, 76.

5. Long and Long, 530.

6. John W. Garrett to Edwin M. Stanton, 3 July 1864, *ORA*, Vol. 37, Ser. I, Part 2, 16.

7. Scott Sumter Sheads and Daniel Carroll Toomey, *Baltimore During the Civil War* (Linthicum, Md.: Toomey Press, 1997), 70.

8. John W. Garrett to Henry W. Halleck, 3 July 1864 (received 2:40 p.m.), *ORA*, Vol. 37, Ser. I, Part 2, 17, 23; Brett W. Spaulding, *Last Chance for Victory: Jubal Early's 1864 Maryland Invasion* (Privately published: 2010), 51.

9. Robert E. Lee to Jefferson Davis, 5 July 1864, *Lee's Dispatches: Unpublished Letters of General Robert E. Lee, C. S. A. to Jefferson Davis and the War Department of The Confederate States of America 1862-65*, Douglas Southall Freeman, ed., New York and London: G. P. Putnam's Sons, 1915, No. 152, 275-276.

10. Christopher C. Augur to James Barnes, 3 July 1864, *ORA*, Ser. I, Vol. 40, Part 3, 30; *Evening Star*, 8 July 1864. Owing to the June 21, 1864 incorporation of the St. Mary's District into the Washington District there was some confusion as to who was in command at Point Lookout. General Butler, who had not been informed of the change, had appointed General Hinks to again take command "because his wounds unfitted him for service in the field." Hinks set out immediately only to be informed of the district change and that General Barnes was to assume actual command. In something of a huff, Hinks sent a dispatch to Butler demanding he be permitted leave to go home. Edward W. Hinks to Benjamin F. Butler, 6 July 1864 (1), *ORA*, Ser. I, Vol. 40, Part 3, 58; Edward W. Hinks to Benjamin F. Butler, 6 July 1864 (2), *ORA*, Ser. I, Vol. 40, Part 3, 58; Benjamin F. Butler to Ulysses S. Grant, 5 July 1864, 11.20 a.m., *ORA*, Vol. 40, Ser. I, Part 3, 18; Edwin M. Stanton to James Barnes, 7 July 1864, *ORA*, Ser. I, Vol. 40, Part 3, 71.

11. Lee's Confidential Dispatches to Davis, 1862-1865, D. S. Freeman, 269, 271, 275, reprinted in Beitzell, *Point Lookout*, 50.

12. Long and Long, 516, 532.

13. Jane Wilson McWiliams, *Annapolis: City on the Severn* (Baltimore and Crownsville, Md.: The Johns Hopkins University Press and The Maryland Historical Trust, 2011), 189; Max. Woodhull to A. R. Root, 3 July 1864, (2) *ORA*, Ser. I, Vol. 37, Part 2, 32; Max. Woodhull A. R. Root, 3 July 1864, (1) *ORA*, Ser. I, Vol. 37, Part 2, 32.

14. Long and Long, 532, 535; Memorandum of Interview with William P. Fessenden, 4 July 1864, in Francis Fessenden, *Life and Public Services of William Pitt Fessenden*, 2 Vols. (Boston and New York: Houghton, Mifflin and Company, 1907), Vol. 1, 324-25; John G. Nicolay and John Hay, *Abraham Lincoln: A History*, 10 vols. (New York: Century, 1890), Vol. 9, 120-21; Abraham Lincoln to John L. Scripps, 4 July 1864, *Collected Works of Abraham Lincoln*, Roy P. Basler, ed. 9 Vols. (New Brunswick, NJ: Rutgers University Press, 1953-1955), Vol. 7, 423-424.

15. "Diary and Other accounts of Prison Life. The Diary of Bartlett Yancey Malone," in Edwin W. Beitzell, *Point Lookout Prison Camp for Confederates* (Leonardtown, Md.: Privately printed, 1972), 59.

16. Christopher C. Augur to William Gamble, 5 July 1864, *ORA*, Ser. I, Vol. 37, Part 2, 62.

17. Hutt Diary, 77.

18. Edwin M. Stanton to James G. Curtin, 4 July 1864, 8 p.m., *ORA*, Ser. I, Vol. 37, Part 2, 58; Edwin M. Stanton to James G. Curtin, 5 July 1864, 3.20 p.m., *ORA*, Ser. I, Vol. 37, Part 2, 74; Henry W. Halleck to Ulysses S. Grant, 5 July 1864, 1 p.m., *ORA*, Ser. I, Vol. 37, Part 2, 59.

19. George G. Meade to Ulysses S. Grant, 5 July 1864, 1 p.m., *ORA*, Ser. I, Vol. 37, Part 2, 60; Ulysses S. Grant to Henry W. Halleck, 5 July 1864, 11.50 p.m., *ORA*, Ser. I, Vol. 37, Part 2, 60; Ulysses S. Grant to George G. Meade, 5 July 1864, *ORA*, Ser. I, Vol. 37, Part 2, 60.

20. John W. Garrett to Abraham Lincoln, 5 July 1864, to *ORA*, Ser. I, Vol. 37, Part 2, 65-66; Philip Sheridan to Henry W. Halleck, 6 July 1864, 10 p.m., *ORA*, Ser. I, Vol. 37, Part 2, 80.

21. James Barnes to Christopher C. Augur, 6 July 1864, *ORA*, Ser. I, Vol. 40, Part 3, 58; *Evening Star*, 8 July 1864; Abstract from returns of the Middle Department (Eighth Army Corps), Maj. Gen. Christopher C. Augur, U.S. Army, commanding, for the month of June, 1864, *ORA*, Ser I, Vol. 37,

Part 1, 697.

22. "Rebel Operations in Hagerstown," *New York Times*, 15 July 1864; Sheads and Toomey, 102; John T. Scharf, *History of Western: Being A History of Montgomery, Carroll, Washington, Allegheny, and Garrett Counties.* 2 Vols. (Philadelphia: Louis H. Everts, 1882 and Baltimore: Regional Publishing Company, 1968 edition), 1:285-286; Jubal A. Early, *War Memoirs,* Frank Vandiver, ed. (Bloomington: Indiana University Press, 1960), 384-386; Richard R. Duncan, "Maryland's Reaction to Early's Raid in 1864," *MHM* (Fall 1969), 251; Spaulding, 41; Bradley T. Johnson, "Riding a Raid, in 1864," in Beitzell, *Point Lookout*, 50; Harry Wright Newman, *Maryland and the Confederacy* (Annapolis: Privately published, 1976), 267; Stephen R. Bockmiller, "It is Not Civilized War . . ." in *The Sentinel*, 150th Anniversary 1864/2014 ((National Park Service: 2014), 17.

23. Long and Long, 534, 535; Henry W. Halleck to Ulysses S. Grant, 6 July 1864, 10 p.m., *ORA*, Ser. I, 40, Part 3, 32; Samuel B. Lawrence to A. R. Root, 6 July 1864, 5:30 p.m., *ORA*, Vol. 37, Ser. I, Part 2, 94.

24. Lew Wallace to E. D. Townsend, -- August 1864, *ORA*, Ser. I, Vol. 37, Part 1, 195-196; Seth Williams to James B. Ricketts, 6 July 1864, 10 a.m., *ORA*, Ser. I, Vol. 40, Part 3, 36, H. G. Wight to S. Williams, *ORA*, Vol. Ser. I, Vol. 40, Part 3, 44; Cooling, 58. For a comprehensive Union perspective of the Battle of Monocacy see Lew Wallace to E. D. Townsend, *ORA*, Ser. I, Vol. 37, Part. 1, 191-192, and Wallace to Townsend, -- August 1864, *ORA*, Ser. I, Vol. 37, Part I, 193-200.

25. D. R. Clendenin to Samuel B. Lawson, 14 July 1864, *ORA*, Ser. I, Vol. 37, Part 1, 219; J. H. Taylor to D. W. C. Thompson, 4 July 1864, *ORA*, Ser. I. Vol. 37, Part 2, 35; Spaulding, 54.

26. Lew Wallace to Henry W. Halleck, 7 July 1864 (received 12:50 p.m.), *ORA*, Ser. I, Vol. 37, Part 2, 108-109; Lew Wallace to Samuel B. Lawrence, 7 July 1864 (received 6:50 p.m.), *ORA*, Ser. I, Vol. 37, Part 2, 110; Clendenin to Lawson, 14 July 1864; Cooling, 58; Bockmiller, 17.

27. Henry W. Halleck to Commanding Officer and Chief Quartermaster, 7 July 1864, 9:42 p.m., *ORA*, Ser. I, Vol. 37, Part 3, 111; Edwin M. Stanton to Lew Wallace, 7 July 1864, 10 p.m., *ORA*, Ser. I, Vol. 37, Part 3, 108. See also John W. Garrett to Edwin M. Stanton, 7 July 1864 (received 7:40 p.m.) *ORA*, Ser. I, Vol. 37, Part 2, 100; Garrett to Stanton, 7 July 1864, 7:15 p.m. (received 7:40 p.m.), *ORA*, Ser. I, Vol. 37, Part 2, 100-101, Garrett to Stanton, 7 July 1864, (received 8:30 p.m.), *ORA*, Ser. I, Vol. 37, Part 2, 101.

28. Edwin M. Stanton to James Barnes, 7 July 1864, *ORA*, Ser. I, Vol. 40, Part 3, 71; Spaulding, 148; Christopher C. Augur to James Barnes, 5 July 1864, *ORA*, Ser. I, Vol. 40, Part 3, 30; Stanton to Barnes, 8 July 1864, 9:30 a.m. (received 10:10 a.m.), *ORA*, Ser. I, Vol. 40, 90; Gideon Welles, to Foxhall A. Parker, 8 July 1864, (telegram), *ORN*, Ser. I, Vol. 5, 459; T. H. Eastman to Foxhall A. Parker, 8 July 1864, *ORN*, Ser. I, Vol. 5, 459. 29. Benjamin F. Butler to E. D. Townsend, 7 July 1864, *ORN*, Ser. I, Vol. 5, 458; Spaulding, 148.

30. Johnson, "Riding a Raid," 51.

31. Ibid.; Duncan, 256.

32. *Confederate Military History: A Library of Confederate States History*, General Clement A. Evans, C.S.A., ed., 12 Vols. (Atlanta, Ga.: Confederate Pub. Co., 1899), Vol. 2, 125; *Lee's Dispatches: Unpublished Letters of General Robert E. Lee, C. S. A. to Jefferson Davis and the War Department of The Confederate States of America 1862-65*, Douglas Southall Freeman, ed. (New York and London: G. P. Putnam's Sons, 1915), 275; Beitzell, *Point Lookout*, 50; Johnson, "Riding a Raid," 51-52.

33. Christopher C. Augur to James Barnes, 8 July 1864, *ORA*, Ser. I, Vol. 40, Part 3, 90.

34. Gideon Welles to Foxhall A. Parker, 8 July 1864, (telegram), *ORA*, Ser. I, Vol. 5, 458; T. H. Eastman to Gideon Welles, 8 July 1864 (received 12:40 a.m.); James Barnes to Edwin M. Stanton, 8 July 1864, 9.30 a.m. (received 10:10 a.m.), *ORA*, Ser. I, Vol. 40, Part 3, 90.

35. James Barnes to Christopher C. Augur, 8 July 1864 (received 1:50 p.m.), 90-91.

36. Ibid., 91; Spaulding, 149.

37. Robert E. Lee, 8 July 1864, (telegram in cipher received at Richmond, 8 July 1864, 7:25 p.m.), *Lee's Dispatches*, No. 155, 278.

37. Bad Humor

1. See Lew Wallace, *Lew Wallace: An Autobiography* (New York: Harper and Brothers, 1906), 2 Vols., and Jubal A. Early, *War Memoirs,* Frank Vandiver, ed. (Bloomington: Indiana University Press, 1960), for personal accounts of the Battle of Monocacy, and Benjamin Franklin Cooling, *Jubal Early's Raid on Washington* (Tuscaloosa: The University of Alabama Press, 1989) and Brett W. Spaulding, *Last Chance*

for Victory: Jubal Early's 1864 Maryland Invasion (Privately published: 2010) for comprehensive overviews of the engagement and the subsequent 1864 Maryland Campaign.

2. Lew Wallace to John W. Garrett, 9 July 1864, *ORA*, Ser I, 37, pt. 2, 139; Lew Wallace to Henry W. Halleck, 9 July 1864 (received 11:40 p.m.), *ORA*, Ser. I, Vol. 37, Part 2, 145; Cooling, 274; Spaulding, 131, 132.

3. Royce Gordon Singleton, *John Taylor Wood: Sea Ghost of the Confederacy* (Athens, Ga.: University of Georgia Press, 1979), 2-5; *ORN*, Ser. II, Vol. 5, 467; M. S. Stuyvesant to Gideon Welles, 18 July 1864 (received 6:10 p.m.), *ORN*, Ser. II, Vol. 1, 467; John Taylor Wood to Jefferson Davis, 9 July 1864, *ORA*, Ser. I, 40, Part 3, 757. Spaulding, 147.

4. Spaulding 149; Daniel Carroll Toomey, *The Civil War in Maryland* (Toomey Press: Baltimore, 1983 124; Bradley T. Johnson, "Riding a Raid in July, 1864," in Edwin W. Beitzell, *Point Lookout Prison Camp for Confederates* (Leonardtown, Md.: Privately Printed, 1972), 52.

5. Cooling, 159; Spaulding, 151, 152; Harry Gilmor, *Four Years in the Saddle* (New York: Harper and Brothers, 1866), 216-217.

6. Johnson, "Riding a Raid," 52-53.

7. Gilmor, *Four Years in the Saddle*, 199; Johnson, "Riding a Raid," 52; "Seventy-Fifth Anniversary of Harry Gilmor's Raid," *The Sunday Sun*, 9 July 1939; "Developments," *Inquirer*, 12 July 1864; *Baltimore Sun*, 24 August 1864; Cooling 160-161.

8. *Daily National Intelligencer*, 11 July 1864.

9. Thomas Swann, Evan T. Ellicott, William E. Hooper, Thomas S. Alexander, Michael Warner to Abraham Lincoln, 9 July 1864 (received 11.50 p.m.), *ORA*, Ser. I, Vol. 37, Part 2, 140; *Collected Works of Abraham Lincoln,* Roy P. Basler, ed., 9 vols. (New Brunswick, NJ: Rutgers University Press, 1953-55), Vol. 7, 437-438; Cooling, 89.

10. John R. Kenly to Samuel B. Lawrence, 10 July 1864, *ORA,* Ser. I, Vol. 37, Part 2, 180; Ulysses S. Grant to Henry W. Halleck, 10 July 1864, 12:30 p.m. (received 9 p.m.), *ORA*, Ser. I, Vol. 37, Part 2, 156; Frank Wells, Defense of Baltimore, 10 July 1864, *ORA*, Ser. I, Vol. 37, Part 2, 180; General Orders No. 1, Edward O. C. Ord, 11 July 1864, *ORA*, Ser. I, Vol. 37, Part 2, 214; Edwin M. Stanton to Lew Wallace, 11 July 1864, 9:30 p.m., *ORA*, Ser. I, Vol. 37, Part 2, 215; Edward O. C. Ord to Ulysses S. Grant, 12 July 1864 (received 13th), *ORA*, Ser. I, Vol. 37, Part 2, 248; Henry W. Halleck to Ulysses S. Grant, 10 July 1864, 3.30 p.m., *ORA*, Ser. I, Vol. 37, Part 2, 157; Henry W. Halleck to Ulysses S. Grant, 13 July 1864, 1 p.m., *ORA*, Ser. I, Vol. 40, Part 3, 207; *Baltimore American and Commercial Advertiser*, 11 and 15 July 1864; *Baltimore Daily Gazette*, 11 July 1864; "The Invasion," *Evening Star*, 12 July 1864; John T. Scharf, *History of Maryland from the Earliest Period to the Present Day.* 3 Vols. (Baltimore: J. B. Piet, 1879. Facsimile edition, Hatboro, Pa.: Tradition Press, 1967), Vol. 3, 628; Richard R. Duncan, "Maryland's Reaction to Early's Raid in 1864: A Summer of Bitterness," *MHM*, Vol. 64 (Fall 1969), No. 3, 259-260.

11. Jane Wilson McWilliams, *Annapolis: City on the Severn* (Baltimore: The Johns Hopkins University Press, and Crownsville: The Maryland Historical Trust Press, 2011), 189; *Annapolis Gazette*, 14 July 1864; *Baltimore Sun*, 11 July 1864; "The Excitement at Annapolis," *The Cecil Whig*, 16 July 1864.

12. Foxhall A. Parker to Gideon Welles, 10 July 1864 (received at Washington 12 m.), *ORN*, Ser. I, Vol. 5, 459.

13. Gideon Welles to Andrew A. Harwood, 27 June 1863, (telegram), *ORN*, Ser. I, Vol. 5, 292; Gideon Welles to Foxhall A. Parker, 10 July 1864, *ORN*, Ser. I, Vol. 5, 459; Gideon Welles to T. H. Eastman, 10 July 1864, *ORN*, Ser. I, Vol. 5, 459.

14. Abraham Lincoln to Ulysses S. Grant, 10 July 1864, 2:30 p.m., *ORA*, Ser. I, Vol. 37, Part 2, 155.

15. Ulysses S. Grant to Abraham Lincoln, 10 July 1864, 10:30 p.m. (received 7 a.m. 11 July), *ORA*, Ser. I, Vol. 37, Part 2, 155-156.

16. A. L. Wells to Christopher C. Augur, [10 July 1864], *ORA*, Ser. I, Vol. 37, Part 1, 248; William H. Fry to J. H. Taylor, 26 July 1864, *ORA*, Ser. I, Vol. 37, Part 1, 248-249; Martin D. Hardin to Joseph H. Taylor, 19 July 1864, *ORA*, Ser. I, Vol. 37, Part 1, 236; J. M. Warner to R. Chandler, 18 July 1864, *ORA*, Ser. I, Vol. 37, Part 1, 239-240; Cooling 109.

17. Duncan, 264, 265; Johnson, "Riding a Raid," 52; "Cutting the Telegraph," *The Evening Telegraph*, (Philadelphia, Pa), 12 July 184, 4th edition; R. Price to A. G. Hennisee, 11 July 1864, 7 p.m., *ORA,* Ser. I, Vol. 37, Part 3, 229-230; Spaulding 154; Cooling, 167-168.

18. "The Invasion of Maryland," *Evening Star*, 12 July 1864; "The Invasion," *The Aegis & Intelligencer*, 15 July 1864.

19. "Raid on the Phil., Wil., and Balt. Railroad"; "The Invasion of Maryland." The Philadelphia *Inquirer* incorrectly identified the gunboat as *Lancaster* "improvised into a gunboat for the protection of the railroad bridge." *The Cecil Whig*, 16 July 1864, reprint from Philadelphia *Inquirer*. *Juniata* is identified on the site at the time by Acting Ensign Philip Sheridan. The commander of the USS *Teaser*, which arrived on the scene on July 12, found her without arms or provisions. Philip Sheridan to Foxhall A. Parker, 20 July 1864, *ORN*, Ser. I, Vol. 5, 470. The train left Washington for Baltimore at 7:30 a.m. and departed the Baltimore station late, at 9:10 a.m. "The Invasion: Particulars of the Burning of the Gunpowder Bridge," *Evening Star* 12 July 1864, reprint of dispatch to the *Baltimore Chronicle*.

20. "Raid on the Phil., Wil., and Balt. Railroad"; "The Rebel Inversion," *Evening Star*, 14 July 1864; Duncan, 127-128; "The Escape of Gen. Franklin," *New York Times*, 15 July 1864; "Developments," *Inquirer*, 12 July 1864; "Seventy-Fifth Anniversary," *The Sunday Sun*, 9 July 1939.

21. "Raid on the Phil., Wil., and Balt. Railroad": "Particulars of the Burning of the Gunpowder Bridge"; "The Invasion of Maryland"; "Incident," *Alexandria Gazette*, 11 July 1864. Another article in the *Baltimore Chronicle*, reprinted in the Washington *Evening Star*, states that the train consisted of "four rattan cars, one ordinary passenger, one Philadelphia baggage, and one Camden and Amboy baggage car, beside the mail car, engine and tender." "Particulars of the Burning of the Gunpowder Bridge," *Evening Star* 12 July 1864, reprint of dispatch to the *Baltimore Chronicle*. Those taken prisoner with General Franklin included Paymaster H. Melville Hanna, Assistant Engineer Clark Fisher of the steamer *Agawam*, Lieutenant George H. Sterling, Franklin's aide, Lieutenant Eaton, Surgeon Delavan Bloodgood of the U.S. Navy, Lieutenant Edmund P. Banning of the Marine Corps and other officers. J. W. Sampson to Thomas T. Eckert, 14 July 1864, *ORA*, Ser. I, Vol. 37, Part 2, 323.

22. "Raid on the Phil., Wil., and Balt. Railroad"; "The Invasion of Maryland"; "Particulars of the Burning of the Gunpowder Bridge."

23. R. Price to A. G. Hennisee, 11 July 1864, 7 p.m., *ORA*. Ser. I, Vol. 37, Part 1. 229-230; Duncan, 266, Toomey 127-128; Gilmor, 195-196, 229; Lew Wallace to Henry W. Halleck, 11 July 1864 (telegram received 2:40 p.m.), *ORN*, Ser. I, Vol. 5, 460; Foxhall A. Parker to Gideon Welles, 16 July 1864, (telegram) *ORN*, Ser. I, Vol. 5, 465; "Developments"; Edward O. C. Ord, to Ulysses S. Grant, 12 July 1864 (received 13th), *ORA*, Ser. I, Vol. 37, Part 2, 247-248; Edward O. C. Ord to Henry W. Halleck, 12 July 1864, 8.30 a.m. (received 9 a.m.), *ORA*, Ser. I, Vol. 37, Part 2, 248; Ord to Halleck, 12 July 1864, 10 p.m. (received 9 a.m., 13 July via Cherrystone and Fort Monroe,), *ORA*, Ser. I, Vol. 37, Part 2, 248; "Raid on the Phil., Wil., and Balt. Railroad"; "Particulars of the Burning of the Gunpowder Bridge"; *Daily National Intelligencer*, 15 July 1864. See *ORN*, Ser. II, Vol. 1, 116, for details on *Juniata*'s outfit and armament.

24. "The Invasion of Maryland"; "Particulars of the Burning of the Gunpowder Bridge."

25. "The Invasion of Maryland."

26. Ibid.

27. William Tell Street to Foxhall A. Parker, 18 July 1864, *ORN*, Ser. I, 5, 466-467.

28. Foxhall A. Parker to Gustavus V. Fox, July 11, 1864, 9:30 a.m., (telegram), *ORN*, Ser. I, Vol. 5, 461; Gideon Welles to J. B. Montgomery, 11 July 1864, *ORN*, Ser. I, Vol. 5, 461; J. B. Montgomery to Foxhall A. Parker, 11 July 1864, *ORN*, Ser. I, Vol. 5, 461; Foxhall A. Parker to Gideon Welles, 11 July 1864 (received 4:15 p.m.), *ORN*, Ser. I, Vol. 5, 462; Parker to Welles, 11 July 1864 (received 1:40 p.m.), *ORN*, Ser. I, Vol. 5, 460; Parker to Welles, 11 July 1864 (received 7:35 p.m.), *ORN*, Ser. I, Vol. 5, 463. The USS *Teaser*, which had originally been charged with going to the Gunpowder, was prevented from reaching her destination by a leaky exhaust pipe.

29. Gilmor, 197-202; "Developments"; C. A. Dana to Ulysses S. Grant, 14 July 1864, 11 a.m., *ORA*, 37, Ser. 1, Part 2, 302; J. W. Sampson to Thomas T. Eckert, 14 July 1864, *ORA*, 37, Ser. I, Part 2, 323; "The Rebel Inversion"; Spaulding, 158.

30. Ord to Halleck, 12 July 1864, 10 p.m.; Gilmor, 201-202; Cooling, 170.

31. Johnson, "Riding a Raid," 52; Cooling, 164; Spaulding, 160.

32. Johnson, "Riding a Raid" 53; Duncan, 266-267; Cooling, 164.

33. Spaulding, 162.

34. Cooling, 165.

35. Duncan, 268; Toomey, 125; John W. Garrett to Edwin M. Stanton, 11 July 1864, *ORA*, Ser I, Vol. 37, Part 2, 212; Johnson, "Riding a Raid," 53; "Affairs on the Railroad," *Evening Star*, 13 July 186; Cooling, 165.

36. *ORA*, Ser I, Vol. 37, Part 2, 212-216, 253; Garrett to Stanton, 11 July 1864; Cooling, 164; Gilmor,

193-196; Johnson, "Riding a Raid," 56; Toomey, 126; *ORA*, Ser. I, Vol. Part 2, 225-226, Cooling, 171.

37. "Communications with Baltimore Interfered With" *Daily National Republican*, Third Edition, 12 July 1864; "The Destruction of the Railroad," *Evening Star*, 12 July 1864. Though Johnson's main force did not pass through Laurel, it was reported that the bridge over the Patuxent had been destroyed. It is presumed the bridge was the B&O railroad bridge, as two public bridges also crossed the river at the town, the Laurel Mills Bridge and the Washington and Baltimore Turnpike Bridge. "The Destruction of the Railroad."

38. "The Destruction of the Railroad"; Johnson, "Riding a Raid," 53; J. B. Fry to Edwin M. Stanton, 12 July 1864, 3:15 p.m. (received 3:20 p.m.), *ORA*, Ser. I, Vol. 37, Part 2, 224; George S. Koontz to Edwin M. Stanton, 12 July 1864 (received 8:45 p.m.), *ORA*, Ser. I, Vol. 37, Part 2, 225; Koontz to Stanton, 12 July 1864 (received 3 p.m.), *ORA*, Ser. I, Vol. 37, Part 2, 225; Cooling 171; Toomey, 126.

39. John Tyler to Sterling Price, 9 July 1864, *ORN*, Ser. I, Vol. 10, 721.

40. John Taylor Wood to Jefferson Davis, 9 July 1864, *ORN*, Ser. I, Vol. 10, 721; Magnus S. Thompson, "Plan to Release Our Men at Point Lookout," *Confederate Veteran* (Nashville, 1912), Vol. 20, No. 2, 69-70, states incorrectly that Wood employed the CSS *Tallahassee* for the operation.

41. Robert E. Lee to Jefferson Davis, 10 July 1864, *Lee's Dispatches: Unpublished Letters of General Robert E. Lee, C. S. A. to Jefferson Davis and the War Department of The Confederate States of America 1862-65*, Douglas Southall Freeman, ed., (New York and London: G. P. Putnam's Sons, 1915), No. 156, 279-280.

42. Jefferson Davis to John Taylor Wood and G. W. C. Lee, 11 July 1864, *ORA*, Ser. II, Vol. 7, 458.

43. Ibid.; Jefferson Davis to G. W. C. Lee (Care of General Whiting), 10 July 1864, 6:15 p.m., (telegram), *ORN*, Ser. I, Vol. 10, 722.

44. Jefferson Davis to John Taylor Wood, 10 July 1864, *ORN*, Ser. I, Vol. 10, 721.

45. Jefferson Davis to John Taylor Wood and G. W. C. Lee, 11 July 1864, *ORA*, Ser. II, Vol. 7, 458.

46. James Barnes to Edwin M. Stanton, 11 July 1864, 9 a.m. (received 10:20 a.m.), *ORA*, Ser. I, Vol. 40, Part 3, 251.

38. The Hottest Day

1. John G. Barnard to C. C. Augur 22 July 1864, *ORA*, Ser. I, Vol. 37, Part 2, 414; Jubal A. Early, *A Memoir of the Last Year of the War for Independence, in the Confederate States of America, Containing an Account of the Operations of His Command in the Years 1864 and 1865* (Lynchburg, Va.: C. W. Button, 1867), 389; Benjamin Franklin Cooling, *Jubal Early's Raid on Washington 1864* (Tuscaloosa: The University of Alabama Press, 1989), 109-110.

2. Martin D. Hardin to Joseph H. Taylor, 19 July 1864, *ORA*, Ser. I, Vol. 37, Part 1, 236; J. M. Warner to R. Chandler, 18 July 1864, *ORA*, Ser. I, Vol. 37, Part 1, 239-240; J. M. Warner to Martin D. Hardin, 12 July 1864, 9.35 a.m., *ORA*, Ser. I, Vol. 37, Part 2, 240; Brett W. Spaulding, *Last Chance for Victory: Jubal Early's 1864 Maryland Invasion* (Privately published: 210), 170.

3. Jubal A. Early, "The Advance on Washington in 1864," *Southern Historical Society Papers*, Vol. 9, Nos. 7 and 8 (July-August 1881), 306; Jubal A. Early, *War Memoirs*, Frank Vandiver, ed., (Bloomingdale: Indiana University Press, 1960 reprint), 389; Cooling, 124; Spaulding, 177; *ORA*, Ser. I, Vol. 37, Part, 215; *ORA*, Ser. I, Vol. 37, Part 1, 240.

4. J. William Jones, *Southern Historical Society Papers*, Vol. I (Richmond, Virginia: 1876), 379; J. H. Oberteuffer, Jr., and E. Hergesheimer to John G. Barnard, 21 July 1864, *ORA*, Ser. I, Vol. 37, Part 2, 415-416; J. M. Warner to R. Chandler, 18 July 1864, *ORA*, Ser. I, Vol. 37, Part 1, 240; Jubal A. Early to Robert E. Lee, 14 July 1864, *ORA*, Ser. I, Vol. 37, Part 1, 348.

5. Early, *War Memoirs*, 395; Cooling, 110.

6. N. P. Chipman to Edwin M. Stanton, 12 July 1864, *ORA*, Ser. I, Vol. 37, Part 1, 235; J. M. Warner to R. Chandler, 18 July 1864; John M. C. Marble to J. M. Warner, 16 July 1864, *ORA*, Ser. I, Vol. 37, Part 1, 241; J. A. Haskin to M. D. Hardin, 18 July 1864, *ORA*, Ser. I, Vol. 37, Part 1, 244; W. H. Hayward to J. A. Haskinse, 17 July 1864, *ORA*, Ser. I, Vol. 37, Part 1, 245; Joseph. N. Abbey to Thomas Goodwillie, 13 July 1864, *ORA*, Ser. I, Vol. 37, Part 1, 247; Montgomery C. Meigs to Joseph H. Taylor, 25 July 1864, *ORA*. Ser. I, 37, Part 1, 256; Ibid., Montgomery C. Meigs [Extract from enclosure], *ORA*, Ser. I, Vol. 37, Part 1, 259; George W. Gile to J. M. Warner, 22 July 1864, *ORA*, Ser. I, Vol. 37, Part 1, 344; Early to Lee, 14 July 1864; Cooling, 112; "The Rebel Force in Front," *Daily National Republican*, 12 July 1864, Third Edition Extra.

7. "Interesting Particulars of the Rebel Invasion," *Evening Star*, 15 July 1864.
8. "The Invasion," *Evening Star*, 12 July 1864.
9. *ORA*, Ser. I, Vol. 37, Part 1, 255; *ORA*, Ser. I, Vol. 37, Part 2, 194, 200, 202, 205; John H. Brinton, *Personal Memoirs of John H. Brinton, Major and Surgeon, U.S.V.* (New York: Neale, 1914), 279; "A Quartermaster's Regiment," *Daily National Republican*, 12 July 1864, Third Edition Extra; "Soldiers From the Hospitals," *Daily National Republican*, 12 July 1864, Third Edition Extra; "Arming the Employees," *Evening Star*, 11 July 1864; "Later," *Evening Star*, 12 July 1864; Cooling, 114;
10. "The Invasion"; "Houses Burned," *Daily National Republican*, 12 July 1864, Third Edition Extra.
11. "The President in the Field," *Evening Star*, 11 July 1864; "From the Front," *Evening Star*, 11 July 1864; Cooling, 125-126.
12. Cooling, 115; Elbert B. Smith, *Francis Preston Blair* (New York: Free Press, 1980), 172-173.
13. "Interesting Particulars of the Rebel Invasion."
14. Spaulding, 177; *ORA*, Ser. I, Vol. 37, Part 2, 215; *ORA*, Ser. I, Vol. 37, Part 137, 240; "Interesting Particulars of the Rebel Invasion."
15. "The Blair Mansion Not Burned," *Daily National Republican*, 12 July 1864, Third Edition Extra; "The Invasion."
16. "Interesting Particulars of the Rebel Invasion"; "Incidents," *Alexandria Gazette*, 14 July 1864; Spaulding, 181; *ORA*, Ser. I, Part 2, 259.
17. "From the Front"; Spaulding, 178; *ORA*, Ser. I, Vol. 36, Part 1, 245, 246: "Later."
18. "Rebels in Force at Silver Spring," *Evening Star*, 11 July 1864.
19. *ORA*, Ser. I, Vol. 37, Part 1, 231; John N. Frazee to J. A. Haskin 16 July 1864, *ORA*, Ser. I, Vol. 37, Part 1, 246; "Dismounted Cavalry," *National Tribune*, 9 August 1900; "The Fight for Fort Stevens," *National Tribune*, 22 January 1914; "Interesting Particulars of the Rebel Invasion."
20. Cooling 124; "The Invasion."
21. ORA, Ser. I, Vol. 37, Part 1, 231; John N. Frazee to J. A. Haskin 16 July 1864, *ORA*, Ser. I, Vol. 37, Part 1, 246; "Dismounted Cavalry"; "The Fight for Fort Stevens"; Spaulding, 179.
22. Spaulding, 179; *ORA*, Ser. I, Vol. 37, Part 1, 231, 246, 344.
23. Cooling, 121; "At Fort Stevens," *The National Tribune*, 2 August 1900; *ORA*, Ser. I, Vol. 37, Part 2, 208, 209; *ORA*, Ser. I, Vol. 37, Part I, 264, 265.
24. "Patriotic Regiments," *Evening Star*, 14 July 1864; *ORA*, Ser. I, Vol. 37, Part 1, 275-276; Cooling 125.
25. *ORA*, Ser. I, Vol. 37, Part 1, 275-276; Cooling 125.
26. "Later."
27. Frazee to Haskin, 16 July 1864; Gile to Warner, 22 July 1864; Cooling, 117-118, 120-121; Spaulding, 179; *ORA*, Scr. I, Vol. 37, Part 1, 231, 246, 344.
28. Cooling, 119; I. G. Bradwell, "On to Washington," *Confederate Veteran*, Vol. 36, No. 3 (March 1928), 95.
29. *ORA*, Ser. I, Vol. 37, Part 1, 238, 241, 344.
30. *ORA*, Ser. I, Vol. 37, Part 2, 208, 209; *ORA*, Ser. I, Vol. 37, Part 1, 264, 265, 273, 275-276; "The Fight for Fort Stevens"; "The Invasion"; "Casualties," *Daily National Republican*, 12 July 1864, Third Edition Extra."
31. "State of the Thermometer," *Evening Star*, 11 July 1864.
32. "The Invasion."
33. "The Probable Time for a Fight," *Evening Star*, 11 July 1864.
34. Spaulding, 180; Johnson, "Riding a Raid," 53; Jubal A. Early, *War Memoirs*, Frank Vandiver, ed. (Bloomington: Indiana University Press, 1960), 392.

39. Just to Show What We Could Do

1. C. H. Cawood to W. N. Barker, 12 July 1864 (forwarded to General Bragg), *ORA*, Ser. I, Vol. 40, Part I3, 769.
2. "The Navigation on the River," *Evening Star*, 11 July 1864.
3. Brett W. Spaulding, *Last Chance for Victory: Jubal Early's 1864 Maryland Invasion* (Privately published: 2010), 149; *ORN*, Ser. I, Vol. 5, 458-460, 464; *ORN*, Ser. I. Vol. 10, 260; *ORN*, Ser. II, Vol. 1, 138, 145, 188, 196, 130-131.
4. *ORA*, Ser. I, Vol. 37, Part 1, 259, 232.
5. "Official," *Evening Star*, 13 July 1864.

6. Jubal A. Early, *War Memoirs*, Frank Vandiver, ed. (Bloomington: Indiana University Press, 1960), 392.

7. Benjamin Franklin Cooling, *Jubal Early's Raid on Washington 1864* (Tuscaloosa: The University of Alabama Press, 1989), 136.

8. Ibid., 139.

9. Cooling 137-38, *ORA*, Ser. I, Vol. 37, Part 2, 232, 238, 242, 246, 247.

10. Cooling, 140; G. W. Nichols, *A Soldier's Story of His Regimen (Sixty-First Georgia) and Incidentally of the Lawton-Gordon-Evans Brigade Army of Northern Virginia* (Kennesaw, Ga.: 1898. and: Continental Book Company, 1961 edition) (Jessup, Ga.: 1890), 172.

11. Cooling 137-138; *ORA*, Ser. I, Vol. 37, Part 2, 232, 238, 242, 246, 247; "The Charge of the Rebels Last Night. They Are Driven a Mile and a Half," *Evening Star*, 13 July 1864.

12. "The Charge of the Rebels Last Night."

13. Ibid.

14. "The Fighting Near Fort Stevens," *Evening Star*, 13 July 1864.

15. Ibid.

16. Bradley T. Johnson, "Riding a Raid in July, 1864," in Edwin W. Beitzell, *Point Lookout Prison Camp for Confederates* (Leonardtown, Md.: Privately Printed, 1972), 53.

17. Ibid., 532; William Painter to Ulysses S. Grant, 12 July 1864 (received 13 July), *ORA*, Ser. I, Vol. 37, Part 2, 234-235; "Affairs on the Railroad-Fighting Near Bladensburg," *Evening Star*, 13 July 1864; George S. Koontz to Edwin M. Stanton, 12 July 1864 (received 8:45 p.m.), *ORA*, Ser. I, Vol. 37, Part 2, 225; "Incidents," *Alexandria Gazette*, 14 July 1864; Harry Wright Newman, *Maryland and the Confederacy* (Annapolis: Privately published, 1976), 305, 306, 309; Cooling, 171.

18. Abraham Lincoln Testimony Concerning Shelling of Houses Near Fort Stevens, 10 October 1864, Forty-eighth Congress, House of Representatives Collection, Box 162, RG 233, NARA.

19. See fullest account of various interpretations of Lincoln at Fort Stevens in John H. Cramer, *Lincoln Under Fire: The Complete Account of His Experience During Early's Attack on Washington* (Baton Rouge: Louisiana Sate University Press, 1948), and Abel A. Safford, "Saw Lincoln at Fort Stevens," *The National Tribune*, April 4, 1912; Cooling, 141, 143-144.

20. "The Charge of the Rebels Last Night."

21. "Affairs on the Railroad," *Evening Star*, 13 July 1864.

22. Cooling, 138; *ORA*, Ser. I, Vol. 37, Part 1, 234-234, 240, 250, 255-259, 271-272; Part 2, 224-225; H. W. Halleck to Christopher Augur, 12 July 1864, *ORA*, Ser. I, Vol. 37, Part II, 225-229.

23. "The Fighting Near Fort Stevens," *Evening Star*, 13 July 1864.

24. Cooling, 145; S. A. McDonald, "Fort Stevens Affair, Part 1," *The National Tribune*, 12 April 1894; Part 2, *The National Tribune*, 19 April 1894; Milton Evans, "Fort Stevens," *The National Tribune*, 30 March 1916; John D. Shuman, "War at Fort Stevens," *The National Tribune*, 7 March 1912; Edward H. Fuller, "Fort Stevens," *The National Tribune*, 22 July 1915; *ORA*, Ser. I, Vol. 37, Part 1, 232, 242, 244, 246, 247, 276-277, 348-349; *ORA*, Ser. I, Vol. 43, Part 1, 60; Frederick David Bidwell, *History of the Forty-Ninth New York Volunteers* (Albany: J. B. Lyon, 1916), 64-65; Cooling, 146-147.

25. "The Charge of the Rebels Last Night"; Daniel H. Bee, "Wounded at Fort Stevens," *The National Tribune*, 11 April 1912; George S. Orr, "Death of Colonel Viscscher," *The National Tribune*, 28 June 1894; Cooling, 148-149; "Prisoners Captured Yesterday," *Evening Star*, 13 July 1864. "The Fighting Last Night," *Evening Star*, 13 July 1864, states that many of the rebels captured belonged to the 22nd and 43rd North Carolina regiments. As there was no 22nd North Carolina Regiment engaged, the error may have been typographical and meant the 32nd, a unit that was present.

26. "The Fighting Last Night"; Cooling, 150. Early declared his losses to be eighty men, most having fallen on July 12. Later casualty estimates were placed at 400 Union, and 200 to 300 Confederates.

27. Johnson, "Riding a Raid," 53.

28. "The Charge of the Rebels Last Night."

29. Ibid.

30. "The Rebel Wounded-What They Say," *Evening Star*, 14 July 1864; Cooling, 178.

31. "Interesting Particulars of the Rebel Invasion," *Evening Star*, 15 July 1864.

32. "The Rebels Have Disappeared from Our Front," *Evening Star*, 13 July 1864; [39] "The Invasion"; "Affairs on the Railroad," *Evening Star*, 13 July 1864; "The Rebels Leave Bladensburg," *Evening Star*, 13 July 1864.

33. *ORA*, Ser. I, Vol. 37, Part 1, 252, 260, 267-268, 280; Newman, 269, 270.

34. *ORA*, Ser. I, Vol. 37, Part 1, 232, 259, 265-266, 267; Ser. I, Vol. 37, Part 2, 233, 258, 259, 260, 261, 284, 285, 291, 350.
35. Harry Wright Newman, *Maryland and the Confederacy* (Annapolis: Privately published, 1976), 270.
36. "The Rebel Inversion," *Evening Star*, 14 July 1864.
37. Spaulding, 189; "The Rebels Have Disappeared from Our Front"; "The Rebel Inversion," *Evening Star*, 14 July 1864; "The Rebel Wounded-What They Say."
38. "Precautionary Measures," *Evening Star*, 13 July 1864.
39. "The Rebel Inversion."
40. Ibid.
41. "Incidents," *Alexandria Gazette*, 14 July 1864.
42. Ibid.
43. "The Rebel Inversion." Union reports, relying upon accounts from the rebel wounded being held as prisoners, tended to greatly inflate the number of sympathizers recruited or impressed. One report stated Johnson had raised about 200 men in Frederick while Gilmor had secured 1,500 men on his ride around Baltimore, a number equal to Johnson's whole force! "The Rebel Wounded-What they Say," *Evening Star*, 14 July 1864.
44. "Interesting Particulars of the Rebel Invasion," *Evening Star*, 15 July 1864.
45. "Arrival of Gunboats," *Evening Star*, 14 July 1864.
46. "Diary and Other accounts of Prison Life. The Diary of Bartlett Yancey Malone," in Edwin W. Beitzell, *Point Lookout Prison Camp for Confederates* (Leonardtown, Md.: Privately Printed, 1972), 59.
47. "The Diary of Charles Warren Hutt, of Westmoreland County, Virginia (Kept While a Prisoner of War at Point Lookout, Maryland – 1864)," in Edwin W. Beitzell, *Point Lookout Prison Camp for Confederates* (Leonardtown, Md.: Privately Printed, 1972), 77.
48. F. A. Parker to Gideon Welles, 14 July 1864 (received 10:40 p.m.), *ORN*, Ser. I, Vol. 5, 464; Malone Diary, 59; Hutt Diary, 77; C. W. Jones, "In Prison At Point Lookout," in Edwin W. Beitzell, *Point Lookout Prison Camp for Confederates* (Leonardtown, Md.: Privately printed, 1972), 92.
49. Ulysses S. Grant to Henry Halleck, 14 July 1864 (received 7:30 a.m., 15 July), *ORA*, Ser. I, Vol. 37, Part 2, 301.
50. Edward Hooker to Foxhall A. Parker, 19 July, 1864, *ORN*, Ser. II, Vol. 5, 467; M. S. Stuyvesant to Gideon Welles, 18 July 1864 (received 6:10 p.m.), *ORN*, Ser. II, Vol. 5, 467; Gideon Welles, Samuel P. Lee, 18 July 1864, 10 p.m., *ORN*, Ser. I, Vol. 10, 281; Samuel P. Lee to B. F. Sands, 19 July 1864, *ORN*, Ser. I, Vol. 10, 287-288; Samuel P. Lee, to O. S. Glisson, 19 July 1864, *ORN*, Ser. I, Vol. 10, 28; Spaulding 154.
51. *Daily National Republican*, 22 July 1864, Second Edition, Extra.
52. William Hoffman to J. A. Hardie, 27 July 1864, *ORA*, Ser. II, Vol. 7, 502; *ORA*, Ser. III, Vol. 5, 169; "Point Lookout," *The Western Democrat*, 26 July 1864.
53. *The Star of the North*, 20 July 1864.

40. A Convention of Maryland

1. A. W. Bradford to A.C. Gibbs, 17 December 1862, *Executive Letter Book*, MDA, reprint in *Maryland Voices of the Civil War*, Charles W. Mitchell, ed. (Baltimore; The Johns Hopkins University Press, 2007), 385; Charles V. Clark, "The Civil War," in *The Old Line State: A History of Maryland*, Morris L. Radoff, ed. (Annapolis: Publication No. 16, Hall of Records Commission, State of Maryland, 1971), 91; Charles Francis Stein, *A History of Calvert County, Maryland* (Baltimore; Published by the author in cooperation with the Calvert County Historical Society, 1976), 180; Harold R. Manakee, *Maryland in the Civil War* (Baltimore: Maryland Historical Society, 1961), 59-60.
3. Proceedings and Debates of the 1864 Constitution of Maryland, CIII, 3, MDA.
4. *Weekly National Intelligencer*, 28 April 1864.
5. Proceedings and Debates, 6, 8.
6. Regina Combs Hammett, *History of St. Mary's County Maryland* (Ridge, Md.: Privately published, 1977), 306; *Port Tobacco Times*, 10 June 1847; 18 March 1848; 29 May 1850; 23 June 1852; 1 April 1858.
7. Hammett 107, 108; *Port Tobacco Times*, 22 November 1860.
8. *Weekly National Intelligencer*, 28 April 1864.
9. Proceedings and Debates, 250-255.
10. Ibid.
11. H. F. Dorton to Foxhall A. Parker, 25 July 1864, *ORN*, Ser. I, Vol. 5, 469-470.

12. H. W. Halleck to James A. Barnes, 12 August 1864, 3 p.m., *ORA*, Ser. I, Vol. 43, Part 1, 778.
13. *ORA*, Ser. I, Vol. 43, Part 1, 637.
14. Ibid.
15. Ibid.
16. *St. Mary's Gazette*, 1 September 1864.
17. Ibid.
18. L[emuel] Wilmer to [William R.] Whittingham, 11 September 1864, MDA, reprint in *Maryland Voices of the Civil War*, 351.
19. Silas Owen to Foxhall A. Parker, 3 September 1864, *ORN*, Ser. I, Vol. 5, 479-480.
20. Foxhall A. Parker to Gideon Welles, 24 September 1864, *ON*, Ser. I, Vol. 5, 482.
21. Manakee, 59-60.
22. Proceedings and Debates, 768.
23. Ibid., 612.
24. Ibid., 612-613.
25. *The New Constitution of the State of Maryland 1864* (Baltimore: Published and Printed by John Murphy & Co., 1864), 16, 40.
26. Stein, 180-181.
27. *The New Constitution*, 22; Stein 181.
28. Stein, 181.
29. Proceedings and Debates, 771.
30. Ibid., 767.
31. *The New Constitution*, 75.
32. Ibid., 74; Proceedings and Debates., 767-769.
33. "The New Constitution of Maryland," *Baltimore Sun*, 22 September 1864.
34. "The Vote on the New Constitution," *Baltimore Sun*, 4 October 1864.
35. Hammett, 126.
36. Foxhall A. Parker to Gideon Welles, 4 October 1864, *ORN*, Ser. I, Vol. 5, 484; William Tell Street to Foxhall A. Parker, 26 September 1864, *ORN*, Ser. I, Vol. 5, 484; William A. Arthur to William T. Street, [nd], *ORN*, Ser. I, Vol. 5, 484-485. Hudgins was among those credited with having captured and burned the New York ship *Alleghanian* in November 1862 near Milford Haven. W. L. Babcock to E. P. McCreay, *ORN*, Ser. I, Vol. 5, 139.
37. *CWNC*, Vol. 4, 119-120; Edward Hooker to Foxhall A. Parker, 19 October 1864, *ORN*, Ser. I, Vol. 5, 486-487; Thomas Nelson to E. Hooker, 17 October 1864, *ORN*, Ser. I, Vol. 5, 487-488.
38. Henry W. Hoffman to Abraham Lincoln, 3 October 1863, MHS.
39. Henry W. Hoffman to Abraham Lincoln, 12 October 1863, MHS.
40. Abraham Lincoln to Henry W. Hoffman, 10 October 1863, *Collected Works of Abraham Lincoln*, 9 Vols. Roy P. Basler, ed. (New Brunswick, NJ: Rutgers University Press, 1953-1955), Vol. 7, 42.
41. "The Maryland Election," *Weekly National Intelligencer*, 20 October 1864; "The Latest Returns," *Weekly National Intelligencer*, 20 October 1864.
42. "A New Constitution for Maryland," *Weekly National Intelligencer*, 3 November 1864; Charles Lewis Wagandt, *The Mighty Revolution: Negro Emancipation in Maryland, 1862-1864* (Baltimore: Maryland Historical Society, 2004), 263.
43. Ibid.
44. Roland C. McConnell, "The Black Experience in Maryland: 1634-1900," in *The Old Line State: A History of Maryland*, 419.
45. "Maryland for McClellan," *Weekly National Intelligencer*, 3 November 1864.

41. Tulip

1. "The Diary of Charles Warren Hutt, of Westmoreland County, Virginia (Kept While a Prisoner of War at Point Lookout, Maryland – 1864)," in Edwin W. Beitzell, *Point Lookout Prison Camp for Confederates* (Leonardtown, Md.: Privately printed, 1972), 82.
2. "Injury to the Tobacco Crop," *Weekly National Intelligencer*, 20 October 1864 [reprint from *St. Mary's Gazette*, nd].
3. Foxhall A. Parker to Gideon Welles, 28 October 1864, *ORN*, Ser. I, Vol., 490.
4. Foxhall A. Parker to Gideon Welles, 1 November 1864, *ORN*, Ser. I, Vol., 490-491.
5. Ibid.

6. Foxhall A. Parker to Gideon Welles, 4 November 1864, *ORN*, Ser. I, Vol., 492.

7. Donald G. Shomette, *Lost Towns of Tidewater Maryland* (Centreville, Md.: Tidewater Publishers, 2000), 230-231; Margaret Klapthor and Paul Dennis Brown, *The History of Charles County, Maryland* (La Plata, Md.: Charles County Tercentenary, Inc., 1958), 128, 129; Kim R. Kihl, *Port Tobacco: A Transformed Community* (Baltimore: Maclay & Associates, 1982), 29-30.

8. Charles B. Clark, "The Civil War," in *The Old Line State: A History of Maryland*, Morris L. Radoff, ed. (Annapolis: Publication No. 16, Hall of Records Commission, State of Maryland, 1971), 92; *Baltimore American*, November 29, 1864. See also William Frank Zorrow, "The Union Party Convention at Baltimore in 1864," in Charles Wagandt, *The Mighty Revolution: Negro Emancipation in Maryland 1862-64* (Baltimore: Johns Hopkins University Press, 1964), 254, 260-283.

9. "Letter from Point Lookout, Md.," *Raftsman's Journal*, 23 November 1864.

10. E. B. Long and Barbara Long: *The Civil War Day by Day: An Almanac 1861-1865* (Garden City, N.Y.: Doubleday & Company, Inc., 1971), 594.

11. Hutt Diary, 84.

12. Foxhall A. Parker to Navy Department, report reprinted in "The Blowing Up of the Gunboat Tulip," *Evening Star*, 15 November 1864; "The Terrible Calamite on the Lower Potomac," *Evening Star*, 14 November 1864; Hutt Diary, 84; J. M. Ellicott, "A Child's Recollections of the Potomac Flotilla," *Chronicles of St. Mary's*, Vol. 10, No. 9 (September 1960), 296.

13. *Chi Kiang #48*, 24 December 1862 in *New York Steam Register*, October 15, 1861 to October 14, 1864. *Chi Kiang* has incorrectly been identified as *Chih Kiang* in Navy Department, Office of the Chief of Naval Operations, Naval History Division, *Dictionary of American Naval Fighting Ships*, 8 Vols. (Washington: U.S. Government Printing Office, 1968), Vol. 7. *Historical Sketches-Letters T through Y*, 329, as a wooden hulled lighthouse tender built by Jowett and Company. Steven Schmidt, "Tragedy on the Potomac: History of the U.S.S. *Tulip*," Master's Thesis, East Carolina University, 1985, 4, n9.

14. "The Terrible Calamite on the Lower Potomac." See also Richard J. Smith, *Mercenaries and Mandarins, The Ever-Victorious Army in Nineteenth Century China* (New York: Kto Press, 1978), 28, 90-97. In June 1863 Ward was listed as the ship's sole owner.

15. *ORN*, Ser. II, Vol. 1, 70, 89, 226.

16. *ORN*, Ser. II, Vol. 1, 226. *Chi Kiang's* New York registry measurements and tonnage, December 24, 1862, do not correspond to those of the Navy's. The New York registry states that she was 240 ton, 100 feet 4 inches in length, 22 feet 10 inches breadth, 11 feet 5 inches depth of hold, with a loaded draft estimated at 8 feet. *Chi Kiang #48*, 24 December 1862 in *New York Steam Register*, October 15, 1861 to October 14, 1864; Schmidt, 5, n.12., n. 13, and 6; *New York Times*, 26 January 1863.

17. Gideon Welles, "Important Circular From the Navy," *Scientific American*, New Series, Vol. 20 (19 March 1864), 197; Schmidt, 10.

18. Parker to Welles, 1 April 1864, *ORN*, Ser. I, Vol. 4, 408-409; R. B. Lowry to Thomas T. Craven, 10 July 1861, *ORN*, Ser. I, Vol. 4, 573; John F. McCutcheon to A. D. Harrell, 28 November 1861, *ORN*, Ser. I, Vol. 4, 759.

19. Samuel Magaw to A. A. Harwood, 28 August 1863, *ORN*, Ser. I, Vol. 5, 323; Schmidt, 11-12; Weekly report, A. A. Harwood to Gideon Welles, 19 October 1863, *ORN*, Ser. I, Vol. 5, 367.

20. List of Stations, Edward Hooker to A. A. Harwood, 21 November 1863, *ORN*, Ser. I, Vol. 5, 374.

21. "The Terrible Calamite on the Lower Potomac," *American and Commercial Daily Advertiser*, 15 November 1864.

22. Schmidt, 9.

23. Ellicott, 296; Foxhall A. Parker to Gideon Welles, November 10, 1864, *ORN*, Ser. I, Vol. 5, 492; Hutt Diary, 84.

24. "The Terrible Calamite on the Lower Potomac"; Foxhall A. Parker to Navy Department, reprinted in "The Blowing Up of the Gunboat Tulip, *Evening Star*, 15 November 1864. The newspaper accounts list an officer named Simons as present, but neither the list of officers and crew that sailed upon *Tulip* on November 11, 1864, noted in the Paymaster's Books, nor the list of officers and men lost, indicate either a Simons or paymaster as being aboard.

25. Foxhall A. Parker to Navy Department, 15 November 1864; "The Terrible Calamite on the Lower Potomac"; Ellicott, 296.

26. R.M. Wagstaff to F. A. Parker, 12 November 1864, *Evening Star*, 15 November 1864.

27. Ibid.; John Davis to F. A. Parker, 12 November 1864, *Evening Star*, 15 November 1864.

28. Ibid.

29. "Gunboat Tulip Blown Up," *Daily National Republican*, 14 November 1864; "The Terrible Calamite on the Lower Potomac."

30. "Gunboat Tulip Blown Up."

31. Ibid.; "The Terrible Calamite on the Lower Potomac;" Wagstaff to Parker, 12 November 1864; *Baltimore Sun,* 11 November 1964.

32. "The Terrible Calamite on the Lower Potomac"; Schmidt 85, n49.

33. The Dr. Miles mentioned was probably Dr. James W. Miles from Chaptico.

34. Schmidt, 15; Ellicott, 293.

35. "The Terrible Calamite on the Lower Potomac"; "Gunboat Tulip Blown Up"; Hutt Diary, 84.

36. Ellicott, 285.

37. Philip Sheriden to F. A. Parke, 12 November 1864, *Evening Star*, 15 November 1864.

38. Schmidt, 16.

39. Ellicott, 296

40. "Navy Yard Affairs—Collision on the Potomac," *Evening Star*, 19 November 1864.

41. Ibid.

42. Schmidt, 17.

43. "The Terrible Calamite on the Lower Potomac."

42. A Melody from Lanier's Flute

1. "The Diary of Charles Warren Hutt, of Westmoreland County, Virginia (Kept While a Prisoner of War at Point Lookout, Maryland – 1864)," in Edwin W. Beitzell, *Point Lookout Prison Camp for Confederates* (Leonardtown, Md.: Privately Printed, 1972), 85.

2. "Arrival of the Officers of the Pirate Florida," *Evening Star*, 16 November 1864.

3. "Ibid.; "The Officers of the Pirate Florida," *Evening Star*, 18 November 1864.

4. John S. Short, "Sidney Lanier, Familiar Citizen," *MHM*, Vol. 35, No. 2 (June 1940), 124-125; Serma Blount, "Sidney Lanier," www.encyclopediaofalabama.org/article/h-2907, accessed June 6, 2017.

5. Ibid.

6. Pend. G. Watmough to David D. Porter, 3 November 1864, *ORN*, Ser, I, Vol. 11, 37; *ORN*, Ser. I, Vol. 11, 741; O. S. Glisson to Gideon Welles, *2* November 1864, *ORN*, Ser. I, Vol. 11, 44.

7. Glisson to Welles, *2* November 1864.

8. Short, 126; Beitzell, *Point Lookout*, 24.

9. "The First Maryland Rebel Cavalry," *Evening Star*, 23 November 1864.

10. Foxhall A. Parker to Gideon Welles, 1 January 1865, *ORN*, Ser. I, Vol. 5, 496; Parker to Welles, 19 December 1864, *ORN*, Ser. I, Vol., 495.

11. J. Barnes to C. C. Augur, 18 December 1864, *ORA*, Ser. I, Vol. 43, Part 2, 801; J. Barnes to C. C. Augur, 19 December 1864 (received 5:55 p.m.), *ORA*, Ser. I, Vol. 43, Part 2, 807.

12. Hutt Diary, 87.

13. "John Bannister Tabb," www.newadvent/cathen/14423c.htm, accessed June 14, 2017.

14. Ibid., *CWNC*, 4:70; Short, 126.

15. Gideon Welles to Foxhall A. Parker, 9 January 1865, *ORN*, Ser. I, Vol. 5, 499, [Enclosure in R. J. Kimball to William H. Seward, 3 January 1865], *ORN*, Ser. I, Vol. 5, 499.

16. Ibid.

17. *ORN*, Ser. II, Vol. 1, 193; Gideon Welles to Guert Gansevoort, 30 July 1864, *ORN*, Ser. I, Vol. 5, 472; Foxhall A. Parker to G. V. Fox, 4 January 1865, *ORN*, Ser. I, Vo. 5, 497; Foxhall A. Parker to Gideon Welles, 4 January 1865, *ORN*, Ser. I, Vol. 5, 497.

18. Gideon Welles to A. H. Kilty, 6 January 1865, *ORN*, Ser. I, Vol. 5, 498; Welles to Kilty, 9 January 1865, *ORN*, Ser. I, Vol. 5, 500; Gideon Welles to F. A. Parker, 9 January 1865, *ORN*, Ser. I, Vol. 5, 501.

19. A. H. Kilty to Gideon Welles, 9 January 1865, *ORN*, Ser. I, Vol. 5, 500.

20. James Barnes to William Tell Street, 26 January 1865, *ORN*, Ser. I, Vol. 5, 505.

21. Ibid.; James Taylor to William Tell Street, 26 January 1865, *ORN*, Ser. I, Vol. 5, 504; Willoughby Newton to James A. Seddon, 9 March 1864, *ORA*, Ser. I, Vol. 51, Part 2, 830.

22. John S. Mosby, *The Memoirs of Colonel John S. Mosby*, Charles Wells Russell, ed. (Boston: Little, Brown, and Company, 1917), 353.

43. They Intend Depredations

1. Report of Captain Thaddeus Fitzhugh, Fifth Virginia Cavalry, *ORA*, Ser. I, Vol. 45, Part 1, 1305-1306.
2 Ibid., 1306.
3. Ibid.
4. Edward Hooker to Foxhall A. Parker, 19 February 1865, *ORN*, Ser. I, Vol. 5, 509; Hooker to Parker, 20 February 1865, *ORN*, Ser. I, Vol. 5, 510; Foxhall A. Parker to Gideon Welles, 25 February 1865, *ORN*, Ser. I, Vol. 5, 510-511.
5. Thomas Nelson to Edward Hooker, 25 February 1865, *ORN*, Ser. I, Vol. 5, 511.
6. W. W. Morris to H. W. Halleck, 26 February 1865, 8.30 p.m., *ORA*, ser. I, Vol. 46, Part 2, 715; Edwin M. Stanton to James Barnes, 26 February 1865, 9 p.m., *ORA*, Ser. I, Vol. 46, Part 2, 715.
7. F. A. Parker to G. Welles, 26 February 1865, *ORN*, Ser. I, Vol. 5, 512; Edward Hooker to F. A. Parker, 1 March 1865, 1 p.m., *ORN*, Ser. I, Vol. 5, 516.
8. Hooker to Parker, 1 March 1865.
9. Edward Hooker to F. A. Parker, 5 March 1865, *ORN*, Ser. I, Vol. 5, 518-519.
10. Foxhall A. Parker to Gideon Welles, 5 March 1865, *ORN*, Ser. I, Vol. 5, 520-521.
11. Foxhall A. Parker to Edward Hooker, 6 March 1865, *ORN*, Ser. I, Vol. 5, 522.
12. Foxhall A. Parker to Gideon Welles, 10 March 1865, *ORN*, Ser. I, Vol. 5, 523; Edward Hooker to Foxhall A. Parker, 8 March 1865, *ORN*, Ser. I, Vol. 5, 523-524.
13. Edward Hooker to Foxhall A. Parker, 14 March 1865, *ORN*, Ser. I, Vol. 5, 527-528; J. H. Eldridge to Edward Hooker, 15 March 1865, *ORN*, Ser. I, Vol. 5, 529; George W. Hyde to Edward Hooker, 15 March 1865, *ORN*, Ser. I, Vol. 5, 530.
14. T. H. Eastman to Foxhall A. Parker, 18 March 1865, *ORN*, Ser. I, Vol. 5, 535.
15. Ibid.
16. Ibid.
17. Ibid.
18. Ibid.
19. Ibid.
20. Ibid., 536.
21. Ibid, 535-536.
22. Ibid.
23. Foxhall A. Parker to Gideon Welles, 29 April 1865, *ORN*, Ser. I, Vol. 5, 536-537.
24. Fitzhugh Report, 1306-1307.
25. Edward Hooker to Foxhall A. Parker, 3 April 1865, *ORN*, Ser. I, Vol. 5, 541.
26. *CWNC*, Vol. 3, 162-163.
27. Ibid., Vol. 4, 116.
28. C. H. Wells to Foxhall A. Parker, 4 April 1865, *ORN*, Ser. I, Vol. 5, 540-541; William H. Seward to Charles Francis Adams, No. 1481, 20 July 1865, *Correspondence concerning claims against Great Britain transmitted to the Sect. of the United States in Answer to the Resolutions of December 4 and 10, 1867, and of May 27, 1868,* (Washington: Government Printing Office, 1869), Vol. 4, 350. The *Baltimore Sun,* 6 April 1865, states the Confederates were about thirty in number.
29. Wells to Parker, 4 April 1865, *ORN*, Ser. I, Vol. 5, 541. The capture of *St. Mary's* was termed by the Baltimore press as a serious loss to Captain Howard, who was part owner of the vessel. "Messrs. Freeland Hall & Co., of this city, lost a lot of goods valued at $350, which had shipped to St. Mary's county by the *St. Mary's.*" *Baltimore Sun,* 6 April 1865.
30. Gideon Wells to Foxhall A. Parker, 4 April 1865, *ORN*, Ser. I, Vol. 5, 541.
31. Seward to Adams, 20 July 1865, *Correspondence*. On 10 August 1865 the United States Ambassador to Great Britain, Charles Francis Adams, requested that the British government return *St. Mary's* to her rightful owner. Six days later the Earl Lord Russell responded that the case was being referred to the "law officers of the Crown," after which *St. Mary's* disappears from the records. Charles Francis Adams to Earl Russell, 10 August 1865, *Correspondence*, Vol. 4, 350-51; Russell to Adams, 16 August 1865, *Correspondence*, Vol. 4, 351.
32. Fitzhugh Report, *ORA*, Ser. I, Vol. 45, Part 1, 1306.
33. *Merchant Steam Vessels of the United States 1780-1868*, William M. Lytle and Forrest R. Holdcamper, comp. (Staten Island, N.Y.: The Steamship Historical Society of America, Inc., 1975), 92; *Baltimore Sun,* 6 April 1865; J. H. Taylor to Foxhall A. Parker, 5 April 1865, *ORA*, Ser. I, Vol. 46, Part 3, 592;

Gideon Welles to Foxhall A. Parker, 5 April 1865, (telegram), *ORN*, Ser. I, Vol. 5, 542; Fitzhugh Report, 1307; *Dictionary of Transports and Combat Vessels Steam and Sail Employed by the Union Army 1861-1862*, Charles Dana Gibson and E. Kay Gibson, comp. 2 Vols. (Camden, Me.: Ensign Press, 1995), 1:144.

34. Fitzhugh Report, 1306.

35. The cannonading was in celebration of the capture of Richmond and Petersburg by Federal forces. The message first reached the Potomac Flotilla flagship *Don* by telegraph at 2:10 p.m., but Fitzhugh's force would not learn of the cause until the following day. Abstract log of the USS *Heliotrope*, 24 April 1864 to 12 June 1865. *ORN*, Ser. I, Vol. 5, 599.

36. Fitzhugh Report, 1306.

37. Ibid.; *Baltimore Sun*, 6 April 1865.

38. *Merchant Steam Vessels*, 96; Fitzhugh Report, 1306.

39. Fitzhugh Report, 1306-1307.

40. Taylor to Parker, 5 April 1865; *Baltimore Sun*, 6 April 1865.

41. One of the recognized men was John Turpin, son of Sewell Turpin of Worcester County, Md. He lived in Poplartown, between Newark and Berlin. The black crewman knew him by having either belonged to or worked for his father. Another of the recognized rebels was Robert Hudgins who lived somewhere about the lower part of the Haven (Milford Haven), in Mathews County, Va. Edward Hooker to Foxhall A. Parker, 13 April 1865, *ORN*, Ser. I, Vol. 5, 546.

42. Fitzhugh Report, 1307; *Baltimore Sun*, 6 April 1865.

43. Ibid.

44. Ibid. The two black witnesses to the capture reported: "They took the boat near the wharf, stopped her, blew the whistle, and the rest came on board in boats, armed with muskets, etc." Hooker to Parker, 13 April 1865.

45. Fitzhugh Report, 1307; Hooker to Parker, 13 April 1865; *Baltimore Sun*, 6 April 1865. A message reaching Colonel F. D. Sewall at Annapolis reported that *De Ford* had been captured by twenty-seven Confederates under Fitzhugh at 2 a.m. and had departed towing two government barges behind her. F. D. Sewell to J. H. Taylor (telegram received 9:20 a.m.), 5 April 1865, *ORN*, Ser. I, Vol. 5, 541-542; Sewall to Taylor, 5 April 1865, *ORA*, Ser. I, Vol. 46, Part 3, 590.

46. Fitzhugh Report, 1307; Hooker to Parker, 13 April 1865; *Baltimore Sun*, 6 April 1865.

47. Ibid.

48. Fitzhugh Report, 1307.

49. *Baltimore Sun*, 6 April 1865; Sewell to Taylor, 5 April 1865, *ORA*, Ser. I, Vol. 46, Part 3, 589; Thomas A. Dornin to Gideon Welles, 5 April 1865, 11:45 a.m. *ORA*, Ser. I, Vol. 46, Part 3, 588; Dornin to Welles, (telegram received 11:40 a.m.), 5 April 1865, *ORN*, Ser. I, Vol. 5, 542. The passengers aboard the *De Ford* set ashore by Fitzhugh were eventually transported to Baltimore aboard the schooner *Hiawatha*.

50. W. W. Morris to E. D. Townsend, 5 April 1865, (received 11:47 p.m.), *ORA*, Ser. I, Vol. 46, Part 3, 591.

51. Samuel B. Lawrence, by command of W. W. Morris, to Captain Vaughan or Lt. Smythe, 5 April 1865, *ORA*, Ser. I, Vol. 46, Part 3, 591; *Baltimore Sun*, 6 April 1865.

52. *Baltimore Sun*, 6 April 1865.

53. Samuel B. Lawrence to John R. Kenly, 5 April 1865, *ORA*, Ser. I, Vol. 46, Part 3, 591.

54. E. T. Nichols to David D. Porter, 5 April 1865, *ORA*, Ser. I, Vol. 46, Part 3, 588; Sewell to Taylor, Annapolis, 5 April 1865.

55. Taylor to Parker, 5 April 1865, *ORA*, Ser. I, Vol. 46, Part 3, 592; Welles to Parker, 5 April 1865, (telegram), *ORN*, Ser. I5: 542; Foxhall A. Parker to James C. Tole, 5 April 1865, *ORA*, Ser. I, Vol. 46, Part 3, 588.

56. Parker to Hooker, 5 April 1865, *ORN*, Ser. I, Vol. 5, 542-543.

57. Foxhall A. Parker to T. H. Eastman, 5 April 1865, *ORN*, Ser. I, Vol. 5, 543; Parker to Welles, 5 April 1865, 1:20 p.m., *ORN*, Ser. I, Vol. 5, 542.

58. Parker to Hooker, 6 April 1865, *ORN*, Ser. I, Vol. 5, 543-544.

59. Abstract log of the USS *Jacob Bell*, 8 March 1863 to 13 May 1865, *ORN*, Ser. I, Vol. 5, 603; Edward Hooker to Foxhall A. Parker, 7 April 1865, *ORN*, Ser. I, Vol. 5, 545; Parker to Welles, 9 April 1865, 12:30 p.m., (telegram), *ORN*, Ser. I, Vol. 5, 546.

60. Hooker to Parker, 6 April 1865, *ORN*, Ser. I, Vol. 5, 544.

61. Parker to Hooker, 6 April 6, 1865, *ORN*, Ser. I, Vol. 5, 544-545.

62. Parker to Welles, 6 April 1865, 5 p.m., (telegram), *ORN*, Ser. I, Vol. 5, 544.

63. Hooker to Parker, 7 April 1865, *ORN*, Ser. I, Vol. 5, 545.

64. Ibid.

65. Abstract log of the USS *Thomas Freeborn*, 22 March 1863 to 17 June 1865. *ORN*, Ser. I, Vol. 5, 619; Abstract log of the USS *Heliotrope*, 24 April 1864 to 12 June 1865. *ORN*, Ser. I, Vol. 5, 599.

66. Parker to Welles, 9 April 1865, 12:30 p.m., (telegram), *ORN*, Ser. I, Vol. 5, 546.

67. Parker to Welles, 7 April 1865, *ORN*, Ser. I, Vol. 5, 547.

68. Welles to Parker, 7 April 1865, *ORN*, Ser. I, Vol. 5, 547.

44. Hail to the Chief

1. David Dixon Porter, *Incidents and Anecdotes* (New York: D. Appleton & Co., 1885), 297-299.

2. "Peace! The End of the Great Rebellion," *New York Times*, 10 April 1865.

3. *Daily National Intelligencer*, 11 April 1865.

4. Elizabeth Keckley, *Behind the Scenes, or, Thirty years a Save and Four Years in the White House* (New York: G. W. Carleton, 1868, reprinted in New York: Arno Press and *New York Times*, 1868), 178.

5. Ibid.

6. George Alfred Townsend, *Katy of Catoctin: Or, the Chain Breakers; A National Romance*. (Centreville, Md.: Cornell Maritime Press/Tidewater Publishers, 1957), 489; "Booth Was Greatly Enraged," *Cincinnati Enquirer*, 21 April 1892.

7. Silas Cobb testimony, CTPitman, 84; Silas Cobb undated statement, Investigation and Trial Papers relating to the assassination of President Lincoln, RG153, M 599, R 4: 172-178.

8. Ibid.

9. Silas Cobb testimony, CTPitman, 84.

10. Ibid., 85.

11. Ibid., 84; Cobb undated statement, M 599, R 4: 172-178.

12. For excellent accounts of the plot to kidnap President Lincoln, see Michael W. Kauffman, *American Brutus: John Wilkes Booth and the Lincoln Conspiracies* (Random House: New York, 2004), 175-186, and Anthony S. Pitch, *They Have Killed Papa Dead: The Road to Ford's Theatre, Abraham Lincoln's Murder, and the Rage for Vengeance* (Hanover, NH: Steerforth Press, 2008), 44-73. See also *Daily National Intelligencer*, 18 March 1865; *Constitutional Gazette*, 18 March 1865; *Daily National Republican*, March 18, 1865 for corroboration of Lincoln's activities.

13. Asa Booth Clarke, *John Wilkes Booth: A Sister's Memoirs,* Terry Alfred, ed., (Jackson: University Press of Mississippi, 1996), 76; "Description of John Wilkes Booth, who Assassinated the President on the Evening of April 14, 1865," *Evening Star,* 17 April 1865; "The Assassination Plot. Booth's Flight," *Evening Star*, 29 April 1865

14. "The Assassination Plot. Booth's Flight," *Evening Star*, 29 April 1865.

15. Thomas Eckhart testimony, AJII, 674; William Doster summation, CTPitman, 314.

16. David Herold statement, 27 April 1865, M 599, R 4: 464; Louis Weichmann statement, 5 May 1865, M 599, R 6; George Adzerodt statement, 25 April 1865, M 599, R 3: 558; Alexander Brawner and Louis Harkins testimony, CTPitman, 153.

17. C. D. Hess, CTPitman, 99; George Wren statement, 19 April 1865, M 599, R 6.

18. Harry Cay Ford testimony, CTPitman, 99; James R. Ford testimony, CTPitman, 100-101; Pitch 85.

19. Harry Cay Ford testimony, CTPitman, 99; Harry Cay Ford testimony, JST, 1: 554; Pitch, 88; John Sleichmann testimony, CTPitman, 73.

20. 20. James Pumphrey testimony, CTPitman, 72; James Pumphrey testimony, JST, 1: 225-226; John Morris statement, 18 April 1865, M 599, R 5; John Morris testimony, CTPitman, 122 and JST, 1: 334-335; Richard Morgan testimony, CTPitman, 122; Richard Morgan statement, JST, 1: 141; W. M. Wermerskirch testimony, CTPitman, 122; H. H. Wells testimony, CTPitman, 158; Thomas Sampson statement, April 19, 1865, M 599, R 2; Richard Morgan testimony, CTPitman, 122.

21. John Deveny testimony, CTPitman, 39; Prentiss Ingram, "Pursuit and Death of John Wilkes Booth," *Century Magazine*, January 1890, 445; Pitch, 106-107.

22. Lewis Weichmann testimony, CTPitman, 113; John Surratt testimony, 1: 391.

23. John Lloyd testimony, CTPitman, 85-87.

24. Ibid., 85-86.

25. George Adzerodt statement, April 25, 1865, M 599, R 3: 558.

26. George Adzerodt undated statement read by Doster, CTPitman, 307.

27. John Matthews testimony, AJII, 782-783.

28. Charles A. Leale. "Report on the Death of President Lincoln," RG112, Records of the Office of the Surgeon General (War), entry 12: Central Office, Correspondence, 1818-1946, 1818-1890, Letters Received, Box 56, NARA; "The Assassination: Statement of an Eye-Witness," *Evening Star*, 17 April 1865; Charles S. Taft, "Last Hours of Abraham Lincoln," *The British Medical Journal*, 231 (June 1865), 569-570.

29. John Sleichman testimony, CTPitman, 73; Edman Spangler statement, 15 April 1865, M 599, R 6: 202-204; Joseph "Peanuts John" Burroughs statement, 24 April 1865, M 599, R 4: 65-70; Joseph "Peanuts John" Burroughs testimony, CTPitman, 74; Leale, "Report on the Death of President Lincoln"; Pitch, 83, 117.

30. Abraham Olin testimony, JST, 1:519; James Maddox testimony, CTPitman, 76; Edman Spangler statement, April 15, 1865, M 599, R 6: 202-204; "The Assassination: Statement of an Eye-Witness."

31. Harry Hawk interview, *Washington Post*, 10 March 1894.

32. Pitch, 103.

33. Harry Rathbone affidavit, 17 April 1865, M 599, R 6; G. W. Post, *Washington Post*, 13 November 1896.

34. Harry Cay Ford, testimony, CTPitman, 99; Harry Cay Ford, testimony, JST, 3: 554; "The Assassination: Statement of an Eye-Witness"; Leale, "Report on the Death of President Lincoln." Though some have claimed that Booth injured his leg by falling from his horse, as he later told Dr. Samuel Mudd, Booth states clearly in his diary: "In jumping broke my leg." John Wilkes Booth Diary, Ford's Theater Collection, Washington, D.C.

35. "The Assassination: Statement of an Eye-Witness"; Joseph Stewart statement, 15 April 1865, M 599, R 4: 59-62.

36. Harry Hawk interview, *Washington Post*, 10 March 1894; William Withers undated statement, M 599, R 6: 469-470; H. P. Wood undated statement on Jacob Ritterspaugh, M 599, R 6: 48-49; Jacob Ritterspaugh statement, CTPitman, 97; "The Assassination: Statement of an Eye-Witness."

37. Clara Harris affidavit, 17 April 1865, in L. C. Baker, *History of The United States Secret Service*, (Philadelphia: King & Baird, 1868, reprinted New York: AMS Press, 1973), 473.

38. John Deveny testimony, CTPitman, 39; Jacob Ritterspaugh testimony, CTPitman, 97.

39. Joseph Burrough's statement, 24 April 1865, M 599, R 4: 65-70.

40. Joseph Stewart statement, April 15, 1865, M 599, R 4: 59-63; Joseph Stewart testimony, CTPitman, 79-80.

41. Samuel Chester testimony, CTPitman, 45.

42. William E. Doster, *Lincoln and Episodes of the Civil War* (New York: G. P. Putnam's Sons, 1915) 268-269; William Bell testimony, CTPitman, 154-155.

43. George Robinson testimony, JST, 1:262; Frederick Seward testimony, JST, 1:261; Fanny Seward Diary, 14 August 1865, R 198, No. 6666, William Seward Papers, LC.

44. Fanny Seward Diary, 14 August 1865; George Robinson testimony, JST, 1: 262.

45. William Bell testimony, CTPitman, 154; George Robinson testimony, JST, 1: 261; "The Assassination. The Murderous Assault upon Mr. Seward," *The Evening Star*, 18 April 1865.

46. George Robinson testimony, 1:262; Seward Diary, 14 August 1865.

47. George Robinson testimony, 1:265; William Barnes testimony, CTPitman, 157.

48. Augustus Seward testimony, CTPitman, 156; Pitch, 127; Tullio Verdi testimony, CTPitman, 157; George Robinson testimony, JST, 1: 263.

49. William Bell testimony, 154.

50. Robinson testimony, JST, 1: 264.

51. Leale, "Report on the Death of President Lincoln"; Pitch 118.

52. Julia Shepherd to her father, 16 April 1865, *Century Magazine* (April 1909), 917; Pitch 118.

53. Pitch, 119.

54. Henry Safford account, *Boston Globe*, 12 February 1909; Keckley, 310; Leale, "Report on the Death of President Lincoln."

55. Ibid.

56. Pitch, 145-146.

57. Ibid., 129-132.

58. G. W. Pope, *Washington Post*, 13 November 1896.

59. Leale, "Report on the Death of President Lincoln."

60. Ibid.; Taft, 569-570.

61. Leale, "Report on the Death of President Lincoln."

62. Edwin Stanton to Charles Francis Adams, 15 April 1865, Edwin Stanton Papers, LC.

63. Elizabeth Blair to Philip Blair, 14 April 1865, in Virginia Jean Lucas, *Wartime Washington: Civil War Letters of Elizabeth Blair* (Urbana and Chicago: University of Illinois Press, 1991), 494; *Daily Morning Chronicle*, April 15, 1865; George Koontz testimony, JST, 1:524; Henry W. Halleck to James Barnes, 15 April 1865, 2.15 a.m., *ORA*, Ser. I, Vol. 46, Part 3, 769; Pitch, 137.

64. Polk Gardiner testimony, CTPitman, 85; Polk Gardiner undated statement, M 199, R 4: 345-347, NARA.

65. John Lee statement, 16 April 1865, M 619, R 456: 473-476; Robert Jones testimony, CTPitman, 144; Lyman Sprague testimony, JST, 3:3 24.

66. Simon J. Martenet, *Atlas of Prince George's County, Maryland 1861: Adapted from Martinet's Map of Prince George's County, Maryland* (Prince George's County Historical Society: Riverdale, Md., 1995), 19.

67. John Lloyd statement, CTPitman, 86; John Surratt Lecture, Rockville, Maryland, 6 December 1870, *Evening Star*, 7 December 1870.

68. John Lloyd testimony, CTPitman, 86; John Lloyd statement, 22 April 1865, box 92, Joseph Holt Papers, LC.

69. Ibid.

70. Samuel Mudd undated statement, M 599, R 5: 227-239; Samuel Mudd statement, 22 April 1865, M 599, R 5: 213-225.

71. Ibid.

72. Ibid.; Swanson, 99.

73. William E. Doster, *Lincoln and Episodes of the Civil War* (New York: G. P. Putnam's Sons, 1915) 268-269; Charles Leale to Benjamin Butler, Charles A. Leale Papers, LC; Leale, "Report on the Death of President Lincoln."

74. Taft, "Lincoln's Last Hours" 635.

45. A Man Named Booth

1. Louis J. Weichmann, *A True History of the Assassination of Abraham Lincoln and the Conspiracy of 1865*, Floyd E. Risvold, ed. (New York: Alfred A. Knopf, 1975), 175.

2. Weichmann, 176; John Clarvoe testimony, JST, 1:697.

3. Anthony S. Pitch, *"They Have Killed Papa Dead!": the Road to Ford's Theatre, Abraham Lincoln's Murder, and the Rage for Vengeance* (Hanover, NH: Steerforth Press, 2008), 205.

4. Louis Weichmann statement, CIPit, 114, 117; Samuel Mudd statement, 8 August 1865, in Clara Elizabeth Laughlin, *The Death of Lincoln: The Story of Booth's Plot, His death and the penalty* (New York: Doubleday, Page & Co., 1909), 216; John Surratt Lecture, Rockville, Maryland, 6 December 1870, *Evening Star*, 7 December 1870; Eliza Holahan testimony, CTPitman, 133; John Lloyd testimony, CTPitman, 86; Pitch, 54, 61.

5. C. C. Augur to John P. Slough, 15 April 1865, 4 a.m. *ORA*, Ser. I, Vol. 46, Part 3, 770.

6. John P. Slough to C. C. Augur, 15 April 1865, 5 a.m. (received 5:20 a.m.), *ORA*, Ser. I, Vol. 46, Part 3, 770; David R. Clendenin to C. I. Wickersham, 16 April 1865, *ORA*, Ser. I, Vol. 46, Part 3, 802; John Nicholson to Charles I. Wickersham, 17 April 1865, *ORA*, Ser. I, Vol. 46, Part 3, 819; J. H. Taylor to James Barnes, 15 April 1865, *ORA*, Ser. I, Vol. 46, Part 3, 769.

7. James Barnes to Henry W. Halleck, 15 April 1865 (received 11:20 a.m.), *ORA*, Ser. I, Vol. 46, Part 3, 769; Henry W. Halleck to James Barnes, 15 April 1865, 2.15 a.m., *ORA*, Ser. I, Vol. 46, Part 3, 769; James Barnes to J. H. Taylor, 15 April 1865 (received 11:40 a.m.), *ORA*, Ser. I, Vol. 46, Part 3, 770; Ulysses S. Grant to Edward O. Ord, 18 April 1865, 10:30 a.m. *ORA*, Ser. I, Vol. 46, Part 3, 825.

8. "The Assassination Plot. Booth's Flight," *Evening Star*, 29 April 1865; John Lloyd testimony, CTPitman, 87.

9. David Dana testimony, CTPoore, 2:68.

10. Samuel Mudd undated statement, M 599, R 5: 213, 225, 227-239, NARA; George Mudd testimony, CTPitman 211; David Dana testimony, CTPoore, 2:68.

11. Ibid.

12. David Dana testimony, CTPoore, 2: 68; George Mudd testimony, CTPoore, 211; E. D. R. Bean, CTPoore, 211; Kauffman, 243. See Kauffman, 449, n.1, for rumors circulating in Bryantown

concerning the identity of the assassin at the time of Mudd's visit..

13. John Hardy testimony, CTPoore, 3: 432 and CTPitman, 228; Frances Farrell testimony, CTPitman 218-219; "The Conspiracy Trials," Testimony of Mr. Farrell, *Evening Star*, 8 June 1865. The diversion from the main road was undoubtedly undertaken to throw off any possible trackers.

14. Samuel Mudd statement, 22 April 1865, M 599, R 5: 213-225.

15. Electus Thomas statement, 21 April 1865, M 599, R 6: 377-379

16. Oswald Swann undated statement, M 599, R 6: 228-229; Oswald [Oscar] Swann statement, 13 May 1865, by acquaintance Joseph Padgett, M 599, R 6: 25; Joseph Padgett statement, M 599, R 6: 15.

17. Booth and Herold arrived at the Cox farm on Easter Sunday between midnight and 4 a.m. Cox claimed 4 a.m. Swann, in his testimony, said midnight. Thomas A. Jones, *J. Wilkes Booth: An Account of His Sojourn in Southern Maryland after the Assassination of Abraham Lincoln.* (Chicago: Laird & Lee Publishers, 1893), 71; Oswald Swann undated statement, M 599, R 6: 228-229.

18. Jones, 71-72; George Alfred Townsend, "How Wilkes Booth Crossed the Potomac," *Century Magazine* Vol. 27, No. 6 (April 1884), 828.

19. Jones, 72. Cox later denied that he let the strangers in because "I heard the news that night of the tragedy in Washington." Samuel Cox, Sr. statement, 28 April 28 1865, Box 92, Joseph Holt Papers, LC.

20. Oswald Swann undated statement, M 599, R 6: 228-229.

21. The location of Booth and Herold's hiding place was given by Thomas Jones in 1889 as "about two hundred yards south of the present village of Cox Station, which is five miles from Pope's Creek, the southern terminus of the Baltimore and Potomac Railroad. An Englishman named Collis, now occupies a house built upon the exact spot where I first be-held the fugitives." Jones, 74.

22. Montgomery C. Meigs to R. M. Newport, 16 April 1865, 8:30 p.m. *ORA*, Ser. I, Vol. 46, Part 3, 806.

23. R. M. Newport to Montgomery C. Meigs, 17 April 1865, 1 p.m., *ORA*, Ser. I, Vol. 46, Part 3, 821.

24. Foxhall A. Parker to Gideon Welles, 23 April 1865, *ORN*, Ser. I, Vol. 5, 558-559.

25. Log of USS *Cactus* May 4, 1864 - May 26, 1865, extract transcript, Tongue Family Collection, Calvert Marine Museum, Solomons, Md.

26. Oswald Swann undated statement, M 599, R 6: 228-229.

27. Jones, 73.

28. Ibid., 65-66.

29. Ibid., 68-69.

30. Ibid., 71, 72-73, 83-84.

31. Ibid., 73.

32. Ibid., 72-74.

33. Ibid., 74, 77.

34. Ibid., 77-78, 80.

35. Townsend, 829; Jones 79-80.

36. Jones, 80.

37. Gideon Welles to Thomas Eastman, 22 April 1865, *ORA*, Ser. I, Vol. 46, Part 3, 902; C. C. Augur to Foxhall A. Parker, 22 April 1865, *ORA*, Ser. 1, Vol. 46, Part 3, 903.

38. Edward F. O'Brien to J. M. Brown, 16 April 1865 (received 6:10 a.m. 17 April), *ORA*, Ser. I, Vol. 46, Part 3, 801.

39. James Barnes to Sylvanus Nickerson, April 17, 1865, *ORA*, Ser. I, Vol. 46, Part 3, 820.

40. James Barnes to C. C. Augur, 17 April 1865 (received 8:45 p.m.), *ORA*, Ser. I, Vol. 46, Part 3, 819-820.

41. Barnes to Nickerson, 17 April 1865.

42. J. H. Eldridge to W. A. Arthur, 17 April 1865, *ORN*, Ser. I, Vol. 5, 555-56; Gideon Welles to Commanding Officer of Naval Force, Hampton Roads, Va., 17 April 1865, *ORN*, Ser. I, Vol. 5, 556.

43. John M. Waite to J. H. Taylor, 20 April 1865 (received 9:30 a.m.); John M. Waite, to J. H. Taylor, 20 April 1865 (received 8:25 p.m.), *ORA*, Ser. I, Vol. 46, Part 3, 870.

44. J. H. Taylor to John M. Waite, 17 April 1865, *ORA*, Ser. I, Vol. 46, Part 3, 818-819.

45. Henry Smith testimony, CTPitman, 121-122, and JST, 1: 331-332

46. Ibid., CTPitman, 122 and JST, 1: 334-335; Richard Morgan testimony, CTPitman, 122; Richard Morgan statement, JST, 1:141; W.M. Wermerskirch testimony, CTPitman, 122; H. H. Wells testimony, CTPitman, 158; Thomas Sampson statement, April 19, 1865, M 599, R 2; Richard

Morgan testimony, CTPitman, 122.

47. William E. Doster, *Lincoln and Episodes of the Civil War* (New York: G. P. Putnam's Sons, 1915), 269; Henry Smith testimony CTPitman, 121- 122 and JST, 1: 333.

48. Henry Smith testimony CTPitman, 121- 122 and JST, 1: 333; W. M. Wermerskirch testimony, CTPitman, 123.

49. William H. Bell testimony, CTPoore, 1: 477-478.

50. Log of *Saugus*, April 17, 1865, Records of the Bureau of Naval Personnel, RG24, NARA.

51. Augustus Seward testimony, CTPoore, 2:9.

52. H. H. Wells interrogation of Mary Surratt, 17 April 1865, M 599, R 6.

53. Hawk was arrested, freed on $1,000 bail, and arrested again under suspicion. Hawk interview, *Washington Post*, March 10, 1894; Henry Hawk statement, April 14, 1865, M 599, R 7: 485-486.

54. *Saugus* log April 17, 1865; John Lee statement, 16 April 1865, M 619, R 456: 473-476; John Lee to President Johnson, 15 August 1865, M 619, R 456: 478-480; I. W. Taylor to General Morris, 17 April 1865, RG 393, Letters Received, Provost Marshal 8th Army and Middle Department, entry 2380, box 1, Part I, NARA.

55. George Mudd testimony, CTPitman, 211.

56. Alexander Lovett testimony, CTPoore, 1: 259, 264, 266-268.

57. Samuel Mudd testimony, CTPoore 2:1028; Sarah F. Mudd, Affidavit, Ewing Family Papers, LC; John F. Hardy, CTPoore, 2: 435-436.

58. Jones, 86.

59. Ibid., 86, 89; John Mathews testimony, AJII, 782-783.

60. Jones, 89; "The Assassination Plot. Booth's Flight," *Evening Star*, 29 April 1865

61. Jones, 89.

62. Townsend, 829.

63. Jones, 81-82, states, that Cox informed him that Herold had put both horses down. See also Townsend, 829. Kauffman, 259, states that Franklin Robey, Cox's overseer, followed by Herold, led the horses to the swamp and shot them because Booth's horse was too easily identifiable.

64. Jones, 89.

65. Ibid., 90, 93.

66. Ibid., 96.

67. Townsend, 830. It was undoubtedly from fear of wholesale revenge by Union authorities against any Confederates available that on April 18, 1865 the inmates at Point Lookout, "through their sergeants of divisions, passed resolutions representing the voice of 22,000 rebel prisoners, expressing their abhorrence of the assassination of the late President and their warm sympathy with the distressed family." General Barnes sent the resolutions to the War Department. *Evening Star*, 20 April 1865.

68. Secretaries of Treasury, War, Postmaster General, Interior and Attorney General to Andrew Johnson, 15 April 1865, M 175, R 223.

69. Edwin M. Stanton to Lafayette C. Baker, 15 April 1865, M 473, R 88: 1018.

70. Jones, 95-96.

71. Ibid., 98-99.

72. Ibid., 100-101.

73. Ibid., 102-105; Townsend, 829-830.

74. Jones, 106-107; Townsend, 830.

75. Jones, 107-109.

76. Ibid., 109-110.

46. In the Barn

1. *Baltimore Sun*, 24 April 1865.

2. John M Waite to J. H. Taylor, 22 April 1865, ORA, Ser. I, Vol. 46, Part 3, 899.

3. John M. Waite to J. H. Taylor, 23 April 1865, 8 p.m. ORA, Ser. I, Vol. 46, Part 3, 910-911.

4. J. H. Taylor to John M. Waite, 22 April 1865, ORA, Ser. I, Vol. 46, Part 3, 899.

5. C. C. Augur to Foxhall A. Parker, 22 April 1865, ORA, Ser. I, Vol. 46, Part 3, 903.

6. J. H. Taylor to N B. Sweitzer, 22 April 1865, ORA, Ser. I, Vol. 46, Part 3, 901.

7. Foxhall A. Parker to C. C. Augur, 22 April 1865 (received 6:50 p.m.), ORA, Ser. I, Vol. 46, Part 3, 903.

8. "Another Report: Booth Attempts to Cross the Potomac," *Evening Star*, April 20, 1865.

9. James Barnes to Edwin W. Stanton, 23 April 1865, *ORA*, Ser. I, Vol. 46, Part 3, 912-913.

10. Gideon Welles to Thomas H. Eastman, 22 April 1865, *ORN*, Ser. I, Vol. 5, 556-557; C. C. Augur to Foxhall A. Parker, 22 April 1865, *ORA*, Ser. I, Vol. 46, Part 3, Sec. 2, 816.

11. David Herold statement, 27 April 1865, M 599, R 4: 464; Thomas A. Jones, *J. Wilkes Booth: An Account of His Sojourn in Southern Maryland after the Assassination of Abraham Lincoln*. (Chicago: Laird & Lee Publishers, 1893), 111.

12. Jones, 111.

13. David Herold statement, 27 April 1865, M 599, R 4: 444, 447; David Herold testimony, PITman, 26 July 1865, PITman, 11 June 1865 appointed, PITman, 10 September 1865, PITman, 7 November 1865.

14. George Alfred Townsend, "How Wilkes Booth Crossed the Potomac," *Century Magazine*, Vol. 27, No. 6 (April 1884), 831.

15. John Wilkes Booth Diary, Ford's Theater Collection, Washington, D.C.

16. David Herold statement, April 27, 1865, M 599, R 4: 464.

17. Log of USS *Jupiter*, Bureau of Naval Personnel, RG 24, NARA.

18. Michael W. Kauffman, *American Brutus: John Wilkes Booth and the Lincoln Conspiracies* (Random House: New York, 2004), 296; Anthony S. Pitch, *They Have Killed Papa Dead: The Road to Ford's Theatre, Abraham Lincoln's Murder, and the Rage for Vengeance* (Hanover, NH: Steerforth Press, 2008), 263.

19. Elizabeth Quesenberry deposition, 16 May 1865, M 599, R 5: 557-559; Kauffman, 297.

20. Quesenberry deposition, 16 May 1865; William Tidwell, James Hall, Winfred Gaddy, *Come Retribution: The Confederate Secret Service and the Assassination of Lincoln* (Jackson: University Press of Mississippi, 1988), 431-432; Jones, 28; Pitch 265.

21. Townsend, 851; William Bryant statement, 6 May 1865, M 599, R 4: 95-97.

22. William Bryant statement, 6 May 1865, M 599, R 4: 95-97; Richard Stuart statement, May 4, 1865, M 599, R 6: 206-212.

23. Richard Stuart statement, May 4, 1865, M 599, R 6: 206-212. Booth would later write a letter to Stuart chiding him for his lack of Southern hospitality and honor, and as an insult sent a small sum of money as payment for the meal eaten.

24. William Lucas statement, M 599, R 5: 135-147.

25. *Black Diamond* was chartered as a second-class steam propeller by the U.S. Quartermasters Department for transport use from December 20, 1862 to September 30, 1863, again on December 1, 1864 for an unknown period, and for the last time on January 1, 1865 until her loss. Charles Dana Gibson and E. Kay Gibson, comp., *Dictionary of Transports and Combatant Vessels Steam and Sail Employed by the United States Army 1861-1868* (The Army's Navy Series), Ensign Press: Camden, Me., 1995, 36; *Evening Star*, 1 and 20 February 1865; *Merchant Steam Vessels of the United States 1790-1868*, William M. Lytle and Forrest R. Holdcamper, comp. (Staten Island, N.Y.: The Steamship Historical Society of America, Inc., 1975), 140.

26. *Alexandria Gazette*, 26 April, 1, 2 May, and 11 November 1865; *Evening Star*, 26 April, 1 and 11 May 1865; *Daily Ohio Statesman*, 27 April 1865; *New York Herald*, 27 April 1865; *New York Times*, 5 May 1865; *Raftsman's Journal*, 3 May 1865. The four known civilians lost on *Black Diamond* while picketing the Potomac to prevent the escape of Booth were Peter Carroll, Samuel N. Gosnell, George W. Huntington, and Christopher Farley.

27. William Lucas statement, 6 May 1865, M 599, R 5: 145-147.

28. William Rollins statement, 20 May 1865, M 619, R 457: 551-561.

29. William Jett testimony, CTPitman, 90.

30. Ibid.

31. Ibid.; Prentiss Ingraham, "Pursuit and Death of John Wilkes Booth," *Century Magazine* (January 1890), 443.

32. William Rollins statement, 20 May 1865, M 619, R 457: 551-561, and 6 May 1865, M 599, R 6-79-82.

33. William Jett statement, M 619, R 5: 94-98; William S. Jett testimony, CTPitman, 91.

34. William Jett statement, M 619, R 5: 94-98.

35. Richard Garrett letter, *New York Herald*, 12 April 1872; John Garrett affidavit, May 20, 1865, M 619, R 457: 500-525.

36. James Owens statement, 28 April, M 619, R 458: 412-415; Samuel Beckwith to Joseph Holt, 18

December 1865, M 619, R 458: 458-461; Samuel Beckwith to Thomas Eckert, 24 April 1865, *ORA*, Ser. I, Vol. 46, Part 3, 937; Pitch, 270-271.

37. Kauffman, 306

38. Everton Conger statement, 27 April 1865, M 619, R 457: 725-729.

39. Boston Corbett statement, 29 April 1865, M619, R 456: 254-262; Stanton proclamation, 20 April 1865, *ORA*, Ser. I, Vol. 46, Part 3, 847-848; Evertson Conger and Luther Baker to Edwin W. Stanton, 24 December 1865, M 619, R 455: 691-703.

40. Boston Corbett statement, 29 April 1865, M619, R 456: 254-262.

41. N. B. Sweitzer to J. H. Taylor, 25 April 1865,12m, *ORA*, Ser. I, Vol. 46, Part 3, 949; Sweitzer to Taylor, (received 2:40 p.m.), *ORA*, Ser. I, Vol. 46, Part 3, 949.

42. A. E. King to John Nicholson, *ORA*, Ser. I, Vol. 46, Part 3, 949.

43. William Jett statement, M 619, R 5: 94-98; David Herold statement, M 619, R 4: 467; William Rollins statement, 20 May 1865, M 619, R 457: 551-561.

44. David Herold statement, M 619, R 4: 467.

45. John Garrett affidavit, May 20, 1865, M 619, R 457: 500-525.

46. Ibid.

47. John Garrett affidavit, May 20, 1865, M 619, R 457: 507-509; David Herold statement, M 599, R 4: 467-469.

48. Richard Garrett statement, 20 May 1865, M 619, R 457: 500-525; Richard Garrett letter to *New York Herald*, 2 April 1872.

49. Richard H. Garrett claim in Committee of Claims, RG 233, NARA; John Garrett affidavit, 20 May 1865, M 619, R 457: 514-17; Herman Newgate affidavit, M 619, R 456: 226-228; Everton Conger testimony, CTPoore, 1: 314.

50. Luther Baker statement, M 619, R 455: 669-70; Conger and Baker to Stanton, 24 December 1865; William Rollins affidavit, 20 May 1865, M 619, 575: 551-561; Edward Doherty to J. H. Taylor, 29 April 1865, M 619, R 456: 274-284.

51. Everton Conger statement, 27 April 1865, M 619, R 455: 725-729; Boston Corbett statement, 29 April 1865, M 619, R 456: 254-262; Conger and Baker to Stanton, 24 December 1865.

52. Luther Baker statement, 27 April 1865, M 619, R 456: 274-284; Edward Doherty to J. H. Taylor, 29 April 1865, M 619, R 456: 274-284. Doherty claims both he and Rollins, who had asked to be arrested because he feared that there were so many still rebels around, remained on horseback.

53. Everton Conger testimony, CTPoore, 1: 313; Everton Conger testimony, M 619, R 455: 726; Luther Baker statement, 27 April 1865, M 619, R 455: 677.

54. John Winter statement, 29 May 1865, M 619, R 456: 229-233.

55. William McQuade statement, 29 May 1865, M 619, R 456: 237-239; David Barker statement, 30 May 1865, M 619, R 456: 244-251.

56. Andrew Wardell statement, 30 May 1865, M 619, 456: 248-251; David Barker statement, M 619, R 456: 244-251.

57. Oliver Lonky affidavit, 29 May 1865, M 619, R 456: 222-223; Edward Doherty statement, 29 April 1865, M 619, R 456: 274-284.

58. John Garrett affidavit, May 10, 1865, M 619, R 457: 515; Luther Baker statement, 27 April 1865, M 619, R 455: 666-689; Luther Baker statement, 27 April 1865, M 619, R 455: 680 Everton Conger testimony, CTPoore, 1: 314; Lewis Savage statement, M 619, R 456: 224; Oliver Lonky affidavit, M 619, R 456: 222; John Winter statement, 29 May 1865, M 619, R 456: 229; Godfrey Hoyt affidavit, M 619, R 456: 236.

59. David Herold statement, M 599, R 4: 470.

60. John Garrett affidavit, May 20, 1865, M 619, R 457: 500-525.

61. David Herold statement, M 599, R 4: 470; John Garrett affidavit, May 20, 1865, M619, R 457: 519-520.

62. Edward Doherty statement, 29 April 1865, M 619, R 456: 274-284.

63. Ibid.

64. Luther Baker statement, 27 April 1865, M 619, R 455: 666-689.

65. Everton Conger statement, 27 April 1865, M 619, R 455: 726; John Garrett affidavit, 20 May 1865, M 619, R 456: 500-252; William Garrett statement, M 619, R 457: 330-331; Everton Conger testimony, CTPoore, 1: 315; David Herold statement, 27 April 1865, M 599, 4: 470-471; Luther Baker, 27 April 1865. M 619, R 455: 680; John Winter statement, 29 May 1865, M 619, R 456: 231.

66. David Herold statement, 27 April 1865, M 599, R 4: 470-471

67. Luther Baker statement, 27 April 1865, M 619, R 455: 666-689.

68. Luther Baker statement, 27 April 1865, M 619, R 455: 681; Boston Corbett statement, 29 April 1865, M 619, R 456: 256.

69. John Garrett affidavit, 20 May 1865, M 619, R 457: 500-525.

70. Andrew Wardell statement, 30 May 1865, M 619, R 456: 274-284.

71. Baker and Dohery both later claimed to have ordered Herold to extend his hands and then pulled him out the barn door. John Garrett and Boston Corbett claimed he came out of his own accord. Edward Doherty statement, 29 April 1865, M 619, R 456: 274-284; Luther Baker statement, 27 April 1865, M 619, R 455: 666-689; John Garrett affidavit, 20 May 1865, M 619, R 457: 500-525; Boston Corbett statement, 29 April 1865, M 619, R 456: 254-262. See Everton Conger statement, 27 April 1865, M 619, R 455: 729 for Locust tree reference.

72. See Everton Conger statement, 27 April 1865, M 619, R 455: 725-729; Boston Corbett statement, 29 April 1865, M 619, R 456: 254-262.

73. Boston Corbett statement, 29 April 1865, M 619, R 456: 254-262; Joseph Barnes autopsy report to Edwin Stanton, 27 April 1865, Ford's Theater Collection; Luther Baker statement, 27 April 1865, M 619, R 455: 666-689. Garrett, who witnessed the scene, stated that when the bullet hit, Booth had raised his arms before falling. John Garrett affidavit, 20 May 1865, M 619, R 457: 500-525

74. Luther Baker statement, 27 April 1865, M 619, R 455: 666-689; Conger and Baker to Stanton, 24 December 1865; Everton Conger statement, 27 April 1865, M 619, R 455: 725-729.

75. Edward Doherty to Andrew Johnson, 23 December 1865, M 619, R 455: 769-775; Herman Newgarten affidavit, 29 May 1865, M 619, R 456: 226-228.

76. Luther Baker statement, 27 April 1865, M 619, R 455: 666-689.

77. Luther Baker statement, 27 April 1865, M 619, R 455: 666-689; Everton Conger statement, 27 April 1865, M 619, R 455: 725-729.

Epilogue

1. The site of the Old Arsenal Penitentiary is on the grounds of Fort Lesley J. McNair, Washington, D.C.

2. Edward Steers, Jr. *Blood on the Moon: The Assassination of Abraham Lincoln* (University Press of Kentucky, 2001). 213-214, 222-223.

3. Ibid., 227.

4. "The Execution," *Evening Star*, 7 July 1865.

5. For an interesting memoir of John Surratt's career, capture, trial and release, and com-mentary on the kidnapping conspiracy, see the John Surratt Lecture, Rockville, Maryland, 6 December 1870, in *Evening Star*, 7 December 1870.

6. Gideon Welles to Foxhall A. Parker, 3 May 1865, *ORN*, Ser. I, Vol. 5, 567.

7. Foxhall A. Parker to Gideon Welles, 5 May 1865, *ORN*, Ser. I., Vol. 5, 567; Foxhall A. Parker to G.V. Fox, 31 May 1865, *ORN*, Ser. I, Vol. 5, 573-574.

8. Gideon Welles to Foxhall A. Parker, 18 July 1865, *ORN*, Ser. I, Vol. 5, 576.

9. Foxhall A. Parker to the Officers and Men of the Potomac Flotilla, 31 July 1865, *ORN*, Ser. I, Vol. 5, 578.

10. *The Civil War Monitor: The American Civil War Almanac* (Penguin Press: nd.), 21.

11. For a complete muster of the 7th, 9th, 19th, and 30th Regiments, USCT, see Maryland Commission on the Publication of the History of the Maryland Volunteers During the Civil War, *History and Roster of Maryland Volunteers, War of 1861-1864* (Baltimore: Guggenheimer, Weil & Co., 1898-99).

12. Roland C. McConnell, "The Black Experience in Maryland: 1634-1900," in *The Old Line State: A History of Maryland*, Morris L. Radoff, ed. (Annapolis: Publication No. 16, Hall of Records Commission, State of Maryland, 1971), 418.

13. See Frederick H. Dyer, *A Compendium of the War of the Rebellion*, (Des Moines, Ia.: The Dyer Publishing Co., 1908), Vol. 2, for a comprehensive breakdown of casualties of U.S. Colored Troops from Maryland and their actions in the Civil War.

14. Today the site of Camp Stanton, part of the Maryland Department of Natural Resources Indian Creek Natural Resources Management Area, lies beneath an open farm field adjacent to Maryland Route 231 and just to the west of the hamlet of Benedict. It is an invisible but still archaeologically

extant site that has, with the exception of occasional relic hunting, generally escaped the ravages of urban growth and development.

15. James H. Whyte, "The Activities of the Freedmen's Bureau in Southern Maryland 1865-1870," *Chronicles of St. Mary's*, Vol. 7, No. 2 (February 1959), 287.

16. *Port Tobacco Times*, 30 December 1870; Regina Combs Hammett, *History of St. Mary's County Maryland*. (Ridge, Md.: Privately published, 1977), 128

17. *St. Mary's Gazette*, 22 May 1867.

18. "Now and Then," *St. Mary's Gazette*, 12 March 1868.

19. Edwin W. Beitzell, *Point Lookout Prison Camp for Confederates* (Leonardtown, Md.: Privately published, 1972), 41.

20. *Alexandria Gazette*, 12 and 13 May 1865; *Merchant Steam Vessels of the United States 1780-1868*. William M. Lytle and Forrest R. Holdcamper, comp. (Staten Island, N.Y.: The Steamship Historical Society of America, Inc., 1975), 156.

21. *Alexandria Gazette*, 12 May 1865.

22. "Departure of Troops," *St. Mary's Gazette*, 25 May 1865; *Alexandria Gazette*, 16 June 1865.

23. "Released Rebel Prisoners," *Evening Star*, June 16, 1865; "Point Lookout," *Evening Star*, June 19, 1865; "Point Lookout," *Evening Star*, 24 June 1865.

24. "The Prisoners at Point Lookout," *Evening Star*, 20 June 1865; *The Soldiers' Journal*, 21 June 1865; "Point Lookout," *Evening Star*, 24 June 1865; "Fortress Monroe," *Evening Star*, 27 June 1865; "Fortress Monroe," *Evening Star*, 5 July 1865.

25. "Point Lookout Nearly Clear of Rebel Prisoners," *New York Herald*, 29 June 1865.

26. "Released Rebel Prisoners," *The New York Herald*, 4 July 1865.

27. "Point Lookout," *Dayton Daily Empire*, 15 July 1865; Beitzell, 41; *ORA*, Ser II, Vol. 8, 705, 991-1002.

28. "The Secretary of State," *Evening Star*, 21 July 1865.

29. Beitzell, 41, 122, 181.

30. Julia A. King, *Archaeology, Narrative, and the Politics of the Past* (Knoxville: University of Tennessee Press, 2012, 145-145.

31. "Asylum for Disabled Soldiers and Sailors," *Daily Ohio Statesman*, 2 December 1865; "Asylum for Disabled Soldiers," *Baltimore Daily Commercial*, 2 December 1865; "Military Intelligence," *Baltimore Daily Commercial*, 14 December 1865; King, 152; "Large Sale of Government Buildings and Other Property at Point Lookout, Md." *Daily National Republican*, 29 December 1865.

32. In 1983 an underwater archaeological survey by Nautical Archaeological Associates, Inc., of Upper Marlboro, Md., along the eroding Potomac River coastline of Point Lookout, resulted in the discover of numerous inundated components of the Camp Hoffman complex. Features of a reinforced earthen fortification, dubbed in modern times "Fort Lincoln", remains of a steamboat wharf, a possible cattle slaughter or rendering site, and a wooden schooner wreck near the shore were identified. The schooner, believed to date to the late 19th or early 20th century, was laden with a number of dressed granite blocks and, when lost, is conjectured to have been engaged in delivering building material for the erection of the 1911 monument. See Donald G. Shomette, "Underwater Archaeological Reconnaissance and Resource Assessment of the Public Beach Nearshore at Point Lookout State Park, Point Lookout, Maryland. Report prepared for Maryland Department of Natural Resources, Annapolis, Md., 1983," for full account of findings.

33. Beitzell, 122-174, 184.

34. "Cape Lookout," *The Daily Exchange*, 14 April 1859.

BIBLIOGRAPHY

Manuscripts

Abraham Lincoln Papers. Library of Congress, Washington, D.C.

Abraham Lincoln Testimony Concerning Shelling of Houses Near Fort Stevens, 10 October 1864, Forty-eighth Congress, House of Representatives Collection, Box 162, RG233, National Archives and Record Administration, Washington, D.C.

Callum, Agnes Kane. Colored Volunteers of Maryland [in the] Civil War, 7th Regiment U.S. Colored Troops. Baltimore, Md.: Mullac, 1990. [Typescript], Calvert County Historical Society, Prince Frederick, Md.

Charles A. Leale. "Report on the Death of President Lincoln," Records of the Office of the Surgeon General (War), entry 12: Central Office, Correspondence, 1818-1946, 1818-1890, Letters Received, Box 56, RG112, National Archives and Records Administration, Washington, D.C.

Charles Leale Papers. Library of Congress, Washington, D.C.

Edwin Stanton Papers. Library of Congress, Washington, D.C.

Eshelman, Ralph E., Donald G. Shomette, and G. Howard Post. "Benedict, Maryland, Cultural Resource Survey and Context Study." Report prepared for the Charles County Department of Planning and Growth Management, July 2009.

Fellix Brannigan Papers, 1861-1863. Library of Congress, Washington, D.C.

Freedmen's Collection. Calvert County Historical Society, Prince Frederick, Md.

Investigation and Trial Papers relating to the assassination of President Lincoln, M599, RG153, National Archives and Record Administration, Washington, D.C.

Letters Received by Office of Adjutant General (main series), 1861-1870, MS619, RG94, National Archives and Record Administration, Washington, D.C.

Letters Received, Provost Marshal 8th Army and Middle Department, Box 1, Part I, RG393, National Archives and Record Administration, Washington, D.C.

Letterbook of U.S. Colored Troops, Office of Adjutant General, RG94, National Archives and Record Administration, Washington, D.C.

Log of USS *Jupiter*, 1865. Records of the Bureau of Naval Personnel, RG24. National Archives and Record Administration, Washington, D.C.

Log of USS *Saugus*, April 18-20, 1865. Records of the Bureau of Naval Personnel, RG24. National Archives and Record Administration, Washington, D.C.

Schmidt, Steven. "Tragedy on the Potomac: History of the U.S.S. *Tulip*," Master's Thesis, East Carolina University, 1985.

Shomette, Donald G. Underwater Archaeological Reconnaissance and Resource Assessment of the Public Beach Nearshore at Point Lookout State Park, Point Lookout, Maryland. Report prepared for Maryland Department of Natural Resources, Annapolis, Md., 1983.

Tongue Family Papers Collection. Calvert Marine Museum, Solomons, Md.

William Seward Papers. Library of Congress, Washington, D.C.

Published Documents, Letters, Papers

The Assassination of President Abraham Lincoln and the Trial of the Conspirators. Compiled and arranged by Benn Pitman. Cincinnati: Moore, Wilstach & Baldwin, 1865.

Basler, Roy P., ed.. *Collected Works of Abraham Lincoln*. 9 Vols. New Brunswick, NJ: Rutgers University Press, 1953-1955.

Berlin, Ira, ed. *Freedom: A Documentary History of Emancipation 1861-1867*. Ser. II (Book 1) *The Black Military Experience*. New York: Cambridge University Press, 1982.

Berlin, Ira, *et al. Free at Last: A Documentary History of Slavery, Freedom, and the Civil War*. New York: The New Press, 1992.

Brinton, John H. *Personal Memoirs of John H. Brinton, Major and Surgeon, U.S.V.* New York: Neale, 1914.

Congressional Globe, 1st Session, 38th Congress, Part I.

Correspondence concerning claims against Great Britain transmitted to the Sect. of the United States in Answer to the Resolutions of December 4 and 10, 1867, and of May 27, 1868. Vol. 4. Washington: Government Printing Office, 1869.

Dowdey, Clifford, ed. *The Wartime Papers of Robert E. Lee*. Boston: Bramhill House, 1961, reprinted New York: De Capo Press, 1987.

Freeman, Douglas Southall, ed. *Lee's Dispatches: Unpublished Letters of General Robert E. Lee, C. S. A. to*

Jefferson Davis and the War Department of The Confederate States of America 1862-65. New York and London: G. P. Putnam's Sons, 1915.

General William Birney's Answer to Libels Clandestinely Circulated by James Shaw, Jr., Collector of the Port, Providence, R.I., with A Review of the Military Record of the Said James Shaw, Jr., Late Colonel of the Seventh U.S. Colored Troops. Washington, D.C.: Stanley Snodgrass, Printer, 1878.

Headley, Phineas Camp. *Massachusetts in the Rebellion: A Record of the Historical Position of the Commonwealth, and the Services of the Leading Statesmen, the Military, the Colleges, and the People, in the Civil War of 1861-65*. Boston: Walker, Fuller and Co., 1866.

Jones, J. Williams. *Southern Historical Society Papers*, Vol. I. Richmond, Va.: 1876.

Lucas, Virginia Jean. *Wartime Washington: Civil War Letters of Elizabeth Blair*. Urbana and Chicago: University of Illinois Press, 1991.

Moore, Frank, ed. *The Rebellion Record: A Diary of American Events*. 12 Vols. New York, 1861-1868: Putnam and Van Nostrand.

Murder of Lieut. Eben White. Letter from the Chief Clerk of the War Department Giving Circumstances of the Murder of Lieut. Eben White by John H. and Webster Southron, *House of Representatives, 43d Congress, 1st Session, Ex. Doc. No. 281*.

The New Constitution of the State of Maryland 1864. Baltimore: Published and Printed by John Murphy & Co., 1864.

Official Records of the Union and Confederate Navies in the War of the Rebellion, 30 vols. Washington: Government Printing Office, 1894-1912.

Poore, Ben Perley, ed. *The Conspiracy Trial for the Murder of President Abraham Lincoln and the Attempt to Overthrow the Government by the Assassination of Its Principal Officers*. 3 volumes. Boston: J. E. Tilton & Co., 1865.

Proceedings and Debates of the 1864 Constitution of Maryland, *Archives of Maryland*, CIII.

Testimony of Captain Philip Reybold before the Angus Commission, Senate Document No. 215, 59th Cong., 2nd sess.: *Report of the Commissioners Appointed by the President to Examine and Report upon a Route for the Construction of a Free and Open Waterway to Connect the Waters of the Chesapeake and Delaware Bays*. Washington, D.C.: Government Printing Office, 1907.

Trial of John H. Surratt in the Criminal Court of the District of Columbia. 2 Vols. Washington, D.C.: Government Printing Office, 1867.

War of the Rebellion: A Compilation of the Official Records of the Union and Confederate Armies. 70 vols. (U.S. Government Printing Office: Washington, 1880-1901).

Books and Secondary Sources

Baker, L. C. *History of the United States Secret Service*. Philadelphia: Published by L. C. Baker, 1867, reprint New York: AMS Press, 1973.

Barbour, James M. *Alexandria in the Civil War*. Lynchburg, Va.: H. E. Howard, Inc., 1988.

Battles and Leaders of the Civil War. 4 Vols. New York and London: Thomas Yoseloff, 1956.

Beatie, Russel H. *The Army of the Potomac*. Cambridge, Ma.: De Capo Press, 2002.

Beitzell, E. W. *Life on the Potomac*. Abell, Md.: Privately published, 1968.

Beitzell, Edwin W. *Point Lookout Prison Camp for Confederates*. Leonardtown, Md.: Privately published, 1972.

Beitzell, Edwin Warfield. *The Jesuit Missions of St. Mary's County, Maryland*. Sponsored by the St. Mary's County Bicentennial Commission: Abell, Md., 1976.

Bernard, George S. *War Tales of Confederate Veteran*. Petersburg, Va.: Fenn and Owen, 1892.

Bidwell, Frederick David. *History of the Forty-Ninth New York Volunteers*. Albany: J. B. Lyon, 1916.

The Biographical Cyclopedia of Representative Men of Maryland and the District of Columbia. Baltimore, Md.: National Biographical Publishing Co., [ca. 1878].

Brewington, M. V. *Chesapeake Bay Log Canoes and Bugeyes*. Cambridge, Md.: Cornell Maritime Press, Inc., 1963.

Brown, George W. *Baltimore and the 19th of April, 1861*. Johns Hopkins University: Baltimore, 1887.

Bruce, Robert V. *Lincoln and the Tools of War*. Indianapolis: Bobbs-Merrill [1956].

Buchholz, Heinrich E. *Governors of Maryland: From the Revolution to the Year 1908*. Baltimore, Md.: Williams & Wilkins Company, 1908.

Burgess, John William. *The Civil War and the Constitution, 1859-1865*. New York: C. Scribner's Sons, 1901.

Butler, Benjamin F. *Butler's Book: A Review of His Legal, Political, and Military Careers.* Boston, A. M. Thayer: 1892.

[Califf, Joseph M.] *Record of the Services of the Seventh Regiment, U.S. Colored Troops from September, 1863, to November, 1866. By an Officer of the Regiment.* Providence, R. I.: Freeman & Co., Printers to the State, 1878. Reprint Freeport, N.Y.: Books for Libraries Press, 1971.

The Civil War Monitor: The American Civil War Almanac. Penguin Press: nd.

Civil War Naval Chronology 1861-1865. Naval History Division, Navy Department, comp. 6 vols. Washington: [U.S. Government Printing Office], 1971.

Clark, Charles B. *The Eastern Shore of Maryland and Virginia.* 3 Vols. New York: Lewis Historical Publishing Company, Inc., 1950.

Clark, Charles B. *Politics in Maryland During the Civil War.* Chestertown: 1952.

Clarke, Asa Booth. *John Wilkes Booth: A Sisters Memoirs.* Terry Alfred, ed. Jackson: University Press of Mississippi, 1996.

Cooling, Benjamin Franklin. *Jubal Early's Raid on Washington 1864.* Tuscaloosa: The University of Alabama Press, 1989.

Cooling, Benjamin Franklin III and Walton H. Owen II. *Mr. Lincoln's Forts: A Guide to the Civil War Defenses of Washington.* Shippensburg, Pa: White Mane Publishing Company, 1988.

Cramer, John H. *Lincoln Under Fire: The Complete Account of His Experience During Early's Attack on Washington.* Baton Rouge: Louisiana Sate University Press, 1948.

Crouch, Tom D. *The Eagle Aloft: Two Centuries of the Balloon in America.* Washington, D. C.: Smithsonian Institution Press, 1983.

Cudworth, Warren H[andel]. *History of the First Regiment (Massachusetts Infantry), from the 25th of May, 1861, to the 25th of May, 1864; including brief references to the operations of the Army of the Potomac.* Boston: Walker, Fuller & Co., 1866.

Dictionary of American Naval Fighting Ships. 9 vols. Navy Department, Office of the Chief of Naval Operations, Naval History Division, Washington: U.S. Government Printing Office, 1959-1991.

Dill, J. Gregory. *Myth, Fact, and Navigators' Secrets: Incredible Tales of the Sea and Sailors.* Guildford, CT: The Lyons Press, 2006.

Doster, William E. *Lincoln and Episodes of the Civil War.* New York: G. P. Putnam's Sons, 1915.

Dyer, Frederick H. *A Compendium of the War of the Rebellion.* Des Moines, Ia.: The Dyer Publishing Co., 1908.

Early, Jubal A. *A Memoir of the Last Year of the War for Independence, in the Confederate States of America, Containing an Account of the Operations of His Command in the Years 1864 and 1865.* Lynchburg, Va.: C. W. Button, 1867.

_____. *War Memoirs.* Frank Vandiver, ed. Bloomington: Indiana University Press, 1960.

Evans, Charles M. *The War of the Aeronauts: A History of Ballooning During the Civil War.* Mechanicsburg, Pa.: Stackpole Books, c2002.

Evans, Clement A. ed. *Confederate Military History: A Library of Confederate States History.* 12 Vols. Atlanta, Ga.: Confederate Pub. Co., 1899, Vol. 2.

Evertine, Carl N. *General Assembly of Maryland 1850-1920.* Charlottesville, Va.: Michie Co., 1984.

Faust, Drew Gilpin. *Mothers of Invention: Women of the Slaveholding South in the American Civil War.* Chapel Hill: University of North Carolina Press, 1996.

Fehrenbacher, Don E. and Ward M. McAfee. *The Slaveholding Republic: An Account of the United States Government's Relations to Slavery.* New York: Oxford University Press, 2001.

Fessenden, Francis. *Life and Public Services of William Pitt Fessenden,* 2 Vols. Boston and New York: Houghton, Mifflin and Company, 1907.

Field, Ron. *The Confederate Army 1861-65: Missouri, Kentucky & Maryland.* Oxford, UK: Osprey Publishing, 2008.

Finley, John H., ed. *Dictionary of American Biography.* 21 vols. New York: C. Scribner's Sons, 1931.

Freeman, Douglas Southall. *Lee's Lieutenants: A Study in Command.* 3 Vols. New York: Simon and Shuster, 1998. Reprint from C. Scribner's Sons, New York, 1942-1944

Gibson, Charles Dana, and E. Kay Gibson. *Dictionary of Transports and Combatant Vessels Steam and Sail Employed by the Union Army 1861-1868.* 2 Vols. Camden, Me.: Ensign Press, 1995.

Gillmer, Thomas C. *Old Ironsides: The Rise, Decline, and Resurrection of the USS Constitution* Camden, Me: International Marine, 1993.

Gilmor, Harry. *Four Years in the Saddle.* New York: Harper and Brothers, 1866.

Glenn, William Watkins. *Between North and South: A Maryland Journalist Views the Civil War: The Narrative of William Wilkins Glenn, 1861-1869.* Bayley Ellen Marks and Mark Norton Schatz, eds. Rutherford, NJ: Farleigh Dickinson University Press, 1976.

Goldsborough, W[illiam] W[orthington]. *The Maryland Line in the Confederate Army.* Baltimore: Kelly, Piet & Co., 1869.

Gottfried, Bradley M., *The Maps of First Bull Run.* New York and California: Savas Beatie, 2009.

Hall, James O. Hall and Gaddy, David Winifred. *Come Retribution: Confederate Secret Service and the Assassination of Lincoln.* Oxford: University Press of Mississippi, 1988.

Hammett, Regina Combs. *History of St. Mary's County Maryland.* Ridge, Md.: Privately published, 1977.

Hartzler, Daniel A. *A Band of Brothers: Photographic Epilogue to Marylanders in the Confederacy.* Westminster, Md.: Heritage Books 2008.

Harvey, Eleanor Jones. *The Civil War and American Art.* Washington, D.C.: Smithsonian American Art Museum, in association with Yale University Press, 2013.

Holland, F. Ross. *Maryland Lighthouses of the Chesapeake Bay.* Crownsville and Colton's Point, Maryland: Maryland Historical Trust Press and The Friends of St. Clement's Island Museum, Inc., 1997.

Holly, David C. *Tidewater by Steamboat: A Saga of the Chesapeake.* Baltimore and London: The Johns Hopkins University Press, 1991.

_____ *Chesapeake Steamboats: Vanished Fleet.* Centreville, Md.: Tidewater Publishers, 1994.

In a Place called Ivy Springs . . . Near the Pines: The History of St. Paul's Episcopal Church, Piney Parish. Waldorf, Md.: September 1992.

Jones, Thomas A. *J. Wilkes Booth: An Account of His Sojourn in Southern Maryland after the Assassination of Abraham Lincoln.* Chicago: Laird & Lee Publishers, 1893.

Keckley, Elizabeth. *Behind the Scenes, or, Thirty Years a Slave and Four Years in the White House.* New York: G. W. Carleton, 186 8, reprinted in New York: Arno Press and New York Times, 1868.

Kent, Michael Gayhart, *Mulatto: The Black History of Calvert County, Maryland.* Privately published: 2019.

Kihl, Kim R. *Port Tobacco: A Transformed Community.* Baltimore: Maclay & Associates, 1982.

Kimmel, Ross M. Kimmel and Musick, Michael P. *"I Am Busy Drawing Pictures" The Civil War Art and Letters of Private John Jacob Omenhausser, CSA.* Friends of the Maryland State Archives: Annapolis, Md., 2014.

King, Julia A. *Archaeology, Narrative, and the Politics of the Past.* Knoxville: University of Tennessee Press, 2012.

Klapthor, Margaret Brown, and Paul Dennis Brown. *The History of Charles County, Maryland.* La Plata, Md.: Charles County Tercentenary, Inc., [nd].

Laughlin, Clara Elizabeth. *The Death of Lincoln: The Story of Booth's Plot, His death ad the penalty.* New York: Doubleday, Page & Co., 1909.

Lewis, George G. and Mewha, John. *History of Prisoner of War Utilization by the United States Army 1776-1945.* Washington, D.C.: Department of the Army, June 1955.

Long, E. B. and Long, Barbara. *The Civil War Day by Day: An Almanac 1861-1865.* Garden City, N.Y.: Doubleday & Company, Inc., 1971.

[Lowe, Thaddeus] *Memoirs of Thaddeus S.C. Lowe, Chief of the Aeronautic Corps of the Army of the United States During the Civil War: My Balloons in Peace and War.* Michael Jaeger and Carol Lauritzen, eds. Lewiston, N.Y.: Edwin Mellen Press, c2004.

Manakee, Harold R. *Maryland in the Civil War.* Baltimore: Maryland Historical Society, 1961.

Marcus, Benjamin, coll. and ed. *Washington During War Time: A Series of Papers Showing the Military, Political, and Social Phases During 1861 to 1865.* Washington, D.C.: Washington City [Press of B. S. Adams], 1902.

Martinet. Simon J. *Atlas of Prince George's County, Maryland 1861: Adapted from Martinet's Map of Prince George's County, Maryland.* Prince George's County Historical Society: Riverdale, Md., 1995.

Maryland Commission on the Publication of the History of the Maryland Volunteers During the Civil War. *History and Roster of Maryland Volunteers, War of 1861-1864.* Baltimore: Guggenheimer, Weil & Co., 1898-99.

Maryland Slave Narratives: A Folk History of Slavery in Maryland from interviews with Former Slaves. Typewritten records prepared by The Federal Writers; Project, 1936-1938. Bedford Mass.: Applewood Books, published in Cooperation with the Library of Congress, [nd].

McCarthy, John P. *Oxon Hill Manor: The Archaeology and History of "A World They Made Together."* St. Leonard, Md. and Crownsville, Md.: Jefferson Patterson Park Museum and Maryland Historical

Trust, 2010.

McPherson, James M. *Tried by War: Abraham Lincoln as Commander in Chief.* New York: Penguin Press, 2008.

McWilliams, Jane Wilson. *Annapolis: City on the Severn.* Baltimore: The Johns Hopkins University Press, and Crownsville: The Maryland Historical Trust Press, 2011.

Merchant Steam Vessels of the United States 1780-1868. William M. Lytle and Forrest R. Holdcamper, comp. Staten Island, N.Y.: The Steamship Historical Society of America, Inc., 1975.

Miles, Nathanial A. Branch, Monday M. Miles, and Ryan J. Quick. *Prince George's County and the Civil War: Life on the Border.* Charleston and London: History Press, 2013.

Miller, Edward A. *Lincoln's Abolitionist General: The Biography of David Hunter.* Columbia: University of South Carolina Press, 1997.

Mills, Eric. *Chesapeake Bay in the Civil War.* Centreville, Md.: Tidewater Publishers, 1996.

Mitchell, Charles W., ed. *Maryland Voices of the Civil War.* Baltimore: The Johns Hopkins University Press, 2007.

Mosby, John S. *The Memoirs of Colonel John S. Mosby,* Charles Welles Russell, ed. Boston: Little, Brown, and Company, 1917.

Newman, Harry Wright. *Maryland and the Confederacy.* Annapolis: Privately published, 1976.

Nichols, G. W. *A Soldier's Story of His Regiment (Sixty-First Georgia) and Incidentally of the Lawton-Gordon-Evans Brigade Army of Northern Virginia.* n.p., 1898 and Kennesaw, Ga.: Continental Book Company, 1961 edition, Jessup, Ga.: 1890.

Nicolay, John G., and John Hay. *Abraham Lincoln: A History,* 10 vols. New York: Century, 1890.

Pitch, Anthony S. *"They Have Killed Papa Dead!": the Road to Ford's Theatre, Abraham Lincoln's Murder, and the Rage for Vengeance.* Hanover, NH: Stereforth Press, 2008.

Porter, David Dixon Porter. *Incidents and Anecdotes.* New York: D. Appleton & Co., 1885.

Quarles, Benjamin. *The Negro in the Civil War.* Boston: Little, Brown, 1969.

Radcliffe, George Lovic Pierce, *Governor Thomas H. Hicks of Maryland and the Civil War.* Baltimore: Johns Hopkins Press, 1901.

Radoff, Morris L., ed. *The Old Line State: A History of Maryland.* Annapolis: Publication No. 16, Hall of Records Commission, State of Maryland, 1971.

Reiner, Karl. *Remembering Fairfax County, Virginia.* Charleston, S.C: The History Press, 2006.

Report on the Highways of Maryland. [In Accordance with an Act Passed at The Session of the General Assembly of 1898, Laws of Maryland 1898, Chapter 454]. Baltimore, The Johns Hopkins University Press, 1899.

Riley, Elihu S. *"The Ancient City." A History of Annapolis, in Maryland. 1649-*1887. Annapolis: Record Printing Office, 1887.

Rodriguez, Junius P., ed. *Slavery in the United States: A Social, Political, and Historical Encyclopedia* 1. Santa
Barbara, Cal.: ABC-CLIO, [2007].

Ross, Fitzgerald. *Cities and Camps of the Confederate State.* Richard Barksdale Harwell, ed. Urbana, Ill.: University of Illinois Press, 1958.

Ruffin, Edmund. *The Diary of Edmund Ruffin.* William K. Scarborough, ed. Vol. 2, (Baton Rouge: Louisiana State University Press, 1976.

Sandburg, Carl. *Storm Over the Land: A Profile of the Civil War.* New York: Harcourt Brace and Company, 1942.

Scharf, John Thomas. *The Chronicles of Baltimore: Being a Complete History of "Baltimore Town" and Baltimore City from the Earliest Period to the Present Time.* Baltimore: Turnbull Brothers, 1874.

_____, *History of Maryland from the Earliest Period to the Present Day.* 3 Vols. Baltimore: J. B. Piet, 1879. Facsimile edition, Hatboro, Pa.: Tradition Press, 1967.

_____, *History of Western Maryland: Being A History of Montgomery, Carroll, Washington, Allegheny, nd Garrett Counties.* 2 Vols. Philadelphia: Louis H. Everts, 1882 and Baltimore: Regional Publishing Company, 1968 edition.

Schneider, Dorothy and Carl J. Schneider. *An Eyewitness History: Slavery in America: From Colonial Times to the Civil War.* New York, N.Y.: Facts on File, Inc. 2000.

Schwartz, Bernard. *A History of the Supreme Court.* New York: Oxford University Press, 1993.

Sears, Stephen W. *George B. McClellan: The Young Napoleon.* New York: Da Capo Press, 1988.

The Sentinel, 150th Anniversary 1864/2014. [Washington, D.C.], National Park Service, 2014.

Sheads, Scott Sumter and Daniel Carroll Toomey. *Baltimore During the Civil War.* Linthicum, Md.: Toomey Press, 1997.

Shingleton, Royce Gordon. *John Taylor Wood: Sea Ghost of the Confederacy.* Athens, Ga.: University of Georgia Press, 1979.

Shomette, Donald G. *Ghost Fleet of Mallows Bay And Other Tales of the Lost Chesapeake.* Centreville, Md.: Tidewater Publishers, 1996.

_____ *Lost Towns of Tidewater Maryland.* Centreville, Md.: Tidewater Publishers, 2000.

_____ *Maritime Alexandria: The Rise and Fall of an American Entrepot.* Heritage Book, Inc.: Bowie, Md., 2003.

Smith, Elbert. *Francis Preston Blair.* New York: Free Press, 1980.

Smith, Richard J. *Mercenaries and Mandarins, The Ever-Victorious Army in Nineteenth Century China.* New York: Kto Press, 1978.

Southern, Eileen, and Wright, Joseph, comp. *African-American Traditions in Song, Sermon, Tale, and Dance, 1600s-1920: An Annotated Bibliography of Literature, Collections, and Artworks.* New York: Greenwood Press, 1990.

Spaulding, Brett W. *Last Chance for Victory: Jubal Early's 1864 Maryland Invasion.* Privately published: 2010.

Steers, Edward, Jr. *Blood on the Moon: The Assassination of Abraham Lincoln.* University Press of Kentucky, 2001.

Stein, Charles Francis. *A History of Calvert County, Maryland.* Baltimore: Published by the author in cooperation with the Calvert County Historical Society, 1976.

Sweetman, Jack. *The U.S. Naval Academy: An Illustrated History.* 2nd ed., rev. by Thomas J. Cutler. Annapolis: Naval Institute Press, 1993.

Thomas, Benjamin P., and Harold M. Hyman. *Stanton: The Life and Times of Lincoln's Secretary of War.* New York: Knopf, 1962.

Tilp, Frederick. *This Was Potomac River.* Alexandria, Va.: Published by author, 1978.

Toomey, Daniel Carroll. *The Civil War in Maryland.* Toomey Press: Baltimore, Md., 1983.

Townsend, George Alfred. *Katy of Catoctin: Or, the Chain Breakers; A National Romance.* Cornell Maritime Press/Tidewater Publishers: Centreville, Md. 1959.

U.S. Bureau of Census. *Negro Population 1790-1915.* U.S. Government Printing Office: Washington, 1918.

Van Horn, R. Lee. *Out of the Past: Prince Georgians and Their Land.* Riverdale, Md.: Prince George's County Historical Society, 1976.

Wagandt, Charles. *The Mighty Revolution: Negro Emancipation in Maryland 1862-64.* Baltimore: Johns Hopkins University Press, 1964.

Wallace, Lew. *Lew Wallace: An Autobiography.* 2 Vols. New York: Harper and Brothers, 1906.

Warner, Ezra J. *Generals in Blue: Lives of the Union Commanders.* Baton Rouge, La.: Louisiana State University Press, 1864.

We Live Here, Too: Slavery in Prince George's County, Maryland, 1860-1864. Clinton, Md.: Surratt House Museum, nd.

Wearmouth, Roberta J. *Abstracts from the Port Tobacco Times and Charles County Advertiser,* 4 vols. Bowie, Md.: Heritage Books, 1990-1996.

Wearmouth, John M. and Roberta J. Wearmouth. *Thomas A. Jones: Chief Agent of the Confederate Secret Service.* Port Tobacco, Md.: Stones Throw Publishing, 1995.

Wills, Mary Ann. *The Confederate Blockade of Washington, D.C. 1861-1862.* Parsons, W.V.: McClain Printing Company, 1975.

Wilson, James Grant and John Fisk, eds. *Appleton's Cyclopedia of American Biography.* New York: D. Appleton and Company, 1889.

Winkle, Kenneth J. *Lincoln's Citadel: The Civil War in Washington, D.C.* New York and London, W.W. Norton & Company, 2013.

Zavodnyik, Peter. *The Rise of the Federal Colossus: The Growth of Federal Power from Lincoln to F.D.R.* Santa Barbara, Calif.: Praeger, [2011].

Articles

Apitheker, Herbert. "The Negro in the Union Navy," *Journal of Negro History,* Vol. 32 (1947).

Blassingame, John W. "The Recruitment of Negro Troops in Maryland," *Maryland Historical Magazine,*

Vol. 58, No. 1 (March 1963).

Bradwell. I. G. "On to Washington," *Confederate Veteran,* Vol. 34, No. 3 (March 1928).

Briscoe, Betty Worthington. "Know Your County," *Calvert Independent* [nd], clipping. Calvert Historical Society, Prince Frederick, Md.

Bockmiller, Stephen R. "It is Not Civilized War . . ." in *The Sentinel,* 150th Anniversary 1864/2014. National Park Service: 2014.

Calhoun, Stephen D. "Col. John Henry Southron 1807-1893," *Chronicles of St. Mary's,* Vol. 40, No. 2 (Summer 1992).

Clark, James Samuel. "A Union Army Reconnaissance Into Calvert County," *Historian.* Calvert County Historical Society: Dunkirk, Md., April 1986.

Douglas, Frederick. "The Proclamation and the Negro Army," An Address Delivered in New York, N.Y., February 6, 1863, in Kate Masur, "'A Rare Phenomenon of Philological Vegetation': The Word 'Contraband' and the Meanings of Emancipation," *Journal of American History,* Vol. 93, No. 4 (March 2007).

Duncan, Richard R. "Maryland's Reaction to Early's Raid in 1864," *Maryland Historical Magazine,* Vol. 64, No. 3 (Fall 1969).

Early, Jubal A. "The Advance on Washington in 1864," *Southern Historical Society Papers,* 7 and 8 (July-August 1881).

Earp, Charles A. "The Amazing Colonel Zarvona." *Maryland Historical Magazine,* Vol. 34, No. 4 (December 1939).

Ellicott, J. M. "A Child's Recollections of the Potomac Flotilla," *Chronicles of St. Mary's,* Vol. 10, No. 9 (September 1960).

Harris, J. Morris. "A Reminiscence of the Troublous Times of April 1861," *Maryland Historical Society Fund Publication,* No. 31. Baltimore: Maryland Historical Society, 1891.

Johnson, Bradley T. "My Ride Around Baltimore In Eighteen Hundred and Sixty-Four," *Journal of the United States Cavalry Association.* Vol. 2. Fort Leavenworth, Kansas, 1889.

Kelley, William J. "Baltimore Steamboats in the Civil War," *Maryland Historical Magazine,* Vol. 37, No. 1 (March 1942).

Lerch, Kathryn W. "Prosecuting Citizens, Rebels, & Spies: the 8th New York Heavy Artillery in Maryland, 1862-1864," *Maryland Historical Magazine,* Vol. 94, No. 2 (Summer 1999).

McConnell, Roland C. "The Black Experience in Maryland: 1634-1900," *The Old Line State: A History of Maryland,* Morris L. Radoff, ed. Annapolis: Publication No. 16, Hall of Records Commission, State of Maryland, 1971.

"New York Seventh Regiment, Our March to Washington," *Atlantic Monthly,* No. 7 (June 1861).

Newman, Harry Wright. "Anne Arundel During the War of Secession," in *Anna Arundel County, Maryland: A Bicentennial History 1649-1977,* James C. Bradford, ed. Annapolis: Anne Arundel County and Annapolis Bicentennial Committee, 1977.

Newton, Blake T. "The White Brothers," *Northern Neck of Virginia Historical Magazine,* Vol. 12, (1982).

Shomette, Donald G. "Infernal Machines: Submarine and Torpedo Warfare in the War of 1812," *Sea History,* 158 (Winter 2012-2013).

Short, John S. "Sidney Lanier, Familiar Citizen," *Maryland Historical Magazine,* Vol. 35, No. 2 (June 1940).

Stone, Charles. "A Dinner with General Scott in 1861," *Magazine of History,* Vol. 9. No. 6 (June 1884).

Taft, Charles S. "Last Hours of Abraham Lincoln," *The British Medical Journal,* 231 (June 1865).

"The Plains: Another Landmark Destroyed," *Chronicles of St. Mary's,* 6:10 (October 1958).

Thompson, Magnus S. "Plan to Release Our Men at Point Lookout," *Confederate Veteran* (Nashville, 1912), Vol. 20, No. 2.

Thomson, David. "Oliver Otis Howard: Reassessing the Legacy of the 'Christian General," *Today's History* (September 2009).

Tidwell, William A. "Charles County: Confederate Cauldron," *Maryland Historical Magazine,* Vol. 91, No. 1 (Spring 1996).

Townsend, George Alfred. "How Wilkes Booth Crossed the Potomac," *Century Magazine,* Vol. 27, No. 6 (April 1884).

Welles, Gideon. "Important Circular From the Navy," *Scientific American,* new series, Vol. 20 (19 March 1864).

Whyte, James H. "The Activities of the Freedmen's Bureau in Southern Maryland, 1865-1870,"

Chronicles of St. Mary's, Vol. 7, No. 2 (February 1959).

Newspapers and Periodicals

The Abingdon Virginian (Abingdon, Va.)
The Aegis & Intelligencer, (Bel Air, Md.).
Albany Journal (Albany, N.Y.)
Alexandria Gazette (Alexandria, Va.)
The Alleghanian (Edensburg, Pa.)
Annapolis Gazette (Annapolis, Md.)
Baltimore American and Commercial Advertiser (Baltimore, Md.)
The Baltimore Daily Exchange (Baltimore, Md.)
Baltimore Daily Commercial (Baltimore, Md.)
Baltimore Daily Gazette (Baltimore, Md.)
Baltimore Sun (Baltimore, Md.)
Boston Globe (Boston, Ma.)
The Caledonian (St. Johnsbury, Vt.)
Cavalier & Telegraph (Cumberland, Md.)
The Cecil Whig (Elkton, Md.)
Century Magazine.
Cincinnati Daily Press (Cincinnati, Oh.)
Cincinnati Enquirer (Cincinnati, Oh.)
Cleveland Morning Leader (Cleveland, Oh.)
The Daily Dispatch (Richmond, Va.)
The Daily Exchange (Baltimore, Md.)
The Daily Green Mountain Freeman (Montpelier, Vt.)
Daily Intelligencer (Wheeling, W.V.)
Daily Morning Chronicle (Washington, D.C.)
Daily National Intelligencer (Washington, D.C.)
Daily National Republican (Washington, D.C)
Daily Ohio Statesman (Columbus, Oh.)
Dayton Daily Empire (Dayton, Oh.)
Delaware Gazette, (Delaware, Oh.)
The Dollar Weekly Bulletin (Maysville, Ky.)
Evening Star (Washington, D.C.)
Evening Sun (Baltimore, Md.)
The Evening Telegraph, (Philadelphia, Pa.)
Freemont Daily Journal (Freemont, Oh.)
The Grand Haven News (Grand Haven Mi.)
Hammond Gazette (Point Lookout, Md.)
Inquirer (Philadelphia, Pa.)
The Jeffersonian (Stroudsburg, Pa.)
The Local News (Alexandria, Va.)
Marlboro Gazette (Upper Marlboro, Md.)
Memphis Daily Appeal (Memphis, Tenn.)
The Nashville Daily Union (Nashville, Tenn.)
Nashville Union and American (Nashville, Tenn.)
National Tribune (Washington, D.C.)
New Orleans Picayune (New Orleans, La.)
The New York Commercial Advertiser (New York, N.Y.)
New York Herald (New York, N.Y.)
New York Steam Register (New York, N.Y.)
New York Times (New York, N.Y.)
New York Daily Tribune (New York, N.Y.)
Orleans Independent Standard (Irasburgh, Vt.)
The Pacific Commercial Advertiser (Honolulu, HI.)
The Planter's Advocate and Southern Maryland Advertiser (Upper Marlboro, Md.)

Port Tobacco Times and Charles County Advertiser (Port Tobacco, Md.)
The Portage County Democrat (Ravenna, Oh.)
Raftsman's Journal (Clearfield, Pa.)
Richmond Examiner (Richmond, Va.)
St. Mary's Beacon (Leonardtown, Md.)
St. Mary's Gazette (Leonardtown, Md.)
Scientific American.
The Soldier's Journal (Rendezvous of Distribution, Va.)
The South (Baltimore, Md.)
The Star of the North (Bloomsburg, Pa.)
The Sun (New York, N.Y.)
The Sunday Sun (Baltimore, Md.)
Vicksburg Whig (Vicksburg, Miss.)
Washington Standard (Olympia, Washington Territory)
Weekly Intelligencer (Fayetteville, N.C.)
Weekly National Intelligencer (Washington, D.C.)
The Western Democrat (Charlotte, N.C.)
The Wyandot Pioneer (Upper Sandusky, Oh.)
The Xenia Sentinel (Xenia, Oh.)

Internet

Biographical Directory of the United States Congress 1774-Present,
    http://bioguide.congress.gov/biosearch/biosearch.asp, accessed June 11, 2013.
John Bannister Tabb, www.newadvent/cathen/14423c.htm, accessed June 14, 2017.
Sidney Lanier, www.encyclopediaofalabama.org/article/h-2907, accessed June 6, 2017.
    www.dnr.state.nd.us/publiclands/aapaxstanton.html

Marshal House Hotel, Alexandria, 87

Marshall, George R. W., 50

Marshall, Mrs. Robert, 279

Marshall, ___, 322

Marston, Gilman, 355, 356, 357, 358, 359, 361, 363, 364, 365, 368, 369, 370, 371, 372, 373, 399, 419, 422, 423, 424, 428, 429, 430, 436, 443

Martin, Luther, 59

Martindale, John H., 256

Martinsburg, WV, 477, 479, 484, 487

Maryland, 1, 3, 7, 8, 10, 11, 12, 15, 16, 17, 18, 19, 20, 21, 25, 26, 27, 28, 29, 30, 31, 32, 33, 34, 36, 37, 38, 39, 43, 44, 45, 46, 48, 49, 50, 51, 52, 53, 54, 55, 57, 59, 61, 63, 64, 65, 70, 74, 75, 76, 79, 84, 86, 89, 100, 101, 103, 104, 105, 106, 107, 108, 109, 110, 111, 112, 113, 115, 116, 117, 118, 126, 128, 130, 136, 137, 138, 145, 152, 153, 154, 155, 156, 157, 158, 160, 161, 163, 164, 165, 170, 171, 172, 174, 176, 179, 180, 181, 182, 183, 184, 185, 196, 197, 198, 199, 202, 203, 204, 205, 206, 207, 208, 213, 214, 215, 216, 217, 219, 220, 221, 222, 223, 227, 229, 230, 231, 234, 235, 237, 238, 241, 256, 263, 264, 265, 266, 267, 269, 272, 275, 276, 277, 278, 284, 287, 289, 301, 302, 303, 305, 308, 309, 311, 312, 313, 314, 315, 317, 319, 320, 323, 324, 325, 332, 333, 344, 345, 349, 356, 364, 377, 381, 382, 383, 384, 386, 387, 388, 389, 395, 396, 398, 401, 402, 404, 405, 406, 414, 415, 420, 424, 437, 444, 445, 451, 452, 455, 456, 457, 467, 468, 469, 470, 471, 472, 473, 475, 476, 479, 480, 481, 482, 483, 484, 485 , 487, 491, 494, 501, 504, 505, 506, 510, 520, 526, 528, 531, 533, 536, 537, 538, 539, 540, 541, 542, 543, 544, 545, 546, 564, 572, 583, 584, 607, 611, 616, 619, 620, 621, 623, 630, 632, 642, 644, 646, 647, 650, 651; Black Code, 9, 23; College of Agriculture, 520; Constitution (1851), 43, 531, 536, 537, 539, (1864), 302, 531, 532, 536, 537, 538, 539, 541, 542, 543, 544; Constitutional Convention (1851), 194, (1864) 424, 482, 494, 531, 541; Democratic Central Committee, 50; Department of Natural Resources, 651; Eastern Shore, 13, 17, 145, 160, 161, 182, 223, 227, 228, 229, 234, 264, 398, 400, 401, 404, 405, 408, 413, 424, 536, 607; General Assembly, 39, 43, 44, 52, 235, [see State Legislature]; Great Seal of, 43; House of Delegates, 43, 50, 52, 110, 126, 180, 181, 198, 392, 532; House Committee on Federal Relations, 43, 180; Land Office, 36; Orphans Court, 646; State Agricultural Society, 55; State Legislature, 1, 38, 52, 54,

130, 180, 197, 198, 228, 232, 310, 424, 533 539 [see General Assembly]; Senate, 14, 43, 44, 52, 392; Tidewater, 15, 68, 223, 245, 482, 625; Western, 43, 349, 351, 381, 479, 480, 483, 485

Maryland Heights, Md., 483

Maryland Jockey Club, 20

Maryland Military and Naval Academy, Oxford, 126

Maryland Point, Md., 60, 74, 86, 99, 102, 105, 106, 111, 156, 217, 259, 278, 294, 309

"Maryland! My Maryland", 32

Maryland State Agricultural Society, 55

Mason, Mistress, 21

Mason, Thomas, 20, 23, 218; plantation, 9, 19, 20, 23

Mason, George, 255

Mason, ___, 320 [see Augusta Heath Morris]

Mason-Dixon Line, 18, 45

Massachusetts, 29, 31, 34, 35, 37, 40, 65, 145, 165, 189, 192, 284, 382, 390, 419, 452, 522, 530, 535, 583, 626

Massachusetts Avenue, D.C., 250

Mathias Point, Va., 86, 89, 101, 108, 109, 113, 114, 115, 116, 118, 119, 121, 125, 130, 131, 157, 158, 159, 163, 165, 171, 173, 175, 176, 177, 178, 184, 199, 202, 204, 205, 206, 208, 219, 220, 237, 238, 243, 244, 245, 281, 296, 621; Neck, Va., 60, 116-117, 171, 172, 292, 517

Mattapany Plantation (Mattapany Sewell), 49, 126

Mattawoman Creek, Md., 107, 217, 221, 222, 226, 235, 237, 242, 243, 249, 258, 259, 274, 275, 280, 281, 282, 289, 607; Muds, 292

Matthews County, Va., 562; Court House, 450

Matthews, John, 586, 609

Mattingly, ___, 279

Mattox Creek, Va., 312, 331, 334, 336, 340, 341, 342, 566, 567

Maury, Matthew Fontaine, 128, 130

Maxwell, James W., 198

Maxwell, John, 449

May, Henry, 198

Mayer, Eldelmiro, 396, 397

Mayo, Joseph, 137

Mayo, Robert D., 116, 121, 122, 125

McCabe, James Dabney, Jr., 180, 181, 183, 184, 198

McCabe, James Dabney, Sr., 180

McCausland, John, 485, 496, 506

McChenny, William, 123

McChesney, John H., 508, 518

McChesney, Robert, 508

McClellan, George B., 159, 162, 164 167, 168, 184, 185, 189, 200, 201, 202, 203, 205, 206,

ABOUT THE AUTHOR

Donald Grady Shomette, a native of Washngton D.C., completed his undergraduate work in art and art history at the Pratt Institute, Brooklyn, New York. He was the recipient of an Honorary Ph.D. in Humane Letters from the University of Baltimore for his contributions to the arts, science, and literature. For more than two decades he served on the staff of the Library of Congress and simultaneously as director of Nautical Archaeological Associates, Inc., an archaeological research organization, which conducted, among others endeavors, the first underwater cultural resources surveys in the states of Maryland, New Jersey, and Arkansas.

As a historian Shomette has served as a consultant for many states, agencies of the U.S. Government, museums, universities, and non-profit establishments. As a marine archaeologist he has worked in the U.S., Canada, and Great Britain under the sponsorship of such institutions as the National Geographic Society, the National Park Service, the U.S. Navy, and various educational foundations and museums.

Shomette is the author of eighteen books, and contributor to three international encyclopedias and two anthologies of history, and most recently an anthology of Southern Maryland poetry. His many scientific and popular articles have appeared in such publications as *National Geographic Magazine*, *History and Technology*, and *Sea History*. For more than a dozen years he served as a lecturer for the Smithsonian Journeys Program in the Great Lakes and along the entirety of the North Atlantic Seaboard of the United States.

Thrice winner of the prestigious John Lyman Book Award for Best American Maritime History, and once winner of the Marion V. Brewington Book award for Best Book of the Year in Naval Literature, Shomette was also honored with the Calvert Prize, the highest award in Maryland for historic preservation. His most recent endeavors have taken him into the field of historic cartography for the National Geographic Society, and into recorded sound and music as a lyricist and music producer.

CPSIA information can be obtained
at www.ICGtesting.com
Printed in the USA
LVHW101506291219
641942LV00022B/1139/P